ANCIENT INDIAN TRADITION & MYTHOLOGY

Translated by

A BOARD OF SCHOLARS

And Edited by

Dr. G.P. BHATT

VOLUME 53

ANCIENT INDIAN TRADITION AND MYTHOLOGY SERIES

[PURĀṆAS IN TRANSLATION]

VOLUMES

ŚIVA 1-4
LIṄGA 5-6
BHĀGAVATA 7-11
GARUḌA 12-14
NĀRADA 15-19
KŪRMA 20-21
BRAHMĀṆḌA 22-26
AGNI 27-30
VARĀHA 31-32
BRAHMA 33-36
VĀYU 37-38
PADMA 39-48
SKANDA, PARTS I-V 49-53

VOLUMES UNDER PREPARATION

SKANDA, PARTS VI-XXV
BHAVIṢYA
BRAHMAVAIVARTA
DEVĪBHĀGAVATA
KĀLIKĀ
MĀRKAṆḌEYA
MATSYA
VĀMANA
VIṢṆU
VIṢṆUDHARMOTTARA

THE SKANDA-PURĀṆA

Translated and Annotated by

Dr. G.V. TAGARE

PART V

MOTILAL BANARSIDASS PUBLISHERS
PRIVATE LIMITED • DELHI

First Edition: Delhi, 1994

ISBN: 81-208-1151-8

Also available at:

MOTILAL BANARSIDASS

41 U.A. Bungalow Road, Jawahar Nagar, Delhi 110 007
120 Royapettah High Road, Mylapore, Madras 600 004
16 St. Mark's Road, Bangalore 560 001
Ashok Rajpath, Patna 800 004
Chowk, Varanasi 221 001

UNESCO COLLECTION OF REPRESENTATIVE WORKS—Indian Series
This book has been accepted in the Indian Translation Series of the UNESCO Collection of Representative Works, jointly sponsored by the United Nations Educational, Scientific and Cultural Organization (UNESCO) and the Government of India

PRINTED IN INDIA

BY JAINENDRA PRAKASH JAIN AT SHRI JAINENDRA PRESS,
A-45 NARAINA, PHASE I, NEW DELHI 110 028
AND PUBLISHED BY NARENDRA PRAKASH JAIN FOR
MOTILAL BANARSIDASS PUBLISHERS PVT. LTD.,
JAWAHAR NAGAR, DELHI 110 007

PUBLISHER'S NOTE

The purest gems lie hidden in the bottom of the ocean or in the depth of rocks. One has to dive into the ocean or delve into the rocks to find them out. Similarly, truth lies concealed in the language which with the passage of time has become obsolete. Man has to learn that language before he discovers that truth.

But he has neither the means nor the leisure to embark on that course. We have, therefore, planned to help him acquire knowledge by an easier course. We have started the series of Ancient Indian Tradition and Mythology in English Translation. Our goal is to universalize knowledge through the most popular international medium of expression. The publication of the Purāṇas in English Translation is a step towards that goal.

Acknowledgements

It is our pleasant duty to put on record our sincere thanks to Dr. R.N. Dandekar and the UNESCO authorities for their kind encouragement and valuable help in the publication of the volumes in this series.

CONTENTS

Publisher's Note v
Editorial ix
Abbreviations xiii

SKANDA PURĀṆA
Book II : VAIṢṆAVAKHAṆḌA
Section II : PURUṢOTTAMA-KṢETRA-MĀHĀTMYA

Chapters

1. A Dialogue between Jaimini and the Sages 1
2. Yama's Prayer 5
3. Story of Mārkaṇḍeya and the Greatness of Yameśvara 9
4. The Redemption of Puṇḍarīka and Aṁbarīṣa 14
5. Puṇḍarīka and Aṁbarīṣa Attain Salvation 22
6. Description of the Land of Utkala 29
7. The Story of Indradyumna 31
8. The Messenger Vidyāpati Returns 39
9. Vidyāpati Reports to Indradyumna 45
10. Dialogue between Nārada and Indradyumna 50
11. Dialogue between Nārada and Indradyumna (Continued) 60
12. Description of the Holy place Ekāmravana (Bhuvaneśvara) 72
13. The Greatness of Kapoteśa and Bilveśvara 82
14. Nārada Consoles Indradyumna and Urges Him to Perform Horse-sacrifices 85
15. Indradyumna's Grief Dispelled: Manifestation of Four-formed Viṣṇu 89
16. Installation of the Idol of Nṛsiṁha 93
17. Indradyumna Performs a Thousand Horse-sacrifices 98
18. The Eternal Banyan Tree Emerges 109
19. The Lord Manifests Himself as Wooden Idol 112
20. Origin of the Indradyumna Lake 116
21. Indradyumna Gets the Royal Shrine Built 122
22. Indradyumna Goes to Brahmā's Abode along with Nārada 126
23. Indradyumna Returns after Visiting Brahmā 130
24. Devas Eulogize the Lord: Padmanidhi's Reception 135

25. The Construction and Installation of the Chariot of the Lord 139
26. Indradyumna Worships the Lord: King Gāla Submits to Indradyumna 145
27. Installation of the Four Deities 149
28. The Lord Adopts the Form of Nṛsiṁha: Dialogue between Brahmā and Indradyumna 158
29. The Lord Grants Boons to Indradyumna 163
30. The Greatness of Pañcatīrtha 168
31. The Procedure for the Sacred Ablution of the Lord in the Wooden Body 181
32. The Rite of Jyeṣṭha Pañcaka 188
33. The Chariot-Procession Called Guṇḍicā Yātrā 194
34. In Praise of the Chariot-Procession 203
35. The Procedure of Preserving the Chariot 207
36. The Festival of the Lord's Retiring to Sleep 209
37. King Śveta Attains Salvation 214
38. The Great Efficacy of Nirmālya etc. 219
39. Festival to be Celebrated during Cāturmāsya 229
40. Prāvaraṇa (Covering) Festival of Nṛsiṁha 235
41. The Festival of Holy Bath on Puṣya Day 237
42. The Festival of the Transit (of the Sun) to Capricorn 239
43. The Festival of the Swing 241
44. Description of the Jyeṣṭhapañcaka Vrata 245
45. The Procedure of Splitting Damanaka Grass 248
46. Celebration of Yātrā by Dakṣa (on Akṣayatṛtīyā) 250
47. Meditation on the Lord in Different Forms 254
48. Popularization of the Lord's Worship by Indradyumna 255
49. The Merit of Listening to a Purāṇa 258

Index 263

EDITORIAL

This Part describes in detail the shrine of Jagannātha at Puri in Orissa, its origin and history which is, incidentally, full of mythological elements, and a number of festivals and processions associated with Lord Jagannātha.

Modern Orissa was formerly known by the names 'Utkala' and 'Oḍhra' (also spelt as 'Oḍra') and the holy region where the shrine is located was called 'Puruṣottama-Kṣetra' or 'Jagannātha-Kṣetra' which are the current names. Utkala, according to the text, is situated between the rivers Svarṇarekhā and Mahānadī, which are still known by these names and reaches as far as the river Ṛṣikulyā (flowing in the Ganjam District) that falls into the Southern Sea, i.e. the Bay of Bengal. It may be mentioned here that the name Kaliṅga which was current in the age of Aśoka is not known to the author of this Section of the Purāṇa. The holy region of Puruṣottama-Kṣetra in this Utkala Deśa is situated in the coastal area of the Bay of Bengal and extends to ten yojanas or 120 kms up to Viraja-Maṇḍala (modern Jājpur or Yājpur on the bank of river Vaitaraṇī, according to Nando Lal Dey). The holy shrine of Lord Jagannātha is located on a hill named Nīlagiri here.

The story in a nutshell goes like this. The hero of the story described in this Part is King Indradyumna who is spoken of as a great Vaiṣṇava of Kṛtayuga born in the Solar Race and belonging to the fifth generation from Brahmā. His capital was Avantī in the country known as Mālava. Being a great devotee of Viṣṇu, he once expressed his eagerness to his priest to know about more famous and meritorious sacred places of the Lord. A stranger present in his Assembly immediately offers to enlighten him and prompts him to visit the shrine of Śrī Jagannātha in Oḍhra Deśa and then disappears. The king then sends the priest's brother Vidyāpati to collect first-hand information about the place.

Vidyāpati starts on the journey and reaches the holy place by a fast running chariot. He is said to have reached Mahānadī the same day at sunset and Nīlādri the next day. Now Avantī, as we know, is at a distance of more than a thousand kilometres from Puri. Is it possible for a chariot, however fast, to cover this distance in such a short time? Most probably the author never visited Avantī and had no idea of the distance.

Anyway, Vidyāpati while climbing Nīlagiri on which the shrine is located happens to meet a devotee Viśvāvasu, a prominent member of the tribal community inhabiting the vicinity of the shrine, who guides him to the shrine and shows the rare, sapphire or black stone idols of Nīla

Mādhava, Lakṣmī, Śeṣa, Sudarśana and Garuḍa and also discloses the secret that the Deity would soon disappear under sand dunes caused by storming winds.

Vidyāpati, the most fortunate one to have had a direct vision of the Deity, then returns to the king and narrates everything to him but holds back the information about the Lord's disappearance which was imminent lest the king would get disheartened. In the meantime the tragedy of the Lord's disappearance has actually occurred.

The king then announces to the people of Avantī and his army to get ready to proceed with all their possessions to Śrīpuruṣottama-Kṣetra and make it their permanent residence. The whole congregation of people reaches the temple of Carcikā (Goddess Durgā) at the boundary of Utkaladeśa where it is greeted by the king of Utkala with all courtesy and Indradyumna is informed about the disappearance of the Deity under sand. The king becomes sad but is assured by Nārada who is accompanying him that the Lord would soon incarnate and the king would be able to see him through the physical eye. Then they resume the journey towards the Nīla mountain which is at a distance of 3 yojanas (120 kms) from the river Gandhavahā flowing by Ekāmravana (modern Bhuvaneśvara) which the vast crowd with all the paraphernalia reaches at noon of the next day, i.e. in $1^1/_2$ days. This again in quite surprising in view of the enormous distance from the starting place! However, the reader of Purāṇas has perhaps by now learnt that there are innumerable such surprises in store for him.

To resume the story, King Indradyumna vows to perform one thousand horse-sacrifices to propitiate the Lord who has disappeared so that he manifests himself again at the holy spot. When the thousandth sacrifice is on he sees mentally while meditating Lord Viṣṇu, Ananta, Lakṣmī on the right of Viṣṇu and the Discus Sudarśana on the left and also God Brahmā in front with palms joined in reverence.

In the meantime servants report having seen a wonderful Banyan tree floating with the top sunk deep and the roots above the waves on the southern seashore where the king has camped to take the valedictory bath in the sea after completing the Yajñas. Nārada reveals that it is the fallen hairs of Viṣṇu that have incarnated in the form of the tree. Thereupon the king worships the tree which is then taken to and installed in the Altar of sacrifices.

At the instance of a heavenly voice the tree is left concealed behind the doors of the Altar for fifteen days during which period an unknown old carpenter (suspected to be the Lord himself) carves out the idols of the

Lord, Balabhadra, Subhadrā and Sudarśana from it. Simultaneously the Mansion, i.e. the palatial shrine of Viṣṇu is constructed and completed at a tremendous cost. It is decided to invite Brahmā for the installation of the idols there and so Indradyumna in the company of Nārada proceeds to Satyaloka for the purpose. Brahmā sends Padmanidhi with them to collect requisite material for the installation ceremony.

Abodes for Brahmā and various categories of invitees, befitting their respective status, as well as three chariots for Viṣṇu, Balabhadra and Subhadrā as per the specifications given by Nārada are constructed in no time by Viśvakarmā, the divine architect.

When all the arrangements are complete, Brahmā's aerial chariot descends. The installation ceremony is carried out with great pomp and show. Brahmā then has a word with Nārāyaṇa in wooden form and recommends King Indradyumna for his blessings. The Lord grants him boons and instructs in detail about celebrating festivals of the Lord's bath (*Mahāsnāna*), the great procession called Guṇḍicā (*Guṇḍicā Mahāyātrā*), of the Lord's waking up (*Utthāna*), going to sleep (*Svāpa*), turning on the sides (*Pārśvaparivartana*), covering of the path (*Mārgaprāvaraṇa*), of Lord's sport in the swing (*Dolā Mahotsava*) and others which have assumed highly ritualized forms and are detailed in 31st and subsequent chapters of this Section.

G.P. Bhatt

ABBREVIATIONS

Common and self-evident abbreviations such as Ch(s)—Chapter(s), p—page, pp—pages, v—verse, vv—verses, Ftn—Footnote, Hist. Ind. Philo.—History of Indian Philosophy are not included in this list.

ABORI	*Annals of the Bhandarkar Oriental Research Institute*, Poona
AGP	S.M. Ali's *The Geography of Purāṇas*, PPH, New Delhi, 1973
AIHT	*Ancient Indian Historical Tradition*, F.E. Pargiter, Motilal Banarsidass (MLBD), Delhi
AITM	*Ancient Indian Tradition and Mythology* Series, MLBD, Delhi
AP	*Agni Purāṇa*, Guru Mandal Edition (GM), Calcutta, 1957
Arch. S.Rep.	Archaeological Survey Report
AV	*Atharva Veda*, Svādhyāya Maṇḍal, Auṇdh
BdP	*Brahmāṇḍa Purāṇa*, MLBD, Delhi, 1973
BG	*Bhagavadgītā*
BhP	*Bhāgavata Purāṇa*, Bhagavat Vidyapeeth, Ahmedabad
Br	*Brāhmaṇa* (preceded by name such as Śatapatha)
BsP	*Bhaviṣya Purāṇa*, Vishnu Shastri Bapat, Wai
BVP	*Brahma Vaivarta Purāṇa*, GM, 1955-57
CC	*Caturvarga Cintāmaṇi* by Hemādri
CVS	*Caraṇa Vyūha Sūtra* by Śaunaka, Com. by Mahīdāsa
DB	*Devī Bhāgavata*, GM, 1960-61
De or GDAMI	*The Geographical Dictionary of Ancient and Mediaeval India*, N.L. Dey, Oriental Reprint, Delhi, 1971
DhS	*Dharma Sūtra* (preceded by the author's name such as Gautama)
ERE	*Encyclopaedia of Religion and Ethics* by Hastings
GP	*Garuḍa Purāṇa*, ed. R.S. Bhattacharya, Chowkhamba, Varanasi, 1964
GS	*Gṛhya Sūtra* (preceded by the name of the author such as Āpastamba)
HD	*History of Dharma Śāstra*, P.V. Kane, G.O.S.
IA	*The Indian Antiquary*

IHQ	*The Indian Historical Quarterly*
JP	*Purāṇa* (Journal of the Kashiraj Trust), Varanasi
KA	*Kauṭilya Arthaśāstra*
KP	*Kūrma Purāṇa*, Veṅkaṭeśvara Press Edn., Bombay; also Kashiraj Trust Edn., Varanasi, 1971
LP	*Liṅga Purāṇa*, GM, 1960; also MLBD, Delhi, 1981
Manu	*Manusmṛti*
Mbh	*Mahābhārata*, Gītā Press, Gorakhpur, VS 2014
MkP	*Mārkaṇḍeya Purāṇa*
MN	*Mahābhārata Nāmānukramaṇī*, Gītā Press, Gorakhpur, VS 2016
MtP	*Matsya Purāṇa*, GM, 1954
MW	M. Monier-Williams' *Sanskrit-English Dictionary*, MLBD, Delhi, 1976
NP	*Nāradīya* or *Nārada Purāṇa*, Veṅkaṭeśvara Press, Bombay
PCK	*Bhāratavarṣīya Prācīna Caritrakośa*, Siddheshwar Shastri, Poona, 1968
PdP	*Padma Purāṇa*, GM, 1957-59
PE	*Purāṇic Encyclopaedia*, V. Mani, English Version, MLBD, Delhi, 1975
PR or PRHRC	*Puranic Records on Hindu Rites and Customs*, R.C. Hazra, Calcutta, 1948
ṚV	*Ṛg Veda*, Svādhyāya Maṇḍal, Aundh
Śat Br	*Śatapatha Brāhmaṇa*
SC or SMC	*Smṛti Candrikā* by Devanna Bhaṭṭa
SEP	*Studies in Epics and Purāṇas*, A.D. Pusalkar, Bharatiya Vidya Bhavan (BVB), Bombay
SkP	*Skanda Purāṇa*
SP	*Śiva Purāṇa*
VāP	*Vāyu Purāṇa*
VR	*Vālmīki Rāmāyaṇa*
VdP	*Viṣṇudharmottara Purāṇa*
VmP	*Vāmana Purāṇa*
VP	*Viṣṇu Purāṇa*
VrP	*Varāha Purāṇa*

SKANDA PURĀṆA

BOOK II: VAIṢṆAVAKHAṆḌA

SECTION II: PURUṢOTTAMA-KṢETRA-MĀHĀTMYA

CHAPTER ONE

A Dialogue between Jaimini and the Sages

Obeisance to Śrī Gaṇeśa. Here begins (description of) greatness of the holy place of Puruṣottama (Jagannātha).

1. After bowing down to Nārāyaṇa and then to Nara, the most excellent one among men, to goddess Sarasvatī as well as to Vyāsa, one shall utter "Jaya"[1] (the Purāṇa).

The sages said:

2-6. O holy Lord, conversant with all the scriptural texts, the knower of the greatness of all the Tīrthas, formerly, when the glorification of the Tīrthas was taken up, it was mentioned by you that a great Tīrtha named Puruṣottama[2] was extremely sanctifying. It is there that the Lord of Śrī abides as a wooden idol in the course of his sports as a human being. On one paying a visit to him he bestows salvation. He directly grants the benefits of all the Tīrthas.

Do recount it in detail to us. By whom was that sacred place created?

Lord Nārāyaṇa is refulgent and self-luminous. He is the Supreme

---

1. *Jaya*: Originally it was the name of Vyāsa's composition on Kaurava-Pāṇḍava War. In course of time it came to be used for all Purāṇas and even the Rāmāyaṇa.

2. *Puruṣottama Kṣetra:* (Jagannātha) Puri, Orissa. It is also known as Śrī Kṣetra, Bhauma Kṣetra, Divya Kṣetra. The Purāṇa regards this region conch-shaped and it is hence called Śaṅkha Kṣetra. Our Purāṇa states that it was originally the area of Śabaras (aboriginals) who worshipped Nīlamādhava.

Puruṣa. How does he stay there in a form made of wood?[1] Do narrate it, O most excellent one among eloquent speakers, O Sage, O Sire of all the worlds. O Brāhmaṇa, we wish to hear it as we have great eagerness and interest in (listening to) it.

Jaimini[2] *said:*

Listen ye all, O sages. It is a great secret.

7. Those who are not the followers of Viṣṇu will not have any devotion to him. By glorifying him the entire darkness disappears.

8-9. Formerly, having heard it from the lotus-like mouth of Śaṁbhu, it has been said by Skanda that the Lord of the universe is omnipresent and sanctifier of all. There are other shrines and holy places which dispel all sins, but this holy place is the very physical body of that great soul. He himself stays here in his (actual) physical form. It is well-known by his own name.

10. All those who wish to stay there, have their sins destroyed. What to say of those who actually stay there and visit Gadādhara (i.e. Viṣṇu)!

11-12. Oh, it is indeed a great holy spot extending over ten Yojanas (i.e. 120 Kms). It has emerged out of the waters of Tīrtharāja ('Chief of Tīrthas' i.e. the Ocean). It is full of sands. In the middle the great mountain Nīlācala shines like a single breast of the Earth. It can be contemplated upon from very far-off places.

13. Formerly the Earth was lifted up (by the Lord) in the form of a Boar; he levelled it up everywhere and rendered it stable by means of mountains.

14-15a. Formerly Brahmā created the entire (universe) of mobile and immobile beings, all the Tīrthas, rivers and oceans. As before he fixed up all the holy spots and thought thus as he had been overburdened with the function of creation:

15b-17a. 'How can I avoid the great task of creation once more?

1. The whole Purāṇa defends the wooden material used for god Jagannātha as 'Dāru-Brahman' (Wooden-Brahman, the Brahman of wooden material).

2. *Jaimini*: Jamini is said to be the author of a section of the Sāmaveda, of (Jaminīya) Brāhmaṇa and Upaniṣad, of the (Pūrva) Mīmāṁsā, of a Gṛhyasūtra and of a late version of Aśvamedha part of Mbh. Most probably there were more than one Jaimini. Mbh, Ādi 67.89 regards him as a disciple of Vyāsa and he was the Brahmā (Superintendent) of King Janamejaya's Serpent-Sacrifice (Ādi 53.6).

The present narrator may be a different person, a namesake of that ancient sage.

How can the creatures afflicted with *Tāpatraya* ('the three types of miseries[1]') be liberated?'

Even as Prajāpati (Brahmā) was musing thus an idea occurred to him: 'I shall eulogize the great Lord Viṣṇu, the sole cause of salvation.'

Brahmā said:

17b-21. Obeisance to you, O Lord holding the conch, the discus and the iron club. O support of the universe, it is from the lotus coming out of your navel that I, the creator of the universe, was born. But, O Lord immanent in the universe, you alone know your own real form.

It is by your Māyā that the entire universe beginning with *Mahat* has been created. *Śabda-Brahman* (i.e. the Vedas which are considered the revealed word of Brahman and hence identical with Supreme Brahman) arose from your breath and became threefold (viz. Ṛg, Yajus and Sāman Vedas). Depending on that only as my source I created the world.

(*Defective Text*) You do not possess any attribute such as grossness, subtleness, longness, shortness etc. Just as the bangles and other (gold ornaments) are identical with gold, so also this universe of mobile and immobile beings is identical with you,[2] O Lord, in spite of different forms on account of the three different Guṇas (Sattva etc.)

22. O great Lord, O Lord of the universe, you are the creator and that which is to be created. You alone are the nourisher and what is to be nourished. You are the support and what is being supported as well as the upholder.

23. With a mind urged by you everyone performs auspicious as well as inauspicious acts. Thereby he attains the suitable goal ordained by you alone.

24. You are the goal, the Lord (the supporter) and the witness, O Supreme Lord. O sire of the mobile and immobile beings, O Lord, the immanent soul of everyone, O merciful one, O Lord of the universe, be pleased with me now (because) I have (submitted to) you as my refuge.

Jaimini said:

25-26. On being eulogized thus by Brahmā the Garuḍa-emblemed Lord, resembling a dark cloud, having the conch, the discus etc. as his symbols, appeared before him seated on the Lord of birds. O excellent

1. The miseries are classified as *Ādhyātmika*, *Ādhibhautika* and *Ādhidaivika*.
2. Brahman or Viṣṇu is also the material cause of the universe.

Brāhmaṇas, his lotus-like face gleamed. His lips throbbed as he was desirous of speaking (something).

Śrī Bhagavān said:

27-30. O Brahmā, it appears that the purpose for which you eulogize me cannot be achieved. The beginningless Avidyā is firmly rooted. It cannot be severed by the bonds of Karmas. How can birth and death cease to be when it (i.e. Avidyā) predominates! Still, O sinless one, if you strive in regard to this, I shall tell you the means whereby it shall occur gradually. O Brahmā, I am you; you are I. The entire universe is identical with me. Think that your interest lies where my interest also lies and not otherwise.

31. There is a region on the northern shore of the sea and the southern bank of Mahānadī. That region bestows the benefit of all the Tīrthas on the earth.

32. O Brahmā, those men of good intellect who reside there enjoy the fruits of the merits earned in the previous births.

33-36. Men deficient in merits, or those who are not my devotees are not born there, O Lotus-born one. From the forest of Ekāmra (modern Bhuvaneshwar in Orissa) and up to the shore of the Southern Sea (the Bay of Bengal) every step is better than the previous one. It is gradually (one step after another) sanctifying. The Nīla[1] mountain that shines on the seashore, is a well-guarded holy spot on the earth, very difficult of access even unto you. It is difficult to be comprehended by Suras and Asuras. It is enveloped by my Māyā. Eschewing all (external) contacts, I dwell there in physical form. I dwell in Puruṣottama after going beyond the perishable and the imperishable.

37-40a. My shrine and the holy place of Puruṣottama is not at all affected by creation or dissolution.[2] After going there, O Pitāmaha, you will see me like this in the form in which you see me now, O Brahmā, the form that is marked by discus etc. Within the Nīla mountain, at the root of the holy fig tree, on the western side there is a pool well-known as Rauhiṇa[3]. I dwell on its bank. Those who see me there

1. The low range of sand-hills on which the temple of Jagannātha is situated (De 141). The epithet 'mountain'(*-giri, -acala, -parvata*) applied to this low sand-hill is a Puranic glorification.

2. Every *Sthala-Purāṇa* claims this eternity to its Kṣetra, be it Purī or Karavīra.

3. Rauhiṇa Kuṇḍa: The tank in the compound of Jagannātha Temple. But the *kuṇḍa* mentioned here is probably lost. Another tank was actually built when the great Jagannātha Temple came up in the 12th cent. CE.

with the mortal eye and those whose sins are washed off by its water shall attain *Sāyujya* with me.

40b-44. Go there, O Lord of exalted magnificence. After seeing me if you go on meditating, another greatness of that sacred place shall become manifest to you. It will appear very strange even to you. It is not revealed by Śrutis, Smṛtis and Itihāsa and Purāṇa. On account of my Māyā it is not visible to anyone. Since you have eulogized me now, everything will be visible and manifest to you by my favour.

By staying there for a day (only) one attains that benefit which is mentioned as the merit acquired by pure souls (by visiting) all the holy Tīrthas, (by performing) rites, Yajñas and charitable gifts. (*Defective text*) By residing permanently there one attains the benefit of a horse-sacrifice.

After directing Brahmā thus, O Brāhmaṇas, Lord Puruṣottama vanished there itself, even as he was looking on.

CHAPTER TWO

Yama's Prayer

Jaimini said:

1. Then Brahmā hastened to the place where the Lord was present. He then saw the Lord in the same form as was seen at the end of the prayer.

2. On seeing the great Lord, he recognized him and became extremely delighted. Then, O excellent Brāhmaṇas, he became the storehouse of excessively wonderful knowledge.

3-7. With his eyes beaming with delight, he began to eulogize when an excellent crow arrived there from somewhere. It plunged into that holy pit full of merciful waters. On seeing Mādhava, the receptacle of mercy, having the lustre of blue gems and jewels,[1] it cast off its physical body of a crow and rolled on the ground. The Lord with the conch, the discus and the iron club stood at his side.[2] On seeing that

1. Nila-mādhava: The ancient form of Jagannātha as originally worshipped by Śabaras was an idol of azure blue stone and not the present wooden form.

2. This crow was named Bhuṣaṇḍa Kāka and is installed near the Rohiṇa Kuṇḍa inside Jagannātha Temple. Th· crow image has four hands holding a disc, a conch-shell, a club and a lotus-like Lord Viṣṇu. In view of this, the line may

achievement of a creature of lower order, not easily accessible even to eminent Yogins, O sages, Brahmā thought that the creation would gradually wear away. He then began to doubt the truth of the Upaniṣadic statement that only humans beings are entitled to salvation. There is nothing in this world which is difficult for a devotee of Viṣṇu to get.

8-11. He was able to see directly the truth of what had been said by the ancient Lord, O excellent Brāhmaṇas. By pronouncing his name a man is liberated from all sins. Is salvation difficult to get, O Brāhmaṇas, on his direct perception? If one casts off one's life mentally meditating on Viṣṇu, one is liberated. What wonder is there that anyone having the direct perception of the Lord attains salvation?

Wonderful indeed is the greatness of the sacred place named Puruṣottama, where, O Brāhmaṇas, even a crow perceived Hari directly.

Rare indeed is this holy spot that releases even ignorant ones. Wonderful is the greatness of this holy spot bestowing liberation on even a crow. What then in regard to those who are always endowed with calmness, detachment and perfect knowledge!

The sages said:

12-17. What did Brahmā do on seeing Mādhava called Nīla, as well as the crow that destroyed all physical bondage within a moment after seeing him?

Jaimini said:

On seeing that wonderful event, Brahmā began to meditate on Mādhava. By that time Pitṛpati (god of Death, Yama) came hurriedly to that place. He was agitated in the matter of retaining his authority. His face indicated distress. He heaved sighs. On seeing Mādhava on the Nīla mountain, he prostrated before him with eight limbs (touching the ground). He eulogized the Lord for the stabilization of his authority.

Yama said:

Obeisance to you, O Lord of the chiefs of Devas, O cause of creation, sustenance and dissolution. All the worlds are fixed and fastened to you like groups of beads strung into a garland. The universe is supported by you, created by you and nourished by you.

---

be interpreted "The crow was transfigured as holder of a conch-shell, discus and iron-club."

18-24a. You always illuminate everything in the form of the Moon and the Sun; I bow down to the Lord of the universe, the source of origin of all the worlds, the abode of the whole Cosmos, the sire of the worlds, the witness of the entire universe, the Lord devoid of beginning and end. Obeisance to the origin of the universe, to the ocean full of the waters in the form of the highest mercifulness, to the Lord whose power transcends the highest, the lowest and what is beyond the highest.

Obeisance to the Lord who is like the Sun unto the frost of the distress of worldly existence. Hail to the kinsman of the wretched ones, to the Lord who has created all other powerful Lords by means of his own Māyā. Obeisance to Him whose ropes (controlling powers) are Guṇas (like Sattva etc.). I bow to the Lord whose robes are yellow and devoid of impurities like the filaments of a lotus flower; to the discus-bearing Lord whose discus cuts off the shoulders of the enemies in great battles.

Obeisance to the Lord who held the Earth uplifted by means of his curved teeth. Obeisance to the Lord, the embodiment of the three Vedas. Obeisance to the Varāha form of Yajña; salute to the Lord whose eyes are the Moon, the Sun and the Fire. Obeisance to the Lord Narasiṁha (Man-Lion), who has driven away the enemies through his fierce form with curved teeth.

24b-30. The creation, sustenance and annihilation of the universe is a graceful sport of his side glance and thereby the creation of the variegated world consisting of beings of higher and lower order takes place frequently. I bow unto that Lord of the lustre of the blue clouds, whose appearance is like that of the precious stone sapphire, whose abode is a cave within the Nīla mountain and who is the storehouse of mercy.

I bow down to the enemy of Mura, the Lord who holds the conch, the discus, the iron club and the lotus, who grants auspiciousness and who dispels the entire mass of sins of those who bow down (to him).

Hail to you whose eyes are consecrated by contact with the outer corners of the eyes of Kamalā, to you whose chest is broad, fascinating to the minds and shining on account of the Śrīvatsa[1] and the gem Kaustubha.

Śrī possesses prosperity and glory by resorting to the pair of lotus-like feet of the Lord. On being resorted to by the people, Śrī grants them separately prosperity and perpetual glory.

Lakṣmī is Prakṛti and is of two different forms, viz. the *Parā* (superior)

1. Śrīvatsa is the curl of hair on the chest of Viṣṇu.

and the *Aparā* (inferior). Because of your desire to create, the Supreme Brahman without any modification or change has been immediately created (transformed) into one characterized by changes. I bow down unto that Lakṣmī who is full of all good characteristics, who is marked with auspicious features and who is permanently stationed on the chest of Viṣṇu.

Jaimini said:

31. Śrīkānta (Lord Viṣṇu) who was thus propitiated by Dharmarāja (Yama) directed Śrī who was at his side with the lute in her hands. The Lord gave the directive by means of the outer corner of his eyes.

32. Honoured by him, Lakṣmī, the destroyer of the misery of worlds, sportingly said to Yama for the sake of the welfare of all the people:

Lakṣmī said:

33. The object with which you eulogize us both in this holy place is indeed difficult to be acquired. This sacred spot of Śrīpuruṣottama cannot be abandoned by us.

34-39a. Even at the close of the Kalpa this abode is sustained by Parameṣthin. Brahmā, the Lords of the Quarters etc. have no jurisdiction over this place.

Fruition of Karmas cannot take place here. (Sins) of men staying here, even if they be wicked, as well as of the creatures of lower order are burned like a heap of cotton in a blazing fire. Formerly you were created as the restrainer of those who, day and night, are fettered by the shackles of sin and merit. But (now) one is liberated from the bondage of Karma by seeing Lord Nārāyaṇa here, who has taken up a physical form and is as beautiful as sapphire. O son of Sun, your authority is restricted to the land of Karma (which is) other than this place. O Yama, do not be disheartened by this restriction being imposed on your jurisdiction so far as this holy spot is concerned.

39b-42. Brahmā, the grandfather (of the universe), is a Lord superior to you. He watches out of curiosity the lower animals attaining identity with Viṣṇu. This Lotus-born Lord knows the ripening of Karmas of everyone. After knowing the greatness of this holy place, he eulogizes Lord Gadādhara. Creatures which come under your jurisdiction do not remain here. O son of Sun, those who are liberated while living and those who are desirous of liberation reside here.

On being addressed thus by her, by Viṣṇu in female form, Yama who was devoid of pride and shyness (?) spoke these words:

Yama said:

43-46. O Mother, what has been ordered by you now has never before been heard by me. I am overwhelmed by ignorance. How can I know the excellent secret? I am deluded by egotism. How can I understand the greatness of that Lord whose form neither Brahmā nor the Vedas know? O Goddess of Suras, it has been commanded by you that this holy spot is the bestower of salvation due to the presence of Vāsudeva. God's will cannot be resisted. Viṣṇu who causes bondage elsewhere grants salvation here.

47-49. He is the creator of hells under my control as well as of heaven. If all those who die here attain salvation, O Mother, tell me in detail all these things: e.g. the area of the holy land; the situation; the benefit of residing there; what are the various Tīrthas that are present here; if there is any thing by way of secret etc.; who is the presiding deity of this (particular) holy spot? Recount all these, so that I can move about fearlessly avoiding (what should be avoided).

CHAPTER THREE

*Story of Mārkaṇḍeya and the Greatness of Yameśvara**

Śrī said:

1. A good understanding due to the proximity of Viṣṇu has been engendered in you. I shall recount to you the wonderful story of this holy spot, O son of Sun.

2-5. Formerly stationed on the broad chest of the Lord, O Yama, I looked out as this universe consisting of mobile and immobile beings,

*The story of Mārkaṇḍeya, the ageless sage, and his vision of *Pralaya* and the existence of the universe within the belly of the young babe lying on a leaf of Nyagrodha tree in the cosmic flood is described in Mbh, Vana 188, BhP XII.8.10, BmP chs 52-56 and elsewhere. But here as in NP chs 54-61 and BmP the main object is the glorification of Puruṣottama Kṣetra. The Kṣetra is unaffected by the Deluge; the Nyagrodha on the leaf of which Viṣṇu lies as a babe stands eternally at this sacred place.

got dissolved in Pralaya. At that time only two (survivors) were there, viz. this holy spot as well as I. At that time the son of Mṛkaṇḍu, the sage who had a span of life extending to seven Kalpas, did not get any place (shelter) to stand, as everything mobile and immobile had perished. He was not happy anywhere. Roving around on that vast sheet of water of dissolution he saw a Banyan tree at a spot resembling Puruṣottama.

6-11. Floating and wading (gradually) he reached the foot of the Banyan tree. Near it he heard the words of a boy, "O Mārkaṇḍeya, come near me. Entering (unto me) cast off your immense misery. Do not be aggrieved."

On hearing those unimaginably wonderful words the sage experienced great surprise. He did not even think of his personal misery.

(The holy spot) was not shattered by the waters of the Deluge; it was not burned by the Kālavahni (the Fire of Destruction), nor was it dried up or carried away by Saṁvartaka (i.e. Cloud of Universal Destruction etc.) in that extremely terrible, vast sheet of water. The holy spot looked like a boat. There a great Banyan tree appeared standing like a sacrificial post.

The Banyan tree was the body of the Lord. This holy spot held on to it. Its branch was not moved by the violent gusts of wind at the time of dissolution. The sage stood beneath it and thought thus:

12-16. 'How does this piece of land appear stabler while all the mobile and immobile beings have perished in the vast sheet of water of dissolution (of the universe). This excellent tree appears to be very tender. Whence is this humble utterance "O Mārkaṇḍeya, come" repeatedly coming without any (visible) source?' Thinking thus he floated on and saw Nārāyaṇa with the conch, discus and iron club in his hands.

O son of Vivasvān (i.e. Yama), he saw me also seated on the lotus of his body. He was helpless on account of water and gusts of wind, but then he regained composure and steadiness.

Delighted in his mind, that sage prostrated before us with eight limbs touching the ground. In order to propitiate the Lord he uttered this prayer:

Mārkaṇḍeya prayed:

17. O ocean of mercy, save me. I have close association with those who follow your lotus-like feet. I possess the wealth of Rudra, Indra and the Lotus-seated Lord. But I am devoid of your devotion and am wretched. I am scorched from all around.

18. O ocean of mercy, save me. I am wretched. Your lotus-like pair of feet served by Brahmā and others have unimaginable power. It is the real primary cause of the acquisition of (future) happiness and prosperity.

19. As a part of your person, this Cosmic Egg appears to be many crores of times (smaller). I have become distressed as this universe has become merged (in you) after having been sustained by you with your graceful charms.

20. The same gold appears different in the forms of bangles etc. The same Sun shining in the sky appears different in the waters contained in different (types of vessels) supporting them.[1] In the same way though you are one and devoid of attributes (yet) you appear in different forms.

21. Though you have no particular and exclusive interest (in any thing), though you are devoid of the will of taking up (any particular form), O Lord of boundless power, you take up physical bodies in every Yuga, conforming to your sympathy with the distressed.

22. Formerly, O Lord of the universe, your lotus-like feet were served by me, not with the understanding of the Ātman, and so I have become victim of the terrible consequences of that action. O ocean of mercy, save me. I am wretched.

23. O great soul, your body of the three Guṇas , that is the agent of the sportive actions of creation, sustenance and annihilation of all the worlds is the cause of *Mahat* etc. Obeisance unto you who are greater than Prakṛti.

24. The form of Brahman is omnipresent. It is very large and immeasurable. It goes on increasing in you. It has assumed the full-grown form. It is the cause of transformation. I resort to it that is my own soul and the soul of the universe.

25. In this extremely terrible, vast sheet of water there is no piece of land for standing, O Lord of Lakṣmī, on account of the showers of the cloud and the violent agitation caused by winds.

26. Save me who have become immersed in the ocean of worldly existence, O Viṣṇu, O Lord of the universe. Redeem me from this, O Govinda, by means of your benign glance from a corner of your eyes.

---

1. Such illustrations and the repeated references to Māyāvāda show the influence of Śaṅkara. Such portions belong to post-Śaṅkara period.

Śrī said:

27. As the Brahmanical sage was eulogizing thus, Lord Nārāyaṇa directly looked at him with benign eyes and spoke these words:

Śrī Bhagavān said:

28-29. O Mārkaṇḍeya, O excellent Brāhmaṇa, you are extremely distressed because without knowing me a very severe penance has been performed by you. Only a long span of life has been the result thereof. See me lying on a leafy cup above this *Kalpavaṭa* (divine Banyan tree). I am in the form of a baby, O great sage. I am Kāla (Time) and the Ātman of everyone. Enter the widened mouth. It behoves you to remain there.

Śrī said:

30-39. On being told thus by the Lord, the sage had expressions of wonder on his face. He climbed (the tree) and saw the form of the baby. He entered his mouth. Through the throat he entered the huge belly of great extent. There the Brāhmaṇa saw the fourteen worlds, Brahmā and others, the Guardians of the Quarters, Suras, Siddhas, Gandharvas, Rākṣasas, sages, celestial sages, the Earth marked by the oceans, different kinds of Tīrthas, rivers, mountains and forests. Cities and towns were seen along with villages and market-towns. The Seven Pātālas[1] were seen and thousands of Serpent-girls too.

He saw Śeṣa holding up all the worlds. He was attended upon by serpents brilliant with exceedingly valuable gems. There were highly praiseworthy mansions set with gems and vessels of nectar. Śeṣa was exceedingly wonderful. He was adorned with a thousand hoods. He was expounding and analysing all the scriptural texts. He was in the midst of his disciples. That great sage saw within the Lord's belly everything that was created by Brahmā and everything that was within the bowels of the Cosmic Egg.

Moving about here and there he never saw the extremity of the belly. He came out of the belly and saw once again Puruṣottama seated as before, when he saw him along with me. With his eyes full of surprise, he bowed down and spoke these words:

1. The seven nether worlds (Pātālas) are: Atala, Vitala, Sutala, Nitala, Talātala, Mahātala and Pātāla.

Mārkaṇḍeya said:

40-41. O Lord, O Lord of chiefs of Devas, what a wonderful thing is this, O Lord? Within the confines free from the Mahāpralaya, creation too is seen. Your *Māyā* cannot be comprehended. How can it be known by me?

Śrī Bhagavān said:

42-44. O sage, know that this wonderful holy spot of mine is eternal.[1] There is neither creation nor dissolution here. There is no worldly existence (with transmigration from body to body).

Know that this holy spot is always of the same form. To those who realize me it gives salvation. This is the holy spot named Puruṣottama. One who has entered this does not go back to stay in a womb (i.e. he gets liberation). He becomes the embodiment of perfect happiness as his form.

On being advised thus by the Lord, the great sage Mārkaṇḍeya became averse to other Tīrthas and said, "I will stay here". He bowed down to the Sire of the world and said with great delight visible on his face:

Mārkaṇḍeya spoke to Viṣṇu with great devotion and faith:

45. O Lord, bless me in this holy spot Puruṣottama. By staying here, O Puruṣottama, I will not be subjected to the control of (the god of) Death.

Śrī Bhagavān said:

46-48. I shall make your stay here, O Brāhmaṇa sage, in the holy spot that is conducive to the achievement of salvation till the annihilation of all living beings. There is no doubt about it. At the end of the Pralaya I shall create (another) eternal Tīrtha for you. On the banks of that Tīrtha you shall perform penance and propitiate my second body Śiva.[2] With my compassion you will certainly conquer Death.

---

1. This eternality is a special feature of this Kṣetra. All *Sthala-Purāṇas* lay the same claim for their specific areas (e.g. Vārāṇasī, Karavīra).

2. As in the Māheśvara Khaṇḍa, this (Vaiṣṇava) Khaṇḍa also affirms the identity of Śiva and Viṣṇu.

Jaimini said:

49-51. Thus Mārkaṇḍeya, the great sage, was formerly granted boons (by the Lord). He resorted to a holy pit dug by the discus of Hari in the north-western quarter of the Banyan tree.[1] He worshipped Maheśvara with great penance. The Brāhmaṇa thus conquered Death immediately. This excellent pit became famous by the name of that sage. By taking the holy bath there and by visiting Śiva one shall derive the benefit of a horse-sacrifice.

Śrī said:

52-55. This holy spot extends to five Krośas[2] (i.e. 5 x 3 = 15Kms) inside the sea. Two Krośas of the great holy spot fall within the shore. It is devoid of impurities. It is scattered with golden sands. It is splendid with the Nīla mountain. The Lord of Viśva (Śiva) is directly identical with Nārāyaṇa. One should restrain sensual feelings and avoid sensual objects and stay on the seashore for worshipping the Lord of the universe. The sixty-fourth Lord (?) is well known as Yameśvara. He destroys the control of Yama. By visiting this Lord and worshipping him, one shall attain the benefit of (the worship of) a crore of Liṅgas.

CHAPTER FOUR

*The Redemption of Puṇḍarīka and Aṁbarīṣa**

Śrī said:

1. The Bull-emblemed Lord who bestows everything dwells on the tip of the holy spot of the shape of a conch on the western border.

2. Nīlakaṇṭha is at the tip of the conch. This spot extending to a Krośa (3Kms) is the very rare, excellent and sanctifying holy spot of Nārāyaṇa himself.

---

1. This is the Mārkaṇḍa (Mārkaṇḍeya) Tīrtha, one of the five important Tīrthas (Pañcatīrthī) at Puri. Mārkaṇḍeśvara (Śiva) is on its bank.

2. VV 52-55 give the usual dimension of this sacred place. But it does not indicate its conch-shell shape mentioned in the next chapter vv 1-5.

* This chapter gives inter alia the locations of important sacred spots (deities, tanks) in the conch-shaped Puruṣottama Kṣetra.

3. The interior of the conch is flooded with the waters of the ocean, the Lord of rivers, up to the root of the Banyan tree.

4-10. The ocean at this place attained the status of the chief of all the Tīrthas because of its contact with the Banyan tree.

Just as the Lord, when perceived, is the bestower of salvation, so also this holy spot is conducive to salvation if a person dies here, and the ocean bestows salvation if a person takes his holy bath here.

Formerly out of anger Rudra cut off the fifth head of Brahmā. He could not get rid of that head (which clung to him). Holding it he wandered over all the regions of the Cosmic Egg. It was only after coming here that he could get rid of the skull.

The Liṅga named Kapālamocana is situated in the second *Āvarta* (turning) of the conch-shaped region (?). One who visits Kapālamocana,[1] worships it and bows down to it, gets rid of the sins of Brāhmaṇa-murder etc. One who dies in the region on the right side of it, is liberated from worldly existence.

My primordial Śakti named Vimalā[2] is in the third (turning) of the conch-shaped Kṣetra. O Dharmarāja, know that it bestows the benefits of worldly pleasures and salvation. He who devoutly worships, bows down to and glorifies it, attains everything desired and on death attains salvation.

11-14. These three are stationed in the naval region, viz. the holy pit, the Banyan tree and the Lord. From the (Tīrtha named) Kapālamocana and as far as the place where Ardhāśinī is installed, should be known as the central region of the conch. It is well-protected by the Discus-bearing Lord.

O Dharmarāja, at the beginning of creation, this Śakti of mine drinks up half of the water that was increasingly accumulated at the time of the Great Deluge. So she is known as Ardhāśinī.[3] He who visits her and bows down to her, enjoys perpetual worldly pleasures.

From the water-front of the seashore to the root on the Banyan tree the region is considered to be the bestower of salvation on insects, birds and human beings on dying here.

---

1. A Tīrtha called Kapālamocana with a similar legend of dropping of a sticking skull is found in many other sacred places in India.

2. This deity existed before the composition of MtP as it refers to its existence as '*vimalāpuruṣottame*' (MtP 13.35). Its temple was built *circa* CE 740-940 during the reign of Kara dynasty (H.K. Mahtab, *Odisā Itihāsa*).

3. A popular etymology of the name of the goddess.

15-21. The interior of this sacred place is highly meritorious. It is desired even by Devas. People see all persons dwelling here as holding discus and lotus.

All the Tīrthas together on the earth, in the firmament and in heaven are three and a half crores in number. They bestow heavenly pleasures and liberation.

This holy spot Puruṣottama is glorified as the king of all those Tīrthas. Among all the sacred places that bestow salvation this one is considered to be one which bestows (liberation called) *Sāyujya*. Those who dwell here do not become afflicted with sorrow due to old age, birth and death.

This holy tank named Rohiṇa[1] is full of water called mercifulness. It exists permanently. Merely by its contact it bestows liberation from bondage. The water within this increases during the period of dissolution and afterwards it dissolves here itself. Hence it is called Rohiṇa.

So do not feel aggrieved due to the loss to your authority here. O king of the dead, you are not the Lord of those who are entitled for liberation.

After instructing Dharmarāja thus Lakṣmī, the mother of the worlds, spoke courteously to Brahmā who was seated in front:

22-26. "O Lord of the worlds, O Brahmā, everything is known (to you). Declare that this holy spot bestows salvation on all creatures. Perform penance with Kāmākhya ('one whose name is Kāma') and Kṣetrapāla (the Guardian of the holy spot) or Vimala in view (*Defective Text*).

Nṛsiṁha (Man-Lion) to the right of the Lord is the embodiment of Brahman itself. He is refulgent after tearing off the chest of Hiraṇyakaśipu.

By simply seeing this deity all the sins will be destroyed. There is no doubt about it. The devotee will be worthy of enjoyment of worldly pleasures as well as salvation. There is no doubt about it.

A person who forsakes his life in front of this deity, shall attain *Sāyujya* with Brahman. Whatever holy rite he performs here, shall have crores and crores of times the merit thereof.

27. This is the shade of the Kalpa tree. It is illuminated by the Sun Nṛsiṁha. On death therein Avidyā (Nescience) perishes with or without perfect knowledge.

1. In Oriya language 'Rohiṇa' means a banyan tree (*Vaṭa*). Its association with the Banyan tree called 'Kalpa Vṛkṣa' gave it the name Rohiṇa. This tank is in the compound of the Jagannātha Temple.

28. Without the perfect knowledge resulting from *Śravaṇa* (listening) and other things prescribed by the Vedānta texts, which is very difficult for the ignorant people to acquire, O Brāhmaṇa, liberation is possible (to them) here.

29. In Avimukta (Vārāṇasī) the great Lord Śiva, the storehouse of mercy, whispers the knowledge of Brahman into the ears of the person who is desirous of salvation. He imparts the means of enlightenment also.

30. By means of that, by practising it intelligently, one shall attain salvation gradually (by degress). Thanks to the greatness of the instructor, his knowledge does not become deficient.

31. Those who give up their lives here shall instantaneously attain liberation from their own forms. O Yama, you need not entertain any doubt in this regard.

32. Those persons of confused minds who are bound by Karmas and those who are subject to coming into and departing from (this world), O son of Vivasvān, never get any faith in this matter.

33. They are as much confounded in their minds as a thirsty person who forsakes the sweet, cool water of Gaṅgā free from impurities and goes to a puddle.

34. (*Defective Text*) Those who leave this excellent holy place and wander over to other holy spots are like those who are satisfied with the sweet smell of a Palāśa flower (merely). The only result they get is weariness.

35. This ocean bestows salvation through holy bath. The Lord bestows salvation through his vision; the Kalpa-tree bestows salvation through its shade and the holy spot bestows salvation on men on their death anywhere (in it).

36. A man is liberated by means of that in which he has devout faith. There is no other Tīrtha like this.

37. He who abandons this Tīrtha and entertains interest in another Tīrtha is certainly deceived by the Māyā of Viṣṇu because he is too greedy and covetous.

38-41. There is no need of giving you more advice. You have directly experienced thus (when) the crow assumed the form of Viṣṇu.

Eight Śaktis have been glorified for the protection of the interior[1] of the shrine and the sacred spot. Formerly for the sake of a wife I was

1. *Antarvedī* is the area between the sea and the Banyan tree. It is the sacredmost spot in Puruṣottama Kṣetra.

meditated upon by Rudra by (undertaking) a severe penance. Gaurī who is going to be his wife has been created by me. She is the abode of all beauty and she came out from my body. At the time she was commanded by me: 'O gentle lady, do something pleasing to me in accordance with my suggestion. Protect the interior of the body shrine all round me by means of your *Mūrtis* (different forms).'

42-45. Out of love for me she stands in the quarters in eight forms: Maṅgalā stands at the root of the Banyan tree. In West stands Vimalā. Sarvamaṅgalā stands in the posterior of the conch (Kṣetra). In North Ardhāśinī and Lambā are stationed. Kālarātri stands in South and Marīcikā is in East. Caṇḍarūpā is well established behind Kālarātri. This holy spot is guarded by these Śaktis of very fierce forms. This is indeed very difficult of access to a man deficient in merits.

46-50. By visiting and glorifying these eight Śaktis all the sins will perish. One shall obtain the benefit of a horse-sacrifice.

On seeing the eight different forms of Rudrāṇī Rudra, Śaṅkara, split himself into eight forms and began worshipping the great Lord.

After propitiating Viṣṇu by means of penance he requested for an excellent boon: 'I shall stay very happily and comfortably wherever you stay, O Lord. Excepting you, O Lord of Kamalā, there is no other cause of bliss and salvation. O Lord, you are my immanent soul. Without you whence is a physical body? Those foolish persons who do not know you, take delight in unclean worldly pleasures. I have sought refuge in you who are like pure (cloudless) sky.' "

Jaimini said:

51-57. The Lord stationed himself in the middle and established Rudra as Kṣetrapāla all round. There are eight Liṅgas of Maheśvara (around), viz. Kapālamocana, Kṣetrapāla, Yameśvara, Mārkaṇḍeya, Īśāna, Bilveśa, Nīlakaṇṭha and Vaṭeśa at the root of the Banyan tree. By visiting, touching and worshipping these Liṅgas one becomes liberated.

Yama has no jurisdiction over those persons who die here in the holy spot. Achieve that object elsewhere, the object for which you came here. Yet the Lord of the universe is willing to dedicate himself to a devotee.

On being devoutly propitiated by Yama the Lord who dispels the distress of those who seek refuge in him, will cover up his Māyā by means of his discus Sudarśana.

In this excellent holy spot covered with golden sands, which could not be abandoned, she deceived Yama and made him proceed to his own abode. She considered it good and thereafter spoke to Brahmā who was present in front.

Śrī said:

58. There will be a king named Indradyumna in Satya Yuga. He will be a follower of Viṣṇu and a knower of sacred texts. He will perform all (types of) Yajñas.

59-62. That excellent king will come here and perform great worship. For the propitiation of the Lord he will perform a thousand horse-sacrifices. The Lord of the subjects will do everything for the sake of his blessings.

One tree will split into four. Viśvakarmā will make the idols out of the wooden pieces. Propitiated by Indradyumna you will be the person who will install them. O grandfather, there will be the installation of idols resembling us.

63. On hearing these words of Śrī the Four-faced Lord and Yama went back to their respective cities with great joy.

64. Remembering the greatness of the holy spot repeatedly they had their hair standing on end all over the body on account of amazement and delight.

65-66. Now, O sages, the Lord still dwells there for the sake of helping the world. He is accompanied by Bala and Subhadrā. It is the same Lord who was propitiated by Indradyumna, the glorious Lord holding the conch and the discus, who resembles a dark-blue cloud and resides in a cave of mount Nīla and has wooden physical body.

67-74. The Lord who destroys the distresses of those who bow down to him, the ocean of mercifulness, is equipped with the discus Sudarśana made of wood.

By visiting him one will be relieved from the strong bondage of sins.

O excellent sages, it is as though all the good and meritorious actions of those who see the Lord (who dispels) the threefold distress like the Moon that dispels heat, have come to fruition simultaneously.

Indeed there are many incarnations of Viṣṇu, both divine and human. (His) wonderful deeds and greatness have been described. On account of great familiarity Suras do not honour human beings (?).

O Brāhmaṇas, the minds of Devas, Asuras, human beings, Gandharvas, Serpents, Rākṣasas and lower orders of beings dwell on Hari in that wooden idol. He is the soul of everyone and he causes happiness unto everyone.

They sustain themselves by this happiness of the Lord having a unique form. One experiences there what the Vedic words of Brahman have said, viz. "It dispels all the miseries of worldly existence and gives imperishable happiness. Therefore Brahman is sung about in the Upaniṣads as 'Dārumaya' (Brahman made of wood). Indeed the idol of wood will never bestow salvation anywhere.

75. O Brāhmaṇas, a natural state cannot be obtained through an artificial one. Salvation is not an artificial one. How can it be the effect of an artificial wood?

76. The blessedness and prosperity of Brahman cannot be achieved without any basis. This excellent abode of Viṣṇu is a great mystery.

77. That idol is supramundane. It was revealed as though it was a worldly one. Where has it been heard or seen that an idol speaks?

78-82. At that time the Lord with wooden idol granted boon to Indradyumna. O sages, seek refuge in Hari, the Lord, without (seeking) anyone else as your shelter. He is the sole asylum for the wretched and helpless ones. He takes us across the ocean of worldly existence.

His feet always deserve to be saluted by the mobile and immobile beings. He is the ultimate resort. Nārāyaṇa is the source of origin of the universe. He is the cause of creation and annihilation. He liberates (us) from all sins. He dispels all miseries. He enhances prosperity and glory. He is the protector of all Yogins. He nourishes all the creatures. He holds up and sustains all the worlds. He is the speech of all the languages. He condemns all the wicked ones. He dries up all marshes (i.e. sins). He resorts to the Nīla Mountain, O sages, seek refuge in the all-pervading Lord, the only support of all.

83. Though he is motionless and wooden-formed, he indulges in graceful divine sports. Even if there is only very little of devotion, he forgives a hundred offences of men.

84. In this connection I shall narrate to you a story of the Supreme Soul abiding in a wooden body out of sport, O sages. That story absolves (one) of sins.

85. There was a Brāhmaṇa and a Kṣatriya who hailed from Kurukṣetra.[1] They became loving friends who moved about taking food together and playing together.

---

1. As stated in v 91 below,their names were Puṇḍarīka and Ambarīṣa. These are imaginary. They are in no way connected with the great royal sage and the Brahmin ascetic of the same name mentioned in the old Purāṇas.

As described in the next chapter, these confirmed sinners were liberated at the sight of Jagannātha. Such is the great merit of merely seeing the Lord.

86-88. They deviated from decent behaviour. They ate forbidden things and got deluded. They did not study the Vedas, nor ever uttered *Vaṣaṭ* (i.e. never performed holy rites). They were devoid of Svāhā and Svadhā (i.e. they gave up sacrificial rites and Śrāddha to Pitṛs). They became ineligible for the practice of religious rites. They were defiled by great sins. They imbibed liquor and rejoiced in the company of harlots. Thought about the next world never occurred to them even in dreams. Behaving in this way they spent half of their life.

89-90. Once in the course of their wanderings they came to a place enclosed for sacrifice. Hearing from afar the hymns and the fascinating words of the scriptures and seeing all those holy rites prescribed in the Śrutis, O Brāhmaṇas, those two irreligious ones developed some faith in the path of piety.

91. They remembered their caste. Puṇḍarīka and Aṁbarīṣa censured their own evil deeds and spoke to each other:

92-93. "How will we cross this vast ocean of our sins incurred by us in this very birth and that too knowingly. It cannot fade away. Even the sacred treatises do not know what extremely rare expiation for the terrible sins that we two have heaped up is available.

94. Still let us ask these Brāhmaṇas in the sacrificial assembly about the redemption. They are well-versed in the Vedas and they have realized Brahman. They will accept us on our prostrating (in front of them)."

95. After deciding thus, they paid their respects to those Brāhmaṇas. They repeatedly confessed their sinful crimes and asked them (about the modes of atonement).

96-99. On hearing their words, those excellent Brāhmaṇas kept their eyes closed. They did not say anything. With great surprise visible on their faces they looked at one another (as though they wanted to say), "Alas, extremely terrible sins have been accumulated by these vicious ones. The sacred texts cannot step in to suggest a suitable atonement. Therefore we are not competent to redeem them."

Among them there was a prominent devotee of Viṣṇu who was the chief of the Assembly. He had destroyed all sins due to the greatness of his devotion to the Lord. He was the most excellent one among those conversant with apt utterances. He laughingly spoke to them:

The Vaiṣṇava said:

100. O Brāhmaṇa, O Kṣatriya, if you desire liberation from the terrible heap of sins, go immediately to Puruṣottama.

101-107. It is the most excellent one among holy spots. It is there that Puruṣottama of wooden idol is present. The Lord had blessed the saintly king Indradyumna on account of his devotion. By propitiating that Lord of the universe, the wielder of conch, discus and iron club you will certainly attain the destruction of your sins or you will get liberation as you please.

He is like a forest-fire unto the mass of cotton (in the form) of the terrible evil deeds. This (mass of sins) cannot be wiped off by means of penance even in the course of crores of births. On seeing that Lord all the sins will be instantaneously destroyed. So do not delay. Go there quickly. Seek refuge in the Lord whose abode is on the peak of the Nīla mountain in the holy land of Utkala (Orissa) on the shores of the southern sea. That Lord, the storehouse of mercy, will grant you the accomplishment of what you desire.

On being directed thus, the Brāhmaṇa and the Kṣatriya became delighted. O Brāhmaṇas, they started towards Puruṣottama by that very path.

CHAPTER FIVE

Puṇḍarīka and Aṁbarīṣa Attain Salvation

Jaimini said:

1. They were disgusted in their minds. They gave up their association with harlots and others. They mentally meditated on Viṣṇu. They took to pure diet and holy rites.

2. After some time, they reached Hari's abode in the Nīla mountain. They took their holy bath in accordance with the directions and injunctions (in the scriptures) in the water of the Tīrtharāja.[1]

3. They stood at the entrance to the palace (i.e the shrine of Jagannātha). They prostrated with eight limbs (touching the ground), O Brāhmaṇas. They looked at the Lord but could not see him.

4. Not being able to see the Lord, their face became pale. They were agitated and anxious. They began the observance of a fast till the Lord could be perceived.

---

1. *Tīrtharāja*: sea, as all sacred rivers join the sea. Here it means the Bay of Bengal on the shore of which stands Puruṣottama Kṣetra.

5. They began to recite the name of the Lord that is conducive to the destruction of sins. On the third night they saw a mass of refulgence.

6. Again for three days they steadfastly continued their fast. In the middle of the seventh night they saw the Lord.

7. By hearing the eulogies of the Devas they became endowed with divine knowledge. After shedding off the slough of sins they saw the Lord directly.

8-13. He had the conch, the discus and the iron club in his hands. He was adorned with divine ornaments. He had placed his lotus-like feet on the back of (i.e. had put on) gem-set sandals. His eyes resembled full-blown lotuses. The Lord had a smiling face. With his left arm he had embraced Lakṣmī who stood on his left. He was seen accepting a folded betel leaf offered by Lakṣmī.

Some of his lady attendants had bejewelled canes in their hands. Others had chowries in their hands. Some held lamps with fragrant oil. Some held lamps with gems and jewels for their wicks in their hands. All of them were well-adorned and were in the prime of their youth. There stood a certain bright-looking (lady) behind him holding a gem-studded umbrella. A certain lady who scorned at (i.e. surpassed) Pramlocā (an Apsaras) by means of her resplendent bodily lustre, held the vessel of incense near his face. It was kept fumigated with Agallochum. The Lord was seen blessing the Devas in front (of him) by means of his eyes over which a lock of hair gracefully swung.

14-20. The Lord blessed with his smiles Siddhas, groups of sages and divine sages, Sanaka and others, who kept their palms joined in reverence, with shoulders lowered in humility. They eulogized the Lord separately. Gandharvas beginning with Nārada were engaged in singing sweet and fascinating divine songs. The Lord attentively listened to them and gracefully blessed them with compassion.

In front of the Lord eminent Vaiṣṇavas, Prahlāda[1] and others, were meditating on his form. The Lord kept their minds attracted towards his person.

The Lord revealed his Cosmic form by means of the Devas and others who were reflected in the Kaustubha jewel that adorned his chest.

From above a shower of divine flowers was falling and the Lord

1. Son of demon Hiraṇyakaśipu. He was a very great devotee of Viṣṇu. It was to save him that Viṣṇu incarnated as Nṛsiṁha and killed Hiraṇyakaśipu. BhP regards him as a great Vaiṣṇava.

stood below. He looked at the group of celestial damsels whose splendour faded on account of the proximity of Lakṣmī. The Lord had many graceful movements of his body and he looked fascinating. On seeing the Lord with such divine grace and charm the Brāhmaṇa and the Kṣatriya became masters of all lores in a moment, O Brāhmaṇas. They circumambulated the Lord of Devas three times. They joyously prostrated (at his feet). With palms joined in reverence they eulogized him with great joy.

Puṇḍarīka said:

21. Obeisance to you, O supporter of the universe, O Nārāyaṇa, the cause of creation, sustenance and annihilation. Salute to you, O supreme soul, O ultimate resort.

22. You alone are the greatest truth, free from origin and destruction. Those who have the vision born of meditation know you as of the nature of eternal bliss.

23. How can those with confounded hearts know you who are pure consciousness, who are the Lord of the worlds, the basis (of the universe), greater than the greatest and absolutely free from impurities?

24. Those whose minds are perturbed on account of their desire to acquire sensual objects are excessively miserable. They are exhausted in the path of coming and going (transmigration of the soul in Saṁsāra). Are they ever happy?

25. Be compassionate and merciful towards me, O Lord. I have sought refuge in you. I am extremely wretched. I am confounded and foolish. I have committed misdeeds. I have fallen into the ocean of worldly existence.

26. In the whole of this world, O Lord, who else is our kinsman? Who is that person showing kindness to the wretched and the helpless even after neglecting his (more urgent) duties?

27. O ocean of mercy, do save me who am perpetually moving up and down like a machine for drawing water, undergoing the torture of high and low movements.

28. You are the person who bestows salvation gracefully and sportingly. Those foolish persons who worship you with *Yogakṣema* (acquisition of what is not acquired and preservation of what is acquired) as their motive are deluded by your Māyā.

29. If your name *Nārāyaṇa* is pronounced even by chance, O Lord of the worlds, it becomes superior even to you.[1] It is the sole means

1. A reference to Ajāmila, a sinner who was liberated by pronouncing the name Nārāyaṇa (BhP VI, Chs 2 and 3). It illustrates the efficacy of God's name.

for achieving the fourfold aim (of life).

30. But you grant different Siddhis through several Yajñas (performed by men). You are the only refuge, O Lord, to those who have fallen into the ocean of worldly existence.

31. In order to take a senseless person to the other shore of the ocean of worldly existence, you are seated in the boat of knowledge with your hands on the oar of mercifulness.

32-33. You alone are powerful enough to grant salvation on being moved by exclusive devotion. Other Devas who have been mentioned in the scriptural texts as bestower of salvation lead (persons) to devotion unto you who like the Pot-born Sage (Agastya)[1] dries up the ocean of misery.

34. Hence, O Lord, be pleased. Grant me a firm devotion unto your lotus-like feet, whereby I can cross the sea of frightful worldly existence that is very difficult to cross (otherwise). I could then spare myself the strain of seeking the help of the Yogic path of eight ancillaries.[2]

35. I have nothing to do with the three things (aims in life) viz. virtue, wealth and love. They are sought after by persons of bad intellect. They are worthless. They give little happiness but great disadvantage. Command me to immerse myself in the ocean of happiness that surges up by meditating upon the pair of your lotus-like feet.

36. After eulogizing thus, the Brāhmaṇa fell at the lotus-like feet of the Lord of the universe saying " Save me, O Kṛṣṇa". His words were drenched (and choked) with tears. He got up again and remained praying with palms joined in reverence.

Ambarīṣa said:

37. Be pleased, O Lord, O soul immanent in everyone, You have innumerable heads and arms. Obeisance to you, O Lord with countless noses, eyes, hands and feet.

38. You are beyond the thirty-six principles.[3] Though devoid of extension, you display and manifest the illusory phenomena of the uni-

1. This exploit of Agastya (drinking-up of all the waters of the sea) is mentioned in Mbh, Vana 105.3-6.

2. The eight *aṅgas* (ancillaries) of Yoga are: Yama, Niyama, Āsana, Prāṇāyāma, Dhyāna, Dhāraṇā and Samādhi.

3. Śaivas and Śāktas add twelve intangible principles to the list of twenty-four principles of Sāṅkhya. The cult of Jagannātha synthesises both Vaiṣṇavism and Śaivism. Hence Jagannātha's transcendence of 36 principles.

verse. You are the abode of the four types of living beings. O Lord with Cosmic Form, obeisance to you.

39-40. You are single-footed, three-footed and firmament-footed. Your feet are Tīrthas. Obeisance to that splendid soul from whose feet Gaṅgā rises and sanctifies the three worlds, whose name is glorified as purifying the sins including Brāhmaṇa-slaughter, and who is the bestower of all auspiciousness.

41. O Lord, all Siddhis are achieved even by glorifying your name, yet out of curiosity the learned men of great intellect seek you.

42. If we resort to it, O Lord, the sacred water from your feet dispels all distresses. Make my devotion to your feet firm and steady. I have been assailed by the three kinds of distress.

43-44. I have no other Lord. Today I have nothing else to request you, prostrating myself before you. O Lord of the universe, I request a thousand times that my devotion to your lotus-like feet may be steadfast as long as I am alive. It is the seed, as it were, of all *Puruṣārthas* (aims of human life).

45. It is due to that devotion that Brahmā accomplished the creation of the universe, that Rudra annihilates everything and that Lakṣmī bestows prosperity.

46-47. O Lord merciful unto the wretched, with my mind dwelling exclusively on you, I request you for that devotion. I am sinking in the mire of the primordial *Avidyā* (nescience) which is very difficult to cross and is very dense. O Lord of the universe, I perish in the absence of a support. There is no other ultimate resort for me than devotion unto you of exalted majesty.

48. The different paths opened up by Śrutis, Smṛtis etc. are causes of delusion. These are incompetent to function if they exclude devotion to you.

49-52a. O Lord, I have no other refuge. Be merciful unto me.

After eulogizing thus joyously he fell down like a rod on the ground near the lotus-like feet of the Lord of the universe, repeatedly uttering "Be pleased".

Then all those Devas duly eulogized and worshipped Keśava. They went back to heaven fully satisfied by his graceful, benign glances (fallen on them).

Puṇḍarīka and Aṁbarīṣa then opened their eyes. Since they were deluded by the Māyā of Viṣṇu, they thought that what they had seen was only a dream.

52b-58. After seeing the divine grace and charm with the mortal eye directly, now they reverted to human feelings and emotions. Then they saw the Lord (in the shrine) seated on the divine throne. He resembled a dark cloud. His eyes were large like full-blown lotus. His lips were red and the nose charming. He was adorned with divine earrings. He held the conch, the discus, the iron-club and the lotus. He wore a garland of sylvan flowers. His chest was stout (and muscular). He had a charming necklace. He was brilliant with a valuable crown. He had on his chest the Śrīvatsa mark and the jewel Kaustubha. He was adorned with divine armlets. He had long arms. He was in complete readiness for saving the wretched and the distressed. He had a golden thread (round his neck) with a big jewel set in the middle. He wore divine yellow garment and had divine garlands and sweet-smelling unguents. He was seated on a golden lotus-like seat. He was closely embraced by Śrī. He dispelled the distress of those who resorted to him. He was an ocean of nectar that had surged up. He was like the Kalpa tree in full bloom bestowing the fruits of all desires.

59-63a. They saw the wielder of plough as a weapon (Balabhadra) seated on his right side. It is he with whom the Lord supports the universe with great strength.[1] He was the king of Serpents adorned with seven hoods. He was as lofty as the peak of Kailāsa. He was white in complexion and resplendent with gold ear-rings. He had a garland of variegated forest-flowers. He wore a divine, dark-coloured, silken robe. Inebriated with liquor, his lotus-like eyes rolled always. His back was slightly bent and the chest projected forward. His body was coiled up. His four arms were brilliant with the conch, the discus, the iron-club and the lotus. He was handsome with different kinds of ornaments. He was a destroyer of the sins of those who bowed down (to him).

63b-68. They saw the gentle lady Subhadrā in between them. She was as pink as saffron.

They saw Lakṣmī who was the abode of all beauty, who was bowed down to by all the Devas. She was stationed in the lotus-like heart of the Lord of Lakṣmī. She was sitting separately. The goddess held an excellent lotus. Her garments and ornaments were of divine nature. She was the destroyer of all sins. She redeemed those who were immersed

1. Balabhadra is an incarnation of Śeṣa, the serpent who supports the Earth. Hence his (Śeṣa's) attributes are applied to Balabhadra. Our Purāṇa, like Harivaṁśa, describes him as a liquor-addict but, strangely enough, he proclaimed total prohibition at Dvārakā at a late stage (Mbh, Mausala 1.29).

in the ocean of worldly existence. She was the source of origin of deities.

They saw the excellent discus of Viṣṇu stationed on his left side. O Brāhmaṇas, it was made out of wood. It was brilliantly embellished in gold.

On seeing Viṣṇu stationed in four forms,[1] that Brāhmaṇa and the Kṣatriya considered their exertion in the early dawn fruitful. Recollecting that charming dream of sport, they were surprised.

69. "This is not a mere wooden idol. It is Brahman itself that shines here." They believed in this utterance of the Brāhmaṇas in the sacrificial assembly.

70-72. 'Where are we (what great difference there is), the great sinners who deserve only tortures; where is this manifestation of Viṣṇu in the assembly of the Suras! We had been fools. Now we have mastered the eighteen lores.[2] Hence this is not an error on our part. It is real knowledge unto us. That has been proved. They had said that the Brahman of wooden form stood at the root of the Banyan tree on the shore of the Tīrtharāja. On seeing it directly, a creature is liberated.

73-75. This Lord of the worlds is that very same (Brahman). He has four forms when he incarnates on the earth. He shines in four forms.

Therefore let us retain our life and stay in his presence. We shall not go elsewhere. We shall be averse to worthless pursuits of lust.'

After deciding thus, O sages, those two became engrossed in devotion to Viṣṇu. Always repeating the names of Nārāyaṇa, they attained salvation.

Jaimini said:

76-77. It is just incidentally that this secret conducive to the destruction of sins has been told. Those who listen to this story of Puṇḍarīka and Aṁbarīṣa and those who recite it always with great joy, go to the abode of Viṣṇu with great joy. They will go to the abode of Viṣṇu with all sins dispelled.

---

1. In Jagannātha Temple at Puri the four images, viz. Jagannātha, Balabhadra, Subhadrā and Sudarśana are worshipped. They as if constitute one object of worship, viz. Jagannātha and are called *caturdhā mūrti*. Hence the epithet *caturdhāvasthita*.

2. Eighteen Lores: Normally four Vedas, six Aṅgas of Vedas (such as Śikṣā, Kalpa etc.), Mīmāṁsā, Nyāya, Dharmaśāstra and Purāṇa constitute 14 lores. To these are added Āyurveda (Science of Medicine), Dhanurveda (Military Science), Gāndharva Veda (Science of Music) and Arthaśāstra (Political Economy) totalling to eighteen Lores.

CHAPTER SIX

*Description of the Land of Utkala**

The sages enquired:

1. In which land is that holy spot Puruṣottama, O excellent Brāhmaṇa, where Nārāyaṇa reveals himself directly in the form of a wooden idol?

Jaimini said:

2. There is a land named Utkala. It is famous and is very sacred. There are many Tīrthas and holy shrines there.

3. The land is situated on the shore of the Southern Sea. The persons living there are models of good conduct.

4-6. The Brāhmaṇas there are given to good behaviour and the study of the Vedas. They perform Yajñas. Ever since the beginning of the creation there have been Vedas and expounders of Vedas and Śāstras (sacred literature). This land is glorified as the home of eighteen Vidyās (lores). At the behest of Nārāyaṇa Lakṣmī dwells in every house (there). The people are by nature shy and humble. They are free from mental agony and physical ailments. They are devoted to their parents. They are truthful in speech and are followers of Viṣṇu.

7. There is no one here who is not a devotee of Viṣṇu. There is no atheist here. All the people are ever ready to bring about the welfare of others. No one is greedy, knavish or wicked.

8. All the people are long-lived. Women consider their husbands gods. They are well-behaved and righteous and they are well-adorned with bashfulness and charity.

9. They have pride in their beauty and youthfulness. They adorn themselves with all kinds of ornaments. They are great experts in the conduct of life, befitting their nobility, chastity, age and decency.

---

*Utkala is a part of modern Orissa. According to our text (vv 27-28 in this Chapter) the country Utkala was situated between the Southern Sea (The Bay of Bengal) and the river Ṛṣikulyā; on the other side it extended from Mahānadī to the river Suvarṇarekhā. According to BmP 47.7 Utkala and Kaliṅga were separate. In Purāṇic age the names Utkala or Oḍra were mostly used for Puri region. Strangely enough, Utkala and Oḍra are not included in the 72 countries of Kaumārikā Khaṇḍa of the SkP unless we presume Oḍḍiānā in the list is Oḍra.

This chapter depicts Utkala as heaven on the earth (Bhūsvarga).

10. The Kṣatriyas there are devoted to their duties. They are scrupulously engaged in protecting the subjects. They are liberal in charitable gifts. They are well-versed in the use of weapons and learning sacred treatises.

11-13. All of them always perform Yajñas with plenty of monetary gifts. Their sacrificial altars have the sacred posts decorated with gold. In their homes guests are worshipped far beyond their expectations. The Vaiśyas are engaged in such activities as agriculture, trade and breeding cattle. They please and propitiate with devotion and also plenty of wealth Devas, preceptors and Brāhmaṇas. If any suppliant goes to any house, he has no need to go to any other house.

14. They are experts in music, poetry, arts and crafts. They are pleasing in speech. The Śūdras there are virtuous and engaged in holy baths, charitable gifts and other pious activities.

15. They serve Brāhmaṇas, Kṣatriyas and Vaiśyas, physically, mentally, verbally and by means of wealth. Persons of mixed castes too are well-established in their respective duties.

16. The seasons do not have any vagaries; the clouds do not shower untimely. There is no damage to plants and vegetation. There is no desert land. Hunger does not afflict the subjects.

17. There is neither famine nor any epidemic (in the land). There is no split or division in the realm. There is no object not available there, if at all it exists on the earth.

18-26. This land is full of all good qualities and different kinds of trees and creepers, viz. Arjuna, Aśoka, Punnāga (Calophyllum inophyllum), Tāla (Palmyra), Hintāla (Phoenix tree), Śāla (Sal tree), Prācīnāmalaka (Flacourtia cataphracta), Lodhra (Svamplocos racemosa), Bakulas, Nāgakesaras, Coconut Palms, Priyālas, Saralas, Himālayan cedars, Dhavas, Calectu, Marmelos, Jackfruits, Wood Apples, Caṁpakas, Karṇikāras, Kovidāras, Pāṭalas,Kadambas, Margosa, Niculas, Mangoes, Embylic Myrobalans, Oranges, Citrons, Nīpakas, Pomegranates, flowering plants of various varieties such as Mandāra, Pārijāta etc., Holy Fig Trees, Agallochum, Sandal trees, Kharjūras (Date Palms), Āmrātakas, Siddhas, Mucakundas (Pterospermunt acerifolium), Kiṁśukas, Tindukas , Saptaparṇas, Aśvatthas, Bibhītakas and various other trees of very charming nature.

There are Mālatīs, Kundas, Bāṇas, Black Karavīras, Ketakīs, Atimuktas, Kubjas, Cardamom, Lavaṅga (cloves), Kaṁkolas, Dāḍimas, Bījapūrakas etc. There are rows of areca-palms and many hundreds of parks and gardens. The land is surrounded by mountains and rivers. This excellent land, O brilliant Brāhmaṇas, is named Utkala.

27-28. This land is situated between Svarṇarekhā and Mahānadī reaching as far as Ṛṣikulyā that falls into the Southern Sea. In this holy spot there are many excellent shrines and sacred temples. Formerly they have been described to you, O Brāhmaṇas, in the course of the pilgrimage by me. This land of Puruṣottama is said to be now *Bhūsvarga* ('Heaven on the Earth').

CHAPTER SEVEN

The Story of Indradyumna

The sages asked:

1-3. O sage, in which Yuga did Indradyumna[1] live? In which land was his (capital) city? How did he go to Puruṣottama and how did he cause the idol to be made? Describe all these truthfully and in detail, O great sage, O omniscient one. We have great eagerness (to hear).

Jaimini said:

4-5. Very well, O excellent Brāhmaṇas, what you ask for is relevant. His (Indradyumna's) ancient anecdote helps to dispel all sins. It is meritorious and splendid. It yields worldly pleasures and salvation. I shall recount it as it happened in Kṛtayuga. Listen ye all, O sages, with great attention and with all the sense-organs under control.

6. There was a great king in Kṛtayuga, O Brāhmaṇas, (named) Indradyumna. That righteous-souled one belonged to the Solar race and was the fifth person (i.e. descendant) from the creator (Brahmā).

7. He was truthful in speech and of good conduct. He was of spotless fame and was the most prominent among sāttvika persons. He protected his subjects like his own children with justice.

8. He was expert in the Science of Spirit (i.e. perfect knowledge of Brahman). He was a hero with increasing (interest) in war. He was always active with devotion to his parents. He always worshipped Brāhmaṇas.

1. This king is different from the Indradyumna who was expelled from heaven for becoming obliterated from public memory (Mbh, Vana, Ch. 199). This Indradyumna is a legendary king of Avantī who built the temple of Jagannātha at Puri. His life story forms an essential part of this Purāṇa.

9. He had mastered the eighteen branches of learning and was like another Bṛhaspati (i.e. Preceptor of gods). In prosperity and glory he was another Indra and in the accumulation of wealth in the treasury he was (another) Kubera.

10. He was handsome with charming features and excellent grace. He was of good behaviour. He was charitable, an enjoyer of pleasures and one of sweet speech. He performed all Yajñas. He was friendly with Brāhmaṇas. He truthfully kept his promises.

11. He was the beloved of men and women like the moon on the full-moon day. (At the same time) he, being the exterminator of his enemies, was too dazzling to look at.

12-14. He was a devotee of Viṣṇu and very truthful. He had subdued anger and the sense-organs. He performed Rājasūya, the most excellent Yajña, and a thousand horse-sacrifices. He was highly glorious, desirous of salvation and devoted to virtue and piety. Thus endowed with all good qualities the king ruled over the earth at the (capital) city named Avantī situated in Mālava[1] country and well known all over the earth. He lived in that city which was rich in all kinds of precious stones and like another Amarāvatī (the capital of Indra).

15. Living there, the king carried on excellent and exceedingly wonderful devotional activities in regard to Viṣṇu mentally, verbally and physically.

16-18. While he was thus (devotionally) active, once, at the time of the worship of the Lord, the consort of Lakṣmī, within the *sanctum sanctorum*, he respectfully addressed his priest who was seated along with learned men, poets, Brāhmaṇas well-versed in the Vedas as well as Astrologers of great fame, "Let that excellent holy spot be known where we can see Jagannātha ('Lord of the worlds') with these (mortal) eyes."

19. On being asked thus by the excellent king, a follower of Viṣṇu, the priest faced the assembly of pilgrims and spoke these words with humility.

20. "O, O ye virtuous ones, experts in the knowledge of holy spots, eager to undertake pilgrimages, what our Lord intends has been heard by you all indeed."

1. Modern Ujjain. Old Purāṇas used it as the name of a country up to *circa* 200 CE. Avantī came to be known as Mālava after 700-800 CE (AGP 158-59). The mention of Mālava as a country here shows that this portion of the Purāṇa was composed after 700-800.

21. After knowing his intention, a certain eloquent person who had visited a number of holy spots said to the king joyously, as he stood there with palms joined in reverence:

22. "O Lord, O king, I have travelled through many holy places on the earth ever since my childhood. These (Tīrthas) have only been heard of by others.

23. There is a land in the subcontinent of Bhārata, famous as Oḍhra Deśa (i.e. Utkala, Orissa). It is on the shore of the Southern Ocean. The holy spot is Śrī Puruṣottama.

24-25. There is a mountain named Nīlagiri there. It is surrounded by forests all round. In the middle thereof is a Kalpa tree (i.e. a Banyan tree) extending to a *Krośa* (3 Kms.). If one enters its shade one dispels the sin of the slaughter of a Brāhmaṇa. To the west thereof is the famous holy pool named Rauhiṇa.

26-28. It is filled with primordial waters (*kāraṇāṁbhobhiḥ*). By means of its mere contact it bestows salvation. On its eastern bank is the body (i.e. idol) of Śrīvāsudeva made out of sapphires.[1] It is directly the bestower of salvation. He who takes his holy bath in the *Kuṇḍa* (holy pool) there and visits Puruṣottama acquires the benefit of a thousand horse-sacrifices and then becomes liberated.

There is an excellent hermitage there, famous as Śabara Dīpaka.[2]

29-30. It is on the western side of the Lord and is encircled by the abodes of Śabaras (hunters). There is a footpath leading to the temple of Viṣṇu . It is there that Jagannātha himself is present holding the conch, the discus and the iron club. The storehouse of mercifulness grants salvation to all living creatures who visit (the Lord).

31. O king, I spent a year there in Śrīpuruṣottama observing holy rites and staying in the forest for the propitiation of the Lord of Devas.

32-33. The divine scent, O great king, of the heaven-dwellers who came there every night for visiting the Lord, is superhuman. Different kinds of prayerful words are heard. Showers of the flowers of Kalpa tree are seen. This greatness is not revealed in any other shrine of Viṣṇu.

34-39. An ancient legend too is heard there, O king. After seeing Mādhava a crow, a being of lower species, became liberated, though it is not authorized to perform any meritorious deed and though it was

1. The idol of Vāsudeva may as well be of black stone as '*nīla*' means 'black' also.

2. Jagannātha appears to be originally a god of a hill-people called Śabaras.

devoid of knowledge, O king. Being thirsty it came to the Rauhiṇa Kuṇḍa in order to drink water. As the time had come, it gave up its life and attained *Sārupya* with Viṣṇu.

Formerly I had been stupid and ignorant. But thanks to his favour, now perhaps Śeṣa is second to me in the knowledge of the eighteen branches of learning. My mind has become free from impurities.

I do not see any Lord other than Viṣṇu. Since you are a devotee of Viṣṇu and are always steadfast in holy rites, I have come to you for the sake of instructing you. Neither wealth nor a plot of land is being requested from you now. This is understood by me as useless. Worship Śrīdhara dwelling there."

40-41. After saying thus that man with matted hair vanished immediately even as everyone was looking on. The king was struck with great wonder. He became excited thinking, 'How can I carry this on?' He spoke to the priest in regard to the accomplishment thereof:

Indradyumna said:

42. This incident is superhuman. After hearing this from a superhuman person my intellect prompts me (to go) to the place where that Gadādhara is present.

43. O excellent Brāhmaṇa, my virtue, wealth and love are under your control. The three aims in life have been accomplished through your grace which was not against me (i.e. you were favourable to me).

44. If now, O excellent Brāhmaṇa, you go on this errand, all the four aims of my life shall be achieved by me.

The priest said:

45. Of course, I shall do this so that you will be able to see with your eyes covered with skin (i.e. your physical, human eyes) Keśava, the Lord who directly confers liberation (from Saṁsāra).

46. I shall endeavour in this matter (so carefully) that we all shall reside in the holy spot (called) Śrī Puruṣottama along with our associates and assistants.

47. What can be a better success than this, O king, in the birth of a human being, if you can directly perceive Mādhava, the Puruṣa beyond Tamas.

48. My younger brother named Vidyāpati will also go now along with your spies who frequently tour many lands.

49-50. He will go there and after visiting the Lord of the universe there on the mountain, he will make a piece of land fit for the residence of your camp. He will soon bring the news (that everything) has been fully arranged. It will be for our welfare.

On hearing his words the king said again:

Indradyumna said:

51-54a. Good, O Brāhmaṇa! Excellent arrangement has been thought of after due contemplation. Even at the outset, on hearing about this, I have decided that I will reside in that holy place in the presence of the Lord. So let your brother go. He will accomplish everything as desired.

After saying this the king entered the inner apartment joyously. At the behest of the king the priest honoured all of them duly and made them go to their respective hermitages.

54b-56. An auspicious hour was fixed by the astrologers. After performing the holy rites (called *Svastyayana*[1])for his safe journey, the Brāhmaṇa bade him farewell. He got into a flower-bedecked chariot along with trustworthy emissaries.

Then, O Brāhmaṇas, seated in the middle of the chariot that Brāhmaṇa Vidyāpati thought thus in his mind:

57. 'Oh! my life is fruitful. My night has dawned into a fine morning since I will be viewing the lotus-like face of the Lord that dispels sins.

58-59. Ascetics strive day and night through various means beginning with *Śravaṇa* (listening) etc. and then see the Lord dwelling in (their) lotus-like heart. I will now see that Discus-bearing Lord directly, the Lord who is residing on the peak of the Nīla mountain, who holds a physical form but who dispels all connections with physical bodies.

60. It is not possible to fix and visualize the form of the Lord through the words of Śruti, Smṛti, Itihāsas and Purāṇas. I will now see that extraordinary form of the Storehouse of Fortune and cross the ocean of worldly existence.

61. To-day I will directly visualize that Lord of the universe who is incomprehensible and immeasurable, who dwells on the mountain and by glorifying whose names the three groups of sins[2] of those who remember him perish.

---

1. An expiatory rite to avert evil. Benedictory mantras are used therein.
2. Sins committed by thought, word and deed.

62. In the case of one who does not meditate on the lotus-like feet of the Lord, the abundant darkness that has settled in his soul does not perish through his Karmas. At every step he will be acquiring more and more misery.

63. The Vedāntic passages say that one may propitiate the subtle spirit dwelling in the soul encased in five sheaths (i.e. those of *Anna*, *Prāṇa* etc.) and enclosed in its own cavity, but one may not realize it. I salute that Primordial Being that can be realized only by its own *Vidyā* (knowledge).

64. I seek refuge in that Lord of the entire universe, each of whose bodily hair supports a Cosmic Egg, who has a thousand (innumerable) heads, feet and eyes, who is ancient and eternal and from whose breath the mass of the Vedas has come out.

65-66. I seek refuge in that Lord who has *Praṇava* (Oṁkāra) for his body, who is devoid of all despicable forms fashioned or superimposed and through whose Māyā this illusory visible world has been created with creation, sustenance and annihilation as its nature. I will directly view that Lord near whom a being of the lower order came casually for the sake of quenching its thirst and attained the *Sārūpya* type of salvation with that very body.

67. Ah! How wonderful it is that one merit of mine acquired in the course of a crore of lives has cropped up indicating my good luck! With these mortal eyes I will see the bulbous root (i.e. cause) of the universe.'

68. Thinking thus, with a delighted mind, the Brāhmaṇa did not notice that a long distance had been covered, thanks to the speed of the chariot.

69-70. After midday had passed and a greater part of the day yet remained, the land named Oḍhra was seen ahead on the way itself. O Brāhmaṇas, this land is an ornament unto the universe.[1] It sanctifies the sphere of the earth.

Thus observing forest regions, mountains, forts etc. on the way he reached the banks of Mahānadī[2] at the time of sunset.

---

1. Such complimentary references to Oḍhra or Utkala (a part of Orissa) throughout the work and a eulogy of that land in one complete chapter (Ch. 6) calling it 'a *Bhūsvarga*' (Heaven on earth), the ornament of the universe show that the author was a resident of Oḍhra.

2. A famous river in Orissa. Formerly it marked the border of Kaliṅga.

71. The Brāhmaṇa got down from the chariot and performed the daily religious rites with sincerity. After performing the evening Sandhyā prayer he meditated on the Slayer of Madhu.

72-75. He spent the night within the chariot itself. Early in the morning, he concluded his daily religious rites and hurriedly crossed Mahānadī.

Contemplating on Govinda as he was seated in the chariot, he set out. On the way he saw, O Brāhmaṇas, the villages of those well-versed in Vedas, who performed Yajñas and were of fiery splendour. The villages were adorned with areca palms. After passing through the Ekāmraka forest[1] the Brāhmaṇa saw the people holding a conch, a discus, an iron-club and a lotus. He thought as though he had taken a new birth and had adopted a divine form.

76. He immediately got down from the chariot and prostrated with eight limbs touching the ground. His eyes became filled with tears of joy. He did not see anything else.

77-78. O Brāhmaṇas, he saw Viṣṇu mentally and externally. He proceeded thus seeing, meditating on and eulogizing Hari. He saw the Nīla mountain covered with forests and adorned with Kalpa and banyan trees. It scraped the sky and destroyed the sins of those who visit it.

79-80. It is the extremely wonderful abode of Hari in embodied form. Climbing on to the top of the mountain, the Brāhmaṇa who was eager to see Mukunda, sought the path all round but could not see one. Therefore he spread Darbha grass on the ground, and controlling his speech slept there.

81. For the vision of the Lord, he sought refuge in him alone. Thereupon he heard a superhuman speech behind the mountain.

82-84. It was the voice of those who were talking together on the subject of devotion to the Lord. Therefore, Vidyāpati became delighted and followed the voice, O Brāhmaṇas. He saw the seat of lighting of the holy shrine?[2] It was known as Śabaradīpaka. All round, it was surrounded by the houses of Śabaras (hunters). The Brāhmaṇa went there slowly and entered the premises with great humility. (There) he saw those devotees of Viṣṇu holding conch, discus and iron-club.

85-88. The Brāhmaṇa bowed down his head and stood there with palms joined in reverence. Then a Śabara called Viśvāvasu, whose body was covered with grey hair and who had completed the worship

1. Forest area round modern Bhuvaneshvar.
2. Probably 'the kṣetra shaped like a lamp' (*kṣetrasya dīpasaṁsthānam*).

of Hari, came out from the middle of the mountain that very moment. He appeared splendid with the remnants of the worship (in his hand). On seeing him the Brāhmaṇa was delighted. He thought thus: 'This leading devotee of Viṣṇu has come here from the abode of Hari. He is tired. He is bedecked with the remnants of the worship. From him I shall get the rare details of Viṣṇu.'

Even as the Brāhmaṇa was thinking thus, he was addressed by the Śabara:

The Śabara said:

89-90. From where have you come to this impassable forest region? You are extremely tired with hunger and thirst. Be pleased to sit here comfortably for a long time.

He gave him *Pādya* and a seat as well as *Arghya*. Viśvāvasu then said to the Brāhmaṇa with humility in his speech, explaining the thing under reference:

91-92. "How do you wish to sustain your life (i.e. satisfy your hunger)? O Brāhmaṇa, with fruits or with cooked food? Whatever is liked by you will be given to you by me, O Brāhmaṇa. It is my good luck, O holy lord. My life has become fruitful since you have come to my house like another Viṣṇu himself."

93-99. As the Śabara said this, the eminent Brāhmaṇa said to him: "O great devotee of Viṣṇu, I have nothing to do with fruits or cooked food. O good Sir, see that the purpose for which I have come from a great distance is fulfilled. I am the priest of king Indradyumna, a resident of the city of Avantī. I have come here desirous of seeing Viṣṇu.

In front of the king there was an assemblage of pilgrims. At that time this was heard. In the context of Tīrthas and holy spots, this was referred to by someone. This holy spot was mentioned in front of the king by a person with matted hair. That Brāhmaṇa mentioned everything in the proper order. It is for this purpose, O gentle Sir, that I have been sent by the anxious king, i.e. to see Hari Nīlamādhava dwelling here. Until I see the Lord and take the news to the king, I shall be observing fast surely. Hence, O gentle Sir, show Viṣṇu unto me."

CHAPTER EIGHT

The Messenger Vidyāpati Returns

Jaimini said:

1-4. On being told thus by the Brāhmaṇa, the Śabara became worried. He thought thus: 'Janārdana who is kept secret is our means of sustenance. Our bad luck appears impending due to which he is to become known to all people.[1] If I do not show (Lord) to this Brāhmaṇa, he will curse me. A Brāhmaṇa is to be honoured by everyone, particularly when he is a guest. If his desires are not fulfilled, both the worlds of mine will be fruitless.

5-10. When this Lord vanishes, when Mādhava becomes invisible beneath the ground, King Indradyumna of exploits comparable to Indra, who is to go to the world of Brahmā along with his physical body, will come here along with his subjects and perform a hundred horse-sacrifices. He will install the four forms of Viṣṇu in wood. If the Brāhmaṇa-guest be highly fortunate, the disappearance of the Lord will be imminent. Hence I will show him Acyuta of Nīlendramaṇi (having the colour of blue sapphire). When a duty has been ordained by fate, no manly effort to avert it is advisable.'

(Pondering over this repeatedly) in his mind the Śabara said to the Brāhmaṇa who was meditating on the immutableViṣṇu in front:

The Śabara said:

11. The news that King Indradyumna will come and reside here has already been (traditionally) heard by us before.

12. You are more fortunate than he, because, O Brāhmaṇa, you will be seeing Nīlamādhava (directly) even prior to him. Come. Let us go to the ridge.

13-16. After saying this, he grasped him by the hand and went to the forest along the path. He climbed up and up along the rugged and rocky path full of difficulties. Only one man could walk along that path at

1. The Śabara correctly and helplessly anticipates the danger that a new advanced culture is going to swallow up the simple primitive culture of the aboriginal Śabaras.

a time. The way was even more difficult to traverse on account of thorns. As the path was nearly enveloped in darkness he guided the Brāhmaṇa by oral directions.

Within two Muhūrtas they reached the bank of the holy tank Rauhiṇa. On seeing it he said to the Brāhmaṇa, "O excellent Brāhmaṇa, this tank is a great Tīrtha named Rauhiṇa. It is the source of all waters. By taking holy bath here one goes to the abode of Lord Viṣṇu, O Brāhmaṇa.

17. To the east of it there is the great Banyan tree like the Kalpa tree with plenty of shade. One who comes within the shade of this tree dispels the sin of Brāhmaṇa-slaughter.

18. Between these two, inside the bushy growth of trees, see directly the Lord of the universe expounded in the Vedāntas.

19. By having a view of him you shall shed off the mass of your sins. After this you will have no grief of falling into the ocean of worldly existence."

Jaimini said:

20-21. The Brāhmaṇa took his holy bath in the Kuṇḍa. Highly delighted in his mind, the extremely intelligent one bent down and lowered his head from a distance. Mentally and verbally he eulogized Hari with concentration and words choked with delight.

Vidyāpati said:

22. O Puruṣa beyond Pradhāna, O all-pervading one, O Lord greater than the greatest, O Lord transforming yourself into the mobile and immobile beings, O highest reality, obeisance to you.

23. O Lord of the universe, you are the only person worthy of being propitiated by means of all holy rites laid down in Śrutis, Smṛtis, Purāṇas and Itihāsas.

24-25. O Supreme Lord, it is from you that the whole of this universe is evolved at the time of creation. O God, it has you as its support and it is protected by you alone. At the end of the Kalpa everything is withdrawn in the space in your belly and it stays there comfortably.[1] O Soul of all, O Immanent Soul, obeisance to you.

26. Salute to you, the Lord of Devas; obeisance to you in the form

1. It is believed that when at the end of the Kalpa the universe is destroyed externally, actually it is taken in the belly of the Lord where with its mobile and immobile beings it remains intact.

of the *Trayī* (three Vedas). Hail to you who always illuminate the universe (assuming) the forms of the Sun, the Moon etc!

27. Obeisance to that sanctifier due to the contact with whose lotus-like feet Gaṅgā becomes filled with all the Tīrthas and purifies all the worlds.

28. Hail to you who enliven the universe and transform the *Havis* (ghee offerings in sacrifices) that have been sanctified by Mantras and been duly poured in the (sacred) fires!

29. Obeisance to that *Ātman* (Soul) identical with Brahman, who is devoid of all blemishes and is an embodiment of bliss, on a part of whom all the worlds subsist.

30. Hail to you, the witness unto the universe, to the form free from impurities, to the Lord of auspicious forms, who are the master of Māyā and devoid of all attachments!

31. Obeisance to you who have all forms, have many (innumerable) feet, eyes, heads, mouths and arms, who conquer everything and who have the forms of all Jīvas.

32. Obeisance to you, O lover of Kamalā (Lakṣmī). Bow to you, O lotus-seated one; obeisance, O Lord with eyes like petals of lotus; save me, O Puruṣottama.

33. Redeem me from this multitude of miseries of worldly existence. I am suffering by transmigrating in this worthless world. I am harassed by ailments and griefs. I have sought refuge in your lotus-like feet.

Jaimini said:

34-35. After thus eulogizing the Lord of Suras, who has Praṇava (*Oṁ*) for his form, the Brāhmaṇa bowed down in front of Hari and repeated the Praṇava Mantra. At the end of his Japa he became calm in his mind. With palms joined in reverence he approached the Lord and stood thinking his objects as being achieved and blessed. Then the Śabara spoke to the Brāhmaṇa :

Viśvāvasu said:

36. O eminent Brāhmaṇa, you are satisfied on seeing the Lord now. It is the close of the day. We shall go home. You are hungry and tired.

37. Residence in the forest suits wild animals. It is not proper for us to stay here. While there is yet sunlight, let us go home.

38. After saying thus, the Śabara caught hold of the hand of the Brāhmaṇa and returned to his hermitage hurriedly, O excellent Brāhmaṇas.

39. Meditating upon the Lord of the universe, the ocean of bliss, the Brāhmaṇa was not at all aware of the pain of hunger, thirst and exhaustion.

40. On account of his joy and indifference to (his) physical body, he did not feel pain when he walked on the uneven and rugged rocky path, very difficult to tread upon on account of a great deal of thorns as well.

41. Going thus, the Brāhmaṇa and the Śabara, both great devotees of Viṣṇu, reached the abode of Śabaras in the evening.

42. There the excellent Śabara duly honoured the Brāhmaṇa who had come as a guest by means of different kinds of dishes.

43. He became satisfied with the royal welcome, honour and services offered by him. He became surprised very much at the rare hospitality of the Śabara.

44-46. 'This Śabara lives in the heart of the forest full of difficulties and inconveniences. He sustains himself with the products of the forest. How then did these dishes befitting kings become available within his house? It is a great mystery.'

As the Brāhmaṇa was wondering thus, the Śabara spoke to him with great humility.

The Śabara said:

47-50. O Brāhmaṇa, have you been relieved of your weariness? Have you got rid of your hunger and thirst? How can city-dwellers get comfort and happiness in the house of forest-dwellers? The customs and manners of city-dwellers are not known to others, especially to Śabaras. Among the persons who live in a royal palace the minister and the priest of a king are the most superior ones. Between these two, the priest should be revered like the king himself. This is approved by the scriptural texts. King Indradyumna is a powerful Emperor. If you are satisfied, O Brāhmaṇa, he will certainly be satisfied.

When the forest-dweller said thus, the Brāhmaṇa became more pleased. He lovingly spoke these words to the Śabara who spoke with wonderful humility:

Vidyāpati said:

51-52. O gentle one, for serving me you have brought superhuman and divine objects not seen even by kings. It is surprising that these divine objects could be in store in the abode of a Śabara. I have increasing curiosity to know this, O gentle one.

The Śabara replied:

53. My mind is not very enthusiastic to reveal this, O Brāhmaṇa. Still because of our devotion to you as guest, O excellent Brāhmaṇa, I shall tell you.

54-59a. Every day, O Brāhmaṇa, multitudes of Devas including Śakra come here taking divine articles of worship and services with them, for worshipping the Lord of the universe. After worshipping the Lord of the universe, after eulogizing and bowing down to him with devotion, they propitiate Puruṣottama by means of vocal songs, instrumental music and dances. Then the excellent Suras return to heaven. These divine articles given to you are the *Nirmālyas* (i.e. remnants of the worship) of the Lord of the universe. You are a learned man. How is it that you are surprised? It is because we have been subsisting on the *Nirmālyas* of Viṣṇu that we are devoid of ailments and old age. All of us are staying here along with our sons and kinsmen with our life span extending to ten thousand years. By consuming the Nirmālya of Viṣṇu the mass of sins perishes. It is not surprising, O excellent Brāhmaṇa, that one shall attain liberation thereby.

59b-63a. On hearing about this rare achievement the Brāhmaṇa experienced a thrill. His eyes became full of tears of joy. He considered himself blessed: 'Ah, this person born as Śabara (can) sees the immutable Lord. Day and night he enjoys the divine pleasures by (subsisting on) the leavings (remnants of offerings) of the Lord. There is none else in the world consisting of the mobile and immobile beings, who can be considered equal to him. There is no other devotee of Viṣṇu on a par with this Śabara of the Nīla mountain. Of what avail is going back home now? Family is a cause of unpleasantness. I shall become an intimate friend of this (Śabara) and shall stay here in the forest region.'

63b-67a. The Brāhmaṇa whose mind was devotedly attached to Śrīkṛṣṇa spoke once more to the Śabara: "If you wish to bless me, O gentle one, my great resolve is that I should form a close friendship with you. Of what use is returning and carrying on the service of the king, which is the cause of unhappiness in the other world? I shall stay here and worship the Slayer of Madhu. Thereby, I shall strive to prevent a subsequent embodiment (i.e. birth) of my soul. Very well, friend!

It is my good luck that I have come into contact with you. Thanks to your favour, I shall cross the ocean of worldly existence that is very difficult to cross.

67b-72. They praise this as an essential thing in this ocean of worldly existence, viz. the friendship with a devotee of Viṣṇu, which takes one across the ocean of misery. By association with the friend, Lord Puṇḍarīkākṣa (Lotus-eyed Lord Viṣṇu) holding the conch, discus and iron club becomes visible once again. When I return, O friend, King Indradyumna will reside here itself in order to propitiate the Lord. He is desirous of building a big Mansion (temple) there pleasing to the Lord. It has been a great vow of the king that he would do a thousand (kinds of) services for the worship of the Lord. This has been promised in his presence. Hence grant me lovingly this permission."

The Śabara said:

73-79. O friend, a traditional legend like that is well-known here. You have said, Indradyumna will come here. But the king will not see Mādhava. Ere long the Lord will be covered with golden sands. The Lord has promised this to Yama that he will vanish. It is a great luck that you are able to perceive the Lord. If the arrival of Indradyumna is imminent, the Lord shall certainly vanish. But, O friend, this fact should not be mentioned by you in front of the king.

After coming here if the king does not see the great Lord, he will undertake a fast unto death. He will then see Gadādhara in a dream. At his behest he will install four wooden idols of the Lord. He will then worship them. As long as the idol is present here our family shall also be present, thanks to the blessings of the Lord. There is no doubt about this.

80-82. Hence, my friend, do not feel sorry in this respect. Everything will be carried out quickly. Now, friend, sleep soundly. In the morning we shall see the Lord in the form (of an idol of) blue sapphire after taking bath in the ocean. We shall find out a place fit for the stay of the king on its shore as you desire, O my friend.

83-86. After discussing this and other things and narrating splendid stories to each other, they slept on a bed of tender leaves and sprouts in a splendid place.

When the day dawned, they took bath in the Tīrtharāja's waters in accordance with the injunctions, bowed down to Mādhava and found out a place for the residence of the king. He took leave of his friend. In accordance with the directions of the king, the Brāhmaṇa got into the chariot and returned to the city of Avantī.

CHAPTER NINE

Vidyāpati Reports to Indradyumna

Jaimini said:

1-8a. When the Brāhmaṇa returned in the evening and when (the place) was crowded with Suras, at the time of the worship of Mādhava, a violent gust of wind blew. It scattered the golden sand everywhere. Thereby the eyes of the Devas became afflicted and they were unable to see Śrīkānta. Then, O Brāhmaṇas, they meditated on Puruṣottama. Those heaven-dwellers remained steady for a Muhūrta in meditation. At the conclusion of their meditation they saw the heap of sand particles and not Mādhava. Nor did they see even Rauhiṇa Kuṇḍa.[1] Then they became agitated. They became extremely anxious and lamented much: "Alas! Alas! What a great misfortune has befallen us all of a sudden! Śrīśa (the Lord of Śrī) who is charming unto the eyes became invisible within a moment. O Puruṣottama, what is the fault that has been seen in us? You have abandoned all your servants simultaneously. You are not to be seen. It is for our sake, O Lord of the universe, that you adopted a physical body. Why do you then leave us helpless in the forest?

8b-16. O Lotus-eyed One, you have abandoned us who are only the glorious powers of your own person. Why do you render us, the heaven-dwellers, as good as dead all of a sudden?

It is because we constitute your own parts that all those who perform Yajñas worship us for propitiating you, O Yajñapuruṣa (Lord, the personification of Yajña). We grant the benefits as directed by you. Your own (Cosmic) Ego forms our body. We sustain ourselves by means of your blessings.

---

1. This might be factually correct. The Coromandal Coast (including the coast of Orissa) is devastated with stormy winds every few years. The small stone idol of those primitive people must have disappeared under some sand-dune. The total disappearance of Rauhiṇa pond shows that the storm was very powerful.

(We are afraid) where are we to flee now that you have become indifferent to us. Of what avail are our abodes in the firmament without being able to see you, O Mādhava?

Without you we shall be unsuccessful and unhappy, roaming about in wilderness. Your face is like the full moon without the spot. It exudes exquisite beauty and happiness. If we are not going to see your face, we shall not go to the heavenly abode. We shall undertake a great penance and stay here itself, observing all holy rites. We shall subsist on the products of the forest. We will grow matted hair and put on bark garments until we can see you, O Lotus-eyed One.

O ocean of natural sympathy and mercy, it behoves you to save us, the wretched ones. We are helpless and in a dejected state of mind. We have resorted to you alone as our refuge.

Being unable to see you, we are sinking in the ocean consisting of grief only. O Lord of the universe, redeem us by means of your auspicious, benign glance acting like a boat."

17. Even as all the heaven-dwellers were talking thus (incoherently) an unembodied speech issued forth:

18-19. "In this matter, O Suras, it does not behove you to engage yourselves in futile efforts. From now onwards the vision of the Lord will be very difficult to get on the earth. One shall attain the same benefit of direct vision by bowing down to this place (where the Lord was originally). Go to Brahmā and know the exact reason."

20-25. On hearing it all the Devas approached Brahmā. When they heard the details of the blessings of Yama and the incarnation of the wooden form, all of them were satisfied in their mind and returned to heaven.

The Brāhmaṇa Vidyāpati who got into the chariot thought thus:

'My purpose has been achieved, since Nīlamādhava was seen. I shall go all round this holy spot and observe. I shall circumambulate this excellent holy spot named Śrīpuruṣottama which has not been visited before. It is exceedingly meritorious and its glorification dispels sins and impurities. I shall then go away quickly.

My friend has advised me that this holy spot on the shore of the sea is adorned by the Nīla Mountain. Those who circumambulate the forest that dispels all sins acquire hundred times the benefit that one gets by circumambulating the earth.'

After thinking thus, the excellent Brāhmaṇa wandered all over the holy spot observing the forest full of different kinds of trees.

26. It was resounded with the chirping of the different kinds of

birds. The humming bees hovered there. The sun's rays did not penetrate it. It was full of groves of shady trees.

27. It was full of the flowers of all the seasons. It had been rendered splendid by creepers, bowers and hedges. It was noisy with the quacking of ducks and the cackling of geese in their different watery resorts.

28. It shone with red lotuses, white lotuses, lilies and full-blown blue lotuses. Neither the water nor the creepers etc. were without flowers.

29. After circumambulating the holy spot quickly, the excellent Brāhmaṇa proceeded ahead observing fast and meditating. The intelligent one reached Avantī by the close of the day.

30. Even while he was far off, the messengers had informed the king about his arrival, O Brāhmaṇas. On hearing it King Indradyumna became exceedingly pleased.

31. After worshipping Janārdana he sat there with a delighted mind along with the learned Brāhmaṇas eagerly waiting for his arrival.

32-34. In the meantime, O Brāhmaṇas, that Vidyāpati hurriedly entered and came in front of the king. The pathway was ceremoniously shown to him by the ushers with canes in their hands, while the gatekeepers went ahead (of him). He was followed by the curious and enthusiastic citizens. He had kept the excellent Nirmālya of the deity called Nīla Mādhava in his hand.

On seeing him the king got up from his excellent seat. Saying "O Lord of the universe, be pleased", he approached him.

35-41. "Today my life has become fruitful by realizing the Karma of this birth, because I see Mādhava here in the form of this Nirmālya garland.

I bow down to the garland that has surpassed the fine fragrance of the celestial trees through the acquisition of a matchless perfume from the head of Mukunda. It (the garland) has made the swarm of bees blind and has destroyed the sins of all the worlds by means of its sweet scent wafted by the wind.

I bow down to the garland consisting of the flowers that have come into contact with the brilliant unguent on the body of Viṣṇu, by coming into contact with the dust issuing from whose lotus-like feet Brahmā and others have attained great wealth.

(I bow down to that garland) which laughs at her co-wife Padmā (Lakṣmī) whose abode is (also) the lotus-like heart (of Viṣṇu) and which is proud of having stayed in the lap of Viṣṇu. (It appears to laugh) by means of the opening flowers.

Where did this brilliant garland stay and acquire greatness (as a result of which) it stayed on the body of the Lord, the storehouse of fortune and prosperity, for a long time pervading (encircling) all his limbs?

Be victorious (O Lord), an ornament unto the peak of the Nīla Mountain, O glorious (Lord) who dispels sins and agony of those who bow down. Save me. I have sought refuge in you."

Saying thus in words choked with tears, the king bowed down his head (till it touched) the ground. He experienced a thrill.

42-47. The Brāhmaṇa Vidyāpati who had destroyed all his sins, stood in front of the king in a divine body meditating on Mādhava.

With his refulgence the highly intelligent one (seemed) to wash off the sins of all the worlds. He spoke thus: "May the Lord whose abode is on the summit of Nīla Mountain bless you. This is the command of the Lord of Śrī, revealed in the form of this garland. You are to visit him who is abiding in the excellent holy spot. He is the bestower of salvation directly."

Having spoken thus, he put the garland round the neck of the king. The king got up and on seeing the garland suspended over his chest, considered that the Lover of Śrī had directly come to his heart. He placed both the hands on his own head with half-closed eyes. With his face wet with tears of joy he eulogized Hari.

Indradyumna prayed:

48. Be victorious, O Lord who are skilled in the art of creation, sustenance and annihilation of all the worlds, who have sportingly assumed the Cosmic Body and who bear the burden of as many Cosmic Eggs as there are hairs (on your body).

49-51. O Immanent Soul of all, O Lord, the dispeller of the agony of those who bow down (to you), O Lord whose lotus-like feet have become variegated due to the crowns of Brahmā, Indra and Rudra, O Lord, always interested in saving the wretched, the helpless and those who have fallen into adversity, O ocean of the waters of sympathy that is genuine (never pretended), O Lord greater than the greatest, O Lord of the universe, O Lord ever affectionate to your devotees, save me, the miserable one. I have you alone as my refuge. I am completely overpowered by the primordial Nescience (*Avidyā*)."

52-56. After eulogizing thus, the king sat on his throne. He was surrounded by householders, religious students, ascetics and forest- dwellers.

He honoured and revered Vidyāpati in the company of Brāhmaṇas who had performed Yajñas and were well-versed in the eighteen *Vidyās* (lores) and who were in the company of many old servants whose leaders were the ministers and (who sat there) silent.

The king made Vidyāpati sit on a high pedestal of honour and asked him the full details beginning with enquiry about his welfare.

With joy and very great attention he enquired about the greatness and features of the holy spot Puruṣottama and of Viṣṇu with blue sapphire for his body.

On being asked about his own experience by the Kṣatriya, the Brāhmaṇa narrated in detail (all his activities) beginning with the entry into the island of Bhillas and ending with the plunge into the ocean. He gave full report about the excellent holy spot.

57-59. He mentioned everything in due order such as the climbing of the Nīla Mountain, the viewing of Nīlamādhava, the holy bath in the Rauhiṇa Kuṇḍa, the greatness of the Banyan tree, the eight beneficent deities such as Nṛsiṁha, the situation of the eight Śaktis and the length and extent of the holy spot as noticed (by him) while driving in the chariot.

60. On hearing that matchlessly wonderful story previously mentioned by that pilgrim, the king became extremely pleased. Delighted in his mind he spoke to him once again:

Indradyumna said:

61-62a. O holy lord, I heard from you what has been already heard. O excellent Brāhmaṇa, now describe unto me the form of Viṣṇu idol of blue sapphire. Describe it as it actually is.

Vidyāpati said:

62b-65. Verily, I shall describe to you the divine idol of the Lord of the universe. By seeing this idol with the ordinary mortal eye one becomes a person deserving salvation. This idol of blue sapphire is very ancient. It is worshipped everyday by Suras, the leaders among whom are Brahmā, Rudra and Indra.

This divine garland is put (on the idol) by Devas in the course of their worship. It never fades, nor is it devoid of its fragrance. Even when many days have passed, this garland is still like this. This garland has originated from the earth.

66. I have destroyed all my sins by eating the divine presents and offerings as well as the Nirmālya, O king. Don't you notice that I have a superhuman splendour?

67. Even if it is swallowed once, hunger, thirst and weakness never harass one. The unseen can be inferred by means of what is seen.

68-69. O king, both worldly pleasures and salvation are present there simultaneously. Old age, ailment, grief and other miseries have no place there. It is the place where the Lord of the universe is directly present. The Lord has a delightful, beaming face. His eyes resemble petals of a full-blown blue lotus. He bestows immortality and salvation on those who resort to him.

CHAPTER TEN

Dialogue Between Nārada and Indradyumna

Indradyumna said:

1. Ever since your birth, O excellent Brāhmaṇa, you have never been there. How did you come to know of the divine information (visit of gods etc.) in Puruṣottama?

Vidyāpati said:

2. There I stood in the evening after approaching the Lord. At that time a cool wind of divine fragrance blew there.

3. A confused noise rose up and was heard from the sky. Gradually it turned out to be a meaningful sound in the form of letters such as "Go, proceed ahead".

4-9a. In the vicinity of Vaikuṇṭha (i.e. Viṣṇu), the assemblage (of Devas) took place, O king, after the mountain had been covered with a shower of flowers by the heavenly beings.

There was an unprecedented sound of lutes, flutes, Mṛdaṅga drums and clapping of hands marking time in music. It got mixed with divine songs.

A thousand presents and offerings were made by the Devas for the propitiation of the Supreme Lord. None of them had ever been visible to men before.

The Devas who could be known only by their hands (i.e. only the hands were seen) duly worshipped the Lord. They delighted the Slayer of Madhu by means of eulogies along with shouts of "Be victorious". Then they (gods) returned to heaven in the same way as they came from it.

After they had departed, my Śabara friend Viśvāvasu gave me the divine food offerings and this garland.

9b-18a. It is invaluable. It never fades. It bestows prosperity, kingship and happiness. It dispels misfortunes, sins and evil spirits. As it is befitting (to you), it has been brought by me.

Listen to the situation of the excellent holy spot of Viṣṇu. Unprecedented skill in workmanship is evident in this pleasing form. It cannot be (adequately) described by a person born on this earth. It has been seen because of your good fortune and manliness. I shall describe it.

This holy spot has the Nīla mountain as its chief centre. All round it is overspread with forests. It is well-known that its extent is five *Krośas* (i.e.5 x 3=15Kms.). It is on the shore of the Tīrtharāja (the ocean) there. It is covered with golden sands.

On the peak of the mountain, there is a large, lofty Banyan tree that is destined to be there for the period of a Kalpa. It extends to three Kilometers. It is devoid of fruits and flowers but is brilliant with sprouts. When the sun moves, its shade does not move.

To the west of it is the Kuṇḍa named Rohiṇa. From the surface of water it is adorned with a flight of steps of blue stone. All the four sides outside it there are paved with crystals. It is very charming and is filled with waters that dispel masses of sins.

In the middle of the eastern platform, in the cool shade of the holy fig tree, there is the Lord holding the discus and the iron club made of blue sapphire-gems.

18b-25a. (The idol) measures eighty-one Aṅgulas (about 2 metres) and is stationed on a golden lotus.

The region of his forehead surpassed the beauty of the crescent moon of the eighth lunar day. His eyes (as if) attempt to censure (denigrate) the splendour of a pair of smiling blue lotuses. He dispels the three types of ever increasing distresses by means of the nectar-rayed moon of his face. He appears very splendid with his nostrils which are like a shining flower of gingelly plant.

Though his body is made of stone, excellent smile bathes his lips. The chin along with the jawbone appears exceedingly charming on account of the cheeks beaming with laughter.

The two corners of the mouth have an unprecedented setup. Dimples are formed in the cheeks due to laughter. The chin and the splendid corners of the mouth are held as models for such (heavenly) artisans as Viśvakarman and others by the Lord.

On either of his ears there is an ear-ring shaped like Makara (crocodile). The face in between these two ear-rings laughs at (i.e. surpasses) the full moon in between Jupiter and Venus (i.e. with these planets on either side).

Through his neck that increases the beauty of his neck ornament, he gives those who look at it, the suspicion that the conch with right-handed curls has given birth to pearls.

25b-30. His shoulders are thick and large. He has four long arms stretching as far as the knees. The region of the chest of the Lord sparkles with white spotless necklaces. There he holds the fourteen worlds reflected in his divine Kaustubha gem.

He is handsome with a small hair line entering the depressed navel as though it were a deep pool. He renders the necklace immovable by the waist having three folds of skin above the navel.

With the waistband studded with jewels and having small bells suspended along with the pearl necklace the buttocks of the Lord shine like leafy cups of beauty of all the worlds.

The pair of pillar-like calves, rendered splendid by means of the pearl necklace hanging down as far as the loins and the yellow robes, supports the auspicious festoons of salvation.

The two feet of the Lord shine on account of the circular and symmetrical knees, the gem-set anklets as well as the garland extending to the forepart of the feet.

31-36. (*Defective text*) The Lord is adorned with necklaces, bracelets, armlets, crown etc. Lord Keśava wields the discus, the lotus, the iron mace and the conch which are the products of perfect knowledge, Cosmic Ego, Supreme majesty and *Śabda-brahman* (Vedas or Oṁkāra or verbal expression of Supreme Knowledge). He illuminates all the cardinal points. Thus he is installed on the Nīla mountain.

By devoutly bowing down to him and seeing him one is liberated from the bondage of the physical body.

Lakṣmī who occupies his left side is embraced by the Lord holding a lotus in his hand. She is engaged in playing on the lute with her eyes fixed to the face of the Lord. She is the abode of all beauty and is adorned with all ornaments.

I saw those two, the parents of the universe, stationed on the mountain. They are silent. With their smiling eyes they bless all those who view them. As they bless all living beings, I thought them to be alive.

Śeṣa with his many hoods forming an umbrella is stationed behind them.

37. In front (the Discus) Sudarśana was seen assuming an embodied form. Behind him I saw Garuḍa stationed with palms joined in reverence.

38. Having seen directly that Lord of Śrī, of wonderful form and features like this, my mind runs back to that place as though dragged with ropes.

39. Only that man who has acquired excellent Karmas in the course of many thousands of births and has all of them ripened simultaneously, sees the Lord.

40. No man is competent to have the vision of Puruṣottama of this nature even by means of holy baths in Tīrthas, austerities, charitable gifts, sacrifices to gods and other holy rites.

41. Those who meditate upon Viṣṇu abiding in the holy place of Puruṣottama, whose form is dark-complexioned and who resembles the sky free from impurities (like clouds etc.) get their bonds cut. They (then) enter the city of Viṣṇu, after attaining which no one feels any grief.

42. If the different kinds of benefits of a man's Karmas brought about by all the eighteen lores are concentrated together, they can come up to a hundredth part (of the bliss) of the vision of Viṣṇu.

43. What more needs to be spoken in this matter, O king? Such is the greatness of the ground of that holy place that whatever be the extent of things coveted by a man's mind, he will acquire all of them and even more, if he merely bows down to the Lord of the Nīla mountain.

44. Only he by whom the Lord of the Nīla mountain has been seen is a donor, performer of sacrifices, speaker of truth, one of pious and righteous conduct—he is the most excellent one in all good qualities and all births.

45. O king, this greatness has been known by me from those attendants of Mādhava, the Lord of the universe, who are present there.

46. In this context the ancient (yet) well known ancedote of the primordial creation coming down by tradition has been heard by me. It is only after that I have come here.

47. At your behest I went there and visited Śrī Puruṣottama. (Everything) has been reported to you. Do whatever you desire to do now.

Indradyumna said:

48-53. I am satisfied (and feel my objects accomplished) on hearing about the Lord's form that dispels sins, from you whose words are trustworthy. O holy Lord, due to my contact with the divine *Nirmālya* my sins acquired in the course of many births have been destroyed. Now I have become a person desiring the vision of the Lord of Śrī. I shall whole-heartedly go there along with the flourishing kingdom. I shall make residence there and build cities and forts.

In order to propitiate the Enemy of Mura I shall perform a horse-sacrifice. Everyday I will worship Śrīnātha (Viṣṇu) with a hundred presents and offerings. I shall propitiate the Sire of the universe by means of holy rites, fasts and other pious observances.

When the Lord will be eulogized by me thus with faithful devotion, the omnipresent Lord Nārāyaṇa who is merciful and considerate towards the wretched will shower with nectarine words me who have become distressed.

54-58. Nārada who is (ever) curious to survey the worlds came there. On seeing that sage, the son of Brahmā, the foremost among the followers of Viṣṇu, coming, the king then hoped that his purpose would be realised.

He got up promptly and received him with the formalities of offering *Pādya* (water to wash the feet), *Arghya* (materials of worship) and *Ācamanīya* (water for formal sipping). With palms joined in reverence he spoke to the sage who was seated in an excellent seat the following words:

Indradyumna said:

Today my Yajñas , charitable gifts, study of the Vedas and penance have become fruitful, since the *alter ego* of Brahmā has come to my abode.

O sage, even though I am satisfied with your blessing in the form of a visit, what behest of yours shall I carry out for pleasing you? What is the purpose for which my abode has been sanctified by you?

Jaimini said:

59. On hearing the words of the king which were tender and full of devotion and humility, the son of Brahmā spoke to the king smilingly:

Nārada said:

60. O Indradyumna, the most excellent one among kings, Devas,

Siddhas and sages along with Brahmā have become pleased with the mass of your flawless qualities.

61. Each of your good qualities is well-founded and makes you worthy enough to remain in the abode of Brahmā. They severally qualify you for it and are desirable ones.

62. I got down (to the earth) to see Nara residing in the hermitage of Badarikāśrama. At the time of meditation of him your endeavour like this has become known.

63-64a. O king, your endeavour is excellent, whereby your mind has been of such a (devotional) nature. O king, devotion unto Mādhava, the Lord of the world, whose abode is in a cave of mountain Nīla, is engendered by practice (of devotion) in a thousand births.

64b-65. By propitiating the Lord of the universe Brahmā of great intelligence created this universe and attained the position of grandfather. As you are born in his lineage, it is proper that your devotion should be such (intense).

66-67a. The devotion to Viṣṇu, the benefit of which is the accomplishment of the four major goals of life, is the result of no small austerity.

The beginningless primordial Nescience (*Avidyā*) which greatly heightens the five kinds of troubles, is firmly rooted (in man). The only remedy to annihilate (it) is devotion to Viṣṇu.

67b-69a. Devotion to Viṣṇu alone is the bestower of happiness on men who wander in the forest of worldly existence which is full of thorns in the form of miseries at every step.

To those who are sinking without support in the ocean of worldly existence where the *Dvandvas* (mutually opposite pairs) rise up like a violent storm and which is difficult to cross, devotion to Viṣṇu is proclaimed (in scriptures) as a boat.

69b-74. By resorting solely to the devotion to Viṣṇu, (which is like) a mother of exalted magnificence, good people are contented in their minds. They never grieve over (anything).

To those noble souls who are exceedingly delighted by drinking the nectar of devotion to Viṣṇu, attainment of the region of Brahmā is only a small benefit.

O king, the great mass of sins of living beings is of three types. In the great forest fire of devotion to Viṣṇu it is burnt like locusts.

Prayāga, Gaṅgā and other important Tīrthas, austerities, *Aśvamedha* (i.e. horse-sacrifice), the most excellent one among all sacrifices, great charitable gifts, observance of holy rites, fasts etc. even in thousands—

if all these are gathered together and multiplied by crores and crores, that will not be equal to, it is proclaimed, a thousandth part of devotion to Viṣṇu.

Jaimini said:

75-76. On hearing about the greatness of devotion to Viṣṇu as explained by the Brahminical sage, the king became desirous of knowing the special nature of devotion to Viṣṇu. The king endowed with (the knowledge of) the use of means of hospitality, spoke these words to Nārada :

Indradyumna said:

77. The greatness of devotion to Viṣṇu has been excellently described (by you), O great sage. A desire to know its form and nature has been in my heart for a long time.

78. Describe the characteristic of *Bhakti* (Devotion), O eminent Vaiṣṇava (follower of Viṣṇu). In the whole of the earth there can be no one else who will explain it. This is known to me.

Nārada said:

79. What has been asked by you, O king, is perfectly sound. I shall recount to you the real characteristics of excellent devotion. Y,ou are the most excellent one of all persons eligible (to hear about) *Bhakti.*

80. This should never be spoken to an undeserving person, a blind one, an internally impure one. It is being recounted by me, O sinless one.

81. Listen to it attentively, O king. Listen to the eternal *Bhakti* in general and *Bhakti* to Viṣṇu in particular.[1]

82. 'He (Viṣṇu) alone is the giver of absolute happiness and the breaker of the series of miseries.' If any one thinks thus and resorts to him (the Lord), it is called *Bhakti.* It is of three types according to three Guṇas and (that which transcends these Guṇas and is thus) attributeless (*Nirguṇa*) is considered to be the fourth one.

83. The devotion of those who are overpowered by lust and anger and who do not see any other means shall be the *Bhakti* of *Tāmasa* variety, O king. It is conducive to the acquisition (of what they desire) as well as magical powers.

1. VV 81-96 give an exposition of Bhakti.

84. The devotion that is resorted to for gaining extraordinary fame or overpowering a rival or incidentally for enjoyment in the other worlds is known as the *Bhakti* of *Rājasa* variety.

85-86a. The devotion is of the *Sāttvika* variety when it is pursued by one who knows the transitoriness of the worldly objects of pleasure and the comparative permanence of those of the other world and who, without giving up the (religious) duties prescribed for one's own caste and stage in life, resorts to devotion only for the sake of self-realization.

86b-90. 'The Lord of the universe himself (is identical with) this universe. There is no other cause (of this universe). I am not different from him. He does not abide separately from me. He is devoid of external attributes and adjuncts. He should be realized through an abundance of love.' This form of Bhakti is very difficult to attain. It is conducive to salvation. It is called *Advaita* (non-dualistic) devotion.

Devotees go to the abode of Brahman by means of *Sāttvikī Bhakti*; to the world of Śakra (heaven) through the *Rājasī Bhakti*. After enjoying the pleasures (of the earth) the devotees of the *Tāmasī Bhakti* go to the world of Pitṛs. They return to Bhūrloka (Earth) and adopt a *Bhakti* other than the previous one. The devotee of *Tāmasa* variety adopts devotion of the *Rājasa* variety; and one of the *Rājasa* type adopts the *Sāttvika* variety. The devotee of *Sāttvika* type attains liberation after non-dualistic contemplation.

91-96. By resorting to any one of these the devotee should go to the path of salvation gradually.

To a person devoid of devotion to Viṣṇu all the holy rites ordained by the Śrutis and Smṛtis: the rites of atonement etc., pilgrimage to Tīrthas, *Kṛcchra* and other forms of penance, nobility of birth, skill in arts etc. are just like a worldly ornament. The only result thereof is pain and strain to the body as in the case of the infidelity of an adulteress.

Even if he is devoid of noble birth and traditional course of conduct, a person of steady devotion who has controlled the sense-organs, is worthy of being praised by the people of all worlds. But not so in the case of a person who possesses eighteen lores but is devoid of devotion, O excellent king. The same holds good in the case of a man of a good caste and holy rites.

Bhakti unto Viṣṇu is not engendered in a man of very little fortune. By acquiring *Bhakti* unto Viṣṇu with great effort, one has his objects achieved and he becomes blessed. He does not perish (spiritually).

That through which one knows the Lord of the universe is glorified as *Vidyā* (learning). That holy rite (Karma) which delights the Lord is destructive of inauspiciousness.

97-99[1]. A man of steadfast holy rites possessing these two (i.e. Vidyā and Karma) is called a devotee of Viṣṇu. By the dust of his feet the whole universe including the mobile and immobile beings, is sanctified. He is competent to create, sustain and annihilate as he pleases. How insignificant then are the simple desires of worldly prosperity or heaven etc.!

There is no difference between these two, viz. Vāsudeva and his devotee. I shall tell you the characteristics of those who are devotees of Viṣṇu.

100-106a. They have calm minds. They are gentle towards all. They have conquered lust and the sense-organs. Mentally, verbally or physically they never desire to harass others. Their minds always melt with pity. They are averse to stealing and inflicting violence. Towards the good qualities of others they are favourably disposed. In activities for the sake of others they rejoice. They are refined and cultured with good conduct. Other's festivities are their own festivities. Without jealousy and rivalry (towards anyone) they see Vāsudeva abiding in all living beings. They are sympathetic with the wretched ones forever. They wish for other people's welfare very much. In the lavish presents and worship of kings they take as much interest as in fondling own sons.

They are afraid of external things (objects of pleasure etc.) as if of cobras. They have for Hari as much love as hundred crores of times the love for sensual objects entertained by persons lacking in discrimination.

They worship Śaṅkara and others with a sense of perpetual duty and they meditate upon them as on Viṣṇu and treat the Manes like forms of Viṣṇu.

106b-110. They do not see anyone as different from Viṣṇu, nor do they see Viṣṇu as being separate from other things. There is separateness in the individual form but there is no separateness in the collective form.

They think thus: 'O Lord of the universe, I am your servant and you are mine. We are not separate. Since the Lord is the immanent soul

1. VV 97 onwards describe Vaiṣṇavas and their characteristics and the contrasts with non-Vaiṣṇavas.

stationed in the heart of everyone, there is no one other than you as the served or the server.'

With this feeling of devotion, they attentively bow down to and always glorify Hari whose lotus-like feet are worthy of being saluted by the Lotus-born Lord (Brahmā). They consider worldly-minded persons as insignificant as blades of grass.

They are clever in rendering help to others always in all the worlds. They consider other people's welfare as their own. If others are afflicted, they are kind and compassionate to them. Vaiṣṇavas are indeed famous as persons with auspicious minds.

111. Vaiṣṇavas are reputed to have the same attitude towards all these: a piece of stone, other men's wealth or a lump of clay; other men's wives or Śālmalī trees with sharp thorns all over them; friends, enemies, brothers and kinsmen.

112. Vaiṣṇavas are famous as having pleasant faces on account of their numerous good qualities. They are ready to cover the weak and vulnerable points of others. They bestow ultimate happiness (on everyone). Their minds always dwell on the Lord. They speak sweet words.

113. Vaiṣṇavas consider the auspicious names of the Slayer of Kaṁsa as destructive of sins. They repeat them with clear and sweet tones. They repeatedly say, "Be victorious, be victorious". They are well known to be negligent of worldly wealth as useless.

114. Vaiṣṇavas are noted for their minds being fixed on the lotus-like pair of feet of Hari. Their intellects are apathetic (towards worldly affairs). They have the same appearance in happiness as well as in misery. They are clever in showing reverence to Hari in their own minds.

115. Vaiṣṇavas have their (limbs such as) shoulders, arms marked with (Viṣṇu's) discus, mace, lotus, conch. They wear as armour the dust particles taken from the feet of Viṣṇu after bowing down to Him. Such Vaiṣṇavas are victorious.

116. Vaiṣṇavas are victorious. They are beautiful with the requisite ornaments and forms through the exceedingly fragrant basil leaf, garland and sandal paste taken from the limb of the Conqueror of Mura in order to woo Mukti (salvation) as it were.

117. Vaiṣṇavas are victorious with false prestige and pride dropped from their pure minds; they are calm with Ahaṁkāra (egotism) perishing quickly; they have destroyed their griefs by worshipping Narahari (Man-Lion), the trustworthy kinsman of Devas.

118. The auspicious conduct and characteristics of those who have

continuous devotion to the Lord have been spoken to you by us. By being listened to these will dispel the impurity of men acquired in the course of a very long time.

119. Wealth is never sought. Nor an antidote against a pain arising in the body. O mind, I shall give you only this, viz. the glorification of the name (of the Lord) in light and soft words and the worship thereof.

120. (As opposed to these) *Avaiṣṇavas* ('non-devotees of Viṣṇu') hate auspicious conduct of (other) men. They themselves indulge in evil conduct and evil thoughts in the minds. They are undisturbed even if great misfortune befalls them. They take delight in sexual enjoyment.

121. Those *Avaiṣṇavas* are inebriated. They do not resort to the Lord even for a moment, although he is the cause of supreme happiness and is present in the lotus of the heart. They always cover up the names of Hari by means of aimless, worthless and futile network of words.

122. They are always covetous of other men's young wives and wealth. They are miserly and always think of filling up their bellies. They invariably think (enviously?) of the greatness of others. Indeed those devoid of devotion to Viṣṇu are human brutes.

123. They are always attached to the company of ignoble persons. They are hideous and highly awful. They assail and hurt others violently. They are not inclined to remember the feet of Narahari. These dirty men are to be shunned from a great distance.

CHAPTER ELEVEN

Dialogue Between Nārada and Indradyumna (Continued)

Jaimini said:

1. On hearing about the excellent devotion to the Lord from Nārada, the son of Brahmā, thus, Indradyumna became highly pleased and spoke to him:

Indradyumna said:

2. Learned men have taught me that association with saintly people is destructive of the ailment of worldly existence. O holy Lord, that has happened to me just now.

3. Viṣṇu, the Supreme Soul, greater than the greatest, has been directly visualized by you. Who else can be a better saintly person than you? And you have come to my abode.

4. By your presence, O holy Lord, my darkness of ignorance has been dispelled. Therefore, my mind prompts me to worship Nīlamādhava.

5-6. Wandering over all the worlds you know the whole of the universe. Therefore, let us get into the chariot and visit Nīlamādhava, the splendid ornament unto the holy spot named Puruṣottama. Many have told me that there are many Tirthas there. If I know them directly from your words, they will be fruitful to me.

Nārada said:

7. Well, I shall show you the holy place and the Tīrthas present in that sacred place. I shall point out Śakti-Śaṁbhus[1] and tell you about the greatness of the holy place.

8. You will directly see the Lord of Devas who bestows his own self on the devotee. You will see him quickly as he will be in fourfold form in order to bless you.

9-10. By visiting him a man becomes a worthy receptacle of devotion.

After concluding their dialogue thus, both of them became pleased and carried out their daily routine of duties. As an auspicious time favourable to the departure, they fixed the fifth day in the bright half of the lunar month Jyeṣṭha, which happened to be a Wednesday. During the night the king and Nārada slept in the same place.

11-16. Then, when the day dawned clearly, Indradyumna, the excellent king, made the following proclamation for the entire kingdom to set out for Nīlādri along with kinsmen and armies and their assets:

"It has been decided that all of us will stay there for the whole of our life. Everyone will continue the same work for livelihood as has been allotted to him here. Let the kings proceed along with their women, ministers and retinue, together with chariots, elephants, horses, foot-soldiers and treasury. Let them be fully equipped and ready. Let the Brāhmaṇas go there along with their sacrificial fires. Let the merchants and traders proceed with their utensils, wares and merchandise. (The following shall proceed:) Those who are experts in politics and

1. Śakti-Śaṁbhus: The various Śakti-goddesses and Śiva-liṅgas installed in the Puruṣottama Kṣetra.

statecraft; experts in (the maintenance of) royal highways; astrologers; astronomers; experts in dances; persons well conversant with administrative work and polity;

17-23. those who are experts in dancing, singing and four types of musical instruments; those who are very clever in the excellent science of medicine for treating elephants, horses and human beings; those who have practical experience in the eighteen *Vidyās* and ancillary subjects; those who have excellence in magic and allied arts; highway robbers; adventurous thieves; those who knock away things even as the victim stands and stares; those who maintain themselves by narrating strange and wonderful tales: those who specially speak agreeably; panegyrists; bards; those who maintain themselves by means of sacred treatises; those who give relief from pain; gamblers; harlots; courtesans; pimps, lechers (lecherous persons); husbandmen; those who breed cows, sheep, goats, camels and mules; those who keep birds; fowlers; those who keep monkeys, tigers, and panthers; snake-charmers; cowherds; hunters; barbarians of various tribes and all others born in the Mālava land who obey my commands. Let them all proceed to their abode on the Nīla mountain with their respective assets. Let them be ready to build their own houses".

24. The king who waited impatiently for the time of the journey, commanded thus. Thereafter he joined Nārada and spoke these words to the astrologer:

25-30. "O astrologer, you have already fixed up the auspicious hour. Whatever is required at the moment in the opinion of the priest, bring all those auspicious articles readily."

O excellent Brāhmaṇas, on being commanded by him that astrologer brought all the required auspicious articles with the assistance of the priest. In the meantime that saintly king sat on his divine throne.

At the outset, the sacred rite of ablution for the sake of (a safe) journey was conducted by the Brāhmaṇas. Separate ablutions were performed repeating the different Sūktas[1] (hymns), viz. *Śrī Sūkta, Vahni Sūkta, Varuṇa Sūkta, Pavamānya Sūkta* and *Abdhi Sūkta.* All of them are contributory to increased auspiciousness. The waters of the different Tīrthas were used. Medicinal herbs and all types of sweet scents were used separately. After the ablution the water was wiped off by

1. These are various Sūktas pertaining to deities Śrī, Agni, Varuṇa, Pavamāna and the Sea.

a silk cloth. With his brilliant body the king shone like smokeless fire.

31-35. The king wore a white cloth. He performed the rite of *Ācamana*. Then he wore the *Pavitra* of Darbha grass. He worshipped the groups of Manes called *Nāndīmukhas* in accordance with the injunctions. He performed the Homas by repeating *Jaya* and *Rāṣṭrabhṛt* hymns, and then the *Gaṇahomas* were performed scrupulously. Śaṅkhas (conchs) were blown; sweet perfumes spread everywhere. He performed the circumambulation of the holy fire that appeared white in colour without any smoke. The flame of the fire curled to the right side. Thereby it appeared to grant directly victory to the king who sought victory.

In order to destroy the vicious influence of Planets and to increase well-being, the king was served with the Grahakuṁbha (water pot consecrated to the Planets) at the end of the sacrifice unto the nine Planets.

The Mantras mentioned in the astrological treatises were repeated in the manner urged by the astrologer.

Thereafter, the auspicious embellishment and dressing rite was begun.

36-42. The silk cloths covered his body like an armour. The (white?) turban was splendid and brilliant with gem-set crown. The ears were adorned with the ring-shaped ear-ornaments (*Avataṁsas*) and gem-set *Kuṇḍalas* (varieties of ear-rings and ornaments). The excellent king wore a neck-ornament of great value and a *Hāra* embellished with a central gem. Then he put on shoulderlets, armlets and rings. He wore round his waist three (fine) gold wires twisted into one waistband and touching the folds of skin above the navel. Then he wore an excellent girdle well set with different kinds of precious stones and having festoon-like clusters of pearls along with golden tinkling bells. He fastened very valuable anklets round his feet. In the mirror held in front of him, he saw his reflection as a well (dressed and) ornamented one.

He remembered Lord Śrīdhara, the slayer of Madhu, Viṣṇu, the abode of auspiciousness and the cause of glorious happiness, as by remembering him sins though multitudinous, perish. He sat facing East on a golden pedestal for the sake of auspicious decorations.

43. At the outset the king wore a garland of seasonal flowers with bright colours and sweet scent after it had been consecrated with Mantras by his own priest.

44. Then he (touched) clay, lamp, fruit, Dūrvā grass, curds and *Gorocanā* (i.e. a bright yellow pigment) after all of them had been sanctified by Mantras. Then he was given (the ceremonious) protection by means of (protective) white mustard.

45. The king then looked at himself (reflected) in the ghee prepared from cow milk. The lion-like king then looked at the reflection in the mirror consecrated by Mantras.

46. Good prospects were wished by the singing of Vedic hymns and loud chanting of Śānti (propitiatory) Mantras.[1]

He was accorded protection while proceeding along the path by means of *Pathisūkta* and Yajur Mantras.

47. The king was filled with heroism and fortitude through the auspicious verses of Purāṇas. His valour was revealed by the bards and heralds through panegyrics.

48. Within his lotus-like heart the king meditated upon the Garuḍa-emblemed Lord who, accompanied by Satyabhāmā, took away the heavenly Pārijāta tree. Then he took (the first) step with his right foot.

49. After circumambulating Sage Nārada who was standing in front, the king went up to the central main door guarded by cane-bearing attendants.

50-51. (As required in royal formalities) the attendants showed him the path. He proceeded with the family sacred Fire (*Agnihotra*) taken ahead (by the priests). There he saw to his right the Brāhmaṇas, standing ready reciting the *Māṅgalya Sūkta* (hymn for auspiciousness). They were brilliant in appearance and wore white silk clothes. They threw fried grains and corn in front of the king along with flowers repeating words of blessings for his welfare.

52. The courtesans stood on the left side busily holding and waving the chowries. They wore shining, gorgeous costumes and bright ornaments. With smiling lotus-like faces they (appeared) exceedingly splendid.

53. O excellent Brāhmaṇas, the king was devout and humble. He honoured Brāhmaṇas with garments, ornaments, garlands, sweet scents and unguents.

54. With the faith that Brāhmaṇas were the Lord Himself, he made those Brāhmaṇas delighted by (thus) honouring them.

55. With the permission of the king the minister gave suitable presents of cash, white doves, swans, a white horse and a white elephant to the courtesans, the bards as well as to the indigent helpless people.

---

1. Śānti Mantras are propitiatory Mantras like (1) *ā no bhadrāḥ* (RV I.89. 1-10), (2) *svasti na indra* (RV I.89.6-10), (3) *śam na indrāgnī* (RV VII.35.1-11) and others. They are used in Śānti-rites on different occasions to avert evil and to pray for good.

56. The king then (intently) looked at the auspicious pitcher filled with water and kept beneath an arch of the stems (with leaves) of plantain tree—the pitcher embellished with mango-sprouts, garlands of white flowers and fruit. He viewed many other auspicious things also. A white umbrella was held above his head to ward off the heat of the sun.

57-58. He heard many musical instruments played, mixed with the sounds of hundreds of conch-shells blown simultaneously. Similarly the king heard auspicious songs and shouts of "Be victorious"

Then he entered the palace to see Nṛsiṁha.

59-63. By remembering that Lord a man becomes recipient of all auspiciousness. Seeing that Lord Nṛhari from a distance, the Lord seated on a divine throne, he (the king) prostrated (in front of him) with the eight limbs touching the ground. With the words of the Upaniṣads he propitiated the Lord. He made obeisance to Durgā who stood on his right side—Durgā who liberates (devotees) from all adversities, looks (at the devotees) compassionately. He paid obeisance to the Goddess just near her feet.

Then the priest took off the auspicious garland from the idol of the Lord and put it round the neck (of the king) and applied sweet scents on his body. He joyously performed the Nīrājana rite (i.e. ceremonious waving of the lights) to the king and covered the head of the king (with a turban?).

The excellent king then circumambulated once again the two deities and placed them in the palanquin. They were kept ahead and he started (on his journey).

64-65a. He came out and saw at the external gate the chariot kept ready. Ten horses with the speed of wind had been yoked to it. The king circumambulated the chariot and got into it along with Nārada.

65b-66a. Various kinds of drums, viz. Ḍhakkā, Mṛdaṅga, Niḥsāṇa, Bherī, Paṇava and Gomukha were sounded. The musical instruments Mādhurī and Carcarī were played. Thousands of conch-shells were blown.

66b-68. There were crores of chariots belonging to the vassal kings. They were kept in rows and rows all round the chariot of Indradyumna. They were equipped with various kinds of weapons. They were adorned with flags and banners. The flag posts were tall. They were fitted with strings of bells made of gold and silver. There wre mirrors too attached to them. They were equipped with various mechanical devices. They had pleasing and majestic rumbling sounds.

69-70. The sounds of the infantry, the horses with the speed of wind and the elephants (were heard). The rumbling sounds of the chariots were mixed with the sounds of the marching of the foot-soldiers, the trumpeting of the elephants and the neighing of the horses. The sounds of the musical instruments too mingled with these. All these were heard by people like sounds of oceans at the time of the close of Yuga.

71. At that same moment the citizens too started equipped with their own requisites along with horses, donkeys, camels and porters.

72. In that tumultuous confusion when the whole nation had set out, swings, palanquins, ponies etc. were seen (proceeding ahead) in rows and rows.

73-76. Hundreds of members of inner apartments of the kings set out from the place. They were surrounded by eunuchs and guarded by officials and great armies. They rode in different kinds of vehicles.

The *Yajvans* ('sacrificial priests') started with their wives after placing the *Agnihotra* (sacrificial) fires and materials in the *Śamyā* vessels in different groups and carrying them in carts.

Bundles of books, utensils for the worship of deities, sacrificial twigs, Darbha grass, pots and pitchers, and the materials for Homa—all these they made other Brāhmaṇas to carry by means of other carts and vehicles.

77-81a. The vassal kings, ministers, servants, priests, Ṛtviks, the king's administrative officials, slaves, those who had been employed in various kinds of services—all these set out with their belongings gathered together. Others went ahead. Those who had been employed in the treasuries took with them the entire treasure (cash etc.) and hastened ahead. The persons who attended upon the king on different occasions, gardeners and others, merchants and traders—all these took with them their respective merchandise and proceeded forth at the behest of the king. Excellent artisans and craftsmen with their guilds started along with the residents of cities, hamlets and rural parts. They had with them all the necessary implements for the practice of their professions or trades.

81b-84. On hearing the sounds of the drums, Bherīs, Paṭahas and Mṛdaṅgas beaten at the time of the journey of King Indradyumna, that pervaded all the cardinal points, all the people staying in rural outskirts became excited. They obeyed the commands of the king and started towards Nīla mountain.

Everyone went along the direct path most suitable to him. At the behest of the king they did not seek the main highway on account of haste. They went along the difficult path leading to Nīla mountain.

85-91. The eminent King Indradyumna, surrounded by residents of the whole city and the four army divisions, who were extremely delighted, shone in his chariot that was in the centre of the series of chariots proceeding ahead in a line of kings. The saintly king had the paraphernalia similar to that of Śakra.

His mind was pleased with the auspicious activities of the ladies of the city, their songs of welcome and good wishes and their showerings of flowers and fried grains—everything increasing the grandeur of the auspicious rite.

He joyously went ahead in the chariot to which horses having the speed of gusts of wind had been yoked, along the dustless path on the surface of the ground that had been levelled as though in quadrangles, and that was very cool under the shade of clouds raised by favourable winds. The way was shown to the king by those persons who had travelled through various lands and who knew thoroughly the ins and outs of the forests.

He went on observing the lands and territories as well as the forest regions on either side of the pathway. He was delighted and his pleasure was evident in his eyes. He reached the shrine of Carcikā[1] (Goddess Durgā) that marked the boundary of Utkaladeśa and was on their way. The deity was decorated with a garland of skulls.

92. The king got out of the chariot at Nārada's behest. With great humility he bowed down to her with the eight limbs touching the ground and with great delight in his mind he eulogized her.

Indradyumna said:

93-97. Obeisance to you, O Goddess, O dispeller of all miseries and adversities. You are glorified through eulogies by Brahmā, Viṣṇu, Śiva and others. You are the cause of all the worlds. O primordial Goddess, O supreme deity, be pleased. O Śivā, without you this universe cannot have any power (or endure) even for a monent. The accomplishment of all undertakings in the mortal world and all auspiciousness is the result of propitiating your feet, O eternal Goddess, and not otherwise. O supreme deity, you are the *Śakti* (power) of Viṣṇu, the Lord of mobile

1. Now this goddess is worshipped at Banki in the Cuttack District of Orissa. The Purāṇa believes the earth as consisting of eighteen continents instead of the usual seven *dvīpas*.

and immobile beings. It is through this *Śakti* that the Lord creates, protects and annihilates the universe. O Goddess, bless me so that with my own eyes I shall see the Lord residing in the Nīla mountain, the sire of mobile and immobile beings.

Jaimini said:

98-105. After eulogizing the Goddess as per advice of Nārada, the king got into the chariot quickly like the Sun climbing the Udaya mountain. Then he started quickly.

(Later on) when his vehicles (horses) became tired, the king halted the army on the banks of the great river Citrotpalā (modern Mahānadī). It was a famous region on account of the caves abounding in minerals. The forest was not at all thick there.

With the intention of performing the requisite rites of the late afternoon, the king entered the bathing Ghat along with his priest after it had been searched thoroughly and found to be devoid of poisonous thorns. The Lord of the subjects took his bath, performed the *Tarpaṇa* rites for Devas and Pitṛs and duly worshipped Viṣṇu.

Thereafter, the king honoured the vassal kings and the ministers and other officers by providing them with seats, resting places etc. Then the glorious king entered the inner apartment along with Nārada and with a delighted mind partook of his food as tasty and juicy as nectar.

When the sun set, the king concluded his evening rites quickly. As the moon rose, the king sat in the middle of the assembly of his subjects and vassal kings.

106. There in that assembly the king shone with all the characteristics of an emperor like the autumnal moon with the full disc in the middle of the luminaries.

107. The poets recited verses describing his fame as pure as nectar. Musicians of sweet and excellent voice sang well-composed songs of praise.

108. Thereafter, the courtesans who were proud of their beauty, youth and graceful charms danced in front (of them) keeping the perfectly correct musical timing, keynote and the proper gesticulations and movements of the body.

109. By means of poetical and prose compositions full of figures of speech and imagery and wonderful groupings of words, the bards and heralds eulogized him whose form and features were the most splendid and perfect in the world.

110. Thereafter the king honoured the prominent Vaiṣṇavas seated in the assembly with sweet scents, garlands and betel leaves which were well-approved and splendid in appearance.

111-112. At the bidding of the king many (vassal) kings had occupied their seats comfortably. King Indradyumna honoured hundreds of them befittingly with those articles which kings deserved.

Then in order to hear the story of the Lord that is destructive of all sins, the king respectfully requested Nārada, a favourite of the Lord, and the most excellent one among sages, who was comfortably seated on a throne he deserved:

Indradyumna said:

113-116. O holy lord, O abode of the Vedas and Vedāṅgas, O beloved one of the Lord, you alone know the life story of Viṣṇu with the vision of knowledge. If you are kind and considerate towards me, O sage, wash my heart with the nectar of the story of Hari as it has become very dirty with mud (sins, ignorance).

While the discourse between the sage and the king thus got mingled with dialogues like these, the doorkeeper, a servant of the Lord of Utkala, entered and reported to the king: "O Lord, the king of Utkala stands near the entrance. He is accompanied by his chief (ministers, officers etc.). He is waiting with presents (in his hands) and wishes to see the lotus-like feet of Your Highness."

117-120. When the saintly king was informed thus by the doorkeeper, he became agitated. O Brāhmaṇas, he had been hearing about the holy spot of Śrīpuruṣottama. Since that holy spot was an ornament to his land, he was eager to listen to what he had to convey. So the king told the gatekeeper: "Without delay usher in the glorious king of Oḍhra land. Indeed, he is devoid of all impurities (sins) by having propitiated Viṣṇu on Nīla mountain. By seeing him all of us shall get our sins destroyed."

On hearing his words the doorkeeper immediately ushered the king (of Utkala) into the assembly of King Indradyumna.

121-124. Immediately the king of Oḍhra entered along with his ministers, followers of Viṣṇu. He bowed down to the venerable pair of feet of Indradyumna with great respect.

The great king (Indradyumna) lifted him up and honoured that Vaiṣṇava by placing him in his own seat. Then he humbly spoke these words:

"O king, O Lord of Oḍhra, Are you happy and well in every respect? I hope the Lord whose abode is on the summit of Nīla mountain is victorious and your pure intellect is fixed on the lotus-like feet of the Lord. You are equal-minded towards all living beings. I hope your mind is devoted to Hari".

125. On hearing his words, the overlord of Oḍhra became extremely delighted and surprised. With palms joined in reverence he spoke these words full of humility:

126. "O Lord, by your blessings I am happy in every respect. How will darkness prevail when the Sun blazes?

127. By the contact of your natural good qualities all the (other) kings have been won over by you. The Earth is blessed with you as her Lord like Amarāvatī with Indra.

128. While you rule over the earth, Dharma (Virtue) is always four-footed. (The words) 'committing forbidden act' can be heard of only in the Vedas, O king.

129. Various qualities of statesmanship and perfection in administration that abide in you, O Lord, serve severally as models to the (other) kings.

130. Even this much of your empire is inaccessible (to others), O most excellent king. The whole earth consisting of eighteen islands (being under your rule) is comparable to a single house.

131. You are fond of all living beings. If Brahmā had not created you, how could people get rid of grief when their sons and kinsmen died?

132. The Śruti says that ordinary kings are parts of Viṣṇu. You are the Lord himself. Who else is a mine of good qualities like you?

133-137. Nīla mountain is on the shore of the Southern Sea. It is surrounded by forests. It is not frequented by ordinary common people. It is there that the deity is present.

Now, it is heard that a storm has scattered sands over the Deity. As a result of it, there is famine, death, pestilence etc. in my kingdom too. Since you have come, there will be welfare all around in my case."

When the king of Utkala concluded his speech thus, O excellent Brāhmaṇas, king (Indradyumna) honoured him duly and sent him off to take rest.

With great dejection he looked at Nārada and said: "O sage, what is this? I begin to doubt that everything for which I had endeavoured has become futile." As he said this, Nārada who is a knower of all the three times, spoke to him:

138. "You should not be astonished at this. The most excellent one among Vaiṣṇavas, you are very fortunate. Indeed the desire of Vaiṣṇavas never goes unfulfilled.

139. You will certainly see Nārāyaṇa who is free from ailments—Nārāyaṇa the primordial deity, who is the cause of all the worlds and has adopted human form.

140-141. For the sake of blessing you he will incarnate on the earth. The entire universe consisting of mobile and immobile beings is under the control of Viṣṇu. He is not under the control of anyone. He is the supreme soul, the eternal one. The Lord can be won over only by means of devotion. He is affectionate to his devotees.

142. It is his Māyā whereby everything beginning with Brahmā and ending with an insect is well protected. How can he, O king, be dependent on others, except devout people?

143-144. The root cause of virtue, wealth, love and salvation is devotion to Viṣṇu. That alone is the means of knowing him. Without it there is no other way. Viṣṇu is really one, but he takes many forms by means of his Māyā. There is no source of happiness except that great soul.

145. There are other deities such as Śiva, Durgā and others. They are engaged in various Karmas. When worshipped, they grant what is desired. They too are dependent on Viṣṇu.

146. That Lord is the immanent soul. He is stationed in the hearts of Devas too. They grant benefits only as much as he directs.

147. O great king, you too are a Vaiṣṇava. You are in the fifth generation from the Lotus-born Lord. You are a master of the eighteen Vidyās (lores). You strictly adhere to good conduct.

148. The earth has been protected by you with justice. You are especially a worshipper of Brāhmaṇas. You will certainly see Viṣṇu in the holy spot by means of your physical eye.

149. In this matter Brahmā too has employed me, O king. When the excellent holy spot is reached, I will tell you everything.

150. Now the night is about to reach the third Yāma (period of 3 hours). Command the (vassal) kings now to go back to their respective apartments.

151. You too should go to the inner apartment and have a sound sleep."

CHAPTER TWELVE

*Description of the Holy Place Ekāmravana (Bhuvaneśvara)**

Jaimini said:

1. When this was said by the son of Brahmā, king Indradyumna, after listening to the words of the sage, pondered with a delighted mind upon them with deep comprehension, and thought that his efforts had borne fruit:

2. 'What a great fortune was acquired in the course of many births! The grandfather of all the worlds is actively participating in my enterprise.

3-4a. He has deputed his son, a living-liberated soul, to assist me. The fulfilment of the tasks of persons conforms to the type of assistance they receive—this old teaching is heard in all assemblies.'

4b-6a. Thinking thus the king dispersed those members of the assembly. Then, O Brāhmaṇas, he grasped the hand of the sage and entered the inner apartment. After duly honouring him, the king spent the remaining part of the night along with him, in the same couch, engaged in mutual conversation.

6b-7. When the day dawned clearly, he concluded the daily routine of religious duties, worshipped the Lord of the universe and crossed Mahānadī. The path was shown by the overlord of the land of Oḍhra who went ahead.

8-10. Accompanied by his army he started towards the holy place Ekāmravanaka (modern Bhuvaneśvara).

After going a short distance he reached the river named Gandhavahā[1] of rapid currents and cool waters.

While he hurriedly crossed the river the king heard from a great distance, the sounds of various drums and musical instruments such as Mṛdaṅga, Muraja, Kāhāla, Carcarī and conchshell. The sound was produced at the time of the forenoon worship of Koṭiliṅgeśvara.[2] It spread everywhere in the great forest.

---

* Vide Brahma Purāṇa, Ch. 39. It gives a more detailed and beautiful description of Ekāmra Kṣetra from a Śaivite point of view.

1. Gandhavahā is the Gandhavatī (modern Gangua) at present flowing in Bhuvaneśvara, It is considered as a sacred river.

2. Koṭiliṅgeśvara is a famous temple at Bhuvaneśvara.

11-13. The king thought that it was (from the shrine) of the Lord residing on Nīla mountain. With great pleasure he enquired of Nārada: "Whence is this sound coming, O great sage? Has (the shrine of) the great Lord residing on the summit of Nīla mountain been reached? It is at the time of his worship that this tumultuous sound is heard. Or, O sage, is there any other deity nearby?" On being asked thus by the king the eminent sage replied:

14-17. "O king, highly inaccessible is the holy spot. It is kept concealed by Viṣṇu. That there is the Lord there, is not known to any man.

You are the most excellent one among lucky people. It is due to your good fortune that the Lord was with great difficulty seen by your priest who has controlled all his sense-organs.

O excellent king, you are equipped with armies having six divisions. Hence, O king, I have begun to suspect that you have undertaken an adventure in a big way.

Nīla mountain is in the third Yojana (i.e. 3x 12 Kms.). This is the holy spot of the Lord of Gaurī named Ekāmrakavana. Not far off, O king, is the place where, being afraid, he sought refuge."[1]

Indradyumna said:

18-20,. Why was the Lord of Gaurī (Śiva) frightened? With whom did he seek refuge?

Why was the Lord who had burned the terrible three Puras (cities of Asuras) formerly by means of a single arrow, frightened? This is very much amazing and I wish to hear about this rare (event).

Bhava is the protector of those who are afraid of worldly existence (bhava). He is extremely sacred. Why was he frightened? Who is powerful enough to conquer (him)?

Nārada said:

21-23. In this connection, O king, I shall tell you an ancient legend. Lord Nīlalohita was won over by Gaurī previously by means of penance. He was under the vow of celibacy. On being afflicted with the arrows of the god of Love, he gave up that vow. He married Gaurī on

1. A Vaiṣṇavite twist to show the inferiority of Śiva to Viṣṇu. The fight between Śiva and Viṣṇu for one King of Kāśi (Kāśirāja) and the subsequent defeat of Śiva and his praise of Viṣṇu and Śiva's departure from Vārāṇasī to Ekāmra Vana (vv 50-79)— all this is invented to show Viṣṇu's superiority.

the Himālaya mountain and sported with that beautiful lady proud of her youthfulness, O king. In the realm of her father he enjoyed all the pleasures desired by Devas (too).

24-30. Once the chaste lady was coming out of her apartment along with (some) noble ladies. She was then gently and smilingly addressed with these words by her mother:

"O noble lady, for the sake of a brideroom a great penance was performed by you in the dense forest. But, O lady of excellent countenance, an old brideroom of unknown parentage and unknown qualities has been acquired by you.

You never leave his presence in day or at night, though he is of such a nature. What is his special excellence, dear girl? Let it be mentioned. What is the return of your husband's favour? You get your clothes and ornaments from me. You stay in my house. O gentle lady; you have been staying here for a long time. You are fondled by your father. You enjoy all your pleasures in your father's house.

We have heard that all the girls in the three worlds go away from their father's house after marriage. They are adorned by their husband and they stay in their husband's house.

I am a mind-born daughter of the Manes. I came from the world of the Manes, O highly fortunate lady. I was married to Himādri.

O lady of roving eyes, you have been spoken thus only jocularly and not out of anger. This should not be mentioned to the Son-in-law. He is considered equal to Viṣṇu."

Nārada said:

31. On hearing these words uttered by her mother, she was deeply pained by the censure of her husband. Though her lips were throbbing with anger, she did not utter a single word.

32. She approached her husband. Though she did not disclose the (actual) words of her mother, she reported lovingly a few harsh words briefly (spoken about him).

33-34. "O Lord, this is not proper for one to stay in one's own father-in-law's house even in the case of the lowliest of men. How can it be otherwise in the case of yours, the sire of the three worlds. Hence I do not like, O Lord, that we should stay here. It is not befitting (to us). Are there no other places proper for you to settle down?"

35. On being told thus by Śivā the Bull-emblemed Lord got on the back of his Bull along with her and hurriedly went to the central land (i.e. land between Himālaya and Vindhya).

36-41a. He crossed all the Tīrthas and went beyond the great sacred place Prayāga, and on the northern bank of Gaṅgā that flows into the Eastern Ocean, he built the city named Vārāṇasī[1] for Gaurī's residence. It is a beautiful city extending to five Krośas (15Kms).

It is splendid with excellent Mansions. It has hundreds of palatial buildings and numerous gardens and parks. There are many Tīrthas there and it is full of people of different kinds. This splendid city had been built by Viśvakarmā at the behest of Dhūrjaṭi (Śiva). It dispels sins by means of holy and cool waves of Gaṅgā.

There in the middle of that city which was rendered splendid by means of golden ramparts and Mansions, which was perfectly built with gemset columns and which fulfilled all wishes and ambitions, Paśupati sported with her like the Slayer of Madhu (Viṣṇu) with Śrī.

41b-43. That city is never left by Viśvanātha (Śiva). So it is well known by the name Avimuktā. It bestows salvation on men. Formerly, O overlord of men, it was resorted to by persons who were afraid of the worldly existence. Gaurī stayed there along with her husband who adorned her in an excellent manner. O king, she did not remember even her mother and father.

44. When many Yugas passed like this, the Lord installed a crore of his Liṅgas there and went to Kailāsa mountain.

45-48. O king, many kings ruled over that city. Formerly in Dvāpara Yuga, there was a king there (commonly) called Kāśirāja. By means of severe penance he propitiated Lord Śaṁbhu with this aim in his mind: 'I will excel in war Acyuta (Kṛṣṇa), the conqueror of kings, the chief of whom is Jarāsandha.'

The Pināka-bearing Lord (Śiva) who was propitiated, granted him that boon: "O suppressor of enemies, you will conquer the Slayer of Kaṁsa in battle. For your sake I shall fight seated on my Bull, along with (my attendants) Pramathas."

49. After securing a boon like this that madly insolent king who (boasted of his) heroism, challenged the Lord (Kṛṣṇa), wielder of the conch and the discus, for a fight.

50. That Lord (Kṛṣṇa) who is the immanent soul (of all), knew the incident of that sort, and sent his Discus for killing Kāśirāja.

---

1. SkP euphemistically gives the credit of building Vārāṇasī to Śiva. As a matter of fact, he usurped this capital city of Divodāsa through Nikuṁbha (vide BdP 2.3.67.31-58).

51-57. The infuriated Discus that was very fierce in appearance, had the refulgence of a thousand suns. It knew the power of the mind of Viṣṇu. It cut off the head of Kāśirāja and burned to ash his army as well as that city.

On seeing that extremely violent action Paśupati(Śiva) became furious. Surrounded by his Gaṇas and seated on his Bull, the Pinākabearing Lord rushed at it. Then Śaṁbhu looked at the Sudarśana Discus at the outset and discharged his Pāśupata missile in front of it, like an ominous calamity.

Formerly Śaṁbhu had secured a boon from Viṣṇu who had been pleased by his devotion: "On being remembered by you I shall invigorate your missile. But if you go against me, it will become lustreless (and ineffective)."

When this Pāśupata missile which was (usually) terrible, became futile and when Vārāṇasī was burned, the Bull-bannered Lord became afraid.

Then he eulogized the Primordial Puruṣottama, the cause of all the worlds.

Mahādeva prayed:

58. O Nārāyaṇa, obeisance to you, the highest abode, O Supreme Soul, O one greater than the greatest, O Lord possessing the properties of existence, knowledge and bliss, O blemishless one!

59. O cause of the universe, O Lord performing the acts of creation etc. by means of the different Guṇas, O Lord concealed by your own Māyā, O self-luminous one, obeisance to you.

60. You are neither within nor without. You are without as well as within. You are far off as well as quite near. You are both heavy and light. You are firm. You are minute as well as very massive. Obeisance to you.

61. O matchless one, obeisance to that Lord in the form of Kāla (Time), the graceful charm of whose sideglance creates crores of Fourfaced Lords (Brahmās) and a Parārdha of mine.

62. Obeisance to that Lord, the soul of the universe, whose body is beyond measurement, and each one of whose hair supports a number of Cosmic Eggs.

63. O Lord, in accordance with your own measurement of time you cause the origin and dissolution (birth and death) of Brahmā and also mark out the periods of Manvantara etc. Obeisance to you.

64. I have been created out of Tamōguṇa, O Lord. I am ignorant

of your power. Hence forgive my offence. Save me. I have sought refuge in you.

65. When (the Lord) who burned down the Tripuras eulogized thus, Adhokṣaja (Viṣṇu) manifested himself after casting off the form of the Discus.

66-68. His face (indicated that he was) delighted. The glorious Lord held the conch, the discus and the iron club. He was seated on Garuḍa as if on a lotus seat. He was adorned with a garland of sylvan flowers. He looked brilliant with necklaces, ear-rings, shoulderlets, crown and other ornaments. Lakṣmī was seated on his left lap. Satyabhāmā[1] was on the right side. His body was as lustrous as a black cloud. Though he was an ocean of mercy, he spoke to the husband of Girijā (who was) frightened, as if he was angry with him.

Śrī Bhagavān said:

69. How has such an evil-mindedness beset you at this time? O Śaṁbhu, for the sake of an insect of a (i.e. an insignificant) king, you have come to fight with me!

70-77. How many examples of my power have not been known to you, O Dhūrjaṭi (Śiva). It is true that your Pāśupata missile cannot be vanquished by Suras and Asuras. The Discus is a form of my anger. It cannot spare even you. Excepting you, who will wander in the world after disregarding me? By performing several austerities formerly you have acquired much strength as a form of mine from my body? Now if you wish to sport about with Gaurī here for a long time, if you wish that this city of Vārāṇasī should stay for a long time (do as follows).

On the shore of the Southern Sea there is a holy spot well known after my name, viz. Śrīpuruṣottama. It is adorned by Nīla mountain. It extends to ten Yojanas (i.e. 10 x 12=120 Kms.) up to Virajā Maṇḍala (modern Yājpur). The holy spot is gradually holier till the river Citrotpalā. The region beyond that as far as the Southern Sea is more and more excellent (sacred) step by step. Nīla mountain is a bestower of salvation. There (my idol) is made of blue sapphire gems. I am stationed there in four bodies (i.e. Jagannātha, Balabhadra, Subhadrā and Sudarśana). To the north of it is the forest named Ekāmraka. O annihilator of Tripuras, stay there fearlessly along with Pārvatī.

1. The author regards Viṣṇu and Kṛṣṇa as identical and brings in Satyabhāmā as Viṣṇu's consort along with Lakṣmī.

78. There you will be crowned as the king of a crore of Liṅgas[1] at my bidding by the Self-born Lord, the creator of all the worlds.

79. This Tīrtha Maṇikarṇika consists of all Tīrthas. Cast off your Ahaṁkāra (ego, pride) here and proceed along with all your followers.

Nārada said:

80. On being told thus by Vāsudeva the Three-eyed Lord bent down his head. With palms joined in reverence he spoke to the Slayer of Madhu:

Mahādeva said:

81. O Lord of Devas, O Lord of the universe, O Lord, O dispeller of the agony of those who bow down (to you), carrying out your behest will be the cause of my welfare, O Lord of the worlds.

82. On account of my stupidity, O Lord, I had been arrogant. There, O Lord, your own blessing is the cause of my fickleness.

83. Since you command me, O Lord of Devas, to proceed to Puruṣottama, I shall carry out your behest reverently and proceed to the auspicious holy place that bestows salvation.

84-85a. Do a favour to me and promise that you alone will protect and sustain my sacred region Puruṣottama. Protect it so that it will never perish hereafter.

85b-86. Thus this sacred place has been established formerly by Mahādeva after duly worshipping Lord Puruṣottama accompanied by Balarāma and Śrī. Here the Lord of Umā has been installed by Brahmā.

87-88. We shall go there and view the destroyer of Puras, the Lord of the Daughter of the Mountain, the Lord who like the sun dispels all the dense internal darkness.

Since this holy place of Śaṁbhu is completely destructive of Tamas, it grants welfare. Since it washes off Rajoguṇa, it is well known as Viraja Maṇḍala.

89-91. Since Sattvaguṇa prevails, Puruṣottama is well known as the bestower of salvation. Whatever other salvation-yielding holy spots there are and heard of by you, O great king, they all bestow liberation here itself. This holy spot, O great king, cannot produce faith in those whose minds are defiled by misdeeds and sins. This is the secret of the Discus-bearing Lord.

1. This explains the epithet of Koṭiliṅgeśvara.

Jaimini said:

92-93. On hearing the words of Nārada the king became delighted in his mind. With his eyes beaming and dilated due to surprise, he spoke to the tiger among sages:

"O Brāhmaṇa, the highly sanctifying holy spot has been properly described to me. It is the place where Umāpati (Śiva) is present and Puruṣottama is the protector. Even if the route is circuitous, we shall certainly go there because this is the right means for the accomplishment of our desired objective."

Jaimini said:

94. Thereafter, O Brāhmaṇas, the sage and the king along with the army reached the holy spot named Ekāmravana at midday.

95. The king took his holy bath in Bindu Tīrtha and worshipped Puruṣottama installed on the bank in accordance with the injunctions. Then he went to the great temple of Koṭīśvara.

96-100. At the entrance, the king duly performed the rite of *Ācamana* (i.e. ceremonious sipping of water) and as he took pleasure (in it he) gifted numerous excellent horses, elephants, gems, garments, ornaments and wealth to Brāhmaṇas, since he was engaged in Sāttvika form of piety.

After taking the holy bath, he worshipped Tribhuvaneśa[1] (Lord of the three worlds) Liṅga (modern Liṅgarāja at Bhuvaneśvara) and derived matchless pleasure as he saw the identity of the Lord with Viṣṇu. He eulogized and bowed down to the Lord with devotion. He sang songs of devotion and played on the Vīṇā.

With palms joined in reverence he sought to propitiate the Lord with his mind exclusively directed towards him. He stood there meditating on the Bull-bannered Lord.

Then the Three-eyed Lord Parameśvara became pleased, O Brāhmaṇas. With each syllable of every word distinctly expressed the Lord spoke to the king directly:

Koṭiliṅgeśa said:

101-103. O great king Indradyumna, a Vaiṣṇava like you is very rare on the earth. Your desire will be perfectly realized after some time.

1. *Ekāmra Purāṇa* and other sources state that Tribhuvaneśvara (Liṅgarāja) was worshipped as Hari-hara (a synthesis of Vaiṣṇavism and Śaivism).

After saying this Śaṁbhu vanished in the very presence of the king. Then he said to Nārada: "O highly fortunate one, carry out what has been commanded by the Self-born Lord along with a horse-sacrifice in that holy spot Śrī Puruṣottama which is the body of Viṣṇu.

104. The interior altar (*antar-vedī*) is highly meritorious. It is like the heart of Viṣṇu. I have been installed in eight forms for the sake of protecting it.

105. I, Nīlakaṇṭha, have been established at the tip of the conch-like[1] (holy-spot) along with Durgā. O eminent Brāhmaṇa. Take this king to that place.

106. Now Hari with the blue sapphire body has vanished. At my bidding build the shrine of Śrī Narasiṁha there.

107-108. There in our presence let the excellent king perform a thousand horse-sacrifices. At the end of those (sacrifices), O excellent Brāhmaṇa, show him that wonderful tree devoid of blemishes and having the form of Brahman. Viśvakarmā will carve four statues therefrom.

109-112a. At the time of their installation Brahmā himself will come so that this king shall get rid of his sins by worshipping Hari by means of horse-sacrifices. Let him go on continuously worshipping Hari for a thousand years. At one end thereof he will see (the Lord) who is the support of all the worlds and destroyer of all sins. On those who visit him the Lord-with-wooden-form will bestow salvation. Neither Brahmā nor you nor I shall know his deeds. He will be pleased only by devoutly carrying out his commands."

112b-113. Nārada bowed down to Mahādeva, the sire of the universe. With palms joined in reverence he said: "(I shall carry out) what has been commanded by you, O Lord. Brahmā too has directed me to carry it out in this manner. Brahmā and you, O Lord, are not different from the Supreme Soul.

114-115. The fortune of this king (is really great). The blessings of you three cannot be even mentally conceived. This Lord, the sanctifier of all living beings, is one whose greatness cannot be even thought of. By his association even the vicious ones can cross the ocean of worldly existence.

116. By how much devotion the Lord is pleased, is beyond the reach of the intellect. By repeating the Vedic passages and other activities people continue to strive for it for a long time. But even an insignificant person attains salvation effortlessly.

1. Puruṣottama Kṣetra is regarded as conch-like in shape.

117-120. The cowherdesses who maintained themselves by (selling) milk and milk products, who spent their days either within the house or wandering about in the forests and who sustained themselves through the forest produces, attained liberation through the enjoyment of love sports.

Śiśupāla who always hated and fought with him attained salvation (even) in the middle of the assembly hall. The hunter pierced the heart (of Kṛṣṇa ?) and attained the goal very difficult to be attained.

Formerly a hunch-backed maiden dragged him to her house by his clothes and enjoyed herself with him whereas the celestial damsels who meditate upon him do not get him at all.

Formerly the Lord granted salvation to a Cāṇḍāla who was very far off but not to a Brāhmaṇa who was well-versed in the Vedas, who was close (to him) and was a great devotee.

121-128. By means of his Māyā the Lord may deceive you as well as Brahmā. Many persons beginning with Gautama still remain in the bondage of physical bodies, suffering from much misery while performing austerities. They cling to their vow of celibacy and they stay till the end of the Kalpa. His acts cannot be comprehended or expressed by saying 'It is like this, it is like that'.

It is not possible to delineate the conduct of this highly intelligent one even by much effort or in the course of a long time.

Many means have been recommended in the scriptural texts for the sake of liberation in the case of learned men. Many of them do worship (by sacrifice). But the most excellent means of all is the residence in (the holy place) Puruṣottama which is certainly conducive to attain *Sāyujya* with the Lord like an excellent companion. That means of attaining this Lord capable of wielding Māyā is invariably connected (with the residence there). The place where Hari placed himself and where he fixed his residence shall become universally known due to the association with Indradyumna. Hence allow me, O Lord of Devas. I shall take this king along with his army to the land at the foot of the mountain and establish him there. I shall then initiate him in the act of the great sacrifice (i.e. horse-sacrifice). Thereafter, O Bull-emblemed Lord, I shall come near your lotus-like feet."

Jaimini said:

129. Saying "So be it", the Lord vanished. The sage drove in the chariot of the king to the excellent holy spot.

130-133. The second day the king reached Kapoteśa.[1] Its length and breadth are the same. It is full of ponds of water and trees. In the eastern boundary was Bilveśa who was stationed on the seashore. His minister indicated that the place was suitable for encamping the army. The excellent king encamped the army in their befitting places. He bowed down to Bilveśvara[2] and Kapoteśa and worshipped them. Accompanied by Nārada the intelligent king got into the chariot. Mentally and verbally, thinking and glorifying Viṣṇu, the resident of Nīla mountain, O Brāhmaṇa, he went to the presence of Hari.

CHAPTER THIRTEEN

*The Greatness of Kapoteśa and Bilveśvara**

The sages enquired:

1. It behoves you to recount to us why this site of Kapoteśa became famous, O great sage. Who Kapota was and who was the Lord, O great sage?

Jaimini replied:

2. Formerly Kuśasthalī became inhospitable for habitation of creatures because it was fully overgrown with Kuśa grass having keen edges and thorns.

3-4. It was devoid of trees. It had no water-reservoirs. It was like an abode of Piśācas (ghosts). Formerly no Deva other than the Lord (Viṣṇu) was worshipped. A desire to compete with (Viṣṇu) and a feeling of rivalry arose in Dhūrjaṭi (Śiva) who thought, 'Let me too be worshipped'. Thinking thus he turned his mind to the devotion of the same Viṣṇu.

5-8. 'I shall propitiate Hari by resorting to a very great penance, staying in a place devoid of all objects. I shall have no personal possessions. What is it that I should speak to the Lord of Ramā? What

1. Kapoteśa temple is now situated at Candanapura at the bifurcation of the rivers Bhārgavī and Mittlānī (on Kāṭhapola Nadī).

2. The temple of Bilveśa is on the eastern side of Puri.

*Kapoteśa is at Chandanpur (Puri) and Bilveśa on the seashore to the east of Guṇḍicā house.

can be the eulogy for Śāradāpati(?)? What else can give satisfaction to the deity who is the lord of the whole universe? Hence no external thing can be of any use to him. Therefore, I shall adopt Antaryāga ('Internal sacrifice' i.e. Mātṛkā Nyāsa etc.) with a pure mind. I shall propitiate Hari, the sire of mobile and immobile beings, the Lord who offers his own soul unto the devotees. By his grace I shall be worthy of being worshipped by all.'

9-10. Thinking thus in his mind, he went to the holy spot Kuśasthalī. He performed a very severe penance near Nīla mountain. Maheśvara avoided all *Dvandvas* (i.e. pairs of opposites e.g. heat-cold, pleasure-pain). He took in only air. Eight-formed[1] though he was, the Lord was reduced to the size of a dove.

11. The delighted Lord granted him supremacy, so that he became equal (to Viṣṇu) in respect of worship, reverence etc.

12. By the power of his penance that holy spot became one comparable to Vṛndāvana, the forest near Gokula. Its interior was rendered splendid by lakes, ponds, reservoirs and rivers.

13. It was full of different kinds of trees and creepers (laden) with fruits and flowers of all seasons. It was resonant with the humming sounds of bees inebriated with honey.

14-15. It was full of different kinds of flocks of birds. It was a comfortable place of resort for all creatures. Since by means of his penance Śiva became (small) like a dove, he came to be called Kapoteśvara[2] at the behest of Murāri (Viṣṇu). It is at his bidding that the Three-eyed Lord always stays here along with Mṛḍānī (Pārvatī).

16. Those who worship, eulogize and bow down to Kapoteśa shall get rid of all their sins and attain Puruṣottama.

17-22. Henceforth I shall narrate the greatness of Bilveśa, O Brāhmaṇas.

Formerly Daityas who were the residents of Pātāla pierced through the surface of the earth and began to harass Bhūrloka. They used to devour people.

When the Lord incarnated as the son of Devakī in order to reduce the burden on the earth, and protected the earth along with the Yādavas and the Pāṇḍavas, he once came to that spot.

---

1. The following are the eight forms of Śiva: (The special name of that form is given in the bracket) 1. Earth (Śarva); 2. Water (Bhava); 3. Fire (Rudra); 4. Wind (Ugra); 5. Ether (Bhīma); 6. The sacrificer i.e. Yajamāna (Paśupati); 7. The Moon (Mahādeva); 8. The Sun (Īśāna).

2. The above is an explanatory legend to support the derivation of the name Kapoteśvara.

He took his bath in the water of the Tīrtharāja (the ocean) and paid obeisance to Nīla Mādhava from a great distance mentally. Then he came to the entrance (of the abode of) Daityas.

He found that the underground passage was awful and impenetrable for human beings. He deluded the worlds with wrong notions (?) and desirous of spreading (the idea of) the venerability of Śiva, he took up a fruit of a Bilva tree and invoked the Three-eyed Lord there. After worshipping the Destroyer of the Puras, Śrīkṛṣṇa eulogized him.

Śrī Bhagavān prayed:

23. Obeisance to you, O Lord beyond the three Guṇas, O Lord who divides the three Guṇas, O Lord, embodiment of the three Vedas, O Lord beyond the three (Vedas). Obeisance to the knower of the three divisions of time (viz. Past, Present and Future).

24. To the Lord with the Moon, the Sun and Fire as eyes, obeisance to the excellent Ātman favourable to Brāhmaṇas. Salute to you, the storehouse of eightfold prosperity, to the eight-formed Lord.

25. Obeisance to the Lord devoid of Tamas, the Lord whose form is beyond darkness, who is immutable and is destructive of darkness and who dispels the darkness of ignorance.

26. After eulogizing his own Ātman by means of his own Ātman, the Lord saw that the passage had become easily penetrable by his favour.

27-29a. Through that passage the Lord went to Pātāla along with his army. There he slew the Daityas who were fierce and powerful and removed the burden (of the earth).

He then came back to the same place. There the Lord worshipped the Bull-emblemed Lord. Desirous of establishing Śiva there in order to block the passage, the highly intelligent Gadādhara (Kṛṣṇa), the Lord who can be won over by devotion, said thus:

29b-33. "O Dhūrjaṭi (Śiva), stay here in the place preventing Asuras from coming out. Who else, O Śaṁbhu, is competent to destroy the army of Rākṣasas?"

After establishing Mahādeva he returned to Dvārakā. Since then Bilveśa became famous on the earth.

O Brāhmaṇas, that Bilveśa is the first creator of the prominent sacred place. By visiting that immutable Lord of Mṛḍānī, the Lord who destroys sins, one shall derive all the desired results. One shall surmount adversity very difficult to cross.

The greatness of Kapoteśa and Bilveśvara has been recounted to you, O sages. Henceforth, what else do you wish to hear?

CHAPTER FOURTEEN

Nārada Consoles Indradyumna and Urges Him to Perform Horse-sacrifices

The sages asked:

1. When they got into the chariot and proceeded ahead, where did Nārada and the king go? What did they do? Describe it to us, O great sage.

Jaimini said:

2. Along with Vidyāpati, the younger brother of the priest, they came near the boundary of the holy place of Nīlakaṇṭha.

3-4. There appeared bad omens on the way. The left eye and the left arm of the king who was going ahead, began to throb and tremble frequently. On seeing them the tiger among kings became dejected. He asked the sage who was a storehouse of all knowledge, the reason thereof.

5-7. "My empire is unassailed. This excellent holy spot has been reached. Our pilgrimage to Mādhava is conducive to auspiciousness. What ominous thing can happen to me today? O sage, tell me truthfully. My left eye throbs and the left arm trembles frequently."

On hearing it Nārada spoke indicating the future task and telling the king the words of welfare and happiness uttered by the Lotus-born Lord.

Nārada said:

8-10. O king, do not get dejected. Generally all auspicious things are impeded by obstacles. When the abstacles are removed, O king, everything shall be splendid in the case of fortunate persons. It is true that you are an emperor. This holy spot is verily the physical body of Viṣṇu. But the deity for whom you have undertaken this pilgrimage has vanished. It was covered up with golden sands in the evening on the day next to that when this Brāhmaṇa Vidyāpati visited it. The deity has gone to his abode in Pātāla and has become very difficult of access in the human world."

Jaimini said:

11. On hearing this dreadful utterance that was as bad as the fall of the thunderbolt, the king fell on the ground unconscious, O excellent Brāhmaṇas.

12. On seeing him fallen thus all the friendly assistants and comrades with the priest as their leader rushed towards him crying out "Alas! Alas!"

13. They frequently sprinkled on his face cold water mixed with camphor. They smeared all his body with sandal paste, agallochum and camphor.

14-15. They quickly fanned him with chowries and fans. Nārada too became bewildered. Performing the yogic process of Dhāraṇā ('Retention') he saved the life of the king knowing that the future good lay therein. After a long time the king regained consciousness by their excellent efforts.

16-19. He got up and fell down at the feet of Nārada, O Brāhmaṇas (and said): "What sin have I committed in a previous birth? It is certainly on account of its ripening that this terrible misery has befallen. O great sage, even in dream no offence has been committed by me mentally, physically or verbally against Brāhmaṇas and cows. O tiger among sages, no holy rite, whether *Nitya*, *Naimittika* or *Kāmya*, prescribed for kings has been omitted by me. O great sage, no insult has been perpetrated by me towards deities, guests, servants, manes, dependents and kinsmen.

20-24. There are fifty (possible) offences against Viṣṇu, O leading Vaiṣṇava; all of them have been avoided by me like huge, furious serpents.

What lucky (and meritorious) act has been done by that younger brother of my priest? He has been able to see Lord Nīlamādhava with the physical eye.

What for did you cause the loss of the kingdom deliberately, even when you knew about this? How is that this was not declared at the time when we set out on the journey?

Why was the abode of Brāhmaṇas well-versed in the Vedas uprooted by me? Why were the lands excellently maintained for a long time abandoned by these people? Ever since the inception of their families the subjects had pursued certain vocations for their livelihood. For my sake they have (now) abandoned them. How will they maintain themselves now?

25. If I do not see Hari, I will put an end to my life. This is my resolve, O Brāhmaṇa. If I die what will be of the subjects?

26. O sage, you are always kind. You advise me as regards the auspicious and inauspicious. Take my son to Mālava and crown him there.

27-29. Let him protect the land with justice. Let not these subjects be subjected to grief. Let all those kings who have come here at my behest return and carry out the directions of my son. I will remain in this holy spot contemplating on Nīlamādhava, I will observe a fast unto death and make the remaining part of my life fruitful."

Jaimini said:

30. As King Indradyumna was lamenting thus, the son of Brahmā made him rise up. Consoling him with kind and gentle words he spoke thus:

Nārada said:

31-35. O king, you are at the head of learned men. You are a Vaiṣṇava and an ocean of courage. How is it that you do not realize that (spiritual) welfare is always attended with obstacles?

This is the greatest good of man that can be acquired only in the course of a hundred births, that one can see with his physical eye the Club-bearing Lord in physical form.

Hari's sportive activity is unrestrained. By whom can it be understood completely? Though I am a living-liberated soul, O king, I do not go beyond his Līlā (sportive activity).

I am a staunch devotee. I stay near the Lord. Still have I not been deceived by him many times? Even by many hundreds of births one cannot resist his Māyā. This endless Māyā of his cannot be comprehended even by the Lotus-born Lord who occupies the lotus coming out of the navel (of the Lord), even though he is in the habit of eulogizing him always.

36. The nature of the master of Māyā has been spoken to you thus, O king. Now I shall tell you especially that you are the most excellent one among fortunate persons.

37-41. All the three forms of his are inclined to bless you.

The creator of the mobile and immobile beings (god Brahmā), the grandfather himself of all the worlds told me thus: "You do go quickly near Indradyumna. He will go to Nīla mountain desirous of seeing Nīlamādhava. After being requested by Yama the Lord has vanished. He must not grieve over it. This (disappearance) cannot be made otherwise. That king, the fifth one in my line, should be spoken to in my words (i.e. conveyed my message) that for his sake I will propitiate Puruṣottama, the Supreme Soul, and will bring him from Śveta island[1] at the end of the thousandth horse-sacrifice. Let that king Indradyumna worship Viṣṇu by means of a thousand horse-sacrifices and stay now in the holy spot of Śrī Puruṣottama.

42-45. At the end, he will see with his (physical) eye Lord Viṣṇu of wooden form. That incarnation of Hari will become famous through him. At that time the bodies (i.e. idols) of Viṣṇu are to be certainly installed by me.

Formerly Lord Hari of bejewelled idol had been in four different forms. The king's priest had seen the Lord and informed the king directly.

The Lord of divine wooden form will incarnate in four forms. Hence, O leading king, do not be grieved. Your desire will certainly be fruitful. There is no doubt about it. Stay here without any worry."

Jaimini said:

46. Thus, O Brāhmaṇas, Nārada consoled the king and restored his confidence. Thereafter he spoke to him once again.

Nārada said:

47. Accompanied by Durgā the Blue-throated Lord (Śiva) is present at the tip of the excellent holy spot having the form of a conch-shell.[2] We shall go there. That is a flat land suitable for horse-sacrifice.

48. In it we shall build a very good structure that will stay firm for a thousand years, for the purpose of the horse-sacrifice. By visiting the Nṛsiṁha idol of the Lord residing on Nīla mountain we shall make our life contented and blessed.

49. At the end of the sacrifice we shall, for the purpose of destroying all obstacles and for increasing the benefit, install an idol worthy of being worshipped by you always.

50. Through excellent sages we shall begin the excellent sacri-

1. Śvetadvīpa: The abode of Viṣṇu. It is supposed to be in the Milk Ocean.
2. Śaṅkha-Kṣetra: Puruṣottama Kṣetra is conceived to be conch-shaped.

fice in a suitable manner. Delaying is not conducive to welfare. Such is the advice of Brahmā.

CHAPTER FIFTEEN

Indradyumna's Grief Dispelled: Manifestation of Four-formed Viṣṇu

Jaimini said:

1-2. Then those Brāhmaṇas left the excellent chariot and walked on foot along with their followers. They approached Nīlakaṇṭha joyously. After worshipping Mahādeva and bowing down to Śrīdurgā they started climbing Nīla mountain[1] with the senses under perfect control.

3. It was overgrown with different kinds of trees and creepers and full of various types of birds. Rugged rocks prevented free passage therein. There was a halo round the mountain.

4. The huge rocks that were tossed about (on the mountain) were hovered around by humming bees causing a confusion of sounds. The waves and waters of the Southern Sea came as far as the ridge of this mountain.

5. It was beyond human imagination and always impenetrable due to the presence of huge serpents. The interior of the mountain was extremely terrible on account of the trumpeting sounds of elephants in their rut.

6. It was always infested with beasts of prey. They never knew an attack (by human beings) with weapons. Many herds of deer moved all around fearlessly.

7. They (i.e. the Brāhmaṇas) were desirous of entering it, but could not see the path leading into it. But due to Nārada's presence they came to know the top of the mountain.

8. They reached the place where the Lord is present in the form of the divine lion beneath the black aloewood tree, dispelling the fear of all adversities.

9. On seeing that Lord crores of the sins of Brāhmaṇa-slaughter

---

1. Purāṇic descriptions are to be cautiously accepted. For example: Svarṇādri in Ekāmra Kṣetra is regarded as the site of Liṅgarāja temple but actually there is no hill there at all. So is the case here.

incurred by men perish. The Lord has a huge open mouth with terrible teeth and tawny-coloured dishevelled manes.

10. He looked fierce with three eyes. The body of the Daitya is kept on his thighs in a supine position. With his claws as frightful as thunderbolt the Lord is (depicted as) tearing the chest of the demon.

11. He has pink lustre with blazing (v.1. lolling) tongue. The Lord bursts into a thunderous laughter. In his arms the conch and the discus were shining. The coronet and the crown dazzled brilliantly.

12. Sparks of fire emit from his eyes, frightening all the quarters. His lotus-like feet have gone deep down into the earth as he has stamped on the ground with great force.

13. Viewing the primordial idol of Hari in the presence of Nārada they looked at the Lord without fear. Free from ailments they bowed down to him from a distance.

14. On seeing the Lord Indradyumna began to believe the words of Nārada. With steady confidence in the future task he said to the great sage:

15. "I am contented (as I have almost fulfilled my task), O great sage; you are the greatest storehouse of knowledge. This Nṛsiṁha is very difficult to be propitiated. He is frightful even to look at.

16. He should be worshipped well by people like you. He should be worshipped from a distance by people like me. I am contented and blessed merely by viewing him. All my sins have been destroyed.

17-19. Since you are nearby, O sage, we stand here fearlessly. The Lord has an excessively terrible form. How can he be propitiated by people deficient in vigour and power? He is excessively frightening in the act of tearing up the king of Daityas, the lord of the three worlds.

Where is that place in which the blue sapphire form of the ocean of mercy had stood originally, O excellent sage, and which bestows salvation by mere sight? Show me that (place) which I consider as the bestower of salvation, O eminent Brāhmaṇa."

20. Thus requested Nārada pointed out to him the sacred place where the Lord stood covered with golden sands.

21. "See this Nyagrodha (Banyan) tree, O king. Its girth is one Yojana and its height is two Yojanas. It will stand till the end of the Kalpa. It bestows salvation on men.

22. One is liberated from the shackles of sins by coming under the shade of the tree. A man who gives up his life at the root of this tree, shall attain salvation.

23. Even by seeing the sinless Nārāyaṇa in the form of the Nyagrodha

tree a man becomes sinless. Then what to say if he worships and eulogizes?

24. It was to the west of the root of this (tree) and to the north of Nṛsiṁha, O king, that Mādhava, the Lord, stood in four different forms.

25-26. He will manifest here once again to bless you. Viṣṇu has his own abode in the Śveta island which is the land of enjoyment of pleasures. Similarly this is known as his own abode in Jaṁbūdvīpa which is the land of holy rites. Since it is a very great secret, its revelation is not approved of.

27. Only one who is eligible to be liberated knows this place, O king. It cannot be believed by (ordinary) men and by vicious people in particular.

28. Another idol of Viṣṇu which was installed here by the citizens, O king, is also a bestower of salvation. What doubt can there be then in the case of an idol installed by the Self-born Lord (Brahmā)?

29. (Manifestation) and vanishing of the Lord of the universe has a purpose behind it. He incarnates in different forms in different Yugas for the sake of blessing the good and pious people.

30. The Lord takes the forms of fish, tortoise etc. When the purpose is served the great Lord vanishes.

31-32. The ocean of kindness is stationed here permanently without any reason. Just as Lord Viṣṇu incarnates elsewhere from the Śveta island, so also stationed here the Lord manifests himself mercifully in places like Dvārakā, Kāñcī, Puṣkara etc. like sprouts from the roots of (mother) tree.

33. Incarnations in the different lands, holy spots, Tīrthas and shrines are (his) partial incarnations. Let there be no doubt in you about it, O king.

34. Īśāna (Śiva) does not forsake this holy spot even for a moment as he does not leave off his own sphere (land). There will be another manifestation, O king, known by you."

35. After saying this, Nārada, the noble soul, pointed out the exact spot. There Indradyumna prostrated himself with eight limbs (touching the ground).

36. Thinking that the Lord was present there personally, he began to eulogize:

Indradyumna prayed:

37. O Lord of Devas, O Lord of the worlds, O destroyer of the

agony of those who bow down (to you), save me, O lotus-eyed Lord. I have fallen into the ocean of worldly existence.

38. You are the only great Lord capable of destroying the mass of miseries. Only worthless, insignificant persons serve worthless and insignificant (deities) with a desire to get a small measure of happiness and comfort.

39. (I pray to you to destroy) the heap of my great sins of three kinds (accumulated) since very early times without a beginning, which cannot be annihilated and which goes on increasing in the course of different births.

40-41a. You are the bestower of salvation on men who see you directly. What of those who are prompted with the feelings of devotion? (They will certainly be liberated.) Those are fools who aver that you who are a storehouse of mercy, are subject to Karma. They do not know that Karma itself has been directed by you.

41b-42. What sins were not committed by the Brāhmaṇa Ajāmila[1] who had neglected everything prescribed for the people of different castes and stages of life? O Lord, he too was liberated by uttering your name. Merely by remembering (you) he was released from those (servants of Yama) with nooses in their hands.

43-44a. All the means of viewing you, O Lord of Devas, have been glorified. Indeed, when you are seen, all the doubts lurking in the heart are dispelled.

When one is free from doubts, certainly all sins and merits disappear.

44b-45. Bless me, O Lord. I am wretched and I seek refuge in you alone.

Even as I was within the womb, all my future events were decided by you. Let my life pass on with them. I beg you only for this.

46. Formerly your idol was stationed here and it has bestowed liberation on even a being of low order. Let me see that form with this mortal eye. I have no other aim in view.

47. After eulogizing the Slayer of Madhu thus with palms joined in reverence, the king bowed down again and lay prostrated on the ground with tears in his eyes.

48. Thereafter an ethereal voice with gentle and clear tone uttered as follows, from the middle of the sky, even as Indradyumna stood listening:

1. For the story of Ajāmila vide BhP VI.1.21-68.

49. "Do not be worried, O king. I shall come within the range of your vision. Carry out the direction of Brahmā as mentioned by Nārada."

50. On hearing that divine utterance as well as what had been spoken by Nārada before, the king gained conviction that the horse-sacrifice must be performed. He decided to do what was pleasing to th Lord.

51-52. With words choked with tears of joy, he spoke to Nārada again: "O sage, what has been commanded by you at the instance of Brahmā, the four-faced Lord, has been approved by this unembodied voice. There is no difference between Brahmā and Viṣṇu, the Lord of the worlds.

53. Indeed you are the son of the Lotus-born Lord. Your words are the words of the Lord. Hence it should be performed because it is conducive to welfare."

CHAPTER SIXTEEN

Installation of the Idol of Nṛsiṁha

Jaimini said:

1. On seeing that the king was cheerful in his mind believing in (the efficacy of) the great sacrifice, Nārada, the delighter of the worlds, spoke to him with great pleasure:

2. "Devas lend a helping hand in the enterprises of meritorious ones. An example thereof is you yourself, as you have the assistance of the Four-faced Lord (Brahmā).

3-4a. Therefore come on. Let us go there to the presence of Nīlakaṇṭha. In front of him, O king, I shall install Nṛsiṁha, the destroyer of all Rākṣasas, the dispeller of all obstacles. The idol shall be facing the West.

4b-5a. The Lord has vanished, but this Nṛsiṁha is visible. The sacrifice in his presence shall yield excellent fruit.

5b-6. You go ahead quickly and get a palace built there. On my remembering (him) the son of Viśvakarman will come there and build the West-facing Mansion rapidly.

7-8. To the south of Nīlakaṇṭha, a hundred Bows' length away (i.e. 400 *Hastas* or about 100 Metres), there is a pretty old huge sandal tree. The land to the west of it shall be the requisite site (for sacrifice), O king. There you do perform a thousand horse-sacrifices.

9-10. You go. I shall stay here for five days and propitiate this divine lion of infinite form of fiery nature. In the return worship, in the idol, I shall install the Lord along with vital breath, sense-organs and mind. Just as one lights a lamp from another lamp, so also (I shall infuse the new idol with the power of the old one) and I shall bring the idol of splendid form."

11. On hearing these words of Nārada the excellent king hurriedly went near the sandal tree.

12-13a. There he saw the son of the Celestial Architect, who had come at the bidding of Nārada. He stood there assuming human form with the necessary implements.

13b-14. On seeing the king desirous of building a shrine, he spoke to him with palms joined in reverence: "O lord, I am conversant with the Science of Architecture. I shall build a temple of Narasiṁha with splendid features." O Brāhmaṇas, the king replied to him laughingly.

Indradyumna said:

15-17. You are no ordinary architect. You are an expounder of the Science of Architecture. This has been spoken by Nārada himself. You are the extremely reputed son of Tvaṣṭṛ.

In this tenantless big forest there was no human habitation before. O Architect, we have come only today; how can we have contacts with architects? You alone can be the architect (of the temple) of Viṣṇu of unmeasured refulgence. You always meditate upon him. You strictly abide by his behest.

18. The sage by whom you have been remembered, will himself come here in a couple of days taking the idol of Narasiṁha with him.

19. Therefore, build a palatial temple of Narasiṁha along with the rampart walls, ornamental gateways etc. It should be a splendid structure facing the West.

20. The king honoured him duly and engaged him in the work of construction. By spending a great deal of money he engaged a number of servants for collecting stones.

21. Thanks to the greatness of the celestial architect, O Brāhmaṇas,

the excellent Mansion-like shrine was complete on the fourth day, though (ordinarily) it could have been accomplished only after a long time.

22-24. When the day dawned clear, the king concluded his daily round of holy rites. Accompanied by his followers he took with him the requisite materials for the installation. While he awaited the arrival of Nārada, presently (mixed) sounds were heard in the sky, viz. those of conchshells, Mṛdaṅga drums, Muraja drums, auspicious songs and instruments of music, the sounds of bells, the trumpeting of elephants and shouts of "Be victorious, be victorious".

25-31. On hearing them Indradyumna and other kings, Brāhmaṇas well-versed in the Vedas and thousands of Vaiṣṇavas stood surprised. While they were thinking like 'These sounds have risen without any (visible) source. No doubt it is a mysterious phenomenon,' a wind blew from the South. There were showers of flowers with great fragrance accompanied by the humming sounds of bees. O Brāhmaṇas, they were drenched with the waters of Gaṅgā.

Immediately after this, Nārada, the son of Brahmā, came with the idol of Narasiṁha, which had been made by Viśvakarman. It had a halo around it. It was highly delightful. It was embellished with many kinds of gems and decorative features. It had divine garlands and robes. Divine scents and unguents had been smeared upon it. It was very beautiful. The holy rite of infusing Prāṇa (vital airs) had been completed herein. It was rendered splendid by celestial women with diamond-studded chowries in their hands. The idol was kept in an excellent *Vimāna* (a decorated carriage, or palanquin) created by the power of penance.

32-37. On seeing the idol, all the kings and the followers of the kings became greatly pleased. 'The Lord had vanished. Has he been brought back by Nārada?' thought all those delighted souls. They praised the sage too. On carefully observing the form of Narasiṁha that was near them, they thought that it was a replica of the earlier idol of Nṛsiṁha. With delighted mind the king stood up in honour thereof. He circumambulated Hari and bent down his head so as to touch the ground. At the behest of the king the sage furnished the palace of splendid characteristics with all the requisites befitting the faithful devotion and affluence (of the king). The idol of the Lord of Devas along with Dharā (Earth) and Ramā (Lakṣmī) was installed on a gem-set altar in an auspicious hour. The idol was infused with Yogic power.

In the company of Vaiṣṇava Brāhmaṇas, the kings and the intelligent Nārada King Indradyumna eulogized it with secret Upaniṣad Mantras, Smṛti Texts, eulogies, and passages from scriptures with great joy.

Indradyumna said:

38-39. O Lord, possessing single, multiple, gross, subtle and minute forms, O Lord beyond the firmament, O Lord with a single form of the firmament, O Lord with the shape of the sky, O pervading one, O Lord stationed in the sky, O Lord mounted on the firmament, O Lord with the sky for the tresses, O Lord with a lotus for womb! O Divine Lion, save me from the ocean of misery. O Lord having the combined splendour of many crores of suns coming out (together), O Lord who are always near at hand and yet stationed far away, O Lord who are neither away nor close by, O Lord with the states of *Bodhya* (i.e. that which should be known) and *Bodha* (i.e. knowledge)!

40. You are both comprehensible and incomprehensible. You can be realised through knowledge, yet you cannot be so realized. You are beyond Māyā. You can be measured, comprehended through inference; you are the cause of everything. You are the maker of everything. You are the knower, protector and annihilator (of all things). O Witness of the universe, obeisance to you!

41-42. (We know) you are the sole cause of the destruction of misery, and not merely the cause; you are born ahead in order to dispel doubts. O Lord with fiery form, (O Lord) with knowledge as form; O light! O Lord, the source of the collection of Stoma sacrifices; O cause of creation! Grant me the excellent perpetual devotion unto your lotus-like feet, the devotion which is the source of the four Puruṣārthas. There are persons who are perpetually engaged in the rites etc. laid down in Śrutis and Smṛtis but are bound within the ocean of worldly existence. They stay here in a wretched condition.

43-45. I seek refuge in you, the Lord with infinite number of feet,[1] hands, eyes and ears, whose garments are the quarters, whose excellent ear-rings are the Sun and the Moon, who have an excellent necklace made of the clusters of stars, who have the wonderfully divine form of Nṛsiṁha (Man-Lion) and who fulfil the desires of devotees.

I bow down to the Lord whose lotus-like feet bloom by the light of the gems of the crown of Brahmā; on the ground of the extremity of the pair of whose lotus-like feet his (Brahmā's) head which is evolved out of the five elements, rolls, and which divine feet the women of the king of Suras bear on their heads.

46. I bow down to that fierce divine lion who destroys the mass of sins of those who resort to his feet—the lion who is an ocean of

1. Purāṇic echo of the Puruṣasūkta (RV X.90).

mercy and by the stroke of whose lotus-like feet all the Cosmic Eggs are shattered.

47. I bow down to Nṛhari who has the three worlds in his belly, who drowns the sound of the thundering clouds by means of his fierce and boisterous laughter, and who routes away the mass of sins by means of the groups of clouds that are scattered when he shakes his thick cluster of manes.

48. Obeisance to you, salute to you, bow to you, O Viṣṇu, O Lord merciful to the poor and the wretched; save me the helpless one. O enemy of Mura, may there be no bondage of physical bodies for me in the prison of worldly existence after attaining you.

49. O Lord, have compassion for me so that at the end of the thousand horse-sacrifices I shall be able to see you of divine form with these physical eyes.

50. O Lord of Yajñas, show me your favour and let me have your proximity, so that my thousand sacrifices may conclude without obstacles.

51. Crores of the heaps of sins of those who eulogize you perish. So it is no wonder that virtue, wealth and love are within their reach. O Viṣṇu, those men who resort to you are the enjoyers of salvation.

52. After eulogizing that Divine Lion thus, the king became delighted in his mind. He fell down on the ground frequently by way of prostrating in front of him.

Jaimini said:

53. That shrine and holy spot of Narasiṁha was built by Brahmā formerly for blessing Indradyumna and for the welfare of all the worlds.

54. There is no doubt about this that those who visit that Nṛsiṁha installed along with Śaṁbhu, do not get involved in the bondage of physical bodies, O Brāhmaṇas.

55. Those who eulogize that Lord in the form of Divine Lion by means of this prayer, obtain whatever is desired by them mentally and even more than that.

56-61. The Lord who gives all desired things grants him salvation.

The Divine Lion was installed in that holy spot by the great sage, the son of Brahmā, on the twelfth day in the bright half of the lunar month of Jyeṣṭha (while it was) in conjunction with the Svātī constellation. Those who visit the Lord on that day obtain more than the benefit of a thousand horse-sacrifices.

Men who bathe the idol with Pañcāmṛta, milk, coconut-water or scented water after offering worship, shall attain the world of Brahmā. They should worship the great Lion with all offerings including milk pudding. Garlands of China-rose flowers as well as splendid garlands of other sweet-smelling flowers should be offered. Incenses, lights, camphor, very fine betel leaves etc. should be offered. Prayers should be recited with excellent words and nice tone. With loud shouts of "Be victorious", he should be circumambulated and bowed down to. Charitable gifts should be made and Brāhmaṇas should be propitiated. By propitiating Narasiṁha thus one shall obtain the world of Brahmā.

62. The first incarnation of the Lion, O Brāhmaṇas, appeared on the fourteenth day of the month of Vaiśākha on a Saturday at the time of dusk in conjunction with Kṛttikā star.

63. If one worships Narasiṁha duly with mental concentration and purity on that day, the heap of sins accumulated in the course of crores of births is burned at the very same instant like a heap of cotton by fire.

64. By visiting, touching, bowing down, falling down (at the feet) and devoutly eulogizing the Lord one is liberated from sins just as a serpent gets rid of slough.

65. He shall not be afflicted with sickness, grief or worries. He shall obtain all desired objects and the benefit of a horse-sacrifice.

66. O Brāhmaṇas, if Yajñas, charitable gifts or other holy rites are performed near him once, they shall have crores and crores of times the benefit by the favour of Narasiṁha.

CHAPTER SEVENTEEN

Indradyumna Performs a Thousand Horse-sacrifices

The sages enquired:

1. After the idol had been installed in that holy spot of Narasiṁha, O sage, what did the king do? Relate it as we are very eager.

Jaimini said:

2-8. At the outset he invited all the Devas beginning with Indra. Then he invited thousands of sages and Brāhmaṇas, persons who had studied the four Vedas along with their six ancillaries, those who could recite the four Vedas by *Padapāṭha* and *Kramapāṭha*, those persons who were experts in the performance of Yajñas, persons who had mastered Mīmāṁsā system of philosophy, those who had very good practical experience in the various holy rites along with the knowledge of Kalpasūtra texts and their glosses, those who were experts in the eighteen lores, those who were proficient in religious texts, those who were spotlessly pure on account of their good conduct, men of noble families, truthful persons. He particularly invited Vaiṣṇavas respectfully. All the kings, Siddhas, Seven Sages, Brāhmaṇas, good Śūdras and the lords of the continents were invited.

The Assembly Hall of the king extended to two Krośas. It had been constructed with stones and plastered with lime and mortar.

In some places the ground was set with precious stones. In some places it was covered with gold plates. In different places the surfaces of the ground were suitably paved with crystals or silver plates.

9-14. There were huge columns of gems covered with silk cloths. The Assembly Hall had a beautiful awning. Garlands of sweet smelling flowers and chowries (were kept there for decoration) with pearl necklaces in between. There were splendid and beautiful windows. The Hall was sprinkled with oil scented with black aloewood and water with sandal paste.

Flowers of all the seasons were scattered everywhere. There were gardens on either side of the chamber with flowers of all the seasons available therein. The tanks had crystalline steps leading into the water adorned with red and white lotuses. Different kinds of aquatic birds such as Cakravākas (ruddy geese), Plavas (a variety of ducks), swans, Sārasas (cranes) etc. moved about here and there in the lakes chirping sweetly. There was cool, sweet, pure, clean and fragrant water in the lakes. There were hundreds of such lakes all round, O Brāhmaṇas. They (had steps etc.) so that people could comfortably get into them and come up. They were splendid in design and pattern. They had plenty of shade. This sacrificial hall of king Indradyumna was exactly like that of Marutta,[1] O excellent Brāhmaṇas. It was beautifully planned and constructed by Viśvakarman.

15-23. On an auspicious day in conjunction with an auspicious con-

1. Marutta, son of Avikṣit: His richly performed sacrifice was personally attended by god Indra and others. God Śiva gave him a Himalayan peak of gold. In his sacrifice all utensils, beds etc. were of gold. His sacrifice became an ideal for successive generations. [vide Mbh Droṇa 55.37-49.]

stellation the king accommodated the members of the assembly in different places. The kings were seated on thrones. The sages, Siddhas and groups of Brahminical sages were seated on very valuable carpets. The Devas were seated on golden pedestals. The (ordinary) Brāhmaṇas were seated on their befitting seats. Others were seated on excellent seats in accordance with their status very comfortably. Śacīpati (Indra, the husband of Śacī) was seated on his own throne set with diamonds and the insignia of his imperial majesty. He was seated in the middle of Devas, kings and sages.

King (Indradyumna) adored and honoured them at the outset by means of divine garlands, scents, clothes, seats etc. along with the priest for the sake of prosperity.

Like an humble and wretched person, the king worshipped him so that even the Lord of the three worlds considered it surprising.

By worshipping the Siddhas, Devas and sages he, like Indra, caused surprise even to Kubera of great affluence. Then he worshipped the Devas who too had much of wealth themselves by means of various services and offerings of presents. The king of the earth was not at all excited in his mind. He adored and honoured the kings with royal dress befitting kings, and they thought, 'Now we shall be kings. It is true that a realm had been acquired by succession but not so lavish a dress as these.'

24. Again he honoured the Vaiṣṇavas by means of presents and offerings as a result of which, though quiescent themselves, they thought that the acquisition of objects was surprising.

25-27. Then, the king in whom Sattvaguṇa predominated, duly worshipped the Brāhmaṇas, Kṣatriyas and Vaiśyas along with the sages. With great excitement he made the ministers worship the others too. He was then delighted. Accompanied by Nārada and his own priest, he humbly approached Mahendra. With palms joined in reverence he spoke to him loudly:

Indradyumna said:

28-33. I seek your favour. This is my wish, O Lord of Devas. Be pleased with me. I wish to worship the Yajñapuruṣa (i.e. Viṣṇu) by means of horse-sacrifice.

Permit me, O Lord. You are the overlord of sacrifices. All those who live in the three worlds obediently carry out your orders. Until the thousand sacrifices are concluded you stay here and be in the middle of the assembly along with the Devas.

O Lord of Devas, I do not wish to perform Yajñas with a desire for your position. O Lord of Devas, you always know the attitude of everyone.

Lord Mādhava was seen by you all here before in physical form during your worship. Now he has vanished beneath the sands.

I will perform a thousand horse-sacrifices in order to get him manifested once again, O Indra, at the bidding of the Four-faced Lord. If the Lord becomes manifested once again, it will be conducive to your welfare too.

34-42. When this was announced by the king, Suras, the chief of whom was Mahendra, remembered the ethereal utterance that was heard immediately after the Lord had vanished and then spoke thus with great delight:

"O Indradyumna, you are a great soul on the earth. Really you are truthful. Your activities now have already been foreseen by us as future occurrences. We shall assist you in this task of sanctifying all the three worlds, in which the creator of the worlds himself has become engaged. While the Lord was entering the inner bowels of the earth here itself, he had sympathetically told us, 'I shall create a wooden body once again'.

Now this is settled. There is nothing displeasing, disagreeable to us or to Indra in this matter. Your endeavour for our good luck is pleasurable to us. Comfortably worship Viṣṇu who is fond of his devotees, O eminent king, by means of the horse-sacrifice to be repeated a thousand times. Though the Lord is fond of his devotees, it is very difficult for us to propitiate him. We shall forsake Deva-hood and with great devotion propitiate the Lord in this holy spot humbly in the form of human beings. A pleasing act performed in the human world brings prosperity."

Jaimini said:

43. When this was spoken by the Devas along with Indra, the king worshipped the Lord with a delighted mind for the sake of beginning the sacrifice.

44-46. He worshipped the Lord and made a thousand offerings in the manner prescribed. Then with great reverence, the king looked at the groups of Pitṛs (Manes), the Brāmaṇas present in the assembly and the performers of the Yajña who had been duly adorned. He kept the tutelary deity Viṣṇu in front along with the sacred fire. He waited thus for the auspicious hour stipulated. When the rite of *Svastivācana* (ceremonial rite preparatory to a sacrifice or any religious observance) was concluded, he stood nearby along with his wife with pure and auspicious apparel.

47. After making the pure Brāhmaṇas perform all the holy rites of *Svastivācana*, *Puṇyāha* and *Vṛddhikarman*,[1] the king who had got ready all the requisite things, formally nominated the Ṛtviks.

48-50. On being chosen they initiated the excellent king along with his wife. When they were urged by the members of the assembly they worshipped the desired objects separately for the sake of initiation (?)

The blazing sacred fire named Āhavanīya was brought to the altar. It appeared like the refulgence of Viṣṇu himself, which is the cause of auspiciousness unto all the three worlds.

They then sprinkled the sanctified water charged with holy spells on the chief horse which had all the splendid characteristics in its limbs. After taking the ceremonial permission of the Lords of the Quarters, they released the horse.

51. The king who had been properly initiated, observed the vow of silence. He sat on the skin of a Ruru deer in the middle of the Assembly Hall like Lord Mṛtyuñjaya (Śiva) himself.

55-57. With a meaningful glance the king ordered that the invitees be fed. At the bidding of the king the minister had got ready all types of vessels for the purpose of their meals. Very valuable vessels studded with gems and jewels were made ready for the Suras to take their sumptuous food.

Vessels of pure gold were brought afresh everyday for the sages, Brāhmaṇas and kings to take their food, O Brāhmaṇas. For ordinary Kṣatriyas and Vaiśyas splendid silver vessels were brought, O Brāhmaṇas. For Śūdras, to take their food, vessels of pure bellmetal were brought.

Everyday after taking their food the people dropped those vessels in pits as though they were the leaves on which food had been served and taken in.

---

1. According to Āpastaṁba Dh.S.I.4.13.8 the three *Svastivācana* etc. mentioned here are a part of *Puṇyāhavācana* and not separate rites. The performer of an auspicious rite worships Brāhmaṇas and requests them to declare the day to be auspicious (*Puṇyāha*) for the performance of the rite. The performer of the rite requests Brāhmaṇas to announce *Svasti*, *Puṇyāha* and *ṛddhi* and they declare '*Oṁ svasti*', '*Oṁ puṇyāham*' and '*Oṁ (karma) ṛdhyatām*'. But the elaborateness and separateness of the performance of these shows the late nature of the Text leaning to *Saṁskāra-ratnamālā*.

Not only those who had been invited to take their food in that Yajña festival but also their sons, grandsons and great-grandsons, nay, everyone in the line, were respectfully fed with cooked food of five flavours at the behest of King Indradyumna.

58-63. All those persons stayed there as though they belonged to one family till the great sacrifice was concluded. The officer-in-charge (for the supervision of all arrangements regarding reception etc.) of the people from a territory was the king of that land. The person to look into the requirements of the kings was Nārada who was impartial in his outlook, was eager to help others and had been particularly requested for that purpose by Indradyumna.

The person to look into the requirements of the leading Suras beginning with Indra and the celestial sages was the excellent king himself.

The king himself ran about here and there to see that the sacrifices were duly completed.

Six different kinds of foodstuffs and beverages were prepared in two ways by men.

In the case of Devas, it was done by men who were experts in the use of magic and spells. In the case of men it was done by those who were well-versed in the culinary art.

Indeed the heaven-dwellers are never aware of hunger or thirst. Their diet is nectar. Even to them that food (served at the festival of Indradyumna) was a wonderful thing because they had not tasted it before.

64. In the mortal world such a food as was distributed in the abode of Indradyumna was rare for men (elsewhere). The only difference between Indradyumna and Indra was that the former's residence was in the mortal world.

65-70. This extremely wonderful show recurred everyday with ever new features. The foodstuffs, their honour and the eagerness for them increased everyday, O excellent Brāhmaṇas.

The different things mentioned below increased as though they competed with one another: sweet scents, flower garlands, musk and other unguents, silk garments and cloths of fine texture and variegated colour, pillows, seats, cushions, bejewelled palanquins and couches, beds, flylaps with gem-set rods, betel leaves along with nutmeg, cloves and comphor, sweet charming songs, different kinds of dances produced by experts of the school of Sage Bharata[1] etc., hundreds of panegyrists and bards fully conversant with the fame and pedigree of their respective

1. This refers to Bharata's *Nāṭya Śāstra* (*circa* 400 CE).

royal families. These and other rare objects were eagerly enjoyed by Devas and human beings.

71-78. Things in one place were more wonderful than elsewhere. There were no inferior things anywhere.

The foodstuff served to the residents of the nether worlds was superior to nectar. After consuming it they never desired to go back to Pātāla (nether worlds).

The cities in Pātāla are illuminated by clusters of gems. They have no necessity for the light of the sun. (They are devoid of sunlight.) The king, therefore, lodged them in cities of that sort for their residence, so that they thought that they were still in Pātāla. They comfortably seated themselves. They ate, played and lay down joyously.

As for Devas, they do not touch the earth elsewhere but in the city of Indradyumna, which was more fascinating than even heaven. They were eagerly engaged in happy sports as they pleased. There they never left the ground.

They say that in Svarga one gets happiness after eagerly desiring for it. But here (in the city of Indradyumna) there was happiness everywhere even without wishing for it.

Men were respectfully and earnestly honoured and fed there. No person was entreated or begged of. How could anyone have been turned back?

The abodes provided by the Emperor were like their own houses for the people. Only in their houses everything that was always available here was not so (readily available) there.

79-80. Whatever object was beyond (even) their expectations there (in their houses) was easily available here in plenty.

When the Yajñas were thus joyously performed for the propitiation of the Lord of Yajñas, every (valuable) thing that the earth had was taken away in the horse-sacrifice of the king. Whatever there was originally was replenished when the earth was adorned with a shower of gold.

81-85a. Thus charitable gifts, honouring and feeding of all the people staying in the three worlds went on everyday in accordance with the injunctions. The people commended the horse-sacrifice and repeated the following verses of praise to one another:

"There has never been such a collection of the materials of a sacrifice like this before. This is exactly in accordance with the injunctions of Brahmā as well as the scriptural texts.

There was never a sacrifice like that of King Indradyumna before. There will never be one like this. There are neither suppliants nor unwilling donors. They have not been invited there."

O Brāhmaṇas, no desire remained unfulfilled even in the case of Devas. The excellent sacrifice of the king with such abundance of supply went on thus. Each of the subsequent sacrifices was better furnished and performed with more ardent faith than the previous one.

85b-90. Those who had written Smṛtis, those who had composed the liturgical texts, those who had expounded the sacred treatises, those who were experts in the performance of Yajñas and those who were adorned with (i.e. possessed) good conduct celebrated everything beginning with fetching the sacred fire and ending with the valedictory bath in the proper order.

The sacrifice performed with the permission of the members of the assembly, O Brāhmaṇas, was conducive to the delight of the king.

There was neither a fault of omission nor of commission in regard to the accent or syllables of the Mantras. Indeed those who had laid down the injunctions were themselves performers of the rites. The atonement has been mentioned in those cases where there is reasonable cause for the same. But there (in the king's sacrifice) there was no mistake in the holy rites, because the Yogins and Karmayogins (those who are well conversant with holy rites) performed the same. The divine Seven Sages were the *Sadasyas* (Members of the Assembly) watching the proceedings of the sacrifice. They could discriminate between merits and demerits and they conducted the holy rites properly. Yājñavalkya and other sages were chosen and nominated as Ṛtviks.

91-94. Those sages were present in the sacred assembly. In the course of their mutual discourse they recited, recounted and related Nyāya Texts, secret Upaniṣadic Mantras, folk-tales and songs with devotion to Viṣṇu as their main theme and anecdotes of Hari's (exploits) that dispel all sins. They expounded them in the assembly of the king.

The joyous Devas, O Brāhmaṇas, the leader of whom was Mahendra, imbibed the Havis in that Yajña personally standing in the middle of the sacrificial fire. They forgot Amarāvatī. They had been away from it for a long time.

95. It is Amṛta (Nectar) that Brahmā had formerly allotted to them as Havis. The Devas were joyous, vigorous and long-lived after consuming it.

96. In other places, apart from the site of the performance of sacrifice, many other objects of pleasure were furnished by Indradyumna. Devas enjoyed all of them.

97. Kings of serpents, the residents of the bottom of Pātāla, en-

joyed more worldly pleasures in the human world than in their own place.

98. They too never desired to go back to Pātāla even mentally. Thus the Yajña proceeded affording great pleasure to everyone in the three worlds.

99-100. In this holy place Puruṣottama at the behest of Brahmā King Indradyumna performed Yajñas in order to propitiate the Lord of the universe. In due order the king concluded a thousand sacrifices short by one. All of them were duly performed in accordance with the injunctions.

101-103. Then the king began his thousandth horse-sacrifice. Day by day, the king acquired more and more spiritual merit. On the night of the sixth day from that of the extraction of Soma juice during the fourth *prahara* (*prahara* = period of 3 hrs.) he meditated on the immutable Viṣṇu.

Very fortunately in the course of his meditation the king saw, as if in direct perception, the island of Śvetadvīpa made of bright crystals.

104-106. He saw the Milk Ocean that stood encircling the island all round. There were great Kalpa trees (all round) that had rendered all the quarters fragrant by the sweet scent of the flowers.

Everywhere within and without those trees, on their fruits, sprouts and barks, there were the bright red-coloured idols of the Lord which were marked with conch and discus and which were brilliantly adorned with all the ornaments. In the middle he saw an excellent Pandal (Maṇḍapa) made of divine jewels.

107. The Pavilion was refulgent with a throne in the centre that shone like the sun and that was studded with gems. It was very fascinating as a gentle, cool breeze blew over the waves of the Milk Ocean.

108-109. In its centre he saw Lord Viṣṇu holding conch, discus and iron club. He resembled a blue cloud. He was adorned with garlands of sylvan flowers. Divine ornaments were worn by him. He seemed to surpass and put to shame all the abodes of loveliness and the houses of beauty and splendour by means of his body.

110-113. To his right he saw Ananta standing, supporting the earth. He had the splendour of a crore of moons. He had the lustre resembling that of the mountain Himālaya. He was charming with the crowned hoods spreading over him like an umbrella. He had a pair of jewel-set ear-rings. He had put on a beautiful blue upper garment. In his four hands shone palm tree (lāṅgala?), plough, conch and discus. He was adorned with necklaces, armlets, bangles and rings. He had a waistband and a girdle. He had decorated himself with divine jewels. His physical body was inebriated due to divine liquor called Hālā. He had pleasing smiles and brilliant eyes.

114-115. He saw Lakṣmī of splendid features stationed on his right side. She had a lotus in her hand and held her fingers in the position of granting of boons as well as freedom from fear. She had the lustre of saffron. She had bright eyes. Her wonderful body was a model for all the young women in the three worlds. He saw her seated in a lotus. She was a pet daughter of the Salt Ocean.

116. He saw Pitāmaha (Brahmā) standing in front of him with palms joined in reverence. He saw the discus of the Lord full of gems stationed on the left side of the Lord.

117. On seeing the Lord of the universe eulogized by Sanaka and other prominent sages in his dream, O excellent Brāhmaṇas, the king became extremely delighted.

118. Standing there in contemplation, he eulogized in words choked with (tears) of joy, the infinite Lord of a fiery form never seen before.

Indradyumna said:

119. Obeisance to you, O support of the universe. Obeisance to you, O soul of the universe. O (cause of) salvation transcending the three Guṇas, O Lord shining with good qualities, obeisance to you.

120. Salute to you with the form of very splendid perfect knowledge devoid of impurities. Obeisance to you having the appellation *Śabda-brahman* (Brahman in the form of sound), O Lord with the universe as your form.

121. Hail to you, O destroyer of the miseries of those who have fallen into (the ocean of) worldly existence and therefore are weary. Obeisance to you who cuts the knot in the heart very difficult to be untied.

122. Obeisance to you, the main pillar of the structure of the fourteen worlds. Salute to the discus-bearing Lord, the architect who fashioned crores of Cosmic Eggs.

123. Obeisance, obeisance, to the Moon rising from the ocean of the nectar of kindness. Obeisance to the ocean of compassion, the sole secret uplifter of the poor.

124. Obeisance to the illuminator of the Sun and other luminous bodies. Hail to the Lord who blazes with a loud report within every heart and burns the sins within.

125. Repeated obeisance to the purifier, to the purest of all pure

ones. Obeisance, obeisance to the weightiest one, to the most excellent one, to the longest one.

126. Obeisance, obeisance to the nearest one, to the most distant one, to the minutest one. Obeisance to you, O Nārāyaṇa, the most excellent one, the holiest one.

127. Save me, O Lord of the universe. Obeisance to you, O kinsman of the poor. After obtaining you as a comfortable boat, I have crossed the ocean of worldly existence.

128-131. When you are seen, O Lord of Ramā, all my distress has disappeared. O Lord, it is certain indeed that those who have attained you having consciousness and bliss for your form, will get their miseries destroyed. It shall be the cause of the outcome of supreme delight.

Save, save me who have sunk in the ocean of worldly existence, whose mind is in a wretched state. When the midday sun blazes in the sky, how can there be darkness!

Still in contemplation, he bowed down to the Lord of the universe eulogizing thus.

At the end of the meditation he woke up and understood everything. At the end of the dream Indradyumna remembered the Supreme Soul by means of his own soul.

132-135a. After seeing this extremely mysterious dream the eminent king considered himself to be one who has fulfilled his task. He thought that all his thousand horse-sacrifices had become fruitful and his good luck was imminent. He thought thus: 'Indeed the words of the Celestial Sage can never be in vain. Now how will the Lord be directly perceptible to me?' In this anxious state the king spent the remaining part of the night. Then he told Nārada the details of the dream experienced by him.

135b-136. Nārada told him: "O king, your grief has come to an end, since you saw the Lord at the time of dawn. A dream at that time, O excellent king, yields the benefit within ten days.

137-139. At the end of the sacrifice the Lord will be visible to you here as Brahmā, the sire of the mobile and immobile beings, conveyed to you through my words.

That Creator of the universe also was seen by you in this dream. Therefore, let the Yajña be performed. Do not divulge this to anyone else.

O tiger among kings, this dream has been brought about by Hari in an inscrutable manner. But only to a fortunate one shall a dream like this occur.

CHAPTER EIGHTEEN

The Eternal Banyan Tree Emerges

Jaimini said:

1-2. Then began the holy rite of *Sutyā*[1] (i.e. extraction of the Soma juice) as a part of the horse-sacrifice of the king. In that activity, O Brāhmaṇas, all the three worlds came to be like one family. All other sounds were drowned by the sounds of the scriptural passages and hymns that touched the vaults of heaven. The Mantras had the prescribed order (without any deviation). Proper accents were given to all the words.

3. Everything desired was given to the poor people without any restriction. That came to be comparable to the Kalpa tree for actors, dancers and bards.

4-9. In the middle (of the sacrificial site) on the southern seashore near Bilveśvara the royal camp was made for the purpose of taking the valedictory bath. The servants who had been appointed there by the king, O Brāhmaṇas, approached the king with great excitement. They reported to the king with palms joined in reverence:

"O Lord, a great tree was seen on the shore of the great ocean. Its top has sunk deep into the sea waves and the roots continue to float above on the waves. It has the colour of madder throughout. It is marked with conch and discus symbols. It was seen by us floating near the bathing house. It is exceedingly wonderful. It is a tree that has never been seen before. It resembles the sun rising with all his rays. It has rendered the entire foreshore fragrant with its sweet scent. It is not an ordinary tree. It seems to be a celestial tree. Certainly it appears that some god has come in the guise of this tree."

10. On hearing the words of the employees the king spoke to Nārada: "They say, an excellent tree has been seen. What does it indicate?"

11-13. Nārada laughingly said to the excellent king: "Let the *Pūrṇāhuti* (final offering of ghee at the end of a sacrifice) be concluded so that

1. Sutyā: This pressing out of Soma is generally done on the last day of the sacrifice and the day therefore came to be called *Sutyā*.

the sacrifice may be fruitful. Your good fortune is imminent as you have already seen in the dream. The hair that has dropped down from the body of the cosmic-formed, imperishable Viṣṇu who has been formerly seen in the Śvetadvīpa has assumed the form of a tree. This partial incarnation of the Supreme Lord shall remain (forever) on the earth.

14-17. The Lord, fond of his devotees, has incarnated in that form. Indeed this tree is not man-made. Except you, O excellent king, O tiger among men, no one on the earth can be fortunate enough to have sight of this holy tree. Thanks to your good fortune, O great king, that it will be the guest of the eyes of the people of all the worlds. It is destructive of all sins. Conclude your valedictory bath near the shore of the sea. Celebrate a very great festival with the auspicious thread (tied round your wrist). Install the Lord of Yajñas in the form of the tree on the great Altar here."

18. After discussing thus both of them, the king as well as Nārada, joyously equipped themselves with all necessary things and went to that place where the lordly tree (was seen).

19-21. On seeing it everyone was extremely delighted. They thought that Brahman itself had come to them. They considered their life fruitful and themselves living-liberated souls of great prosperity.

King Indradyumna too sank in the ocean of nectar. This king, a beloved of the Lord, saw the tree in the same manner as the Lord of the universe whom he saw in the dream, with four branches as four arms. The excellent king thought that his exertion had become fruitful. O Brāhmaṇas, he got rid of his grief caused by the disappearance of the Blue-sapphire Mādhava.

22-27. With tears of joy welling in his eyes the king bowed down again and again to the tree. He brought it up through the Brāhmaṇas as it was tossed about by the waves.

Conch-shells were blown. Kāhāla trumpets were sounded to the accompaniment of Muraja, Ḍhakkā and Paṭaha drums. Songs were sung. Musical instruments were played. Thousands of people shouted "Victory to you". Handfuls of sweet-smelling flowers were repeatedly showered from the sky. Vessels of incense fumigated with black aloewood were taken round. The tree was fanned with chowries having rods studded with gems and jewels, held and waved by courtesans of great beauty in the prime of their youth. It was rendered splendid by means of flags and banners made of divine silk cloths. It was surrounded by a number of saintly kings, vassal kings, the cavalry and the infantry.

It was saluted (and panegyrized) by the bards and eulogized by great sages.

28. The Brāhmaṇas, priests, learned men and scholars well-versed in the Vedas prayed to it. It was attended upon by kings, persons born in the families of Vaiśyas as well as good Śūdras.

29-32. It was eulogized with various hymns from the Vedas, Smṛtis and Purāṇas.

They took that heavenly tree of Viṣṇu that was eulogized, that had been beautified with garlands and sweet scents and that had come to the terrestrial world surrounded (by various things) to the great Altar that had been wonderfully and tastefully decorated with canopies and completely covered without leaving any space in between. At the bidding of Indradyumna they installed it on the Altar. At the instance of Nārada the king worshipped it. The excellent king worshipped it with thousands of offerings and services of divine nature.

At the end of the worship he asked Nārada, the excellent sage:

33-35. "Of what sort shall the idols of Viṣṇu be? Who will carve it?" On hearing that the sage said: "The size is of unimaginable greatness. Who knows his extraordinary activity? Even the creator of all the worlds is in doubt regarding it."

While Nārada and the king were discussing thus, an unembodied divine speech was heard from the firmament.

36-43a. The speech was heard by all those who were present there with great surprise:

"The Lord is not under the influence of any person. He is beyond the path of discourse and contemplation. He will directly incarnate in the great Altar which shall be kept well-concealed. Let that be covered for the next fifteen days. Let this old carpenter who is present here with weapons (and instruments) in his hands be allowed to go in and let the doors be closed carefully thereafter.

Let there be instrumental music as long as the carving work goes on. If the sound of chiselling or carving is heard it will result in deafness and blindness. He who hears it will go to hell and his line may become extinct.

No one shall enter the place nor peep in. If anyone other than the employee looks in, there is great danger to the king, the realm and the person who looks in. Both of his eyes will become blind.

Hence as long as the idol is completely carved and chiselled no one shall look into the premises. If the work is concluded, the Lord himself shall announce it. Whatever is to be done for the sake of the happiness of all the worlds the Lord himself will announce."

43b-46. On hearing these words Nārada and others desired to do what had been mentioned by Viṣṇu himself. By that time the carpenter too came there. He said to the king, "With the wood of divine form I shall fashion all those things seen by you in the dream."

After saying this Lord Nārāyaṇa who himself took the form of the old carpenter for the sake of deceiving (ordinary) men, vanished behind the Altar.

CHAPTER NINETEEN

The Lord Manifests Himself as Wooden Idol

Jaimini said:

1. Thereafter the king did what the goddess (the ethereal voice) had said: He attended to everything.

2-8. As days passed on, a divine fragrance was experienced. There was a shower of the flowers of Pārijāta that was very rare in the world of human beings. There was the sound of divine music. The songs were very sweet. There was a shower of (tiny drops of) waters of the celestial Gaṅgā, very beautiful and splendid in the form of small drops. The sweet aroma of the ichor of Airāvata and other elephants was experienced. It was unbearable to wild elephants but very pleasing to (other) living beings. All those Devas who had come for the sake of the Yajñas were free from ailments, O Brāhmaṇas. On seeing Hari becoming visible they worshipped him. Just as they worshipped Mādhava before, so also they worshipped the tree of Viṣṇu. In the course of the worship of Devas divine symbols appeared. On the fifteenth day the Lord completed the work. In the manner explained by me before the Lord manifested himself in four forms. It has been described to you before. He was seated in the divine throne along with Bala, Subhadrā and Sudarśana.

Janārdana has conch, discus, iron club and lotus shining in his hands.

9-15. Balabhadra has the shape of a serpent. He holds iron club, mace, discus and lotus. He has seven hoods in the form of an umbrella shining with crowns and also ear-rings.

Subhadrā of charming face, granting boons and immunity from fear (through the positions of her fingers) holds a lotus (in her hand). This is the manifestation of Lakṣmī who has been the embodiment of the consciousness of everyone. Indeed in the course of the incarnation as Kṛṣṇa she was born of the womb of Rohiṇī (?)* and had the forms of Bala and Bhadrā (i.e. Subhadrā) since she contemplated on the form of Bala. She could not bear even for a moment separation from the Lord of sportful incarnation. There is no difference at all between Kṛṣṇa and Bala.

Since they were born of the same womb, the story in the Purāṇa says that she is the sister of Baladeva. So is the way in which ordinary people also mention it.

This is the case when she has the male form (?). In the female form as Lakṣmī she stays everywhere. By a male name she is Lord Viṣṇu and by a female name she is Kamalālayā ('lotus-aboded one'). Among Devas, lower animals, human beings etc. there is none greater than they.

16. Who else other than the lotus-eyed Lord can bear the fourteen worlds? Ananta bears them with the tips of his hoods. He is called Bala.

17. His sister Śrī is glorified in the form of his Śakti. The discus Sudarśana is always present in the hand of Viṣṇu.

18. It is at the tip of the branch and stationed in the middle of the pillar (?). That is the fourth form (of the Lord). Thus the four forms were revealed by him.

19. When the fourfold divine form of the Lord was completed, the ethereal voice said once again for helping the worlds:

20. "Cover these idols completely. Through paints give appropriate colour to everyone of them in an aggreeable way.

21-24. Viṣṇu must be dark-coloured like a blue cloud. Bala should be white like a conch or the Moon. The discus Sudarśana should be red. Subhadrā should be tawny-coloured like saffron. She should be beautifully adorned with different ornaments and the curves and contours should be properly depicted.

If these idols are seen as wooden pieces, they are conducive to sin. They should be carefully concealed with cloths, resin-like exudations or bark garments. Hence at the very outset get all these covered with the barks of this very tree by craftsmen who are experts in their respective jobs. Every year they must be adorned and embellished after removing the previous ones.

---

* But in Mbh. Ādi. 217 she is Devakī's daughter.

25-28. Without the bark-garments and the unguents it is divine and eternal (?)

If anyone were to remove the unguent inadvertently, there will be famine and pestilence in the kingdom. His line of progeny will become extinct. O king, they should not be ever seen by you without a covering. O great king, if they are seen so by ordinary men, they will cause fear. Hence they should be seen in agreeable colours and smeared with many unguents.

By seeing the lotus-eyed Lord in agreeable colour with beauty, grace and elegance, one is liberated from sins accumulated in the course of crores of Kalpas.

29-34. Make them variegated and aggreeable, O great king. You will get wonderful objects desired by you. The Lord has manifested himself with a desire to bless you. Since he is pleased with you, he will grant all the four aims of life to all living beings.

On Nīla mountain, about a hundred Hastas (i.e. about 45 Metres) to the north-west of the Kalpa tree (Banyan tree), and on the northern side of Narasiṁha in a large piece of land get a Mansion built. It should be large and firm. It should be a thousand Hastas high (i.e. 450 Metres). There install the Lord.

Formerly when the Lord was on that mountain, a Śabara named Viśvāvasu, an excellent devotee of Viṣṇu, used to worship Mādhava. Your priest became an intimate friend of his on that occasion. Only the descendants of these two should be employed, O great king, in the job of smearing the unguents or adorning the Lord in future festivals."

35-41a. After speaking this the divine speech ceased.

On hearing what was instructed by it the excellent king became extremely delighted within himself. He unveiled the great Altar. At that time all of them saw Lord Kṛṣṇa, son of Vasudeva, Rāma, Subhadrā and Sudarśana. The Lord was seated on a gem-set throne. All the idols were charming in their features with the unguents smeared and the limbs duly adorned. He saw Lord Kṛṣṇa with a kind and beaming face. The chest was broad and projecting forward. He had long brawny arms capable of uplifting the poor. His eyes resembled full-blown lotuses. There was a gentle smile on the broad lips. By his mere glance he could dispel the mass of sins of those who view him. He was seated in the lotus-posture. He was embellished with divine ornaments. He was surrounded by his own refulgence. Even in that wooden form he was free from impurities. He resembled a blue cloud. He was the destroyer of all distresses.

41b-44. He saw Baladeva with a face giving boisterous laughter. He had extensive circular hoods and eyes rolling on account of (the intake of) liquor. He was the rising king of serpents with a thick and muscular chest. He had a slight depression on his back. He had his body coiled up. He appeared like the peak of Kailāsa with an Arjuna tree in full bloom on its top. He held plough, discus, lotus and iron club. He had a garland of sylvan flowers. He was remarkably resplendent with necklaces, ear-rings, armlets, coronets and crowns.

45-47. He saw in between them Lakṣmī (who was) Subhadrā of gentle form,[1] the source of origin of all the Devas, the goddess who took the (devotee) across the ocean of sins, whose face was like a full-blown lotus, who held a lotus and gesticulated granting of boons and immunity from fear (by means of her fingers), who was the abode of beauty, grace and charm, who shone splendidly with ornaments and whose body was tawny-coloured like saffron. She appeared like another Lakṣmī in person. She was installed on the left side of Viṣṇu.

48-50. He saw the discus (Sudarśana) that had been made out of tips of the branches. It resembled the rising Sun. It had sharp edges. It was excessively refulgent, O Brāhmaṇas.

On seeing all of them the king became immersed in the ocean of bliss. He was confused as to what he should do. He was not capable of sustaining his own body.

The excellent king stood just like a stump with palms joined in reverence. With the eyes slightly closed he simply shed tears (of joy).

51. The excellent sage spoke to the lord of the earth, with a smile on his face: "That for which you exerted yourself has taken effect now.

52-53. It is evident now, O tiger among kings, that you are the only person fortunate on the earth. See this Lord of the universe with large eyes resembling lotus, Hari, the ocean of blessings unto the devotees, the storehouse of all knowledge. The Yogins of restrained minds strive forever to see him.

54-56. Men see him for a moment with great concentration. That Janārdana has taken up a wooden body and has become directly perceptible, O king, in order to bless you.

Worship this Lord of the earth. Eulogize the ocean of kindness. On

---

1. It is not known why the Purāṇa confuses Subhadrā with Lakṣmī. Subhadrā's sister-wife relation with Kṛṣṇa reminds one of the Rāma-Sītā (sister-wife) relation in the Pāli *Dasaratha Jātaka*.

being eulogized, O king he will grant you everything that you desire in your mind."

CHAPTER TWENTY

Origin of the Indradyumna Lake

Jaimini said:

1. On being enlightened and urged by Nārada thus, the king eulogized in the following words, the compassionate Lord of the worlds.

Indradyumna said:

2. O Enemy of Mura, your lotus-like feet have not been worshipped (by me) in the course of previous lives. Therefore, I am subjected to the terrible effects of Karmas. O ocean of mercy, save me; I have become wretched.

3. How great are your lotus-like feet free from impurities, sunk beneath the crowns of Brahmā, Rudra and Indra and how small am I, a despicable and wretched fellow encompassed by masses of faeces, blood, flesh, urine and bones and everything (outward) covered by skin!

4. How can I know you, O Lord, because I am sick and wearied by wandering through worthless worldly affairs! Indeed, O Lord of Devas, only they do know you, they whose birth is illuminated by the light (of knowledge) born of misery.

5. O Lord, much misery has been experienced by me as a result of the sins committed in the course of many births. I have experienced many types of emotions too. The small happiness that has resulted from (a small quantity of) merit acquired is like (a little of) honey mixed with a mass of bitter things.

6. For the sake of happiness I performed holy rites, as a result of which I experienced worldly pleasures which have ultimately turned into misery. There is no other person as miserable as I.

7. O Lord, if only I had mentally worshipped you before, though my eyes had been directed towards other worldly objects, I could not have had the numerous births with all sorts of miseries to be experienced again and again.

8-9. I was born as a master as well as a slave; I have enjoyed various statuses and states such as a father, son, lover, mother, rich man, one worthy of being killed, one taking to violent means, husband, wife, lower animal, Sura etc. Ups and downs of diverse nature have been experienced on many occasions by me rolling in the courtyards of various worlds. O Enemy of Mura, this is not a desirable thing, because it involves keeping away from your lotus-like feet.

10-11. My treasury, this army surrounded by the entire wealth of the earth, amiable women in hundreds in their prime of youth with great charm and beauty, my royal circle rid of all thorns (i.e. troublesome elements) and my Empire—all these are extremely burdensome to me because I am deprived of your knowledge like a brute. O ocean of compassion, remove this burden forever, as it is always attended by distress.

12. O Lord merciful towards the wretched one, an elephant was liberated because it had remembered you.[1] It behoves you to save me with an attitude of compassion, O Lord, because I whirl and whirl like a waterwheel here.

13. In this situation which is similar to one in which a log of wood has got caught up in a rapid current, I do not have any kinsman (to help) other than you. The sinful intellect that has been fettered by feelings of affection and that has become emotionally fixated on worldly objects, should be broken away (by you).

14-17a. By day or night let not my (mind) move away from your lotus-like feet. This alone is my pressing request.

Fortunately during thousands of births, some have attained you, the ocean full of existence, knowledge and bliss. Do they find even an iota of happiness in the jugglery of mundane affairs, the source of many miseries?

Where is the bondage of Karmas, which cannot be broken on account of hundreds of knots causing much misery but very little of pleasure? Where is your lotus-like foot which is infinite, which has neither beginning nor end and which is the sole thing that grants pleasure?

Your Māyā is like an ocean. *Mamatā* (sense of possession, my-ness) is a whirlpool therein. Evil actions are like crocodiles in the middle of (the dangerous) pits. I have fallen into that ocean. I have no support. Take me to the shore by your benign, graceful side-glance.

17b-21a. I have abandoned what is conducive to my welfare. I am ever wandering to accomplish what is desired by others who have re-

---

1. Reference to Gajendra-mokṣa in BhP VIII, Ch. 3.

sorted to me to achieve their own ends. So I have become confused and stupid. O Lord who are compassionate by nature, save me.

Save me, O Viṣṇu, who are the only person worthy of being saluted to in the whole universe. I am running after insignificant things too much without attaining you, the root cause (of all), the great Lord. I am subjected to great stress and strain. I am extremely wretched.

O Lord of the universe, to be known only through Vedānta, O immutable one, you are competent to destroy masses of sins. Hence you are the sole cause of happiness. Still I have abandoned you (to seek happiness elsewhere), O Viṣṇu. Save me, a mean-minded fellow that I am.

The entire group of four kinds of living beings is asleep in the night of delusion created by you. In the end it is enlightened when the Sun of your knowledge rises. I seek refuge in you.

21b-25. You alone are the creator of all the worlds by successive turns. Your form is encircled by thousand of hoods. O most excellent one among *Balins* (powerful ones), I seek refuge in you, the Lord and master.

O Lord, you create and annihilate the worlds through your own Śakti seated in your lotus-like heart (chest). I bow down to the pair of feet of that support of the worlds in the form of Bhadrā (Subhadrā), the source of origin of Devas.

The group of these Cosmic Eggs is evolved out of the clusters of the rays of your discus, O Lord. It is in contact with your hand. It is pleasing to view. The name of that discus is Sudarśana. It is destructive of Daityas' army. I bow down to you.

After eulogizing thus, the excellent king prostrated with eight limbs (touching the ground). He continued: "Save me, O Lord of the universe. O kinsman of the helpless ones, save me mercifully. I am sinking in the ocean of worldly existence. I am wretched. I am overcome with Tamoguṇa (darkness)."

Nārada said:

26. Be victorious, be victorious, O Nārāyaṇa, O Lord engaged in taking (devotees) across the boundless ocean of worldly existence; O Lord whose divinity is being contemplated upon by Sanaka, Sanandana, Sanātana and other excellent Yogins; O Lord, in the activities of whose Māyā all the elements and living beings are superimposed (or transformed); O Lord of three principles; O Lord who hold three staffs (powers),

whose divine knowledge is being praised by the Vedic Mantras, viz. *Triṇāciketa,*[1] *Trimadhu*[2] and *Trisuparṇa,*[3] who are identical with the Vedas, who are fond of Garuḍa on whom you are seated, who are fond of your devotees, who are the sole favourite of your devotees, whose form is hidden (and separated) by your own cluster of Māyās, who are Cosmic-formed, who are the illuminator of the universe, who have faces all round,[4] who have eyes all round, who have ears all round who have feet, heads and necks all round, who have hands, noses, tongues, skin, hair tresses and penises all round, who are identical with all the worlds, who are conducive to the happiness of all the worlds, who render help to all the worlds, who are bowed down to by all the worlds, who have graceful elegance, who are bowed down to by crores of Brahmās, Rudras, Indras, Maruts, Aśvins, Sādhyas, and groups of Siddhas; O sire of the three worlds including the entire Suras and Asuras; O Lord not knowable to anyone, repeated obeisance to you, obeisance to you.

Jaimini said:

27-28. Other kings who were there, learned priests well-versed in the Vedas, sages, Brāhmaṇas, Kṣatriyas, scholars, Vaiśya classes—all these eulogized the lotus-eyed Lord and Bala along with Subhadrā by means of hymns, prayers, Purāṇa passages, and ordinary poems.

29. Then Indradyumna said to the sinless priest that he should (make arrangements) for the worship of Vāsudeva duly accompanied by offerings.

30. That excellent king himself worshipped them in due order in accordance with the injunctions (and reciting) the proper Mantras following the instructions of Nārada.

31. With the twelve-syllabled Mantra[5] he worshipped Balabhadra, by worshipping whom Dhruva obtained the most excellent abode.

32. With the great and sacred *Puruṣa Sūkta* famous in the Vedas, the king worshipped Nārāyaṇa in accordance with his ability.

---

1. One who has kindled the Nāciketa fire thrice.
2. The 3 Ṛcs—*madhu vātā ṛtāyante* etc. in RV I.90.6-8.
3. Two groups of three mantras are given this name:
   (i) *Ekaḥ suparṇaḥ* etc. RV X. 114.4-6. (ii) *brahmametumām* etc. Tait. Āraṇyaka X. 48-50.
4. Cf. Śvetāśvatara Upaniṣad 3.16; also BG 13.13.
5. The twelve-syllabled Mantra is *Oṁ namo bhagavate vāsudevāya*. But Dhruva, according to BhP IV, Chs. 8-12, got his pre-eminent position by devotion to Viṣṇu, and not to Balabhadra.

33-36. He worshipped Subhadrā with the *Devī Sūkta*[1] and discus Sudarśana with the *Sudarśanī Sūkta.*

After worshipping them devoutly in accordance with his affluence the excellent king gave charitable gifts with great devotion to eminent Brāhmaṇas in order to get the full favour (of those deities).

The king gave *Tulāpuruṣa* gift (things weighed against himself) and other great gifts. As a part of the horse-sacrifice, he gave crores of cows then. He gave cows with and without ornaments. O excellent Brāhmaṇas, a great pit was formed as they dug up with their hoofs. That pit was filled with the waters poured when charitable gifts were made. That became a Tīrtha of great merit.

37-40. If a man takes his holy bath there and offers libations to Pitṛs and Devas in accordance with the injunctions, he will undoubtedly get the merit of a thousand horse-sacrifices.

That lake was named after King Indradyumna.[2] It became very famous. If a man offers rice-balls here to his Pitṛs, he uplifts twenty-one generations of his family, and is honoured in the world of Brahmā. There is no Tīrtha greater than this because this has originated from part of the horse-sacrifice. Perhaps Gaṅgā may be equal to the lake Indradyumna. Thereafter the king began the construction of the Palatial Temple.

41-46. In an auspicious season, in a splendid, auspicious hour as proclaimed by astrologers, on a day in conjuction with a good constellation, he worshipped Nārada and other eminent Brāhmaṇas. The excellent king made them recite the Mantras connected with the holy rites of *Svastivācana* and *Karmardhi*,[3] and remembering the Lord of the universe he offered *Arghya* on the site of the palatial temple. He requested the Earth to give him a piece of land for the duration of the life of the Stars and the Moon. Along with the *Vāstuyāga* (i.e. sacrifice for the building site) he worshipped the artisans and masons.

With plenty of songs and instrumental music great celebrations were held. To the poor, the helpless and the disabled people, he gave everything they desired.

With due honour he bade farewell to the kings whose sins had been destroyed by viewing the incarnation of Hari and who were contented and blessed.

---

1. *Devī Sūkta* is *Vāgāmbhṛṇī Sūkta* (RV X. 125) and *not Śrī Sūkta.*
2. Indradyumna 'lake' is not a naturally formed reservoir of water like Cilikā but only a tank at Puri.
3. *Svastivācana* and *Karmardhi* are the same as *Puṇyāhavācana.*

Then the excellent king presented sums in crores and crores to the stonecutters for bringing stones from many different countries.

47-51. The king joyously said this in the Assembly: "Everything that I had acquired by my heroic exertions from the eighteen continents has now been dedicated to the grace of the Lord of the universe. In the context of the campaign of victory, whatever strain I might have undergone shall become fruitful by supplying the necessary funds for the Mansion of Viṣṇu.

What shall be more fortunate unto me than this that I am propitiating Hari, the sire of mobile and immobile beings, with my wealth and glory acquired with my own pair of arms?

Śrī is always present in the lotus-eyed Lord. But I have many Śrīs originating from his blessings. What can the Lord do with it? (?)

The glory of that person who is a recipient of the benign glance of the Discus-bearing Lord of Devas is multifaced.

52-53. The eighteenfold goddess dances at the tip of the tongue of the Lord of the universe, by propitiating whom Vidhi attained the status of Brahmā (the Creator), Rudra that of Maheśvara (Great Lord) and Śakra that of the Lord of Heaven. I shall worship that eternal deity worthy of being worshipped by all the worlds.

54. The sin that had accumulated in three heaps has been vanquished by that noble soul by whom Kṛṣṇa was duly worshipped along with ancillary and subsidiary rites.

55. (*Defective Text*) This holy spot is the body where the Lord resides as the Cosmic Ego. His appearance and disappearance and continuous existence all are eternal.

56-59. One who worships the sire of the worlds who is directly embodied here shall achieve everything directly. He will be the recipient of the fourfold aim of life.

The prosperity of the kingdom has been acquired by me after spending much and undergoing a great deal of strain. That was solely due to the blessings of this Lord. Let that be fruitful at his lotus-like feet.

By means of the wealth taken from the ocean-girt earth I shall worship the Lord with all offerings. Until the effects of Karmas come to an end, let my imperialistic campaign be fruitful.

Of what avail is my wealth if I do not dedicate it to Viṣṇu along with my body and become rid of sins? Of what avail is my exertion if the necessary adjuncts for Vāsudeva are not secured by me?

CHAPTER TWENTYONE

Indradyumna Gets the Royal Shrine Built

Jaimini said:

1. As the saintly king said thus, a certain Brāhmaṇa who had mastered Ṛgveda and acquired the knowledge of Vedānta, gladly spoke to the king these words:

2. "Wonderful indeed is the mass (greatness) of your fortune, whereby the Lord has manifested on the earth in a wooden body. Śruti says that his sincere and regular worship bestows salvation on those who are deluded because of the ignorance of Ātman.

3-11a. The tree had been floating on the other side of the ocean. By worshipping (the idols made out of it) and adoring the super-human Lord very difficult to be propitiated, people attain liberation which is difficult to attain.

Nārada himself, who is a storehouse of the knowledge of Brahman, has told you that the knowledge of this (Lord) cannot be had from anything other than the words of Vedānta. Indeed the activity of Viṣṇu cannot go on without the Vedas. Whether it is the creation of others or manifestation of himself, the Lord honours the authority of the Vedas.

If he were to act without Śruti, who will accept it as authoritative? Hence, O king, this incarnation is also noted in the Vedas.

Do not think that it is an (ordinary) statue. It is the Puruṣa comprehensible through the Vedānta and sung about in the Sāman songs. It is the cause of spiritual welfare (Mokṣa) unto men.

Merely by its sight our dense darkness has subsided. There are Śrutis shedding light on the worship of this (idol).

The worship of this is praiseworthy, if it is employed for a good cause. Oh! the men living in the sub-continent of Bhārata have got their sins reduced and destroyed because Janārdana, the bestower of salvation, has appeared before them. There too this Oḍhra-land (Orissa State) is the most excellent one, because people living there see the Lord in the form of Brahman with their physical eyes.

11b-17a. The mysterious path of Śrutis and Smṛtis has become perplexing through rituals. Those who go by that path whirl in great agitation like a waterwheel. The Lord, the embodiment of knowledge and consciousness, is the cause of attainment of the true status (i.e. salvation). Even without such means as Śruti etc. he is the bestower of the greatest bliss and salvation.

To the vicious people who undergo great distress on account of the continuous departures and arrivals (i.e deaths and births), this wooden idol of Viṣṇu is the bestower of happiness, and a good kinsman.

The rules and regultaions mentioned in Śrutis and Smṛtis are not binding here, O king. He is the bestower of salvation on even Cāṇḍālas, should they happen to come within the range of (his) vision.

Even if a man is no devotee but views him as a blind follower, he shall obtain full merit of thousands of horse-sacrifices.

If a person strictly adheres to holy observances and worships devoutly with steady mind, he will undoubtedly attain *Sāyujya* with Brahman.

17b-22. How ineffective is the means (ritual act) which is full of exertion, easily perishable, temporary in nature, yielding only insignificant results and characterized by return (i.e. rebirth); and how great is this Brahman constituted of wood which burns heaps of sins like a forest fire burning out trees! It is merely by its sight that it bestows salvation—the state of aloofness characterised by existence, knowledge and bliss!

Repetition of the Vedic passages and other rites are very difficult to be performed by vicious souls. What can be achieved through them by noble souls, is granted by this (Lord) coolly without any excitement.

In the other holy spots the Lord is far away from the residents of the mortal world. But (here) the Lord is always present in his own holy spot as the bestower of salvation.

Hence, O illustrious king, stay here with your army and men. You are the most learned and a great devotee. Worship him along with all ancillary and subsidiary rites."

Jaimini said:

23-28. On hearing those words of the Brāhmaṇa Nārada became delighted in his mind. (He said:) "What is said by the excellent Brāhmaṇa, a follower of the Vedic path, is relevant. The collection of the Vedas issued forth at the beginning of creation from the breath of Brahmā. There the purport of the Upaniṣads has become revealed now.

The meaning of the same, only Prajāpati, the lotus-born lord, knows. Now I have understood it, O king, directly from him. Everything has been performed at his bidding. Propitiate this (Lord) as much as you desire and stay here. I am going to Brahmā; I shall inform him that the manifestation of the Enemy of Mura has been brought about.

By spending a big sum get the (Lord's) Mansion built, O king. After installing Narasiṁha in the Temple, you will be liberated."

Jaimini said:

29-33. On hearing it the king replied to the sage: "O great sage, I am desirous of going to Brahmā along with you.

It is by his grace that the Lord of the universe has been made the guest of our eyes. I shall tell him about the Palatial Shrine for the installation of Viṣṇu. I shall request him that the festival of the installation within the Mansion should be celebrated in (his) presence. Then the Grandfather (i.e. Brahmā) shall come from Brahmaloka and celebrate the great festival of the Lord here in the Mansion (Temple). Hence, O sage, take me also to the presence of Brahmā. We shall conclude the rite of installation in the inner sanctuary in the Mansion. O sage, stay here and complete it. We shall proceed thereafter. Kindly wait for some time."

34-41a. Then the king engaged several experts in sculpture in cutting stones as well as in construction activities. He honoured them with gifts and respectfully requested them to attend to every aspect of the job.

O Brāhmaṇas, the neatly constructed Mansion rose up everyday like the moon during Śuklapakṣa (bright fortnight), growing bigger and bigger. The Mansion rose up very tall in a short time. It was impossible to count the number of stones used in the construction.

The money was spent in crores. There also it was impossible to calculate the expense. All the people in the subcontinent of Bhārata who owned allegiance to King Indradyumna were engaged in this. All those who were engaged worked jointly with mutual co-operation. The great delight of those engaged in the work gave rise to a loud clamour filling the vaults of heaven and the quarters.

41b-46. The Goddess of prosperity and fortune was pleased with the sincerity, faith, devotion, and the Sattva quality of the king. Along with the fame of the king the glory increased, O Brāhmaṇas.

The Mansion of Viṣṇu was excessively refulgent. In some places it was covered with gold and inlaid with different kinds of gems. In some places where crystals were used in the construction it had the lustre of the antumnal sky. The walls in some places were built of blue stones and the Mansion appeared like the sky covered with black clouds. As the beautiful Mansion of Viṣṇu was thus perfectly finished, the excellent king duly performed the rite of *Garbhapratiṣṭhā* (installation of the idol in the inner sanctuary of the temple). In order to ward off stroke of lightning, cracks in the structure and other calamities, gems etc. were suitably fitted in the manner prescribed in the treatises on architecture. The king then suitably utilized many other costly articles acquired by his heroic exertions in the construction of the Mansion.

47-54. The Mansion that was being constructed was such as could not be even mentally imagined by kings in the three worlds. It increased the fame (of Indradyumna), O Brāhmaṇas. Even Devas who live till the end of the Kalpa could not visualize it. Ādityas spoke to one another thus:

"A Mansion like this has never been constructed anywhere on the earth or in heaven. His excellent intellect is wonderful. It has taken this lofty form. It craves for the lotus-like feet of the Lord with faith and sincerity. Who are such wise kings on the earth who see such supra-mundane activities or perform them? Emperors may defeat all the enemies and establish their suzerainty. They may have hoarded much wealth in crores and crores, but is it possible for those kings to perform a thousand horse-sacrifices as performed by this king unto the Lord of heaven. Before this it has not been performed. A thousand horse-sacrifices have not been seen or heard of, but they have been performed by this king. In the course of those sacrifices the residents of all the three worlds stayed on the earth along with this king and enjoyed the pleasures.

55-59. As he performed the sacrifices, his assembly appeared like the world of Brahmā. The three Vedas were present there in embodied form. Dharma had all the four feet. Suras who can realize their desires by merely thinking of them have become struck with wonder there in regard to this excellent Mansion. The king has intelligently planned this (and got it constructed) but no other person resident in all the three worlds could even imagine this. What can be inaccessible to this king who has the help (and guidance of) Nārada and Brahmā, the creator of all the worlds, the Lord of all the Devas!

Or to a devotee of Viṣṇu what is desired to be done cannot be far off (inaccessible). O Brāhmaṇas, there is no difference between Viṣṇu and his devotees."

At the conclusion of the construction of the Mansion the king said to Nārada, the eminent sage:

60-66. "Everything which was impossible for Suras and Asuras has been accomplished by me, because I have been meditating on Viṣṇu directly in an exclusive way. The Lord said to me formerly, 'The palatial building is ever in me' " (?) After saying this he fell at the feet of Nārada and bowed down to him.

Nārada raised the excellent king and honoured him: "O king, there is no difference between you and me really. For your sake the Lord of the universe has directly manifested himself. Do worship him. Now you are a living-liberated soul. Your mind is attached to his lotus-like feet. What more than this has to be acquired by a person with single-minded devotion?

O king, what cannot be achieved through Tīrthas, Mantras, Japas, charitable gifts, sacrifices with plenty of monetary gifts, holy rites, study of Vedas and austerities, O great king, has been acquired by you through devotion. Henceforth you need not grieve. Let your mind remain in the path of devotion.

67. After staying in this world for a long time, O great king, propitiate the Lord of the universe by means of offerings and great festivities.

68. If you are desirous of seeing Brahmā, if you wish to go to the Lord, he will instruct you in the various festivals and processions.

69-71. The Lord himself will grant you boons. After the Palatial Shrine has been inaugurated by the Self-born Lord I shall also come along with the Seven Sages. Then we can go to the sinless world of Brahmā. Except you who is fit for going to the world of Brahmā?"

After saying this to the king Nārada rose into the sky.

CHAPTER TWENTYTWO

Indradyumna Goes to Brahmā's Abode along with Nārada

Jaimini said:

1-4. The king told him:

"O sage, why should the journey be a secret one? Here we have the flower-chariot that has a velocity more than that of the mind. We shall get into it and go. Kindly wait for a short while, when I shall instruct the officers in-charge of the Palace after circumambulating the Lord and then come back, O excellent sage."

Nārada heard his words and believing in the utterance of the king held him by the hand and entered the great Altar. They repeatedly bowed down to Kṛṣṇa along with Balarāma and Subhadrā. Nārada then requested for permission to go to the world of Brahmā.

5. Indradyumna too circumambulated Hari after praying to him mentally, verbally and physically. With great eagerness he bowed down to him with the eight limbs (touching the ground). O Brāhmaṇas, with palms folded in reverence, he requested for permission to go to the world of Brahmā.

6-10. Both of them, the sage and the king, went in the divine vehicle. After circumambulating the Sun that was in the centre of the sky, they went up and up crossing the zone of the Pole Star. They were looked at by Siddhas residing in Janaloka with bent and immediately uplifted faces. They were very joyously conversing mutually.

The conduct of the Lord is conducive to the removal of dirt and purification of the mind. Just as the excellent sage, a living-liberated soul, wandered over all the worlds without his movement obstructed anywhere, so also this resident of the mortal world. Thanks to the favour of Viṣṇu, the king proceeded ahead quickly.

In the whole of the Cosmic Egg there was nothing which could not be attained by him if it could be attained by a devotee of Viṣṇu. Or he would attain salvation. Both of them were honoured and adored by the Siddhas residing in Maharloka.

11-17. Indradyumna did not remember his earthly residence while gradually rising up and seeing (the liberated souls), the sole receptacles of happiness, devoid of *Dvandvas* (mutually opposed pairs like heat-cold etc.) and having many types of human aims realized at the very time when the desires arose. The only thing that he remembered was the Mansion he built in the land of Karmas on the earth for the propitiation of the Lord. He thought about it as follows: 'Will it be completed or not? Now that I have come to the world of Brahmā I wonder whether it has been attacked by the enemies. The servants and attendants may have lost interest or respect because of their covetousness of wealth. The artisans and masons may be slow in their jobs even after taking the full amount of wages. As I have come to the abode of Brahmā, they may not complete the construction. Until I return to the earth with the four-faced Lord Brahmā, the Mansion will not be complete, as I am far off. Those who had come here before had not returned to the earth once again. Perhaps the vassal kings of wicked minds are thinking thus. Will the enemies seize my realm?'

While the king was thinking thus with a worried mind, the sage, the storehouse of the past and future knowledge, spoke to him:

18-21. "What do you think, O great king, thus with a distressed mind? The place where we have come to is not one where one should be worried. Agonies and ailments never prevail here; neither death nor old age find a place here. What else then is the cause of misery? O highly fortunate one, you are blessed. You have achieved your objectives because you have come to the world of Brahmā here in your human body itself. You have seen Hari directly. Those who have come here do not worry about various worldly affairs that are fit to be discarded."

As the eminent sage spoke thus, the king spoke to him:

22-24. "O Brāhmaṇa, I do not worry about the kinsmen and the members of the family of the king. I have started construction of the Mansion of the Lord. Knowing that I have come away here, it is possible that the servants and the attendants do not carry out their tasks further. What has been started by me should be completed certainly, O sage. Thinking of a possibility of obstacles coming in the way, O holy Lord, my mind has become unhappy." On hearing his words the sage said laughingly:

25-31. "You are on a par with Brahmā. You are not an ordinary king. You have never been offended or assailed by anyone on the earth. What is that which has been performed by your predecessors or by yourself which can cause any loss to creation or sustenance? You have come to the world of Brahmā. Your exploits and reputation spread in the three worlds like the Sun and the Moon. In your affairs the Four-faced Lord renders you assistance. Why should there be any suspicion of obstacles in those affairs, O tiger among king?

(*Defective Text*) He who is a direct enemy of yours is far off (?) O great king, Śakra who is the lord of the three worlds is seated in the middle of the assembly. Particularly in regard to the Mansion of the Lord of the worlds, O king, which man will even mentally desire (to harm the temple). Let there not be any doubt in you in regard to that.

Look ahead, O king, there is a mass of refulgence with the lustre of a crore of the moons. It generates delight all round like a crore of the oceans of nectar. Know that this mass of refulgence belongs to the abode of Brahmā."

32-43. Conversing thus they reached the world of Brahmā. Even from afar they heard the sound of recitation of the Vedas issuing from the mouths of Brahminical Sages. The words, the letters and their sequences were clearly audible. Itihāsas, Purāṇas, metres, liturgical texts and songs—all were audible without any mix-up of the sounds or words. They were brilliant and they were heard distinctly. "O tiger among kings, know this as the city of Brahmā. The assembly is seen yonder where the Four-faced Grandfather of the worlds is comfortably seated along with the leading Brāhmaṇa Sages. He is attended upon by many living-liberated souls of variegated nature and sound consciousness. Those who come here do not return to the turmoils of the ocean of worldly existence. The word *sat* is another name of Brahmā. This is his excellent world. Hence it is famous as Satyaloka. There is nothing above it.

Slightly above this and beneath the hemispheroidal lid of the Cosmic Egg is the world of Vaikuṇṭha, O king. It is there that the liberated ones dwell. It is there that Janārdana, the Lord of Yogins, worthy of being contemplated upon by Yogins, himself dwells. Consciousness is his body. The Lord is of the nature of highest bliss. After attaining him they do not return to the path of worldly existence where death prevails. For the sake of his own salvation Brahmā always attends upon him along with the living-liberated ones.

At the end of the tenure of life allotted to him he too resorts to him along with these. He is the creator of the worlds. He assumes the forms of fish, tortoise etc. He is the creator of the worlds, the protector and the annihilator in the form of Rudra."

Saying thus to Indradyumna he reached the abode of Brahmā. Within a moment he went to the entrance and the *Prakoṣṭha* (a room near the gate) where Śakra and other Guardians of Quarters stood waiting.

44-48. They were standing there engaged in meditation for a long time. The overlords of Manvantaras were denied entry by the gatekeeper as though they were ordinary people.

On seeing Nārada accompanied by Indradyumna that gatekeeper humbly bowed down to him, bending down his neck: "O holy lord who takes pleasure in wandering over all the fourteen worlds, O master, your father's assembly does not look nice without you.

Of course, there are Gautama and other excellent sages, Brāhmaṇas, well-versed in the Vedas; still the assembly of Brahmā is not delightful. Though the night may have many stars, yet it is through the Moon that it shines well."

Praising him thus, he humbly granted him permission to enter.

CHAPTER TWENTYTHREE

Indradyumna Returns after Visiting Brahmā

Nārada said:

1-6. O gatekeeper, this is a saintly king of great fame (named) Indradyumna. He is an emperor and the foremost among devotees of Viṣṇu. He has come to see Brahmā. Let him go ahead if you give him permission.

On being told thus Maṇikodara said to Nārada: "O holy lord, he who has accompanied you, does not seem to be an ordinary person. Let this resident of the mortal world wait for a short while over there where you see the Guardians of Quarters, Pitṛs and overlords of the Manvantaras. You will kindly go in and inform the Lotus-born Lord and then admit him in. After going near the entrance to the Assembly Hall, he will go in along with the Guardians of Quarters.

The Four-faced Lord is now listening to singing with concentrated mind. It is necessary for us employed as doorkeepers to wait for the proper opportunities. I am only a slave to you and to your father. Be pleased. Do not be angry with me."

7-12. On being told thus Nārada went in and bowed down to Brahmā, the Lord of the worlds, and prostrated with the eight limbs (touching the ground). Then the king's (arrival) was reported to him.

With a side-glance he commanded him to fetch Indradyumna. The Lord did not say anything because he was attentively listening to the song. His mind had been attracted by the divine songs and music. After understanding the gesture Nārada brought the excellent king in.

Thereupon he was closely observed by Śakra and others. Seeing Pitāmaha, the creator of the worlds, from a distance, O excellent Brāhmaṇas, the king thought him to be Hari himself of the wooden idol.

The king went ahead slowly bowing down, with palms joined in reverence, eulogizing him, falling down (by way of prostrating) and going on with faltering steps due to fright and awe of the place. At the bidding of Nārada the king stood a little away.

Listening to the meritorious holy anecdotes of the Lord of the Daughter of the Ocean that were being sung, O great Brāhmaṇas, the Four-faced Lord remained seated for a short while.

13-16. He was fanned by Sāvitrī and Śāradā (who stood) on either side. The Self-born Lord was eulogized by the Vedas assuming pure bodies.

He began calculating the units of time such as Kalā, Kāṣṭhā, Nimeṣa etc. up to the cycle of Yugas.

In the case of persons who have gone to his (Brahmā's) world, there is no old age, birth or death; there is no change of form, colour, feature etc. There is neither mental affliction nor physical ailment; there are no divisions such as Manvantara etc., cycles of Yugas etc. There is nothing like the close of a Kalpa etc. He is the Supreme Lord himself.

At the close of the song, he spoke to the king laughingly:

17-20. "O noble Indradyumna, you are the beloved of the Lord himself. This world named Satya which is inaccessible to others has been known by you (i.e. reached by you).

Sages who have destroyed their sins and are desirous of coming here, stand engaged in penance till the ultimate annihilation of all living beings.

This is the abode of the wonderful qualities of sentience etc. of all the living beings created in the fourteen worlds."

Thereafter he honoured the excellent king. The extremely delighted Grandfather knew his object; still he asked him:

21. "Why have you come here? What is in your heart? Tell me. When I am seen, there is nothing which cannot be obtained. Is it nectar that is desired by you?"

Indradyumna replied:

22-29. You are the Immanent Soul, O Lord. How can there be anything not known to you? Still the question put by you, O Lord, indicates your compassion for me.

Obeying your behest humbly as conveyed by your son (Nārada), I performed a thousand horse-sacrifices. At their close the Lord of everything past, present and future appeared before me in wooden form.

It is on account of your plentiful blessings that I am able to see such a Lord, the lotus-eyed one. That is why I came to your world.

O Lord, construction of a palatial shrine unto that Lord has been begun by me. If you yourself were to go over there and install the Lord of the universe. O creator of the worlds, your blessings to me shall be fruitful.

It is for this purpose, O Lord of the universe, that I have come to your world to see your lotus-like feet in the company of Nārada.

Be pleased with me. Do this. You alone are the Lord of the worlds.

You alone are that Lord of the worlds (viz. Jagannātha). There is no difference between you two, O Lord. You are the installer and the installed. You are the knower and what is to be known.

Jaimini said:

30-37. At the end of his entreaty thus the great sage Durvāsas bowed down to him and fell (at his feet) with eight limbs (touching the ground). Then he stood near with palms joined in reverence. Stooping low down due to humility, he spoke to Brahmā, the Sire of the worlds:

"O Lord, O creator of the worlds, the Guardians of Quarters along with Pitṛs and overlords of the Manvantaras have been standing at the gate for a long time like wretched people, as they have been prevented by the gatekeeper. Hence command (the gatekeeper). Let them see your lotus-like feet."

On hearing the words of Durvāsas then the Lord of Devas laughed and spoke these words: "Indeed there is no occasion for these people, but since they are deluded, they are jealous of Indradyumna. This king is a living-liberated soul. He has destroyed all Karmas and masses of sins. He is the fifth one in my line of progeny. He is a Vaiṣṇava eagerly devoted to Viṣṇu.

But these people have attained their life aims of enjoyment of pleasures by the performance of holy rites. Indeed Devas seek an entry here only by performing penances. By my blessings, these have come here for attending upon me. Still, permitted by you, let them come to see me."

Thereupon, by the words of Durvāsas those Devas entered.

38-45. They bowed down to Brahmā from a distance, near the singers (and saw) Indradyumna, the king, conversing with palms joined in reverence.

As the Guardians of Quarters bowed down to him, the Lord of the universe blessed them with his benign glance and respectfully continued to speak to Indradyumna:

"It is true that a Mansion was built by you for the installation of the Lord. But this is not that time. O king, neither your kingdom nor your successors exist now.

In the course of the time when the songs were sung, much of your time has passed. Indeed a Manvantara consists of seventyone divine Yugas (i.e. cycles of four Yugas according to human reckoning). Your dynasty has become extinct. Crores and crores of kings have passed away. The Lord and the ultimate Mansion—these two alone remain. Now it is the first Yuga of the Second Manu Svārociṣa. Since you have stayed near me, there is neither death nor old age (to you). There is no change of seasons nor the flow of time.

Hence, O great king, go to the earth. Make the Lord and the Mansion your own and come here quickly. Or I shall go over there immediately after you.

46-49. You first go to the earth. By the time you gather together the essential things in plenty, O highly fortunate one, I too shall come."

After commanding Indradyumna thus, the Lord, the Grandfather (of the world), spoke to the Devas who stood in front of him stooping down their necks in humility with palms joined in reverence. They were awe-struck and their eyes were fixed to the feet of the Lord. The Lord then spoke with affectionate but grave words, O Brāhmaṇas: "Why have you all heaven-dwellers come here simultaneously? What is your task that has to be carried out by me? Tell me without delay."

Jaimini said:

50. On hearing these words of Brahmā the Devas became rid of their fever (i.e. worry). All of them became delighted. They spoke to Lord Brahmā thus:

The Devas said:

51-54. How did that Lord of Blue Sapphire (body) who had been formerly worshipped by us on Nīla mountain vanish? How did he assume the wooden body now and manifest himself at the close of the sacrifice of King Indradyumna? It is to know the reason for this that we have come here to propitiate your lotus-like feet. Be pleased. Kindly tell us.

When this was requested by the Devas, the Lotus-seated Lord (said): "O Devas, this is a great secret. Previously it was never disclosed to anyone. All of you have come together. You have been waiting for a long time. So I shall tell you this excellent secret of the Suras.

55-62. In the previous Parārdha (half of a full day of god Brahmā) Janārdana of blue sapphire body occupied the holy spot of Śrī Puruṣottama and did not leave it. Now this is my second Parārdha. Manu, the son of the Self-born Lord (Svāyaṁbhuva), was functioning in the Śvetavārāha Kalpa. That was the time of morning of the first day. In the middle one of all the worlds (i.e. on the earth), the Lord of wooden body will stay on for the duration of my whole life honouring (us).

The Lord is my Ātman, O Suras, and I am identical with him. In this universe consisting of mobile and immobile beings, there is nothing apart (outside) from us both.

Resorting to *Yoga Nidrā* (Yogic Slumber) the Lord Puruṣottama lies down on his couch in the Śveta island in the middle of the Milk Ocean. He is the root of all the worlds, the primordial cause. His hair (on the body) are called Kalpadrumas. They are marked with conch and discus.

This tree is stationed in their middle. O Suras, it is presided over by the Super-sentience. It is the *Satyapuruṣa* (the Real Person) arising from the waters of the ocean.

63-68. In order to enjoy the pleasures of the three worlds, Janārdana of the wooden body was meditated upon (and worshipped) by pursuing the path of devotion in the course of many thousands of births.

I have been distressed much on account of the repeated creation, sustenance and annihilation. Therefore, the Lord was requested by me formerly for the destruction of the terrible worldly existence, for the annulment of all Karmas, for the liberation of all in all the worlds.

The various activities connected with the practice of Yoga such as *Dhāraṇā* (Retention), *Dhyāna* (Meditation) etc. are very difficult. Lord Puruṣottama manifested himself for the sake of granting salvation without all these difficult practices.

This holy spot is the mysterious body of this Lord. This cannot be discussed (specially) or thought of by means of the testimonies that apply to ordinary holy rites (?)

The Lord is the bestower of the fourfold aim of life in accordance with how one conceives him. He can be meditated and worshipped in the manner (the devotee chooses).

Persons who have destroyed the masses of their sins gradually by visiting him on the earth, become purified souls and they deserve salvation."

Jaimini said:

69. On hearing these nectar-like words of the Lotus-born Lord, the Devas were delighted. They thought thus within their contented minds:

70. 'Our Deva-hood is not permanent. We shall cast it off and go to the earth. In this holy and most excellent shrine, we shall worship the Lord with great self-control.'

71-73. On seeing the Suras with faces beaming with pleasure, Brahmā (said): "The Lord has manifested in order to bless Indradyumna. His idol has already gone there. It will speak of itself (everything). The Lord favourably inclined towards his devotees will grant many boons.

I will go to the Mansion of Indradyumna in order to install the Lord. You will also go there.

74-77. Let Indradyumna go first in order to gather together the requisite things for the installation. All of you shall be divested of your official duties. You shall assist him there.

Now the first Manvantara has passed, O Suras. Accompanied by Indradyumna, O excellent Suras, you shall all go there. He is the maker of the palace and the idols. Hence he is the owner. So let him gather together all the necessary articles along with his assistants.

If his progeny or any one connected with him remembers, Padmanidhi will go at my behest to the earth.

78-80. He will go there for the sake of gathering together all the articles for the installation."

On seeing the Śrī (glory, splendour, prosperity) of Brahmā, Indradyumna was delighted in his mind and struck with great wonder. He bowed down to the Sire of the universe. Obeying his behest with a low bow, he came down to the earth along with the Devas whose tenure of duties had come to an end. Brāhmaṇas were duly encouraged (for performing the holy rites).

CHAPTER TWENTYFOUR

Devas Eulogize the Lord: Padmanidhi's Reception

Jaimini said:

1-5. After coming (to the earth) with an anxious mind on account of the delay (in returning), he prostrated before the Lord like a long staff. Hair standing on end through excessive joy covered his body as though it was an upper garment. (He said:)

Indradyumna said:

Obeisance to the Lord friendly to Brāhmaṇas; to the Lord conducive to the welfare of cows and Brāhmaṇas; to the Lord who destroys the miseries of his suppliants; to the Lord who is the sole cause for the acquisition of the fourfold aim of life.

Oṁ, Obeisance to Vāsudeva who is in the form of Hiraṇyagarbha, Puruṣa and Pradhāna; to the Lord, the embodiment of pure knowledge.

Uttering the prayer thus, the king had his eyes filled with tears of joy. Circumambulating the Lord, he bowed to him again and again.

Then the Devas who had gone there, joyously bowed down to the Lord and eulogized him with palms joined in reverence.

The Devas said:

6. The Puruṣa has a thousand (innumerable) heads, a thousand eyes and a thousand feet. He pervades the entire earth and stands ten Aṅgulas above*.

7. He is being sung as the Puruṣa, the Supreme Brahman and the great Ātman. The past, present and the future everything is Puruṣa himself.

8. His greatness is this much. This Puruṣa, the Lord, is very great. The collection of all living beings constitutes his one *pāda* (i.e. one-fourth part). His (remaining) three *pādas* (parts) are immortals in heaven.

9. The Vedas were born of you. From you was born the Yajña-Puruṣa. Horses were born of you, cows and sheep too.

10. Brāhmaṇas were born of your mouth; Kṣatriyas were born of your arms. Vaiśyas were born of your thighs. Śūdras issued forth from your feet.

11. From your mind the Moon was born and from your eyes, the Sun. The Wind flowed from (was born of) your ears along with the vital airs and the Carrier of *Havya* (i.e. Fire) from tongues.

12. Ether emerged forth from your navel; Firmament from your head; the Earth was born from your feet and the eight Quarters came out from your ears.

13. The Seven *Paridhis* (sacrificial sticks laid round the sacred fire) issued from you and so also the twenty-one *Samits* (sacrificial twigs). The mobile and immobile beings of all species came forth from you alone.

14. You alone are the lord of all the worlds; you alone are the protector. In a fierce form, O great Lord, you alone are the annihilator.

15. You alone are Yajña and part of Yajña. You are the lord of Yajña, greater than the greatest. You are the great Śabda Brahman (Sound as the Supreme Being or the Vedas).

---

*Cf the Puruṣa Sūkta (RV X.90). The eulogy is a Purāṇic version of RV

16. You are the independent king, Emperor. O Lord of the worlds, O ruler of the universe, you are *Virāṭ* (of Cosmic form). You are beneath. You are above. You are at the sides. O Lord identical with the universe, everything in the world has been pervaded by you.

17. Yājñikas (performers of Yajñas) who worship you, obtain the highest abode. You alone are the consumer and what is consumed. You are the *Havis* offering, the *Hotṛ* (oblator of *Havis*) and the *Havana* (the act of offering *havis* into the fire); you are the bestower of benefits.

18. You are the enjoyer of the benefit of all holy rites, O Lord; you are identical with all holy rites. You are the implements of all holy rites; you are the bestower of the benefit of all holy rites.

19. You are the inspirer to perform Karmas. You are the bestower of perfection in Virtue, Love and Wealth. Excepting you, who else is the bestower of salvation? O Hṛṣīkeśa, obeisance to you.

20. Obeisance to the infinite one having a thousand (innumerable) forms; to the lord having a thousand feet, eyes, head, thighs and arms; to the eternal Puruṣa having a thousand names. Hail to the Lord, the sustainer of thousands of crores of Yugas!

21. We have fallen off from the posts of authority; we have resorted to you as our refuge. O Lord, save us, O lotus-eyed one. Be the asylum unto the helpless ones.

22. O Lord, you are the sole refuge to the creature fallen into the ocean of worldly existence. There is none equal to you in your creation, who can protect the distressed ones.

23. O Lord, you are the father of the universe, the sole refuge to the distressed one, to the helpless one. You are the protector, the nourisher; O Lord, you alone are the person to prevent all calamities.

24. Save us, O Viṣṇu, O Lord of the universe, save us, O Supreme Lord. O lover of Kamalā, excepting you who else is competent to protect us?

25. O immanent soul, obeisance to you. O storehouse of all splendour, obeisance to you.

26. Eulogizing thus, those Devas bowed down again and again, O excellent Brāhmaṇas, and came out along with Indradyumna.

27. They then went to the Shrine of Śrī Narasiṁha, fell (at his feet), bowed down with great devotion and worshipped Nṛkesarī (the Man-Lion).

28. Then, along with Padmanidhi they went to the summit of the mountain Nīla where the excellent Mansion (had been built). They

went there for the purpose of getting all the requisites together.

29. There they saw the excessively lofty (Mansion) pervading the entire sky. (It caused the suspicion) whether it was the rising Vindhya mountain getting ready to obstruct the movement of the Sun.

30. It pervaded all the quarters. It sparkled with its wonderful structure. Although much time had elapsed, it retained its grace and wonderful outline.

31-32. Then Indradyumna, the devotee of Viṣṇu, thought thus: 'From here I went to the Satyaloka formerly while it was being constructed. After a long time the completed Mansion, the perfect palace, has come into my view. It is only due to the grace of the Lord and not to human endeavour.

33. There is the end of a Manvantara when even the Sun, Moon and Indra are annihilated? Still this rare Mansion continues to stand (perfectly).

34. These Mansions built by human beings are like anthills. They crumble down and they are overgrown with trees. In a short while, their life expires (and they crumble down).

35. It is on account of the compassion for me of the Lord that Hari's abode has been preserved.' Then he spoke threse humble words to his assistants:

36-39. "Know that the Mansion of the Lord has been constructed by me. The Lord himself manifested there with a wooden body. At that time an unembodied ethereal voice spoke to me: 'Get the Mansion for the stay of the Lord of the universe constructed on the peak of Nīla mountain. It shall be a thousand Hastas high. For the ceremony of the installation of this, the Lotus-born Lord himself will come here along with Siddhas, Brahminical sages and Devas.' How can it be known what requisites are to be gathered together?"

When (Indradyumna) said thus, those Devas, divested of their authority, spoke to him:

Devas said:

40. We too do not know that. Our preceptor Guru (Bṛhaspati) is not within our power now. He is engaged in the welfare of heaven.

Padmanidhi said:

41. O Lord, according to the behest of Brahmā, I have come here along with you. What is to be done by me here? What is the object expected (by you all)?

Jaimini said:

42. While they were conversing thus, Nārada, who had been previously sent by Brahmā and who was an expert in all sacred treatises, stood in front of them.

43. (Brahmā had said to him) "O sage, collect together all the requisite things in accordance with the injunctions of the scriptures. At your bidding Padmanidhi will fetch everything."

44. On seeing the son of Brahmā all of them joyously stood up. The excellent king adored him by means of *Ṣaḍarghya Pūjā* (worship in which the Arghya is offered six times) too.

45. Those Devas who were having human forms, bowed down. Indradyumna told him about the articles necessary for the rite of installation:

46. "O excellent sage, I do not know what specific things should be collected together, as I have been abandoned by my priest for a long time. Hence, O Brāhmaṇa, command whatever is to be done and the sequence thereof."

CHAPTER TWENTYFIVE

The Construction and Installation of the Chariot of the Lord

Jaimini said:

1-7. On this being said, Nārada thought over everything in the light of the injunctions of the scriptures. He wrote everything in the proper order on a leaf and informed the king.

After hearing the contents of the leaf and pondering over it again and again, the king handed it over to Padmanidhi saying: "O Padmanidhi, whatever is written here, you collect together. Make the hall full of gold; embellish it with gold. Let there be the following abodes: the divine abode of Brahmā, the abode of Brahminical sages free from impurities, and abodes for the residence of Indra and other Suras, of Siddhas, of the residents of the mortal world, of the prominent sages, of the kings, of the residents of the nether worlds, of the serpent kings, O Padmanidhi, of the residents of the three worlds. Every house should be furnished with suitable seating arrangement.

O Padmanidhi, carry it out with great promptness. Till the time of gathering the materials together Viśvakarman also will assist you."

As Indradyumna was ordering thus, the sage said to him; "This must be done apart from the collection of the requisites with spaces apart (in different places).

8. Three excellent chariots[1], perfectly fitted with gold and adorned with silken cloths, jewel-studded necklaces etc. of great value, should be made. They must be big and strong.

9. The chariot of Śrī Vāsudeva should be marked with Garuḍa emblem. Let a lotus-emblem be placed on the top of the chariot of Subhadrā.

10. The chariot of Viṣṇu should be carefully fitted with sixteen wheels, that of Bala with fourteen, and that of Subhadrā with twelve.

11. The width of the chariot of the Discus-bearing Lord shall be sixteen Hastas (i.e. 16 x 45=720Cms); that of Bala fourteen and that of Subhadrā twelve.

12. (*Defective text*) He is the place of rest of all the worlds. His idol is made in a sitting posture. If he were to move, the worlds will perish. Hence there is no movement (? vehicle).

13. Let him see the universe consisting of the mobile and immobile beings in the mirror of knowledge. Hence there is a clean mirror always in his hand which is free from impurities.

14-15. The Palm-tree is called *Tāla* because it is stationed in *Tala* (surface of the earth). The Lord is always marked with it. Hence that alone should be made the emblem devoid of impurities, of the incarnation of Śeṣa as Balabhadra. So he is known as *Tāladhvaja* (having palm tree as the emblem). Or the plough alone shall be made the excellent emblem of the Lord with one in his hand.

16. O king, the Lord should not be made to stay in an uninstalled chariot, Mansion, pavilion or city. That shall be fruitless.

17. Hence at the outset, the installation of the chariot of Hari should be made. Let the requisites thereof be collected together. It should be carried out by me.

18. This is the command of my father. I have come here immediately after receiving this command".

On hearing these words of his, three chariots were made.

19-22. The three chariots were made by Viśvakarmā in a single day through the money and articles acquired by Padmanidhi.

1. VV 8-18 and up to 22 describe the chariots meant for Vāsudeva, Balabhadra and Subhadrā.

The axles, wheels, pillars, flagstaffs, emblems etc. were very splendid. The chariots were spacious and fitted with ornamental festoons.

They were beautiful with different kinds of wonderful features. There were carvings of couples in wonderful combinations and there were small images placed in different parts.

Half of them was completed with gold coverings. They were comparable to the chariot of the Sun-god himself. They had a loud rumbling sound like that of clouds. They had the qualities of attracting the eyes. They were yoked with hundreds of white horses having the speed of wind.

They were installed by Nārada in accordance with the injunctions of scriptures in an auspicious Lagna (Sun's entrance into a Zodiacal sign), in a *Muhūrta* (good time of the day) on a good Tithi (Lunar day) as instructed by Astrologers.

The sages said:

23-24. O holy lord Jaimini, speak out. You are omniscient. You are honoured by us. What is the procedure whereby the chariot of Hari should be installed? Tell us as it should be, so that we may know the details of the procedure.

Jaimini said:

25. I shall tell you the procedure whereby it was installed by the noble-souled Nārada and which was seen by me formerly.

26-29. A splendid hall shall be made to the north-east of the chariot. A pavilion shall be made in its middle. A square altar shall be made there, O Brāhmaṇas. It shall be free from impurities. The sides shall measure four *Hastas* (4 x 45=180 Cms.) and the height shall be one *Hasta.* On the night previous to the installation, in an auspicious hour, the auspicious rite of *Svastivācana* shall be performed after which the sprouts shall be fixed (the rite of *Aṅkurārpaṇa*) after offering oblations to the thirty-two Devas in accordance with the injunctions.

In the morning, a holy mystic picture of circle, lotus or Svastika should be made on the Altar. A water-pot shall be placed thereon.

30-36. A decoction of five trees (i.e. exudation from the barks) shall be poured into it. The intelligent devotee shall pour into it the holy waters of Gaṅgā etc. along with clay and tender shoots, all types of scents, five precious stones, all medicinal herbs. After filling it thus in accordance with the injunctions the preceptor shall sit facing the

East. He should be pure (in mind and body). Remembering Viṣṇu he should thereafter fill it with *Pañcagavya*.[1] The pot shall be covered with a silk cloth. There shall be splendid and sweet-smelling garlands round its neck. Fruits and tender leaves must be placed upon it. The auspicious thread must be tied. There the idol of Narasiṁha, free from ailments, the Lord of Devas, should be put. The devotee shall then recite the Mantrarāja (Oṁ etc.) and pray duly with offerings etc. for the sake of favour after invoking Hari therein. Then, O Brāhmaṇas , he should worship duly with external offerings of various kinds. To the north-west of that water-pot one thousand and eight Homas shall be performed by the preceptor by means of sacrificial twigs, ghee and *Carus*. The residue of the offerings shall be put in the middle of the pot at the end.

37. The chariot should be decorated beautifully by means of banners, garlands of sweet-smelling flowers etc. All the parts of the chariot should be sprinkled with water mixed with sandal paste and sweet scents.

38-39. Black aloewood should be fumigated. Conch-shells and Kāhāla trumpets should be sounded. Samīraṇa (Wind-god) shall be installed in the flag of Nṛsiṁha. Then after duly worshipping with red garlands having sweet-smelling flowers the following Mantra should be recited and Suparṇa (Garuḍa) be prayed to:

40. "I salute Suparṇa, the golden-coloured lord of birds, who is the cause of the life of the universe, who is a body of Viṣṇu, who is the vehicle as well as the emblem of Viṣṇu, on thinking about whom the foetuses in the wombs of the multitudes of Serpent females are aborted immediately, whose face is marked with the red dirt and the fat of serpents severed by means of his fierce, moving beak, who is of the nature of the Vedas and who is free from impurities."

41. Reciting the Vedic Mantras in chorus, blowing conch-shells and playing on various musical instruments and uttering the excellent Sūkta (along with others), the priest should place Suparṇa on the top of the chariot.

42. Then a water-pot should be waved about it and on all the sides of the chariot. Accompanied by a Brāhmaṇa, the Mantrarāja should be recited three times and the chariot should be sprinkled with water.

1. *Pañcagavya*: A collection of five products of cow, viz. milk, curds, ghee, urine and dung.

43. Then the *Pūrṇāhuti* (final oblation into fire) should be offered. Monetary gifts should be given to Brāhmaṇas and the preceptor. Thereby, that preceptor will become pleased.

44-47. At the end, the devotee should feed Brāhmaṇas with milk puddings, honey and ghee.

The installation of the chariot of Balabhadra shall be done while reciting the twelve-syllabled Mantra. The Mantra for the ploughshare emblem shall be the one beginning with "The plough is thunderbolt. It protects" etc. Or the twelve-syllabled Mantra is also glorified.

The chariot of Subhadrā shall be installed with Lakṣmīsūkta . The lotus-emblem shall be raised and unfurled after reciting this Mantra: "O seat of residence of Śrī, You have originated from the whirlpool of the navel of the Enemy of Mura. You have assumed the form of the group of Cosmic Eggs. You are the seat of the Four-faced Lord. Be steady."

48-53a. There is this much of difference. The *Havis* should be offered five times for each of the three separately. Everything connected with one should be completely performed separately. After installing the chariots the devotee should offer as gifts gold, cows, clothes, grains and money with great devotion to the Lord.

The Lord should be placed in the installed and well-decorated chariot in accordance with the injunctions along with the singing of Vedic Mantras.

There should be auspicious utterance of "Be victorious" to the accompaniment of various musical instruments. Chowries should be waved. Incenses should be burnt. Flowers should be showered.

The deity should be taken towards the chariot by Brāhmaṇas, Kṣatriyas or Vaiśyas. The chariot should be carefully drawn by tamed horses of good features, or by bullocks or by men of great devotion to Viṣṇu.

53b-60a. All the people should be fed to their heart's content, pleased with different kinds of food, unguents etc. Offerings should be made above the chariot to the Devas, O Brāhmaṇas, while reciting *Balimantras*:

"May you all accept the offerings, O Devas, Ādityas, Vasus, Maruts, Aśvins, Rudras, Suparṇas, serpents, evil spirits, Planets, Asuras, Yātudhānas, all the deities present in the chaiot, Guardians of Quarters, protectors of the worlds and Vināyakas causing obstacles. May the great divine sages grant welfare to the universe. Let these prevent all obstacles. Let them not be inimical. Let Daityas and groups of goblins be satisfied and gentle."

Thereafter, the Lord is taken along the level ground which reciting the following Mantras: Gāyatrī pertaining to Viṣṇu,[1] the sacred Sūkta (hymn) of Viṣṇu and the Mantras Vāmadevya, holy *Mānastokya* (RV I.114.8) etc. and *Rathantaras.*

Then there shall be the loud utterance of *Puṇyāhavācana* along with the sound of musical instruments.

The chariot of the Discus-bearing Lord should be taken very slowly and affectionately.

60b-65. O excellent Brāhmaṇas, I shall now describe the evil portents in regard to the chariot:

If the shaft breaks there is danger to Brāhmaṇas; if the axle is broken there is destruction of Kṣatriyas; if the beam of the balance breaks there is destruction of Vaiśyas; if the pin of yoke breaks there is danger to Śūdras. If the axle pin breaks there shall be drought; if the pedestal breaks there is danger to the subjects. If the wheel of the chariot breaks it forewarns that the army of enemies shall invade. If the flagstaff falls, O Brāhmaṇas, another person shall certainly become the king. If the idol breaks one can predict that the king will die. If the chariot is shattered there shall be destruction in the whole of the realm.

If these and other inauspicious portents occur the offering to the deities should be made once again; so also the *Śānti Homa* should be performed. The Brāhmaṇas should be fed once again or food-grain should be given to them.

66-69. The sacred fire should be kindled in the north-eastern quarter of the chariot. *Homa* should be performed by means of sacrificial twigs with ghee, honey, *Ājya* (i.e solid ghee, or any substitute such as oil etc.) smeared at the roots and the tips.

The sacrificial twigs should be from Palāśa tree, O excellent Brāhmaṇas. The devotee should be initiated by means of the Mantrarāja. The devotee should perform the *Homa* by means of the Mantra of initiation. There should be special result from everything. At the end of the *Homa* he should perform *Śāntivācana* rite:

70. "Hail to the Brāhmaṇas; let there be the welfare of the king always. Hail to the cows; let there be welfare unto the subjects. Let there be peace to the whole universe.

71-74. May there be welfare unto the bipeds; let there always be peace unto the quadrupeds. Welfare unto the subjects; so also let there be welfare unto our soul.

1. Viṣṇu Gāyatrī:
nārāyaṇāya vidmahe/vāsudevāya dhīmahi/ tan no viṣṇuḥ pracodayāt//

Let there be calmness unto the Lord, Bhūḥ, Bhuvaḥ, Svaḥ (names of the three worlds) and auspiciousness. Let there be peace, let there be auspiciousness; let there be welfare all round us.

O Lord, you are the creator of the universe; you alone are the nourisher; O Lord of Devas, protect the subjects. O Lord of the universe, create peace."

O king (?), one should perform the rite of *Grahaśānti* (pacifying the Planets) etc. after knowing the evil Planets of the person undertaking the journey.

CHAPTER TWENTYSIX

Indradyumna Worships the Lord: King Gāla Submits to Indradyumna

Jaimini said:

1. The deities were brought near the Mansion without any untoward incident via the level ground in accordance with the proper procedure in an auspicious hour.

2. Then a very great chamber, the biggest among all the chambers, was built with various colours and studded with gems at the behest of Indradyumna by Viśvakarman.

3. In that chamber all the things required for the installation and worship, viz. *Havis*, sacrificial twigs, Darbha grass, different kinds of foodstuffs were acquired and provision for different kinds of music and dances was made.

4. At the time of the installation, O Brāhmaṇas, there was greater prosperity and affluence than what was there before in his empire.

5-9a. At the time there was a king on the earth named Gāla. He had made a stone image called Mādhava and installed it in the Mansion and he had been worshipping it deriving prosperity thereby.

The excellent king (Indradyumna) got a smaller Mansion built. After removing the stone idol from there with great respect, he got it installed in the smaller palace (shrine).

The king (Gāla) heard about this through messengers (and spies) and became furious. He came to Nīla mountain along with his army.

On seeing the materials required for the installation gathered together, which could not be obtained by human beings even in dream, King Gāla became wonder-struck in his mind. He remained (thinking thus in his mind):

9b-13a. 'What is this? What is the news? Who is making all these?' He carefully gathered the following information: Indradyumna had divine powers. That king was the original builder of the Mansion of the Lord. He had then come from the world of Brahmā along with the Devas, Padmanidhi and the preceptor Nārada in order to install (the Lord). It was he who had gathered all the requisite materials. Brahmā, the excellent Sura, would be coming (presently) for the purpose of the installation.

After getting all the details and knowing the divine activities, (King Gāla) considered himself blessed and one who had fulfilled the tasks. He knew that it was an extremely wonderful thing in his kingdom.

13b-20a. (He thought thus:) 'A holy rite more conducive to welfare, has never been performed before, nor will it ever be. So I shall stay near him and follow the details or procedure. I shall celebrate festivals every year after knowing the mode of these.

On account of the increase of my ill luck so long I did not know about Janārdana of this wooden body, the form of Brahman itself. So I have not served him (till now): thereby my very birth has become fruitless.

I should bow down to this Indradyumna, the Sire of the universe. He is the most excellent one among the great devotees of the Lord. He has come here from the world of Brahmā.

I should seek refuge in him. By seeing the Lord Nārāyaṇa directly after the installation in the Mansion I should certainly attain salvation. After installing Lord Viṣṇu he will transfer him to me. Why does one who has gone to the world of Brahmā, stay (long) on the earth? He will instruct me about the offerings and services. He will gather together the treasure of the Lord (entrust it to me) and will certainly go to the abode of Brahmā along with him.'

20b-27. Then Gāla, a devotee of Viṣṇu, had deliberation with his ministers. He joyously and humbly went near Indradyumna. Even after seeing him from afar he fell (on the ground) by way of prostration.

With palms joined in reverence King Gāla gazed at the head of Indradyumna with awe and went near him slowly. (Then he said:)

"O lord, you are the king of kings. You are the man who has gone to the world of Brahmā. You are a living-liberated soul (and hence) an

Īśvara (Lord). How can I (adequately) eulogize you? I am only an insect of a king. I did not know your greatness. I had repeated consultations with my ministers and came to fight with you. O lord, I have now seen your great superhuman manliness and a wonderful position (equal to that) of Indra.

After seeing this I have come to the conclusion that a great task like this can be accomplished by only one who has returned from the world of Brahmā and whose behest is carried out by the great treasurer Padmanidhi. O excellent one among Suras, all the Devas staying in the three worlds are under the control of your command, Let your mind be favourably inclined towards me."

Jaimini said:

28-33. As Gāla, the great king, pleaded thus (King Indradyumna) said thus smilingly: "O king, why do you expatiate? You too are a devotee of Hari. You are an Emperor. The ownership of the earth is common to all kings living on the earth. Now you are the sole ruler of the earth. All the rites of men and Maruts (i.e. Devas) are subject to the king's approval.

A king is constituted by Brahmā with parts of the eight Guardians of Quarters. A king deficient in merit cannot be eagerly devoted to the protection of the subjects. But you, O tiger among kings, particularly follow the excellent path and obtain fame and virtue here. You are a (real) Vaiṣṇava. One who installs the idol of Hari in accordance with the injunctions in the Mansion does not get involved in the bondage of physical bodies. He goes to the great region of Viṣṇu.

34-39. You yourself have installed this idol of Mādhava made of wood,* O king. It has all splendid features and it is directly the bestower of salvation.

Your holy rite has become accomplished without any obstacle. A Manvantara has passed in my case. I have no doubt in regard to this. The self-willed Four-faced Lord has been requested for the purpose of installation. How can one other than he install it? O excellent king, it is the direct incarnation of the Lord in the wooden form. How can another install it in the Palatial Shrine? If Brahmā blesses me with his presence, I shall install Janārdana in fourfold form and entrust him to you and go. You will serve (and worship) him. Whatever the Lord

* The reading should have been 'made of stone.

himself or Brahmā directs in regard to the daily offerings and services, processions and festivals of the Lord of the universe, the king, the righteous protector of virtue, shall carefully carry it out."

40-42. On hearing what had been earlier thought of by himself, King Gāla obtained great delight to know that it had been ordered by Indradyumna himself.

Like an obedient servant King Gāla stood near him. Whatever Indradyumna ordered, he immediately carried out.

Thus Lord Indradyumna who had gathered together all the requisites, who sat on the throne and was surrounded by Devas, shone like Indra.

43-48. Then various auspicious sounds arising from the divine Dundubhi drums were heard. The sounds of Mṛdaṅga drums, flutes, lutes etc., bell-metal cymbals and trumpets were heard.

There were the trumpeting sounds of Airāvata and other elephants in the sky. All round, the shouts of "Be victorious" were heard mixed with showers of flowers.

Drops of the waters of the celestial Gaṅgā mixed with Mandāra flowers (fell down). The fragrance of divine garlands, unguent and incense spread in every direction. There were the sounds of the clusters of tinkling bells from the aerial chariots of Devas.

Then, O Brāhmaṇas, a mass of refulgence appeared filling the space between heaven and earth. It dazzled the eyes of everyone present on the earth.

It was seen in front by the subjects with rows of eyes lifted up. Then gradually the excellent aerial chariot of Brahmā came into view.

It was carried on the shoulders by hundreds of golden swans. It was attended upon in front by the Guardians of Quarters with their hands busily engaged in waving chowries.

49-51. The rivers Jāhnavī and Yamunā held the fly-flaps which they waved all round with their hands. The umbrella was held by the Moon and the Sun standing on either side.

Thanks to the slow movement of the wind, the garment was moving slightly. In the midst there was the Lord of the Subjects (Brahmā) who was eulogized by Gautama and other Brahminical sages who knew the esoteric things.

He was seen being eulogized by Indradyumna and others. He was eulogized by multitudes of Devas with shouts of "Be victorious".

52-56. Raṁbhā and other heavenly courtesans danced with great awe. The songsters Hāhā and Hūhū and others continued to sing.

Groups of Siddhas and Vidyādharas sang the songs of his praise respectfully on their lutes. He was attended upon by ascetics who stood a little away with palms joined in reverence.

By their wonderfully variegated talks Sāvitrī and Śāradā delighted him very much. Who else is competent to delight him?

The waters of Jāhnavī and Yamunā were sprinkled on his body.

Gandharvas, Siddhas and others, the chief of whom was Nārada, O Brāhmaṇas, had a staff in their hands. They were seen standing humbly in the flight of stairs in the divine chariot. There was a great rush of Devas moving about in the sky.

57. Nobody cared which Deva went where and by which path. The Heaven-dwellers vied with one another in going about here and there.

58-62. Due to their great rush many fell down from their vehicles. The creator, protector and annihilator of all the worlds, the Lord himself who was identical with the universe, proceeded ahead. Who cared for the greatness of these Suras therein?

On seeing him, the king stood humbly with devotion and awe. He had his palms joined in reverence. Along with those Devas, King Gāla and others, the chief of whom was Nārada, he fell on the ground in prostration with the eight limbs touching the ground.

Then he stood up with great devotion and delighted mind. Owing to thrill (of joy of devotion) his hair stood on end all over the body. He considered himself one whose task was accomplished.

Gazing at Brahmā, the pure Lord, the king stood in front of the Lord of the universe with palms joined in reverence. He was immersed in the ocean of bliss.

CHAPTER TWENTYSEVEN

Installation of the Four Deities

Jaimini said:

1-8a. A ladder made of gold and set with gems was suspended from the sky. The top of it was fixed to the footrest of the Lotus-born Lord in the aerial chariot.

The bottom of it touched the earth for facilitating the descent of Brahmā. Each one of the rungs was four *Vyāmas* (the distance between the tips of the middle fingers when both the arms are extended on either side) long and thick.

The Lord appeared at once between the aerial chariot and the Mansion like a rainbow giving out rays (of light) (and was) looked at with wonder by the people.

With gem-set staffs in their hands the kings of Gandharvas ceremonially pointed out the path to him saying, "This is the path, O Lord, come."

The Lord extended his hands to those of Durvāsas and Nārada (on either side) and descended down the steps sanctifying the universe with his eyes.

He smilingly looked at the chariots and well-adorned Mansion and the sacrificial chamber that extended from horizon to horizon, was rendered splendid by gem-set pillars, caused wonder even to Śakra and that was filled with all the requisites gathered together. He got down from the aerial chariot, being eulogized all round by Devas, kings and Brahminical sages with their palms joined together and kept over their crowns.

8b-11. The quarter blessed by the benign side-glance of the Lord was filled with crores of *Añjalis* (palms joined together in reverence) held over the heads. On seeing Indradyumna bowing down at his lotus-like feet, Brahmā said in courteous words, a gentle smile slightly separating his lips, pointing with his finger to the Devas, Pitṛs, ascetics, Brahminical sages, Siddhas, Vidyādharas, Yakṣas, Gandharvas and celestial damsels who had all gathered together in one place and were simultaneously filled with joy.

12-14. "See how your good luck, O Indradyumna, has captivated all the worlds! For your sake all of them have joined once together keeping me at the head."

After saying this he hastened to the chariot of Nārāyaṇa. Bowing down to the Lord of the worlds and circumambulating three times, Brahmā sank into the ocean of bliss with hair standing on end all over his body. With faltering notes he eulogized his own perceptible soul himself.

Brahmā said:

15-17. Obeisance to you. Obeisance to me.[1] Repeated obeisance to you and to me. I am you. You are me. You are this entire universe

1. The prayer shows identity or oneness between the devotee and the god, here Brahmā and Viṣṇu.

consisting of mobile and immobile beings.

The entire universe beginning with *Mahat* (the 'Great Principle') is the sport of your Māyā. It is superimposed on you, O Soul of the universe.[1] It has been transformed by you alone.

All this apparent world originated because of the absence of your knowledge. When you are realized everything will perish as in the case of the illusion of serpent in a piece of rope.

18. This (visible) world cannot be described in terms of the distinct categories of *Sattva* and *Asattva* (existent and non-existent). O Lord without a second, O self-luminous one appearing as the universe, obeisance to you.

19. The entire joy (derived) from objects of pleasure is just a part of yours who are the embodiment of natural (genuine) delight. All beings sustain their lives on a part (of that delight of yours).

20. O Lord devoid of the extensive manifestation of the worlds, O Lord without form or shape, O Lord without aberrations, O Lord without another support, O Lord who are gross and subtle, huge and minute, O Lord devoid of grossness and subtlety!

21. O Lord transcendental to the Guṇas (yet) the support of the Guṇas, O Lord the soul (the source) of the three Guṇas, obeisance to you.

22. I am deluded by your Māyā. I am devotedly engaged in creation only. Even today I do not get perpetual bliss. Obeisance to you, O immanent Soul.

23. I am born of the lotus in your navel. I remain there itself permanently eulogizing (you). I am incompetent to transgress your Māyā; who else can be (so) competent?

24-25. Just as in the middle of this Cosmic Egg I have been created (and engaged) in the activity of creation, so also there are crores of Cosmic Eggs and Crores of Brahmās created in succession. Not a single Brahmā among these numbering three and a half crores knows you in reality just as I standing in front of you.

26. Obeisance to you whose greatness is beyond contemplation, Obeisance, obeisance to you in the form of *Cit* (Knowledge, Consciousness); obeisance to the overlord of Devas. Obeisance to you, the Lord of Devas.

27. Obeisance to you with divine and non-divine forms; obeisance

1. The influence of Śaṅkara's Advaitism—his Māyāvāda, the theory of *adhyāsa* (superimposition) etc. is found not only in the prayer but elsewhere also in this Purāṇa.

to you with divine form; obeisance to you devoid of old age and death; obeisance to you, the embodiment of (god of) Death.

28. Obeisance to you of the form of blazing fire; to the Death unto the (god of) Death; to the lord who destroy the death of those who resort to you; to the lord of the form of innate bliss; to the lord fond of devotion; repeated bows to the mother, to the father, of all the worlds.

29. Obeisance to the lord dispelling the agony of those who bow down (to you); obeisance to the lord, perpetually endeavouring (for the same). Obeisance, obeisance to you the ocean of natural sympathy in regard to the poor and the wretched.

30. Obeisance to you the transcendental one; to the lord in the form of the greatest; obeisance to you who are the shore beyond; obeisance to the shoreless one (taking the others) to the other shore; obeisance to you in the form of Brahman.

31. Obeisance to you of the truthful form; to the greatest cause. Obeisance to you devoted to the greatest reality pervaded by an uninterrupted series.

32-33. Obeisance to the annihilator of the distress of those who bow down; to the only Sun of your own Soul. O Lord, O Lord of the worlds, do that for which you had been prayed to formerly at the time of your acceptance of the responsibility of creation (?), O embodiment of innate bliss. What is inaccessible to me, if you are pleased, O Lord?

34-35. I have been rendered different from you in a sportive way, O ocean of mercy.

One who wanders within the prison of the universe enveloped by the darkness of ignorance, does not find any way out for the sake of liberation other than you.

36. Obeisance, obeisance to you, the only one worthy of being saluted in the world, O Lord whose lotus-like feet are worshipped by Suras and Asuras; obeisance, obeisance, O Lord, the only moon dispelling distress. Obeisance, obeisance, O Lord with abundance of welfare and excellent knowledge.

37. Obeisance, obeisance, O Lord transcending speculation, O Kalpa Tree bestowing even the unattainable desires; O Lord who are always ready to remove the mass of misery of the distressed and helpless ones who bow down.

38. Be pleased, O lord of worlds, to those immersed in the ocean of misery. O merciful one, save (us) by means of the graceful charm of your benign side-glance.

* * *

39. After eulogizing the glorious Lord of the worlds thus by means of words full of the meanings of Vedic passages, Brahmā went to see the Plough-wielding Lord, who held up the earth and had incarnated (as Balabhadra).

40-41. After bowing down with great devotion he eulogized Balarāma joyously:

"O Lord of Devas, the sky is your head; O Lord, water is your physical body, the earth constitutes your feet, fire is your mouth and wind is your breath, the lord of herbs (i.e. Moon) is your mind, the Sun is your eye.

42. O Lord, the quarters are your arms. Obeisance to you, the mirror of knowledge. Obeisance to the plough-wielding lord, the original pillar of all the fourteen worlds.

43. Obeisance to the dispeller of the mass of sins of those who seek refuge in your lotus-like feet. Obeisance to the lord with innumerable faces (mouths), eyes, ears, feet (?), eyes and arms.

44-45. Obeisance to the Sun for the mass of darkness that is firmly rooted and that has no beginning, O lord identical with the three Vedas; obeisance to the destroyer of the threefold defect; to the lord with three incarnations; to the lord holding up the sphere of the earth which is like a cluster of gems in the hoods; obeisance to the lord in the form of Kāla, fire and Rudra; obeisance to you, the great Rudra.

46a. Obeisance to you, asleep in the middle of the umbrella of the hoods with the body as the bed (?)

46b-47. When the water of the great ocean gets increased (during Pralaya), when the three worlds become one, you alone lie there as Śeṣa, O lord, adorned with a thousand hoods. Under the pretext of having clusters of gems on the hoods, you have gathered together all the living beings.

48. You alone are the lord of everything; you are the creator, protector, devourer and supporter of everything always. Myself and others are only a means unto you.

49. It is spoken in the Vedāntas that Lord Nārāyaṇa is not different from you, O lord. You resort to difference for some reason.

50. You are the bed; he is the person lying on; you are the person covering and he is the person covered. He who is Viṣṇu is Rāma and he who is Rāma is Kṛṣṇa alone.

51. There is no difference between you two; be pleased. You are identical with the worlds."

At the end of this prayer he bowed down to the great Lord Balarāma.

52a. Then he went over to the chariot of Subhadrā in order to see the goddess of the worlds. (He prayed:)[1]

52b-57. "Be victorious, O mother of the universe, be pleased, O great goddess.

You are the maker of the effect and the cause; obeisance to you, the omnipotent one.

O goddess, you have entered the hearts of all who are of the nature of knowledge and delusion!

O Bhadrā, you are always the bestower of the *Kaivalya* type of liberation. I bow down to you, the source of origin of Suras. O goddess, you are the Māyā of Viṣṇu enchanting the mobile and immobile beings.

You are seated in the lotus of the heart. You follow the feelings and inclination of Viṣṇu. You alone are Lakṣmī, Gaurī, Śacī and Kātyāyanī.

O goddess identical with everything, whatever object there is at any place whatsoever, whether it is real or unreal, you are the Śakti thereof. Who is competent to eulogize you?

Be victorious, O Subhadrā, O gentle lady, you are the bestower of welfare on all. You are Bhadrakālī of auspicious and inauspicious forms. Obeisance to you.

58-62. O goddess, you are the mother of all the worlds. Indeed Nārāyaṇa is the father. You are everything (in the universe) in the female form. Lord of the universe is everything in the male form. There is no difference between you two. There is nothing greater. We have been engaged by you, the Māyā of Viṣṇu. We always wander about, O goddess, carrying out your behest. You are the profession, the predilection and the great hunger. You alone are the sleep.

You are the hope. You fill in all quarters. You are the fulfiller of the hopes and ambitions of everyone, O goddess, you alone are the cause of bondage and of salvation.

O goddess bestowing every knowledge, O eternal one, you are the wish-yielding Kalpa-creeper to all devotees. Save me by means of the benign glances of the corner of your eyes. I bow down to your lotus-like feet."

63-67. After eulogizing that deity in the form of Bhadrā he went over to the discus of Viṣṇu, Sudarśana, stationed in the chariot nearby.

1. In vv 52-62 Subhadrā is regarded as Viṣṇu's Śakti or Māyā and hence her identification with different goddesses like Lakṣmī, Gaurī etc. and her oneness with Viṣṇu in this prayer.

He bowed down to the discus that is (i.e. assumed) the fourth form of Viṣṇu.

After bowing down with great devotion, he recited the following prayer:

"O Sudarśana of great flames, (O lord) having the lustre equal to that of a crore of Suns, (O lord) pointing out the path to Vaikuṇṭha to those who are blind due to the darkness of ignorance, obeisance to you. O eternally charming one, O abode of the wealth of Vaiṣṇavas, I bow down to that form of Viṣṇu, the vigour of which cannot be checked or restrained."

After bowing down and eulogizing the deities (thus) the Lord turned away from the chariots.

By the way pointed out by Indradyumna and Nārada he climbed Nīla mountain because he was desirous of seeing the Mansion.

68. He went near the Mansion along with the Devas, O Brāhmaṇas. He saw the beautiful hall mentally approved by him.

69. In its middle he seated the Devas, serpents, kings, Brahminical sages, Yogins, Brāhmaṇas, Vaiṣṇavas and ascetics.

70. The Lord himself sat on an excellent divine throne having a footstool offered by the king.

71. At the bidding of Brahmā, the king chose Bhāradvāja (?), the great sage, in order to perform the prosperity-yielding holy rites: *Śāntika* (peace-giving) and *Pauṣṭika* (nourishing).

72-73. Those Devas who were required to be present at the time of the installation, in the holy rites of offering oblations and worship, in the Homas and those who were to be meditated upon occupied the four quarters at the bidding of the Lotus-born Lord. They were excellently adored with sweet scents, flower garlands, embellishments and ornaments.

74. Then the holy rite was begun by the intelligent Bhāradvāja(?) in the presence of the Lord of Devas and all the heaven-dwellers.

75. After worshipping the creator of the worlds at the very outset along with all ancillary and subsidiary rites, the king joyously performed the worship of all the residents of the three worlds.

76-77. Thereupon all the residents of the three worlds who were worshipped by him looked at the immutable Brahmā himself seated in the middle and also the Lord of the worlds visible in the form of Brahman. By the favour of Indradyumna they attained the state of living-liberated souls.

78-83. After performing the inauguration of the Mansion which was very fascinating, wherein a great flag was unfurled on a lofty flagstaff and which was (as though) the body of the Lord, Bharadvāja requested Brahmā to infuse life (into it). Then Brahmā stood up. He performed the holy rite of *Svastyayana* himself accompanied by Nārada and other sages, learned Brāhmaṇas, kings, Kṣatriyas, Nāgas (serpents) and great ascetics.

Divine songs were sung in sweet voice by Gandharvas in tunes befitting the auspicious occasion. Celestial damsels began to dance. The hymns of good omen[1] (*Śākunas)* were recited by the Brāhmaṇas. The sound prevailed everywhere when conch-shells were blown, Kāhāla trumpets, Muraja and Bherī drums and various other musical instruments were played. Then all of them went into the chariot and lowered (the idols) from the chariot down the flight of stairs.

84-85. They lowered (the idol of) Nārāyaṇa, free from ailments, very slowly and gracefully. They were very alert and attentive. They had good concentration. They had perfect self-control along with great devotion. They held (the idol) placing their hands (gently) at the sides, arms, head and feet. They placed it on cotton-beds and took it near the Mansion.

86-89. From above the flowers of the divine Santāna tree were showered. The following prayer was sung:

"Be victorious, O Kṛṣṇa, O Lord of the universe. Be victorious, O destroyer of all sins. Be victorious, O Lord who adopted the wooden body sportively. Be victorious, O bestower of the desired benefit. Be victorious, O Lord, the graceful uplifter of those who sink in the ocean of worldly existence; Be victorious, O immutable one.

Be victorious, O ocean of mercy. Be victorious, O Lord, the ultimate resort of the distressed ones.

Be victorious, O Acyuta; be victorious, O Ananta; be victorious, O Īśāna; obeisance to you."

The Lord was eulogized with these prayers by the Self-born Lord Brahmā. Nārada too eulogized, playing on his lute.

90-92. Two gem-set umbrellas were held (one) above the head (and the other) behind the back by the Moon and by the Sun with great devotion. Divine incense was burnt. (Celestial damsels) embellished

1. This is a *Khila* (supplementary) Sūkta after RV II.42. It begins with: *kanikradaj januṣam prabruvāṇa* etc. RV II.43. is also recited to remove the evil due to the cries of certain birds.

by their youthful charms stood on either side in rows with chowries (in their hands). They were eager to wave them gracefully. All of them joined together with great enthusiasm and took (the idols of) Sudarśana, Subhadrā and Balabhadra.

93-94. A pavilion had been constructed with gem-set pillars at the entrance to the Mansion. The idols were placed there with a circular mirror in front for ablution. Gem-embellished water-pots were filled with holy waters from the Tīrthas scented with perfumes.

Reciting *Śrī Sūkta*[1] and *Puruṣa Sūkta*, (RV.X.90), O excellent Brāhmaṇas, Lord Brahmā performed the rite of ablution of the idols for the benefit of all the worlds.

95. Then the deities were adorned and rendered splendid with sweet scents and garlands. The creator of the world himself performed the rite of Nīrājana (waving of the lights). Then the Lord repeated the Mantras and placed them on a gem-set throne.

Brahmā said:

96. O Lord, the support of the entire universe, established in all the worlds. O Lord with good reputation, O omnipresent one, be settled in the Mansion.

97-102. When you are installed, O Lord, all of us are also stabilized. Let this installation rite be fulfilled at your bidding and thanks to your grace.

After installing the Lord of the worlds, and touching his lotus-like heart, he repeated the *Mantrarāja* (Leading Mantra) in the Anuṣṭup metre a thousand times.

O Brāhmaṇas, the rite of installation was performed on the eighth day in the bright half of the month of Vaiśākha on a splendid Thursday in conjunction with the Puṣya Star.

That day is very auspicious. It is destructive of all sins. The holy bath, charitable gifts, penance and Homa—all these yield everlasting benefit.

Those who see Kṛṣṇa, Rāma and Subhadrā on that day, sanctified by devotional feelings, will certainly become liberated.

1. It is a very popular *Khila* Sūkta after RV V. 87 but it is separately recited as an independent Sūkta.

When the eighth day in the bright half of the month of Vaiśākha is in conjunction with Thursday and Puṣya constellation, Viṣṇu should be worshipped. This worship is conducive to the destruction of the sins of a crore of births.

CHAPTER TWENTYEIGHT

The Lord Adopts the Form of Nṛsiṁha: Dialogue between Brahmā and Indradyumna

Jaimini said:

1-8. By the power of the Mantra Indradyumna and others saw Lord Narasiṁha as having a mysteriously wonderful appearance.

He appeared to lick up the entire universe all round by means of his blazing tongue. He was like Kāla (god of death), fire and Rudra[1] rising up as if to swallow everything.

He pervaded the entire space between heaven and earth with his intensely blazing refulgence. The Lord had innumerable eyes, mouths, necks, hands, feet and ears.

Everything is mysterious and wonderful with the Lord. He was the only storehouse of splendour. They were frightened and excessively bewildered. They could not even eulogize the Lord.

On seeing him (the Lord) like this, then, Nārada asked his father:

Nārada said:

O holy Lord, how does this (Lord) shine like this? It was for blessing (the world) that he took the incarnation. But on the contrary, he has become terrifying. All have become inert due to fear. They are apprehending universal annihilation now.

O Lord of the worlds, you alone know the graceful sports of the Lord.

On hearing those words of Nārada, the Lotus-born Lord's face

1. Or like fire at the destruction of the universe (Kālāgni) and Rudra.

beamed with smiles. He spoke these interesting words rendering comfort unto all:

Brahmā said:

9-13. Foolish persons who do not know the reality are likely to disregard or to be indifferent to the Lord after seeing the Lord incarnated with wooden body, though he is directly Brahman itself. Hence, the Lord was consecrated with the Mantrarāja (king of Mantras) by Brahmā (Parameṣṭhin) so that they too may understand. This Mantra was the same as was formerly used by Parameṣṭhin so that the Lord could tear the demon (i.e. Hiraṇyakaśipu).

(Therefore) this idol attains such a form as is very difficult to view and terrifies. This idol is the highest point of perfection of Viṣṇu of unmeasured splendour.

By worshipping this idol péople will attain the goal from which a return is impossible.

Facing Nṛsiṁha, he joyously recited this prayer:

14. "Obeisance to you, O sole Lion-God, O excellent one among Devas. Obeisance to you, O Lord, the sole lion for the elephants of the mass of sins. Obeisance to you, O Lord, the Lion that takes (the devotees) across the ocean of misery. Obeisance to you, O highly refulgent Lord, O divine Lion!

15. Salute to you, O wonderful Lion, of all forms. Obeisance to you, O Lion (capable of) liberating from pain. Obeisance to you, O Nṛsiṁha, of divine form and body. Hail to you, O most excellent one among heroes, O unique Lion!

16. Obeisance to you, O Lion capable of tearing the Daitya; obeisance to you, O Lion, the overlord of all the Devas; obeisance to you, O Sole Lion in the forest of the Vedāntas. Obeisance to you, the Sole Lion in the cave (heart) of Yogins.

17. Obeisance to you, O Lion, O sole Lion of piety and virtue, Obeisance to you, the Lion on the summit of Nīla mountain."

Jaimini said:

18-21. (*Partially defective Text*) After eulogizing the Divine Lion thus Brahmā began to initiate Indradyumna in the Mantrarāja.[1] He

1. VV 18-26 describe the power of Nṛsiṁha Mantra.

made a Talisman (Amulet) of the Divine Lion and placed it on him (the king). This Mantra has been directly mentioned in the Atharvaṇa (Veda). Those who are devoted to the Vedāntas call this Vaiṣṇava Nirvāṇa (salvation to the followers of Viṣṇu). All the four Vedas are always established in it. It is by learning this Mahāmantra ('Great Mantra') from this Four-faced Lord himself that Lord Svāyaṁbhuva Manu carried on creation formerly. The qualities (super-natural powers like) *Aṇimā* (Minuteness) etc. are its secondary benefits.

22. In order to acquire all the four aims of human life this great Mantra alone is enough. What to speak of insignificant petty desires!

23. This great Mantra alone bestows the benefit of all Yajñas; it is the bestower of all the Tīrthas; it is the bestower of the benefits of all charitable gifts and holy rites.

24. Just as this Lord in the form of the Divine Lion destroys all the groups of sins, as the forest fire burns up a heap of cotton, so also (does) the great Mantra.

25-26. It is by practising this that ascetics dispel the ailment of worldly existence. The moment one receives this and masters this, evil spirits, adverse Planets, epileptic fits, Demons, Ḍākinīs (witches), goblins, vampires, ghosts, serpents etc. flee away. They are not capable of even to look at him.

27-30. Then Indradyumna received the King of Mantras (the most important Mantra) from the Four-faced Lord and viewed the Lord thus: Nṛsiṁha has quiescent body. Lakṣmī has resorted to his chest. He holds the discus and the Pināka bow*(?) The Moon and the Sun constitute his eyes. The pair of lotus-like hands extend up to the knees. The nose is prominent. He is comfortably seated in a thirtytwo-petalled lotus full of Mantra syllables, which shines with OṀ in the middle for its pericarp and which has been placed above the seat of Yogic tablet (slab). He has a boisterously loud laughter. He is looking towards the lotus-like face of Śrī. His lotus-like face is adorned with manes.

31. Behind the Lord, he saw Balabhadra in the form of an umbrella as he had extended his thousand hoods of shining features with divine gems. He held the plough and the palm tree.

32. On seeing Puruṣottama of such a form the king was delighted. With his mind struck with wonder, he asked the Lotus-seated Lord:

---

* '*cakraṁ pinākaṁ dadhatam*' may be emended as follows: '*cakraṁ śārṅgaṁ ca dadhatam*', as *Śārṅga* is the name of Viṣṇu's bow and *Pināka* that of god Śiva.

33. "O holy Lord, wonderful indeed is the act of the Slayer of Madhu. O Creator of the worlds, how is it possible for us to understand him?

34. At the end of the sacrifice he adopted that form made of wood. You alone, O Lord, placed him within the Mansion, the Lord who had been in the chariot.

35-37. Formerly that ethereal voice told me that the Lord would have a fourfold form from the tree of superhuman origin[1] (*apauruṣeya taru*).

Now only one is seen. He has been well-installed. Is this Māyā or reality? O Lord, tell me exactly if you consider me worthy of hearing about it, O Creator of all the worlds."

On hearing this, (Brahmā) replied to the excellent king who was in doubts.

Brahmā said:

38. The first idol of the Lord, O king, was in the form of Narasiṁha. It was proclaimed by Nārāyaṇa to you on account of my blessings.

39. O tiger among kings, do not consider this an ordinary statue, an idol of wood. This is indeed the form of the Supreme Brahman.[2]

40. Since it is naturally capable of dispelling all the miseries and bestowing unending bliss, this idol of wood itself is called Supreme Brahman.

41. Thus as the Lord of wooden body is the creator of all the worlds, he created (revealed) his own self in accordance with the four Vedas.

42. There is no difference between these two, viz. the Brahman of sound (Vedas) and the Supreme Brahman. At the time of universal dissolution this is one. Difference comes at (the time of) creation.

43-45. Indeed, O king, *Śabda* (sound, words) and *Artha* (meaning) are interdependent. If there is no meaning (object), there is no word. If there is no word, nothing is known.

Hence the four Vedas constitute the object. The words and the

1. This is the tree which was seen floating on the sea and it was out of this tree that the idols of Jagannātha etc. were carved.

2. In vv 38-56 god Brahmā emphasizes the greatness of the wooden images of Jagannātha etc. The wooden images are the Supreme Brahman. Brahmā advises Indradyumna to propitiate that Wooden-Brahman (*Dāru-Brahman*).

meanings are like this. The wielder of plough (i.e. Balarāma) is in the form of Ṛgveda. Nṛsiṁha is in the form of Sāma Veda; this Bhadrā is in the form of Yajus and the discus is known as Atharvaṇa. The Vedas are four when different, but constitute one entity when they do not differ.

46. Hence, let there not be any doubt in you. The Lord is one as well as manifold. In the other incarnations too this happens like this. This is the rule.

47. The difference and non-difference of the Lord of the universe have been explained to you, O king. Wherever (i.e. in whatever way) your mind feels contented, follow it up with devotion.

48. This Lord has all the forms. The Lord is identical with all the Mantras. He bestows benefit in accordance with the manner in which he is worshipped.

49-50. Just as a piece of gold can be turned into any (ornament) as one wishes and calling it by a particular name (of the ornament) yields the pleasure and contentment thereof, so also, O king, the Lord has manifested himself here along with his greatness. One attains Siddhi as much as one has faith.

51. Mentally, verbally and physically and with a pure conscience propitiate Govinda here, the Lord assuming the wooden body.

52. For the sake of the acquisition of the benefit in the form of the four aims of life, worship this Lord Viṣṇu as you desire by means of this prominent Mantra.

53-56. There has never been a greater Mantra nor will there ever be one. The Lord is so fond of his devotees that Viṣṇu worshipped by means of this becomes pleased instantaneously and gives even his own city. Of what avail are Yajñas, Tīrthas, holy rites, charitable gifts and penances unto him who adores Viṣṇu of wooden body stationed on Nīla mountain?

I shall tell you the truth, O king. Listen to this attentively. By seeing the immortal Brahman stationed on Nīla mountain in the guise of a wooden statue, at the root of the banyan tree, on the shore of the sea, one shall certainly be liberated.

CHAPTER TWENTYNINE

The Lord Grants Boons to Indradyumna

Jaimini said:

1-4. After saying this to the tiger among kings, the Lotus-seated Lord took away the lion form of Viṣṇu that had formerly manifested in the form of light and touched the heart for the sake of the welfare of the worlds.

The four idols that were seen before at the time of placing them down from the chariot were seen again seated on thrones. Brahmā then worshipped Balabhadra with the twelve-syllabled Mantra. He worshipped Nārāyaṇa, free from ailments, with the Puruṣa Sūkta, (Subhadrā) with the Devī Sūkta and the discus with the twelve-syllabled Mantra. After worshipping he submitted the request (to the Lord) to bless the king.

Brahmā said:

5-8. O Lord, O Lord of the chiefs of Devas, O bestower of blessings on devotees, Indradyumna has been a devotee of yours in the course of a thousand births. At the end he saw you.

Indeed, O Lord, seeing you is the cause of *Sāyujya* with you, although he wishes to worship you through the yoga of devotion. So command him to meditate on you through the yoga of devotion, through holy rites, different kinds of offerings and services to be performed in different places on different occasions.

Desirous of imbibing the nectarine juice of your command issuing from your lotus-like mouth, O Lord of the universe, the king looks at you without winking.

Jaimini said:

9. On being requested thus directly by the Lotus-born Lord, the Lord, though he had only the wooden body, laughingly said thus in a majestic tone:

The holy idol said:

10. O Indradyumna, I am delighted with your devotion and holy rites performed without selfish motive. So much of wealth has never been spent by any person other than you.

11-12a. I shall grant you this boon, O king, that your devotion to me shall be steady. You have spent crores and crores and built my shrine, O great king. Even if it cracks and crumbles, this spot will not be abandoned by me.

12b-18. Even if any other person later, on another occasion, were to build the Mansion, the credit surely shall go to you only. It is due to my love for you that I will stay there. I affirm repeatedly that it is true. I am speaking the truth to you. Even when the Mansion crumbles, I will never abandon this spot. With this wooden body I shall stay here for the period till the second Parārdhaka (the later half of the life) of Brahmā comes to a close.

In the second set of four Yugas of Svāyaṁbhuva Manu, in the first Jyeṣṭha month of the Kṛta Yuga,[1] I was born in the Jyaiṣṭhī (i.e. on the full-moon day in Jyeṣṭha). That is the auspicious birthday of the incarnation.

On that day the sacred ablution should be performed on my idol in accordance with the injunctions for great ablutions. O great king, it should be done profusely with the waters (of the Tīrthas) scented with perfumes.[2] This holy rite will destroy the sins acquired in the course of a crore of births. The benefit of all the Tīrthas and sacrifices and the benefit of all charitable gifts (shall be acquired).

19-21. Benefit is acquired, O great king, even by those who view this.

There is a well to the north of the Banyan tree.[3] Indeed it is filled with all the Tīrthas. It was originally dug up for the purpose of bathing. It has been covered a little by the (falling) earth. I incarnated afterwards. Clear it and bring it to light. It should be consecrated on the fourteenth lunar day after offering oblation in accordance with the injunctions to the Kṣetrapāla (Protector of the holy spot) who protects it and to the Guardians of the Quarters.

22. Brāhmaṇas should take water therefrom with golden pots to the accompaniment of the sweet sounds of conch-shells, Kāhāla trumpets, Muraja drums etc.

23. On the morning of the full-moon day, in the month of Jyeṣṭha,

---

1. Two words '*daśeti kratusaṁsthitiḥ*' in the original appear to be irrelevant.
2. *sādhivāsam:'adhivāsa'* is also interpreted as 'the necessary arrangement for festive religious duties performed on the previous day'. Then the translation will be . . . "on that day . . . for great ablution along with the *Adhivāsa* ritual".
3. The Kalpa tree which stands in the compound of Jagannātha Temple.

the devotee should perform the ablution of Rāma, Subhadrā and me along with Brahmā. Thereby he will obtain my world.

24. The man who sees me being bathed then, O excellent king, does not become bound with bodies thereafter.

25-29. In the north-eastern corner a sturdy stage [raised platform] be made and placed. It should be well-adorned. A canopy should be put up above it. It should be sprinkled with sandalpaste water. Along with Rāma and Subhadrā I should be bathed and taken there. He who sees me proceeding ahead facing South with great devotion, shall certainly obtain whatever he wishes for.

O king, after placing me (installing me), for fifteen days one should never see ugly or beautiful things (?) By performing this holy ablution of Jyeṣṭha one is liberated from all sins.

30. O lord of the earth, you should celebrate 'the great procession named Guṇḍicā.[1] The very glorification of this liberates a man from sins.

31. The fifth day of the lunar month of Māgha and the eighth day in the bright half of Caitra—these are the best days for the great festival named Guṇḍicā.

32. Particularly the second day in the month of Āṣāḍha in conjunction with Puṣya constellation is conducive to salvation. The festival shall be celebrated on the specified lunar day even if the constellation does not coincide. It is pleasing to me always.

33. On the second day, in the bright half of the lunar month of Āṣāḍha, in conjunction with Puṣya constellation, the devotees should place Rāma and me along with Bhadrā on the chariot.

34. For the performance of the great festival, many Brāhmaṇas should be propitiated. The Guṇḍicā pavilion should be where I was born before.

35. At that time the great Altar of your thousand horse-sacrifices was there. There is no spot here on the earth more meritorious than that.

36. There is no other place on the earth more pleasing to me than that place where you performed *Homas* for five hundred years to propitiate me.

37-38. Just as this Nīla mountain is highly pleasing to me now on

1. Another name for *Ratha-yātrā*.

account of your Mansion (built) at the instance of the Four-faced Lord, so also in the Nṛsiṁhakṣetra the great altar of your sacrifice, the place of my birth, is eternally pleasing to me.

39. I have stayed there for a great deal of time. I have great pleasure therein. This Lotus-born Lord is my Ātman. My Ātman has been installed by him in the Mansion.

40. Due to his request and your devotion I shall stay here permanently. I shall go (there) for nine days. Then I will come here.

41-42a. There, O great king, is your lake consisting of all the Tīrthas. On its shore I shall stay for seven days with a desire to bless (people). Men who see me stationed there go to my abode.

42b-44a. There are three and half crores of Tīrthas in all the three worlds together. Due to my presence near the lake all those Tīrthas flow into that lake. By taking holy bath there and by seeing me duly with devotional feelings they do not undergo any longer the pain in the womb of a mother.

44b-45. When I return on the ninth day facing the South, the devotees shall see me. Those who see me then, shall attain the benefit of a horse-sacrifice for every step. They being on a par with Indra enjoy the pleasures and in the end enter me (i.e. become one with me).

46. My getting up, my going to sleep, turning on the sides, covering of my path and meritorious bath—all these are occasions for great festivals.

47-50. On the full-moon day in the month of Phālguna, O king, the festival of my sport in the swing (dolā) should be celebrated. Those who see me worshipped facing the South and sporting in the swing shall be liberated from Brāhmaṇa's slaughter and other sins. There is no doubt about it. Worshipping me in these two (festivals), seeing me and bowing down to me, the devotee shall obtain the benefit of eight thousand horse-sacrifices for each.

On the thirteenth day in the bright half of Caitra, the festival of *Karmaprapūraṇam* (filling in the Karmas) shall be celebrated. I shall be worshipped with *Damana* (Artemisia Indica) flowers on the fourteenth day in the bright half of the month of Caitra. All the sins of those people shall be destroyed.

51-52. The third day in the bright half of the month of Vaiśākha is called Akṣayatṛtīyā. On that day I shall be smeared with excessively splendid unguents. It shall please me. Those who celebrate my festivals regularly shall attain all the four aims in life. Each of these is glorified as the bestower of the fourfold aim of life.

Jaimini said:

53. After granting boons to Indradyumna, O Brāhmaṇas, the Lord said to Brahmā with smiles on his lotus-like face:

54. "O Four-faced One, everything has been accomplished for your delight. Your wish is my wish. Certainly there is no difference between us.

55. This incarnation has been taken by me as a result of your former request to me while I was in the form of Mādhava.

56. By seeing me here, by worshipping me and by casting off their life here, all of them are gradually liberated along with you. Again they will attain *Sāyujya.*

57. If a man wishes something and serves me here, he will certainly obtain it.

58. Let the king in (your) company go now to Satyaloka. Let the Devas go to heaven. I stay on here as long as you live."

59. Then those excellent Brahminical Sages and Suras became delighted. After bowing down their heads to the Lord they went to their respective abodes.

60. The Lord, the Lord of the universe having the form of the idol remained silent, delighting all the men.

61. The righteous-souled Indradyumna, the devotee of Viṣṇu, steadfast in his holy rites, followed the Lotus-born Lord. At his behest he returned.

(Brahmā said:)

62. Celebrate well all the processions and festivals commanded by the Lord. When this Lord of the universe is pleased, all the mobile and immobile beings are pleased.

63. The lord of the earth received this behest of the Lotus-born Lord with bent head. Accompanied by Nārada and Padmanidhi he celebrated all the festivals beginning with Jyeṣṭhasnāna (taking the holy bath in the month of Jyeṣṭha) gorgeously.

CHAPTER THIRTY

The Greatness of Pañcatīrtha

The sages enquired:

1. What was the manner in which he (Indradyumna) performed the rite of ablution of the Lord of Śrī on his birthday? O sage, describe all the other festivals too duly.

2-3a. Everything had been spoken to you formerly by Nārada, O excellent sage. Indeed that sage, the son of Brahmā, knows Brahman that is beyond *Tamas* (darkness of ignorance). Restate all those things of Indradyumna accurately, O sage. We are eager.

3b-5. Wonderful indeed is the luck of Indradyumna, the king, O sage. At the end of that much of the holy rite this great miraculous event happened to him.

It has never been seen or heard that a wooden idol could grant boons directly like a human being, as though it had an animate body. The more we remember the story of the Lord, the more it is destructive of sins.

6. Rare indeed among the residents of the mortal world is such a life as that of that king. To us who listen to it, O great sage, there is not satiety at all.

7. Therefore, O holy lord, recount to us in due order the various processions and festivals that are destructive of all sins. It is certain that one will (go to) and stay in Vaikuṇṭha by seeing them.

8. Since the persons who (originally) spoke about the greatness of the processions was the Slayer of Madhu himself, therefore recount it to us, O highly fortunate one, with the desire for the welfare of all the worlds.

Jaimini said:

9-11. I shall recount the (mode of) the holy bath in the month of Jyeṣṭha, O sages. Listen to it now.

On the tenth day in the bright half of the month of Jyeṣṭha, the devotee should get up early in the morning with perfect control over his speech. He should perform the holy rite of *Saṅkalpa* (i.e. ceremonial pronouncement of the pious resolve of the religious act to be performed) in accordance with the injunctions regarding the

Pañcatīrtha.[1]

With great purity the man should go to Mārkaṇḍeyāvaṭa ('holy Pond of Mārkaṇḍeya') and perform the rite of Ācamana. After bowing down to Śaṅkara he should stand in front of the Lord with palms joined in reverence (and pray:).

12. "O excessively fiery one of a huge body, O Lord comparable to the fire at the close of the Kalpa, it behoves you to grant me permission. Obeisance to you, to Bhairava."

13. He should then enter the holy waters and bathe, O Brāhmaṇas, repeating the five Vedic Mantras pertaining to Varuṇa,[2] or the Aghamarṣaṇa Sūkta[3] three times. After (the preliminary) bath, he should recite the following Mantra at the end and take his bath duly.

14-15. "Obeisance to the quiescent Śiva, the dispeller of all sins. O Lord of Devas, I am taking my bath. Let my sin perish. O Enemy of Tripura, obeisance to you. O Lord, O destroyer of the eyes of Bhaga,[4] save me. I have been swallowed by sins and hence I am insentient. I have sunk in the ocean of worldly existence."

16-18. After taking the bath thus, he should come out and wear washed cloth and apply Puṇḍraka (the parallel marks with sacred ash). He should duly perform the Tarpaṇa rite to Devas, sages and Pitṛs.

He should then enter the temple of Śiva and touch the scrotum of the Bull, O Brāhmaṇas, with the following Mantra. He shall get the benefit of all the sacrifices.

"You are Dharma on its four legs. You are Yajña; your horns are golden. Your body is the set of the three Vedas. O Lord of cows, you are the vehicle of the Trident-bearing Lord. I bow down to you."

19. Thereafter the devotee should worship the Bull-vehicled Lord with Aghora Mantra (Maitrayaṇī Saṁhitā 2.9.10). Then he should touch the excellent Liṅga with the Ṛks called *Pañca Brahman*.

20-23a. He shall touch the Liṅga with the thumb and Śakti with the

1. *Pañcatīrtha*: According to our text the five Tīrthas in Puruṣottama Kṣetra are: (1) Mārkaṇḍa Tank, (2) Mārkaṇḍeśvara, (3) Jagannātha, (4) Indradyumna Tank and (5) the Sea (Bay of Bengal). These are supposed to grant salvation. But according to present-day belief, Mārkaṇḍa Tank, Śvetagaṅgā Tank, Maṇikarṇikā, the Sea and Indradyumna Tank collectively make the Pañcatīrtha.

2. According to Kātyāyana, the Varuṇa Mantras for recitation at the time of bath is "*imaṁ me varuṇa* etc. (Vāj. Saṁhitā 21.1-4).

3. Aghamarṣaṇa Sūkta is RV X.190.1-3.

4. This refers to the occasion of destruction of Dakṣa's sacrifice. But it was Vīrabhadra and not Śiva who blinded Bhaga (BhP IV.5.20).

fist. By worshipping in accordance with the injunctions and by eulogizing the Lord, the enemy of Tripura, one gets the excellent benefit of ten Aśvamedhas (Horse-sacrifices).

By taking the holy bath in Mārkaṇḍeyāvaṭa and by seeing Lord Śaṅkara one obtains the complete benefits of Rājasūya as well of Horse-sacrifices. After death the man obtains *Sālokya* (i.e. residence in the same world as that of Śiva) with Śiva. Thereafter he acquires knowledge and by the favour of the Lord of the universe he obtains salvation gradually.

23b-28. Then the devotee should silently go towards Nārāyaṇa, the destroyer of pain, as well as to the excellent Nyagrodha tree which is (another) form of Viṣṇu and which is situated to the south (of Nārāyaṇa). It is destructive of the mass of sins of sinners by a mere sight of it.

After seeing it the devotee should bow down meditating on Puruṣottama. Thereafter he should circumambulate it reciting this Mantra:

"O Kalpa (i.e. Banyan tree[1] living till the end of the Kalpa), you are immortal. You are always the great abode of Viṣṇu. Destroy my sins. Obeisance to you. Obeisance to the Kalpa tree of unmanifest form existing even during the great deluge, and the sole support of all the worlds. Obeisance to you."

At its root the devotee should eulogize and repeat the names of Janārdana with great devotion to him. He is liberated from the sins arising from hundreds and crores of births.

29-35. Merely by passing through its shade a man becomes free from sins. Thereafter, the devotee should bow down to Suparṇa in the form of the vehicle of Hari. He should stand in front of Hari, bowing down with devotion to Viṣṇu with great joy and with palms joined together in reverence (and pray):

"O Lord in the form of the vehicle, O embodiment of the Vedas, O abode of the universe, O Lord with a body consisting of three parts, O Lord in the form of Yajña, the pervader of the universe, obeisance to you who are to be pleased."

By eulogizing Garuḍa thus he becomes liberated from the sins incurred in the course of many births.

He should be restrained in mind, words and body and proceed ahead thinking about the Lord. After entering the temple he should circumambulate the Lord three times. He should worship him with Mantra-

1. This banyan tree is in the compound of the great Jagannātha temple.

rāja, Puruṣasūkta or the twelve-syllabled Mantra, whichever he is interested in.

Kṣatriyas and Vaiśyas all are authorized to worship. To the others seeing the Lords with devotion and repeating the names of both of them (? of Rāma and Kṛṣṇa) will suffice.

The devotee should worship the great Lord in the manner laid down in the case of *Pañcopacāras*[1] (five offerings and services). With palms joined in reverence he should recite this prayer:

36-40. "O Lord of Devas, O Lord of the worlds, O Lord taking (the devotees) across the ocean of worldly existence , O Lord blessing the devotees, protect me always, as I bow down at your feet.

Be victorious, O Kṛṣṇa. O Lord of the universe, be victorious. O destroyer of all sins, be victorious, O Lord whose lotus-like feet are worthy of being worshipped by the entire universe. Be victorious, O Lord of crores of Brahmāṇḍas, O Lord whose breath constitute the Vedas, O supporter of the entire universe. O Supreme Soul, obeisance to you. Be victorious, O Lord bowed down to by the multitudes of Devas beginning with Brahmā, Indra and Rudra, O dispeller of agony. Be victorious, O abode of the entire universe. O Immanent Soul, obeisance to you. Be victorious, O ocean of genuine mercy, O lover of the distressed and the poor. O sole refuge of the wretched and the helpless, O witness unto the universe, obeisance to you.

41-43. O Lord of Devas, I am fettered by the Guṇas (i.e. Sattva etc. as well as ropes) of your Māyā. I am helpless. I have fallen into the waters of the ocean of worldly existence, which cannot be crossed, which has whirlpools of delusion, which cannot be crossed on account of the *Ṣaḍūrmis* or six waves (viz. grief, delusion, death, old age, hunger and thirst), which is terrible with evil actions as crocodiles, in which there is no place of refuge nor any support, which is devoid of intrinsic essence and which has miseries for its foams. Redeem me, O Lord of Devas, with the benign glance of the corners of your eyes. I am sunk therein, O excellent one among Suras, O doer of excellent favour.

1. *Pañcopacāra Pūjā*: The Upacāras (ways of serving the deity) are normally sixteen (Ṣoḍaśopacāra Pūjā). But if one can't afford these, the Pañcopacāras (five Upacāras), viz. *Gandha* (applying sandalpaste), *Puṣpa* (offering flowers), *dhūpa* (incense-burning), *Dīpa* (waving a light before the deity) and *Naivedya* (offering food etc.) are essential.

44-48a. You are the only kinsman, O Lord of the universe, to those who are afraid of the worldly existence. Hunger and thirst are (the tormentors) of Prāṇa (vital airs); grief and delusion (are the tormentors) of the mind and old age and death (those of) the body. Among your creation, there is none who protects the poor people like you. You have incarnated, O Lord, with the intention to bless the worlds. Since all your desires are fully realized, O Lord, what else can be the reason (for the incarnation) on the earth? After attaining your lotus-like feet, O Lord of the universe, there is no worry at all, since your lotus-like feet are the sole means for the acquisition of the fourfold aim of life. By seeing them all the worlds obtain all they desire."

48b-49. Then the devotee should worship the Plough-emblemed Lord by the Mantra of Śeṣa, twelve-syllabled Mantra, or the name, or the Praṇava etc. He should concentrate his mind, fall down (at his feet) and propitiate him:

50. "Be victorious, O Rāma, delight unto the good, having a body consisting of existence, knowledge and bliss. O Lord devoid of the mud of *Avidyā*, obeisance to you of pure form.

51. Be victorious, O Lord devoid of any strain or weariness through supporting the burden of the entire universe. You hold the plough always for dragging the three types of distress.

52. O Lord with clean lotus-like eyes for the protection of the wretched who seek refuge in you, O Lord, you alone are competent to wash off the entire sins of others.

53. O delighted one, O ocean of mercy, O kinsman of the poor and the downtrodden, obeisance to you. O Lord by whom the earth consisting of the mobile and immobile beings is held up on the tip of hood.

54. Redeem me from the boundless ocean of worldly existence, very difficult to cross. O supreme one among the greatest and the smallest ones, O greatest Lord, obeisance to you."

55. After thus eulogizing Bala, the king of Serpents, holding the threshing rod, the devotee should worship the primordial cause of all the worlds (Subhadrā) of splendid eyes.

56. After eulogizing that Jayā (i.e. Subhadrā), O Brāhmaṇas, the devotee should fall at her feet and propitiate her (with the prayer): "Be victorious, O Goddess. O great Goddess, be propitious, be pleased, O Goddess taking (devotees) across the ocean of worldly existence.

57. O source of origin of happiness of those who resort to you, be victorious, O cause of satisfaction. You are the effect of those which are in the form of effects, the cause of all causes.

58. You are the supporter of all who are being supported; I bow down to you, the primordial one, stationed in the region of the chest of Viṣṇu, the sharer of half the body of Śaṁbhu.

59. You are stationed in the lotus-like face of the Lotus-born Lord, I bow down to the favourite one of all the worlds.

You alone are the matchless Śakti of the Supreme Ātman in regard to the activities of creation, sustenance, destruction etc.

60. Without you even he is not competent (to do anything). You are the mother of all the worlds, the Māyā of Viṣṇu, the ascetic lady.

61a. I bow down to that Subhadrā of gentle form, the Goddess who has been the original cause."

61b. Thereafter, the devotee should pray to Puruṣottama for sea-bath:

62. "Obeisance to you, O Lord Viṣṇu who pervade the universe consisting of the mobile and immobile beings. O Lord, let the rite of my taking the holy bath in the sea achieve the result without obstacles.

63. Obeisance to you, the Lord of all the worlds, holding conch, discus and iron club. Grant me, O Lord, the permission to resort to your Tīrtha."

64. Thereafter he should go towards the sea silently thinking about Viṣṇu. With great concentration and mental purity, he should request for and receive the permission of Ugrasena stationed on the path:

65-66. "O Ugrasena of great might, O strong one of fierce exploits, you have resorted to the seashore after receiving the boon from (the Lord) who is extremely delighted. O Lord, the bestower of complete benefit on those who take their holy bath in the Tīrtharāja (i.e. the Sea), I shall take the holy bath in the sea. It behoves you to grant me permission."

67-68. Thereafter, O excellent Brāhmaṇas, he should go to Svargadvāra (Gateway to Heaven)* whereby Devas come into the holy spot Puruṣottama which is heaven on the earth, for the purpose of seeing the Lord of the earth day by day. (The gatekeepers should be prayed to:) "I bow down to you both stationed on the path of descent from heaven.

69. Take me too up above, O witness unto the rites of good people; you two are born of the waters of the ocean. You are the most excellent ones. You are endowed with all good qualities.

70. I shall go between you both. Do open the gate unto heaven."

---

* A place on the seashore at Jagganātha Purī.

After praying thus the devotee should go to the sea, the Tīrtharāja (King of Tīrthas).

71-74. By seeing the sea even from afar the devotee is certainly liberated from a great sin.

After washing the hands and feet the devotee should perform the rite of *Ācamana* (ceremonial sipping of water). He should sit facing the East on a clean seat and draw the mystic diagram in front of him. It shall be a square with four entrances. There shall be Svastika designs in the four corners. In its middle he should draw the diagram of a splendid eight-petalled lotus. Then the eight-syllabled Mantra should be fitted (i.e. spiritually deposited) in the hands and on the body. The Nyāsa (symbolic assignment of the part of the body to the deity) of six parts of the body with six syllables has been proclaimed by the wise (experts), and the remaining two should be assigned in the belly and on the back.

75-78a. The thirty-two syllables of the Mantra should be fixed in due order in the pair of feet, pair of calves, pair of thighs, pair of buttocks, pair of sides, navel, back, pair of arms, heart, neck, armpits, lips, ears, eyes, cheeks, nostrils, eyebrows, forehead and head.

After performing the several Nyāsas individually the devotee should with mental concentration and purity perform a *Vyāpaka* (pervasive, collective) Nyāsa with all the syllables.

Reciting the Mūla Mantra he should perform twenty-five Prāṇāyāmas each consisting of the three units (i.e. Pūraka, Kuṁbhaka and Recaka). Then he should put on the mystical symbols regarded as protective *Kavaca*, the coat of mail (i.e. ceremonial and imagined by means of the Mantras). It is divine and destructive of all sins.

78b-82. "Let Govinda protect me in the East; Vārijākṣa (the Lotus-eyed) in the South; let Pradyumna protect me in the West; Hṛṣīkeśa in the North; Narasiṁha in the South-East; Madhusūdana in the South-West; let Śrīdhara protect in the North-West and Gadādhara in the North-East. Let Trivikrama protect me from above and the Lord having the form of Boar protect me from below. Let the Lord holding conch, discus and iron club protect me in all directions everywhere.

Let Nārāyaṇa protect my mind and Garuḍadhvaja the consciousness. Let Janārdana in the form of the three Guṇas protect my intellect and ego. Let the destroyer of the groups of Daityas always protect the sense-organs."

83-87. After binding the armour thus the man becomes devoid of sins.

With the sixteen types of offerings and services mentally conceived the man should worship Puruṣottama in accordance with the injunctions, O Brāhmaṇas. The Lord should be invoked in the mystic diagram. The Lord of Devas, remover of suffering, should be worshipped in accordance with the injunctions with the offerings increased in accordance with his capacity.

The devotee should meditate upon the Ātman of the Tīrtharāja and the Lord of Devas. Then with palms joined in reverence, he shall recite this Mantra:

"Obeisance to you, O Sudarśana, having the lustre of a crore of Suns. Point out the path to Viṣṇu, to me who am blind with the darkness of ignorance."

After praying thus, O Brāhmaṇas, the devotee should kneel near the waters of the sea and with great devotional feelings, he should bow down (and pray):

88-93. "O Lord of all Tīrthas, obeisance to you, to Viṣṇu in the form of water, the life of all creatures, the greatest cause of salvation. Agni (fire) is your source of origin as well as Ilā (earth). The navel of the immortal Viṣṇu impregnates your body (?) I approach your form having no other cause, and richly endowed with bliss, after entering the waters."

He should enter the waters reciting this Mantra, O Brāhmaṇas. Meditating on the Lord of the worlds, he should invoke the Tīrtharāja, the Lord of waters standing in front in order to grant the benefit unto those who take the holy bath. He should invoke with the *Aghamarṣaṇa Sūkta* along with that of Nārāyaṇa, repeating them three times or by means of the five *Varuṇa Sūktas*. The invocation etc. is conducted only once. They are the six ancillaries in the rite of ablution.

94-97. The rite of invocation has been mentioned before. Now *Sannidhāna* (bringing near) is being mentioned. The rite of bringing near is for the acquisition of the benefit desired by the bather: For purity within he should perform the rite of *Ācamana* drinking the Mantra-charged (water). For the sake of purity of external limbs he should cleanse by means of Kuśa-water. For purity both within and without he should sprinkle his head thrice with water filled in the cavity of folded palms sanctified by means of water sanctified with Mantras. In the ocean, there is no *Japa* (i.e. repetition of holy names) within the waters.

He should take holy dips three times with the conviction that his sins committed in crores of births have been washed away in that water. He should meditate on the Lord, the destroyer of sins. He should (then) come up, perform the Ācamana rite and duly request for the destruction of sins reciting this Mantra:

98-102. "You are Agni, O Lord of the worlds. You are the depositor of semen virile. You are the kindler of love. You are the chief one of all elements, the Lord of living beings, O immutable one. You are the source of origin of nectar, O Lord of waters, the source of origin of Devas. Dispel all my sins, O Lord of all Tīrthas. Obeisance to you. Let all the sins formerly committed by me in the course of thousands and crores of births perish. Give me the eternal Brahman."

After taking the holy bath, he should come to the shore, perform the *Ācamana* rite with restraint on speech and wear two white clothes. He should apply brilliant Puṇḍraka marks or the markings of conch, discus, iron club and lotus with devotion.

103. The devotee should propitiate Devas and Pitṛs duly meditating upon them with the belief that they are the Lord himself, O Brāhmaṇas, perfectly without the least excitement in the mind.

104-105. Thereafter the devotee should draw the mystic diagram as before, facing the North. With the *Mūla Mantra* as well as the following Mantra, he should worship devoutly Nārāyaṇa, the Four-armed Lord holding conch, discus and iron club either in the company of Dharā and Ramā or alone, O excellent Brāhmaṇas. After meditating on the Lord contented with the Yāga, within his mind, he should invoke the Lord externally:

106. "O Supreme Bliss! Come. O Lord pervading the universe and identical with the universe, be present in the mystic diagram for blessing (us).

107. This universe consisting of the mobile and immobile beings is established here. You alone, O Lord, are stationed within it. I shall conceive it as a seat unto you.

108. Your lotus-like feet were washed by Dharma in the form of Brahmā. Gaṅgā arising therefrom sanctifies the universe. I shall give (that) *Pādya* unto you.

109. With their hands raised up and placed against their crest jewel set with highly precious stones, Brahmā and others meditate upon your lotus-like feet. To you, the invaluable one, the abode of the universe, I offer this *Arghya*.

110. The Tīrtharāja (Sea) was drunk up (by you) in the form of Agastya. To you I give the sweet-scented water as Ācamanīyaka (i.e. water for the rite of *Ācamana)*.

111. He who coming in contact with (demon) Madhu dragged him

in order to take out all his sins—to him I offer *Madhuparka*[1] in the form of water.

112. With water I bathe that Lord who assumed the form of Boar and redeemed this Earth that had been submerged in the waters of the great deluge.

113. To cover up everyone I offer two splendid clothes to the Lord who in his cosmic form has crores of Cosmic Eggs as a covering.

114. I allot this sacred thread to that Lord of Yajñas without whom even a Yajña that has been performed is certainly (no better than what is) not performed.

115. I assign ornaments unto that ornament of the universe by coming into contact with whose body the ornaments themselves shine splendidly.

116. Sweet scents and unguents (are offered) to that Lord, by coming into contact with the air from whose body sandal trees become richly endowed with scented juice.

117. I assign the garland of flowers to that Lord, by thinking about whom people get their sins destroyed and acquire fair-mindedness and gentleness.

118. I offer sweet-scented excellent incense to that Lord, by keeping whom steady in the mind one stops getting scorched by the fire of worldly existence.

119. I offer this light unto that Lord who is brilliantly lit and by whose lustre the entire universe is illuminated.

120. I offer this food to that Lord who eats up the entire universe consisting of mobile and immobile beings and who creates it again after being nourished with this.

121. Excellent betel-leaf (is offered) to that Lord, the red lustre of whose mouth that emits natural sweet fragrance, enchants the celestial beauties.

122. I bow down to that Sire of the universe,[2] the ocean of mercy, who destroys the frequent movement in the courtyard of (or arena of) worldly existence, of one who performed circumambulations."

123. All these Mantras with the services and offerings have been

---

1. It is strange that *Madhuparka* (a respectful offering of a mixture of honey to a respectable guest) is connected with the demon Madhu! Is it the identity of the first word in *Madhu-parka* and of the name of the demon Madhu that led the author to connect them together?

2. VV 122-143 give the complete procedure of Lord's worship with the prescribed *Upacāras*.

stated separately. The devotee should meditate upon the Lord stationed outside oneself after invoking him (duly).

124-127. After offering a gem-set throne, the devotee should meditate on the Lord as seated thereon. The *Pādya* shall be offered at the pair of feet resembling lotuses. By reciting the Mūlamantra the water for *Pādya* should be consecrated with Śyāmāka rice-grains, lotuses, Dūrvā grass and Aparājitā (a plant used as an amulet).

The water for *Arghya* should be taken in a gold, silver or copper vessel or in a conchshell and consecrated duly with water, sandalpaste, flowers, barley grains, Dūrvā and Kuśa, fruits, white mustard and gingelly seeds. The water should be sprinkled on the head of the Lord with the tips of Dūrvā and Kuśa leaves. If there is anything remaining, it should be poured on the ground. (So) the injunction regarding *Arghya* has been recounted.

128. For the sake of *Ācamana*, the devotee should give water consecrated with nutmeg, cloves and Kaṅkolas. Thereafter he should give Madhuparka.

129. The water for bathing should be mixed with honey, ghee and curds of cow's milk. It should be placed in a pure bell-metal vessel. It should be covered with another similar vessel. It should be well consecrated and fruits should be added.

130. The two splendid clothes should be made of machine-made silk or homespun silk or of cotton. They should be given in accordance with one's capacity. There should be no dishonesty or fraud involved in the purchase of the same.

131. He should place according to his capacity such ornaments as necklace, armlets, crown, garlands etc. in the proper places on the body of the Lord.

132. The sacred thread offered to Hari should be of silk or cotton, O Brāhmaṇas, and it should be consecrated with sweet scents and sandal-paste.

133-135. The anointing shall be done with camphor, sandal, musk and saffron.

The garland or wreath of the Lord should be of Tulasī (holy basil) leaves or the flowers of jasmine, lotus, Caṁpaka, Aśoka, Chura, Punnāga, Nāga Kesára, Keśara and other sweet-smelling flowers. Loose flowers not wreathed into a garland should be offered on the head of the Lord.

136. The garland that reaches the forepart of the feet is called *Mālā*. *Mālya* (wreath) extends from the neck to the thighs. *Garbhaka* (nosegay) is placed in between the tresses and the devotee should shower flowers

in handfuls on the head of the Lord.

137. *Dhūpa* (incense) should be sweet-scented containing *Guggulu* (fragrant gum-resin), *Uśīra* (a fragrant grass), ghee, honey and sandal powder. The light offered with ghee from cow's milk is the most splendid one. It should also be offered with a camphor tablet or gingelly oil.

138-140. The *Naivedya* should consist of well-cooked rice. It should be unbroken, swollen and puffed up. It should be made fragrant with ghee. Cow milk and curd should be added. It should be accompanied by ripe plantains and sugar. There should be different kinds of side dishes, pickles and pies. Many varieties of fruit should be used. They should be sweet-smelling, juicy and fresh. The *Naivedya* unto the Lord of Devas should not be less than a *Prastha*. Less than a *Prastha* is not recommended.

141. *Ācamanīyaka* should be offered with *Dhūpa*, light, Naivedya, Snāna (water for bath), Arghya, Madhuparka, clothes, and sacred threads.

142-143. On other occasions only water well-consecrated, should be offered by way of formality. At the end of Naivedya too Ācamanīyaka should be offered. O Brāhmaṇas, the sweet-smelling sandal should be ground with one's own hands. Thereafter betel leaves shall be offered along with camphor, cloves, nutmeg, cardamon and Areca nuts.

144. After repeating the *Mūlamantra* one hundred and eight times with the mind not dwelling elsewhere, the devotee should eulogize, circumambulate and pray to Puruṣottama.

145. "O Lord of Devas, O Lord of the universe, O Lord making all the Tīrthas function, you are identical with all the Tīrthas, O Lord identical with all the Devas.

146. By your grace I have taken the holy dip in the Tīrtharāja. Let that be successful, O Lord, be the bestower of the benefit as mentioned.

147. The Lord of the rivers and you, O Lord, are undoubtedly in the liquid form. Save me. I have sunk in the abode of sins. Obeisance to you."

148. One who worships the Lord of Devas, Nārāyaṇa, remover of all suffering, thus and takes the holy dip in the Tīrtharāja shall obtain the benefit of all the Tīrthas.

149. The benefit that is acquired by gifting away crores of cows, by performing crores of sacrifices, by feeding crores of Brāhmaṇas and by making crores of charitable gifts by men of holy rite, is obtained by means of this.

150. Meditation, charitable gifts, penance, *Japas*, *Śrāddhas* and worship

of deities—everything performed on seashore shall have crores and crores of times the benefit.

151. (Pitṛs think like this) Would that in our family there were one who took holy dip in the sea. He will propitiate Devas and Pitṛs by offering water libation with gingelly seeds.

152. Even if a person attempts to take the holy dip in the sea, all his evils cry aloud, all his sins become excited and bewildered and all undesirable things flee.

153. The sin committed in other Tīrthas perishes on the seashore. The sin committed on the seashore perishes when sea bath is taken.

154. On seeing a person always engaged in taking sea bath, the servants of Yama flee to all the ten directions like deer on seeing a lion.

155. Even Yama (the god of death) is frightened on seeing him. He bows down to and worships him. He is not competent enough to stand in front of him then, in front of that man of meritorious rites.

156. Devas always desire thus: 'May we obtain human life. We shall then have our bodies purified by having the holy dip in the sea.'

157. The heap of sinful activities may well-nigh be as big as Meru and Mandara. It shall be burned by the holy dip in the sea like a heap of cotton by fire.

158. At the time of holy bath one should always remember Lord Nārāyaṇa in the waters, particularly so in the sea which is directly the form of Viṣṇu.

159. A slayer of a Brāhmaṇa, a drink-addict, a slayer of cows or a person who has committed the five sins—all these undoubtedly get redemption on account of the holy dip in the sea.

160. The holy bath in the sea excels the charitable gifts of crores of tawny-coloured cows. By taking a plunge into the sea once one should redeem a crore of the members of one's family.

161. There is no doubt about this that one obtains all those benefits and merits which accrue from all the Tīrthas and all the shrines if one takes the holy bath in the sea.

162. He who wishes for a successful birth, life and learning should proceed towards the sea and propitiate Pitṛs as well as Devas.

163-166. It is easy to learn all the four Vedas, ancillary subjects and their different modes of recitation such as *Pada*, *Krama* etc.; it is easy to make different kinds of charitable gifts in Kurukṣetra; the holy expiations of Cāndrāyaṇas, Kṛcchras etc. and the penances are also easy; Yajñas beginning with Agniṣṭoma and involving many monetary gifts are easy to perform; but offering libations to Pitṛs with the waters of sea is very rare.

If the libation is offered for a month and the rice-balls are dedicated at seashore, all the Pitṛs become contented with the libation in the sea and propitiated by the rice-balls of Śrāddha rite. They get into aerial chariots resplendent like the Sun and immediately go to the eternal world of Brahman.

167-168. In the beginning and in the end one should worship the Lord of the universe in accordance with the injunctions. The man should then take ablution in the Tīrtharāja. He will be one who deserves salvation. Thereafter he should perform the rite of *Tīrtha Visarga* (dismissal of the Tīrtha). The person should be pure in mind. He should bow down to Rāma, Kṛṣṇa and Subhadrā and meditate on their forms.

CHAPTER THIRTYONE

The Procedure for the Sacred Ablution of the Lord in the Wooden Body

Jaimini said:

1-2. Feeling contented that he has accomplished what has to be accomplished, the devotee should thereafter go towards the lake Indradyumna which originated as a part of the horse-sacrifices. It is on its bank that Hari dwells in the form of Narasiṁha (Man-Lion). After praying to Narasiṁha, he should take his bath therein in accordance with the (prescribed) injunctions.

3-7. "Obeisance to you, O Narasiṁha. In your excellent holy place, by your favour, the excellent king Indradyumna performed a thousand horse-sacrifices. I have come to take my holy bath in the lake that originated as a part of the horse-sacrifice. Grant me permission (to do so), O Lord."

After performing *Śauca* (bodily cleanliness), *Ācamana* and other routine rites, he should go to the bank of the Tīrtha, stand with palms joined in reverence and pray reciting this Mantra:

"The surface of the ground was dug up by the hoofs of a crore of cows that formed part of the horse-sacrifices. It was filled with their froth and urine as well as the waters (used in the rite) of charitable gifts. You sanctify everything. I have come to take bath in your sacred waters filled with (the waters of) all the Tīrthas. Remove all the sins by this bath, that had arisen in the thousands of my previous births."

8. Entering the waters, O Brāhmaṇas, he should repeat the five Vāruṇa Mantras and bathe. Within the waters, the *Aghamarṣaṇa* Mantra should be repeated three times.

9-10. The devotee should then repeat the following Mantra three times and take three dips in that water, O Brāhmaṇas:

"O Tīrtha born of the limbs of the horse-sacrifice, O destroyer of all sins! May the sins incurred in crores of births perish by taking a bath in you."

He should then remember Hari in the form of Narasiṁha by (uttering) Viṣṇu Gāyatrī.

11-15. Waters are called Nārā because they are sons of Nara. This is the first resort of his. Hence the devotee should remember Hari in the waters.[1]

Then the man should propitiate Devas, sages and Pitṛs in accordance with injunctions. He should then go to Narasiṁha seated facing the West.

By seeing Saṁbhu whether already in existence or artificially prepared as well as Hari facing the West, one is rid of sins originating from crores of births.

The devotee should worship Narasiṁha by means of Atharvaṇa Mantra. Indeed this Mantra-Rāja ('King of Mantras') was established formerly by Nārada.

This has been used for worship for a long time by him as well as by Indradyumna. In regard to the Lord in the form of Narasiṁha, O Brāhmaṇas, there is no other Mantra like that.

16. Lord Narasiṁha becomes delighted merely by the utterance of this (Mantra). It is by means of this Mantra that the Lord with wooden body (idol) was installed by Brahmā.

17-22. The devotee should worship Lord Narasiṁha with all the offerings and services mentioned before. *Japā* (China rose) flowers of tawny colour and other sweet-smelling flowers also should be used. The devotee should smear Narasiṁha with (fragrant ointments of)

---

1. Cf. the explanation of the term 'Nārāyaṇa:
āpo nārā iti proktā, āpo vai nara-sūnavaḥ/
tā yadasyāyanaṁ pūrvaṁ tena nārāyaṇaḥ smṛtaḥ//
—Manu I.10.

sandal paste, Agallochum and camphor. The following should be the *Naivedya*:

Milk pudding along with sugar and cow's ghee, sweetmeats fried in ghee with pieces of camphor, *Saṁyāvas* (cakes prepared from wheat-flour), pies prepared in ghee, different kinds of fruits and cooked rice along with sugar and curds.

By seeing, touching, bowing down and worshipping Narasiṁha a man obtains his own desires. There is no doubt about it. Whatever he mentally desires, such as Devahood, Lordship of immortal beings, Gandharvahood, power and mastery over others, ability to win over others and becoming an Emperor, he obtains the same undoubtedly.

23-26. The procedure of Pañca-Tīrtha has been recounted to you, O Brāhmaṇas, as you had asked (for it). After performing (such worship) for five days, the man of holy rites engaged in devotion to Viṣṇu will not subsequently enter the body consisting of the five elements (i.e. he is liberated).

On the full-moon day, early in the morning, the devotee should take his holy bath in accordance with the injunctions mentioned before. He should take in only pure food, should control his sense-organs and observe the holy fast of taking food once a day only. Thus he observes the vow for the pleasure of the Deity. He should continue this for five days. Thereafter, he should enter the Mansion and see Puruṣottama reclining on the couch. By seeing Rāma (Balabhadra) and Subhadrā too he is liberated from all sins.

27-28. If a person sees Hari on the full-moon day in the month of Jyeṣṭha, as he is being bathed by sweet-smelling water taken from the well consisting of all the Tīrthas, no contact with any sin or sinner can have any adverse effect on his soul.

Now, I shall describe the procedure for those who want to take out processions (of the Lord). O sages, listen to it.

29-34. On the fourteenth day itself, a sturdy and splendid cot made of wood and straw should be got ready. Or it may be made of stone and smeared completely with lime and mortar. It must be durable, O excellent Brāhmaṇas. It is intended for the ablution of the Lord. The devotee should not use trickery in spending for this. The place must have different kinds of trees all around. It must be cool with gentle wind blowing from the South. It must be consecrated on the open grassy land where the waves of the sea lash gently. There must be a lofty canopy rendered splendid by means of costly clothes. But the covering should be so fine that Devas can have a clear view.

Devas, sages etc. come there along with Brahmā for bathing the Lord of the universe. They take with them the waters from the celestial Gaṅgā adorned with Pārijāta flowers. Brahminical sages and Devas accompanied by Brahmā bathe the Lord seated on the couch. They bathe him at the behest of Parameṣṭhin.

35-38. This Lord should be adored by Heaven-dwellers with the words 'Be victorious' and eulogies. Hence the couch should be embellished with wreaths and chowries as well as gem-set necklaces of various sorts. Festoons must be made with attractive silk cloths. It must be sprinkled with sandal-water rendered fragrant with sweet scents and incense. After installing the couch the devotee should place pots made of gold to the south of it. They should be filled with water taken out from the well. In the hall it should be duly consecrated and perfumed.

39. The devotee should fill the pots with excellently scented water repeating *Pavamāna Suktas.*[1] This rite shall be performed at midnight on the fourteenth day. It has been so prescribed.

40-42. Brāhmaṇas, Kṣatriyas, Vaiśyas and others who are honoured and respected by the king should slowly carry (or take in a palanquin) Hari along with Balarāma as they are continuously fanned with chowries and hand-fans. While bathing Lord Viṣṇu, the unguents applied previously should not be removed from the body of the Lord. By applying the sweet-smelling unguents, the idol should be made stronger in the limbs everyday. Indeed one with weak limbs cannot make others strong.

43-51a. The devotees carrying the Lord should be careful. They must not commit any mistake. If they are careless and if the Lord, the enemy of Mura, or Bala or Subhadrā were to fall down, it indicates danger to the king or to the realm. There will be harm to those who let the idol fall down. Their children will be extremely miserable.

Those wicked souls will have certainly to go to hell. Those who are deluded and do not have any faith or belief and say, "How can a wooden idol remain for a long time", are inimical to the Lord. They will be excluded from all holy rites and will fall into hell. A number of arguments to create disbelief in regard to righteous and pious activities can be advanced by deluded persons, atheists, ungrateful persons and damned souls. Everything depends on the invisible merit of the person concerned. The idol appears to be made of different things in accordance with the merit of these persons. At the end, the Mansion (Temple), the idol etc. perish.

1. *Sūktas* in RV IX.

This is not made by anyone. Nor has that tree been grown by anyone. That which grants boons is certainly not considered to be this idol.

In the Manvantaras that have gone by, when the idol was made, the devotional feelings of the people and of the Devas used to increase. Such were the divine devout feelings of all the kings too, O Brāhmaṇas.

51b-55a. The Lord, the receptacle of mercy, manifested himself in the Svārociṣa Manvantara. In the Vaivasvata Manvantara, in the twenty-seventh cycle of the sets of four Yugas, at the close of the Dvāpara Yuga, both Kṛṣṇa and Arjuna came here. Performing the holy rites, they stayed here for three days. With great devotion they worshipped the Slayer of Madhu (Jagannātha), eulogized him and then returned to Dvārakā.[1] No one who has adopted human body, knows the reality. The incarnations of Viṣṇu take place in every Yuga and after establishing piety and righteousness, they merge into the original region (of the Lord).

55b-59. He was formerly requested by Brahmā who was told by the Lord that he, Lord Viṣṇu, would be staying for the period of a Parārdha in wooden form. Viṣṇu, on being meditated upon with pure Sattva qualities, is a bestower of boons forever.

The achievement of one will be in accordance with one's faith. Even if he errs in his belief, a person who is a devotee of steadfast mind, derives the rare benefit befitting his endeavour from him. Formerly, everything in regard to the liberation of Aṁbarīṣa was narrated to you.

Therefore, have very firm devotion towards the Lord of the universe in the form of the supreme Brahman and stay in the holy place of Puruṣottama.

60-66. Hence this excellent couch of Śrīkṛṣṇa should be carried with great devotion. The devotees should serve Ṣubhadrā and Balabhadra with royal honour.

The umbrellas should be lifted up. The chowries are used for fanning. The incense from Agallochum spreads everywhere. Different kinds of musical instruments resound majestically in all the directions. When the triple symphony of songs, dances and musical instruments fills the abode, when the darkness is dispelled by means of rows and rows of lamps, and when the great festivities increase, anticipating some negligence (on the part of those who carry the Deity) the Lord is kept

1. This incident is unsupported in the Mbh and BhP. If Jagannātha is Kṛṣṇa, this reference is a bit confusing.

covered by means of excellent silk cloth of fine fabric while being taken over a long distance. Due to the speed of the movement, the sire of the worlds comes to a supine position. The Devas who observe repeatedly, begin to suspect if the Lord is about to ascend to heaven. They chant (loudly), "Be victorious, O Rāma. Be victorious, O Kṛṣṇa. Be victorious, O Bhadrā."

Thus the Lord is gracefully taken to the place of the couch by Brāhmaṇas and others at midnight in the course of the holy ablution on his birthday, on the full-moon day in the month of Jyeṣṭha.

67-70. The sound of the Devas vying with one another is heard in the firmament. The sounds of the divine Dundubhi drums mixed with the shouts of 'Be victorious' are heard. Then the embodiment of Brahman placed on the couch, is covered along with the idol intended to be worshipped. All the limbs except the face are covered with excellent cloths. The Lord is worshipped as per the formalities and services mentioned before, excepting the offer of *Naivedya.*

With the proclamation of Śānti (Mantras) the devotee should bathe the leading Suras (deities) by means of the pots kept ready with perfumed water duly consecrated by repetition of the Mantra *Samudrajyeṣṭhāḥ* (RV.VII.19-1) to the satisfaction of those who bathe (the deity) and watch.

71. Those men who stand there and watch (the Lord) being bathed, shall not take bath in the waters of the womb any longer (i.e. will not be reborn but attain liberation).

72. Those who are eager in their mind to witness the procession, those who joyously witness the ablution of the Lord in the month of Jyeṣṭha, do not sink in the ocean of worldly existence.

73. The beginningless mass of sins whether committed intentionally or unwittingly, of those persons who witness the ablution of Hari, perishes instantaneously.

74-78. It is true. It is (definitely) true, O eminent Brāhmaṇas. I am speaking the truth. It subdues all distresses. It is destructive of all sins and impurities, if the ablution of Śrīpati is devoutly witnessed on the full-moon day in the month of Jyeṣṭha.

All those sins which necessitate expiation, of those persons who witness the ablution of Hari, perish. There is no other holy rite greater than this which liberates one without exertion, viz. the ablution of Hari that is witnessed on the birthday of Hari in the month of Jyeṣṭha.

Holy baths, charitable gifts, penance, Śrāddha, Japa, Yajña etc.—all these performed regularly in crores of births and multiplied by a crore, do not equal the merit of witnessing the ablution of Hari.

79. If a person witnesses with great devotion, the ablution of Viṣṇu even once a year, O Brāhmaṇas, he does not come to grief in getting liberation from *saṁsāra*.

80-82. O Brāhmaṇas, if a person witnesses the ablution of Hari, it is as meritorious as the performance of meritorious sacrifices with sincerity, offering sumptuous monetary gifts, as offering great charitable gifts (*Mahādānas)*, as the feeding of crores of Brāhmaṇas, as the performance of crores of Śrāddhas at Gayaśīrṣa and other holy spots, as the performance of penances in Tīrthas etc. at the auspicious hours and as the holy ablutions taken crores of times in crores of Tīrthas in the *Yogas* (auspicious hours) such as *Ardhodaya*[1] etc.

83. It is true. It is (nothing but) the truth. I am speaking the truth, O prominent Brāhmaṇas. There is no other holy rite more conducive to welfare as this in the view of śāstras.

84. He who sees Puruṣottama being bathed while stationed on the couch, gets hundred times the benefit of taking holy bath. There is no doubt about it.

85. He who witnesses the Lord of the universe stationed on the couch and getting wet after the bath, becomes one whose mind is wet with thick mass of bliss. He does not incur any sin.

86. By seeing Acyuta stationed on the couch one obtains that benefit which has been mentioned in regard to the rite of witnessing the ablution.

87. The only Lord of the universe is stationed there in three forms, O Brāhmaṇas. The witnessing of the ablution of each of these yields worldly pleasures and salvation.

88-91. He who joyously proclaims "Be victorious, O Rāmabhadra", "Be victorious, O Bhadrā", "Be victorious, O Kṛṣṇa, the Lord of the universe", at the time of the holy ablution, attains salvation, O excellent Brāhmaṇas.

The devotee should joyously and sincerely distribute monetary gifts separately to those persons who have consecrated and added scents and perfumes to the waters intended for the rite of ablution. With great faith, the devotee should give sumptuous food, garments and ornaments to the Brāhmaṇas. He should satisfy the poor and helpless ones. Those

1. *Ardhodaya*: When in the month of Pauṣa or Māgha there is Amāvāsyā (new-moon day) with Śravaṇa Nakṣatra and Vyatīpāta Yoga, it is called *Ardhodaya*. (Mbh quoted in *History of Daharmaśāstra* vol. I, p.261).

who arrive to witness the rite of ablution are certainly liberated souls while alive.

92-96. For the delight of Hari the king should honour them according to his capacity. If a man or a woman occupies a good seat and takes a bath with the water left over after the ablution, he or she gets great merits, which I shall describe.

One who is afflicted with a chronic malady becomes strong and vigorous. He shall conquer premature death. A woman who has no son or whose son is dead or who is barren, shall get a son. A poor man shall become rich and the most handsome of all the people in the world. A pregnant woman will deliver a son of great merits and longevity. A righteous-souled man certainly gets the merit of witnessing the ablution, which is said to be the merit of taking holy bath in Gaṅgā and all the other Tīrthas.

CHAPTER THIRTYTWO

The Rite of Jyeṣṭha Pañcaka

Jaimini said:

1. Henceforth I shall describe (the procedure) of visiting the deities facing South.[1] In this the benefit of a horse-sacrifice is obtained at every step.

2. Therefore, the devotee should worship (the Lord) with different kinds of divine foodstuffs and offerings and services in accordance with his capacity as well as with scents and wreaths.

3-6. The devotee should worship Rāma, Kṛṣṇa and Subhadrā with various offerings and services such as songs, dances etc., and shows of various kinds accompanied by faith.

Excellent Brāhmaṇas should be honoured with garments, sandal-paste, wreaths, etc. Similarly the Brāhmaṇas, devotees and great Bhāgavatas (followers and devotees of the Lord) should be honoured.

Thereafter, those deities should be taken (in procession) facing the

1. 'Dakṣiṇāmūrti' are the three deities, viz. Jagannātha, Balabhadra and Subhadrā when they proceed to the South. See vv 5 ff. below.

South. As in the previous case of Hari, a great festival should be celebrated. One who sees Hari proceeding ahead facing the South along with Subhadrā, is not an ordinary man.

7. Devas who come for (seeing) the ablution, remain in the sky crowding together even after the ablution of the Sire of the universe is over, in order to see Hari, the destroyer of worldly existence, facing the South and proceeding ahead.

8. A person who sees (the Lord) facing the South and proceeding ahead, attains (the benefit of) all those rites prescribed in treatises on Dharma.

9. He who sees the Lord, the enemy of Mura, proceeding ahead, facing the South after the ablution, obtains the entire merit accruing from seeing the ablution (itself).

10-11. After performing the rite of Nīrājana (i.e. waving of lights in front of the idol of God) to the Lord of Ramā along with Rāma and Bhadrā and making them enter the Mansion, no one shall see (the deities) at all. This has already been said in detail by me, O Brāhmaṇas.

The sages asked:

12. O holy Lord, O most excellent one among those who know, speak to us what you said (before) that one invariably attains the benefit by seeing the Jyeṣṭhāsnāna.

Jaimini said:

13. I shall narrate to you that holy rite called Jyeṣṭhapañcaka.[1] Nothing greater than this has been spoken by sages who have mastered the scriptural texts.

14. This is the most excellent one among the *Vratas* mentioned in Śrutis, Smṛtis and Purāṇas. This has been proclaimed at the outset by Parameṣṭhin Brahmā.

15-17. Since it is the greatest of all important *Vratas*, it is well-known as Jyeṣṭhapañcaka.The ocean is the bestower of great benefit. The Lord is the bestower of great benefit.

---

1. *Jyeṣṭha Pañcaka*: Name of a Vrata extending for five days from the 10th day in the bright half of Jyeṣṭha up to the full-moon day of Jyeṣṭha. The pun on *Jyeṣṭha* (in v 15) meaning 'The Seniormost' and the month of the same name is used for the glorification of the Vrata, The Vrata extends over five days and hence is called '*Pañcaka*'.

The merit of seeing (the Lord) for a year is obtained from *Mañcaka* (Couch) alone. What is to be obtained from Mañcaka, one gets in Mahājyaiṣṭhi.[1] What has been mentioned by me before, O Brāhmaṇas, as the benefit accruing from witnessing the holy ablution, one gets it entirely in Mahājyaiṣṭhī. There is no doubt about it.

The sages said:

18. Recount (to us) Mahājyaiṣṭhī where the holy bath yields great benefit. O holy Brāhmaṇa, our eagerness in regard to that is very great.

Jaimini said:

19-22. On the fifteenth day in the bright half (i.e. on the full-moon day) of the month of Jyeṣṭha, in conjunction with a Thursday as well as when the Moon and Jupiter occupy the same part of the constellation Jyeṣṭhā, when all these astronomical combinations are present, it is called Mahājyaiṣṭhī. It is destructive of all sins.

All the holy places, all the Tīrthas, the seven oceans, sacrifices, the group of great charitable gifts (*Mahādānas)*, penances, the eighteen types of *Vidyās* (Lores), different kinds of holy rites, pious rites of *Śānti* (propitiatory rite to avert evil) and *Pauṣṭika* (a rite promoting welfare) and the Sāṁkhya and Yoga (systems of philosophy)— all these collectively go to the holy place Srīpuruṣottama.

23-24. They as a group say to everyone of those who go to the holy spot: "To which one fortunate enough to witness the holy ablution in the month of Jyeṣṭha (shall we render services)? We shall enter the holy spot in the Mahājyaiṣṭhī, vying with one another." During that great period of astronomical combination they go to the excellent holy place of the Lord.

25. Mahājyaiṣṭhī is extremely meritorious. It increases the pleasure of the Lord. By worshipping the Lord of Devas, the ocean of mercy, on that day and by seeing him bathed, one is liberated from the mass of sins (or the sheath of sins).

26. Henceforth, I shall recount to you the holy rite of Jyeṣṭha Pañcaka. So also I shall tell you the different benefits that can be obtained by observing this *Vrata*.

27. The devotee should perform austerities on the tenth day after

1. *Mahājyaiṣṭhī*: See vv 19-22 below for the description of the *Vrata*. Also vv 26-70.

taking his bath in accordance with the injunctions early in the morning. He should then choose a Vaiṣṇava, a leading Brāhmaṇa, as his preceptor.

28-31. In this excellent *Vrata* he should take a pure *Saṁkalpa* thus: "O Lord of Devas, O Lord of the universe, O Lord taking (the devotee) across the ocean of worldly existence, beginning from today and until that great Mahājyaiṣṭhī day, I shall observe the holy rites, O Keśava, for propitiating you.

The holy ablution shall be performed in all the Tīrthas. There shall be *Vratas* and feeding everyday. At least one of your five forms shall be worshipped each day, O Lord, in all the three Sandhyā-periods (i.e. morning, noon and dusk), O Holy Lord, let this holy observance successfully conclude by your favour."

32. Thereafter, he should take his bath in the five Tīrthas and return home. On the ground he should draw the mystic diagram of an eight-petalled lotus along with the pericarp.

33-34. In its middle (of the pericarp) he should place a pot filled with waters from the Tīrthas. It must have fruits and sandal-paste in it. A copper vessel must be kept above it. There must be a pot filled with raw rice-grains. Round it a cloth should be wrapped. Place into it (the idol) of Lord Madhusūdana made of gold.

35-38. The limbs of the Lord should be auspicious and splendid. It must be calm and quiescent (in appearance). It should be accompanied by (the idol of) Śrī on the left. On the right, it must be accompanied by Garuḍa touching the Lord from behind. He holds in his hand the conch and the discus is held aloft. The Lord occupies a lotus-seat.

The devotee or his preceptor should worship the Lord with all offerings and services, O Brāhmaṇas. He should devoutly offer a garland of blue lotuses to the Lord. If the worship is performed thus on the tenth day, it is conducive to the destruction of ten crores of sins. With palms joined in reverence he should pray repeating this Mantra:

39. "O Lord of Devas, O slayer of Madhu, obeisance to you, O lover of Mādhavī. Protect me, O ocean of mercy, I have fallen into the ocean of worldly existence."

40-41. On the eleventh day the devotee should worship Nārāyaṇa who has four arms, who holds the conch, the discus and the iron club, who is stationed in the lotus and is made of five gold coins or half thereof. He should worship the Lord with a garland of lotuses.

The *Naivedya* offered should consist of milk pudding, sugar and plantain fruit. After offering different kinds of *Naivedya*, the devotee should joyously pray:

42-43. "O Nārayaṇa, obeisance to you. O Lord taking (the devotees) across the ocean of worldly existence, save me, O lotus-eyed one, affectionate to those who seek refuge in you."

The Lord who is worshipped shall destroy all that worst heap of sins committed with the eleven organs (mind and ten conative and cognitive organs) and accumulated in the course of births without any beginning.

44-47. On the twelfth day, the devotee should worship the Yajñavarāha made of gold. Sandal-paste, agallochum and camphor should be applied as unguent and a garland of Caṁpaka flowers should be offered.

After offering as *Naivedya* different types of sweet pies with cream, fresh butter and various other kinds of foodstuffs accompanied with fruits, the devotee should recite this verse of prayer:

"You lifted and held up the Earth sunk in the ocean of Deluge. Are you not powerful enough to lift me up? I have fallen at your lotus-like feet. Therefore, O Govinda, redeem me; I have sunk in the ocean of grief."

A year consists of twelve months. The Lord who is worshipped on the twelfth day, destroys greater and lesser sins committed in the whole of the year as well as in the births prior to this.

48-51. On the thirteenth day the man should devoutly worship Pradyumna holding the conch, the discus and granting boons and immunity from fear (by the positions of the fingers) on the mystic diagram of the lotus. The replica shall be made of four gold coins. The offering and services should be as mentioned before. The garland should be brilliant, consisting of Aśoka and Pāṭalī flowers and fixed with pearls.

The *Naivedya* offered should consist of cooked rice and pleasant ripe fruits. After the *Naivedya* has been offered, the devotee should bow down and pray with palms joined in reverence. He should remain pure (in body and mind).

"O Lord Pradyumna, assuming the form of Kāma, O fulfiller of all desires, let our desires be fruitful, obeisance to you, O protector of desires".

52-57. On the fourteenth day the devotee should worship Narasiṁha of golden features. He is brilliant with manes and is delighted by Lakṣmī stationed in the region of his chest. He has kept his mouth wide open and laughs boisterously. He is stationed on the mystic diagram of a lotus on the Yogic silk cloth[1] (?). The Lord has sharp claws. He is the

1. *Yoga Paṭṭa* generally means 'a cloth thrown over the back and knees of an ascetic during abstract meditation' Here it is used in relation to Narasiṁha.

dispeller of all calamities. He has splendid characteristics and is made of four gold coins. As before, the devotee should, with great devotion, worship the Lord with all the offerings and services. Garlands of Japā flowers (China rose) and jasmine flowers should be offered and handfuls of flowers be strewn on the feet. The Lord shall then be prayed to as follows, after circumambulation and obeisance:

"Just as with a desire for the welfare of all the worlds you tore up Hiraṇyakaśipu, so also, on being worshipped, destroy the mass of my sins."

After requesting Lord Narasiṁha thus and after prostrating on the ground like a staff, the devotee should conclude his *Vrata* lasting for five days. He should offer five lamps during the day and five during the night.

58-59. At the end of feeding, he should, with great sincerity and faith, give the Brāhmaṇas five pairs of clothes, five umbrellas, five pairs of footwear, along with sacred threads and five pots each with five fruits.

60-64. He shall propitiate Vāsudeva by keeping awake at night, singing songs and making various offerings or by reading the Purāṇas. In the morning of the full-moon day he should take his bath and go to Śrīkṛṣṇa.

The priest should worship Rāma, Kṛṣṇa and Subhadrā in accordance with the injunctions. He should get the ablution (of the Lord) duly performed and see the same. Then he should take his bath once again in the sea as prescribed in the scriptural texts and return home. He shall kindle the sacred fire in a place to the west of the spot where the images of Viṣṇu were worshipped within the pots with due recitation of the Mantras. He should kindle the fire there in accordance with the injunctions and then perform all the rites in that sacred fire with the respective Mantras.

65-69. The names should be uttered with Praṇava (Oṁ) prefixed and the dative case terminations suffixed and followed by the word *namaḥ* (obeisance)[1]. The Mūlamantra of the deities shall be used with the word *svāhā* at the end during the rite of *Homa*. Keeping each of the deities in view, *Homas* should be performed with *Caru*, ghee, twigs of a banyan tree and of a Palāśa tree, separately. Afterwards, a hundred flowers should be used for *Homa* (to each of the deities the flower pertaining to it should be offered). After offering the *Pūrṇāhuti* the

1. It plainly means : oṁ (*jagannāthāya, balabhadrāya* or *subhadrāyai*) *namaḥ* and at the time of Homa 'oṁ (*Jagannāthāya* etc.) *svāhā*'—these are to be uttered.

devotee should give monetary gifts to Brahmā (the Brāhmaṇa presiding over the sacrificial and other rites).

To the preceptor he should give gold and a cow. The horns (of the cow) should be covered with gold, the hoofs with silver and various other subsidiary things also should be given. Charitable gifts of very valuable clothes should be made, so that the preceptor is pleased. The devotee should give the idols with all the adjuncts.

70. The devotee should feed the Brāhmaṇas with milk puddings along with sugar-candy and ghee. This excellent *Vrata* is called *Jyeṣṭha-pañcaka.*

71-74. By devoutly performing this holy rite a man obtains the benefit of witnessing the ablution. He obtains the same entirely, O Brāhmaṇas. There is no doubt about this. The Ekādaśī (Eleventh day) that falls in between is proclaimed as *Nirjalā* ('Devoid of water' i.e. even water is not drunk on that day). The fast observed on that day alone in accordance with the injunctions and with great devotion, is as good as fasts observed on all the Ekādaśīs during the whole of one's life. By performing this great holy rite one shall obtain the benefit of all the *Vratas.* Whatever he may desire he shall attain certainly.

CHAPTER THIRTYTHREE

The Chariot-Procession Called Guṇḍicā[1] *Yātrā*

Jaimini said:

1. Henceforth I shall describe the great festival of the Great Altar,[2] whereby even a person blind with ignorance, shall go to the resplendent region.

---

1. Guṇḍicā-House is at a distance of a mile and half from the Jagannātha temple. It is called Mahāvedī as Indradyumna performed one thousand horse-sacrifices here. It is regarded as the birthplace of the Trinity—Jagannātha, Balabhadra and Subhadrā—as their images were carved out by the divine carpenter within the Mahāvedī. Jagannātha promised Indradyumna that he would annually stay for seven days here near Indradyumna Lake (vide Supra Ch. 29.40-41).

As our text shows, Jagannātha worship was originally current among Śabaras, the aboriginals of that Orissan region. In their language, *Kun*= He, and *Dījā*= 'The stem of a tree'. So Kuṇḍījā> Guṇḍijā> Guṇḍicā shows the Śabara origin of the festival.

2. Mahāvedī i.e. the Guṇḍicā-House.

2-8. The third day in the bright half of the lunar month of Vaiśākha is destructive of sins. If it is in conjunction with the constellation Rohiṇī, the king should perform the *Saṁkalpa*-rite (for the following *Vrata*):

Remaining pure (in body and mind), he should choose a preceptor as well as one or three carpenters whose work has been seen (and found all right). He should choose the carpenter with great respect, offering garments, ornaments etc. for the purpose of *Vanayāga* (sacrifice in the forest).

Along with the carpenter he should go to the forest full of excellent trees. (The preceptor) who is conversant with Mantras should repeat *Mantrarāja* and kindle the fire in the middle of the forest. He should then offer one hundred and eight *Āhutis*. He should (then) smear the roots of the trees severally with ghee mixed with the residue of ghee from the *Homa*.

He should offer oblation to the Guardians of Quarters, and animals unto the Kṣetrapāla. Then he should offer a hundred *Āhutis* to the larger forest-tree in the form of cooked rice mixed with milk.

Thereafter, the preceptor should take up the axe. Repeating the Mantra and meditating upon Garuḍa-emblemed Lord (Viṣṇu), he should cut off small bits from the roots of the trees and the places where the sacred ghee was smeared.

9. In the midst of sounds of musical instruments and auspicious songs the preceptor, after engaging the carpenter there, should return home.

10. Or (he should stay there) and when the logs of wood are (hewn) and kept in their places ready for the work of making the chariot, he sould consecrate them in accordance with the injunctions for the consecration mentioned (in the scriptural texts). He should perform the rite in the fire assigned (for it).

11-17. After making the chariot, he should celebrate the great festival of Vighnarāja (Gaṇeśa).[1] He should make the chariot of Viṣṇu equipped with sixteen iron wheels, very strong and durable. Each of the wheels should have sixteen spokes. The axles and the pole-shafts should be sturdy. It shall have wonderfully carved images all round, with separate cabin-like apartments.

There should be various wonderful features marked by great crafts-

1. Gaṇeśa is the controller of all obstacles. So he is worshipped at the beginning of every auspicious rite or act.

manship. It should be embellished with pieces of sugarcane. There shall be four ornamental arched gateways. The four door panels should be splendid. The chariot should be twenty-two Hastas high (22 x 45 Cms). It should be adorned with flags. It should be decorated with different golden plates marked by great craftsmanship. The emblem in the form of Garuḍa should be made of red sandalwood. The beak should be long. The body should be stout. He should be adorned with ear-rings. He should be depicted as biting a serpent with the tip of the beak. He should be adorned with all types of ornaments. He keeps his wings spread and is (as if) ready to fly up in the sky. He is (strong enough) to suppress the arrogance born of power of the multitudes of Daityas and Dānavas. The entire body should be rendered splendid by covering it with gold plates.

18a. Thus, he should make the chariot of Hari well-decorated with splendid seating arrangement.

18b-20. He should make the chariot of Balarāma with fourteen wheels. The excellent chariot of Subhadrā should be made with twelve wheels.

The Palm-tree emblem of Balarāma should have seven leaves. The lotus emblem of the Goddess should be made of Padmakāṣṭha (wood of *Cerasus puddum*). After getting the chariots made, the king should install them as before.

21-27. The king should perform every rite in accordance with the scriptural prescriptions with suitable Mantras. He should have faith in Brāhmaṇas. Brāhmaṇas are declared (in Smṛtis) as the mobile (living) bodies of the Lord of the universe.

These well-built three chariots of the three deities should be installed on the day of Viṣṇu (i.e. eleventh day) in the bright half of Āṣāḍha that yields auspicious results.

After installing them in a luxurious manner as before, O Brāhmaṇas, they should be well-guarded so that no unclean person, a bird, a human being, a cat, or a mongoose etc. should climb it.

Within three days therefrom the rite of *Aṅkurārpaṇa* should be performed in the pavilion made to the north of the chariots, as a part of the festival. If unusual events occur, the rite of *Śānti* (pacification for averting evils) mentioned before should be performed.

The street should be cleaned and kept neat so that it will be (easy) to go to the Great Altar. The zone on either side of the path should be decorated with hedges etc., fruits, bunches of flowers, wreaths, silk-cloths and chowries, so that it would appear as though there is a forest region in full bloom there.

28. The ground should be made level facilitating a smooth walk. It should be free from mud. Cleaned of all impurities, it should be rendered fragrant. Rubbish from places even away from the path, should be removed.

29-34. The king of pure holy rites should gather together all the requisite items. There should be placed containers of incense at every step rendering the quarters sweet-smelling. Sandalwood-water should be sprinkled. Water should be sprayed by means of mechanical devices. Many kinds of seasonal flowers should be collected there for showering. Important actors, dancers and songsters, courtesans proud of their prime of youth and of beautiful features adorned with ornaments (and similar persons) should be engaged. There must be various kinds of drums such as Mṛdaṅgas, Paṇavas, Bherīs, Ḍhakkās etc. There must be many flags, festoons, banners etc. of diverse kinds and picturesque designs. There must be many flagstaffs made of gold and silver. There must be different kinds of ensigns and vehicles for transport on the surface. Well-caparisoned elephants and horses must be ready at hand. Thus equipped with every essential thing, the king should celebrate the grand festival with great joy and earnest devotion.

35. He should worship the Lord at the time of early dawn on the second day in the bright half of the month of Āṣāḍha in conjunction with Puṣya constellation.

36. Accompanied by Brāhmaṇas, Vaiṣṇavas, ascetics and saints, he should beseech the Lord of Devas with palms joined in reverence, to be ready for the procession.

37-39. "O Lord, just as you had done in the case of king Indradyumna formerly, be pleased to proceed towards the Guṇḍicā Pavilion victoriously in the chariot.

Let the ten quarters be sanctified by the benign glance of the corner of your eye. Let the mobile and immobile beings attain the abode of highest good.

Indeed, O Lord, this incarnation has been taken (by you) with a desire for blessing all the worlds. Therefore, O Lord, set foot on the ground and come joyfully."

40. Then he should scatter camphor powder and flowers (over the chariot). Brāhmaṇas shall recite *Śākuna Sūktas* (Ṛgveda II.42, 43) on the way.

41. Some should sing songs of auspiciousness. Some should shout "Be victorious", "Be victorious". Some should loudly recite the Mantra beginning with *jitam te* (you have won).

42-44. The chief of panegyrists, bards and heralds should joyously sing the meritorious praise (of the Lord). On either side there should be a row of chowries with golden handles. (Young ladies) should gracefully wave them, while their bangles produce sweet enchanting sounds. Black Agallochum is put in gold vessels and fumigated. The entire environment and all the quarters are rendered fragrant.

In the course of that victorious procession of Govinda the sweet sounds of flutes, lutes and other musical instruments such as Carcarī, Jharjharī, Mādhurikā etc. are heard.

45. At this time, when all these go on, Brāhmaṇas take away Kṛṣṇa along with Rāma. Kṣatriyas and Vaiśyas take away Subhadrā.

46. A series of umbrellas is held aloft adorned with pearl strings and silk festoons. Flags with staffs covered with gold and set with gems are held on either side of the Enemy of Mura (Kṛṣṇa).

47. The king, the people of the four castes, other ordinary persons, the poor, the great ones etc. all appear as equal to one another.

48. If they are tired anywhere on the way, they should place the deities on cotton mattresses placing the feet gently down and go towards (follow) the chariot.

49-53. In the midst of great festivities and loud sounds of music the people should hold the Lord of the universe in the hands, turn the excellent chariot and place Rāma, Kṛṣṇa and Subhadrā in the middle of the chariot.

It (the chariot) should be decorated with a pavilion lighted with excellent moonlight. It should be decorated with clusters of strings with tinkling bells. It should be adorned with wreaths and chowries. The space within should be fumigated fully with the incense from the essence of black Agallochum. The excellent deities should be kept on cotton beds. They should then be adorned with different kinds of garments, ornaments and wreaths.

Prompted by devotional feelings, they should then be worshipped with due offerings and services luxuriously provided. No other procession of Viṣṇu is seen to be greater than this.

54. Here the Lord of the three worlds himself goes ahead in the chariot every year, honouring the earlier command (i.e. commitment).

55. Those who joyously and devoutly witness the Lord stationed in the chariot and proceeding ahead in the course of the great festival of Mahāvedī shall dwell in the region (of the feet) of Hari.

56. It is true. It is true. I promise, O excellent Brāhmaṇas, that it is the truth. There is no other festival honoured by the scriptural texts

and yielding greater good than this.

57. Just as this is a sportful procession of Viṣṇu by means of chariots, so also it is a great festival of the Great Altar. Devas come down here from heaven and go back as possessed of power (?)

58. What more can I say about the greatness of that festival of the Enemy of Mura? Merely by glorifying him the sins incurred in the course of hundreds of births perish.

59-60. By witnessing Puruṣottama, Subhadrā and Balabhadra seated in the chariot and proceeding towards the Great Altar, the devotee dispels the sin committed in crores of births. No doubt need be entertained in this regard. By crossing the shadow of the chariot the sin of Brāhmaṇa-slaughter perishes.

61. He whose body comes into contact with its dust, shall get rid of the three types of collections of sins. He shall attain the benefit accruing from the holy bath in the celestial Gaṅgā.

62-63. If the path of the chariot becomes muddy due to the shower of waters from clouds, it becomes capable of removing all impurities and sins, thanks to the divine vision of Kṛṣṇa(?)

Those excellent Vaiṣṇavas who prostrate there, get rid of all the dirt (sins) amassed in the course of the beginningless time and shall attain salvation.

64. Undoubtedly he (such a Vaiṣṇava) derives the benefit of gifting away a crore of cows, or (giving away in marriage) ten thousand virgins and that of performing a thousand horse-sacrifices.

65. Devas, the chief of whom is Śakra, follow those persons who follow Kṛṣṇa even out of curiosity (to witness) the procession.

66. It is proclaimed that they will obtain the benefit of a horse-sacrifice for every step, if they witness the eternal *Dārubrahman* (i.e. the Brahman in wooden form, viz. Jagannātha) and the chariot proceeding ahead.

67-68. Expounders of the Vedas eulogize the Lord, the bestower of salvation, by means of the Vedic mantras. Others eulogize the Lotus-eyed One by means of prayers composed by themselves or through passages from the Itihāsas, Purāṇas etc.

Those who eulogize thus become rid of sins. By adopting the Yogic path of the followers of Viṣṇu they rejoice along with Nārada and others.

69. Those who eulogize the Lord with shouts of *Victory* in front of Vāsudeva, conquer different kinds of sins. There is no doubt about it.

70. Even if a person is devoid of sweetness of voice and cannot sing, even if a person is ignorant of the proper pause in music and beating of the time and rhythm—but if that excellent man dances and sings (before the Lord), he shall undoubtedly attain salvation by his contact with excellent Vaiṣṇavas.

71. He who goes along with the Lord glorifying (and repeating) the names or follows the Lord, shall undoubtedly derive the benefit thereof.

72. He who devoutly and repeatedly says, "Be victorious, O Kṛṣṇa", "Be victorious, O Kṛṣṇa" as Lord Kṛṣṇa proceeds towards the city of Guṇḍicā, shall never again attain the misery of staying in the womb of a mother.

73-75. If a person stands in front of the chariot and fans Puruṣottama with flyflaps, fans, bunches of flowers and blue bodices, he will be fanned by celestial damsels and adorned by Gandharvas (and eulogized) by the Devas who follow him. He will be seated in the throne of Mahendra. He will then enjoy all types of matchless pleasures till the annihilation of all living beings. At the end of it he will attain the world of Brahmā and (finally) attain salvation.

76. Those who shower flowers in front of Kṛṣṇa will attain all the desires and ambitions entertained by them.

77. Devas shall bow down their heads before them and circumambulate those persons who accompany the chariot and repeat the thousand holy names (of the Lord).

78-85. Those who are as valiant as Viṣṇu, will go to the abode of the Lord.

At that time which is highly meritorious and resorted to even by Devas, sages and Pitṛs, the one and only Brahman attended by his own Māyā becomes three.

The Lord of the universe himself in his wooden form gets into the chariot eagerly and proceeds ahead during the great festival of the Great Altar. Wherever the Lord of the universe goes riding in the chariot sportfully, there the people of the earth should celebrate the great festival at the same time.

Casting off their prestige, Devas, the leader of whom is Indra, will form lines on either side and carry on the procession with their respective divine retinue and attendants.

Lord Brahmā too will go ahead of them. Lord Brahmā, the maker of the fourteen worlds, who is a great Lord, returns from (his own) world of Brahmā and eulogizes the Lord of the universe who goes in the chariot during the great festival. He eulogizes with Vedic prayers and hymns. At every step he bows down to the eternal Lord.

86. Although there is no difference between the Lotus-born Lord and Kṛṣṇa, this is the greatness of the great festival that all of them become followers.

87. In the world there is no greater Yoga than the great festival of the Great Altar, the Yoga that dispels all the sins and bestows the benefit of all the Tīrthas.

88. Keeping Kṛṣṇa in view, if a man makes the gift of anything there, it will have everlasting benefit. It will be equal to Merudāna.[1]

89. Whatever holy rite is performed in front of the Lord of Devas, who proceeds towards the abode of Guṇḍicā, shall become inexhaustible (in benefit).

90. If different kinds of presents or varieties of foodstuffs are dedicated to the Lord or to Brāhmaṇas for the delight of the Lord, those offerings will have inexhaustible merits. They will yield all desires.

91-92. Those who go ahead in front of Hari and witness his lotus-like face (repeatedly) and bow down at every step as well as get themselves dust-ridden and muddy, will get rid of their unbreakable armour of sins acquired in the course of crores of births and attain the benefit of salvation in a trice. They then go to the splendid abode of Viṣṇu.

93. They derive the benefit of all the sacrifices, Tīrthas and charitable gifts. There is no other festival more meritorious than this in regard to those persons who have devotional feelings towards the Lord.

94-95. Thus Lord Kṛṣṇa in the company of Subhadrā and Rāma goes ahead riding in the excellent chariot and illuminating the four quarters. He destroys the sins of all embodied beings through the wind that comes into contact with his glorious limbs. The glorious Lord is merciful and he sanctifies the devotees.

96. Though he is a natural bestower of salvation, he carries on the activities of processions for the sake of inspiring faith in ignorant persons who have no faith.

97-103. The procession goes ahead with multitudes of Devas and human beings (accompanying the Lord). On the way, at midday, the sun is excessively hot, scorching foreheads. With all the followers tired, he stands in the middle of the road. He is covered with dust and looks exhausted. There, in order to suppress the (effect of) sunlight, the people

---

1. Dāna or religious gifts of the heaps (of any one) of the following: *dhānya* (corn), *lavaṇa* (salt), *guḍa* (jaggery), *hema* (gold), tila (sesame), *kārpāsa* (cotton), *ghṛta* (ghee), *ratna* (precious stones), *rajata* (silver), *śarkarā* (sugar).

should sprinkle the glasses with Pañcāmṛtas and cool waters perfumed with flowers and camphor. They should fan the Lotus-eyed Lord, Subhadrā and Rāma with chowries and cool fans, the tips of which are drenched in water.

They must worship Puruṣottama and offer these things: cool drinks, pleasant and juicy sugar candies, date fruits, coconuts, different kinds of plantain fruits, various milk-products, jack fruits, palmyra fruits, sugarcane juice, tasty and sweet fruits of different kinds, perfumed cool water, betel-leaves with ripe fruits, camphor, cloves etc.

104-108. O excellent Brāhmaṇas, those who see Janārdana at that time and worship him in accordance with their capacity, do not get the weariness arising from worldly existence. They become the residents of the world of Brahmā, O excellent Brāhmaṇas.

Excellent men shall circumambulate the three deities stationed in the three chariots three, four or seven times. Then, they should bow down ten times. At the end, they should stand with palms joined in reverence. They should eulogize the great Lord, the Lord of Devas, with those prayers with which the lotus-born Lord Brahmā eulogized the Lord and the other deities stationed in the chariots. Those men who do thus, definitely go to the world of Brahmā, O Brāhmaṇas.

109. Then in the afternoon, they should take the Lord of Devas fanned by the southern wind, slowly to the accompaniment of vocal music as well as the sweet sounds of flutes, lutes etc.

110-113. The bards and panegyrists should sing sweet songs. There must be continuous showers of flowers and waving of flyflaps and chowries. When the Lord proceeds ahead thus, the sun may set. At that time thousands of lamps should be lit. The remaining part of the path shall be traversed in the light of these lamps. There will be great rush and crowd of people eager to see the Lord at the time of getting down from the chariot and going up the pavilion. The people should keep the Lord in the charming pavilion named Guṇḍicā.

114-116. The pavilion should be well-lit with the charming moon-light. It should be adorned with charming wreaths and chowries. It must have gem-set pillars. The middle should be raised into an Altar paved with gold. There must be an enclosure all round. It should be brilliant with fresh whitewash and plastering. There must be good flight of steps. It must have four splendid doors. It must have all the grandeur of the three worlds. It was here that the great Lord appeared on the Great Altar of the great sacrifice, in the wooden form.

CHAPTER THIRTYFOUR

In Praise of the Chariot-Procession

Jaimini said:

1-4. The Lord is seated to the south of the lake that formed part of the horse-sacrifices as well as to that of Nṛsiṁha. It appears as if the Lord incarnates once again. He shines in his divine form. He is too dazzling to be gazed at by Suras and Asuras. At that time the Lord of the universe should be worshipped by means of various offerings and pleased with songs and dances. One should propitiate the Lord by offering different kinds of flowers, sweet scents and unguents, fumigation of black Agallochum and lamps with scented oil. Thus the devotee should please the Lord of the worlds by means of many offerings and services.

5. Janārdana shall stay on the shore of the Bindutīrtha[1] for seven days. Formerly the Lord himself had granted this boon to the king:

6. "Every year I shall stay on the shore of your Tīrtha, O great king. While I stay there, all the Tirthas will be present therein too.

7-11. Devotees should take their holy bath in accordance with the injunctions in that Tīrtha which sanctifies all the groups of Tīrthas. He who (then) sees me along with Rāma and Subhadrā for seven days while I am housed in the Guṇḍicā pavilion, shall attain *Sāyujya* (absorption) with me."

Therefore the devotee, whether a man or a woman, should take the holy bath in the auspicious and extremely meritorious Tīrtha which is destructive of all the sins. It (the Tīrtha) is the sole bestower of the benefits of all the Tīrthas and causes delight unto Viṣṇu.

After the bath he should offer libations to Pitṛs and Devas carefully in accordance with the injunctions. Then he should worship and bow down to Narasiṁha installed on the shore. After completing the rites of purification and *Ācamana* he should go to the Great Altar, worship as before or bow down with great devotion. The devotee who does this for seven days is not an ordinary man or woman (but becomes superhuman).

12. At the bidding of the Enemy of Mura (Kṛṣṇa) he attains *Sāyujya* with Viṣṇu. Seeing him during day is meritorious (but doing so) at

1. The same as Indradyumna Lake.

night will give ten times the merit.

13. Whatever holy rite is performed in the presence of the Lord of the universe on a modest or large scale, shall become (multiplied) crores and crores of times more.

14. The devotees may give charitable gifts of Tulāpuruṣa[1] or other great gifts. But even if one (thing) is given, O Brāhmaṇas, it is as good as the gift of everything.

15. When Kṛṣṇa goes to the Great Altar, all charitable gifts are on a par with Meru; all people are equal to Vyāsa, O Brāhmaṇas. This *Yoga* is rare indeed (*Yoga* = an astronomical combination).

16. *Ardhodaya* and other Yogas expounded by Skanda do not deserve even a sixteenth part of the Yoga called *Mahāvedī*.

17. Henceforth I shall describe the excellent holy (*Śrāddha*) rite of Pitṛs. Even if one performs Gayāśrāddha throughout one's life, one shall not get a benefit (as from this).

18-19. All the Manes, all the grandfathers whether stationed in heaven or in hell or re-born as animals or human beings, about one hundred famous members (of the family) desire that their scions should perform this. That procedure I shall recount to you. Listen to that excellent one, O sages.

20-26. Maghā is the constellation (specially favourite) of the Pitṛs. It is highly pleasant and delightful (to them). If the Śrāddha is offered by the sons joyously in this constellation, it delights (Pitṛs). The fifth lunar day is also excellent. (If available) in Śrāddha, it is conducive to prosperity. If both of these coincide, the day is extremely meritorious. If the Śrāddha rite is performed on that day by the sons, the Pitṛs will be uplifted.

If at the Tīrtha inclusive of (i.e. comprising) all Tīrthas the Śrāddha is devoutly performed in the presence of the Enemy of Mura, in the most sacred area between Nīlakaṇṭha and Nṛsiṁha and on the extremely rare Yoga (specific astrological time), he redeems a hundred men (ancestors) of his family and is honoured in the world of Brahmā.

The period of *Kutapa*[2] (early afternoon), when the sun is gentle, is extremely praiseworthy. One should offer a gold piece keeping the

1. The donor is to be weighed in a balance with gold or other valuable articles in the other pan and the articles equal in weight with the donor are to be given to Brahmins. This is called *Tulāpuruṣa*.

2. This is the eighth Muhūrta of the day (MtP 22.84). *Kutapa* and the following four Muhūrtas form the proper period for Śrāddha.

Manes in view. If he cannot afford it, he should remain pure and duly perform the rites of libation with gingelly seeds. Thereby he gives excellent satisfaction to Pitṛs.

Or he should feed Brāhmaṇas or give them the cost of the foodstuffs. Or he should feed one meritorious person and give him a thousand (cost of the foodstuffs of a thousand Brāhmaṇas?).

27. At this particular Yoga no discrimination regarding merit (eligibility) and non-merit (ineligibility of the Brāhmaṇa to be invited to Śrāddha) be made. O Brāhmaṇas, on that extremely rare Yoga, all Brāhmaṇas are on a par with sages.

28-30. The fifth day in the bright half of the month of Āṣāḍha, the constellation Maghā and the contact (installation) of the Lord of the universe with the Great Altar—when all these three come together and at the excellent lake of Indradyumna—this Yoga is known as *Catuṣpāda* (four-footed). It bestows everlasting benefit unto the Pitṛs.

By performing a Śrāddha then no one gets despondent in regard to the holy rites of Pitṛs.

Listen to another thing, O Brāhmaṇas. I tell it to you on this occasion.

31-32. On the new-moon day in the month of Nabhasya[1] (or Bhādrapada i.e. August-September) or on the four Yugādi (i.e. anniversary of the beginning of the Yugas) days, the devotee should perform Śrāddha of the Pitṛs at the lake formed as part of the horse-sacrifice (i.e. Indradyumna Lake). It will then have the same benefit as that of a thousand Gayā Śrāddhas faithfully performed. In this matter there need be no doubt at all.

33-36. A charitable gift offered and *Homa* and *Japa* performed during the seven days when Kṛṣna stays here in the Pavilion is destructive of all sins. The subsequent day is superior to the previous one.

The third day in the bright half of Āṣāḍha is the most excellent day. On that day the devotee should take the holy bath early in the morning, on the bank of Indradyumna Lake, in the excellent holy spot of Nṛsiṁha. After the due performance of the rite of *Saṁkalpa*, the man should take up this *Vrata* called *Vanajāgaraṇa*. It increases the pleasure of the Lord. It suppresses all the sins and yields the benefit of all *Vratas*.

1. The text reads *nabhasyadarśe* i.e. the new-moon day of Nabhasya (Bhādrapada). The new-moon day of Bhādrapada is specially meant for offering Śrāddha to Pitṛs and is hence called '*Sarvapitrī amāvāsyā*'.

37-39. On all these seven days, the devotee should take three baths per day. He should light lamps fed with cow's ghee or sesamum oil. He should observe the vow of silence. He should place these lamps in front of Hari and keep them lighted day and night. During the day time he should observe silence and during the nights he should keep a vigil. He should repeat the Mantra of the Lord at intervals between the daily routine of duties while observing this *Vrata.*

40. He should observe fast also during the seven days. After the seven days have passed, on the eighth day he should get up early in the morning and perform the installation.

41. After taking the holy bath in the same excellent Tīrtha, he should return home. In the previous mystic diagram of Sarvatobhadra he should place the pot.

42-44. He should invoke Hṛṣīkeśa there and worship by means of the offerings. To the west of it, on the ground duly consecrated, he should kindle the sacred fire in accordance with the injunctions mentioned in the Gṛhyasūtras.

He, surrounded by Brāhmaṇas, should perform the rites of fire-worship. He should offer sacrificial twigs, ghee and the Caru into the fire a thousand times by way of Homa or each of them a hundred times. It is laid down that the Homa should be performed with the Vaiṣṇava Gāyatrī.

45. After feeding (the Ācārya), he should offer monetary gifts and give a cow, garments and gold (to him). At the end he should feed the Brāhmaṇas for the satisfaction of the Witness of the universe.

46. By performing this important Vrata in accordance with these injunctions, O Brāhmaṇas, he obtains all the four aims of life. Whatever one desires shall be obtained.

47. If a woman possessing sincere faith performs this rite of the great festival of the Altar, she will also obtain the benefit thereof.

48. The merit acquired by a person observing the vow is the same as that of the person who participates in the festival of the chariot-procession.

O excellent Brāhmaṇas, everything has been said to you. Be happy.

CHAPTER THIRTYFIVE

The Procedure of Preserving the Chariot

Jaimini said:

1-3. Henceforth I shall describe the procedure of protecting the chariot, whereby terrible goblins, ghosts and others as well as hideous supernatural beings do not harm the chariots. O sages, (I shall tell you) what will be approved by you all.

Everyday the devotee should worship Kṛṣṇa and other deities stationed on the flags with sweet-smelling flowers, raw rice-grains, wreaths, excellent offerings and services, songs, dances etc. as well as incense, lamps and food-offerings.

4. Oblation should be offered to the Guardians of the Quarters everyday with rice cooked in milk. Excellent oblations should be offered to goblins, ghosts and evil spirits.

5. With great efforts (and care) those chariots should be kept in a condition fit for the riding (of the deities). It should be seen that no man or domestic animal climbs on them. Particularly birds whose habitation is inauspicious should not be allowed to occupy them.

6-11. On the eighth day the chariots should be kept facing the South. The devotee should adorn (the deities and the chariots) with cloths, wreaths, flags, chowries etc. On the morning of the ninth day the Devas should be installed in them luxuriously.

This South-facing journey of Viṣṇu is very difficult to be accomplished. That journey (procession) should be carried out with great effort, devotion and faith.

Just as the previous (procession), so also this—both of these yield salvation. Both these—the journey (procession) and re-entry of the Lord, are considered to constitute one festival alone.

Those who are conversant with tradition and mythology say that this journey is of nine days' duration. This three-limbed (three-staged) journey (procession)[1] should be attended to in full. To those who do so, the great festival of the Great Altar will yield complete benefit.

12. Those who watch Kṛṣṇa while returning from the Guṇḍicā Pa-

1. *Tryavayavā Yātrā:* The procession of three limbs i.e. stages, viz. (1) Journey from the temple of Guṇḍicā; (2) Return journey from Guṇḍicā to Nīlācala; (3) The visit of Dakṣiṇāmūrti (i.e. turning the chariots to the South).

vilion with face to the South and seated in the chariot along with Balarāma and Subhadrā, attain liberation.

13. That kind of benefit derived by those who witness the splendid Lords Rāma and others seated in the chariot with their faces to the North, is also obtained by those who see them (Rāma and others) facing the South.

14. If anyone sees (the Lord) going on foot or in the chariot facing the South, his birth is blessed, for at every step he obtains the merit of a horse-sacrifice.

15. The devotee should attend to the Lord in front with eulogies, prostrations, showers of flowers, different kinds of dances, offerings and services with fans, umbrellas, chowries and presents of various kinds.

16-17. Those who see Hṛṣīkeśa, the Lord who is like the wish-yielding Kalpa tree, who grants salvation to men merely by his sight, along with Subhadrā and Balarāma coming to Nīla mountain seated in the chariot and facing the South, are noble souls. They go to Hari's abode, Vaikuṇṭha.

18-20. While Hari returns to his palace on Mount Nīla with his face to the South, those devout believers who eulogize him and prostrate themselves before him who is the abode of all the Tīrthas and is like a wish-yielding tree donating (anything and) everything, do not return to this world (after death). They get established in Brahmā's region.

21. O sages, this great festival of the Great Altar has been described to you. By glorifying this a man becomes free from impurities (and sins).

22. The man who gets up early in the morning and recites this or listens to this or retains this in his memory, shall go to the world of Śakra.

23-24. If anyone makes a replica or a picture of Hari, places it on the chariot and carries out this procession with faith and devotion, that man shall obtain the merit of the festival of Guṇḍicā by the favour of Viṣṇu. He then goes to the abode of Vaikuṇṭha. There is no doubt about this.

25-26. A person should perform this Yātrā (procession) in accordance with his affluence, devotion and faith. By sponsoring or witnessing this one ceases to be afflicted and worried. This holy and great secret has been revealed by Brahmā.

CHAPTER THIRTYSIX

*The Festival of the Lord's Retiring to Sleep**

Jaimini said:

1-2. Henceforth I shall describe the excellent festival of (the Deity's) going to bed.[1] With Āṣāḍhī as the starting point, Hari's sleep covers the four months of the rainy season from Āṣāḍhī (eleventh day in the bright half of Āṣāḍha) when the sun goes to the Zodiac of Cancer to Kārttikī (eleventh day in the bright half of Kārttika). This is the most meritorious period for the propitiation of Hari.

3-5. If a person stays in the holy place Śrī Puruṣottama even for a single day during the period of these four months in the presence of Hari, know that his merit is what has been mentioned for the stay in Kāśī for many Yugas performing pious observance and holy rites. If a person passes all the days of those rainy months in the meritorious holy spot in the presence of the Lord of the universe devoid of impurities within, he will directly obtain the merit of a thousand horse-sacrifices.

6. A person who bathes in the holy waters of the ocean, sees Śrī Puruṣottama and devoutly performs holy rites during the four months (of the rainy season), never has any grief from anywhere.

7. Stay in the holy place Śrī Puruṣottama during the four months, and direct view of the Lord—these two are the means of salvation.

8. Hence a man should give up all the rites ordained in the Śrutis or Smṛtis and make efforts to stay in the meritorious holy spot Śrī Puruṣottama.

9. The Lord remains asleep on the couch of the serpent's (Śeṣa's) body during these four months. The Sire of the universe is not present then in any of the other sacred places.

10. But he stays here visibly as though in his abode of Vaikuṇṭha.

---

* Anthropomorphism and anthropopathism are a special characteristic of *Saguṇa Bhakti*. The Lord is treated as a human being and he wants sleep, turns his side during sleep, suffers from colds and requires medicine—all this is sincerely done in the spirit of Saguṇa Bhakti to the Lord. This is amply illustrated in our Text.

1. This festival of Lord's going to sleep is one of the twelve Yātrās of Jagannātha. The eleventh day in the bright half of Āṣāḍha is called Śayanī Ekādaśī. The Lord is supposed to go to sleep on this day to be awakened on the eleventh day in the bright half of Kārttika which is called 'Prabodhinī' (the awakener). And the period of four months between these Ekādaśī days is called 'Cāturmāsya'.

During all the twelve months the Lord is in his embodied form here. If he is seen with one's eye especially during these four months, he is the bestower of salvation.

11. By seeing the Lord on a single day during these four months (*Cāturmāsya*) one obtains that merit which is acquired by seeing Viṣṇu everyday while staying here all through the other eight months.

12-17. By staying in the holy spot of Śrī Puruṣottama for the whole period of four months one acquired the merit of staying in all holy places on everyone of those days. The Lord grants (befitting) benefit for staying in the holy place for a whole year.

A man may be engaged in all kinds of evil actions. He may be fallen from all kinds of decent conduct and behaviour. He may be excluded from all pious and devout rites. But if that sinful man stays in Puruṣottama during one set of (these) four months, he dispels all the sins. He becomes free from impurities both within and without. By the favour of Narasiṁha he shall go to the abode of Vaikuṇṭha.

Hence with all his devout feelings a man should stay in Puruṣottama during those four rainy months sanctified by Viṣṇu's sleep. He may or may not do anything else, notwithstanding that his life becomes fruitful.

18. The devotee should celebrate the great festival of (the Lord's) sleep on the eleventh day in the bright half of the month of Āṣāḍha. A pavilion should be made and an excellent bedchamber should be built there.

19-26. In front of the Lord, the bed must be spread over a gem-set couch along with a pillow and a bedsheet of soft China silk. Camphor-powder should be scattered over the bed and splendid awning should be made. The enclosure all around should have no holes. It shall be sprinkled with sandal-paste. There must be a good doorway. The bed should be even. It should be decorated with various pictures and paintings.

There should be only one bedchamber. The devotee must have ready with him three images (of the three deities). They should be made of gold, silver, brass or stone according to one's faith. The succeeding is better than the preceding one. During midnight the images (specially made ones) should be placed at the foot of the respective deity. They should then be worshipped. The remnants (of worship) must be deposited on them. At the the end of the worship the devotee should meditate on the identity of those images with Kṛṣṇa and others.

"Come, come, O Lord, the sole life of all the worlds, for sleep during these four months for the increase of prosperity of everyone."

After praying thus to the deities the devotee should take the three garlands from the deities and place them on the special movable images of the three deities. To the accompaniment of auspicious prayers and songs, they should be taken to the door of the bedchamber and kept there for three Ghaṭikās.

27-33. The images should be bathed with Pañcāmṛta separately, weighing more than 100 Palas for each. They should be smeared with fragrant sandal-paste and adorned with robes, ornaments etc. After duly worshipping them, the devotee should repeat this Mantra with palms joined in reverence:

"O Lord of the universe, worthy of being saluted by all the worlds, engaged in protecting the universe! O Lord, sleep during these four months of the advent of clouds, for the sake of the welfare of the worlds. Worshipped along with Śakra, suppress all evils and calamities. Come, come to the bedchamber. O Lord sleep here comfortably."

After praying thus to the Lord of Devas, the devotee should make Puruṣottama go to sleep. He should firmly close the door of the bedchamber of Viṣṇu. After making the Lord of the worlds sleep one obtains excellent happiness.

When Janārdana is asleep during the four rainy months, the devotee should pass those four months in performing many holy rites and pious observances. The man with devotion shall dwell in the world of Viṣṇu for the period of a Kalpa.

Even as I recount the holy rites and vows to be observed during *Cāturmāsya*, listen to them, O sages.

34-37. The man of devotion should give up resting on bedsteads and couches. Except in the stipulated period after the monthly menstural discharge (of his wife) he should not carnally approach even his wife. He should give up meat, liquor, food of another person, *Paṭolas* (a kind cucumber)*, *Mūlaka* (radish) and brinjal. He should keep away from all forbidden foodstuffs. He should avoid *Masūra* (a kind of pulse), white mustard, *Rājamāṣa, Kulattha* and Āśudhānya. In the beginning of the month of Śrāvaṇa he should gradually avoid greens, curds, milk and pulses. No one other than a king, ascetics and cowherds should put on leather footwear. If it happens that one could not perform holy rites during the four rainy months, he should perform the holy rites in the

* Known as *Paḍvaḷ* in Marathi.

month of Kārttika for overcoming that sin.

38-44. He should repeat this prayer in the morning, midday, evening and at the conclusion of holy rites:

"Obeisance to Kṛṣna, to Hari. Repeated obeisance to Keśava. Salutation to Narasiṁha, to Viṣṇu, to the conqueror of sins."

He will burn all his terrible sins acquired in the course of many births like fire burning a heap of cotton.

If a person observes restriction in his diet, takes food only once a day, or takes in only the remnants of the offering unto Viṣṇu,or takes in food only during the night throughout the period between Āṣāḍhī and Kārttikī, heaven is the least gain unto him.

The devotee should avoid oil-bath, midday nap and slander-mongering.

The man should undertake the Vrata (vow) on the eleventh day in the bright half of the month of Āṣāḍha, on the day of the transit of the Sun to the Zodiac Cancer or on the new-moon day in the month of Āṣāḍha.

After worshipping Lord Madhusūdana, the destroyer of all sins, and after taking the *Saṅkalpa* in front of him in regard to the Vrata, worship, Japa etc. the man of holy rites should pray to the Lord, the supreme Bliss, with palms joined in reverence:

45. "O Lord, the vow of the four months has been taken up (by me) by your favour. O Keśava, let it be accomplished without obstacles through your grace.

46. If I were to die when this vow is yet incomplete, O Adhokṣaja, even then let it be complete by your favour."

47. After praying thus to the Lord of Devas the man who is observing the vow should strictly adhere to the rites mentioned before and pass the four months with his mind dedicated to Viṣṇu.

48-53. At the end of every month he should perform Pāraṇa (formal conclusion of the austerities) for the pleasure of Kṛṣṇa. The devotee should feed Brāhmaṇas with sweet sumptuous food after worshipping the Lord of the universe.

If one is incapable (of doing it every month), he should conclude the excellent holy rite of Kārttikī day. On that day he should worship the Lord of the universe, abiding in the holy fire. Thereafter, he should propitiate prominent Brāhmaṇas with sweet milk-puddings and honour them with devotion as unto Viṣṇu. In accordance with his capacity he should give gold and garments.

A man not capable of the full (-timed) austerities should perform the austerities in the month of Kārttika as mentioned before.

There are various Vratas[1] (austerities) of Viṣṇu such as *Kṛcchra, Cāndrāyaṇa* etc. One who passes (the month) subsisting on milk only or vegetables (greens) only shall enjoy extensive worldly pleasures and then attain salvation.

54. If the vratī (vower) is incapable of even this austerity, he should observe the excellent vow of Bhīṣma-Pañcaka to propitiate the Lord of Devas. He shall sustain himself with forest products (take fruits, roots etc. naturally produced not cultivated, but no cooked food).

55. This *Vrata* is said to be conducive to the delight of the Lord. It supresses all sins. It yields the attainment of the world of Viṣṇu as its fruit. It is conducive to longevity, reputation and wealth. It accomplishes all desired things.

56-58. O sages, this secret has been disclosed to you. Listen to another. Know that these and many other Vratas are fruitless in the case of those devoid of devotion to the Lord.

One attains all the benefits by devotion to Viṣṇu alone—the benefit of great sacrifices, the excellent benefit of (pilgrimage to) Tīrthas, charitable gifts and all penances of the Sāttvika type.

59-60. Those noble souls who witness the excellent festival of retirement to bed (of the Lord) do not rest in the womb of any mother.

Those who sponsor the great festival, should make a promise of taking up this *Vrata* in front of the Lord at the conclusion of the festival. After performing the rite of Pāraṇa sufficiently well they are honoured in the world of Brahmā.

---

1. Observances such as *Kṛcchra, Cāndrāyaṇa* and others. *Kṛcchra* is of different types (for details vide HD IV 132-133). In Cāndrāyaṇa morsels of food are to be increased and decreased as per waxing and waning of the moon. (Hence the name *Cāndrāyaṇa.*) In this observance one morsel of food is to be eaten on first day of the bright half, two morsels on the second day and so on till fifteen morsels are to be consumed on the full-moon day. On the first day of the dark half fourteen morsels are to be eaten reducing the quantity by one morsel everyday and ending in complete fast on the new-moon day. (For details see HD IV 135-136.)

CHAPTER THIRTYSEVEN

King Śveta Attains Salvation

Jaimini said:

1-7. Henceforth I shall describe (the rites to be performed during) the excellent Dakṣiṇāyana (transit of the Sun to the South). The period of time extending to twenty Kalās just before the transit of the Sun is the most auspicious time for the performance of holy rites by men devoted to duties.

As in the case of the (ceremonial) going to bed of the Lord, O Brāhmaṇas, the devotee should bathe the Lord with *Pañcāmṛta*. He should smear the entire body of the Lord with agallochum, camphor and sandal-paste. He should worship the great Lord with sweet scents, wreaths, ornaments, charming garments, lamps and different kinds of foodstuffs and offerings. He should wave a lighted camphor near the face of Hari. Then the Lord should be duly saluted after the offering of blades of Dūrvā and raw rice grains following the Nīrājana rite of waving the lights. Women should sing auspicious songs and shout *Hulā-Hulā*.[1] They should dance too.

Janārdana will give hundred times the merit of the worship to a person who witnesses Puruṣottama having been worshipped and being worshipped. Those who see the Lord of Śrī being worshipped during the Southern Transit (of the Sun) get rid of all their sins and go to the world of Viṣṇu.

8. Whether the festival of procession of Hari is celebrated on a small scale or on a grand scale, it always bestows salvation. The Lord seen on the different days is certainly the bestower of salvation.

9. It is to inspire faith in the ignorant, O Brāhmaṇas, that these festivals of procession have been declared by the merciful Viṣṇu. They dispel the sins of sinners.

10-11. Those who regard that merit is (always) created by undergoing strains are base persons.

In order to prepare the food-offering for the Lord of Lakṣmī the kitchen should be consecrated well. After kindling the Vaiṣṇava sacred

1. This inarticulate sound is uttered by women in Orissa on joyous occasions—an evidence of the author of this section being an Orissan.

fire, the excellent *Caru* should be prepared. It should be made the means of cooking the Vaiśvadeva[1] oblation unto the Lord.

12-17. The preceptor devoted to the holy rites prescribed in Śrutis and Smṛtis, and employed by the king, should with great (mental and physical) purity, perform the Homas in the sacred fire to Brahmā, the Lord of house-site, the Lord of the subjects and Viṣṇu, the maker of the universe.

The preceptor employed by the king should be a scrupulous performer of the religious rites prescribed in Śrutis and Smrtis.

Thereafter, Bali (oblations) should be offered and offerings should be made as follows:

To the Dvārapālas[2] (Caṇḍa and) Pracaṇḍa in the North-East; to the Kṣetrapāla, Virūpa and the Lord of birds in the South: to Durgā and Sarasvatī in the South-West. As per injunctions the offering of oblations to Mahālakṣmī and Mahendra is made in the Eastern Quarter. The offering of oblation to the attendants of Viṣṇu and to the Lord of Paśus (i.e. Śiva) shall be made in the North. (The Bali should be offered) to Nārada in the West; to the Fire-god in the South-East, to Viśvasākṣin (witness unto the universe, the Wind-god?) in the North-West; to the Wind-gods in the forms of the five vital airs and to the maker of the universe in the middle. In every rite of offering the oblations water should be offered in the beginning and in the end.

18. After offering the oblations the excellent cooking should be conducted in that fire to prepare *Caru* to be offered in the worship of the Lord in all the three *Sandhyās* (dawn, noon and dusk).

19. The different foodstuffs form part of the consecration of the *Caru*. The king should not engage brilliant persons of the (first) three castes.[3]

20. He should engage clean Śūdras of noble birth or persons of the labour class.[4] This is the common practice. It is certainly Śrī herself who cooks.

21-27a. Nārāyaṇa in his embodied form always eats what is cooked

1. It is an offering to all deities made by presenting oblations to Fire (before one takes one's meals).

2. Caṇḍa and Pracaṇḍa are the two doorkeepers of Viṣṇu. Hence the dual, *pracaṇḍābhyām* as Caṇḍa is understood in the compound.

3. The existing reading *traivarṇiko* obviously having no relevance should be corrected as *traivarṇikān* to give this meaning.

4. The Purāṇa thus testifies to the Śabara origin of Jagannātha cult, though modern scholars from Cunningham onwards attribute it to the Buddhist influence.

by her. Indeed that *Naivedya* is nectar itself. By keeping it on the head one can dispel all sins. If it is eaten, it destroys great sins arising from drinking liquor etc. If it is inhaled, it destroys mental sins; if it is looked at, it dispels sins arising from sight; if it is tasted, it dispels auditory sins; if it is touched, it destroys sins committed through touching as well as those arising from false utterances: by applying it over the body, it dispels all bodily sins: it burns them, there is no doubt about it. Indeed, the food offered to Hari is exceedingly sacred. If a person uses it in the rites of Manes as well as deities, Pitṛs and Suras are pleased with him. They go to the world of the Slayer of Madhu. Among *Havyas* and *Kavyas*,[1] O Brāhmaṇas, there is nothing more pure and sacred. Heaven-dwellers assume the forms of men and eat it. In it there is great attachment of the Discus-bearing Lord of Devas.

The Story of King Śveta

27b-32. Formerly there was a great king named Śveta in Tretāyuga. He observed all holy vows and had great devotion to Puruṣottama.

Everyday he joyously got ready different kinds of food-offerings of the same type as the food-offerings got prepared by Indradyumna. There were many kinds of foodstuffs, well-prepared dishes of all the six tastes. There were wonderful varieties of wreaths, sweet scents and unguents. There were songs and instrumental music and dances of divine charm. On different occasions Hari was given royal reception and service. Everything involved great expenditure and strain and reflected devotional feelings. The food-offerings of different varieties mentioned in the sacred writings of Vaiṣṇavas were got prepared by that king (who was like) the sun for the lotuses (in the form) of learned men.

33. Once, on a certain day in the morning, the king went (to the shrine) to see Hari at the time of worship. He saw the Lord being worshipped.

34. After bowing down to the Lord of Devas, the excellent king stood near the entrance to the Mansion (Temple) joyously, with palms joined in reverence.

35-42. On seeing the excellent offerings got prepared by himself as well as a thousand gifts arranged in front of Hari, the king thought thus in his mind and he fell into a reverie. He mused thus: 'Does Hari

---

1. *Havyas* and *Kavyas*: Offerings to gods are *Havyas* and to Pitṛs are called *Kavyas*.

accept the food-offerings prepared by human beings? The external Yāga (i.e. gross sacrifice) defiled by sentimental feelings is certainly not for the joy of that Hari who cannot be adequately adored even by Devas by means of divine offerings and whom men of restraint and holy rites worship by means of mental offerings.' Even as he thought thus, the king saw the Lord seated in the divine seat eating the food and drinking the beverage served by Śrī. She was adorned with a divine garland. She had divine silken robes and unguents. She seemed to fill the abode of Suras with the charming tinkling sound of her anklets set with very valuable gems. She was serving the juices eagerly with a gold ladle. The Lord was surrounded by many persons of similar personal features. They were also taking food. On witnessing that mysterious scene, the king thought himself contented and blessed. He opened his eyes. Then also he saw what he saw before. From that time onwards the king obtained great delight.

43-44. He regularly ate only what was first offered to the Lord. He performed holy rites and very great penances. For the destruction of untimely death in his kingdom and for the salvation of those who died, he used to recite the Mantrarāja. At the end of a hundred years he saw Narasiṁha, the wish-yielding Kalpa-tree to those who resort to him, the Lord who dispelled sins.

45. The Yogic lotus-posture was his abode. Śrī was stationed on his left. All his limbs were adorned with divine objects. His body was as pure as crystal.

46. He was being eulogized by Devas as well as Siddhas and liberated souls. His face was beaming with smiles. He (the king) was confused, surprised and frightened. With words choked with excessive delight he blurted out, "O Lord, be pleased." Uttering these words he fell on the ground.

47. On seeing the sinless king who was emaciated on account of penance and was bowing down, Narasiṁha, the Lord affectionate to his devotees, spoke thus:

Śrī Bhagavān said:

48. Get up, O dear one, know that I am the Lord delighted with your devotion. There is nothing which cannot be obtained when I am pleased. Hence let it be prayed for by you.

49. On hearing these words of the Lord the king got up. With palms joined in reverence he humbly spoke these words to Janārdana.

Śveta said:

50-51. O Lord, if you are pleased with me, it is a rare blessing. I shall attain your *Sārūpya* ('identity of form') and stand in your presence. As long as I continue to be a king, let no one in my kingdom meet untimely death. In case the death is timely, let him attain salvation.

52-57. On hearing it, the Lord said to the excellent king Śveta: "O Śveta, your desire shall be fulfilled. Get up and be on my right side. You will enjoy your kingdom with all its luxuries for a thousand years. Through the (consumption of) remnants of the offerings unto me your remaining sins too shall be destroyed. With a mind devoid of impurities you will attain *Sāyujya* with me.

Between the Banyan tree and the ocean is the very rare spot of (i.e. affording) Salvation. Facing me, the first incarnation of Viṣṇu in the form of Fish, stay there with a body as pure as crystal. You will be well-known in the terrestrial world by the name Śvetamādhava.

If human beings, lower animals or even insects were to cast off their lives in between you two, they shall certainly attain salvation.

58-59. Even the immortal Devas wish to die there. How much more would human beings! To the north of you there is a lake that dispels sins. The devotee should take bath there and sip its water. If a person becomes purified by seeing both of you on its southern shore and casts off his life, he becomes liberated.

60. All (the area) round this holy place, every bit of it, yields salvation. In order to inspire faith in the ignorant, the important spot is said to be efficacious.

61. All the people in your kingdom who eat my *Nirmālya*[1] (remnants of offerings) will never have untimely death."

1. Nowadays it means the dry boiled rice which is offered to Lord Jagannātha in the preceding day. This dry rice is also regarded as sacred *Mahāprasāda*.

CHAPTER THIRTYEIGHT

The Great Efficacy of Nirmālya etc.

Jaimini said:

1. After granting the boon thus to King Śveta formerly, O Brāhmaṇas, Hari who was stationed within the Mansion, vanished.

2-3. Śrī, the cause of creation, sustenance and annihilation of all the worlds, the matchless Śakti of Viṣṇu, is the person serving the nectar-like well-cooked food and Lord Nārāyaṇa consumes it. Enjoyment of its remnants and leavings is the cause of the destruction of all sins.

4. There is no object on the surface of the earth which is so meritorious as that. It does not become defiled due to contact with sinful persons.

5-8. Due to the presence of Padmā (Lakṣmī) all of them are proclaimed to be pure and clean. That *Nirmālya*, present in the abode of Viṣṇu, does not become defiled even if fallen persons etc. touch it. It is (pure) like Viṣṇu himself. Widows who perform holy rites, people of all castes and stages of life, the initiated performers of Agnihotra sancrifices, the poor, the miserly, a householder or a master, natives or foreigners—all those who come there, become sanctified by eating. In the matter of consuming the *Nirmālya* of Viṣṇu no one should display any false prestige.

9. Whether due to devotion, or covetousness or out of curiosity or as a means to satisfy hunger, if the Nirmālya is eaten to the full, it dispels all the sins.

10. It mitigates all ailments; it increases sons and grandsons; it dispels poverty. It is excellent and splendid, bestowing learning, longevity and prosperity.

11-15. The partiality of Viṣṇu of unmeasured splendour is present therein. Those who find fault with that nectar-like *Nirmālya* are fools vainly considering themselves learned. The Lord himself remains ready to punish them. He never brooks the guilty. Indeed calamity certainly befalls those people against whom he raises his rod of punishment. They will be cooked in the terrible hell Kuṁbhīpāka.

No sale or purchase (of the *Nirmālya*) is to be encouraged, O Brāhmaṇas. If a person takes this vow, 'I will never eat anything before eating the *Nirmālya* of the Lord of the universe' and eats it everyday keeping up his vow, that man shall get rid of all sins. His mind shall become pure.

There is no doubt that he will go to the pure region of Viṣṇu in due course.

16. Even if (Nirmālya) is kept for a long time, even if it is dry, even if it is taken to far-off places, it can be eaten as it is. All these are destructive of sins.

17. If that food-offering of the Lord drops down from a dog's mouth while it was being carried off, the same may be eaten even by a Brāhmaṇa. What need one say of others!

18. As soon as it is received, it must be eaten by a person whether he is observing a fast or not, whether he is bodily pure or not, even if he does not follow the code of good conduct, or is mentally sinful. No doubt need be entertained in this respect.

19. The Naivedya offering of the Lord of the universe and the water of Gaṅgā —both these are equal. If they are looked at, one obtains heaven etc.; if they are partaken of, all the sins are destroyed.

20. What is cooked by the Mother of the universe in the well-consecrated Vaiṣṇava fire, the Discus-bearing Lord eats everyday in all the Yugas, Manvantaras etc.

21. In the whole of the earth consisting of the seven continents there is no presence of Hari like it is on Nīla mountain, which he offers under the pretext of a human act.

22. The Supreme Brahman in the form of a wooden idol perceptible to everyone shines (here), O sages. It is neither seen nor heard anywhere (else).

23-28. Unto that Brahman in the form of *Pravṛtti* (Activity), Śrī, Śakti in the form of *Pravṛtti* prepares and serves the Havi. The Lord of the universe eats it. The remnants thereof can dispel sins. What is surprising in this, O Brāhmaṇas, if it is spoken as the cause of salvation?

Persons deficient in merit do not believe in it. This is glorified in the Yugas when the Vedas and conventional norms hold sway.

No one knows its greatness, particularly in Kaliyuga. In the terrible Kaliyuga,[1] opposition to Dharma (righteous conduct) has three-fourths share. Dharma has only a single foot left. It moves about only in some rare places because it is afraid (of Kali). All the people are inherently

1. Most of the Purāṇas draw a gloomy picture of Kali Age. See Mbh, Vana, Chs. 188, 190; BrP Chs. 229-230; MtP 144.32-47; BhP XII Chs. 1, 2; VP VI.1. Most probably that was the state of society when Purāṇas came to be written. The present state of society is however no better.

given to falsehood. They are hypocrites and knavish. Generally they are averse to virtue. They are addicted to eating and sex. They never meditate, perform penance or observe a holy rite.

29. All people are mostly unrighteous, violent and excessively greedy and rapacious. They themselves will not do anything. They are satisfied when they slander others.

30. Due to their mean-minded interests they put obstacles in other people's activities.

31. They neglect beautiful women lawfully married to them in their household. They are of brutish activities seeking contact with other people's wives of ignoble and censurable activities.

32-37. There is no Agnihotra or other holy rite anywhere. It has become a means of livelihood to Brāhmaṇas to whom it should have been a means of attaining the other world.

A holy rite does not yield (the desired) benefit if it is performed by one who has learnt the Vedas without the requisite holy rites, by means of wealth acquired unjustly and fraudulently.

Generally in Kaliyuga kings are averse to their duty of protecting their subjects. They are ever eager to exact taxes. They are extremely sinful and behave like thieves.

All the people indulge in mixing up different castes (through intermarriage) in Kaliyuga mostly behaving like Śūdras. Kings themselves become robbers and Śūdras minions of kings.

The holy rites laid down by Śrutis and Smṛtis are not properly performed in the prescribed way in the fourth Yuga, O Brāhmaṇas. They are not (hence) capable of yielding good results in the other world.

(In Kaliyuga) the virtue of practising charity is the highest and no other virtue is considered praiseworthy. One should wish for the welfare of the twice-born by words, thoughts and deeds.

38-41. Thus spake the Lord: "The Brāhmaṇa is my body. I am pleased with that person with whom Brāhmaṇas are pleased."

One should behave equally towards both, Brāhmaṇas and Janārdana. The words that Brāhmaṇas utter, are what the Lord himself would utter.

Whatever may be the mode of his living, Brāhmaṇa is the preceptor of all castes. That Lord too, the Lord of Devas himself, is fond of Brāhmaṇas.

Janārdana incarnates always for the sake of Brāhmaṇas. In every Yuga, he punishes the wicked ones for the sake of protecting them.

42. At the beginning of the creation the Four-faced Lord created

Brāhmaṇas. Afterwards all the other castes were severally born in their families.

43. Hence, in Kaliyuga, these two are the goal and resort unto all, viz. Brāhmaṇa and Viṣṇu. Hari is the goal unto Brāhmaṇas.

44. Here Hari alone is the goal unto all, when Kaliyuga approaches. He is remembered and glorified in Śālagrāma and other holy spots.

45. In that holy spot on Nīla mountain which is like the physical body of the Kṣetrajña, the Lord who has assumed physical body under the guise of the wooden idol, is the soul immanent in all beings.

46. For the destruction of the evils of Kali, he is usually the bestower of salvation on men of evil actions who pay a visit, offer eulogy and partake of the leavings of his food.

47. A man whose body is smeared with the leavings of the food of the Lord of Suras, whose food is the same (leavings of Lord's food) and whose mind is directed towards that, is never polluted by sins.

48. Food-offering is made to other idols too of the Lord and it is what purifies. But the leaving of the food is what liberates.

49-51. It is only here that the Lord eats (food himself); in other places he glances with his eye. Formerly the Lord was requested by Yogins who surrounded (him), "We shall overcome your Māyā by enjoying the Nirmālya and leavings of food."

He is the bestower of lilberation easily (without any strain) on persons whose sense-organs have become calm.

He sports with Śrī through the activities of sitting, lying down, partaking of food etc. together. Let this be remembered that the activity of the Lord in this respect is what the purport of the Veda is.

52. The Lord never transgresses the Vedas. Indeed his incarnation in every Yuga is for the sake of protecting the Vedas.

53. How can the Lord who is the authority, act contrary to that? If he were to act against it, the whole universe will be (behaving) like that.

54-55. Indeed it is on account of its regular practice (by people) that the Veda has become the authority.

Formerly an excellent Brāhmaṇa (named Śāṇḍilya) hailing from Madhyadeśa (Central Region) came here.[1] He was completely free from impurities on account of his decent and decorous behaviour. He had

1. This story (vv 55-100) illustrates the great sanctity and efficacy of the Lord's Naivedya.

mastered the topics of all scriptural texts. He was always calm. He always got his sense-organs under control in thought, words and deeds. He was a householder.

56. In accordance with the procedure regarding the rites to be performed at the (particular) Tīrthas, he worshipped the Lord. He maintained the sacred fires. He spent here three days engaged in worshipping Viṣṇu with great purity.

57. Since there is the injunction in the scriptural texts that the remnants of Yajña should be partaken of by householders, he did not take the remnants of the offering unto the Lord suspecting that it must have been cooked by another (inferior person).

58. 'It should be consecrated by Devas; (otherwise) how can it be suitable unto the Lord? Because it is unsuitable, the Naivedya should certainly be unacceptable,' He thought.

59. When the Naivedya was not accepted with the Brāhmaṇa, all his attendants too did not eat the Naivedya (food-offering).

60. Thereupon, he became afflicted with diseases. His body ached and he became excessively distressed. He was dumb-founded along with his family because he had offended the Lord.

61. He mentally thought, 'How is it that without any cause the whole family has been afflicted with this pain (as if) breaking all the limbs?'

62-63. He went on thinking thus, when at the end of three days an idea struck him: 'An affliction and ailment like this cannot befall everyone at once. In what way have we offended this Lord Puruṣottama? It cannot be deliberate. What then is the cause of this sickness of mine?'

64. After deliberating thus frequently, he meditated on Lord Nārāyaṇa. At the end of the meditation (that Brāhmaṇa) the expounder of the real meaning of scriptural passages eulogized (the Lord).

Śāṇḍilya said:

65. All the fourteen lores, the bases for the determination of virtue, are your utterances which have come out of your lotus-like mouth.

66. This is the conclusion of all the scriptural texts that one should practise Dharma only according to them. It is for the sake of the protection of that Dharma that you incarnate in every Yuga.

67-73. One who transgresses that (Dharma) is certainly one who offends you. O Lord of the chiefs of Devas, I never transgress the code of conduct (of Dharmaśāstra) mentally, verbally and physically. Even in regard to wealth and love I do not transgress Dharmaśāstra.

O Lord, I have come here to burn down the mass of sins accumulated in the course of many thousands of births by means of the forest fire of your sight.

What was the offence committed by me, adhering, O Lord, to your own path prescribed in scripture? A dreadful ailment with no apparent cause afflicts all the limbs.

Whether knowingly or unknowingly, if any offence has been committed by me against the lotus-like feet of yours, O Lord, O ocean of mercy, forgive it. The ground alone is the support to those who have slipped in their steps on the ground.

You alone are the refuge, O Lord, to those who commit offences against you. You alone do forgive my sin arising from an offence against you.

A wound (eruption etc.) caused by (bodily) heat is cured by applying fire (remedial heat). So, O Lord, subdue by means of your graceful glance from the corner of your eyes, this deplorable condition arising from the seeds of sins. The evil action has begun to bear fruit. Your benign glance is the sole cause of salvation. I have fallen into the ocean of grief. Redeem me, O Lord of the universe.

74-77. How can a man who has come within the range of your vision be in a pitiable state? O ocean of natural mercifulness, one who has come within the range of your vision is always immersed in the ocean of bliss. He does not bemoan nor does he yearn.

My fortune is by no means meagre. I have seen you with my own eyes. If there is any obstacle in my getting salvation, it is certainly terrifying. So be pleased, O Lord of the universe, towards me, your attendant though a habitual offender. In view of our relationship as Master and Servant, do forgive my offence.

At the end of this prayer, the affliction of his body immediately disappeared.

78-80. He saw Govinda, Nṛsiṁha fond of his devotees. He was seated on a divine throne. He was adorned with divine ornaments. He was found taking up in his lotus-like hand the excellent cooked food offered by Śrī and dropping the remnants of the mouthful frequently into the (various) vessels.

Lakṣmī went on placing in his hand (various food items) with graceful smiles and coquettish glances. Whatever was handed over to him he went on eating without any hurry.

81. On seeing this, Śāṇḍilya, the excellent Brāhmaṇa, became surprised. He remembered his own offence in not taking up the Naivedya. (He eulogized thus):

82. "What a great difference! I am a knower of a limited things while you are the storehouse of all knowledge and the creator of the principles of *Mahat, Ahaṁkāra*! (There cannot be any comparison between us.)

83. O Īśa, how can those who are deluded by your Māyā know your unbridled, indefinable wish manifesting itself in the form of creation and annihilation?"

84. As he eulogized thus, the Lord, Nṛsiṁha, scattered the remnants of the morsels all over the body of the excellent Brāhmaṇa with his own hand that was *Ucchiṣṭa* (not washed after eating anything).

85-86. When he was sprinkled with them which he felt comparable to nectar, the Brāhmaṇa joyously shone with divine body. He was as lustrous as a sage who is a living-liberated soul.

"Only devotees know the greatness of devotion. A barren woman never experiences the severity of labour pain."

87. Saying this he took up the leavings of the Supreme Soul from his body and ate them. The eminent Brāhmaṇa well-versed in the Vedas considered himself one who has attained his goal in life.

88-90. 'Ordinary code of conduct (Dharma) is not much (highly) thought of in this holy spot. This is the greatest Dharma which has been proclaimed by the Lord himself. Dharma has its source of origin in the conduct of life. Acyuta is the Lord of Dharma.' Thinking thus, the Brāhmaṇa himself took a handful of the remaining food to the members of his family. At that time his reverie broke. He got up from his sleep. With a great surprise he realized that it was a dream.

91. He thought, 'This alone is my offence that I slighted the Lord without knowing the wonderful greatness of taking in the Naivedya.

92. (*Defective verse*) The lotus-like feet of the Lord are the eighteeen and fourteen Cosmic Eggs. The devotee who washes His feet with the liquid in the form of Dharma actually sanctifies himself with that water.

93. In this holy spot it is a great mystery that the Lord eats what has been cooked by human beings, the Lord whom Śakra and others worship with excellent divine items of food offerings.'

94. Wondering thus, O Brāhmaṇas, he took the Naivedya acquired in dream and respectfully sanctified his family through it.

95. Thereupon all of them became free from ailments. They be-

came delighted in their minds. Their power of expression became excellent. They considered it their rebirth. They praised the excellent holy place:

96. "In the whole of the earth consisting of seven continents there is no other holy spot like this, where by giving the leavings of his food the Lord liberates men from their sins.

97. This sacred place has the same greatness as Puruṣottama. It is extremely rare since heavenly and worldly pleasures as well as salvation come within the reach (of the devotee).

98. Those who are distressed in the forest of worldly existence and fortunately come here, become completely satisfied by different kinds of enjoyment. They will easily attain the path of salvation."

99. Excessively delighted, they began to talk like this to one another. They fed one another with the remnants of food offered unto the Lord to their heart's content.

100. Thereupon, all of them became free from impurities, O Brāhmaṇas. They had the lustre of the midday Sun. They shone like gods, free from sins and devoid of fever.

101. O excellent Brāhmaṇas, the efficacy of tasting the Naivedya has been recounted to you. Even by hearing thus the greatest of sinners is liberated from a great sin.

102. We are not competent to recount the full benefit of taking the Nirmālya. It is worn by the body which is directly the form of Brahman.

103. Flowers, sandal paste, wreaths of flowers etc. which are being worn by the limbs (of the Lord), when taken away from the idol at the proper time, are called Nirmālya.[1]

104. If the Nirmālya is worn on the head and if (the unguent etc.) is smeared on the body, it yields the benefit of the holy bath in all the three and a half crores of Tīrthas. If it is eaten, it is destructive of all the sins including that of defiling the preceptor's bed.

105. This idol of Viṣṇu is to be smeared with unguents. The following unguent is much better than others. Sandalwood, agallochum, camphor, musk, saffron etc. are its constituents.

106. Indradyumna got a special unguent ready by means of sandalwood and black aloe-wood ground into a paste and applied it to the body of Vāsudeva.

---

1. This verse explains the term *Nirmālya* and the articles to which it is applied.

107. Everyday it was applied, O excellent Brāhmaṇas, and it was removed at the end of the year. When the unguents become devoid of stickiness their sight is not praiseworthy.

108. If the unguent were to fall in the middle (of the year) it should be made into a paste once again and applied. Other types of unguents are not recommended. This alone is approved for the limbs of Viṣṇu.

109. Formerly a prince of confused mind saw Viṣṇu wet in body with sandal paste. The prince coveted it due to its fragrance.

110. The officer engaged there wanted to please him. He peeled off the unguent from the Lord's body (idol) and gave it to the prince who applied it to his chest.

111. That portion of his body became afflicted with white leprosy immediately. The officer who gave him the unguent contracted leprosy on his hand.

112. Hence it is laid down that the unguent that has alreay been (on the body of the Lord) for a year is the most meritorious. It is the most important of the Nirmālyas. If it is inhaled it destroys sins.

113. Formerly there was a Daitya named Damanaka.[1] He had become very powerful due to Māyā. He harassed people. He could move through the waters of ocean.

114. The Lord too could wield Māyā. At the request of Brahmā the Lord took up the incarnation of Fish and entered the ocean.

115. He searched for and found (the demon). He dragged him to the shore and thrashed him on the surface of the earth. The excellent Dānava fell on the fourteenth day in the bright half of the month of Madhu (i.e. Caitra).

116. By the contact of the hands of the Lord he became a fragrant grass of the same name, i.e. *Damanaka* (Artemisia indica). The Lord accepted it with a surprised mind.

117. He made a garland of it and wore it on his chest along with the garland of sylvan flowers. He thought that its fragrance should stay as long as the object exists.

118. Its fragrance excels the fragrance of all the flowers. Its colour also became very splendid like that of the body of the Lord.

119. A garland made of this is extremely conducive to the pleasure of the Lord. Even if it becomes dry, even after the lapse of a long time, it never becomes defiled.

1. The legend of Damanaka is given to explain why this fragrant grass (Artemisia indica) is worn by the Lord on the 14th day of the bright half of Caitra. In Maharashtra Damanaka is used for worshipping Śiva on this day.

120. If any person wreathes a fine garland of it and offers it to the Enemy of Damanaka, he will give great pleasure to Viṣṇu. It bestows salvation.

121. He who devoutly wears the garland after removing it from the body (of the Lord), certainly attains the merit of a thousand horse-sacrifices.

122. If a person takes away the garland of holy basil leaves from the idol of Viṣṇu and wears it over his head, round the neck or on the chest, he acquires without any strain the merit of as many horse-sacrifices (as there are leaves therein).

123. If a person eats the leaves of Tulasī Nirmālya of Hari, he is honoured in the world of Viṣṇu for as many thousands of births as they (the leaves) are.

124. If a person eats the Naivedya (cooked rice mixed with Tulasī leaves), he attains the merit equal to the drinking of Soma juice for every such morsel.

125. One who eats it throughout one's life shall certainly attain salvation.

126. The remnants of *Arghya* etc. of Viṣṇu, the *Ācamana* water, the *Pādodaka* (water with which the feet are washed), *Snānavāri* (water after the bath is performed)—all are destructive of sins.

127. They yield the merit of ablution in all the Tīrthas; they are destructive of evil spirits; they destroy ill-luck, sins and demons; they dispel goblins, vampires etc.

128. They are excellent dispellers of the fault (evil) of touching impure things like dead body etc.; they bestow the benefit of all initiations and holy rites; they increase prosperity.

129. They prevent premature death; they destroy the collection of ailments; they destroy the mass of sins of consuming liquor, cow's meat etc.

130. If a man sprinkles these waters on his body and then hears of sūtaka (child birth), he is not polluted thereby. He still remains a person having the right to perform all holy rites.

131. If one takes a vow to take all these or anyone throughout one's life and takes it in smaller or greater quantities, one shall become liberated due to Viṣṇu's favour.

132. Thus the Lord stays there with a desire to bless the worlds. He sports with Śrī. He is the Lord who liberates spontaneously.

133. In this excellent holy spot named Puruṣottama, the Lord is the bestower of salvation through the following: the Nirmālya, the water

with which the feet are washed, the food offering, charitable gifts, seeing the Lord, bowing down to him, worship and making present.

CHAPTER THIRTYNINE[1]

Festivals to be Celebrated during Cāturmāsya

The sages requested:

1-2. O sage, the greatness of the Lord of the universe has been heard from you; that of Nirmālya etc. also was heard in the proper order. We wish to hear, O Brāhmaṇa, the benefits of other Yātrās (festivals) too. To us who (wish to) listen to it, relate it accurately as you had originally intended.

Jaimini replied:

3. Puruṣottama exists for the welfare of all the worlds in every respect, and (for the purpose) produces different Guṇas and activities in various forms.

4-7. For the sport in various graceful forms, the Lord who is identical with the universe, becomes diverse souls.

Without Ahaṁkāra (Ego) there is no (experience of) the fruits of Karmas, O excellent Brāhmaṇas.

It is through the Ego that the people are bound in the prison called the worldly existence. Man does everything after being equipped with Buddhi (Intellect) and Ahaṁkāra (Ego). In accordance with the Guṇa (quality) of the Intellect, he obtains the benefit, auspicious or otherwise. Intellect is of three kinds according to the Guṇas.

Those who are *Sāttvikas* are good men shunning the fruits (of the Karmas). They perform holy rites for propitiating the Lord. They are desirous of liberation.

8. People of the *Rājasa* type perform various rites with a feeling of rivalry with others, or for the sake of reputation, or for fruits. They

1. This chapter deals with the following festivals:
   i) Pārśva-paryāyaṇa (Turning over the side) on the 11th day of the bright half of Bhādrapada.
   ii) Utthāpana (Waking up) on the 11th day of the bright half of Kārttika.

spend much wealth over it and strain themselves much.

9. People of the *Tāmasa* type are blind followers of others. They are devoted solely to perceptible results. They want benefits following from their acts. Thus they perform various rites.

10. When meditated, seen or remembered, the Lord of the universe is always a bestower of salvation on *Sāttvika* people. He is the sanctifier of everyone. There is no doubt about this.

11. The *Rājasas* and the *Tāmasas* are foolish souls desirous of results. They think that performance of rites etc. gives benefits.

12. Many of them, O Brāhmaṇas, join together and perform a small ceremony. To them that action or rite which involves great strain, pain and misery is the bestower of benefits.

13. In order to uplift them, for the purpose of convincing the vicious ones, O Brāhmaṇas, one should celebrate different kinds of Yātrās (festivals, processions etc.) every year.

14. The holy ablution on the birthday and the festival of the Great Altar have been recounted. These two great *Yātrās* are destructive of the sins by (their) glorification.

15. The sight of the Lord facing the South and the festival of retiring to bed are destructive of all sins. They are the festivals to be celebrated during the period of the Southern Transit.

16. Henceforth, I shall describe the festival of the turning on the other side of the Lord of the universe, who is lying down, the Lord who turns even the Yugas.

17-19. On the eleventh day in the bright half of the month of Bhādrapada (August-September), the devotee slowly goes towards the door of the bedchamber of Viṣṇu. He enters and bows down to the Lord of the universe, who is happily asleep on the couch. He should go to him slowly and cover him up (with a sheet) and worship with various offerings. Bowing down to his feet with devotion, he should eulogize with secret (mystical) Upaniṣad passages. He should repeat the following Mantra and make the Lord sleep facing the North:

20-24. "O Lord of Devas, O Lord of the universe, O Lord who turns the Kalpas! This universe consisting of mobile and immobile beings is turned by you, by your will and activities such as keeping awake, dreaming and sleeping. It is for the welfare of the universe that you are asleep. Turn over on the other side.

This is the time for the change, for the protection of the universe. At your bidding this Śakra is eagerly standing by your flagstaff to see your lotus-like feet. He is showering water through the clouds. He floods the surface of the earth as a means for the protection of the subjects."

The devotee should pray to the Lord of Devas repeatedly twice like this and propitiate him. He should fan the Lord with fans and chowries and serve him.

25-27. He should smear all the limbs of the Lord with sweet-smelling sandal paste. He should offer as Naivedya the following things: Tasty sugarcane juice and its products, milk products, palatable barley preparations, different kinds of fruits, tasty pickles, other sidedishes, sweet pies prepared in ghee, milk puddings of various types, ripe arecanuts and well-dressed betel leaves. These should be offered at the door of the bedchamber of the Lord. The devotee should offer these slowly and with great devotion.

28-30.On that day, if the devotee meditates on the form of Hari, it will yield great merit. Whatever is done for the sake of the Lord, such as holy bath, charitable gift, Japa, Homa, penance, keeping awake, fasting and other observances, shall have everlasting benefit. At the conclusion of the *Vrata*, Brāhmaṇas should be propitiated. By performing this *Vrata* with all its ancillaries, one shall attain the world of Viṣṇu. Whatever he desires in the mind, he shall certainly obtain.

31. This festival recounted to you is *Pārśva Paryāyaṇa* (Turning on the other side). It bestows everlasting happiness on all the worlds without any difficulty.

32-36. Henceforth listen to the great festival of *Utthāpana* (waking up).

At the outset, the Lord of the universe is worshipped in the great festival named *Kaumudī* (Moonlight) by means of games of dice etc., flowers, garments, wreaths and unguents.

Then on a full-moon day during the night the devotee should worship Hari with great festivities by means of ground-flour cakes, coconuts and other articles of worship.

Then in the morning the devotee should declare his intention to perform the holy rite during the month of Kārttika. Till the eleventh day in the bright half of Kārttika, he should continue the *Vrata*. On that day he should awaken the Lord of the universe who is sound asleep. As before, he should perform the worship of the Sire of the universe at midnight. He should repeat the following Mantra joyfully and awaken the Lord gently:

37-42. "O Lord of the chiefs of Devas, O mass of refulgence, O Lord of the universe, look, all are sleeping due to your Māyā. Look at them with your eyes that take away the splendour of full-blown lotuses. This universe seen by you will attain the greatest sanctity. Then all the holy rites laid down in the Śrutis and Smṛtis can certainly be performed."

After awakening the Lord thus, the devotee should take him to the Dance-pavilion to the accompaniment of playing of flutes and lutes and other musical instruments, the eulogies of the heralds, bards and panegyrists, auspicious sounds, the sounds of conchshells, Kāhāla trumpets and Muraja drums, dances, songs and shouts of "Be victorious".

After anointing him with scented oil, he should bathe Puruṣottama with Pañcāmṛta, coconut juice and the juices of fruits. Thereafter, he should smear the Lord with perfumed embylic myrobalan and paste of barley.

43-48. He should rub the body (of the Lord) with powdered Tulasī and smear it with fragrant sandal-paste. Then the Lord should be bathed with waters rendered fragrant by means of flowers as well as by camphor. Waters should be sprinkled by means of Kuśa blades. The Lord should be then bathed with waters rendered fragrant by means of perfumes from bejewelled vessels.

Those who joyously see the Lord being bathed thus, wash off their dirt (sins) firmly fixed and acquired in the course of many births.

Thereafter, O Brāhmaṇas, the devotee should apply perfume on the chest of the Lord of the universe.

Then the entire body from head to foot should be smeared with saffron, agallochum, musk and camphor mixed with sandal-paste. These should be ground into a paste with waters mixed with tumpet flowers and the liquid extract of black aloe-wood. A garland of jasmine flowers should be put on the Lord and dusted with powdered camphor. After worshipping Viṣṇu with great offerings and services, the rite of Nīrājana should be performed. With palms joined in reverence the devotee should pray with greatest joy:

49-54. "This entire universe consisting of mobile and immobile beings has you alone for its refuge, O Lord. Sanctify it by means of your benign nectarine glances, O Sire of the universe."

He should spend the remaining part of the night by having shows, dances and songs. He who sees Lord Gadādhara who has got up from the bed, shall destroy the slumber of delusion and attain the peaceful enlightenment. Whatever other desires he may have in his heart of hearts, he shall attain all those desires.

He shall attain the merit of a thousand horse-sacrifices and even something more. He shall attain the merit of gifting away a crore of tawny-coloured cows, well adorned. He shall attain the greatest merit of taking the holy bath in all the Tīrthas. The *Pāraṇā* (concluding rites) of the vow of the four months should be performed on the Kārttikī day. (The devotee should give away) the idol of Dāmodara made of gold (a gold coin called) Niṣka or one made in accordance with one's capacity or one made of Śālagrāma stone.

55-58. Then the devotee with restrained self should worship the Discus, (another) form of the Lord. A separate excellent pavilion should be made and decorated or a part of the house may be decorated well with garlands, chowries and canopies. The floor and the walls should be well plastered and the pillars adorned with silk cloths of various colours.

He should fumigate with the incense of black aloe-wood the entire portion of the splendid house (or pavilion). In its middle he should draw the mystic diagram of Svastika-design with splendid colours. He should place an ivory cot within it. A silk mattress should be spread over it. The devotee should place Puruṣottama upon it.

59-62. The Lord should be in the form of Dāmodara with four arms and having the conch-shell and the lotus in his hand. He is to be depicted as embracing Lakṣmī with his left hand, Lakṣmī seated on a lotus and stationed on his chest. With his right hand he makes the gesture of granting boons to devotees.

His nose, forehead, eyes, pair of ears etc. are excellent. The Lord has a broad chest. He is endowed with every graceful and handsome features. He is charming with all kinds of ornaments. He has divine yellow garments.

Lakṣmī is depicted as having a lotus in her hand and offering betel leaves (to the Lord). After bathing the Lord with Pañcāmṛta the devotee should cover him up with two cloths.

63. He should worship him with offerings and services as elaborate as his affluence can allow. He should light copper lamps or earthen lamps with cow's ghee.

64. He should have a hundred light trees where the wicks burn with oil. He should worship there Brahmā and the celestial sages headed by Nārada.

65. He should worship Brāhmaṇas too, (the visible) forms of Dāmodara, and honour them with pairs of cloths, wreaths and scents, foodstuffs of various kinds and fruits as well.

66. The worship of Dāmodara here should be done in the manner in which worship involving ablution in the Tīrtharāja (the sea) is done.

67-73. He should worship Brahmā and others with the Mantra "TAD VIṢṆOḤ" ("THAT OF VIṢṆU") (RV I.22.20) etc. He should celebrate a great festival to the accompaniment of songs and instrumental music on flutes, lutes etc. There should be reading of the Purāṇas and keeping awake for the whole of the night. After the day has clearly dawned, he should perform the rites in the sacred fire. For the sake of general welfare he should perform Homas with *Samits* (sacred twigs), ghee and *Carus* while reciting the eight-syllabled Mantra (viz. *oṁ namo nārāyaṇāya*). To propitiate Śrī he should perform the Homas with fried grains mixed with honey and sacrificial twigs while reciting *Śrī Sūkta*.

In propitiating Brahmā and others, he should perform Homas one hundred and eight times. Eight of the oblations should be offered one by one with gingelly seeds. Thereafter he should offer Homas for Brahmā, Nārada, Dakṣa, Vasiṣṭha, Gautama, Sanatkumāra, Atri, Bharadvāja, Kaśyapa, Durvāsas, Agastya and Mahādeva. All these are well-known Vaiṣṇavas. They are the forms of Viṣṇu. There is no doubt about it.

By performing the worship of these Brāhmaṇas Viṣṇu can be pleased instantaneously. At the conclusion of Homa he should break his fast and make monetary gift to the preceptor.

74-79. He should give a cow also adorned with gold. With great devotion clothes and foodgrains also are to be given for the satisfaction of Vāsudeva. He should then feed Brāhmaṇas. Along with all offerings and services, a replica of Dāmodara should be given to the preceptor with the recitation of the following Mantra:

"Oṁ, Dāmodara, O Lord of the universe, the whole universe is identical with you. All these have you as their support. You are Dharma, the sanctifier of all. It is by your grace that the vow has been completed. Let it be perfect. Dāmodara is the giver. The Bull-emblemed Lord is the receiver. The Lord of the universe is being given. Let the preceptor of the universe be pleased with me."

Repeating this Mantra, he should give the excellent god to the preceptor. After concluding everything he should worship, eulogize and propitiate him with devotion.

If the preceptor is pleased, Mādhava becomes pleased. Thereafter, he should gift away the different articles to Brāhmaṇas.

80-81. Thereafter he should take his food along with the near and dear and kinsmen of good culture. After completing this holy rite in accordance with the injunctions, he should be richly endowed with the benefits as mentioned. He shall attain the world of Viṣṇu. There is no greater *Vrata* than this in the Śrutis, Smṛtis and Purāṇas.

82-85. Merely by performing this the man will feel that he has done his duty. Other *Vratas* are not as pleasing to Viṣṇu as this, O Brāhmaṇas. By performing this excellent holy rite one obtains that merit which one gets by giving thousands of vessels full of gingeily seeds, thousands of thousands of cows, a hundred deerskins, and ten thousand virgins, O Brāhmaṇas. He obtains the merit of taking holy baths in three and a half crores of Tīrthas. The man gets whatever he desires.

CHAPTER FORTY

*Prāvaraṇa (Covering) Festival of Nṛsiṁha**

Jaimini said:

1. By celebrating or by witnessing the *Prāvaraṇotsava* (the festival of covering the Lord) with devotion on the sixth day in the bright half of the month of Mārgaśīrṣa, one shall attain the world of Viṣṇu.

2. I shall describe the procedure for the same now, O sages. Listen to it. A devotee conversant with the holy rite should perform the preliminary consecration of the cloth on the night of the fifth day.

3-6. He should make a lotus design with eight petals in the pavilion in front of the Lord. He should worship the Guardians of the Quarters in the various directions. He should worship Kṣetrapāla, Gaṇādhipa, Caṇḍa and Pracaṇḍa outside the diagram in the four directions. He should place the pot in the middle and sprinkle it with the water from the cloth. He should recite the Mantra *dyutā nas tvā* etc. (*Taittirīya Saṁhitā* 5.5.9.4) and cover it with the divine cloth. In its middle he should place well-fumigated cloths twenty-one in number repeating the Vaiṣṇava Mantra. With another cloth he should carefully cover that. Touching it and remembering Puruṣottama, he should recite this Mantra:

7-9. "Viṣṇu is the immutable Lord who envelops the worlds with his refulgence. O Cloth, worn by him you stay in the residence of the Lord of the universe."

---

*This Festival takes place on the 6th day of the bright half of Mārgaśīrṣa. This is clothing the Lord for the winter.

He should make arrangements for its protection with the Mantra *indraghoṣas tvā* etc. (*Taittirīya Saṁhitā* 1.2.12.2).

He should worship it with sweet scents and flowers. Then he should worship the Lord. He should smear all types of unguents and spend the night in the midst of dances and songs.

10. Thereafter, at the time of dawn, about the time of morning junction, he should worship the Lord once again as before, with great concentration and purity of mind.

11-14. Then he should bring the lot of cloths that have been worshipped out (of the Pavilion). While being taken out, they should be in the same covered state in the cotton or silk cloth covering, O Brāhmaṇas.

They should be taken out in procession with umbrellas, flags, banners, waving of the chowries, songs, instrumental music, dances, scattering of flowers etc. He should circumambulate the Mansion (shrine) three times and then go round the Lord three times.

Then the covering cloth should be pulled off and the bundle of cloths should be consecrated by exposing it to the vision etc. (of the Lord). Each of the deities should be covered with seven cloths. All the limbs excepting the face should be thus covered with cloths affording protection against chilliness, O Brāhmaṇas.

15. Betel leaves are offered as Naivedya along with camphor creeper. After worshipping the Lord with Dūrvā blades and raw rice grains the rite of Nīrājana should be performed.

16. Those who cover Nṛsiṁha with excellent cloths during the advent of winter and those who witness the festival of covering will never be covered by delusion.

17. They will never experience the fear arising out of the mutually opposed pairs as well as chill wind. This is the *Prāvaraṇa* festival of Viṣṇu, the Lord of Devas.

18-19. Those who witness this devoutly shall attain all desires. For the sake of the Lord blankets etc. as protection against chillness should be given to Brāhmaṇas, preceptors, other Devas (?) as well as to the poor and the helpless. These should be given to them after honouring them joyfully. The delighted Lord grants him an excellent boon.

CHAPTER FORTYONE

The Festival of Holy Bath on Puṣya Day

Jaimini said:

1-2. I shall describe the festival of the holy bath on the Puṣya day[1] as approved by Brahmā formerly. The devotee should perform the festival of the holy bath on Puṣya day in the month of Pauṣa, when the full moon coincides with the Puṣya constellation. On the eleventh day the offering of germinating seeds[2] should be done in the North-East.

3-6. Thereafter, worship should be continued everyday of the idol of Hari in the abode (Temple) of Hari. Every night an oblation should be offered with dances, songs and other offerings and services.

The pots should be consecrated in the preliminary consecration rite on the night of the fourteenth. These pots should be eighty-one in number. There should be twenty-one gold pots too, filled with cow's ghee. In front of Hari the devotee should make the mystic diagram of *Sarvatobhadra*. In their middle he should fix an auspicious mirror with a broad base. In the night everyone should keep awake with elaborate arrangements for dance, music etc.

7-13. In the morning, O Brāhmaṇas, the devotee should perform the holy rites in the sacred fire for those deities. With sacrificial twigs of Palāśa (*Butea frondosa*), *Caru* as well as ghee oblations with their Liṅga Mantras are offered to Brahmā, Viṣṇu and Śiva a thousand times for each. At the conclusion of the *Homas* with the respective Mantras and Symbols (of the deities), he should worship Puruṣottama reflected in the mirror. Thereafter, he should charge the pots with the Mantras of *Puruṣa Sūkta*.

Reciting the same, he should bathe Puruṣottama with an unbroken flow of water.

Reciting the *Pāvamānīyaka* hymns he should bathe the Devas and again reciting *Śrī Sūkta*.

Thereafter, he should bathe the Lord with the pots of ghee reciting the *Vaiṣṇavī Gāyatrī*. Then he should worship the Lord with scented

---

1. This festival of the bath ceremony of the Lord is performed on the full-moon day of Pauṣa, when the Moon coincides with the Puṣya asterism in the sky.

2. As is seen in the procedure of the Yātrās, this rite is to be performed at the beginning of religious functions.

water dropping in a thousand streams (i.e. water is poured from a pot with many holes pierced therein) while reciting ***Śrī Sūkta.***

Thereafter, the Nirmālya should be cast off. He should then smear the body of the Lord with scents and sandal-paste. He should then adorn the Lord with ornaments in the proper places so that their charm shall be displayed. Thereafter, he should adorn (the Lord) with sweet-smelling flower-garlands.

14-18. He should place the eight weapons beginning with the discus in front of the Lord. After holding the gem-set umbrella aloft, he should worship once again Puruṣottama accompanied by Lakṣmī, O Brāhmaṇas, with rich offerings. Then the conch-shells should be blown for their pleasing and resonant sounds. Beautiful courtesans should be employed for the waving of chowries constantly. There should be auspicious songs, dances etc. The bards should recite eulogies and panegyrics. The Brāhmaṇas should repeatedly give shouts of "Be victorious".

The devotee should then worship Keśava with three handfuls of Dūrvā blades and raw rice grains. He should then perform the *Nīrājana*[1] rite to the Lord of the universe by means of lamps with wicks burning with cow's ghee in gold vessels of great purity along with camphor.

19-20. Excellent betel leaves kept in a gold vessel should be well prepared and offered slowly near the mouth (of the Lord) one by one.

Monetary gifts should be given to the preceptor and the Brāhmaṇas should be honoured.

21-23. Those who joyfully witness the festival of the holy bath on the Puṣya day shall realize all their desires fully and go to the region of Viṣṇu. A king dislodged from his kingdom shall regain the realm. He shall even become an Emperor. A lady having no son or with a dead child shall get a son with a long life.

Puṣyasnāna (Puṣya bath) festival is destructive of poverty. It is conducive to wealth. It is a producer of Brahminical splendour. It has been glorified unto you. Now listen to the *Uttarāyaṇa.*

CHAPTER FORTYTWO

The Festival of the Transit (of the Sun) to Capricorn

Jaimini said:

1. Desirous of going to the North, when the Sun enters the Zodiac of Capricorn, O excellent Brāhmaṇas, it is the period of *Uttarāyaṇa* (Northern Transit).[1]

2. When a period of twenty *Kalās* yet remains for the actual transit (of the Sun), that time is extremely meritorious and favoured by Pitṛs, Devas and Brāhmaṇas.

3-5. The man (i.e. the devotee) should take bath in the waters of the ocean at that time, worship Nārāyaṇa, bow down to the Kalpa tree and enter the shrine. He shall circumambulate the temple three times and worship Śrī Puruṣottama by means of the Mantrarāja. Similarly he should worship Bala and Subhadrā with their respective Mantras. By seeing the Lord in *Uttarāyaṇa* (the Northern Transit of the Sun) one is liberated from the bondage of physical body.

6-9. I shall describe the procedure. It is great and sacred. Listen to it. On the day previous to Saṁkrānti (the Transit) the devotee should place well-pounded fresh grains of rice in a spot to the east of the Mansion (Shrine) and perform the rite of consecration (*adhivāsa*). He should cover the grains of rice with a new cloth and worship with Dūrvā blades, mustard and flowers. Thereafter he shall mutter: "May Kṛṣṇa protect you."

When a *Yāma* (3 hours) of that night has passed, the replica (the movable idol) of the Lord of the universe should be taken to the presence (of the Lord) and the identity (of the two) should be meditated upon. With the remaining offerings he should worship with great concentration.

10-15. The *Nirmālya* cloths and garlands should be placed on the replica which should be taken round the three deities three times elaborately.

It should then be placed in a palanquin and brought to the door of the Mansion. Imitating the graceful movements of the Lord in his incarnation as Trivikrama when he measured the three worlds with his steps, the replica should be taken round the Mansion three times. At

1. It appears that in order to emphasize the identity of the Lord with Time (Kāla) these festivals are celebrated on important turning points in the year's Calendar.

the end, it should be waved slowly and elaborately on the lap[1] (?). There should be hundreds of lights to dispel the covering of darkness. The circumambulation should be done with paraphernalia of umbrella, flags, banners etc. to the accompaniment of dances, songs and instrumental music.

The noble souls who have destroyed their sins by seeing the Lord, need not have markings of symbols on their body nor the imprints of red hot iron.

Those who follow Lord Trivikrama who proceeds ahead during that festival, obtain the merit of a horse-sacrifice for every step.

16-21. By seeing the first circumambulation the devotee is absolved of the five sins. By seeing the second circumambulation, O Brāhmaṇas, he is liberated from sins of defiling act or contacts with a woman in menstruation. By seeing the third circumambulation he is certainly liberated from the sins of honouring undeserving persons. The fourth circumambulation liberates him from the minor sins.

Again in the morning, the devotee should smear the Lord of Devas with scents and sandal-paste. After duly adorning him with robes, wreath and ornaments, he should worship the Lord as per procedure with all offerings and services elaborately in accordance with his capacity. After concluding the *Nīrājana* rite to the Lord of Devas, he should take the rice grains that have already been consecrated and put in gold pots, to the Lord. They must be mixed with curds, ghee and sugar candy. Small pieces of coconut and ginger should also be put therein. They should be taken to the Lord after circumambulating the Mansion three times. Sweet scents, flowers and raw rice grains also should be put over them. They should be placed in front of the Lord in rows.

22-25. He should then pray thus: "O Lord of the universe, you are the very life of all living beings. You are their progenitor. These rice grains are identical with you. They have been produced by you alone, O Lord.

O Lord who have assumed the body proper for blessing the worlds, O great Lord, accept these things got ready for propitiating you.

If you are satisfied, all the worlds will become powerful by means of this. The holy utterances like Svāhā, Svadhā and Vaṣaṭ will be competent to nourish the Heaven-dwellers. The universe is nourished by them alone. O Lord of the universe, protect the universe consisting of mobile and immobile beings and pervaded by you.

---

1. Probably a misprint for '*ante*' as '*aṅke*' does not fit in the context.

26-27. After praying thus to the Lord of Devas he should offer paddy blades as *Naivedya.*[1] Similarly he should offer *Naivedyas* of foodstuffs made with rice along with pots of sweet-smelling curds mixed with camphor, sugar candy, pepper powder etc. He should devoutly worship the Brāhmaṇas standing in front of the Lord of Devas.

28-30. Those cooked rice grains and other things should be given to them with great devotion, thinking them to be the Lord himself.

In a former Kalpa, after procreation was over, Kaśyapa celebrated this festival for propitiating the Lord. Those who witness this festival first celebrated by Kaśyapa shall become happy with all their desires realized always, O Brāhmaṇas. They never bewail. After staying along with Devas they will attain salvation at the end of the Kalpa.

31-34. O sages, he should consecrate the kitchen and the fire here itself. He should perform Vaiśvadeva sacrifice everyday. In the consecrated fire Ramā cooks the food everyday for feeding the Lord. She is in invisible divine form. Charitable gifts of *Tulāpuruṣa* etc. in the course of this highly meritorious festival of the Supreme Soul will have crores and crores of times the benefit. Holy bath, charitable gifts, penance, *Homa*, study of the Vedas and the libation to Pitṛs in the course of Uttarāyaṇa festival, will have everlasting benefit.

CHAPTER FORTYTHREE

*The Festival of the Swing**

Jaimini said:

1. In the month of Phālguna the devotee should celebrate the excellent festival of the swing, wherein Govinda plays and sports for the purpose of blessing the worlds.

---

1. The offering of newly harvested corn (rice) to the Lord seems to be one of the motives of the agricultural community in celebrating this festival.

*The festival of the swing (Dolā-Yātrā) indicates the midday position of the *Ahorātra* year, of which the eleventh day of the bright half of Bhādrapada (*Pārśva-Parivartana* Festival) is regarded as the midnight in Orissa. Jagannātha's identity with Kāla (Time) is hereby emphasized. There is one change in today's Dolā-Yātrā as compared with that in our Purāṇa. King Rāmacandra Deva, the Abhinava Indradyumna, who re-established the glory of Jagannātha after Kālā Pahāḍ's invasion, introduced some changes such as building a permanent swing-altar etc. One important point to be noted is the influence of the Bhāgavata Purāṇa. Vṛndāvana is as if transplanted at Puri and Govinda (Kṛṣṇa) participates in the Dolā-Yātrā.

2. He (the devotee) should get a replica made of the Lord of Devas. It should be named Govinda. In front of the Mansion a pavilion should be made.[1] It should be a tall one with sixteen pillars.

3. It should be square in shape with four doors. It should be provided with an altar. There should be charming awning. It should be rendered splendid with wreaths, chowries and banners.

4. There should be a fine seat on the altar. It shall be made of the wood of Śrīparṇī (Gmelina arborea). The lovely festival should be celebrated for five or three days.

5. On the previous fourteenth day in the month of Phālguna, early in the night, O Brāhmaṇas, there should be a fire festival on the east of the Pavilion intended for the festival of swing.

6. That is blessed by Govinda. It is glorified as an ancillary of the Yātrā (festival, procession). A preceptor should be chosen and the fire should be kindled with sacrificial twigs by rubbing them together.

7. The ground should be cleaned and consecrated duly. The mass of tall grasses should be trimmed and the ground should be made even. Fire should be deposited there.

8. After worshipping in accordance with the injunctions, *Homa* should be performed in accordance with the procedure laid down for Kūṣmāṇḍa. After worshipping Govinda, he should be (perched on the swing and) swung (at regular intervals).

9-10. This fire should be preserved carefully till the conclusion of the festival. In the early morning *Yāma* (3 hours) of the fourteenth day, the splendid idol of Govinda should be placed in front of Hari (Hari's replica—Pratyarcā) and then Puruṣottama be worshipped. With the remaining portion of the offerings and services the devotee should worship the replica too.

11. Thereafter, O excellent Brāhmaṇas, the cloth and the garland should be taken away and be placed on the replica while reciting the Mantra and meditating upon the Supreme Refulgence.

12. Thereupon, that replica (idol) becomes Puruṣottama himself. That replica should be placed in a bejewelled palanquin and taken to the Pavilion of holy bath.

---

1. It means, at the time of the Purāṇa, there was no permanent structure for this Yātrā. The present structure was built in the 16th century CE by King Rāmacandra Deva who is aptly designated as 'New Indradyumna'.

Preparation of a statue of Govinda is for recreating the scene of Vṛndāvana and Kṛṣṇa's playing Holi and colour with Gopīs.

13. There the festival should be celebrated with playing of different kinds of musical instruments, blowing of conch-shells, shouts of "Be victorious", hymns etc. and showers of flowers.

14. There should be umbrella, flags and banners, chowries and fans. There should be continuous burning of lamps.

15. At that time Devas with Brahmā as their leader come there along with multitudes of sages in order to witness the great festival of Govinda.

16. The idol should be placed and consecrated on the excellent seat and then worshipped with offerings and services. In accordance with the injunction governing the great ablution the devotee should perform the rite of ablution.

17. The ablution should be performed with Pañcāmṛtas (the five sweet things, viz. milk, sugar, ghee, curds and honey) or with any one of them. At the end of the ablution he should bathe (the idol) with perfumed water while reciting *Śrī Sūkta*.

18. The Lord should be sprinkled and adorned with robes, wreaths and ornaments. After performing the *Nīrājana* rite and worship the idol should be taken round the Mansion (shrine).

19. The idol should be taken round the Mansion seven times. Then the Lord should be brought to the Pavilion of swing through the street well adorned with buntings, banners and festoons and other embellishments. The idol should be moved round seven times beneath the lower part of the Pavilion.

20. (It should be moved round) seven times over the upper part and seven times on the altar with pillars. At the conclusion of the festival again it should be moved twenty-one times.

21-25. This sport of the Lord was proclaimed by Brahmā orally and celebrated by the saintly King Indradyumna formerly in the beautiful forest in Vṛndāvana abounding in trees bending with plenty of fruits and flowers and resonant with inebriated bees, sweetened by the cooings of the cuckoo, full of many kinds of birds. The place should be splendidly decorated. It should be fumigated with incenses of various kinds as well as black aloewood. The quarters should be rendered fragrant by means of the sweet smell of Ketakī flowers in full bloom. It shall be made beautiful with jasmine, Aśoka, Punnāga and Caṁpaka trees. The Maṇḍapa erected in the middle of that forest should have charming festoons and ornamental gateways. It must be adorned with wreaths, cloths and chowries.

26-32. In its middle the Lord should be placed in a bejewelled couch in a palanquin. The Lord should have a gem-set crown. His chest is rendered splendid by a sparkling pearl necklace.

His ears are brilliantly illuminated by means of ear-rings made of valuable gems. He is charming and fascinating on account of divine ornaments worn in their proper places so as to enhance the beauty and splendour.

He is stationed in the middle of a full-blown lotus. He is accompanied by Śrī, the mother of the universe.

He holds the conch, the discus, the iron club and the lotus. He wears the garland of sylvan flowers. He is exceedingly delighted. His nose is splendid. He is refulgent with a stout, muscular chest.

He is eulogized by Devas including Brahmā, who are stationed in the firmament in front (of the Lord), who have bent down their heads and joined their palms together in reverence and who devoutly shout the slogan "Be victorious".

He is worshipped by Gandharvas, celestial damsels, Kinnaras, Siddhas, Cāraṇas etc. including Hāhā and Hūhū who sing divine songs and vie with one another in dancing, singing and playing instruments. They are joyously viewing the Lord so that they appear to be worshipping him with thousands of lotus-like eyes.

33. The devotees should scatter fragrant sandal powder all round in all the quarters. They should place down the idol of Govinda and worship (him) with various offerings and services.

34-35. The devotee should imagine the Lord of the universe as being positioned in the middle of cowherd lasses at the root of a Kadaṁba tree—the Lord who went on sporting with graceful charms, jocular remarks and various amorous gestures in the middle of the forest and who was taken in vehicles drawn playfully by cowherdesses and cowherds. Thinking of Jagannātha thus, he should scatter scented powder over the Lord.

36-38. Scented powders of red, yellow and white colours should be scattered in the various quarters along with camphor. The Lord should be adorned and adored with divine robes, divine garlands, divine scents, excellent incenses etc.

There should be sweet songs and hymns. Chowries should be waved to and fro. The Lord in the swing should be slowly swung seven times. Those who see Kṛṣṇa then shall undoubtedly attain salvation. The five sins like that of the murder of a Brāhmaṇa shall be destroyed.

39. The devotee should swing the Lord thus three times. It dispels all sins. The Lord blesses men who are devoutly engaged in this. He

is the sole cause of enjoyment of pleasures and salvation.

40. All his graceful activities both intentional and spontaneous, destroy masses of sins. They dispel *Avidyā* (Ignorance), the root cause (of Saṁsāra).

41. If a person sees this on a second occasion lesser sins like slaughter of a cow etc. are dispelled. On the third occasion all the sins are destroyed. There is no doubt in this regard.

42. By seeing the Lord being swung one is liberated from all sins and troubles caused by spirits, animals and deities.

43. It is certain that by celebrating this festival an ordinary king will become an Emperor; a Brāhmaṇa shall master all the four Vedas and become blessed with perfect knowledge.

CHAPTER FORTYFOUR

*Description of the Jyeṣṭhapañcaka Vrata**

Jaimini said:

1-7. I shall recount to you a *Vrata* lasting for a year. On the first day of the year, on the full-moon day in Phālguna (the *Vrata* begins).

There are twelve *Mūrtis* (forms) of Hari, the Primordial Lord. They are well known by the names of Viṣṇu etc. Those *Mūrtis* should be worshipped in turn every month.

(Out of these) One *Mūrti* should be worshipped everyday in the course of a month. There are twelve flowers and twelve fruits to be offered severally like this. The flowers are : Aśoka, Mallikā, Pāṭala, Kadaṁbaka, Karavīra, Jāti, Mālatī, Śatapatra (Lotus), Utpala, Vāsantī, Kunda and Punnāgaka. The devotee should joyously offer these flowers in due order.

The fruits to be offered in due order are : Pomegranate (*Dāḍima*). coconut, mango, jackfruit, dates, palmyra fruit, old embylic myrobalan,

---

* This chapter shows how twelve different Mūrtis (Idols) of Jagannātha are worshipped one per month with their specific flowers and fruits. Viṣṇu is the Vedic Sun-god. As the Sun is regarded to have twelve different forms, each one being related to a different month, this Jagannātha-Viṣṇu is conceived to have twelve forms. But this is given the Purāṇic garb of a Vrata—the Mūrtipañjara Vrata.

śrīphala (bilva fruit), orange, arecanut, karmaṅgaka (Carissa carandas) and jātīphala (nutmeg).

8. After offering different types of food consisting of lambatives, sweet juices etc., the devotee should offer seat and other services and then eulogize the Sire of the universe.[1]

9. "O Lord of the universe, O omnipresent one, O Lord of things past, present and future, save me. O lotus-eyed one, O Viṣṇu, save me from the ocean of worldly existence.

10. Formerly in the terrifying vast expanse of the ocean water without any support you killed Madhu for the sake of protecting the universe. O Slayer of Madhu, protect me.

11. You took three steps and killed the huge army of Daityas. You (thus) protected the three worlds. O Trivikrama, obeisance to you.

12. You assumed the form of a dwarf having the (Vedas) Ṛk, Yajus and Sāman within. With your wonderful form you enchanted (everyone). Obeisance to that Māyā-wielder.

13. You hold Śrī perpetually on your chest. You grant prosperity to the devotees. Obeisance to you, O Śrīdhara.

14. You are the presiding deity of all sense-organs. You are always the Lord of sense-organs. You are the sole cause of the happiness of devotees. O Hṛṣīkeśa, obeisance to you.

15. This universe consisting of mobile and immobile beings has originated from the lotus coming out of your navel. It is the permanent seat of the Creator. O Padmanābha, obeisance to you.

16. This universe consisting of mobile and immobile beings is bound by the three Guṇas belonging to you. Such a Lord has been bound with ropes by a cowherdess (Yaśodā). O Dāmodara, obeisance to you.

17. You killed the demon Keśin who caused havoc in all the three worlds. You are the master of all types of happiness. O Lord Keśava, protect me.

18. You are the creator of the worlds. You are the first cause of the worlds. Brahmā created living beings (with your guidance). O Viṣṇu of unimaginable greatness, O Nārāyaṇa, obeisance to you.

19. The universe is deluded by your Māyā that has no beginning. Obeisance, obeisance to Mādhava, the embodiment of all Dharmas.

20. You are accessible to the wise ones through perfect knowledge. You are the bestower of the goal on those who are helpless. By your favour, O Govinda, let my *Vrata* be concluded (successfully)."

1. This prayer gives the etymologies of the different names of Viṣṇu (Jagannātha).

21. Every month, at the conclusion of the worship the devotee should pray with these Mantras with great devotion, with palms joined in reverence. He should thus pray to Janārdana at the end of worship.

22. Thus the devotee should perform this *Vrata* (named) *Mūrtipañjara* ('Cage of the *Mūrtis*') for a year. In order to get full benefit he should perform the rite of installation.

23. The devotee should make gold images of the twelve *Mūrtis* of Viṣṇu in accordance with his capacity. These *Mūrtis* should be placed in twelve pots.

24-26. Those pots should be covered with mango leaves separately and draped with white cloths. They must contain perfumed water with tender leaves (of mango) put in them. In the mystic diagram, Sarvatobhadra, square in shape, these pots should be placed in the eight cardinal points and the *Mūrtis* should be worshipped in them separately by means of the twelve-syllabled Mantra (viz. *oṁ namo bhagavate vāsudevāya*) with offerings and services. At the outset, O Brāhmaṇas, all of them should be bathed in Pañcāmṛtas.

27-31. The following things must be provided for: songs, instrumental music, dances etc., worship of Brāhmaṇas, twelve pairs of cloths, twelve umbrellas, twelve pairs of shoes, fans, waterpots, beds, footstools, sweet scents, wreaths, good betel leaves, rings, ear-rings etc.

Lamps should be burned with ghee. They must be twelve in number. The night should be spent thus.

In the morning, the rites in the sacred fires should be performed.

For each deity three hundred Homas should be offered with sacrificial twigs, ghee and Carus. The Homas with gingelly seeds should be offered one thousand and eight times while uttering the *Vyāhṛtis* (viz. Bhūr, Bhuvaḥ Svaḥ).

At the end of the Homas he should partake of (the *Naivedya*) and give monetary gifts to the preceptor. Twelve well-adorned tawny-coloured cows should be given.

32-33. Thereafter, the devotee should feed one hundred and forty-four Brāhmaṇas. The devotee should gift away to the preceptor all those twelve images along with their pots, canopies, chowries, etc. with due courteous offerings and services. By performing this Vratarāja ('the king of holy rites') the devotee shall realize all desires.

34. Twelve festivals have been glorified including *Guṇḍicā* festival of *Viṣṇu*. By performing this Vrata one obtains the same merit as one gets by viewing those festivals of Viṣṇu.

35. By the favour of the Lord of Devas the devotee shall attain the

region of Indra, overlordship of the entire earth, and the eight supernatural powers.

36. Nārada performed this extremely meritorious *Vrata* for twelve years and the sage became a living-liberated soul.

37. Other Vaiṣṇavas too performed this many times formerly. There is no other *Vrata* more pleasing to the Lord than this.

38. It is conducive to virtue, fame, and longevity. It is favourable to Brāhmaṇas. It causes increase in the family. You all are the sages of restrained souls; you do perform this excellent *Vrata*.

CHAPTER FORTYFIVE

*The Procedure of Splitting Damanaka Grass**

The sages said:

1-2. O sage, this *Vrata* named *Mūrti Pañjara* has been heard of (by us). It causes joy within. It is great with its own grandeur. You spoke of twelve meritorious festivals of which the Lord is very fond. Two of them yet remain (to be told). Recount them to us, O great sage.

Jaimini replied:

3. I shall recount the festival named *Damanabhañjikā* ('Splitting the grass, Artemisia indica'). This is a Spring Festival. If it is performed or witnessed, Puruṣottama becomes pleased.

4. O Brāhmaṇas, previously I have spoken about the grass named *Damanaka*. The devotee should bring it along with its root on the thirteenth day in the bright half of the month of Caitra.

* Damanaka (Artemisia indica) is a fragrant variety of grass which is used in the worship of Viṣṇu (Jagannātha) and Śiva on the 14th day of the bright half of Caitra. The legend to justify this, viz. the killing of a demon called Damanaka and the boon granted to the dying demon to wear him on his person by Viṣṇu is mentioned already. This chapter gives formal recognition to this as a festival 'Damanabhañjikā' (splitting of Damana) with its usual Tāntric formalities. Caitra being the first month of the spring season, this is called the Spring Festival.

5. In its (Mansion's) middle he should make a splendid mystic diagram named *Padma* (Lotus). A replica of the Lord should be worshipped and then kept within it.

6. The image must be accompanied (by the images of) Śrī and Satyabhāmā. The devotee should worship them in accordance with the injunctions. He should perform this rite of the Lord of Devas at midnight.

7. Formerly it was at midnight that the Lord thrashed Damanāsura. After thrashing him, he attained great pleasure. This grass has originated from his body.

8. On the same *Trayodaśī* (thirteenth day) the devotee should consider the grass to be the Daitya. With palms joined in reverence he should utter these sentences:

9-10. "Formerly you killed the Daitya Damanaka who was a thorn unto the three worlds. He has become transformed thus and stands in front of you. At that time when this was produced you felt pleased, O Mādhava. May you have now too the same pleasure in splitting Damana".

11. After saying thus the devotee places the grass in a hand of the Lord. Then he should spend the remaining part of the night by means of dances, songs etc.

12. When the sun has risen, the Lord and the grass should be taken to the presence of the Lord of the universe, O excellent Brāhmaṇas.

13-14. Thereafter, he should worship the Lord of the universe as before by means of offerings and courteous services:

"After killing Hiraṇyakaśipu and putting round your neck the entrails taken out of his body, you became delighted. Similarly, O Lord, this Damana grass is given into your hand by me for the sake of your delight."

15. After uttering this the devotee should place the splendid fragrant grass on Hari's head. At that time one who is distressed through the worldly miseries joyously sees Hari's lotus-like face beaming with pleasure and therefore attains excellent happiness.

16. The devotee should take away that blade of grass from Viṣṇu's head and place it on his own head. He shall be rid of all sins. He shall then certainly dwell in the city of Viṣṇu.

CHAPTER FORTYSIX

Celebration of Yātrā by Dakṣa (on Akṣayatṛtīyā)*

Jaimini said:

1. Henceforth I shall describe a Yātrā that will yield everlasting salvation without strain to (even) the dull-witted whose mind is tied to the imprints of previous Karmas.

2. (The holy rite is to be performed) at midnight on the second day in the bright half of the month of Vaiśākha. The pavilion should be square-shaped. It should be plastered and provided with an altar.

3-4. There should be made a screen all round with a well-washed cloth. The pavilion must have a splendid flight of stairs. It must have a beautiful awning.

In the middle of the pavilion the devotee should place an extremely excellent seat. It should be covered with a cloth. A gold vessel should be placed upon it.

5-8. To the west of the gold vessel a Brāhmaṇa should be comfortably seated. He must be pure and clean. He should take the following articles in another vessel: twenty-five *palas* of sandal-paste, black aloewood more than a *pala*, saffron half the quantity of aloewood, incense half the quantify of saffron, musk and camphor together equal to the incense. All these should be ground into paste with the juice of trumpet flowers. Two *palas* of excellent black aloewood oil should be mixed with them. All these should be stirred together and poured into the first vessel.

9. He should cover it up with the leaves of Ketaka plant and wrap it with a silk cloth. Repeating the Mantra "*gandhas te somam*" etc. he should protect it with *Garuḍamudrā*.

10. Thus all these things should be consecrated and placed in the pavilion. At the time of dawn it should be taken to the presence of Kṛṣṇa.

---

* Akṣaya Tṛtīyā is the third day in the bright half of Vaiśākha. It is supposed to be the first day of *Kalpa* (*Kalpādi*) as well as that of Yuga and, Jagannātha-Viṣṇu being an embodiment of Kāla (Time), the day has a special significance. From the point of Saguṇa Bhakti Jagannātha must be protected from the coming Summer which is so hot. It is by application of cool sandal-paste that Jagannātha is worshipped on this day.

11. With chowries, umbrellas and (the blowing of) conch-shell etc. the shrine should be circumambulated. The replica is then placed in front of the Lord. He should then worship Puruṣottama.

12. Then the covering cloth should be taken away and (the materials) should be looked at with the divine (?) vision. He should then sprinkle it with water while reciting the Mantrarāja and stir it by beating etc.

13. The Lord should be worshipped with fragrant flowers and raw rice-grains. Repeating *Śrī Sūkta* he should smear the idol (with the paste). The entire body of the Lord of Śrī should be so smeared with gentle touches.

14. Devotees of Viṣṇu shout the slogan of "Be victorious" and praise Hari. Learned men eulogize him with different hymns and passages from the Upaniṣads.

15-20. He should propitiate the Lord of the universe with flutes, lutes etc., various dances, songs and (playing of) musical instruments, fans, chowries, umbrellas and other kinds of offerings and services.

On the third day also the Lord should be smeared (with the paste) at the outset. Merely by thinking about the Lord the embodied ones get all their distresses destroyed. The same Lord, O Brāhmaṇas, destroys (all distresses) on being seen. The greatness of Viṣṇu cannot be comprehended (perfectly) by saying that it is like this or that.

Robes of fine texture, wreaths, different kinds of foodstuffs and beverages, tasty milk-products and other materials should be repeatedly offered. Then the devotee should worship the Lord with well-prepared betel-leaves.

Those men who devoutly see Kṛṣṇa at that time will never return to earthly existence even after hundreds and crores of Kalpas. They will attain the form of Viṣṇu and dwell in the region of Viṣṇu.

21-23. In a former Kaliyuga, O Brāhmaṇas, the Prajāpati (Patriarch) named Dakṣa was moved with pity on seeing men suffering from distresses coming from bodies and other sources. He went there and celebrated the great festival in the manner described by me. He was the first person to do so. On the third day in the bright half of the month of Vaiśākha he applied sandal-paste on the body of the Lord and joyously repeated this prayer:

Dakṣa prayed:

24-31. O Supreme God, O Lord of Devas endowed with natural bliss,

O Lord of the universe free from impurities, save us. We have become immersed in the ocean of worldly existence. These men are suffering from different kinds of distresses. O Kṛṣṇa resembling cloud, they are like dry grass. Nourish them with nectar and your splendid glance with a feeling of compassion for me too. Obeisance to you.

O Lord of the worlds, it is to redeem those who are confounded with the sins of Kali that you have taken this incarnation within the cave of this Nīla mountain.

O Lord, merciful to the wretched and the helpless ones, you alone are competent to burn down the mass of great sins that has taken root over a long time and cannot be easily got rid of.

Seeing you is a great Yoga (but it is) devoid of the usual eight limbs such as *Yama* (Restraint) etc. It is the means for accomplishing the fourfold aim of life. Those who are inclined towards it do not become grief-stricken in the forest of worldly existence that is very difficult to cross and that causes great terror.

O Lord of Devas, self-knowledge is not the liberator without the assistance of (good) Karmas. But this, your sight, O Lord, shall liberate (devotees) without (performance of) Karmas.

O Kṛṣṇa, be victorious. O Lord, be victorious. O Imperishable One, be victorious. O Immutable One, be victorious. Be pleased. Bless these wretched, confounded and foolish people.

32. After praying thus and repeatedly saying "Be pleased, O Lord; be pleased, O Lord; be pleased, O Lord", he fell at the lotus-feet (of the Lord) like a rod.

33-36. Thereupon the Lord spoke to the Prajāpati (Dakṣa) in clear, well-modulated tone:

"O dear one, get up. The boon that is desired by you is very difficult to get. Yet it is granted to you. It shall undoubtedly take place by my favour. It is known to you that my blessing is very difficult to get by persons deficient in merit. You are born of my own limbs. You have prayed to me (pleasing me) through my festival. Hence I shall grant you a favour as a token of my pleasure.

Those who devoutly and joyously witness this celebration of everlasting benefit, shall obtain whatever they mentally wish for at that time.

37. Just as the application of sandal-paste removes bodily heat, so also this festival of mine, O Dakṣa, is destructive of the three types of distress.

38. With your mind urged and directed by me, you have celebrated this festival. This has certainly been thought of by me for the sake of the uplift of the distressed ones.

39-40. O Prajāpati, I shall definitely grant you everything that has been desired by you. These twelve great processions and festivals beginning with *Guṇḍicā* are very sanctifying. Each of them yields salvation. All of them are conducive to the increase of virtue, wealth and love.

41. If a person devoutly witnesses even one of these, he shall cross the ocean of the worldly existence by means of that one alone and shall go to the region of Viṣṇu."

Jaimini said:

42-44. After saying this to the Prajāpati the Lord vanished.

Believing everything faithfully, Dakṣa, the Prajāpati, stayed on that mountain for a year and witnessed all the great festivals at his behest. He was born as an omniscient Brāhmaṇa in the excellent family of Kauśika. He made people celebrate all the great festivals.

45. These festivals have been recounted for the sake of convincing people of deficient intellect. This Sire of the universe is that Supreme Brahman itself. He has been propitiated by the Lord of Suras for the sake of blessing all the worlds.

46-49. Whatever may be the form in which he comes into our view, he is certainly the bestower of salvation. Even to women he grants all the desired objects. There is no doubt about it.

The Lord is true to his promise. The Slayer of Madhu dwells there. On seeing him one surmounts all difficulties and griefs originating from the ocean of worldly existence.

Of what avail are holy rites, penances, gifts, *Kṛcchras* (varieties of expiatory rites) and sacrifices? Of what avail is Yoga with its eight limbs? Of what avail are Sāṁkhya and other (systems of philosophy)?

One should take bath in the waters of the ocean in the holy spot of Śrī Puruṣottama and witness with his physical eyes the Brahman in wooden form dwelling at the root of the banyan tree. Thereby one is liberated from the bondage of physical bodies.

CHAPTER FORTYSEVEN

Meditation on the Lord in Different Forms

The sages said:

1. O holy Lord, conversant with all scriptures, a wonderful account about the greatness of the festivals of the Lord, destructive of sins, has been heard.

2. Now tell us how this Lord grants prosperity on meditation of his glorious attributes by those who desire prosperity. How is he the bestower of all desired objects?

Jaimini said:

3. All the mobile and immobile beings of the universe are the *Vibhūtis* (glorious attributes) of Viṣṇu. That one Supreme Lord is the bestower of prosperity and glory. He is the Supreme *Vibhūti* too.

4-5. It is not possible to measure his greatness by saying "It is this much". What one gets or becomes is determined by the degree of his devotion to God and his mode of worship. The single path for acquiring all the four aims of life beginning with Dharma is that Lord of wooden form.

6. The path of virtue and piety is incomprehensible. It has become (too) narrow due to numerous restrictions imposed by precepts. O excellent Brāhmaṇas, no one is competent to come to a decision as to its (of Dharma) exact nature.

7. Artha (Wealth) and Kāma (Love) have always gross features. They have their origin in Dharma. The Lord increases all these three without any strain.

8. Indeed Dharma itself is Lord Viṣṇu. This universe has its root in Dharma. Janārdana is the Lord of Dharma and of the universe.

9. If a man's devotion is well-established in him (the Lord) who is identical with the aims of life, he becomes a contented soul in every respect. He is not affected by (unfulfilled) yearnings. He never feels grief-stricken.

10. If he is worshipped in the form of Śakra,[1] he bestows the wealth and glory of all the three worlds.

---

1. VV 10-15 describe the specific merits derived from worshipping the different forms of the Lord such as Śakra, Brahmā etc.

If Hari is meditated upon in the form of Brahmā, he causes increase in family.

11. In the form of Sanatkumāra he grants long life. Meditated upon in the form of Pṛthu he bestows employment and riches.

12. Worshipped as Vācaspati he bestows the benefit of bathing in Gaṅgā and other sacred waters. Meditated upon in the form of the Sun he dispels internal darkness.

13. Worshipped as the Moon he will give matchless fortune. One who meditates upon the Lord in the form of Vākpati, becomes conversant with the principles of the eighteen Vidyās (branches of learning).

14. This Lord identical with the universe, when meditated upon in the form of the Lord of Yajñas, shall bestow the benefits of performing horse and other sacrifices. He is the eternal Lord.

15. Meditated upon in the form of Kubera he will grant immense prosperity.

16. Such is the Ocean of Mercy dwelling on that Nīla mountain. He has come in embodied form under the guise of the Lord with wooden form to bless the wretched and the helpless.

17. Go there, O Brāhmaṇas; stay there with mental and bodily purity and concentration. Seek refuge in the pair of lotus-like feet of the Lord of Śrī.

18. If you wish for perpetual enjoyment of pleasure here and hereafter and, in the end, final emancipation in the form of complete isolation from matter, go to that place.

CHAPTER FORTYEIGHT

Popularization of the Lord's Worship by Indradyumna

The sages said:

1-2. At the conclusion of the installation of the Mansion, what boons Hari granted to Indradyumna as well as the twelve great festivals that he ordered—all these we have heard directly from you. Thereafter, what did the highly intelligent king who continued to remain a devotee of Viṣṇu, do?

Jaimini said:

3. After receiving the boons directly from the Lord of the universe,

who is the Brahman incarnate, that excellent man considered himself blessed and one who had fulfilled his task (in life).

4. He celebrated all those festivals, the bestowers of merit and emancipation, in accordance with the command (of the Lord). He worshipped the Sire of the universe in diverse ways and with many offerings and courteous services.

5. Then he instructed king Gāla about the various things that the Lord had commanded along with the procedures for the same. And he spoke these sweet words full of righteousness and justice:

Indradyumna said:

6. O king, you are a man of vast learning. You abide by the practice of virtuous deeds. You entertain devotion to the Lord in thought, words and deeds.

7. The Lord does not command merely for the sake of instructing a single person. He is the preceptor of both mobile and immobile (beings). The entire universe has become his disciple.

8. With the aim of blessing me the Lord of the universe incarnated. For the sake of uplifting men of distressed minds he will stay here for a long time.

9. Carry out his behest with devotion and faith. O king, do not think that he is a mere idol.

10. It has been perceived directly by you that all the three worlds came to the earth at the time of the entry into his Mansion by the Lord of the universe.

11. All the Devas headed by Brahmā came simultaneously along with the Lord in his cosmic form. We all became bewildered, unable to know what we should do.

12. This Lord who has assumed the wooden form is himself identical with mobile and immobile beings. Know him to be the Kalpa tree, the bestower of all desires on the earth.

13-15. Whatever may be the form in which one worships him, one attains the fruit of one's desire. Though they strive much, ascetics do not obtain him. He is stationed beyond the darkness. He is of the form of some unique luminous being. He is the sole path of Yogins, of pious ascetics, of the purest persons having sublimated their sexual energy, of those who are endowed with single-minded devotion.

During Summer one attains the greatest pleasure by immersing oneself in a vast water reservoir, cool, deep and majestic. In the same manner one gets the height of bliss in this ocean of mercy.

16-18. When Puruṣottama has been approached (realized), one gets rid of the misery in the form of the three types of suffering. Neither mother nor father, neither a friend nor a wife nor a son can be of as much assistance as he to those distressed persons who have sought refuge in him. So serve him. He bestows the benefits of worldly enjoyment as well as salvation. Make the citizens and the general public celebrate those festivals elaborately.

19. This is the usual path of virtue among kings, O excellent king, that what is initiated by the earlier one is kept up and perpetuated by the later one.

20. Worship Nṛsiṁha, O king of kings, with offerings and services leading to great prosperity. Worship him at the three sandhyās (morning, noon and evening) everyday and attain the greatest bliss.

21. They say that the preservation of what is done and achieved by others is superior to what is done by oneself. If a person maintains what is handed over by others, it is indeed superior to what is given by himself.

Jaimini said:

22. With palms joined in reverence that excellent king Śveta accepted his suggestion with a bowed head like a garland of great quality (or value).

23. The saintly King Indradyumna propitiated Puruṣottama. Accompanied by Nārada that glorious king went to the world of Brahmā.

24. Thus the excellent, meritorious greatness of the sacred place has been recounted to you. So also the greatness of the Brahman in wooden form permanently dwelling there.

25. If a person devoutly listens to this, as it is being read, O excellent Brāhmaṇas, he will get the entire benefit of performing a thousand horse-sacrifices.

26. The *Ardhodaya* is a great astronomical combination glorified by Skanda. The merit of the glorification of Viṣṇu's greatness is crores of times greater than that.

27. He who listens to this every morning, shall be on a par with one who gifts away a hundred tawny-coloured cows. He shall obtain the benefit of ablution in the holy waters of Gaṅgā and Puṣkara.

28. It is conducive to wealth, fame and longevity. It is meritorious. It increases progeny. It yields the benefit of being established in heaven. It is destructive of all sins.

29. This is the secret mentioned in Purāṇas. It is well-guarded. It should never be mentioned to anyone except a Vaiṣṇava.

30. The following are Avaiṣṇavas: Those who indulge in evil arguments, those who have imperfectly learned the Vedas and the Āgamas, atheists, hypocrites, those who always see only defects in others. Their lives are furitless. From them this should be kept secret.

CHAPTER FORTYNINE

The Merit of Listening to a Purāṇa

The sages said:

1-6. O holy Lord Jaimini, O master of the Vedas and their ancillaries, with your blessing everything has been heard by us. The greatness of the Lord of the universe, of the prominent sacred place and all the festivals has been heard by us.

The merit of consuming the leavings (remnants) of the food of the Lord, the rare story of the life of King Indradyumna, the form of Nīlamādhava and the revelation of the Brahman in wooden form—all this has been heard by us as it issued forth from your lotus-like mouth.

O most eloquent one, from you alone we wish to hear the merit of listening to a Purāṇa. We are joyful and eager for the same.

O holy Lord, tell us in detail. What is its mode? By whom should it (be read). If you have mercy on us, it behoves you to relate as it is.

Jaimini said:

7. Very well, O excellent sages. What has been asked by you with great joy is nice; I am exceedingly pleased. It makes me thrilled with joy.

8-10. So I will speak everything. Listen attentively. When a devotee is ready to listen to a Purāṇa, he should first perform the rite of *Saṁkalpa* in accordance with his capacity.

He should choose a Brāhmaṇa (i.e. narrator of the Purāṇa) for the purpose of listening. He (i.e. the Brāhmaṇa) should be born of a pure family. He should not have any limb mutilated. He should be calm and of the same branch of Veda as oneself. He should be one's own priest. He should be a knower of the true meaning of all the scriptures. He should be invited with (the offer of) extremely splendid ornaments, robes, sandal-paste, wreaths etc.

11-16. With palms joined in reverence the devotee should pray to the Brāhmaṇa:

"You are Viṣṇu. Viṣṇu is yourself. There is no difference at all. Let my undertaking be free from obstacles by your favour. Be pleased."

The Brāhmaṇa invited should be made to sit on an auspicious and costly seat. He should put a garland round his neck. There must be a flower besmeared with sandal-paste (placed) on the head. Since at that time that Brāhmaṇa is considered to be on a par with Vyāsa, he should be requested to worship the book which is in the form of Viṣṇu. This is called *Vyāsapūjā*. The Brāhmaṇa should perform it with sandal-powder, aloewood and flowers. There should be different kinds of tasty foodstuffs etc. With great devotion the rule of offering the seat should be observed everyday.

Now I shall describe the characteristics of the listener. Let it be heard.

17-18. The devotee should make arrangements for seating the people who may be coming one after another, O Brāhmaṇas. For that purpose he should set apart a number of seats.

He himself should sit on another seat. He should be eager in his mind to listen. Or he should sit on the ground cleansed and purified duly along with the others.

19. He should sit in front of Vyāsa. But his seat should not be higher (than that of Vyāsa). He should have taken his bath. He should be joyful. He should wear two white clothes.

20. He should perform the rite of *Ācamana*. He should have the markings of conch-shell, discus etc. He should meditate on Viṣṇu mentally. He should have great faith.

21. Faith in the Purāṇa, the Brāhmaṇa, the Lord, the employment of Mantras, Tīrtha, utterance of elderly people etc. is beneficial.

22-23. Hence, O excellent sages, all merit has belief as its cause. One should avoid the following: conversation with heretics, futile talk and all kinds of worries. In this manner, O Brāhmaṇas, he should joyfully listen to it everyday.

24-25. When the reading is concluded, the people should give their appreciation by clapping their hands repeatedly and utter words such as "Be victorious, O Kṛṣṇa, O Lord of the universe, O Hari etc." The sound of the same should rise to the sky and be heard everywhere. This should be done everyday to propitiate the Enemy of Mura.

26. Then, when the (reading of the) book is completed the devotee should be eager to propitiate Viṣṇu. He should adorn the Brāhmaṇa equal to Vyāsa by good clothes, wreaths, sandal-paste etc. as well as ornaments. O Brāhmaṇas, he should do everything with great devotion.

27-31a. He should give monetary gifts according to his capacity and in accordance with the injunctions. Listen now from me as to who should give what. Kings should give elephants along with their ornaments. Kṣatriyas too should do likewise. Indeed they are considered equal to king.

Brāhmaṇas should give books and bamboo-boxes for the worship of Viṣṇu. In accordance with their devotion, they should give gold, silver, foodgrains and clothes.

Vaiśyas should give horses hailing from the Sindhu land and fully caparisoned with gem-set ornaments etc. They should give milch-cows with all (auspicious) characteristics and give them along with their calves. Other pious persons can give other things such as gold etc.

31b-33. Righteous Śūdras should also give gold etc. with great joy in their minds. They can give clothes, gold, foodgrains, gems, cows etc. all adorned with different kinds of ornaments. They should be giving plenty of milk or they may be pregnant. Monetary gifts should also be made so that the preceptor may be pleased.

(The listener) should give in accordance with his capacity, O Brāhmaṇas; he should not be unnecessarily stubborn or niggardly in spending.

34-35. *Śānti* (conciliation) rites, *Pauṣṭika* (nourishing) rites, *Vratas*, marriages, rites for the achievement of salvation, listening to the Purāṇas, *Yajñas* etc., performing charitable acts and different kinds of *Vratas*—these should never be devoid of monetary gifts (*dakṣiṇā*). Otherwise they will be fruitless.

36-38. Asuras appropriate the merit of that holy rite. The beauty of a woman (is futile), if it is bereft of the love of a husband. Archers (are deemed unfit), if they show their backs and run away from battle-field. If a horse is not capable of running, it is considered defective, O Brāhmaṇas. A man may be a knower of all the scriptures but dumbness (on his part) makes it (his scholarship) defective. In the same manner all holy rites devoid of monetary gifts are fruitless.

39. Since the mass of sins is destroyed by *Dāna* (gift), therefore it is called *Dakṣiṇā* by persons conversant with scriptures, O Brāhmaṇas.

40-41. Then Brāhmaṇas should be fed with articles prepared in accordance with one's capacity. There should be camphor, sugar-candy, ghee, milk-puddings, foodstuffs of six kinds and beverages tasty like nectar etc. To them also gold, clothes etc. should be given.

42. Thus the mode of listening to a Purāṇa has been entirely described to you. If it is followed, it shall be fruitful. Now, O excellent sages, what else do you wish to hear?

The sages said:

43-45. Oh! It is our great fortune that the fruit and mode of listening to a Purāṇa destructive of the mass of sins, has been heard by us directly along with its sub-divisions and ancillaries from your lotus-like mouth.

We are blessed. We are meritorious. We are free from ailments in this world. Now, O sage, according to our capacity Dakṣiṇā is given to you for the sake of getting the merit. Be pleased to accept it.

46. After saying this those sages who had no possession or assets whatsoever gave him sacrificial twigs, Kuśa grass, flowers, fruits , raw rice grains etc. They became liberated thereby. With great delight they went to the excellent holy region.

:: End of Puruṣottama-Kṣetra-Māhātmya ::

INDEX

Adhokṣaja 77
Ādityas 125
Agastya 25, 234
Aghamarṣaṇa Sūkta 175
Ajāmila 24 ftn, 92
Altar, festival of the Great 194, 199, 200, 201, 207
Altar, Great 196, 203
Ambarīṣa 20 ftn, 21, 26, 28, 185
Ananta 113
Antarvedī 17 ftn, 80
Architect, the son of the Celestial 94
Ardhāśinī 15, 18
Ardhodaya 187, 204, 257
Arjuna 185
— tree 115
Artha 254
Asuras, prevention of 84
Aśvamedha 55
Atala 12 ftn
Atri 234
Attributeless 56
Avaiṣṇavas 60
Avantī 32
Avidyā 4
Avikṣit 99 ftn
Avimukta/Avimuktā 17, 75

Badarikāśrama 55
Bala 19, 112, 113, 239
Balabhadra 27, 119, 140, 160, 163, 183, 199
——, chariot of 143
Baladeva 115
Balarāma 127, 153, 162, 184, 208
Balarāma, chariot of 196
Banyan 10, 12, 15, 18, 28, 33, 40, 49, 51, 164
Basil leaf/leaves 59, 228
Bhaga 169
Bhakti 56
Bhakti, Rājasī 57
Bhakti, Sāttvikī 57
Bhakti, Tāmasī 57
Bhakti, three types of 56
Bharadvāja 156, 234
Bharata 103
Bhauma Kṣetra 1
Bhava 73
Bhillas 49
Bhīṣma-Pañcaka 213
Bhuvaneśvara 72
Bilva, fruit of a 84
Bilveśa 18, 83, 84
Bilveśvara 82, 109
Bindutīrtha 79, 203
Boar 2, 177
Body, wooden 162
Boon 75
Brahmā 5, 6, 8, 12, 15, 46, 55, 71, 76, 78, 91, 93, 97, 105, 106, 108, 116, 121, 124, 125, 126, 127, 128, 129, 130, 132, 133, 135, 139, 146, 147, 150, 153, 157, 159, 163, 165, 168, 184, 208, 227, 233, 234, 243, 255
Brahmā, abode of 55
Brahmā, son of 54, 72
Brahmā, world of 97, 120, 125
Brahmaloka 124
Brāhmaṇa 102, 136, 144, 221, 222, 233, 236, 260
Brāhmaṇa-slaughter 15, 40, 89
Brahman in wooden form 199
Bṛhaspati 32
Bull 76

Caṇḍa 215, 235
Cāṇḍāla 81 123
Caṇḍarūpā 18
Cāndrāyaṇa 213
Carcikā 67
Carpenter, Nārāyaṇa as 112
Cāturmāsya 210 ftn
Catuṣpāda 205
Cause 43
Chariot, protecting the 207
Citrotpalā 68, 77
Conch 59
Conduct, evil 60
Coromandal Coast 45
Cowherdesses 81
Cows, Brāhmaṇas and 86
Crow 33

Dakṣa 234, 251, 253
Dakṣiṇāmūrti 188 ftn

Dakṣiṇāyana 214
Damanabhañjikā 248
Damanaka 227, 248, 249
Dāmodara 233, 234
Dāru-brahman 161 ftn, 199
Dārumaya 20
Deluge 10
Devakī, son of 83
Devi Sūkta 120, 163
Devotion, Advaita (non-dualistic) 57
Devotion, characteristics of excellent 56
Devotion, steady 57
Dharā 95
Dharma 254
Dharmarāja 8, 16
Dhūrjaṭi 75, 82
Dīpaka 33
Discus 59, 75, 76, 77, 233
Divodāsa 75 ftn
Divya Kṣetra 1
Dolā-Yātrā (festival of the swing) 241 ftn
Dove, Śiva as a small 83
Durvāsas 132, 150, 234
Dvārakā 91
Dvārapālas 215

Egg, Cosmic 11, 36
Ego, Cosmic 52
Ekādaśī 194
Ekāmra 4
Ekāmraka 37
Ekāmrakavana 73
Ekāmra Kṣetra 1
Ekāmravana 79
Ekāmravanaka 72
Enjoyment, delight in sexual 60

Father-in-law's house, stay in 74
Festival of the holy bath 237
Festival of (the Deity) going to bed 209
Fish 227
Four-faced Lord 19

Gadādhara 8, 34, 44, 84
Gajendra-mokṣa 117 ftn
Gāla 145, 146, 147, 148, 256
Gaṇādhipa 235
Gandhavahā 72
Gandhavatī 72 ftn
Gaṇeśa 195
Gaṅgā 17, 55, 112, 120
Garbhaka 178
Garbhapratiṣṭhā 125
Garuḍa 53, 196
Garuḍamudrā 250
Gaurī 18, 73, 75
Gautama 129, 148, 234
Gayāśrāddha 204
Gāyatrī, Vaiṣṇava 206
Gāyatrī, Vaiṣṇavī 237
Gāyatrī, Viṣṇu 144 ftn
Govinda, festival of 243
Grahakuṁbha 63
Guṇḍicā 165, 201, 207, 253
Guṇḍicā, festival of 208, 247
Guṇḍicā-House 194 ftn

Hāhā 148, 244
Hair of Viṣṇu 110
Hālā 107
Hari 59, 112
Hari-hara 79
Himādri 74
Hiraṇyakaśipu 23, 159, 249
Horse-sacrifices, a thousand 88
Hṛṣīkeśa 206, 208
Hūhū 148, 244
Hunch-backed maiden 81
Hunter 81

Idol, wooden 28, 168
Indradyumna 19, 20, 31, 38, 39, 42, 44, 47, 60, 61, 66, 67, 69, 72, 81, 88, 90, 92, 97, 100, 103, 104, 105, 110, 111, 124, 127, 129, 130, 131, 132, 133, 135, 138, 140, 145, 147, 148, 158, 168, 169 ftn, 194 ftn, 216, 226, 243, 257, 258
Indradyumna lake 120, 194 ftn
Īśāna 18, 91

Jagannātha 22, 32, 33, 169 ftn, 185, 194 ftn
——, wooden images of 161
——temple 28 ftn
Jāhnavī 148
Jaimini 2
Janamejaya 2
Janārdana 115, 122, 203, 211, 221, 254
Jarāsandha 75
Jaya 1 ftn

Journey, three-limbed (three-saged) 207
Jyeṣṭhāsnāna 167, 188, 189

"ailāsa 27, 115
Kāka, Bhuṣaṇḍa 5
Kālarātri 18
Kālavahni 10
Kalpasūtra 99
Kalpa-tree 17
Kāma 254
Kāmākhya 16
Kamalālayā 113
Kaṁsa, Slayer of 59, 75
Kāñcī 91
Kapālamocana 15, 18
Kapoteśa 82, 85
Kapoteśvara 83
Karmaprapūraṇam, festival of 166
Karmas 4
Karmas, Fruition of 8
Kāśī 209
Kāśirāja 75, 76
Kaśyapa 234, 241
Keśava 34
Koṭiliṅgeśvara 73
Koṭīśvara 79
Kṛcchra 57, 213
Kṛṣṇa 113, 114, 121, 127, 153, 157, 185, 188, 193, 198, 201
Kṣatriyas 102, 136, 260
——, destruction of 144
Kṣetrapāla 18, 195, 235
Kubera 32, 255
Kuṁbhīpāka 219
Kurukṣetra 20, 180
Kuśasthalī 82, 83
Kutapa 204

Lakṣmī 16, 52, 77, 115, 192, 224, 233, 238
Lakṣmīsūkta 143
Laṁbā 18
Liṅgarāja 79
—— temple 89
Lion, Divine 97
Lord, Blue-throated 88
Lord, Discus-bearing 78
Lord, Four-faced 93
Lord, Lotus-born 8, 59
Lord, Pināka-bearing 75
Lord, Plough-weilding 153
Lord, Self-born 126
Lord, vanishing of the 91
Lord-with-wooden-form 80
Lores, eighteen 28
Lotus 59
Love sports 81

Mace 59
Mādhava 5, 6, 33, 34, 39, 44, 45, 53, 55, 85, 114, 145, 234
Mādhava, Blue-sapphire 110
Mādhava, Nīla 84
Madhu, Slayer of 43, 75, 78, 92
Madhuparka 177
Mahādeva 78, 80, 234
Mahājyaiṣṭhī 190, 191
Mahānadī 31, 36, 37, 68, 72
Mahāprasāda 218 ftn
Maharloka 127
Mahātala 12
Mahāvedī 194 ftn
Mahāvedī, festival of 198
Mahendra 100, 101, 105
Maheśvara 14, 121
Mālā 178
Mālava 32, 87
Mālya 178
Mamatā 117
Maṅgalā 18
Māṅgalya Sūkta 64
Maṇikarṇika 78, 169 ftn
Maṇikodara 130
Mansion 125
Mantra, Aghora 169
Mantra, Aghamarṣaṇa 182
Mantras, Śānti (Propitiatory) 64
Mantras, Vāruṇa 182
Manu, Svāyaṁbhuva 160, 164
Marīcikā 18
Mārkaṇḍa tank 169 ftn
—— Tīrtha 14 ftn
Mārkaṇḍeśvara 169 ftn
Mārkaṇḍeya 9 ftn, 12, 13, 14, 18, 145
Mārkaṇḍeyāvaṭa 169, 170
Marutta 99 ftn
Māyā 4, 7, 17, 18, 24, 26, 36, 71, 81, 87, 117, 151, 154, 161, 171, 173, 200
Māyā, master of 87
Māyāvāda 11 ftn
Merudāna 201

Milk Ocean 106
Mīmāṁsā 99
Missile, Pāśupata 76, 77
Mokṣa 122
Moon 255
Mṛḍānī, Lord of 84
Mṛkaṇḍu, son of 10
Mṛtyuñjaya 102
Mukunda 37
Mura, Enemy of 124
Mūrtipañjara 247, 248

Nāndīmukhas 63
Nārā 182
Nārada 23, 54, 60, 62, 64, 68, 70, 79, 80, 85, 86, 88, 90, 91, 93, 94, 95, 100, 108, 109, 110, 111, 112, 119, 120, 123, 125, 126, 127, 129, 130, 139, 141, 146, 149, 150, 158, 167, 215, 248
Narahari 59
Narasiṁha 94, 95, 97, 98, 124, 142, 158, 161, 181, 182, 192, 193, 210
Narasiṁha, temple of 94
Nārāyaṇa 10, 12, 20, 24, 28, 54, 161, 163, 219
——, chariot of 150
Nescience 48, 55
Nikuṁbha 75 ftn
Nīla (mountain) 4, 14, 15, 19, 20, 22, 35, 37, 43, 46, 48, 49, 51, 52, 66, 69, 70, 73, 88, 89, 114, 133, 137, 145, 159, 162, 165, 208, 220, 222, 255
——, Lord of 53
Nīlācala 2
Nīlagiri 33
Nīlakaṇṭha 14, 18, 85, 93
Nīlalohita 73
Nīlamādhava 1, 5, 38, 39, 46, 49, 86, 87, 88, 258
Nīrājana 240
Nirmālya 43, 54, 219, 220, 226, 228, 238, 239
Nitala 12 ftn
Nṛhari 65
Nṛsiṁha 16, 49, 88, 90, 93, 142, 159, 162, 203, 224, 225, 236, 257
Nṛsiṁhakṣetra 166
Nyagrodha 9 ftn

Oḍḍiānā 29
Oḍhra 33, 36, 69
Oḍhra-land 122
Oḍra 29 ftn

Padmanidhi 137, 139, 140, 146, 147, 167
Palm-tree 196
Pañcagavya 142
Pañcāmṛta 97, 211
Pañcatīrtha 169, 183
Pañcopacāras 171
Parameṣṭhin 159
Parameśvara 79
Pārśva-paryāyaṇa 229 ftn, 231
Paśupati 76
Paśus, Lord of 215
Pātāla 12 ftn, 86, 104, 105, 106
Pātāla, Lord went to 84
Pātālas 12 ftn
Pavamāna Sūkta 184
Pāvamānīyaka hymns 237
Pavilion 106
Penance, severe 83
Pināka 160
Pitāmaha 107
Pracaṇḍa 215, 235
Pradyumna 192
Prahlāda 23
Praṇava 36, 41
Prāvaraṇa 236
Prāvaraṇotsava 235
Prayāga 55
Principles, thirty-six 25
Proclamation 61
Pūjā, Ṣaḍarghya 139
Puṇḍarīka 20 ftn, 21, 26, 28
Puṇḍarīkākṣa 44
Puṇyāha 102
Puṇyāhavācana 102
Purāṇa, Ekāmra 79
Puruṣa 122
Puruṣasūkta 157, 163, 171
Puruṣottama 4, 6, 12, 13, 16, 29, 31, 33, 43, 45, 49, 50, 53, 78, 81, 88, 106, 134, 160, 173, 199, 209, 210, 214, 223, 229, 233, 235, 237, 238, 239, 251, 253, 257
Puruṣottama Kṣetra 1, 9, 80 ftn, 80
Puṣkara 91
Puṣyasnāna 238

Quarters, Guardians of the 12, 129, 130,

132, 147, 148, 195, 207, 235

Rajoguṇa 78
Ramā 95, 114, 153, 157, 165, 188, 193, 201, 203
Rāmacandra Deva 242 ftn
Rāma-Sītā 115 ftn
Rambhā 148
Rauhiṇa 4, 33, 34, 40, 45, 49
Rice, boiled 218 ftn
Rohiṇa Kuṇḍa 5 ftn, 16, 51
Rohiṇī 113
Rudra 15, 18, 116
Rudrāṇī, eight different forms of 18

Śabara 42, 43
Śabara Dīpaka 37
Śabaras 33
Śabda-brahman 52, 101, 107
Śacīpati 100
Sage, Celestial 108
Sages, Seven 99, 105, 126
Śakra 121, 128, 129, 230, 254
Śaktis, eight 17
Śākuna Sūkta 197
Śālagrāma 222
Śambhu 75, 97, 978
Sanaka 23, 107, 118
Sanandana 118
Sanātana 118
Sanatkumāra 234, 255
Śāṇḍilya 222, 225
Sands, golden 85, 90
Sands, Lord Mādhava vanished beneath the 101
Śaṅkha-Kṣetra 1, 88
Śāradā 130, 149
Sarvamaṅgalā 18
Sarvatobhadra 206, 237, 247
Sattvaguṇa 78
Satya 131
Satyabhāmā 64, 77
Satyaloka 129, 138
Sāvitrī 130, 149
Seed, offering of germinating 237
Śeṣa 12, 27
Sheaths, five 36
Śiva 75 ftn, 84
Śiva, eight forms of 83 ftn
Sleep, festival of 210
Ṣoḍaśopacāra 171 ftn
Śrīkānta 8, 45
Śrīkṛṣṇa 43, 84
Śrī Kṣetra 1
Śrīnātha 54
Śrīpuruṣottama 8, 46, 69, 77, 88
Śrī Sūkta 157, 238, 243, 251
Śrīvāsudeva 33
Storm 70
Subhadrā 19, 27, 112, 113, 114, 115, 118, 127, 157, 163, 165, 183, 188, 193, 198, 199, 201, 203, 208, 239
Subhadrā, chariot of 140, 143, 154
Sudarśana 18, 53, 112, 113, 114, 115, 118
Sudarśana Sūkta 120
Śūdras 102, 136, 144, 260
Sutala 12 ftn
Sutyā 109
Svargadvāra 173
Svarṇādri 89
Svarṇarekhā 31
Svārociṣa 132
Svastivācana 102 ftn
Svāyambhuva 133
Śveta 216, 218, 219, 257
Śvetadvīpa 88, 91, 106, 110
Śvetagaṅgā tank 169 ftn
Śvetamādhava 218
Śvetavārāh Kalpa 133

Tāladhvaja 140
Talātala 12
Tamōgṇa 77
Tāpatraya 2
Thoughts, evil 60
Tīrtharāja 22 ftn, 28, 51, 84, 174, 175, 176, 181, 233
Tree 80
Tree, a great 109
Tree, Viṣṇu's hair assumed the form of a 110
Tribhuvaneśa 79
Tribhuvaneśvara 79
Trimadhu 119
Triṇāciketa 119
Tripuras 77
Trisuparṇa 119
Trivikrama 239, 240
Tulāpuruṣa 120, 204, 241
Tulasī 228

Tvaṣṭṛ, son of 94

Ucchiṣṭa 225
Unguent, removal of 114
Utkala 22, 29
Utkala, king of 69, 70
Utthāpana 229 ftn, 231

Vācaspati 255
Vaikuṇṭha 50, 129, 168, 208
Vaiṣṇavas 59
Vaiśyas 102, 136, 260
——, destruction of 144
Vanajāgaraṇa 205
Vārāṇasī 75, 76
Varuṇa Sūkta 175
Vasiṣṭha 234
Vāsudeva 58, 78, 121, 193
——, chariot of 140
Vaṭeśa 18
Vedas 123
Vidhi 121
Vidyā 58
Vidyāpati 34, 35, 37, 46, 47, 48, 49, 85
Vimalā 15, 16, 18
Vīrabhadra 169
Viraja Maṇḍala 78
Viśvakarman 99
Viṣṇu 8, 9, 17, 34, 43, 49, 54, 55, 61, 71, 82, 83, 88, 93, 100, 101, 110, 112, 113, 114, 121, 122, 124, 127, 130, 146, 153, 185, 215, 219, 222, 226, 227, 228, 234
Viṣṇu, Bhakti unto 57
Viṣṇu, characteristics of those who are devotees of 58
Viṣṇu, city of 53
Viṣṇu, devotee of 58
Viṣṇu, devotion to 56
Viṣṇu, idol of 123
Viṣṇu, mansion of 124
Viṣṇu, Nirmālya of 43
Viṣṇu, non-devotees of 60
Viṣṇu, tree of 111
Viṣṇu, wooden idol of 123
Viṣṇu of wooden forms 88
Viṣṇu's superiority 73
Viśvakarmā 19, 75, 80, 140
Viśvakarman 52, 93, 140, 145
Viśvakarman, idol of Narasiṁha made by 95
Viśvāvasu 37, 38, 41, 51, 114
Vitala 12 ftn
Vṛddhikarman 102
Vṛndāvana 83

Wooden Brahman 161 ftn

Yajñapuruṣa 45, 100
Yajñas, Lord of 104
Yajñavarāha 192
Yama 8, 18, 19, 44
Yameśvara 14, 18
Yamunā 148, 149
Yātrā 208, 250
Yātrā, Tryavayava 207
Yātrās 229
Yoga, eight aṅgas of 25 ftn
Yogakṣema 24
Yoga Nidrā 134
Yoga Paṭṭa 192 ftn
Yugādi 205

ANCIENT INDIAN TRADITION & MYTHOLOGY

Translated by

A BOARD OF SCHOLARS

Edited by

Dr. G.P. BHATT

Late Prof. J.L. SHASTRI

VOLUME 8

ANCIENT INDIAN TRADITION AND MYTHOLOGY SERIES

[PURĀṆAS IN TRANSLATION]

Volumes Released

ŚIVA 1-4
LIṄGA 5-6
BHĀGAVATA 7-11
GARUḌA 12-14
NĀRADA 15-19
KŪRMA 20-21
BRAHMĀṆḌA 22-26
AGNI 27-30
VARĀHA 31-32
BRAHMA 33-36
VĀYU 37-38
PADMA 39-48
SKANDA, PARTS I-XXI, 49-69
VĀMANA 72

Volumes Under Preparation

SKANDA, PARTS XXII-XXIII, 70-71
BHAVIṢYA
BRAHMAVAIVARTA
DEVĪBHĀGAVATA
KĀLIKĀ
MĀRKAṆḌEYA
MATSYA
VIṢṆU
VIṢṆUDHARMOTTARA

THE BHĀGAVATA PURĀṆA

Translated and Annotated by

DR. G. V. TAGARE

PART II

MOTILAL BANARSIDASS PUBLISHERS
PRIVATE LIMITED • DELHI

Reprint: Delhi, 1979, 1986, 1993, 2002, ***2007***
First Edition : Delhi, 1976

ISBN: 978-81-208-0201-8

MOTILAL BANARSIDASS
41 U.A. Bungalow Road, Jawahar Nagar, Delhi 110 007
8 Mahalaxmi Chamber, 22 Bhulabhai Desai Road, Mumbai 400 026
203 Royapettah High Road, Mylapore, Chennai 600 004
236, 9th Main III Block, Jayanagar, Bangalore 560 011
Sanas Plaza, 1302 Baji Rao Road, Pune 411 002
8 Camac Street, Kolkata 700 017
Ashok Rajpath, Patna 800 004
Chowk, Varanasi 221 001

UNESCO COLECTION OF REPRESENTATIVE WORKS— Indian Series
This book has been accepted in the Indian Translation Series of the UNESCO Collection of Representative Works, jointly sponsored by the United Nations Educational Scientific and Cultural Organization (UNESCO) and the Government of India

PRINTED IN INDIA

BY JAINENDRA PRAKASH JAIN AT SHRI JAINENDRA PRESS,
A-45 NARAINA, PHASE-I, NEW DELHI 110 028
AND PUBLISHED BY NARENDRA PRAKASH JAIN FOR
MOTILAL BANARSIDASS PUBLISHERS PRIVATE LIMITED,
BUNGALOW ROAD, DELHI 110 007

PUBLISHER'S NOTE

The purest gems lie hidden in the bottom of the ocean or in the depth of rocks. One has to dive into the ocean or delve into the rocks to find them out. Similarly, truth lies concealed in the language which with the passage of time has become obsolete. Man has to learn that language before he discovers that truth.

But he has neither the means nor the leisure to embark on that course. We have, therefore, planned to help him acquire knowledge by an easier course. We have started the series of *Ancient Indian Tradition and mythology* in English Translation. Our goal is to universalize knowledge through the most popular international medium of expression. The publication of the Purāṇas in English translation is a step towards that goal.

PREFACE

The present Volume contains the *Bhāgavata Purāṇa* Part II (Skandhas 4-6) in English translation. It is the eighth in the series of fifty Volumes on *Ancient Indian Tradition and mythology*.

The project of the series was envisaged and financed in 1970 by Shri Sundarlal Jain, the Veteran enterprizer in the field of Oriental Publication and the leading partner Messrs Motilal Banarsidass. Hitherto eight Volumes of the Series (that is, four Vols. of the *Śiva Purāṇa*, two Vols. of the *Liṅga Purāṇa* and two Vols. of the *Bhāgavata Purāṇa*, Skandhas 1-6) have been published and released for sale.

The present translation is based on the Sanskrit text of the *Bhāgavata Purāṇa* published by Messrs Kṣemarāja Śrīkṛṣṇadāsa Veṅkateśvara Press, Bombay. This text, constructed on the Collation of mss and supported by the oldest Commentator Śrīdhara Svāmin, is fairly accurate. But we have also recorded the translation of all the additional verses accepted as genuine in the authoritative commentaries of Rāmānuja and Madhva Schools, that are not found in the text of Śrīdhara Svāmin.

The *Bhāgavata Purāṇa* deals with a variety of subjects—geographical, historical, philosophical, religious and the like which need elucidation. This task could not be accomplished by a mere translation. We have, therefore, provided footnotes on the topics. On the philosophical verses, especially, we have recorded different interpretations of the commentators belonging to different schools of thought, viz. those of Śaṅkara, Rāmānuja, Madhva, Nimbārka, Vallabha and Caitanya (Gauḍīya School of Vaiṣṇavism) and also two eminent Marathi Commentators—Kṛṣṇa Dayārṇava and Ekanātha. In the accomplishment of this task we have also utilized the commentaries published in the Bhāgavata Vidyā Peeth Ahmedabad Edition and the Vrindavana edition of this Purāṇa.

In order to help the reader understand the background of the subject matter we have prefixed to part I a critical and comparative introduction which discusses, among other topics, the date, authorship, philosophy, religion, general characteristics and the commentators of this Purāṇa. A List of Abbreviations is also prefixed to Part I, while a general index will be included in the last part of this work.

Before closing, it is our pleasant duty to put on record our sincere gratitude to Dr.S.K. Chatterjee, Dr. V. Raghavan, Dr. R.N. Dandekar, Shri K.R. Kripalani, and the authorities of the UNESCO for their kind encouragement and valuable help which render this work more valuable to scholars than it would otherwise have been. We must also thank the learned translator and annotator Dr. G.V. Tagare for his untiring zeal and sustained efforts in bringing out this Volume within scheduled time, in spite of untold obstacles.

Finally, we avail of this opportunity to state that any critical suggestion and advice for improvement are welcome and will receive proper consideration from us.

—Editor

CONTENTS

Skandha IV

Chapters

1. The progeny of Svāyambhuva Manu's Daughters 421
2. The Rift between Śiva and Dakṣa 429
3. Śiva dissuades Satī from attendance at Dakṣayajña 435
4. Satī's Self-immolation by yoga 438
5. Destruction of Dakṣa's Sacrifice 444
6. Appeasement of Rudra—Revival of Dakṣa 447
7. Completion of Dakṣa's Sacrifice 455
8. Story of Dhruva 468
9. Viṣṇu's boon and Dhruva's Coronation 478
10. Dhruva invades Alakā 489
11. Svāyambhuva Manu dissuades Dhruva from fighting 492
12. Kubera's Boon and Dhruva's attainment of Viṣṇu's realm 498
13. Dhruva's descendants : King Aṅga's abdication 504
14. The story of Vena : Pṛthu's Birth 510
15. Birth of Pṛthu and his Coronation 515
16. The Eulogy of Pṛthu by Bards 519
17. Pṛthu subjugates the Earth 522
18. Milking of the Earth 527
19. Pṛthu's Conquest : His Horse sacrifice and Conflict with Indra 530
20. Pṛthu initiated by Viṣṇu 536
21. Pṛthu explains Dharma to his subjects 543
22. Sanatkumāra's Sermon to Pṛthu 552
23. Pṛthu's penance and ascension to Heaven 563
24. Pṛthu's Descendants and the Hymn of Rudra 569
25. The Story of Purañjana—Introduction 583
26. Purañjana's Hunting Expedition and His Queen's wrath Pacified 591
27. Invasion of Caṇḍavega—The Episode of Kālakanyā 595

28. Purañjana's Rebirth as a woman and Attainment of Liberation 599
29. The Purañjana allegory explained 608
30. The Story of Pracetas—their marriage with Māriṣā and the birth of Dakṣa 621
31. The Story of Pracetasas : Their Renunciation and Liberation 628

Skandha V

Chapters

1. The Life of Priyavrata 634
2. The History of Agnīdhra 643
3. The History of Nābhi—Incarnation of Ṛṣabha 647
4. The miraculous history of Ṛṣabha 651
5. Ṛṣabha's discourse on the Path of Liberation 654
6. Ṛṣabha quits his body 661
7. The Life of Bharata 665
8. Bharata reborn as a deer 669
9. Bharata reborn as a Brāhmaṇa, saved by Bhadrakālī 674
10. Bharata's Life : King Rahūgaṇa accepts discipleship 680
11. Bharata imparts spiritual Knowledge to Rahūgaṇa 686
12. Dialogue between Bharata and Rahūgaṇa 690
13. The Saṁsāra—a forest : An allegory 694
14. Explanation of the Allegory of Saṁsāra—Forest 700
15. Description of Bharata's Dynasty 708
16. Mythological Geography—The Terrestrial Globe 711
17. Descent of the Gaṅgā 716
18. Description of Various Continents 722
19. Description of Kimpuruṣa and Bhārata Varṣas 730
20. Description of the remaining six Dvīpas 737
21. Stellar Region 745
22. Description of the moon and other Planets 748
23. Description of Viṣṇu-pada—the position of Dhruva and Śisumāra Cakra 752
24. Rāhu's Position and Subterranean Regions 755
25. Description of Saṅkarṣaṇa—the Serpent Śeṣa 761
26. Description of Hells 764

Skandha VI

Chapters

1. The Story of Ajāmila 773
2. Exposition of the Bhāgavata Dharma; Efficacy of the Lord's name and Ajāmila's Ascension to Viṣṇu-loka 782
3. Yama explains Viṣṇu's greatness 789
4. History of Dakṣa, the son of Pracetas 795
5. Dakṣa curses Nārada 803
6. Progeny of Dakṣa's Daughters 809
7. Bṛhaspati's insult and his abandonment of Preceptorship 813
8. Nārāyaṇa-Kavaca 818
9. Slaying of Viśvarūpa. Approach of gods to Dadhīci 824
10. Indra-Vṛtra fight 833
11. Indra-Vṛtra fight 837
12. Vṛtra slain by Indra 840
13. Indra's Triumph 845
14. Previous Birth of Vṛtra—King Citraketu 848
15. Consolation of Citraketu 854
16. Citraketu's Realization of Lord Ananta 858
17. Citraketu cursed by Pārvatī 866
18. Birth of the Maruts 871
19. Details of the Vow—Puṁsavana 880

FOURTH SKANDHA

CHAPTER ONE

(*The Progeny of Svāyambhuva Manu's Daughters*)

Maitreya said:

1. Besides (his two sons Priyavrata and Uttānapāda) Manu had three daughters from Śatarūpā. They became well known as Ākūti, Devahūti and Prasūti.

2. The king, with the consent of Śatarūpā, gave Ākūti to (the progenitor) Ruci in marriage, on condition of *Putrikā dharma*[1] (even though) Ākūti had brothers.

3. The venerable progenitor Ruci, full of the spiritual glory of Brahman, begot through her a twin—a son and a daughter, by virtue of his supreme concentration (of mind on the Lord).

4. Of the two, the male child was Viṣṇu himself who had assumed the form of Yajña). And the female child was called Dakṣiṇā ('sacrificial fee') who was a part of Lakṣmī (the goddess of fortune) inseparable (from Viṣṇu)[2].

5. (As per stipulation in the marriage) Svāyambhuva Manu brought to his house his daughter's son of pervasive glory. With great delight, Ruci (also) joyfully accepted Dakṣiṇā (as his child).

6. Lord Yajña, the Lord of all Sacrifices (or *mantras*) married her (Dakṣiṇā) who was in love with him. He felt

---

1. *Putrikā-dharma* : When a daughter is given in marriage on the explicit condition that the first male child of the daughter shall be the (adopted) son of the giver, it is called *Putrikā dharma*. This was done by one who had only daughters and no son. The obvious object was securing the continuity of one's race. VJ. explains that although Manu had sons, he laid down this condition as he knew that Lord Viṣṇu would be born to Ākūti. He wished to secure Viṣṇu's higher grace by becoming his adopted father.

2. *anapāyinī* : ŚR., VR. VC. point out that Dakṣiṇā was an *aṁśa* (part) of Lakṣmī. Hence the marriage of *Yajña* and *Dakṣiṇā*, though born as brother and sister, is not objectionable. VJ. takes the word to mean 'One who has neither birth nor death'. Like Nārāyaṇa, Lakṣmī manifested herself to others as an *āvirbhāva*.

delighted and had twelve sons by hér, who too was highly pleased.

7. These twelve sons were : Toṣa, Pratoṣa, Santoṣa, Bhadra, Śānti, Iḍaspati, Idhma, Kavi, Vibhu, Svahna, Sudeva, Rocana.

8. In the epoch (*Manvantara*) called Svāyambhuva, they (these sons of Yajña and Dakṣiṇā) officiated as gods, and were (collectively) called *Tuṣitas*; Marīci and others were the seven sages (*Saptarṣis* of that era) while Yajña, the incarnation of Hari, occupied the post of Indra (the rulership of gods).

9. Priyavrata and Uttānapāda, the sons of Manu, were endowed with great power and splendour. They, their sons, grandsons (both from sons and daughters) and their descendants ruled throughout the period (of this *Manvantara*)*.

10. Oh Vidura, Manu gave his (second) daughter Devahūti to Kardama (a Lord of created beings). (History) relating to them has been already heard by you as narrated by me.

11. Venerable Manu gave (his third daughter) Prasūti (in marriage) to Dakṣa (another Lord of creation), a mind-born son of Brahmā. Their progeny has very widely spread all over the three worlds.

12. Now, hear as I tell you about the sons and grandsons of the nine daughters of Kardama who became the wives of the Brāhmaṇa Sages (born of Brahmā) and about whom I have spoken to you.

13. Kalā, the daughter of Kardama and the wife of the sage Marīci, gave birth to two sons—Kaśyapa and Pūrṇiman whose descendants have fully populated (filled) the world.

14. Oh conquorer of enemies (Vidura), Pūrṇiman was the father of (sons) Viraja and Viśvaga and (a daughter called) Devakulyā who washing the feet of Hari became the heavenly river Gaṅgā (in her next birth).

*According to VP. 3.2.48 every Manvantara (epoch of a manu) has the following batch of office bearers: (1) Manu, (2) seven sages—Saptarṣis, (3) gods, (4) The ruler of gods—Indra, (5) Ruling progeny of Manu. To these Bh.P. 12,7.15 adds : (6) Incarnations of Hari. The dignitaries of these posts in the Svāyambhuva Manvantara are mentioned in the above verses.

15. Anasūyā, the wife of Atri, gave birth to three illustrious sons, viz. Datta (god Dattātreya, the sage), Durvāsas and the Moon-god, each of whom was separately born (as a manifestation of the portion) of Viṣṇu, Rudra and Brahmā (respectively).

Vidura said :

16. Oh Preceptor, please narrate to me for what purpose these (three) most eminent gods who are severally the cause of the creation, preservation and destruction (of the world), were born in the house of (the sage) Atri.

Maitreya said :

17. When the sage Atri, the foremost of the knowers of Brahman, was urged by god Brahmā (to undertake the work of) creation, he along with his wife went to one of the principal mountain ranges, Ṛkṣa[3] and was engaged in the performance of austere penance.

18-19. The mountain was covered with the forest of *Palāśa* and *Aśoka* trees which were beautified with clusters of flowers. All around, it was resounded with the echoes of the waterfalls of the river Nirvindhyā. On that mountain, the sage controlled his mind by means of Prāṇāyāma (breath-control) and stood for one hundred years on one leg, defying heat and cold (and such other pairs of opposites), and subsisted on air.

20. He contemplated (and prayed in his mind): 'I take shelter under him who alone is the Lord of the World. May he bless me with progeny just like himself.'

21-22. Seeing that the three worlds were being distressed by the fire produced by the fuel of (the sage's) breath-control (Prāṇāyāma) and issuing from the head of the sage, the three Lords (of the world, Brahmā, Viṣṇu and Śiva) went to the hermitage of the sage—the three Gods whose glories were extensively eulogised by celestial damsels, sages, Gandharvas

3. *Ṛkṣa*—The eastern part of the Vindhya range extending from the Bay of Bengal to the sources of the Narmadā and the Śoṇa—including the mountains of Chhota Nagpur and Gondwana in which the Mahānadī rises—GDAMI 168-69.

(celestial musicians), and (demigods like) Siddhas, Vidyādharas and Nāgas.

23. The sage got his mind illuminated by the simultaneous manifestation of the three gods. (To show them respect) he stretched up his body (while standing on the leg), and saw those prominent gods.

24. (He paid them homage) by prostrating himself fully (before them) on the ground, like a stick. With articles of worship in the hollow of his palms, he respectfully received the gods who were severally riding a swan, Garuḍa and a bull and were characterised by their speciality (viz. possession of a Kamaṇḍalu, Sudarśana discus and a trident).

25. They directly expressed their pleasure by their gracious looks and smiling faces. The sage closed his eyes as they were dazzled by their (gods') brilliance.

26. With his mind concentrated on them and with folded palms he praised, in sweet words of deep significance, the three gods who are the supreme-most in all the worlds.

Atri said :

27. You are (obviously the celebrated gods) Brahmā, Viṣṇu and Śiva who in every Yuga (kalpa), assume forms with the help of the *guṇas* (attributes) of Māyā, trifurcated for bringing about the creation, maintenance and dissolution of the universe. I bow to you all. (Kindly tell me) which of you has been invocated by me here.

28. In this hermitage, I have concentrated (contemplated) only on one glorious Lord by various means, with a desire to get a child. It is a great surprise to me how (all of) you who are beyond the range of the mind of bodied beings, have come here. Be pleased to tell me the mystery.

Maitreya said :

29. Oh Lord (Vidura), hearing this speech of the sage (Atri), the three prominent gods laughed. They replied to the sage in soft gentle words (as follows) :

The gods said :

30. "Oh Brahman ! As you have willed it, so shall it exactly happen and not otherwise. You are of true resolve. We

three form that Principle (called the Lord of the world) which you are contemplating.

31. Oh sage! May you be blessed! from our aṁśa (parts) now you will beget sons who (themselves) will be celebrated in the world and spread your reputation as well."

32. Having granted their desired boon, the Lords of gods who were properly worshipped by the couple, returned from that hermitage while they (Atri and Anasūyā) stood looking on (agape).

33. Thus Soma was born with a portion of Brahmā, Datta, the master of Yoga, with that of Viṣṇu, while Durvāsas with the portion of Śaṅkara. Now listen (to me), about the progeny of Aṅgiras (another mind-born son of Brahmā).

34. Śraddhā, the wife of Aṅgiras gave birth to four daughters viz. Sinīvālī, Kuhū, Rākā and the fourth Anumati.[4]

35. Besides these he (Aṅgiras) had two sons—Utathya who was the venerable Lord himself and Bṛhaspati (the preceptor of gods) the eminent knower of Brahman. They became celebrities in the Svārociṣa Manvantara.

36. By his wife Havirbhū, Pulastya (another mind-born son of Brahmā) had a son called Agastya who was abdominal fire in another birth and also (another son) Viśravas, the great ascetic.

37. Of Viśravas and his wife Iḍaviḍā was born god Kubera (the god of Wealth), the king of Yakṣas. Rāvaṇa, Kumbhakarṇa and Vibhīṣaṇa were born (to him) by another wife (Keśinī).

38. Oh talented Vidura, Gati, the pious wife of Pulaha, gave birth to three sons, viz. Karmaśreṣṭha, Varīyān and Śahiṣṇu.

39. Even Kratu's wife, Kriyā, bore sixty-thousand (thumb-sized) sons known as Vālakhilyas—all brilliant with the splendour of Brahman.

4. These are the deities presiding over the 14th and 15th day of the bright and dark fortnights who came to designate those days. Thus Sinīvālī is the day preceding the new moon day. On this day the moon rises with a scarcely visible crescent, while Kuhū is the 15th day or the last day of the lunar month when the moon is invisible. Rākā presides over the full moon (15th) day, while Anumati is the 14th day in the bright half—Vide ASD under these heads.

40. Oh tormentor of enemies (Vidura), by his wife Ūrjā (Arundhatī) Vasiṣṭha had seven sons of whom Citraketu was prominent. They all were pure-hearted Brāhmaṇa-sages.

41. They were Citraketu, Surociṣ, Virajas, Mitra, Ulbaṇa, Vasubhṛd yāna and Dyumat. He had other sons such as Śakti and others (by another wife).

42. Citti (or Śānti), the wife of Atharvan, got a son, Dadhīci alias Aśvaśiras who took the vow (of austere penance). (Henceforth) hear from me the race of Bhṛgus.

43. The distinguished sage Bhṛgu begot by his wife, Khyāti, (two) sons—Dhātṛ and Vidhātṛ, and a daughter, Śrī, who was devoted to the glorious Lord (Viṣṇu).

44. (The sage) Meru gave his daughters Āyati and Niyati (in marriage) to these (sons of Bhṛgu) severally. Of them (Āyati and Niyati) were born Mṛkaṇḍa and Prāṇa (respectively).

45. Of Mṛkaṇḍa was born Mārkaṇḍeya, and of Prāṇa, the sage Vedaśiras. Kavi, (another) son of Bhṛgu, had the venerable Uśanas (Śukrācārya, the preceptor of Daityas) as his son.

46. All these sages peopled the worlds by their descendants. I have narrated to you, Oh Vidura, the account of the progeny of Kardama's grandsons (from daughters' side)—an account which immediately removes the sins of the faithful and reverential listener.

47. Dakṣa, another (mind-born) son of god Brahmā, married Prasūti, the daughter of (Svāyambhuva) Manu[5]. He begot, by her, sixteen fair-eyed daughters.

48. The Lord (Prajāpati Dakṣa) gave thirteen of his daughters to Dharma, one to Agni, one to all Pitṛs combined, and one to god Śiva, who cuts the bonds of Saṁsāra.

49*. Śraddhā, Maitrī, Dayā, Śānti, Tuṣṭi, Puṣṭi, Kriyā, Unnati, Buddhi, Medhā, Titikṣā, Hrī and Mūrti—these (thirteen) are the wives of Dharma.

50*. Śraddhā gave birth to Śubha (auspiciousness), Maitrī to Prasāda, Dayā to Abhaya, Śanti to Sukha, Tuṣṭi to Mud (a daughter) Puṣṭi to Smaya.

5. Vide supra 4.1.11 above.

Vide infra p. 427, note

51-52*. Kriyā bore Yoga, Unnati, Darpa; Buddhi, Artha; Medhā, Smṛti (a daughter); Titikṣā, Kṣema and Hrī, a son called Praśraya. Mūrti who was the fountain-head of all excellent qualities, gave birth to sages Nara and Nārāyaṇa.

53. When these two (sages) were born, the universe rejoiced with great pleasure. The minds (of men), the quarters, winds, rivers and mountains—all became calm and serene.

54. Trumpets were blown in the heavens; showers of flowers rained; sages offered their prayers. Gandharvas and Kinnaras sang joyfully.

55. The celestial nymphs and goddesses danced; highest bliss reigned everywhere. (There was auspiciousness everywhere). All divinities like Brahmā (and others) attended upon (Nara and Nārāyaṇa) with eulogistic prayers.

Gods said :

56**. Salutations to the Supreme Man who, manifested in himself this universe created by his own Māyā power, just like the phenomenal appearance (e.g. a city of Gandharvas) in the (cloudy) sky, and who appeared today, in the house of

---

*Dharma (Religion or Piety) is always associated with virtues or certain pious mental states. These are described as the wives of Dharma and his progeny from them.

**(i) By his Will or Māyā power, this created universe is supported on Brahman, but it does not affect the Brahman, just as colours blue, white etc. of the clouds, do not stick to the sky. Or the changes of form, such as that of a god or a subhuman being with which *jīva* is associated (when it is born in that particular *yoni*), do not affect the real nature of Ātman. The Lord has manifested himself as sages under the roof of Dharma in order to instruct the distinctness of Ātman, Brahman, from the form of god, man etc., and to lead to liberation by this knowledge. We bow to that Supreme Person.—VR.

(ii) His own Māyā has arranged (created) this universe on the support of Ātman like the cluster of clouds in the sky. For shedding light (explaining the nature) of the Ātman, he has manifested himself.—VC.

(iii) Just as different kinds of cavities, (*ghaṭākāśa*, *maṭhākāśa*) are in the sky, similarly the universe is arranged (created) in Yourself. Just as the sky is neither different from, nor circumscribed by, these cavities or vacuums, so also the Lord is neither affected nor delimited by the universe. The illustration of the sky is taken to emphasize the unattachedness and not unreality.—GD.

VB. has not written his commentary on this skandha.

Dharma, in the form of sages (Nara and Nārāyaṇa), for revealing the true nature of the Self.

57. May the Lord, whose real nature is to be inferred by the Śāstras, condescend to look on us, the gods, who have been created by him, by means of Sattva, for the protection of the world from the disturbances in the orderly existence of the world—his eyes which are overflowing with mercy and which surpass the beautiful lotus, receptacle of Śrī (or the home of Lakṣmī).

58. Oh child (Vidura), the two divine sages who were thus extolled and worshipped by the (multitude of) gods, blessed them by their look, and left for mount Gandhamādana.

59. Verily, those two part (-manifestations) of Lord Hari, have incarnated in this world as Kṛṣṇa, the descendant of Yadu, and the dark-complexioned Arjuna of the Kuru race, for relieving the burden of the earth.

60. And Svāhā, the wife of Agni, gave birth to three sons—Pāvaka, Pavamāna and Śuci—all of whom are the deities presiding over Agni, and who subsist on sacrificial offerings.

61. They gave birth to fortyfive fires. These fortyfive fires, their three fathers (Pāvaka, Pavamāna and Śuci) and one grandfather (god Agni) make fortynine fire-gods.

62. These are the fire-gods in whose name *iṣṭis* (small sacrifices) called Āgneya (pertaining to Agni) are performed during Vedic sacrificial sessions, by persons, well-versed in the Vedas.

63. The manes (Pitṛs) are* (1) Agniṣvātta, (2) Barhiṣad, (3) Saumya and (4) Ājyapa. They are either Sāgnaya (receiving libations of water through the sacred fire) or Anagnaya (receiving libations directly without *agnaukaraṇa*). Svadhā, the daughter of Dakṣa was their wife.

64. Svadhā bore to them two daughters—Vayunā and Dhāriṇī. Both of them were well-versed in scriptural knowledge and spiritual knowledge, and they expounded the same.

*These are main divisions of the Pitṛs : (1) Those who joined the manes by following only *Smārta karmas* are *Agniṣvātta*; (2) Those who joined forefathers after performing *Agnihotra* and Vedic sacrifices are *Barhiṣadas*; (3) Those who drink Soma in sacrifices and become Pitṛs are *Somapas* or Saumyas; and (4) Those who partake of ghee in sacrifices are *ājyapa*.

65. Though Satī, the wife of Śiva who was like him in qualities and character served him, she had no son.

66. (For) when she was quite young, she cast off her body of her own accord by Yogic process, as she was angry with her father who was antagonistic to her innocent husband, Śiva.

CHAPTER TWO

(*The Rift between the God Śiva and Dakṣa**)

Vidura said :

1. Dakṣa was affectionate to his daughter. Why did he disregard his own daughter Satī and cherish hatred towards Śiva who was the foremost among the virtuous ?

**Introductory* : Chapters 2 to 7 (both inclusive) treat of the legend of Dakṣa's sacrifice. It is a very popular legend and is found in MBH. Shānti. 284 (283 is a different episode), the Va. P. Ch. 30 (which repeats verbatim the MBH. text), to mention a few pre-Bhāgavata texts.

The development of the conception of Dakṣa in the Vedic period is traced in PCK 407 and *MP-a Study* 54-8. This solar deity of the Vedic age seems to have developed into two Dakṣas in the Purāṇic period : (1) Dakṣa Prajāpati of the Svāyambhuva Era (*Manvantara*) and (2) Dakṣa Prācetasa of the Sāvarṇi Era. The MBH and subsequently Va.P. mix up these two Dakṣas and the story of the destruction of the sacrifice of the first Dakṣa is described to have happened in the case of the second (Prācetasa) Dakṣa.

According to the BH.P. the cause of rift between Dakṣa and Śiva is due to Dakṣa's insult by Śiva (Bh. P. IV. 2, Br. P. I.1.64). But in MBH. and Va.P. it is the argument between Dakṣa and Dadhīci as to the relative superiority of Śiva and Viṣṇu which led Dakṣa to ignore Śiva during the sacrifice.

It is possible that this legend represents the conflict between the *pravṛtti dharma* characterised by the orthodox sacrificial culture and the *nivṛtti dharma* emphasizing renunciation and Yoga. The latter may be pre-Aryan as the relics of Yogins and Śiva worship are found in the Indus valley. But it is an overstatement to say that this legend is a symbol of the struggle between monarchy and republics as stated by Dr. T.S. Rukmani (*A Critical Study of the Bh.P.* 100-2).

2. Who would and how could one hate the god Śiva who is a great divinity to the world of the movables and immovables; who bears enmity towards none, and who is tranquillity incarnate; and who is delighted in his own blissful self ?

3. Oh Brahman ! Narrate to me what led to the enmity between the son-in-law (Śiva) and the father-in-law (Dakṣa) which made Satī give up her life with which it is difficult to part.

Maitreya said :

4. Formerly during the sacrificial session of the Prajāpatis (progenitors of the world) were assembled great seers and sages, all classes of gods including divinities presiding over the sacred fires, along with their attendants.

5-6. When Dakṣa who was brilliant like the Sun entered, he dispelled the darkness of the great assembly-hall by his splendour. Seeing him, all the members of the assembly, including the presiding deities of fire, were overwhelmed with his brilliiance, and stood up from their seats. Only Brahmā and god Śiva did not stand up.

7. The leaders of the assembly reverentially received Lord Dakṣa. He bowed down to god Brahmā, the creator of the universe and with Brahmā's permission, he took his seat.

8. Finding that Śiva (the Delighter of the world) was already seated and had ignored him, Dakṣa did not tolerate this. Looking askance at him, as if to consume him with the fire (of his wrath), he burst forth :

9. "Listen to me, Oh Brāhmaṇa Sages, along with gods and divinities of fire, I explain to you the mode of behaviour of good people. This is not out of jealousy or ignorance (that I speak).

10. This (god Śiva) is shameless, and has detracted the glory of the protectors of the world. This haughty fellow who does not know what should appropriately be done, has polluted the path followed by the good.

11.* He has been like a disciple unto me, as he, like a virtuous person, took the hand of my daughter who is like Sāvitrī, in the presence of Brāhmaṇas and sacrificial fire.

*Some annotators interpret this as the praise of Śiva.

12.* Having married (lit. taken the hand of) my daughter, this monkey-eyed fellow did not show due courtesy, even by words, to me whom he should have respected by standing and by bowing.

13.** To this proud, impious fellow who has given up performance of religious acts, and has violated all the bounds (of religious propriety), I gave my young daughter though reluctant to do so, as one would be to impart the sacred beautiful word (Vedas) to a Śūdra (who is not eligible to receive Vedic lore).

(i) Conforming to the traditional religious practice (at the time of his marriage), he took the hand of my daughter who is pure like Sāvitrī, in the presence of Brāhmaṇas and the sacred fire. He is, however, of the status of non-disciple i.e. worth bowing. He is a *jīvan-mukta*, and is, therefore, above formalities—GD.

(ii) Being omniscient, Śiva knew from the beginning my unworthiness which remained undisclosed till today. Hence he did not pay respect to me who am like (but not really) a good person. It is due to the virtuousness of my daughter like Sāvitrī that he married her, in the presence of Brāhmaṇas and the sacred fire—VC. & VD.

*Out of his grace, he (Śiva) satisfies the desires of persons who are passionate etc., like monkeys. He deserves to be respected by us, by standing and paying obeisance. But fie upon me ! I did not show even verbal courtesy to him—VC. & VD.

(ii) He is anxious about the redemption of people who, like a monkey, take interest in sensual pleasures. To remove the pride of the egotist Dakṣa, he established relationship with him by marrying his daughter. To eliminate his ego, Śiva incited him by not paying even verbal respect to him, though Dakṣa, as a father-in-law, should have been shown due courtesy—GD.

**(i) All religious activities are lost in Śiva as he is the Brahman. Nothing is more pure than he. He is not proud nor has he crossed any bound of propriety—VC.

VC. presumes an *avagraha* before *mānine* and *bhinna-setave*.

(ii) He is so great that even the desire to give my daughter in marriage to him did not occur to me, as comparatively my daughter was not worthy of him. It was due to the advice of Brahmā that I overcame that shyness. Śiva accepted her out of respect to Brahmā's word. Śiva is *Śūdra* i.e. one who removes grief by his favour and advice (*śucaṁ śokaṁ kṛpayā jñāna-bhaktyādyupadeśena drāvayatīti śūdraḥ* / As this belongs to 'Pṛṣodarādi' group 'c' in 'śuc' is lost and -u- is lengthened as -ū-. As to violation of etiquettes, Śiva being the Brahman, all *kriyās* (religious and other actions) are lost in him. He is absolutely pure and worthy of the highest respect. He is beyond the limits of ordinary *jīvas*. Hence the duties prescribed by the Vedas, do not apply to him.

14.* Surrounded by spirits and hosts of goblins, and with his hair scattered, he wanders in nudity, laughing and crying like a madman, in the terrible abodes of ghosts (crematories).

15.** He is bathed in the ashes of funeral pyres, and is adorned with the garlands on corpses and with human bones. He is Śiva (auspicious) in name only, but is (actually) inauspicious. He is (always) intoxicated and loved by drunken people. He is surely the Lord of devilish spirits (*pramathas*), and ghosts which are the personification of *tamo-guṇa*.

16.*** Alas! It was at the instance of god Brahmā, that I gave my virtuous daughter to such a fellow who is destitute of purity (and cleanliness), and of wicked heart, the lord of goblins (called *unmāda*).

Maitreya said :

17. Having thus reproached Śiva who sat all the while quiet (without retaliation), the enraged Dakṣa touched water (sipped it in *ācamana*) and proceeded to curse him.

18. "When sacrifices are offered to gods, this Śiva, accursed of the gods, shall not (henceforth) get his share (in

---

*VC. states that Śiva's behaviour like a mad person is his *līlā* (sports) out of godly ecstasy.

(ii) GD. : The bounds of Vedic injunctions are not applicable to a votary who has realized the Brahman. The show of madness is for the purpose of teaching the world, to renounce worldly bonds of wife, sons, property etc. Rudra performs penance, while he externally behaves like a mad person.

Cf. Supra III. 14.26.

**ŚR. explains the eulogistic aspect thus :

He, being the Brahman, no *kriyās* are possible in him. There is nobody more pure than he. I was diffident about offering my daughter (a human being) to this great god, but did so to establish relationship. There is none more auspicious than he. That he is the Lord of goblins, evil spirits etc. shows how kind he is to his devotees. He removes their *tāmasic* nature and protects. He is compassionate to the wicked in his heart. Hence he is *dur-hṛd*. I am glad (*bata*) that as per advice of Brahmā, I overcame shyness, fear etc., and gave my daughter to him.

***VR. rightly criticises the absurdity of giving double, i.e. contrary interpretations, one a praise, the other a censure of Śiva. Pertinently he asks the propriety of uttering a curse on Śiva if Dakṣa praised him so highly.

the sacrificial offerings) along with Indra, Upendra (Viṣṇu) and other gods".

19. Oh Vidura, though Dakṣa was prohibited (from uttering the curse) by prominent members of the assembly, he pronounced it, on Śiva (the Lord of the mountains). In great rage, he left the place and retired to his abode.

20. Having come to know about the curse, Nandīśvara, the leader of Śiva's followers, with his eyes reddened with anger, uttered a terrible curse upon Dakṣa and the Brāhmaṇas who approvingly listened to Śiva's denunciation.

21. "He who, being ignorant, highly thinks of this mortal frame, and hates the Lord (Śiva) who does not bear enmity against anybody, cherishes the notion of difference, and has his face turned away from the Truth.

22. With the desire of gratifying low sensual pleasure, he (Dakṣa) is attached to householder's life which is full of deceptive psuedo-religious practices. His intellect is confused by *arthavāda* in the Vedas, and he is engrossed in kārmic ritual (pertaining to sacrifices and other such acts).

23. With his intellect wrongly concentrated on the body as the Soul, and having forgotten the real nature of the Soul, Dakṣa is as good as a beast. He will be intensely addicted to women, and will soon have the head (face) of a goat.

24. This dullard (Dakṣa), who regards the *avidyā* (ignorance) consisting of performing of sacrifices and other religious acts, as the real knowledge, and those who followed him (approved of him) in his censure of Śiva, shall continue in the *saṁsāra* (the cycle of births and deaths).

25. The enemies of Hara (Śiva) shall be infatuated with (and attached to) *karmas*, as their minds will be agitated by the churning (rod) of rich promises (viz. happy life in heaven) alluring like the smell of wine given in the flowery language of the Vedas.

26. Brāhmaṇas will eat anything and everything (without considering whether it is permitted by *Śāstras*). They will be devoted to learning, *tapas* (penance) and *vratas* (vows) for the sake of their own livelihood. They shall wander a-begging in this world, taking delight in property, (pleasure of) the body and sense organs."

27. Hearing him pronounce this curse upon the Brāhmaṇa community (as a whole), Bhṛgu uttered a counter-curse which is an irrevocable punishment inflicted by Brahmanical power.

28. "Those who observe the vows to propitiate god Śiva, and those that follow them, shall be the heretics and the opponents of true Śāstras.

29. They shall lose their (sense of) purity, shall be dull-witted. They shall wear matted locks of hair and bones, and smear themselves with ashes. They shall enter the cult of Śiva worship where wine shall be the divinity.

30. As you denounce the Vedas and Brāhmaṇas who, like protective dams, lay down fixed laws restricting men (for preservation of the society), you have embraced hereticism.

31. This is the only auspicious, ancient path for the people (viz. the path laid down by the Vedas). The ancients (our forefathers) have followed it, and Janārdana is its standard authority.

32. It (Veda) is the Supreme Brahman, absolutely pure. It is the eternal path of the good. Condemning this, you shall embrace hereticism wherein the Lord of goblins is the divinity".

Maitreya said :

33. While Bhṛgu was uttering the curse, Lord Śiva, being slightly disconsolate at heart (for what had happened), left (the assembly hall), along with his followers.

34. The progenitors of the world also completed the sacrificial session of one thousand years-sacrifice in which Lord Hari was the deity to be propitiated.

35. At the conclusion of the session, they took their concluding bath (*avabhṛtha*) in the confluence of the Gaṅgā and the Yamunā. Purifying themselves thus, they returned to their respective homes.

CHAPTER THREE

(*Śiva dissuades Satī from attendance at Dakṣa-Yajña*)

Maitreya said :

1. A long time elapsed while the son-in-law (Śiva) and the father-in-law (Dakṣa), continued their lasting enmity to each other.

2. When Dakṣa was installed as the chief of all Lords of creation by Brahmā, the highest of gods, he felt puffed up with pride (An additional factor to exclude Rudra from sacrifice).

3. Having performed the Vājapeya sacrifice, and disregarded Īśvara and others who were thoroughly proficient in Brahma-Vidyā, he (Dakṣa) began the best of sacrifices, called Bṛhaspatisava (as the Śruti enjoins this sacrifice, after the performance of the Vājapeya).

4. In that sacrifice, all Brāhmaṇa sages, heavenly sages, Pitṛs (and other) divinities were welcomed with auspicious formalities. Their wives, along with their husbands, were given auspicious reception (Those divinities, whose wives attended, were thus worshipped again).

5. Goddess Satī, the daughter of Dakṣa, came to know about the grand festival of her father's sacrifice, from the talks of the heavenly beings, while they were passing through the sky.

6-7. She saw that beautiful women of demi-god tribes (e.g. Gandharvas, Yakṣas) of rolling eyes, clad in rich garments, and wearing *padakas* (a gold ornament) round their necks, and burnished ear-rings, going with their husbands, in heavenly cars, from all directions. Seeing them flying past her own mansion, she in her eagerness, spoke to her consort, god Bhūtapati (the protector of all beings).

Satī said :

8. "It is reported that the great sacrificial festival of your father-in-law, Prajāpati Dakṣa, has now commenced. Oh beautiful Lord, let us go there, if you so desire, as these gods are also going thither.

9. My sisters, desirous of seeing their kith and kin, will certainly go there with their husbands. I wish to receive along with you, the presents which will be offered by my parents.

10. Oh Śiva, really I am eagerly longing to see there, my sisters worthy of their husbands, my aunts and my mother whose heart is full of (lit. wet with) affection, and the greatest of the sacrifices being conducted by leading sages (or the flag or sacrificial post of the sacrifice raised by great sages).

11. Oh unborn Lord ! This wonderful universe consisting of three *guṇas* (*sattva*, *rajas*, *tamas*), appears created in you by your own Māyā.[6] (Hence you have no curiosity to go). I am, however, a poor woman who do not know your real nature. I, therefore, strongly desire to see my native place.

12. Oh birthless Lord, look at those other women (in no way related to Dakṣa), richly adorned, going with their husbands in crowds. Oh Śitikaṇṭha the sky looks beautiful by the movements of their aerial cars white like sweet warbling swans (Kala-haṁsas).

13. Oh great God, how can the body (including mind) of a daughter remain unmoved, after hearing about a festival in the father's house ? Even though uninvited, people go to the houses of their friends, their husbands (masters), their preceptor and parents. (The formality of invitation is superfluous in these cases).

14. Oh immortal Lord ! Be gracious unto me. You are compassionate. You should really grant me this desire. I have been located in half of your person by you who possess perfect wisdom. Do this favour as entreated by me, to you."

The Sage said :

15. Thus earnestly entreated by his beloved wife, Śiva, who was so affectionate to his friends and relatives, was (pain-

---

6. Militant Vaiṣṇava commentators like VR., VJ. refuse to give the credit of creation to Śiva. Instead of taking *aja* (unborn) as a vocative addressed to Śiva, they take *ajātma-māyayā* as one compound and interpret : 'The universe that is created by the unborn Lord Viṣṇu by his Māyā'. According to them, Śiva being a great Yogin, has the direct perception of the universe and hence no curiosity to see the festival of Dakṣa's sacrifice.

fully) reminded of the shaft-like bitter words, cutting to the quick, which Dakṣa spoke to him in the presence of (other) progenitors of the universe. He, however, replied to her with a smile.

The Lord Śiva said :

16. Oh charming lady, you have put it nicely when you said that people go to their relatives, even though they are not invited. But that is only when their vision (outlook) is not prejudiced by their powerful ego about the body being the *ātman*, and by their wrath (against such a visitor).

17. Learning, penance, wealth, beautiful personality, youth and (high) pedigree are good qualities in the case of the good, but are like a curse to the most wicked. When these attributes destroy the memory and knowledge of the wicked, they increase only the arrogance, as these wicked people cannot realize the glory of the great.

18. One should never go to the house of such persons, of unsteady minds, regarding them as relatives—persons who look upon the visitors (to their house), with crooked mentality, with frowning eye-brows and angry eyes (looks).

19. A person whose body is (deeply) wounded with arrows of the enemies, does not feel the tortures to that extent, as he who is cut to the quick by the harsh words of his own relatives of crooked minds. For the former can (at least) get sleep, but the latter suffers day and night, with a tormented heart.

20. Oh beautiful lady (of charming eyebrows), I do certainly agree that you are the most beloved of all the daughters of Dakṣa (the Lord of created beings) of eminent rank. You wlll not however receive (proper) attention or respect from your father, because of your relations with me, whom he hates intensely.

21. At the sight of the prosperity (glory, possession of *siddhis*) of great persons who stand (unconcerned) like a witness to the minds of *jīva* (i.e. are devoid of *ahaṁkāra*—ego), his heart is boiling with jealousy, and his senses are over-anxious for gratification. But being incapable of attaining to their

eminent position easily, he hates them intensely as the Asuras hated Hari.

22. Oh slender-waisted lady, the mutual exchange of respects, viz. going forth to receive, expressing modesty, paying obeisance is properly done by the wise *bhāgavatas* (devotees of the Lord) only. They do it all mentally to the Supreme Person Vāsudeva, who abides in the heart of all, but not to him who regards the Soul and the body as identical (and expects the external observance of formalities directed to his body).

23. The absolutely pure *sattva* (heart or the attribute called *sattva*) is designated as Vāsudeva; for it is in the *sattva* that Supreme Man Vāsudeva is manifested (and realized) in his real (unveiled) form. It is in the *sattva* (absolutely pure mind) that I pay obeisance[7] to him who is beyond sense perception.

24. Therefore, Oh beautiful lady, you should not see Dakṣa and his followers—even though Dakṣa is your father, the protector of your body, Dakṣa is my enemy. When I went to attend the sacrifice performed by the Prajāpatis, he expressed his hatred, by using abusive language to me, even though I was innocent (not at fault at all).

25. If you go there ignoring my advice, no good will betide you thereby. When a person of well-established reputation suffers insult from his relatives, the indignity leads immediately to his death.*

CHAPTER FOUR

(*Satī's Self-immolation by Yoga*)

Maitreya said :

1. Having said this much, Śaṅkara became silent, as he anticipated the destruction (death) of his wife's body, in either case (whether he permits her to go or refuses to do so).

7. v.l. *manasā*—deeply meditate upon him in mind.—ŚR.

*Cf *sambhāvitasya cākīrtir maraṇād atiricyate*/ BG. 2.34

Satī who was eager to see her friends and relatives, but was afraid of Śaṅkara, became indecisive (two in mind). (Like an oscillating pendulum) she went out (to see her relatives), and returned (for fear of Śiva).

2. Satī was troubled in her mind by the thwarting of her desire to see her kith and kin. Out of affection, she burst into tears and wept in utter despondence. She trembled in rage. She looked in wrath at the peerless Śiva, as if she would burn him.

3. Then she lost her judgment, due to her womanly nature. Heaving heavy sighs, and with her heart tormented by grief and anger, she went to her parents' house, leaving him (Śiva) who is beloved of saintly persons and who, out of love, had given half of his body to her.

4. Thousands of followers of the three-eyed-god (Śiva) including personal attendants and Yakṣas like Maṇiman, Mada and others, and with Nandikeśvara at the head, hastily yet fearlessly (or with saddened heart at her disobedience to Śiva), went after Satī who set out all alone, with quick pace.

5. They made her ride the best of the bulls (Nandikeśvara). They accompanied her, taking with them Sārikās (singing birds), balls, mirrors and lotuses (for her entertainment), a white umbrella, *chowries*, and garlands (her insignia of royalty) and musical instruments like kettle-drums, conchs and flutes.

6. She entered the place of sacrifice where Vedic hymns were loudly chanted by Brāhmaṇas, keenly competing with each other in reciting Vedic *mantras*[8]; where Brāhmaṇa sages and divinities were in attendance; where on sides were (seen) vessels and utensils made of clay, wood, iron, gold, *darbha* grass and hides.

7. Being afraid of the sacrificer (Dakṣa), who treated her insultingly, nobody except her mother and sisters, dared to welcome her, on her arrival. They (her mother and sisters),

---

8. *ā-brahma-vaiśasam* : OR 'Where the sacrificial act of killing the animal is sanctified by the loud chanting of Vedic hymns.'—ŚR.

RR. brands this as 'coarse' (*aślīla*) and prefers the explanation given above. All commentators do the same.

however, eagerly and rapturously embraced her, with their throats choked with tears of affection.

8. Satī who was not welcomed by her father, did not accept the hospitality and the seat of honour respectfully offered to her by her mother and maternal aunts. Nor did she pay attention to her sisters' affectionate enquiries about her health etc.

9. Seeing the sacrifice being performed without offering the due share to Rudra, and the insulting treatment meted out to Lord Śiva by her father, the great goddess Satī, who herself was not given proper reception at the sacrificial assembly, became enraged, as if she would burn the worlds in anger.

10. By her divine lustre, the goddess Satī controlled the hosts of goblins (who accompanied her) who sprang to their feet (to destroy the sacrifice). But within the hearing of the whole world, she censured (Dakṣa), the enemy of Śiva who was proud of his exertions in the path of smoke (i.e. was puffed up with performance of great sacrifices), in accents faltering with anger.

11. "Who else than you would behave inimically towards the Lord, who is above enmity ? To him nobody is superior in the world. Though he is the beloved Soul of all embodied beings, nobody is dear or hateful to him. He is the cause of all.

12*. Oh Dvija ! Persons who are jealous like you, discover faults in the virtues of others (and not merits) are called mean. Those who, occupying a middle position, note merits and demerits as they are, are regarded as great. Good people note only the merits and not the weaknesses (and these are greater). The greatest ones do not see the defect at all, but they magnify even the minutest good points.

13. It is no wonder that out of jealousy, there is always the malicious condemnation of the great among unrighteous persons who look upon this inert material body as the Soul. The glory (of such slanderers) is obscured by the dust of the

---

* *Literally* : Oh Dvija ! People like you detect (see) faults even in the good qualities of others; but no good person does this. Those who magnify even the trifling merits in others are the greatest of all. You have however found fault with them (great persons).

feet of those great men. Hence it befits these (slanderers to revile the good Souls)?

14. Alas! Your honour has become inauspicious, as you hate god Śiva, whose fame is holy and commands inviolable, and whose name of two syllables (Śi-va) if incidentally uttered by the tongue even once, destroys all the sins of men (who utter it).

15. Your honour is hating (Śiva), that friend and protector of the universe. His lotuslike feet are resorted to by the bee-like minds of the great (sages like Sanaka etc.), who long to taste the winelike honey of Brahmānanda (bliss of being absorbed in Brahman)—Feet which shower blessings upon people desirous of worldly objects (irrespective of their worthiness to receive them.)

16.* You say that god Śiva is inauspicious—*a-śiva*—in his dress and behaviour. If that be so, do not gods etc. other than your honour, (such as Brahmā and others) who wear on their heads flowers etc. fallen from his feet,' know that he is auspicious (śiva) only in name but is really inauspicious—Śiva who with his dishevelled matted locks of hair, dwells in the cremation grounds in company of goblins, and who decorates himself with the flower-garlands, ashes (of funeral pyres) and skulls lying there?

17. When the Supreme Lord (Śiva), the protector of religion, is blasphemed by restraintless people, one should shut one's ears and leave the place if he is powerless (to kill the slanderer or die in the action). If he is powerful enough, he should, by force, cut off the vituperative tongue which utters such evil words, and lay down his own life (if necessary for that). Such is the course of righteous duty (*dharma*).

18. I, therefore, shall not retain this body which is born of you, the slanderer of Śiva. For, the wise people say that the remedy for eating of the impure food taken in through ignorance, is to vomit it out.

---

*VR. is hard put to it to reconcile this verse with the injunction in the *Sāttvata-tantra* that no god other than Nārāyaṇa should be respected (*nānyaṁ devaṁ namas-kuryāt* etc.). He says that injunction is restricted to those who are trying for *mokṣa*. He concludes :

sarva-devatānām brahmātmakatvena-anusandhānaṁ tvaviruddham-eveti na virodhaḥ /

19. The mind of the great sage who finds joy in his own Self, does not necessarily follow Vedic statements (regarding injunctions and prohibitions). Just as the movements of celestial beings and men are different (the former through the sky and the latter on the earth) a person who follows his own course of duty, should not find fault with another following a different path.

20. It is true that *karmas* of two kinds—*pravṛtta* (sacrificial acts etc.) and *nivṛtta* (self-control, renunciation etc.) are prescribed in the Vedas, severally, for two distinct types of men—one characterised by attachment to worldly objects and the other, by absence of it. Both the types of *karmas* cannot be found (practicable) simultaneously in the same agent. But no duty of doing a *karma* of any kind devolves upon the Brahman (god Śiva).

21. (You need not entertain the pride that you are affluent and Rudra is a pauper for), the mystic powers (*siddhis* like *aṇimā* etc.) possessed by us, can never be yours, oh father. They are not found (attained) in sacrificial halls (by performance of sacrifices). The cause of our (attainment of) powers is unmanifest (as they depend on our will). They are enjoyed by Avadhūtas (knowers of Brahman who have renounced everything). While your path is extolled by creatures following the path of smoke (*karma-mārga*) who are gratified with the food offered in sacrifices.

22. Now enough of this impure body born of you who have sinned against (offended) Lord Śiva. I have been ashamed of my kinship with an unworthy father. Fie upon the birth from a man who vilifies the great Souls.

23. When (out of joke) Lord Śiva (the bull-bannered god) refers to your *gotra* by addressing me as "Dākṣāyaṇī" (Dakṣa's daughter), I immediately lose all joyfulness and smiles, and become extremely pained at heart. Therefore, I shall give up this body (corpse) begotten of you."

Maitreya said :

24. Oh vanquisher of enemies ! Having thus addressed Dakṣa in the sacrificial hall, she sat silently on the ground with her face to north. She wore a yellow garment. She

touched water (i.e. sipped it as in *ācamana*), and closing her eyes, she entered the *yogic* path (for casting off her material body).

25. Steady in her *yogic* posture, she controlled *prāṇa* and *apāna* equally at the navel. Forcing up the vital air called *udāna* from the mystic plexus at the navel (*maṇipūra cakra*), she gradually brought it up and steadied it along with intellect at the mystical plexus in the heart. The pure, sinless lady brought it through her throat to (*ājñā cakra*), the mystical plexus in the midregion of the eyebrows.

26. Thus, out of her anger against Dakṣa, she desired to cast off her body which was many times lovingly placed (and caressed) on his lap by god Śiva, the most exalted amongst the great. The strong-willed lady instituted the *yogic* contemplation (*dhāraṇā*) of fire and wind in her limbs (body).

27. Then meditating on the bliss of the lotus-like feet of her lord, the preceptor of the world (Lord Śiva), Satī (was so absorbed that she) perceived nothing else. She destroyed all impurities. And her body was soon ablaze with fire produced by her *samādhi* (*yogic* concentration).

28. There arose a tremendous uproar of grief ('alas ! alas !!') both in the heaven and on the earth by those who witnessed the great miracle. "Alas ! provoked by (her father) Dakṣa, Satī, the beloved spouse of Lord Śiva, had thrown away her life.

29. Oh ! Look at the enormous wickedness of the Lord of Creation (Dakṣa) from whom are born all creatures, mobile and immobile. His high-souled daughter who always deserved honour, had to give up her life, due to insults inflicted by him.

30. This Dakṣa of intolerant (jealous) heart, the hater of the Brahman, will reap great infamy in this world. This enemy of god Śiva did not prevent his own daughter, while she prepared for death, on account of the disrespectful treatment meted out to her."

31. While the people were criticising thus, at the sight of the miraculous self-immolation of Satī, her attendants rose with their weapons to kill Dakṣa.

32. Having noticed the vehemence of the on-rushing attendants of Śiva, venerable Bhṛgu offered oblations in the

sacrificial fire called *dakṣiṇāgni* reciting the *mantras* of Yajur-veda efficacious to kill the destroyers of the sacrifice.

33. While the priest *adhvaryu* (viz. Bhṛgu) poured the oblation, gods called Ṛbhus who had secured share in the *soma* juice by their austere penance, rose up in thousands, (from the sacrificial pit) with great force.

34. Beaten by the gods who were armed with fire brands and who were resplendent with Brahmanic lustre, all the attendants of Śiva, *pramathas* and *guhyakas* dispersed in various directions.

CHAPTER FIVE

(Destruction of Dakṣa's Sacrifice)

Maitreya said :

1. Having learnt from Nārada, the report of the death of his wife (Satī) on being insulted by Prajāpati Dakṣa, and of the total rout of the army of his attendants by the Ṛbhus in that Sacrifice, Śiva's anger knew no bounds.

2. Śiva (the god with matted locks of hair) got enraged, and bit his lips. He pulled out a matted lock of hair which dazzled with terrific splendour, like the flash of lightning, and a flame of fire. He suddenly sprang to his feet, and with a loud laughter and roar, dashed it on the ground.

3. From it (was born Vīrabhadra), of colossal size, who touched the skies, by his stature. He had a thousand arms. His complexion was like a dark cloud. He had three eyes brilliant like the Sun. He had sharp fangs. His locks of hair were shining like burning flames of fire. He wore a garland of skulls and held various weapons aloft (for striking).

4. Śiva, the Supreme Lord, the master of *bhūtas*, commanded Vīrabhadra who, with folded hands, requested for an order. "Oh Rudra, as you are my part (manifestation, you need not be afraid of Brahmanic power). You be the leader of my army, oh warrior, and destroy Dakṣa along with his sacrifice".

5. Being thus commanded by wrathful Śiva, he circumambulated the all-powerful god of gods. Oh Vidura, he then regarded himself capable of withstanding the might of very powerful warriors, by his irresistible force.

6. He was followed by the attendants of Rudra who were roaring loudly. He himself thundered most terribly. Raising his trident which was capable of killing even the god of Death, he dashed forth, with his feet jingling with ornaments.

7-8. Having seen (a cloud of) dust in the northern direction, the sacrificial priest, the sacrificer (Dakṣa), members of the sacrificial assembly, Brāhmaṇas and their wives began to speculate : "What darkness is this ? From which place is the cloud of dust (coming) ? Winds are not blowing. Nor can these be robbers, as king Prācīnabarhiṣ of iron rule, is still alive. Cows are not driven home so hastily. Whence is this dust ? Is the world now due for dissolution (*pralaya*)?"

9. Ladies of whom Prasūti was prominent, commented with a troubled heart : "This is the consequence of the sin committed by Dakṣa, the Lord of Creation, who slighted his innocent daughter Satī, in the presence of his other daughters.

10. It may be due to Dakṣa's offence against Rudra who dances at the end of the universe, with his locks of matted hair scattered about, and with the elephants supporting the directions pierced on the prongs of his trident, and with his bannerlike hands holding up the missiles (for discharge), tearing down the directions, by thunderlike peals of laughter.

11. When he is full of rage, can anyone fare well, even if he be god Brahmā himself who provoked his (Rudra's) wrath —Rudra, who is of irresistible splendour, full of wrath, unbearable to look at when he knits his eyebrows in angry looks, and who has scattered the whole group of constellations with his terrible fangs."

12. While people with perturbed eyes, were speculating thus wildly, there were thousands of omens portending misfortune to Dakṣa, frequently appearing in the sky, and on the earth.

13. Oh Vidura, in the meanwhile the big sacrificial pandal was rushed at on all sides, and occupied by the followers of Rudra with their weapons held up in their hands. They

were short in stature, dark and brown (in complexion) and their faces and stomachs were like crocodiles.

14. Some broke the *Prāgvaṁśa* (the beam resting on the eastern and western pillars of the sacrificial hall). Others broke the apartment of the sacrificer's wife (This is to the west of the sacrificial hall). Some broke the assembly hall in front (of the sacrificial hall). Some broke the store-room of the materials for sacrificial offerings; others, the cottage of the sacrificer himself, and the kitchen.

15. Some smashed the sacrificial utensils; some put out the sacrificial fire; some urinated in the sacrificial pit, and some cut down the zonelike construction around the sacrificial platform.

16. Some struck the sages; others threatened the wives of the priests, etc.; others seized gods who were near by and trying to run away.

17. Maṇiman bound Bhṛgu; Vīrabhadra, Prajāpati Dakṣa; Caṇḍīśa, god Pūṣan; Nandīśvara caught hold of Bhaga.

18. All the sacrificial priests, along with the members of the assembly and gods, saw this. Being severely pelted with stones, they ran quickly, helter-skelter in all directions.

19. Glorious Vīrabhadra pulled out mustaches and the beard of Bhṛgu, while he was offering the oblations with *sruva* (a ladle) in his hand, as he had laughed derisively in the assembly showing his beard (when Dakṣa insulted Śiva).

20. Out of anger, venerated Vīrabhadra knocked down Bhaga and pulled out his eyes, as in that sacrificial session of the assembly (while Dakṣa censured Śiva), he made signs with his eyes to Dakṣa.

21. He knocked out the teeth of Pūṣan as Balarāma did to the king of Kaliṅga, as he laughed, showing his teeth, while the great god Śiva was vilified by Dakṣa.

22. The three-eyed Vīrabhadra (threw down Dakṣa and) seating himself on Dakṣa's chest, he tried to cut his head by a sharpedged weapon, but he was unable to do so.

23. Hara (Vīrabhadra) was greatly wonderstruck to find that the skin of Dakṣa was not cut by weapons charmed with Vedic *mantras* called *astras*. He (who is a form of Paśupati) deeply thought what to do.

24. Observing the way in which animals are killed in the sacrifice, the Lord of Paśus (Souls) severed by that method the head of Dakṣa, the sacrificer, whom he made the animal to be sacrificed.

25. There arose a shout of applause 'well done', 'bravo' from the *Bhūtas*, *Pretas* and *Piśācas* (members of Vīrabhadra's army) who praised that act of gallantry. The reverse was the case in others (i.e. in Dakṣa's camp).

26. Full of rage, Vīrabhadra threw Dakṣa's head in the sacrificial fire called *Dakṣiṇāgni*, as an oblation. Having burnt down the sacrificial edifice, he returned to Kailāsa, the home of Guhyakas.

CHAPTER SIX

(*Appeasement of Rudra—Revival of Dakṣa*)

Maitreya said :

1-2. Thereupon all the hosts of gods who were defeated by the armies of Rudra, had got their bodies hacked and hewn with tridents, spears (*paṭṭiśa*), swords, maces, iron bars and clubs. Being overwhelmed with fear, they, along with the sacrificial priests and their associates, approached god Brahmā, bowed down to him, and narrated in details this incident.

3. (As) worshipful Brahmā and Nārāyaṇa, the Soul of the universe, had long back foreseen it, they did not go to the sacrifice of Dakṣa.

4. After giving them hearing, Brahmā said, "the desire to retaliate against a person of superior might, even though he has offended you, cannot generally lead to the welfare (of the weak retaliator).

5. Here, however, you have committed the offence against Śiva, inasmuch as you excluded him from the sacrifice, even though he had a rightful share (in the sacrificial offerings). Now, with a pure chastened heart, you resort to his lotuslike feet and obtain his grace, for he can be easily propitiated.

6. You, who wish for the revival (and completion) of the sacrifice, should immediately beg the pardon of the god, who is cut to the quick, by words of abuse (by Dakṣa), and is bereaved of his beloved wife. If he is enraged, the whole world along with its protectors, will cease to be.

7. The Lord Rudra is absolutely independent. Neither I nor Yajña (Indra of that era), nor you nor sages or any embodied being, knows his real nature and the extent of his strength and power. (This being the case) who can be certain of the means to be adopted (for his propitiation)".

8. Having advised the gods, thus, Brahmā accompanied by them (gods), Pitṛs, Prajāpatis set out from his own region (Satyaloka) to Kailāsa, the chief of the mountains, the favourite abode of god Śiva, the destroyer of the Tripuras.

9. Mount Kailāsa is inhabited by gods who have attained superhuman powers (*siddhis*) by their (superiority in) birth, or by drugs, penance, *mantra* (incantation of mystic power) or the practice of *Yoga*. It is always crowded with Kinnaras, Gandharvas (celestial musicians) and celestial damsels.

10. Its summits are made up of various kinds of gems; they are variegated with different kinds of metallic ores; they are covered with various kinds of trees, creepers and shrubs. They abound in different kinds of wild beasts.

11. With its streams of crystal clear water, and its peaks and caves, the mountain is a pleasure-haunt for *siddha* women, to sport along with their lovers.

12. It is resonant with the cries of the peacocks, melodious humming of bees intoxicated with honey, loud notes of cuckoos and warbling of birds.

13. It seems to invite birds, by the highly raised boughs of wish-yielding trees. It appears to be in motion by the wandering of elephants. It is, as if, speaking with the murmuring of flowing springs.

14-15. It is beautified with trees such as (the heavenly) Mandāra and Pārijāta; with Saralas, Tamālas, Sālas, Tālas, Kovidāras, Asanas, Arjunas, mango-trees, Kadambas, Nīpas, Nāgas, Punnāgas, Campakas, Pāṭalas, Aśokas, Bakulas, Kundas, and Kurabakas.

16-19. It is ornamented with lotus flowers of golden

hue (and hundred petals), excellent cardamom creepers, Mālatī (Jasmine), Kubjas, Mallikās, Mādhavīs; and also with (fruit) trees (such as) Panasa, Audumbara, Aśvattha, Plakṣa, Nyagrodha, Hiṅgu, Bhūrja; with herbs and plants like betel nuts, Rājapūga (a kind of arecanut palm), rose-apple trees, date-palms, Jambū, mango-trees and others, with Priyāla, Madhuka, and Iṅguda (soapnut trees). It was adorned with various kinds of bamboos called Veṇu and Kīcaka; it was beautified with swarms of birds which were sweetly singing on the banks of the lakes rich in the beds of lilies and lotuses of various kinds.

20. It was abounding in deer, monkeys, boars, lions, bears and Porcupines, Gavayas (a species of ox) Sarabhas (a mythological eight-footed animal), tigers, *ruru*-deer, buffaloes and other beasts.

21. It was infested with a number of beasts called Karṇāntra, one-footed animals, horse-faced animals, wolves, musk-deer; and it presented a charming sight with its sandy banks of lotuslakes, surrounded by gardens of plantain trees.

22. It was surrounded by the Nandā (the Ganges) whose waters have been all the more hallowed by the ablutions of Satī. At the sight of that mountain of Lord Śiva, gods were filled with wonder.

23. There (on the mountain), they beheld the famous and beautiful city of Alakā, with its garden called Saugandhika, where grew the species of lotus, bearing the same name (Saugandhika).

24. Along the outskirts of the city, flow the two rivers Nandā and Alakanandā, which are highly sanctified with the dust of the ever-hallowed feet of Viṣṇu.

25. Oh Vidura, when celestial women get tired of their amorous sports, they descend from their heavenly cars into these rivers. They then plunge and sport therein, sprinkling their mates with water.

26. (Being tempted by the fragrance of saffron), elephants, though not thirsty, drink the waters of these rivers, yellow on account of the fresh saffron washed (from the breasts of celestial women) during their baths, and make the female elephants also drink it.

27-28. Alakā, the capital of the Yakṣa king (Kubera), which was swarmed with hundreds of aerial cars made up of silver, gold and highly precious stones, and inhabited by Yakṣa women, looked like the sky, overcast with clouds and streaks of lightning. They (Brahmā and others) bypass the capital of Kubera, and the Saugandhika forest, which was beautified with wish-yielding trees with variegated flowers, fruits and leaves.

29. (Therein) the cooking and warbling of cuckoos and other birds, harmonised with the melodious humming of bees. It was full of lakes with lotus beds, which were the most favourite haunts of swans of melodious notes.

30. (In that forest) the breeze blowing over the Haricandana trees against which wild elephants have rubbed their bodies, created frequently more agitation in the wives of Yakṣas.

31. There were tanks beautified with lotuses, with steps of *vaidūrya* gems, built around them. It was enjoyed by Kiṁpuruṣas. Having seen the forest, the gods saw a banyan tree near by.

32. It was hundred *Yojanas* in height; its branches extended seventy-five *Yojanas*, on every side; it had a permanent shade on all sides; it had no nests on it, and it warded off the Sun.

33. Beneath that tree, which induced great concentration of mind (*mahā-yoga*), and which is the resort of people seeking liberation, the gods beheld Śiva, seated like the god of Death, free from anger.

34. (They saw) Śiva of a very tranquil personality. He was attended upon by great serene Yogins like Sanandana and others and also by Kubera, his friend, and the master of Guhyakas and Rākṣasas.

35. (They saw) the Supreme Lord Śiva, the friend of the universe, who is following the path of *upāsanā*, concentration and Yoga meditation[9], practising it out of affection for the welfare of the people.

---

9. *Vidyā-patham*—(i) The path of *bhakti* supplemented by paths of knowledge (*jñāna*) and of *karma* (action)—VR.

(ii) One who propagated (and thus resorted to) the paths of *vidyā*, *tapas* and *yoga*—VC.

(iii) VJ. reads *dhyāyantam* for *carantam* and treats it as adj. quali-

36. His body had the golden hue of evening clouds. He wore the marks which are desirable of ascetics e.g. sacred ashes, a club, matted hair and the hide of a deer. He bore the crescent moon (on his forehead).

37. He was seated on a seat of *darbha* grass. He was expounding to Nārada the nature of the eternal Brahman, while other saints were listening.

38. He placed his left lotuslike foot on the right lap, and placed his left hand on the left knee (i.e. in the Vīrāsana posture[10]). A rosary of beads was round his right wrist, and he assumed *tarka mudrā*[11].

39. The sages, along with the protectors of the world, folded their hands and bowed to god Śiva (Lord of Mountains). Śiva who was absorbed in the meditation of being one with the blissful Brahman; who wore a *Yoga-kakṣa* (a strap to secure the position of the left knee)[12]; and who was the foremost among the contemplators.

40. Knowing that god Brahmā (Self-born god) had come, he (Śiva) whose feet had been respected by the Lord of gods and *asuras*, rose (from his seat) and bowed to him with his head, as the most adorable Viṣṇu did to Kāśyapa (in Vāmana incarnation).

---

fying Śiva and takes other adjectives to qualify Viṣṇu. So according to VJ. : They saw Śiva who was contemplating on Nārāyaṇa who is the disinterested friend and well-wisher of the universe, and confers auspiciousness on the people, and who is the preceptor in and object of knowledge, penance and Yoga which he is practising.

(iv) GD. explains: Śiva practises the path of *upāsanā*, mental concentration and *Yoga*. He practises *upāsanā* out of affection for the world, to confer on it auspiciousness. He is the well-wisher of the world of which he is the creator, preserver and destroyer. Being the Lord of the world, he takes care of its welfare.

10. It is described as under :

eka-pādam athaikasmin vinyased ūru-saṁsthitam /
itarasminstathā bāhuṃ vīrāsanam idam smṛtam //

11. *Tarka-mudrā* or *Jñāna-mudrā* : Joining the tips of the thumb and the index finger, and straightening the other fingers after joining them together. This position of the hand is *tarka mudrā*.

12. Probably it might be a wooden support called *kubḍī* in Marathi. Yogis keep it under their armpit to support the erect posture of their body during contemplation.

41. So also the hosts of other Siddhas, along with great sages, who were (sitting) around Śiva, did the same. God Brahmā who was thus bowed (to by them), spoke, as if with a smile, to Śiva (the god who wears the crescent moon on the head), who was still in a respectful pose (bowing).

Brahmā said :

42*. I know you to be the Lord of the universe. You are the same undifferentiated Brahman which is the cause of both the Śakti (*prakṛti* or the divine energy) and Śiva (the *puruṣa*) who are both the womb and the seed of the world.

43. Oh Lord, it is you who carry on your sport through Śiva and Śakti who are essentially one (*sarūpayoḥ*)[13], and create, protect and destroy the universe, as a spider does with his cobweb[14].

44** You have created the institution of sacrifice through Dakṣa, as a string or instrument for the preservation of the

*(i) Parabrahman is the inner controller (*antar-yāmin*) of Rudra who is merely an *āveśa* type of incarnation of Parabrahman. Therefore Rudra is identified with the Parabrahman and the attributes of the latter are applied to him. Hence this is the eulogy of Parabrahman—VR. (ii) VJ. says that these verses are in praise of Narasiṁha (Viṣṇu) for the same reason as above. (iii) VC. regards that the author has followed *Śaiva-mata*, in this panegyric.

13. VR. accepts the v.l. *svāṁśayoḥ* : Śiva and Śakti are the parts or *aṁśas* of the *viśiṣṭa* mentioned as *sva*. This verse is addressed to Parabrahman who is the *antar-yāmin* of Rudra. *Prakṛti* and *Puruṣa* form the body of Parabrahman. VR. expounds the stand of *viśiṣṭādvaita* with reference to god and the world etc. in this com. (ii) VC. explains this reading: Śiva is god's *aṁśa*. *Śakti* is Śiva's shadow. Hence they are equated here. VJ. accepts the v.l. *Svarūpayoḥ*. He regards this verse as addressed to Viṣṇu who is the *antar-yāmin* of both Śiva and Śakti. They are not one in essence with Viṣṇu. He uses them as instruments for the creation etc. of the universe.

14. Cf. *yathorṇa-nābhiḥ sṛjate gṛhṇate ca* /—Muṇḍaka Up. 1.1.7.

**Oh bestower of *dharma* and *artha* (religious merit and wealth)! For the attainment of *puruṣārthas*, you have created the institution of sacrifice by efficacious (*dakṣa*) *sūtra*. The bounds of *varṇa*, *āśrama* etc. are fixed by you. Brāhmaṇas adopt strict religious vows and faithfully follow these limitations or commands—VR.

(ii) VC. and SD. state that here Brahmā implies that as Śiva had destroyed the sacrifice of Dakṣa who followed Vedic injunctions laid down by Śiva, it was Śiva's responsibility to see to it that the sacrifice was completed.

three Vedas which bestow *dharma* and *artha* (religious merit and wealth)[15]. It is you who have ordained the boundaries (of the course of conduct) of the world-boundaries which Brāhmaṇas, who have adopted religious vows, follow with faith.

45. Oh auspicious Lord! You confer heaven (*svarga*) or final beatitude (*Mokṣa*) on those who perform auspicious deeds, and assign the terrible dark hell to the perpetrators of evil deeds. Why is it that the same act in the case of some persons, gives the contrary result? (Why should Dakṣa who followed the Vedic path, and accordingly tried to perform a sacrifice as per Vedic injunction, meet with that fate?)

46*. Verily anger cannot generally[16] overwhelm pious people as it would do in the case of brute (-like ignorant persons. For these (righteous people) have offered their hearts to your feet, and visualise you in all beings, and see all beings as one with(their Soul)[17]. (If your righteous devotees are above anger, how is it that you, their god, can be wrathful?).

47. A person (of exalted status) like you, ought not to kill those who perceive differentiation in their hearts; who fix their eyes on *karmas* (ritualistic acts) only; being of wicked minds, they are always jealously burning in their hearts at the prosperity of others; who being naturally disposed to hurt the

15. *dharmārtha-dugha* : Alternatively ŚR. takes it as a Voc.—*dugha*. Oh Lord Śiva who give religious merits and wealth ! For the attainment of *dharma* and *artha* you have created etc.

(ii) VJ. takes this as instr. sing. and explains it as qualifying Dakṣa. According to VJ. : Dakṣa's sacrifice was disturbed by Hari, as Dakṣa treated Śiva disrespectfully. Śiva was superior to Dakṣa even as a devotee. Hence Hari disturbed the sacrifice, as the boundary or etiquette to be observed was crossed by Dakṣa.

*(i) It is impossible that your wrath can be the cause of such a contrary result. The righteous persons entertain no anger against good people (ŚR.) (ii) VJ. takes this verse as addressed to Viṣṇu, and explains that Brahmā does not attribute any anger to Viṣṇu. If the devotees of Viṣṇu are not overwhelmed with anger, there is no possibility of finding resentment in Viṣṇu.

16. *Prāyeṇa*—Śiva might have been angry as there are exceptions in such people, e.g. Sanaka's anger on Jaya & Vijaya —VC.

17. *apṛthag-didṛkṣatam*—Those who positively see things as they are —VJ.

feelings of others, wound them by harsh words. For such (wicked) persons are doomed by the Providence.

48*. If persons who have their minds deluded by the unfathomable Māyā of Viṣṇu, and who consider the universe as different from God, offend the righteous at any time or place, they regard it (the offence) as caused by the Providence. Out of compassion they (the righteous) definitely show mercy to them, but do not show their prowess for their destruction.

49. Oh Lord! you have your intellect uninfluenced (untouched) by the irresistible Māyā of the Supreme Man, and hence you are Omniscient. You should therefore show grace to persons whose minds are affected by the Māyā, and hence, whose minds follow (the path of) ritualistic *karmas*.

50. Oh Lord! Be pleased to revive (recommence) the sacrifice of Dakṣa, the son of Manu—the sacrifice which remained incomplete as it was wrecked by you when the petty minded priests who conducted the sacrifice did not offer you, your due share (in it).

51. May this sacrificer (Dakṣa) be alive again. May Bhaga get back his eyes as before. Let Bhṛgu grow his beard and mustaches. Let Pūṣan have his teeth as before.

52. Oh Rudra (Manyu)! By your grace may gods and sacrificial priests, the limbs of whose bodies have been wounded and broken by weapons and stones, be restored to health immediately.

53. Oh Rudra! Whatever will remain after the completion of the sacrifice shall be your share[18]. Oh destroyer of the sacrifice, let this sacrifice be consummated today, with this share assigned to you.

---

*VJ. This verse is addressed to Rudra so that he should not entertain any anger against Dakṣa : 'In this world, minds of persons like Dakṣa, are overpowered by Māyā—the binding power of Viṣṇu. How is it that when the persons of incorrect perception, offend or hate the good, righteous persons like you do not feel compassion for them, and oblige them by toleration ? For the ignorant have acted so, due to their previous *karmas* and under compulsion of Lord's will.

(ii) SD. & GD. : The righteous persons take the offence done to them as due to their own *karmas*, and feel compassion for the wicked, for their future life in hell.

18. Literally : Oh Rudra ! May all that has remained of the sacrifice be your share.

CHAPTER SEVEN

(*Completion of Dakṣa's Sacrifice*)

Maitreya said :

1. Oh Vidura (of mighty arms)! God Śiva who was thus entreated by Brahmā, was highly pleased. With a loud laugh, he said, "Listen".

Śrī Mahādeva said :

2. Oh Lord of the created beings, I do not refer to (pronounce), nor do I recollect the misdemeanour of the ignorant who are overwhelmed with Lord's Māyā. I have only meted out punishment there (to the offenders).

3. The head of Prajāpati Dakṣa which has been burnt, may have the face of a he-goat. Let god Bhaga look at his own portion of offering in the sacrifice, through the eyes of Mitra god.

4. Let god Pūṣan who eats flour only eat the offering of flour with the teeth of the sacrificer. The gods, who have offered to me the remaining portion of the sacrifice, will have all their limbs restored, properly.

5. Let *Adhvaryus* and other sacrificial priests who have lost their arms use the arms of gods, Aśvins; while those who have lost their hands should work with those of god Pūṣan. Bhṛgu will have the beard and mustaches of a he-goat.

6. Oh Vidura, when all beings heard the speech of the most bountiful god Śiva, their hearts were fully satisfied, and they exclaimed 'Well done, well done'.

7. Thereupon, gods along with sages, (cordially) invited god Śiva (to help the consummation of the sacrifice), and went again to the site of the sacrifice, along with Śiva and Brahmā.

8. Having accomplished completely whatever Lord Bhava instructed them to do, they joined the head of the sacrificial animal (he-goat), to the trunk of Dakṣa.

9. While the head was being joined (to Dakṣa's body), Śiva cast a gracious look at it, (and lo!) Dakṣa got up as though from sleep, and saw Śiva in front of him.

10. Prajāpati Dakṣa whose mind had been turbid with hatred against Śiva (god with a bull on his banner), became

free from that impurity (hatred), like a pool (the waters of which become clear and translucent) in the autumn.

11. He (Dakṣa) had a mind to offer praise (to Śiva). But recollecting his daughter who was no more, his throat got choked with tears of affection and anxiety, and he could not utter a word of praise.

12. The wise Prajāpati Dakṣa who was overwhelmed with affection, controlled his mind with difficulty. He then praised Lord Śiva, with sincere devotion.

Dakṣa said :

13. "Oh venerable Lord! Even though you were disrespected by me, a great favour has been shown to me by you, in meting out a (corrective) punishment. Both you and Hari are never different to even fallen Brāhmaṇas. How can you be so to those who follow religious vows (i.e. the sacrificial duties).

14. For the preservation of the Vedas and knowledge of Ātman[19] you created out of your mouth[20] Brāhmaṇas who possessed learning and practised penance and religious vows[21] at the beginning (of the world). Oh great god, you therefore protect Brāhmaṇas in all calamities like a herdsman protects his cattle with a staff.

15. May the Lord who, though insulted in the assembly with arrowlike piercing words of abuse, by me, who was ignorant about the true knowledge (of his real nature), ignored them, and with his gracious look (at me) saved me who was falling down for having reviled the most worshipful person—May that venerable Lord be pleased with his own (merciful) act (as it is beyond my capacity to repay this obligation)."

---

19. *Brahmātva-tatavmavitum*. To protect the continuity of the knowledge that everything mobile and immobile is in reality Brahman, GD.

20. *mukhataḥ*—chiefly (VC.).

21. Or : Manifesting yourself as Brahma at the beginning of the world.—ŚR. VR. : You are the four-faced Brahmā who created Brāhmaṇas for the preservation of the true knowledge about *Paramātman* and *jīva* by your own realization and instruction, at the beginning of the *kalpa*. VJ. accepts the v.l. *brahmātmatām prathayitum*. For proclaiming that you are the protector of the Vedas (Brahman). Or : You are the special abode of Brahman (Hari) perfect in all highest attributes.

Maitreya said :

16. Having thus apologised to Śiva (who showers blessings on devotees), he (Dakṣa), with the permission of god Brahmā, restored the continuity of sacrifice, with the help of preceptors and sacrificial priests and fire.

17. For the continuity of the sacrifice and for purification (from the pollution resulting) from the touch of warriors (such as, Pramathas), the best of the Brāhmaṇas offered in three plates Puroḍāśa (oblation made of ground rice) dedicated to Viṣṇu.

18. Oh King (Vidura), while, along with the sacrificial priest (*adhvaryu*) who stood holding the oblation in hand, the sacrificer (Dakṣa) meditated upon Hari with pure heart (so earnestly that) Hari manifested himself.

19. Then eclipsing their (of the members of the assembly) splendour by his lustre which illumined the ten quarters, he was brought there by Garuḍa whose two wings were the two Sāma hymns[22] (viz. *Bṛhad* and *Rathantara*).

20. He was of blue complexion and wore a zone of gold. He was adorned with a (gold) crown brilliant like the Sun. His countenance was beautified with locks of hair, dark like black-bees, and with ear-rings. With a conch, a lotus, a discus, an arrow, a bow, a mace, a sword and shield in each arm adorned with gold ornament, he looked (beautiful like a blossoming Karṇikāra tree).

21. His consort (Lakṣmī) was resting on his bosom (in the form of *Śrīvatsa*). He wore a garland of forest-flowers (*vanamālā*). He delighted the universe even with his slight winsome smile and looks. On his sides were waving fans and *chowries* (white) like royal swans. He appeared beautiful with a moonlike white umbrella over his head.

22. Seeing him arrive, all gods and others of whom Brahmā, Indra and Śaṅkara were prominent at once stood up and bowed to him.

23. Their splendour was eclipsed by his. With their tongues faltering through his awe, they folded their hands on their heads, and attended upon him (respectfully).

22. *Stotra-Vājinā*—(i) Who was expert in singing the hymns (VR).
(ii) VJ. reads *Stotra-nirjita* : Who has secured Hari's grace by singing Sāma hymns.
(iii) Cf. *bṛhad-rathāntare pakṣau*—Kauṣītaki Up. 1.5.

24. Even though his glory was beyond the reach of their capacities (as they are his partial manifestations), Brahmā and others began, to the best of their knowledge, to sing the glory of him (Viṣṇu) who manifested that form to confer his blessings.

25. Dakṣa himself took with him the articles of worship in an excellent receptacle[23]. Joyfully singing his praise with his hands folded, devoutly he sought the protection of the Lord of Sacrifices, who is the Supreme preceptor of the Prajāpatis and who was surrounded by attendants like Nanda and Sunanda.

*Dakṣa said** :

26. In your own essence (essential form)[24], you are pure, untouched by states of mind (e.g. wakefulness etc.). You are absolutely one (without a second), and (hence) above fear and of the nature of pure consciousness. You have negated Māyā[25] and are completely self-dependent. But when you take incarnations (as Rāma or Kṛṣṇa) by the same Māyā, you appear to abide in Māyā tainted with impure matter.

The officiating sacrificial priests said :

27**. Oh Lord, untainted by merits or demerits (or by

---

23. *gṛhīta-uttamam* : Taken as adj. qualifying *Yajñeśvara* it means : Viṣṇu who out of grace, accepted the excellent receptacle of presents from Dakṣa. But VR.'s interpretation is better : 'Viṣṇu who is the best of all the means which lead to *puruṣārthas*'.

* As ŚR. points out, the following eulogy of Viṣṇu contains a variety of metres.

24. *pratiṣiddhya māyām* etc. : VJ. The word *Māyā* signifies inert, unintelligent *prakṛti* the material cause of the world and not unreal jugglery (*indrajāla*). The verse means : You have distanced the unintelligent Prakṛti. You have created Mahat (and other principles) and grossest bodies called Puruṣa from it. You are called Puruṣa as you are the inner-controller (*antar-yāmin*) of these bodies. The ignorant Māyā-vādins regard you affected by Prakṛti like the Jīva.

25. *sva-dhāmni* (i) In Vaikuṇṭha—JG.

(ii) Of the nature of the highest bliss—SD.

**(i) VJ.: It is through the gracious looks of Sadāśiva which blossomed (created) in us the real knowledge that the ritualistic act, viz. this sacrifice that we are performing, is an act of worshipping you. It leads to devotion and other pious qualities. This is logically proved by three

upādhi or *māyā*) ! Due to the curse of Nandīśvara[26], we were strongly attached to ritualistic duties, and we did not know your real nature. We have known this sacrifice (*yajña*) as your form—the sacrifice which is established by (and expounded in) the three Vedas[27]; which implies (i.e. creates) religious merit (*apūrva*) ; for the purpose (of accomplishing) which, the definite instructions for the arrangement of specific deities in specific places, have been laid down (Or for this purpose, you have assumed different forms such as Indra).

The assistant priests said :

28. Oh Lord (who affords protection to all)! This caravan of ignorant people who are overburdened with the heavy load of their body (misconceived as their Soul), and their house (mistaken as their own), and who are tormented with desires (passions), is traversing the path of *saṁsāra* (lit. path of births) which is devoid of any shelter; (and) is difficult to travel on account of great hardships; which is under the strict watch of the terrible serpent called Death (to devour) them; which has the (enticing) mirage of the objects of senses; which is full of pitfalls of pleasures and pains (and such pairs of opposites); which is fearful on account of carnivorous beasts in

---

modes of proof, viz., *Pratyakṣa* (perception), *anumāna* (inference) and *āgama* (authoritative word or the Veda). For accepting the oblations due to you, but offered to gods like Brahmā etc., you dwell in them. This is the decisive proof.

You, being the Supreme God, are object of *apūrva* (merit) which accrues from the performance of sacrifice. We thought that the act of sacrifice is for Indra and other deities. Hence our ignorance about you.—VJ.

VC : When we did not comprehend your real nature, how can Dakṣa do so ? We knew the sacrifice only as your form.

GD : Due to the imprecation of Nandīśvara, we could not understand that you underlie the forms of the deities of Rudra etc. Hence we ignored Rudra's share in the sacrifice, and proceeded with it. Now we realize that it is you who have assumed all forms.

26. Vide Supra IV.2. 24-26.

27. *tri-vṛt*—(i) Vedas of which three *pramāṇas* (modes of proof) viz. *pratyakṣa* (apprehension by senses), *anumāna* and *āgama* (Vedic testimony) are given.—VJ.

the form of the wicked; and which is encircled by the wild fire of grief—when will this crowd resort to your feet for shelter ?

Rudra said :

29. Oh bestower of boons! Your excellent feet which confer all the *puruṣārthas* here (in this very world), are definitely worthy of worship with reverence, even by the sages who are not attached to worldly pleasures. I have fixed my mind on your feet. Even, if the ignorant people call me an apostate (fallen from the path of established rules of conduct), I do not mind it due to your supreme grace.

Bhṛgu said :

30. Brahmā and other embodied beings have been deprived of their knowledge of Ātman by your mysterious Māyā. They sleep (i.e. are immersed) in the darkness of ignorance, and do not even now comprehend your real nature lying within them (as *antar-yāmin*). May you, who are the Soul and friend of your suppliants, be gracious unto me.

Brahmā said :

31. What man perceives through his sense-organs which cognize difference between the objects, is not your (real) nature. You are the basis of knowledge, the objects of senses and the (three) *guṇas*, you are (hence) quite distinct from the illusory phenomenon of Māyā.

*Indra said** :

32. Oh Acyuta! Even this form of yours which creates the world and which is delightful to the mind and the eyes, is a real one (even though it is perceptible)—your form which is distinguished with eight mighty arms holding weapons in readiness, to destroy the enemies of gods.

The wives of the Priests said :

33. (In days of yore) the institution of sacrifice was established by god Brahmā as your worship. It has been now

*According to ŚR. here Indra contradicts Brahmā by stating that the form of Viṣṇu that is visible to them is real even though it is perceived through a sense-organ.

ruined by Paśupati (Śiva) out of his ire against Dakṣa. Therefore, Oh embodiment of sacrifice, be pleased to sanctify with your lotuslike charming eyes, this sacrifice of ours which has been made (desolate) like a cremation-ground devoid of joy and auspiciousness.

The sages said :

34. Inscrutable are your ways, Oh Lord, for you perform an act of your own accord but are not affected thereby. People worship the Supreme goddess Lakṣmī for their prosperity. But you do not think highly of her, though she waits upon you of her own accord.

Siddhas said :

35. This elephant in the form of our mind which is scorched in the forest-conflagration of afflictions, and is distressed by the thirst (of sensual pleasures/desires) has plunged in the pure, nectarlike river of your stories. It does not (even) remember the wild-fire of *saṁsāra*. Nor does it come out of it like one who has attained Brahman.

Dakṣa's wife said :

36. Oh Lord! Auspicious (indeed) is your appearance here. Please be gracious unto us. I bow to you. Oh Lord of Śrī (Lakṣmī), may you and your consort Lakṣmī protect us. Oh Supreme Lord, a sacrifice, though complete in all its parts (e.g. *prayāja*, *anuyāja*), does not appear beautiful (i.e. really complete), like the trunk of a man without its head.

Guardians of the worlds said :

37*. Are you (in your real form) seen (by us) with our

---

*The different interpretations are interesting :

(i) ŚR. : To those of pure heart, you appear in pure *sāttvic* form. But to us whose senses can look externally only you are simply a *jīva* invested with a material body of five elements. You (i.e. your real form) are not perceptible to our senses. Fie upon our life !

(ii) VR. : The attribute *bhūman* (all pervasive) distinguishes the Lord from *jīva* which is atomic in size (*aṇu-svarūpa*) and also from *prakṛti*. "It is due to your mystical power called *māyā* that *ātman* and the material body are falsely regarded as one, and *jīva* is wrongly taken to be identical

eyes (senses) which can perceive things in the wrong light?[28] (No) you are the seer from within (as *antaryāmin*) by whom the phenomenal world is seen. For, Oh infinite Lord (*bhūman*), it is certainly your Māyā that you appear to be (as if) the sixth (*jīva*) associated with the (material body composed of) five *bhūtas* (elements).

Yogeśvaras (Masters af Yoga) said :

38*. Oh Lord! There is none who is more beloved to You than he, who does not see (regard) himself different from You, the Para Brahman (lit. the *ātman* of the universe). However, Oh merciful Lord, please be gracious to those (Your devotees) who resort to You with unswerving devotion (like loyal servants to their masters).

---

with the Lord (*Īśa*). You are different from *jīva* and *acit* (five *bhūtas*) but you appear as the sixth (i.e. *jīva*) due to your *māyā*".

(iii) VJ.'s alternative explanation : Oh how lucky we are that you who can be apprehended with the divine eye (of knowledge), are visible to our sight.

(iv) VC. : Though you are the Seer, it is through your Grace that you can be seen. The apprehension of our senses which are accustomed to grasp their objects, is not real. It is your Māyā that you appear to be vested with material body with you as the sixth (distinct from the five *bhūtas*). Jarāsandha and others who thought your real form (Śrī-vigraha) to be material, have not seen your real self, though they have just seen you, for they remained impervious to your sweetness.

(v) GD. : The sense organs are incapable of apprehending you. It is your Will due to which you became visible to us.

28. *asad-grahaiḥ*—(i) By us who are strongly attached to body and its belongings, and who look upon the body as the *ātman*—VR.

(ii) By our eyes or senses which are habituated to apprehend inauspicious sounds, objects etc.—VD.

(iii) By senses which comprehend their objects—VC.

(iv) By senses, mind, intelligence (and other *vṛttis*) which have attachment to this transient *saṁsāra*—SD.

*(1) RR. and VD. clarify that devotees (servants of God) are more dear to him than mere possessors of knowledge (*jñānin*).

(2) VR. accepts the v.l. *bhṛtyeśatayā* for ŚR.'s *bhakteśatayā*, and points out that 'master-servant relation' given here conflicts with the interpretation which supports the identification of the *jīva* with God, as such identity between *jaḍa* and *ajaḍa* is sheerly impossible. Thus VR. interprets : There is none more dear to you than he who does not regard himself existing independently of you, and who sees that he is a part of Lord's body, as such his existence is inseparable from God.

39*. By means of your Māyā in which are exhibited many and different varieties of *guṇas* by the destiny (*adṛṣṭa*) of the *jīvas*, you give rise to a notion of diversity about yourself (by assuming the form of Brahmā, Viṣṇu etc.) for the creation, maintenance and destruction of the universe. But in your own real, essential state, you are free from the illusive notion of difference and its cause, the *guṇas*. We bow to you who are such.

Brahmā (*Śabda-brahman or Vedas*) *said* :

40. I pay my obeisance to you who have assumed the *sattva* attribute and are (hence) the source of (*puruṣārthas* like) Dharma (*artha* etc.), but are still destitute of attributes. Yur real nature is incomprehensible to me as well as to others.

Agni said :

41. I, whose flames are brightly enkindled by your light, bear the offerings soaked in ghee, in every good sacrifice. I bow to you who are sacrifice incarnate, and the protector of sacrifices—you who are five-fold in form[29] and are duly worshipped by five hymns[30] of the *Yajurveda*.

The gods said :

42. You, the first Puruṣa who, formerly, at the end of the kalpa, withdrew in your stomach the universe which is the

---

(3) SD. : (the first half). Those who know that *jīvas* who are your parts (*aṁśas*) are different *inter se* and from you, and that they are still not different from you as you are the Soul of the universe (and an *aṁśin*), are dearest to you.

*VR. : Obeisance to you who have given rise to differentiation about the Soul (*ātman*) such as god, man etc. through your Māyā. Your Māyā assumes the forms of Brahmā, Śiva etc. with you abiding in them. Your essential nature always keeps away the attributes (e.g. *sattva* etc.) which lead to misapprehension.

29. The five forms of sacrifice are : (i) *Agnihotra*, *darśa*, *Pūrṇamāsa*, *Cāturmāsya* and *Paśusoma* (ŚR., VC., SD., GD.).

(ii) VR. lists : *Dakṣiṇa*, *Āhavanīya*, *Gārhapatya*, *Sabhya* and *Āvasathya*. (iii) VJ. enumerates : *Yajña*, *Yojña puruṣa*, *Yajñeśa*, *Yajña-bhāvana* and *Yajña-bhuj*, as the five forms.

30. The five hymns mentioned are : *āśrāvaya*, *śrauṣat*, *yaja*, *ye yajāmahe* and *Vaṣaṭ*.

effect caused by you, lie down on the excellent bed of Śeṣa (the king of serpents), over the cosmic waters (after the deluge). You, the path of realizing whom is sought after by the Siddhas in their hearts, today move in the range of our sight and protect us, your servants.

Gandharvas said :

43. Oh God, these progenitors like Marīci and others, the hosts of gods like Brahmā, Indra and others of whom Rudra is the foremost, are merely the parts of your part (manifestation), Oh highest Lord! We always pay obeisance to you whom this universe is a toy-box.

Vidyādharas said :

44. Oh Lord, (even) after entering into the human body which is the means of (attaining) the (highest human) objective, viz. *Mokṣa*, a person thinks his material body as 'I' and 'mine' due to Your Māyā. This wicked-minded fool hankers after the unreal pleasures of the senses, even though he is reproached by his relatives. He who drinks the nectar in the form of stories about you, will be able to shake off the delusion about his body.

The Brāhmaṇas said :

45. You are the Sacrifice. You are the sacrificial offering. You are the sacrificial fire. You are certainly the incantations (sacred *Mantras* recited at the time of offering the oblations to fire), the sacrificial fuel, the *darbha* grass, and sacrificial utensils. You are the *sadasya* and the *ṛtvij* (the superintending and officiating priests forming the assembly at the sacrifice). You are the couple (the sacrificer, and his wife), the divinities (to be propitiated in the sacrifice), the *agnihotra* (the act of offering oblations to fire), the *Svadhā* the sacred oblations offered to *Pitṛs*), the Soma juice, the clarified butter (to be offered to the sacrificial fire) and the sacrificial animal.

46. Oh Lord, whose body is constituted of three Vedas, you are the embodiment of sacrifice (and of the will and the activity of the performance of sacrifice. Formerly you assumed the form of a mighty boar. While Yogins were eulogizing you, you, with a roar, sportively brought the earth on your

tusk (to the surface of waters), from the Rasātala, just as a big elephant would playfully do to a lotus plant.

47. May you (who are) of so great a glory, be gracious unto us, who long to see you, as our auspicious undertaking (of performing sacrifice) is interrupted. Oh Lord of Sacrifices, when your name is sung by men, all obstacles to sacrifices vanish. To you we offer our obeisance.

Maitreya said :

48. Oh blessed Vidura ! While Viṣṇu the protector of sacrifices was being eulogized, the wise Dakṣa recommenced the performance of the sacrifice that was interrupted by Rudra (Vīrabhadra).

49. Oh sinless Vidura ! The Lord who is within all (as *antaryāmin*) and (thus) the enjoyer of the oblations offered to all, expressed pleasure at the offering of his share (of *tri-puroḍāśa*). Addressing Dakṣa, He said :

The Lord said :

50*. I am the prime cause of the universe. I am its Soul and the Lord[31] and the witness (of all). I am the self-refulgent one, not subject to any condition (*upādhi*)[32]. I am Brahmā and Rudra (the creator and destroyer of the universe).

51**. Oh Brāhmaṇa (Dakṣa), having entered my own Māyā constituted of three Guṇas, it is I, who create, protect

---

*The gist of VR.'s lengthy commentary is as follows:

I, Brahmā and Śiva (the latter two) who constitute my body and who have (thus) no independent existence, (as I am their *antaryāmin*) are the cause of the world. I am the Lord of myself and abide as the controller from within, in all *jīvas* (*ātmeśvara*). Being bereft of name or form (as a god or a man) I am simply a witness or onlooker (*upadraṣṭā*). I am free from the defects or limitations of *Prakṛti* and *Puruṣa* such as lack of intelligence, limitedness, affliction. (*aviśeṣaṇa* is not a negative concept as the Lord is) *svayaṁ-dṛk*—possessor of all excellent attributes.

31. *ātmeśvara*—(i) The Lord of all *jīvas*—VJ.

(ii) Having none superior or Lord to him—SD.

32. *aviśeṣaṇaḥ*—(i) The best of all (*sarvottama*)—VJ.

(ii) With nobody equal or superior to me—SD.

(iii) Free from all attachment—GD.

**(1) VR. : I alone am the cause of the effect called universe consisting of *cid* (sentient) and *acid* (non-sentient). By my will, I enter my

and destroy the universe, and assume the name (Brahmā, Viṣṇu, Rudra) suitable for the function.

52. It is only the ignorant persons who view Brahmā, Rudra and all creatures as distinct from me who am the one Brahman without a second (either of the same or different kind, and who am the absolute, the Supreme Soul (*paramātman*).

53*. Just as a man never entertains the idea that his own limbs like head, hands etc. belong to others, similarly a person devoted to me does not regard other creatures as distinct from him.

54**. Oh Brāhmaṇa ! He who sees no difference between the three (Brahmā, Viṣṇu and Śiva) who are essentially one and who are the Souls (*antaryāmins*) of all creatures, attains real peace (*Mokṣa*).

Maitreya said :

55. Thus enlightened by the Lord (Viṣṇu), Dakṣa, the foremost among the Prajāpatis (first) worshipped Hari by his special sacrifice (*tri-kapāla-puroḍāśa*), and (then) other gods

---

Māyā and protect the world, and create it through Brahmā, and destroy it through Rudra. I assume the names Brahmā, Viṣṇu and Śiva according to the function performed.

(2) VJ. : I enter the unintelligent Prakṛti under my control. With *rajo-guṇa* as the material cause, I create Brahmā, enter into and abide in him and create the world . . . . In this way, by my form as Viṣṇu and my *aṁśas* in Brahmā and Rudra, I carry on the functions of the creation etc. It is a wrong notion that Brahmā or Rudra creates or destroys the universe.

(3) SD. : God is essentially free from *vikāras*. His modifications etc. are due to his Śakti. It is by means of his *aṁśa* that the creation etc. take place, and God assumes the particular name suitable for the function.

*VR : Even a man who wrongly identifies his body with his Soul, does not regard that the limbs of his body (which cannot exist independently of his body) as belonging to another person or have an existence apart from his body. Similarly, a person devoted to me, does not think that creatures can have an existence independent of me (*Brahman*).

**VR tries to interpret this verse as supporting the tenets of the Viśiṣṭādvaita school. The gist of his lengthy erudite Com. is as follows :

'The existence of the three (Brahmā, Viṣṇu and Rudra) is dependent upon Viṣṇu who is really independent and exists by himself, and the existence of Brahmā and Rudra is in Viṣṇu's power.

also in both ways (i.e. through principal and secondary types of sacrifices).

56. With a concentrated mind, he waited upon Rudra, by offering the share due to him (viz. the remains of the sacrifice). By performing the concluding rite called *udavasāna*, he offered oblations to gods who were eligible to drink Soma and also to others. Thus, after completely performing the sacrifice, he (Dakṣa) along with the priests (participants in the sacrifice), performed the sacred ablution called *avabhṛtha*.

57. Even though Prajāpati Dakṣa attained Siddhis (divine powers or knowledge) by his own merits, the divinities blessed him with devotion to Dharma only and returned to heaven.

58. We hear that Satī, the daughter of Dakṣa cast off her previous body, was born of Menā, the wife of Himavān (the presiding deity of the Himālayas).

59. Just as Śakti (the Divine Power) which lies asleep (dormant, during the period of *Pralaya*) again resorts to Puruṣa (God, at the beginning of creation), Ambikā (Satī, of the previous life) who was devoted to Rudra exclusively as her only resort[33], sought again the same beloved (Rudra) as her husband.

60. This deed of Lord Śambhu (Śiva) who destroyed Dakṣa's sacrifice, was heard by me from Uddhava, the great devotee of the Lord and the disciple of Bṛhaspati (preceptor of gods).

61. Oh Vidura (descendant of Kuru), a person who, every day, devotedly listens to and recounts this sanctifying work of the Supreme Lord (Rudra)—the work which enhances glory, confers longevity and purges all sins—shakes off sin (of himself and his listener).

62*. Oh Vidura, Śiva again obtained as his wife Satī, (now) the daughter of Menā. God Śiva enjoyed himself with her for a hundred years.

63. Realizing that she is incapable of bearing his semen, Dhūrjaṭi (Śiva) discharged it out into the sky, and the river Gaṅgā bore it.

33. *ekagatim* : VR. takes this as adj. qualifying Rudra : 'Rudra who was brooding over her only'.

*The verses 62-65 are commented upon by VJ. only.

64. (Finding the Gaṅgā too weak to bear it), Agni swallowed it (through *svāhā*) into a bush of reeds. There was born god Kumāra whom the six Kṛttikās (the stars constituting the Pleiades) adopted as their son.

65. By sucking their milk with six mouths, the child came to be known as Ṣaṇmukha (six-faced god). The gods then appointed him—the terror of all Asuras,—as the commander of their army.

CHAPTER EIGHT

(*Story of Dhruva*)*

Maitreya said :

1. Sanaka and others (viz. Sanandana, Sanātana and Sanatkumāra), Nārada, Ṛbhu, Haṁsa, Aruṇa and Yati—these sons of Brahmā did not take to the life of a householder, and observed life-long celibacy.

* From the 8th verse of this chapter, we find the famous story of Dhruva, so popular in Purāṇas and later literature. V.S. Agrawala (*MP—a Study* 58-9) traces this story to RV. X. 72.3-4. Agrawala interprets it as 'the Sun', while Siddheshwar Shastri Chitrav takes it to mean 'the tree' (*RV. Marathi translation*, p. 671). In MBH, Dhruva is a holy name which if remembered, wards off difficulties (*Anuśāsana*. 150.78). The *Vā. P.* (2.62.75-83) briefly refers to the story of Dhruva of the Cākṣusa Manvantara, but therein, it is god Brahmā and not Viṣṇu who confers on him the eternal astral position. The nucleus of the story of Dhruva in the Bh. P. is obviously the one given in *V.P.* I. Chs. 11 and 12. But there are some important differences. For example :

(1-2) In the *VP.*, Nārada plays no part in Dhruva's spiritual guidance. The seven sages initiate Dhruva with the *mantra* : *Om namo Vāsudevāya* and *Not Oṁ namo bhagavate Vāsudevāya* as given in the *Bh. P.* (vide verse 54).

(3) In the *VP.* 1.12.13-30, gods tried to disturb Dhruva's meditation by their Māyā. In the *Bh. P.* there is no such distraction.

(4) The eulogy of Viṣṇu sung by Dhruva in the *VP* 1.12. 53.75 is a Paurāṇic version of the *Puruṣa Sūkta* (RV.X.90). But the beautiful classic eulogy in the *Bh. P.* IV.9.6-17 is quite independent.

The *Bh. P.* seems to have revised and enlarged the story of Dhruva as given in the *V.P.*

2. Oh Vidura (destroyer of enemies), Adharma's wife, by name Mṛṣā (falsehood) gave birth to a twin—Dambha (Hypocrisy) and Māyā (deceit). Nirṛti (the Evil spirit presiding over the South-West) who was childless adopted that couple (as Dambha married his sister Māyā).

3. Oh man of great wisdom (Vidura)! To them (Dambha and Māyā) were born Lobha (Avarice) and Nikṛti (Wickedness). Of these (Lobha and Nikṛti) were born Krodha (Anger) and Hiṁsā (Violence); of these again (were born) Kali (Quarrel) and his sister Durukti (Abusive language).

4. Kali begot Bhaya (Fear) and (the daughter) Mṛtyu (Death) through Durukti. Of this couple (Bhaya and Mṛtyu) was born a twin, viz. Niraya (Hell) and Yātanā (Extreme tortures), Oh righteous-most Vidura.

5· Oh sinless one! I have described to you briefly the *Pratisarga* (secondary creation or the creation that leads to *Pralaya*). Having heard this sacred account thrice, one shakes off the impurities from his Soul.

6. Oh Scion of Kuru! I shall now describe the race of Svāyambhuva Manu of sacred renown, born from the part of (Brahmā who himself was) Hari's *aṁśa* (part).

7. Priya-vrata and Uttāna-pāda, the sons of Manu, the consort of Śatarūpā, were engaged in the protection of the world, as they were endowed with an *aṁśa* (a part of protective energy) of Lord Vāsudeva.

8. Uttānapāda had two wives—Sunīti and Suruci. (Of the two) Suruci was more beloved of her lord, and not the other (Sunīti) whose son was Dhruva.

9. One day, while the king was fondling Suruci's son Uttama by placing him on his lap, he did not like Dhruva who also wished to climb up his (Uttānapāda's) lap.

10. To Dhruva, her co-wife's son who was thus trying to climb (his father's lap), the extremely proud Suruci jealously spoke, while the king was listening :

11. 'Oh child, even though you are the king's son, you do not deserve to ascend the royal throne, as you were not borne by me, in my womb.

12. It is a pity that you are but a child, and you do

not verily know that you were borne in another woman's womb. Hence you desire for an unattainable object.

13. If you cherish a desire for the king's throne, you propitiate the Lord (*Puruṣa*) by penance, and by His grace, get yourself borne in my womb (secure birth as my son)."

Maitreya said :

14. Being cut to the quick by the harsh words of his stepmother, Dhruva, like a serpent beaten with a stick, heaved heavy sighs with anger. Leaving his father who was merely looking on tongue-tied, he went away crying to his mother.

15. Sunīti took up on her lap, the child which was (heavily) sighing with quivering lips. She was extremly distressed to hear from the inmates of the harem, the words of her co-wife.

16. Being scorched by grief like a forest creeper by the (encircling) forest conflagration, the young queen lost her heart and wept bitterly. Remembering the words of her co-wife, tears flowed out from her lotuslike beautiful eyes.

17. Heaving long sighs, and being unable to see the end of the misery (miserable state), the young lady spoke to her child, "Oh child! Do not blame others for the misery. A person experiences the same suffering which he has inflicted on others.

18. What Suruci said was true as you were borne in the womb of and were brought up with the milk of my unfortunate self whom the king is ashamed of recognising as his wife (nay even his maid servant).

19. Oh child! Remain above jealousy. Abide by the true path even though it is advised by your step-mother. If you desire the highest seat (throne) like Uttama, propitiate the feet of Adhokṣaja (god Viṣṇu).

20. It is by worshipping the lotuslike feet of Lord Viṣṇu who has assumed the *sattva guṇa* for the protection of the universe, that god Brahmā attained to the position of parameṣṭhin (the most exalted among gods), which is worthy of being bowed to by sages, who have controlled their minds and breath.

21. So also, your grandfather, the venerable Manu, with complete faith in him as the *antaryāmin* of all, worshipped

him, by performing sacrifices with liberal sacrificial fees (*dakṣiṇā*). He obtained earthly and heavenly happiness, and the highest bliss in Mokṣa, unattainable by other means.

22. Oh child, resort to him who is kind to his servants (devotees), the path of whose lotuslike feet should be sought by people desirous of Liberation (Mokṣa). Adore the *Puruṣa* (Supreme Man) by firmly fixing him in your mind by being exclusively devoted to him, and purified by performance of righteous duties.

23. My child! I find none other than the lotus-eyed God who can redress your grievance. The Lord is sought after by goddess Lakṣmī with a lotus in her hand, but who herself is sought by all others (like god Brahmā etc.).

Maitreya said :

24. Having heard the words thus spoken out to him, guiding him how to attain his objective, Dhruva controlled his mind by his will power, and left his father's capital.

25. When Nārada heard this and came to know what he (Dhruva) desired to do, he touched his (Dhruva's) head with his purifying hand, and said to himself in wonder :

26. "Oh, how wonderful is the spirit of the Kṣatriyas who cannot put up with the loss of respect; for even though (Dhruva) is but a child, he has taken to heart, the vile speech of the step-mother."

Nārada said (*to Dhruva*) :*

26.A "Oh child! Where are you going alone leaving behind your home full of prosperity ? I can perceive, Oh child, that you are indignant at the insulting treatment (meted out to you) by your own relatives."

Dhruva said :

26B. "Did you perceive this, Sir, by your power of contemplation developed by Yoga ?[34] I cannot console my heart which is wounded by the words of Suruci."

---

* 26 A and 26 B are additional verses in the text of the Bh. P. commented by VR. and VJ.

34. You have seen everything by your Yogic power born of contemplation. Although you can perceive everything, I, however, tell it to you. —VJ.

Nārada said :

27. Oh child, we do not find that (the sense of) honour or dishonour is developed now (at this early stage) in a child (like you), who is (normally and) naturally fond of play and (such) other things.

28* Even though the sense of distinction between honour and dishonour is developed, there are no other causes of dissatisfaction and misery for a man except his misapprehension. For in this world, people are different in their weal and woe as a result of their (past) *karmas*.

29. Therefore, observing the ways of the Almighty, a wise man should remain contented with whatever has been allotted to him by the Providence, Oh child.

30. Moreover, the Lord whose grace you aspire after by the path of *Yoga* as advised by your mother, is in my opinion, very difficult to be propitiated by men.

31. Though the sages have been seeking his path by intense *Yogic* meditation, and by remaining free from attachment through many births, they have not been able to find it.

32. Hence please return home. This persistence of yours is futile. You may try for your good (or final beatitude), at the proper time (viz. in advanced age).

---

* (1) VC : Insults or those who inflict them (upon us) are the creations of our misapprehension. From the point of *jñāna-yogins*, the *vikalpa* (the difference between honour and dishonour) being non-existent, the misery (resulting from mal-treatment) or the persons who cause it have no existence. In the case of *bhaktas* (*bhakti-yogins*) and *karma-yogins*, they consider that as everything in this world happens according to our past *karmas*, they should not blame anybody else except their own fate.

(2) In the first half VR. prefers to read *vikalpe avidya-māne'pi* instead of *vidyamane'pi* : In the same *ātman* there is no difference of categories like man, god etc. But it is the false identification of *ātman* with the body (of man, god etc.) which causes dissatisfaction.

In the later half :VR. prefers to read *lokāḥ* for *loke*. *Lakas* i.e. sentient beings are different (as men, gods etc) as a consequence of their past *karmas*.

(3) VJ. affirms that there is a difference in the world as friend or foe; but it is due to misapprehension that dissatisfaction or troubles to mind are caused. People are different from each other, according to their past actions (*karmas*).

33. An embodied being, who reconciles himself to the pleasure or pain (happiness or misery) meted out to him by Providence, reaches the end of the darkness of ignorance (i.e. attains *Mokṣa*).

34. One should feel delighted to see a person of superior merits; should feel compassion to one who is inferior; and should desire friendship with one's equals. (In this way) one is not overwhelmed with afflictions.

Dhruva said :

35. This path of tranquillity has been graciously shown by your venerable Self, to persons whose hearts are affected with pleasure and pain. But it is beyond the ken of persons like us.

36. It, however, does not dwell (i.e. impress) in my heart which is shattered by sharp arrow-like words of Suruci—heart of mine who am undisciplined, and have inherited terrible martial (*Kṣatriya*) spirit.

37. Oh Brāhmaṇa (sage Nārada), I desire to secure (lit. conquer) a place which is the highest and the most exalted of all in the worlds, and which had never been attained either by forefathers or anybody else. Be pleased to tell me a good path (leading to it).

38. You are the son of the Lord Parameṣṭhin (Brahmā). Certainly it is for welfare of the world, that your honour roam over (the world) like the Sun, playing on (your) *Vīṇā* (lute).

Maitreya said :

39. Hearing this excellent reply, the venerable Nārada was pleased with the child. Out of compassion, he then spoke to him the (following) excellent words in reply.

Nārada said :

40. The path pointed out to you by your mother will verily lead to the highest good. The course is no other than Lord Vāsudeva. Adore him with a mind completely devoted to him.

41. If one wishes to be blest with good fortune known as Dharma, Artha, Kāma and Mokṣa (righteousness, wealth,

sense-pleasure and Liberation from Saṁsāra), worship of Hari's feet, is the only course for attaining it.

42. Therefore, Oh Child, God bless you! You go to the holy bank of the Yamunā where there is the sacred Madhuvana which is ever permeated with Hari's presence.

43. You bathe in the holy waters of the Yamunā three times (morning, mid-day and evening) a day; perform religious duties (e.g. bowing to god) proper for (a child like) you; be steady in a suitable easy posture (like *Svastikāsana*) on a seat (of *Kuśa*-grass etc.).

44. Gradually remove the impurities fickleness etc. of *Prāṇa*, *Indriyas* (sense-organs) and the mind by threefold *Prāṇāyāma* (breath-control consisting of *Pūraka*, *Kumbhaka* and *Recaka*). With a steady and a concentrated mind, you should meditate upon Lord Hari.

45. Hari is disposed to show his grace. His face and eyes are ever graciously cheerful. He has a well-shaped nose, beautiful brows and charming cheeks. He is the most beautiful of all gods.

46. He is ever youthful with beautiful limbs, red lips and reddish eyes. He is the only resort of all suppliants (devotees), the dispenser of infinite happiness (or the reservoir of all *Puruṣārthas*, the protector and the ocean of mercy.

47. He is distinguished by the mark called Śrī-Vatsa. He possesses all the characteristics of the Supreme Man. He is dark blue like a cloud, and wears a Vanamālā (about his neck); and his four arms are distinguished with *Śaṅkha* (a conch), *Cakra* (a discus), *gadā* (a mace) and *Padma* (a lotus).

48. He is adorned with a crown, (a pair of) ear-rings, armlets and bracelets. His neck adds to the beauty of the *Kaustubha* gem. He wears yellow silken garments.

49. He wears a girdle furnished with small tinkling bells round his waist, and is adorned with anklets of burnished gold. He is extremely beautiful, serene, and enhancer of the delight of the mind and the eyes.

50. Having occupied the pericarp of the lotus in the form of his devotees' heart, with his feet beautified by a row of gemlike nails, he presents himself to the mind of his worshippers.

51. With a steady, concentrated mind, one should con-

template Hari, the formost among the bestowers of boons, as (having a) smiling (face) and looking with affection (to the devotees).

52. The mind which contemplates the extremely auspicious form of the Lord in this way, is soon filled with highest bliss[35] and does not revert (to *saṁsāra*).

53. Oh Prince, hear from me the most secret *mantra* (mystic formula to be continuously repeated mentally during meditation). Any person who repeats it for seven days (and nights) can see the heavenly beings (moving through the skies).

54. The Mantra is *Oṁ namo bhagavate Vāsudevāya* (salutation to venerable Vāsudeva who is the embodiment of *OM* or *praṇava*). Judging the appropriateness of the articles of worship with due regard to time and place, a wise man should perform the worship of the Lord with various material substances, repeating all the while this *Mantra*.

55. He should worship the Lord with sacred waters, garland of flowers, roots, fruits etc. found in forests, sprouts approved for worship (e.g. *durvā*-grass-blades), garments and leaves etc. of *Tulasī* so dear to the Lord.

56. Having secured an image of substances like stone or through the medium of the earth, water etc. as a substitute for the image, the sage should perform the worship of the Lord. He should be controlled in mind[36] and speech; should be serene and should subsist on moderate quantity of forest products (life fruit, roots etc.).

57. He should meditate upon the glorious deeds which the Lord of hallowing fame, will perform in the incarnations which He assumes at his will and pleasure, by the force of his incomprehensible Māyā.

58. Whatever articles (or forms) of worship are adopted by the ancients for his adoration, should be offered to the

35. v.l. *nivṛtti*: renunciation. 'The mind is immediately filled with renunciation (of worldly objects)'.

36. v.l. *ādṛtātmā*—with a devout mind—VR.
āhṛtātmā—One who has controlled his mind by withdrawing it from sensual pleasure.

Lord embodied in the Mantra, by means of repeating the same Mantra (of twelve letters).

59-60. When the Lord is thus being worshipped with body, speech and mind with acts of devotion, he enhances the Divine Love in men who properly perform his devotion sincerely. He confers upon them the bliss cherished by them as beneficial, in the form of Dharma, Artha etc.

61. He (the devotee) should be indifferent to sensual pleasures. With a highly intensive practice of *Bhakti-yoga* (path of devotion) and with his mind exclusively devoted to God, he should worship him directly for Liberation from *Saṁsāra*.

62. The Prince, who was thus advised, circumambulated Nārada. After bowing down to him (Nārada), he went to the holy Madhuvana which was adorned with Hari's footprints.

63. When Dhruva went to the forest for penance, the sage Nārada entered (Uttānapāda's) harem. He was received with due worship by the king. Seating himself comfortably, he spoke to the king.

Nārada said :

64. Oh King, what is it that you think about so long, with a withering face? Is there any deficiency in your *Dharma* (religious duties), *Artha* (wealth and prosperity) and *kāma* (fulfillment of desires)?

The King replied :

65. Oh sage My wise and noble son of five years has been exiled along with his mother by me, who became heartless due to my submissiveness to (her) co-wife.

66. Oh Sage May not the wolves prey upon my helpless child lying in the forest, fatigued and famished, with his lotus-like face faded.

67. What a pity! Look at the wickedness of a fellow like me who am under the thumb of a women. I am an extremely vile fellow, I did not welcome him while he affectionately wished to climb my lap.

Nārada said :

68. Oh King ! Do not worry about your child at all. He is protected by the Lord. You do not know his greatness. His glory will spread over the whole world.

69. Oh King! After achieving a feat difficult even for the Protectors of the world, your powerful son will soon return enhancing your glory.

Maitreya said:

70. Having thus heard the speech of the divine sage Nārada, the King Uttānapāda discarded his royal fortune and anxiously brooded over his son only.

71. There (in Madhuvana), Dhruva had his bath in the Yamunā. Remaining self-controlled, he fasted that night. With a concentrated mind, he worshipped the Supreme Man according to the instructions of the sage.

72. He passed one month in the worship of Hari, eating at the end of every third night fruits called *kapittha* (wood-apple) and *badara* (jujub), just enough to maintain his life.

73. The second month also he continued the worship of the Lord, eating every sixth day withered blades of grass, leaves etc.

74. He spent the third month in propitiating the Lord of hallowing fame, with perfectly concentrated mind, drinking water only, on every ninth day.

75. With perfect control over his breath, he passed the fourth month in contemplating the Lord, subsisting on the air, on every twelfth day.

76. When the fifth month arrived, the Prince controlled his life-breath and meditating upon Brahman (the Supreme being) stood motionless like a post.

77. He withdrew his mind which is the basis of the sense-organs and their objects from every side (external objects). He meditated upon the form of the Lord in his heart and perceived nothing else.

78. While he was having the *Dhāraṇā* (steadfast fixation of mind on the Supreme Brahman, the support of Mahat and other principles and the controller of Pradhāna and Puruṣa, all the three worlds began to shake.

79. When the child of the King (i.e. Dhruva) stood on one leg, the earth, being pressed down by his great toe, became semi-inclined to one side, as a ferry-boat carrying a big elephant does at every step, according as he raises his right or left leg.

80. Dhruva controlled his life-breath and the (working) of) his senses and began to meditate on Hari, the Soul of the universe as not being different from himself. While he was contemplating thus, the worlds along with their protecting deities became greatly distressed at the stoppage of their breath, and they resorted to Hari for refuge.

Gods said :

81. We do not know the reason of this sudden and simultaneous stoppage of breath of all beings, mobile and immobile. We have sought refuge under you who alone can afford shelter to us. Therefore save us from this calamity.

The Lord said :

82. Do not be afraid. I shall dissuade the child (Dhruva) from this austere penance. You return to your respective abodes. The son of King Uttānapāda has identified his Self with me (as the Soul of the universe). This has led to the stoppage of your breath.

CHAPTER NINE

Viṣṇu's boon and Dhruvā's Coronation.

Maitreya continued :

1. Gods, whose fears were thus dispelled, bowed down to Viṣṇu (God of very great valour or God of long strides in His Trivikrama form). When they returned to heaven, even Lord Viṣṇu (the Cosmic Man of thousand heads), being eager to see His devotee, sped to Madhu-vana riding on Garuḍa.

2. Verily, Dhruva found that the lightening-like brilliant form of the Lord which he visualized as manifested in the

lotus of his heart, due to his intellect sharpened by his intense yoga, suddenly disappeared. (Opening his eyes) he saw him standing outside in the same state (form).

3. Awed at his presence (lit. sight), the child bowed to him, bending down his body and prostrating himself before him like a stick. While looking at him, he was as if drinking him (with his eyes). He was, as if, kissing him with his mouth, and embracing, as it were, with his arms.

4. Hari who dwells in the heart of Dhruva as well as those of others, knew that the child which folded its palms before him, desired to praise him, but did not know how to express himself. Out of grace, He touched him on the cheek with his conch, the embodiment of the Veda.

5. Immediately (at the touch of Visnu's conch) Dhruva whose eternal abode was reserved, was inspired, with the divine speech and realized decisively the real nature of the Supreme Soul (*Brahman*) and the *jīva*. Being full of devotion and love, he calmly (and without faltering) began to praise the Lord whose great glory is heard everywhere.

Dhruva said :

6. Salutations to you, Venerable Lord, the *antaryāmin* of all. You are the Lord of all powers. Having entered into me by your power of intelligence, you reactivate the power of my speech which was lying dormant, and enliven the activities of my (cognitive and conative) sense organs like hands, feet, ears, tactile sense and others.

7. Oh Lord! You are really only one. Having created the entire universe consisting of *Mahat* and other principles by your power called Māyā consisting of *guṇas* of infinite varieties, you enter as *an antaryāmin* (Inner[38] Controller) in it, and appear as many in the apparent *guṇas* of Māyā (in the

37. *sva-dhāmnā*—(i) By your will power and knowledge—VR.
(ii) By your being *antar-yāmin*
v.l. *sva-dhāmnaḥ*—VR.'s Text. : Prāṇas and sense-organs wherein Paramātman abides.

38. *Puruṣa*—*antaryāmin* (Inner Controller)—ŚR., VC., GD.
Jīva-śarīrakaḥ/ God dwelling in *Jīva*—VR.
One who abides in the body—VJ.

form of the presiding deities of organs of senses), just as the fire (though one) appears of different forms in relation to the different shapes and sizes of the wood (fuel).

8. Oh Lord! God Brahmā has completely submitted to you for refuge. By the knowledge conferred by you, he saw (i.e. created this universe like a man awakened from sleep. Oh friend of the distressed? How can your feet which are the shelter of the liberated persons, be forgotten by one who is grateful to your benevolent acts (such as resuscitating all the sense-organs etc.).

9. Your Māyā has really deluded their intelligence who worship you—a veritable wish-yielding tree (capable of) liberating persons from the cycle of births and deaths—for other purpose, and desire physical pleasures enjoyable by this body which is as good as a corpse—pleasures which men can get even in the hell.

10. Oh Lord! The bliss that embodied beings enjoy from meditating upon your lotus-like feet, or from listening to the stories of your devotees, is not available in the Brahman who is essentially blissful. How can it be enjoyed by beings who fall from the celestial cars struck down by the sword of Death.

11. Oh Infinite Lord! Bless me with the intimate companionship of those great persons, who bear constant devotion to you, and are of pure (desireless) heart. Thereby, being intoxicated with drinking the nectar in the form of stories about your honour's excellent attributers, I shall easily cross[39] the terrible ocean of *saṁsāra*, teeming with great calamities.

* VJ. construes differently: The bliss is not enjoyable by the *Jīva* who is in contact with Brahman by meditation etc.—Brahman whose greatness lies in its absolute independence. There is no need to speak of persons who, having attained the heaven (*Svarga*), move in the celestial cars, for the heaven is subject to destruction by the impending sword of Kāla or death.

39. *neṣye* : (i) VJ. notes a pun here (I) Cross over and (II) shall not return to (*na+iṣye*).

(ii) VC. & VD. : defeat, overcome. Just as the god of death cannot touch a person who has drunk nectar, the ocean of *saṁsāra* dare not affect me who am drunk with your nectarlike stories.

12.* Oh Lord with a lotus in the navel! Those who closely associate themselves with (your devotees) whose hearts are longing for the fragrance (excellent attributes) of Your lotuslike feet, do not remember (even) their mortal frame which is extremely dear to them, much less their sons, friends houses, wealth and wives which are connected with it.

13.* Oh unborn Lord! I know only your grossest form (the *Virāṭ rūpa*) consisting of the world teeming with beasts, trees, birds, reptiles, gods, demons human beings etc.—the world characterised by *sat* and *asat* and produced by a number of principles like *Mahat*. I do not know, Oh Supreme Lord, your other form which is beyond this, where speech and mind cannot reach.

14. I bow to that glorious Lord, the Supreme Man, who at the end of Kalpa (at the time of the dissolution of the universe) withdraws this entire universe in his stomach. He, the friend of Ananta (the serpent Śeṣa) turns his eyes (inwards) upon him self (in *Yoga-nidrā—Yogic* sleep), and lies (asleep) on his coils. It is in the interior part of the gold lotus (comprising all worlds) which sprouted in the oceanlike navel of the Lord, that the resplendent god Brahmā appeared.

15. (As contrasted with the *jīva*) you are the eternally free, absolutely pure, omniscient, intelligent spirit, essentially unchangeable, First Person (existing before the creation and

* VJ. construes the first half differently :

Those who think of their own sons, friends, house, wealth, and wives, do not remember you who are (really) the dearest of all and who are the First Being.

* VR. takes objection to ŚR's interpretation as he is knowable by Śāstras. He combines *na-yatra-vādaḥ*, and separates *param-a-vedmina*, and interprets : 'Not that I cannot, by your grace, comprehend your subtle form about which there is a controversy...' VR. gives another interpretation of *na-yatra-vādaḥ*—'The controversy whether it is *prākṛta* (produced of *Prakṛti*) does dot arise'.

(ii) VJ. adopts the v.l. *na-yatra-vācaḥ* and explains :

It is not possible for me to know your subtle form which the goddess of speech (which implies Lakṣmī, Brahmā and other divinities) who sees him everyday, cannot comprehend due to his infiniteness.

SD. states : I do not know fully even your gross form. Need it be said that I cannot comprehend your subtle form ?

after the dissolution of the universe), possessor of divine attributes, and the controller of the triad (of guṇas or worlds or Vedas or divisions of time.). For you are the seer of the different states of the mind by your unobstructed vision. For the maintenance of the universe, you stay as (Viṣṇu) the presiding deity of sacrifices. You are thus totally distinct from *jīva*

16.* I take resort to you who are that *Para Brahman* in whom various powers of contradictory character, such as knowledge and others, incessantly yet causelessly manifest themselves in succession—that *Para Brahman* who is the cause of the universe, the indivisible whole[40], infinite, beginningless and endless, of purely blissful nature and unchangeable.

17. Oh Lord! You are the embodiment of the highest bliss. To those who are devoted to you that way (without cherishing any desires), your lotuslike feet themselves are the real blessings which are far superior to other worldly boons such as sovereignty and others. Oh noble Lord, you are however, so eager to confer your grace that like a mother-cow which nourishes and protects (against wolves etc.) its newly born calf, Your Lor hip protects us, your miserable devotees, who cherish worldly desire.

Maitreya said :

18. Verily, on being thus highly extolled by the intelligent (Dhruva) of noble heart (intent), the Lord who loves his devotees, applauded him and spoke thus.

The Lord said :

19. Oh Young prince, I know what you cherish in your heart. You are a strict observer of religious vows. May you

* (i) Mutually contradictory potencies exist in their qualitative capacity in the Lord, and they *carry out* their different functions in proper order—JG.

(ii) The lord is the receptacle of mutually exclusive powers. But they manifest themselves *in due succession* for the maintenance of world order (e.g. creation, sustenance, dissolution etc.)—VR.

40. *ekam*—who is both the material and efficient cause, the protector and destroyer of the universe—VR.

be blessed. I bestow on you your cherished object even though it is unattainable (to others).

20. Oh blessed one, (I confer to you) that resplendent eternal place which is not attained to by anyone else. On it is based the entire circle of stellar luminaries like planets, stars and constellations of stars.

21. The circle of luminous bodies like stars etc. are fastened to the eternal post offered to Dhruva like a team of oxen to the central post in the threshing ground. The place given to Dhruva will survive even the destruction of three worlds in intermediate *Kalpas*. The stars presided over by Dharma, Agni and others and those by seven sages (*Ursa Major*) revolve round it (always) keeping it to their right.

22. When, at the time of his retirement to the forest, your father makes over (the kingdom of) the earth to you, you who are firmly established in *Raja-Dharma*, and with your senses (faculties) unimpaired, will protect the earth for a period of thirty-six thousand years.

23. When your brother Uttama is missing in a hunting expedition, his mother, brooding over him in mind, will enter a forest-conflagration while in search for him in the jungle.

24. As you know it, Sacrifice is my beloved form. Having, worshipped me by performance of a number of sacrifices with liberal *dakṣiṇas* (sacrificial fees), and having enjoyed here the real blessings, you will fix your heart on me, at the end.

25. Then, you will attain to my place which is bowed to by all the worlds and which is above that of the sages (*Ursa Major*)—a place from which there is no return (*to saṁsāra*).

Maitreya said :

26. Lord Viṣṇu (whose banner is Garuḍa), who was

* It (this eternal place) continues to exist even after the destruction of those who live for a Kalpa. Just as a team of oxen employed to thrash out corn by trampling over it, is fastened to a post in the middle of the thrashing ground, and the bulls go round it, the stars presided over by Dharma, Agni, Kaśyapa, Śukra (Venus) and the forest dwelling sages (*Ursa Major*) along with stars and constellations, revolve round it, keeping it to their right. (SD).

worshipped (by Dhruva) promised to give his own realm (to him), and returned to his own abode, while the boy stood gazing in wonder.

27. Although he got his wishes gratified by obtaining his cherished object through the service of the feet of god Viṣṇu, Dhruva was not very much pleased. He also returned to the city (his father's capital).

Vidura asked :

28. How is it that Dhruva, who knew the real (value of) *Puruṣārthas*, regarded himself as unsuccessful in obtaining them even when, within (the period of) a single birth he secured the promise of the supreme abode of Hari, by worshipping his feet—a place extremely difficult to attain to by persons actuated with desires.

Maitreya replied :

29. Dhruva whose heart was pierced with sharp arrow-like words of his step-mother, (pointedly), remembered those words, and did not desire to attain the Final beatitude from the Lord who confers *Mukti* (Liberation). Hence, he became full of regrets (as the bitterness about his step-mother disappeared at the Lord's blissful presence.)

Dhruva said (to himself) :

30. I attained within a period of six months the asylum of the Lord's feet which life-long celibates like Sananda and others could realize by Yogic meditation extending over a span of many lives (i.e. births). Alas ! I, whose mind was fixed on diversity (or on worldly pleasures), have receded from them.

31. Oh ! Look at the folly of a luckless fellow like me. Alas ! Having reached the feet of the Lord who can terminate *saṁsāra* (the cycle of births and deaths), I begged for what was ephemeral.

32. My judgment was possibly deluded by jealous gods who attain to positions lower than mine[41]. Hence, I, the

41. Or : who are to fall from their position as gods.

wicked-most fellow, did not follow the true and salutary advice of Nārada.

33* I became deluded by Divine Māyā. Like sleeping man experiencing (fear at the sight of tigers etc. in) dreams while (in reality) there is nobody else (except the dreamer), I entertained a perverted view—a notion of difference[42], even though the second is non-existent (i.e. only the *ātman* exists everywhere—one, without a second), and mistaking my brother as an enemy, I got afflicted at heart with jealousy.

34. In vain have I solicited this kingdom of the world or eternal astral position, (as it is) like the medical treatment administered to a person whose life has ended. Having propitiated by penance, the Soul of the Universe who is so very difficult to propitiate, and who alone is capable of terminating the *saṁsāra*, I, a luckless fellow, begged of him *saṁsāra* only.

35. Alas ! From the Supreme Lord who offered his own blissful state, I, whose fund of good merits is exhausted, stupidly begged for pride (i.e. sovereignty etc. the cause of pride), just as a penniless fellow begs unhusked grains from an emperor.

36. Oh Vidura, people like you who are devoted to the pollen dust in the lotus-like feet of Lord Kṛṣṇa, and whose hearts are satisfied with whatever they get by chance (or by

* Other interpretations :

(i) Like a man in sleep, I am under the influence of the divine Māyā which is difficult to overcome. Due to her influence, I mistake my body for the real Soul (*Ātmnā*) and think that I have got independent existence, even though, in reality, there is nothing which is not under the control of Brahman. Hence, under the misconception that my brother is my enemy, I am afflicted with this heart-burning.—VR.

(ii) I am influenced by Hari's binding power—Māyā, just as a person asleep (steeped in ignorance) fails to see things in correct perspective, but takes a perverted view, I mistakenly look upon brother Uttama as my enemy, and am afflicted at heart by this misconception, even though Hari is the only independent, omnipotent Lord without a second. —VJ.

(iii) From point of *ātman*, I and my brother Uttama are *jīvas* (the *taṭastha-vṛtti* of the Lord), and from physical point of view, our bodies are composed of five *bhūtas*. In spite of this, I am deluded by Māyā to look upon him as an enemy.—VC.

42. *bhinna-dṛk*—who thinks of a *puruṣārtha* other than the Lord.—J

his will), do not really seek for any personal objective (*puruṣārtha*), except his service.

37. When King Uttānapāda heard that his son Dhruva was coming he did not believe in it, thinking as if it were like the news of the return to life of a dead man, and thought to himself, "How could an unfortunate person like me be so lucky ?"

38. He, however, put faith in the words of the Divine Sage Nārada. He was overwhelmed with joy. Being highly pleased with the person who brought the news, he presented him a costly necklace of pearls.

39-40. He mounted a chariot decked with gold and drawn by excellent horses. Surrounded by Brāhmaṇas, elderly members of his family, ministers and kinsmen, he, being eager to see his son, immediately set out of his capital, while conches were being blown, kettle-drums sounded, Vedic hymns chanted and flutes played upon.

41. Adorned with gold ornaments, his queens, Sunīti and Suruci, accompanied by prince Uttama, went forward in palanquins to receive him.

42-43. The king saw him (Dhruva) coming, near the garden. Being overwhelmed with love, he hurriedly got down from the chariot and quickly approached him. The king, whose heart was full of anxiety for a long time (for his missing son), was heaving deep sighs, and clasped in his arms his son Dhruva who was absolved of all the bonds of sins by the touch of Lord Hari's feet.

44. Then, the king whose most cherished desire (to see Dhruva safe) was fulfilled, smelt again and again the crown of Dhruva's head, and bathed his son with his cool tears (of joy).

45. Dhruva, the foremost among the pious people, respectfully welcomed by all, bowed at his father's feet and was addressed with blessings. He paid respects to his mothers by bowing his head.

46. Suruci (Dhruva's step-mother) lifted up the child that bowed down at her feet. She clasped it to her bosom and with her throat choked with tears, she blessed, 'May you live long'.

47. Just as water automatically flows to a lower level,

all creatures bow to him with whom Lord Hari is pleased, on account of his qualities like universal friendliness and others.

48. Overwhelmed with love, both Uttama and Dhruva embraced each other. With their hair standing on the end at the touch of each other, they constantly shed tears of joy.

49. His mother Sunīti hugged her son (who was) dearer to her than her life. Feeling happy at the touch of his body, she was relieved of her mental anguish.

50. Oh warrior Vidura ! Milk flowed out from her breasts which were then constantly bathed in the tears of joy (flowing) from the eyes of the hero's mother (Sunīti).

51. People praised the queen, "luckily your son, who was missing for a long time, has returned to remove your mental affliction. He will now protect the world (lit. the globe of the earth).

52. You have really propitiated the Lord who removes the afflictions of his suppliants, and by constantly meditating on whom, heroes (wise men) have conquered death which is very difficult to overcome".

53. While people were thus caressing Dhruva, the king placed Dhruva along with his brother, on a female elephant, and joyously entered his capital, amidst their cheers (lit. praise).

Description of the decorations in the city

54. There, at different places brilliant alligator-shaped festoons were hung; plaintain-trees and young areca-nut trees, with bunches of fruit were set up.

55. At every door (were placed) vessels full of water with lights burning on them, and decorated with leaves of mango trees, pieces of cloth, wreaths of flowers and strings of pearls hanging round their necks.

56. The ramparts, gates and mansions which beautified the city were decked in gold, and the tops (of the buildings) were shining like the pinnacles of celestial cars.

57. Its quadrangles, royal roads and streets were swept clean, and sprayed over with (scented) sandal-water. It was spread over with fried rice, unbroken rice *akṣatas*, flowers, fruits and other articles of worship.

58-59. Wherever Dhruva was seen on the road, the ladies of the city, out of affection, gave him auspicious benedictions. They showered on him white mustard, unbroken rice, curds, water, blades of *durvā* grass, flowers and fruits. While listening to their sweet strains, he entered his father's palace.

60. Fondly caressed by his father, Dhruva lived in the best of mansions built of most precious stones, like a god in the celestial region.

61.* There that palace was furnished with beds white and soft like the foam of milk, on ivory bed-steads chased with gold. The seats were highly precious and the furniture was made of gold.

62. There, on the walls of crystals and very costly emeralds, were shining jewel-lamps held by statuettes of beautiful damsels made of precious stones.

63. The gardens were beautiful with various species of celestial trees on which couples of birds were warbling and the swarms of intoxicated black-bees were humming sweetly.

64. There, the tanks in the garden had steps of cat's-eye (*Vaidūrya*). They contained white and blue lotuses and lilies, and were resorted to by swarms of swans, ducks, ruddy geese and cranes.

65. The royal sage Uttānapāda was highly wonder-struck at seeing his son's most wonderful prowess, of which he heard (only the reports).

66. Seeing that Dhruva had come of age, and was acceptable to his cabinet of ministers, and was loved by the subject the king coronated him as the Lord of the earth.

67. Realizing that he had grown old, the King, contemplating over the nature of the Soul, became unattached to worldly pleasures, and left for the forest.

---

* This verse and the following three verses are repeated. Cf. Supra 3.33. 16-19—the description of Kardama's mansion.

CHAPTER TEN

(*Dhruva invades Alakā*)

Maitreya said :

1. Dhruva married Bhrami, the daughter of Prajāpati Śiśumāra. They had two sons, Kalpa and Vatsara.

2. And by his second wife Ilā, the daughter of Vāyu, the mighty Dhruva begot a son by name Utkala who was covetable to women like a jewel.[43]

3. But Uttama, who was yet unmarried, was killed in a hunting expedition, in the Himālayas, by a more powerful Yakṣa. His mother, Suruci, also followed his course.

4. Having heard of his brother's death, Dhruva was filled with wrath, revenge and sorrow. Mounting his victorious chariot, he marched against the abode of Yakṣas, the city of Alakā.

5. Proceeding to the northern direction, he saw, in a valley of the Himālayas, the city, Alakā, crowded with Yakṣas, and frequented by the followers of Rudra (Such as goblins, spirits).

6. The stout-armed Dhruva blew his conch, resounding the sky and all the quarters. Oh Vidura, thereby the demi-goddesses (women of the *Yakṣa* tribe) became greatly terrified and looked bewildered.

7. Incensed at the blast of the conch, the mighty and great warriors among the *Yakṣas* sallied forth from the city, and with uplifted weapons, fell upon him.

8. While the *Yakṣas* were dashing towards him the great warrior[44] with a formidable bow, simultaneously hit each one of them with three arrows.

9. With those arrows planted on their foreheads, all of

---

43. *yoṣid-ratnam*—(he got) a daughter who was like a jewel among women—ŚR. VJ. accepts the v.l. *yogeśvaram*—(the son Utkala) who was the master of *Yoga* and possessed supernatural powers (*siddhis* like *aṇimā*).

44. *mahāratha*—An expert who, riding his chariot, can engage ten thousand archers simultaneously.

eko daśa-sahasrāṇi yodhayed yas tu dhanvinām |
astra-śastra-pravīṇas' ca, vijñeyaḥ sa mahārathaḥ ||

them felt definitely vanquished, and verily appreciated that heroic deed.

10. Being enraged like serpents trodden under feet, the *Yakṣas* also, desiring to do the double of what he did, simultaneously shot at him double the number of arrows (six each).

11-12. Then fired with anger, and desirous of retaliation those one lakh and thirty-thousand *Yakṣas* showered on him, his chariot and charioteer iron bars, swords, darts, spears, axes, lances, double-edged swords, *bhuśuṇḍi* missile and arrows with variegated feathers.

13. At that time, being covered with the heavy volley of weapons, Dhruva, the son of Uttānapāda, could not be seen, just as a hill is hidden by a thick shower of rain.

14. Immediately arose the cry 'Alas ! Alas' from the Siddhas who were witnessing the fight from the sky. 'This Sun of Manu's race, drowned in the ocean of *Yakṣa*-army, is killed'.

15. While Yakṣas and Rākṣasas (Yātudhānas)[45] were shouting and proclaiming their victory, the chariot of Dhruva came into view, like the Sun from behind the mist.

16. Twanging his divine bow, he struck terror in his enemies. He shattered to pieces their volley of missiles, like strong wind dispersing the army of clouds.

17. Sharp arrows discharged from his bow, pierced through the armours of the Rākṣasas into their bodies, just as thunderbolts (*vajras*) into the mountains.

18-19. When they were mowed down with Dhruva's arrows of *bhalla* type, the battlefield was covered with their heads adorned with beautiful ear-rings; with their thighs resembling golden palms; with arms beautiful with bracelets; with precious necklaces, armlets, crowns and costly turbans, and it appeared attractive to warriors

20. Most of the survivers of the Rākṣasa army who escaped death, got the limbs of their bodies cut off with the arrows of Dhruva, the foremost among the Kṣatriyas, and they

45. The Bh. P. mixes up Yakṣas and Rākṣasas, as Alakā was inhabited by all kinds of demigods and their army was composed of these.

fled away from the field of battle, like the elephant-leaders discomfited in their fight with a lion (king of beasts).

21. At that time, Dhruva, the best among Manu's race, did not see anyone with a weapon in hand, on the great battlefield. Though he desired to see the city of the enemies, he did not enter it. 'A man cannot know the intentions of those expert in black magic'.

22. Telling this to his charioteer, Dhruva of wonderful chariot, apprehended an attack from the enemies and remained alert. He heard a noise like the roaring of the sea, and saw on all sides dust raised by a strong wind.

23. In a moment, the sky was overcast on all sides by a host of clouds accompanied with flashes of lightening and terrible thunders rattling, in all directions

24. They (the clouds) showered blood, phlegm, puss, excreta, fat and urine. Headless bodies fell down from heaven before him, Oh sinless (Vidura)!

25. Then a mountain appeared in the sky; and from all directions were showered maces, iron clubs, swords, pestles along with a volley of stones.

26. Serpents with thunderous hissing and emitting fire from eyes with rage, rushed at him. Intoxicated elephants, lions and tigers attacked him in multitudes.

27. Terrific like the ocean at the time of deluge, at the end of a Kalpa, a loudly roaring terrible sea, engulfing the earth on all sides with waves, approached him.

28. By means of their special power of black magic, the Asuras (Yakṣas)of cruel disposition, created many kinds of such phenomena which strike terror into unthinking men.

29. Hearing that insuperable type of black magic had been employed against Dhruva by the Asuras, sages assembled there praying for his welfare.

Sages said:

30. Oh Dhruva, son of Uttānapāda ! May the glorious Viṣṇu (wielder of the *Śārṅga* bow), your God who removes afflictions of the suppliants, destroy your enemies—the Lord by

uttering or hearing whose name, people easily overcome death which is so very difficult to conquer.[46]

CHAPTER ELEVEN

(*Svāyambhuva Manu Dissuades Dhruva from Fighting*)

Maitreya said:

1. Hearing this speech of the sages, Dhruva sipped some water as *ācamana*, and set to his bow the missile created by Nārāyaṇa.

2. Oh Vidura, just as afflictions disappear at the dawn of the (highest) knowledge, the manifestations of the black magic created by Guhyakas, immediately vanished, while the missile was being set on the bow.

3. Even while he was fixing on his bow the missile devised by the sage Nārāyaṇa, shafts with gold-plated heads and feathers resembling the wings of swans, shot forth from it, and penetrated the enemy's forces like peacocks entering a forest, with a terrible cry.

4. Assailed on every side, in the battle, by those sharp-pointed arrows, the Yakṣas (*Puṇyajanas*) got enraged. With their weapons raised, they rushed towards him on all sides, just as cobras with their hoods raised, would attack Garuḍa.

5. Even as they were attacking him in the battle, he cut down their arms, thighs, necks and stomachs, and sent them to that highest region, to which sages with lifelong celibacy attain, penetrating their way through the sphere of the Sun.

6. His grandfather Manu saw that the innocent Yakṣas were being slaughtered in great numbers by Dhruva, of a wonderful chariot. Out of compassion, he, accompanied by

46. VC. and VD. add : What of dispelling the Māyā of Yakṣas. Hereby, they (sages) suggested him to use the missile *Nārāyaṇāstra*.

sages, approached Dhruva, the son of Uttānapāda and spoke thus:

Manu said:

7. Oh child, enough of this sinful rage which is a gateway to Tama (hell)—rage, (blinded) with which you have killed these innocent Yakṣas.

8. Oh child! This act of slaughtering innocent demigods (Yakṣas) commenced by you, is censured by the good. It is not becoming to our race.

9. Being enraged at the murder of your brother, whom you dearly loved, a great number (of Yakṣas) have been killed by you, for the crime of one (Yakṣa), on your suspicion of their involvement in it.

10. To massacre creatures like beasts, mistaking the gross body for the Soul (*ātman*)—this is not the way of the righteous who are devoted to Hari (the Lord of sense-organs).

11. Having propitiated Hari who dwells within all creatures[47], and who is difficult to be pleased, and looking upon all living beings as (a part of) your own self,[48] you have secured for yourself the highest realm belonging to Lord Viṣṇu.

12. You are constantly remembered by Hari, and are highly respected by his devotees. How is it that you, who should instruct others by your (exemplary) righteous conduct, have committed this censurable act?

13. It is by patience, compassion and friendliness[49] and the attitude of equality[50] to all beings that the glorious Lord, who is the Soul (*ātman*) of all, becomes propitious.

---

47. Or : who is the abode of all creatures.

48. *Sarva-bhūtātma-bhāvena* : (i) Looking upon Hari as the indwelling Soul of all creatures. — VR.

(ii) Hari as *antaryāmin* of all creatures abides in all beings.—VJ.

(iii) Identifying yourself with all creatures. — VC.

(iv) Realizing that all creatures, mobile and immobile are your own Self. — GD.

49. GD. thinks that the qualities are to be shown to the superiors, the inferiors and equals respectively. Thus patience to elders etc.

50. *samatvena* — (i) To regard that all beings are essentially equal, as the Lord dwells within each of them. — VR.

(ii) To show enmity to enemies and friendliness to friends is equality. — VJ.

14. When the Lord is thoroughly pleased, a man becomes free from all the *guṇas* of *Prakṛti*. Liberated from the stage of *Jīvahood* (i.e. his subtle *Liṅga Śarīra*), he attains to the blissful Brahman.[51]

15. The male and the female are the products of the five gross elements developed in the forms of bodies. It is by their cohabitation that the creation of men and women takes place here in this world.

16. Oh king, it is due to the intermingling of *guṇas* caused by the *Māyā* (power) of the Supreme Lord that the creation, preservation and destruction of the world, take place.

17. The Supreme Man who is devoid of all attributes (like *sattva*, *rajas* etc.) is merely an apparent cause—therein that the universe consisting of manifested and unmanifested things, is in a state of flux like iron moved (by the presence of a magnet).

18.* The Supreme Lord whose power and energy is distributed by the disturbance in the equilibrium of *guṇas* caused by his potency called Time, verily creates (the universe) without being its agent, and destroys it himself not being the destroyer. Inscrutable, indeed, is the working of the Almighty.

---

51. *nirvāṇa* (i) Characterised by the highest bliss. — VR.

(ii) (Brahman) which is free from body or full of bliss — VJ. VJ. strongly objects to the concept of merger with Brahman as Liberation (*mukti*) will be *śūnya*.

(iii) the highest (beyond *atiśayas*)—SD.

(iv) Beyond *saṁsāra* — GD.

* *The first half*:

(i) The Lord's power is differently distributed in different species of beings such as a man, a god etc., and according to the various degrees of happiness or unhappiness to be experienced according to their *Karmas*. His potency is so divided due to His power called Time, which causes commotion among the *guṇas*. — VR.

(ii) OR: For the sake of creating disturbance in the balance of *guṇas* for the creation etc. of the universe, he divides his power, i.e. He assumes the form of Brahmā, Viṣṇu and Rudra. — VR.

(iii) VJ. accepts the v.l. *yogaśaktyā* for *kāla-śaktyā*.

It is by his power of Yoga that the Lord exhibits his power, and carries out the function of creation etc. through his three *guṇas*. Due to his effortlessness in creation he is regarded as non-creator. Though he

19* He is a creator, as he makes men beget men. As he destroys the destroyer (robbers etc.) by means of death (through kings and others), he is called the destroyer—Time. But the Almighty Himself is endless (immortal), beginningless, unchangeable and subject to no dimunition.

20.** The Supreme Lord has nobody as his own or none as his enemy; (for) he enters all beings equally as (i.e. in the form of their) death. Not being their masters (due to their *Karmas*), all creatures follow[52] him in his course, just as particles of dust follow the blast of wind.

21. The All-pervading Lord cuts short or prolongs the life of a creature according to its destiny (previous *karma*), while he himself, being above these changes, abides in his natural state.

22. Oh King (Dhruva)! Some call him Karma; others,

---

destroys the universe, he has no enmity against anyone. Hence he is not regarded as destroyer. — VJ.

The Lord is the cause of the creation etc. of the universe, but his workings defy our comprehension. The creation etc. of the world is due to the power of Time which creates commotion in *guṇas*. — SD.

* Though he himself is endless (immortal), he brings about the end (of the world) as Time. Though he is without a beginning and imperishable, changeless, he brings about the beginning (of all). He is the creator by making men beget men and destroys the destroyers (robbers etc.) through death.

(ii) VR. points out that the Almighty whose form is Time, does not directly create or destroy but does so through the father or death.

** (1) The Lord who is untouched by *saṁsāra* (or whose body is death), enters the bodies of all creatures as *antaryāmin* for controlling them according to their *karmas*. Nobody is his friend or enemy. (All are equal to him). All creatures, not being their masters (but subject to their previous *karmas*) follow the Lord who runs (i.e. controls them according to their *karmas*) just as particles of dust helplessly follow the wind. (The dust particles may fall at any place or pit, the wind is impartial to all the particles) — VR.

(2) Though God enters all beings as Death, creatures get different fruits according to their *karmas* despite God's equality, just as the wind treats all particles of dust equally, though some of them fall in darkness, light, water or fire. — VC.

52. *anudhāvanti*—(i) do the actions — SD.
(ii) take births — GD.

Nature; some, Time-spirit; others, Destiny; while others, the *Kāma* (desire) of men.

23. Verily nobody knows the design (purpose) of the Unmanifest Immeasurable Lord who is the source of innumerable potencies (like *Mahat* etc.). Oh child who can then know the Lord Who is one's own origin?

24. Oh dear son! These Yakṣas (the servants and followers of Kubera) are definitely not the slayers of your brother. For, oh child, it is the Destiny (*daiva*) alone, which brings about the birth or death of men.

25. It is he only who creates the universe. Nobody else but he alone protects and destroys it. In spite of this, he is not affected by *guṇas* (attributes) and *karmas*, as he is free from *ahaṁkāra* (ego).

26. This Soul of created beings, their Lord and creator gets united with his Māyā power and creates, preserves and eats up (i.e. withdraws within him) the created beings.

27. Dear child! Completely submitting all your Self, seek the shelter of the Deity who is the final resort of the world, and who is the death itself (to the unrighteous, non-devotees)—Deity to whom creators of the universe bear offerings, just as bulls controlled by a string passed through their nostrils, carry the loads (of their) masters.

28. Cut to the quick by the (harsh) words of your stepmother, you, as a child of five, went to the forest leaving back your mother. By your penance, you propitiated Lord Viṣṇu who is beyond the ken of senses, and secured (for you) a position at the head of the universe.

29. Oh dear child, with your mind (lit. sight) turned inward (on your self),[53] seek the Supreme Lord who dwells in the heart that is free from enmity[54];—the Lord who is beyond attributes (*guṇas*); one (without a second), imperishable, eternally liberated and in whom this phenomenal world of

53. *ātmadṛk* — Or one who looks upon all as himself.
(ii) With your mind concentrated on the Supreme Self.

54. *mukta-vigrahe* — Adj. qualifying *ātmani*,
(i) the Soul which is indivisible (without parts).
(ii) VJ. reads: *vimukta-vigrahair vyapāśritam* : Who is resorted to by Yogis who have become free from physical bodies.

differences, though unreal, appears to exist[55].

30. (While seeking the Lord), You practise intense devotion to the Almighty Lord who abides in all as *antaryāmin*; who is infinite, pure and absolute bliss, and is possessed of all powers. Then you will gradually cut asunder the knot of *avidyā* (nescience) which has grown very strong by (brooding over the notions that this is) 'I' and 'Mine'.

31. Oh King, by your deep and extensive study of the *śāstras*, control your anger which is a formidable hindrance to attaining to the final beatitude, just as you would control a disease with a medicine. May God bless you!

32. A wise man who wishes to attain the state of fearlessness for himself, should not allow himself to be overpowered by that passion (anger). For people get afraid of a person who is overwhelmed with anger.

33. Inasmuch as you, being enraged, have killed Yakṣas thinking that they were the slayers of your brother, you have committed a grave offence against Kubera, the brother (i.e. friend) of god Śiva (the Lord of the mountains).

34. Oh child, while the wrath of the exalted Souls (like Kubera) does not vanquish our race, you try immediately to propitiate him by paying him obeisance, and offering humble apologies.

35. Having thus admonished his grandson Dhruva, who bowed down to him, Svāyambhuva Manu returned to his city along with the sages.

---

55. In the *jīva*, the worldly difference of being a god or a man is not part of his essence, but it is seen on account of meritorious or sinful *karmas*. It is not that way *mithyā*. This difference is unreal (*asat*), as it is always changing—VR..

CHAPTER TWELVE

(*Kubera's Boon and Dhruva's Attainment of Viṣṇu's Realm*)

Maitreya said:

1. Learning that Dhruva's anger had been appeased and that he had desisted from slaughter, the divine Lord of Wealth (Kubera) who was being eulogised by Cāraṇas, Yakṣas and Kinnaras, arrived there, and spoke to him (Dhruva) who folded his hands (to pay respects to Kubera).

Kubera (*the donor of riches*) *said*:

2. Oh sinless Kṣatriya Prince ! I am extremely pleased with you, as at the behest of your grand-father, you have given up the feeling of enmity which is very difficult to renounce.

3. (The fact of the matter is that) neither you have killed the Yakṣas nor did they slay your brother. It is none but *Kāla* (the power of God called Time), which is responsible for the creation and destruction of created beings.

4. Just as a notion in the state of dreaming is false and meaningless, so is the notion of difference as 'I' and 'You' which arises in man due to his ignorance, and on account of continuous thinking of the physical body as the Soul. Bondage of *saṁsāra* and miseries are due to this notion.

5. Oh Dhruva! Please return now. God bless you. For the sake of Liberation from *Saṁsāra*, adore Lord Adhokṣaja (Viṣṇu) who manifests himself in the bodies of all creatures, and consider that he is the *antaryāmin* (indwelling Soul) abiding in all beings[56].

6. For terminating *Saṁsāra* (the cycle of births and deaths), please worship him whose feet are worth resorting, and who destroys *saṁsāra*, and who, though associated with his own *māyā-śakti* constituted of the three *Guṇas* (attributes—*Sattva*, *Rajas and Tamas*), is yet aloof from it.

7. Oh son of Uttānapāda, we have learnt that you are very close to Viṣṇu's (God with a lotus in His navel) feet. Oh King Dhruva, as you deserve to receive a boon, ask of me freely and without any hesitation, any boon at will, cherished by you in your heart.

---

56. Or: considering all beings as your own self.

Maitreya said:

8. The great devotee of the Lord, that highly intelligent Dhruva, who was thus induced by Kubera (the king of Kings) to ask for a boon (from him), sought to be blest with the constant remembrance of Hari, whereby one effortlessly goes beyond the darkness (of ignorance or *saṁsāra*) which is very difficult to cross.

9. With a glad heart, Kubera (the son of Iḍaviḍā), having conferred that boon (on Dhruva), immediately disappeared while Dhruva was gazing. He also repaired to his capital.

10. Thereafter, by performing sacrifices with liberal donations and sacrificial fees, he worshipped the Lord of Sacrifices who is both the donor of the fruit of religious *karmas*, and is himself the reward of the religious duties (sacrifices). He performed them with proper materials as per ritualistic technique and with due offerings to Gods.

11. Bearing an intense flow of devotion to Acyuta (Viṣṇu) who abides in all as their Soul, yet is distinct from them, he visualised the All-pervading Lord as dwelling within himself and in all other beings.

12. The subjects considered him as their father (protector)—him, who was of such noble character, friendly to Brāhmaṇas, compassionate to the afflicted, and the protector of the bounds of religion.

13. Exhausting the fund of his meritorious deeds by enjoyments of pleasures, and the balance of inauspicious deeds by performing sacrifices and other religious acts, he governed the sphere of the earth for thirtysix thousand years.

14-15. In this way, the great-Souled king of perfectly controlled senses, passed a long time in performing a number of sacrifices which result in the attainment of the Trinity—of *Dharma*, *Artha* and *Kāma*. He then regarded this universe as being illusory—constructed by Māyā on the basis of the Soul, like the dream city of Gandharvas created by *Avidyā* (Māyā or Nescience), and abdicated the throne in favour of his son.

16. Comprehending that his own body, wife, children, friends, army, rich treasury, harem, beautiful places of sport and recreations and the whole sphere of the earth engirdled by

the ocean, are subject to destruction and hence transitory, he proceeded to Viśālā (*Badarikāśrama*).

17. Having performed ablutions in the sacred waters thereof, he purified his mind (by observing *yama* and *niyama*, the code of Yogic discipline). Having steadied himself firmly in a *yogic* posture, and controlled his breath (through *prāṇāyāma*), and restraining his senses by his mind, he concentrated his mind on the gross (Cosmic) form of the Lord, viz. the *Virāṭ-rūpa*. In course of meditation, the consciousness of the distinction between the meditator and the object of meditation, was lost. Being absorbed in meditation, he forgot the thought of that gross (Cosmic) form also.

18. He cherished constant devotion to the venerable Lord Hari. He was now and then overwhelmed with tears of joy. His heart melted (with emotions for the Lord), and his hair stood on their ends all over the body. He detached himself from his gross body, and did not remember that he was so-and-so (Dhruva).

19. Dhruva noticed an excellent heavenly car descending from the heavens, illumining the ten directions like the rising full moon.

20. Later on, in that heavenly car, (he saw) two prominent gods in the prime of their youth. They were four-armed of dark complexion and with eyes (beautiful) like red lotuses. They were richly attired, and were adorned with crowns, pearl necklaces, armlets and beautiful ear-rings. They stood leaning against their maces.

21. Comprehending them to be the attendants of Hari (the God of excellent renown), he stood up (to show respect). Forgetting the due procedure of worship in the hurry of that (agitated) moment, he folded his hands uttering the names of Hari, as he thought them to be the chief attendants of Viṣṇu (the slayer of the demon Madhu).

22. Sunanda and Nanda, the esteemed servants of Viṣṇu (the lotus-navelled god) approached him (Dhruva) who had concentrated his mind on Kṛṣṇa's (Viṣṇu's) feet; had folded his palms and bowed down his neck in humility.

Sunanda and Nanda said :

23. Oh King! May you be extremely blessed! Your honour, who, while yet a child of five, had pleased the Lord by your penance, listen to our speech attentively.

24. We both are the attendants of the God with the Śārṅga bow (Viṣṇu) who is the sustainer of the whole world. Both of us have arrived here for taking you to the Lord's abode.

25. You have successfully attained to the region of Viṣṇu which is extremely difficult to secure, and to which sages, (the *saptarṣis—Ursa Major*) not being able to reach, merely look up from below. Now occupy that place round which (luminous bodies like) the Moon, the Sun (and other luminaries), planets, constellations of stars and (independent) stars go, keeping it to their right.

26. Dear (Dhruva), take your abode in the realm which has never been occupied by your forefathers. That highest region of Viṣṇu is adorable to all worlds.

27. Oh long-lived one, you should now ascend this excellent aerial car, despatched to you by Viṣṇu who is the foremost among persons of meritorious renown.[57]

Maitreya said:

28. Having heard the extremely sweet (honey-dripping) words of the two prominent deputies of Lord Viṣṇu, Dhruva, the beloved devotee of Viṣṇu[58], took his bath, performed his daily auspicious duties, paid his obeisance to sages and received their blessings.

29. Having circumambulated that excellent heavenly car, he worshipped it. He bowed down to both the attendants of Viṣṇu. Assuming a form brilliant like gold, he desired to get into the car.

30. At that time, when the son of Uttānapāda (Dhruva) saw that the god of Death had come, he placed his foot on the head of that god (of Death)[59] and mounted that wonderful aerial mansion.

---

57. *uttama-śloka*.

58. *Urukrama* : Viṣṇu, so called because in the Vāmana incarnation he took very long strides to occupy the three worlds from Bali.

59. ŚR. narrates the episode thus: When Dhruva was about to enter that heavenly car, the God of Death arrived there, bowed to him and

31. At the very moment, drums and musical instruments like Paṇava, etc. were sounded. Prominent Gandharvas sang his praise. Showers of flowers fell on him from above.

32. As he was about to fly to the heavenly regions, Dhruva suddenly remembered his mother Sunīti, (saying to himself), 'How am I to proceed to the inaccessible celestial region, leaving my poor mother behind?'

33. Having understood this wish of Dhruva, the two excellent gods showed to him the brilliant queen-mother Sunīti—going ahead of him, in an aerial car.

34. At every stage on way, Dhruva was being showered with flowers and praised by gods seated in their heavenly cars; and he went past planets, one after another.

35. Then he (Dhruva) who was blest with an eternal position, went by the *devayāna* path (or by the celestial car sent to him by the Lord), beyond the three worlds and the astral positions of the seven sages (*Ursa Major*), and reached the abode of Viṣṇu which lies beyond them.

36. It (Viṣṇu's abode) shines brilliant by its own splendour. It illuminates these three worlds (the earth, the heaven etc.) by its light. The people who are not compassionate unto living beings never attain to this realm. Only those who always perform auspicious deeds, reach there.

37. Those who are of tranquil mind, who look upon all beings as equals, whose minds are cleansed of all sins and impurities (like *rajas* and *tamas*), who are pleasing to all beings, who look upon Acyuta (Viṣṇu) as their dear relative—those easily reach the abode of Viṣṇu.

38. In this way, Dhruva, the son of Uttānapāda who was solely devoted to Kṛṣṇa (Viṣṇu), became as if a refulgent crest-jewel of the three worlds.

39. Oh Vidura (descendant of Kuru)! Riveted to this (Dhruva's) post, the whole group of heavenly luminaries revolve round it ceaselessly, just as (pairs of) bullocks tied to a post in the middle of the threshing ground, go round with great speed (for threshing out the corn by trampling).

---

requested him to accept him. Dhruva welcomed him, requested him to sit down for a moment; and remembering Lord Viṣṇu placed his foot on the head of that God (Death) and accended into the heavenly car.

40. Having seen the great glory of Dhruva, the venerable sage Nārada, playing on his lute, sang the (following) verses at the sacrificial session of Pracetas:

Nārada said:

41. Despite their knowledge of the means, Brāhmaṇa sages, the expounders of Vedas, are not able to reach the attainment secured by the dint of his austere penance, by Dhruva, the son of Sunīti who looked upon her husband as god. How can then, kings attain to it?

42. As a child of five, he went to the forest with his heart afflicted by being wounded with the arrow-like words of his stepmother. Abiding by my advice, he conquered i.e. won the favour of the unconquerable Lord who is overpowered only by the excellent qualities of his devotees.

43. Can an ordinary Kṣatriya on the earth even imagine to reach after many years to the exalted position occupied by Dhruva who, as a child of five or six years, secured it by propitiating Lord Viṣṇu within a few days?

Maitreya continued:

44. I have narrated to you everything that you asked me here about the life-story of Dhruva of excellent fame—the life story which is held in high regard by the righteous.

45. If heard and recited, it (Dhruva's life story) leads to wealth, glory and longevity; it is meritorious and brings in great auspiciousness; it helps to attain to the celestial region and to reach even the eternal abode; it leads to godhood; it is extremely praiseworthy, and cleanses all sins.

46. By constantly listening with faith and devotion the lifestory of Dhruva who was dear to Lord Acyuta (Viṣṇu), devotion unto the Lord will be engendered, which will lead to the destruction of all miseries.

47. Here this story is a sacred fountain of greatness for those who seek it. When it is heard, virtues like good-naturedness generate in the listeners. Those who desire bravery and splendour get it developed (in them by listening to it). It bestows respectability on the noble-minded (listeners who aspire after it).

48. One should recite both in the morning and in the evening, the glorious life, with a concentrated attention, of Dhruva of sacred glory, in the assembly of the Brāhmaṇas.

49-50. Or one who resorts to the sacred feet of Hari, should narrate to the faithful (audience, the life of Dhruva) on the full-moon day or the new moon day, the twelfth day of a fortnight or when the moon passes by the constellation of stars called Śravaṇa or on *dina-kṣaya* or on (the astronomically inauspicious *yoga* called) the Vyatipāta, or on the Saṅkramaṇa day (when the Sun crosses the sign of the zodiac) or on Sundays. He should cherish no desire and be self-contented; thereby he attains Liberation.

51. Gods bestow favours on the merciful man who is helpful to the afflicted and who imparts this knowledge (which is like) nectar in the pathway to God, to persons who are ignorant of the Truth.

52. Oh Vidura (the foremost descendant of Kuru), I have narrated to you this biography of Dhruva who is well-known for pious deeds, and who, as a child, abandoned his toys and mother's house, and resorted to Viṣṇu.

CHAPTER THIRTEEN*

(Dhruva's descendants : King Aṅga's Abdication)

Sūta said:

1. After listening to (the account of) Dhruva's ascension to the Vaikuṇṭha region as described by Maitreya, Vidura

---

* Chs. 13-15 give the following genealogy of Dhruva —

Bhrami = Dhruva = Ilā

Kalpa | Vatsara (Svarvīthi) | Utkala

Vatsara (Svarvīthi)
|
Puṣpārṇa (and others, 6 sons in all)
|
Vyuṣṭa (and others, 6 sons in all)
|

whose devotion to Lord Viṣṇu (Adhokṣaja) was intensified, proceeded again to make further queries.

Vidura said:

2. Oh strict observer of religious vows (Maitreya)! Who were those Pracetasas? Whose children were they? To whose familyline were they known to belong? Where did they have the sacrificial session?

3. I regard Nārada as a great devotee of the Lord, and as one who has directly realized the Almighty. It is he who has expounded (in the Pañcarātra Āgama) the *Kriyā-Yoga* (Yoga of practical devotion), in the form of the detailed procedure of worshipping Hari.

4. They say that while the Lord, the presiding deity of sacrifices, was being worshipped (by performing sacrifice) by men (Pracetasas) who were devoted to their righteous duties, Nārada, who was full of devotion, extolled him.

5. Oh Brahman, you should please narrate to me in details, all the stories of the Lord which have been related there, in that sacrifice by the divine sage (Nārada), as I long to hear them.

Maitreya said :

6. When the father (Dhruva) retired to forest, Dhruva's (eldest) son Utkala did not wish to ascend the imperial throne and to enjoy the imperial glory.

7. From his very birth, he was of tranquil mind, unattached and of impartial outlook. He saw his Soul as pervading the world and the world abiding in his Soul.

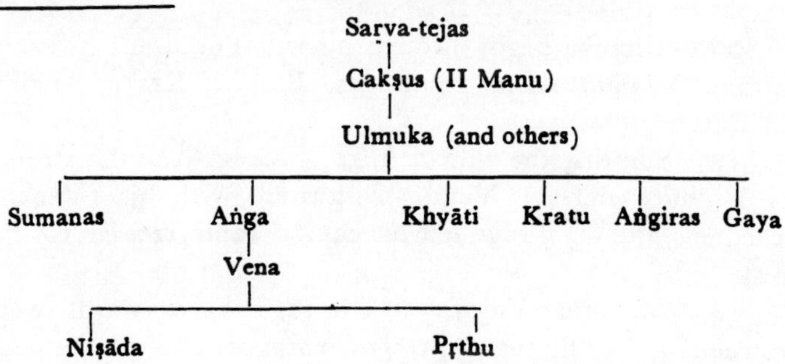

8-9. By the fire of the uninterrupted practice of *Yoga*, Utkala had burnt down all the impurities of the past actions in his mind. He realized that the individual Self is the same as the tranquil Brahman in whom all differences dissolve and disappear, and who is the embodiment of the joy of pure knowledge, absolute bliss, existing everywhere. Knowing thus his own real Self, he ceased to perceive anything different from it.

10. To ignorant persons on the road, he (outwardly) appeared to be a stupid, blind, deaf, mad or a dumb man, though (in reality) he was mentally not like any of these. He was like a fire that had ceased to send out flames.

11. Considering him to be a dull idiot, the elders of the family along with the ministers, coronated the younger brother Vatsara, the son of Bhrami, as the ruler of the earth.

12. Svarvīthi, the beloved wife of Vatsara, gave birth to six sons, viz., Puspārṇa. Tigma-ketu, Iṣa, Ūrja, Vasu and Jaya.

13. Puṣpārṇa had two wives—Prabhā (Day-light) and Doṣā (Night). Prātar (morning), Madhyandina (Mid-day) and Sāyam (Evening) were the sons of Prabhā (Day-light).

14. Pradoṣa (night-fall or the first part of night), Niśītha (Midnight) and Vyuṣṭa (Dawn or the late part of the night) were the three sons of Doṣā (Night). Vyuṣṭa begot from (his wife) Puṣkariṇī a son called Sarva-tejas.

15. He got from his wife Ākūti a son, Cakṣus the Manu (after Svāyambhuva Manu). Manu's queen Naḍvalā gave birth to (twelve) sinless sons.

16. (They were) Puru, Kutsa, Trita, Dyumna, Satyavat, Ṛta, Vrata, Agniṣṭoma, Atirātra, Pradyumna, Śibi and Ulmuka.

17. Ulmuka begot through his wife Puṣkaraṇī six excellent sons by name Aṅga, Sumanas, Khyāti, Kratu, Aṅgiras and Gaya.

18. Sunīthā, the wife of Aṅga, gave birth to the strong-willed (but wicked) Vena. Disgusted with his (Vena's) wickedness, the royal sage left his capital (and retired to the forest).

19. Oh child (Vidura)! The sage whose words were (destructive) like thunderbolt, got enraged and pronounced

a curse on him. (As a result of the curse he fell dead). They churned again the right hand of his dead body.

20. When there was no King, in that period, the subjects in the world, were troubled by robbers. Then Pṛthu, the first Lord of the earth (so called as he was the first founder of cities, habitations etc.) was born embodying in him an *aṁśa* or portion of Nārāyaṇa.

Vidura said :

21. How is it that the high-souled, pious king, who was a treasure-house of virtues and so friendly to Brāhmaṇas got such wicked progeny, that he had to leave his capital in sadness and grief.

22. Or for what offence did the sages, who were well-versed in Dharma-Śāstra, directed their curse against King Vena, who had vowed to punish the evil-doers.

23. As the king, in the capacity of the protector of his subjects, possesses the energy and the splendour of (Indra and other) world-protectors, in his own superior glory, he should not be disrespected by the subjects, even though he be at fault.

24. Oh Brahman, as you are the foremost among the knowers of *para* and *avara*[60], please narrate to me, a devout devotee, the deeds of the son of Sunīthā.

Maitreya said :

25. The royal sage Aṅga performed a great Horse-Sacrifice (Aśvamedha). But in that sacrifice, the deities though invoked by the priests well-versed in the Vedas, did not turn up (to receive their share of the sacrificial offerings).

26. Then the sacrificial priests who were wonder-struck told the sacrificer (King Aṅga), "the deities do not accept the sacrificial oblations though poured into the fire."

27. "Oh King, the materials for oblations are unpolluted and pure and have been devoutly procured by you. The Vedic incantations are not inefficacious, since they are chanted and used by persons of steadfast vows.

60. *para* and *avara* : Variously interpreted as 'past and future', Parmātaman and products of Prakṛti, etc.

28. We do not know if the slightest disregard is shown to gods here (in this performance of sacrifice) as a result of which gods who witness the performance of this sacrificial act, do not partake of their share of oblations".

Maitreya said :

29. Hearing the words of Brāhmaṇas, the host, the performer of the sacrifices, Aṅga became deeply grieved. With the permission of the members of the assembly, he broke his silence in order to ask them the reason of the non-acceptance of oblations.

30. "Oh Members of the sacrificial assembly ! Here (in this sacrifice) deities even though invoked, do not attend. Nor do they accept their cups of Soma. Be pleased to tell me what censurable act has been committed by me."

The Leaders of the Assembly spoke :

31. Oh King, there is not the slightest sin committed by you so far in this life. There is however one sin of your previous life on account of which you are thus issueless.

32* Oh King, the Lord, the enjoyer of sacrifices, when worshipped, will vouchsafe a son to you who are so desirous to have one. Try that way to have good progeny. May God bless you.

33. If Lord Hari, the presiding god of the sacrifices himself, is directly invoked by you for a child, all sacrificial deities (the residents of heaven) will automatically accept their respective share of oblations.

34. Hari confers upon men (his devotees) whatever desires are cherished (and sought) by them. The attainment of the desired objects, however, depends upon the manner (and devoutness) of the worship (of the Lord)."

35. Thus resolved, the Brāhmaṇas offered *puroḍāśa*[61] to Viṣṇu in the form of *Śipiviṣṭa*[62], for securing progeny to that king.

---

* With a view to ensuring that deities should be pleased to accept oblations from you, you should try to secure a child to you. — ŚR.

61. *Puroḍāsa* — a sacrificial oblation made of ground rice and offered in a *kapāla* or vessel. ASD. 341.

62. *Śipiviṣṭa* (i) 'One who has entered the sacrificial animal (the beast to be sacrificed) in the form of Sacrifice'. ŚR. quotes a Śruti

36. From that sacrifice arose a person adorned with gold necklace and clad in immaculate garments, bringing with him in a gold vessel ready made *pāyasa* (rice boiled in milk).

37. With the assent of the Brāhmaṇas the generous-minded King accepted the boiled rice in the hollow of his folded palms, smelt it and gave it to the queen joyfully.

38. Having eaten that food which had the efficacy of creating a male child, the issueless queen varily became pregnant from her husband, and in due course of time gave birth to a son.

39. Since his childhood, the boy was attached to his maternal grandfather Mṛtyu who inherited a portion of Adharma. Hence he became unrighteous.

40. Taking up his bow and wandering as a hunter in the jungle, this wicked boy killed innocent deer. Hence people (after seeing him) would cry out "This is Vena"[63] (the tormentor).

41. This extremely ruthless, hard hearted boy used to slay violently like beasts, boys of his own age playing on the playground.

42. Seeing that his son was so wicked, and finding that he (the king) was not successful in disciplining him in spite of different kinds of punishments, the king became sorely dejected at heart.

43. (He thought) 'Most probably the householders who are issueless must have worshipped god for they are spared the unbearable agony caused by a wicked child.

44-45. Indeed what wise man will think highly of the embarrassing bondage called (his own) son if he brings evil reputation (to his father) among men and implicates him in serious unrighteousness, if he creates conflicts with all and causes unending mental torture (to his father) making his home-life full of distress.

---

which means that Viṣṇu resides in the sacrificial animal as the spirit of the sacrifice. This form of Viṣṇu is invoked in the sacrifice specifically performed to get a son. (Putra-kāmeṣṭi).

(ii) Or: from whom rays are emanating—VR.

63. ŚR. derives the name from *ven* — 'to harass' or 'to make others full of anxiety.'

46. (In a way) I regard a bad child preferable to a good child as it is a cause of many sorrows. And a man gets disgusted with his home which is full of troubles.

47. The king who was thus dejected at heart, could not get any sleep. At midnight he got up and leaving Vena's mother asleep[64] and unnoticed by other men, he departed from the palace abounding in prosperity.

48. When the subjects, royal priests, ministers, friends and relatives of the king learnt that the king had departed in disgust, they became overwhelmed with excessive grief. They searched for him all over the world (without success), just as Yogins on the wrong path do in search of the unmanifest Supreme Man hidden in their heart[65].

49. Being unable to trace any trail of the king and having thus failed in their attempts to do so, the subjects returned to the capital. Bowing to assembled sages, they reported with tearful eyes the disappearance of their king, oh Vidura (discendant of Puru).

CHAPTER FOURTEEN

(*The Story of Vena : Pṛthu's Birth*)

Maitreya said :

1-2. Bhṛgu and other sages who were solicitous about the well-being of the people, saw that men are reduced to brute-level at the time of anarchy. Those sages, well versed in the Vedas, invited Sunīthā, the mother of the hero (Vena), and coronated Vena as the Lord of the Earth, even though he was not approved by ministers or people.

---

64. ŚR. thinks that the king disguised himself while Vena's mother was sleeping.

65. ŚR. states that the king was somewhere in the town while they were searching for him outside all over the world.

3. Having heard that Vena, the very high-handed iron ruler, had ascended the throne, robbers hid themselves immediately like rats afraid of a serpent.

4. After occupying the king's place he who became proud and self-conceited, regarded himself invested with the powers of the eight protectors of the world automatically, and contemptuously treated the great sages.

5. He, who thus became blind with pride, and haughty like an elephant uncontrolled by goads, mounted his chariot and wandered over the earth shaking heaven and earth.

6. With the sound of drums, he promulgated everywhere, "Oh Dvijas, you shall never perform worship, and shall give no donations and shall not perform sacrifices". Thus he prohibited religion everywhere.

7. The sages, seeing the ill-behaved conduct of Vena, and considering the public calamity, assembled at a sacrificial session and said.

8. "A great danger has arisen to people from both sides—from robbers and the king, like (that to ants who find themselves in the middle of) a piece of wood burning from both sides.

9. This unworthy prince was made a king on account of the fear of anarchy. But today danger has arisen even from him. How can the welfare of beings be ensured ?

10-11. Vena who is born from the womb of Sunīthā, is hereditarily wicked. Just as the nouriṣhing of a snake with milk is dangerous even to the man who so feeds it, Vena who has been appointed as the protector of the subjects verily desires to destroy them. Let us (however) persuade him (to behave properly) so that his sin may not touch us.

12-13. Despite our full knowledge of Vena's wicked conduct and sinfulness, we made him the king. If, in spite of our gentle persuasions, that unrighteous fellow does not abide by our words of advice, let us burn him by our spiritual power, although he is already burnt by the reproach of the people". Having decided thus, the sages, concealing their anger, approached that Vena, and pacifying him with conciliatory words, spoke.

Sages said :

14. "Oh Great King ! Please note that what we propose to urge for your consideration will, Oh child, increase your longevity, prosperity, power and glory.

15. Righteous duty (*Dharma*) practised in thought, word, deed and understanding, bestows on ordinary people worlds which are free from sorrows and the eternal abode (*Mokṣa*) to those who perform it without any attachment (to its fruits).

16. Oh brave king, let not your *Dharma* (duty) of ensuring security and well being of the subjects, be neglected (and lost) by you. For when it is lost (disregarded), the king falls from his rulership.

17. Oh king, a king who protects his subjects from wicked ministers and from thieves (and other miscreants) and takes revenue (from them as prescribed in *Śāstras*), leads a happy life.

18-19. Oh illustrious King ! The Lord creator of all beings, the Soul of the universe is pleased with the king who obeys his commands, and in whose kingdom and capital city, the glorious presiding deity of the sacrifice is worshipped according to their *dharma*, by persons who follow the duties of their respective *Varṇa* (social class) and *āśrama* (stage of life).

20. What is unattainable, when the Lord of the rulers of the worlds (e.g. god Brahmā etc.) is pleased ? For all the worlds along with their protecting deities devoutly offer worship to him.

21* Oh King ! It behoves you to approve of, and be

---

* VR.: The Lord controls all worlds, their presiding deities and sacrifices which lead to the attainment of godhood. He is the embodiment of hree Vedas which explain what .is and is not the righteous duty (*dharma*). The Vedas prescribe both the ways of sacrifices and of penance. It is for the sake of your Liberation or prosperity that the inhabitants of your country perform different kinds of sacrifices. You should therefore follow their example.

SD.: You should direct the inhabitants of your country to perform their respective duties—the inhabitants who according to their abilities of the *pravṛtti* and *nivṛtti* type, worship the Lord who protects all the worlds, gods and sacrifices, and who is the embodiment of three Vedas which give the knowledge of sacrifice, and who is the sacrificial materials and the penance, the knowledge leading to Liberation. It is thus that you will get prosperity here and Liberation hereafter.

conciliatory to the inhabitants of your country[66] who, for your prosperity, worship, by performance of various sacrifices, the Lord who is the Controller of all worlds, gods and sacrifices—the Lord who is the embodiment of three Vedas and of all sacrificial materials, and who is the object of penance.

22. Oh brave king, if gods who are parts (*aṁśas*) of Hari, are properly worshipped and well-propitiated by performance of sacrificial sessions by the twice-born Brāhmaṇas, Kṣattriyas and Vaiśyas, they will confer whatever is desired by you. It is not, therefore, proper to disrespect them (by prohibiting sacrificial and religious performances).

Vena said :

23. Verily, all of you are foolish. You regard non-righteousness (*adharma*) as righteousness (*dharma*). What a pity ! Abandoning the husband who gives you means of subsistence, you wait upon a paramour.

24. Those fools who disregard the supreme Lord in the form of a king, do not obtain any good either here or hereafter.

25. Who is this *Yajña-puruṣa* (the presiding deity of sacrifices) for whom you cherish such (intense) devotion like characterless women who, being absolutely devoid of love for their husbands, cherish it for their gallants.

26-27. Gods like Viṣṇu (the protector of the universe), Brahmā (the creator of the world), Śiva (the destroyer of the universe), Indra, Vāyu (Wind), Yama (god of death), the Sun (-god), the rain-god, the god of Wealth (Kubera), the Moon (-god), the (presiding deity of the) Earth, the Fire (-god) and Varuṇa (the Lord of Waters)—these and other gods who are competent to confer boons or pronounce curses reside in the person of the sovereign ruler. The Monarch is thus the embodiment of all gods.

28. Therefore, Oh Brāhmaṇas ! Being free from jealousy, you worship me with your religious rites. Give me all

---

66. *svadeśān* : (i) The persons whom you command — the sacrificers. VR. (ii) The Brāhmaṇas on whom donations or gifts are conferred —VJ.

your offerings (taxes etc.). What other person than me, deserves to be propitiated (honoured) for it ?

Maitreya said :

29. Even though so humbly entreated, the wretched sinner was of such a perverted mind and had gone so astray on the wrong path, that he did not accede to their supplications, for he had lost all auspiciousness.

30. Oh Vidura ! When he, priding himself as very learned, insulted these twice-born (Brāhmaṇas), and spurned their request made in the interest of the public good, the Brāhmaṇas got angry with him.

31. "Let him be slain; let this wicked fellow of terrible nature be killed. If he lives (any longer), he will soon reduce the world to ashes.

32. This shameless fellow vilifies Viṣṇu, the Supreme Deity of Sacrifices. This man of wicked conduct does not deserve the exalted seat of a monarch.

33. Or who else other than this base unlucky Vena alone, will revile Viṣṇu after attaining to such sovereignty over world through His grace."

34. With their rage flared up, the sages who thus decided to slay him, killed by their hissing (*huṃ*) sound, Vena who was already dead by his vilification of god Viṣṇu (Acyuta).

35. When the sages departed to their hermitages, Sunīthā who was full of grief, preserved the dead body of her son by means of incantations (mantras) and medicines.

36. Once upon a time, those sages, having performed ablutions in the Sarasvatī, and after offering oblations to the sacrificial fire, were sitting on the bank of the river, talking about the stories of the Lord.

37. Observing the appearance of terrible ill omens striking terror into the world, they (wishfully) said : "May no evil befall the protectionless earth from robbers".

38. While sages were thinking thus, there arose in all directions clouds of dust from the rushing of the thieves and miscreants who ran amuck plundering (wherever they went).

39. They came to know that the serious trouble to the

world was caused by those free booters who plundered the wealth of the people, and by those who tried to kill each other, as the king (Vena) was dead.

40. When anarchy prevails, the state becomes weak and the country is infested with robbers. Though they (sages) were powerful enough to control, they did not check the people as they saw the evil (involved therein).

41. "Even if a Brāhmaṇa who should view all beings equally and should be tranquil, neglects (to protect) the afflicted, his penance leaks away like water filled in a pot with a hole.

42. The race of the royal sage Aṅga should not come to an end, as it is in this family that there were many kings of unfailing prowess, yet completely dependent on Keśava (Viṣṇu)".

43. Having resolved thus, the sages churned forcibly the thigh of the deceased king. Therefrom appeared a dwarfish man.

44. He was black as crow, had very short limbs and small arms, protruding chin, short legs, flat nose and blood-red eyes and red hair.

45. To him who bowed to them, and meekly asked them, "What I should do", they asked him to sit down (*niṣīda*). Therefore, Oh Vidura, he became *niṣāda* (by tribe).

46. As soon as he was born, he took upon himself the heinous sins of Vena. His descendants the *naiṣādas* took refuge in mountains, jungles, etc.

CHAPTER FIFTEEN

(*Birth of Pṛthu and his Coronation*)

Maitreya said :

1. Thereupon, a couple (a boy and a girl) was born from the arms of the sonless king, when they (the arms) were being churned by the Brāhmaṇas.

2. Having seen the birth of the couple, the sages who were well-versed in the Vedas, became highly pleased to know that it was an *aṁśa* (portion or digit) of the glorious Lord and spoke.

Sages said :

3. This (Pṛthu) is a manifestation of that *aṁśa* (portion) of Lord Viṣṇu which protects the world[67]. This (girl) is the portion and incarnation of Goddess Lakṣmī who is never disunited from the Supreme Man (Viṣṇu)*.

4. As to this male child, he will be the first and foremost among kings, the enhancer of their glory. As his fame will spread far and wide, he will be known as Pṛthu, the great king.

5. And this beautiful, resplendent lady with finely set teeth who is the ornament of ornaments and virtues, will be called Arcis and will be Pṛthu's consort.

6. It is with the object of protecting the world that this *aṁśa* (portion) of direct Hari himself, is born. And this is verily the Goddess Lakṣmī who is inseparable from him and ever (absolutely) devoted to him.

Maitreya said :

7. Brāhmaṇas eulogised him; the foremost among the Gandharvas sang (his glory); Siddhas poured down showers of (heavenly) flowers; the celestial damsels danced.

8. The heavens were reverberating with sounds of musical instruments like conchs, trumpets, timbrels and drums. There assembled all the gods, sages and *pitṛs* (manes) of all grades.

9-10. With gods and kings of gods, Brahmā, the father of all the worlds, arrived there. Observing the mark of Viṣṇu (the wielder of the mace) on (Pṛthu's) right palm, and the lotus-mark on the soles of Pṛthu's feet he concluded that he (Pṛthu) is verily the part (*kalā*) of Viṣṇu; for he on whose

---

67. *Viṣṇoḥ kalā* : (i) The special *āveśa* type of *avatāra* — VR.
(ii) Who was filled with the presence of Viṣṇu.—VJ

* Here ends Ch. 14 of the Bh.P. as per VJ.'s text. Some texts omit ses 2 and 3.

palm the *cakra* (discus) mark is uncrossed by any other line, is the *aṁśa* (portion) of the Lord.

11. His coronation ceremony was commenced by Brāhmaṇas who were well-versed in Vedas (and expert in the Vedic rites and rituals of the ceremony). From all directions, people brought all the materials necessary for the coronation ceremony.

12. Rivers, seas, mountains, snakes, cattle, birds, beasts, deer, the sky, the earth and all beings brought tributes to him.

13. When the emperor, arrayed in excellent royal robes, and richly adorned with ornaments, was thus installed, along with the well-adorned queen, consort Arcis, he shone like another Fire-god.

14. Oh warrior, Kubera (the god of wealth) brought to him an excellent throne of gold; Varuṇa (the Lord of Waters), a royal umbrella radiating moon-white rays and dripping with water;

15. Vāyu (the Wind-god) presented him two *chowries* (special types of fans made of the tufts of hair on the tails of particular kinds of wild cows); Dharma, a garland, the very embodiment of glory; Indra (the King of gods), an excellent crown; Yama (the god of death and controller of the world), a sceptre to govern the world.

16. God Brahmā bestowed upon him an armour of Vedic incantations (or Vedic knowledge); the goddess of learning, an excellent necklace; Lord Hari, the Sudarśana disc, and his consort Lakṣmī, undiminishing prosperity and affluence.

17. Rudra gave him a sword engraved with ten moon-like marks, while Pārvatī, gave him a shield bearing the marks of a hundred moons; the Moon-god presented him immortal, indefatigable, undaunted horses made of nectar, while Tvaṣṭṛ gave him extremely artistic and beautiful chariot.

18. The Fire-god gave him a bow made from the horns of goats and oxen; the Sun-god supplied him with his solar-ray-like arrows. The earth presented him sandals with mystic (Yogic) powers; and the sky, an ever fresh flower garland.

19. The demigods that move through the sky bestowed on him the arts of dancing, vocal and instrumental music, and

the mystic power of vanishing. The sages gave him their never-failing efficacious blessings, and the Ocean-god, a conch born from him.

20. The oceans, mountains and rivers gave the high-souled King roads of communications by chariots. Then bards (Sūtas) minstrels (Māgadhas) and heralds (Bandins) began to sing his panygeric.

21. Knowing their intention, Pṛthu, the chivalrous son of Vena, laughed and spoke to them in a voice deep like the thunder of clouds.

Pṛthu said:

22. Oh Sūta ! Oh Māgadha ! Oh gentle *Bandin* ! What is the basis of your panygeric of me whose qualities are yet to be manifested in the world ? You should address it to me when my merits will be acknowledged by the public. Your words of praise in my case should not prove untrue.

23. Oh bards of sweet words ! Therefore, after a lapse of some time (when we perform some exploits worth singing), you may compose as many panygerics about my glory as you like. But when praise-worthy attributes of Lord Hari of excellent glory are there for glorification, good people do not eulogise ordinary (contemptible) men (like me).

24. What man with the capability of acquiring high merits will allow the bards to sing of qualities that are actually non-existent in him ? The dullard who fools himself that those (non-existent) virtues may be manifest in him (later), does not see that he becomes thereby a butt of public ridicule.

25. Really competent persons and illustrious persons abhor the praise, (even though they possess the qualities so praised, and are known for them). Truly modest and noble-minded persons shrink from the praise of their uncomplimentary show of valour.

26. Oh bard ! We are still unknown in this world for the performance of any exploit. (As we have not performed any great deed which can be extolled), how can we, like fools, allow you to sing of our glory.

CHAPTER SIXTEEN

(*The Eulogy of Pṛthu by Bards*)

Maitreya said :

1. The bards were satisfied at heart by hearing his nectarlike words. Being urged by sages, they began to extol the king who was speaking thus.

2. We are competent to describe fully your glory as you are the Supreme God who have incarnated in this world by your Māyā (power). The intelligence of even masters of speech (like god Brahmā and others) has been perplexed in describing the exploits of you who are born from the arms of Vena.

3. We are, however, devoutly interested in the nectarlike stories of Pṛthu, of glorious renown, who is an incarnation of an *aṁśa* (part) of Hari. We are instructed by sages. We broadcast far and wide the praiseworthy deeds, according to the instructions of the sages.

4. This (king Pṛthu) is the foremost among the upholders of religion. He makes the people act according to *Dharma* (righteous path). He is the protector of the established institutions of religion and morality. He is the punisher of those who are antagonistic (to religion).

5. (Though) he is one, he bears in his person the bodies (i.e. the powers and functions) of the guardians of the world from time to time, as per needs (of the situation) for the public good, both here and hereafter.

6.* He is impartial to all beings. This mighty monarch collects taxes and tributes at proper times, and releases (the fund) at the opportune time (like famine etc.), just as the bright Sun (evaporates the waters in the summer and returns it as showers of water in the rainy season).

7. The behaviour of the king is like the goddess of the earth. The compassionate son of Vena (i.e. Pṛthu) always bears the faults of the distressed beings, though they may encroach upon him.

* From this verse onwards the king's execution of the functions of the eight protectors of the world (*lokapālas*), is described.

8. He is veritable Hari who has assumed the body of the king. When the rain-god withholds showers of rain, he would like Indra, easily protect the subjects whose life was in danger.

9. He pleases the world with his moon-like face—the embodiment of nectar—beaming with charming smiles and brightened with affectionate looks.

10. His ways are inscrutable; his acts are secret and unsurmisable; his intentions are too deep to be comprehended; he strictly guards his wealth; he is the sole receptacle of infinite greatness and innumerable excellent attributes; like Varuṇa, the Lord of Waters, Pṛthu's true nature is unfathomable (hidden from the public view).

11. He is (like) the fire born from (the friction of) the *araṇi* (piece of Śamī wood) in the form of Vena (for he was born after churning Vena's arm). He is (even mentally) unapproachable to his enemies. His overwhelming power is irresistible by his enemies. Though he be near, he is as if at a great distance (as he is well-guarded by his security force) It is impossible to overpower him.

12. Though he sees the overt and covert activities of human beings through his intelligence service (spies), he behaves as if he is indifferent (to praise or blame). He is thus like the vital air, the Soul that witnesses, as if unconcerned, the inner and outer activities of all.

13. He is so firmly established in the path of *dharma* (royal duties) that he never punishes anyone if he does not deserve punishment even though he be the son of his personal enemy; and that he would punish his own son, if found guilty (and worth punishing).

14. His unchallenged *cakra* (sway, march of his army or the path of his chariot) extends from the *Mānasottara* mountain[68] to all regions where the Sun-god shines by his rays.

---

68. *Mānasottara.*—A hill of Puṣkaradvīpa to the east of Meru. Devadhānī, the city of Indra and other cities are there; like the wheel of an oilmill, the wheel of Sūrya's chariot is said to rotate on the hill as its axis (PI.2. 686), A.B.L. Awasthi's identification of this mount with the northern portion of Mānasādri, the neighbouring hill overlooking Mānasa lake (*Studies in Skanda Purāṇa*, p. 138) is purely conjectural.

15. He will delight and bring happiness to all people by his acts. It is on account of his acts of promoting happiness (and welfare of the people) that his subjects will call him *rājan* (lit. one who pleases, i.e. the king).[69]

16. He is firm in his vows; true to his words; a friend of Brāhmaṇas (who are devoted to the studies of Vedas); a servant of aged people; the shelter of all beings; paying respect (where due) and kind to the afflicted.

17. He shows the same regard and respect to other women as he would to his mother. He treats his wife as if she were half of his own person. He is affectionate to his subjects like a father. He behaves (respectfully) like a servant, to those who are well-versed in the Vedas.

18. He is most beloved to all creatures as if he was their own Self. He enhances the delight of his friends and well-wishers. He is especially attached to the company of those who are free from worldly attachments. He wields his rod of punishment against the evil-minded (miscreants).

18A*. By dint of his great personal power, he will make the good earth produce all the plants (as one milks the cow). He will make this earth flat by the end of his bow.

19. But really he is directly the Supreme Lord himself who has incarnated by his *kalā* (portion, part)—the Supreme Lord who governs the three worlds; is the unchangeable perpetual inner controller of all beings; even the apparent multiplicity created in whom by nescience is rendered substanceless (and unmeaningful) when he is realized.

20. This matchless warrior, the King of kings, is the sole protector of the sphere of the earth, from the *Udaya* mountain with a bow in hand, and seated in his triumphant chariot, he will go round the earth from right to left, just as the Sun does.

---

69. Cf. *Yathā prahlādanāccandraḥ pratāpāt tapano yathā /*
Tathaiva so'bhud anvartho rājā Prakṛti-rañjanāt //

Raghuvaṁśa. 4.12

* This verse is included here, being authenticated by VR., VJ., SD. and BP. who have commented on it. It is found in the Southern recension of the Bh. P. But ŚR., RR., VD. GS. and GD. have ignored it in their comments.

21. Kings, as well as the guardians to the quarters of the world, will certainly pay tribute to him at every place. Their queens will regard this first king as Lord Viṣṇu (the god whose weapon is *cakra*—discus), and sing of his glory.

22. This King of kings, the protector of subjects with a view to providing means of livelihood to his subjects, will milk the earth in the form of a cow. Like Indra, he will break down the mountains with the point of his bow, and level the earth as if in a sport.

23. Twanging his irresistible *ājagava* bow in the battle, when he, like a lion with his tail erected, traverses the earth, the evil-doers will hide themselves in all directions.

24. He will perform a hundred horse-sacrifices (*aśvamedha*) at the source of the river Sarasvatī. While the last sacrifice will be performed, Indra (the performer of hundred *aśvamedha* sacrifices) will steal away his sacrificial horse.

25. He will meet the venerable Sanatkumāra alone in the garden of his palace. He will propitiate him (Sanatkumāra) with devotion. He will get from him the pure knowledge which leads one to attain to the Supreme Brahman.

26. Wherever he will go, Pṛthu, of celebrated glory and enormous prowess, will hear various songs and ballads and praise based on his[70] exploits.

27. His *cakra* (sway, army, wheels of his chariot) will be unobstructed and unchallenged. After conquering all the quarters of the earth, he will remove the evil-doers of the world by his heroic lustre. He will be the supreme master of the world whose great glories will be sung by the chiefs of gods and demons."

CHAPTER SEVENTEEN

(*Pṛthu subjugates the Earth*)

Maitreya said:

1. King Pṛthu, the illustrious son of Vena, who was thus eulogised for his excellent attributes and exploits, satisfied

70. *ātmāśrita* : pertaining to Viṣṇu (ŚR.).

those bards by honouring them with gifts as desired by them and by appreciating them.

2. He honoured all the classes of people of whom the Brāhmaṇas were foremost, and also his servants, ministers and family priests, the citizens as well as the rural public, various trade guilds and other prominent subjects.

Vidura asked :

3. Why did the goddess of the earth who can assume multifarious forms assume the form of a cow? When Pṛthu milched her who became the calf and what was the milk-pail?

4. How is it that he levelled the goddess of the earth who was by nature uneven? For what purpose did the god Indra carry off his sacrificial horse?

5. Oh Brāhmaṇa (Maitreya)! To what state did the royal-sage attain after getting initiated in the knowledge of the Brahman and its personal experience[71] from the venerable Sanatkumāra, the best among the knowers of Brahman?

6-7. I am a votary devoted to you as well as to Lord Kṛṣṇa (Adhokṣaja). Your honour should narrate to me many other deeds of Lord Kṛṣṇa of sanctifying glory, connected with the account of his former manifestation as Pṛthu. Kṛṣṇa in the form of Pṛthu has milched this cow in the form of the earth.

Sūta said :

8. When he was thus urged by Vidura to narrate the story of Vāsudeva, Maitreya, who was pleased with him in mind, praised him and replied.

Maitreya said :

9. Dear child (Vidura)! When Pṛthu was coronated and was called as the protector of the public, the subjects with their bodies emaciated with hunger due to barrenness of the earth, approached Pṛthu, the protector and appealed.

10. "Oh King! We are oppressed by the gastric fire

---

71. *Jñānaṁ savijñānam* — In B.G. III. 41, Śaṅkara explains *jñāna* as 'knowledge of the self and other things acquired from the scriptures and the teachers' and *vijñāna* as 'the personal experience—*anubhava* of things so taught'.

just like the wood with fire in its hollow. Today we have approached you for shelter, as you are installed as our king who will provide us with means of livelihood, and are worthy of seeking asylum.

11. Oh King of kings! You are verily the protector of the people and the bestower of the means of livelihood. Therefore, while we have not perished from starvation, Your Majesty should endeavour to supply food to us who are famished with hunger."

Maitreya said :

12. Oh great Kuru ! Having listened to the heart-rending lamentations of his subjects, Pṛthu contemplated deeply for a long time, and at last came to perceive the cause of the scarcity.

13. By his reasoning power he came to the conclusion (that the earth had held up the seeds of herbs, plants and food-grains within herself). Being indignant, he took up his bow and fitted an arrow on it aiming at the earth, just as the enraged destroyer of Tripura (Śiva, did against Tripura).

14. When the earth saw the king with his weapon uplifted, she began to tremble. She assumed the form of a cow and in terror began to run fast like a terrified female deer chased by a hunter.

15. The enraged son of Vena, with eyes blood-red with wrath, and with the arrow fitted to his bow, chased after her whithersoever she ran (for shelter).

16. Running to all the directions (cardinal points) and intermediate directions (e.g. South-east, South-west etc.), to the heaven and the earth and in the space between them, the goddess Earth saw him chasing her everywhere with uplifted weapon.

17. Just as people do not get protection from death, she did not get any asylum in the world against Pṛthu, the son of Vena. Terrified, she returned with a troubled heart.

18. And she spoke to the illustrious king, "Oh Knower of Dharma ! you are kind to the afflicted. Determined as your majesty is on the protection of creatures, protect me as well.

19. Such as you are, why do you intend to kill me who am afflicted and innocent ? How could a person who is regarded as expert in (the niceties of) Dharma, strike women ?

20. Oh King ! Beings (people) do not at all strike the females even though they have committed an offence. Much less would persons like you who are merciful and compassionate to the helpless, do so, Oh King.

21. How can you support yourself and these subjects of yours on the surface of (cosmic) waters after destroying me—a strong boat wherein the whole universe is established ?"

Pṛthu said :

22. "Oh Earth ! I want to kill you as you disobey my commands—You partake of your share in the sacrifices, but you do not yield us wealth.

23. It is not that punishment is disapproved in the case of a wicked cow which every day eats fodder but does not yield milk from her udders.

24. You are dull-witted. You have confined in yourself the seeds of plants etc. created already by god Brahmā. You do not allow them to grow, thus you set me at nought.

25. I shall pacify the afflictions of these subjects who are famished with hunger and are distressed, with your flesh cut down by my arrows.

26. To kill a vile self-conceited fellow—whether a man, a woman or an impotent person—who is merciless to others, is no killing at all, in the case of kings.

27. You are obstinate, arrogant and have assumed a false form of a cow. Having shattered you to sesamum seed like pieces with my arrows, I shall support these subjects by the dint of my Yogic power."

28. The earth began to tremble. She bowed to him who like the god of death[72] bore a form which was wrath incarnate, and spoke to him with folded hands.

The Earth-goddess said :

29. "I pay my obeisance again and again to the Supreme Man who manifested his various forms by his Māyā (power),

---

72. ŚR. explains that the body of the god of death is not made of anger.

and appears to be composed of the (three) *guṇas*, though (in reality) by the realization of his essential nature; he has been ever free from the waves of love, hate (etc.) born of *ahaṁkāra* (his false identification) with regard to matter (*adhibhūta*), action (*adhyātma*) and the agent (*adhidaiva*).

30. That Supreme Being, the very Creator who created me as the abode of all *jīvas* (living beings) and as the support of the four classes of creatures composed of the *guṇas* of Prakṛti, has come, with uplifted arm, to strike me down! To whom else can I resort now for shelter?

31. He who, at the beginning of creation, created this world of mobiles and immobiles by his supra-logical Māyā Power which rests on him (for support) is said to be now ready to protect it by dint of the same Power. Devcted to righteousness (and its promotion) as he is, how does he desire to kill me?

32. The Almighty, though one, appears as many on account of the other, i.e. the Māyā Power. He created god Brahmā and made him evolve the universe. Alas, the intention of the Lord cannot at all be fathomed by people whose minds are distracted by the invincible Māyā.

33. I bow to the Highest Person, the Creator (of the world) who manifests and withdraws his powers (suitable for the occasion or purpose), and who brings about the creation (preservation and destruction) of the universe by means of his potencies in the form of substance (i.e. five gross elements—*mahābhūtas*), action (senses and deities presiding over sense-organs), the principle of intelligence (*buddhi*) and ego (*ahaṁkāra*).

34. Oh birthless Almighty! It is Your Majesty who as the primeval Boar verily lifted me up from the waters of *Rasātala*, with the intention of establishing the world created by you and consisting of five gross-elements, sense-organs and the inner organ (the heart).

35. Today that very Boar (the upholder of the earth) has appeared as the hero (Pṛthu) who desires to protect his subjects who have resorted to me as on board a ship on the surface of the waters. Your Majesty whose arrows are terrible, certainly desires to kill me for the sake of milk.

36. Oh Warrior! The intention of sovereign rulers (like

you) is certainly not comprehended by people like us, whose paths of minds are deluded by the Māyā which creates the universe consisting of three *guṇas*. I pay my respects to those kings who bring glories to all."

CHAPTER EIGHTEEN

(*Milking of the Earth* (*in the form of a Cow*)

Maitreya said :

1. Having thus praised Pṛthu whose lips were quivering through rage, the goddess of the earth steadied her mind herself (by her reasoning and will power) and addressed the king again, although she was afraid (of him).

2. "Oh King ! Please control your wrath completely.[73] Please consider what I tell you. For like a bee, a wise man takes the essence from everything.

3. Expedients for the accomplishments of the welfare of men in this world as well as in the next, have been discovered and employed by the sages who have realized the truth.

4. Anyone belonging to the later periods, who properly and with faith adopts the measures demonstrated by the ancients, easily accomplishes his objectives.

5. Even if a learned person,[74] disregarding those expedients adopted and tested successfully by the ancients, tries to accomplish those objectives in his own (independent) ways, his objects are never realized, despite his frequent efforts and experiments.

6. Oh King ! It has been observed by me that the herbs and plants which were produced by god Brahmā formerly, were being enjoyed by the wicked who did not undertake religious observances.

7. When I was left unprotected and uncared for by rulers of the people like you (i.e. Vena and other ordinary kings), and when the world was infested with thieves, I swallowed up those herbs and plants (to preserve them within me) for the performance of sacrifices.

---

73. Restrain your anger so as to offer me protection (ŚR.).

74. If the text is read as *avidvān*, 'one who in his ignorance' etc. (ŚR.).

8. Due to a lapse of a long period, those plants and herbs within me have become diminished and weak. You should, therefore, try to take them out by some expedient known to be effective in such matters.

9-10. Oh mighty-armed hero ! Oh protector of creatures ! If Your Lordship desires (to provide) nutritious food coveted by creatures, please arrange for a calf, a suitable vessel (milk-pot) and a milk-man competent to draw (my) milk, so that, being full of affection, I shall yield for you all your desired objects in the form of milk, Oh warrior.

11. Oh mighty king ! Make me a level plain so that the waters showered by god Indra may stand on me, even after the rainy season is over. God may bless you."

12. Accepting the agreeable and wholesome words of advice of the goddess of the earth, the king made (Svāyambhuva) Manu as the calf, and milked all the herbs and plants (such as cereals etc.), in his own hand.

13. Similarly, other wise men also extracted essence of everything everywhere. Then others (fifteen including sages) drew out their desired objects from the cow (earth) tamed by Pṛthu.

14. Oh most righteous Vidura ! Then the sages made Bṛhaspati, the calf and drew from the goddess (earth) milk in the form of the holy Vedas, into their own sense-organs (viz. ears, speech and mind).

15. The gods made Indra a calf, and extracted in a vessel of gold Soma-juice, and (nectarine) milk giving mental vigour, splendour, energy and physical strength.

16. (The demonic tribes) Daityas and Dānavas made Prahlāda, the foremost among the Asuras, as the calf, and milked from her wine and decoction (spirituous liquors) in a vessel of iron.

17. (The celestial *artistes*), Gandharvas (heavenly musicians) and Apsaras (heavenly nymphs) made Viśvāvasu the calf, and extracted the milk in the cup of lotus-flower and it became the special Gāndharva honey giving sweetness of voice and beauty.

18. The venerable manes (Pitṛs), the presiding deities of the Śrāddha ceremony performed in memory of the departed

souls, made Aryaman (the head of the Pitṛs) as the calf, and reverentially drew milk in an unbaked earthen vessel and it became *Kavya* (food for the manes).

19. The Siddhas (Semi-divine beings) made Kapila the calf, and extracted in the vessel of the sky the eight superhuman powers (*Siddhis*) exercisable by mere will. The Vidyādharas (a tribe of demigods) drew the milk in the form of the art of moving through the sky (in the same vessel with Kapila as the calf).

20. Others (such as *Kimpuruṣas*, a semi-divine tribe) noted for their power of conjuring tricks (*māyins*) made Maya the calf and got from her, magical powers possessed by wonderful beings who can become invisible at will.

21. The Yakṣas and Rākṣasas (demonic beings), Bhūtas and Piśācas (ghosts and fiends) who feed upon raw flesh made the Lord of ghosts (Rudra) as the calf, and extracted in a skull the wine of blood.

22. In the same way, hoodless reptiles, scorpions, serpents and snakes made Takṣaka (the chief of Nāgas) a calf, and drew poison as the milk, in their mouths as the vessels.

23-24. Herbivorous beasts made the bull of Rudra the calf and drew grass as their milk, in the vessel in the form of the jungle. The carnivorous beasts with big tusks and feeding upon raw meat, with the lion (the king of beasts) as the calf, drew in (the vessel in the form of) their body flesh (as their milk). The birds who used Garuḍa (the chief of birds) as the calf, had mobiles (like worms and insects) and immobiles (life fruits) for their milk.

25. With the Banyan tree as the calf, the trees extracted their own respective juices as the milk. Mountains had the highest (mountain) Himālaya as the calf and milked various minerals (as their milk) in (the vessels in the form of) their ridges.

26. All species of beings used their own chiefs as the calf and extracted severally in their own vessels the milk specifically useful as food to their own species, from the earth which yielded all desired objects when she was tamed by Pṛthu.

27. Oh Vidura (son of the Kuru family)! In this way, Pṛthu and others who subsisted on food obtained from the earth

different kinds of milk in the form of their specific food, using different kinds of calfs and milk-pots.

28. Thereafter Pṛthu, the lord of the earth, was highly pleased with the earth-goddess who yielded all desired objects, and affectionate as he was to daughters, he regarded her as his daughter, out of paternal affection.

29. The mighty son of Vena, the king of kings, crushed to pieces mountain-peaks with the ends of his bow and made the surface of the globe of earth almost level.

30. The illustrious son of Vena was a father unto his subjects, as he provided them with means of livelihood. He then constructed on the earth, at different places, suitable houses for them.

31. He founded a number of villages, towns, cities, forts and castles of different types. He built abodes for cowherds and cowpens and planned camping grounds, quarries. He provided agricultural habitations and hamlets on hillsides.

32. Before the time of Pṛthu, there was no such planning and construction of cities, towns etc. in this world. During his reign subjects began to live comfortably at various places (in rural and urban areas) with a sense of security.

CHAPTER NINETEEN

(Pṛthu's Conquest)

(Pṛthu's Horse-sacrifices and Conflict with Indra)

Maitreya said:

1. The king (Pṛthu), thereupon, consecrated himself with the intention of performing one hundred horse-sacrifices at Brahmāvarta, the land of Manu, where the Sarasvatī flows towards the east.

2. Anticipating that Pṛthu would excel his record performance of sacrifices, glorious Indra grew jealous of Pṛthu's grand festival of sacrifices.

3. In that festival of sacrifices, the glorious Lord Hari, the Soul of all beings, the revered father of all the world, and

the ruler of the universe, was perceived directly as the Lord of the sacrifices by all.

4. He was accompanied by Brahmā, Śiva and protectors of the world along with their followers. His glories were being sung by Gandharvas (celestial musicians), sages and troupes of Apsaras (heavenly nymphs).

5-6. Semidivine beings like Siddhas and Vidyādharas, Daityas, Dānavas, Guhyakas and others and Lord Hari's prominent attendants headed by Sunanda and Nanda, Kapila, Nārada, Datta and the great masters of Yoga like Sanaka and others—all devotees of the Lord who were eager to serve the Lord, accompanied him.

7. Oh descendant of Bharata (Vidura)! In that sacrifice the earth which supplies the materials for oblations in the sacrifice acted as a wish-yielding heavenly cow, and gave as milk, all the objects desired and required by the sacrificer Pṛthu.

8. The rivers flowed flooded with all kinds of sweet juices like those of sugarcane, grapes etc. as well as with milk, curds, food, ghee and butter-milk. Trees of gigantic dimensions which oozed out plentiful honey bore fruits abundantly.

9. The oceans brought to him heaps of precious stones as tributes; mountains, four kinds of food; all people along with their protectors[75] paid tributes to him.

10. The mighty Indra grew jealous of this great prosperity of Pṛthu who regarded god Viṣṇu as his Master, and created obstacles in his way (to sabotage his scheme of hundred horse-sacrifices).

11. While Pṛthu, the son of Vena, was propitiating Viṣṇu, the Lord of Sacrifices, with the last (hundredth) horse-sacrifice, the jealous Indra carried away the sacrificial horse, himself remaining invisible.

12. The venerable sage Atri noticed him hurrying through the sky in the disguise of a heretic who mistakes unrighteousness for righteousness and the guise served him like an armour.

13. As directed by Atri, the son of Pṛthu, who was a great warrior, pursued Indra to kill him, and shouted to him in rage "Halt! Halt".

75. *lokapālāḥ*—Protectors of the world like Indra—GD.

14. Seeing Indra in that sage-like form with matted hair and body besmeared with sacred ashes, the son of Pṛthu thought him to be Dharma (piousness, religion) incarnate, and did not (feel disposed to) shoot an arrow at him.

15. When the Prince returned without killing Indra, Atri urged him again to slay him, saying, "Oh child, kill this great Indra, who is the meanest of gods as he had obstructed your father's sacrifice".

16. Thus incited (by Atri), the son of Pṛthu, got furious and chased Indra who was fleeing through the sky as Jaṭāyu[76] (the king of vultures) pursued Rāvaṇa.

17. The King of the Heaven (Indra) gave up his own form and the sacrificial horse and disappeared. Taking with him his own sacrificial horse, the hero (Pṛthu's son) returned to (the place of) his father's sacrifice.

18. Witnessing his miraculous deed, the great sages conferred on him the (significant) epithet *Vijitāśva* (conqueror of the horse), Oh Lord (Vidura)!

19. The mighty Indra created very thick darkness under the cover of which he stole again the horse tied with a gold chain from the sacrificial post with the circular wooden ring called *caṣāla* on its top.

20. Atri (again) pointed out Indra hurrying through the sky. But the warrior (Pṛthu's son) did not molest him as he was carrying a human skull and *Khaṭvāṅga* (a club with a skull at the top) in his hands (like a Kāpālaka).

21. Being urged by Atri, however, he indignantly fixed an arrow (on the bow) aiming it at Indra. The king of heaven (Indra) gave up the sacrificial horse, and his guise (as Kāpālika) and stayed invisible.

22. Taking the horse with him, the hero (Pṛthu's son) returned to (the place of) his father's sacrifice, while people of poor understanding accepted the censurable guise assumed (and left) by Indra.

23. Whatever forms were assumed by Indra with the in-

76. *Jaṭāyu*—A son of Aruṇa and Gṛdhrī; king of vultures and younger brother of Sampāti. He tried to prevent the abduction of Sītā by Rāvaṇa, and was killed by Rāvaṇa's treachery. His funeral was performed by Rāma.

tention of carrying away the consecrated horse, were the marks of sins. Here the word *khaṇḍa* is used in the sense of "mark".

24-25. In this way while carrying away the horse with the intention of interrupting Pṛthu's sacrifice, Indra assumed and abandoned deceitful disguise of nude ascetics (Digambara Jainas), red-robed ascetics (Buddhists) and others (such as Kāpālakas). Minds of men, through their misapprehension (of the true teachings of the Vedas), are generally attracted to these pseudo-religious sects as the true religion, as they are charmingly presented with excellent eloquence.

26. When the illustrious king Pṛthu of great prowess learnt this, he got infuriated. He took up his bow and aimed an arrow at Indra.

27. Finding that Pṛthu was determined to kill Indra and appeared of irresistible vehemence and terrible to look at, the sacrificial priests prevented him urging, "Oh highly intelligent and wise king, it is not proper to kill anything else here (at the sacrifice) except the consecrated beast (as enjoined by Vedas).

28. By the force of Vedic incantation of undiminished power, we shall now invoke (and forcibly bring) Indra, the Lord of Maruts who has interrupted your object (of performing this sacrifice) and has lost his glory by your high reputation. Oh King, we shall then forcibly offer your enemy as an oblation to fire."

29. Oh Vidura ! Having thus addressed Pṛthu, the master of the sacrifice, his sacrificial priests, with the ladle (*Śruc*) in their hands, indignantly proceeded to pour oblations in the sacrificial fire, when the self-born god Brahmā appeared and prevented them (from doing so saying).

30. "Indra whom you wish to kill by means of the sacrifice, should not be killed. For Indra designated as Yajña is the manifestation of the Almighty Lord (himself), and gods whom you offered oblations are (mere) forms of Indra."

31. Oh Brāhmaṇas ! consider this great violation of Dharma (leading to propagation of heretic sects) perpetrated by Indra who desires to interrupt the king's performance of the sacrifice. (He may again encourage heretic doctrines to the detriment of the world.)

32. Therefore may Pṛthu who has performed ninety-nine sacrifices be more famous than Indra" (Brahmā then addressed to Pṛthu) : "As Your honour knows the path leading to Liberation, the sacrifices which you have so magnificently performed are enough.

33. May you be blessed (despite the non-completion of this sacrifice). Both you and Indra are the embodiments of Viṣṇu of excellent renown. Hence, it is not proper to cherish anger against the great Indra who is your own self.

34. Oh great king ! Please do not worry about this (interruption or non-completion of the sacrifice). Listen to our words with respectful attention. The mind of the person who contemplates to accomplish what has been frustrated by the Fate, certainly gets extremely infuriated and enters blinding darkness of delusion[77] (and does not get peace).

35. Let this sacrifice be stopped now for there is obstinacy in gods.[78] It is here (due to this sacrifice) that Dharma was violated by heretics created by Indra.

36. Have a look at these people who are being enticed away by attractive heretical doctrines propagated by Indra who maliciously plotted against your sacrifice and stole away the sacrificial horse.

37. Oh son of Vena ! You are a part of Viṣṇu incarnated on this earth now from Vena's body to protect the religion[79] of the people suitable to the present times—religion that declined by the misdeeds of Vena.

38.* Oh sovereign ruler of the people ! Such a ray of

---

77. v.l. *mano'ti-kaṣṭam* : The mind falls into the darkest hell. This suggests both the reason and undesirable consequences of such attempts against the gods.—VJ.

78. You should give up your prejudice against gods, for the gods, if enraged, will obstruct rainfall and famine will devastate the land.—VJ.

79. Religious tenets based on Vedas and orthodox philosophic systems like Sāṁkhya, Yoga etc.—ŚR.

* VJ. differs : As you have incarnated yourself for the protection of religion, you should consider that your performance of the intended hundredth sacrifice will be an insult to Indra (Prajāpati) and as such you should not perform it. You should completely fulfil the desire of Indra that you should not complete the hundredth horse-sacrifice. Taking into account the all-round auspicious effects of not opposing Indra's will, you

Viṣṇu as you are, you consider the origination of the universe[80] and fulfil the purpose of the proginators of the world (like Bhṛgu and others who created you.) Oh Lord ! destroy the formidable heretic path—the illusion created by Indra which is the source of pseudo-religious sects".

Maitreya said:

39. Being thus advised by Brahmā, the creator of the world gave up his insistance on the performance of the hundredth sacrifice, adopted a friendly policy to Indra, and made peace with him.

40. Those gods who were propitiated in the sacrifice and were disposed to confer blessings bestowed boons upon Pṛthu who had performed many auspicious deeds including the concluding ablution (*avabhṛtha*) at the end of the sacrificial session.

41. Oh Vidura ! The Brāhmaṇas whose blessings were efficacious, and who were faithfully paid the sacrificial money and honoured, became satisfied and pronounced their blessings on the first monarch (Pṛthu).

42. Oh mighty-armed king ! All the manes (*Pitṛs*), gods and sages who were invited by you, have attended and have been worshipped by you paying proper respects and gifts."

---

obey the desire of the creator of the universe (viz. myself) that you should perform only ninety-nine sacrifices. By this sacrifice or religious conduct you should destroy the formidable heretic path which is the illusion created by Indra—a source of pseudo-religious creeds.

80. VC. and SD. interpret *bhava* as the 'good' of the universe.

CHAPTER TWENTY

(*Pṛthu initiated by Viṣṇu*)

Maitreya continued :

1. Even the glorious Lord Vaikuṇṭha (Viṣṇu), the all-pervasive Master and Enjoyer of sacrifices, was highly pleased with sacrifices (performed by Pṛthu). (Manifesting himself) along with Indra, he addressed Pṛthu as follows :

The Lord said :

2 This (Indra) has verily caused obstruction to your hundredth sacrifice. (As) he is begging apology for the same, you should (now) pardon him.

3. Oh King ! The best ones among men who are highly intelligent and righteous, cherish no illwill against creatures (even though) they have offended them, inasmuch as the physical body (so offended) is not the Soul (Hence the irrelevance of retaliation).

4. If persons like you are deluded by divine Māyā, service of elderly people (rendered by you) for a long period, has turned out to be mere fruitless labour.

5. A wise man who has realised that this body is the product of *avidyā* (ignorance about the real nature of the Self), *kāma* (desire) and *karma* (actions of the previous life), cherishes no attachment for it.

6. What wise man who has no attachment to his body will cherish a feeling of mineness to house, offspring or even wealth produced by the body?

7*. The Self (*ātman*) is a changeless one, pure, self-luminous, free from *guṇas*, the substratum of the attributes (of

---

* GD. draws a clear contrast between Self (*ātman*) and the body in his com. as follows:

This Soul is different and distinct from the physical body. The Soul is one while bodies are many. The Soul is pure while the body being composed of five elements (*bhūtas*) is impure. The Soul is self-effulgent, self-luminous, while the body is dull, dead. The Soul is beyond *guṇas* but the body is the product of *guṇas* and hence dependent on them. The Soul is the substratum of *guṇas*. The Soul is all-pervasive while the body is limited (by spatio-temporal relations). Due to its all-pervasiveness the

knowledge, bliss etc.), omnipresent (and hence) unveiled by anything, (a detached) witness, and possessing no other Soul,[81] and distinct from the body[82] (which, in contrast with the Soul, changes with childhood, youth and age; is impure, unintelligent; is constituted of *guṇas* and dependent on *guṇas* which produce it; is limited, covered over by houses etc., and is an object of sight; and possesses a Soul distinct from it).

8. The man who thus knows the Soul abiding in him, is established in me. Though he dwells within (the domain of) Prakṛti, he is not affected by its attributes.

9. Oh King! He who, possessed of deep faith (in me) and with no desire of any fruit, always worships me according to his prescribed religious duties (according to his *Varṇa* and *āśrama*) gets his mind gradually purified.

10. When he gets serenity of mind, he becomes unassociated with *guṇas* (worldly objects), and attains pure vision (true knowledge). He enjoys eternal peace, and the absolute Brahmahood which is a state of unconcernedness and equipoise like me.

11. He who realizes this Supreme unchangeable Soul to be quite unconcerned though presiding over the material body,

---

Soul is uncovered while the body being of limited dimensions can be covered with dress. The Soul being consciousness by nature and witness to all, is a seer, but the body being a dead material is subject to perception. The Soul is void of another Soul, mind (inner organ), while the body is the receptacle of the Soul. In this way the knowledge of the identity of *jīva* (individual Soul) and *Īśvara* (God)—knowledge which is a means to liberation is explained.

(2) VR. explains the concept of Soul held in the *Viśiṣṭādvaita School*:

The Soul which resides in different types of celestial human or subhuman bodies is one, due to his inherent knowledge which is one (common). He is pure while the body is filthy. He is self-luminous, free from qualities like love, hate, the Seat (substratum) of attributes like knowledge, bliss. Though he is atomic he is all-pervasive due to his knowledge of *dharma* etc. He is not covered by environments such as house, dress etc. He is a direct seer (of his own body, sense-organs) but the body is an object of perception possessing qualities like love, hate, coverable (by clothes etc.). The Soul enters the body and sustains it and while the body is the object to be so sustained. Hence it is distinct from the body.

81. *nirātmā*—Having no controller superior to him.—VJ.

82. *anātmanaḥ paraḥ*—Superior to and distinct from *jīvas* who are devoid of good attributes—VJ.

the sense organs of cognition and action and the mind, attains the highest bliss.[83]

12. *Saṁsāra* (cycle of birth and death) which is a product of the *guṇas* (of *Prakṛti*) pertains to the *liṅga śarīra* (subtle body) which consists of subtle elements, subtle conative and cognitive sense-organs and their presiding deities and the mind—the reflection of *ātman*. That body is distinct from the Soul. Learned persons who are deeply attached to me are not affected by pleasure or pain, while experiencing prosperity or adversity.

13. Oh valiant King! Being equally undisturbed by pleasure or pain, looking upon the excellent, the middling and the vilest as equals, and having subdued all the sense-organs and the mind, you carry out the duty of protection of all the world with the cooperation of all the people (ministers etc.) appointed by me.

14. Protection of the subjects is the only way to the final beatitude in the case of a king, as he obtains in the next world one sixth of the meritorious acts performed by his subjects. But if he collects only taxes and does not protect his subjects he loses his own merits and becomes responsible for the sins of his subjects.

15. (Considering this) if you are mainly devoted to the righteous duty (*dharma*) as approved by the foremost Brāhmaṇas and handed down by tradition and if you are completely detached from (the *puruṣārthas* like) *dharma* (*artha* and *kāma*) you will protect this earth and will be their beloved king. In a short while, you will see Siddhas (like Sanaka, Sanandana) who will come to visit you.

16. Oh ruler of men! Ask for whatever boon you like from me. I am bound to you on account of your virtues and character. I am not easily available by the performance of sacrifices, austere penances or by *Yoga*, as by nature I like to dwell with those who are even-minded and look upon all as equals."

---

83. v.l. *abhayam*—Liberation (*Mokṣa*).

Maitreya said :

17. Thus advised by the All-pervading god Viṣṇu, the preceptor and the Lord of the universe, Pṛthu, the conqueror of the world respectfully received Hari's command with his head.

18. He affectionately embraced Indra (the performer of hundred sacrifices) who, being ashamed of his own act, was touching his (Pṛthu's) feet (to beg his pardon), and gave up enmity with Indra.

19. Thereupon the venerable Lord (Viṣṇu), the Soul of the universe, was offered worship by Pṛthu who clasped his lotus-like feet with overflowing devotion.

20 The god whose eyes were like petals of lotus and who is a well-wisher and friend of pious saints, was about to leave. But looking at him (Pṛthu), he lingered on to confer his grace, and did not depart.

21. The first monarch (Pṛthu) could not see Hari as his eyes were full of tears. Nor could he speak as his throat was choked with tears. With folded hands he stood, embracing Hari in his heart.

22. Then wiping out his tears, he beheld with unsatisfied eyes the Supreme Man who stood before him touching the ground with his feet[84] and placing His palm on the elevated shoulder of Garuḍa (the enemy of serpents). Pṛthu spoke to him (as follows).

Pṛthu said:

23. Oh Omnipresent Lord ! From you—the Supreme Lord of gods like Brahmā who can confer boons on others—what wise man would seek for boons craved after by persons dominated by ego (*ahaṁkāra*), the product of *guṇas* (or enjoyable to those who regard the material body as Self). Oh bestower of Mokṣa (Liberation), I do not seek them as they are available even to embodied beings in Hell, Oh Lord.

24. Oh Lord ! I do not desire even that Mokṣa (final

84. Normally gods do not touch the earth with their feet. This action of Hari indicates that he was so overwhelmed to shower his grace on Pṛthu that he forgot himself and touched the ground with his feet—ŚR.

beatitude) (if there be no opportunity to taste) the honey from your lotus-feet, which surges from within hearts of great saints and oozes out of their mouths. Bless me with ten thousand ears for hearing your glory. This is the boon (I seek).

25. Oh Lord of excellent fame ! The breath laden with small drops of the nectar of your lotus-like feet which issues from the mouth of great saints, restores the knowledge of the Self to false Yogins who have forgotten the Path of Truth. Hence enough of boons to us (as there is absolutely no possibility of us—devotees being affected by passions like love, hate etc. Bhakti comprises within it the bliss of liberation).

26. Oh Lord of excellent renown ! If, by a lucky chance, one happens to listen even once, to your auspicious glory in the assembly of noble saints, how can an appreciator of virtues forget it—unless he is a brute. For the goddess Lakṣmī earnestly seeks your glory with a desire of assimilating those virtues (or concentrating in her all *puruṣārthas* or objectives of man's life).

27. Hence, being full of ardent desire, I would, like Lakṣmī (the lotus-handed goddess) be eagerly devoted to you, the Supreme most Person, the receptacle of all excellent attributes. May there be no jealousy[85] between us who are vieing with each other for the service of one and the same Lord, and have concentrated our minds on your feet alone.

28.* Oh Lord of the World ! There may arise jealousy in the mind of Lakṣmī, the mother of the worlds, as we have

---

85. As there was between Indra and myself for the performance of sacrifices—ŚR.

* (i) VR. gives an additional interpretation :

Oh Lord of the world ! The fruit of sacred duties like sacrifices bestowed on us by Prakṛti the mother of the universe is unimportant and disastrous as it leads to Saṁsāra. But you are so magnanimous and kind to the poor and distressed that you do not see any wrong in it and you elevate that insignificant act of sacrifice yielding ordinary commonplace fruit to the dignity of the means leading to Mokṣa (Liberation). For such commonplace fruits are trifles to one who is satisfied in one's natural Self.

(ii) VJ. differs. The gist is as follows :

The danger that there would arise a quarrel between Pṛthu and Lakṣmī a desire to share her work (of rendering service to you). However you who are compassionate to the poor and distressed, magnify (the value of) our insignificant services. Of what account (importance) is she (Lakṣmī) to you who are satisfied in your own natural Self.

29. (As you are kind to the poor and pitiable) pious persons (who are free from attachment) resort to you (even after attainment of knowledge). You are above the deluding effects of the *guṇas* of Māyā.[86] We do not know whether the righteous souls cherish any ulterior motive other than the act of remembrance and contemplation of the feet of the Lord.

30. That you addressed the words, "Seek a boon" to me who am your devotee, your words are, I think, deluding to the world. If the world is not bound by the cords of Your speech (Vedic injunctions) who could be so deluded again as to perform the usual (ritualistic) actions.

31.* Oh Supreme Lord ! An ignorant[87] man is indeed

(as is natural in common rivals) is not possible as both of them were devotees of the Lord :

Oh Lord of the universe ! There will be naturally an injurious rivalry among persons under ordinary kings. But there is no cause for such rivalry amongst us (Lakṣmī and myself). In our actions, viz. your worship, what we do is very little. You magnify it as you are compassionate to the poor. Conferring blessings even for a small act does not however mean that you change an atom-like insignificant act into a mountain.

(iii) VC. regards this a characteristic of a warrior-devotee. I shall face opposition with mother Lakṣmī. We desire to perform her work, viz. service of your feet. Let her rest on your bosom. As a son, I shall serve your feet. I am not afraid that Lakṣmī, as compared with me, is more ancient and great. But as you are kind to the weak and meek, you magnify our insignificant service. As I am confident of my power, I am not concerned with Lakṣmī's pleasure or displeasure.

86. From the minds of your devotees, you dispel the delusion caused by the *guṇas* of *Māyā*.—VR. and VD.

* (i) VR. : Being deluded by your Māyā, a person becomes devoid of true knowledge. If such ignorant person fortunately adores you and requests you for *artha*, *kāma* etc.—objects other than you,—he remains separate from you. This means, Oh Lord, you have compromised your own greatness. Just as a father guards the interests of his minor and ignorant child, you should do what is good for him (even without his request to do so).

(ii) VC. : You should not test your devotee by asking him to select a boon, for people are likely to select other material things. You should therefore, yourself do what is good for us according to you.

(iii) GD. : Oh Lord ! This ignorant person is separated from your real Self by your powerful Māyā. Hence he seeks from you son's property and other things. You further entice him by telling him to choose a boon, just as a father etc.

87. *abudhaḥ* : If the word be taken as *budhaḥ* the verse means : It is indeed by your Māyā that man is separated from you, his real Self.

separated from you—his real Self—by your Māyā. Hence he covets after something else (like *artha, kāma* etc.). Just as a father, of his own accord (without being requested by the child to look after his interests), looks after the good of his child, you yourself also should do what is good for us.

*Maitreya said** :

32. The Omniscient Lord who was thus eulogised by Pṛthu, (the first monarch of the earth) said, "Oh King! May your devotion in me remain (constant). Fortunately, you have such a (firmly devoted) mind towards me, as would enable one to get over my Māyā which is so difficult to cross.

33. Therefore, Oh Protector of the People, you carry out my commands carefully. People who abide by my commands are blessed with happiness here and hereafter."

Maitreya said :

34. Having thus gladly received the deeply significant compliments of the royal sage Pṛthu (the son of Vena), and being worshipped by him, Acyuta (the imperishable Lord) blessed him (with his grace) and thought of departing.

35-36. Gods, sages, manes (Pitṛs), Gandharvas, Siddhas, Cāraṇas, Serpents, Kinnaras, Apsaras, men, birds and various creatures and the attendants and followers of Viṣṇu were regarded as Viṣṇu (The Lord of Sacrifices) and were honoured with devotion by respectful address, donation of wealth, folding of palms by the king—after which they departed.

37. Carrying away (as it were) the mind of the royal sage as well as that of his preceptor, Lord Acyuta (Viṣṇu) also returned to his own abode (Vaikuṇṭha).

38. Having paid obeisance to the Lord, the god of gods, who though unmanifest by his nature, (out of grace) revealed himself to Pṛthu and became invisible again, Pṛthu returned to his capital.

Hence even though he be wise or learned, he longs for other things (such as sons etc.).

* Verses 32 and 33 are not commented by ŚR but are annotated by VR., GD. and others.

CHAPTER TWENTY-ONE

(*Pṛthu explains Dharma to his subjects*)

Maitreya said :

1-3. (Pṛthu retired to his capital city)—the city was decorated everywhere with wreaths of pearls and garlands of flowers, with silk drapery and decorative arches of gold, and with extremely fragrant incense (burning). Its streets and squares were besprinkled with water scented with sandal and *agaru* (agallochum). They were beautified with flowers, *akṣatas* (unbroken rice pigmented with red *kuṁkuma*), fruits, tender barley-shoots, parched grains of rice, and illuminated with lamps. It was adorned with plantain trees as well as with young arica plants laden with fruits and flowers, and was beautified with wreaths of tender leaves of (mango and other) trees.

4. His subjects, along with beautiful girls wearing bright gold earrings, went forward to greet him with lamps, materials of worship, and all other auspicious articles (such as curds) prepared (for the occasion).

5. In the midst of blowing of conchs and sounding of kettledrums and chanting of Vedic hymns (by Brāhmaṇas), the warrior who was untouched by pride, in spite of the singing of his eulogies, entered his palace.

6. The highly renowned king was honoured everywhere on his way. He (in return) honoured the residents of his city as well as his subjects from rural areas. He was pleased with them, and granted them the boons they liked.

7. Performing many such and other achievements, the most adorable king of great virtues and pious conduct, governed this globe of the earth. After establishing his pure reputation, he ascended to the highest abode (Vaikuṇṭha).

Sūta said :

8. Oh Śaunaka (Leader of the sacrificial assembly in the Naimiṣa forest)! Vidura, the great devotee of the Lord respectfully adored Maitreya, (the son of Kuṣīrava), who was eulogising the primal king's (Pṛthu's) worldwide renown of all excellent attributes which was glorified by highly virtuous people. He spoke to him (Maitreya, as follows):

9. Pṛthu who received adorations from all gods, and who bore in his arms the mighty and heroic lustre of god Viṣṇu wherewith he milked the earth (in the form of a cow), was coronated by Brāhmaṇas.

10. What wise man will not listen to the glories of Pṛthu on the remnants of whose valorous achievements, all the rulers of the world, the guardian deities and the people, still subsist to their hearts' content—Please, therefore, narrate to me in details his pious deeds.

Maitreya said :

11. Dwelling in the land (*doāb*) lying between the rivers—the Gaṅgā and the Yamunā, Pṛthu enjoyed only those pleasures which came to his lot, as a result of the fruition of his past deeds, as he desired to exhaust (the stock of) his merit (and not due to addiction to pleasures).

12. His writ ran unobstructed everywhere. He wielded his sceptre (sovereignty) over seven island-continents[88]—with the exception of Brāhmaṇas and devotees of Hari (who was like their progenitor).

13. Once upon a time, he was consecrated for the performance of a great sacrifice. There assembled, Oh Vidura, a congregation of gods, Brāhmaṇa sages and royal sages.

14. When all the respectable persons were duly honoured according to their merits and positions, he (Pṛthu) stood up in that assembly, like the moon in the midst of stars.

15. He was tall with muscular long arms; he was fair in complexion; his eyes were reddish like a red lotus; his nose was shapely; his countenance, beautiful. He was gentle in appearance; his shoulders were rounded. His rows of teeth and smiles were beautiful.

16. That powerful monarch had a broad chest, full, bulky loins, stomach shaped like a *pipal* leaf and beautified with three folds; his navel was deep and circular like a whirlpool, his thighs were like pillars of gold, and the fore part of his feet was slightly plump (elevated) and prominent.

---

88. They are : Jambu, Plakṣa, Śālmali, Kuśa, Krauñca, Śāka and Puṣkara.

17. He had fine, curly, dark and glossy hair on the head. His throat was (marked with three spiral lines) like a conch. He wore two costly silk garments, one around his waist and one around his upper part of the body.

18. Due to his sacrificial vow, he laid aside his ornaments. So the natural splendour of the limbs of his body became manifest. He looked dignified with (upper part of) his body covered with the skin of a black-antelope, and with Kuśa grass in his hand he had completed the prescribed religious acts (of that time).

19-20. He looked around with his calm, soothing, affectionate eyes. With a view to thrilling the assembly with joy, the Lord of the earth delivered the following address which was pleasant to hear, couched in beautiful figurative expressions, polished, deep in significance, unagitated and calm. He was, as if, briefly narrating, at that time, his own experiences for the benefit of all.

The King said :

21. "Oh members of this assembly, please listen to me. May auspiciousness betide you all righteous people who have come here. Persons desirous of knowing (the true nature of) Dharma—righteousness—should state (fully) their concept (of Dharma) before the righteous people. (Hence I speak out to you my concept.)

22. I have been installed here as a king to govern and dispense punishment (to anti-social elements), to protect the people, to provide them their means of livelihood, to control them severally within their respective spheres of duties.

23. May those regions which yield whatever one desires and which are reached—according to the knowers of the Vedas—by persons with whom (Lord Hari), the Witness of the previous deeds of all persons, is pleased, be attainable to me, by my performance of this duty.

24. The monarch who collects taxes without imparting instruction to his subjects in their respective religious duties, shares their sins only, and forgoes his own good luck.

25. My dear subjects! You should, therefore, (continue to) perform your own righteous duties, fixing your mind on

god Viṣṇu, and remain free from jealousy. It will be in the interest of the subsistence of your king hereafter, as well as in your own. You would thereby be rendering a great favour to me.

26. Oh purehearted and sinless *Pitṛs* (manes), gods and sages, kindly give your hearty approval (to my request): 'May the doer, the preceptor and the consenter of any action share equally its fruit in the next world.'

27. Oh most worthy men, Mīmāṁsakas! According to some (believers in God), there exists the Lord of sacrifices (the dispenser of the fruit of *karmas*). For here and in the next world, there are seen some rare regions full of moonlight (meant for enjoying pleasures), as well as bodies brilliant like moonlight (which are the mediums for enjoying worldly pleasures as a result of *karmas*).

28-29.* In the opinion of Svāyambhuva Manu, Uttānapāda, even of king Dhruva, the royal sage Priyavrata, my paternal grandfather Aṅga and such others, as well as that of god Brahmā and Lord Śiva, as also that of Prahlāda and even of Bali (whom Viṣṇu pushed down to subterranean regions), Gadādhara (Lord Viṣṇu) must necessarily be postulated as the dispenser of the fruit of *karmas*.

30.* With the exception of Mṛtyu's daughter's son (i.e. Vena) and others who are deluded about religion, and deserve to be pitied (lamented), others believe that there must be one common cause (i.e. God) who mainly dispenses the three *puruṣārthas* (viz. *Dharma*, *Artha* and *Kāma*), heavenly bliss and Liberation.

31. The relish and desire of serving the Lord's feet, increase with the passing of each day. Like the river (Gaṅgā) flowing out from his (Viṣṇu's) toe, this ever-increasing desire

* These verses refute the view of Pūrva-mīmāṁsā (and that of other heretic doctrines attributed to Indra's Māyā) about the non-existence of God. The *karma* doctrine must be accepted to explain the variety and inequality in the world. Karma, by itself, is inert (*jaḍa*) and deities like Indra, Varuṇa are themselves dependent (*paratantra*). For the dispensation of the fruits of *karma* and for explaining inequality in the world, we must postulate an independent God possessing powers of doing, undoing and changing differently : *ataḥ svātantryeṇa kartum akartum anyathā-kartuṁ samarthena Parameśvareṇa bhāvyam* /—ŚR.

to serve, washes off instantaneously the sins, accumulated through all the past lives, in the minds of people who are tormented with pains and afflictions.

32. A person who takes shelter at His feet, gets all the impurities in his mind washed off, develops special powers of non-attachment and self-realization, and does not return to *saṁsāra* (the cycle of births and deaths) which brings with it all miseries.

33. With faith in sure achievement of your goal (Liberation) according to your capacity and merit, and without any hypocrisy, you worship him only—whose lotus-like feet yield all your desires—with (i.e. dedicating to him) all duties pertaining to your vocations, and with all the powers of mind, speech and body (i.e. performance of meditation, prayer and worship), and with duties (of your respective caste and stage of life—*varṇa* and *āśrama*).

34.* Though, by nature, he is pure knowledge and consciousness, and devoid of any attribute, he manifests himself here as sacrifice possessing innumerable attributes (or essential requirements etc. of sacrifice), such as rice (and other sacrificial materials), qualities (of things such as whiteness, blackness), actions (such as threshing, winnowing of grains), words (*mantras* used in sacrifices), purpose (for which acts are meant), the

* (i) VC. : Verses 34 and 35 state that *karma* is essentially impure, inert (*jaḍa*) and *rājasa* (characterised by the *guṇa*, *rajas*). But if it is, devoutly dedicated to God, it is transformed into pure *sāttvic* nature, and yields fruit. Hence the author advises *karma* mixed with *bhakti* (devotion).

(ii) VJ.: This verse illustrates the term *Svakarmabhiḥ* in the previous verse (33). Nārāyaṇa described in *Ait. Up.* 1.1. is attained to by a righteous person who performs sacrifices of many kinds, and of many attributes (or requirements), such as materials (*puroḍāśa* etc.), qualifications viz. good heredity or birth from particular parents (of the sacrificer), actions i.e. Vedic incantations for gods like Indra, Agni, by the sacrificial priests, the interest of these gods in the sacrificer, and the characteristics of gods, e.g. Indra, holdidg a *Vajra* (or god Nārāyaṇa, the wielder of Sudarśana disc). By this sacrificial act, the mind gets purified, and the higher knowledge which terminates the *saṁsāra*, dawns on the sacrificer. It is by such deeds that Janaka and others attained final beatitude (B.G. 3.20).

(iii) SD : *Karmas* dedicated to God lead to God-realization. God is devoid of bad attributes (*aguṇa*) and possesses innumerable auspicious attributes (*aneka-guṇaḥ*).

intention or object (of performing the sacrifice), the efficacy (of sacrificial materials so used), and means (by which the sacrifice is known, e.g. *agniṣṭoma*).

35.* Just as fire in (a piece of) wood appears as possessing all the characteristics (e.g. size, shape etc.) of the (piece of) wood, the Omniscient Lord (though essentially the Highest Bliss itself) appears as intellect or consciousness (which identifies itself with the external objects) in the body, which is a product of *Pradhāna* (Prakṛti or Primordial Nature), *Kāla* (the Principle of Time which sets in commotion or agitation the *guṇas* of *Prakṛti*), *Vāsanā* (impressions unconsciously left on the mind by the past actions which give rise to pleasure or pain) and *dharma* (merit or demerit constituting the fate or *adṛṣṭa* of an individual) and manifests himself as the fruit of religious acts (e.g. a sacrifice).

---

* (i) The previous verse identifies God with sacrifice. In this verse, the fruit of sacrifice is stated to be the manifestation of the Lord—ŚR.

(ii) VR. : This verse identifies the Lord with Jīva, the enjoyer of the fruit of *karma*, as well as the fruit of the act itself (*atha karma-bhoktṛ-jīva-rūpatvaṁ tat-phala-rūpatvaṁ cāha*). The Lord is the innerdweller (*antaryāmin*) of *jīvas*. As such, through the medium of *jīva*, he gets the experiences of external objects in relation to body (due to *dharma-bhūta-jñāna*, the theory of attributive consciousness of the Self). The body is the product of *Pradhāna*, *Kāla*, *Vāsanā* and *adṛṣṭa*. The Lord is hence regarded as the fruit of sacrifice, (such as Svarga). But despite these experiences, the Lord is not contaminated by the blemishes etc. of the *karmas*, just as fire appears to share the characteristics (e.g. length, curvature etc.) of the burning wood, (and yet actually it shares none of them).

(iii) VJ. : Nārāyaṇa, the Omniscient Lord enters Jīva who, having renounced everything, retains a formal relation with Jīva. The pious persons (*jīvas*) know that Nārāyaṇa is the fruit of the righteous acts, and the dispenser of the fruits as well, according to *Brahma Sūtra—phalam ata upapatteḥ* (3.2.39 acc. to *Madhva bhāṣya*).

(iv) VC. : God realization is the fruit of *karmas* dedicated to God. After such dedication of *karmas*, God, out of his grace, manifests himself. But this degree of god-realization varies directly with the intensity of faith, devotion, knowledge in the dedicated one's acts to the Lord, even as the fire differs with the quality of the wood like *sandal*, *agaru*, *khadira*. (The first two give out sweet fragrance while the last does not.)

(v) GD. : This All-pervading Lord who enjoys the experience of happiness of intellect—due to contacts of the objects to the body, is also realized to be the fruit of acts (such as sacrifice etc.)

36.* Oh! How blessed I am that my subjects of firm vows, always worship Hari by performing their prescribed religious duties in this world—God Hari who is the preceptor (or Father) and the Supreme Lord of divinities who receive oblations in sacrifices. These (subjects) render me great favour.

37.** At no time may the martial lustre of the ruling princely families, born of great military power and effluence, dominate over the race of Vaiṣṇavas, the votaries of the unconquerable god (Viṣṇu) and that of the Brāhmanas who (though lacking in opulence) are resplendent on account of their forbearance, austere penance and learning.

38. Even Lord Hari, the most ancient person, the foremost among the greatest (of gods like Brahmā) is gracious unto Brāhmaṇas. It is by paying obeisance to their feet that he got Lakṣmī (the goddess of wealth) who never forsakes him and great glory that hallows the world.

39. The Absolutely independent Supreme God who resides in the hearts of all and to whom Brāhmaṇas are dear is certainly pleased by service rendered to them (Brāhmaṇas). Therefore, may the Brāhmaṇa race be served sincerely, and with all your hearts, by persons who are self-controlled, disciplined and devoted to the righteous duties (prescribed in the Bhāgavata way of life) pleasing to him.

40.*** By constant association with and service of the

---

* Pṛthu hereby confirms the religious tendencies of his subjects who with a firm resolve worship the Lord (ŚR. and others) but VJ. treats this as a compliment to Brāhmaṇas who as teachers and pupils are born from Hari's mouth, and always conduct their religious duties, and as such, they should be worshipped.

** (i) VR. : The verse indicates that Brāhmaṇas and Kṣatriyas should mutually respect and favour each other : 'May not the votaries of Viṣṇu, the Brāhmaṇa caste which stands resplendent with its forbearance, austerities and such other virtues, be provoked by the Princely houses puffed up with pride in their power and affluence'. VJ. endorses the same view.

(ii) VC. : For firm establishment of devotion to god, this verse prohibits the insubordination to Vaiṣṇavas and Brāhmaṇas.

***ŚR. : This verse removes the following doubt :

(i) If one always serves Brāhmanas, the performance of sacrifices—offering oblations to gods in sacrificial fires—will be neglected. This laxity in religious duties will not lead to purity of mind and the final beatitude which depends on it.

Brāhmaṇa (caste), the mind soon attains purity and serenity, (and consequently) the person, automatically (without any effort to get knowledge or Yogic practice) attains the highest bliss and final emancipation. Is there any better mouth of gods who receive oblations through fire than the Brāhmaṇa race? (The fruit of sacrifices and of knowledge is obtained by service of Brāhmaṇas).

41. The infinite Lord who is essentially knowledge incarnate and the indweller of all creatures, does not verily relish so much the oblations offered to the sacrificial fire which is devoid of consciousness, as certainly those offered with faith, into the mouths of the Brāhmaṇas in the names of adorable divinities (like Indra, Varuṇa) to be invoked in sacrifices, by the knowers of the Truth.

42. With a view to understanding the true import of the Vedas in which the universe is clearly reflected as in a clean mirror, they (Brāhmaṇas) bear (in their memories) the pure and eternal Vedas with faith, austere penance, auspicious conduct, control of speech unrelated to Vedic studies, self-control and concentration of mind. (Hence Brāhmaṇas are superior to fire due to their knowledge of Vedas).

43. I would like to bear on my crown the dust from the lotus-like feet of those (Brāhmaṇas), for, the sin of the man who wears this dust, immediately disappears, and all excellent attributes abide in him, Oh noble ones.

44. Affluence (in every respect) and accomplishments of desires seek to follow a man who is the receptacle of excellent qualities, looks upon character as his wealth, is full of gratitude, and resorts to wise elderly people. May the race of Brāhmaṇas, and that of cows, Lord Viṣṇu, along with his votaries (and followers) be gracious unto me."

(ii) VR.: By service of Brāhmaṇas, the deities to be propitiated by performance of sacrifices are served.

(iii) VJ.: The Brāhmaṇa caste is in constant contact with the Lord. By serving them, one obtains serenity of mind and immediately attains to the highest bliss, the final beatitude (Mokṣa). By service of Brāhmaṇas, one gets the fruit of performance of sacrifices, knowledge.

Maitreya said:

45. All *Pitṛs* (manes), gods and Brāhmaṇas felt highly pleased at heart with the king who spoke thus. Those pious souls expressed their approbation and praised him.

46. True is the Vedic text that a man attains to the higher worlds by means of a son. For the sinful Vena (Pṛthu's father) who was killed by Brahmanical curse, has crossed over the dark Hell (through Pṛthu).

47. And Hiraṇyakaśipu also was about to enter the dark hell for reviling the Lord, but crossed over it through the power of piety of Prahlāda (his son).

48. Oh foremost warrior, father of the earth ! May you live long for eternal years, as you cherish such devotion to Lord Viṣṇu, the sole ruler of all worlds.

49. Oh King of holy fame! With you as our ruler, we regard ourselves as having today Lord Viṣṇu as our ruler, as you reveal to us the narratives of Viṣṇu whose renown saves others from infernal regions and who is favourable to Brāhmaṇas.

50. Oh Lord! It is the nature of the great, whose hearts are full of pity, to love their subjects. Hence, it is no wonder that you exhort your dependants this way.

51. Oh King ! You have brought us today across the hell—we who, losing their insight due to our past deeds designated as Fate,—have been wandering in Saṁsāra.

52. Salutation to you, the most powerful Person with dominant Sāttvic attributes, who inspiring the Brāhmaṇa race by your force support the Kṣattriya race and *vice versa*, and inspiring both Brāhmaṇas and Kṣattriyas support the universe by virtue of your own power.

CHAPTER TWENTY-TWO

(Sanatkumāra's Seımon to Pṛthu)

Maitreya said :

1. While people were thus extolling Pṛthu of mighty prowess, there approached four sages, brilliant like the Sun.

2. Attended upon by his servants, the king saw those lords of sages descending from the heavens. They were recognized to be Sanaka and others by their lustre which absolved the worlds of sins.

3. Just as the lord of sense-organs (*jīva*) rushes forth to the objects of senses, Pṛthu, the son of Vena, along with the courtiers and attendants, immediately stood up (and went forth to the sages), as if to recover his vital breaths which sprang forth at their sight.[89]

4. When the sages accepted preliminary reception (*arghya*)[90] and occupied the seats (offered to them), the courteous king, who was hypnotised with their august presence, bowed down his head out of modesty, and worshipped them with due formalities.

5. (To purify himself) he sprinkled the hair on his head with (the sanctifying drops of) water with which he washed their feet. He, thereby, observed the course of conduct of the virtuous, to show respect to them.

6. The king was endowed with deep faith and self-discipline, and was full of joy. He addressed those elder brothers of Lord Śiva, who occupied seats of gold, and were looking like sacrificial fires in their respective altars.

Pṛthu said :

7. "Oh! What meritorious deeds I must have performed that I have the privilege of seeing you, the abodes of auspicious-

89. As ŚR. explains, it is the belief that when an elderly person comes, the vital breaths of young people immediately go forth to receive them. The youth catches back his vital breath, by immediately standing up to show respect, and by bowing down before the elders.

90. *arghya*—Water and other articles respectfully offered to gods or venerable persons. ASD. 51.

ness, who are very difficult to be perceived even by masters of *Yoga*.

8. What is very difficult to attain here and hereafter to a person unto whom Brāhmaṇas (like you), and gods Śiva and Viṣṇu along with their attendants are gracious!

9. Just as *Mahat* and other principles (or Brahmā, Manu and other makers of the world)—which are the causes of the universe, do not visualize the Omniscient *ātman* (Soul), people do not at all see you even though you roam over the world (to help them to attain their *puruṣārthas*).

10. Verily, blessed are those saintly householders who, though penniless, have in their houses materials for worship such as water, mat of (*darbha*) grass, accommodation (or floor), the master of the household and his dependants ready (for receiving) the worthies.

11. (Unwelcome) like the trees which are haunted by poisonous serpents, are the houses which, though fully furnished with all kinds of riches, are not hallowed by the holy water used for washing the feet of Viṣṇu's devotees.

12. Welcome is your arrival, Oh preeminent Brāhmaṇas who, determined to secure liberation, have been faithfully and with resolute mind, observing great vows (like lifelong celebacy) since your very childhood. (Or.....Brāhmaṇas whose course of observances of vows is followed by other ignorant persons desirous of Liberation).

13. Oh spiritual Masters! Is there any hope of good for us who regard the (achievement of) objects of senses as the goal of life and who, by our own deeds, have fallen into the *saṁsāra*, the bed of miseries.

14. The etiquette of enquiring after welfare of the guests is not applicable (or desirable) in the case of your honours, who are absorbed in the bliss of the *ātman* (Soul), and who are above the thoughts of welfare or otherwise.

15. You are the friends and well-wishers of the distressed. With full faith in you, I, therefore, wish to enquire of you how one can speedily achieve the *Summum bonum* (Mokṣa) in this *Saṁsāra* ?

16. It is obviously certain that the unborn Lord Nārāyaṇa who shines as the Soul of the self-knowing sages, and

who manifests himself (in the heart of the devotees), goes about in the world, in the form of Siddhas (like you), for showering his grace upon his votaries."

Maitreya said :

17. Having heard Pṛthu's beautifully worded, logical, deeply significant, brief, melodious speech, Sanatkumāra slightly smiled, and verily replied with pleasure.

Sanatkumāra said :

18. "With the welfare of all beings at your heart, a good enquiry has been made by Your Majesty, even though you know its answer, Oh great King! For such is the nature of the righteous.

19. The meeting of the righteous is highly approved by both (the speakers and the members of the audience) for, their dialogues and enquiries increase the happiness of all.

20. Oh King! Your honour has definitely a constant and abiding love for eulogizing the excellent attributes of the lotus-like feet of Lord Viṣṇu (the enemy of demon Madhu). Such constancy of love is difficult to be found in others. Such love (if generated) completely shakes off the sticky dirt of inner passions and desires in the heart (which is difficult to remove).

21. In the Śāstric texts which have made a thorough enquiry (about the good of beings), it has been positively decided that perfect non-attachment to things other than the Soul (e.g. one's own body), firm and constant love of attributeless Brahman and the Self—these constitute the means of the final beatitude of men.

22-25. Attachment for attributeless Brahman and non-attachment to the entire non-self material world (*un-ātman*), both effect and cause are easily generated by intense faith, performance of righteous duties towards the Lord,[91] the desire

91. *Bhagavad-dharma-caryayā*—In the case of all (even uninitiated ones): (i) By performing the five *mahāyajñas* and other round of religious duties for propitiating the Lord—VR.

(ii) By religious duties according to one's own caste and stage of life (*varṇāśrama*)—VJ.

(iii) GD. emphasizes the dedication of these religious duties to the Lord.

to know (the details about the Truth), firm faith in the spiritual path of *Yoga*,[92] meditation about the Lord of *Yoga*,[93] and constant listening to the holy stories of the Lord of hallowed renown; by cessation of desire to associate with the *tāmasa* people who take pleasure in wealth, and with the *rājasa* people who revel in the enjoyment of sensual pleasure, and by non-attachment to the filthy lucre and to sense-gratification which are highly valued by them, through love of seclusion[94] for enjoying the blissfulness of the Self (*ātman*) except on occasions when the drink of the nectar of Hari's excellent glories is available;[95] by practising non-violence, by following the course of conduct prescribed for the highest ascetic order called the *paramahaṁsas*, by drinking the highest form of nectar in the form of Lord Hari's stories, by eschewing desires and by observing rules of self-discipline called *yama* (abstention) and *niyama* (observance),[96] by refraining from slandering (and condemning other paths of God-realization prescribed in scriptures), by desirelessness, and by endurance of

92. *ādhyātmika-yoga-niṣṭhayā*—In the case of the initiated ones : With faith in the meditation as a part of adoration of the Lord as enunciated by the spiritual preceptor —VR.

93. Service of great Yogis like Kapila—GD.

94. *vivikta-rucyā*—Taste limited to food uncontaminated by the touch of other caste; by the delight and satisfaction one gets in the realisation of the Soul—VR.

95. By attending the congregations when Hari's *līlās* are sung—VC.

*By renunciation of objects of sensual enjoyment which are as if the pleasure-garden to the body and sense-organs, by non-acceptance of flower-garlands, cosmetics, women which are agreeable to them, by the sense of enoughness (*alaṁ-buddhi*) about carnal pleasures enjoyable by the body —VJ.

96. Patañjali gives the following list of *Yamas* and *niyamas* :

(i) *Yamas* (abstentions)—Abstinence from injuries, from falsehood, from theft, from incontinence and from acceptance of gifts (VSP. ii. 30).

(ii) *niyama* (observance) : Cleanliness, Contentment, Self-castigation, Study and Devotion to Īśvara (VSP. ii.32).

VJ. quotes from *Yājñavalkya Yoga Śāstra* 10 *Yamas* but as given in ASD 455 the lists include 10 or 12 Yamas according to different authors. ASD 290 quotes the following 10 *niyamās* :

Śaucam ijyā tapo dānaṁ svādhyāyo 'pastha-nigrahaḥ/
Vrata-mauno'pavāsaṁ ca snānaṁ ca niyamā daśa//

opposite states (such as heat and cold, pleasure and pain); by devotion to Hari that blossomed for the constantly glorifying Lord Hari's excellences which form the ornaments to the ears of his devotees through faith and deep devotion.

26.* When his attachment and delight in Brahman becomes firmly established, a man seeks a spiritual preceptor. Just as fire ignited from *araṇī* (a piece of wood of the Śamī tree used for kindling fire by friction) consumes its own source (the piece of wood from which it arose), the man, by force of his knowledge and non-attachment burns down his subtle body consisting of five subtle elements[97] and enveloping his Soul, in such a way as to render it unrevivable.

27**. When the screen or sheath (of the subtle body enveloping the Soul) which, till then intervened between the Super-Soul (*Paramātman*) and the Soul, is destroyed,[98] the

---

97. *Pañcātmakam* : (i) Consisting of five *kleśas* viz. *avidyā* (nescience), *ahaṁkāra* (ego), *rāga* (attachment), *dveṣa* (hatred) and *abhiniveśa* (instinctive clinging to worldly life and bodily enjoyment and the fear of being deprived of this—ASD.39) ŚR. and GD. VC. endorses this view while SD. supports the first interpretation given.

(ii) Consisting of five Kośas (sheaths) which lying one within the other make the body enshrining the Soul. They are : (1) *annamaya*, (2) *manomaya*, (3) *Prāṇamaya*, (4) *Vijñānamaya* and (5) *ānandamaya*. *Sarvopaniṣat-sāra*, however, gives *Prāṇamaya Kośa* the 2nd place before *Manomaya Kośa*.

* According to VR., firm fixation of love in Brahman leads to the grace of spiritual preceptor (and not vice versa). With the force of knowledge, renunciation and the love or delight in Brahman, a man burns down the seed of *karmas* (both merit and sin) which is the cause of the body (and *Saṁsāra*).

VJ. explains that the heart is an external *upādhi* (condition or attribute) and its burning does not harm and not the Soul or seed so enveloped by the external sheath.

98. What interrupted the knowledge of the relations between the Supreme Soul and the *jīva*.

** VJ. differs: When the 'heart' and its attributes e.g. knowledge, disappear, the *jīva* does not perceive any difference—within and without like a blind person. When in the Saṁsāra, there is a screen between the Supreme Lord and the *jīva*, there exists a semblance of knowledge like doubt, as in a dream. But when the subtle body is lost, the *jīva* also will disappear. And the Saṁsāra with its modicum of knowledge is preferable to the vanishing of the *jīva*. Who would then bother about Liberation (Mukti)?

person becomes freed from all the attributes[99] pertaining to the subtle body which has been burnt down. (Thenceforth) he does not perceive (his subjective states of pleasure, pain etc.) which are within him,[100] nor objects (e.g. a pot, a piece of cloth) which are external to him, just as a man awakened from a dream does not see the objects he had been perceiving in his dream.[101]

28. (It is in the state of wakefulness and dream) while this *upādhi* (conditioning) of mind continues, that man can perceive himself (the seer), objects of senses and what is beyond them both (viz. *ahaṁkāra* which establishes relation between them—the seer and the seen), and not otherwise (as in sleep).

29. (For example), if, anywhere, (reflecting) condition —*upādhi* like water,[102] mirror or such other condition is present, a man can see the difference between himself (the object of reflection) and the other thing (his own reflection) and not in the absence of the reflecting medium.

30. The mind of those who brood over objects of worldly enjoyment is distracted by their senses which are attracted to objects of worldly pleasure, and thereby the in-

---

99. The attributes like love, hate which deserve to be shed off (heya-guṇāḥ)—VR.

100. All internal blemishes, e.g. love, hate etc.—VR.

101. ŚR. explains: Just as a person who in a dream sees himself to be a king attended upon by an army of soldiers, sees no more his kingship and the army when the dream is over.

S.D.: In the dream the externals are friend, foe etc. and the internals are the honour, dishonour etc. meted out by them. These disappear when the dream is over.

102. *jalādau*—But VR. reads *jaḍādau* and interprets: *jaḍa* is the inert body. When the limiting condition like this inert body continues as interruption, the *jīva* experiences separateness from his Self and the Supreme Soul. But in Liberated stage this limitation of the body ceases, he sees no such difference between the two.

VC. thinks that this *upādhi* (limiting condition) is destroyed by knowledge and the *jīva*, by his powerful love of God enjoys the blissful nature of the Lord.

SD. thinks that the extreme difference between the Soul (*ātman*) and Brahman is due to ignorance. When real knowledge dawns, he realizes the Brahmahood in *ātman* (*ātmano Brahmātmakatvam paśyati*).

tellect loses its power of thinking and discrimination, just as the water from a pool is (imperceptibly) sucked up by the roots of a clump of grass.[103]

31. As a consequence of the loss of the reasoning capacity memory is lost. The loss of memory[104] results in loss of knowledge and wisdom. The wise people call this loss of wisdom as the covering of the Self through one's own Self.

32. In this world, there is no worse loss of his self-interest to a man than the loss of his own Self (through himself) for whose sake every other thing in the world becomes dear (lit. on whom depends the dearness of every other thing in the world).[105]

33. Constantly brooding over wealth and objects of senses leads to the loss of all *puruṣārthas* (goals to be achieved in life). Having thus lost knowledge of Brahman and worldly knowledge, he enters(= is born in) immobile *yonis*—births e.g. a vegetable).

34. A person who desires to cross the dense darkness (of *Saṁsāra*), should not entertain attachment to anything whatever. For that attachment is extremely harmful to *Dharma*, *Artha*, *Kāma* and *Mokṣa* (the four *puruṣārthas*).

35. Even among these objectives of life, *Mokṣa* (Liberation) is acknowledged as the highest goal of life. For, the remaining goals of life, are always subject to the fear of death.

36. For the *jīvas* of the higher order (like Brahmā) and lower order like us who are created after the equilibrium of the three *guṇas* of *Prakṛti* was disturbed (at the time of creation), there is no security and happiness, as all their blessings and hopes (of attaining their objectives) are ruined by the All-powerful Time.*

---

103. *stamba*—The canal or outlet from a tank—VJ.

104. *bhraśyatyanu smṛtiś cittam* / VR. connects the words *anu-smṛtis* and interprets it as 'the sense of the proper time for *upāsanā* or *Yoga* (*anusmṛtir upāsanam, Yoga-kālānusandhānam* /)

105. Cf. *ātmanas tu kāmāya sarvam priyam bhavati* /

—*Bṛhad. Upa.*4.5.6.

* After verse 36, VJ. gives the commentary on 3 verses which are not noted by other commentators. The Bhāgavata Vidyā Peeth, Ahmedabad edition does not give the text of those verses but only the commentary. Hence they are not included here.

37. Therefore, Oh King, you realize that you are (the same as) the Lord (the only existing reality)—the Lord who manifests himself and directly shines everywhere in the Self as *antaryāmin* (the inner controller) in the hearts of all mobile and immobile *jīvas* who are covered (i.e. invested) with body, sense-organs, vital airs, intellect and ego (*ahaṁkāra*).

38.* I take shelter with the Supreme Soul who is eternally free, extremely pure, highly enlightened, Reality itself and who has overpowered the *Prakṛti* (primordial nature) contaminated by Karmas (of various *jīvas*), and in whom appears this universe of superior and inferior things (or of cause and effect) as Māyā, which disappears due to (the dawn of) discriminating wisdom like (the dispelling of) the misapprehension of a garland of flowers as a serpent.

39.** You (therefore) take resort to Lord Vāsudeva as your asylum[106]—Lord Vāsudeva, through devotion (and concentration) on the splendour[107] of petal like toes of whose lotus-feet the saintly devotees so easily cut the knot of the egotism (*ahaṁkāra*) formed at the heart by *karmas*, that even recluses and ascetics who have cleared their mind[108] (of all worldly thoughts and kept it vacant) and have controlled their senses, are unable to do so.

---

* VR. emphasizes the point that the Lord is not directly affected by Karmas, ignorance etc., but it is through the *jīva* (*kṣetrajña*) which is his body (as he is the *antaryāmin*) that he experiences these.

106. *araṇam*. VD. treats this as a pun : *a-raṇam* who is beyond fight; If you do not resort to Vāsudeva, you will have to battle with your sense-organs which by their brute majority will defeat you.

107. *vilāsa*—beauty which increases every moment—VC., VD.

108. *rikta-matayaḥ*—Whose minds have no support of the Lord—GD.

** (i) The above verses expound the path of knowledge which is difficult. Hence these two (39 and 40) verses describe *bhakti* (the path of devotion)—ŚR., VC.

(ii) VR. treats the last two lines of the verse as qualifying the saintly devotees who meditate on nothing else but the Lord and who control themselves.

(iii) VC.—*Vilāsa-bhaktyā*—through the devotion to the ever-increasing beauty of petal-like toes of the lotus feet of Vāsudeva and *bhakti* i.e. devotion, is both the means and the end.

OR : Through worshipping in a rich way; or
Trough meditation over or memory of his toes.

40. There is a great trouble here to those who have not resorted to the Lord as a boat for crossing the ocean of *saṁsāra* which is infested with crocodiles in the form of sixfold [passions viz. *kāma* (desire), *krodha* (anger), *lobha* (avarice), *mada* (conceit), *moha* (delusion), *matsara* (jealousy) or the mind and five senses]. For they desire to cross it (*saṁsāra*) by painful means (e.g. practice of Yoga). You should therefore make the adorable feet of Lord Hari as a boat and reach the other end of this impassable ocean of *saṁsāra* easily without any difficulty."

Maitreya said :

41. The king to whom the real nature of *ātman* (Soul) was thus expounded by Sanatkumāra, the son of god Brahmā, the knower of Brahman, praised him appropriately and enquired.

The king said :

42. Oh venerable Brāhmaṇa! Lord Hari is compassionate to the afflicted. He had formerly conferred his grace upon me. You all have now come to consummate it.

43. Your venerable Selves, merciful as you are, you have translated into reality the blessing in its entirety. Everything that I possess, including my own self, belongs to the saintly souls who have graciously returned it to me as a favour. What can I give to you?

44. My life, wife, sons, houses with all their furnishings, kingdom, army, earth, treasury—everything is offered to you although it already belongs to you.

45. And a person who is well-versed in Vedas and Śāstras really deserves to command an army, (to rule over) a kingdom, to direct military operations and to govern all the world.

The duties pertaining to God being the reverse of *saṁsāra*, the knot of *ahaṁkāra* formed by *karmas* is very easily cut asunder, while the recluses control their senses—an impossible task, an evidence of their dull-wittedness. It it easy for the righteous *Bhaktas* to destroy *ahaṁkāra* but it is not possible for *sannyāsins* to achieve, for they being vacant-minded are 'intellectless' while the *bhaktas* have their mind filled with God. Bhaktas enjoy the beauty etc. of God to the full.

46. A Brāhmaṇa eats his own food, wears the clothes belonging to him and offers his own belongings. It is through his (Brāhmaṇa's) grace that Kṣattriyas and others enjoy their own food.

47. You are past-masters in the Vedic lores. In your discourse about *ātman* (and other spiritual matters), you have succinctly and definitely explained to us the nature of the Lord as above. Abounding in mercy as you are, may you be forever pleased with your action of redeeming the afflicted. Who can return your obligations except by folding his palms in reverence or (become an object of ridicule in his supposed attempts to repay your kindness)."

Maitreya said :

48. Those masters of *ātma-yoga* (the Yogic path of self-realization) were worshipped by the first monarch Pṛthu. They appreciated his righteous character and rose up to the heavens while people were looking on (agape).

49. Pṛthu (the son of Vena), the foremost among great Souls, became firmly established in his Soul due to concentration achieved by their instruction in the spiritual lore. He felt as if[109] he had achieved all his desires in life.

50. It was as an offering to Brahman that he performed all his actions at the proper time, at the proper place, to the best of his ability, according to proper formalities, according to his means and property.

51. Thus with concentrated mind, he consigned the fruit (of his deeds) to Brahman. He remained unattached by regarding his Self as distinct and beyond Prakṛti, a mere witness to all actions.

52. Just as the Sun (remains unattached and unsoiled by the objects on which it shines), the king, though leading the life of a householder and endowed with imperial majesty and splendour, remained free from egotism (*ahaṁkāra*), and hence unattached to the objects of the senses.

53-56. While he was, in this way, doing his prescribed duties properly and in time, with his heart fixed on his *ātman*

109. *iva*—Being a true devotee, his real satisfaction was in devotion. This is implied by *iva*—VD.

(Self), he begot through his queen Arcis five sons who were resembling and agreeable to him. They were Vijitāśva, Dhūmrakeśa, Haryakṣa, Draviṇa and Vṛka. But Pṛthu was a part of Lord Viṣṇu. For the protection of the created world, only Pṛthu combined in him (and manifested) powers of all *lokapālas* (protectors of worlds like Indra, Varuṇa), from time to time as was necessary (according to the exigency of the situation). He bore significantly the title *Rājā* by delighting his subjects with his thoughts, words and deeds, and pleasing Soma-like (*saumya*) qualities as if he was another king Soma (the Moon or the Soma—juice—which has *rājā* as its epithet). Like the Sun (evaporating water from the earth and collecting it in clouds), he levied taxes from the world only to give it back to the people (for their welfare) and governed them (as the Sun gives light and heat to them).

57. By his majestic splendour he was unassailable like Agni (Fire-god); he was unconquerable like the great Indra; in forebearance he was like the earth; he was like the heaven (*Svarga*) in granting desired objects to his subjects.

58. Like the rain-god he showered to the satisfaction (of his subjects) all that they desired; like the (unfathomable) sea, he was too deep to be understood; in his firmness he was like Meru, the king of mountains.

59. He was comparable to Yama-dharma, in dispensing punishment; in marvellousness (in scenes, findings of ores etc.), he was like the Himālayas. He had rich treasure like Kubera (The god of wealth). He possessed immense undivulged treasures like Varuṇa.

60. In physical strength, force and energy and in his ability to move anywhere he was like Vāyu. In his irresistibility he was comparable to god Śiva.

61. He was a compeer of the god of Love in beauty; in spiritedness he was like a lion; in fatherly affectionateness he was like Manu; while in his lordship over man, he was like god Brahmā.

62. He was Bṛhaspati in his knowledge of Vedas, while in self-control he was like Lord Hari himself. While he was comparable to himself only in his devotion to cows, Brāhmaṇas, preceptor, votaries of Hari and in qualities like modesty, humility, good nature and work for the benefit of others.

63. As his glory was loudly sung by people everywhere in the three worlds, he reached the ears of women just as Rāma entered the ears of the saintly people.

CHAPTER TWENTY-THREE

Pṛthu's penance and ascension to Heaven

Maitreya said :

1-3. The self-controlled son of Vena, (Pṛthu), the protector of subjects, had made the arrangement of fostering his creation, (viz. by founding of agriculture, and of human habitation like cities, villages etc.). He provided for the livelihood of the mobile and immobile creatures. He supported the practice of religion (*dharma*) by pious people. He carried out the mission of the Lord for which he was created in this world. One day, finding himself to have grown very old, he entrusted to his sons his daugther-like earth which was as if crying due to separation from him. Unattended by any one (servant), he retired to the penance-forest along with his queen while the subjects became depressed in mind and disspirited.

4. Without any interruption in the observance of rules of self-discipline, there too he began to practice a course of austere penance, highly approved by *Vānaprasthas* with the same zeal and determination which he showed formerly in the conquest of the world.

5. He lived upon bulbous and ordinary roots and fruits, and occasionally on dry leaves. For some fortnights, he took water only, and thereafter, he subsisted on air (only).

6. In the summer, the warrior-sage practised *pañcāgni sādhana* (in which one has to sit in the Sun and in the midst of four burning fires in four directions around). In the rainy season, he exposed himself to the downpour of rain. In the winter he stood immersed in cold water upto the neck and slept on the bare-ground (all through the year).

7. He practised endurance, controlled his speech and sense-organs, he observed celibacy and mastered *prāṇāyāma*

(breath-control). He practised the most austere type of penance with a desire to propitiate Lord Kṛṣṇa.

8. Due to the practice of that austere penance, which gradually reached perfection, his balance of Karmas became exhausted and he became pure in mind. By means of *Prāṇāyāma* (breath-control), all the six passions were completely subdued and the bondage (of *vāsanā*) was cut asunder.

9. Pṛthu, that prominent person, worshipped the Supreme Man by that very highest Yoga which venerable Sanatakumāra explained to him as the best path to *ātman*.

10. As the righteous king was performing the duties sacred to the Lord and was unceasingly exerting himself with faith, he developed complete devotion to the glorious Brahmaṅ exclusively.

11. His (Pṛthu's) mind became purely Sāttvic (without any admixture of other guṇas like *rajas* and *tamas*) through adoration and service of the Lord. He attained to knowledge combined with renunciation—knowledge which became sharpened by his devotion which went on increasing continuously through constant remembrance and comprehensive realization of the Lord's greatness. It is with such knowledge that he tore off the sheath called *jīva*[110]—the knot of egotism (*ahaṁkāra*) in the heart—which is the basis of doubts and misapprehensions.

12. When his concept of self-body identification was dispelled and he realized the real nature of his Soul, he became desireless and disinterested even in the mystic *yogic* powers (like *aṇimā*, *laghimā* etc.) that were acquired by him. He gave up the attempt to attain the knowledge wherewith he

---

110. *Jīvakośa*—the subtle body (*liṅga śarīra*) with its internal and external organ —VJ.

VC.: To Pṛthu, whose mind became purely *Sāttvic* by service of the Lord, the knowledge of the science of Brahman (*Brahma vidyā*) combined with non-attachment, manifested itself. Real votaries of God are so much attracted by the sweetness of *Bhakti* that they discard *Brahma vidyā* which automatically comes to them, and they destroy without any effort their subtle body (*liṅga deha*) through their intense devotion. It was the impatience of Pṛthu to go to Lord's region to serve him directly that he accepted *Brahma vidyā* to destroy his *upādhi* (limiting condition) of *jīva kośa*.

tore off his sheath (called *jīva* or egotism which is source of doubt). For so long even a recluse (exerting on the path of *Yoga*) does not feel devotion and attachment for the stories of Lord Kṛṣṇa, he will not cease to be attracted by the Yogic discipline (and mystic powers attained by *Yoga*).

13. Thus at the time of the end of his life,[111] the great hero concentrated his mind firmly in the Supreme Soul and stabilising himself in Brahman,[112] he cast off his mortal coil.

14. He closely pressed both his heels on his anus. He slowly forced up his vital airs (from the *mūlādhāra cakra*).[113] He held vital airs up (progressively) at the navel and then at heart, chest, the throat and the head, i.e. the place between the eyebrows, (i.e. through the following *cakras* or mystical plexuses : *Maṇipūra, manas* or Solar plexus, *anāhata, viśuddha* and *ājñā*).[114]

15-16. By degrees he conducted up his breath upto the crown of his head and made it occupy *Brahma-randhra* (the aperture in the crown of the head through which the Soul escapes on its leaving the body). Freeing himself from all desires, he merged the wind element in the body with the outer Vāyu element, the earth element (solidity in the body) with the Pṛthvī (earth) element, the vacuum (in the appertures constituting sense-organ) with the cosmic element *ākāśa* (ether) and the liquid in the body with the element water—each in its own source. (For his own knowledge) he then contemplated the merger of cosmic elements (as follows:)—earth into water, water into fire, fire into wind and wind into the cosmic *ākāśa* (which is the product of *Tāmasa ahaṁkāra*—ego of *Tāmasa* type). This process is called *Laya-cintana* contemplation of (the happening of) the process of absorption.

---

111. *kāle*—When the fund of his *karmas*—Prārabdha—was exhausted —VR., VJ.

112. *Brahmabhūtaḥ*—(i) He became like Brahman by the manifestation f eight attributes—VR.

(ii) He realised that he depended on Brahman—VJ.

113. A mystical plexus situated between the anus and the organ of generation.

114. For details about these *cakras* vide : Sir John Woodroff—*Serpent Power*; and Leadbeater—*The Chakras*.

17.* He absorbed the mind (implying presiding deities as well) into the senses,[115] the senses into the subtle elements from which they severally emerged. These (the ether, the senses and mind merged into subtle elements as described above) he carried higher still and he contemplated the above objects along with *ahaṁkāra* (I-ness) as merged in the Mahat *tattva* (the principle of cosmic intelligence).

18.** He (Pṛthu) merged the Mahat, the ground of all *guṇas* (evolutes) into *jīva* conditioned by Māyā. By the power of his knowledge and renunciation, Pṛthu—still a *jīva* conditioned by Māyā—became established in the pure Brahmahood and cast off the conditioning Māyā attached to the Self.

19. His wife, the great queen Arcis, though too delicate to touch the bare ground with her feet, followed him to the penance-forest.

20. Though she (queen Arcis). became extremely emaciated due to her intense devotion in participating in the austere observances (such as sleeping on the bare ground) and religious duties of her husband, by rendering personal services

---

115. For the mind is drawn by the senses in the world of varied experiences and hence it is said to be absorbed in them.

* VJ. interprets this according to the general law of merger (*laya*) viz. the effects are to be absorbed into the cause. Thus the senses are merged into the *Taijasa-ahaṁkāra*. Its presiding deities in those of the presiding deities of *Vaikārika ahaṁkāra* and their bodies into the *Vaikārika ahaṁkāra*. The elements *Pṛthvī* etc. along with their qualities like smell, touch etc. are absorbed in the *Tāmasa ahaṁkāra* (*bhūtādi*). These three types of *ahaṁkāras* (along with senses etc.) merge into the *Mahattattva* (Principle of cosmic intelligence). And Rudra, the presiding deity of *ahaṁkāra*, is absorbed into god Brahmā, who presides over the *Mahat*.

** VR: (The last two lines): Pṛthu who was practically free from the effects of the *karmas*, realised the Supreme Being in himself. By dint of his knowledge and renunciation, he became free from the remaining *karmas*. He thus became liberated, established in his own essential nature.

VJ. refutes the idea of Liberation of *advaitins*. The process of Pṛthu's liberation was as follows: Pṛthu merged Brahmā, the presiding deity of the *Mahat* into Lakṣmī and the principle *Mahat* into unintelligent Prakṛti. Lakṣmī with Prakṛti was absorbed into Hari. By force of his knowledge and dispassionateness, Pṛthu did this and attained the *Sāyujja* form of Liberation.

VC. : Pṛthu became a Pārṣada (attendant) of the Lord in Vaikuṇṭha.

GD. : Pṛthu was able to abandon his subtle body (*Liṅga-śarīra*).

to him and by leading the sage's way of life (such as subsisting on roots, fruits etc.). She did not feel any affliction, as she was satisfied with the loving regard and affectionate touch of her beloved husband's hand.

21. Having observed that the body of the protector of the earth, her own beloved husband, became completely devoid of consciousness, life etc., the pious lady wept for a while and got it placed on the funeral pyre on the ridge of the mountain.

22. She bathed in the waters of the river, performed the prescribed rites. Having given libations of water to the departed Soul of her husband, the performer of noble deeds, she paid obeisance to the celestial gods who had assembled there to witness her self-immolation, she went round the fire three times and meditating on the feet of her husband, entered the burning funeral pyre.

23. Seeing the chaste lady perform self-immolation after her husband, Pṛthu, the great hero, thousands of goddesses who were competent to confer boons, began to praise her, along with their consorts.

24. They showered flowers on that peak of the mount Mandara. While the celestial trumpets were blowing, they spoke (in praise of her) to each other.

Goddesses said :

25. "Oh ! What a blessed wife is this who, with all her heart, served her husband, the king of kings, just as Lakṣmī does to the Lord of Sacrifices (Nārāyaṇa).

26. Following her husband Pṛthu, this chaste lady really proceeds to regions higher than ours. Look ! Arcis is going up beyond us, by virtue of her noble deed incomprehensible to the unrighteous.

27. What is verily difficult to be achieved by those mortals who, though the span of their life on the earth is uncertain, attain to spiritual knowledge (of actionlessness) leading to the region of the Lord (Liberation).

28. He is definitely deceived—a veritable enemy of his own Self who after great difficulty attains to the life as a human being, capable of leading to Liberation (Mokṣa), is attached to objects of pleasure."

Maitreya said :

29. While the heavenly damsels (goddesses) were praising her, Arcis (the queen of Pṛthu) reached the region of her husband—the region which Pṛthu (the son of Vena) whose mind was concentrated on Lord Viṣṇu (Acyuta) and who was the foremost amongst those who realized the Soul, attained.

30. Of such glory and prowess was king Pṛthu, the Suprememost mighty monarch. I have described to you the history of the king of noble deeds.

31. He who, with faithful and attentive mind, reads, listens to or recounts this extremely holy life of Pṛthu, would attain to the region of Pṛthu.

32. By reading this, a Brāhmaṇa would become preeminent in Brahmanic lore, a Kṣattriya, the ruler of the world, a Vaiśya, the leader of his guild and a Śūdra (listening to it) would attain the most preeminent position (like a man of Sūta community).

33-34. After hearing this account thrice with faith and reverence, a man or a woman, if devoid of issue, becomes blessed with the best progeny, and if penniless, he/she becomes the wealthiest; An obscure person, attains good renown; a dull-witted one would become a scholar; this is a means of securing prosperity to men, averting evils and inauspiciousness.

35. It blesses with wealth, glory, longevity, heavenly blessings and removes the impurities of the Kali-age. Those who aspire after full achievement of the four *puruṣārthas* (goals of life) viz. Dharma (righteousness), Artha (wealth,) Kāma (enjoyment of life) and Mokṣa (Liberation), should regularly and with faith listen to this story of Pṛthu which is the best means of securing *puruṣārthas*.

36. A king intending to undertake the conquest of the world starts his expedition after listening to this, the kings against whom he marches will receive him with tributes as was done to Pṛthu.

37. Even though one gets auspicious fruits mentioned above from listening to Pṛthu's life, one who gives up all desires and bears pure, motiveless devotions to the Lord, should listen, narrate and read this holy life of Pṛthu, the son of Vena.

38. Oh Vidura (the son of Vicitravīrya), the story of Pṛthu which reveals the greatness of the Venerable Lord has been narrated to you. A mortal who devotes his mind to it, attains to the goal achieved by Pṛthu.

39. A person who devoutly listens to or narrates the story of Pṛthu everyday, becomes free from attachment and develops intense love and devotion to the Lord whose feet serve as a boat to cross the sea of worldly existence (*saṁsāra*).

CHAPTER TWENTY-FOUR

(*Pṛthu's Descendants and the Hymn of Rudra**)

Maitreya said :

1. Vijitāśva, the son of Pṛthu, was an emperor of great renown. He was affectionate to his brothers. He distributed to each of his younger brothers each direction (of his kingdom to rule).

2. The sovereign gave the eastern quarter to Haryakṣa; assigned the southern direction to Dhūmrakeśa; he appointed

* This chapter gives the following genealogy of Pṛthu.

Pṛthu

- Vijitāśva alias Antardhāna
  - Havirdhāna
    - Barhiṣad or Prācīnabarhis
      - Pracetas (10 sons of the same name).
    - Gaya
    - Śukla
    - Kṛṣṇa
    - Satya
    - Jita-vrata
  - Pāvaka
  - Pavamāna
  - Śuci
- Haryakṣa
- Dhūmrakeśa
- Vṛka
- Draviṇa

V.P. confirms this genealogy except about the number of Pṛthu's sons According to V.P. 1.14.1, Pṛthu had only two sons Antardhāna and Vādin. Vṛja and Ajina instead of Satya and Jita-vrata are the brothers of Prācīnabarhis (V.P. 1.14.2). The hymn of Rudra is a new contribution in the Bh.P. and it is not in V.P.

(his) brother named Vṛka to the western quarter, and gave the fourth direction (the North) to Draviṇa.

3. Vijatāśva obtained from Indra the power of making invisible movements and came to be designated as Antardhāna. He had three sons by (his queen) Śikhaṇḍinī who were highly beloved by all.

4. They were former firegods by name Pāvaka, Pavamāna and Śuci who were born (as human beings) by the curse of Vasiṣṭha, and who subsequently regained their godly status by practice of Yoga.

5. Antardhāna who did not kill Indra even though he knew that Indra stole the sacrificial horse,[116] got Havirdhāna (a son) by his (another wife) Nabhasvatī.

6. Looking upon kingly duties, such as exacting tributes, inflicting punishment, levying taxes, as harsh and ruthless, he relinquished them under the pretext of undertaking a long sacrificial session.

7. Even there (while engaged in the sacrificial session), the king who realized his Self, worshipped the Supreme Soul who is perfect and annihilates the afflictions of his devotees, and attained to His region, by pure and perfect meditation.

8. From Havirdhāna, (his queen) Havirdhānī begot six sons viz., Barhiṣad, Gaya, Śukla, Kṛṣṇa, Satya and Jitavrata.

9. Oh descendant Kuru (Vidura)! Barhiṣad, the eldest son of Havirdhāna, the most fortunate lord of men (*Prajā-pati*) was a pastmaster in sacrificial lore as well as in the science and practice of Yoga.

10. (He was called Prācīnabarhis as) the surface of the whole earth was covered over with Kuśa grass with their ends pointing to the east, for he went on performing sacrifices (successively) one after another, each close to the place reserved (used) for the previous sacrifice.

11. On the advice of Brahmā, the god of gods, he married Śatadruti, the daughter of the presiding deity of Seas. She was still a girl but beautiful in every part of the body. In the marriage ceremony, when she went round the fire, beauti-

116. Vide Supra IV. 19-20.

fully decorated with ornaments, the firegod (himself) became enamoured of her, as he did in the case of Śukī.[117]

12. Gods, demons, celestial singers (Gandharvas), sages, Siddhas (a tribe of demigods), men and serpents were captivated by the young married girl, with the melodious jingling of her anklets ringing in all directions (while she walked).

13. Prācīnabarhis had ten sons called Pracetas, from Śatadruti. All of them bore the same name, observed the same vows and were equally well-versed in religion (or Dharmaśāstra).

14-15. When ordered by their father to beget children, they entered the ocean to perform penance. They propitiated the Lord of Penances (Hari), by undergoing austere penance for ten thousand years. With perfect self-control, they (all the while) meditated on and worshipped him, repeating (to themselves) what was imparted to them by Lord Śiva, whom they saw (revealed to them) on the way, conferring his grace on them.

Vidura said :

16. Please narrate to us, Oh Brāhmaṇa, how the meeting between the Pracetasas and Lord Śiva took place on the road, and tell us what advice of deep import was he pleased to impart to them (out of his grace).

17 Sages, freeing themselves from all attachments have been meditating on Lord Śiva as their coveted goal. Hence contact with the Lord is very difficult, for embodied beings in this world, Oh Brāhmaṇa sage.

18. Though finding delight in his Self, Venerable Lord Śiva accompanied with his terrible Śakti (power of destruc-

117. v.l. *stukīm*—A slender continuous stream of ghee poured into the fire.

Śukī—According to all commentators, except VJ., this refers to the episode when the seven Sages were conducting a sacrificial session, Fire-god was overcome with passion at the sight of their wife. Svāhā, the wife of Agni (Fire-god) assumed the form of that lady and satisfied him. She then assumed the form of a female parrot (*Śukī*) and deposited his semen in a clump of grass. VJ. thinks that Śukī was a princess who was abducted by the Fire-god through lust, while she was going round the fire. In the case of Śatadruti, he could not physically do so. Hence he loved her on the mental plane only.

tion) moves about in the world for the proper maintenance of the world-order.

Maitreya said :

19. Receiving their father's command reverentially (lit. on their heads), the pious Pracetasas set their minds zealously on practising penance and proceeded towards the West.

20. They saw a very big lake, slightly smaller than the sea in expanse. It was crystal-clean like the mind of the noble Souls, and abounded in happy acquatic beings.

21. It was (as it were) a rich mine of blue and red lilis, lotuses that blossom by night, by day and by twilight and blue lotuses (*indīvara*). It was resounded with the warblings and notes of (waterbirds like) swans, cranes, ruddy geese and ducks (Kāraṇḍava).

22. It was surrounded by lush growth of trees and creepers which were thrilled with[118] the sweet musical humming of intoxicated bees. It presented (as if) a festive occasion (celebrated) by the winds, by scattering of the pollen from lotuses, in all directions.

23. The Princes were wonderstruck to listen to the celestial, classical[119] vocal music of Gandharvas ravishing the mind—music which followed[120] the playing of instrumental music of tabors (*mṛdaṅga*) and Paṇava.

24-25. At that very moment, they noticed Śiva, the foremost among gods, coming out of that lake, along with his attendants. His complexion was like a mass of red-hot gold. His throat was blue-coloured. He had three eyes. His smiling countenance showed his inclination to shower his grace (on his devotees). His glory was being sung by the followers of gods (like Gandharvas and Kinnaras). As curiosity was

---

118. VR. thinks that the ends of creepers intertwining trees were the hair standing on their ends in the case of the trees which heard the music. While VC. and GD. regard the thick clusters of buds on them as the result of the thrill of the music.

119. *mārga* and *deśī* are styles of singing. *mārga* is the classical style (cf. Vālmīki Rāmāyaṇa I.4.36 *agāyatāṁ mārgavidhānasaṁpadā*).

120. v.l. *mṛdaṅga-paṇavādyavat*—accompanied by playing on *mṛdaṅga* and *paṇava*.

aroused in them, the Princess bowed down to him as soon as they saw him.

26. The Venerable Lord (Śiva) who removes the afflictions of his devotees (seeking his shelter), and who loves righteousness, was pleased with those (Princes) who were experts in religion, possessed high moral characters and who were happy (to see him). He spoke to them.

Śrī Rudra said :

27. You are the sons of Vediṣad (Barhiṣad). I know what you intend to do. May you be blessed. (It is) for conferring grace on you that I have revealed myself to you.

28. He is certainly dear to Me, who, completely submitting himself, has directly resorted to Venerable Lord Vāsudeva who is beyond the subtle Prakṛti consisting of the three attributes (*Sattva*, *rajas* and *tamas*) and also the entity called *jīva*.[121]

29.* A person conscientiously and firmly devoted to his own righteous duties, attains to the position of god Brahmā after hundred births, and reaches me if possessed of still more excessive merits. But a votary of Lord Viṣṇu, after the end of this mundane body, attains to the region of Lord Viṣṇu which is beyond *saṁsāra*, just as we (Rudra and other divinities) do after the termination of our office (and dissolution of our subtle bodies).

30. You, votaries of the Venerable Lord (Viṣṇu), are as dear to me as the Lord himself. And to the devotees of the Lord, no body else than me, is more dear anywhere.

31.** This is a sacred and highly auspicious hymn leading to the Final Beatitude. This should be constantly repeated

121. : He is superior to the principle known as Lakṣmī designated here as *jīva* and *tamas*.

*VJ. differs :...after enjoyment of the status or region of Brahmā, the *jīva* goes to Lakṣmī which is not subject to change. It is in the *Pralaya* stage that all come to the Omniscient Lord.

** Please listen to what I tell you. It should constantly be repeated (to oneself). It explains how the Supreme Soul is distinct from Prakṛti and Puruṣa. Hence it is sacred and auspicious inasmuch as it secures the *Puruṣārthas* (Dharma, Artha, Kāma) and is a means to Liberation. Hence I am narrating it to you—VR.

secretly (in strict privacy). I shall now relate it to you. Please listen (attentively)

Maitreya said :

32. Lord Śiva whose heart is full of compassion and who is fully devoted to Nārāyaṇa, spoke (the following words) to the Princes who were standing with folded palms before him.

33. "Victory to you, Oh Lord! Your victory is for the attainment of the blessedness of the Self, by the pre-eminent ones among those who have realized the Soul. May I too (thereby) attain to the state of blessedness! You eternally abide in the highest blissful nature. Hence I bow to you, Supreme Soul who is immanent in all.

34.* Salutation to the Lord who has a lotus (constituting the universe) springing up in his navel; who is the controller (lit. Soul) of the subtle elements (*tanmātras*) and the sense-organs; who is (the first and foremost *Vyūha* or manifestation of the Lord called) Vāsudeva,[122] (the presiding principle or the ruler of *citta*—Reason); who is absolutely tranquil, self-refulgent, the unchangeable Supreme Soul abiding in (and controlling) all beings.

35.** Obeisance to Saṅkarṣaṇa (the second *Vyūha*, the presiding deity of *ahaṁkāra* or ego) who is unmanifest, infinite, the destroyer of the universe (by fire emanating from his

* VC : Oh Lord with a lotus in his navel; My physical body is born of Brahmā who was created from the lotus springing up from your navel. Make me inclined to your devotion. Oh Vāsudeva, the presiding deity of *citta* (mind), make my mind serene and tranquil. Fill it with your light and urge it on to your devotion.

122. *Vāsudevāya*—To the Principle that abides in all and yet is unsoiled by their defects.

** VR: (I) bow to Saṅkarṣaṇa who withdraws within himself the universe; Who consumes the world by fire blowing out of his mouth; who is too subtle to be distinguished by name and form but who is unmanifest and hence is himself unwithdrawable. Salute to Pradyumna (the 3rd *Vyūha*-Manifestation of the Lord), who enlightens the world by instruction in the *Śāstra* called *Vedas* which teach the means to all the Puruṣārthas (objectives in human life); who controls all the beings by abiding in them simultaneously.

mouth at the time of *Pralaya*—the dissolution of the universe); (I) bow to Pradyumna (the third *Vyūha*) who awakens the universe (to the highest knowledge),[123] and who presides over Buddhi (intelligence).

36.* I pay my respects again and again to (the fourth *Vyūha*) Aniruddha who is the ruler of the mind which controls the sense-organs (e.g. the eye, the ear etc.).[124] I bow to him (i.e. You) who as the Sun god[125] pervades the universe with his light[126] and who is unaffected by increase and decrease.[127]

37.** I bow to him who is the gateway to the heaven as well as to the Liberation (Mokṣa); who ever abides in pure hearts.[128] I pay obeisance to the Fire-god (whose energy is gold), who is the means of performing sacrificial activities (for which services of four sacrificial priests, viz., *Hotā*, *Adhvaryu*, *Udgātā* and *Brahmā* are essential) and who promotes the continuity of the (tradition of the) sacrifice.[129]

---

123. *Viśva-prabodhāya*—Who is perfect in wisdom or who 'awakens' the universe—VJ.

124. *Hṛṣikeśendriyātmane*—Master of sense-organs and whatever belongs to Indra who presides over the mind and senses—VJ.

125. *paramahaṁsāya* : (i) One who destroys from himself as well from his devotees the impurities of Karmas whether merit or sin—VR.

(ii) One who completely removes the doubt of his devotees like Sanaka and others by imparting real knowledge to them—SD.

126. *pūrṇāya*—(i) Who pervades (everything) both internally and externally—VR.

(ii) Who assumed full-fledged incarnations like Nṛsiṁha, Rāma—SD.

127. *nibhṛtātmane*—One whose all desires are fulfilled or achieved —VR.

VR. records a v.l. —*nirvṛtātmane*—One who is unaffected by sorrow.

* VC. (2nd half) : Oh Lord, the Soul of the Sun-god ! Direct my eyesight to the beauty of your (the Lord's) personality. May the inherent light of this Sun purify me. I bow to you. Cf. supra III 26.28.

** Just as you direct others to the path of *karma*, direct my power of speech for performing your *kīrtana* form of devotion.

128. *Śuciṣad*—(i) Hence is called *haṁsa*—ŚR.

cf. *Haṁsaḥ śuciṣad/Kaṭha Up.* 5.2 also *Mahānārāyaṇa* 9.3; 17.8 and *Nṛsiṁha-Pūrva-Tāpinī Upa* 3.1, vide Jacob's UVK (*Upaniṣad Vākya Kośa* p. 1067).

(ii) Who dwells in the pure hearts of Yogis—VR.

(iii) One who abides in the Fire—VJ.

129. *tantave*—(i) Who is of the form of or identical with *Yajña*—VR.

(ii) Who secures the continuity of the race, or All-pervading—VJ.

38.* Salutation to him who, as Soma is the food of manes (*pitṛs*) and gods, is the Lord of Three Vedas (viz. *Ṛg*, *Sāman* and *Yajus*), and is the semen (essence) of sacrifice. My obeisance to you who in the form of water, give satisfaction to all *jīvas*.

39.** I bow to him who is the body of all the Souls (*ātmans*) or living beings; who is in the form of the earth; who forms the Cosmic Body (Virāṭ); who, as the Vāyu—the deity of vital airs and wind—sustains the three worlds, and forms the power of the mind, senses and body.

40.*** I pay obeisance to him who as ether (through its attribute called Sound) serves as an index (to the existence)

---

* (i) VR. : I bow to him who as an Inner Controller dispenses fruits of *karmas*; who as the food of Pitṛs and gods brings satisfaction to them; who is the protector of three Vedas and is the fruit (seed) of sacrifices; thus he reveals the means of attaining to heaven (*Svarga*—including worldly pleasures on the earth) and *Mokṣa*; who is the giver of pleasures to *jīvas* from the contact with objects of senses and all kinds of tastes.

(ii) VC: Oh Lord in the form of Soma, the food of *Pitṛs* and gods ! By repaying the debt (obligations) to gods, sages and *Pitṛs*, please fix up my heart in devotion (to you) and may the lustre of Soma purify me Oh Lord in the form of fluids! Please develop in me taste for your essential sweetness. May my tongue and humids in my body be purified. I pay obeisance to you.

(iii) GD : The Lord, in the form of *rasa* (fluids) is bowed to create proper ability in the tongue to taste the sweetness of divine grace.

** (i) VR : Salutations to him whom everything insentient and all sentient beings serve as a body; who is gross (*Virāṭ*) and of the form of Pṛthivī and its characteristic quality—fragrance.

(ii) VJ : Obeisance to him who abides in everyone as the Soul, thumb-like in stature; and who staying within the earth makes her most important.

(iii) VC : Oh Hari in the form of the Earth ! Direct my sense of smell to your divine fragrance and my body to your service. Oh Hari in the form of Vāyu ! Make my sense of touch appreciative of the tenderness of your person and make my body, senses and mind capable of worshipping you.

*** (i) VJ: Bow to him the correct means of knowing whom is *Śāstra* or *Veda*; or who is the cause or source of *Puruṣārtha* (the highest objective in human life); who is unattached like *ākāśa* (ether); who sanctifies all; who is light itself; who abides in all deities or who gives sacred regions like *Svarga* etc.

of all things and are the basis of the concept of differentiation between the internal and external. I bow to him who forms the regions of great refulgence (called *Svarga* etc. and which are attained by great meritorious acts).

41. I bow to you who are both *Pravṛtti karma* (acts pertaining to worldly activities or *saṁsāra*) leading to the region of manes (Pitṛs), and the *Nivṛtti karma* (the discontinuance of worldly acts) the means of attaining to the region of gods. (Bow to you) who are the god of Death, (which is) the fruit of unrighteousness which causes pain.

42. Salutations to you, Oh Lord! You are the source of all blessings. You are the Manu (or all-knower and the embodiment of *Mantras*). I bow to you in the form of Kṛṣṇa who is the highest righteousness incarnate and whose intelligence is unobstructed (anywhere); who is the ancientmost Puruṣa (person), the master of the path of knowledge (Sāṅkhya) and of Yoga.

43. You are the Lord Rudra who is the presiding deity of *ahaṁkāra* (ego) and who possesses the threefold potencies (of being the doer, the instrument and action). I bow to you (Oh Brahmā!) who are the embodiment of knowledge and action, and who are the source of (four kinds) speech (viz. *parā, paśyanti, madhyamā* and *vaikharī*). My obeisance to you.

44. Be pleased to bless us who are earnestly desirous of seeing you, with your vision which is highly adored and esteemed by the devotees of the venerable Lord (i.e. you). Please reveal to us your beautiful form which is so dearest to your votaries, and which, forming the objects of enjoyment of all senses simultaneously, delights them all (*or* which delights all senses by its numerous qualities).

45. Your form is lovely, bluish and resplendent like the rainy cloud. With its four long graceful arms and winsome face with beautiful and well-shaped features, it is as if a synthesis (lit. a treasure-house) of beauty in everything.

46. Your form has eyes (charming) like the inner petals of lotus, beautiful eyebrows and shapely nose, excellent rows

(ii) VC. : In these verses one's own elements, senses and mind are made prone to the devotion of the Lord. After adoring Lord, the Lord is bowed to as having the form of the Vaikuṇṭha.

of teeth, attractive cheeks and mouth with symmetrical ears beautifying it.

47. With side-long looks as if smiling with love, your form is beautified with flowing locks of hair. It is clad in silken garments, (yellowish) like lotus-filaments, and is adorned with a pair of polished earrings.

48. It is also decorated with a brilliant crown, bracelets, wreaths of pearls, anklets and a girdle. It is extremely magnificent by its conch, discus, mace, lotus, garland of sylvan flowers and excellent jewels (of various kinds).

49. Its shoulders which resembled those of a lion, are shining with lustre of necklace, earrings (and other ornaments). Its neck appears beautiful with the refulgence of the *Kaustubha* gem. Its bosom on which rests permanently the goddess Śrī (in the form of *Śrīvatsa*) far outshines the (dark coloured) touchstone bearing a streak of gold on it.

50. Its belly is like the leaf of an *aśvattha* (Indian fig-tree) in shape, and appears beautiful with its threefold heaving due to his inhalation and exhalation of breath. Its navel is so deep like a whirlpool that it is as if withdrawing again the universe (to its source) through it.

51. On the dark-blue waist (of Your form) the (yellow) silken loin-cloth fastened with a girdle of gold, appears all the more resplendent (by contrast in colours). Your form is extremely handsome to look at due to (its pair of) symmetrical and beautiful feet, shanks, thighs and depressed knees.

52. You dispel the darkness (of ignorance) in our hearts by the rays of light emanating from the nails of your feet (toes) which are beautiful like the petals of autumnal lotus. Pray reveal to us your form, our asylum, which removes the fear (of your devotees). Oh Master! You are the preceptor to guide us who are groping in the dark.

53.* This form of yours should be constantly meditated upon by those who earnestly desire to purify their hearts. For

---

* (i) VR. : Pray reveal unto us your form as an object of meditation (and not *sākṣātkāra*—perception). The Yoga of meditation leads to the Yoga of devotion.

(ii) VJ. : Self-purification means liberation from *saṁsāra*. For this mere performance of our righteous duties according to our *varṇa* (caste) the path of devotion brings fearlessness (or final beatitude) unto those who perform their respective religious duties.

54. You are difficult to be attained by all embodied beings (who are not your devotees). You are sought after and respected by the ruler of heaven—*Svarga*. You are the goal of them who exclusively seek Self-realisation. You are accessible only to them who are full of devotion.

55. You are very difficult to be propitiated. Having propitiated you, with exclusive devotion which is difficult to be found even in the righteous people, who will covet for anything else than an asylum at your feet?

56. Even though the god of death destroys the universe by the movement of his eyebrow—an index of his majestic power and energy—he does not wish (to exercise his authority on) him who has resorted to your feet as shelter.

57. I do not regard the heaven (*Svarga*) as well as final Beatitude (*Mokṣa*) as equivalent to companionship for the duration of half a moment with the devotees attached to the Lord. What of the blessings of mortals.

58. Now, let this be the favour conferred on us: May we be blest with the association of those who have washed away their sins internally by immersing their Souls in the (stream of the) glory of the Lord, and externally by bathing in the sacred waters of the Gaṅgā flowing from the Lord's holy feet which absolves one of all sins, and who are compassionate to all beings and have their minds free from passions like love, hate etc., and are endowed with virtues like straightforwardness.

59.* The contemplative sage whose mind is completely purified by being blest with the path of devotion (in associa-

and *āśrama* (stage of life) is not enough. This observance of duties developing into and combining therewith intense devotion leads to Liberation.

(iii) VC.: Mere knowledge of *karmas* is not sufficient. *Bhakti-yoga* is absolutely necessary for those who observe their respective religious duties. A *Sādhaka* desirous of removing his *avidyā*, should meditate upon this form till a gets a vision of it.

* VC.: The mind is specially purified in the association of your devotees. Such pure mind enjoys the beauty of your sports (*līlā*). The ten defects or 'offences' against *bhakti* (devotion) or *nāma* (God's name) do not arise. The goddess of Bhakti confers her blessings and such a contemplative Soul visualizes God's sports in his pure heart

tion with such devotees of God) and is neither distracted by external objects nor lost in the dark cave of ignorance,[130] soon perceives your real nature easily and properly.

60.* You are that superbly effulgent *Brahman* in whom this universe is manifested and who appears shining in everything and who is all-pervading (and unaffected or unattached) like the sky.

61. Oh Lord! Your Māyā assumes various numerous forms. By this (Māyā) you create, sustain and again destroy the world as if it were real. But you remain changeless (all the while). Your Māyā creates the notion of difference (in others), but has no control or effect on you, the Supreme Soul. Hence we know you to be absolutely independent.

62. This form of yours is indicated as their controller by the *bhūtas* (five elements e.g. Earth, Water, Fire etc.), (conative and cognitive) sense-organs and the mind. Those (*karma*)—*yogins*[131] (the followers of the Path of Action), who devotedly worship this very form properly, by means of various ritualistic acts, for the attainment of *Siddhi* (final emancipation), are verily the past masters in Vedas and Āgama-Śāstra (Tantric-lore).

63. You are the only One, primeval Person with your potency (called Māyā) lying dormant. When it is activated through her, (the three *guṇas* viz.) *sattva*, *rajas* and *tamas* become differentiated (and combined). From it are evolved this universe (consisting of) (the principle of cosmic intelligence called) *Mahat*, *ahaṁkāra* (ego), (elements such as) the sky,

---

130. VJ. reads differently : Whose mind enters the Soul who abides in cave of the heart.

*VJ: This verse points that Brahman (the support) and the universe are different; that his supreme effulgence shows that he is unaffected by ignorance or nescience and his comparison with the sky indicates his limitlessness.

131. *yoginaḥ*—(i) VR.: For Liberation (*Mokṣa*) the followers of the path of knowledge (*jñāna-yoga*) devoutly worship this form of the Lord, by performance of righteous duties specifically prescribed for their *varṇa* and *āśrama*. They do these properly and without any attachment or longing for the fruit of the action.

(ii) Followers of *Bhakti-yoga*—GD.

wind, fire, water and earth, as well as gods, sages, multitudes of living beings.

64* By a portion of yourself, you have entered the bodies of four types[132] which you have created by your (Māyā) power. It is, therefore, that they call him *Puruṣa* i.e. one who abides in the body. He is the *jīva* who through his senses enjoys the (drops of) honey (insignificant pleasures) collected by bees[132a]. (This shows his negligible nature.)

65. Though you are as described above, your real nature is inferrable (as its direct perception is not possible). (At the time of the dissolution of the world) you exhibit very terrific velocity sweeping off one element by another; You (ultimately) destroy the world just as a hurricane of irresistible force scatters away and sweeps off a multitude of clouds.

66. Just as an alert serpent, licking (its lips) with hunger, suddenly seizes a rat, you, as vigilant Death, suprisingly catch hold of a person who, absorbed in the anxiety of what to do and how to do, has become extremely negligent, is extremely addicted to sensual pleasure and has grown over-greedy.

67. What wise man who regards his life (lit. body) wasted by disregarding (i.e. not remembering) you, will give up your lotus-like feet—feet which my father Brahmā has been

---

* VR. : The Lord is known as Puruṣa as he is the *antaryāmin* of *jīva* in whom he enters and controls.

VJ. : By a slight portion he enters the bodies of four kinds (e.g. viviparous, oviparous etc.) and through the senses of the *jīva* he enjoys only the essence of bliss. Hence as he abides in the body, he is known as Puruṣa.

VC.: The word *sāragha* indicates that the so-called pleasure is really pain (the sting of bees).

SD. : He who enjoys the insignificant pleasures of senses, the fruit of actions, is called *jīva* and is bound and he who abides in the body and is free, is the *Puruṣa*.

132. *caturvidham* : ŚR. enumerates them as follows :—(i) *jarāyuja* (viviparous); (ii) *aṇḍaja* (oviparous); (iii) *svedaja* (sweat-born); (iv) *udbhija* (germinating as a plant). According to VR. they are :—(1) gods; (2) men; (3) subhuman beings; (4) immovables.

132a. Cf. *dvā suparṇā sayujā sakhāyā*. . ...
tayor anyaḥ pippalaṁ svādvatti etc. —*Muṇḍ. Up*. 3.1.1.
Śvet. Up. 4.6.

adoring through fear (of bondage of *saṁsāro*) and which the fourteen Manus have been worshipping without arguments (with implicit belief).

68. Oh Brahman! Oh Supreme Soul! The whole universe is overwhelmed with the fear of Rudra (the destroyer of the universe). To us who are wise, you are our asylum completely free from fear.

69. Oh Princes! While you carry out your righteous duties with a pure heart and with your mind concentrated on the Lord, you repeat this (hymn). May God bless you!

70. (Please do) worship Hari, extolling and contemplating him again and again, as Hari is the Supreme Soul abiding in you as well as in all other beings.

71. Please commit to memory the hymn called *Yogādeśa* which you have received from me. Observing the vows of a sage's life and concentrating your minds, all of you study this reverentially.

72. With a desire to create the world, the venerable god Brahmā, the Lord of all the progenitors of the universe, formerly taught this (hymn) to us, his sons e.g. Bhṛgu and others who were intent on augmenting procreation.

73. When we, all the progenitors of creatures, were urged to create beings, we dispelled our ignorance by (repeating) this hymn and procreated various species of beings.

74. Hence, if a person who is devoted to Vāsudeva, repeats this hymn with faith and concentrated mind, he would before long obtain blissfulness.

75. Knowledge leading to the final beatitude is the highest of all blessings. It is by the boat of knowledge that one easily crosses the impassable sea of misery (i.e. *saṁsāra*).

76. He who with perfect devotion and concentration, studies this hymn in praise of the Lord sung by me, propitiates Lord Hari himself who is otherwise so very difficult to be pleased.

77. As the Lord is the sole receptacle of all blessings, a man with a steady mind who highly delights the Lord (by praising him) with this hymn sung by me, immediately gets whatever blessings he likes.

78. A man, who, rising up early at dawn, and with a heart full of devotion, hears this or recites this to others with folded palms, is released from the chains of *karmas*.

79. Oh princes! By repeating with concentrated mind this praise of the Highest Person, the Supreme Soul, sung by me, you do perform this great penance at the end of which you will obtain your desired object.

CHAPTER TWENTY-FIVE

*(*The Story of Purañjana—Introduction*)

Maitreya said :

1. Having thus instructed Pracetasas, the sons of Barhiṣad, Lord Śiva who was devoutly worshipped by them, immediately disappeared at that very spot, while the Princes were simply looking on.

2. Repeating the hymn in praise of the venerable Lord, as sung by Rudra, all the Pracetasa princes standing in water, practised penance for ten thousand years.

3. Oh Vidura! In the meanwhile (while Pracetasas were undergoing austere penance) the compassionate Nārada who knew the reality about the Supreme Soul, (visited and) reasoned with (their father) Prācīnabarhis who was attached to and was preoccupied in ritualistic Vedic acts, (as follows) :

4. "Oh King! What bliss do you attempt to secure by the performance of ritualistic acts? That which removes miseries and secures happiness is (called the real) bliss. And (according to the wise) such beatitude is not expected from the *karmas*."

* The story of Purañjana is an allegory on *jīva* and Paramātman. (Cf. the allegorical reference to the *jīva* and *Śiva* as two birds occupying the same tree, one enjoying the fruits and the other staying aloof—*Muṇḍ. Up*. 3.1.1 and *Śvet. Up*. 4.6) The commentators explain the allegory at every step in details.

It is interesting to compare the interpretation of the allegory given by the commentators with that given by the author of the Bh. P. himself in chapter 29 (infra).

The King said :

5. "Oh blessed Sir ! My mind is distracted by the ritualistic *karmas*. I do not know the supreme bliss. Please initiate me in that pure knowledge whereby I can be free from (bonds of all) *karmas*.

6. In the householder's life which is characterised by deceitfulness, a person looks upon his sons, wife and wealth as the sole objectives in life. Such ignorant persons, wandering in the pathways of *saṁsāra* (transmigration of the Soul), never attain the Supreme Bliss.

*Nārada said** :

7. Oh Lord of men ! Have a look at those multitudes of living beings mercilessly slaughtered by you in thousands, as beasts (consecrated) for sacrifice.

8. Remembering your cruelty(to them), they are waiting for you. When you will be dead, they, with their ire aroused, will pierce you(through and through) with their steel-like horns.

9. On this point, I shall narrate to you this ancient legend. Listen to the story of Purañjana as I tell you.

10. Oh King, there was a king of wide fame, by name Purañjana (i.e. *Jīva*). He had a friend called Avijñāta (i.e. the Supreme Soul) as his activities were unknown.

11. The king wandered over the earth[133] in search of an abode.[134] When he did not find any suitable asylum, he became rather dejected.[135]

12. Seeking after pleasures, he did not approve of any of the cities that existed on the earth as suitable for the realization

* By his Yogic powers Nārada showed to the King the huge multitudes of beasts slaughtered by him for sacrifice—ŚR.

133. *Pṛthivī*—This indicates the universe—ŚR., VR. *karma-bhumī*—VJ.

134. *Śaraṇam*—Body through which the *jīva* gets experience in life.

135. Although he (the *jīva*) gets sensual pleasures in all births, he is not satisfied as non-attachment, which is the means of the Liberation (*Mokṣa*) is not possible in non-human births. Hence his dejection—GD.

of those pleasures.[136]

13.* Once upon a time, he saw, on the table land in the southern range of the Himālayas, a city having nine gates and possessing all the characteristics of a good city.

14.** It was surrounded by ramparts, gardens, watch-towers, moats, windows, arched gateways. It was crowded on all sides with houses with crests of gold, silver and iron.

15. It appeared resplendent like Bhogavatī,[137] in beauty, with floors of its mansions studded with precious stones like sapphires, crystals, cat's eyes, pearls, emeralds and rubies.

16. It appeared beautiful with assembly halls, court-yards, main roads (highways), gambling houses, markets, resthouses, flags and fluttering banners and platforms built of coral.

17. Outside the city, there was a park full of celestial trees and creepers. There was a lake resounding with warbling sounds of birds and humming of bees.

18. The bank of the lotus pond was richly beautified with trees the foliage and branches of which were fluttering with the cool breeze laden with spray from the cascades and blowing over the flower beds.

19. It was safe and free from molestation as the multitudes of wild animals infesting it were observing ascetic vows (e. g. non-violence etc.). The traveller feels that he is invited there, by the cooing of the cuckoos.

20.*** In that garden, he (King Purañjana) saw a young

136. There is no possibility of enjoying all the earthly and heavenly pleasures in non-human species. Hence his disapproval—ŚR. Cf. *tābhyo gām ānayat tā abruvan na vai no'yam alam* etc. *Ait. Up.* 2.2.

*In Bhāratavarṣa, to the south of the Himālayas, he saw the city (human body) which was free from disabilities and handicaps like blindness, deafness–ŚR.

**The limbs or sense-organs of the body are the ramparts etc. The plexuses (*cakras* like *ādhāra* etc.) are the houses. The three types of turrets or house-crests are the *guṇas* viz. *sattva*, *rajas* and *tamas*—ŚR.

137. *Bhogavatī* : Literally—a place for enjoyment of pleasures, but it is generally derived from *bhoga* 'serpent's body'. It is the name of the city of snakes in the lower-regions, famous for its beauty.

***The lady is the intelligence (*buddhi*) and the ten attendants are the conative and cognitive sense-organs and the hundred (i.e. hundreds of) activities or *vṛttis* of each are the wives.—ŚR.

damsel of superb beauty coming there by chance. She was accompanied by ten servants each of whom was the husband of hundred ladies.

21. She was guarded on all sides by her bodyguard, a serpent with five hoods.[138] She was sixteen years of age, beautiful or capable of assuming any form she liked. She was in search of a husband.

22. The girl had a shapely nose, beautiful rows of teeth, lovely cheeks, attractive face and was wearing lustrous earrings in her symmetrical ears.

23. She put on a reddish-brown garment round her waist with a girdle of gold around it. The dark-complexioned[139] lady with well formed hips walked with her feet making a tinkling sound with the adorning anklets.

24. Out of bashfulness, she was (now and then) covering with the end of her garments. her symmetrical, closely knit, round (spherical) breasts indicating the advent of youth. She was walking (in the stately gait) like an elephant.

25. Being (as if) wounded with the arrows of her charming side-long glances, shot from the bow of her eyebrows making lively amorous movements, the hero (Purañjana) spoke in soft winsome tones to the girl who looked all the more lovely by her bashful smiles.

26. "Who are you, Oh beautiful lady with eyes like the lotus-petals? Whose (relative) are you? Whence have you come here? Oh timid lady, please tell me what you desire to do here on the outskirts of the city?

27. Who are these ten attendants commanded by the formidable warrior, forming the eleventh? Who are these beautiful damsels? Who is the serpent who goes ahead of you, Oh lady with beautiful eyebrows?

28. Are you the goddess Hrī, Pārvatī or Sarasvatī (the goddess of speech) or the goddess Lakṣmī leading the life of a sage in this secluded forest seeking a husband who must have surely got all his wishes fulfilled as your feet are desired

---

138. This is *Prāṇa* of five vital functions—ŚR.

139. ŚR. quotes the following from the *Chānd. Up.* to explain the darkness of complexion : *annamayaṁ hi somya mana iti yat kṛṣṇam tad annasya* /

by him ?[140] If you be the goddess Lakṣmī, where has the lotus been dropped from your hand ?

29. Oh lady with beautiful thighs, you are surely none of these deities as you touch the earth (with your feet). You should, therefore, adorn this city along with me (who am) an excellent warrior of great exploits, just as goddess Lakṣmī as the consort of Lord Viṣṇu (the Lord of Sacrifices) graces Vaikuṇṭha (the highest region).

30. Please show favour to me, Oh graceful lady, as the mind-born god of love, prompted by you with the playful movement of your eyebrows and your bashful smile expressing love, is harassing me by piercing my heart with your side-glances.

31. Oh lady with bright smiles ! Please raise up and show me your sweet speaking face with beautiful eyebrows and eyes of bright, charming pupils—your face which is covered with locks of long dark-blue hair—as it is not turned to me through bashfulness."

Nārada said :

32. Oh warrior! The lady was infatuated with Purañjana, the hero[141] who was courting her so impatiently and (in response) greeted him with a smile

33. "Oh prominent man, we do not know properly who is your or my progenitor. No, do we know the family or the name (by which we are called?)

34. We know that we are here today, now. We do not know beyond that. Nor do we know who created this city which is my abode, Oh warrior.

35. Oh respectful one, these men and women, who are my friends, stay awake while I am asleep. So does this serpent guarding this city.

36. Leave aside the details about my name, family etc. Oh destroyer of enemies, I am glad that you have come.

---

140. According to most commentators: But the alternate explanation "who must... wishes fulfilled as his feet are desired by you" is worth considering.

141. ŚR. presumably reads *vīkṣya* and interprets *dṛṣṭvā* (having seen).

God bless you! Whatever sensual pleasures you desire, I shall secure for you with the help of my kinsmen.

37. Please occupy this city of nine gates, enjoying for hundred years all the sense-pleasures which I shall secure for you, Oh Lord.

38. For, whom else than you should I really please—him who is ignorant of erotics or pleasure, void of learning or wisdom, careless about tomorrow's work (i.e. his life here) and heedless about his life hereafter, a sheer brute.

39. Here (in the life of a householder) one attains to *puruṣārthas* called *dharma* (righteousness), *artha* (wealth) and *kāma* (pleasures of the senses). It is here that one gets the joy of getting progeny, immortality (i.e. Liberation—*Mokṣa*), fame and regions which are free from sins, sorrow—which even recluses do not know.

40. They, the sages of old, say that in this world, the stage of householder's life is the only asylum for the well-being of manes (*pitṛs*), gods, sages, men and all other beings and of the householder himself.

41. Oh warrior, what girl in my position (lit. like me) would not accept as a husband a famous, munificent, good-looking, loving personage like you.

42. Oh mighty-armed hero! What woman's heart in this world would not cling to your arms which are (tender yet powerful) like the body of a serpent?—You move about in the world in order to remove the mental anguish of the helpless by your smiling looks full of compassion."

Nārada said :

43. Oh King (Prācīnabarhis)! In this way the couple entered into a mutual agreement there. They then entered the city and lived in happiness for a hundred years.

44. Sweetly eulogised by bards everywhere, and playing in company of women, he entered the (swimming-) pool in the hot season.

45. For (the convenience of) the movements from and to the outer regions, of whosoever (unknown) was the master of the city there were seven gateways in the upper (i.e. front-)

part of the city (viz. two eyes, two ears, two nostrils and a mouth) and two in the lower part (the anus and the penis).

46. There were five doors to the east (front, viz., two eyes, two nostrils and one mouth), one to the South (the right ear), one to the North (the left ear) and two to the west (viz. the penis and the anus). I shall describe to you the names of these, Oh King.

47.* To the East were constructed adjacently a pair of gates called *khadyotā* (fire-fly) and Āvirmukhī (of manifest face—bright light). Through them he (king Purañjana) accompanied by his friend Dyumat, used to visit the country called Vibhrājit.

48.** A pair of adjacent gates called Nalinī and Nālinī were also built to the east. Through them he (Purañjana) in company of Avadhūta, goes to the region called Saurabha (Fragrance).

49.*** The fifth gate to the east was called Mukhyā (the main). In association with Rasajña and Vipaṇa, the king of the city goes through the gate to the countries of Āpaṇa and Bahūdana.

50.† On King (Barhisad)! Through the southern gate of the city called Pitṛhū, Purañjana, in accompaniment of Śrutadhara used to go to the country called Southern Pañcāla.

51.†† By the northern gate of the city, known as *Devahū*, Purañjana along with Śrutadhara, used to go to the country called Northern Pañcāla.

52. To the west of the city was the gate called *Āsurī* (pertaining to *asuras*—people indulging in sensual pleasures). In company of Durmada, Purañjana used to go to the country called Grāmaka (low or vulgar pleasures).

---

* Description of the eyes.

** Description of the nose.

*** Herein *Āpaṇa* signifies speech, and *Bahūdana* denotes variety of food. *Vipaṇa* thus stands for the organ of speech and *Rasajña*, for the capacity of the tongue to taste—ŚR.

† The right ear is the Southern gate leading to the region of Pitṛs by the path of ritualistic *karmas*. It hears the *karma-kāṇḍa*, the path of the *karmas*. Due to its association with *Pitṛ-yāṇa* the right ear is called *Pitṛhū*. *Pañcāla* here is the science of *Pravṛtti mārga*.

†† *Devahū* is the left ear. It leads to the region of gods by following the *Devayāna* Path.

53. There was another gate to the West. It was called *Nivṛti*. Through it Purañjana went to the country called *Vaiśasa* (terrible), in company of Lubdhaka (a miser).

54. Out of the citizens (there were) two viz. *Nirvāk* (speechless) and *Peśaskṛta* (possessing no aperture). With these the lord of senses made movements of walking and doing.

55. If he goes to his harem (viz. heart) along with (his friends) *Viṣūcīna* (the chief of attendant in a harem), he experiences delusion, calmness and (excitement of) joy, from wife and children.

56. The unwise king (Purañjana) who was thus deeply attached to *karmas* (action) and whose mind was completely given up to sensual pleasures, was enraptured and whatever the queen wished to do, he acted accordingly.

57. Sometimes when she used to drink wine, he used to drink and get intoxicated. Sometimes when she took meals, he took it with her ; when she chewed, he did the same.

58. Sometimes when she sang, he used to sing; sometimes he wept when she shed tears; sometimes he followed her while she laughed ; sometimes when she chattered, he prattled.

59. Sometimes when she ran, he ran; he stood when she stood. When she lay in bed, he did so; sometimes when she sat up, he also sat up.

60. Occasionally, when she heard, he heard; when she saw, he also saw it; sometimes she smelt, he also smelt; when she touched, he used to touch.

61. Sometimes when the wife cried in sorrow, he wept after her like a man in distress; when she rejoiced, he rejoiced; on her being delighted, he was delighted.

62. In this way, he was deceived by the queen and lost his original nature (such as non-attachment to everything). The ignorant King though unwilling, simply imitated (the acts of his queen) helplessly like a domesticated monkey kept for amusement.

CHAPTER TWENTY-SIX

Purañjana's Hunting Expedition and His Queen's Wrath Pacified

Nārada said :

1-3.* One day, Purañjana, clad in the armour of gold and equipped with a mighty bow and an inexhaustible quiver (of arrows) and accompanied by his eleventh general, mounted his chariot fit for speedy marches. It was yoked with five horses; had a pair of shafts, two wheels, one axle, three flag-staffs, five cords, only one rein, one charioteer, one seat, two central poles to which yoke is fixed, five covered litters and sevenfold protection, capable of five kinds of movements and provided with instruments of gold. He set out for the forest called *Pañca Prastha* (Forest of five hills).

---

*ŚR., VR. SD., GD., GS., BP. regard verses 1-10 as the description of Purañjana in the state of dream. Only VJ. thinks this as a state of wakefulness (*jāgrad-avasthā-praveśa*).

According to ŚR., the allegory becomes clear when we understand the following:

The chariot=His body in the dream.
Five horses=five cognitive senses.
Two shafts=The notions of I-ness and Mine-ness.
Two wheels=merits and sins.
One axle=Pradhāna (Primordial Nature).
Three flagstaffs=*Sattva*, *rajas* and *tamas*.
Five cords=Five vital breaths (Prāṇa, apāna etc.).
One rein=the mind.
One charioteer=The intellect.
One seat=the heart.
Two poles=grief and delusion (*Śoka-mohau*)
Five recesses=Five objects of senses.
Seven-fold protection=Seven constituents of the body.
Five kinds of movements=Five conative organs.
Gold armour=*Rajoguṇa*.
The big bow=Attachment.
The inexhaustible quiver=Infinite tendencies associated with ego (*ahaṁkāra*).
One general=The Mind.
The Pañca-prastha forest=Five objects of the senses (e.g. sound, smell etc.)

VJ. explains differently (only differences are noted here):

While coming to the state of wakefulness, Purañjana entered the stage through the five senses for the purpose of possessing various objects.

4.* Being carried away by the passion for game, the proud king left behind his wife who did not deserve that treatment. Taking a bow and arrows, he started a-hunting there.

5. Taking to Asura (demonic) way of life, he became hard-hearted and merciless. He killed (all) the wild animals in the jungle with his sharp arrows.

6.** Even if a king is extremely fond (of hunting), it is restricted by the *śāstras*, that (it is only) on religious occasions like special *Śrāddhas* as specified in the *Śāstras* and not for routine *Śrāddhas* that theking may kill just the required number of sacrificial animals in the jungle (and not more).

7.*** Oh Chief of Kings! A learned person who does his acts as prescribed by the *Śāstras* is not thereby affected due to the knowledge arising from the performance of that act.

8. Otherwise a person who does acts (in violation of the restrictions of Śāstras), becomes full of egotism and falls in the stream of *guṇas* (i.e. *saṁsāra*). Losing his faculty of discrimination and judgment, he goes down[141a] (to lower grades of existence).

9. In the forest, there took place destruction of the afflicted animals whose bodies were shattered by arrows with variegated feathers—a sight unbearable to those whose hearts were full of compassion.

10.† After hunting down hares, hogs, buffaloes, bisons, deer, porcupines and many other (animals) irrespective of their fitness for being offered for sacrifice, he got exhausted.

His bow is the sacred syllable OM. The inexhaustible quivers are *Pravṛtti* and *Nivṛtti*. Purañjana is the leader of the army of eleven (10 sense-organs, mind). One axle is the Vāyu—the common 'thread' or force impelling all activities. Five recesses or knots are the *nāḍīs* or 'tubes' through which five vital breaths (*prāṇas*) circulate through the body.

*Purañjana ignored his reasoning faculty altogether and with a mad attachment to sensual pleasures, indulged in them indiscriminately—ŚR.

**The allegory being thus clear, its application to each and every verse is not given here as it is unnecessary. Commentators, however, emphasize the inner meaning minutely rather than the story element.

***These show how one should do one's duties without being bound down by their effects and how an ignorant person impelled by passions gets involved in *saṁsāra*.

141a. *adho*—to hell—VR., GD.

† The hunted animals are the permitted and prohibited pleasures enjoyed by the *jīva*.

11.* Then being exhausted with hunger and thirst, he retired from hunting and returned to his palace. Having taken bath and proper (sumptuous) meal, he lay on bed and was relieved of fatigue.

12.** He got himself beautified with scents, cosmetics, flower garlands etc. Having got his person well adorned, he set his heart on the queen (his intelligence of *sāttvic* type).

13.*** In his youthful pride, the King who was satisfied and in a gay mood, got his mind overcome with the passion of love, he missed his (charming) wife who helped him discharging his duties as a householder.

14. Oh King Prācīnabarhis! Being rather frustrated, he asked the ladies in the harem, "Oh beautiful ladies, are all of you and your mistress, the queen, well as before?

15. The splendour and wealth of the house do not appear as brilliant as before (because) if the house is bereft of the mother or the wife who treats her husband as a god, it is like a broken chariot (without wheels etc.). What wise man will stay in it, like a miserable wretch?

16. Where is that charming lady who, at every step, illuminated my intelligence and lifted me up (by cheering me), while I was being drowned in the sea of miseries?"

---

*According to ŚR., VR. and others, after describing the state of dream in verses 1-10, the author describes the happy life of a man with *sāttvikī buddhi* to the end of the chapter.

VJ. regards the remaining chapter as the description of the state of sleep thus: Being thoroughly tired of gross and violent mental' activities, he retired from the state of wakefulness to his asylum viz. *hṛdaya-nāḍī*. Removing the dust of enjoyments in the stage of wakefulness and eaten his meals (his own blissful nature), the *jīva* sleeps fully relieved of fatigue.

**VJ. : This describes the preparation before going to sleep. Materials of decoration are for the worship of the Lord (the *antaryāmin*) to whose presence the *jīva* goes in deep sleep. His thought of the queen is the change from deep sleep to the dream-state.

***When the *jīva* is under the influence of *rājasī buddhi*, he will not find this *sāttvikī buddhi*—ŚR.

(ii) In the dream-state the *jīva* does not find the conclusive understanding about Hari (*niścaya-jñānaṁ no'paiti*)—VJ.

The ladies replied :

17. "Oh King (Lord of men), we do not know what your beloved intends to do. You see (for yourself) that she is lying on the bare ground, Oh destroyer of enemies."

Nārada said :

18. Purañjana who had lost all his knowledge (power of discretion and judgment) through his fondness for his wife, became highly agitated and distressed to see her lying stretched (that way) on the ground.

19. With an aching heart, he tried to soothe her with soft, pleasing words. But he did not get any indication (in her behaviour) that it was a feigned anger of his beloved queen towards him (due to love).

20. Being expert in the art of conciliation, the hero gradually cajolled her, touched her feet and seating her on his lap he caressed her.

Purañjana said :

21. Really unfortunate are those servants on whom, though they have committed an offence, their masters do not inflict any corrective punishment, thinking that they (servants) are after all under their control, Oh beautiful damsel.

22. Punishment is a supreme grace shown by the master to his servants. Oh slim lady, it is only an intolerant fool who does not understand this as a friendly act.

23. Oh high-Souled lady with beautiful teeth and charming eyebrows ! Please show to us who are your own, your face with prominently shapely nose and soft, sweet accented speech—face bright with smiling looks, bent down with the weight of love and bashfulness, adorned with bee-like dark locks of hair.

24. Oh queen of a warrior (like me) ! I shall instantly inflict punishment on him who has committed any offence against you unless he be an earth-god (*Brāhmaṇa*) or a devotee of Lord Viṣṇu. Verily I shall see to it that he is not free from fear, much less joyous either in the three worlds or (even) beyond (wherever he may go, he shall die out of fear from me).

25. Never have I seen (before) your face without its *tilaka* mark (on the forehead) or your countenance so dull,

cheerless, terrific with anger, unwashed and gloomy. Nor have I ever noticed your lovely breasts soiled with (tears of) grief and your lips red like *Bimba*-fruit, bereft of their saffron-colour.

26. Therefore be gracious unto me, who, being mad with the passion for hunting, have committed the offence of going out to hunt as per dictates of his whim (without taking your permission). What woman wishing to have a union would not accept for the proper duties her lover who has always been under her control and who has lost his patience by the vehemence of passion of love.

CHAPTER TWENTY-SEVEN*

(Invasion of Caṇḍavega—The Episode of Kālakanyā)

Nārada said :

1. In this way, bringing Purañjana under her complete control by her womanly charms, Purañjanī (the queen of Purañjana) enjoyed her life, giving delight to her husband, Oh great king.

2. When the queen who took her full bath and beautified herself with auspicious decorations, approached the king fully satisfied and with bright countenance, he hailed her with joy, Oh king (Prācīnabarhis).

3. Embraced by her, he threw his arms about her neck. He lost his reasoning capacity by the amorous sweet words of the queen in privacy. As he was thus possessed by the young lady day and night, he did not grasp the inexorably rapid course of time.

4. The magnanimous prince, being overwhelmed with lustful passion, lay on a very costly couch with the queen's arm as a pillow. He regarded her as the supreme objective in life (puruṣārtha) and he did not think of his real transcendental self[142] (or Brahman) as he was overpowered with *Tamas* (ignorance).

---

*This chapter describes the general course of *saṁsāra* with Purañjana as the representative *jīva*.

142. Or alternatively he did not know what was his and what was another's.

5. Oh king of kings! While he was enjoying pleasures thus with his mind clouded with passion, his youth passed away as if it were half a minute.

6.* The emperor Purañjana begot through (empress) Purañjanī eleven hundred sons. But he lost half of his life then.

7. Oh Lord of creatures! He (also) begot eleven hundred and ten daughters called Paurañjanīs. They brought glory to their parents and were endowed with qualities like good character and generosity.

8.** That king of Pañcālas (Purañjana) got his sons, (all) capable of continuing the race of their forefathers, married to suitable brides and his daughters to proper bridegrooms.

9. And his son had each a hundred sons who have verily propagated the race of Purañjana in the Pañcāla country.

10. By the formation of a strong attachment (lit. sense of mineness) to (sons and grandsons), the shareholders in his property, house treasures and dependants (e.g. ministers, servants), he became firmly attached to the sense-objects.

11. Being prompted by various desires he became consecrated for sacrifices and worshipped gods, manes (*pitṛs*), Lord of the goblins with sacrifices terrible on account of slaughter of beasts, as your honour has done.

12. In this way, he remained remiss about his duties (spiritually) beneficial to him, and had his mind strongly attached to his family. Verily there came the period of life (old age) which is repellent to persons addicted to women.

13. Oh King Prācīnabarhis! There was a King of Gandharvas, known as Caṇḍavegà (signifying the complete year). The powerful king had a force of three hundred sixty Gandharvas (Gandharvas standing for days).

---

*Here 'eleven' signifies the ten sense organs and the mind. 'Hundreds' means innumerable activities of senses.

Daughters are the mental activities.

**Jīva, the Lord of five senses, married his sons i.e. sense-activities to suitable brides, i.e. thoughts about what is beneficial or otherwise. His daughters i.e. mental activities were associated with virtues like modesty or proper objectives of pleasure.

14. Paired to(i.e.wedded to)them were similar (equal number of) Gandharva women (i.e. nights) some dark, some fair or white (according to the fortnights). By their rotational raids, they plundered the city furnished with all desired objects, since its creation.

15. When those attendants of Caṇḍavega began to plunder the city of Purañjana, Prajāgara, the serpent-guard resisted them there.

16. That powerful presiding deity of the city of Purañjana, single-handedly fought with seven hundred and twenty Gandharvas (male and female) for one hundred years (which is the duration of man's life).

17. When his relative—the guardian-serpent—began to lose strength by his single-handed fight with many, Purañjana, along with kingdom, capital and relations felt very much distressed with great anxiety.

18. In the capital city of Pañcāla he indulged in drinking and was under the thumb of women. While he used to receive taxes collected by his retainers, he was not aware of the danger.

19. Oh king Barhiṣad(Prācīnabarhis)! There was a certain daughter of Kāla[143] (the Time-spirit) who, being desirous of having a husband, toured over the three worlds. But nobody welcomed her.

20. Due to her misfortune she was well-known over the world as Durbhagā (the unfortunate). She was (once) sought after by the royal-sage, Puru, to whom she gave a boon.[144]

21. One day while she was wandering, she met me when I descended from Brahmā's region (*satyaloka*) to the earth. Being infatuated with passion, she sought me even though she knew that I had taken a vow of lifelong celibacy.

22. Getting enraged (at my refusal), she gave me an extremely unbearable curse ; 'Oh Sage, as you have set your

143. *Kālakanyā*=Old age.

144. This refers to Puru's acceptance of the old-age of his father Yayāti to himself in exchange of his youth. Yayāti returned his youth to his son and made him the sovereign king after him.

P.I. 2,374.

face against my importunity, you will never stay at one place.'

23. The girl whose desire was so frustrated then followed my advice and approached the king of Yavanas,[145] by name Bhaya (Fear or Death), and courted him as a husband.

24. "Oh brave warrior! I woo you, the leader of the Yavanas, as my coveted husband. The hope entertained by the creatures in you is never falsified.[146]

25. Good people feel regret for those two (types of) foolish and perverse natured people who neither give nor accept what is offered without any request and which is worth giving or receiving according to custom or Vedic precept.

26. Therefore, Oh good Sir, accept me who am offering myself to you. Please be gracious to me. It is the bounden duty of man to be compassionate with the afflicted."

27. Having heard the speech uttered by Kāla-kanyā (the daughter of Kāla), the lord of Yavanas, who desired to carry out the secret work of gods (viz., to bring about the death of living beings)[147] spoke to her with a smile.

28. "With the help of my Yogic vision born of my power of meditation, I have foreseen and selected a husband for you (even if) this world does not welcome you as you are both disagreeable (undesirable) and inauspicious.

29. Adopting unmanifest and imperceptible way of movement, you enjoy (each and every being in) the world created by *karma*. You go in company of my army (of diseases and anxieties) and you will bring about the destruction of all living beings.

---

145. Yavanas signify physical pains and mental anguish.

146. VC. takes *bhūta* as 'the devotee of god' and interprets :

'The purpose of the devotees of the Lord is never frustrated'. Nārada intended that the 'Fear' (*Bhaya*) should grow old and weak by the marriage of Kāla-kanyā with him. His purpose should be achieved by my marrying you.

(ii) As *Bhaya* means *Kāla* (Death or Time) VD. adopts the second meaning 'Time' and explains: "A plan or determination made at the opportune (auspicious) time always bears fruit. I court you as you are the giver of fruit (success in undertaking) to all."

147. Death is kept secret by gods, lest people should renunciate the world.—ŚR.

30. This Prajvāra (Fatal fever created by Viṣṇu) is my brother. You be my sister. Accompanied by both of you and my formidable soldiers (physical and mental ailments) I shall range this world imperceptibly."

CHAPTER TWENTY-EIGHT

(Purañjana's Rebirth as a Woman and Attainment of Liberation)

Nārada said :

1. Oh King Barhiṣman (Prācīnabarhis)! Those soldiers of king Bhaya (i.e. diseases) who were the agents of fate, roamed over this earth accompanied by Prajvāra and the daughter of Kāla.

2. And all of a sudden, they swooped on the city of Purañjana on the D-day (on a certain day) and besieged the city, rich in earthly enjoyments, and guarded by the old serpent (i.e. the Prāṇa in old age whose physical activities became sluggish).

3. The daughter of Kāla also enjoyed perforce the city of Purañjana. Whatever man was overpowered by her, would at once become powerless.

4. The Yavanas (i.e. diseases) entered the city through all the gates from all directions and excessively ravished it, while it was being enjoyed by her (the body of the *jīva* is battered by repeated attacks of various diseases).

5. The city being (thus) devastated, Purañjana who identified himself with it as his own Self, and whose mind was troubled by his sense of mine-ness for his family (viz. intelligence, the mind, sense-organs etc.) underwent agonies of various kinds.

6. Clasped in the arms of the daughter of Kāla, bereft of his splendour and affluence, the wretched Purañjana whose mind was engrossed in sense-pleasure, lost his power of judgment and was forcibly deprived of his powers (viz. of making physical movements) by Gandharvas and Yavanas.

7. He saw that his capital city was completely razed and found that his sons, grandsons, attendants and ministers were antagonistic and disrespectful to him and his wife had lost love for him.

8. He found that he was in the clutches of the daughter (of Kāla) and that the Pañcālas were infested with enemies. He was lost in boundless anxiety and could not find any remedy against it.

9. The miserable king still hankered after the pleasures which were made stale (due to dyspepsia etc.) by the daughter of Kāla. He lost his affection for his son etc. here and his spiritual position hereafter, and continued in fondling his wife and sons.

10. Very reluctantly did the king proceed to abandon the city which was over-run by Gandharvas and Yavanas and was ravaged by the daughter of Kāla.

11. (At that time) there arrived Prajvāra (i.e. the high fatal fever) the elder brother of Bhaya (the chief of Yavanas). With a desire to render service to his brother, Prajvāra burnt down the entire city. (This indicates high temperature of the body).

12. When the city was aflame, the head of the family (Purañjana) along with his wife, children, dependents and citizens was greatly tormented.

13. When the city was occupied by the daughter of Kāla and his own home was surrounded by Yavanas, the guard of the city was greatly distressed when he was attacked by Prajvāra. (When the aged man is about to die, his body is in grip of diseases and the jīva is tormented every moment.)

14. When the serpent Prajāgara was not able to defend the city any longer there, he was violently trembling with severe agonies and he wished to escape from it (like a serpent) from the hollow of a tree ablaze with fire.

15. Oh King! When his limbs became weak and disabled and his prowess was thwarted by Gandharvas and he was surrounded by the inimical Yavanas, he verily wept bitterly.

16-17. The householder (Purañjana) entertained a false notion about his house etc. When the time of separation from his wife arrived, he became very miserable. Possessed with egotism and a false sense of mine-ness about his daughters, sons, grandsons, daughters-in-law, sons-in-law, attendants and whatever (little) remained of his house, treasures and belongings, he thought:

18. "When I have departed to the next world, how will this mistress of the family, being bereaved of her lord and lamenting for the children, carry on her life?

19. She is so devoted to me that she does not eat food until I have taken mine; nor does she take her bath till I have bathed. She gets terribly afraid, when I am angry; when reproached by me, she keeps quiet through fear.

20 When I become thoughtless, she brings me round (lit. wakens me) to the proper path. When I proceed on a long journey, she becomes emaciated through grief. True, she is the mother of heroic children. But how will she desire to carry on the householder's life (without me)—she will certainly die.

21. How can my miserable sons or supportless daughters possibly live when I am gone, as they are like unto passengers on a boat broken in the midst of the sea."

22. While he was thus lamenting like a mean-minded fellow which was unbecoming to him (as he was really the Brahman himself, the Yavana king called Bhaya with a determination to capture him, drew near him.

23.* When he was being dragged like a beast to his (destined) place by the Yavanas, his followers being extremely grieved, over-anxious and afflicted ran after him.

24. When the serpent which was blocked (by the Yavanas) escaped from the city to join (his master Purañjana) the city was completely razed and reduced to its elements.

25. Though Purañjana was forcibly dragged by the powerful Yavana, he was so much overpowered with *tamas* (ignorance) that he did not remember (Avijñāta) who was his former well-wisher and companion.

26. The sacrificial beasts which were ruthlessly slaugh-

* When the *jīva* is being taken to his next birth predetermined by his *karmas*, his subtle-senses etc. follow him—ŚR., VR.

Cf. *tam ut-krāmantam prāṇo nūtkrāmati prāṇam anūtkrāmantaṁ sarve prāṇā anūtkrāmanti*—*Bṛhad. Up.* 4.4.2.

tered by him, remembered his cruelty and getting enraged cut him down with axes (or axe-like sharp horns).

27. He sank in bottomless darkness (hell). He lost his memory. Due to his sinful contacts with women, he suffered unbounded afflictions for eternal years.

28.* As he brooded over that very (virtuous) wife at the time of death, he was born later as a most beautiful damsel, the princess of (the pious king) Rājasiṃha of Vidarbha.

29.** The Pāṇḍya king, Malayadhvaja, the conqueror of the cities of enemies, vanquished other kings in the battle and married the princess of Vidarbha who was offered as prize for bravery.

30.*** He begot from her one daughter of dark-blue eyes, and seven sons younger to her who became the kings of Draviḍa countries.

---

* ŚR. and VR. explain that brooding over a woman at the time of death results in birth as a woman. Purañjana thought of his virtuous wife at the time of his death and due to his good merits he was born in the pious family of Rājasiṁha of Vidarbha and got married to Malayadhvaja, a devotee of Viṣṇu. Both explain the pun on *Vidarbha.*

This allegory is explained differently by different commentators :

** (i) Purañjana was thus associated with a great devotee of Viṣṇu. For Malayadhvaja signifies an eminent votary in the southern country—Malaya—famous for Vaiṣṇavism. Pāṇḍya means one who deserves Paṇḍā—intellect capable of deciding the truth.—ŚR., VR.

(ii) Malaya-dhvaja—one whose mind has attained serenity etc. by service of Hari. By means of *yama, niyama* he defeated and subdued his passionate senses (the inimical kings). He is Pāṇḍya—one endowed with discriminatory intelligence. *Para-purañjaya*—conquerors of *viṣayas* or objects of senses. *Vaidarbhī*—keen intellect. Purañjana and Purañjanī brooded over each other at the time of their death and were born as Pramadottamā and Malayadhvaja—VJ.

(iii) SD. : *Malayadhvaja*—famous in Bhāratavarṣa.

Para-Purañjayaḥ—One who conquers, i.e. attains to Vaikuṇṭha.

Vīrya-paṇām—One available by good merits.

Jīva who was infatuated with *Buddhi* (Intelligence) changed one body after another, once upon a time finds a spiritual preceptor leading to *Mokṣa* (Liberation).

*** Allegory explained :

(i) ŚR., VR., GD. : *ātmajā*—Liking for the service of Lord Kṛṣṇa.

Draviḍa-bhūmi : The Draviḍa country is protected by devotion of the type of Śravaṇa etc.

31. Oh King, each one of them had hundred million sons, whose descendants will enjoy this earth for one Manvantara and more.

32. Agastya married the first-born daughter who was constant in observance of vows.[148] Through her was born Dṛḍhacyuta who had sage Idhmavāha as his son.

33. The royal sage Malayadhvaja distributed the land, among his sons. With a desire to propitiate Lord Kṛṣṇa he retired to the Kulācala mountain, viz., Malaya.

34. The Princess of Vidarbha with bewitching eyes abandoned her palaces, sons and pleasures and ran after the Pāṇḍya king (Malayadhvaja) like the moonlight following the Moon.

35. There flow three rivers viz., Candravasā, Tāmraparṇī and Vaṭodakā in that region. Every day he washed off both his internal (mental) and external (bodily) impurities with the holy waters of the rivers.

36. He performed austere penance by subsisting on bulbous roots, seeds, roots, fruits, flowers, leaves, blades of grass and water. (Thereby) his body got gradually emaciated.

37. He conquered the pairs of opposites like cold and heat, wind and rain, hunger and thirst, agreeable and disagree-

---

In association with devotees of Viṣṇu, a desire to serve him is created and it is followed with seven kinds of *bhakti* or devotion viz. *Śravaṇa* (study of scriptures), *Kīrtana* (singing Lord's praise), *Smaraṇa* (remembering him—his name), *Pādasevana* (serving his feet) *arcana* (worshipping him), *vandana* (laying oneself prostrate before him). The Draviḍa country is famous for votaries of Viṣṇu.

(ii) VJ. names the seven sons as follows : *Virāga* (renunciation), *Vinaya* (discipline), *Dāna* (charity), *Dhairya* (courage), *Aspardhana* (non-jealousy), *Viveka* (discrimination), *Dama* (self control.

148. Different interpretations of the allegory :

Agastya : (i) The mind (ŚR., VC., GD., SD.) (ii) One desirous of *Mokṣa* VR. (iii) A devotee of Viṣṇu (VJ.).

Dṛḍhacyuta : (i) Devoid of any desire for even hereafter such as *Satyaloka*—ŚR.

(ii) Who has absolutely no attachment for sons etc. (VJ).

(iii) One not attached to any pleasure here and hereafter—VC,. SD., GD.

Idhmavāha : (i) Desire to worship the feet of the spiritual preceptor for initiation and obtaining the Lord's grace–ŚR., VR.

(ii) Desire to be a pupil of a spiritual preceptor—VJ.

able, pleasure and pain, viewing them' with equanimity of mind.

38. He burnt down his passions by austerities and knowledge. He conquered his senses, breath (*Prāṇa*) and mind by observing religious vows and rules of self-discipline called *Yama* and *Niyama*. He reflected over the identity of his Soul with Brahman (lit. He united his Soul with Brahman).

39. He sat motionless like a post at one and the same spot for a period of a hundred celestial years. As he bore intense love and devotion to Lord Vāsudeva, he ceased to be conscious of anything else (even of his body).

40.* He realised within himself, the Self as pervading (and illumining) his own body and mental activities and being distinct and different from them. Just as in a dream, one is witness to (and is therefore different from) mental activities (for example the scene of oneself being beheaded in the dream). And hence he verily ceased to participate (in any activities).

41-42.** Oh King! By the light of pure knowledge which radiates its light in all directions—knowledge which was imparted to him by venerable Hari as his preceptor—he realized himself as within (i.e. identical with) the Supreme Brahman

---

*(i) Malayadhvaja realized Paramātman, the Seer, to be different due to his pervasiveness and his body as ephemeral as a dream and devoted himself solely to Paramātman—VR.

(ii) He reasoned with himself and realized the Supreme Soul as present within his own Self and as all pervasive yet distinct from everything else. Thus renouncing *saṁsāra* he became liberated while alive (*jīvan: muktyavasthām āpa*)—VJ.

(iii) Due to *smaraṇa-bhakti* (constant remembrance of God) he felt deep love for the Lord. And he realized him to be shining everywhere in all directions. But feeling him to be distinct and different from himself, he was overcome with the intense feeling of separateness and was fainted in a swoon—VC.

(iv) He realized his Self as knower and his body etc. as transient. He became unattached to everything else except his Self.

**(i) In his religious meditation (*upāsanā*) he realised that his individual Soul (*antaryāmin*) to be identical with the Supreme Brahman. He continued his *upāsanā* to the end of his life.—VR.

(ii) He set aside the false view about the identity of *jīva* and Paramātman—VJ.

and the Supreme Brahman within himself that way. Ultimately he lost this consciousness (of identity) and (like a fire, fuel of which is burnt down) he automatically ceased to belong to *saṁsāra* (i.e. became liberated).

43. Oh King! At that time the Princess of Vidarbha (Malayadhvaja's queen) who looked upon her husband as a god, renounced all pleasures and affectionately waited upon her husband Malayadhvaja, the knower of the highest form of religion.

44. Clad in dark garments, emaciated by observance of vows and with her hair on the head matted, she appeared in the company of her husband like a smokeless flame near flameless fire (of live charcoals).

45. Not being aware of the expiry of her beloved-most husband who was firm in his sitting posture (even after death), the lady approached him and waited upon him as before.

46. When, while serving the feet of her husband she did not feel any warmth, therein she got terrified in her heart like a doe which has strayed away from her herd.

47. Finding herself miserable and friendless, she was overcome with grief and lamented (her fate). Bathing her breasts in tears, she wept loudly in the jungle.

48. "Arise, Oh royal sage, arise. You should protect the earth engirdled with seas, as she is afraid of robbers and apostate and wicked Kṣatriyas"

49. Lamenting thus loudly, the lady who followed her husband to the forest, fell at his feet wailing and shedding profuse tears.

50. She piled up a funeral pyre of fuel. Placing her husband's body on it, she set it on fire. Weeping (all the while) she determined to follow him in death (by burning herself along with his body).

(iii) He realised that the whole—the Supreme Brahman, comprised of the part (the individual Soul) and vice versa. He (thereby) gave up thoughts about *Saṁsāra* and became liberated —SD.

(iv) Oh ! How wonderful is the power of *Bhakti* as *Mukti* (Liberation) is dependent on *Bhakti*—GD.

51. (At that time) there appeared an old friend of hers, a Brāhmaṇa who had mastered his Self. Soothing the lady with sweet consoling words, he spoke to the weeping lady (as follows) :

The Brāhmaṇa said :

52. Who are you? Whose (daughter) are you? Who is this man lying down for whom you are weeping? Don't you recognize me as your friend with whom you used to roam about formerly (before the creation of the universe) ?

53. Friend! (Even if you do not recognize me) do you remember yourself as having a friend called Avijñāta and that you being given to earthly pleasures, left me in search of some place.

54.* Oh noble Sir ! You and I were swans, friends, living in the Mānasa lake. For a period of one thousand years (while the great deluge lasted), both of us were without any abode.

55. Oh brother ? You whose original nature was that, left me and with your heart set on carnal pleasures, you went down to the earth. While roaming there, you saw a place built by a certain woman (Māyā).

56. It was provided with five gardens, nine gates, one guard, three surrounding walls, six families (of merchants), five market places. It was constructed with five materials, and was ruled by a woman.

57. The gardens are the objects of senses; the nine gates are the openings (viz. two eyes, two ears, two nostrils, one mouth, the penis and anus) for Prāṇa (who alone works as a

---

*(i) *Haṁsa* means one who has annihilated all agitations or emotions (*hinasti nirasyati vikārān iti haṁsaḥ*). They are by nature deathless and untouched by pleasures of senses. Enjoyment of pleasure to *jīva* is due to *upādhi* (conditioning) —VR.

(ii) Oh learned one ! Both of us are *haṁsas* which are by nature free from all impurities. Our abode is the Mānasa lake (i.e. knowledge). We have lived together for thousands of years. The memory of previous birth is aroused as a result of the accumulated merits. —VJ.

(iii) *mānasam* etc. : Our abode was the heart in the subtle body (*sūkṣmaśarīragataṁ hṛdayam*) —SD.

guard). Fire, water and food are the surrounding walls, and the group of five sense organs and the mind are the families (of merchants).

58. The market places were the five conative organs; the five elements constituted the imperishable materials and the power i.e. Intelligence was the ruler. Under her dominance the man who enters this abode loses his Self consciousness in deep sleep.

59. Being overcome with (the charms of) the woman there, you enjoyed yourself in her company and forgot the memory of the previously known fact (your original status of being the Brahman). It is due to your association with her that you have been reduced to this wretched condition, Oh Lord.

60. You are not the daughter of the king of Vidarbha. Nor is this warrior your friend. Nor are you the husband of Purāñjanī by whom you were interned in the city of nine gates.

61. It is really the illusion created by me that you regard the man (Purañjana in the previous birth) as the virtuous woman—(Vaidarbhī in this birth). You are neither. We are *haṁsas* (pure spirits). Please see (realize) our real nature (course).

62. I am identical with you. You are not other than me. Please note that you and I are one. Wise men never see even the slightest difference or distinction between us.

63. Just as a man finds his one Self as divided in two in (his reflection in) the mirror and in the pupils of eyes, similar is the difference between us two.

64. In this way, the *haṁsa* (swan) from the Mānasa lake i.e. *Jīva* who was awakened (was made to realize his original state) by his fellow swan, became established in his own real nature. He regained the memory of his original nature which was lost due to his separation from him.

65. Oh Barhiṣman! This knowledge about the Self has been explained to you in an indirect manner; for the venerable Lord, the creator of the universe, likes to remain beyond the ken of senses.

CHAPTER TWENTY-NINE

(The Purañjana allegory explained)

Prācīna-barhis said :

1. Oh divine sage ! (The implication of) your speech is not clearly understood by us. Sages (with spiritual knowledge may) grasp it (correctly) but not we who are deluded by ritualistic *karmas*.

Nārada explained :

2. One should understand Purañjana (creator of the city) as the embodied Soul (or *jīva*); for it is he (*jīva*) who builds his own city, i.e., body, having one, two, three, four or many feet or no foot at all.

3. The friend of *Puruṣa* (*Jīva*) who is called *Avijñāta* (the Unknown) is *Īśvara* (Himself), for he is not known by men as being endowed with names, actions or attributes.

4. When the *Jīva* desired to enjoy all the attributes of the *Prakṛti* (i.e. material objects of pleasure) in their entirety, he thought that (out of those bodies) the human body, provided as it was with nine entrances, two hands and two feet, as the most suitable one.

5. One should understand the young damsel Purañjanī as the intellect (*Buddhi*) which creates the notion of I-ness and mine-ness. It is by presiding over (i.e. identifying himself with) *Buddhi* that the *Jīva* in this body enjoys sense objects by means of sense-organs.

6. The male companions (of Purañjanī) are the group of (ten) conative and cognitive sense-organs which bring about knowledge and action. (Her) female friends are the activities of the senses. The (five-hooded) serpent is the *Prāṇa* (vital breath) with its five-fold activities.

7. One should understand *Bṛhadbala* (the eleventh powerful hero attending upon Purañjanī) as the Mind, the leader (and controller) of both kinds of senses and that the *Pāñcālas* are the five sense-objects, in the midst of which is situated the city of nine gates.

8. Two eyes, two nostrils, two ears, the penis and the anus are the four pairs of adjacent gates, with the mouth (as

the nineth). Out of these *Prāṇa* goes out (to the particular sense object) in association with (the faculties of that) particular sense-organ.

9. The pairs of eyes, nostrils and the mouth are the five gates in the east (i.e. the front of the head). The right ear is regarded as the south gate and the left ear as the north gate.

10. The two opening gates in the lower parts of this are the western gates and these are called here the anus and the penis. *Khadyota* and *Āvir-mukhī*, the two gates that are constructed at the same place adjacently in this city, are (known as) the eyes. By means of the power of seeing possessed by these, the Lord of the body (Purañjana or *Jīva*) perceives forms and colours which are called here the *Vibhrājit* country.

11.* *Nalinī* and *Nālinī* are the two nostrils, and smell has been called the *Saurabha* country. The faculty of smelling is designated *Avadhūta* (the companion of Purañjana). The gate called *Mukhyā* is the mouth. The organ of speech is (Purañjana's companion) *Vipaṇa* and the organ of taste is (the name of Purañjana's friend) *Rasajña* or *Rasavid.*

12. *Āpaṇa* or the market signifies here as (the region of) speech activity while *Bahūdana* means the varieties of food. The right ear is the Southern gate known as *Pitṛhū* and the left the Northern gate is remembered as *Devahū.*

13. The scriptures (*Śāstras*) which treat of the path of worldly activities (i.e. ritualistic *karmas*) and those which deal with abstention from such *karmas* and renunciation, are designated as the country of Pañcālas. Hearing to these through the faculty of hearing is called here *Śrutadhara* (the companion of Purañjana), the *Jīva* may proceed by the path of manes (*Pitṛs*) or of the gods.

14. The organ of generation is the western gate called *Āsurī*; the act of sexual intercourse is the region known as *Grāmaka.* The procreative ability (in the organ) is spoken of as *Durmada* (who was Purañjaña's friend). The anus is de-

* The order of verses from 11 to 30 in the text before VR. and to some extent before VJ. is different.

signated as *Nirṛti* (the other western gate or the postern passage).

15. The hell is the region called *Vaiśasa*, while the power of the organ to defecate (through the anus) is called his friend *Lubdhaka*. And now, hear from me who the two blind ones are. They are (the pairs of) hands and feet with the help of which one makes movements and does work.

16. The harem is the heart and the mind is called *Viṣūci* (*Viṣūcīna*)—the principal officer over the harem. By the mind's attributes (like Sattva etc.), the Jīva attains to the state of infatuation, serenity or joy.

17. According as the *Buddhi* (intellect) is disturbed (in the dream state) or affects (the senses in the waking state) the *Jīva*, though (by nature) a mere witness, is tainted with her (*Buddhi's*) attributes, and is made to feel as if he is affected by those changes (directly)

18* The body is the chariot with horses in the form of senses, yoked to it. It (apparently) moves with the unimpeded speed of the year, though (actually) it is motionless. Good and evil actions are its two wheels. The three attributes (*sattva*, *rajas* and *tamas*) constitute its flagstaffs and the five vital airs (*Prāṇas* or *asus*) are its five cords.

19.** The mind is its rein (to control the horses); the Intellect is the charioteer; the heart is the seat; the pairs like pleasure and pain are the poles to which the yoke is rivetted; the objects of five senses are the weapons (for attack); the seven constituents of the body (viz. blood, flesh, fat,. bones etc.) are its protective covers.

20. Ākūti (the five organs of actions, e.g. hands, feet, etc.) is its external motion. The *Jīva* vigorously runs after the mirage (-like objects of pleasure) with his army of eleven sense-organs (five cognitive and five conative sense-organs plus mind—the internal organ). He takes pleasure in five types of slaughter (i.e. wrongful enjoyment of five types of sense-ob-

---

* These verses echo the following from *Kaṭha Up*. 1.3.3-4

***Ātmānaṁ rathinaṁ viddhi, śarīraṁ ratham eva ca /*
Buddhiṁ hi sārathiṁ viddhi, manaḥ pragraham eva ca //
Indriyāṇi hayān āhur viṣayāns teṣu gocarān /
Ātmendriya-mano-yuktam bhoktetyāhur manīṣiṇaḥ//

jects by his five senses). The year which records the passage of time is *Caṇḍavega* (the king of Gandharvas).

21. Here the three hundred and sixty male Gandharvas under his command are the days and an equal number of female Gandharvas are the nights. By their turns, they take away the life of man by rotation.

22. *Kāla-Kanyā* is the old age incarnate. People do not greet her. Death, the king of Yavanas, adopted her as his sister for the (help in the) destruction of the world.

23. Mental anguishes and physical pains and diseases are his active Yavana soldiers. *Prajvāra* means the two types of fever (one accompanied with cold and the other with high temperature which is said to have a swift career to harass living beings.

24. Thus for a period of one hundred years, the embodied Jīva, covered as he is by dark ignorance, is being tormented in his body with various types of afflictions caused by supernatural agencies, (*adhidaivika*), elements (*adhibhautika*) and his body (*adhyātmika*).

25. Though he is essentially attributeless, he superimposes on himself the attributes of *Prāṇa* (such as hunger, thirst), the qualities of sense-organs (e.g. blindness, deafness) and the attributes of the mind (for example : passions of love, hate etc.). He lies confined to the body brooding over trifling pleasures of the senses and he continues to perform actions under the (influence of the) false notions of I-ness and mine-ness.

26. When the Jīva, though by nature self-luminous (i.e. self-knowing), does not recognise (himself to be) the glorious Supreme Preceptor, the Soul, he gets attached (and bound) to the attributes of *Prakṛti*.

27. Regarding the attributes as referring to his own self, he then helplessly commits actions which are white (*sāttvika*), black (*tāmasa*) and red (*rājasa*) and is born in various species of life according to the nature of his actions.

28. By his white (i.e. *sāttvika*) actions, he sometimes attains to worlds (like *Svarga*) which are full of light. Sometimes (by his red i.e. *rājasa* actions) he goes to regions which result in (i.e. lead to) sufferings and require exertion through

activities. And sometimes (by *tāmasika* actions), he takes birth in regions which are full of darkness (i.e. ignorance) and grief.

29. This *Jīva* with blind (i.e. deluded) intelligence is sometimes (born as) a male, a female, an impotent person, a god or a man or as a subhuman being according to his previous actions and the (dominant) attribute of *Prakṛti*.

30-31. Just as a poor starving dog which goes from door to door, gets (beating with) a stick or cooked rice (according) as destined by fate, the *Jīva*, with his heart full of desires, wanders, by paths which are high (as prescribed by religion) or low (as prohibited by scriptures), through higher (celestial) worlds, lower (infernal) regions or the middle (human) world and experiences pleasure or pain as ordained by fate.

32. There is no immunity to the *Jīva* even from one type of miseries which are caused by superhuman agencies like gods (*adhi-daivika*), by other beings (*adhi-bhautika*) and these relating to one's body (*adhyātmika*). Even if the remedy (against them) is sought, it is temporary and is (again) of the nature of misery.[149]

33. Just as a man carrying a heavy load on his head, places it on his shoulder (for relief), so are all remedies (of the nature of misery itself).

34. Oh sinless King ! Mere act (without the knowledge of the truth and accompanied with some desire) cannot be the effective final remedy against (the miseries etc. resulting from) another act (*karman*) as both are the outcome of *avidyā* (ignorance). It (such attempt to terminate one *karma* by another) is like a dream within dream (wherein there is an exchange of dream-consciousness but no termination of dreams as in wakefulness).

35.* Just as a person wandering in the dream-land with his mind which as *liṅga śarīra* (subtle body) forms the limita-

149. There is no remedy against misery, the only remedy being the worship and contemplation of God—VR.

* VR. : The state of being a god, a man is not inherent in the nature of the Soul. It is due to the working of the mind that one falsely identifies the Soul with the body and experiences miseries. But they are like dream experiences.

tions of the Soul (and experiences fear, misery etc. till he wakes up from the dream to realize the unreality of that experience), the *saṁsāra* (transmigration of the Soul in the miserable world) does not come to an end (while his sleep of ignorance continues) in spite of the non-reality of the phenomenal world.

36. It is ignorance (or Mind—*manas*) that causes the uninterrupted chain of miseries[150] (or transmigration) to the Soul which is essentially the real existence. The chain of *saṁsāra* is cut asunder by Supreme devotion[151] to the Preceptor (Hari)[152].

37. When the *Yoga* of (self-less, disinterested) devotion to Lord Vāsudeva[153] is established in the proper manner[154], it (automatically) causes renunciation (of worldly pleasures) and manifests knowledge.

(ii) VJ.: The transmigration of the Soul (*saṁsṛti*) does not cease to be till one does not realise Hari directly (*arthe avidyamāne*) just as dream experiences continue till one awakes (to find that those experiences were unreal.)

As Madhva regards this world as real, VJ. takes pains to explain that the analogy between the dream and the world shall not be stretched too far and that 'the absence of knowledge of the reality-as-it is' is the common factor between the experiences in the dream and in the world and not the non-reality of the world. The implication of *hi* is that, if a person, born in *saṁsāra*, does not attain to the real knowledge of Hari, his *saṁsāra* is purposeless and fruitless.

(iii) GD.: Just as waking up from sleep is the only remedy against the miseries one experiences in dreams, realization of the Self is the only remedy against *avidyā* (nescience); other remedies cannot cut the vicious circle of the transmigration of the Soul and consequent miseries which are caused by 'I-ness' and 'mine-ness'.

150. *anartha*—The illusion about the identity of the body with the Soul—SD.

151. *paramayā bhaktyā*—Devotion which is superior to austerities, vows, ritualistic acts and even the knowledge of the Soul—SD.

152. Devotion to Hari which generates knowledge should be performed as it terminates *Saṁsāra*—VJ.

153. Who is knowledge and renunciation incarnate and is the controller of the universe and giver of knowledge—GD.

154. *Sadhricīnena* : (i) by burning down all evils in the mind by the fire of Breath-control—VJ.

(ii) By person who is free from worldly desires—VJ.

38. That *Bhakti-yoga* dependent as it is on the stories of Lord Acyuta, will be mastered before long by him who always listens to those stories with faith or devoutly studies them every day, Oh royal sage.

39. Oh King ! (He can listen to those stories) in places where pious and pure-hearted votaries of the Lord narrate and listen to the glorification of the attributes of the Lord with eager hearts.

40. There (to the congregation of the devotees) flow forth from all sides rivers (entirely) of pure nectar (in the form) of stories of Lord Viṣṇu (the destroyer of demon Madhu) sweetly sung by noble souls. Oh King ! Those who drink those (nectar-like stories) with intent ears and without being surfeited, are never touched (affected) by hunger, thirst, fear, sorrow and delusion.

41. (In the absence of the company of the pious), being always harassed by these natural troubles, the world of beings (i.e. men) does not cherish any real love for the ocean of nectarlike stories of Lord Hari indeed !

42-44. Brahmā (the chief among the progenitors) himself, the venerable Lord Śiva (the Lord of mountains), Manu, Dakṣa and other lords of creation, Sanaka and life-long celibates, expounders of the Vedas like Marīci, Atri, Aṅgiras, Pulastya, Pulaha, Kratu, Bhṛgu, Vasiṣṭha—these and others ending with me—all masters of speech could not, to this day, see the Supreme Lord, the Seer of all, though (we have been) trying to visualize him by means of penance, *upāsanā* (worship) and meditation.

45* Those who meticulously study the meaning of the Vedas which are of very great expanse and fathomless in the depth of meaning, and worship him in his limited form (such as Indra etc.) the characteristics of which (viz. wielding a

---

* (i) VR : The realization of god is possible by worshipping (*upāsanā*) him only and not by mere knowledge or by *karma* (ritualist act) only.

(ii) JG. & VC : Persons devoted to ritualistic acts (*karmas*) only, never realize God.

(iii) SD : The Veda directs persons not favoured by the Lord, to perform ritualistic acts (e.g. sacrifices) for attaining the Heaven and not to the worship and service of the Lord.

Vajra etc.) are detailed in the Mantras (Vedic text), do not know the Supreme Lord.

46. When the Lord who is being meditated upon in the heart by a person, shows his grace unto the meditator, the person (so favoured) withdraws his mind, howsoever deeply attached (it may be) to the ways of the world, and to the ritualistic acts prescribed in the Vedas.

47. Oh Barhiṣman ! Do not therefore look upon as real the acts (ritualistic *karmas*) which appear as real through ignorance. These acts are pleasant and attractive to listen to, but they do not even touch (i.e. have any relation with) the ultimate Reality.

48. Those whose intellect is occupied with *dhūmra-mārga* (the path of ritualistic acts like sacrifices etc.)[155] call the Vedas as prescribing the ritualistic acts only. They have not grasped the truth about the Veda. For they have not realized that the Ātman (the Soul) which is their own essential Self, is implicitly intended in the Vedas. These (devotees of the path of Karma) do not know the region where god Viṣṇu (Janārdana) dwells (much less Janārdana himself).

49. Having encircled the entire sphere of the earth with *darbha*-grass by spreading them with their ends to the East, you have become haughty, (and) proud by slaughtering a great many beasts (in sacrifices). You do not know what is *karma* and what is superior to *karma*. The act that pleases Hari is the real *karma*. And the knowledge which leads to the fixation of the mind in Hari is the real knowledge.

50. Hari is the Soul of the embodied beings as well as their Ruler. He is their independent cause (the material cause of the universe). The soles of his feet are the real asylum to all, for in them lies the well-being (and security) of all men here.

51. Verily he is the most beloved one, the Soul (*Ātman*). By resorting to him, there is not the slightest fear or misery (as in the cases of others). He who knows this, is indeed the learned one. He who is learned is the (real) preceptor and he is (veritable) Hari himself.

155. Or whose intelligence has been smoky and impure—ŚR.

Nārada said :

52. In this way, your question is completely answered, Oh excellent one among men! Now listen to me carefully as I tell you, a secret yet definitely ascertained truth.

53. Find out the deer which ignoring the blood-thirsty wolves (which are waiting) ahead and unmindful of (the coming of the arrow) shot from behind by a hunter to pierce it, strolls about in a flower-garden enamoured of its female associate, grazing tender grass and with its ears spell bound with the music of humming beas.

54. Oh King! You should look upon yourself as the doomed deer whose heart is pierced with a hidden arrow discharged by the hunter, viz., the god of Death, who chases you unperceived from behind. You who, in the house resorted to by women who are similar to flowers (in their ephemeral youthful charms which fade away very soon), seek after the most insignificant dose of sensual pleasures of taste and sex which are extremely minute like the fragrance and honey in flowers and are the result of ritualistic acts (*karmas*) performed with a motive, for attaining a particular object. Co-habiting with women and with your mind firmly attached to them, your ears are extremely charmed by the sweet conversation with women and others—conversation which is extremely attractive like the sweet honey of swarms of bees. You are enjoying yourself in the house, completely oblivious of the small components of time amounting to days and nights which, like a pack of wolves ahead of you, prey upon your life.

55. Having carefully considered your own behaviour (as being) like that of the deer (in the above verse), you, who are so conditioned, restrain your mind in the interior of your heart, and the stream-like outgoing tendencies of your ears (and other senses) in your mind. Renounce the householder's stage of life (lit. women's house) with its talk about extremely lustful and lascivious gatherings; (Do try to) please the Lord who is the shelter of *jīvas* (*haṁsas*) and withdraw step by step (from everything else)."

The King said :

56. "Oh Brahman ! What Your venerable Lordship has spoken has been heard and reflected over by me. The sacrificial priests do not know this. Would they not have spoken (about it to me) if they had known it ?

57. You have thoroughly resolved a great doubt raised by them (my preceptors) in this matter (pertaining to the Soul). (But a doubt still lingers). For even sages are deluded in the realm which is beyond the range of senses, Oh Brāhmaṇa sage. (The Vedists say :)

58. Leaving in this world the body with which a person begins to perform acts (*karmas*), he enjoys the consequent fruits (of those *karmas*), elsewhere (in the next world) through a different body.

59. This doctrine of the Vedists (the knowers and advocates of Vedic *karmas*) is heard everywhere. (But how is it possible when the two bodies viz., the performer of an action and the enjoyer of the fruit of that action are different?) (The second doubt is :) As soon as an act prescribed in the Vedas is performed, it disappears and does not become visible. (Thus due to the cessation of an act, its consequent fruit is an impossibility)".

60. A person enjoys the fruits of an action in the next world with the same subtle body with which he performs the act (in this world), and thus, there is no interruption (i.e. change of the subtle body and the mind).*

61. Just as a person (in a dream) forgets his identity with this body (which is) lying and breathing, and experiences (in the dream) impressions of actions recorded in the mind, similarly (he experiences the fruits of his actions committed here) with another body similar (to the previous one) or belonging to another kind (as of a god or of a sub-human being).

62. Whatever body the jīva assumes by saying in his mind that 'these (wife and sons) are mine' and 'I am this body (e.g. a Brāhmaṇa)' he accepts (the responsibilitiy of) the

* ŚR. adds :—Due to the persistence of the subtle mental body even after the destruction of the physical body, there is no logical discrepancy in this.

karmas committed by that body and thereby (he gets) a subsequent birth.

63. Just as (tendencies of) the mind (that direct activities) are inferred by the behaviour and activities of both the conative and cognitive sense-organs so are the acts committed by the body in the previous birth, inferred from the natural inclinations of the mind.

64. What is never and nowhere experienced or seen or heard by this (present) body, is sometimes experienced (in dream etc.) according to the form as it is impressed on the mind (in the previous birth).

65. Therefore, Oh King, definitely believe that the *jīva*, dependent as he is on his subtle body consisting of *vāsanās* (*karmic* impressions left on the mind), had a previous body which has undergone that type of experience. For the mind is incapable of touching (perceiving) an object which is not experienced by it (previously).

66. May you be blessed! It is (the high and low propensities of) the mind which speak of the previous births of man as well as predict whether he will be born in a higher or lower form of life.[156]

67. Sometimes some impossibilities[157] with reference to place (e.g. a sea on the mountain top), time (e.g. stars by daylight) and action (e.g. getting one's self beheaded) are seen or heard in the mind (in dreams). (As these are impossible experiences even in previous births) these are to be inferred to be due to disturbed sleep etc. and these do not contradict the above (statement in verse 65.)

68. All objects which are within the ken of sense-perception enter the mind according to their (particular) order and in groups and disappear (after being so experienced). Hence (it is that) all persons possess a mind (with impressions of the past).

---

156. *nābhaviṣyataḥ*—will not be born again or will be liberated —VC.

157. VJ. explains these impossibilities as due to mixing up of impressions. VC. explains the possibilities of these with reference to other times, places etc. For example : the sea is on the top of (the submerged) mount Maināka, stars appear in complete solar eclipse, disturbance in the humids or components of the body may give rise to strange dreams.

69. (Normally these objects appear in a serial order but some times all of them present themselves simultaneously).

When the mind is firmly established in pure Sattva (uncontaminated with *rajas* and *tamas*) and is in the presence of the venerable Lord (in meditation), the whole universe shines forth united with the Lord, like the dark planet Rāhu appears on the disc of the Moon (at the time of lunar eclipse). (It is the experience of Yogins that sometimes all objects simultaneously flash on the pure mind).

70. (Thus the doubt that the performer of an act and the enjoyer of its fruits are different is dispelled by the proven continuity of the same subtle body) as the notion of 'I' and 'mine' about the physical body which conditions the *jīva*, will persist (i.e. will not cease to exist) so long as this beginningless subtle body which is the result of the conglomeration of intellect (*Buddhi*), mind, the senses (and their) objects and the triad of *guṇas* (*sattva* etc.), continues.

71. Due to suspension of the passage of Prāṇa (i.e. of sense-activity) in deep sleep, unconsciousness, extreme anguish (due to bereavement of the near ones), as well as in high fever and at the time of death, the sense of 'I-ness' is unmanifest (dormant).

72. Just as the moon (though existent) is not seen in the night of the new-Moon day, due to underdevelopment of senses and organs in the embryonic stage, and even in infancy the notion I-ness does not clearly manifest itself in the eleven sense organs (ten sense-organs *plus* the internal organ—the mind) as it does in the case of a full-grown youth.

73. Just as (in spite of the unreality of the objects and events in dreams) the unpleasant happenings in the dream do not cease to be (till one is awakened), the *saṁsāra* (the cycle of the transmigration of the Soul) does not come to an end in the case of one who broods over the objects of pleasure, even though the objects are (in reality) non-existent.

74. Thus the subtle body (*liṅga*) is constituted of five subtle elements; is extended by the development of sixteen modifications (viz. 5 Prāṇas + 1 mind + 10 Indriyas—sense); is a product of three *guṇas* (*sattva*, *rajas* and *tamas*). When

it is united with consciousness, it (the whole aggregate) is called *jīva*.

75. It is through the subtle body that the *jīva* takes over or casts off (different) bodies. And it is by this that he experiences delight, sorrow, fear, misery or happiness.

76. Just as the caterpillar does not go away (from its first foot-hold on the blade of grass) and moves on (only after getting a firm foothold on another blade), the *jīva*, even while dying, does not let go his identity with its previous body (which he is giving up even at the point of death).

77. While he does not attain to another (i.e. the next) body by the exhaustion of the *karmas* (which were the cause of the previous dying body), the mind alone is the cause of birth and death (i.e. the *saṁsāra*) of beings, Oh King.

78. When, brooding over sensual pleasure (enjoyed by it), the *jīva* frequently indulges in *karmas* for achieving them. As a result of those *karmas* he, being subject to *avidyā* (nescience or ignorance), gets bound up with *karmas* of the body and the like.

79. Hence, in order to free yourself from the bondage of *avidyā* you worship Hari with all your heart, looking upon the universe as identical with him, for everything : the creation, maintenance and withdrawal of the universe is due to him."

Maitreya said :

80. Venerable Nārada, the chief votary of the Lord, explained to him the real nature of the swans (*jīva* and the *Paramātman*) and bidding good bye to him, he then went to the realm of the *Siddhas*.

81. The royal sage Prācīnabarhis passed on instructions (to his minister for conveying them) to his sons for the protection of his subjects and retired to the hermitage of Kapila for performing penance.

82. In that hermitage, the warrior, being free from attachment and with thoroughly concentrated mind, worshipped the lotus-like feet of Govinda with earnest devotion and attained a personality similar to the Lord.

83. Oh sinless Vidura, he who will listen to or make

others listen to this spiritual allegory sung by the divine sage Nārada, is emancipated from his subtle body.

84. He who gets by heart, while it is being sung, this self-purifying account which was issued from the mouth of a great divine sage and which purifies the world by the glories of Lord Mukunda (Kṛṣṇa) and which brings in the highest reward, becomes free from all bondages and does not wander in the *saṁsāra*.

85. This is what I understood of this wonderful allegory about the Soul. I have narrated to you about *saṁsāra* by the alllegory of the householder's life and have dispelled the doubt as to how the fruit of *karmas* is enjoyed in the other world.

CHAPTER THIRTY

(*The Story of Pracetasas—Their Marriage with Māriṣā and the birth of Dakṣa*)

Vidura said :

1. What well-being did the sons of Prācīnabarhis mentioned by you, accomplish by propitiating Hari through repeatedly reciting the hymn sung by Rudra, Oh Brahman.

2. Oh pupil of Bṛhaspati (Maitreya)! Meeting by a lucky chance god Śiva (the Lord of mount Kailāsa), the Pracetasas who won the grace (lit. became favourite personal attendants of the Lord of *Kaivalya* or Liberation.[158] must have certainly attained to their highest goal in life (viz. Liberation or *Mokṣa*). Please tell me: Have they attained it here or hereafter?

Maitreya said :

3. Pracetasas who wished to carry out the order of their father remained under the waters of the sea (-like

158. i.e. Viṣṇu—VJ.

lake)[159] and propitiated the creator of all bodies (i.e. Viṣṇu) by worshipping him with repeated recitation (of the hymn sung by Rudra) and by practising austerities.

4. At the end of (the penance covering) ten thousand years, the Eternal Supreme Man (Lord Viṣṇu) manifested himself to them in a purely *sāttvika* form, completely pacifying their trouble of penance by his soothing splendour.

5. Like a (dark-blue) cloud on the peak of mount Meru (which is of pure gold) he rode over the shoulders of Garuḍa. He wore a yellow garment and had the Kaustubha gem in his necklace. By his splendour he dispelled the darkness from all directions.

6. His cheeks as well as his entire face appeared refulgent with bright gold ornaments (shedding a spectrum of variegated light of the precious stones set in ornaments). He wore a brilliant crown. He was wielding (lit. was attended upon by) eight weapons[160] (in his eight hands). He was waited upon by his attendants, sages and prominent gods (like Brahmā); His glory was being sung by the celestial singer Garuḍa with the fluttering of his (*Veda-*) wings.

7. The First (Ancientmost or Supreme) Man was garlanded with a wreath of forest-flowers (*vanamālā*) which vied in beauty with the goddess Lakṣmī who beautified the central space (His chest) encircled by His eight long and mighty arms. He looked with compassion at the sons of Barhiṣmat (the Pracetasas) who sought his protection, and addressed to them in deep voice like the rumbling of clouds.

The Venerable Lord said :

8. May you be blessed, Oh Princes! Due to your strong mutual love, you are following the same religious observances. I am highly pleased with you by your brotherly affection. You seek a boon from me.

9. A man who will daily remember you at dusk and

159. Vide supra 4.24.20; 4.25.2.

160. VR. enumerates them : a conch, the disc—*Sudarśana*, the mace *Kaumodakī*, a lotus, the Śārṅga bow, an arrow, a sword, a shield. He defends the inclusion of a lotus as weapon by *chatri-nyāya*.

dawn, will love his brothers like his own self and will cherish friendliness to all living beings.

10. I shall bestow whatever boon is desired from me and brilliant intellect as well, to those who every morning and evening praise me with concentrated mind, with the hymn (which Rudra sang).

11. Since you have, with gladness, accepted and carried out the command of your father, your enviable glory will spread all over the worlds.

12. You will have a glorious son who is not inferior to Brahmā (the creator) in excellent attributes and who will fill (i.e. populate) the whole of these three worlds with his progeny.

13. Oh Princes ! A lotus-eyed girl was born to (a heavenly nymph called) Pramlocā from (a sage by name) Kaṇḍu. When the girl was abandoned (by her mother) (the presiding deity of) trees took charge of her.

14. When she, being hungry, began to cry, king Soma (the Moon god) who was moved with compassion, put his index finger overflowing with nectar, in her mouth.

15. You are commanded to increase population by your father who is (now) my follower. Therefore, marry that beautiful girl (with fine hips) without delay.

16. All of you are observers of the same vows (e.g. protection of subjects) and are of similar disposition (good-naturedness, high moral character etc.). She will completely dedicate her heart to you all and hence will have the same disposition and observe the same vows. (Hence there will be no conflict). May this beautiful lady (with a slender waist) be your wife.

17. Without any diminution in physical vigour, you will enjoy the earthly and heavenly pleasures through my grace, for a period of one million celestial years.

18. Then through your firm devotion to me, the impurities (such as lust, hate) in your heart will be burnt. Being disgusted with the hell (-like pleasures of this world and the next), you will attain to my abode.

19. Even in the case of those men who enter householder's life, if they dedicate all their actions to me and spend

their time in talking and hearing about my stories, the householder's life does not result in a bondage to them.

20. By listening to the discourses about me, by those who are well-versed in the Vedas, I, the Omniscient Lord, enter the heart of those devotees as if I become new one (every moment). This entry (i.e. my manifestation) into the heart itself is the realization of Brahman, for those who reach me are not deluded, grieved nor are elated.

Maitreya said :

21. When Lord Viṣṇu (Janārdana), the conferrer of the objectives in human life (viz. *dharma, artha, kāma* and *Mokṣa*) and the best Friend of all, spoke to them thus, Pracetasas, whose impurities of *tamas* (ignorance) and *rajas* (emotions and passions) have been perfectly cleansed at his sight, bowed him with folded hands and addressed to him with their voice choked (with tears).

Pracetasas said :

22. "Many salutations to the Lord who destroys all types of misery and whose excellent attributes and names have been considered (by the Vedas and knowers of the Brahman) as the means of attaining the highest good. Obeisance to him who surpasses the mind and speech in speed[161] and whose path is beyond the ken of all the senses.

23. In your own essential nature, you are pure, serene (and joy incarnate). The unreal appearance of duality in you is due to (the function of the) mind. For the creation, sustenance and dissolution of the universe, you have assumed forms (of Brahmā, Viṣṇu and Śiva) through the *guṇas* (attributes viz. *Sattva, rajas* and *tamas*) of the Māyā. Our salutations to you.

24. Obeisance to Hari who is essentially pure *sattva* (unmixed with *rajas* and *tamas*), and knowledge about whom terminates the *saṁsāra*. Bow to Vāsudeva, Kṛṣṇa, the Lord of all *Sātvatas*.

25. Hail to you who have a lotus sprouted in the navel. Bow to the Lord, the wearer of a wreath of lotuses. Salutations

161. Cf. *tad dhāvato'nyān atyeti tiṣṭhan* / Īśa. 4.

to the God with lotus-like feet. Obeisance to you, Oh lotus-eyed God!

26. Salutations to you who wear spotless, pure yellow garments like the filaments of the lotus. We bow to you who are the abode of all beings and a seer or witness of them all.

27. You have manifested to us who are afflicted with miseries, your form which annihilates all these kinds of trouble. What more grace could be shown? (This is the highest favour shown to us).

28. Oh destroyer of inauspiciousness ! Only this much is to be done by the masters who are kind and compassionate to the poor that they should remember at the proper time, that the indigents are their own. (But in our case you have done much more than that in manifesting yourself to us).

29. Such remembrance (of the poor) brings peace and happiness to beings. Abiding as you are as *antaryāmin* (Inner Controller) in the hearts of even the most insignificant creatures, how is it that you do not know the blessing desired by us who are your devotees ?

30. To us whom you are not only a guide to Liberation but a goal desired by us, the very fact that the Lord is pleased with us, is itself a boon sought by us.

31. We, however, seek a boon from you, Oh Lord, who are beyond the cause of causes i.e. *Prakṛti* (the prime cause of the universe). As there is no limit to your excellences or glories, you are extolled as Ananta (Infinite).

32. When the *Pārijāta* tree is easily found (by a lucky chance), a bee does not resort to any other tree. (Similarly), when we have found shelter at your feet directly, what other things should we seek ?[162]

33. So long as we, being dominated by Māyā, are wandering here in the *saṁsāra* due to the force of our actions (*karmas*), may we be blest in every life with the companionship of devotees attached to you.

34. We do not consider (the pleasures in) heaven or even the final beatitude as equivalent to the companionship of

162. Alternatively: (i) Why should we beg for other contemptible things?

(ii) If we are to seek anything there is no end to desires—ŚR.

your devotees (enjoyed even for a single moment). What of blessings like kingdom etc.) coveted by mortal beings?

35. In the company of Your votaries, sweet purifying stories (of the Lord) which pacify the thirst of desire are extolled. There is absence of enmity against all beings. Nor is there any fear to anybody.

36. There (in the company of devotees) the glorious Lord Nārāyaṇa Himself, the goal of Sannyāsins, is again and again extolled through sacred stories, by persons who are free from attachment.

37. Will not the association of your devotees who with a desire to purify the sacred places, move about on foot, be liked by a person afraid (of *saṁsāra*)?

38. Oh Lord! It is due to a moment's contact with your friend, god Śiva (Bhava) that we have today attained to you direct—you who are our goal and the best physician who cures the incurable malady of (the cycle of) births and deaths.

39-40. Oh Lord! (we seek the second boon:). Whatever we have properly studied, whatever troubles we have taken for propitiating the preceptors, Brāhmaṇas and elderly people by our compliance, the respects we paid to noble persons, friends, brothers and to all living beings without any jealousy, the austere penances we have performed without food, submerged in water for a very long period—may all this, we beseech you, contribute to the entire satisfaction and pleasure of yours—you who are the Omnipresent, the Supreme Man.

41. Manu, god Brahmā (the self-born), glorious Lord Śiva and others who have purified their hearts with penance and knowledge, praise your greatness even though they could not grasp the fullest extent of your glory. Hence we extol you according to our humble capacity.

42. Obeisance to you, the Supreme Man, who are equal to all and pure (unsoiled by Māyā). Salutation to you, glorious Lord Vāsudeva, who are pure *sattva* incarnate."

Maitreya said :

43. Thus extolled by Pracetasas, Hari who is affectionate to his devotees (lit. those who seek his shelter) and is of

irresistible prowess, became pleased with them and conferred that boon (saying 'So be it'.). Even though their eyes were not satiated by looking at him and they did not wish his departure, he returned to his abode.

44. Then the Pracetasas came out from the water of the sea (-like lake). Seeing the earth (wildly) covered with trees that had grown so tall as to obstruct the way to heaven, they flared up with wrath.

45. For rendering the earth tree-less, they then angrily breathed out from their mouth fire and wind, just as Saṁvartaka or Kālāgni Rudra does at the time of the dissolution of the universe.

46. Seeing the trees being thus reduced to ashes, god Brahmā appeared and pacified the sons of Barhiṣmat (Pracetasas) by reasoning.

47. Then the surviving trees which were terrified, acted upon the advice of god Brahmā and offered their daughter to Pracetasas.

48. In compliance of the command of god Brahmā, they (Pracetasas) married Māriṣā (the daughter of the trees). Dakṣa, the former mind-born son of Brahmā (lit. one born of the unborn Viṣṇu), was born of her, on account of his (Dakṣa's) insulting the great god Śiva (formerly).

49. At the advent of the Cākṣuṣa Manvantara (the sixth aeon), when the previous creation was annihilated by the force of time[163] it was this Dakṣa who directed by the Lord, created the progeny as desired by him.

50. While he was being born, he eclipsed with his own splendour the light of all luminous bodies. He came to be called Dakṣa, the competent, on account of his precision and proficiency in the performance of ritualistic acts.

51. (The beginningless) god Brahmā installed him (as a Prajāpati—the protector of the creation) and appointed him to procreate and protect the creation. Dakṣa (in his turn) employed all other Prajāpatis—progenitors of creation—to perform their respective jobs.

---

163. When Dakṣa's previous body was destroyed through the force of time (ŚR.).

CHAPTER THIRTYONE

(*The Story of Pracetasas : Their Renunciation and Liberation*)

Maitreya said :

1. Then (at the end of one million years of enjoying earthly and heavenly pleasures), superior knowledge dawned on Pracetasas. Remembering the words of Lord Viṣṇu (vide supra 4.30. 18), they entrusted their wife to the care of their son (Dakṣa) and immediately left their house (as recluses).

2. On the western sea-shore, at the place where (the sage) Jājali[164] attained the final beatitude, they resolved to engage themselves in (the sacrificial session in the form of) the enquiry about the Soul which leads to the realization that the Soul abides in all beings.

3. Nārada who was worthy of being praised by gods and demons (alike), saw them (Pracetasas) who controlled their vital breath, mind, speech and sight. Being the masters of their yogic (bodily) posture, their bodies were firm, unagitated and straight. They concentrated their minds on the Supreme, perfectly pure Brahman (unalloyed with Māyā).

4. Seeing him come, they (respectfully) stood up, bowed to him by lying prostrate before him and received him joyfully. They worshipped him with due formalities. When he was comfortably seated, they addressed to him.

Pracetasas said :

5. "Welcome is your arrival, Oh divine Sage! How glad we are that you have appeared before us today. Oh Brahman, your moving about (in the world) is like the movement of the Sun, for dispelling the fear of the people.

6. Whatever enlightenment was given to us by glorious Śiva and Lord Viṣṇu has been almost forgotten by us due to our strong attachment to house (householder's life).

---

164. Jājali—An ancient sage famous for austere penance. When he felt pride about his spiritual attainment, he was directed to go to a merchant named Tulādhāra. The merchant enlightened him in spiritual matters after which Jājali attained Mokṣa (liberation).
—*MBH. Śānti.* 261-64; *PCK.* 371

7. Therefore, please kindle in us the light of the knowledge of the Soul which reveals the reality and by (realizing) which we shall easily cross the impassable sea of *saṁsāra*".

Maitreya said :

8. When enquired thus by Pracetasas, the venerable sage Nārada whose mind was merged in Lord Viṣṇu (of glorious renown) spoke to those kings.

Nārada said :

9. That life, those acts, that period of time, that mind, that speech of men are of some real worth in the world, if Hari, the Soul and Ruler of the universe is served by them.

10. If Lord Hari, who blesses us with self-realization is not attained, of what benefit is the three-fold birth, viz., through pure sinless parents, initiation ceremony and consecration (for the performance of sacrifice) ? What is the use of the (performance of) ritualistic duties enjoined by the three Vedas or a span of long life like that of gods' ?

11. Of what avail are the learning, austere penance, eloquent speech or the capacity to attend many things simultaneously ? Of what use is the keen intellectual capacity or physical power, high efficiency of senses ?

12. Of what use are the Yoga (consisting of breath control etc.) the Sāṁkhya (the knowledge of non-identity of the Soul and the body), the Sannyāsa (the life of a recluse) and the study of the Vedas and observances of other vows and renunciation.

13. For, as a matter of fact, the Self is the highest of all blessings (as they are liked and desired for the sake of the Self). Lord Hari is the Soul of all living beings. He is Self-giver (i.e. he manifests himself by the removal of *avidyā* or he gives form, power etc. similar to him to his votaries like Bali). He is dear (as he is by nature the highest bliss).

14. Just as watering the roots of a tree nourishes the trunk, branches, sub-branches (leaves and flowers of a tree, and just as the nourishment of the life (with food etc.) leads to the strengthening of the senses and organs of the body (and

not by applying food to those parts), so the worshipping of Acyuta (Lord Viṣṇu) is the worship of all.

15. Just as in the rainy season, waters (rain-drops) emanate from the Sun (the evaporator of waters which form the clouds and are the cause of subsequent rain-fall) and return to it again (as water vapour) in the summer, and just as the bodies of the mobiles and immobiles spring up from the earth and return to it, so does this universe of animate and inanimate things—the stream of *guṇas*—(emerge from and) merge in Hari.

16* This universe is the absolute, unconditioned essence of the universal Soul. (It is not different from him as it is

---

*(I) VR. affirms the reality of the world as the universe has no separate existence except as the body of the Lord. Just as the light of the Sun and the Sun are inseparables, the whole universe is an inseparable attribute—the body of the Supreme Soul. Once, at the time of the creation, the universe appears as gross and at the time of the dissolution it becomes too subtle to be perceptible but its reality of existence persists, like the power of the sense-organs which are active in a waking state and inactive in sleep when illusions regarding the matter (the five elements) and the cognitive and conative sense-organs and one's being god, man etc. are lost.

(II) VJ. reads differently. Briefly stated : Referring to *harāveva guṇapravāhaḥ* in the above (15) verse, he refutes that Hari is conditioned by the *guṇas* or their products. This world wherein Hari dwells and which he has created is quite distinct and cannot condition him—the only relation between Hari and the universe is that of the supporter and the supported or the 'phantom city of Gandharvas' and the sky. Hari is essentially knowledge brilliant like the light of the Sun. And His wisdom dispels all illusions regarding the body (*dravya*), power etc. When due to accumulation of merits, the breath and other *Vṛttis* cease to work externally and begin to function internally, and awaken the *jīva*, and the illusions about the false identity of the Soul and the body, thinking one's self to be an independent doer and that of being the master of one's senses, are removed, the real Form of the Lord is manifested.

(III) SD. : The analogy of the Sun and the water (in the above No. 15—verse) may be misconstrued to show that the universe and the Lord are totally different. This verse refutes that misinterpretation. The relation between the Lord and the world is like that between the Sun and its light, viz. identity-cum-difference. It is identical yet different. Just as the powers of the sense-organs are manifest in wakefulness and dormant in sleep, so is the creation and dissolution of the universe. How can the *jīva* be released from the *prapañca* (universe) so related with Brahman ? It is by propitiation of Hari, the Soul of the universe, that illusions causing *saṁsāra*, viz. (i) the feeling of I-ness and mine-ness about one's

evolved from him) just as the light of the Sun is not different from the Sun in spite of the once (i. e. temporary) appearance of the phantom phenomenon called 'the city of Gandharvas' Just as the powers of the cognitive and conative organs function during wakefulness and lie dormant during sleep (the universe which appears at the time of the creation from the Lord, dissolves itself in the Lord at the end of Kalpa.). In reality, in the Lord, there is absence of the effects of three types of ego (viz. ego due to matter, action or thought or the types of ego known as *tāmasa*, *taijasa* and *vaikārika*)and the misapprehension of diversity (caused by it).

17* Just as clouds, darkness and light appear in the sky and also disappear in their turn (but do not stick to the sky), similarly, Oh King, the potencies called *sattva*, *rajas* and *tamas* appear in Brahman (without affecting it) and the flow (of creation and destruction of the universe) continues (undisturbed).

18. Therefore, adore (and meditate upon) the Lord directly as being not different from you. Hari is the one undifferentiated Soul of all embodied beings. He is Time (the effi-

---

body, house etc. (ii) regarding ritualistic acts leading to heaven as leading to Mokṣa, (iii) wrongly believing in the teachings of Kapila, Kaṇāda, Buddha as true and leading to salvation.

(IV) GD. explains the position of *Brahma vāda* as follows : Hari being the material cause of the universe, the latter cannot be different from Hari. At the time of the creation it evolves from the Lord, the Soul of the universe and it is not different from him just as the light of the Sun is not distinct from it. The evanescence of the universe and the eternity of the Lord are not contradictory, for just as the power of the senses functions during the state of wakefulness and becomes dormant in sleep (but the power still persists in both the stages) the world appears at the time of the creation and ceases to be so at the time of dissolution. (It is however not destroyed). The creation of the universe and the supported-supporter relation between the universe and the Lord do not act as his limitations, for the Lord is a cause of extraordinary and miraculous nature and above popular analogies. He is free from the illusory contact of five elements, eleven sense-organs and their presiding deities.

*VR. insists on the reality of the universe : the appearance and disappearance of clouds, darkness and light do not imply their unreality. Similarly, the manifestation and disappearance of *sattva*, *rajas* and *tamas*, the three potencies of *Prakṛti* with relation to Brahman do not mean that they are unreal.

cient cause), *Prakṛti* (Primordial Nature, as the material cause), the Supreme Ruler (as the creator). By his own prowess (or lustre) he has destroyed (i.e. remained unaffected by) the flow of *guṇas*.

19. By compassion to all living beings, and by remaining contented with anything whatever and by pacifying urges of the senses by remaining detached from the objects of the senses, Hari becomes pleased in no time.

20. Hari, the imperishable Lord, is invited by continuously growing contemplation to the pure hearts of pious people who have dispelled all the cravings. He does not wish to move out of the space of the heart, for he remembers his obligations to his devotees.

21. Hari loves the poor people who regard him as their only wealth; for he can appreciate the sweet bliss in their devotion which is motiveless and is solely concentrated on him. Hari does not accept worship from such crooked-minded persons who out of pride for their own scholarship, opulence, parentage and achievements, despise indigent yet righteous people.

22. He is not attached to Śrī (his wife—the goddess of wealth and beauty) even though she (always) waits on him. Nor does he attend to kings and gods who entreat her favours. For he himself is absolutely perfect (bliss etc.). But he is (always) subservient to the will of his servants (devotees). (This being the case) how can anyone with a feeling of gratefulness abandon him?

Maitreya said:

23. In this way, sage Nārada, the son of Brahmā (the Self-born god) narrated (these and) other stories of Lord Hari to Pracetasas and returned to the region of Brahmā.

24. Having heard the glories of Hari as narrated by Nārada, and which remove the sins of the world, they (Pracetasas) meditated upon his feet and attained to his region.

25. Oh Vidura, I have now narrated to you everything that you requested me to tell, viz. the dialogue between Pracetasas and Nārada containing the glorification of Hari.

Śrī Śuka said:

26-27. This dynasty of Uttānapāda, the son of Manu has been described to you, Oh best of Kings! Now listen from me the race of Priyavrata (Uttānapāda's elder brother) who obtained the spiritual lore from Nārada and who after enjoying (i.e. ruling over) the earth, divided his kingdom among his sons and attained to the Lord's abode.

28. Having heard this sanctifying story about the invincible Lord Hari, as described by Maitreya (Kauṣārava), Vidura was overwhelmed with emotions. With his eyes flowing with tears, he installed the feet of the Lord in his heart and held (i.e. bowed to) the sage's feet with his head.

Vidura said:

29. Oh great Yogin! Compassionate at heart as you are, you have shown me today the other shore of the ocean of darkness (i.e. ignorance) where dwells Lord Hari who is realized by votaries who are solely devoted to him.

Śrī Śuka said:

30. Having bowed to him (Maitreya) and taking his leave, Vidura who was desirous of seeing his relatives returned with peaceful mind, to Hastināpura.

31. Oh King! He who would listen to the account of kings who have dedicated their minds to Lord Hari, would be blest with (lit. obtain) longevity, affluence, glory, family-bliss (sons, grandsons etc.), sovereignty and eternal happiness (or godhood).

FIFTH SKANDHA

CHAPTER ONE*

(*The Life of Priyavrata*)

The king (Parīkṣit) said :

1. Priyavrata was a devotee of the glorious Lord. As such he was merged in the highest bliss of the Soul (*Ātman*). How is it that he took delight in the life of a householder as it is the root of the bondage of *karmas*, and obscures one's real nature (by diminution of knowledge), Oh omniscient sage ?

2. Oh most excellent Brāhmaṇa ! It is definitely unbecoming that men like him, who have given up all attachment, should cherish such intense attachment to family life (including Vedic rituals, children, wife etc.).

3. The high-souled persons whose minds have found happiness and delight under the shade[165] of the feet of Lord Viṣṇu of excellent renown, cannot definitely entertain an intense desire for family life, Oh Brāhmaṇa sage !

4. (It is possible that due to the power of fate, some persons who found delight in the Soul, may get attached to family life). But there is my great doubt as to how he (Priyavrata) attached to his wife, home, children etc., could ttain Liberation, and could cultivate an unswerving devotion to Lord Kṛṣṇa, Oh Brahman !

---

*This *Skandha* presents the third characteristic—*Sthāna*—of this Purāṇa (SD., VD., GD.). At the end of the last *Skandha* 4.31.26-27 it is mentioned that Priyavrata was at first initiated into spiritual lore by Nārada, but he entered householder's life and after enjoying the kingdom of the earth, he renounced it and attained final beatitude. King Parīkṣit asked the question here.

165. *chāyā* : (i) Which removes (i.e. cools down) hot tormenting passions—ŚR.

(ii) Which removes *saṁsāra* and three types of misery—VR. VC.

(iii) Shade characterised by knowledge which removes torments of *saṁsāra*—VJ.

Śrī Śuka said :

5. Certainly, what you said is correct. But persons whose mind is possessed by (being soaked in) the honey of the lotus-like feet of the Lord of Śrī, Lord Viṣṇu of excellent renown[166] do not generally abandon their own blessed path of listening to the stories of the Lord, most loved by the great ascetics (*parama-haṁsas*) and the votaries of the Lord, even though their path might be temporarily obstructed (by some difficulties).

6. Oh King ! It is widely known that Prince Priyavrata was a great devotee of the Lord. By serving the feet of Nārada, he easily got insight into the real nature of the Soul. When he intended to dedicate his whole life to the abstract contemplation of the Supreme Soul, he was called upon by his father (Svāyambhuva Manu) to protect or to assume the responsibility of governing the world, as he (the Prince) was the sole receptacle of a host of excellent qualities (as pre-requisites of a ruler) as prescribed in the scriptures. By the *Yoga* of uninterrupted meditation, he (the Prince) had already resigned all the functions of his senses and organs solely to Lord Vāsudeva. He foresaw that by accepting office (of the king), his Self will be obscured by the duties and functions of the government, even though they be (essentially) unreal. Hence, even though the command of the father is not to be disobeyed, he did not welcome the order (to be a king).

7. Thereupon, the Self-born god Brahmā, the first among the gods, who correctly comprehends the intentions and desires of (everybody in) the world by his continuous thinking (and solicitude) for promoting the prosperity of the creation (world) which is the product of (three) *guṇas*, came down from his region (*Satyaloka*), surrounded by all the Vedas *incarnate*, and his retinue (consisting of Marīci and others).

8. During his journey through heavens, he was being worshipped at several points by great gods, riding their celestial cars. On his way through the sky, he was being eulogized by *troupes* of divine *artistes* like Gandharvas, Sādhyas, Cāraṇas

166. *uttamaśloka*—Who is glorified by excellent gods like Brahmā—VR.

and by Siddhas and sages. Illumining the whole valley of *Gandha-mādana* by his moon-like splendour, he approached the Prince.

9. (ŚR. asks us to understand that at this time, while Nārada was instructing Priyavrata, Manu also had come to take the Prince to his capital).

There, recognising by the vehicle—swan—that it was his father Lord Hiraṇya-garbha (Brahmā), Nārada rose up hastily and waited upon him with articles of worship, and along with the father and the son (Manu and Priyavrata), and offered prayers to him with folded hands.

10. Oh King Parīkṣit (Oh descendant of Bharata), Lord Brahmā, the Primeval Man, who was offered worship (by Nārada), and whose various excellent qualities, arrivals on the earth from Satyaloka (to confer boons), and glorious victories, were highly extolled in appropriate words, cast a smiling look, full of compassion at Priyavrata and spoke :

The Lord (Brahmā) said :

11. Oh Child ! Try to understand carefully this truth that I am telling you. You should not find fault with the self-refulgent inscrutable God (who is beyond the ken of intelligence). For, we (I Brahmā, Marīci and other sages), god Rudra, your father (Svāyambhuva Manu), this great sage (Nārada)—all of us, being totally under his control, carry out his behests.

12. No embodied being can undo what is decreed by him, through austere penances, knowledge of *Śāstras*, the power of Yoga (or Yogic powers like *aṇimā*, *laghimā*), his intellectual capacity, wealth, religious acts, or with the help of another (powerful person) or with his own capacity.

13. Dear Priyavrata ! All living beings always maintain association with the body which is ordained by the unmanifest Lord, for (undergoing) birth, death, doing actions, (experiencing) sorrow, delusion, fear, pleasure and pain.

14. We are tightly bound together to the cord in the form of his Word (the Vedas), with the unbreakable strings in the form of *guṇas* (like *sattva*), and actions (suitable for one's own position and stage—*varṇa* and *āśrama*—in life), Oh child !

We all offer worship to the Supreme Lord like quadruped animals (controlled) with a string woven through their nostrils, carrying loads for the bipeds (men).

15. For, dear Priyavrata, we accept whatever form of existence (e.g. gods, subhuman beings) is assigned to us by the Lord, according to our attachment to *guṇas* (*sattva* etc.), and actions (*karmas*); experience pleasure or pain (as ordained by him) like the blind led by a person endowed with eye-sight.

16. Even though a person is liberated, he should maintain his body, experiencing the fruits he is destined to reap, but without identifying himself with the body, just as a man, awakened from sleep, remembers the experienced dream (in a detached manner without identifying himself in the dream condition). He does not seek after attributes which lead to next body (birth).

17. (He answers the objection : as there cannot be detachedness in the householder's life due to one's indulgence in pleasure, one should renounce it and resort to forests). The fear of *saṁsāra* (cycle of births and deaths) persists in the case of a person who has not controlled his senses, even though he (leaves his house and) wanders from forest to forest (out of fear of attachment). (For) he stays in the forest beset with his six (internal) enemies (viz. uncontrolled mind and five cognitive senses). On the other hand, what harm can the householder's life possibly do to a wise man who has subdued his senses and who is absorbed in the bliss of his Soul.

18* He who wishes to subdue his (above-mentioned) six enemies, should first enter the householder's life, and intensively try to do so, like a king who, resorting to his stronghold, (first) overcomes his powerful enemies. When the enemies have been weakened, the wise man may go about (to another *āśrama*—stage of life) at will.

---

*VJ. : A person desirous of subduing his enemies in the form of senses should first stay in the householder's stage of life. After getting satiated (*alam buddhim prāpya*) by enjoying pleasure, he should try for his final beatitude. In the householder's life, however, he should stay in the stronghold, viz. devotion to the Lord and curb his powerful enemies viz. senses eager for enjoyment, by restraining himself from enjoying pleasures and thus bring the senses under control. When the desire of sense-enjoyment recedes, the wise man may fearlessly proceed (with the Lord's devotion).

19. But you have already fortified yourself in the castle in the form of the lotus-like feet of Lord Viṣṇu (the god with a lotus sprouting from his navel), and have conquered the six enemies. Therefore, (you should) now enjoy the blessings bestowed upon you by the Supreme Person, and then renouncing all attachment, you should resort to your essential nature (viz. the Self—*ātman*).

Śrī Śuka said :

20. (Priyavrata) the great devotee of the Lord who was thus addressed (by Brahmā), bent his head low, with a sense of his own smallness (before god Brahmā) and respectfully acquiesced in the command of the venerable Preceptor of the three worlds (viz. Brahmā), with the words 'Yes Sir'.

21. Venerable Brahmā was worshipped with due formalities by Manu. And while Priyavrata and Nārada were looking on calmly (without any rancour for the frustration of their original plans), he retired to his abode, meditating upon the Supreme Brahman, his own asylum, who is beyond the range of speech, mind and actions (*avyavahṛtam*).

22. Manu also got his desired object (of retiring to forest after appointing his son to the throne), fulfilled by the great god Brahmā With the consent of the great divine sage Nārada, he installed his son to protect and stabilise his sway over the whole of earth. As for himself, he (Manu) renounced his desire of householder's life which is like an unfordable poisonous lake of sensual enjoyments.

23. In this way, it was by the will of the Supreme Lord that Priyavrata, the Lord of the world was invested with powers to execute his duties (of kingship). He burnt down the impurities in his heart, by dint of constant meditation of the pair of feet of the Lord, the Supreme First Person, Whose supreme glory is capable of destroying the bondage of the whole world. Pure as he (Priyavrata) was, he governed the kingdom of the earth in order to show his regard to the great (god Brahmā and others, by carrying out their command to rule).

24. Then, he married the daughter, by name Barhiṣmatī, of Viśvakarmā, the Lord of created beings. And as

known to all, he got by her, ten sons, all of whom were great like him in character qualities, capacity of work, beauty of form and prowess, and a daughter, youngest of all, by name Ūrjasvatī.

25. All of them were named after the fire-god—Agni—(viz.) Agnīdhra, Idhmajihva, Yajñabāhu, Mahāvīra, Hiraṇyaretas, Ghṛtapṛṣṭha, Savana, Medhātithi, Vīti-hotra, Kavi.

26. Out of these Kavi, Mahāvīra and Savana were lifelong celibates. Since their infancy, they cultivated acquaintance (i.e. took to the study of) the science of the Soul (spiritualism) and adopted the order of Paramahaṁsas (the highest type of recluses).

27. (While) in that (order of Paramahaṁsas), those great sages who were habituated to self-control and tranquillity, uninterruptedly meditated upon the beautiful lotuslike feet of the venerable Lord Vāsudeva who is the abode of all species of living beings and the place of refuge for those who are afraid (of death or *saṁsāra*). They realized the Lord within their heart which becomes thoroughly purified by the power of steadfast and supreme Yoga of devotion (born of that ceaseless contemplation). And freeing themselves from the conditioning gross body, they became absolutely identical with the Lord who is Soul of all beings.[167]

28. By another wife also, he had three sons (named) Uttama, Tāmasa and Raivata, each of whom ruled over a *Manvantara*.

29. While (three of) his sons were practising self-control, the Lord of the earth ruled over the world for one hundred and ten million years.[168] (During his reign) the enemies of righteousness were deterred by the twang of the bow-string pulled by his mighty pair of arms possessing enormous power whereby all his heroic undertakings became successful without any obstruction. The high-minded king enjoyed (the plea-

167. VR. interprets *pratyag* as *jīva* 'individual soul' and *bhūta* as 'insentient bodies' (*a-caitanya-śarīrakatvam*). Thus VR. explains : They (the Princely Sages) realized that the individual Soul (*Jīvātman*) is like a body to and not separable from the Supreme Soul (Paramātman). Thus they attained to a state like him (*Sādharmyam*).

168. *arbuda*=Ten crores (1000,000,00) years.

sures of life) as if he had not realised his true Self or had his judgment clouded by queen Barhiṣmatī's expression of daily increasing raptures in greeting him with her amorous womanly charms, her smiles and side-glances half-concealed by bashfulness and by witty conversations.

30. (Once he noticed that) even to the extent of the world (upto the Lokāloka mountain), over which the Sun shines during his circumambulation round Mount Meru (the mount of gods), it gives light to half the surface of the earth while leaves the other half to be enveloped in darkness. He did not approve of it. As his super-human power was enhanced by the adoration of the Lord, he decided to turn even the night into the day, by (riding in his) luminous chariot, equalling the Sun in speed. Thus, like a second Sun, he made seven circuits closely following the Sun (on the heels).

31. Verily, the wonderful moat-like tracks left by the fellies of the wheels of his chariot, became the seven seas which divided the earth into seven island continents (*dvīpas*).

32* They (*dvīpas*) are called Jambū, Plakṣa, Śālmali, Kuśa, Krauñca, Śaka and Puṣkara. As regards their dimensions, each succeeding island-continent is double in area as that of the previous one, and is surrounded by an ocean separating it (from the other).

33** The seven oceans are respectively of salt-water, juice of sugar-cane, wine, clarified butter, milk, curds and pure

---

*This concentric division of the earth in seven island-continents is mentioned by Patañjali (2nd cent. A.D.), and is common to *Viṣṇu P.* (2.4), *Mārkaṇḍeya P.* (54.6), and with a variation in *Matsya P.* (121, 122) and *Agni P.* 108.1.3. The arrangement is briefly as follows : (1) Jambūdvīpa surrounded by an ocean of salt water. Beyond this ocean and encircling is *Plakṣa-dvīpa* which is double the area of Jambūdvīpa. (2) Plakṣa-dvīpa is surrounded by the ocean of sugar-cane juice which in turn is engirdled by (3) Śālmalidvīpa. The ocean of wine surrounds this *dvīpa* and is encircled by (4) Kuśadvīpa with the ocean of clarified butter around it. (5) *Krauñcadvīpa* surrounds this ocean and is itself engirlded by an ocean of milk. (6) *Śākadvīpa* surrounds the ocean of milk and is itself encircled by ocean of curds (7) *Puṣkaradvīpa* surrounds this ocean of curds and is encircled by the ocean of fresh (sweet) water.

**N. L. De in GDAMI. 179, identifies the seven seas or oceans as follows : (1) Salt water sea—The Indian ocean surrounding Jambūdvīpa or India; (2) *Kṣīra* (Milk ocean)—Shirwan alias the Caspian Sea; (3)

(fresh) water. They serve as moats to each of the island-continent. They are equal in extent to the continent they encircle. Each one of the oceans is in a serial order, the outer boundary of the continent surrounded by it. Priyavrata (the consort of Barhiṣmatī) severally installed as ruler, dutiful sons by name Agnīdhra, Idhmajihva, Yajñabāhu, Hiraṇyaretas, Dhṛtapṛṣṭha, Medhātithi, Vītihotra—each being the ruler of one of the continents such as Jambūdvīpa and others.

34. He gave his daughter called Ūrjasvatī in marriage to Uśanas (Śukra, the preceptor of demons), and of her was born Devayānī also called Kavya-suta (the daughter of Kavi, i.e., Śukra).

35. Such heroic achievements are not impossible in the case of devout men who, by the (efficacy of the) dust of the feet of Lord Viṣṇu (who as Trivikrama took the universe in his long strides), have conquered the six senses (five cognitive senses and the inner organ—mind) or six anxieties (such as physical hunger and thirst, grief and delusion, old age and death). For if, a man even from the lowest caste, utters but once the name (of god Viṣṇu), he immediately shakes off the shackles of *Saṁsāra*.

36. In this way Priyavrata, a possessor of immeasurable strength and prowess, once felt disgusted with himself as he found himself to be dissatisfied with the contact with the product of *guṇas* (in the form of his kingship and worldly enjoyment) which fell to his lot, even after his resorting to the feet of (the) celestial sage Nārada, and said this (to himself):

Surā (Wine)—a corruption of Sarain or the Caspian Sea forming the south-eastern boundary of Kuśadvīpa; (4) *Ghṛta*—derived from the Erythraean Sea or the Persian Gulf forming the boundary of Śālmalidvīpa or Chaldia, i.e. Assyria; (5) *Ikṣu* (sugar cane) a variant of the Oxus. The river is taken as a sea (cf. Sindhu means both the sea and the river). It forms the southern boundary of Puṣkaradvīpa or Bhushkara i.e. Bokhara. (6) *Dadhi* (curds) is a hyper Sanskritisation of Dahi (Dahae)—a scythian tribe living in the upper Jaxartes on the shore of the Aral Sea. Hence *Dadhi* is the Aral Sea. (7) *Svādu* (sweet water)—a corruption of Tchandun, a river in Mongolia i.e. Plakṣadvīpa. These identifications are still controversial. Vide—Baladeva Upadhyaya—*Purāṇa Vimarśa* pp. 317-331. D.C. Sircar—*Studies in GAMI* pp. 17-25.

37. "Alas! What a (terrific) iniquity has been perpetrated by me! I have allowed myself to be pushed by my senses into the dark terrible pit of sensual objects produced by Avidyā. Now enough of this. Fie upon me who became a beast of recreation (i.e. monkey) to this woman" Thus he censured himself.

38. He regained his power of discretion and thinking, by the grace of Hari, the Supreme Deity. (Hence) he divided the earth proportionately among his dutiful sons (as per injunctions of the Dharma Śāstra). He abandoned, like a dead body, his queen with whom he enjoyed pleasures, renounced his great imperial wealth and grandeur. By the power generated by the realization of the stories and pastimes of Hari, he became disgusted (with *Saṁsāra*) in his heart, and he followed again the spiritual path shown to him by the divine sage Nārada.

These are verily the verses composed of old to eulogize the glory of Priyavrata:

39. Who else than the Lord Himself can perform the great achievements of Priyavrata who, while dispelling the darkness (of the night by riding in his refulgent chariot), created seven oceans by the deep tracks of fellies of his chariot.

40. For the happiness and convenience of beings he divided the earth (in seven island-continents). He fixed the boundaries (in each *dvīpa*) by means of rivers, mountains and forests.

41. Devotees of Lord Viṣṇu were dear to him. He regarded as hellish, the glories and affluence acquired in the Pātāla (subterranean world), the celestial world and the human world as well, through powers of *karma-yoga*.

CHAPTER TWO

(The History of Agnīdhra)

Śrī Śuka said :

1. When his father (Priyavrata) was thus absorbed (in the *yoga* of devotion as advised by Nārada), Agnīdhra, who abided by his (father's) commands, kept the injunctions of Dharma in view, and accordingly protected properly his subjects, the inhabitants of Jambūdvīpa, like his own children.

2. Once upon a time, he, being desirous of attaining to *Pītṛloka* (the region of manes, by having a son), went to perform penance in the valley of mount Mandāra which was the sporting ground of beautiful celestial damsels. He collected all the articles required for worship, and with concentrated mind, he propitiated the venerable Brahmā, the lord of the progenitors of the universe.

3. Having understood his intention, the glorious First-born god Brahmā, deputed to him a celestial damsel called Pūrvacitti who was a singer in his assembly.

4. And leisurely did she stroll to the garden adjacent to Agnīdhra's hermitage. The garden appeared extremely beautiful with its lotus-ponds of crystal-clear water, which were resounded with the variegated sweet warblings of acquatic birds like water fowls *Kāraṇḍavas* (a kind of duck), swans etc. And the water-birds were (in their turn) aroused by the resounding melodious notes of the pairs of herbacious and terrestrial birds, perching on golden creepers which entertwined the mass of branches of densely grown forest trees of various kinds.

5. The Prince caught up the sound of the beautiful anklets jingling at every step she wove in a charming, amorous pattern in her graceful advance. He slightly opened the pair of his lotus-bud-like eyes which were till now closed in religious meditation, and perceived her closely.

6. Like a female bee (kissing a flower), the heavenly nymph was enjoying the sweet smell of flowers not far from him. She was making room for the god of Love (the flower-weaponed god) in the minds of men by her gait, sportiveness, bashful and modest glances, sweet voice and charming limbs which profusely delighted the minds and eyes of gods and men (alike).

Her full (pitcher-like) breasts, braids of hair and girdle were slightly agitated by her quickened steps out of fear, when she was assailed by a swarm of bees blind and inebriated with the fragrance of her breath (in the form) of words which dropped from her mouth, and which being accompanied with a smile, were sweet like nectar and intoxicating like wine. Agnīdhra fell under the strong influence of the god of love (with a crocodile on his banner), who got an opportunity to enter his heart the very moment he saw her, and like a stupid[169] fellow, he addressed her (as follows):

7. "Oh great sage ! Who are you and what do you propose to do on this hill ? Are you some indescribable power of the worshipful, Supreme Deity ? Oh friend ! Do you carry a pair of stringless bows (namely your eyebrows) for your purpose, or do you hunt after careless uncautious beasts (like me who are not self-controlled) ?

8. (Referring to her amorous side-glances). These two arrows of your glorious self are winged with lotus-petals (in the form of your eyes). They are gentle, beautiful without feathers, yet of extremely sharp teeth (points). We do not know at whom you wish to aim them in this jungle. May your valour be for the good of dull-witted persons like us.

9. (Referring to the black bees moving about her due to the fragrance of her body). These disciples of your worship are reciting (Vedic hymns) around you, and by incessantly singing the Sama verses with a full understanding of its mystic doctrine they are glorifying the Lord. Just as all sages eagerly resort to their particular (traditional) branch of the Vedas, all these (black bees) eagerly resort to the showers of flowers that are dropped down on all sides from your braid of hair.

10. (Listening to the jingling of the anklets). Oh Brahman ! We can hear only the sweet notes of the *tittira* birds which are encaged (in your anklets), but their form is not visible. Whence did you get the Kadamba-flower-like splendour (of the garment), round your hips which are engirdled by a fire-like shining zone.

11. (Referring to her full conical breasts). Oh Brāhmaṇa

169. He is called stupid as he failed to distinguish betwean a man and a woman, and addressed the nymph as if she was a man.

(twice-born one)! What is stored in your beautiful horns which you carry (with difficulty on your bosom), despite your slender waist, and on which my eyesight is firmly resting? The saffron—coloured fragrant paste applied to your horn is such as has filled my hermitage with sweet smell, Oh beautiful one.

12. Oh best friend! Please show me your region, the inhabitants whereof bear on their bosom such wonderful pair of limbs which (delight yet) agitate the minds of ascetics like us, and who have on their countenance such a wonderful treasure of sweet words, amorous gestures, nectar and the like.

13. (Pointing to the betel leaves which she was chewing) What is the food on which you subsist? By eating (chewing) that there blows forth a fragrance like that of an oblation offered into the sacrificial fire, Oh dear friend. You are a part (*aṁśa* or *kalā*) of god Viṣṇu, for like Him, there are (ear-rings with) two unwinking crocodiles in your ears. Your countenance is like a lake with its bewildered eyes which are a pair of fish in agitation; with your rows of teeth appearing beautiful like a row of swans and with the mass of curly hair like swarms of black bees moving about you.

14. This ball which, when hit by your lotuslike hands' moves about in all directions, makes my eyes roll about. You are not aware of the loosened braids of your curly hair. Alas! The dissolute wind, addicted to licentious pleasure, is taking off your lower garment.

15. Oh ascetic (rich in penance)! Your beauty wrecks the penance of those who are engaged in austerities. By what kind of penance did you secure it (your beauty)? My friend! (Come on) You should perform penance in my company. Or it may be that god Brahmā (who desires to extend creation), has been verily pleased with me (and has sent you to me).

16. I shall not let you go, my beloved, who are conferred on me by god Brahmā. Neither my mind nor even my sight, fixed on you as they are, would like to depart. Oh friend with beautiful horns, be pleased to take (lead) me, your devoted servant, wherever you like. May your faithful companions follow me (Or, may the female deer which are the companions in the forest go by the right side—as an auspicious omen".

Śrī Śuka said:

17. In this way, Prince Agnīdhra who was highly expert in the art of courting beautiful ladies and was blest with god-like intelligence, thoroughly propitiated the celestial damsel in a language which cleverly expressed his intention.

18. And she whose heart became strongly atttached to him on account of the intelligence, noble character, beauty, youth, splendour and liberality of that prominent hero (lit. the lord of warriors), enjoyed in the company of the lord of Jambūdvīpa, earthly and heavenly enjoyment for a pretty long time (lit. a period of a myriad of myriad years.)

19. The great king Agnīdhra, they said, got by her nine sons by name Nābhi, Kimpuruṣa, Harivarṣa, Ilāvṛta, Ramyaka, Hiraṇmaya, Kuru, Bhadrāśva, Ketumāla.

20. Having given birth to nine sons, one per year, and leaving them in the palace, Pūrvacitti again rejoined her service with god Brahmā.

21. Those sons of Agnīdhra, from their birth, inherited well-built body and (enormous) strength by the grace of their (heavenly) mother. When the patrimony was duly divided among them by their father, they enjoyed severally (kingship of) the different divisions of Jambūdvīpa which were also named after them[170].

22. King Agnīdhra was not still satisfied with enjoyment of pleasures. Everyday he brooded over nothing else but that celestial damsel. By performance of acts prescribed in the Vedas, he attained the same region as hers—a region where departed forefathers enjoy themselves.

23. On the demise of their father, the nine brothers married the nine daughters of Meru, whose names were Merudevī, Pratirūpā, Ugradaṁṣṭrī, Latā, Ramyā, Śyāmā, Nārī, Bhadrā, Devavītī.

170. VR. notes that Bhāratavarṣa is later named after king Bharata. Previously it was known as Ajanābha, after king Nābhi.

CHAPTER THREE

(*The History of Nābhi—Incarnation of Ṛṣabha*)

Śrī Śuka said :

1. Being desirous of progeny, Nābhi, along with childless Merudevī[171], worshipped the venerable Lord of Sacrifices, with concentrated mind.

2. Although the Lord of charming personality is difficult to be attained to by the use and accomplishments of all the means of sacrifices such as wealth, suitable place, time, appropriate *Mantras* (incantations), competent sacrificial priests, and payment of liberal sacrificial fees he is affectionate to his devotees. Hence, when he (king Nābhi) was devoutly and with pure heart, performing the sacrifice, his (the Lord's) heart became eager to accomplish the object desired by his devotee. Although his charming personality is absolutely independent, he manifested his form with beautiful limbs, ravishing the mind and sight, at the time of conducting the *Pravargyas* (the ceremony preliminary to the Soma Sacrifice).

3. And lo! The Supreme Lord appeared as a self-refulgent personality with two pairs of arms. He was clad in tawny coloured silk garment. He had the splendid *Śrī-vatsa* mark on his chest. He was characteristically distinct by the great conch (Pāñcajanya), lotus, Vanamālā (a garland of forest flowers), discus, the immortal jewel Kaustubha, mace and others. At this the priests officiating at the sacrifices, the directors of the sacrifice and the sacrificer waited upon him very respectfully with *arghya* offering water to wash the guest's hands. They received him bending down their heads respectfully, just as poverty-stricken persons would do when receiving a rich treasure-trove.

The Sacrificial Priests said:

4. "Oh most adorable (God)! (Even though you are perfect in every respect) you be pleased to accept of your own accord, the worship offered (to you) by us, your servants.

---

171. Marudevī in Jaina tradition (Hemacandra's *Triṣaṣṭi Śalākā Puruṣa Carita* (TSPC).

We are unable to praise you as your form is incomprehensible. Hence we are taught by the saintly persons to express our obeisance to you again and again. You transcend Prakṛti and Puruṣa. What man, whose mind is absorbed in *saṁsāra,* the product of the *guṇas of Prakṛti* and hence incapable, can describe fully the nature of the Supreme Ruler of *Prakṛti* and *Puruṣa* by means of name, form or colour belonging to modern gross creation called *saṁsāra* which can hardly touch you).

5. One cannot do anything more than to extol only, a part of those multitudes of the excellent and the most auspicious attributes which destroy the sins of all human beings.

6. You are thoroughly pleased indeed, Oh Supreme One, through worship offered to you lovingly, by Your followers—worship consisting of water, pure white shoots, tender *Tulasī* leaves and sprouts of *dūrvā* grass, and accompanied by sincere prayer in faltering tone.

7. We do not see if you have to achieve any covetable object of yours through this elaborate sacrifice enriched with a number of component parts (formal rites).

8. You are the highest bliss, the embodiment of all the mutually complementary *Puruṣārthas* (highest objectives in human life) which flow from yourself uninterruptedly, directly and to an unlimited extent. But Oh Lord, this sacrifice signifies as merely (an inadequate) means of propitiating you in the case of us who covet blessings (of *Puruṣārthas.*)

9. Oh Supreme Person ! You are superior to supreme gods (like Brahmā). We are ignorant. We by ourselves do not know what is our highest good. Nor have we worshipped you properly (with due formalities). But just as others (philosophic teachers approach the laity for enlightening them, even though not duly received), out of your exceedingly profuse compassion, you reveal yourself here to us and bestow upon us your glory known as Final Liberation as well as the objects coveted by us.

10. However, (the very fact) that you have now manifested yourself to the vision of your own people (devotees), at the sacrifice of the royal sage (Nābhi), is itself a veritable boon, Oh most worshipful God, the foremost among those who confer boons !

11. Oh Lord! The description of the host of your excellent attributes is a source of the highest auspiciousness even to sages who have completely burnt down their impurities by the fire of knowledge intensified by non-attachment, and have consequently become similar to you in nature, and enjoy themselves in their Self. (But even such sages have not visualized you). Hence your excellent virtues are continuously (and repeatedly) sung by them.

12. (Though we have been favoured with your audience, we seek one boon of you. May your names descriptive of your excellent qualities and annihilating all sins, be ever uttered by us (lit. be within the range of our speech), even when we are unable to remember you, while stumbling, hunger-stricken, falling, yawning and in wretched conditions and even when attacked by fever and at the moment of death as well.

13. Moreover, this royal sage is desirous of progeny. He looks upon progeny as a covetable object in human life. He covets to have progeny like you. Hence, like a beggar approaching Kubera, the Lord of Wealth—for obtaining mere husk, he beseeches you, the Lord who are competent to give all blessings including pleasures in Heaven and Final Beatitude.

14. Is there any such person in this world who has not waited upon the feet of the high-souled ones and still is not overcome by your invincible Māyā of inscrutable ways and whose intellect and understanding has not been clouded by her and whose nature has not been overwhelmed by the vehemence of the poison in the form of sense objects of pleasure?

15. You have been invited here for an insignificant object. This act of ours who are dull-witted enough to regard progeny as the highest object in human life, is really an insult to you who are the Lord of unlimited achievements. Be pleased, Oh God of gods, to forgive us all who are ignorant ones as you are equal (in kindness) to all."

Śrī Śuka said :

16. The glorious Lord Viṣṇu was thus being praised in a hymn composed in prose. The feet of that foremost of gods were bowed to by the priests who were (in their turn) paid obeisance by (king Nābhi), the ruler of a 'sub-continent

(which later became famous as Bhārata-varṣa). He (the Lord) spoke graciously as follows :

The Lord said :

17. "Oh sages ! It is admirable that a very embarrassing and difficult boon viz. the son of this (king) should be like unto me, has been sought from me by you whose words are not futile and ineffective. For being matchless (one without a second), I alone am similar to me. Nevertheless, the words of Brāhmaṇas should not prove untrue inasmuch as it is my own mouth that is represented by the race of Brāhmaṇas who are like gods among the twice-born ones.

18. Therefore, no compeer to me being available, I shall exhibit a part of mine by incarnating (on the earth) through (king Nābhi), the son of Agnīdhra."

Śrī Śuka said :

19. Within the hearing of queen Merudevī the Lord addressed this to her consort and disappeared.

20. Oh king Viṣṇudatta[172] (Parīkṣit) ! The glorious Lord who was thus propitiated by the great sages in that very sacrifice, and who desired to oblige the monarch, descended as the son of Merudevī in the king's harem. He assumed a white (pure, *Sāttvic*) personality with a view to demonstrating to the world the sacred vows to be observed by (nude *Śramaṇas*) or recluses clad with air, performing austerities with a pledge to observe life-long celibacy[172a].

---

172. So called because he was restored to life by Kṛṣṇa—vide supra 1.12, 7-10.

172a. This obviously refers to Digambara Jaina sages despite ŚR.

CHAPTER FOUR

(*The miraculous history of Ṛṣabha*)

Śrī Śuka said :

1. It is reported that after the incarnation, Lord Ṛṣabha had all the characteristic marks of the Supreme Lord (such as the marks of thunderbolt, goad etc.) manifest (on the soles of his feet), from his very birth. His majestic splendour was everyday enhanced by qualities like impartiality and equality towards all, control of internal and external senses, non-attachment to sense-pleasures, domination and control over all beings, and possession of great spiritual powers. The king's counsellors, subjects, god-like Brāhmaṇas very eagerly wished to have him as the protector of the earth.

2. On account of his Supreme-most personality which was extolled in laudatory verses by poets, his abundant vigour, physical strength, splendour, glory, dominance and valour, his father significantly named him Ṛṣabha (the most excellent).

3. The mighty Indra became jealous of him, and did not rain in his continent (Ajanābha, later known as Bhāratavarṣa). When apprised of it, Ṛṣabhadeva, the Master of yoga pooh-poohed it with a laughter, and profusely showered rains over his *Varṣa* (continent) called Ajanābha, by his mystic (yogic) power.

4. Being blessed with a worthy child as desired by him, Nābhi was transported with rapturous joy, and affectionately fondled the glorious Lord, the most ancient Person who, of his own free will had assumed a human form. His (Nābhi's) mind was overpowered with Māyā. He fondly caressed him with faltering words choked with emotion : 'Oh child, my daddie' and felt exceedingly happy.

5. King Nābhi who regarded the mandate of the public as authoritative, came to know the love and loyalty of all, from common man to the minister (commanded by Ṛṣabha), installed his son for the protection and preservation of the boundaries (standards) of religious conduct. Having entrusted him to the care of Brāhmaṇas[173] he, accompanied by Merudevī,

173. According to Jinasena, Nābhi installed Ṛṣabha as an emperor when he was grown up and married. MPS (*Tri-ṣaṣṭi-lakṣaṇa Śrī Mahā Purāṇa—Saṅgraha*—K.B. Nitwe, Ed. 1899) 16.32.

retreated to Viśālā (Badarikāśrama), where he propitiated the venerable Lord Vāsudeva (alternatively) known as Nara and Nārāyaṇa, through severe penance which caused no trouble to others, and through the *yoga* of profound meditation. In due course, he attained to his greatness, viz., the state of *jīvanmukta* (being liberated while alive).

Oh descendant of Pāṇḍavas (king Parīkṣit)! The two following verses are sung in his (Nābhi's) praise :

6. What other man can perform the righteous deed as done by the royal sage Nābhi, due to the purity and piety of which act, Hari became his child ?

7. Who else than Nābhi could be so devoted to Brāhmaṇas, who, being propitiated by sacrificial fees, by their spiritual power, made the Lord of Sacrifice manifest himself (to him) in his sacrifice ?

8. After his coronation, Lord Ṛṣabha-deva regarded his own continent as *Karma-kṣetra*[174] (a land fit to perform acts leading to the Heaven and Liberation), and showed (the model of life) how one should stay in the preceptor's house (for education). He obtained the permission (to enter householder's life) from his preceptors who were given boons (as fees) of their choice. For teaching the duties of a householder's life he married Jayantī[175] who was given (in marriage) by Indra. He performed both types of duties as prescribed in the scriptures (of *Śrutis* and *Smṛtis*). He begot through her (queen Jayantī) one hundred sons who were like unto him.[176]

9. Out of those (sons), the eldest was the great *yogī*, Bharata, who was endowed with highly excellent attributes. It is on account of him that this continent came to be called Bhārata[177].

---

174. Jinasena interprets *karma-bhūmi* as a country in which the order of Agriculture and other six ways of livelihood had been fixed by Ṛṣabha (MPS 16.249).

175 According to Jinasena, he married Yaśasvatī and Sunandā with the consent of Indra. These two were the Princesses of Kaccha and Mahākaccha (MPS. 15,69, 70).

176. Jain tradition confirms the number of sons as 100, but the names are different (MPS. 16.4).

177. Jain tradition endorses this derivation :

taṁ nāmnā Bhāratam Varṣam
iti hāsīj janāspadam /

MPS. 15.59.

10. After him were born nine sons viz. Kuśāvarta, Ilāvarta, Brahmāvarta, Malaya, Ketu, Bhadrasena, Indra-spṛś, Vidarbha and Kīkaṭa—these were the leaders of (other) ninety (sons).

11-12. Kavi, Hari, Antarīkṣa, Prabuddha, Pippalāyana, Āvis, Hotra, Drumila, Camasa and Karabhājana—these nine who demonstrated to the world, the sacred duties of votaries of the Lord, were themselves eminent devotees of the glorious Lord. We shall describe to you later on (in Skandha XI) their pious life imbued with the glory of the Lord, and leading a fund of tranquility, in the dialogue of Vasudeva and Nārada.

13. The eightyone younger sons of Jayantī who were obedient to their father, and of great modesty, profound scholars of the Vedic lore, habitual performers of sacrifice and of extremely pious deeds, became Brāhmaṇas (i.e. were given to meditation on Brahman).

14. The venerable Lord called Ṛṣabha was completely self-dependent. By his nature, he was eternally free from evils. He enjoyed absolute joy. Though he was the Ruler of the universe (God himself), he performed actions as if he were the opposite (an ordinary human being). He taught the ignorant by his behaviour, the traditional righteous duties. He was equal and impartial, friendly and merciful. He laid down the rules of conduct to people in the householder's stage of life, by his achievement of righteousness, wealth, fame, progeny, (earthly) joy and liberation.

15. Whatever is done by the heads (the leading persons) is followed by the world.[178]

16. Even though he knew for himself the confidential, esoteric Vedic lore containing the religious duties of all (people), he governed the people by expedients called *sāma*, (conciliation) *dāna* (gift or, bribery), *daṇḍa* (punishment), *bheda* (sowing discords) as advised by Brāhmaṇas.

17. As per counsels of Brāhmaṇas, he worshipped the Lord by performing for a hundred times, sacrifices, each provided with all the requisites with reference to the materials,

178. *Yad yad ācarati śreṣṭho . . . . lokastad anuvartate*/ BG. 3.21.

place, time, age (of the sacrificer), faith, (proper) sacrificial priests, and the several gods to be invited.

18. While Lord Ṛṣabha was protecting this continent (Bhārata-varṣa), no man, at any time, desired or expected anything whatsoever from anybody else, as if it was non-existent (and hence beyond desire or expectation); nor did he cast a wistful glance at another's possession—except the ever-increasing intense love for their Lord.

19. Once upon a time, while touring (through his kingdom) Lord Ṛṣabha came to Brahmāvarta.

With a view to admonishing his sons in that conference of great and prominent Brāhmaṇa sages, he spoke thus to his sons even though they had their minds controlled, and their conduct governed by affection and modesty—he did so, within the sight and hearing of his subjects.

CHAPTER FIVE

(Ṛṣabha's discourse on the Path of Liberation)

Ṛṣabha said :

1. (My) dear sons ! This human body in the world of embodied beings, does not deserve to be devoted to pleasures which lead to misery, and which are fit for animals (like dogs and swine) feeding on excrement. It is fit for penance devoted to the realization of the Lord, and which purifies the mind; and pure mind leads to the infinite bliss of absorption into Brahman.

2. The wise say that service rendered to the great is the gate to final liberation, while association with those who are attached to women, is the entrance to hell (or *saṁsāra*). They are (really), the great who are of balanced mind, serene and composed, free from anger, friendly and righteous.

3. They (only are the great) who regard love unto me as the highest objective of human life, and who entertain no liking for people who are engrossed in maintaining their bodies

only, and have no attraction to houses (householder's life) and are devoid of desire for anything beyond the bare necessities of life (lit. maintenance of the body).

4. When one attempts to gratify one's senses (with their objects of pleasure), one certainly (loses discretion and) becomes wreckless, and commits sins only. I do not approve of (the repetition of) such (sinful) acts which (having been perpetrated in the previous existence) caused the body which, though really (unreal and) transitory, became a source of trouble to the Soul.

5. So long as one does not enquire into the real nature of the soul, it remains obscure[179] due to ignorance[180]. So long as the actions (*karmas*) are being performed, the mind persists in its disposition to activity (*karmas*) and a mind so disposed binds down the Soul to the body.

6. In this way, while (the real nature of) the Soul remains obscured by *avidyā* (nescience), the previous *karmas* (of man) tend his mind to perform more activities. He is not liberated from the bonds of the body, so long as he does not entertain love and devotion to me (Vāsudeva).

7. When one (the *jīva*) becomes careless about one's own interest, and even though possessing the power of discrimination does not realise the activities and functions of organs of sense as unreal and unconnected with him, he fails to bear in mind his real nature. Ignorant as he is, he gets into a householder's life (lit. a home with the provision of sexual enjoyment) and undergoes misery (of three types) therein.

8. They (the learned ones) call this stage of matrimonial union of a man with a women as the knot of their mutual hearts which reciprocally binds them. (This is in addition to the knot of the identification of their body with the Soul,—the knot which exists already in their individual hearts. It is this marital knot that deludes a man to regard the house,

179. *Parābhavaḥ*—The real nature of the soul is dominated over by the body.—ŚR. (2) Is dependent on *karma* (VC., VD.). (3) Misery. —VS. (4) Involved in *Saṁsāra* characterised by the recurrence of birth and death (SD.).

180. Cf. *Jñānāgniḥ sarva-karmāṇi bhasmasāt kurute*/BG. 4.37.

landed property, sons, relatives and wealth as being himself or his own.

9. When this strong knot of the heart, viz., the mind which continues to be hard by the past *karmas* (of the *jīva*), becomes loose, (then alone) a man becomes absolved of the (deluding) man-wife relation. He (then) shakes off *ahaṁkāra* (ego, the cause of the bondage), becomes free, and attains to the highest position, viz., *Mokṣa*.

10. Through devotion to me, the pure Self and preceptor; through service unto me; through freedom from thirst (for worldly enjoyment), by endurance of the pairs of opposite states like pleasure and pain; through understanding that the life of *jīva* is subject to miseries everywhere (even in the other world); through an enquiring spirit (into the nature of the truth); through penance and abstention from *karmas* (performed) for attainment of desires:

11. By actions done for my sake; by (listening to and recounting) my stories all the time; through association with persons who regard me as the only Deity; only by glorifying my excellent attributes; throu ˙ ˆeedom from the feeling of enmity, by impartiality and e indedness, through tranquillity and self-restraint; and through a desire (and attempt) to dispel the (false) notion of the identity of the Self with the body, house (property etc.), Oh sons.

12. Through proper studies in the scriptures dealing with the Soul (*ātman*); by living in seclusion; through control of breath, senses, organs and the mind; through absolute faith in the truth (or scriptures and the word of saintly people); through observance of strict celibacy; through eternal vigilance in performance of sacred duties; through control of speech (for abstention from studying the false doctrines and for observing silence).

13. Through clearsightedness realizing my presence everywhere, through wisdom illumined with Śāstric knowledge and experience; by means of deep concentration, a clever man, endowed with courage, perseverance and discrimination should strive to get rid of the subtle body, the limiting condition known as ego (*ahaṁkāra*).

14. One should always remain vigilant and by the

means, as taught (by the *śāstras* or the preceptor) should completely cut asunder the bondage in the form of the knot (of (*ahaṁkāra*) in the heart which has been caused by Nescience (*avidyā*); for that (knot) is the reservoir of all (previous) *karmas*. Having done so, he may cease to adopt these means.

15. A king, a teacher or a father who desires to attain to my region or regards my grace as the highest object in life, should thus instruct his subjects, pupils or sons who are ignorant of the Truth. (If they do not abide by his teaching) he should not get angry with them. Deluded as they are with the path of *karma* (as the path of real happiness), he should not direct them to perform *karmas*. What[181] advantage would a man reap by misdirecting the blind (i.e. ignorant ones to perform action (*karmas*) with a desire to get their fruit) and make them fall into the abyss (*of saṁsāra*).

16. People (involved in *saṁsāra*) have no insight (to know) in what lies their own (real) good. (Hence) they, being overwhelmed with (a powerful) lust for enjoyment of pleasures, desire for objects of sensual enjoyment. They entertain enmity with each other, for a particle of (insignificant pleasure). Deluded as they are, they have no idea of the unending misery (as a result of such hostility).

17. Seeing an ignorant person steeped in Nescience, what learned and compassionate person who himself knows the Truth, will misdirect him to the wrong path, just as one does not lead astray a blind man who has missed his way.

18. He who would not, or is incompetent to, liberate a a person (whether he/she be a pupil, relative, an offspring or a wife or a devotee) from involvment in *saṁsāra*, is not a real preceptor (even though he may claim to be so) or a real relative, father or mother or husband or a deity. [ŚR. followed by VC., SD., GD. and BP. explains the implication as follows : If a preceptor would not or is incapable of leading his pupil to Liberation, he should not claim preceptorship and accept anyone as his pupil, and the pupil should disown such a teacher and leave him. Similarly, a man should not procreate a child or a mother should not accept one in her womb if he or she

181. VR. offers no comment on this line, presumably due to the deletion of the line *kam ...... garte* in his text of the Bh. P.

is incompetent to guide the child to Salvation. There is no sin in disowning such a father or mother as was done by Prahlāda in the case of his father and Bharata about his mother Kaikeyī. Such a deity is not a real deity and should not accept worship from a devotee and the devotee should ignore such a deity as was done by Khaṭvāṅga].

19. This body of mine (which, by my free will, appears human in form) is beyond comprehension (as I am not an ordinary human being). For my heart is definitely pure unalloyed *sattva* wherein abides righteousness (*dharma*). Since non-righteousness has been already expelled by me far behind, the noble ones call me Ṛṣabha (the most excellent).

20. All of you are born from my heart (which comprises of nothing but pure *sattva*). You should, therefore, without entertaining any jealousy, serve your brother, the noble-minded Bharata. That will render service unto me and will be (the real execution of duty of) protecting the subjects.[182]

21. Among the (animate and inanimate) created beings, creepers (which spread by themselves) are extremely superior. Higher than these (creepers) are reptiles (and other mobile creatures like insects) which can move from place to place ; better than these are beasts which are gifted with intelligence ; superior to them are the human beings ; higher than men are *pramathas* (goblins, spirits) to whom are superior Gandharvas (celestial singers) and Siddhas (a demi-god tribe endowed with supernatural power) ; higher than these are followers of gods (such as Kinnaras).

22. Higher than these are Asuras (demons) to whom gods, whose leader is Indra, are superior ; greater than these are Dakṣa and other sons of god Brahmā ; among them Bhava (Lord Śiva) is the greatest. Brahmā is superior to god Śiva whose power or birth is derived from Brahmā; I am superior to him (Brahmā, and I regard Brāhmaṇas adorable as my own God.

182. VJ. thinks that this is an exhortation to serve Hari. He interprets: You should sincerely resort to Hari who is mightier than the mighty, loves to support the subjects and is the shelter of all. Through your loving devotion to me, Liberation is just on the palm of your hand. Bharata to whom you serve will be serving me who abide in the subjects whom he protects.

23. Oh Brāhmaṇas ! As I do not regard any other being as comparable equal to Brāhmaṇas, I cannot see any being superior to them. I do not enjoy the oblations offered to the sacrificial fire with that much relish, as I enjoy to the full, the food liberally offered by men to these Brāhmaṇas with faith.

24. It is the Brāhmaṇas who have maintained in this world my glorious, ancient, eternal body (the Vedas). In them are found the eight great excellences such as) most sanctifying *sattva*, tranquillity of the mind, control of senses, Truthfulness, grace, asceticism, the spirit of endurance and knowledge of the reality. (Who can be then superior to Brāhmaṇas?).

25. Though destitute of everything, Brāhmaṇas who cherish deep devotion to me seek nothing of me, although I am superior to the Supreme-most god (Brahmā), possess infinite power etc. and am competent to confer heavenly blessings and Liberation (*Mokṣa*). How can they crave for any other blessing (like kingdom etc.)!

26. Oh my sons, at every step, you should look upon all mobile and immobile beings as my place of residence. That alone will be my real worship by you whose mind (sight) is unprejudiced by jealousy etc.

27. My propitiation is therefore the dedication of the activities of the mind, speech, sight and other sense-organs to me. Without such propitiation one shall not be able to free himself from the noose of death in the form of great delusion."

28. The divine Lord whose name was Ṛṣabha and who was the greatest well-wisher of all, exhorted his sons, even though they were well disciplined, as the exhortation was meant for the world as well. Possessor of great power as he was, he exemplified the path. He intended to exemplify the path of the Paramahaṁsas (recluses of the highest order) which is characterised by devotion, knowledge and renunciation, of great sages who are habituated to tranquillity and self-control and who have desisted from the path of *karma*. Having installed on the throne for the protection of the earth, Bharata, the eldest of his hundred sons, who was (himself) a great devotee of the Lord and devoted to the votaries of the Lord as well,

retained the possession only of his body and renounced everything else in the house. With the sky as his clothing, and with scattered dishevelled hair like a madman, he enshrined within himself the Āhavanīya fire, and set out from Brahmāvarta.

29. He took a vow of absolute silence and kept quiet even though spoken to by men. Behaving like a stupid, blind, dumb, deaf person or like a ghost or a mad person, he put an appearance of an Avadhūta (a sage who has renounced all worldly attachments and connections) who has lost all the sense of his body.

30. With his mind remaining unperturbed, he wandered all alone over the world. (While wandering) in cities and towns, mines and hamlets, flower gardens and the habitations at the foot of mountains, military camps and cowpens, settlements of cowherds, caravans, hills and forests, hermitages of sages and such other places wherever he went, on every road he was maltreated by the dregs of human society. He was threatened, belaboured, was urinated over, spat at, pelted with stones, showered with dust, subjected to stinking odours and to words of abuse. Like an elephant harassed by flies, he ignored these, as he never assumed any ego-hood as being his own self or as belonging to him the unreal habitat in the form of the body which is wrongly called real. He was established in his own essential glory, realising both being and non-being.

31. His hands, feet and broad chest were very delicate; his long and big arms, shoulders and neck, charming face and other limbs of the body were beautifully disposed. His beautiful face was brightened up with a spontaneous smile as he was by nature charming; he appeared beautiful with his reddish, large and refreshing eyes which were like petals of full blown lotus; his cheeks, ears, neck and nose were shapely and captivating; by the superb gracefulness of his face, he made the god of Love enter into the hearts of the damsels of the town; his face was adorned with profuse ringlets of matted and golden locks of hair overhanging it. His uncared-for body covered with dust (like an *avadhūta*), he appeared to be possessed by a devil.

32. When the Lord found that this world was opposed to his practice of Yoga, he regarded it reprehensible to offer any

resistance to it. He accepted the vow to lead the life like an *ajagara* (python). It was in a lying position that he ate, drank, chewed, passed urine, execrated till his limbs were daubed with faeces.

33. The wind perfumed with the fragrance of his faeces filled with sweet smell the whole country within a radius of ten *yojanas*.

34. Similarly, adopting the mode of life of a bull, deer and a crow, he behaved like a bull, a deer and a crow and drank, ate, chewed, urinated while going, staying, sitting or lying down.

35. In this way Lord Ṛṣabha, the dispenser of Liberation, adopted various modes of life useful for the practices of yoga. He had no environment like a physical body to prevent his mind i.e. power of direct cognition. He realised his highest bliss in all-pervading *ātman* who is Lord Vāsudeva, the inner controller of all beings. He was, by nature, fully possessed of yogic power such as travelling through the space, acquiring the speed of mind, the power of becoming invisible and of entering the body of another, the faculty of seeing objects distant in time and space and such other powers. Oh King, he did not welcome at heart these super-natural powers which came to him unsolicited.

CHAPTER SIX

(*Ṛṣabha quits His body*)

The King said :

1. The Yogic powers which accrue unsolicited to persons who realise bliss in their Self and who have burnt down the seeds of their *karmas* (leading to future bondage), through the fire of knowledge, inflamed and fanned by yoga, do not lead to miseries. (Then why did Ṛṣabha not like them?)

The sage (*Śrī Śuka*) *said* :

2. Your observation is true. But there are some intelligent persons in this world who are not at all prepared to trust

their fickle mind like a wily hunter would do about a deer (even though trapped by him).[183]

It has also been observed thus:

3. One should never form friendship with (i.e. place trust in) the fickle and changeful mind. It is through such (blind) trust in the mind that the penance of Śiva (at the sight of god Viṣṇu in the Mohinī form)[184] or that of great ascetics (like Saubhari[185]) which was accumulated for a long period, was totally lost.

4. Just as a faithless wife would give entry (to her paramours in her husband's house to get him murdered), the mind of a *yogin* who has formed friendship with it, always leaves loopholes to lust and other enemies (like anger, delusion etc.) to enter.

5. What wise man would regard his mind as obedient and trustworthy to him, for it is the mind which is the source of lust, anger, pride, greed, sorrow, delusion, fear and which binds him down with *karmas*?

6. Though he (Lord Ṛṣabha) was the ornament of all the protective deities of the world, his divine grandeur remained unnoticed due to his strange stupid-like dress, speech and behaviour like an *avadhūta* (an ascetic who has renounced all worldly attachments and connections). He desired to give up his body with a view to instruct the *yogins* in the method of quitting this mortal body. He realised that the Supreme Spirit directly abiding in him was absolutely one with him without a second. Being free from the continuity of the *vāsanās* or effects of past deeds, he became free from his subtle body, shedding off his (conceptual) identification with the *liṅga śarīra* (subtle body).

7. The body of Lord Ṛṣabha who was free and detached from his subtle body, roamed over the world through the semblance of egotism caused by virtue of the unconscious effects of his yogic powers. As willed by Providence, he tra-

183. Or just as a dealer (merchant) would not trust a deceitful *Kirāta*—ŚR.

184. Vide infra 8.12.24-32

185. Vide infra 9.6.39-52.

versed Koṅka, Veṅka, Kuṭaka and South Karṇāṭaka[186] countries. In the jungle near mount Kuṭaka, he holding a piece of stone in his mouth and with dishevelled hair, wandered like a madman.

8. Then a fearful forest conflagration created by the friction of bamboos tossed by the velocity of winds, burnt down the forest along with his body.

9. Verily, in the Kali Age, when unrighteousness will rule supreme, there will be a foolish king named Arhat, ruling over the territories of Koṅka, Veṅka and Kuṭaka. Learning about the strange way of the life of Ṛṣabha, he will (try to) study and adopt it. As a result of the accumulated sins of the previous life of the people, as fate would have it, he (Arhat) being deluded, will give up the path of his own *dharma* which is free from fear or danger in every way. Out of his whim, he will propagate the wrong, and absurd way of the heretics.

10. By that (propagation of the heretical creed), in the Kali Age, wretched people, being deluded by the Māyā potency (power of delusion) of God, will (neglect and) be devoid of the purity, cleanliness and good conduct enjoined upon them by their scriptural injunctions. With their intelligence stupefied by the Kali Age wherein unrighteousness predominates, they, of their respective individual free will, will adopt wrong and corrupt vows involving contempt of gods, abstention from bath, *ācamana* (sipping of water before religious ceremonies etc.), neglect of cleanliness, plucking out hair (from the head instead of shaving) and such others. They will generally condemn the Vedas, Brāhmaṇas, Lord Viṣṇu (the presiding deity of sacrifices) and the world.

11. Believing in the blind tradition about the new way of life chosen by them but which is unsupported by the Vedas, they of their own accord will fall into dark abysmal hell.

12. This incarnation (of Lord Viṣṇu as Ṛṣabha) was

---

186. VR. and VJ. identify Koṅka with Koṅkaṇa, the narrow strip of land between the Western ghats and the Arabian sea. Veṅka is probably Veṅkaṭādri, the Tirupathi hill.

VJ. states: Ṛṣabha travelled from the land irrigated by the Bhīmā and Southern Karṇāṭak a to Saurāṣṭra and thence to the east of Nagpur where near the 'Uttarā' river there is the Kuṭaka hill. Obviously VJ. is guessing. N. L. De identifies Kuṭaka with Gadag in Dharwar district. GDA. MI. 112.

intended for instructing people (who are) immersed in the *Rajoguṇa*, in the way of Liberation.

They (people) sing the (following) verses describing Ṛṣabha's excellent qualities:

13. Oh! This sub-continent (Bhāratavarṣa) is the sacredmost in all sub-continents (*Varṣas*) and island-continents (*dvīpas*) of the earth which is engirdled with seven seas; for people hereof sing of the auspicious deeds of Murāri (Lord Viṣṇu, slayer of the demon mura)—deeds associated with his (Viṣṇu's) incarnation.

14. How lucky is the race of Priyavrata of pure and sacred glory! In it (Viṣṇu), the Ancient Person took an incarnation (of Lord Ṛṣabha). The First Personage observed that path of religion which became the cause of Liberation (lit. non-action).

15. Is there any other *yogī* who can even mentally follow the direction of this birthless Lord (Ṛṣabha)? For the yogic powers, to attain which other Yogis strive covetously, were discarded by him as unreal and illusory, even though the powers automatically accrued to him.

16. Thus has been narrated to you the pious (and sanctifying) life of the Lord, by name Ṛṣabha, who was the most venerable to all the Vedas, the worlds (people), gods Brāhmaṇas and cows. It completely cleanses all impious actions of men (who devoutly listen to or recite it). It is the abode of the highest auspiciousness and supreme bliss. He who, with rapt attention and increasing faith, listens to it or recites it to others, unswerving devotion into venerable Vāsudeva is developed in them.

17. It is in *bhakti* (devotion and not in *yoga* etc.) that wise men continuously steep their Soul, tormented as it is with the scorching heat in the form of miseries of the worldly life (*saṁsāra*) full of manifold sins. They do not at all evince any regard or desire for the final beatitude though it is the highest *Puruṣārtha*, (objective in human life), despite its being automatically obtained. For, being worshippers of the Lord, they have ipso facto completely achieved all the *Puruṣārthas* (highest objects of human pursuits).

18. Oh King ! Of you Pāṇḍavas and Yadus; the vene-

rable·Lord is the protector, preceptor, the deity to be worshipped, a friend and well-wisher, the controller of your family, and occasionally even a servant (e. g. an ambassador to the Court of Duryodhana). May it be as it is. But Lord Krsna (Mukunda) awards Liberation to his worshippers, but not loving devotion (to him).

19. Salutation to the venerable Lord Ṛṣabha who is free from desires due to his eternal realization of his own Self, and who, out of compassion for the world, explained the fearless nature of the self to the people (or the world) whose mental capacity is lost in sleep (ignorance) for a long time, as it is engrossed in desires of the body and its property.

CHAPTER SEVEN

(*The Life of Bharata*)

Śrī Śuka said:

1. When Bharata, the great devotee of the venerable Lord, was by his volition ordained to protect the earth by Lord Ṛṣabha, he became fully engaged in complying with his will (viz. protection of the world). He married Pañcajanī, the daughter of Viśvarūpa.

2. Just as *Ahaṁkāra* (ego, the source of all *bhūtas*) creates the subtle elements (*tanmātras*), through her he begot five sons who were entirely like himself.

3. (They were:) Sumati, Rāṣṭrabhṛt, Sudarśana, Āvaraṇa and Dhūmraketu. It is after him that this continent (*Varṣa*) which was (erstwhile) called Ajanābha, came to be designated as Bhārata.

4. The Lord of the earth had a wide knowledge, and like his father and grandfather was devoted to his duties (as a king). Like them, with great (filial) love, he protected the subjects who were engaged in their respective duties.

5. He worshipped the venerable Lord who is of the form of *Yajña*[187] and *Kratu* by performing punctually[188] and with

187. A sacrifice conducted without the use of Yūpa or a sacrificial post is Yajña and that with the use of a sacrificial post is a *Kratu*—ŚR.

188. i. e. at the proper time in the morning, at noon and in the evening.

ardent faith, sacrifices, both big and small such as Agnihotra, Darśa, Pūrṇamāsa Cāturmāsya and those performed with the offering of a beast as well as with Soma sacrifices in their completely detailed forms as well as their modifications. Being properly authorised he got them performed through the four classes of sacrificial priests, viz., Hotā, Adhvaryu, Udgātā and Brahmā.

6. While different sacrifices were being performed wherein all the accessory rites and actions were being conducted with meticulous care (by Adhvaryus, with ghee, rice, *puroḍāśa* and other oblations in their hands for offering to the fire) Bharata (the sacrificer) mentally dedicated the entire Apūrva[189] (the prospective transcendental effect) of the fruit of the sacrificial act which is designated as Dharma, to Lord Vāsudeva, the Lord of the sacrifices. He is the doer, as he is the director and controller of deities (lit. objects) of all the Mantras which are symbols of all the gods. In this way, he cleared the impurities (like love, hate) of his mind by his cleverness and wisdom (of dedicating the fruit of sacrifice to Lord). The sacrificer (Bharata) contemplated the gods who partook the offerings from the hands of the Adhvaryus, as resting on the various limbs of the Sacrificial deity (viz. Lord Vāsudeva).

7. In this way, in Bharata's heart, thoroughly purified by such exemplary (faultless) performance of (sacrificial) actions, developed intense devotion which went on increasing

---

189. *Apūrva*: (A) Lit. Something new, not known before. It is 'a Force set in motion by the action of sacrifice, this Force being the Direct Instrument whereby, sooner or later, the Action brings about the Result' (G.N. Jha—*Pūrva Mīmāṁsā in its Sources*, p. 231). Jha discusses the details of this (*Apūrva*) theory and the differences between the Prābhākara and Bhāṭṭa Schools of the Mīmāṁsā (ibid., pp. 226-35).

(B). Jhalkikar defines Apūrva as the special potency developed by performance of sacrifice and leading to heaven. (*Yāgādijanyaḥ svargādijanakaḥ Kaścana-guṇa-viśeṣaḥ*/*Nyāyakośa*, p. 48-49). He further states that *Prārabdha-karma* of Vedāntins, *dharmādharma* of the Nyāya Schools, *adṛṣṭa* of the Vaiśeṣikas and *Puṇya* and *Pāpa* of followers of *Purāṇas* are the same as *apūrva*. Śaṅkara criticises this theory that it is non-spiritual and if God is said to act according to *apūrva*, it becomes identical with the Vedāntic view that God acts with reference to the law of *Karma* (*Śārīra Bhāṣya* 3.2.41).

daily with forceful ardour. The devotion was unto the Supreme Spirit (Brahman) who, within the inner space of Bharata's heart, manifested himself in the form of the Supreme Man, Lord Vāsudeva who was distinguished with the characteristic *Śrī Vatsa*, the *Kaustubha* gem, a garland of forest flowers (*Vanamālā*), the discus (*Sudarśana*) and the mace (called *Kaumodakī*) and others. Lord Vāsudeva who stays steady (as if drawn in portrait) in the heart of his devotees, stood effulgent in Bharata's mind (as well).

8. In this way he spent one thousand myriad (Ten million) years. Having understood that the time of exhaustion of the fund of his *karmas* (resulting in enjoyment of kingship) had arrived, he proportionately divided the ancestral property and kingdom which was till then enjoyed by him, to his sons. Abandoning his home which was the abode of all kinds of wealth and prosperity, he retired as recluse to the hermitage of Pulaha.[190]

9. They say that, out of affection and grace for his votaries who stay there (at Pulahāśrama), Lord Hari, verily even now manifests himself to his devotees in the form desired by them.

10. That eminently holy river called Cakra-nadī (the Gaṇḍak) hallows all the places in that hermitage with wheel-like circular pebbles with navel-like dimples on both the sides.

11. It is indeed said that in a grove adjacent to Pulaha's hermitage, he performed, all alone, the worship of the Lord with different kinds of flowers, tender leaves of various kinds, especially of the Tulasī-plant and with water, and offered to him (as *naivedya*) bulbous roots, roots and fruits. He ceased to have any desire for objects of senses and cultivated perfect tranquillity of the mind and attained to supreme bliss.

---

190. *Pulahāśrama*—ŚR., SD., GD. call it *Harikṣetra*, while VR., VJ., BP. identify it with *Śāla (li) grāma*. N. L. De locates it somewhere near the source of the Gaṇḍaka. However, he points out that (Jaḍa) Bharata's hermitage was situated on the Kakaveni river on the north of Redigrama and that of Pulaha in the latter village. —GDAMI. 174.

The place is confirmed by *Padma P.* Pātālakhaṇḍa, Ch. 78 and *Brahma Vaivarta, P.* 2.13.

12. By such type of uninterrupted worship of the Supreme Man, his heart melted with the pressure of his increasing love for God and became slack in making any efforts (as if hypnotised); due to ecstatic joy, the hair stood on their end all over his body; his eyes became bedimmed with tears of joy which flowed profusely due to his love and solicitude (to realize the Lord). His consciousness and thought activity was drowned in the deep lakelike heart overflowing with supreme joy due to the increasing intensity of devotion caused by his constant contemplation of the red-lotus-like feet of his beloved Lord. And he forgot (even) the worship of the Lord that he was performing.

13. He had thus undertaken the sacred vow of propitiating the Lord. With the deer-skin for his clothing and with his mass of tawny, curly matted hair, wet on account of his ablution in the morning, noon and evening, Bharata appeared charming. He praised the glorious Lord, the golden (Self-effulgent) Supreme Man manifested in the orb of the rising Sun by means of Ṛgvedic hymns addressed to the Sun, thus :

14.* The light of the Sun-god (the Creator of the universe) which dispenses the fruit of actions, is transcendental to

---

* (i) VR. : We take shelter with the brilliantly luminous form of god Viṣṇu—Viṣṇu who is beyond the sphere of Prakṛti and whose knowledge is ever manifesting, eternal and limitless. He created this universe by His Will (-power). He entered again his own creation, along with Jīva, charged with his power (or it is by his Will-power and knowledge that he entered the universe consisting of the sentients and insentients). He sees (protects) the Jīva who hankers after the objects of senses and who enjoys the fruits of his action by his intelligence leading to the miseries of the cycle of births and deaths.

(ii) VJ. : You transcend (i.e. are superior to and beyond) Prakṛti or are free from *rajas*. You are the maker of the world. You have perfect knowledge of everything. Being established by the Vedas, you are the offspring of the Vedas. The Lord created this universe by his mental power. By his power, he entered the universe and stayed there as the controller. You put an end to miseries. You are the Lord of all *jīvas* who are full of cravings (of all kinds). We eulogize you.

(iii) SD. : This verse elucidates the meaning of Gāyatrī. The main idea is: "Lord Vāsudeva is the creator of the universe. To his brilliantly shining golden form, we take shelter."

Prakṛti (lit. is beyond *rajas*, is purely *Sāttvic* unalloyed with *rajas* and *tamas*). It created this (phenomenal universe) by its will (power) only, and having entered it (as the *antaryāmin*—the Inner Controller), it protects, by its intellectual capacity, the *jīva* who seeks its help. We resort to that light which actuates our intellect.[191]

CHAPTER EIGHT

(Bharata reborn as a deer)

1. Once upon a time, after finishing the necessary (bodily) acts (e.g. urination), Bharata bathed in the great river (the Gaṇḍkakī) and completed his routine of general and special religious duties. He then sat on the bank of the river, repeating the sacred syllable *Om*, for a period of three *muhūrtas*.[192]

2. At that time, Oh King, there approached near the river, a female deer, all alone, to satisfy her thirst.

3. Exactly at that time, while she continued to drink water with avidity, there arose, not far from the place, a terrifically loud cry of a roaring lion, panicking the world.

4. The female deer was timid by nature. Hearing it, with frightened looks, she became panicky at heart, with the

---

(iv) GD. : This verse brings out the following characteristics of the Lord :

(1) The creator of the universe; (2) the protector of the world, (3) Being a witness—aloof and above the world; (4) Being the inner controller as follows:

(1) His lustre being identical with the Lord's form created the universe with his mental power. (2) From him does the wealth i. e. the fruit of Karmas, issue. (3) Having re-entered the universe, he, by his *cit-śakti* (intellectual capacity) sees the Jīva hankering after pleasures. (4) He motivates the intellect, organs of senses and vital airs among beings.

191. Cf. also

tat savitur vareṇyam bhargo devasya dhīmahi|
dhiyo yo naḥ pracodayāt| RV. 3.62.10.

192. *muhūrta*—a period of 48 minutes.

fear of the lion. With her eyes swimming and thirst unquenched, she suddenly leapt across the river through fear.

5. When the doe which was carrying leapt over, the foetus in her which became dislodged through terrific fear, got discharged from her organ of generation and fell into the river.

6. That devoted female companion of a black antelope was afflicted with exhaustion caused by the abortion, (unusually) long jump and fear (of the lion), she strayed away from her herd, rushed into a cave and fell dead.

7. The royal sage Bharata noticed that the helpless young one of the deer was being carried away by the current. Out of compassion, he picked it up, as it was abandoned by its relatives, and took it to his hermitage, as it was motherless.

8. They say that he developed intense attachment for it, feeling the young deer to be his own. Day by day, he got engrossed in its feeding, protection (from wolves etc.), caressing and pleasing it (with scratching etc.). When he got so fondly attached to it in the course of some days, his daily righteous duties along with *yamas* (moral observances like non violence—*ahiṁsā* etc.), worship of the Supreme Lord and others, became neglected one by one, and soon all of them were abandoned by him.

9. (Bharata said to himself) : "Alas ! What a pity ! This poor unfortunate young deer has, due to the velocity of the rotation of the wheel of Time, been separated from its kith and kin and friends, and has resorted to me as a shelter. It regards me only as its father, mother, brother and relative and as a companion in its herd. Nor does it know anyone else. It has placed its absolute trust in me. I know the gravity of the sin in letting down a person seeking my protection. Hence it is up to me that I, with envy towards none, should look after the feeding, protection, satisfaction and fondling of this young deer which completely depends on me."

10. For certainly, self-restrained and tranquil-minded noble worthies who are friendly to the poor and wretched, disregard even their bigger interests for such (compassionate acts).

11. In this way he felt attachment to it. His heart was

bound down with affection for the fawn while he was sitting, sleeping, wandering, standing, eating and doing such other acts.

12. When he wanted to bring the (blades of) Kuśa grass, flowers, sacrificial sticks, leaves, fruits, roots and water, he went into the forest along with the young one of the deer, as he apprehended danger to the life of the fawn from wolves and dogs.

13. When due to its innocent nature, it became stuck up at various places on the way, he, with his heart overwhelmed with excessive affection, bore it on his shoulder, out of pity for it. In this way, by placing it on his lap, hugging it to his bosom and by fondling it, he derived the highest pleasure.

14. Even during the course of performing his religious duties, he used to rise up frequently at intervals to have a look at it, and with his heart reassured, the Lord of the Bhārata varṣa) continent expressed his blessing with the words, "may you be safe from all sides, my child".

15. On other occasions (when he did not see the fawn), he felt excessively anxious about it like a miser who has lost his wealth. With extreme anxiety and full of tenderness and compassion, his heart was tormented, with the pangs of separation from the fawn. Being overcome with great infatuation and lamenting for the young deer, verily, it is said that he used to lament (lit. express himself) as follows :

16. "Oh ! Is it possible ? Will that pitiable motherless young one of the deer place its confidence again in me who am, alas ! ignoble, of deceitful and cruel nature like a cunning Kirāta and who have done no meritorious acts ? Will it return (to me) forgetting and forgiving my faults by its inherent goodness and purity of heart like a saintly person ?

17. Shall I be able to see it (again), protected by God, and safely grazing tender leaves of grass in the garden of the hermitage ?

18. (How strongly I wish) that no wolf, or dog or any other gregarious animal (like boar) or solitary wanderer (like a tiger) eats it.

19. The glorious Lord (the Sun), which rises for the weal of the whole world and which is the Soul of the triad of

Vedas (the Ṛg, Yajus and Sāman) is (now) certainly setting. But still the fawn, the charge entrusted to me by the female deer, has not arrived.

20. Would that the princely young deer return and delight me who have done no righteous deed, and remove the anxiety and sorrow of his near and dear ones, by its manifold beautiful, pleasing, sportive fawn-like activities?

21. When in joke, I close my eyes in sham meditation, out of anger resulting from affection, it would approach me hesitatingly with awe. And with the tips of its horns soft like drops of water, it would strike at me.

22. When it is chided by me for polluting (by nibbling) the Kuśa grass on which the sacrificial offerings are placed, it being extremely afraid, immediately desists from its sport (sportiveness) and stays steady without moving its limbs, like a boy-sage with all his senses controlled. Oh! What wonderful penance must have been practised by this fortunate earth!"

23. (After saying the above words, he went out and found the prints of the hooves of the deer and said): "By means of the rows of the imprint of tiny, charming, auspicious-most hoofs of the docile young one of the black-antilope, the earth indicates the track of the treasure-trove (viz. the lost fawn) to me, a wretched person, who am afflicted due to my being deprived of my wealth (the youny deer). And having got herself beautified with those foot-prints, she becomes transformed into a sacrificial place[193] for the twice-born ones (*dvijas*) aspiring after *Svarga* (heaven) and *Mokṣa* (the final beatitude).

24. (Looking at the Moon that has arisen, he imagined that the deer-like spot on the disc of the Moon was his fawn). Maybe that, out of compassion, the glorious Lord of stars who is kind to the poor and afflicted, protects, from the fear of the lion, this fawn whose mother is dead and which has strayed away from its hermitage (shelter).

25. Or it may be that with its cool, soothing and (due to affection) profusely flowing drivel in the form of rays, the

193. ŚR. quotes a Smṛti text to support the sanctifying effect of the foot-prints of black antelopes rendering that place fit for performing sacrifices : *yasmin deśe mṛgaḥ kṛṣṇas tasmin dharmān nibodhata*/Cf. Manu 2.23.

Moon soothes me whose land-lotus-like heart is scorched by the flames of the forest conflagration of the fever (torments) of separation from my child (-like fawn), and who, in search of the fawn, am following the young one of the doe."

26. In this way, the heart of Bharata was overcome with wishes which could not be accomplished. By the force of his own destiny (lit. fruition of his deeds done in previous birth) which appeared in the form of that fawn, Bharata the *Yogī* and the sage, swerved from the yogic practices[194] and his acts for propitiating the glorious Lord. How else there would be such an intense attachment to the young one of a deer—an animal of a different species—in Bharata who formerly considered his own sons—with whom it is so very difficult to part—as veritable impediments in the attainment of Liberation and separated himself from them. In this way, the practice of Yoga, commenced by the royal sage Bharata, got interrupted. He forgot the real nature of the Soul (or himself) while feeding, protecting, pleasing and caressing the young deer. Meanwhile just as a serpent rushes to the hole of a rat, the inevitable time of death, of terrific speed, arrived.

27. Even at that time, he wistfully fixed his glance on the deer which like unto a son was mourning by his side. With his heart fixed on the fawn, he left this world. He did not lose the memory of his previous life along with his dead body, but like other (ordinary *jīvas* with such obsessions at the time of death*) got the body of (birth as) a deer.

28. Even in that life as a deer, by virtue of his (endeavouring at) propitiation of the Lord (in his previous birth) he remembered the cause of his birth as a deer and being greatly tormented with repentance, he said:

29. "Alas! How painful it is! I strayed away from the path of the knowers of the Supreme Self. With great fortitude I divested myself from attachment of every kind and resorted

194. VR. includes under these the three kinds of *Yoga* viz. *Jñāna-yoga*, *Karma-yoga* and *Bhakti-yoga* and these are regarded as the three kinds of austerities which Bharata practised.

*Cf. *yaṁ yaṁ vāpi smaran bhāvaṁ tyajatyante kalevaram / taṁ taṁ evaiti* to a secluded sacred forest. Self-controlled as I was, I completely devoted and concentrated my mind on the venerable Lord Vāsudeva who is the (*antaryāmin*) inner controller of all, I utilized fully all the time, every moment of which was devoted with energetic efforts to the listening to the excellences of the Lord, reasoning and pondering over them, extolling his virtues, worshipping him, constantly remembering him. That mind of my ignorant self in a moment flowed (was attracted) to a young one of a deer from far afar''.

30. Thus being full of deep remorse, he left his mother-deer. And from Kālañjara[195] hill (his birth place), he returned again to the hermitage of Pulastya-Pulaha at Śālagrāma, a holy place consecrated to the Lord, a place favourite with sages who have attained self-control and serenity of mind.

31. Even there, he waited for the termination of his life (lit. death). He was so terribly disgusted with attachment that he lived all alone. Subsisting on dry leaves, grass and creepers he was counting (his days) for the exhaustion of (his *karma* which was) the cause of his birth as a deer. (Ultimately) he cast off his body of a deer immersing half of it in the sacred waters of the Gaṇḍakī.

CHAPTER NINE

(*Bharata, reborn as a Brāhmaṇa, saved by Bhadrakālī*)

Śrī Śuka said:

1. Then (after Bharata's quitting his body as a deer, the story of Bharata proceeds as follows).

There lived a certain holy Brāhmaṇa, foremost in the clan of Aṅgiras. He was possessed of self-control and tranquillity of mind. He was noted for his austerities, study of the Vedas, liberal hospitality, contentment, endurance, modesty, knowledge of rituals, non-jealousy, knowledge of the Supreme

195. Kālañjara in the Badausa Sub-division of Banda district-N.L. De—GDAMI. 84.

Self (as being different from the body) and felicity (as a result of righteousness). (From his elder wife) he got nine sons, all similar to him in scholarship, nobility of character, righteous conduct, handsomeness and liberality. From his younger wife was born a twin—a son and a daughter.

2. They say that the male among the twins was Bharata, the great votary of the Lord, the foremost among royal sages. He cast off the body of a deer and as the last incarnation (before final beatitude) was born as a Brāhmaṇa.

3. In this birth also, he was terribly afraid of attachment to his relatives. He specifically contemplated in his mind the pair of the lotus-feet of the glorious Lord who cuts asunder bondage of *Karma* of those who listen to, meditate upon and extol the excellences of the Lord. He remembered the series of his previous incarnations through the grace of the Lord and being apprehensive of his fall (as in his previous life), he presented himself to the world as being an insane, stupid, blind and deaf person.

4. With his heart deeply attached to his son through filial affection, the Brāhmaṇa verily performed all the sacred ceremonies (*Saṁskāras*) up to *Samāvartana*[196] as prescribed in the *Śāstras*. To his son whose *upanayana* ceremony (for investiture of the sacred thread for the beginning of the study of the Vedas) was performed, he taught him well the rules of conduct such as the Śāstric way of personal purity of performing *ācamana* (sipping water before and after meal and while performing *sandhyā* etc.) and other rules of performing sacred duties, even though they were not to the liking of his son; for (according to Śāstric injunctions) a son must be instructed (in the observance of religious duties) by his father.

5. And he (Bharata) also used to behave in the wrong

196. *Samāvartana* was originally a ceremonial bath after finishing Veda study. It marked the termination of studenthood. Some texts on *dharma Śāstra* regarded it as a subordinate element (*aṅga*) of marriage. The Brāhmaṇa did not want to get the stupid son married. Hence he completed the purificatory ceremonies upto *Samāvartana*. For details of this ceremony vide Kane *Hist. of Dharma Śāstra*, pp. 402-415.

way,[197] contrary to the instructions[198] (of his father) in his father's presence. The father intended to instruct him in the Vedas (in the month of Śrāvaṇa). But in spite of his continuous instructions during the months of the spring (*Caitra* and *Vaiśākha*), and the months of the summer (*Jyeṣṭha* and *Āṣāḍha*) he could hardly teach the boy the three-footed Solar-hymn (known as *Gāyatrī mantra*), along with *Vyāhṛtis* (the mystic syllables *bhūḥ, bhuvaḥ* and *suvaḥ*) with the sacred syllable OM at the beginning.[199]

6. In this way, the Brāhmaṇa's heart was fixed on his son who was his own self. He stuck fast to the false notion that a son must be made learned at all costs. He taught Bharata all the duties of *upakurvāṇa*[200] celibate, viz., cleanliness and purity, Vedic studies, observance of vows, self-discipline, service of the preceptor, worship of the sacrificial fire and others, even though Bharata had no regard for them. But he could not realise his ambition. In the meanwhile, the Brāhmaṇa who, due to his attachment to domestic life, remained negligent (about his spiritual good) was taken away by the ever vigilant death.

7. Having entrusted the twin children that were born from her, to the care of her co-wife, the younger pious wife of the Brāhmaṇa died after him (by immolating herself on his funeral pyre) and attained to the region of her Lord.

8. When the father died, (Bharata's) brothers who were ignorant of his superhuman power and greatness, and who, being (totally) ignorant of the higher knowledge (viz. that

---

197. GD.: The word *iva* implies that whatever a knower of Brahman does, is right and true, though it may appear strange to ordinary people.

198. VC. illustrates: He used to take *ācamana* before going for urination and not after. GD. explains: the words *u ha* express wonder at the necessity of compliance to his father's request when Bharata had realized Brahman.

199. i.e. in spite of instruction for four months, Bharata could hardly pronounce the following Gāyatrī Mantra:

Om, bhūr bhuvaḥ suvaḥ tat Savitur vareṇyam /
bhargo devasya dhīmahi, dhiyo yo naḥ pracodayāt //

200. *upakurvāṇa*—A Brāhmaṇa in a state of pupilage (Brahmacārin) who wishes to pass on to the state of a householder.

of the Self or Brahman), regarded knowledge of the three Vedas (i.e. *karma-kāṇḍa* enjoined therein) as the highest knowledge, thought him to be dull-witted and desisted from their duty of teaching their brother.

9. When he was addressed by ignorant bi-ped brutes (e.g. men) as madman, a stupid or a deaf fellow, he replied to them suitably (according to the implications of the epithets given by them). When he was made to work according to the will of another person, he worked. He used to partake whatever food he got, in return for wages or forced labour (without wages), by way of begging or unsolicited, whether it be little or plenty, savoury or otherwise, but (he never ate) for the gratification of his senses. For he attained the knowledge of his Self which is not the product of any cause but is self-existent, of the nature of extremely pure bliss; and he never identified himself with his body in pleasure or pain caused by pairs of opposites (like heat, cold, respect, disrespect).

10. Stout and muscular as he was, he wandered about barebodied like a bull, in cold (the winter) and heat (the summer), in stormy winds and showers (the rainy season). He lay down on the bare ground to sleep; had not massaged his body (with oil); nor did he ever take a bath. Under the coating of the dirt (so accumulated on his body), his spiritual glory remained unmanifested just as the brilliance of a big gem is obscured by a coating of dust. His loins were covered with a dirty cloth. With his dirty-most sacred thread, he was (contemptuously) ridiculed as 'a nominal Brāhmaṇa', 'an unworhty Brāhmaṇa' (a Brāhmaṇa by caste only), by persons ignorant of his real greatness.

11. When, however, he wished to have food (for his livelihood) in return (as wages) for work, from others, he was employed even by his brothers in farm work, on agricultural farm. He did it but he did not (care to) know whether the ground was level or uneven or whether he worked less or more (in proportion to the wages). He swallowed, as if it were nectar, the broken rice, oil cake, husk, worm-eaten grains (called Kulmāṣa), charred rice sticking to the bottom of the boiling pot (offered as remuneration for work).

12. Now, on one occasion, a certain chieftain of robbers

(of Śūdra caste) desirous of having a child, was about to offer a man as a sacrificial beast to goddess Bhadrakālī.

13. The animal (i.e. the man brought for being sacrificed) providentially escaped. The servants of the chieftain who ran in all directions on the track of the (luckily escaped) victim in (the darkness of) the night, could not catch the 'beast', even at midnight owing to thick darkness. By chance (however) they saw the famous scion of the Aṅgiras family in the Vīrāsana posture guarding the fields against deer, boars and other beasts.

14. Observing him to be of defectless limbs and feeling pretty sure that it will serve their master's purpose thereby, they bound him with a rope and brought him to the temple of the goddess Caṇḍikā (Bhadrakālī), their faces blooming with joy.

15. The Paṇis (robbers) bathed him in their own ritualistic way, covered him with new (unwashed) piece of cloth, decorated him with ornaments, pigments, garlands, a sandal-paste mark on the forehead etc., fed him (to his fill). Taking with them burning incerse, lamps (torches), wreaths of flowers, fried grains, tender shoots and sprouts and offerings of fruits according to their traditional ritual of human sacrifice and in accompaniment of loud music, singing of panegyrics and beating of drums and the musical instrument called *Paṇava*, they made the human (sacrificial) animal sit before the goddess Bhadrakālī.

16. The robber chieftain of the Vṛṣalas (Śūdras) wishing to worship the goddess Bhadrakālī with the wine in the form of human blood of the man sacrificed as a beast, took a very terrible sword charmed with the specific incantation (of Bhadrakālī[201]).

17. The nature of the Vṛṣalas (Śūdras) was dominated by *rajas* and *tamas*. Their minds grew haughty due to the *rajas*, the pride of wealth. In utter disrespect for the family

---

201. VD. quotes it as follows :

gṛdhrakarṇi, virūpākṣi, lamba-stani, mahodari /
hana śatruṁ triśūlena kruddhasya piba śoṇitaṃ //

He gives an alternate incantation:

Kāli-kāli, Mahā-kāli etc.

of Brāhmaṇas, (who are) the leaders possessing (and preserving) the Vedas, the rays of the venerable Lord, they strayed wilfully on the wrong (sinful) way and sported in acts of violence (as an amusement). The goddess Bhadrakālī noticed the terrible-most act of immolating the son of a Brāhmaṇa sage who had become one with Brahman, and who was above enmity, and a friend of all beings—the killing of whom is not permissible[202] even in (such an) imminent danger wherein violence is allowed. With her body fiercely scorched with the extremely unbearable Brahmanic lustre, the goddess suddenly exploded forth from the image.

18. In extreme wrath and indignation, her terrible face with her branch-like arched eyebrows thrown up in agitation, her dreadful, curved jaws and the movement of her blood-red eyes, showed that she was as if bent on destroying this world. In terrible rage, she roared forth a thunderous laugh. Springing forward, she cut off the heads of those wicked sinners with that very sword (with which the king was to slay Bharata) and drank to her fill, along with attendants, hot wine of the blood gushing forth from their throats. Intoxicated with over-drinking of that blood-wine, she sang at the topmost pitch of her voice in company of her attendants, and danced and played with the ball-like lopped heads.

19. In this way, verily, a malevolent aggressive black magic to kill the great-souled ones totally rebounds against the exorciser.

20. Oh Viṣṇudatta (King Parīkṣit) ! It is not a great miracle in the case of the great devotees of the Lord who are free from all attachment to the world (*Parama-haṁsas*) that they remain unperturbed even if the calamity of getting beheaded is impending; for they have resolved the formidable knot in their heart—the knot viz., the identification of their Self with their body—and who are well-wishers of all the beings in their heart

---

202. VD. quotes an Āgama text prohibiting human sacrifices in general and of a Brāhmaṇa in particular. The quotation from the Black Yajurveda indicating human sacrifice does not involve actual killing as explained by the annotator. A.B. Keith, the translator of the Black Yajurveda, also shows that actual human sacrifices were not current in Vedic times. (*The Religion & Philosophy of the Veda and Upaniṣads*—pp. 347-48).

and are above all enmity. They have resorted to the feet of the Lord and are protected from all sides by the venerable Lord Himself directly, by the ever-vigilant weapon called the discus of Time and through various forms (like Bhadrakālī here).

CHAPTER TEN

(Bharata's Life : King Rahūgaṇa accepts discipleship)

Śrī Śuka said:

(The following incident took place when Rahūgaṇa, a King of Sindhu-Sauvīra, was going to the sage Kapila for instruction in philosophy).

1. One day, while Rahūgana, the King of Sindhu-Sauvīra,[203] was proceeding (to Kapila), the captain of the palanquin-bearers who was in search of a palanquin-bearer, providentially found this excellent Brāhmaṇa (viz. Bharata). (He thought that) this stout, young man of sturdy constitution was fit to carry any load like a bull or a donkey. Bharata was taken perforce along with others who were already so employed to carry on the forced labour without remuneration even though he (Bharata) did not deserve it, that exalted personage carried the palanquin.

2. The gait of the great Brāhmaṇa who (in order to avoid injury to others) walked after carefully looking the ground ahead to the length of arrow, did not conform to that of other men (bearing the palanquin) Rahūgaṇa felt the jolts of the irregular movement of the palanquin. He spoke to the men (palanquin-bearers), "On bearers, walk properly. Why is the vehicle (palanquin) borne so irregularly?".

203. *Sindhu-Suavīra*—Names of two adjacent countries, Sindhu and Sauvīra. Ancient Sauvīra was situated to the east of the lower Indus and included Multan on the north. According to Alberuni, Sauvīra included Multan and Jahrawar. Sindhu lay to the west and Sauvīra to the east of the lower Indus. D.C. Sircar GAMI 33 and 113. For other identification see N.L. De : GDAMI, p. 183.

3. Hearing the taunting words of the master, they, afraid in their minds of the application of the fourth remedy[204] (viz. corporal punishment) to them, humbly submitted to him.

4. "Oh Lord of men! We are not negligent. We are properly carrying (the palanquin) in complete obedience to your majesty's commands. Though employed just afresh (just now), this (new) fellow does not walk quickly. Hence we are not able to carry the palanquin with him."

5. He (King Rahūgaṇa) realized that the contagious fault (disease) even of one man certainly becomes the fault of all who come in contact with him. Though he had waited upon the elderly (wise) person, his original (Kṣatriya) nature overpowered him. His intelligence was clouded (lit. covered) with *rajo-guṇa*. Getting slightly enraged, he spoke (sarcastically to Bharata) whose Brāhmanic lustre remained unmanifested like fire (covered with ashes).

6. "Alas! What a pity, brother! You are obviously very much exhausted. Your honour alone has carried the palanquin to a great distance for a long time, and these other co-bearers are as good as non-existent. You are neither stout nor possessing a well built body. And you are overcome with old age, oh friend!" Though he was thus severely reproached in an insulting manner, he (Bharata) who had never superimposed the false notion of I-ness and mine-ness on his final body which was created by nescience (*avīdyā*) as a combination of gross matter (five elements), attributes (ten sense organs), (effects of past) actions (merits and sins) and the mind—an unreal configuration of aggregates and who was on the verge of merging into Brahman[205], silently carried the palanquin as before.

7. Later on, when the palanquin was borne irregularly again, Rahūgaṇa flared up in rage and said, "Oh! What does

---

204. *upāyāḥ sāma dānaṁ ca bhedo daṇḍas tathaiva ca |*
samyak prayuktāḥ siddhyeyur daṇḍas tvagatikā gatiḥ ||
Yājñavalkya Smṛti 1.346

Conciliation or negotiation (sāman), bribery (dāna), sowing dissension (*bheda*) and punishment (*daṇḍa*) are the stratagems or expedients to deal with enemies (in the case of Kings).

205. Brahma-bhūta—(i) One whose mind is absorbed in Brahman—VJ.

(ii) One who has realized the identity of his self and Brahman by the cessation of *avidyā*—GD.

this mean? You are (as good as) dead though alive. Disdaining me (who am your lord), you transgress the command of your lord. Like unto Yama, (the god with a rod) who metes out punishment to people, I shall administer the corrective remedy to you, a negligent fellow, so that you will come to your senses."

8. The venerable Brāhmaṇa who was to be absorbed into the Supreme Spirit (*Brahman*) was the well-wisher of all beings (even those who offended him), the very self of them all. Totally free from pride, he spoke with a slight smile to Raḥūgaṇa who indulged in a good deal of irrelevant bragging. This way Rahūgaṇa who was puffed up with the pride of being the lord of men, who being inebriated with arrogance and infatuation born of *rajas* and *tamas* contemptuously disregarded the whole community of the votaries of the Lord (who are beloved of him) by insulting Bharata, who, though (in conceit wrongly) considered himself to be learned, had little knowledge of the modes of behaviour of masters of yoga.

The Brāhmaṇa said:

9* What you stated (about fatigue, bearing palanquin alone for a long distance, etc. in 6 above) is a fact. There is no sarcasm (therein) Oh warrior![206] If there be anything like a burden, and if it be borne by a body called bearer, and if the body has any relation with me, then the taunt would apply to me. (But that is not the case due to the unreality of the burden and the bearer and their non-relation to me—the self). So also if a station is to be reached by the goer, there

* (i) What you spoke is true from the popular point of view. But if there be a burden to the bearer, the consequent fatigue is possible; it however is not applicable to me as I am not carrying anything. If there be some station to be reached there would have been distance to be covered but such movement is obviously non-existent in my case. The epithet 'fat' may be applicable to the body which is a conglomeration of *bhūtas* and not to me in the language of those who have realized the Self (*ātman*) —VR.

(ii) VJ. endorses the same interpretation in different words.

206. v.l. *addha*—directly, in the real sense of the term.

would be (the existence of) the way[207]. Only the fools and never the wise, apply the epithet 'stout' to the Soul. For this description is applicable to the (body which is) the conglomeration of *bhūtas* etc. (and not to the Soul).[208]

10. Corpulence and emaciation, (bodily) pains and (mental) worries, hunger and thirst, fear, quarrelsomeness, desire, old age, sleep, attachment, anger, arrogance and griefs—all these apply to one who is born with a body, but not to me (who am the self and not the body).

11. (As for your words, "You are as good as dead though alive", I say that): Simultaneousness of life and death is the law found applicable to everything that is a product (and hence subject to transformation, and not limited to me) for all products have a beginning and an end. (As for your charge of transgressing your orders), Oh praiseworthy king! If the relation as servant and master were real and permanent, then only would the relation between order and its execution be real. (But if you lose your kingdom and I become a king, the whole relation will be reversed).

12* (If you think that I am a servant so long as you are the king) we do not find the slightest ground for the notion of the difference as king and his servant, except conventional verbal usage. Who is then the ruler and what it is to be governed (servant)? However (if you still entertain the notion of being the ruler) please tell what we should do for you.

---

207. Just as you concentrate in ruling your kingdom, pay similar attention to what I say—GD.

208. I am by nature the Supreme Soul to which the epithet 'stout' is slanderous,—VC.

* (i) VJ. goes out of his way to prove the superiority of Hari to Rudra while explaining this verse :

Master-servant relation is reversable in the case of men but not so in the case of gods. This unchangeable lordship among gods is conferred on Rudra by Hari—the real Ruler. The ignorant subjects of Sindhu call you a ruler. But this is a conventional verbal usage. You are in no way superior to other *jīvas*. However granting that you are the ruler, please tell us what should be done for you.

(ii) GD. waxes eloquent to establish the Śuddhādvaita thesis : The pure Brahman (unsoiled by Māyā etc.) is the reality and not the master-servant relation. He does not differ in the interpretation.

13* (Bharata presents a dilemma to show that the King's threat of punishment is wide of mark. If I be a *mukta* —beyond bondage of *saṁsāra* what purpose and to what extent, can be served by your treatment (punishment) or lessons to me who am established in the self, though appearing like a lunatic, intoxicated or dull-witted person. (If I be not a *mukta* the proposed punishment or lesson to a person who is obstinate or insane is (as useless as) grinding flour, Oh warrior[209]."

Śrī Śuka said:

14. In this way, Bharata replied (each and every) statement (of the king) after recapitulating them. The great sage was tranquil and self-controlled by nature. Nescience—the cause of false identification of the body with the Soul, had ceased in him. He wanted to exhaust by sufferance (the effect of) the *karma* that was bearing fruition, and (thence) he continued to bear the vehicle of the king.

15. By the force of his genuine right faith, the king of Sindhu-Sauvīra countries became eligible to enquire into the Truth. Having (carefully) listened to the speech of the Brāhmaṇa which was calculated to resolve the knot (of ignorance) at one's heart and which was approved of (and supported by) many treatises on Yoga (self-knowledge), he got down (from the palanquin) in haste, and prostrated himself (before him) with his head at the sage's feet. Beseeching forgiveness (for his rudeness), and completely free from the pride of his royalty, he said:

16. "Who are you of the great Brāhmaṇas who go about in disguise, as you wear the sacred thread? Who are you among the *avadhūtas* (like Dattātreya and others, if you be an *avadhūta*) ? Whose son are you ? What is your native place ? Why have you come here ? If you have come for our spiritual well-being, are you not the sage Kapila ?

---

* VJ. : Bharata explains to the king that despite his appearance like a mad person etc., he is totally immersed in Lord Hari; and as such, the punishment proposed is useless; for he has completely detached himself from his corporal body.

209. Your prowess may have been effective elsewhere, but is vain against me.

17. I am not afraid of the thunderbolt of the lord of gods (Indra), of the trident of the three-eyed god (Śiva), or of the rod of Yama (the god of death). I do not fear the missiles of (the fire-god), the Sun-god, the wind-god and the lord of wealth (Kubera). But I am terribly afraid of disrespecting the Brāhmaṇa race.

18. Hence please tell me. You are free from attachment. Though you possess infinite power, you conceal your superior wisdom and prowess, and roam about like a dull-witted person. Oh pious sage, your words are couched in yogic terms (or conveying the advice of great yogis) as such, are not capable of being comprehended by our minds. (Or-Even persons of keen intellect cannot grasp the significance of your speech couched in yogic terms).

19. "What is the true asylum in this Saṁsāra"? To ask this, I am now proceeding to Kapila who is master of yoga, and the supreme preceptor of sages who have realized the true nature of the Self; who is Hari incarnate and has incarnated in this world by his power of supreme knowledge.

20. It may be that perhaps your honour verily be Kapila himself, who is going about incognito, for observing the condition of the people. How can a person attached to house-(holder's worldly) life, with intellect blinded (by infatuation), fathom the ways (of behaviour) of the masters of yoga?

21. (The king raises objections to Bharata's speech given above*).

I have experienced fatigue through activity (e.g. fighting in battle). By inference I presume that your honour must have felt the same when carrying a load while walking. The course of the phenomenal world must be real at the bottom; for, otherwise it is impossible to carry water etc. with a non-existent pitcher.

* ŚR. expounds the logic in the king's speech by detailing the syllogisms as follows :

He who does work, feels exhausted.

e.g, I feel exhausted in fighting etc.

You have carried the burden of my palanquin. Therefore you must have been exhausted. Hence, your statement that you did not feel fatigue (verse 9) is illogical.

22. The heat of fire applied to the vessel is conducted to the water (in the pot); the heat of the water leads to the softening of the grains of rice from inside. Due to the contact with the body, sense-organs and the life-breath and the mind, the state of *saṁsāra* affects the *jiva*, as the states of environments affect each other.

23. (As to the impermanence of the master-servant relation mentioned by you:)

The king is (for that particular period at least) the (real) controller and protector of the subjects. He who is the servant of Acyuta does not grind the already ground material flour. (His performance of duties is not wasted). For by carrying out his righteous duties he propitiates Lord Acyuta and gets rid of his sins.

24. Oh friend of the distressed, be pleased, therefore, to cast a friendly glance at me who, out of my intoxicating pride of being the ruler of men, have treated with contempt the best of saints,so that I may be able to cross over the sin of showing disrespect to the the righteous people.

25. (The king refers to Bharata's words that he was not insulted etc., and says)

There may not be any change (perturbation of mind) in you who are a well-wisher and friend of the universe and who, out of his sense of equality to all, are completely devoid of attachment (even to your body). But a person like me—even though he be Rudra, the bearer of trident, will certainly perish in near future as a result of his showing disrespect to the exalted."

CHAPTER ELEVEN

(Bharata imparts spiritual knowledge to Rahūgaṇa)

The Brāhmana said:

1. You are (really) ignorant. You (simply) give verbal expression to the arguments (which are apparently similar to those) of the learned. You will not, therefore, be (considered

as) pre-eminent (in any way) among those who are supremely wise; for the sages never speak of mundane relations (e.g. the master-servant relation) along with their investigation into (the nature of) Reality. (You regard master-servant relation as real but the sages do not recognize it as such.

2.* (Similarly the ritualistic way—*Karma-Kāṇḍa*—described in the Vedas is also not true. In the highly glittering flowery descriptions in the Vedic texts pertaining to the detailed study of the minute rituals connected with the householder's life, no light is definitely thrown on the exposition of the truth which is pure (i.e. free from the contamination of injury (*hiṁsā*) etc.) and good (i.e. devoid of passions like love, hate) as a rule (persons who dedicate all their *karmas* to God are eligible for such exposition of truth).

3. Not even the most authoritative Vedic (Upaniṣadic) texts can directly impart the comprehension of the Truth to a person who on the analogy of (the unreal, evanescent and hence worthless pleasures enjoyed in) a dream does not conclude that the (dreamlike) pleasures in the house-holder's life (and those in heaven accruing from sacrifices) are by themselves worth casting off.

4. As long as the mind of a man is under the dominating influence of *sattva*, *rajas* or *tamas*, it goes on producing unchecked merit or sin through his sense-organs of perception and action.

5. The mind (which, as an *upādhi* of *ātman*, is designated as *ātman*) is a store-house of impressions unconsciously left by the good or bad actions in the past life; it is attached to objects of pleasures; it is tossed about by *guṇas*; it is affected by passions; it is the chief among sixteen constituents (elements, sense-organs etc.) of the *Liṅga Śarīra* (the subtle body). It assumes different forms (man, beast etc.) under different names, and extends (i.e. causes) higher or lower form of life in the various kinds of physical bodies.

* (i) VR.: Persons interested in performance of ritualistic *karmas* cannot be interested in pure knowledge. And in the former (i.e. *karma-kāṇḍa*) portion of the Vedas, no decisive conclusion is reached.

(ii) VC.: Mīmāṁsakas do not regard an objective (*puruṣārtha*) higher than heaven attained by *karmas*. Exposition of truth to such unqualified persons is a waste. For this truth is above the taint of passions and free from injury.

6. The mind, the limiting condition created (and imposed upon the Soul) by *Māyā*, entices it (the *jīva*) in the cycle of saṁsāra.[210] By embracing the Soul associated with it, it subjects the *jīva* to pleasure, pain and other[211] (viz. delusion), inevitable fruits of *karmas* at the proper time (of fruition).

7. So long as the mind exists, this phenomenon of waking and dream states manifests itself within the range of perception of the *kṣetrajña*. It is hence that they (the wise ones) say that the mind is the cause of the lower state viz. *saṁsāra* (the product of *guṇas*) and of the higher state viz. *Mokṣa* (liberation), which is beyond the range of all *guṇas*.

8. If the mind is attached to objects of senses (which are the products of *guṇas*) it leads the creature to misery (viz. *saṁsāra*). If it is free from and unattached to them, it takes the *jīva* to eternal happiness (*in Mokṣa*). Just as a lamp which emanates flames mixed with soot while it consumes its wick soaked in ghee, otherwise (after the consumption of ghee) betakes itself to its original state, the mind, which is attached to objects of senses and (consequent) activities, resorts to various courses and returns to its true original self, when unattached (to them).

9. The courses (of the activities) of the mind are eleven —five in relation to the organs of action, five with reference to the senses of perception and its own sense of I-ness. And they say that conative organs, the subtle elements and the body are (respectively) the eleven grounds (receptacles) for these (courses), Oh Warrior.

10. Smell, form, touch, taste and sound (the five objects of cognitive organs), evacuation (of bowels), copulation, locomotion, verbal expression, and manipulation and the eleventh is the body which is accepted as mine; (And in the case of the ignorant who have completely identified themselves with the body, the I-ness is the twelfth course (of the mind) with the body as its object or bed (In the city viz. body, the *jīva* sleeps i.e. abides with *ahaṁkāra* and is hence called *puruṣa*).

---

210. *saṁsṛti-cakra-kūṭaḥ*—The *jīva* stands firm like a mountain-top in the whirlpool or cycle of *saṁsāra*. —VR.

211. v.l. *vyatimiśra*—a mixture of pleasure and pain. —VJ.

11* These eleven modifications (tendencies) of the mind multiply into hundreds, thousands and multi-millions with reference to objects, nature of things (the variety of the causes of the products), the effect of previous experience, unmanifested effect of *karmas* (acts), the agitating factor Time. They owe their existence to the *Kṣetrajña* (the Supreme Soul) and not to each other or to their own Self. (Or: The *Kṣetrajña* or *jīva*, being above changes, these *vṛttis* do not proceed from *jīva*; nor do they spring from their mutual action and reaction nor from themselves. Hence all these are *mithyā*—unreal).

12. The Supreme Soul who is pure and unaffected, stands as a witness to the continuous stream of states of the mind which are sometimes manifest (in the waking and dream states) and sometimes unmanifest (as in deep sleep)—the mind, an *upādhi* of *jīva*, a creation of *Māyā*, and of impure activity.

13. The Supreme Soul is all-pervading, the prime cause of the perfect (in all respects), ever-present, self-luminous (not depending on anything for the proof of its existence), devoid of birth (and death), the Ruler of gods like Brahmā, Nārāyaṇa (the abode of the world of beings), the venerable Lord (of six excellences), Vāsudeva (the receptacle of all beings) and Himself the Inner-dweller and Controller of all *jīvas* by His *Māyā* power.

14. Just as the air, entering in the from of breath controls both the mobile and the immobile beings, so does the Supreme Lord Vāsudeva, the all-pervading Soul, enter this universe (as the Inner Controller).

15. Oh Lord of men! A man continues to wander in the *saṁsāra* so long as he has not shaken off *Māyā*, by the dawn of knowledge, and became free from attachments and conquered

* (i) VR. emphasizes that *kṣetrajña* here should be interpreted as *jīva*—the individual Soul. He however admits that the interpretation of *kṣetrajña* as Nārāyana is possible.

(ii) VC : Due to infinite variety of objects (e.g. sandal, saffron) and variety of natures liking these, and differences in mind due to wickedness etc., destiny or fate and stages in life (childhood, youth etc.) these states or *vṛttis* of mind are infinite. But they owe this variety to God of infinite powers, and not to themselves individually or mutually.

the six enemies (viz. passions like lust, anger, avarice etc.) and has not realized his true Self.

16. (He continues to wander) so long as he does not understand that the mind, the conditioning environment of the Soul, is the field of the miseries of *saṁsāra* (the cycle of birth and death), and the source of a continuous series of griefs, delusions, diseases, passions, avarice and hatred and the creator of the feeling of mine-ness.

17. Therefore, being very careful and armed with the missile in the form of the feet of Lord Hari, Who is the preceptor, kill this enemy (in the form of the mind) of formidable power who has grown in strength through your negligence and who, though unreal in itself, is capable of deluding you about (the true nature of) your Soul.

CHAPTER TWELVE

(*Dialogue between Bharata and Rahūgaṇa*)

Rahūgaṇa said[212] :

1.* Salutations to you again and again—you, who are the Prime Cause of the universe (God himself) who has assumed a human form (for the protection of the world), and who, in the light of supremely blissful self-realization, have regarded your body as insignificant. I bow to you, Oh Master

212. Verses 1-4 are an echo of the query made by Rahūgaṇa to Bharata in the same context in V.P. (*Viṣṇu Purāṇa*) 2.14.2-6.

* VJ. notes that this apparent praise of the Brāhmaṇa is really a eulogy of the *antar-yāmin*. VR. and others generally echo ŚR., but VR.'s alternative explanation is interesting :

"Salutations . . . you who are the Supreme Self incarnate who have assumed human form for the protection of persons like me. In your self-realization, you have banished hatred against persons (like me) who have offended you, and who have concealed your realization of the Eternal, Supreme Soul under the guise of the contemptuous dress of a depraved Brāhmaṇa".

of Yoga, who have concealed your realization of the Eternal (Supreme Soul) in the guise of a depraved Brāhmaṇa.

2. My vision (power of understanding) has been thoroughly poisoned (perverted) by the bite of the serpent in the form of (my) false identification of the self with this worthless body. Your speech acts like a nectarine medicine on me, just as a sweet palatable specific medicine (does) to a patient suffering from high fever or the ice-cold water (or the water of the Gaṅgā (is soothing) to a person scorched by the heat of the summer.

3. I shall, therefore, refer my doubts to your honour later on. My mind is full of curiosity. Now, be pleased to explain to me, in easily intelligible language, your speech which was couched in *Yogic* terms, about the (knowledge of the) Soul.

4. Oh Lord of Yoga ! My mind fails to grasp (in bewilderment, the significance of) your statement that the (actual) act (of carrying a load) and its effect (the resultant fatigue) though visible (directly), are limited to (and not contradicted in) practical life (*vyavahāra*), but they will not easily stand the test of philosophic investigation.

Brāhmaṇa replied[213] :

5. That which has come to be known as 'this person' (the palanquin bearer) is a modification of the earth which moves over the earth due to some (inexplicable) cause, Oh King ! Above the feet of this (modification of the earth called 'this person') are two ankles, two shanks, two knees, two thighs, the waist, the chest, the neck and the two shoulders (one above the other).

6. On the shoulder is the wooden palanquin wherein is seated an (empty) designation called 'the King of Sauvīras'— which is nothing but another modification of the earth. You identify yourself with it (that modification of the earth). Be-

---

213. Verses 5 and 6 are echoes of VP. 2.13.66-67.
Bhūmau pāda-yugaṁ tvāste jaṅghe pāda-dvaye sthite |
ūrvor jaṅghā-dvayāvasthau tadādhāraṁ tathodaram||66||
Vakṣasthalaṁ tathā bāhū skandhau codara-saṁsthitau |
skandhāśriteyaṁ śibikā mama bharo'tra kiṁkṛtaḥ||67||

ing blinded with arrogant pride, you feel that you are the king of the Sindhu country.

7. You are hard-hearted as you caught hold of these pitiable (palanquin-bearers) who are already highly afflicted with hardships and have forced them to labour without remuneration. Still you brag about as being 'the protector of the people'. Shamelessly insolent as you are, you will not look respectable in the assemblies of the wise.

8*. We know that all the mobile and immobile creation is always born out of and re-assimilated into the earth only. The difference in name is due to the difference in its product or functions[214]. Let it be investigated if there be any other real cause or basis deducible from its effect and work (functions).

9. (The substance) that is denoted by the word 'earth' is unreal as (will be) explained thus (hereafter). The earth (in its ultimate analysis) disaggregates itself into atoms. The atoms, the aggregates of which combine to form the particular (element viz. the earth) are hypothetical, postulated by mind (of the theorists) through ignorance. (As a matter of fact, they do not exist. Hence the unreality of the earth).

10. Similarly, know that what is thin or fat, small or big, cause or effect, sentient and non-sentient or that which has a second (i. e. all the duality), is brought about by the *Māyā* (the unborn), under the name of substance (viz five elements), nature (the changeability of the phenomenal world), the inclination (determined by the impressions unconsciously left on the mind by past actions, i. e., *vāsanā*), the time factor (disturbing the equilibrium of *guṇas* leading to creation) and the destiny (*karma*).

---

* VC : We know that all things mobile and immobile are created out of the earth and get disintegrated into the earth. All these modifications are not different from the earth. Please tell us if you have any reasoning or logical argument to show if there be any real cause other than mere verbal designations of its effects and functions.

214. cf. *vācārambhaṇaṁ vikāro nāmadheyam mṛttiketyeva satyam*/—Chāndogya Up. 6.1.4.

11*. Knowledge alone is pure (unsoiled by passion or actions), absolutely real, one (without any difference) devoid of any aspect of in-ness or out-ness, perfect and full, direct (self-manifesting), unchangeable, designated by the appellation *Bhagavat* (the venerable possessor of six excellences such as Lordship of the Universe etc.). They (the sages) called it ('knowledge') by the term 'Vāsudeva'.

12. Oh Rahūgaṇa! This knowledge (or Brahman) is not attained through austere penance, or through Vedic sacrifices or through charitable distribution of food or through performance of duties prescribed for a householder (such as honorary social service) or through the study of the Vedas or through propitiation of (the presiding deities of) water, fire and the Sun, except (i. e. it is attainable only) by being sprinkled over with the dust on the feet of the exalted Souls (while rendering service to them).

13. For here (in the congregation of these exalted persons) the discourses on the excellent attributes of the Lord are always held. These prohibit all talks of vulgar worldly topics. By listening daily to these (holy discourses) the pure mind of the seeker of Liberation is concentrated on Lord Vāsudeva.

14. I was formerly a king called Bharata who, freeing himself from the bondage of attachment to all things seen or

---

* (i) VR. : The Ātman or the Self is knowledge or consciousness. It is unsoiled by *Karma* (actions) and passions; it is the only highest objective to be attained (by man). It is absolutely one whole with no aspect of in-ness or out-ness. It is all-pervading, real, eternal, self-realizing (or direct) unaffected by the six miseries (such as hunger, thirst, sorrow, delusion, old age and death). It is *Vāsudeva* also called by the appellation *bhagavat*.

(ii) VJ. regards these as the attributes of Hari, the Supreme Self. He derives the term 'Vāsudeva'—*vas*—'to dwell', although he concedes the popular etymology 'the son of Vasudeva'.

GD. explains : 'Knowledge' means 'Brahman'. In the path of *Bhakti*, it is designated as *bhagavat*, the venerable Lord (the possessor of six excellences) and 'Vāsudeva'. It is essentially existent and of the nature of the highest bliss and consciousness or knowledge. Being direct (being Self-hood by nature) one need not go elsewhere to attain it. It is perfectly serene as it is devoid of birth, death or othar troubles. It is 'pure' i.e. absolutely unconnected with any attachment. It is beyond the limitation of space as the states of outness or inness are inapplicable to it.

heard (i. e. objects obtainable here and hereafter) endeavoured the propitiation of the Lord, but was frustrated (in my object of God-realization) through my attachment to a deer and was born as a deer.

15. Due to the efficacy of my devoted worship of Kṛṣṇa that memory (of my previous birth) was not lost even in my form (i. e. birth) of the deer. Oh Warrior ! Hence, being unattached to and afraid of association with the society, I roam about without disclosing my real personality.

16. Therefore a man should, in this very world, completely cut off (the ties of) delusion by the sword of knowledge obtained through the blessed company of the great Souls who are free from attachment. Having revived the memory (consciousness about God) by recounting and hearing (meditating upon) the glories of Hari, one reaches the end of this long road of *Saṁsāra* and attains to the Lord.

CHAPTER THIRTEEN

(*The Saṁsāra—a forest*: An allegory)

The Brāhmaṇa said :

1. Like unto a company of merchants intent on acquisition of wealth, this (well-known) multitude of *jīvas* desirous of and solely devoted to the attainment of pleasure[215], was put by the Prakṛti or Māyā, on the path (of Pravṛtti—active worldly life) which is unending and so difficult to traverse. It (the multitude of *jīvas*) sets its eye (attention) on[216] the activities actuated and dominated by (the attributes) *sattva*, *Rajas* and *Tamas*. While wandering (in search of pleasure) in the forest of *Saṁsāra* (worldly existence), it does not find any bliss.

---

215. BP. *artha* :—*dharma*, *artha* and *kāma*—the three *puruṣārathas* (highest ideals in life).

216. VJ. : It (the multitude of *jīvas*) regards them as its own and identifies them with the Soul.

2.* In that forest these six bandits (viz. sense-organs) perforce rob the caravan captained by an evil-minded leader, Oh king. Just as wolves carry away the sheep, jackals (in the form of relatives), finding entrance into their camp, carry off a careless member (devoid of spiritual outlook).

3. In the forest, impregnable with the dense growth of a mass of creepers, grass, clumps of trees and bushes the caravan was harassed by sharp stinging gnats and mosquitoes (In the householder's life full of passions and actions, a man is harassed by wicked people). At some places they find the city of Gandharvas in the sky (the phenomenon is fictitious; so is one's body), while at other places, they witness fleeting spirits in the form of fire brands.

4. Oh (King Rahūgaṇa!) With their intellect (mind) naturally anxious to find some dwelling-place, water and wealth, the company of merchants ran here and there in the jungle. And at some places, with eyes blinded with dust, it does not distinguish the directions darkened with the dust whipped up by whirl-winds (Here the whirl-wind stands for a woman who raises erotic sentiments which blind man to the existence of the dieties presiding over directions who stand witness to his actions).

5. With their ears acutely pained by the shrill cries of unseen crickets (i.e. back-biting by evil-minded persons) and with their minds agitated by the hooting of the owls (i.e. harsh words, scolding directly addressed by enemies, persons in authority), they resort to unholy trees[217] (i.e. irreligious persons) when tormented with hunger. At some places (when thirsty) they run after the mirage[218] (i.e. fruitless objects of worldly pleasure).

---

* ŚR., VR., VC., SD., GD., BP., state that although the allegory is explained in the next chapter, they are briefly explaining it for reader's understanding the text of these verses.

217. This refers to the superstition that the shade of the *vibhītaka* tree (*Terminalia Belerica*) is inauspicious by day and that of Pippala tree by night and that of the wood apple tree, day and night—VD.

218. i.e. are attracted to the centres of the non-believers in Vedas—pākhaṇḍa śramaṇas—VJ.

(ii) beg at the doors of notorious misers—VC.

6. At some place they go towards beds of dry rivers (only to get their limbs bruised by falling, instead of getting water); being short of food they beg it from one another. At some places they approach the forest conflagration only to get scorched; at other places, they find to their despair that they are deprived of their life (-like wealth) by Yakṣas.[219]

7. At some other places, it, being deprived of its possession by the powerful government officials (or village chiefs expert in robbery) becomes mentally despondent. Overcome with grief and bewildered, it faints away. At some places, it enters an imaginary city of Gandharvas (the company of loving near relatives) and feels overjoyed for a while, as it is really happy.

8. At some places, being desirous of scaling a mountain (i.e. attempting a great undertaking) it proceeds with the soles of its feet pierced with thorns and cut with gravel and sits down depressed in spirit. Tormented at every step by the inner (gastric) fire (or hunger), and with the (unbearable) responsibility of maintaining) a large family, it gets angry with its own people.

9. Sometimes being swallowed up by the boa-constrictor (viz. sleep) it lies like a dead body abandoned in a jungle and is not conscious of anything. Sometimes bitten down by fierce venomous snakes, it becomes blind and falling into a well with its mouth hidden with overgrown grass and plants, it lies immersed in darkness (i.e. misery and ignorance).

10. At times (when) it seeks after honey of low quality (i.e. courting another man's wife) it is harassed and humiliated by bees (i.e. is insulted and beaten up by her husbands). If it (caravan members) is successful in that attempt with great difficulty, others rob it perforce, and while it is engaged in fighting with them, others carry off that booty.

11. And sometimes, (at some places), it (the caravan of merchants) sits down incapable of protecting itself against

219. ŚR. explains : The dry riverbeds are the schools of the non-believers which lead to misery in the other world. The forest-fire is the household where the *jīva* is tormented with miseries. The *Yakṣas* and Rākṣasas are the government servants who squeeze out life-like wealth of men.

(lit. warding off) cold, heat, storm and showers of rain; at some other places they sell among themselves whatever they have with them and become enemies of each other by fraudulent money-dealings.

12. Now and then, being destitute of wealth, and devoid of bedding, blanket (to sit on), house and conveyance, they beg it from others. But not getting their desired objects, they cast a coveting glance at another man's property and get insulted.

13. (Though) they develop hostile relations with each other by mutual (fraudulent) monetary transactions, they enter into marital relations with each other. Thus they proceed along their path, famished through suffering great difficulties, financial losses and other calamities (and feelings of hatred).

14. The caravan of merchants proceeds on its journey leaving behind those that are dead, at various places, and taking with them the new born babes. Nobody has as yet returned to its starting place. Nor does anyone (howsoever powerful) betake to yoga which lies at the terminus (of the road), Oh Warrior.

15. All those resolute and highminded warriors who have conquered the great elephants guarding the eight directions and who, claiming the earth as their own, have contracted hostility (with each other), shall lie dead on the battlefield. But they do not attain to the place (the region of Viṣṇu) where the recluse (the Saṁnyāsin) who has been free from enmity, reaches.

16. At some places, it (the caravan) clings to the arms (tender shoots) of creepers (i.e. rests on the tender arms of women); it longs to listen to the indistinct chirping of birds which have resorted to them (i.e. listen to the sweet indistinct warbling of children clinging to their mothers). And it feels strongly attached to them. Occasionally, at other places, it is afraid of a multitude of lions and makes friends with cranes, herons and vultures (Being afraid of death, they enter the fold of vile, cruel heretics).

17. Being deceived by them, it (the company of merchants tries to enter the flock of swans (i.e. knowing the futility of the false faiths, it tries to enter Brāhmanic fold). But

not liking their pious way of life (i.e. not finding the Brāhmanic way of life to their liking), it approaches the monkeys (i.e. takes to the monkey-like behaviour of depraved people). By the (amorous) sports natural to that species, it (the caravan) gets its senses gratified (with sensual pleasures) and forgets the (approaching) end of life, while looking at the faces of each other.

18. Amusing himself in the trees (i.e. worldly objects observed in life), he fondly loves his children and wife. Being powerless in their own bondage, he becomes void of judgment due to the lust for sexual enjoyment. Some times falling into a valley due to inadvertence, he catches hold of a creeper and remains in a hanging position, afraid of elephant (below) (i.e. due to the meritorious acts done in previous life, he continues to live in fear of impending death).

19. If, by a lucky chance, he anyhow overcomes this calamity, he again enters the company of merchants (i.e. takes to the path of *pravṛtti* or active worldly life), Oh vanquisher of enemies. A person who is set on this path (of *Pravṛtti*) by Māyā (the unborn) continues to wander in *saṁsāra*. No such person has as yet perceived the highest *Puruṣārtha* (viz. *Mokṣa* or liberation).

20. Oh Rahūgaṇa ! Even you are also set on this track (by Māyā). You lay down your sceptre (or desist from violence to living beings) and make friends with all beings. With your mind unattached to worldly pleasure and arming yourself with the sword of knowledge sharpened by (dedicated) service to Hari,[220] get to the other end of this road (of *saṁsāra*).

The King said :

21. Oh ! The birth as a man is the most glorious of all births in other species. Of what use are other births even in the heaven, where the association with high-souled people like you whose minds are purified by (singing and listening to) the glories of Lord Hṛṣīkeśa (the Ruler of sense-organs—Viṣṇu), is not available to the full ?

220. VR. interprets *Sevā* as 'the propitiation of the Lord by observing duties prescribed for one's caste (*varṇa*) and stage of life (*āśrama*) and *jñāna* as constituting the worship of the Lord.

22. It is no wonder (at all) that pure devotion to Lord Hari is generated in the hearts of those whose sins have been destroyed by the dust of your lotus-like feet (when constantly served for a long time). For my thoughtlessness and ignorance, rooted as it was in fallacious reasoning, has been completely removed by association with you for a short time (a *muhūrta*).

23. (As it is not known in what form the knowers of Brahman move about in the world, the King pays his respects to them all). Salutations to Brāhmaṇas (knowers of Brahman), who are advanced in age, to those (who are) infants, to the youthful ones, to all down to young boys ! May (blundering) kings like me receive blessings from Brāhmaṇas who wander over the earth as *avadhūtas* (ascetics who have renounced all worldly attachment), giving no indication of their greatness.

Śrī Śuka said :

24. Oh Parīkṣit (son of Uttarā) ! In this way, verily, (Bharata) the son of a Brāhmaṇa sage, who was endowed with the highest glory, explained, out of very great compassion, the real nature of the Self to (Rahūgaṇa) the King of Sindhu, even though he had insulted him. His feet were respectfully bowed by Rahūgaṇa with great remorse. Bharata, whose mind like that of an overful ocean, was unperturbed by waves in the form of senses, wandered over this earth.

25. Even the king of Sauvīra (Rahūgaṇa) who realized the real nature of the Supreme Self as taught by a saintly person (like Bharata), repudiated the false notion of identifying the Soul with the body—a notion superimposed on the mind by Nescience (*avidyā*), Oh King ! Such is, therefore, the greatness of those who resort to the devotees of the glorious Lord.

The King Parīkṣit said :

26. Oh great devotee of the Lord ! The path in the form of *Saṁsāra* of the individual souls has been described in indirect and allegorical language by you who possess very wide and varied knowledge. It will not be easily comprehensible

to people who are not of trained mind. Hence, the same (allegory) which is difficult to understand, be pointed out (explained) by using the proper explanation.

CHAPTER FOURTEEN

(Explanation of the Allegory of Saṁsāra—Forest)

He (Śrī Śuka) said :

1. Characterised and influenced by special attributes like *sattva* and others, auspicious, inauspicious and mixed types of *karmas* (actions) are being committed by *jīvas* (individual Souls) who wrongly identify the body with the Soul. The group of six senses (five cognitive senses and the mind) act as the portals or media of experience of the beginningless *saṁsāra*, consisting of association with and separation from the series of different bodies, created as a result of those karmas.

Just as a caravan of merchants, intent on making money, loses its way to find itself in a wilderness, this company of *jīvas* (individual Souls) has been set on this difficult path (of *saṁsāra*), hard to travel like a mountain pass, by Māyā (the deluding potency of the Lord) which functions under the Supreme Ruler Viṣṇu. It (the multitude of *jīvas*) finds itself in the wilderness of *saṁsāra*, in-auspicious-most like a funeral ground. It (i. e. the *jīvas*), experiences the fruit of their *Karmas* wrought by means of their bodies. Although all their activities are obstructed by numerous difficulties and rendered fruitless, they do not still betake themselves to the path of bees (votaries of the Lord) who resort to the lotus-like feet of Lord Hari in the form of the preceptor—feet which pacify all the afflictions and agonies of *Saṁsāra*. It is in the forest of *Saṁsāra* that what are called the six senses (mind and five senses) act as veritable robbers in practice.

2. For whatever little wealth a person acquires through great hardships, should be utilised for the sake of *Dharma*. The

wise say that this *Dharma*, characterised by the propitiation of the Supreme Person Himself, is conducive to one's beatitude in the other world.

But the wealth of a man of perverted intellect and uncontrolled senses, which should have been used for the sake of this *Dharma* (worship of God), is wasted in house-holder's life on vulgar pleasures of sight, touch, sound, taste and smell (the five objects of sensual pleasures and in low desires and resolutions (mental tendencies), even as a company of merchants with an unworthy leader of uncontrolled mind is robbed of money.

3. And here (in the wilderness of *saṁsāra*) the so-called members of the family such as wife and children, are nothing but wolves and jackals in actions. They carry away the carefully-guarded wealth of the close-fisted householder, despite his watchfulness and unwillingness (to part with his wealth), like a lamb well-protected (in a pen).

4. For just as a field, the seeds (of weeds, grass etc.) in which are not burnt down, again becomes densely over-grown with a thicket of shrubs, grass and creepers at the time of sowing, even though it is (regularly) ploughed annually, in the same way, the householder's life is a field of *karmas* wherein the seeds of *karmas* are never destroyed. This householder's life is certainly a box of desires (in which seeds of *karmas* are never completely annihilated, just as the smell of camphor persists even after the exhaustion of camphor-tablets from the camphor-box).

5. While there, (in the householder's stage of life), his wealth which is the very external life-breath of man, is squeezed (lit. sucked) by vile people comparable to gnats and mosquitoes, and (food-grains) by locusts, birds, thieves, rats and others. At times, wandering on this road (of *saṁsāra*), his mind becomes eclipsed with ignorance (*avidyā*), lust or desires and actions. Hence being possessed of erroneous views, he looks upon the human world which is as unreal as the (optic illusion of) the city of Gandharvas, to be factually real.

6. There (in the *saṁsāra*), with a passionate desire for vicious habits of drinking, eating, sexual intercourse and the like, he sometimes pursues mirage-like (unreal) pleasures.

7. Sometimes, just as a man intensely longs for (the warmth of) fire, runs after the fire-goblin—the will of-the-wisp, he with his mind overpowered with the attribute *rajas* which is of the same colour as that of gold, ardently yearns to acquire gold which is the abode of all evils and is a kind of excreta of fire.

8. And again, with an earnest desire for dwelling-places, water, wealth and other numerous amenities of life and means of livelihood, it (the company of merchants) runs about here and there in the forest of *saṁsāra*.

9. Sometimes (when) placed on her lap, by a bewitching young woman who is like a whirlwind,his mind is instantly enveloped in ignorance, due to the force of *rajas*, and transgresses the boundaries of virtue[221]. With his eyes filled with the dust of lust, his mind is too much charged with passion to cognize (the existence of) the presiding deities of the directions (who watch him).

10. Occasionally, he perceives spontaneously for a moment the unreality of worldly objects. But as he identifies the Soul with his body, he loses his memory) about the nature of the Soul. With his memory (mind) thus led astray, he intensely pursues those very sense-objects which are (illusory) like mirage.

11. Sometimes, its (the company of merchants) ears and heart are intensely troubled by the extremely harsh and fiercely vehement threats administered directly, like hooting of the owls, by king's officers and indirectly (behind one's back) like the shrill cries of crickets, by enemies.

12. When he has exhausted his fund of merit acquired in the previous life, he is (in the process of) dying though nominally alive. He runs after (for help to) those who are as good as dead though living, and whose wealth is not useful to them either in this world (as they do not enjoy themselves with it) or in the next world (as they do not donate it and earn merit), and who are comparable to poisonous trees and creepers like *kāraskara*, *kākatuṇḍa* and to wells full of poisonous water.

---

221. like goblins at night according to v.l. accepted by ŚR., VR.

13. Sometimes, with his mind perverted due to association with evil persons, he takes to the path of heretics which leads him to miseries here and hereafter—(an act which is) like falling into the rocky bed of a waterless river.

14. When he cannot get food for himself even by harassing others, he proceeds to devour those possessing even blades of grass belonging to his father or son or to "eat up" his own father or sons.

15. Sometimes, he reaches home which is like a forest-conflagration—a home devoid of enjoyable objects, full of a series of miseries. There, being scorched with the fire of deep anguish, he becomes extremely depressed in spirits.

16. To him, wealth was dearmost—a veritable life itself. Sometimes he is deprived of it by demon-like officers of the king who have turned hostile (to him) through change of time. He falls in a swoon or appears like a dead man devoid of any symptom of life.

17. Sometimes, imagining as real, the unreal appearance of his (deceased) father, grandfather in fulfilment of his desire, he enjoys (a momentary) pleasure as in a dream.

18. Sometimes he desires to ascend (i.e. perform in a thorough manner) the mountain of extensively detailed duties prescribed for the householder's life. But his mind being distracted with worldly miseries, he sinks into despondency and feels afflicted like one entering (and traversing) a tract full of thorns and sharp-edged gravel.

19. Sometimes, his power and energy being sapped by the (gastral) fire (of hunger raging) within his body, he gets angry with the members of his family.

20. Again, being seized (swallowed) by the boa-constrictor in the form of sleep, and sunk in the blinding darkness (of ignorance), he remains asleep, as if in desolate forest, and he is unconscious of anything else like a dead body cast off by the relatives.

21. Sometimes his larger tooth in the form of his egotism is being broken by venomous reptiles, viz. wicked persons. He does not get sleep even for a moment. His consciousness gets dimmer and dimmer as his heart is (deeply) agitated and

disturbed. And like a blind man, he falls in a dark, covered well (of ignorance and misery).

22. Sometimes, (he is) on the look out for small drops of honey in the form of sensual pleasure. While he is in attempting to snatch away another man's wife or property, he is beaten to death by the King or the husband or the master (of the property) and falls into the bottomless unsurmountable hell.

23. Hence, sages say, that *karman* of both forms (whether Vedic or non-Vedic) performed in this (path of *Pravṛtti*) sows the seeds of future series of births (of the doer).

24. If he (the *jīva*) escapes the bondage (or punishment meted out by the King, the woman's husband or the master of the property), one Devadatta wrests the prize away from him and from him (another fellow), one Viṣṇumitra, takes it away and so on endlessly. (None retains permanently the objects of enjoyment.

25. And sometimes being incapable of warding off miserable conditions like biting cold winds and others caused by super-human agencies, or by elements (or created beings) or pertaining to his body, he sinks down despondently in unending anxieties.

26. Sometimes while transacting business among themselves, if he deceitfully takes away a petty amount, say, twenty *cowries* or even less than that, he incurs the enmity of others due to deceitful dealing in money.

27. On this path (of *pravṛtti*), there are these obstacles (viz. financial losses, difficulties etc. enumerated in Ch. 13.13) and also other ones viz. pleasure and pain, lust and hatred, fear and pride, negligence and madness, delusion and greed, envy and jealousy, insult, hunger and thirst, anxieties and diseases, birth, old age, death and others.

28. Sometimes, (when) embraced with the creeper-like (tender) arms of the woman who is the *Māyā* (deluding divine potency of the Lord) incarnate, he loses his power of judgment and wisdom. He becomes anxious at heart to construct a pleasure-house for her. His heart becomes transported by the (sweet) speech, (affectionate) looks and (winsome) behaviour of his wife and sons, daughters who resorted to him for protec-

tion. Thus, being of uncontrolled mind, he sends himself to the abysmal hell of blinding darkness.

29. Sometimes he gets terrified in his heart at (the thought of) the discus (viz. *kāla*—Time, death) of the Supreme Ruler, Lord Viṣṇu—the discus is alternatively designated as Time and consists of divisions beginning from the minutest point to the period covering two *Parārdha* years (the life-span of god Brahmā). With inexorable velocity consisting of ages (childhood, youth, old age), this unwinking (watchful) discus mows down all created beings from god Brahmā down to a clump of grass while they are (helplessly) looking on. But disrespectfully ignoring the Supreme Lord, the presiding Deity of Sacrifice whose weapon is this eternal discus of Time, he on the basis of unauthoritative canon of the heretics, resorts to the deities of the heretics which are no better than kites, vultures, cranes on the banyan trees (in extending protection against death and hence) which are discarded in the religion of Aryas.

30. When he was devastatingly deceived by those heretics who are themselves deluded, he (returns and) stays within the Brāhmanic fold.

He, however, does not like their pious way of life, propitiation of the glorious Lord of Sacrifices with acts prescribed in the *Vedas* and *Smṛtis* after performance of the thread investiture ceremony. As he is impure (and hence ineligible) to perform duties enjoined by the Vedas, he resorts to the Śūdra community which like the species of monkeys, indulges in copulation and maintenance of the family.

31. Even in that community, he behaves as he likes, without any restraint. The low-minded fellow forgets the limit of his (span of) life in vulgar gratification of senses such as looking at the faces of each other (mutually by husband and wife).

32. Sometimes he enjoys himself in the householder's life which, like trees, yields pleasures pertaining to this world only. He is fond of children and wife and like a monkey[222], he delights in sexual enjoyment.

222. GD.: "Just as a monkey addicted to sexual enjoyment, becomes negligent (about his safety) and is caught by the hunter while it is indulging in that enjoyment on the trees and is unable to get himself released."

33. Enjoying and suffering pleasures and pain on the path (of *pravṛtti*), he falls into the veritable dark vale of ailments and other calamities and stays (there) constantly in the fear of the elephant in the form of death.

34. Sometimes, when incapable of protecting himself against innumerable miseries such as heat and cold—miseries caused by supernatural agencies, the elements or creatures or by his own body or mind—he sinks (lit. sits) despondently worrying over endless sense-objects.

35. Sometimes, entering into business transactions among themselves, he acquires some wealth through fraudulent monetary dealings.

36. Sometimes, when his wealth is spent up he becomes destitute of (normal necessities of life such as) a bed, a seat, food etc. He then makes up his mind to snatch away the objects which he covets but has not succeeded to acquire till then. Hence, in due course, he is subjected to insult etc. by the public.

37. Although their mutual hostility is enhanced by their covetousness for wealth, they enter into matrimonial relations or break them according to their tendency resulting from actions to the previous life.

38. On this road of *Saṁsāra*, if one is afflicted with innumerable sufferings and obstacles and succumbs to calamities or death, he is definitely abandoned then and there. They take with them the new-born children. They sometimes weep, fall in a swoon, are afraid, quarrel, cry and are overjoyed, sing and are bound down. They are avoided by saintly people and are thus denied pious company. In this way, they continue to go ahead. This caravan of men has not yet returned to the starting point of this journey (viz. God) which the sages say, is the terminus of the road (of *Saṁsāra*).

39. For, he who gets knowledge of and takes to the discipline of Yoga, does not definitely return to the universe or *saṁsāra*. It is only the meditative persons who have renounced all forms of violence (to all creatures) and are firmly given to self-control (and consequent serenity), and who have detached their minds (from worldly objects), reach the Supreme (Self).

40. Even the royal sages who have conquered the elephants guarding all directions and perform sacrifices, do not attain it. Asserting their claim on the earth that it is their own and entering into hostilities for it (its possession), they lie dead on the battlefield, leaving their bodies on the earth (claimed by them) and depart. (These also do not reach the other end of *Saṁsāra*).

41. Supporting themselves by catching hold of the creeper of *karma* and getting out, with great difficulty, from the miserable hell, he is again present on the way of *Saṁsāra*, and rejoins the caravan of men. Similar is the case of men who have gone up to the Heaven.

Thus do they sing of Bharata !

42. Just as a fly cannot, even in its imagination soar up along the path of Garuḍa (high up in the sky), no other King in this world can even mentally follow the path of the high-souled royal sage Bharata, the son of Ṛṣabha.

43. Even while he was a youth, he longed to serve the Lord of hallowing renown (or of Supreme glory), and abandoned like excreta, his wife and children, friends and kingdom, so endearing to the heart and (hence) so difficult to renounce.

44. It is quite befitting on the part of the king (Bharata) that he did not long for the (kingdom of the) earth, sons, relatives, wealth and wife—so difficult to renounce. Nor did he wish for Śrī (the Goddess of Fortune), coveted by great gods, even though She waited for having a gracious look from him. For in the view of the great (Souls) whose minds are devotedly attached to the service of Viṣṇu, even the Final Emancipation is of little account.

45. "Salutations to Lord Hari who is himself the personified *Yajña* (sacrifice), the defender of righteousness, punctilious observance of scriptural injunctions, Yoga *incarnate*, the head (the ultimate, chief principle) of the *Sāṁkhyas*, the controller of the *Prakṛti* (the personified Will or Māyā of the Almighty), who is the shelter of all created beings)", so nobly praised he, at the time of casting off his body as a deer.

46. One who faithfully listens to, recites or praises the history of the royal sage Bharata whose spotless virtues and pure actions are appreciated and eulogised by devotees of the

Lord—the history which brings in good fortune, long life, riches, renown and leads to (the attainment of) the Heaven and Final Beatitude secures all blessings, of his own accord and needs nothing from others.

CHAPTER FIFTEEN

(Description of Bharata's Dynasty)*

Śrī Śuka continued :

1. As already narrated (supra 7.3), Bharata had a son called Sumati. He followed the path of Ṛṣabha. In the Kali Age, heretics (non-believers in the Vedas) outside the Aryan fold, will set him up, according to their wicked and perverted intelligence, as a deity n ot described in the Vedic

* The Bharata Dynasty may be conveniently summarised as follows:

1. Bharata
2. Sumati
3. Devatājit
4. Devadyumna
5. Parameṣṭhī
6. Pratīha Prastotā Udgātā
7. Pratihartā
8. Bhūmā Aja
9. Udgītha
10. Prastāva
11. Vibhu
12. Pṛthuṣeṇa
13. Nakta
14. Gaya
15. Chitraratha Sugati Avarodhana
16. Samrāṭ
17. Marīci
18. Bindumān
19. Madhu
20. Vīravrata
21. Manthu Pramanthu
22. Bhauvana
23. Tvaṣṭā
24. Viraja
25. Śatajit etc. 100 sons

texts. (They will think him to be an incarnation of Lord Buddha).

2. By (queen) Vṛddhasenā, he had a son by name Devajit (conqueror of gods).

3. Then, through Āsurī (Devajit's wife) was born to him a son, Devadyumna; he had by Dhenumatī, a son, called Parameṣṭhī; and then Parameṣṭhī begot on Sauvarcalā a son called Pratīha.

4. Having taught the knowledge of *ātman* (to many), he himself became thoroughly purified, and directly realized the Supreme Soul.

5. From Pratīha, through (his wife, another) Suvarcalā, three sons beginning with Pratihartā were born; all of them were well-versed in the sacrificial lore. Pratihartā begot on (his wife) Stuti, two sons Aja and Bhūman.

6. Bhūman had by Ṛṣikulyā a son called Udgītha. He had (a son named) Prastāva from Devakulyā. Prastāva had a son called Vibhu, through (queen) Niyutsā; Vibhu had Pṛthuṣeṇa from Rati; Pṛthuṣeṇa begot Nakta from Ākūtī. From Nakta and (his wife) Druti was born the eminent royal sage Gaya of noble reputation. Gaya who attained the status of a *Mahāpuruṣa* (an exalted personage) by his possession of characteristics (of greatness) such as self-control, was an *aṁśa* (part or ray) of Lord Viṣṇu himself who, for the protection of the world, assumed a form consisting of pure *Sattva*.

7. He followed his righteous duty as a king by protecting his subjects, supplying them with the means of livelihood, providing them with (amenities of) recreation behaving tenderly with them and by governing them per legal precepts. He dedicated with absolute faith his sacrificial and other pious acts to the glorious great personage viz. the Brahman who is higher than the highest.

By constantly serving the feet of those who have realized Brahman and by cultivating path of devotion to the Lord, his mind and intellect became extremely pure. His mind became completely free from the false identification of the non-Soul (viz. the body and its belongings) with the Soul. Though he realized within him the identification of his Self with Brahman, he was totally free from pride and as such he protected the earth.

8. Oh descendant of Pāṇḍavas ! Persons well-versed in Purāṇic history sing the following stanzas about him.

9. "What other king, except the one in whom a ray of the Lord has been manifest, can equal Gaya in his achievements ? Who else is there like him, a performer of great sacrifices, so highly respected by all, possessor of extensive scholarship, a defender of religion, one so highly blessed with the Goddess of Fortune, a leader of the assembly of the learned and a devoted servant of the saints.

10. The virtuous daughters of Dakṣa (such as Śraddhā, Maitrī, Dayā) whose blessings always prove true, accompanied the presiding deities of holy rivers (like Gaṅgā) sprinkled him with water (at the time of his coronation) in ecstatic joy. The king, himself was free from desire. But just as the milk begins to flow out of the udders of a cow at the sight of its calf, so at the sight of his excellent virtues, the earth yielded like a cow, milk in the form of the desired objects of his subjects.

11. Though he (Gaya) was above desires, Vedas and the rites prescribed therein blessed him with all enjoyments. (Inimical) kings who were honoured by him with a volley of arrows in the battle, brought him tributes. The Brāhmaṇas who were honoured by him with sumptuous sacrificial fees and donations while performing religious acts, allotted to him one-sixth of their total merit.

12. In his sacrifices, liberal libations of Soma juice were offered. While Indra (the king of gods) became intoxicated (with Soma juice), the glorious Lord who is the Soul of the Sacrifices appeared in person and accepted the fruit of the Sacrifice offered (by the king) in the spirit of unswerving devotion rendered absolutely pure by (unflinching) faith.

13. By pleasing whom (i.e. the Lord) the whole universe from god Brahmā upto gods, men, sub-human beings, creepers and grass, become the Self-same Lord, the very Soul of the universe, who, though ever blissful by nature, became evidently satisfied and delighted at Gaya's performance of sacrifice.

14. Gaya begot on Gayantī three sons, Citraratha, Sugati and Avarodhana. Out of them, Citraratha had by queen Ūrṇā a son called Samrāṭ.

15. From Samrāṭ, thorough Utkalā, was born Marīci. From Marīci and Bindumatī was born Bindumān; he had by Saraghā (a son) named Madhu; Madhu begot Vīravrata on Sumanas; from Vīravrata and queen Bhojā were born Manthu and Pramanthu; of Manthu, through Satyā, sprang Bhauvana; of Bhauvana and Dūṣaṇā was born Tvaṣṭā; from Tvaṣṭā through Virocanā came Viraja; and Viraja had by Viṣūcī a hundred sons, of whom Śatajit was the eldest, and also a daughter.

About Viraja is sung the following stanza :

16. Viraja, the last born son (in the race of Priyavrata) adorned the dynasty of Priyavrata by his glory, even as Viṣṇu embellishes the host of gods.

CHAPTER SIXTEEN*

(*Mythological Geography—The Terrestrial Globe*)

The King said :

1. The whole extent of the globe of the earth on which the Sun shines and where the Moon with the hosts of stars is visible, has been described by you.

2. Within that area, seven seas were formed by the seven (moat-like) ruts, furrowed by the wheels of (king) Priyavrata's

* This and the following chapters deal with geography. Most of the material is common to other Purāṇas. Purāṇic geography is not all imagination, vide V.S. Agrawala : *M.P.—A Study*, pp. 184-215, D. C. Sircar's SGAMI., pp. 17-118, N. L. De's GDAMI. The concept of the earth with four continents (*catur-dvīpā Vasumatī*) and the details of the lands, mountains, rivers etc. tally a great deal with the details in the East, West and South Asia. The 'Greater India' of to day was regarded not merely an extension of India but a part of one unit separated by seas. (Vide B. Upadhyaya—*Purāṇa-Vimarśa*, pp. 338-341.

chariot. You have verily suggested, venerable Sir, that the divisions of this earth in seven distinct island-continents is due to those (seas). I am now desirous to know all about the dimensions and characteristics of those continents, in detail.

3. For, the mind, when concentrated on the Lord's gross form—the physical universe, a product of three *guṇas*, becomes capable of entering into and fixing on the attributeless, subtle-most, self-refulgent, transcendent *Brahman* known as Lord Vāsudeva. Oh Preceptor, may you be pleased to describe to me the same.

The sage (Śrī Śuka) said :

4. Oh great King ! No human being, even if it be blessed with the longevity of gods, can adequately comprehend even by mind or (can express) by speech, the extent of Lord's great glories (viz. the universe) displayed through the (product of) three *guṇas* of His *Māyā* Potency. We, therefore, shall mainly describe to you the special features of the terrestrial globe, with the names, position, extent and characteristics.

5. As for this (*Jambūdvīpa*) island-continent (in which we live), it forms the central innermost (the seventh) layer of the lotus-like earth. It is one lakh *yojanas*[223] (eight lakh miles) in extent, and is circular in form like the leaf of a lotus.

6. In this *dvīpa*, there are nine continents (*varṣas*) each nine thousand *yojanas* in extent. They are clearly separated from each other, by eight mountain-ranges forming the boundaries of each (of the *dvīpas*).

7. The inner-continent called Ilāvṛta forms the centre of these continents. At the navel (centre) of this (*Ilāvṛta*) continent stands the all-gold mount Meru, the king of all of mountains. It is as high as the extent of his (Jambū) *dvīpa*. It forms the pericarp of the lotus in the form of the earth. It is thirty-two thousand *yojanas* in extent at the top, and sixteen thousand *yojanas* at its foot, and its root lies under the earth's surface to the same extent viz. sixteen thousand *yojanas*. (i.e. it is 84000 *yojanas* in height from the surface of the earth)

8. To the northern side of Ilāvṛta, are three mountain ranges one after the other—viz. Nīla, Śveta and Śṛṅgavān.

223. Yojana—8 miles.

They form the boundaries between the continents called Ramyaka, Hiraṇmaya and Kuru. They stretch in eastern and western directions upto the salt ocean, and are two thousand *yojanas* in breadth. Every outer range (of mountains) is shorter only in length by a little over of one tenth of the next interior range (their height and breadth is the same).

9. In this way, to the south of Ilāvṛta, are the mountain ranges Niṣadha, Hemkūṭa and the Himālayas. They run from the east (to the west) and are ten thousand *yojanas* in height, like Nīla and other mountains (mentioned above). They form the boundaries of Harivarṣa, Kiṁpuruṣa and Bhārata respectively.

10. Similarly, the West and East of Ilāvṛta, upto the mountain Nīla and Niṣadha, run the mountain-ranges called Mālyavat and Gandhamādana, each two thousand *yojanas* in length. These (two mountains) form the boundaries of ketumāla and Bhadrāśva.

11. As side supporters on its four sides to Mount Meru, are the (four) mountain-ranges, Mandāra, Merumandāra, Supārśva and Kumuda--each ten thousand *yojanas* in length and height.

12. There stand respectively on these four mountain-ranges, four great trees, viz. the Mango, the Jambū (rose apple), the Kadamba and the Banyan, like the flags of these mountains. They are more than one thousand *yojanas* in height extending over the same by their branches. The trunk (of each) is one hundred *Yojanas* in circumference.

13. And there are four lakes, of Milk, honey, sugarcane juice and fresh water (one per mountain). The demigods who drink of these acquire natural *yogic* powers, Oh prominent Bharata.

14. There are also four celestial gardens (on them), viz. Nandana, Caitraratha, Vaibhrājaka and Sarvato-bhadra.

15. While listening to their eulogies sung by bands of demigods (like Gandhrva, and Kinnara), prominent gods, heading the bevies of celestial beauties, indulge in sports, in those celestial gardens.

16. From the top of the celestial mango tree eleven hundred *yojanas* in height, fall nectar-like sweet mangoes, as

big as mountain peaks, on the upper side of the Mountain Mandāra.

17. A river, named Aruṇodā(a river of deep red water) is formed. It is so called because it carries as water extremely sweet, fragrant, scented abundant reddish juice of the mangoes (falling from the tree and) bursting open. It falls down from the crest of Mount Mandāra and waters the eastern part of Ilāvṛta.

18. When the damsels of Yakṣa tribe, the female attendants of goddess Pārvatī, enjoy the sweet juice of Aruṇodā, their person becomes so fragrant that the breeze coming in contact with them gets charged with perfume, and it diffuses that perfume over an area of ten *yojanas* (in radius).

19. In this way rose-apples, as big as elephants, and containing very fine seed, fall from a very great height and burst open. The river Jambū formed out of their juice, falls from the peak of Mount Merumandāra, ten thousand *yojanas* in height, down to the ground and irrigates the whole of Ilāvṛta, lying south of the river.

20. The clay on both the banks of that river gets saturated through and through, with that juice (of rose-apples). With the chemical change wrought by the action of the wind and the Sun (on it), it (the clay) is transmuted into gold known as Jāmbunada and it is always used for ornaments by celestial beings.

21. How wonderful ! The gods and other heavenly beings along with their consorts, wear that (variety of) gold in the forms of various ornaments such as crowns and diadems, bangles, girdles and other ornaments.

22. There grows a big Kadamda tree on the Supārśva mountain. From its hollows flow out five currents of honey each five *āyāmas*[224] in dimension. They fall from the tops of Supārśva, they spread joy to the region of Ilāvṛta lying to the west of those currents.

23. The wind (breath) issuing out of the months of those who drink from those currents (of honey), spreads fragrance on an area of one hundred *yojanas* (in radius).

---

224. *āyāma*—Vyāma—a measure of length equal to the space between the tips of the fingers of either hands when the arms are extended (*Vyāmo bāhvoḥ sakarayos tatayos tiryagantaram*/—ŚR.)

24. Similary, there stands a banyan tree called *Śata-valśa* on mount Kumuda. From the branches (lit. arms) of that tree flow forth all streams, capable of yielding whatever one desires, such as milk, curds, honey, clarified butter, raw sugar, (delicious) food, garments, beds, seats or chairs, ornaments and others. These streams fall down from the summits of mount Kumuda and flow in the northern part of Ilāvṛta.

25. Subjects (beings) who make use of these river-waters never suffer afflictions from wrinkles, baldness, fatigue, perspiration, bad odours, old age, diseases and death or from cold, heat, paleness and other troubles. They enjoy the highest bliss all through their life.

26. Like filaments on the seed-vessels in a lotus, around the base of Meru, on all sides, there are twenty mountains viz. Kuraṅga, Kurara, Kusumbha, Vaikaṅka, Trikūṭa, Śiś ira, Pataṅga, Rucaka, Niṣadha, Śinī-Vāsa, Kapila, Śaṅkha, Vaidūrya, Jārudhi, Haṁsa, Ṛṣabha, Nāga, Kālañjara, Nārada and others.

27. Mounts Jaṭhara and Devakūta are to the east of Meru. They extend to the north for eighteen thousand *yojanas* in length, and two thousand *yojanas* in breadth, and in height. Similarly to the west (of Meru) stand two mountain-ranges, Pavana and Pāriyātra. To the south are situated Kailāsa and Karavīra which extend to the east. To the north (of Meru) stand Mount Tṛśṛṅga and Makara. Enclosed by these eight mountain-ranges, the mountain of gold (Meru) shines like (sacrificial) fire surrounded by blades of Kuśa grass. (to demarcate its boundaries).

28. Those (who are in know) say that on the summit of Meru, at the very centre, is situated Śāta-Kumbhī, (the city of gold), the capital of god Brahmā. It covers an area of a ten thousand *yojanas*[225] and is square in shape.

---

225. *ayuta-yojana-sāhasrīm*: I followed the text as it is. I doubt the interpretation as the area "a thousand times ten-thousand *yojanas*", although some respectable commentators like GD. interpret it this way without suspecting any contradiction between the area of the plateau on Meru and the city built over it, as the area of the plateau on Mount Meru is only 32,000 *yojanas*, vide Bh. P. Supra verse 7 above, which states *Mūrdhani dvātriṁśat-sahasra-yojana-vitataḥ*. ŚR. is conscious that the dimen-

29. Surrounding that city (capital of god Brahmā), there are eight suburbs (or cities) of the eight guardian deities of the world (such as Indra, Varuṇa etc.),[226] They are after the model of Śāta-Kumbhī, and are built in a style befitting their masters, each city being one fourth in extent of Lord Brahmā's capital.

CHAPTER SEVENTEEN

(*The Descent of the Gaṅgā*)

Śrī Śuka said :

1. In the sacrifice performed by Bali, the Lord (Viṣṇu) himself appeared as Trivikrama.[227]

Standing there (on the ground, he wanted to measure three feet of land donated to him by Bali. He covered the whole of the earth by his right foot. He raised the left foot to

---

sion given here conflicts with that given in the VP. 2.2.30 which states fourteen thousand *yojanas* as the area covered by Brahmadeva's capital.

catur-daśa sahasrāṇi yojanānāṁ mahāpurī/
Meror upari Maitreya Brahmaṇaḥ prathitā divi//

This is plausible in view of the area of the plateau on the summit of Meru which is 32,000 *yojanas*. ŚR.'s explanation that the dimensions differ with different *Kalpas* is not satisfactory. VR. interprets this as *ayuta-yojana-vistarām* i. e. ten thousand yojanas in area. VJ. regards *Śatakoṭi* as the name of Brahma's capital. GD. does not suspect any contradiction between the area of the plateau on Meru and the city built over it. He explains: *ayutāni yāni yojana-sahasrāṇi/* BP. explains: *ayuta-yojana-sāhasrīm* as *ayuta-sahasra-yojana-vistārām* but hastens to add, *atra bhāgatyāga-lakṣaṇayā yuta-sabda-varti-sahasrārtha-tyāgo bodhyaḥ.*

226. GD. and others enumerate the suburbs of Brahmadeva's capital as follows: To the East, Indra's capital Amarāvatī, to the South-East, Fire-god's headquarters Tejovatī, to the South, Yama's city Saṁyaminī, to the South-West, Kṛṣṇāṅganā of Nirṛtas, to the West, Varuṇa's capita Śraddhāvatī, to the North-West, Vāyu's headquarters Gandhavatī, to the North, Kubera's town Mahodayā, and to the North-East, Lord Śiva's capital Yaśovatī.

227. This refers to Vāmana incarnation of Viṣṇu, vide *infra* 8.18-20 (Skandha VIII. Chs 18-20)

measure the heavenly regions) by his foot-step, the upper crust of the shell of the Cosmic egg got cracked by the nail of the big toe of his left foot. Through that opening, rushed in the stream of waters, covering externally the cosmic egg. While washing the lotus-like feet of the Lord, she (the water of the stream) became reddish by the pollen-like dust (on the Lord's feet). She washed away the dirt, in the form of the sins of the whole of the world, by her touch, and yet, herself remained pure (unpolluted by sins). She was, at first, designated directly as *Bhagavatpadī* (Born from the feet of the Lord) to the exclusion of other epithets e.g. Jāhnavī, Bhāgīrathī which may imply any other less important source). After a long period of time measured in thousands of *yugas*, she descended on the top of the celestial regions which the sages call *Viṣṇu-pada*.

2. There (at the *Viṣṇupada*), verily, Dhruva (the son of Uttānapāda) of steadfast vows, the great votary of Lord Viṣṇu, even now bears (i.e. sprinkles) on his head her waters, with utmost reverence. "This water flows from the lotus feet of our family deity". (With this feeling) every moment his heart gets deeply saturated with ever-increasing devotion. Overcome with ardent longing (for the Lord), he forgets himself. Tears of pure love flow down from his half-closed lotus-bud-like eyes, and his whole person bristles with hair standing on their ends through ecstasy.

3. Thenceforth (in the next stage), the seven sages (inhabiting the constellation called *Ursa Major*) who know the greatness of this stream, regard it as the ultimate achievement of their austere penance, and even today, receive it with great reverence on the matted hair (of their heads), as persons desirous of Liberation (*Mokṣa*) would receive Final Emancipation due to their achievement of unswerving devotion unto the glorious Lord Vāsudeva, the Soul of all beings. They have grown indifferent to other *Puruṣārthas*, and even to Self-realization.

4. Later on, it (the stream) descends by the path of gods (i.e. sky), teeming with multitudes of thousands of crores of celestial cars, to the sphere of the Moon. After flooding

the lunar sphere, the stream (of the *Bhagavatpadī*) flows down to the city of Brahmā (on the summit of Mount Meru).

5. There, on mount Meru, it is divided into four branches under four names :—Sītā, Alakanandā, Cakṣu and Bhadrā,[228] and it (i.e, these branches) flows towards four quarters and enters into the ocean, the Lord of big and small rivers.

6. From the city of god Brahmā, the Sītā[229] flows down from the peaks of mountains like mount Kesara and others and descends on the summit of mount Gandhamādana. Flowing through the continent of Bhadrāśva it falls into the salt ocean on the east.

7. In the same way, Cakṣus (the Oxus or Amu-Daria) comes down from the summit of mount Mālyavān. It rushes with unabated velocity towards Ketumāla,[230] and enters the ocean on the west.

8. And to the north, the Bhadrā descends from the peak of Meru. Passing from the summit of one mountain to that of another, it jumps from the peak of mount Śṛṅgavat. It traverses the Northern Kuru region, and ultimately falls into the ocean on the northern direction.

9. Similarly, the Alakanandā flows down from the south of the city of Brahmā. Passing over from many a mountain peak, one after another, it reaches mount Hemakūṭa. (Thence) it rolls down, with very great velocity, to peaks of the Himālayas. It flows through Bhāratavarṣa on the south and falls into the sea. Men who come for ablutions in this river, easily acquire the merit of performing great sacrifices like the Aśvamedha, Rājasūya and others, at every step.

10. There are hundreds of other big and small rivers flowing through every continent, all daughters of Meru and other mountains.

11. (There are types of *Svargas* or celestial places according to their location in the heavens, on the earth and in

---

228. The Yarkand river on which the town of Yarkand is situated—N.L. De—GDAMI p. 31.

229. *Sītā*—N.L. De identifies it with the Jaxartes or Sir-Daria (GDAMI, 187). The identification may be correct for the Sitā of the *Brahmāṇḍa Purāṇa* (ch. 51). But the Sītā in the Bh. P. flows *to the east, through China* (*Bhadrāśva*). Hence it is not the same as *Sir-Daria*.

230. *Ketumāla-varṣa*—Turkestan and the lands watered by the Cakṣu or Oxus—N.L. De—GDAMI. p. 99.

the subterranean regions. The celestial spots on the earth are mentioned here).

The wise say that of all these continents (*varṣas*), Bhārata is the only continent which is a *karma-kṣetra*[231] (i.e. a land where men can make or mar their destiny by their actions or a land of religious acts). The remaining eight continents are called celestial spots on the earth which serve as places of enjoyment for celestial beings who return from the heaven with some balance of merit unexhausted.

12. In these continents, the longevity of the inhabitants is ten thousand human years. They are just like gods. They are endowed with the strength of ten thousand elephants; blessed with adamantine frame of the body and power, eternal youth, abundance of sense pleasures and extra-ordinary capacity for conjugal enjoyment, the couples are extremely happy. Their wives show signs of pregnancy only once in the final year of their life of sexual pleasures. In these continents, the Time has characteristic of the Treta Age.[232]

13. In those continents, verily, the lords of gods who are richly worshipped with sumptuous gifts by the leaders of their respective retinue, enjoy themselves at will, to their heart's content, in valleys of these mountains dividing the continents (*varṣas*)—valleys which are teeming with hermitages and mansions and abound in charming forests beautified with creepers and the supporting trees with branches bent low with

---

231. The idea that Bhārata-varṣa is a *karma-bhūmi* or *karma kṣetra* is common to most *purāṇas*. MP. 114.6-7 and MKP. 57.60 explain *karmabhūmi* as a land which contained within it the seeds of all pious actions and their fruits, and people in this land were entitled to go to heaven or *Mokṣa* or the earth. Other *purāṇas* repeat the same belief, e.g.

(i) *Prithivyām Bhāratam varṣam karmabhūmir udāhṛtā* /BRP. 27.2.

(ii) *Bhāratam nāma yad varṣam . . . .*
tat karma-bhūmir nānyatra, samprāptiḥ puṇyapāpayoḥ /MKP. 55.21-22.

(iii) *na tatrāpi Bhāratam varṣam karma-kṣetram uṣanti ha* / Devī Bh. P. 8.7.34.

232. According to ŚR. and other commentators, the Tretā Yuga is a period of sensual enjoyment. In the Kṛta Age all are engaged in meditation. In Dvāpara and Kali, people are overwhelmed with miseries.

flowers, bunches of fruit and tender foliage of all seasons. And with their mind and eyes fascinated with the attractive movements, bewitching smiles and sportive glances—all pregnant with love—of the most charming celestial beauties, they (the Lords of gods) amuse themselves at will with acquatic sports and other forms of diversions, in lakes of crystal-clear waters resounding with the warbling and cries of royal swans, water-fowls, ducks (*kāraṇḍavas*), cranes, rudy geese (*cakravākas*) and other birds which are delighted by the fragrant lotuses of various kinds, and (waters) resonant with the humming of different species of black-bees.

14. In all the nine continents, Lord Nārāyaṇa, the Supreme Person still maintains his presence in his various manifestations (*vyūha*) with the object of showering his grace on the inhabitants thereof.

15. In the Ilāvṛta continent, Lord Śiva is the only one male; no other male person who knows of the curse of the goddess Pārvatī enters it. I shall narrate to you later on (Infra IX Skandha) why a male person entering it (Ilāvṛta continent) is transformed into a woman.

16. There, Lord Śiva is served in every respect by one hundred million thousands of female attendants headed by goddess Pārvatī. He (Lord Śiva) is engrossed in the meditation upon the conceptualized image of Saṅkarṣaṇa, his own source, and presiding deity over the attribute *tamas*, the fourth manifestation of the glorious Lord Vāsudeva, the Supreme Person of Four forms (viz. Vāsudeva, Pradyumna, Aniruddha and Saṅkarṣaṇa). He sings of the following prayer.

17. "Salutations to the Supreme Person[233], the symbol of *Parabrahman*, the source of the manifestation of all attributes, (though himself) unmanifested and Infinite[234]. Hail[235] to him.

18. Oh adorable Lord! I take resort to your lotus-like feet which afford shelter to all. You are the Supreme abode

---

233. *mahā-puruṣāya*—Whose sport is the creation, maintenance and destruction of the universe—VR.

234. *anantāya*—(i) Śiva meditates upon the serpent Śeṣa along with Viṣṇu who is his inner controller—VJ.

(ii) Above the distinction of time, place etc.—GD.

235. The repetition of *Namaḥ* at the beginning and the end of the sentence shows that *namaḥ* or 'salutations' is applicable to all the adjectives included in the sentences—GD.

of all (the six) divine excellences (such as sovereignty over the universe, Omniscience and others). To your devotees you have fully manifested yourself as one who terminates their *saṁsāra* (the chain of births and deaths); but you create (i.e. continue) Saṁsāra (in the case of those who are not devoted to you.

19. What person intent on subduing his senses (and desirous of attaining liberation will not respect you whose vision—unlike that of ours who cannot control the vehemence of anger—is not, even in the slightest degree, affected by the *guṇas* of Māyā (i.e. worldly objects which are the products of the three attributes or *guṇas* of Māyā) and by the activities of the mind and sense, while you supervise them for government and control.

20. To a person of wrong perception,[236] you appear, through your Māyā Potency,[237] intoxicated and terrible with eyes reddened under the influence of spirituous liquors (though as a matter of fact, your form is pure, unalloyed *sattva*, beyond the power of karmas and auspicious). At the touch of your feet, the Nāga damsels get their mind and senses excited and are hence unable to proceed with your worship due to bashfulness (and the feeling that you, the omniscient know their mental agitation).

21. The goddess Lakṣmī and sages or Vedic Mantras declare him (i e. you) to be the prime cause of the creation, preservation and destruction of this (universe) but as you are Infinite, you are above these states. You do not feel even like a mustard seed where the sphere of the earth is lying somewhere on one of your thousand heads.

22. The principle called *Mahat* (Cosmic Intelligence) was his (i.e. your) first body (manifestation) constituted of (three) *guṇas*. It is based on *sattva* (in the form of *citta*—reasoning faculty), and is said to be (the same as) the glorious

---

236. *a-sad-dṛśaḥ*—(i) Who is strongly attached to this unreal or worthless body as his own Self (VR., BP.).

(ii) Whose vision is devoid of the knowledge about your form. excellences etc. (SD.)

237. *Māyayā*—Due to ignorance (of a person with incorrect view about the Lord—VR.

Brahmā (the deity presiding over it). It is from Brahma that I (Rudra) was born. I create through my power (viz. *Ahaṁkāra*—I-ness) consisting of three (*guṇas*) the deities (presiding over the sense-organs and mind—the *sāttvika* variety of *ahaṁkāra*, the gross elements (the *tāmasic* type) and cognitive and conative sense-organs (the *rājasa* kind of *Ahaṁkāra*).

23. We—these aforesaid *Mahat* (principle of Cosmic Intelligence), *ahaṁkāra* (Ego), *vaikārika*, (the abovementioned deities), the elements (the principles of *ākāśa*, *vāyu* etc.) and the (aforesaid) senses—remain under his control like birds cordoned together with a string and carry on this process of creation through his (your) grace.

24. This person (the *Jīva*) deluded by the world, the product of (three) *guṇas*, may possibly know Māyā, (his i.e. your) creation, which binds (the *jīva*) with *karmas* but it (the *jīva*) will never easily know the means of getting over it. My salutations to him who comprises within him the creation as well as the dissolution of the universe (and which as such are his form).

CHAPTER EIGHTEEN

(*Description of Various Continents*)

Śrī Śuka continued :

1. So also, there live in the continent of Bhadrāśva, a son of Dharma, Bhadraśravas by name, and the foremost members of his retinue (who are the heads of important families and great votaries of the Lord). They establish in their hearts, with supreme concentration of mind, the beloved form of the glorious Lord Vāsudeva himself, called *Hayaśiras* who is righteousness incarnate. (While muttering the *mantra* : *Om namo bhagavate dharmāyā'tma-viśodhanāya namaḥ*. They sing the following prayer :

Bhadraśravas and his people pray :

2. "Salutations to the glorious Dharma, the embodiment of righteousness, represented by the sacred syllable OM, the purifier of the mind (and *jīva*).

3. Oh wonderful ! How mysterious and strange are the ways (acts) of the Lord ! (Thereby) this world perceives Death, the destroyer of all, and yet fails to cognise it (as such) (For) a man contemplates (to commit) a sin for the enjoyment of insignificant, unreal pleasures and wishes (to continue) to live on the wealth of his father and the son (the old and the young), even after cremating him.

4. The learned persons, assert (on the authority of *Śāstras*) that the world is evanescent. The masters of spiritual science who have realized the Self within them, see (actually) that it is so. They, however, are deluded by your Māyā (Potency), Oh birthless Lord ! (One above the cycle of birth and death). Highly miraculous (and inscrutable) is your working (giving up all the labour of Śāstric studies and meditational processes) I (simply) pay my obeisance to you.

5. The Vedas attribute to you the authorship of the creation, preservation and destruction of the universe, even though you are not the doer, nor conditioned in any way (by Māyā). This is quite reasonable. There is nothing wonderful in your case as (through your Māyā) you are everything, and the cause of all effects, though factually you are essentially different from all things.

6. He (i.e. you) assumed the form of Man-horse (*Hayagrīva*), and recovered from the nether-worlds the Vedas which were concealed there by the demon (Madhu), at the end of the Yuga (i.e. the time of the dissolution of the universe) and returned them to the suppliant sage Brahmā. I bow to him (you) whose will is never futile."

7. And in (the continent called) Harivarṣa, the Lord abides in the form of Man-lion (Nṛsiṁha). I shall describe to you the reason of his assumption of that form later (in Skandha VII). That beloved form is propitiated by Prahlāda along with the inhabitants of that continent (Hari-varṣa) —Prahlāda who is the abode of the excellent qualities of exalted Souls, a great devotee of the Lord, whose virtuous charac-

ter and behaviour purify the race of Daityas and Dānavas, and who is unsurpassed in uninterrupted and undivided devotion (unto the Lord). He (along with the men of that Varṣa), recites the following prayer :

8. "Salutations to Lord Narasiṁha who is denoted by the sacred syllable OM. I bow to the Light of all lights. Oh Lord, manifest yourself completely. Oh Lord of adamantine claws and adamantlike fangs, completely burn down our latent deeds and desires. Please swallow up all the darkness (of our ignorance). We offer our worship to you (*Oṁ svāhā*). Please confer on me the state of absolute fearlessness. *Oṁ kṣraum* (a mystical syllable sacred to Lord Narasiṁha).

9. May the universe be blissful and happy! May the wicked give up their wickedness and be pure-minded! May all beings wish well of each other! May our mind resort to (the path of) goodness. May our thoughts as well as that of other beings enter into and concentrate on Lord Viṣṇu, without any ulterior motive.

10. May we be unattached to our home, wives, children, wealth and kinsmen. If there be any attachment (at all in us) may it be to the votaries who love the Lord. He who is satisfied with bare means of subsistence, achieves Liberation at no distant future. Not so does one who likes (the objects of) senses.

11* The holy waters remove the external dirt of the body by constant ablutions. But the birthless glorious Lord who enters into the mind through the ears of those who having got into the company of devotees, frequently listen to the extra-ordinary, hallowing exploits of Lord Viṣṇu, removes the impurities of the mind. Who will not then, wait upon such votaries?

---

* VR. gives an alternative explanation :

The company of his beloved votaries confers the capacity to meditate over the Lord and his extra-ordinary exploits. Those who properly dwell upon his hallowing fame constantly find that the Lord has occupied their minds through the ears (through constant listening to his exploits) and he purifies the mind of (mental) dirt. What man will abstain from listening to and meditating upon Lord Viṣṇu's exploits?

12. Gods with all their excellences (like knowledge, righteousness) abide in the heart of a person whose devotion unto the Lord is not motivated by any desire. How can a person not devoted to Hari possess the qualities of the great Souls, if he runs after worthless external objects of senses, attracted by desires.

13. For the glorious Lord Hari himself is the beloved Soul of all embodied beings just as water being the mainstay of its life is beloved to the fish. Howsoever a person may be otherwise great, if he forgets Hari and is attached to the householder's life, his greatness is like advancedness in age (and not in excellences) as in the case of married couples.

14. Hence, Oh Asuras, you renounce the householder's life which is the root cause (i.e. original source) of passions, attachment, despondency, wrath, pride, desire, fear, humiliation and anguish and which continues the cycle of births and deaths and take shelter at the feet of Lord Narasiṁha, the abode of fearlessness.

15. Even so in the continent called Ketumāla, the glorious Lord abides in the form of the god of Love, with the desire of pleasing the goddess Lakṣmī (his consort) and the rulers of that continent (*Varṣa*) viz. the sons (presiding deities of the day) and the daughters (female deities presiding over the night) of Prajāpati, *Saṁvatsara* (a year) whose number equals the days and nights comprising the full span of human life (i.e. 100 years × 360 days per year = 36000). The embryos (of these daughters) are discharged still born at the end of every year as the minds of the daughters are agitated and terrified at the dazzling splendour of the mighty missile (Sudarśana) of the Supreme Being (Viṣṇu).

16. He (Kāmadeva) delights his own senses while bringing ecstatic joy to goddess Lakṣmī with the splendour of his lotuslike face which is enchanting on account of his beautiful brows which are slightly raised, and by his playful glances and winsome gentle smiles, the charmingness of which is heightened by his extremely graceful gait.

17. At night, in the company of the presiding deities of night, the daughters of Prajāpati Saṁvatsara and at day time accompanied with their husbands (the male deities pre-

siding over the day), goddess Ramā (Lakṣmī) propitiates the blissful form[238] of the Lord, and recites this (the following *mantra*).

18. "Om ! Hrām, Hrīm, Hrūm[239] Om. Salutations to the glorious Lord Hṛṣīkeśa (the Ruler of Senses) symbolised by the sacred syllable Om. You are distinguished by all of your excellent special attributes. You are the Supreme Master of my conative organs and cognitive senses and of my internal organ (consisting of mind, ego, intelligence and understanding) along with their specialities (objects and functions).. You are the Ruler of sixteen *Kalās* (eleven senses and five objects—this is the 'subtle body'.) You are the Vedas incarnate. You are the food that sustains the body. You are the blissful *summum bonum* itself. You are all-pervading and the source of mental strength, physical potency and power. You are the Beloved Lord, Love personified. I bow to you here and hereafter (with the *bīja mantra*: Om ! Hrāṃ, Hrīṁ Hrūṁ !).

19. By observing (various) vows, (unmarried) women propitiate you, the Lord of all senses, and beseech from you another person as a protector (i. e. husband). But they (the earthly 'protectors' or husbands) are really incapable of protecting their beloved child, wealth or life and are hence themselves poor dependents.

20. He is the real husband or protector who himself is above fear from any quarter, and protects, in all respects, other persons stricken with fear. You alone are such a master. You do not regard anything more joyful than the realization of your own self, (otherwise you would not have any independence, if your happiness depended on someone else). There would be fear from each other (if there were more than one independent rulers).

21. A woman who knows that you are such a Lord and loves to offer worship to your lotus-like feet (without entertaining any desire for something in return), secures all her desired objects. But if you are worshipped and sought for a desired

238. *Māyā-mayaṁ rūpam*—The form which he can assume at will—VJ.

239. Mystical syllables regarded as the seeds of *Mantras*, the utterance of which is supposed to be extremely efficacious. These *bīja-mantras* show the influence of Tāntrism on the Bh.P.

boon, you grant that desired object only. Oh Lord, if, however the sought-for-object (granted by the Lord) is lost or exhausted (in enjoyment), she feels tormented.

22. God Brahmā, Śiva, gods, demons and others whose heart is attached to object of senses, perform austere penance for winning my favour. But no person, except one who is exclusively attached to your feet, attains to me and is favoured by me. For, Oh Invincible one! My heart is set on you (hence, being dependent on you, I glance with favour your devotees only).

23. Oh Acyuta (Lord Viṣṇu)! Your lotus-like hand is lauded as a showerer of desired objects. Be pleased to place that praiseworthy hand of yours on my head—your hand which you have placed, out of grace, on the crown of the head of your devotees. Most excellent Lord ! You bear me as an emblem on your chest (which shows that you do not entertain any disrespect for me). But strangely enough you show mere respect to me but extend your highest grace to your votaries). Who can comprehend the working of your divine Māyā ?"

24. In the Ramyaka continent, its ruler, Vaivasvata Manu, to whom the Lord manifested his beloved Fish incarnation formerly (while he was in the birth of King Satyavrata), even still adores him with intense; constant devotion and praises him as follows:

25. "Salutations to the Divine Lord denoted by (the syllable) Om ! I bow to him who is the life-giving principle; is pure *Sattva* incarnate; and is (the fountain head of) the power of the senses, the power of the mind and the strength of the body ! I pay my obeisance to the Great Fish[240]

26. Though you move about inside (as the vital breath of all beings), and outside (as the atmosphere or wind), making a loud noise (in the form of Vedas), your form is (invisible to and hence) unseen by all the guardian deities of the world. Just as a person controls a wooden doll (by means of strings), you, the Supreme Ruler, have brought this universe under your control, by (the strings in the form of pres-

240. For the Fish-incarnation of the Lord see *infra* Skandha VIII. 24.

criptions and prohibitions given under) the designation of Brāhmaṇas.

27. (You, being the vital breath, are the real Protector and Controller of the creation). Discarding you (the vital breath of all), the guardian deities of the world, being feverish with jealousy, tried but could not protect both severally and jointly, the bipeds and quadrupeds, reptiles and the immobiles —in fact whatever is seen in the world.

28. Oh birthless Lord ! Piloting this earth, the abode of herbs and creepers, along with me (Manu, then in birth of Satyavrata) you sported enthusiastically and vigorously on the ocean of deluge surging with heavy billows. I bow to you who are the controller of all multitudes of beings in this universe."

29. In Hiraṇmaya continent also, the Lord abides assuming the form of the Tortoise. Aryaman, the ruler of the manes (departed forefathers), along with the inhabitants of this continent (*varṣa*) worships this most beloved form (of the Lord) and continuously repeats the following Mantra:

30. "Salutation to the glorious Lord, the (Divine) Tortoise, designated by the symbol Om. Your form is specially characterised by pure *Sattva*. Your position is beyond perception (due to your submarine activities). Bow to you who are above the limit of Time. Obeisance to you who are Omnipresent and the support of all.

31. This visible objective universe which appears in innumerable forms and which cannot be enumerated due to its being an illusion, is really your own form (inseparable from you and) manifested by your Māyā. I bow to you whose form is thus indescribable.

32. It is you alone that are designated as a mammal, a sweat-born being, an oviparous being, a plant, a mobile or immobile creature, a god, a sage, a departed ancestor (*Pitṛ*) a goblin, the world as perceived by senses, the celestial region, the sky, the earth, a mountain, a river, an ocean, an island-continent, a planet and a star.

33. The number (viz. twentyfour principles) has been presumed by sages (like Kapila) in you, even though you possess innumerable specialities, names, forms or shapes. In

the light of true knowledge, the number (automatically) disappears. I bow to you who are of the nature of real knowledge or the real essence of the Sāṅkhya doctrine."[241]

34. Assuming the form of a boar, the glorious Lord, the presiding deity of Sacrifice, stays in the region called the Northern Kurus. The goddess of the Earth along with the Kurus (the inhabitants of that country) adores him with unswerving devotion. She constantly repeats the following, the most sacred, secret mystical *mantra*:[242]

35. "I pay obeisance to the Supreme Lord symbolised by the sacred syllable Om—the Lord who can be truly comprehended only through the *mantras* (Vedic texts); who is of the form of both types of sacrifices—performed with or without the use of sacrificial posts; every limb of whose person is constituted (of different kinds) of great sacrifices[243] (e.g. *aśvamedha*). Salutations to you, Oh Supreme Person. I bow to him (who as a performer of sacrifices) is of pure actions, and who is called *triyuga* (manifest in three *yugas*, due to the absence of sacrifices in the *Kṛta* Age, or their neglect and discontinuance in the *Kali Age*.

36* Just as learned experts (in sacrificial lore) ignite fire latent in pieces of (Śamī) wood, by means of friction, so do sages, eager to see you (i.e. your real form) lying concealed in actions and their results (due to their attachment), find you out in (the discipline of) body and the senses which are the product of *guṇas*. They discover you with the help of the churning rod in the form of the discriminative faculty of the mind. I bow to you who manifest your real form this way.

---

241. VR : Salutation to you who are object of true knowledge which removes the idea of the limited numbers (viz. twentyfour).

242. *Oṁ namo Bhagavate mantra-tattva-liṅgāya Yajña-kratave mahādhvarāvayavāya mahā-puruṣāya namaḥ karma-śuklāya tri-yugāya namaste* /

243. In explanation of the different limbs of this Lord of Sacrifices VR. quotes : *sruktuṇḍa āsīt, sruva īśa nāsāyor iḍodare camasāḥ karṇa-randhre* / Supra Bh.P. 3.13.36.

* Learned persons who know the Reality as propounded in the Vedānta realize, after deep thinking, your real form unmanifest yet the controller of the body and its sense organs, a product of three *guṇas* by means of their mind or reasoning faculty . . . . I salute to you who are designated differently as Indra etc. when invoked in sacrifices—VJ.

37. You, the Supreme Self, are discerned to be an independent absolute reality, distinct from the products of the Māyā, viz. gross matter (elements), sense-activities, the presiding deities of senses, the body, the controller (Time) and ego, by those whose intellect has been sharpened and discerning through deep contemplation and the practice of the (various) stages of *Yoga* (*Yama*, *Niyama* etc.).

38. By means of its *guṇas*, Māyā, though inert (*jaḍa*), brings about the creation, preservation and destruction of the universe through his presence, just as a piece of iron moves about (due to the presence of) a load-stone with its face towards it. This is meant only for the *jīvas* (by you) and not desired for himself. I bow to you who stand a mere witness to the *guṇas* and the working of the *Māyā*.

39. You are the primeval Boar, the cause of the universe. Just as an elephant crushes its rival elephant, you killed the demon (Hiraṇyākṣa) in the battle. Placing me on the tip of your tusk, you emerged from the lowest region in the ocean of deluge, playing (all the while) like an elephant. I pay my obeisance to you the Omnipotent Lord."

CHAPTER NINETEEN

(*Description of Kimpuruṣa and Bhārata Varṣas*)

Śrī Śuka said :

1. In the continent called Kiṁpuruṣa, the greatest votary Hanumān, who feels pleasure and delight in being near the Lord's feet, worships with uninterrupted devotion—along with the Kiṁpuruṣas (the inhabitants of that continent)—the Primeval Being, the glorious Lord Rāma, the beloved of Sītā and the elder brother of Lakṣmaṇa.

2. (There) he listens with rapt attention the most auspicious story of the glorious Lord, his master, melodiously sung of by Ārṣṭinemi and the Gandharvas. And he sings the following to himself :

3. "I bow to the Lord of hallowing reputation who is symbolized by the syllable Om. I salute the Lord who possesses noble qualities, excellent character and conduct. I pay obeisance to him who has perfectly controlled his mind and who is deligent in the service of his subjects. Hail to him who is the touchstone (the utmost limit) of excellent renown. Salutations to the Supreme Person, the king of kings who is a great devotee of Brāhm aṇas.

4. I take shelter with him who is pure consciousness and knowledge incarnate, absolutely one (without a second); who, by his innate divine power, has dispelled (and transcended) all the states (e. g. wakefulness, sleep) caused by the three *guṇas* (of Māyā) and is (hence) perfectly serene; who is (totally) different from the phenomenal world and is above (all) names and forms; who is not touched by egoism, yet is realizable (as Brahman) by wise persons of pure mind.

5. The incarnation of the Almighty Lord, in a mortal body, in this world, is not merely for extirpating the demon race but for teaching (the ideal way of life) to human beings. Otherwise, how could the omnipotent Ruler who abides in his innate blissful self, seem to be distressed for Sītā.

6. Verily, the glorious Lord Vāsudeva (i.e. Rāma) is not at all attached to anything in the three worlds, (for) he is the Soul and the most intimate friend of the wise people (who have subdued their Self). Hence, he cannot suffer from infatuation for a woman (viz. Sītā). Nor would he exile Lakṣmaṇa (for his technical breach of order by allowing sage Durvāsas for Rāma's audience).

7. Neither birth (in a noble family) nor beauty nor eloquence nor (brilliant) intelligence, nor the charming personality pleases (lit. is a cause of satisfaction to) him. For the elder brother of Lakṣmaṇa (Rāma) has formed friendship with us, dwellers in the forest who are bereft of these qualities.

8. Hence, whether a god or a demon or a monkey or a human being—whoever he may be—should take shelter with all his heart, with Rāma who is Lord Hari in the human form, and he remembers all good deeds done to him. And he carried (the people) in the Northern Kosala (with him) to Heaven."

9. In the continent of Bhārata also, the Lord under the name Nara-Nārāyaṇa, remaining in an unmanifested form, continues to perform penance to the end of the *Kalpa*. (It is) for compassionately bestowing his grace on self-controlled persons. His penance is such as enhances righteousness, knowledge, renunciation, mystic powers, sense-control, freedom from I-ness (*ahaṁkāra*) ultimately consummating in self-realization.

10. The revered (sage) Nārada intended to initiate the sage Sāvarṇi (the prospective Manu presiding over the future *Manvantara*) in the *Pañcarātra* doctrine (describing the glories of the Lord) along with Sāṅkhya philosophy and practice (or *karma-yoga*—unattached practice of *karmas*) as expounded by the Lord (himself). He (Nārada) along with the inhabitants of all classes (*varṇas*) and stages of life (*āśrama*) in (this) Bhārata, adores him with the feeling of utmost devotion and sings (mutters) the following (*mantra*) :

11. "I pay respects to the glorious Lord who is symbolised by the sacred syllable OM. (I bow to him) who is perfectly serene by nature and (absolutely) free from *ahaṁkāra* (ego). Salutations to the foremost sage Nara-Nārāyaṇa who is the property of the property-less. I bow again and again to him who is the preceptor of *Parama Haṁsas* (the highest order of recluses) and who is the Master of those (saintly persons) who find delight in the Soul.

12. I bow to him who is (completely) detached and (hence) is not bound by the egotistical feeling of being the creator or even though he is the Master of the creation (etc. of the universe); who is distinct (from the body) for though he resides in the body, he is not affected by the bodily conditions, (and needs like hunger, thirst etc.); who is (an impartial) witness whose vision is not biased by the *guṇas* like *Sattva*, *rajas* and *tamas*.

13. Oh Lord of Yoga ! This is stated to be the highest proficiency in Yoga by revered god Brahmā (*Hiraṇyagarbha*) that, at the time of death, one should give up one's (Soul's) identification with this evil body and fix his mind in you who are attributeless (or untouched by the *guṇas* of *Māyā*).

14. (It is only) a fool who, being addicted to the pleasures both of this world as well as those in heaven, feels anxiety for his son, wife and wealth (at the time of death). If like (such) a fool, a learned person be afraid of the death of this contemptible body, all his (intensive) studies (in *Śāstra*, of this learned person) is no better than (wasteful and onerous) labour.

15. Therefore, Oh Lord Viṣṇu, confer on us that (*bhakti*) *Yoga*—which is your natural attribute—whereby we can quickly cut asunder (and give up) the feeling of identity and mineness felt for this contemptible physical body due to Your Māyā—i.e. a bond very difficult to sever."

16. Even in this continent of Bhārata, there are many rivers and mountains, namely, Malaya, Maṅgalaprastha, Maināka, Trikūṭa, Ṛṣabha, Kūṭaka, Kollaka, Sahya, Devagiri, Ṛṣyamūka, Śrī-Śaila, Veṅkaṭa, Mahendra, Vāridhāra, Vindhya, Śuktimān, Ṛkṣagiri, Pāriyātra, Droṇa, Citrakūṭa, Govardhana, Raivataka, Kakubha, Nīla, Gokāmukha, Indrakīla, Kāmagiri and other hundreds and thousands of mountains. There rise in these (mountains) innumerable big and small rivers.[244]

17. The peoples of Bhārata-varṣa touch with their body (use for their personal needs) the waters of these rivers, the names of which purify them even by pronouncing (their names).

18. The great rivers (in Bhārata varṣa) are : Candravaśā, Tāmraparṇī, *Avatodā*, Kṛtamālā, Vaihāyasī, Kāverī, Veṇī, Payasvinī, Śarkarāvartā, Tuṅgabhadrā, Kṛṣṇā, Veṇyā, Bhīmarathī, Godāvarī, Nirvindhyā, Payoṣṇī, Tāpī, Revā, Surasā, Narmadā, Carmaṇvatī, Sindhu; two mighty rivers : Andha (Brahmaputra) and Śoṇa—Mahānadī, Vedasmṛti, Ṛṣikulyā, Triśāmā, Kauśikī, Mandākinī, Yamunā, Sarasvatī, Dṛṣadvatī, Gomatī, Sarayū, Rodasvatī, Saptavatī, Suṣomā, Śatadru, Candrabhāgā, Marudvṛdhā, Vitastā, Asiknī, Viśvā and other great rivers.

---

244. For the identification of these mountains and rivers etc. mentioned here and in the next two verses, vide D.C. Sircar—SGAMI, pp. 48-74 and N.L. De—GDAMI under relevant heads.

19. It is in this very continent only that men who are born here can, through the white (*sāttvic*), red (*rājasa*), and black (*tāmasa*) acts commenced by them, attain to the numerous celestial, earthly and hellish existences (births) according to the serial order of their *karmas*; for all (everyone) get the proper type of birth according to (the nature of) their *karmas*. And the Liberation is achieved by the (unattached) performance of the duties prescribed for each class of society.

20. Liberation is characterised by Yoga of motiveless devotion solely directed to the glorious Lord Vāsudeva, the Supreme Soul who abides in all beings as their self; is above prejudices and defects (like love, hate), and beyond the range of speech, and not dependent on any other support. It is attainable by intimate association with great personages, viz. devotees of Lord Viṣṇu—association which can be formed when the knot of ignorance which leads to different kinds of births, is cut down completely. For gods sing this very praise of human life as the means of attaining all *puruṣārthas* (highest goals in human life).

21. Oh ! What (wonderful) meritorious deed has been done by these ! Or Lord Hari of his own accord has bestowed his grace on them. In the land of Bharata, these have got birth in the human species which is useful as a means of serving Lord Mukunda. How strongly we yearn for this !

22. Of what use are the performances of sacrifices, austere penances, observances of vows, charitable donations—all so very difficult to perform ? Or of what avail is this worthless attainment of heaven (as a result of merits earned) where the remembrance of the lotus-like feet of Nārāyaṇa is wiped out in the excessive enjoyments of sensual pleasures.

23. It is preferable to attain (birth in) the land of Bhārata with its momentary span of life to achieving those regions where beings are blessed with a life span of a *Kalpa* but whence return to birth (in *saṁsāra* is inevitable . For the wise resolute mortals (in Bhārata-varṣa) dedicate at Hari's feet, their acts in a moment and attain to the region of Hari, free from the fear of *Saṁsāra*.

24. The region, even if it be the residence of god Brahmā, the Supreme Controller of gods, is not worth resort-

ing, if there be no river of nectar in the form of discourses on Lord Viṣṇu, flowing, and if there is no saintly votaries of the Lord entirely depending on it[245], and where sacrifices in the form of the worship of the Lord of sacrifices, accompanied with the celebration of festivals (like music and dancing based on his episodes) are not performed.

25. But those *jīvas*, who, even after getting birth here, in the human race, endowed with the power of knowledge and discrimination, the capability of doing actions to attain it, the plentitude of substances necessary for securing it, do not verily exert to attain to Liberation whence there is no return to the mundane existence, enter again into the bondage (of *saṁsāra*) like forest birds (which after getting freedom from the fowler's net carelessly play on the same tree on which they were formerly caught and thus get into the bondage again).

26. (How blessed are the inhabitants of Bhārata varṣa). When in performing a sacrifice, they (people of Bhārata) set apart for various deities their due share of oblations and with faith offer these oblations to the sacrificial fire in the proper manner, reciting the relevant *mantras* and offering the substances according to prescriptions laid down, he is the One Lord, perfect in all respects and a bestower of blessings but who, invoked under different names gladly accepts them.

27. It is true that when prayed, the Lord confers the desired object to him who implores him for it. But certainly he does not confer on them the real blessing as they are again brought to the position of a supplicant. But to those who adore him without any ulterior motive, he, of his own accord, offers his foliage-like tender feet which cover (satisfy) all their desires.

28. If after exhausting our merits in enjoying celestial life, there be some balance of merit accruing from a duly performed sacrifice, a religious discourse preached or any other pious act done, we pray for a birth in the continent called Ajanābha (Bhārata Varṣa) retaining our remembrance of the

245. Or Votaries of the Lord who are the sources (i.e. the participants) of the nectarine discourses on Hari.

Lord. For glorious Lord Hari extends his blessings to those who worship him*.

Śrī Śuka said :

29. Oh King ! Some people describe eight minor sub-continents attached to Jambū-dvīpa. They are said to have been created by the sons of Sagara who excavated the earth on all sides in their search for the sacrificial horse.[246]

30. They are as follows: Svarṇa Prastha, Candra-Śukla, Āvartana, Ramaṇaka, Mandāraharina, Pāñcajanya, Siṁhala and Laṅkā.

31. In this way, the divisions of the Jambūdvīpa into continents have been described to you (exactly) as I was taught.

---

* D.S. Yande's edition of the Bh.P. gives the following eight verses as additional, recorded in some editions. ŚR. has not commented on them. But they are translated here in case their genuineness be proved in some subsequent critical edition of the Bh. P.

1. Hence even gods desire to be born on this earth in the Bhārata Varṣa with a view to accumulating noble, inexhaustible, pure, auspicious merit.

2. They wish : "When shall we be able to be born in the land of Bhārata ? When can we attain to the highest abode of Viṣṇu by (our) great merit ?

3. When can we, by charitable donations, performance of various kinds of sacrifices, and austerities, adore Lord Hari who is reposing in the cosmic ocean, and reach his abode which the wise sages visualize(directly).

4. The noble Soul who, by nature, is inclined to sing in praise of Hari, or is dear to his votaries or who renders service to his great devotees, deserves to be paid respects by us.

5. The great person whose mind is keenly interested in hearing the exposition of the Vedas as well as in listening to the Purāṇas or in the company of the pious persons, deserves our obeisance.

6. After being born in Bhārata, if a person is averse to pious acts, he (is like a person who) discards a pitcher(full) of nectar and desires to have a pot of poison.

7. He who, abandoning the worship of Vāsudeva, indulges in various acts, (is like a person who) neglecting a wish-yielding cow, desires to drink the milk of the *arka* plant."

8. In this way, the denizens of heaven eulogize the land of Bhārata. Those who, attaining birth herein, indulge in sensual pleasures, are really deluded by the Māyā of Lord Hari.

246. Vide infra ix.8. 8-9.

CHAPTER TWENTY

(Description of the remaining six Dvīpas) *

Śrī Śuka said:

1. Hereafter the division of *Plakṣa* and other *Dvīpas* into *Varṣas* is being detailed, with special reference to their dimensions, distinguishing characteristics and relative position.

2. Just as mount Meru is surrounded by *Jambūdvīpa*, this *Jambūdvīpa* is engirdled by the salt sea of the same dimension as the *dvīpa* itself. Just as a moat is surrounded by an outlying garden, the Salt Sea is enclosed by a *dvīpa* called Plakṣa, which is double in dimension of the Salt Sea. There stands the great Plakṣa (the Indian fig) tree equal to the Jambū (Rose apple) tree (in Jambūdvīpa). It is of gold and it gave its name to the *dvīpa*. At its foot, dwells the god of fire, of seven tongues. Its ruler is Idhmajihva, the son of Priyavrata. He divided his *dvīpa* into seven continents. Having entrusted them to his sons bearing the same name as that of the Seven Varṣas, he became liberated from *saṁsāra* by practising union with the Soul.

3. The continents (Varṣas) are called Śiva, Yavasa, Subhadra, Śānta, Kṣema, Amṛta and Abhaya. It is said that there are seven wellknown mountains and seven famous rivers in each (continent).

4. The seven mountains forming the borders of the Varṣas are Maṇikūṭa, Vajrakūṭa, Indrasena, Jyotiṣmān, Suparṇa, Hiraṇyaṣṭhīva and Meghamāla. The principal rivers are Aruṇā Āṅgirasī, Sāvitrī, Suprabhātā, Ṛtambharā and Satyambharā. The four classes of people (*varṇas*), called Haṁsa, Pataṅga, Urdhvāyana, (and) Satyāṅga use the waters of these rivers and wash away (the effects of) their *rajas* and *tamas*. They live a thousand years; their form is (free from fatigue, sweat etc.) like that of gods, and they beget progeny like them. With the rituals prescribed in the three Vedas, they worship the Ātman, the glorious Lord—Sun, the gate of heaven, who is described in the three Vedas.

---

* Some commentators like GD. seem to have followed a text with different order of verses. Here the text adopted by ŚR is accepted.

5*. (They meditate upon him as follows:) "We resort to the Sun-god who is the manifestation of the ancient god Viṣṇu; who is the presiding deity of *Satya* (righteousness to be practised) and *Ṛta* (the divine law), the Vedas, the dispenser of good and evil fruits."

6. In the five continents (*dvīpas*) commencing with Plakṣa, all persons, without any distinction are, from their very birth, blessed with long life, soundness (conative and cognitive) of sense-organs, virility, lustre, physical power, intellectual capacity and bravery.

7. *Plakṣa dvīpa* is encircled by a sea of sugar-cane juice equal in extent to the (*Plakṣa-dvīpa*) itself. So also Śālmalī-dvīpa, double in dimension (of the sea of the sugarcane juice) stands shining with the sea of wine equal to Śālmalī *dvīpa* in width, surrounding it.

8. Here (in Śālmalīdvīpa) stands the Śālmalī (the silk cotten) tree which has the same dimension as that of the Plakṣa tree. The sages proclaimed that on that tree is the nest (abode) of the worshipful Garuḍa, the King of birds who praises the Lord with his wings consisting of the Vedas. And this tree is regarded as the origin of the name of the *dvīpa*.

9. The Lord of the dvīpa, Yajñabāhu, the son of Priyavrata, divided the seven subdivisions (*Varṣas*) of that *dvīpa* among his seven sons who gave their names severally to the (seven) Varṣas, viz. Surocana, Saumanasya, Ramaṇaka, Devavarṣa, Pāribhadra Āpyāyana and Avijñāta.

10. In those *Varṣas* (continents), the continental mountains (forming the boundaries) and the rivers are seven each. (The names of the boundary-mountains are:) Svarasa, Śataśṛṅga, Vāmadeva, Kunda, Mukunda, Puṣpa-varṣa and Sahasra-śruti. And names of the rivers are: Anumati, Sinivālī, Sarasvatī, Kuhū, Rajanī, Nandā and Rākā.

11. Men in this Varṣa are divided in classes designated as Śrutadhara, Vīryadhara, Vasundhara and Īṣandhara; with

---

* VR. : *ṛta*—meritorious act. *mṛtyu* and *amṛta*—Bondage and Liberation. *pratna*—the beginningless cause of the universe. This excludes *jīvas* etc. which have a beginning. *Satya*—unchangeable.

Translation : "We take asylum with the unchangeable Sun-god who forms the body of Viṣṇu who is the beginningless cause of the universe and the cause of bondage and liberation and leads *jīvas* to the course of *dharma*."

Vedic hymns they worship the glorious *ātman*, the Moon-god who is Veda incarnate.

12. "May the Moon-god who, dividing (the month into) dark and bright fortnights, by his rays distributes food to the manes, gods (respectively in the dark and bright fortnight) and to all created beings, be our ruler"[247].

13. Likewise beyond the Sea of Wine (Suroda) and double its size, lies Kuśa-dvīpa which, like the previous (Śālmalī) *dvīpa*, is surrounded on the other side by the Ocean of Ghee of dimension equal to it (Kuśadvīpa). In that *dvīpa* stands a dump of Kuśa grass planted therein by the Lord. It has given its name to the *dvīpa*. It (the clump of Kuśa grass) is refulgent like another Fire-god, and it illuminates all directions by the lustre of its tender shoots.

14. The (first) ruler of that *dvīpa* was the son of Priyavrata, Hiraṇyaretas by name. Dividing his *dvīpa* proportionately (in seven parts) he distributed them to his seven sons namely Vasu, Vasudāna, Dṛḍha-ruci, Nābhi-gupta, Stutyavrata, Vivikta and Vāmadeva, and he himself took to austere penance.

15. In those *Varṣas* the boundary mountains and rivers are well-known to be severally seven: Cakra, Catuḥśṛṅga, Kapila, Citrakūṭa, Devānīka, Ūrdhva-roma, Draviṇa mountains, and the Rasakulyā, Madhukulyā, Mitravindā, Śrutavindā, Devagarbhā, Ghṛtacyutā and Mantramālā rivers.

16. With the waters of these rivers, the inhabitants of Kuśadvīpa denoted by (the classes—Varṇas) Kuśala, Kovida,

---

247. (i) VR. emphasizes that but for the division into dark and bright fortnights by the Moon-god, there would have been no food-offerings to the manes and gods. May the Moon-god bring happiness (*amṛtam* = *sukham*) to us.

(ii) VJ. : May the inner controller of the Moon-god whose rays are full of nectar, distribute Soma to manes and gods and food to us all in both dark and bright fortnights. May he bring happiness (*somam* = sukham) to us.

(iii) BP. attributes the division into dark and bright fortnights to the Moon-god. By his rays he distributes food to the manes (in the dark fortnight) and to gods (in the bright fortnight). May that Moon-god be our king and bring us happiness.

Abhiyukta, Kulaka (corresponding to our Varṇas like Brāhmaṇa etc.) worship the glorious Lord in the form of Fire by their proficiency in sacrificial rituals (or skilfulness in work).

17*. (They pray): "Oh Fire-god! You are the carrier of oblations directly to the Supreme Brahman (Lord Hari). Worship the Supreme person by sacrifice (sacrificial oblations) offered to gods who are the limbs of the body of the Cosmic Man (just as what is offered to the part of the body e.g. a hand is as good as given to the person himself)."

18. Similarly, beyond the Sea of Ghee (Ghṛtoda), there is the *Krauñca-dvīpa* twice as extensive (as Ghṛtoda) and encircled by the Ocean of Milk (Kṣīroda) equal to it (Krauñca-dvīpa) in dimension, just like Kuśa-dvīpa by the Sea of Ghee (Ghṛtoda). Here the chief mountain is called Krauñca which gives its name to the *dvīpa*.

19. Though the projecting ridges and bowers were devastated by the weapon (javelin) of Kārttikeya, it (Krauñca) became free from fear as it was sprayed over by the surges of the ocean of Milk and was protected on all sides by god Varuṇa.

20. Even in that Dvīpa was its (first) ruler, a son of Priyavrata, Ghṛtapṛṣṭha by name. He divided his (Krauñca) *dvīpa* in seven continents. In those continents bearing the names of his sons, he installed his seven heirs (sons) as the rulers of those Varṣas, and he himself resorted to the lotus-like feet of the glorious Lord Hari (the destroyer of the Bondage of Saṁsāra) who was his *Antarātman* (Inner Controller) and whose glory was supremely auspicious.

21. The sons of Ghṛtapṛṣṭha are : Āma, Madhuruha, Meghapṛṣṭha, Sudhāman, Bhrājiṣṭha, Lohitārṇa and Vanas-

---

*Other interpretations are : (i) VR. : "Oh Fire-god ! You form a part of the body of the transcendental Brahman. You are the carrier of sacrificial oblations to gods and thereby to the Inner Controller in the bodies of gods. Convey our sacrificial oblations offered to gods who are but limbs of the body of the Supreme Man, to him who is also the *Antarātman* (Inner Controller)".

(ii) VJ. : "Oh Omniscient (Fire-God) ! You are the carrier of sacrificial oblations to Śrī Nārāyaṇa as well as to gods who are members of his Person. Staying near us, you make us worship Śrī Hari (called Yajña) by the performance of the act called Sacrifice."

pati. The mountains demarcating the *Varṣas* are seven, viz. Śukla, Vardhamāna, Bhojana, Upabarhin, Nanda, Nandana, and Sarvatobhadra. And the rivers are known to be seven only, viz. Abhayā, Amṛtaughā, Āryakā, Tīrthavatī, Vṛttirūpavatī, Pavitravatī and Śuklā.

22. The inhabitants of that Varṣa (classified into Varṇas) called Puruṣa, Ṛṣabha, Draviṇa and Devaka (corresponding to the Varṇas such as Brāhmaṇa, Kṣatriya) use the sacred, purifying waters of those rivers, and propitiate the Lord in the form of water, by offering water with the hollow of their joined palms filled with water.

23. (They pray the waters thus :) "Oh waters! You are endowed with powers by the Supreme God. Hence, you purify the three worlds, viz. the heaven, the earth and the intervening space. As you are naturally capable of destroying all sins, purify our bodies as we touch you."

24. Similarly beyond the ocean of milk (*Kṣīroda*) and surrounding it lies the Śākadvīpa, thirtytwo lakh *Yojanas* in extent. It is encircled by the sea of liquid curds equal to it in length. Herein stands a tree called Śāka which has given its appellation to the *dvīpa*. And its extremely fragrant smell perfumes the (whole of the) *dvīpa*.

25. Even of that *dvīpa* also, a son of Priyavrata named Medhātithi is the (first) ruler. He also divided it in seven continents (Varṣas) bearing the names of his sons. In them, he installed, as rulers, his sons, viz. Purojava, Manojava, Pavamāna, Dhūmrānīka, Citrarepha, Bahurūpa, Viśvadhara by name. And concentrating his mind on Lord Ananta, he himself entered Penance-forest (for performing austerities).

26. In these continents, the boundary-mountains and (main) rivers are only seven each. The mountains are Īśāna, Uruśṛṅga, Balabhadra, Śatakesara, Sahasrasrota, Devapāla and Mahānasa. The rivers are Anaghā, Āyurdā, Ubhayaspṛṣṭi, Aparājitā, Pañcapadī, Sahasrastuti, Nijadhṛti.

27. The inhabitants of that continent, (classified in Varṇas) called Ṛtavrata, Satyavrata, Dānavrata and Anuvrata who have washed off their *rajas* and *tamas* by Prāṇāyāma (breath-control) propitiate the glorious Lord in the form of Vāyu through perfect concentration of mind.

28. (They pray as follows :) "May the glorious Lord who is the Inner Controller of all beings, and who, entering (the body in the form of the chief vital breath), sustains all the beings by his five functions of inhalation and exhalation, and under whose control the whole of the universe exists, protect us."

29. So also beyond the ocean of (liquid) curds is situated *Puṣkaradvīpa* which is double the extent (of the ocean of curds), and which is encircled by the sea of sweet water equal in dimension to it (*Puṣkara-dvīpa*). Herein grows a gigantic lotus of hundred million petals of burnished gold, shining like the flames of fire. It was intended to be the throne of Lord Brahmā (who has a lotus-flower as his seat).

30. In the middle of the *dvīpa*, stands only one mountain called Mānasottara. It demarcates the boundary between the eastern and western continents (*Varṣas*). It is ten thousand *Yojanas* in its height and length. Here (on this mountain), in the four directions, are built the four capital cities of Indra (and other) guardians of the world. Over it (the *Mānasottara* mount) revolves the (other) wheel, in the form of a year (*Saṁvatsara,*) of the chariot of the Sun-god. It goes round mount Meru within the limit of a day and night of gods (each of which consists of six months of human beings).

31. The ruler of that continent was the Prince of Priyavrata, named Vītihotra. He had two sons Ramaṇaka and Dhātaki by name. He installed them as the rulers and protectors of the Varṣas, and like his elder brothers, he devoted himself solely to the service (worship) of the Lord.

32. The inhabitants of that continent propitiate the Lord in the form of god Brahmā, with (mental) acts leading to the region of Brahmā (the *Sālokya* type of liberation), and recite the following (*Mantra*) :

33* "We pay obeisance to that serene glorious Lord who is (regarded as) the fruit of all righteous actions, and a con-

*(i)VR. : Salutations to Lord Hiraṇyagarbha! May people differentiated by castes (*varṇas*) and stages in life (*āśramas*) worship with unswerving devotion (*ekāntam=avyabhicaritam*) that which forms the body of the Supreme Brahman, and is known through Vedas, and which is full of activities like the creation of the world etc., as the one reality.

crete means which leads to (the knowledge of) the Brahman; whom all people should adore (with the master-servant relation); who is established in the one Supreme Reality (Brahman) and is (hence) one without a second."

The sage (Śuka) continued :

34. Beyond that sea of sweet water and encircling it, is a ring of mountain-range called Lokāloka which divides the *Loka* i.e. the region illuminated by the light of the Sun, and the *Aloka*—the region which gets no light of the Sun.

35. Beyond the ocean of Fresh water, there is a tract of land which is in extent as wide as the distance between the mountains Mānasottara and Meru. Beyond that stretches a land of gold which is (shining) like a sheet of mirror. Nothing that goes or is dropped there ever returns and hence it is avoided by all living beings (as it is reserved for gods).

36. The mountain is called Lokāloka, as this mountain stands between the regions lighted by the Sun (*Loka*), and those not lighted by him (*Aloka*).

37. The mountain-chain has been laid beyond and round all the three worlds, by the Almighty Lord. It is so high and extensive that rays of the innumerable heavenly luminaries from the Sun to the Pole-star illuminate only the three worlds on this side (of the mountain), but cannot penetrate to the other side.

38. This much disposition of the world with reference to its (details of) dimensions, characteristics and relative position has been considered by sages. The whole of the terrestrial globe is calculated as fifty crore Yojanas in extent, out of which the land from Meru to the Lokāloka mountain occupies onefourth (i.e. twelve and half crores of Yojanas).

39. The Lords of elephants viz. Ṛṣabha, Puṣkaracūḍa, Vāmana and Aparājita have been posted in four cardinal points over (and beyond) that (Lokāloka mountain), by the

(ii) VJ. : Oh Lord ! Your form, possessing all auspicious characteristics, is realized by the performance of sacrifices. People adore your being manifested in the form of Brahmā, as distinct from the rest of the world, and absolutely one without a second.

(iii) VC. : *ekānta* : One whose absolute devotion is in the Lord.

Self-born god (Brahmā), the preceptor (or the eldermost one) of the whole of the world. They are the cause of (i.e. have the responsibility of) maintaining the stability and balance of all the worlds.

40. For infusing and increasing the various powers of the elephants and the guardian deities (like Indra) who are (the manifestations of) his own part, and for the welfare of all the worlds around, the glorious Lord, the supremely Exalted Person, the Lord of all great Powers, the Inner Controller (of all), abides on all sides on the great mountain (Lokāloka.) He manifests his form of pure (unalloyed with *rajas* and *tamas*) *sattva* distinguished by (his excellences like) Supreme righteousness, knowledge, renunciation, sovereignty and the great eight-fold mystic powers. With his powerful arms adorned with his superb weapons, he stays surrounded by his prominent attendants like Viśvaksena and others.

41. It seems that the Lord has assumed the above-described form to the end of this Kalpa, for the protection and maintenance of the careers of the different worlds evolved by his *Yoga-māyā* (mystical creative potency).

42. By the extent of the area falling with (i.e. on this side of) the Lokāloka mountain, the extent of Aloka (regions not receiving solar light) which is beyond the Lokāloka mountain, is explained. The sages say that the extremely holy region lying beyond Aloka can be travelled only by masters of Yoga (as was done by Kṛṣṇa to bring back the dead son of a Brāhmaṇa—vide infra Bh. P. X).

43. The Sun is located in the middle position of the great Egg of the universe which is at the centre of the space between the earth and the vault of the sky. The distance between the Sun and the circumference of the universe is twentyfive crore of Yojanas.

44. As the Sun was in this inanimate egg of the universe, he got the epithet *Mārtaṇḍa*. He is also called *Hiraṇyagarbha* as he was born of the golden Egg (of the universe).

45. It is by the Sun really, that the cardinal points, the sky, the celestial region, the earth, regions of pleasure (*bhuvar-loka* and *svar-loka*) and Liberation, the infernal regions and the

nether worlds (e.g. Atala, Vitala etc.) and all others, are divided.

46. The Sun god is the Soul, and the deity presiding over the eyesight of gods, sub-human beings, men, reptiles and plants as well as of all species of living beings.

CHAPTER TWENTYONE

(The Stellar Region) *

Śrī Śuka said :

1. To this extent (viz. 50 crore *Yojanas* diameter and 25 crore *Yojanas* height) has, the disposition of the terrestrial sphere, been described, with reference to its dimensions and characteristics.

2. Experts in this (science) describe the dimensions (etc.) of the heavenly sphere with reference to this (extent etc. of the sphere of the earth, as being symmetrical in dimensions) just as the size etc. of one of the two halves of beans is known from that of the other half. Between the two (the heavenly sphere and the globe of the earth) is the *Antarikṣa* (Intermediate region) which is joined by the two (by the earth from below and the heaven from above).

3. Situated in the centre (of the sky), the glorious Lord of luminaries gives warmth to the three worlds with its heat,

* This chapter deals with the old astronomical ideas current at the final redaction of this Purāṇa. It is a popular statement of a scientific subject. We find similar topics discussed in *Devī-bhāgavata* VIII 5-20, *Matsya P.* 124-128, VP. II. 8-12 and the astrological aspect in *Garuḍa* P. 59-64, *Agni P.* 121 etc. The statements given in these Purāṇas are to be taken broadly, as modern astronomical exactness should not be expected in such works. Thus the increase and decrease in the duration of days and nights and the rate of this variation as given in verse 4 here is roughly correct, though actually it is not so uniform mathematically. Other statements are to be taken in a broad sense. The commentators profusely quote from Purāṇas, Tantras on old astronomy which cannot be summarised here.

and illumines them with its lustre. It proceeds by slow, rapid and regular movements known by the (technical) terms *Uttarāyaṇa* (the period of the Summer Solstice, when the Sun appears moving to the North of equator), *Dakṣiṇāyana* (the period of the winter Solstice, when the Sun moves to the south of equator) and *Vaiṣuvata* (period of Vernal or Autumnal equinoxes), and also in higher, lower and middle positions, according to seasons.

4. When the Sun traverses the signs of *Meṣa* (Aries) and *Tulā* (Libra), the days and nights are of equal duration. When it traverses the five zodiacal signs from *Vṛśabha* (Taurus) to *Kanyā* (Virgo), the days go on lengthening and the duration of the night goes on decreasing one *ghaṭikā* (24 minutes) per month.

5. When it traverses the five signs from *Vṛścika* (Scorpio) to *Mīna* (Pisces), days and nights are in the reverse order (and days go on decreasing and nights increasing).

6. Days go on increasing in duration, till the *Dakṣiṇāyana* begins, while nights do the same, till the commencement of *Uttarāyaṇa*.

7. The learned say that a distance of nine crores and fiftyone lakh *Yojanas* is thus traversed by the Sun in its revolution round the Mānasottara mountain. (They say that) on that mountain, to the east of Meru, is situated the capital city of Indra (presiding deity of the eastern direction), called Devadhānī; to the South (of Meru) is the capital of Yama (the presiding deity of the Southern direction) by name Saṁyamanī; to the West, the city of Varuṇa (the god presiding over the Western quarter), called Nimlocanī; and to the North is the capital of Soma (presiding deity of the northern direction), named Vibhāvarī. When the Sun passes through these cities, there is Sunrise, Midday, Sun-set and Midnight on the four sides of Meru (respectively). These serve as the special time of activity and cessation of activities for living beings.

8. To the dwellers on Mount Meru, it is always the Mid-day. And though the Sun (with its face towards the stellar sphere, actually moves to the eastern direction) with Mount Meru on its left side, it appears (to move to the West and) to keep the Meru on its right (because the wind called

Pravaha which always blows with the Meru on its right, forces the stellar spheres including the Sun which goes from east to west to move in the opposite direction[248].

9. It is said that just on the diametrically opposite side of that point where the Sun rises (or appears in view), it sets (goes out of view). If at any point, it troubles people with heat and makes them perspire, exactly on the opposite side of the point, it makes them sleep (as it is midnight). Those who see it shining (brightly in their place), do not see it when it is at the (diametrically) oppoiste point.

10. When it starts from the capital of Indra, it traverses in fifteen *ghaṭikās* (six hours) the distance of two crores and a quarter, twelve lakhs and a half and twentyfive thousand (i. e. 23775000) *Yojanas*, and arrives at the city of Yama.

11. In this way, it proceeds to the city of Varuṇa, to that of the Moon-god and again to the capital of Indra (all the cities are equidistant). So also, in the stellar region, all planets such as the Moon and others, rise as well as set together along with the stars.

12. In this way, the chariot of the Sun which is the Vedatriad incarnate, covers in a *muhūrta* (48 minutes) a distance of thirtyfour lakh and eight hundred *Yojanas* and travels through the four capital cities (in the abovementioned serial order).

13. It is traditionally said that the chariot has one wheel in the form of a year with twelve spokes (i. e. twelve months), six tyres (viz. six seasons) and three navels (three parts of four months each). Its axle-tree is fixed (at one end) to the top of Mount Meru and the other end is placed on the Mānasottara mountain. Fixed to it, the wheel of the Sun's chariot rotates like the wheel of an oil mill over the Mount Mānasottara.

14. Into that axle, there is another axle-tree measuring onefourth of the first. It is like the axle of an oilpress with its upper end joined to the Polestar.

---

248. *Nakṣatrābhimukhatayā svagatyā Meruṁ vāmataḥ kurvannapi, pradakṣiṇāvartapravahākhya-vāyu-bhrāmyamāṇa-jyotiṣcakra-vaśāt pratyahaṁ dakṣiṇataḥ karoti* —ŚR

15. The seat of the chariot is thirty-six lakh Yojanas in extent. The yoke of the Sun's chariot is of the same extent. Yoked to it by Aruṇa, are seven horses bearing the names of (Vedic) metres (viz. Gāyatrī, Bṛhatī, Uṣṇik, Jagatī, Triṣṭubh Anuṣṭubh and Paṅkti). And they carry the god Āditya (the Sun).

16. They say that, entrusted with the duties of a charioteer, sits Aruṇa in front of the Sun-god, but with his face turned towards the west (i.e. to the Sun-god to show respect).

17. Appointed to sing the Vedic hymns, the sages called Vālakhilyas, sixty thousand in number and of the size of the fourth part of a thumb,—who are placed in front of the Sun—sing the praise of the Sun-god.

18. And other sages, Gandharvas (celestial musicians), *Apsarasas* (Divine damsels), Nāgas (serpents), Yakṣas (demigods), Yātudhānas (demons) and gods—fourteen in all if taken one by one, and seven if taken in pairs—have different and varied names. And they, two at a time, serve the Lord, the Self in the form of the Sun, bearing different names; they perform their several duties and serve the Ātman in the form of the glorious Sun, every month. (For details vide infra 12.11, 33-34).

19. The circumference of the terrestrial sphere is nine crores and fifty lakh *yojanas*. Out of this, he crosses the distance of two thousand and two *yojanas* in a moment.

CHAPTER TWENTY-TWO

(Description of the Moon and other Planets)

The King (Parīkṣit) enquired :

1. Your revered Self has described that while the glorious Solar deity, facing the stellar sphere moves forward (through the signs of the zodiac) with Meru and Pole Star to the left but appears to traverse keeping Meru and the Pole-Star on its

right side (vide supra 21.8). How are we to reconcile (and understand) that statement ?

He (*Shrī Śuka*) *said* :

2. When a potter's wheel is rotating, the movement of ants and other (insects etc.) which dwell on it is quite different (and independent from that of the wheel even though they are carried along with it), for they are found in the different parts of the wheel (even while it is in motion). Similarly, (although) the wheel of Time consisting of constellation of stars, signs of zodiac as a whole, revolves with great velocity, keeping Mount Meru and the Pole-Star to the right, the Sun and other planets depending on it (i. e. the Time-Wheel), their course of movement is also different (from that of the Time-Wheel with which they move); for they are observed in conjuction with different constellations of stars and signs of zodiac (at different times).

3. He (the Sun) is the very same glorious Lord Nārāyaṇa, the First Person (the Prime cause of the universe). He is enquired into by learned sages with the help of the Vedas. For the well-being of the people and for the purification (and timely performance) of ritualistic acts, he divided his body which is an embodiment of three Vedas, into twelve parts. He creates the respective characteristics (such as heat, cold) in the six seasons like the spring etc., for enjoying fruits of Karmas.

4. In this world, people who follow the path of duties prescribed for different classes of society (*Varṇa*) and stages in life (*āśrama*), in the three Vedas, devoutly worship him through different rituals, high or low, as laid down in the Vedas, and through the practice of Yogic meditation with faith, attain the eternal bliss.

5. Now, this Soul of the worlds[249] (or living beings), viz. the Sun moves along the Wheel of Time in the middle of the sky, midway between the earth and the heaven and enjoys twelve months known by the signs of the zodiac as (twelve) divisions of the year. The learned teach that a month consists of two fortnights (one bright and the other dark), or a day and night (of the Pitṛs) or a period required (by the Sun) for traversing two constellations and a quarter in the space

249. Cf. S*ūrya ātmā jagatas tasthuṣaśca*/RV. 1.115.1.

It is (further) instructed that the season (*ṛtu*) is that period (division) of the year in which the Sun traverses one sixth part (of his orbit).

6. And the period which he (the Sun) takes to traverse one half of his path through the sky is called an *Ayana*.

7. The learned have laid it down that the period in which the Sun, with his slow, rapid and moderate motions, completes his circuit in the orbit (through the whole extent of the sky) along with heavenly and earthly spheres, is called *Saṁvatsara*, *Pari-vatsara*, *Iḍāvatsara*, *Anuvatsara* and *Vatsara*. (*Vide Supra* 3.11.14).

8. Similarly the Moon is observed to be a hundred thousand *Yojanas* above the rays (orb) of the Sun. As it is faster in velocity (than the Sun), it goes ahead (of the Sun). It covers in two fortnights the circuit made by the Sun in one (complete) year; in two days and a quarter of that distance which the Sun traverses in a month; and in one day the distance the Sun requires a fortnight to cover.

9. It is by the waxing of its digits in the case of gods and in the waning of its rays in the case of manes that the Moon makes the day and night of gods and manes, by means of its first (bright) and the second (dark) fortnights.[250] The Moon (as the king of plant-life and as such a food-giver) is the very life (-breath) of all species of living beings and (hence is called) the life. He is in conjunction with each of the constellation of stars for thirty *Muhūrtas* (24 hours).

10. And this glorious person comprising of sixteen digits (in his fullness) viz. the Moon, is the presiding deity over

---

250. The construction of the SK. text is significant. It wants to emphasize the Śruti text :

Tasmād āpūryamāṇāḥ pakṣe yajante /

which enjoins worship etc. of gods in the bright fortnight and the injunction *apara-pakṣe pitṛṇām* about the suitability of the dark-fortnight for the worship etc. of the manes. GD. points out the contradiction of the statement 'bright and dark fortnights make the day and the night of gods' in the above verse with that of *supra* 3.11.12. which states 'the *ayanas* are called the day and night of the Svarga'. He reconciles by explaining that the bright fortnight is called the day of gods for it is regarded as suitable for the worship etc. of gods and the dark fortnight as the night of gods due to its unsuitability for worship and other functions pertaining to gods.

the mind, the ruler (and giver) of food and an embodiment of nectar. The sages describe him as one with all, as he is, by nature, the nourisher of the life of all gods, manes, men, goblins, beasts, birds, reptiles, plants and creepers.

11. The Almighty god has placed twentyeight constellations inclusive of Abhijit[251], three lakh *Yojanas* above thc Moon. They are fixed by him on the Time-Wheel. Hence they revolve with Meru on their right side.

12. Above these (constellations) at a height of two lakh *Yojanas*, is observed Venus. It revolves with rapid, slow and even velocity like the Sun, and is found either ahead of or at the rear of or along with the Sun. As it (overcrosses the constellation in the serial order and thus) marches rapidly, it generally brings showers of rain and is always favourable to the world. And (in combination with some other constellations) it is observed to counteract the unfavourable influence of planets (like the Mars obstructing rainfall.

13. The Mercury (Budha) becomes described (in its variations of motions etc.) by the description of the Venus. Budha or the Mercury, the son of Soma (the Moon) is observed to be two lakhs of *Yojanas* above the Venus. It generally sheds beneficent influence. When it surpasses the Sun (and becomes independent), it indicates dangers like stormy winds, cloudy weather, drought and other calamities.

14. Two Lakh *Yojanas* higher up (than the Mercury) (i.e. eleven lakh *Yojanas* higher than the earth) is the Mars traversing each sign of the zodiac in three fortnights, it completes its revolution through the twelve signs, unless it takes retrograde course. It is an inauspicious planet in general portending evil.

15. At a height of two lakh *Yojanas* above the Mars is the glorious Bṛhaspati (Jupiter). Unless it takes to retrograde course, it moves through each sign of the zodiac in one year. It is generally favourable to Brāhmaṇas.

16. The Śanaiścara (the slow-mover i.e. the Saturn)

---

251. ŚR. notes that this constellation is supposed to be on the conjunction of the Uttarāṣāḍhā and Śravaṇa constellations. It is supposed to be an independent constellation due to its astrological implications. In his support, he quotes a Śruti passage : *Abhijin nāma nakṣatram upariṣṭād Aṣāḍhānām adhastāc Śroṇāyāḥ* /

is observed to be two lakh Yojanas above Bṛhaspati (Jupiter). Lingering for thirty months in one house of the zodiac, it takes as many (thirty) years to complete its revolution through all the signs of the zodiac. It generally portends evil and anxiety to all.

17. At a height of eleven lakh *Yojanas* from the Saturn are seen the (seven) sages (the *Ursa Major*). Always contemplating (and wishing) the good of the world, they go round the most exalted region of Viṣṇu, keeping it to their right.

CHAPTER TWENTY-THREE

(*Description of Viṣṇu-pada*—the position of Dhruva *and Siśumāra Cakra*)

Śrī Śuka said :

1. Now at a height of thirteen lakh *Yojanas* above the *Ursa Major*, lies what they call the highest abode of Viṣṇu. Here dwells the Supreme Votary of the Lord Dhruva, the son of Uttānapāda. The stars presided over by Agni, Indra, Kaśyapa Prajāpati and Dharma respectfully go round him keeping him on their right,—all moving simultaneously (as stars). He is still the support of those whose span of life is upto the end of a *Kalpa* (till the time of deluge).

2. He (Dhruva) alone shines perpetually as he is decreed by God to support like a post all the hosts of luminaries, planets, constellations of stars, etc. which are set in motion by the ever vigilant almighty Time of incomprehensible velocity.

3. Just as oxen, employed in treading ears of corn, are tied to the post in the middle of the threshing ground, with strings short, long and medium in length, walk round in their respective spheres in three circles (at a distance of short, long

and midway between the two according to the length of the string with which they are fastened), similarly posts of celestial bodies, planets etc., fastened to the Wheel of Time in the inner circle or in the outer circle, and impelled by the Wind (called *Pravaha* in supra 21.8), and with Dhruva (the Polar Star) as their support (central pivot), go on revolving to the end of the *Kalpa*, in three courses (marked by the periods of *Uttarāyaṇa* or northerly course, *Vaiṣuvata* i.e. along with the equator and *Dakṣiṇāyana* or Southward course). Just as clouds and birds like hawks with the support of air and piloted by their past actions move about (afloat) in the sky, similarly, the host of these heavenly luminaries which are *jīvas* which are favoured with those shining bodies by the union of matter and spirit and whose velocities (and directions of motions) are controlled by their past actions, do not fall to the ground.

4. Some persons describe this system of heavenly luminaries as being supported by the mystical Yogic powers of Lord Vāsudeva who has assumed the form of a Gangetic porpoise.

5. The Pole-star is located at the end of the tail of this porpoise that lies coiled with its head downward. (Just below it) on the tail are located the four stars called Prajāpati (the sage Kaśyapa) Agni (the Fire-god), Indra (the King of gods) and Dharma (the presiding deity of righteousness). At the root of the tail, are fixed the star, Dhātā and Vidhātā, and the Seven Sages (the *Ursa Major*) on the hip; on the right side of its body which coils from left to right are located the fourteen constellations of Stars (from *Abhijit* to *Punarvasu* which mark the northern course (*Uttarāyaṇa*) and the fourteen constellations marking the Southern Course (*Dakṣiṇāyana*)—viz. from the *Puṣya* to *Uttarāṣāḍhā*—are located on its left side. This is just like the porpoise whose coiled body has equal number of members on its either side. (He mentions further details of the positions of the constellations:). On its back is the Ajavīthī (the group of constellations called Mūla, Pūrvāṣāḍhā and Uttarāṣāḍhā) and the heavenly Ganges (the Milky Way) is at its belly.

6. (The constellations) *Punarvasu* and *Puṣya* are located on its right and left loins; *Ārdrā* and *Āśleṣā* on its right and left

hind-legs; *Abhijit* and *Uttarāṣāḍhā* on its right and left nostrils; *Śravaṇa* and *Pūrvāṣāḍhā* at its right and left eye respectively while *Dhaniṣṭhā* and *Mūla* are at its right and left ears. (The group of) eight constellations beginning from *Maghā*, which mark the Southern Course (*Dakṣiṇāyana*) are located on the ribs of its left side while the eight constellations from *Mṛgaśirṣa* (the Orion) and others marking the northern course (*Uttarāyaṇa*) are on its ribs on its right side, but in the reverse order (i.e. from *Pūrvābhādrapadā* to *Māgaśirṣa*). One should locate the remaining two, viz. *Śatabhiṣā* or *Śata-tārakā* and *Jyeṣṭhā* on its right and left shoulders.

7. (One should locate) the star *Agasti* on its upper chin and (the star called) *Yama* on its lower chin; the Mars in the mouth and the Saturn on its generative organ and the Jupiter on its hump, the Sun on its chest and *Nārāyaṇa* at the heart; the Moon in the mind; the Venus in the navel, the pair of Aśvinīkumāras on the nipples (of its chest), the Mercury in its inhalation and exhalation, (the shadow-planet) Rāhu at the throat and Ketus at all members of the body and the (remaining) stars all over the hairs of its body.

8. This is verily the manifestation of the form of glorious Lord Viṣṇu consisting of all gods. Silently and with concentration of mind one should watch it every evening and adore it with the following Mantra :

"We bow to the Supreme Personage, the Lord of all gods, (who assumed the form of) the Time Wheel, the support of all heavenly bodies, We meditate upon him."

9. This form of the Supreme God embodying all planets, constellations of stars and other heavenly luminaries washes off the sins of those who repeat the above Mantra three times (morning, mid-day and evening) a day. The sin committed in the past, present and future of a person who bows to him or remembers him three times a day is destroyed immediately.

CHAPTER TWENTY-FOUR

(Rāhu's Position and the Subterranean Regions)

Śrī Śuka continued :

1. According to some (experts in *Śāstras*) at a distance of ten thousand *Yojanas* below the Sun, Rāhu makes his revolution like a lunar mansion. Though himself a wretched Asura, a son of Siṁhikā, it was through the grace of the Lord that he attained the status of a planet, even though he did not deserve it. We shall describe his birth and deeds later on (in the VI and VIII Skandhas), Oh child.

2. They say that the sphere of the burning Sun is ten thousand Yojanas and that of Rāhu, thirteen thousand Yojanas. Rāhu continues to entertain a grudge against the Sun and the Moon since their interruption (in his opportunity of drinking nectar by exposing his demonic identity), and attacks them on full-moon and new-moon days.

3. Having come to know of it, the venerable Lord has deployed his favourite missile called Sudarśana by the sides of them both. Rāhu stands for a period of Muhūrta facing the discus of irresistible blazing splendour which constantly revolves round them (the Sun and the Moon). Overcome with sorrow, trembling with his heart full of fear, he goes back even from a distance. It is this occurrence that people call an eclipse.

4. Below that (region of Rāhu), at a distance of the same (ten thousand) Yojanas, lie the regions of Siddhas, Cāraṇas (Heavenly singers) and Vidyādharas (celestial artists).

5. Below these is the space serving as a sporting ground of the hosts of Yakṣas, demons, goblins, spirits (*pretas*) and ghosts. It extends downwards to the level where the wind blows or the clouds are met with.

6. Below that, at a distance of one hundred yojanas lies this earth up to the height to which the prominent birds such as swans, vultures, hawks, eagles and others are soaring.

7. Description of the earth with respect to its situation and arrangement (of its continents etc.) has already been

given (to you). Below the earth there are seven sub-terranean regions, each at a distance of ten thousand *Yojanas* from the other, and equally so (ten thousand *Yojanas*) in length and breadth. (Their names are :) Atala, Vitala, Sutala, Talātala, Mahātala, Rasātala and Pātāla.

8. In these subterranean regions are veritable heavens. Therein reside Daityas, Dānavas and Serpents (sons ef Kadrū) in extremely rich mansions, gardens, parks and play-grounds which surpass the heavenly world in their exuberance of sensuous enjoyments, affluence, joy and richness. They are householders whose affectionate wives, children, relatives, friends and servants always enjoy a highly delightful life. Their desires are never thwarted even by the lord of gods. They divert themselves with their skills in Māyā (miraculous powers).

9. Oh great King! Maya, (the architect) of miraculous powers has built cities in these regions. They (the cities) shine resplendent with wonderful mansions, defence-walls, gates, town-halls, temples, big quadrangles and houses constructed with excellent precious-stones of various types, and with palatial buildings of the lords of these subterranean regions, the terraces of which are teeming with couples of Nāgas (serpents) and Asuras (demons) and with pigeons, parrots and *sārikās*.

10. The gardens thereof also superbly excel the splendour of the land of gods, with their glorious beauty, giving delight to minds and senses :—Beauty of trees embraced by tender creepers, the branches of which (trees) are weighed down with clusters of flowers and fruits and lovely foliage of ponds and lakes full of translucent waters teeming with couples of various species of birds; (these are charmingly vocal) with the varied sweet warblings of birds that have made their homes in the beds of lilies, lotuses, Kalhāra—blue and red lotuses—and lotuses with hundred petals, in the water of those lakes (etc.) when they (waters) get agitated by the leaping of fishes—all these provide feast to one's senses.

11. It is said that here (in this netherworld) no fear is noticed (to have been caused) due to the divisions of time such as day and night.

12. The crest jewels on the hoods of great serpents dispel all the darkness there.

13. Due to the intake of herbs, saps, elixirs, food, drinks and bath of miraculous efficacy, the inhabitants of these regions do not suffer from mental worries and physical ailments. They are immune from wrinkles, grey hair and old age. Nor are they affected by paleness of body complexion, bad bodily odour, perspiration, fatigue, nervousness or bodily changes due to age (from childhood to old age).

14. These blessed souls have no fear of death from any source except from the Lord's power, called the discus (Sudarśana), the Lord's might.

15. When it (Sudarśana) enters those regions the embryos in the wombs of Asura women are miscarried or aborted through sheer terror.

16. Now in region called Atala resides the demon Bala, the son of Maya. The learned say that he has verily created ninetysix varieties of Māyā (magical tricks) some of which are still practised by jugglers. As he yawned, three groups of women—*svairiṇīs* (who enter into sexual intercourse with men of their caste), *kāminīs* (who copulate with men not belonging to their caste) and *Puṁścalīs* (the most fickle minded of the Kāminī group)—came forth from his mouth. They administer a liquid preparation called *Hāṭakarasa* to a man who enters their subterranean region and make him sexually capable. They give him amorous pleasure at their will indeed, by their sportive seductive smiles, lovely conversations, embraces, etc. When the elixir is imbibed, the man feels that he is a veritable god endowed with mystical powers and possessing the physical strength of ten thousand elephants. He goes aboasting like one mad (blind) with intoxication.

17. Below that (*Atala*), in the subterranean region called Vitala, dwells god Śiva, designated as Lord Hāṭakeśvara, surrounded by his retinue, the legions of goblins. With the object of multiplying the creation of Prajāpatis (proginators) he, under the name Bhava (the procreator), remains united with his divine consort, Bhavānī (Pārvatī). From him has issued the great river called *Hāṭakī* which is charged with the energy of them both. There, the Fire kindled by Wind, drinks

vigorously that water of the river. What is spit out by Fire is the gold called *Hāṭaka.* Males and females in the harem of the kings of Asuras wear that gold in the form of ornaments.

18. Below that (*Vitala*), in the region called *Sutala,* lives (the demon king) Bali, the son of Virocana of wide fame and hallowing renown. He was deprived of his sovereignty over the three worlds by Lord Viṣṇu who, with a desire to oblige the great god Indra, was born of Aditi and approached Bali, in the form of a dwarf celibate (*Brahmacārin*). It was by the Lord's grace that he was accommodated here, and is again blest with overflowing wealth and prosperity not possessed by Indra and others. Immune from all fears he even now continues to propitiate the most adorable Lord by performing his righteous duties.

19. It is not at all the direct result (fruit) of the donation of land (viz. three worlds) that Bali was blest with the sovereignty and fortune in the subterranean world : the gift that was duly given with absolute faith and devotion, with utmost reverence and perfectly serene mind to the glorious Lord Vāsudeva, the Supreme Soul, the principle of life and the inner controller of all species of living beings, the holiest and the most worthy recipient who has ever approached. Bali's donation was thus a gate-way directly leading to liberation (*Mokṣa*).

20. (The learned sages say) that if a person who while losing his control (and becoming helpless or unconscious) utters but once his name while sneezing, falling or tumbling down or in any such condition, he instantaneously cuts asunder the bonds of Karma, for removing which people desirous of attaining to the Final Beatitude, try various other means (except remembrance of his name and are not successful).

21. The sovereignty, prosperity etc which implies mere worldly pleasure—*viṣayānanda*—cannot be the fruit of the bestowal of the Land, viz. three worlds on the Lord as it was given to the Lord as being his own Self—the Lord who is the Self of all beings and who dedicates his own Self to his devotees and to those who have realized him.

22. As a matter of fact, the Lord has not really confer-

red any favour on him[252] (i.e. Bali). He extended to him sovereignty, pleasures of senses which are of illusory nature and which, on the contrary, deprive him of the constant remembrance of Himself. (But Viṣṇu's presence near him as a door-keeper is the real fruit).

23. It is quite well-known that when it was found by the Lord that there was no other alternative (to deprive Bali of his sovereignty of the three worlds), He adopted the pretext of begging (three paces of land for sacrifice). When Bali was deprived of the sovereignty of three worlds (and had nothing with him) except his body, and was securely bound down with the cords of Varuṇa and was thrown into a mountain-den, he (Bali) actually exclaimed the following words:

24. "It is a pity that Indra, learned as he is, is certainly incapable of knowing his real interests—This Indra who has appointed the sage Bṛhaspati as an advisor to counsel him in all matters, ignored him[253], and instead of requesting for the service of the Lord (Upendra) begged for himself through the Lord (Vāmana or Upendra) my blessings viz., the sovereignty of the three worlds. (When the Lord is pleased, he is to be sought and not the worthless kingship of three worlds). Of what value is this Lordship of three worlds which terminates at the end of a *manvantara* which is quite an insignificant part of Time which is of infinite duration.

25. (Only my grand-father Prahlāda knew his real interest) for though after his father's (Hiraṇyakaśipu's) death, he was offered by the Lord (*Nṛsiṁha*) the throne of his father which had no danger from any quarters (then), my grand-

---

252. *amuṣya*—this vague pronoun has confused the commentators. VC., VD., GD. think that this implies Indra and the translation will be : "Nor did the Lord confer any real favour on Indra, for he extended to him......himself". Though ŚR. mentions no name after *amuṣya*=*amum* "him", his quotations from Parāśara.

Vāsudeve mano yasya japa-homārcanādiṣu /
tasyāntarāyo Maitreya, Devendratvādikam phalam //

probably hints at Indra which VD., VC., SD., GD. endorse. I think that in the present context *amuṣya* refers to Bali as interpreted by VR., J.G., & BP. as it is a continuous discussion about Bali. I however concede that *amuśya*=Indra is not impossible though rather out of context.

253. VD. : Even that Bṛhaspati is not clever inasmuch as he did not advise Indra properly and etc.

father (Prahlāda) preferred his service only to the throne as he knew that it was something different from the Lord.

26. He (Prahlāda) was a noble Soul while a person like me has his passions unsubsided, nor is blessed with the grace of the Lord. How can such a person hope to approach the path trodden by him (Prahlāda)?"

27. His (Bali's) history will be narrated to you in details later on (in the VIII Skandha). At his (Bali's) door, the glorious Lord Nārāyaṇa, the Preceptor of the whole world (who hence deserves to be adored and not to be made to stand guard), whose heart is full of compassion for his devotees, stands with a mace in his hand. (It was) by him that Rāvaṇa (the ten-headed demon) who came there in the course of his expedition of conquering all the quarters (of the world), was kicked away to a distance of ten crores of Yojanas, simply by his toe.

28. Below that region (*Sutala*), in *Talātala*, dwells the king of Dānavas, by name Maya, the Lord of three cities. His three cities having been burnt down by the venerable Lord Śiva (the destroyer of the enemy cities or of the demon Tripura), with the desire to bring about the happiness of three worlds, he secured this position through his (Śiva's) grace. This great master of all experts in magic is protected in every respect by the great god (Śiva) and hence, being free from the fear of Sudarśana (Viṣṇu's discus), he is greatly respected (by the inhabitants of Talātala).

29. Below that, in the subterranean region *Mahātala*, there lives the tribe of many-hooded serpents called *Krodhavaśa*. Their prominent members are Kuhaka, Takṣaka, Kāliya, Suṣeṇa and others, all possessing huge bodies. They, however, live in fear of Garuḍa (the over-Lord of kings of birds), the vehicle of the Supreme Person. It is on a few occasions that they sport in company of their wives, children, friends and members of their families.

30. Lower still, in *Rasātala*, there dwell the descendants of Diti and Danu (the two wives of Kaśyapa, the proginator), called Paṇis who are also known as Nivātakavacas, Kāleyas and the residents of Hiraṇyapura. These enemies of gods are from their very birth, very powerful and daring in spirit. They live

like reptiles in holes as their arrogance of power is subdued only by the refulgent discus Sudarśana of the glorious Lord Hari whose majestic splendour spreads over all worlds. It is traditionally learnt that they are afraid of Indra due to the Vedic text uttered by the female dog, Saramā, the messenger of Indra[254].

31. Still lower down is the region called Pātāla. With Vāsuki as their king, there reside the chiefs of the Nāga (Serpent) race like Śaṅkha, Kulika, Mahāśaṅkha, Śveta, Dhanañjaya, Dhṛtarāṣṭra, Śaṅkhacūḍa, Kambala, Aśvatara and others possessing extensive hoods and extremely impetuous by temperament. It is reported that the big effulgent crest jewels on the hoods of serpents possessing five, seven, ten, hundred and thousand heads, dispel by their splendour the mass of darkness in the hollow of the nethermost world (*Pātāla*).

CHAPTER TWENTYFIVE

(*Description of Saṅkarṣaṇa—the Serpent Śeṣa*)

Śrī Śuka said:

1. At the lowest extreme below Pātāla, at a distance of thirty thousand *Yojanas*, abides a part-manifestation of the Lord which is dominated by the *Tamas* only. It is also well-known as Ananta. Followers of the Sātvata School call it Saṅkarṣaṇa as, being characterised by ego and presiding over by 'I'-ness, it brings about the unification between the subject (the Seer) and the object (the seen).

2. This terrestrial globe, supported on one out of the thousand heads of the Lord who manifested himself as Ananta, appears like a mustard seed.

---

254. ŚR. mentions the Vedic legend that when the Paṇis stole the cows and concealed them under water, Indra sent the female dog Saramā to trace them. She discovered them but when Paṇis tried to have a treaty type of understanding with her, she cursed them : *Hatā Indreṇa Paṇayaḥ Śayadhvam*—"Oh Paṇis ! Lie down (dead) slain by Indra !"

3. It is said that when He desires to withdraw (destroy) this world at the (predestined) time, from between his agitated eyebrows knit in wrath, yet charming, was manifested Rudra (god of destruction) called Saṅkarṣaṇa (one born of Saṅkarṣaṇa). He manifested his eleven forms, each three-eyed and holding a trident.

4. When the kings of serpents along with prominent devotees (Sātvatas) bow down with intense and unswerving devotion (his feet), they certainly look with an overjoyed mind, their most attractive faces with cheeks beautified with the splendour of their refulgent ear-rings, in the reddish, spherical nails, shining like rubies, on his pair of lotus-like feet.

5. Seeking blessings from him only, they say, that unmarried Nāga princesses besmear with pigment of *aguru*, sandal wood and saffron, his bright, long, fair-complexioned, beautiful, charming arms like silver-pillars, beautifully set up in the sphere of his beautiful body. Their minds being agitated with the touch of his body, they put on winsome smiles as the god of Love stealthily enters their hearts. They really cast bashful glances at his lotus-like face as his reddish eyes swim with inebriation and cast a merciful glance at them.

6. He is that very glorious Lord Ananta, the ocean of infinite excellences, the primeval Deity. Restraining the vehemence of His impetuosity and wrath (as it is inappropriate and unnecessary for the maintenance of the worlds), he abides for the well-being of all the worlds.

7. He is being contemplated upon by hosts of gods, demons, reptiles (Nāgas), Siddhas, Gandharvas, Vidyādharas and sages. Due to continuous exhilaration under intoxication his eyes were swimming restlessly. He was giving delight (lit. feeding) the leaders of His attendants and gods with his nectar-like winning speech. Clad in blue garments and wearing only one ear-ring, he has placed his blessed, beautiful hand on the top of (his special weapon) the plough. Just as the majestic elephant (Airāvata) of the great Indra is decorated with a girth of gold, the glorious Lord of gracious and beneficient deeds wears his *Vanamālā* (a wreath of forest flowers) called *Vaijayantī*[255], the

255. *Vaijayantī* wreath consists of the shoots of the *Tulasī* (Basil) plant, flowers of *Kunda, Mandāra, Pārijāta* and lotuses.

charm and gracefulness of which was heightend with the melodious humming of the bees inebriated with the sweet scented honey of fresh and new Tulasī blossoms of unfading beauty.

8. When this (Saṅkarṣaṇa) (as traditionally described by one's spiritual guide) is listened to and meditated upon, he enters the hearts of those who seek Liberation (from Saṁsāra). He instantly cuts asunder the knot of ignorance (avidyā), fored at (his devotee's) heart, due to the impressions created in the sub-conscience by the beginningless *karmas* and consisting of the attributes (or modes of Prakṛti) viz. *sattva*, *rajas* and *tamas*. The venerable sage Nārada, the son of god Brahmā, accompanied by Tumburu (the famous celestial singer), described (in a musical composition his glorious prowess, in the assembly of god Brahmā.

9. Who can comprehend the way[256] (the truth) of the Lord (who is Brahmā himself)—the Lord by whose glance (i.e. desire to create) *sattva* and other attributes of Prakṛti[257] which are respectively the cause of the creation, preservation and destruction (of the universe) became capable (of executing their function); whose form is eternal (infinite) and beginningless, for One as he is, he contains in himself the universe characterised by many-ness.

10. Out of unlimited grace for us, he assumed a form consisting of (pure) *sattva* unalloyed with *rajas* and *tamas*, wherein appears the unmanifest and manifest[258] universe. The Lord who possesses unbounded energy like a lion, exhibited his faultless sports (e.g. creation of the universe etc.) for attracting the minds of his devotees.

Tulasī-Kunda-Mandāra-Pārijātāmbujais tu yā
Pañcabhir grathitā mālā Vaijayantīti kathyate ||

256. *vartman*—(i) The truth about—ŚR.
(ii) The working of—VJ.
(iii) The reality about or the way of attaining to—VC., GD.

257. VR., BP. note that the factual order implied herein is *rajas*, *sattva* and *tamas* as the creation, maintenance and destruction of the universe are mentioned in a series in the text.

258. *Sadasad* (*idam*) : (i) Intelligent and unintelligent—VR.
(ii) Subtle and gross—VJ.
(iii) Manifest and unmanifest.

11. Even if a person either in distress or fallen from the righteous path accidentally or in joke utters his name as heard (from the spiritual teacher or any other person), he instantly annihilates completely the sins of (other) men. Hence to whom else than the glorious Lord Śeṣa, will a man desirous of Liberation, resort?

12. On one of the heads of the thousand-headed Lord lies like an atom, the terrestrial globe with all its mountains, rivers, seas and the living beings (inhabiting it), owing to the infiniteness of the immeasurable and innumerable exploits of the Almighty Lord, who can, even if endowed with a thousand tongues, hope to count completely all his herioc acts?

13. Of such prowess is the glorious Lord Ananta. His energy and excellent attributes and potencies are limitless. Unsupported by anyone else, he stays at the bottom of the earth bearing it easily for the preservation and wellbeing of the entire creation.

14. These are, verily, the regions to be attained to by people desirous of enjoying pleasures. These are created to accord with their respective *karmas*. These are described to you as it was traditionally taught to me (by my preceptor).

15. Oh King! I have described to you according to your queries, these various, high and low regions attained by men as a fruit of the *karmas* performed by them. On what other topic should I discourse now?

CHAPTER TWENTY-SIX

(Description of Hells)

The King enquired:

1. Oh great Sage! How is it that there is such a diversity (in regions attained to by people) in the word?

The Sage (Śrī Śuka) replied:

2. The courses (and results) of *karmas* are varied according to the faith of the performer of the action which

differs according to the (dominance of) particular mode of *Prakṛti* (e.g. *sattva*, *rajas* and *tamas*) influencing him.[259] All these are attained (at different times) by everyone (in more or less degree according to the influence of a particular *guṇa*).

3. Thus in the case of perpetrators of unrighteous atcs of a prohibited character, the fruits according to them are of dissimilar nature according to the variety of the faith of the perpetrator. Now we shall describe in details (some prominent states out of) the thousands of hellish states which are the results of the (commission of) prohibited sinful acts committed by those who indulge in desires (of various kinds) due to the influence of *avidyā* (ignorance) dominating them from time immemorial.

The King asked:

4. Are the infernal regions some particular parts of this world ? Or are they somewhere outside the worlds or are they somewhere in the space inside these worlds ?

The Sage (*Śrī Śuka*) *replied*:

5. They (the infernal regions) are within the three worlds. They lie in the Southern direction below the earth and above the waters. And in this direction reside the groups of Pitṛs (manes) called Agniṣvātta and others. Meditating on God with utmost concentration, they continue to invoke auspicious blessings on their descendants.

6. It is reported that it is really true that the venerable, king of the manes (*pitṛ*), Yama (son of the Sun-god) who never violates any command of the Lord, dwells here along with his retinue. And to the departed souls brought to his region by his messengers he inflicts punishments in proportion and according to the gravity of the sin committed.

7. Some learned have enumerated that there are twentyone—hellish regions. Oh King, I shall now serially describe them to you according to their name, form (or function) and character (nature of the sin expiated.) They

259. Cf. the characteristics of the *sāttvic*, *rājasa* and *tāmasa* acts (BG. 18.23-25) and the three types of the performers of acts (BG. 18. 26-28).

are as follows: Tāmisra, Andha-tāmisra, Raurava, Mahā-raurava, Kumbhī-pāka, Kāla-sūtra, Asipatra-vana, Sūkara-mukha, Andha-kūpa, Kṛmi-bhojana, Sandaṁśa, Tapta-sūrmi, Vajra-kaṇṭaka-śālmalī, Vaitaraṇī, Pūyoda, Prāṇa-rodha, Viśa-sana, Lālābhakṣa, Sārameyādana, Avīci and Ayaḥ-pāna. Moreover, (there are seven in addition) viz., Kṣāra-kardama, Rakṣogaṇa-bhojana, Śūlaprota, Daṇḍaśūka, Avaṭa-nirodhana, Paryāvartana and Sūcimukha. These twentyeight infernal regions are the places where (*jīvas* are subjected to) tortures of various kinds.

8. The person who takes away another person's wealth, children or wife, is certainly bound down with mortal cords of death and is forcibly hurled into the Tāmisra hell by the terrible servants of Yama. In that hell of utter darkness, the being is subjected to various kinds of torment such as denial of food and water, belabouring with cudgels, holding out threats, and ultimately overcome with torment he instantaneously drops down unconscious.

9. In the same way, a person who enjoys the wife (property etc.) of another person by deceiving him, is thrown into the Andhatāmisra hell. Here the embodied being who is subjected to tortures loses his sight and consciousness due to torments, just like a tree the roots of which are being cut down. Hence they call this hell 'Andha-Tāmisra' due to its blinding effect.

10. Verily, he who wrongly identifies his body with his Soul and regards his wealth (wife etc.) as his own and every day contributes to the nourishment and comforts of his family by maliciously treating other beings, falls, after leaving his body etc. in this world, into the Raurava hell due to the sin (perpetrated in his malicious dealings).

11. The creatures which have been tortured and killed by him in this world, are born in the world as Rurus and while he (their murderer) undergoes torments inflicted by Yama, kill him in the same way (as done to them by him). *Ruru* is the name of a creature much more cruel than a serpent. Hence this hell is called Raurava.

12. Similar is the hell called Mahāraurava. He who is given solely to the nourishment of his body by any unscru-

pulous means etc.) enters this hell. Here the Rurus are *Kravyādas* (carnivorous, flesh-eaters) which kill him for the sake of his flesh.

13. In the hell, called Kumbhīpāka, the servants of Yama fry in boiling oil that hard-hearted man who cooked living beasts or birds in this world and was censured for his cruelty even by cannibals (or demons).

14. He who bears malice towards his parents, Brāhmaṇas and the Vedas is hurled into the hell called Kālasūtra. It is a plain of a copper-sheet ten thousand *Yojanas* in area. The sheet of copper is heated by fire from below and the Sun from above. The creature is being burnt within and outside his body by hunger-thirst. Due to restlessness, he sometimes sits, sometimes lies down and rolls and sometimes stands up and begins to run about. Thus he suffers for as many thousand years as there are hair on a beast's body.

15. They (servants of Yama) throw in the hell called *Asipatravana* (a forest of trees with sword-like leaves) a person who, while in this world, abandons his Vedic way of life even when there was no calamity and embraces a heretic sect. They strike him with a whip. And while he runs hither and thither (to avoid whipping), all the limbs of his body are cut down by the two-edged sword-like leaves of the palm trees thereof. Crying with excruciating pain, "Alas ! I am killed", he falls in a swoon at every step. A renegade from one's own faith he reaps the fruit (punishment) suitable for the sin of embracing a heretic creed.

16. In this world, verily, a king or a king's servant inflicts punishment on those who did not deserve it (being innocent), or subjects a Brāhmaṇa to corporal punishment, that sinful fellow falls into the hell Sūkaramukha in the next world. While his limbs are being crushed with very powerful hands like a sugarcane (in a crusher) in this world, he laments in a piteous tone and sometimes he becomes unconscious like innocent persons confined in jail by him (while) in this world.

17. But a person whose course of life in this world is prescribed by God and who is capable of understanding agony caused to others, causes pains to creatures whose feeding upon

human bodies is determined by God but which are incapable of being aware of causing pains to others, falls into the hell *Andhakūpa*. He is hated and troubled there by beings like beasts, deer, birds, reptiles, mosquitos, lice, bugs, flies and others. Being harassed on all sides in the darkness, his sleep and mental peace are disturbed. Being devoid of rest, he wanders in darkness even as the *jīva*, the embodied soul, lives restlessly in a diseased body.

18. A person who, without performing five daily great sacrifices[260] (prescribed for a householder) eats whatever comes to his lot without sharing that with others (stranger-guests, his elders, dependents etc.) is spoken of as (comparable to) a crow. After his death, he falls in the most wretched hell called *Kṛmibhojana*. There he is born as a worm in a pool of worms, of hundred thousand Yojanas in extent. Being himself preyed upon by worms, he continues to feed himself on worms. He who thus enjoys his earnings without offering (a portion of it) to others or to gods, subjects himself to these torments for as many years (one hundred thousand) as the Yojanas of the extent of that hell or till his sin is expiated.

19. He who, in this world, without being in (a justifiable) emergency or calamity, steals or robs by force the gold, jewels etc, of a Brāhmaṇa or of any other person, gets the skin of his body cut with red-hot iron balls or tongs by the servants of Yama in the other world, Oh King.

20. To a man who indulges in a sexual intercourse with a woman whom he should not have approached or to a woman who does so with a man unworthy of such an approach, the

---

260. The following are the 'great sacrifices' enumerated in the *Manu-smṛti* 3.70-71 :

(1) *Brahma-yajña*—Propitiation of ancient seers-ṛṣis by teaching and learning of the Vedic lore

(2) *Pitṛ-yajña*—Propitiation of one's forefathers by offering libations of water or *Pitṛ-tarpaṇa*.

(3) *Deva-yajña*—Propitiation of gods by offering oblations in sacrificial fire.

(4) *Bhūta-yajña*—Offering a portion of one's meals to sub-human creatures.

(5) *Nṛyajña*—Sharing one's food with a stranger who by chance comes to the door for food or shelter (*atithi-pūjana*).

servants of Yama lash them with a whip and make the man or woman embrace the red-hot iron image of that woman or man respectively.

21. He who (indiscriminately) indulges in sexual intercourse with all (including sub-human beings) is placed on a silk-cotton tree with thorns of adamants in the hell (called *Vajra-kaṇṭaka Śālmalī*) in the next world, and is dragged (down on those thorns).

22. Those persons who are born as Kṣatriyas or officers of king who are of noble descent (and have joined the heretic sect) transgress the bounds of religion, fall into the (river) Vaitaraṇī after death. Those transgressors of the restrictions (laid down) in religion are being bitten (eaten) by the aquatic animals of that river which forms the moat of the infernal regions. They are not disunited with the Soul but are sustained with life by their sins. Remembering the result of their sin, they continue to be tormented in the river which carries a flood of excretion, urine, pus, blood, hair, nails, bones, fat, flesh and marrow.

23. Those who (though born in higher caste but) keep low-caste women, neglect purity, righteous conduct and self-discipline and shamelessly lead a beastlike life, fall after their death in (the hell called *Pūyoda* which is) a sea full of pus, excretion, urine, phelgm and dirt and eat nothing but these most detestable things.

24. The Brāhmaṇas and others who keep a pack of hounds and donkeys, find delight here in hunting and kill animals on occasions other than those prescribed in the *Śāstras*, become, after death, targets of the discharge of arrows by the servants of Yama who pierce them with arrows (in the hell named *Prāṇa-nirodha*).

25. Verily those hypocrites who kill beasts in sham sacrifices in this world, fall in the *Vaiśasa* hell in the next world. There the Lords of that hell torture them and finally cut them to pieces.

26. The sinful twice-born (*dvija*) who, being blind with passion makes his wife of his own caste drink his semen, is thrown in the next world in a stream of semen (in the *Lālābhakṣa* hell) and is made to drink semen.

27. In this world the dacoits (who loot the property of others), perpetrators of arson and poisoning—be they kings or king's servants and soldiers—plunder villages or caravans of merchants, servants of Yama (in the form of) seven hundred and twenty hounds with teeth like adamant voraciously eat them up when they die (and enter the *Sārameyādana*).

28. Again, a person who utters any lie at the time of deposing evidence, money-transactions (e.g. barter, sale, purchase) or donating a gift, enters after death a supportless hell called *Avīcimat.* In that hell, he is hurled down headlong from a (steep) mountain top one hundred Yojanas in height to a place with rocky surface appearing as water. Hence, it is called *avīci-mat* (A place with hard surface but appearing like water with ripples). His body is shattered to very small pieces but he does not die. He is again taken up and hurled down.

29. If a Brāhmaṇa or his (Brāhmaṇa) wife or anyone who has taken a sacred vow, drinks wine through mistake or if a Kṣatriya and a Vaiśya (who are not eligible to drink Soma) drink the Soma juice, they are taken to the hell (called *Ayaḥ-pāna*) where, the servants of Yama, pressing a foot on their bosom pour molten iron into their mouth.

30. If a person belonging to the lowest strata of the society does not duly pay respect to those that are superior in birth (heredity), performance of austerities, learning, righteous conduct, caste and stage of life, out of esteem for himself, he is as good as a dead (while alive). After death, he is hurled down with head downwards into the hell called *Kṣāra-kardama* where he is subjected to endless tortures.

31. (When) men who, in this world, verily propitiate (gods like Bhairava) by offering human sacrifice and the women eat the human victim so offered, the human beings so sacrificed become a battalion of demons (Rākṣasas) in the region of Yama (in the hell called *Rakṣo-gaṇa-bhojana*). There Rākṣasas torture their former slayers in many ways, cut them into slices with their axes like butchers, drink their blood, dance and sing merrily just as those who ate them (as human victims) did on the earth.

32. Those persons who, in this world, attract by means

of allurement innocent people in the forests or in villages and inspire confidence in them to come near and then torture them in various ways by transfixing them on an iron pike or by binding them with ropes even though they strongly desire to survive—such (cruel) persons after death, at the time of being tortured by Yama (in the hell called *Śūlaprota*) are transfixed on iron pikes. When they are distressed with hunger and thirst, they are attacked and pecked on all sides by hellish birds like Kaṅka, Vaṭaka of sharp beaks. It is then they remember their own sins.

33. Those people who are of a ferocious nature like serpents, torment other beings in this world, they fall even after death in a hell called *Dandaśūka* where serpents with five and seven hoods (mouth) approach them and devour them like mice.

34. Those who actually confine living beings in dark holes, granaries or caves in this world, (the servants of Yama) in the other worlds shut them up into similar places (in the *Avaṭanirodhana hell*) full of poisonous fire and smoke.

35. A householder who in this world often gets angry with and looks with burning eyes at the guests who have arrived at his door, gets his sinful eyes forcibly plucked out by birds of adamantine beaks like vultures, crows, *kaṅka Avaṭa*.

36. If a person, in this world is proud of his wealth and full of egotism, looks askance at others and is suspicious about all, and if his heart and mouth are withered by the anxiety of the expenditure or loss of that wealth and if, without any peace of mind he guards his treasure like a goblin, after death he becomes transformed into a devil for he accumulates sin in earning, supplementing and preserving wealth. He falls into a hell called *Sūcīmukha.* There the servants of (Yama-) dharma, like tailors, stitch the body of this devil-like protector of wealth, on all sides.

37. Oh Protector of the earth ! There are hundreds and thousands of such and the like hells in the abode of Yama. Some of them have been described here and some are not. All persons following an unrighteous path, enter into them in due course. Similarly, those who follow (the path of) religion

enter elsewhere (in the heaven). They are again reborn to this world with some balance of sin and merit with them.

38. The path of *Nivṛtti* (cessation from worldly activities) has been propounded to you in detail at first[261]. Of this extent is the Brahmāṇḍa (egg-shaped universe) which is divided into fourteen regions in the Purāṇas. It is the grossest form of the glorious Lord Nārāyaṇa, the Supreme Person. It comprises of the attributes of his Māyā (viz. *sattva*, *rajas*, *tamas*). He who full of faith and devotion reads, listens to and recites to others this account as narrated by me, begets in him faith, devotion and pure intelligence and realizes the incomprehensible Supreme Self.

39. Having listened to the gross as well as the subtle form of the glorious Lord, a self-controlled person, after successfully concentrating the mind on the gross form, should gradually comprehend the subtle form by his intelligence.

40. Oh King! In this way the disposition of the world with its divisions (*dvīpas*), sub-divisions (*Varṣas*), the rivers, mountains, the sky (aerial region), the seas, the nether-world, the subterranean regions, the quarters and the hells as well as the heavenly bodies and various regions have been described to you by me. It is the gross form of the Lord, the asylum of all species of beings.

---

261. Viz. *Vaiśvānaraṁ yāti* etc. in Supra 2.2.24—ŚR.

SIXTH SKANDHA

CHAPTER ONE

(*The Story of Ajāmila*)

The King (*Parīkṣit*) *said* :

1. The path of cessation from *karmas* (*nivṛtti*) has been already described in detail, by your respectable self, in the beginning.[262] By that path, Brahmā (i. e. the region of Brahmā) is gradually attained through different stages[263] (such as passing through the abode of fire-god etc.). The Liberation is attained along with god Brahmā.

2. And (you have also described in detail)—the path characterised by worldly activities (*pravṛtti*), the object of which is to attain happiness in heaven and other pleasures which are themselves the product of *guṇas*[264] and which, in the case of *jīvas*, not disassociated with *Prakṛti*[265], results in constant re-embodiment of the *jīvas* for repeated enjoyments of such pleasures.[266]

3. The various infernal regions which are characterised by unrighteousness (as their cause) have been described in detail (in the fifth Skandha). And the first period of Manu, (presided over and hence) named after Svāyambhuva Manu, has also been described (in the fourth Skandha).

---

262. *Vide Supra* 2.2.24 in *Vaiśvānaraṁ yāti* and 3.32.5 in *Ye svadharmān na druhyanti*.

263. *Karma-yoga* : (i) Through the path of action (*Karma*), knowledge (*Jñāna*) and devotion (*Bhakti*)—VR.

(ii) Remembrance of the Lord, visualization of the various members of the Lord's Person and visualization of the full divine form—VJ.

(iii) Birth in a good family, residence at a holy place, association with saintly persons (S.D.)

(iv) *dhyāna* (contemplation), *dhāraṇā* (concentration) and *samādhi* (realization of identity with Brahman.) GD.

264. *traiguṇyaṁ svargādisukhaṁ tadeva viṣayaḥ prāpyaṁ yasya—ŚR.*

265. *alīna-prakṛteḥ—avinaṣṭa prakṛti Sambandhasya/—VR.*

266. *guṇa-sargaḥ—bhogārthaṁ dehārambha-rūpaḥ* (*yo mārgaḥ*)—ŚR.

4-5. The dynasty of Priyavrata and Uttānapāda and the life-stories of (both of) those kings (have been narrated by you). You have also described the (division of the earth in important) island-continents (*dvīpas*), their subdivisions (*varṣas*), oceans, mountains, rivers, gardens, the disposition of this spherical earth with reference to its divisions, their special characteristics and dimensions and also those of heavenly bodies and subterranean regions, as they were created by the Almighty Lord.

6. Oh illustrious holy sage ! Now be pleased to explain in detail, the way which may save a man from falling into the infernal regions of various unbearable tortures.

Śri Śuka said :

7. If a man does not perform expiation (as prescribed in the *dharma śāstra*), in this very life, for the sin committed by him with his thought, word and deed, it is said that he definitely goes to the hellish regions after death. And those regions of severe tormentations have been described to your honoured self by me.

8. Hence, before one is overtaken by death and not incapacitated in body (or while one is not entangled in difficulties) one should immediately (after the commission of the sin), try to atone for the sin, with a controlled mind, according to the gravity or simplicity of the nature of the fault, just as a physician expert in diagnosis of the disease, promptly adopts remedies or dosage of the medicine (according to the nature of the disease).

The King said :

9. In spite of the full knowledge that (commission of) a sin is against his interest as evidenced by what he has seen (viz. punishment meted out by the king for an offence) and has heard (for example internment in hellish region as described in Purāṇas), he loses the control over himself, commits it repeatedly after the act of expiation. Hence (under these circumstances), how can there be any (real) expiation at all, if the tendency to commit sins, persists.

10. Sometimes he refrains from committing a sin; on

other occasions, he does it again. Hence, I think that the act of expiation is meaningless like the washing of an elephant (which besmears its body with dust again after washing).

Śrī Śuka said :

11. It is not laid down that there is the total and final annihilation of sin by the action of expiation (such as bodily mortification), for only the ignorant (i.e those who wrongly identify body with the Soul) are eligible for it. (But as the ignorance about the Soul and non-Soul—*avidyā*—is not dispelled, the particular sin may be atoned for, and the man again relapses into sinful ways). Knowledge (i.e. self-realization) alone is the real expiation (as it removes the ignorance—*avidyā* which is the real root-cause of the sin).

12. Just as diseases do not attack a person who eats only wholesome food, (on the contrary they recede gradually if they had already affected that person), a person who observes regular spiritual discipline (e.g. penance) becomes, step by step, eligible for the *summum bonum* (which annihilates sin and leads to realization of the self), Oh King.

13-14. Through concentration of the mind and sense-organs, practice of (eightfold) celibacy, the control of the mind and external organs, charitable gifts, truthfulness, purity (both bodily and mental), the vows of non-violence etc. and observances like *japa* (muttering the sacred syllable OM), the wise (who bear with equanimity the pairs of opposites like pleasure and pain) who understand (real principles of) righteousness and are full of faith, rid themselves of the most grievous sin committed by thought, word or action, just as the fire destroys even a big cluster of bamboos.

15. Just as the Sun completely dispels the mist, a few persons absolutely devoted to Lord Vāsudeva, annihilate their sins thoroughly (from its very root of *avidyā*) merely through their unswerving devotion to the Lord (without performing penance etc. But the number of such devotees is scarce).

16. Oh King ! A sinner is not purified to that extent through performance of penance and expiatory acts as a person who has dedicated his life to Lord Kṛṣṇa (and regards Kṛṣṇa as

his last resort, without worrying over the punishment in hell) does so by rendering service to his devotees.

17. Certainly this path (of devotion) is the correct and the best one in this world, as it is blissful (annihilating all miseries), and quite safe (with no danger or fear from anything). Kindly-disposed and desireless devotees of Lord Nārāyaṇa are found on this path (to help one in need, but there is nobody to do so in the paths of knowledge and action).

18. Oh King of Kings! Performance of all acts of expiation do not thoroughly purify a person who has set his face against Lord Nārāyaṇa, even as all the rivers (taken together) cannot purify a pitcher of wine.

19. Those who have even once in their life here, set on the lotus-like feet of Lord Kṛṣṇa, their mind which felt an attachment for (and not knowledge or complete comprehension of) his excellent qualities, have by this (very temporary attachment and devotion) performed all expiatory acts. And they never see Yama (god of death) or his servants with a noose in their hands, even in their dreams.

20. And on this topic, the learned one narrate (by way of illustration) this ancient legend consisting of a conversation between the messengers of Viṣṇu and those of Yama. Listen to it from me.

21. In (the city of) Kānyakubja (modern Kanauj), there lived a certain Brāhmaṇa called Ajāmila. He married a maid-servant and got polluted through his association with a female slave, and he neglected the pious way of life (including the religious duties prescribed for a Brāhmaṇa).

22. He maintained his family by adopting a reproachful way of life consisting of holding captives for ransom, gambling, committing frauds and thefts. That sinful fellow tortured creatures (before killing).

23. A long period consisting of eighty-eight years of his life thus elapsed in maintaining himself that way, and fondling the children of that Dāsa woman.

24. The old fellow (Ajāmila) had ten sons (by that woman). The youngest of them was a boy named Nārāyaṇa. He was extremely doted over by his parents.

25. He (Ajāmila) had set his heart on that sweet lisping child. The old man was highly delighted while witnessing the child's plays.

26. Bound by filial love for child, he used to feed it while he was eating, make it drink at the time of his drinking. In this way, the fool did not know that the hour of his death had arrived.

27. Thus, the ignorant Ajāmila led his life. When the time of death actually arrived, he thought of his young son called Nārāyaṇa.

28. (Then) he saw that three extremely terrible male figures with wry faces, and with the hair on their bodies standing erect, and with nooses in their hands, had come to take him away.

29. With his senses greatly agitated, he called out in a prolonged loud voice, his son named Nārāyaṇa who was absorbed in his play-things at a distance.

30. Having heard the repetition of the name of Lord Hari, their master, uttered by the dying man, the servants of Nārāyaṇa immediately rushed forward, Oh great King.

31. Angels of Viṣṇu (intercepted and) forcibly stopped the messengers of Yama who were dragging (the *jīva* of) Ajāmila, the husband of the maid-servant, from the interior of his heart.

32. Thus prevented (from carrying out their duty) the messengers of Yama demanded, "Who are you who thus defy the order of Yama, the god presiding over righteousness.

33. Whose servants are you ? Whence have you come ? Why do you prevent his being taken away ? Are you gods or demigods or are you some prominent Siddhas ?

34. (Please do not get offended for our ignorance about you). All of you have eyes like lotus-petals, wear yellow silken garments and are adorned with diadems, ear-rings and shining lotus garlands.

35. You are all in the full bloom of youth. All of you possess four beautiful arms. (Each of) you appears majestic with (your lustrous) bow, quiver, sword, mace (*gadā*), conch, discus and lotus.

36. By your personal splendour, you dispel darkness

from all quarters and out-shine the lustre of others. Why do you prevent us, the obedient servants of Yama, the protector of the moral law?"

Śrī Śuka said :

37. When the obedient servants (who execute the commands) of Lord Vāsudeva were asked thus by the messengers of Yama, they laughed heartily, and replied as follows to them, in a voice deep like the thunder.

The Messengers of Viṣṇu replied :

38. If you are really the executors of the orders of the King of Righteousness, tell us what is the true nature of righteousness and what is the distinguishing character of Dharma.

39. How (on what principles) is punishment given? What (who) is regarded as the proper object? Who deserve punishments? Whether all of them are punishable or some of them?

Servants of Yama replied :

40. What is ordained in the Vedas is *dharma* or righteousness. What is against the prescription of the Vedas is *a-dharma* (*un*-righteousness). We have heard it traditionally said that the Vedas are Nārāyaṇa incarnate and they, being the breath (flowing out naturally from the nostrils) of the Lord[267] are self-existent.

41. It is the Lord (Nārāyaṇa) by whom all these living beings which are constituted of the attributes *sattva*, *rajas* and *tamas* and which are severally discriminated and distinguished by their qualities (e.g. quiescence), designations (Brāhmaṇa, Kṣatriya etc.), activities (study, teaching etc.) and forms (social classes, stages of life—*varṇas* and *āśramas*), are supported properly in his own Form (Being).

42. The Sun-god, the Fire-god, the Sky, the Wind-god, cows, the Moon-god, the twilights, days and nights, cardinal points, the presiding deities of Water and the Earth, Time and (the god) Dharma—all these are the witnesses (of the acts) of the embodied beings.

267. Cf. *asya mahato bhūtasya niḥśvasitam etad yad Ṛgvedaḥ* /

43. (Acts of) unrighteousness as evidenced by these is judged to be the proper reason for awarding punishment. All the perpetrators of (evil) actions deserve punishment according to the nature of their acts.

44. Oh sinless ones! Actions, meritorious or sinful are being done by active persons as they are associated with attributes (like *rajas*, *tamas*). For nobody invested with a body can be actionless.

45. The same person enjoys the fruit of the same sinful or a meritorious act in the next world in the same manner and to the same extent according to the manner and extent to which that (sinful or meritorious) act has been done by him in this world.

46. Oh great gods! (As you know it by your omniscience) Just as here (in this world) there is found a three-fold variety[268] in living beings due to the diversity in the peculiar qualities (or mixtures of *sattva*, *rajas*, and *tamas* attributes exhibited in their pious, sinful or mixed acts), the same may be inferred about them in the next birth[269]. (Otherwise such a diversity cannot be explained).

47. Just as the present period of time is the index of the characteristics of the other periods that precede and follow it[270], similarly the present life (of human beings, prognostically) indicates the righteous and sinful actions committed in the past and (likely to be committed) in the future existences as well.

48* Staying in his own capital (Saṁyaminī), the god Yama-dharma clearly visualizes by his mental power, the pre-

268. ŚR. states that this is the *arthāpatti* (circumstantial inference) to explain re-birth. He explains the three-fold variety as follows :

1) of quiet, ferocious or dull nature.

2) experiencing a happy, miserable or mixed type of life.

3) of righteous, vicious or mixed nature.

According to VJ., they are the best, worst and middle types of beings according to dominance of guṇas—*sattva*, *tamas* and *rajas*.

269. In the next world.—VR.

270. Just as the present season, e.g. the spring indicates the characteristics regarding flowers, fruits etc. of the past and future Spring-seasons.—ŚR., VJ.

*(i) ŚR. : The Inner Controlling Self (*antaryāmin*) staying in the city in the form of body etc.

(ii) VR. thinks that this verse refers to the Supreme Soul who stays as *antaryāmin*.

(iii) VJ. : Lord Nārāyaṇa staying in the body of the living beings, sees the past and future form, as also the merits and sins of the *Jīva*.

vious form (e.g. god, sub-human being or the merits, sins etc.) of the *jīva* (departed Soul), and deeply reflects what the *jīva's* future state should be, by his reasoning capacity; for his Lordship is omniscient like god Brahmā,

49. Just as a sleeping person in the dream-state regards that he is identical with the body manifested in the dream, and does not know his body in the pre-dream state or the body to be assumed in the next dream, similarly the ignorant *jīva* conditioned by *avidyā* knows his present body as manifested by the actions of his previous existence and not the previous form assumed in the past incarnation nor the future body (of his future existence) due to the loss of memory of his past lives.

50. With five conative organs, the *jīva* carries out his (physical) functions (e.g. locomotion, exchange); with five cognitive senses, he perceives (knows) the five objects of senses. The single *jīva*, the seventeenth, combined with the sixteenth, i.e. the mind[271] experiences all alone, three-fold objects presented by the cognitive senses, conative organs and the mind.

51. This subtle-body (*liṅgam*) constituted of the sixteen parts (enumerated above) and possessing three potencies (of the attributes *sattva*, *rajas* and *tamas*) is beginningless. It continues to hold down a man in *saṁsāra* which gives him joy, grief, fear and sufferings.

52. The ignorant embodied being who has not subdued the group of six (viz. five cognitive senses and the mind is forced (by his subtle body) to perform actions despite his unwillingness. Like a silk-worm covering itself in its cocoon, he covers (entangles) himself in the net of *karmas* and fails to see the way out.

53. Verily, nobody can ever remain actionless even for a moment; for everyone is helpless and is forced to do some act by passions like attachments etc. born of (the three) attributes (viz. *sattva*, *rajas* and *tamas*) which are the results of the impressions of past actions.[272]

(iv) SD. : It is the Supreme God (*Parameśvara*) abiding in the body yet unaffected by birth etc. connected with the physical body, dispenses the fruits of merits and sins through god Yama and he never interferes.

271. And the other fifteen constituents are the ten sense-organs, five subtle *bhūtas* forming the bases of objects of senses—ŚR.

272. This is *verbatim* the same as BG. 3.5

54. With *avyakta* (unmanifested destiny—*adṛṣta*) as the instrumental cause, the gross physical body and the subtle *liṅga-śarīra* are formed. According to the powerful impulses of the *jīva*, he becomes moulded like his mother's form or like his father's personality.

55. This contrary state of the *Puruṣa* (viz. involvement of the (*puruṣa* into *saṁsāra*, miseries suffered despite the Soul's blissful nature, due to his false identity with his body) was due to the contact with *Prakṛti*. It (this contact) dissolves completely within a short time through his devotion to God.

56. This (Ajāmila) was really studied in the Vedic lore; (was) the very abode of good nature, righteous conduct and virture; was a strict observer of vows, gentle, self-controlled truthful, master of mystical formulae, pure (both in mind and body).

57. He used to serve his preceptors, the sacred fire, the guests and elderly relatives advanced in age. He was untouched by pride (full of humility), a friend to all living beings, a man of few words; he was a saintly person, not jealous of anyone.

58. One day, this Brāhmaṇa who obediently used to carry out his father's orders, went to the forest. He returned therefrom taking with him fruits, flowers, sticks for sacrificial fire and *Kuśa* grass.

59-60. On his way back, he saw a certain shameless, libidinous Śūdra who had drunk wine (called *Maireya*—distilled from meal) in the company of a harlot whose eyes were also swimming due to intoxication. With that woman who was standing by him, with the knot of her *Sari* loosened (hence in a semi-naked condition), the shameless Śūdra was courting, and singing and joking nearby.

61. Seeing her embraced in arms which were erotically painted with unguents, Ajāmila was instantaneously infatuated and succumbed to passionate love.

62. Despite his attempts to control himself with all (the power of) his reasoning capacity and scholarship, he was unable to stabilize his mind and calm down his heart, which was agitated by the god of Love.

63. Being possessed by the devil in the form of passionate

desire for her, he lost (the balance of) his mind. Brooding over her in his mind, he desisted from performing his prescribed religious duties.

64. With his entire ancestral property, he tried to propitiate her by vulgar carnal pleasures (appealing to her) so that she may be pleased with him.

65. The sinful fellow whose judgment was paralysed by the side-glances of that wanton woman, soon abandoned his regularly wedded young Brāhmaṇa wife who was born in a good family.

66. This stupid fellow (after squandering his ancestral property) got money from any place, by fair means or foul, and maintained the family of this woman (now his housewife).

67-68. Inasmuch as this fellow violated all the Śāstric injunctions and led a licentious life censured by noble persons, and lived a sinful life for a long time in an impure condition and eating dirty (polluted by a harlot's touch) food, we (servants of Yama-dharma) shall therefore carry this sinner who did nothing for expiating his sins, to the presence of Yama (the god wielding the rod of punishment). There he will get purified through (undergoing the prescribed) punishment.

CHAPTER TWO

(*Exposition of the Bhāgavata Dharma*; *Efficacy of the Lord's Name and Ajāmila's Ascension to Viṣṇu-loka*)

Śrī Śuka said :

1. Having thus carefully heard the exposition addressed (to them) by the messengers of Yama, the angels of Lord Viṣṇu who were pastmasters in philosophy and ethics, replied to them, Oh King.

The messengers of Viṣṇu said :

2. Oh What a pity ! Injustice (or unrighteousness) influences the assembly of those who should see through (the real

nature of (righteousness. There, punishment is wrongly inflicted by these (custodians of righteousness) on persons who are not sinners and do not (hence) deserve it.

3. To whom can created beings go for a shelter, if injustice particularly enters into their fatherly protectors and teachers like rulers who are expected to be well-disposed, righteous and impartial?

4* Whatever a superior person does is emulated by other common people. Whatever he sets up as a standard or regards as an authority the masses (ordinary people) follow it.

5. A common man, like unto a brute, does not understand, of his own accord, what is righteousness and unrighteousness. Placing his head confidently on the lap (of a fatherly protector like Yama-dharma), he sleeps resting without any anxiety.

6. How is it proper that if the latter is really deserving of confidence of all beings and has some compassion (and scruples), he can be so treacherous to one who has completely surrendered himself in faith, and cherishes friendship, and is unaware (verging on unconsciousness).

7. That this man (Ajāmila), even in a helpless stage uttered the name of Hari which (not only expiates sins but) leads to the Final Beatitude, has atoned for all the sins committed by him even in crores of his past incarnations.

8. For, by the very act that he uttered the four syllables NĀ—RĀ—YA—ṆA (while calling his son 'Oh Nārāyaṇa come'), this sinner has already completely atoned for all his sins.

9-10** A thief, a wine-drinker, perpetrator of treachery to one's friend, a murderer of a Brāhmaṇa, one who violates his preceptor's bed (i.e. has illicit relation with one's preceptor's wife), the slayer of a woman, a king, a parent or a cow and other types of sinners—to all these sinners, the utterance of the name of Viṣṇu is the most effective expiation, for Lord's

* A verbatim quotation from BG. 3.21.

** VR. and VC. write long discourses on the importance of God's name which may be read in the original. V.J. points out that the condition precedent is that the name of the Lord is to be uttered with ardent devotion.

mind gets attracted to the sinner uttering his name (or the sinner's mind is attracted to the Lord).

11. A sinner is not so thoroughly purified to that extent, by performing the expiatory acts and observances of vows prescribed by the masters of the Vedic lore (like Manu and others), as by the utterance of the mere syllables of the names of Hari (without adding 'I bow to'), as his name is suggestive of the excellences of the glorious Lord. (The effect of Lord's name does not exhaust and disappear immediately after dispelling the sin as is the case with the penances like *Kṛcchra* and *Cāndrāyaṇa*.[273]

12. For if the mind again runs (is attracted) to the evil path even after going through the process of expiation, that act of atonement is not thorough (in destroying sin). For those who desire to annihilate (the effects of) their (sinful) acts, repeatedly extolling the merits (by uttering the names) of Hari is the sure remedy, as it (actually) purifies the mind.

13. Hence, do not carry him (the *jīva* of Ajāmila) by the wrong way (the sinner's path leading to Yama's abode). He has completely expiated all his sins. (When even a syllable of the Lord's name is sufficient to annihilate all sins), he has uttered the complete name of the Lord when he was about to die (and there is no time and hence possibility of committing a sin after articulating the Lord's name).

14. (As to the objection that Ajāmila called his son and and not Viṣṇu, Viṣṇu's messengers explain). The experts in *Śāstras* say that utterance of the Lord's name even if taken to denote another person, or in a friendly joke or as an insertion during the recitation of a song, or in (an outward, apparent) disrespect[274], completely annihilates all sins.

15. If a person unconsciously (and involuntarily) utters the Lord's name (Hari or any other) while he falls, tumbles down, gets maimed, is bitten (by a serpent), heated (by fever etc.) and struck (by a stick), he does not deserve to be tormented in hell.

16. (Proportionately) heavy (difficult) and easy processes of atonement for sins of grievous and light natures have

273. VC. adds—This is the omnipotence of the Almighty Lord.

274. But real disrespect for God's name is a great sin.

been thought over and laid down by the great sages (like Manu and other writers on the *Dharma-Śāstra*). (But there is no such differentiation in case of Lord's name, as by merely remembering Lord Viṣṇu, one is absolved of all sins).

17. Those (different kinds of) sins are washed away by the austerities, charitable acts, mutterings (of prayers or *mantras*) and such other (expiatory) processes. But the heart of the sinner (or the subtle residual forms of the sins called impressions or *saṁskāras*) are not thereby purified. Even that is achieved by the service of the feet of the Lord. (All the sins are annihilated by the very name of Hari, but *vāsanā* or the impressions unconsciously left on the mind by past actions are wiped out by the vision of Lord Viṣṇu—the Great Man etc.).

17a*. This Dharma, characterised by the repetition of the name of the Lord, is the highest and the ancientmost, and has been thus laid down. If practised, it purifies the mind day by day, like clothes washed on every day.

17b*. As the individual soul (*jīva*) has no independence in relation to the acts he performs, the expiatory acts cannot completely purify the *jīva's* mind (due to his dependence on God's will). Desisting from forbidden acts, he should therefore worship Hari by continuous singing and repetition of his name.

18. Irrespective of a man's knowledge or ignorance (about the efficacy and potentiality of the Lord's name for purifying thoroughly all the sins), if Lord Viṣṇu's name is sung or muttered repeatedly, it burns down all the sins of man, like fire (even though ignorantly thrown by a child on a heap of fuel) burns the fuel completely.

19. Just as a medicinal drug of the highest potency, even though taken by chance, without being aware of its efficacy, is bound to show its remedial effects, similarly the sacred formula (*mantra*) consisting of the Lord's name, even when muttered by chance, without knowing its highest purificatory power) shows its efficacy (in annihilating all sins). (Inherent power or potency does not require faith etc. in showing its efficacy).

---

*17a & 17b are additional verses in VJ's text.

*19a. Oh messengers (of Yama)! If you still entertain any doubt about the righteousness (of this), you consult (enquire) with your Lord, for the glorious god Yama knows the most secrets of (what is the real) *Dharma*.

Śrī Śuka said :

20. Oh King! Having thus logically and convincingly explained the path of the Lord (the *Bhāgavata dharma*) and after liberating him (Ajāmila's *jīva*) from the noose of Yama, they (Viṣṇu's messengers) got him released from (the clutches of) Death.

21. The messengers of Yama who were thus (discomfited and) expelled, approached god Yama and faithfully reported the whole matter to King Yamadharma, Oh vanquisher of enemies!

22. Being completely extricated from the noose of Yama, the Brāhmaṇa overcame his fear, and became his own former normal self.[275] Feeling delighted at their sight, he bowed to the servants of Viṣṇu with his head.

23. Perceiving that he was desirous to speak to them, the servants of Lord Viṣṇu instantaneously disappeared on that very spot, while he (Ajāmila) was (simply) looking on, Oh sinless King.

24. Ajāmila also heard separately from the conversation of the messengers of Yama and of Viṣṇu (Kṛṣṇa), the (ritualistic) Dharma as propounded in three Vedas and based on *guṇas* as the fruit of this Dharma, viz. celestial pleasures are a product of *guṇas*), and also the Pure Dharma pertaining to (and consisting of absolute devotion to) the Lord, and transcending the three *guṇas*.

25. Having heard the great glories of Lord Hari, he immediately conceived earnest devotion to the Lord. Remembering his evil past, he felt deeply remorsed.

26. "Alas! How extremely deplorable it was of me who could not subdue my (lower) Self, and procreating myself in the form of sons from a Śūdra woman, I have desecreted my Brahminhood.

---

* An additional verse in the text of VR. and VJ.

275. Resumed his previous pious way of life.—VJ.

27. Fie upon me who am condemned by good people as a sinful wretch, a dark stigma on my family—I who abandoned my virtuous young wife, and went to an unchaste wench given to drinking.

28. Alas! An ungrateful vile fellow that I am, I have forthwith deserted my supportless, poor, aged, afflicted parents who had no relative to protect them.

29. I, who am of that nature, shall obviously fall into that terrible-most hell wherein lustful violaters of the path of righteousness undergo tortures inflicted by Yama.

30. Was this a dream or was it a reality that I witnessed a miracle here? Where have the noose-bearers who dragged me (out of my body) today, gone now?

31. Again, where have gone those four beautiful-looking Siddhas (demi-gods) who released me while I was being taken noose-bound, down to the subterranean (infernal) regions?

32. In spite of my being a wretched person (in this birth), there must have been some auspicious (deed done in previous birth) inasmuch as I had the vision of those foremost gods and due to which my mind feels serene and peaceful now.

33. Otherwise (but for such auspicious acts in my previous birth) the tongue of an impure, sinner like me who kept a Śūdra woman, could be capable of uttering, at the time of death, the name of Lord Viṣṇu.

34. Oh! What a contrast between a shameless rogue and a sinner like me! I have violated (destroyed) my Brāhmaṇahood and the auspicious name of the Lord 'Nārāyaṇa'.

35. Though I be such, I who have controlled my mind, cognitive and conative organs and breath, shall endeavour that way whereby I shall not plunge myself in the blinding darkness in the form of transmigration of the Soul.

36. Having freed myself from the bonds (for household and relatives) due to *avidyā* (wrong identification of the body with the Soul), lust (for enjoyment of pleasures) and actions (binding the doer to this world and the next), I shall be a friend to all beings, serene, friendly, compassionate and self-controlled.

37. I shall liberate myself who am completely possessed

by Lord's Māyā in the form of a woman (my Śūdra keep) by whom, wretched as I was, I was made to dance and play like a deer kept for amusement.

38. Having given up the notion of 'I' and 'mine' with reference to my body, (belongings, property etc.) and with my thought concentrated on the real substance, I shall fix my mind on the Lord. My mind has been purified by singing of the name of the Lord (and other modes of *bhakti*)."

Śrī Śuka said :

39. In this way, through a moment's association with the pious (servants of Viṣṇu), he felt a thorough aversion to worldly life (and its pleasures) and freeing himself from all ties (to his mistress, children and property), he proceeded to Gaṅgādvāra.

40. Settling down in that sacred place (the abode of God), he betook himself to (the path of) Yoga. He withdrew (from worldly pleasures) all his senses and organs, and concentrated his mind on the self.

41. Then, he dissociated his self from (the product of) the *guṇas* viz. the body, sense-organs etc., and by concentrating his mind, he fixed it on the Supreme Brahman, which is the essential form of the Lord and is the embodiment of consciousness, and bliss.

42. When his mind and intellect were thus (thoroughly) stabilised in the Brahman, the Brāhmaṇa visualized before him those very male figures (messengers of Viṣṇu), and recognizing them as those as having been seen before, he stood up and bowed down his head (to pay respect).

43. After that vision, he cast off his body at the sacred place (Haridvāra) in the Gaṅgā and immediately assumed the (angelic) form of the attendant of the Lord.

44. Along with the servants of Lord Viṣṇu, the Brāhmaṇa ascended the heavenly car made of gold and proceeded through heavens to the abode of the Lord of Śrī (i.e. Viṣṇu).

45. (Ajāmila), the husband of the maid-servant (of a low caste), who had thereby deluged (violated) all religious duties and flouted his vows (of fidelity to his wife etc.) and had (thus) fallen from Brāhmaṇahood by his reprehensible acts (like stealing) and was consequently being hurled into the hell

(by Yama's servants), was released (from the noose of Yama) the very moment he uttered the name of the Lord.

46. There is no better efficacious remedy to cut down the roots of sin, for persons wishing *Mokṣa* (Liberation from *Saṁsāra*) than the continuous chanting of (the glories and) the name of the Lord of hallowing feet (god Viṣṇu). By having recourse to remembrance (and repetition) of the Lord's name, the mind is not attached again to acts (*karmas*); but by any other (expiatory) acts (except the chanting of the Lord's name) it becomes tainted with *rajas* and *tamas*.

47-48. He who listens with deep faith and reverence this esoteric legend which is capable of destroying (all) sins and he who devoutly recounts it (to others), never, verily, goes to hell, nor is even eyed by the servants of Yama. Howsoever inauspicious (and sinful) the mortal may have been (in this world) he is greatly honoured in the region of Viṣṇu.

49. By (merely) calling out the name of Hari addressed to his son at the time of his own death, (even a sinner like) Ajāmila attained to Lord Viṣṇu's abode. What should be said of a person who takes his name with faith and devotion. (He would certainly ascend to Viṣṇu's abode).

CHAPTER THREE

(*Yama explains Viṣṇu's greatness*)

The King asked :

1. What did the god Dharmarāja (Yama, the presiding deity of righteousness), to whose authority this world is subject, and whose order was thus flouted by the servants of Viṣṇu (Murāri) reply to his servants, on hearing their report of that incident ?

2. Oh Sage ! The quashing of the penalty or order of god Yama was never heard of at any time or from any person. It is my firm conviction, Oh Sage, that nobody else than you, can clear this doubt in the popular mind.

Śrī Śuka said (in reply):

3. Oh King! The servants of Yama whose attempts (to execute Yama's order) were foiled by the messengers of Viṣṇu represented to their Lord Yama, the master of the city of Saṁyaminī.

Yama's messengers said :

4. Oh Lord! How many controllers are there of the world of living beings who perform three types of action (meritorious, sinful and mixed)? And how many are there who can dispense (lit. are the cause of the manifestation of) the fruits thereof?

5. If there be a number of rulers invested with the powers to dispense justice (lit. wielding the rod of punishment) who would (i.e. nobody would) suffer death, i.e. the result of sin leading to hell or enjoy nectar (i.e. the fruit of merit conferring celestial happiness) [in case these rulers of the world disagree], and who would not suffer both, i.e., hell and heaven, (in case they agree, one condoning an act and conferring heavenly bliss, and the other condemning the same act and dispensing suffering in hell, and both consenting to each other's decision).

6. (It may be argued that there is no hitch, if several rulers dealing severally with the acts of these large numbers of beings are postulated. But in the case of postulating a plurality of rulers for dealing with vast numbers of beings engaged in multifarious activities, rulership will be (reduced to) nominal formality like that invested in tributary princes under an emperor (the real absolute ruler being different).

7. (Due to the untenability of plurality of controllers) you are, therefore, (according to us) the only one Supreme ruler of all beings including the gods. You are the sole controller and the judge to decide the good and evil actions of beings and the dispenser of reward and punishment (lit. wielder of the rod of justice to award heaven and hell).

8 Such as you are, your authority (lit. awarding of punishment) is null and void and has ceased to exist in the world today; for your order has been superseded (lit. tricked off) by four wonderful Siddhas (demi-gods).

9. While, in compliance of your order, a sinner was being taken by us to the torture-houses (infernal regions), they perforce cut asunder your nooses (fastening the sinner) and liberated him.

10. As soon as the word 'Nārāyaṇa' was uttered (by the sinner), they hastened in saying, "Do not be afraid". So we wish to know from you who they are, if you think it is in our interest to know them (otherwise by showing disrespect to them through ignorance, there may be a trouble to you).

Śrī Śuka said:

11. Thus enquired, god Yama, the controller of all created beings was pleased, and calling upon mentally, the lotus-like feet of Hari, replied to his messengers.

Yama said:

12. Quite different from me is the Supreme Ruler of the mobile and immobile creation. (Who transcends it. As his servant, I control the mobile beings, especially the human beings among them and more especially the sinners among men, while he is the Supreme Ruler of all). Into him the universe lies woven warp and woof, like a piece of cloth. It is from his parts (*aṁśas* viz, gods Brahmā, Viṣṇu and Rudra) that the creation, sustenance and destruction of the universe take place. The whole world remains under his perfect control like a bullock controlled by a string pierced through its nostrils.

13. Just as one keeps bullocks tethered together to a long rope, he binds people to his word (viz. the Vedas) by designating them (into classes as Brāhmaṇas, Kṣatriyas etc.) and prescribing to each his respective duties. These people who are thus tightly regulated by their denominations and duties are afraid of him and bear him worship (by scrupulous performance of their prescribed work).

14-15. I (and the guardian deities of other cardinal points like) the great Indra, Nirṛti, Varuṇa, the Moon-god, the Fire-god, God Śiva, the Wind-god, as also the Sun-god, Brahmā, the (twelve) sons of Aditi (the monthly rotational solar presidents during a year), the Viśve-devas, the (eight) Vasus, demi-gods called Sādhyas, the (fortynine) Wind gods, the group of (eleven) Rudras along with the Siddha tribe of demi-gods, and other progenitors of the universe (like Marīci), rulers of gods (i.e. ruler-like highly respected persons like Bṛhaspati), Bhṛgu and others who are not tainted with *rajas* and *tamas*—all these though dominated by the attribute *sattva* but are touched (deluded) with his Māyā do not understand his intentions—What of others? (Others can never fathom it).

16. *Jīvas* (individuals) verily cannot visualize him or comprehend him by means of their cognitive senses, mental faculties or vital breaths (which actuate the conative organs) or by means of speech (or Śāstras composed of words) even though he exists within their hearts and pervades them all (as the inner controller), even as the forms (which are the objects of the sight) cannot visualize the faculty of vision (which reveals them). He is beyond them all.

17. Generally, the messengers of Hari, the Supreme Soul, the self-dependent Supreme Ruler, the transcendent Lord of the Māyā go about in this world. They have attractive personalities and the same form, attributes and disposition as of their Lord.

18. The messengers of Viṣṇu are worshipped by gods. Their most wonderful forms cannot be easily perceived. They protect the mortal devotees of Viṣṇu from enemies, from me and from all (sides and people) as well.

19. The (secret of the) doctrine as enunciated by the Lord himself could not be comprehended by (persons dominated by the attribute *Sattva* like the sages, gods and prominent *Siddhas*. How can it be understood by demons and men—much less by demi-gods like Vidyādharas and Cāraṇas.

20-21. We twelve—god Brahmā, (the heavenly sage) Nārada, god Śiva, Sanatkumāra, Kapila (the founder of the Sāṅkhya doctrine), Manu, Prahlāda, Janaka, Bhīṣma, the demon Bali, Śuka (the son of Vyāsa) and we ourselves—know the essence of the Dharma (the esoteric doctrine) as expounded by the Lord. It is extremely sacred, pure, secret and difficult to comprehend. One who knows it attains immortality (Final Liberation—Mokṣa).

22. That alone has been remembered (prescribed in the

Dharma Śāstra) as the highest Dharma (sacred duty) of all men in this world, viz., that they should cultivate devotion unto the Lord through the utterance of his name (and other forms of *bhakti*).

23. Look at the great efficacy of the utterance of Hari's name, my boys. It is due to that, that even (a great sinner like) Ajāmila was rescued from the clutches (lit. noose) of death.

24. That even a great sinner like Ajāmila, while on the point of death (when one's faculties could not be concentrated on the Lord), simply shrieked out (and not devotionally chanted) for his son (and not for Lord Viṣṇu) as 'Nārāyaṇa' and attained Liberation shows that (mere utterance of Lord's name—*nāmābhāsa*—is enough to annihilate all sins and that glorification of the Lord's attributes and deeds and chanting of the Lord's name—all these are not required for mere destruction of the sins (but they are needed for cleanly wiping out the impressions (*vāsanās*) left over by sins.

25. (As this esoteric doctrine was grasped by only a dozen persons and remained a great secret to others, these great men) like Manu(most probably did not know that) the (efficacy of Lord's name) is this (as described above). Alas! Their mind is sufficiently deluded by the goddess Māyā. Their intellect is focussed on (and entangled in) the three Vedas promising in flowery language attractive fruits (of sacrifices and other rituals). And they engage themselves in great exhibitory performances of sacrificial acts. (The exhibitory attraction of sacrifices as contrasted with the chanting of the Lord's name in a solitary place, or due to their lack of faith in the efficacy of the Lord's name leads people to performance of sacrifices etc.

26. Having reasoned in this way, persons of good intelligence certainly perform with concentrated mind, acts (such as chanting of the Lord's name etc.) conducive to the loving devotion to the Lord of infinite attributes. They do not deserve punishment at my hands (as they are sinless). Even if sin is committed (inadvertently) by them, it is destroyed by their singing the glory and chanting the name of the Lord (who is widely sung by the Vedas).

27. Do not (even) approach those good souls who have resorted to the Lord and entertain equal outlook toward all and whose holy stories are (therefore) sung by gods and Siddhas. For they are protected by the mace of Hari and neither we nor the Time-spirit is competent to punish them.

28. Bring (only) those wicked persons who are averse to the sweet fragrant honey of the lotus-feet of Mukunda (Lord Viṣṇu) which is incessently tasted by multitudes of Paramahaṁsas (ascetics of the highest order, or noble Swans) who possess nothing of their own and are expert connoisseurs of sweetness (of Lord's lotus-feet). Bring also those who have set their hearts on their households, which is the way to hell.

29. Bring those fellows (to me) whose tongue does not describe the excellent attributes of the Lord or utter his name; whose mind does not remember his lotus-like feet; whose head does not even once bow down to Lord Kṛṣṇa and who have rendered no service to Lord Viṣṇu.

30. May the Venerable Lord Nārāyaṇa, the Ancient-Person, pardon me for the offence committed by my men who are his men. For his devotees who are ignorant, folding of palms in reverence to the great persons is the way of requesting forgiveness. I bow to the perfect Person."

31. The singing of Viṣṇu's name and glory is, therefore, auspicious and blissful to the whole world. Oh King of the Kuru race! Please understand this to be a thorough expiation of the greatest[276] of sins.

32. The mind is not purified to that extent by observance of vows (e.g. fasting) as it does by the properly-developed devotion of those who constantly listen to and sing of the great exploits of Lord Viṣṇu.

33. He who has tasted the sweet honey in the lotus-like feet of Lord Kṛṣṇa does not find pleasure again in objects offered by Māyā which he has contemptuously discarded as leading to sin and miseries (of hell). But the other person who is ignorant about the blissfulness of devotion is overcome with passions, desires to wipe out the sin in his heart by performing

276. *mahatām*—Or 'Of great persons'. Translate : 'It deserves to be observed by great persons for the complete expiation of their sins, Oh Parīkṣit.'

another *karma* which in its turn leads to (the creation of) another sin (like the proverbial bath of an elephant which covers itself with dust after coming out of water.

34. Oh King ! The servants of Yama were not wonder-struck in the mind as they remembered (their realization by personal experience) the greatness of Lord Viṣṇu as described to them by their master (Yama). Being afraid of persons who have resorted to Viṣṇu (Acyuta) they do not dare even to look at them since that day onwards.

35. The venerable Agastya (the sage born from a pitcher) who was seated (on the peak of) Malaya mountain, worshipping god Viṣṇu, narrated to me this secret historical legend.

CHAPTER FOUR

(*History of Dakṣa, the son of Pracetas*)

The King (*Parīkṣit*) *said*:

1. You have briefly described the genesis of gods, Asuras (demons), men, serpents, beasts and birds during the (first) Manvantara period presided over by Svāyambhuva Manu.

2. I desire to know from you the details of that creation (as to) how and with what power the transcendental, glorious Lord brought for the subsequent creation, Oh venerable sage.

Sūta said:

3. On hearing this excellent query from the royal sage (Parīkṣit), the great Yogī Śuka, the son of Bādarāyaṇa, expressed his appreciation and spoke unto him, the noblest of sages.

Śrī Śuka said:

4. When the ten Pracetasas, sons of king Prācīna-barhis emerged from within the sea (-like lake) they saw that the earth was covered with trees.

5. Being enraged at the trees and with their wrath flared up by austere penance, they blew out fire and wind through their mouth, with the intention of burning down the trees.[277]

6. Finding the trees being reduced to ashes by them both (the fire and the wind), the great Moon-god, the ruler of the vegetable kingdom, addressed them with a view to appeasing their anger.

7. "Oh highly fortunate Princes! It does not behove you to bear enmity to the poor trees. You are regarded as the protectors of the beings the special promotion of whose growth should be your concern and desire.

8. Oh Princes! The immutable glorious Lord Hari, the ruler of progenitors of all creatures has created the trees and the annual plants (cereals) for fruits and food-grains (or the food of the manes and food for gods).

9. The immobile ones (trees, plants etc. i.e. their produce like fruits and flowers) are food for the mobile creatures; the footless (i.e. grass etc.) the food of those having feet; the handless ones (e.g. the fish) are the food of those endowed with hands; and the quadrupeds (e.g. deer, boar etc.) are the food of the bipeds (human beings).

10. Oh sinless ones! Inasmuch as you are commanded by your father (Prācīnabarhis) and by the god of gods to procreate beings how is it proper for you to burn down trees (which form the food of creatures).

11. Please follow the path of the righteous which was adopted by your father, grandfather and great-grandfather and control your intensified wrath.

12. The parents are real friends (guardians of interests) of children; the eyelashes are of the eyes; the husband is of a woman; the king is of the subjects; the householder is the true friend of the mendicants and the teacher or the wise person is that of the ignorant. (The protectors of beings are hence the true friends of the creatures; you should not therefore, destroy the food or the means of livelihood of your subjects).

13. The Soul that dwells within the bodies of the creatures is Lord Hari, the Supreme Controller; please note

277. Vide Supra 4.30.44ff.

(carefully) that the entire creation is his abode. Hence, it is thus that he will be propitiated by you.

14. He, who, with a desire to know the real nature of the Soul, controls (within himself) sudden explosion of wrath within the cavity of his heart, goes beyond the *guṇas* which are the cause of the miseries of Saṁsāra).

15. Enough of the helpless trees that are (so far) consumed with fire. (Spare the remaining ones). May the surviving trees and yourselves live in bliss. Here is this excellent girl (Māriṣā by name) brought up by the trees. May she be accepted by you as your wife."

16. Having pacified them (the Pracetasas) thus and having offered that beautiful daughter (with fine hips) of the Apsaras (Pramlocā) to them in marriage, the king Soma (the Moon-god) returned. They then married her according to religious rites.[278]

17. Dakṣa, the son of Pracetasas, they say, was born of her from them. The three worlds are fully populated by his progeny (and their descendants).

18. Now listen to me attentively how Dakṣa who was so affectionate to his daughters procreated beings by his mind (mental faculty) as well as with his semen (physical body).

19. In the beginning, it was by his mental faculties that he procreated these beings, viz., gods, demons (*Asuras*), men and such other creatures dwelling in the sky, on the earth and in the water.

20. Finding that this creation of beings was not growing prolific, the progenitor (of creation) approached the hills near the foot of the Vindhya mountain and performed very austere penance.

21. There was an extremely holy lake efficacious to destroy sins. It was called Aghamarṣaṇa (efficacious to wash off sins). He bathed three times a day (in the morning, midday and evening) in the lake and propitiated Lord Hari with his austere penance.

---

278. Vide supra 4.30. 13-16. As Soma brought her up by nectar from his index finger, he had the fatherly right to offer her in marriage. As Lord Viṣṇu commanded them all to marry her, religious sanction was automatically received for this polyandric marriage.

22. He praised the glorious Lord Viṣṇu with the *Haṁsa-guhya* hymn. I shall now recite that hymn with which Hari was pleased with Dakṣa.

Prajāpati (Dakṣa) said:

23. I pay obeisance to the transcendental Lord whose power of consciousness is not unreal; who is the controller of *jīva* (the individual Soul as reflected through the three *guṇas* of Māyā) and the Māyā (the cause or the basis of such reflection); whose form or true nature is invisible to those who look upon *guṇas* or objects of senses as real; who is beyond all the means of knowledge (e.g. inference etc.) who is beyond limit of time and space, and Self-effulgent.

24. I bow to the Supreme Lord who is the friend of the *jīva* inhabiting the same city (body) along with him but of whose friendliness (in activating the sense-organs and the mind) the *jīva* is not aware. He is the seer of the world (and hence unseen by the world) just as a *guṇa* (the object of cognition) cannot perceive the possessor of the *guṇa* (viz. the cognitive ability of the cognizing sense).

25. The body, the vital breaths, the senses, the internal organs or mental faculties, the five *bhūtas* (gross elements) and their *tanmātrās* (subtle forms e. g. sound, touch etc.) do not know either themselves or the others and their presiding deities who are beyond them all (as all these have no consciousness). The *jīva* (being consciousness by nature) knows all the *guṇas* (the root cause of the above-mentioned list). But the *jīva* who knows them (the above) does not know the Omniscient Lord who is Infinite. Him I praise.

26. When the mind which cognizes the world of names and forms ceases to function due to the loss or obsolescence of all cognition and memory, in the state of *samādhi* or complete absorption in the self, he (the Supreme Brahman) reveals himself through his inherent existence, consciousness and bliss. I offer my salutations to him whose abode is the pure heart.

27. With their purified intellect, the self-controlled, discerning persons discover (and meditate upon) him (as distinct from *ahaṁkāra*) as enthroned in the innermost heart,

even though he lies unmanifest by his nine powers[279] (viz. Prakṛti, *mahat* or cosmic intelligence, *ahaṁkāra* or ego, mind and *tanmātras* (five subtle *bhūtas*) and (by mind, five gross elements and ten sense-organs) and influenced by three *guṇas* (viz. *Sattva*, *rajas*, and *tamas*). (The above-mentioned wise persons do so) just as the experts in sacrificial lore separate (by friction) the sacrificial fire latent in the (piece of) wood by reciting the fifteen Sāmidhenī verses[280] (in the course of churning out fire).

28. He is realized as the highest bliss in meditation by the negation of Māyā which creates all distinctions and differences. Verily he bears every name, and assumes all forms. He possesses within him innumerable potencies which are beyond the power of words to describe. (May the Lord be gracious unto me).

29. Whatever is described in words, concluded (to be true) by the intellect, perceived by the senses or imagined by the mind, is only a phenomenon of the (three) *guṇas* and cannot be his essential nature; for he is verily characterised by the creation or dissolution of *guṇas* (i.e. their product, the universe).

30. It is Brahman on which everything depends; from it everything is caused; it has created everything from itself with itself. Everything is for it and belongs to it. Whatever it makes and causes others to make is Brahman. It is the ultimate cause of all causes both earlier (e.g. god Brahmā) or later. As the primary cause, it is known to have preceded all causes. It is one without a second, whether of its own kind or of another category. It is Brahman to whom I bow[281].

31. (If Brahman is the cause of the universe, why do

---

279. VJ. mentions a different list of nine potencies, viz., *Vimalā, Utkarṣaṇī, Jñānakriyā* etc. and the three powers (*trivṛdbhiḥ*) are Will, Knowledge and Action (Kriyā).

280. Viṣṇu is called the fifteenth Principle (*Pāñcadaśya*). The remaining fourteen are: Ten sense-organs (*indriyas*), mind, intelligence (*buddhi*), vital airs (*Prāṇa*) and *Pradhāna*. Viṣṇu controls these—VJ.

281. VR. takes the Viśiṣṭādvaita position in which Īśvara is the Soul and *jīva* and *jagat* (unintelligent matter) form his body. The different cases in this verse show the intimate relation of Īśvara with others.

the different schools of thoughts like the followers of Mīmāṁsā, Nyāya, indulge in disputation?). It is his potencies (such as Māyā) which have verily become the grounds (causes) for disputations and concurrence for various eloquent theoreticians (of different schools of thought) and which (in spite of the exhortations of the knowers of the truth to these disputants) delude their minds now and again. I bow to him, the omnipresent Lord of infinite excellences.

32. (Yoga, as a science of divine worship, conceives of God as a cosmic person with Pātāla, subterranean regions, as his feet, while Sāṅkhya which is the Science of Knowledge or self-realization regards him as formless without any hands or feet.) The Yoga and Sāṅkhya systems of philosophy which proclaim faith in one and the same Reality predicate the existence and nonexistence of (two) distinct and mutually contradictory attributes to be subsisting in the same Reality (viz. possession and non-possession of feet etc.). But the common basis on which they agree and (is thus beyond dispute) is the existence of God—a Reality beyond dispute. It is the great thing—Brahman (to whom I bow).

33. May that glorious Supreme Lord of infinite attributes be gracious unto me—the Lord who though above material names and forms, invested himself with (absolutely pure *sāttvic*) forms by incarnating himself, and assumed names by his (wonderful) deeds, for the sake of bestowing his grace on those who seek shelter at his feet.

34. May that Supreme Ruler grant me my desired object (s)—the Supreme Lord who abiding in all bodies as the (formless) Inner controller, manifests himself in the forms of different deities to people according to the tendencies (formed by impressions of the actions of their previous births) and their paths of worship of recent origin, just as a breeze of wind (though itself devoid of the characteristics of the earth, viz. fragrance or colour) bears different kinds of smells according to the fragrance of the flowers with which it comes into contact or looks whitish, the attribute of dust mixed with it.

Śrī Śuka said :

35. Thus praised (with the hymns), the glorious Lord who is affectionate to his devotees manifested himself to Dakṣa

while he was extolling him in the sacred lake called Aghamarṣaṇa, oh foremost Kuru.

36. Riding with his feet flung on both the shoulders of Garuḍa, he wielded in his extraordinarily long and mighty arms a discus, a conch, a sword, a shield, an arrow, a noose and a mace (in each respectively).

37. He was clad in yellow silken garment with complexion dark like a cloud, his countenance and eyes were beaming with pleasure and joy. His person was adorned with *Vanamālā* (a garland of forest-flowers) and bore the mark called Śrīvatsa and the valuable gem Kaustubha.

38. He wore a very costly crown and bracelets and radiant pair of crocodile-shaped ear-rings. He was adorned with zones, rings, bracelets, anklets and armlets.

39. The Lord of the three worlds manifested a beautiful form captivating the three worlds. He was surrounded by Nārada, Nanda and other attendants and by protectors of the worlds (like Indra, Varuṇa). He was eulogized by Siddhas, Gandharvas and cāraṇas (the celestial singers and others) who followed him singing.

40. On seeing that most wonderful form (of the Lord), the progenitor Dakṣa was overcome with awe, but his heart was overjoyed. He lay prostrate before him on the ground (like a rod) and bowed to him.

41. Just as rivers are overflooded by streams, his senses were too full with intense joy to be able to speak. Thus, on account of excessive joy he could not utter a word.

42 Lord Viṣṇu who knows the minds of all created beings spoke thus to the progenitor devotee Dakṣa who had laid himself prostrate that way before him and was desirous of procreating progeny.

The Venerable Lord said :

43. Oh highly fortunate son of Pracetas! You have achieved the objective of your austere penance inasmuch as you have cherished supreme devotion unto me through your unswerving intense faith in me.

44. Oh Lord of created beings! I am pleased with you as the growth of the universe is the aim of your penance. It is

also my desire that there should be all round growth and prosperity of all created beings.

45. God Brahmā, Śiva, you all Prajāpatis (Lords of created beings), Manus (progenitors of human beings who preside over certain epochs or *Manvantaras*) and the foremost deities—all are my special incarnations for the prosperity and procreation of created beings.

46*. Oh Brahman (Dakṣa) ! Contemplation (accompanied with disciplines of *Yama* and *niyama*) is my heart. The spiritual lore (the internal repetition of *Mantras* with the specific technique of *nyāsa* etc. which results in concrete meditation and my realization) is my body. The activities pertaining to contemplation is my form. Accurately performed sacrifices are the limbs of my body. The merit (accruing from the well-performed sacrifices) is my Soul. Gods (the recipients of oblations in the sacrifices) form my very life.

47. At the beginning of creation, I alone existed (without any activity). There was nothing else as internal (the seer or knower) or external (the seen or the object of knowledge). I was pure consciousness and unmanifested. There was (as if) deep sleep (no activity) everywhere.

48. In me who am Infinite and endowed with an infinite number of attributes, there evolved through Māyā (constituted of three *guṇas*) this universe (a product of *guṇas*). At that time the selfborn Brahmā, the First Person (the creator of all) arose (along with the universe).

49. When the great god Brahmā, though supplied with my energy, became engaged in the work of creation, he felt that he was not sufficiently competent for it.

50. Then as per my command, the god Brahmā performed very austere penance. Empowered by it, he created nine progenitors of created beings including you (in your previous birth) in the beginning.

---

*. VR., SD. explain that Lord wants to emphasize the importance of contemplation, sacrifices etc. as they are dear to him.

GD. explains that the Lord reminds Dakṣa of his previous birth and proficiency in sacrifice by calling him 'Brahman'.

51. Oh dear child! Here is the daughter of the progenitor of creatures, Pañcajana. Her name is Asiknī. Accept her as your wife, Oh Lord of created beings.

52. You have to follow the righteous course of sexual union between a duly married couple. You will procreate progeny in large numbers from her who will also observe the same righteous duty (of sexual intercourse between the duly married) like you.

53. All created beings after you will be born through sexual intercourse with women, under the influence of my Māyā and they will offer worship.

Śrī Śuka said:

54. Having addressed him [thus, Lord Hari the prime cause of the universe vanished on that very spot like an object seen in a dream, while Dakṣa was looking on.

CHAPTER FIVE

(*Dakṣa curses Nārada*)

Śrī Śuka said:

1. Being imbued with the energy of Viṣṇu, Dakṣa became powerful and begot through that (above-mentioned) Pāñcajanī ten thousand sons called Haryaśva.

2. Oh King! All those sons of Dakṣa were of the same nature and similarly righteous in conduct. When they were commanded by the father (Dakṣa) to beget children, they went to the western direction.

3. They went to a sacred lake called Nārāyaṇa-saras[282] situated in the area where the river Sindhu meets the sea—a holy place resorted to by a number of sages and Siddhas.

4. At the very touch of that (sacred water of the) lake, their hearts were cleansed of all impurities and they found their

282. A lake at the mouth of the Indus at the western extremity of the Runn of Kacch, 18 miles south-west of Lakhpat—CDAMI 138.

mind attracted to the righteous way of life of the Paramahaṁsas (the highest order of ascetics).

5. Being restrained by the command of their father for begetting prolific progeny, they practised severe austerities. It is then, they say, that the celestial sage Nārada saw them.

6. And he (Nārada) spoke unto them:

'Oh Haryaśvas! How is it that without seeing the limits of the earth you want to create children. You are certainly childish (foolish). It is a pity that protectors (of the subjects) as you are, you are really childish.

7-9. Without seeing a kingdom inhabited by only one man, and without knowing the hole with (apparently) invisible outlet, the woman who can assume different forms (at will), and the man who espouses a harlot, a river flowing in both directions, a wonderful house constructed of twentyfive materials, at one place a swan telling miraculous tales, an independent, revolving (strong, sharp) disc made of adamants and razors, and without properly understanding the implication of the command of your omniscient father, how will you proceed with your job of creation?

Śrī Śuka said:

10. Having heard the enigmatic words of the divine sage (Nārada), the Haryaśvas, with their ow ninborn reasoning capacity, began to investigate with their intelligence.

11. The earth (*bhū*) is that field (or the *liṅga-śarīra*—the subtle body—which causes pleasure, pain, merit, demerit etc. like an agricultural farm yielding crop of cereals) designated as *jīva*. The subtle body is (practically) beginningless (existing from times immemorial) and it acts as a bondage to the Soul. Without seeing how it becomes extinct, what is the use of impious *karmas* (which do not lead to Mokṣa).

12. The only one (man in the country) stands for the Sole Almighty ruler (of the universe). He is (beyond and) witness to all mental states, viz., *viśva*, *taijasa* and *prājña*) and hence is called the fourth—the omnipresent. He is self-dependent supreme (the cause of everything else). Without seeing that birthless (eternally free) Lord, what purpose can be served by acts not dedicated to him?

13. Just as a person who has gone to the subterranean heaven (*pātāla*) does not return (to the earth in the same body), a man does not return to *saṁsāra* after attaining to the self-illuminating Brahman within him. To a man who has not realized (lit. is ignorant of) the Inner Light—Self-effulgent Brahman, worthless *karmas* (which may lead to heavenly happiness and other transitory pleasures) are of no avail.

14. Like a loose wanton woman wearing various attractive forms and gifted with (many attractive) qualities, the intellect of man assumes shapes of objects of lower type of pleasures (like form, taste and other objects of senses) and is influenced by *guṇas* (like *rajas*, *tamas*). To a person who has not put an end to (i.e. transcended) such a multiple-interested intellect, what can be achieved through hot pursuit of such activities?

15. What can be achieved through acts done without discernment and knowledge by a *jīva* (man) who does not understand the loss of his independence (and non-attachment) by his association with such (above-mentioned) intellect and is like a husband of a loose wife, follows her ways (characterised by pleasure and pain).

16. What can be gained from activities influenced by Māyā which causes both the creation and destruction (and is like a river flowing both ways). (In order to prevent people fallen in it from reaching the banks) it rushes forth with great velocity (assuming the form of anger, egotism etc.) at the ghats, and its banks (in the form of penance, learning etc.).

17. Puruṣa (the Inner Controller abiding in the body) is a wonderful basis and mirror[283] reflecting the twentyfive categories (enumerated by Sāṁkhyas). Of what use are the acts (done with a false sense of independence) by one who has not realized that he (Puruṣa) presides over the body (the aggregate of the categories—a collection of cause and effect).[284]

---

283. ŚR. reads *adbhuta-darśana* 'One who is of wonderful form' (*āscarya-rūpa*).

284. Sāṅkhyas differ : According to Īśvarakṛṣṇa, Prakṛti is uncreated (without any cause). The next seven categories from *mahat* to *tanmātras* are both cause (of the next category) and the effect (of the previous category) and the next sixteen : mind, 5 gross elements, 10 sense-organs are effects only. Puruṣa is neither the cause nor effect.—Sāṅkhyakārikā 3.

18. (This explains *kvacid haṁsaṁ citrakatham* in verse 8 above). What purpose will be served by acts oriented to the external phenomenal world if one neglects (the study of) the *śāstra* (philosophic teaching) which establishes the existence of the Almighty Ruler by distinguishing between the intelligent principle (the Soul) and inert matter and shows the (nature of) bondage and (Final) Liberation (like a swan drinking milk only from the mixture of milk and water) ?

19. (The explanation of *kṣaurapavyaṁ svayam bhramim*—verse 8 above).

The wheel of Time which is relentlessly and eternally revolving is sharp like razor-blade. It is absolutely independent (and hence uncontrollable). It destroys the whole creation. To him who does not know this (nature of Time), of what use are the worthless acts (done under the false presumption that their fruits are eternal).

20. (The inner significance of verse 9 above).

How can anyone who does not understand the precept of desisting from worldly activities, given by his father, the *śāstra* (which gives him the second birth by the *upanayana*, investiture of the sacred-thread-ceremony and tenders salutary advice) and who entertains faith in the path of worldly activities (*Pravṛtti-mārga*) based on *guṇas*, go ahead with the work of creation? (As Dakṣa ceases to be a father after *upanayana*, you can disregard his order without incurring a sin if you follow the precept of *śāstra*, your father, and follow the path of renunciation—*Nivṛtti-dharma*).

21. (Being convinced by Nārada) Haryaśvas unanimously resolved thus, and circumambulating him (Nārada, by the right side as a mark of respect) went the way (to liberation) from which there is no return, Oh King!

22. The sage Nārada, who has concentrated (lit. entered) his undivided mind in the lotus-like feet of Lord Viṣṇu (Hṛṣīkeśa—the Master of sense-organs) as revealed in *Svara-Brahman* (*Brahman* in the form of notes of the musical scale on his lute), went about (his own way in) the world.

23. Having heard that his sons, so excellent due to their righteous character, have disappeared and are lost to their original duty (of procreating children) due to the advice of

Nārada, Dakṣa was tormented with sorrow and lamented that even to have good children can be a source of grief.

24. Being much consoled by god Brahmā, Dakṣa again procreated by Pañcajanī a thousand sons called Śabalāśva.

25. Even they (Śabalāśvas) who were commanded by the father to beget progeny, took to religious vows and went to the (sacred) lake Nārāyaṇa where their elder brothers attained perfection (i.e. god-realization).

26. With their minds and hearts perfectly cleansed of all impurities (sins) at the touch of those sacred waters, they practised austere penance muttering (all the while) the sacred syllable OM (a symbol of the Supreme Brahman).

27. For several months, they subsisted on water, and for many months, on the air only. They propitiated the Lord of all *Mantras* (the glorious god Viṣṇu), repeating this (following) sacred *mantra* :

28. "OM. Salutations to Lord Nārāyaṇa, the Indwelling Controller, the Supreme Soul, whose place of manifestation is the extremely pure *sāttvic* heart and who is absolutely free from all blemishes. We meditate upon him."

29. The sage Nārada approached even those (sons of Dakṣa) who made up their minds to renew creation and spoke to them the enigmatic words similar to those addressed to their (elder) brothers, Oh King of Kings.

30. "Oh sons of Dakṣa! Listen carefully to the precept as given (lit. addressed) by me. You find out the path followed by your elder brothers (for whom you are so full of affection).

31. A brother who knows the path of righteousness, follows the great path trodden by his brothers and with merit as his friend, he enjoys (celestial) life in the company of the Marut—(wind) gods (noted for their fraternal affection)."

32. Oh noble King! having addressed this much, Nārada whose audience is never unfruitful, departed. They (Śabalāśvas) also followed the (spiritual) path of their (elder) brothers.

33. Having resorted to the exalted and agreeable path attainable to those whose senses and minds are turned within (away from the external world)—the path that leads to

the realization of the Supreme Brahman—they, like the nights that have passed, never return to this day.

34. Noticing at this time, a number of evil portents, the Prajāpati Dakṣa came to know that Nārada had ruined his sons.

35. Overwhelmed with grief for his sons, he got enraged with Nārada. (To prevent Dakṣa from turning into a recluse, Nārada approached him). Finding Nārada, he exploded (lit. spoke to him) with his lower lip quivering with rage.

Dakṣa said:

36. Oh wicked fellow donning the garb of holy man! You have done a great harm to good people like us, in showing the path of mendicants to my young (good-natured) children.

37. Oh sinful person! You have deprived (my sons) of the bliss in both the worlds (here and hereafter), as they have not repaid their debts to the sages, gods and manes and have not investigated the nature of *karmas*.

38. Merciless and prejudicer of the mind of children as you are, you are bringing stigma to the glory of Lord Hari, and shameless as you are, you still move among the attendants of Hari.

39. With the exception of you who are verily a traitor to friends and who sow enmity between friends, all the devotees of Hari are really ever eager to shower grace on living beings.

40. Renunciation cannot in this way be generated in the minds of men by you who have disguised yourself as an Avadhūta even though you have no knowledge. Though you regard that self-control (automatically) severs the bonds of affection (it is wrong).

41. A man cannot realize how objects of sensual pleasures cause painful consequences, without personally experiencing them. Therefore, one does not get disgusted to that extent if his mind is unsettled by others (in that matter), as a person would who has undergone the experience himself.

42. We have tolerated the unbearable wrong you have done to us, householders, who have vowed to perform Vedic *karmas* with a wish to get heavenly bliss.

43. You are a destroyer of the continuity of my race. As you have again done a wrong to us, you will not get a resting place while wandering through the worlds (Oh fool).

Śrī Śuka said:

44. Nārada who was highly respected by the pious people accepted the curse saying, 'Very well'. He is called really a *Sādhu* (pious soul) who though competent to retaliate, bears up the wrong done to him.

CHAPTER SIX

(Progeny of Dakṣa's Daughters)[*]

Śrī Śuka said :

1. Then comforted by the self-born god Brahmā, Prācetasa Dakṣa begot on Asiknī sixty daughters who were affectionate to their father.

2. He gave ten daughters (in marriage) to Dharma, the presiding deity of righteousness, thirteen to sage Ka (Kaśyapa), twenty-seven to the Moon-god, two each to sages Bhūta, Aṅgiras and Kṛśāśva and the rest to Tārkṣya, another name of Kaśyapa.

3. Now, hear from me their names along with those of their offspring whose children and children's children (descendants) have populated completely the three worlds.

4. (The names of Dharma's wives are) : Bhānu, Lambā, Kakubh, Jāmi, Viśvā, Sādhyā, Marutvatī, Vasu, Muhūrtā, Saṅkalpā. Now listen to (the names of the sons).

5. From Bhānu was born Devarṣabha. His son was Indrasena. From Lambā was born Vidyota who gave birth to (deities presiding over) cloud.

6. Saṅkaṭa was born from Kakubh. His son was Kīkaṭa, from whom were begotten the spirits presiding over

the fortresses on the earth. Svarga was the son of Jāmi. From him was born Nandi.

7. From Viśva were begotten the Viśvedevas who are said to be childless. Sādhyā gave birth to a group of gods known as Sādhya whose son was Arthasiddhi.

8. From Marutvatī were born (the forty-nine) Maruts (wind-gods) and Jayanta who was a part manifestation of Vāsudeva and whom they know as Upendra.

9. From Muhūrtā were born the race of gods called Mauhūrtikas who verily bestow upon living beings fruit appropriate to the particular period of time (when an act is performed at that time).

10. Saṅkalpā gave birth to Saṅkalpa (the deity presiding over thought process). It is declared that the god of love is born of Saṅkalpa. Vasu gave birth to eight sons called Vasus. Hear from me their names (now).

11. (Their names are): Droṇa, Prāṇa, Dhruva, Arka, Agni, Doṣa, Vasu, Vibhāvasu. Droṇa begot from his wife Abhimati children called Harṣa, Śoka, Bhaya and others (the presiding deities of joy, sorrow, fear etc.).

12. Prāṇa begot Sahas, Āyus, Purojava from his wife Ūrjasvatī. Dharaṇī (the earth), the wife of Dhruva, gave births to various towns and cities.

13. Vāsanā was the wife of Arka (the Sun-god). Their sons like Tarṣa and others were well known. Dhārā was the wife of the Vasu called Agni, and their sons were Draviṇaka and others.

14. And Skanda was the son of Kṛttikā (another wife of Agni). From him were born Viśākha and others. Doṣa had by Śarvarī, a son called Śiśumāra (the deity of the stellar sphere) who was an *aṁśa* (digit) of Hari.

15. From Āṅgirasī, the wife of Vasu, was born Viśvakarmā, the architect of gods. The name of his wife was Ākṛti. From her were born Cākṣusa, (the sixth) Manu. Viśvedevas and Sādhya gods were the sons of Manu.

16. From Vibhāvasu, Uṣā gave birth to Vyuṣṭa, Rociṣa and Ātapa. From Ātapa was born Pañcayāma (the deity presiding over the day-time) who keeps created beings awake and alert to their duties.

17-18. Sarūpā, the wife of Bhūta, gave birth to crores of Rudras (the deities entrusted with the duty of destruction), the chief among them were the eleven, namely, Raivata, Aja, Bhava, Bhīma, Vāma, Ugra, Vṛṣākapi, Ajaikapāda, Ahirbudhnya, Bahurūpa and Mahān. From Bhūtā, another wife of Bhūta, were born the terrible Bhūtas and evil-spirits (called Vināyakas) who were the attendants of Rudras.

19. Svadhā, the wife of Prajāpati Aṅgiras, gave birth to the manes (*Pitṛs*). Satī, another wife of Aṅgiras, accepted the Veda called Atharva—Aṅgiras—as her son.

20. Kṛśāśva begot from his wife Arcis, Dhūmrakeśa as the son, and on Dhiṣaṇā four sons, viz. Vedaśiras, Devala, Vayuna and Manu.

21-22. Tārkṣya which was another name of the sage Kaśyapa, had four wives, namely, Vinatā, Kadrū, Pataṅgī and Yāminī. Pataṅgī gave birth to birds; Yāminī to locusts. Vinatā had a son called Garuḍa who was the vehicle of directly the Lord of Sacrifices (Viṣṇu). She had another son called Aruṇa (the thighless) who is the charioteer of the Sun-god. Kadrū, mothered serpents of various species.

23. Oh descendant of Bharata ! The presiding deities of Kṛttikā and other twenty-seven constellations of stars, were wedded to the Moon, but due to the curse of Dakṣa, he was affected by consumption and had no issue from them.

24. Having propitiated Dakṣa again, he regained his digits which decreased in the dark half of the month but had no children. Now, listen to the auspicious names of the mothers of the world (viz. Kaśyapa's wives).

25-26. The following are the names of the wives of Kaśyapa who gave birth to this world; Aditi, Diti, Danu, Kāṣṭhā, Ariṣṭā, Surasā, Ilā, Muni, Krodhavaśā, Tāmrā, Surabhi, Saramā and Timi. From Timi were born aquatic beings; from Saramā, tiger and other carnivorous animals.

27. From Surabhi, were created buffalo, cow and other beasts with cloven hooves; from Tāmrā, hawks, vultures and other birds of prey; from Muni, the bevy of celestial demsels.

28. Oh King ! Serpents like Dandaśūka and others were the offspring of Krodhavaśā; the vegetable kingdom, of Ilā, and the Yakṣas and Rakṣasas of Surasā.

29. The Gandharvas (celestial singers) were born of Ariṣṭā; beasts with uncloven feet (e.g. horses, donkeys etc.), of Kāṣṭhā; Danu had sixty-one sons. Listen to the names of the prominent ones in them :

30-31. (They are :) Dvimūrdhan, Śambara, Ariṣṭa, Hayagrīva, Vibhāvasu, Ayomukha, Śaṅkuśiras, Svarbhānu, Kapila, Aruṇa, Puloman, Vṛṣaparvan, Ekacakra, Anutāpana, Dhūmrakeśa, Virūpākṣa, Vipracitti and Durjaya.

32. As is reported, Namuci married Suprabhā, the daughter of Svarbhānu. The mighty Yayāti, the son of Nahuṣa, was wedded to Śarmiṣṭhā, the daughter of Vṛṣaparvan.

33. Danu's son Vaiśvānara had four daughters who were very beautiful to look at. They are : Upadānavī, Hayaśirā, Pulomā and Kālakā.

34. Out of them, Upadānavī was married to Hiraṇyākṣa and Hayaśirā to Kratu. Oh King, Kaśyapa married Pulomā and Kālakā, the two daughters of Vaiśvānara.

35. The great sage Kaśyapa married them as he was directed to do so by god Brahmā. The sons of Pulomā were the Dānavas known as Kālakeyas who were famous for their warlike nature.

36. Out of them, sixty-thousand sons known as Nivātakavacas who used to disturb sacrifices, were killed by your father's father single-handedly, while he paid a visit to Svarga and wanted to please Indra.

37. Vipracitti begot on his wife Siṁhikā one hundred and one sons. The eldest of them was Rāhu who got a position in the planetary system, along with the remaining hundred sons who were named Ketu.

38. Now, listen from me in due sequence, the details of the race of Aditi wherein the Almighty God Nārāyaṇa incarnated by his own *aṁśa* (digit).

39. The sons of Aditi were : Vivasvān, Aryaman, Pūṣan, Tvaṣṭṛ, Savitṛ, Bhaga, Dhātṛ, Vidhātṛ, Varuṇa, Mitra, Indra and Trivikrama (Vāmana). (These are the presiding deities of the orb of the Sun each month).

40. The highly fortunate Saṁjñā, the wife of Vivasvat, gave birth to Śrāddhadeva, the Manu and a twin called the

Yama god and (his sister) Yamī. That very Saṁjñā became a female horse and gave birth to the twin gods Aśvinīkumāras, on this earth.

41. Chāyā (another wife of Vivasvat) gave birth to Śanaiścara, the presiding deity of the planet Saturn, and Sāvarṇi Manu. She gave birth to a daughter also called Tapatī who chose in marriage Saṁvaraṇa as her husband.

42. Mātṛkā was the wife of Aryaman. Their sons were called Carṣaṇi (for they possessed wisdom of what should and what should not be done). From them were evolved the human kind by god Brahmā.

43. Pūṣan was childless. He got his teeth broken formerly as he exhibited his teeth in laughing at Śiva when he was enraged at Dakṣa, and Pūṣan had to subsist on flour.

44. The girl Racanā, the younger sister of the Daityas, became the spouse of Tvaṣṭṛ. From them were born sons namely Saṁniveśa and the mighty Viśvarūpa.

45. The host of gods selected him (for preceptorship) even though he was the nephew (sister's son) of their enemies, as they were forsaken by their preceptor Bṛhaspati who was insulted by them.

CHAPTER SEVEN

(Bṛhaspati's Insult and his abandonment of Preceptorship)

The King said :

1. Please tell me, Oh venerable sir, why the gods were forsaken by their own preceptor and what was the fault of the disciples (gods) against their teacher.

Śrī Śuka said :

2-6. Indra transgressed the path followed by the good, due to his arrogance of overlordship of the three worlds. (Once) surrounded by Maruts, Vasu, Rudras, Ādityas, Ṛbhus, Viśvedevas, Sādhyas and the Aśvinikumāras, and attended upon and praised and sweetly extolled by Siddhas, Cāraṇas, Gandharvas, by sages, the knowers of Brahman, Vidyādharas, heavenly damsels, Kinnaras, birds and Nāgas (serpents), he (Indra) was seated on the throne equipped with a white umbrella, beautiful like the orb of the full Moon, and with *chowries*, fans and other insignia of supreme royalty. He looked extremely splendid with (his wife) Śacī occupying half the throne.

7-9. When he did not welcome the great preceptor of gods and of himself, by offering him due formalities of respect such as standing up, offering a seat, on his arrival; he (Indra) did not rise at all from his seat, even though he saw the great sage Bṛhaspati who was adorable both to gods and demons, coming to his assembly; the wise and powerful descendent of Aṅgiras (Bṛhaspati) who understood that the violation of good manners is due to the arrogance of affluence and power, came out of the assembly and quietly returned to his house.

10. At that very moment, Indra became aware of the disrespect shown by him to his preceptor, and he, of his own accord, censured himself publicly in the assembly.

11. "Oh what a pity ! What an unrighteous and wicked deed has been committed by me, of poor intellect : being intoxicated with the arrogance of wealth and power, my preceptor has been disrespectfully treated in this assembly.

12. Who will covet for the prosperity and wealth of the Lord of the celestial regions, if he be wise ? for I who am the Lord of gods of *sāttvic* nature was dragged into the demonic state of egotism by that prosperity.

13. Those who lay down that the occupants of the highest position should not rise to receive anyone, do not know the highest code of conduct.

14. Those who believe in the words of those who show the wrong course and themselves sink in the dark infernal regions, verily, go down (to the abysmal depth of hell) by boarding a raft of granite rock, as it were.

15. Now with all my crookedness shed off and touching with my head the feet of that Brāhmaṇa, the preceptor of gods, and possessor of unfathomable intelligence, I shall propitiate him."

16. While Indra was musing thus, the venerable Bṛhaspati went out of his mansion and disappeared with his superb spiritual power.

17. The glorious Lord of the celestial region, looked on all sides for the whereabouts of his preceptor, but could not trace him. Anxiously considering (what will happen to them all, in the absence of the protection of the preceptor) Indra, though he commanded the loyalty of all gods, did not get the peace of mind.

18. As soon as all the demons got the report of it (the desertion of gods' side by Bṛhaspati), they followed the advice of Śukra. Haughty as they were, they carried a war against gods with their arms raised.

19. Gods whose heads, thighs and arms were deeply wounded by the sharp arrows discharged by the demons, went along with Indra, with their heads lowered in humility, to god Brahmā for protection.

20. The venerable birthless self-born god Brahmā saw them afflicted and harassed that way. Consoling them, the god spoke out to them in his supreme grace.

God Brahmā said :

21. What a pity it is, Oh great gods ! Out of arrogance of power and wealth you have certainly committed a very unjust and inauspicious deed in not respectfully welcoming a self-controlled Brāhmaṇa who was imbued with the spirit of Brahman.

22. It is the result of your unrighteousness that you gods, rich and powerful as you are, are defeated at the hands of your enemies who were extremely weak.

23. Oh Indra ! Look at your enemies who became extremely powerless due to disrespect shown by them to their preceptor, have again grown in strength due to their devoted propitiation of their preceptor Śukra. They, who regard Śukra as their deity, may capture even my abode (Brahmaloka).

24. The demons who are well instructed in their objectives by Śukra and whose secret designs are not divulged, have the slightest regard for the celestial region. (They can easily

conquer it). Inauspicious results do not befall kings who are protected by Brāhmaṇas, Lord Viṣṇu and cows.

25. Therefore, take resort to Viśvarūpa immediately. That Brāhmaṇa, the son of Tvaṣṭṛ, possesses self-control and (a wealth of) penance. If respectfully treated by you, he will accomplish your objects, if you put up with (some of) his acts (of partiality to demons).

Śrī Śuka said :

26. Oh King ! Gods who were thus advised by god Brahmā, were relieved of their feverish anxiety. They approached the sage Viśvarūpa, the son of Tvaṣṭṛ, embraced him and addressed him thus.

Gods said :

27. We have approached your hermitage as unexpected guests. May you be blessed, Oh child. Please accomplish the wish of your elders (uncles) as demanded by the occasion.

28. It is the highest duty of virtuous sons to serve their parents, even though the sons themselves have got children. It is much more so in the case of celibates, Oh Brahman.

29. The preceptor who invests the sacred thread and initiates in the Vedas, is the embodiment of the Vedas. Father is god Brahmā (the creator) incarnate. A brother is as if an image of Indra, the chief of gods. The mother is a veritable earth personified.

30. A sister is the embodiment of tenderness. An unexpected visitor is the soul of *dharma* (the god of righteousness). And the guest staying with us is the god of Fire incarnate and all beings are the representations of the Supreme Soul of Lord Viṣṇu. (Therefore, one should look upon all beings like himself).

31. Oh child, you should carry out our request and remove by your penance the afflictions of us, your elders, who are suffering from defeat at the hands of our enemies.

32. We select you, who are possessed of Brahmanic power, and a Brāhmaṇa deserving respect, as our preceptor, so that we shall easily and thoroughly vanquish our enemies by the virtue of your spiritual power.

33. They (the wise) do not censure the act of bowing at the feet of younger persons for the accomplishment of their objects. Mere age is not the ground of superiority when one is wanting in Vedic knowledge.

The Sage (Śuka) said :

34. The great sage Viśvarūpa who was so earnestly entreated by the gods for accepting priesthood, became pleased and spoke to them in soft words.

Viśvarūpa said :

35. Priesthood has been condemned by the righteous ones as leading to the loss of spiritual power. But, Oh masters, how a person like me who deserves to be commanded by Lords of worlds like you, can refuse your request, for compliance (of your orders) is in my real interest.

36. To those who decide not to possess anything, grain that is gleaned after the removal of corn from the fields and the grains of corn found after the market-day is over, form the wealth. I have performed my righteous duties with that wealth. Oh suzerine Lords, how should I accept the reproachful priesthood which pleases only those who are wretched in intellect.

37. I, however, do not refuse what has been requested by elders like you. Whatever insignificant is desired by you, I shall accomplish it, at the cost of my life and means.

Śrī Śuka said :

38. The great ascetic Viśvarūpa who was thus solicited for accepting priesthood promised them (the gods) thus, and carried out his duties of priesthood, with perfect concentration.

39. The (spiritually) powerful sage snatched the fortune of the enemies of gods even though it was protected by the incantations and spells of Śukra, and by the prayer (lore) of Viṣṇu, i.e. by *Nārāyaṇa Kavaca*, gave it to Indra.

40. The noble-minded Viśvarūpa initiated Mahendra in that lore, and Indra, the thousand-eyed god, became powerful and protected by that lore, vanquished the armies of demons.

41.* Indra, the leader of all gods, entered the spiritual coat of armour called *Nārāyaṇa Kavaca* and always scored victories over the demons, like a lion over ordinary beasts, Oh child.

CHAPTER EIGHT

(*The Nārāyaṇa-Kavaca explained*)

The King enquired:

1-2: Oh venerable Sir, please teach me the protective prayer of Nārāyaṇa which serves as an armour, and protected by which, Indra, the god with thousand eyes, sportfully but thoroughly vanquished the soldiers of the enemies with their horses and chariots, and enjoyed the sovereignty of the three worlds, and protected by which he conquered his enemies who attacked him with raised arms, in the battle.

Śrī Śuka replied:

3. The priest Viśvarūpa, the son of Tvaṣṭṛ, when solicited, explained to the great Indra, the protective prayer called Nārāyaṇa Kavaca. Listen to it with concentrated mind.

4-6. "When a danger is impending, a person should wash his hands and feet, and sip water as *ācamana*. He should put on a ring of the Kuśa grass round his finger, and sit with his face turned to the North. Thus purified and observing silence, he should perform *Nyāsa*, consecrating the various parts of the body and hands with the *mantras* or sacred formulae (one of eight syllables viz. *Oṁ namo Nārāyaṇāya* and the other of twelve syllables, viz. *Oṁ namo bhagavate Vāsudevāya*). He should put on the armour (protective covering) sacred to lord Nārāyaṇa, by contemplating the Lord (with the eight-syllabled *mantra—Oṁ namo Nārāyaṇāya*) located in the feet, in the knee-joints, the thighs, the stomach, the heart and the chest, the mouth, the crown of the head (thus spiritualizing the

*VJ's text adds this verse.

whole body with the protective *mantra* of Nārāyaṇa) or perform the same in the reverse order (technically known as *Saṁhāra Nyāsa*).

7. He should then perform the *karanyāsa*—the spiritualization of the hands—with the secret incantation or *mantra* consisting of twelve syllables (*Oṁ namo bhagavate Vāsudevāya*). He should deposit spiritual power beginning with the sacred syllable *Oṁ* and ending with *ya* in his fingers and joints of the thumbs.

(The method of spiritual insulation against dangers with the mantra *Oṁ Viṣṇave namaḥ* is explained).

8. He should deposit OM (the first syllable of the mantra *Oṁ Viṣṇave namaḥ*) in the heart, *vi* on the crown of the head, *ṣ* in the middle of the eyebrows, and *ṇa* in the tuft of the hair on the head.

9-10. The syllable *ve* should be used (to spiritualize) the two eyes and *na* be deposited in all joints (of the body). He should contemplate the syllable *ma* as the missile. He should direct in all (the ten) directions the syllable *maḥ* (ma with a *visarga*), and ending with the sound phaṭ (for casting the spiritual protection on all sides, to shut out evil spirits—the words to be used while snapping the middle finger and the thumb are maḥ astrāya phaṭ). Thus a wise man becomes the mantra *Oṁ Viṣṇave namaḥ* incarnate.

11. He should then meditate on the Supreme Lord endowed with six potencies (viz. sovereignty of the universe, righteousness, glory, affluence, supreme knowledge and detachment from the world) and should contemplate himself as identical with him. He should then repeat the following mantra viz., *Nārāyaṇa kavaco* as the embodiment of learning, energy and penance.

12. May Hari, designated by the sacred syllable OM, afford me protection on all sides and in every respect—Hari who has placed his lotus-like feet on the back of the king of birds, viz., Garuḍa; who possesses eight spiritual powers (*siddhis-aṇimā* etc.) and who is endowed with eight arms in which he wields eight weapons, viz. conch, discus, a shield, sword, mace, arrows, bow and a noose.

13. May Viṣṇu in the form of the Fish (Incarnation)

protect me from aquatic animals and the noose of Varuṇa in waters. May Vāmana who has assumed the form of a young boy by his magic power protect me on land. May Trivikrama who has assumed the cosmic form protect me in the skies.

14. May the mighty Lord Nṛsiṁha (the Man-Lion form of Viṣṇu), the vanquisher of the king of demon-forces (Hiraṇyakaśipu), at the release of whose tremendous peals of roaring laughter, the cardinal points reverberated violently, and the embryos (from the wombs of Asura women) were discharged, protect me, in dangerous situations like jungles, battle-fronts and others.

15. May the boar-incarnation of Lord Hari, who uplifted the sphere of the earth with his tusk, and who is the embodiment of Sacrifice (yajña) protect me on the road (while travelling). May Paraśurāma shield me (from dangers) on mountain-peaks and may Rāma, the elder brother of Bharata, along with Lakṣmaṇa, protect me in long journeys (or foreign lands).

16. May Lord Nārāyaṇa shield me from black magic and commissions of mistakes of all kinds. May the sage Nara protect (me) from pride; Datta, the Lord of *yoga*, guard me against pitfalls in the practice of yoga. May Kapila, the controller of (*sattva*, *rajas* and *tamas*) *guṇas* protect me from the bondage of *karma*.

17. May Sanatkumāra save me from the god of Love; May the horseheaded God (Viṣṇu), from (neglecting in payment of obeisance to (images of) gods situated on the way. May the prominent divine sage Nārada, from the (thirty-two)[285]

285. VD. quotes from Pañcarātra, the list of 32 transgressions in the worship of god Viṣṇu. They may be translated as follows :—

(1) To enter a temple in a vehicle or without removing even wooden sandals; (2) to neglect serving in celebrations (the *utsavas*) of gods; (3) to fail to bow to an image of god after seeing it; (4) to bow to god in an impure condition (as in the mourning period); (5) to salute with one hand (instead of folding both the hands); (6) merely to circumambulate the image of the deity without stopping to bow to it, after completing each circle; (7) to sit with legs stretched before god's image; (8) to squat raising one knee and encircling them with hands before the deity: (9) to take meals in front of the deity; (10) to sleep before deity; (11) to tell a lie in the deity's presence; (12) to talk loudly; (13) to speak between each other: (14) to cry loudly and (15) to quarrel before the god's

transgressions in worshipping the Supreme person. May Hari in the Tortoise-form save me from all kinds of hells.

18. May Lord Dhanvantari (the physician incarnation) protect me from unwholesome food; may Lord Ṛṣabha, the subduer of his mind, from the pairs of opposites (pleasure-pain, heat-cold) and from fear; may Yajña, from the censure of the world; Balabhadra, from the death and violence at the hands of others (or from Yama); Lord Śeṣa, the king of serpents, from the revengeful race of serpents (called Krodhavaśa).

19. May venerable Vyāsa (Dvaipāyana) guard me against ignorance, Lord Buddha save me from heretical doctrines and negligence of duties; may Kalki who has specially taken this noble incarnation for the protection of Dharma (righteousness), protect me from the Kali age, the dirtiest of all aeons.

20. May Lord Keśava protect me with his mace in the morning (the 1st sixth part of the day); may Kṛṣṇa who has taken a flute in his hands, protect me in the *Saṅgava* period (next sixth part of the day); may Nārāyaṇa with his javeline held up (protect me) in the forenoon; may Viṣṇu with the discus Sudarśana in his hand, shield me at mid-day.

21. May god Madhusūdana, the wielder of the terrible bow, protect me in the afternoon; may god Mādhava of three forms (Brahmā, Viṣṇu and Rudra), in the evening. May Hṛṣīkeśa protect me in the first sixth part of the night; and Padmanābha alone during the second part and even at midnight.

---

image; (16) to trouble or (17) to favour another; (18) to speak cruel words in the presence of the Deity; (19) to cover one's self with a blanket; (20) to speak ill of others (21) or to eulogize others in god's presence (22) to utter obscene words; (23) flatuence or breaking wind; (24) to offer ordinary material for worship when one can afford the better; (25) to eat without offering it as *naivedya* to the Deity; (26) not to offer fruits or flowers peculiar to and available in the sesaon to god first before distributing them to others; (27) to offer a fruit etc. a part of which has been already eaten or taken by others; (28) to sit with one's back turned towards the Deity; (29) to bow to other persons before offering obeisance to the Deity; (30) negligence in greeting one's preceptor and failure to speak to him; (31) self-extolment and (32) scandalising any deity in the presence of god Viṣṇu's image.

22. May the Supreme Ruler bearing the Śrī-Vatsa mark protect me in the latter part of the night, and god Janārdana, carrying the sword, at about dawn (the fifth part of the night); may god Dāmodara at dawn; and Viṣṇu the Lord of the universe who manifested himself as Time (or the destroyer of all) protect me during twilights.

23. The discus Sudarśana, the rim of which is fierce like fire raging at the time of the destruction of the universe, whirls about when discharged by the Lord. Oh Sudarśana do completely and thoroughly burn down the inimical forces to ashes just as fire, helped by the friendly (favourable) wind, immediately consumes (heaps of) dry grass.

24. Oh mace (Kaumodakī)! You are dear to the invincible Lord. The sparks discharged by you are as formidable as the blow of Indra's Vajra (or thunderbolt), thoroughly crush down to powder all the evil spirits like Kūṣmāṇḍa, Vināyaka, Yakṣas and Rākṣasas, goblins and *grahas* (spirits harassing children). Reduce to powder all my enemies.

25. Oh excellent Conch Pāñcajanya: Blown by Lord Kṛṣṇa you, by your terrific blast, shock the hearts of enemies with convulsions of fear. May you drive away demonic spirits like Yātudhānas, Pramathas, ghosts, Mātṛkā (female spirits posing as mothers) Piśācas, Brahma-rākṣasas, and other evil-eyed spirits.

26. Oh sharp-edged excellent sword Nandaka! When directed by the Lord cut down to pieces all the army of my enemies. Oh shield brilliant like hundred Moons (decked with hundred moon-like buttons), cover up the eyes of the enemies, destroy the sight of the evil-eyed enemies.

27-28. May all the *grahas* (planets) and comets, Ketus, human beings, reptiles, carnivorous animals, Bhūtas (goblins), and sins which caused us fear, who stood in the way of our welfare, go immediately to utter destruction through the missile in the form of the utterance of the Divine name and form.

29. May the mighty Lord Garuḍa who is the embodiment of the Veda and who is extolled in *Bṛhad, Rathantara* and other *Sāma* hymns and Viṣvaksena protect us from all dangers with (utterance of) their names.

30. May all the names, forms, vehicles, arms of Lord

Hari protect us from all dangers. May his excellent attendants guard our intellect, *Indriyās* (cognitive and conative powers), mind and vital airs.

31. The glorious Lord himself factually constitutes everything gross and subtle, with or without forms. By the force of this truth may all our troubles come to an end.

32. To those who have realised the identity of the Lord with themselves, the Lord himself stands undifferentiated. But he with his own Māyā wields powers known as ornaments, weapons and insignia.

33. On the strength of the same factual reality, may the omniscient glorious Lord Hari protect us everywhere at all times, with all his manifestations, as he is omnipresent.

34. May the glorious Lord Narasiṁha who dispels the fear of the world by his roar and who eclipses the brightness of all luminaries by his all-absorbing brilliance and splendour, protect us in all directions, in the corners of directions, in the upward and downward directions, on all sides, from within and from without.

35. Oh Indra, this spiritual armour imbued with the power and spirit of Nārāyaṇa has been taught to you. Equipped with this spiritual armour, you will easily conquer the leaders of the Asura hosts.

36. Whomsoever does the wearer of this (*Nārāyaṇa Kavaca*) see with his eyes or touch with his feet, he is instantaneously freed from fear.

37. From no quarter does fear affect him who possesses this mantra. Neither from kings, robbers, evil planets (and such other wicked powers) nor from ferocious animals like tigers has he anything to fear.

38. In ancient times, there was a Brāhmaṇa of Kuśika *gotra* who had this sacred mantra mastered by him. He cast off his body by yogic process in a desert.

39. Once upon a time Citraratha, the Lord of Gandharvas, surrounded by ladies crossed in his aerial car the place of the death of the Brāhmaṇa.

40. Immediately he fell down along with his heavenly car with his head downwards. On the advice of sage Vālakhilya, he collected together the bones of the Brāhmaṇa and

immersed them in the Sarasvatī where it bends to the East. He took his bath and returned home amazed (at this instance).

Śrī Śuka said :

41. He who listens to this *Kavaca* at the opportune time (of fear, danger etc.) and devoutly fixes his mind on this Mantra becomes free from fear in every respect, and is reverentially respected by living beings.

42. Indra, the performer of hundred sacrifices, learnt this sacred lore (*Nārāyaṇa Kavaca*) from Viśvarūpa. He conquered the demons in the battle and enjoyed the sovereignty of the three worlds.

CHAPTER NINE

(*Viśvarūpa killed. Gods defeated by Vṛtra, advised to approach Dadhīci*)

Śrī Śuka said :

1. Oh Parīkṣit (the scion of the Bharata race), we have heard the report that Viśvarūpa had three heads, one used to drink Soma, the other wine, and the third used to eat food

2. They say that in sacrifices, he directly offered the share of gods to them with due respect declaring loudly their names (e.g. *Indrāya idam*—this is the share of Indra), for gods were his forefathers.

3. Himself being the sacrificer, he managed secretly to offer the share in the sacrifices to the Asuras also, for due to his affection to his mother, he oblated some share to them.

4. Indra, the king of gods, noticed his contempt and faithlessness to gods and his sham righteousness. Being afraid (lest Asuras should be powerful) he immediately cut down his (Viśvarūpa's) heads in wrath.

5. The head that used to drink Soma became the bird Kapiñjala; the head drinking wine, a sparrow (Kalaviṅka); the head eating food became the Tittiri bird.

6. Even though Indra was powerful enough, he accepted the sin of assassinating a Brāhmaṇa with both his hands folded. But at the end of the year for self-purification of the elements constituting himself, he distributed that sin proportionately in four parts to the earth, water, trees and young women.

7. They say that the earth accepted the fourth part of the sin on condition that pits excavated in it are (automatically) filled up (in due course). Barren soil is the form of the *Brahmahatyā* which became manifested in the earth.

8. The trees accepted one-fourth of the sin on condition of the boon that a chopped part of the trees will grow with greater force. *Brahmahatyā* is seen exhibited in trees in the form of gum.

9. Women took over one-fourth of the sin on condition of getting the boon that they would ever cherish the passion of love (even during pregnancy). This sin (of killing a Brāhmaṇa) appears in the form of menstrual discharge from month to month in them.

10. The waters accepted the (remaining) one-fourth of the sin on condition of increasing the quantity of the substance with which it is mixed. The sin appears in the form of bubbles and foam on the water. He who throws away the bubbles etc. removes that sin from water.

11. Tvaṣṭṛ whose son was slain (by Indra) then performed a sacrifice for the birth of an enemy, the killer of Indra: "Oh enemy of Indra grow in strength and kill the enemy (Indra) without delay" (prayed Tvaṣṭṛ).

12. Then arose from Dakṣiṇāgni or *Anvahārya-pacana*, a demon terrific in appearance like the god of death, at the end of the destruction of the worlds, at the end of Yugas.

13. Everyday he increased in size, in all directions, to the extent of the distance covered by the shot of an arrow. He looked like the burnt top of a mountain and was bright like the mass of evening clouds.

14. His hair of the head and beard was red like heated copper and his eyes were fierce like the mid-day Sun.

15. He, as it were, held the vault of the heaven pierced

with his brilliant trident. He was dancing and roaring and was shaking the earth by his gait.

16. By his deep valley-like mouth he was as if drinking the surface of the sky, and was licking the stars with his tongue, and was as it were swallowing the three worlds.

17. He was now and then yawning his mouth which displayed his terrible tusks—seeing him people were stricken with panic and ran away to all the ten directions.

18. That most ferocious wicked demon was called Vṛtra as he, the son of Tvaṣṭṛ, covered the whole world with the darkness, by the shadow of his person.

19. The prominent leaders of gods, along with their armies, attacked him, and discharged at him streams of their respective divine missiles and arms. But he swallowed them up completely.

20. The gods were thereby amazed. All of them got despondent. With their splendour eclipsed, they approached Nārāyaṇa, with their minds composed, as he is the *antaryāmin*, the inner controller.

21. May we get protection from him (the Supreme Lord) of whom even the god of Death (or the god presiding over Time) is afraid—the god of death to whom the five elements (constituting the universe) viz., the wind, the sky, the fire, the water and the earth, and three worlds (along with their denizens) and (the rulers of the worlds like) god Brahmā and others and we (ordinary) gods pay homage out of great fear.

22. Like an ignoramous person desiring to cross the sea with the help of a dog's tail, is he who approaches for protection to someone else than him (the Supreme Lord) who is absolutely free from egotism (or curiosity), perfectly serene and passionless, all whose wishes are fulfilled through the realization of his own blissful self and is unconditioned by limitations.

23. The same god, in his fish incarnation, to whose broad big horn Manu fastened his boat in the form of the earth and crossed the danger of deluge, will certainly protect us, his dependants, from the danger caused by Vṛtra, the son of Tvaṣṭṛ—a danger which is difficult to be got over.

24. Formerly (at the beginning of the creation of the universe) god Brahmā, the self-born deity, was all alone. He was all but fallen from his lotus (-abode, growing out of the navel of Viṣṇu) in the terrible waters of the deluge, by the roars of the heavy billows whipped up by stormy winds. But he got over from that danger by (the grace of) Viṣṇu. May the same God be our protector.

25. That Supreme Sovereign, though all alone, has created us by his Māyā. It is through his grace and by imitating him that we carry on the work of creation. We each being proud as independent rulers, cannot see his form, though he is present before us.

26. When he finds that we are excessively harassed by our enemies, he, though eternally existent, by his Māyā takes incarnation by assuming forms of gods (e. g. Vāmana), sages (e. g. Paraśurāma), sub-human beings (e. g. Varāha, Nṛsiṁha), and human beings (Rāma, Kṛṣṇa), in every yuga-period and protects us, regarding us as his own.

27. To that God alone we shall all resort for asylum as he is worthy of it. He is our own Deity (object of worship). He manifests himself as the universe and yet is different from it. As the ultimate cause of it, he is himself both *Pradhāna* and *Puruṣa*. The Supreme Soul will positively confer happiness and prosperity on us who are his devotees.

Śrī Śuka said :

28. While they were praying thus, Oh great King, the Lord revealed himself in their hearts, as wielding a conch, disc and a mace.

29-30. On seeing the Lord whose eyes were like full-blown autumnal lotus, and waited upon on all sides by sixteen attendants (like Sunanda and others) who were just like himself (wielding conchs, discs etc.) with the exception of *Śrīvatsa* mark and the *Kaustubha* gem, all of them were overwhelmed with joy, and lay prostrate before him on the ground like a stick, and rising slowly, began to praise him.

The gods said :

31.* Salutations to you whose power (to confer Svarga and other blessings) is (revealed in) the sacrificial performance. Hail to you who are our Age (The Time-Spirit) defining the time limit of the fruits of sacrifices etc. to be enjoyed. Bows to you who hurl your disc (at our enemies to destroy them). We salute you who are addressed with a number of blessed epithets.

32. Oh Lord ! One who is born posterior to the Creation (of the universe) is incapable of knowing the highest nature which transcends the *guṇas*. We can merely bow to you who are the controller of the three courses of *guṇas* (or the modes of existence as gods, human and sub-human beings).

33. Bow to you, Oh Lord, who are designated by the syllable OM ! Oh Nārāyaṇa (occupant of Cosmic Waters), Vāsudeva (the Abode of the worlds), the most ancient person, the supreme person, possessor of supreme glory and auspiciousness, the supremely blessed and merciful, the absolute (one without a second), the support of the world, the only protector of the universe, the ruler of all, consort of Lakṣmī (the goddess of fortune and bliss) !

When the ascetics of the highest *paramahaṁsa* order deeply meditate upon you by means of the highest concentration of the mind through eight-fold yogic processes the real *dharma* of the *Paramahaṁsas*, viz., the adoration of the Lord, becomes manifest and realized in their pure hearts. Thereby the door of darkness of their hearts is broken open and you stand revealed as the inherent bliss of the Soul, in the regions of their hearts.

---

* VR. : Hail to you who have empowered sacrifices and made them the cause of creation, and who bless (us) with longevity for performance of sacrifices and other forms of worship. You wield the disc Sudarśana for the protection of your devotees and the remembrance of whose glorious name is efficacious enough to ward off danger immediately.

VJ. : We salute you who are the creator of sacrifices. You keep *jīvas* bound in *saṁsāra*. You continue the cycle of creation and destruction again and again. You incarnated as Sudarśana (for the protection of the world). You are addressed with various sanctifying names. (We bow to you).

34. You create, protect and destroy this universe constituted of (*sattva*, *rajas* and *tamas*) *guṇas* though you yourself are without any support, body or form, without any expectation of cooperation and help from us (the divinities presiding over various organs etc.) and without undergoing any transformation (within yourself). The cause of this sport of yours is simply beyond (our) comprehension.

35. Moreover, we do not properly understand whether your worship, like Devadatta (an ordinary person who builds a house and helplessly experiences joys and sorrows while staying therein) enters (as an *antaryāmin*) the various bodies (which are the products of *guṇas*) and depending upon other (*karmic*) forces helplessly reap the fruit of good or bad actions or whether you are an unconcerned witness (of such happenings) remaining delighted in yourself and naturally unruffled with your spiritual essence undiminished.

36. As a matter of fact, there is no contradiction in both the positions which are compatible in Your Lordship who are endowed with infinite variation of excellences, the absolute ruler of unfathomable greatness. You are far beyond the range of controversies of modern disputants who are strongly prejudiced as their minds are bewildered by the study of heretic scriptures teeming with doubts, (false) reasoning, wrong conclusions, (untrustworthy) authorities and bad logic. Your real essential Self is absolute, transcending all the products of Māyā. What is there that cannot be predicated of you, who, remaining concealed under Māyā, make the Māyā create any impossibility and your real self is free from both the above (contradictory) propositions. (There is no contradiction as there is no duality in you).

37. Just as a piece of rope appears to be a serpent (garland etc.) to those whose minds are prepossessed with the false notion of a serpent etc., (but appears factually a piece of rope to the right thinking men), you show yourself according to the views of the right-thinking persons or of prejudiced wrong-thinkers.

38. Again, the Lord is certainly the real essence of every existing thing and abides in all things. He is the ruler of all. He is the cause of all the causes (*Prakṛti* or *Brahma*) of

the whole of the universe. The illuminating power of the objects (intellect, senses) indicates the *jīva* but not him as he abides in all, as the Inner Controller (*Sarvāntaryāmin*). He is the only true existence conclusively left over (proved) by the process of elimination of double negation (*neti neti*).

39. Oh slayer of (the demon) Madhu! By tasting but once a small drop of the nectar-like sweet ocean of your glories, incessant stream of rapturous joy begins to flow uninterruptedly in the heart of great devotees. It makes them forget the apparent trifling bits of pleasures of senses actually seen (enjoyed on the earth) or heard (of as available in the heaven)—the devotees whose hearts find incessant and ecstatic delight in the Lord who is beloved friend of all beings and is the Soul (the Inner Controller—*antaryāmin*) of the entire universe. Under these circumstances, how is it that the saintly persons (devoid of love, hate etc.) who are skilful in achieving their high purpose (viz. Liberation) and who look upon you as their dear friend and a well-wisher, give up the service of your lotus-like feet whereby there is no return to the *Saṁsāra*, the transmigration of the Soul.

40. Oh Lord whose manifestation and mansion are the three worlds (or Oh Soul and the abode of the three worlds)! Oh God who dominate the three worlds (or who covered the universe in three steps)! Oh Guide of the three worlds whose majestic charm captivates (the minds of) the worlds! Even the demons like the sons of Diti and Danu and others are your glorious forms. Considering (however) that this is not the appropriate time for (giving free rein to) their (destructive) activities, you as a wielder of the rod (of punishment), dispense punishment (to them) proportionate to (the gravity of) their offence by assuming, through your Māyā Power, forms of gods (e.g. Vāmana), men (e.g. Rāma, Kṛṣṇa), beasts (such as Boar or Varāha), half-man half-beast (e.g. Narasiṁha, Hayagrīva), aquatic animal (e.g. the Fish or the Tortoise). In the same way, Oh glorious Lord, if you deem it fit, kill this son of Tvaṣṭṛ (viz. Vṛtra).

41. Oh Father! (Nay) Oh grand-father! Since we are yours and have completely submitted to you, and since our heart has been firmly attached (lit. fettered) with the bond of

love (evolved) through (our) meditation on the pair of your lotus-like feet, and as you have accepted us as your own by the revelation of your person, be pleased to cure the fever (torments) of our hearts, by your bright, charming, soothing, smiling looks which are rendered still more gracious by your compassion and with the nectarine drops in the form of sweet words proceeding from your lips, Oh Faultless one !

42. Oh glorious Lord ! To what extent can we respectfully communicate to you our specific entreaty any more than the sparks of fire (which emit little light) can bring illuminasion to the god of Fire ? (as a matter of fact, it is superfluous). For you indulge in your pastime with the divine Māyā which is the instrumental cause of the creation, maintenance and the destruction of the whole world, and you, as Brahman as well as *Antaryāmin* (the Inner Controller of bodies) reside within the hearts of all the multitudes of beings, and from without as *Pradhāna* (the Primordial matter) you are their material cause, and thus experience the peculiarities of the place, time, body and conditions (of all beings). With your body (untouched and untainted) like the sky, you are a detached witness of the thoughts of all. You are the transcendental *Brahman*, the Supreme Soul.

43. (You are omniscient). Hence please accomplish for us of your own accord (without waiting for being requested for it by us) that object (of ours) desiring which we have resorted to you and have sought refuge under the shade of your lotus-like feet which removes the fatigue of the transmigration of the Soul resulting from various sins. And you are the glorious Lord and the Supreme Teacher.

44. Therefore, Oh Lord, kill Vṛtra who has already swallowed up our powers as well as missiles, Oh Kṛṣṇa, and is now devouring the three worlds.

45. Salutations to you Hari, the reliever of sufferings—to Hari who is absolutely pure and abides in the cavity of heart remaining witness to the intellect etc. You are the eternal Bliss incarnate. Your glory is resplendent. You are beginningless and are cherished as a treasure by the virtuous. To wanderers in *Saṁsāra* seeking refuge with you, you are the

final destination to be reached at the end of *Saṁsāra*, the excellent fruit to be coveted.

46. Oh King ! Being thus reverentially and earnestly praised by gods, Lord Hari listened to the prayer offered to him and being highly pleased, he addressed them (as follows:).

The Lord said :

47. I am highly pleased with you, Oh great gods, for the knowledge enshrined in your eulogy which will awaken the memory of transcendental nature of their real Self among the beings and engender in them devotion unto me.

48. What is difficult to be attained when I am pleased, Oh great gods ? But he who knows the truth and cherishes devotion to me, does not covet for anything else than Myself.

49. The miserly fool who looks upon the products of the *guṇas* as real, does not know what is really good for himself and he who confers those objects (products of *guṇas*) on them at their request is of the same description (is equally ignorant).

50. A wise man, knowing for himself what the highest good is, does not prescribe the (path of) *Karma* (ritualistic actions) to the ignorant, just as an excellent physician does not allow the ailing patient unwholesome food even if he (the patient) may desire it.

51. May good betide you, Oh Indra ! Without delay you all go to Dadhyaṅ (Dadhīca or Dadhīci), the foremost of sages and beg of him his body which has been reinforced by *Brahma-Vidyā*, observance of vows and austerities.

52. Dadhyaṅ has completely realized his identity with Pure Brahman (untainted by Māyā or has mastered the *Pravargya*). He initiated the gods Aśvinikumāras in that knowledge which came to be called *Aśva-śiras*—horse headed (as at the time of imparting the knowledge, the sage Dadhyaṅ had a horse's head instead of a human one.[286] That Brahma-lore conferred immortality (*mokṣa* while alive) on those gods.

---

286. Purāṇic quotations in the commentaries of ŚR., VR. etc. give the story as follows :

When Aśvinikumāras sought initiation in *Brahma-vidyā* from Dadhyaṅ, the sage was engaged in some religiuos rites. He told them to see him on

53. Dadhyañ, the son of Atharvan, taught the impregnable protective armour (called the *Nārāyaṇa kavaca*) full of my essence and imparted it to Tvaṣṭṛ. Tvaṣṭṛ gave it to his son Viśvarūpa who in turn taught it to you.

54. The sage is well-versed in Dharma (righteousness). When begged by Aśvinikumāras (your physicians) he will offer his body (i.e. the limbs of the body) to you. Then with the (bones of the requisite) limbs, the most powerful weapon will be forged by Viśvakarman (your artisan). With that weapon imbued with my power, you will cut the head of Vṛtra.

55. When he (Vṛtra) is killed, you will regain your former glory, missiles, weapons and wealth. May you be happy ! Nobody can trouble or destroy those who are devoted to me.

CHAPTER TEN*

(*With Vajra forged, Indra fights*)

Śrī Śuka said :

1. The glorious Hari, the protector of the universe, thus instructed Indra and disappeared at that very spot, while the gods, with unwinking eyes, were simply gazing.

2. Oh Bhārata (Parīkṣit) ! Solicited by gods thus (as per instructions of the Lord), the great-hearted sage of

---

some other occasion as he was then busy. In the meanwhile, Indra came to the sage and advised him not to impart Brahma-vidyā to Aśvins as they were merely physicians and hence unqualified. He further threatened to behead him, in case he initiated them in that lore. When Aśvinikumāras approached the sage and learnt of Indra's threat, they proposed a surgical operation in which the sage's head would be replaced by a horse's head and requested him to teach through the horse's mouth. In case Indra beheaded the horse's head, they would substitute his original human head. The sage preferred to keep his word and not his head. He allowed the Aśvins to perform the operation and imparted to them the Brahmavidyā with a horse's head on his shoulders.

* JG—No commentary on this chapter.

Atharvan Clan was delighted and addressed them jokingly (with a smile), as follows:

3. "Oh gods! (Presiding deities of the senses as you are) can you not imagine the excruciating and unbearable pain caused to embodied beings at the time of death—a pain that deprives them of consciousness.

4. In this world, (one's own) body is the dearest thing coveted by living beings who have a desire to live. Who can dare to donate it even to Viṣṇu, should he beg for it ?"

Gods said :

5. Oh Brahman! Is there anything which is difficult to part with in the case of great persons like your honour, who are compassionate to all beings, and whose noble deeds are worthy of being praised by people with hallowing reputation.

6. There is no doubt that persons who are solely devoted to achieve their own objects, do not (care to) understand the danger faced by others (the donors). If they could realize it, they would not beg for it. (In the same way, the donor also does not appreciate the difficulty of the seeker of his help). If the donor were (aware of the seeker's danger and) capable of granting it, he would never say "No". (Hence understand our danger and grant our request).

The sage said :

7. It is with a desire to hear from you the (exposition of) Dharma (righteousness) that you were replied that way (by me). Here I cast off my body which is dear to you (due to its utility) as (some day) it is sure to leave me.

8. Oh Lords! A person who does not desire to earn religious merits out of compassion to living beings or aspire after glory by means of this ephemeral body, deserves to be pitied even by immobile creatures.

9. That one should sympathetically feel sorrow or delight at the grief or joy of other beings, is the eternal law of righteousness (*Dharma*) practised by persons with holy renown.

10. Alas! What a pity! that a mortal does not show benevolence (by helping others) with his wealth, sons and relatives and his body—all of which are transient, of no use to him and (actually) belong to others.

Śrī Śuka said :

11. In this way, Dadhyañ, the scion of the Atharvan Clan, made up his mind and uniting his individual Soul with the glorious transcendental Brahman, gave up his ghost.

12. He controlled his senses, vital airs, mind and intellect and fixed his gaze on the Reality. He severed all bonds and established himself in union with the Brahman, and (in the process) was not aware of the falling away of his body.

13. Then Indra was equipped with Vajra (the thunderbolt) forged out of the bones of the sage, by Viśvakarman (the chief artisan of gods). He (Indra) was endowed with the Lord's power and felt himself mighty.

14. Surrounded by all the hosts of gods and eulogised by assemblies of sages, he shone riding his excellent elephant (Airāvata), to the delight of the three worlds.

15. In order to cut him down, Oh King! he attacked vehemently Vṛtra who was surrounded by the leaders of Asura forces, just as wrathful Rudra does in the case of the god of Death (at the end of the world).

16. Then ensued the most ferocious fight between the gods and the demons, on the bank of the Narmadā, at the beginning of the Tretā Age (in the first round of four yugas in this *manvantara*).

17-18. The demons, headed by Vṛtra, did not tolerate the sight of Indra armed with Vajra and resplendent in his original glory and surrounded by Rudras, Vasus, Ādityas, Aśvinikumāras, manes, Fire-gods, Wind-gods, Ṛbhus, Sādhyas, and Viśvedevas, on the battle-field.

19-21. Namuci, Śambara, Anarvā, Dvimūrdhā (a two-headed demon), Ṛṣabha, Ambara Hayagrīva (a demon with horse's head), Śaṅkuśiras, Vipracitti, Ayomukha, Puloman, Vṛṣaparvan, Praheti, Heti, Utkala, and the sons of Diti and Danu and Yakṣas, Ogres in their thousands, of whom Sumāli and Māli were prominent—all armoured and decorated with gold ornaments—resisted the vanguard of Indra's army which was unapproachable even to the god of Death.

22-23. The haughty and furious demons were fearless and unbewildered. With a lion-like roar, they attacked gods with maces, iron bars, arrows, barbed shafts and javelins.

They covered the leaders of gods with volleys of weapons and missiles like pikes, axes, swords, *Śataghnīs* (cylindrical pieces of wood, 4 cubits long and studded with iron spikes) and *Bhuśuṇḍis* (a Śataghnī-like weapon with iron spikes, one exceeding the other in length), on all sides.

24. The gods, covered with net-like volleys of arrows showered on all sides with one arrow closely following the other, were rendered invisible like luminaries behind the screen of clouds in the sky.

25. The streams of the volleys of missiles and weapons did not reach or touch the soldiers in the army of gods, for they were cut down to pieces in thousands on their way in the sky, by gods with quick hands.

26. When their stock of missiles and weapons was exhausted, they showered the army of gods with mountain peaks, trees and stones, and the gods cut them to pieces as before.

27. Finding that the gods were unhurt and safe despite the volleys of weapons and missiles, and unaffected by trees, shower of stones and different mountain peaks, the demons led by Vṛtra were filled with consternation.

28. Just as abusive language employed by the vulgar against the exalted persons does not disturb them, all the efforts repeatedly made against the army of gods by the demons became ineffectual, as Lord Viṣṇu was favourable to them.

29. The demons who were not devoted to Hari, had their arrogance and pride of fighting crushed, when they found that all their efforts had become infructuous. With their *morale* deeply affected, they thought of fleeing from the battle-field deserting their leader at the initial stage of fighting.

30. The self-possessed warrior Vṛtra saw that his followers are running away. Finding his army broken through terror and fleeing, he laughed loudly and spoke.

31. The heroic person spoke the following words appropriate to the occasion and agreeable to the high-minded souls:

"Oh Vipracitti, Namuci, Puloman, Maya, Anarvan, Śambara, listen to me.

32. This death is inevitable to whoever is born. No escape from any side from this, has been devised (by any one). If the attainment of heaven and glory could follow death, who would not court such a desirable and welcome end ?

33. Two modes of death are approved of (by the great), but they do not easily come to one's lot, namely, (1) he who, engaged in the Yogic process, controls his vital airs, concentrates himself on Brahman and casts off his body and (2) one who, in the fore-front of battle, gives up his body on the battlefield (the bed of warriors), without turning his back."

CHAPTER ELEVEN

(*Vṛtra, Hari's devotee, fights*)

Śrī Śuka said :

1. Oh King, while he (Vṛtra) was explaining the course of righteousness to the demons, they were struck with terror, and were bent on fleeing, and hence paid no heed to the words of their leader.

2-3. The great Asura, found his army of demons being shattered and scattered like a leaderless mob by gods to whom time was favourable and got enraged. The enemy of Indra, being indignant, was deeply pained, and warding the gods off, he spoke to them scoldingly, Oh King.

4. "What are you gaining by striking on the back of the fleeing soldiers who are no better than the excreta of their mothers ? The slaughter of the cowards does not contribute to the glory or lead to heaven those who pride themselves as valiant.

5. Oh insignificant fellows, if at all you have faith in fighting or some courage at heart and have no longing for sensual vulgar pleasures, try to stand before me at least."

6. The wrathful demon possessed of vast strength and formidable figure, threatened the army of the gods thus and gave out a loud roar which made people lose their consciousness.

7. By that terrible roar of Vṛtra all the hosts of gods verily fell unconscious on the ground as if struck down by a thunderbolt.

8. Just as a leader of a herd of elephants in the period of his youthful madness, tramples over a bed of lotuses, Vṛtra of irrepressible passion for fighting, shaking the earth by his might and with his trident raised, trampled under his feet the army of gods which was terrified and lying with closed eyes.

9. Indra, the wielder of Vajra, saw him and got extremely enraged. He hurled his heavy mace at his enemy who was rushing towards him. But Vṛtra sportively caught it in his left hand while it was coming with irresistible force.

10. The enemy of Indra, possessing terrible prowess, was extremely enraged and by that very mace, he struck the vehicle of the great Indra, viz., the elephant Airāvata on its forehead (its temples). All present in the battlefield warmly appreciated this feat (of Vṛtra).

11. Airāvata which was smitten down by Vṛtra's mace, reeled down like a mountain struck by a thunderbolt. With blood coming out of its mouth, it retreated along with Indra for a distance of seven bows, as it was extremely afflicted with its mouth deeply wounded.

12. The great-souled Vṛtra did not hurl his mace against Indra who was deeply dejected in spirits as his vehicle, viz., the elephant was stunned. Indra whose wounded elephant recovered from its pain, by the touch of Indra's hand dripping with nectar, again took his stand (against Vrtra).

13. Oh King of kings, seeing Indra, his enemy the murderer of his brother, armed with the Vajra (thunderbolt) itching for a fight, he remembered Indra's wicked sinful deed (the murder of his brother) and filled with grief and infatuation he laughed and spoke.

Vṛtra said :

14. How glad I am that you, my enemy, the murderer of a Brāhmana, the slayer of your own preceptor and my brother, have stood before me. Oh most wicked fellow, how lucky is it that I shall discharge my debt by piercing your stony heart with my trident within a short time.

15. Just as a sacrificer desirous of heaven mercilessly lops off the head of a sacrificial beast, you cut off the heads of our innocent elder brother who had realized his Self, was a Brāhmaṇa and your preceptor, and who, reposing full confidence in you about his safety, was engaged in a sacrifice.

16. Being destitute of shame, grace, mercy and glory, you are fit to be censured by man-eaters for your misdeed. With your body painfully torn up by my trident and uncremated the vultures will devour you.

17. I shall propitiate the lords of goblins (*Bhairavas*) along with their retinue, by piercing the necks with my sharpened trident, of those ignorant followers who obey a wicked fellow like you, and who attack me with their missiles raised.

18. Oh valiant Indra, if you will cut off by force my head with the Vajra, I shall have discharged the debt of all beings (by my body) and shall attain to the regions (lit. the dust of the feet) of the high-souled ones.

19. Oh Lord of gods, why do you not hurl your unfailing Vajra on your enemy who is stationed before you. Do not entertain any doubt that like your mace, the Vajra will be ineffectual like a request made to a miserly fellow.

20. Oh Śakra, this Vajra of yours is sharpened and strengthened with the power of Lord Viṣṇu and the austerities of Dadhīci. Kill your enemy by that thunderbolt which is prompted by Viṣṇu's power, because where there is Hari, victory, fortune and excellences are to that side.

21. Concentrating my mind on the lotus-like feet of Lord Saṅkarṣaṇa as directed by him, with the ties of attachment to sensual pleasures cut asunder by the force of your Vajra, I shall cast off my body and attain to the region of sages.

22. He does not confer on persons whose minds are absolutely devoted to him, the wealth and affluence of heaven, the earth, and the netherworlds as it engenders passions, fear, anxiety, arrogance, discord, misery and physical pain.

23. Oh Indra, our Master causes obstructions in the efforts for attaining the three objects of human life, (viz, Dharma, Artha and Kāma). The grace of the Lord is to be

inferred from such obstructions, for it is the lot of those votaries who have given up everything for him (and have nothing of their own). This is extremely rare in the case of others.

24. (Contemplating over the Lord, Hari, Vṛtra addresses :) Oh Lord Hari, let me be again the servant of the servants of your devotees whose sole refuge is your feet. May my mind ponder over the excellences of the Lord of my life. May my speech extol them and may my body render service to you.

25. Oh treasury of Bliss and Grace ! I do not aspire after the post of Dhruva which is above the heaven; nor the position of god Brahmā, nor absolute sovereignty over the whole world or the overlordship of a subterranean region, nor do I covet for supernatural yogic powers nor for Liberation (which terminates the cycle of births and deaths)—if it means separation from you.

26. Oh lotus-eyed God, my mind eagerly yearns to see you, just as the unfledged young ones of birds anxiously wait for their mother or young calves tormented with hunger wish for the milk from the udders (of the mother cow) or a beloved lady dejected due to the absence of her lord who has gone to a distant country (waits for her beloved).

27. Bless me with friendship with the devotee of the Lord of excellent renown, while I am wandering in the cycle of Saṁsāra (transmigration of the Soul) as an effect of my *karma* (deeds). I may not form friendship with people whose minds are attached to their bodies, children, wife and house (property) due to the force of your Māyā.

CHAPTER TWELVE

(*Vṛtra slain by Indra*)

The Sage (Śuka) said:

1. In this way, Vṛtra who was eager to lay down his life (body) in the battle, and who thought death preferable to victory, seized his trident and attacked the Chief of gods, just

as the demon Kaiṭabha did against the Almighty Lord Viṣṇu, on the Cosmic waters of the deluge, Oh King.

2. Then, whirling with force his trident with prongs, dazzling like the fire of *Pralaya* (the dissolution of the universe), he hurled it at the great Indra. The valiant Vṛtra roared aloud and exclaimed in wrath, "Killed are you Oh wicked fellow".

3. Seeing that (trident) darting through the sky with a whirling motion, and unbearable to look at like a dazzling planet or meteor, Indra remained unperturbed. The wielder of thunderbolt i.e. Indra cut it with his Vajra of hundred joints, along with Vṛtra's arm which was long and stout like the body of the serpent lord Vāsuki.

4. Vṛtra whose arm was cut, became extremely enraged and dashing at Indra, he dealt a blow both to Indra and his elephant on the cheek. And the bolt slipped down from the hand of Indra.

5. Gods, demons, the companies of Cāraṇas and Siddhas applauded the most marvellous feat of Vṛtra, but seeing the critical plight of Indra, they shouted loudly in great anxiety, "Alas, Alas".

6. Being very much ashamed, Indra did not pick up his bolt which slipped from his hand in the presence of the enemy. To him Vṛtra said, "Oh Indra, take up your Vajra and kill your enemy. This is not the time for despondency".

7. With the exception of the Omniscient, beginningless, Eternal Person, the Controller of the creation, maintenance and destruction of the universe, victory does not always favour the belligerents equipped with weapons anywhere, as there are some occasions when their bodies are controlled by others (destiny).

8. It is due to the control of God (in the form of Time) that the worlds along with their guardian deities live and act, in spite of their will, like birds caught in a net. Hence it is the Time-spirit alone which is the cause of victory and defeat.

9. Not knowing that the Time (or god) is the cause of the power of the mind, the potency of the sense organs, physical strength, vital breaths, immortality or Liberation and death that people regard this gross body of theirs as the cause (of victory).

10. Just as a wooden doll or a mechanical toy-deer is controlled by the showman or the mechanism, similarly all the *bhūtas* (beings or elements) are subject to the control of god.

11. In the absence of his grace, neither the individual Soul, nor Prakṛti (primordial matter), nor *Mahat* (cosmic intelligence), nor ego, nor elements, nor the cognitive and conative organs or the mind is individually or aggregatively capable of the creative and other activities (pertaining to the universe).

12. He who is ignorant of this, regards his incapable Self as capable of doing this. But it is really the Lord who creates or evolves beings or elements from *Bhūtas*, and devours them through carnivorous beasts or withdraws the elements at his own sweet will.

13. It is at the favourable time that length of life, affluence, glory, power and blessings fall to the lot of man. They are reversed against them even against his will.

14. Therefore, one should be balanced, irrespective of glory and infamy, victory or defeat, pleasure or pain, life or death.

15. He who knows that *Sattva*, *Rajas*, and *Tamas* are the modes of Prakṛti and not the qualities of the Soul, and that the individual Soul is merely the witness of their working, is not subjected to the bondage of *Saṁsāra*.

16. Oh Indra, look at me. I am defeated and deprived of the weapon and my arm in the battle. I am however endeavouring to the best of my ability to take your life.

17. This battle-field is like a gambling house where life is the stake, arrows are the dice and the vehicles like horses, elephants etc. are the board. Here it is not known who will be triumphant and who is defeated (to the last of the fight).

Śrī Śuka said:

18. Having heard the straightforward and guileless speech of Vṛtra, Indra expressed his respect. Picking up his Vajra and overcoming astonishment (at his charitable disposition), he laughed heartily and spoke.

Indra said:

19. Oh son of Danu, you are really a Siddha (one who has attained enlightenment) as your tenor of thought is such. You are a real devotee, with all your being, of the Lord, a friend of the universe.

20. Your respectable self has verily crossed the Māyā (deluding power) of Viṣṇu which infatuates the world, as your honourable self has given up his demonic nature and attained the level of exalted Souls.

21. It is certainly a great wonder that you who are *Rājasic* by nature, entertain unflinching faith and devotion in the glorious Lord Vāsudeva who is the embodiment of Sattva.

22. He who cherishes devotion to the glorious Hari, the bestower of Mokṣa, has as if sported in the ocean of nectar. Of what account are to him waters of the ditches and the pools (i. e. pleasures in the heaven)?

Śrī Śuka said:

23. Oh King, discoursing this way with a desire to ascertain the nature of Dharma (righteousness), those two leading veterans in fight, Indra and Vṛtra, possessed of extraordinary prowess, fought on.

24. Vṛtra, the vanquisher of enemies, whirled his terrible bludgeon made of black iron and hurled that dreadful weapon with his left hand at Indra, Oh noble king.

25. But the god with his bolt of hundred joints, simultaneously cut down that iron bludgeon as well as Vṛtra's hand which was like the trunk of an elephant.

26. The demon with both of his arms cut at the roots and streaming forth profuse blood shone like a mountain with wings chopped, and dislodged from the sky by being struck down by the wielder of thunderbolt.

27-29. With his lower jaw touching the earth and his upper jaw brushing the heavens, and with his mouth deep like the sky and with his lusty serpentlike tongue and with his large teeth looking like the god of Death, he was as it were swallowing the three worlds. With his extremely gigantic body he was shaking the mountains with his violent motion, and like a big mountain moving on feet, he was pounding the earth. He thus assailed Indra and swallowed him up along with his vehicle namely the elephant Airāvata.

30. (Vṛtra swallowed them) as a big serpent of immense strength and indomitable power swallows up an elephant. Gods along with the protectors of the worlds and great sages observed Indra being swallowed up by Vṛtra and wailed despondently "Alas, how unfortunate"!

31. Though Indra was swallowed up by the chief of demons, he entered Vṛtra's belly. Protected as he was by the armour of the Supreme Person (Nārāyaṇa Kavaca) and by his Yogic powers and Māyā, he did not die.

32. Ripping open the abdomen of Vṛtra by his Vajra, the powerful vanquisher of Bala, came out of it and by his power lopped off the enemy's head, like the peak of a mountain, by his Vajra.

33. Whirling very rapidly and cutting on all sides the neck of Vṛtra, Vajra felled it on the ground at the proper time of Vṛtra's death in as many days (360) as are required for the heavenly bodies like the Sun for two *Ayanas* (the apparent motions of the Sun from the northernmost to the southernmost point and vice versa.

34. At that time kettle-drums were sounded in the sky, Gandharvas, Siddhas along with companies of great sages, joyously showered flowers on Indra glorifying him with panegyrics describing his great feat of killing Vṛtra.

35. Oh vanquisher of the enemies, while all people were looking on, from the body of Vṛtra there came forth a light (his effulgent Soul) and merged in the Supreme Being, transcending the universe.

CHAPTER THIRTEEN

(*The Triumph of Indra*)

Śrī Śuka said :

1. When Vṛtra was killed, all the three worlds along with their guardian deities, with the exception of Indra, became immediately free from feverish anxiety and felt felicitous at heart.

2. Without bidding good-bye to Indra, gods, sages, manes, Bhūtas, demons and the followers of gods returned to their respective regions. Then dispersed Brahmā, Rudra, Indra and others. [According to GS, Indra did not return to Svarga. The very moment he killed Vṛtra, the sin of killing a Brāhmaṇa (*Brahma-hatyā*) assailed him and Indra had to fly away hurriedly and hide himself in the Mānasa lake. Indra's restoration took place after his performance of a horse sacrifice].

The King said :

3. Oh Sage, I wish to hear the cause of Indra's unhappiness whereby gods became happy, while Indra suffered agony.

Śrī Śuka said :

4. All gods along with sages who were agitated over the prowess of Vṛtra, begged Indra to slay him, but Indra being afraid of *Brahma-hatyā* did not wish to do so.

Indra said :

5. The sin of killing Viśvarūpa, a Brāhmaṇa, was graciously shared by women, the earth, the water and trees. Where can I wipe off the sin of killing Vṛtra, another Brāhmaṇa ?

Śrī Śuka said :

6. Having listened to him, the sages assured him, "May good betide you ! We shall help you in performing a horse-sacrifice. Please do not get afraid (of *Brahma-hatyā*).

7. Worshipping Lord Nārāyaṇa, the Supreme Man, the universal Soul and the Controller of the Universe, by perform-

ance of the Horse-sacrifice, you will be absolved of the sin of massacring the world. What of one Brāhmaṇa like Vṛtra.

8. By singing the Lord's name, a person who slays a Brāhmaṇa or his own father, or a cow, or his own mother, or a preceptor, a sinner who eats a dog, or is of the lowest caste, becomes purified.

9. If with faith and reverence, the great sacrifice called *Aśvamedha* (Horse-sacrifice) be performed with our co-operation, you will not be affected by sin, even if you kill all the mobile and immobile creation along with Brahmā. Then what of killing a wicked demon like Vṛtra?

Śrī Śuka said :

10. Thus strongly impelled by Brāhmaṇas, Indra killed his enemy Vṛtra. As soon as Vṛtra was killed, the sin of slaying a Brāhmaṇa attacked Indra.

11. Indra suffered agonies by that and did not get any peace of mind, for to selfrespecting persons, excellences like sovereignty do not give any pleasure if they bring censure.

12-13. He saw the *Brahma-hatyā* chasing after him. She was like a Cāṇḍāla woman in form. Her body was trembling with age and she was a victim of consumption. She put on blood-stained garments. With her grey hair scattered, she was asking Indra to stop and stand. She was polluting the atmosphere on the road with her breath stinking like rotten fish.

14. The thousand-eyed god ran in all directions in the sky, Oh Lord of the earth. He speedily rushed to the north-east and entered the Mānasa lake, Oh king.

15. He stayed within the fibres of a lotus therein without getting any subsistence, for he had the fire-god as his purveyor of food.[287] He remained unperceived in the water for one thousand years, pondering over his absolution from the sin of *Brahma-hatyā*.

16. During that period (of Indra's absence), Nahuṣa who possessed the capacity of a ruler due to his knowledge,

---

287. ŚR. points out the impossibility of fire-god's entry into water. VC. & GS. attribute his non-entry to the guards of Rudra, for Agni purveys oblations of Varuṇa.

austerities and strength of yoga, governed the third heaven. But as his intelligence became blind by the arrogance of affluence, and power was reduced to the state of sub-human being (boa constrictor) by Indra's wife, Śacī.[288]

17. Then Indra whose sin was warded off by meditation over the protector of Truth, namely, Lord Viṣṇu, returned as he was invited by Brāhmaṇas. His sin of *Brahma-hatyā* was deprived of its power by Rudra, the god of that direction, and it did not assail him as he was protected by Lakṣmī, spouse of Viṣṇu.

18. The Brāhmaṇa sages approached him and consecrated him according to religious formalities for the performance of the Horse-Sacrifice by which Hari is propitiated.

19-20. When the Supreme Person who embodies within himself all the divinities, was thus worshipped by the great Indra, in the Horse-Sacrifice which was performed duly through the Brāhmaṇas who were expositors of the Veda, the huge mass of sin of slaying Vṛtra the son of Tvaṣṭṛ was reduced to naught by that very worship of the Lord just as the frost is evaporated by the Sun.

21. By performance of the Horse-sacrifice according to scriptural injunctions through sages like Marīci who conducted it on proper lines, Indra worshipped the ancient Supreme Person, the presiding deity of sacrifices and thus being completely free from sin (of *Brahma-Hatyā*), became as great as before.

22. This great narrative which celebrates the glory of Lord Viṣṇu of hallowed feet, absolves one of all sins. It extols the virtues of devotion and the greatness of the devotees of the Lord, and describes the purification of the great Indra from *Brahma-hatyā* and his final victory.

---

288. Nahuṣa thought that as he was Indra, former Indra's wife would be ipso facto his own. When Śacī received an invitation from Nahuṣa, she, as per advice of Bṛhaspati, requested him to come to her in a palanquine borne by sages like Agastya. Nahuṣa while being borne thus, in his eagerness, touched Agastya with his leg and asked him to hasten (*Sarpa, Sarpa*). Agastya being thus insulted cursed him to be a serpent.

23. Wise persons should always read this narrative. They should listen to it on the days of *Parvans* e.g. the new-moon-day and the full-moon-day. It contributes to the prosperity and glory, removes sins, bestows victories over enemies, is conducive to auspiciousness and confers long life.

CHAPTER FOURTEEN

(*The Previous Birth of Vṛtra—King Citraketu*)

Parīkṣit said:

1. Oh Brāhmaṇa sage, how is it that the sinful Vṛtra who, by nature, was predominated by *Rajas* and *Tamas*, entertained unflinching devotion to the glorious Lord Nārāyaṇa.

2. Even in the case of gods who are constituted of pure Sattva and in that of pure-souled sages, generally devotion to the feet of Viṣṇu is not engendered.

3. In this world there are beings which are as numerous as the particles of dust. Among them, it is very few like the human beings who can practise righteousness.

4. Oh best of the Brāhmaṇas, there are generally very few among them who seek Liberation from Saṁsāra. Out of thousands of seekers of Mokṣa, it is only one who can get rid of attachment (to sensual pleasures etc.) and attain liberation.

5. Out of the crores of Siddhas who are free from attachment and have realized the Self, a person who is absolutely devoted to Nārāyaṇa and of serene mind is very difficult to find, Oh great sage.

6. But how is it that Vṛtra, the fiend incarnate, the tormentor of all the worlds, was thus so steadfast in devotion to Kṛṣṇa (Lord Viṣṇu) in the heat of fierce battle.

7. On this point, we entertain a great doubt and wish to hear eagerly about it, Oh Master, for he gratified god Indra by his heroism on the battlefield (and did not remember God out of Indra's fear).

Sūta said:

8. The venerable Śuka welcomed the relevant and interesting query of the devout king Parīkṣit and replied as follows:

Śrī Śuka said:

9. Oh King, listen attentively to this legendary history as heard by me from the mouth of Vyāsa, Nārada and even of Devala.

10. It is traditionally reported, Oh King, that there was a sovereign ruler of the world called Citraketu, in the country called Śūrasena. To him the earth yielded whatever he desired.

11. He had ten million wives. Though he was capable of procreation, he did not get any issue from them.

12. Though he was endowed with handsomeness, generosity, youth, noble lineage, deep learning sovereignty, affluence and other excellences, the husband of barren ladies was overweighed with anxiety.

13. Neither his affluence nor his queens of beautiful eyes or the universal sovereignty of the earth became a source of delight to him.

14. Once upon a time, the glorious sage Aṅgiras, during his course of wandering over the world, arrived by chance to his palace.

15. The king honoured him with due formalities such as respectfully standing, offering articles of worship, and with a collected mind, he sat near the sage who was fully entertained as a guest and was seated comfortably.

16. The great sage respectfully showed every courtesy to the king who was sitting near him on the ground and bowing down modestly. Addressing him as 'Mahārāja' (Oh great King), he spoke to him as follows:

Aṅgiras said:

17. Are you in good health? Are your subjects and yourself well? Just as the individual Soul (man) is protected by seven constituents (viz. *Mahat*, *Ahaṁkāra*—ego and the five subtle elements), the king is protected by the constituent elements of the state, namely ministers, allies, treasures, ter-

ritories, fortifications, and militia and his own office of kingship.

18. By placing oneself under the control of Prakṛtis, the king should enjoy sovereignty and regal prosperity. Similarly the Prakṛtis (ministers, subjects etc.), with their grievances removed, become enriched and benefited by king.

19. Are your wives, subjects, ministers, servants, members of trade guilds, councillors, citizens, country people, tributary princes, and sons obedient to you?

20. He who has controlled his mind has all these (mentioned above) obedient to him. All the worlds along with the guardian deities offer to him dutifully due honour and worship.

21. It appears that your mind is not pleased with you or with others. I find that your countenance is overshadowed with anxiety as you presumably have not achieved your object or desire.

22. The king who was thus subjected to various alternative questions by the sage who knew (everything) by intuition, bent down with modesty, and then addressed the sage, with a desire for progeny, Oh King.

Citraketu said:

23. Oh worshipful sage! What is not known to yogins (like you) who have destroyed their sins, what lies within and without embodied beings, by means of their penance, spiritual knowledge and concentration?

24. But as I am prompted by your worship who knows what is weighing on my mind, it is with your permission that I am speaking it to you.

25. (My) sovereign power and affluence which are covetable even to the guardians of the world, do not give me any delight. Childless as I am, these are like other things (such as garlands, sandal-paste etc.) to a person overwhelmed with hunger and thirst.

26. Oh highly blessed one, kindly therefore protect me who along with my ancestors, am on the verge of falling into a dark abysmal hell. Please do that unto us whereby we shall cross this hell which is difficult, by blessing us with progeny.

Śrī Śuka said:

27. The venerable, merciful son of Brahmā who was thus entreated, caused *caru* (rice cooked in milk) to be prepared for Tvaṣṭṛ and worshipped Tvaṣṭṛ with its oblations.

28. The seniormost queen both in age and status among the queens, was Kṛtadyuti by name. The Brāhmana gave the remainder of the sacrificial offerings to her.

29. Then the son of Brahmā told the king, "Oh king, one son will be born to you. He will give you both joy and grief". Saying thus, he departed.

30. Queen Kṛtadyuti conceived a son through Citraketu by the eating of that *caru*, just as (the constellation) Kṛttikā bore a son to the Fire-god.

31. Her foetus which was begotten by the king of Śūrasena gradually developed every day, just as the Moon waxes in the bright half of the month.

32. In due course, after the arrival of the proper time, a son was born, giving great joy to the inhabitants of Śūrasena who heard the news.

33. The king who was overjoyed, purified himself by taking a bath and adorned himself. He made the Brāhmaṇas pronounce pious benedictions and caused them to perform the *jātakarma* ceremony.

34. He gave them gold, silver, garments, ornaments, villages, horses, elephants and six crores of cows.

35. Like a showering rain-cloud, the noble-minded king showered other persons with objects desired by them for the future affluence, glory and longevity of the prince.

36. Just as a penniless person develops love for his hard-earned money, the father, a royal sage, developed, day after day, great affection for his son who was got after great difficulty.

37. To the mother Kṛtadyuti, the affection caused by infatuation developed into intense love, but it created feverish desire for a child in her co-wives.

38. By fondling the child every day, Citraketu showed so much intensive love to his wife who gave birth to a child, that he ignored others.

39. Those co-wives tormented and reproached themselves out of envy, the misery of childlessness and the indifference of the king.

40. Fie on the childless accursed woman who is not loved in the house of her husband and is treated with contempt, like a maid-servant, by other co-wives blessed with children.

41. What agony can there be to maid servants who are constantly waiting upon their master and whose services are appreciated by him ? We are unfortunate like the maid-servant of maid-servants.

42. The co-wives, in this way, developed intense hatred, as they were burning due to the wealth in the form of child to their co-wife and their very existence being not approved by the king.

43. The women who lost their good sense through hatred and became cruel-hearted administered poison to the prince, in their unappeasable hatred for the king.

44. Kṛtadyuti was quite innocent about the grievous sin committed by her co-wives. Looking at him (her son) she thought him to be asleep and went about in the house.

45. The clever woman realizing that the child had slept for a pretty long time ordered the nurse, "Oh auspicious lady bring the son to me".

46. The nurse approached the sleeping child and saw him with the pupils of his eyes turned upwards and bereft of breathing, senses and life. (She cried out) "Oh I am undone" and fell down on the ground.

47. Then hearing her painful shriek and violent beating of the breasts with her hands, the queen entered in haste and approaching the child, she saw that it had met with sudden death.

48. Overpowered with grief, she fell on the ground and with her hair and garments in disorder, she lost her consciousness.

49. Then all the men and women who were in the harem of the king heard the wailing. Coming there, they equally shared her grief and became extremely distressed and even those who perpetrated that heinous crime pretended to weep.

50. Hearing that his son died from an unknown cause, the king lost his eye-sight. He staggered with faltering steps on the way. The king who was surrounded by his ministers and Brāhmaṇas fell in deep swoon, due to his grief which was infinitely intensified by love.

51. The king fell at the feet of his dead son. His (king's) hair and garments fell in disorder. He heaved heavy sighs. His throat was choked with tears and he was not able to speak.

52. Observing that her husband was overwhelmed with grief as the son, the only scion of the family, was dead, the virtuous queen burst out into lamentations of various sorts enhancing the afflictions of the subjects and the ministers.

53. Bathing her breasts decorated with paintings of saffron and sandal-paste, by means of tears mixed with collyrium, and with her dishevelled hair dropping flowers (used for hair decoration), she cried out loudly and in diverse tones like a female osprey.

54. "Oh Creator, you are extremely foolish, for you act contrary to your (process of) creation, because here the elderly people survive when the young ones die. If you are of a contrary nature, then you must be an eternal enemy of all creatures.

55. If there be no order in the birth and death of embodied beings, it may be due to their own *Karmas*. But the tie of affection which you have engendered for the growth of your creation, is cut asunder by you, due to the death of the child.

56. (Addressing the child) Oh dear child ! It is not proper for you to abandon a wretched and helpless (mother like) me. Please have a look at your father who is tormented with grief. It is through you that we shall easily cross the dark hell which is impassable for childless persons. Please do not go far away, with the merciless god of Death.

57. Oh child, get up. These young children, your friends, are calling you to play. Oh Prince, you have slept for too long a period. You must have been famished with hunger. Enjoy breast-feeding and remove the grief of our relatives.

58. Unfortunate as I am, I have not (as usual) seen your lotuslike face with cheerful looks and innocent smile, Oh

child. Or is it that you are taken away by the merciless (Yama) and have gone to the other world from which there is no return, for I do not hear your sweet words."

Śrī Śuka said :

59. While she was bewailing her dead son through such various laments, Citraketu became extremely tormented with grief and cried at the top of his voice.

60. While the husband and wife were thus lamenting, the subjects, both men and women, who were devoted to them verily wept aloud and everything was lifeless.

61. Knowing that everybody was reduced to such wretched plight and lost all consciousness and were leaderless (for consolation) the sage Aṅgiras came along with Nārada.

CHAPTER FIFTEEN

(*Consolation of Citraketu*)

Śrī Śuka said :

1. Bringing back to consciousness the king, with their soft and wise words, the sages Aṅgiras and Nārada spoke to the king who was overpowered with grief, and was lying like a dead person by the side of the dead child.

2. "What can be your relationship, in the previous and the present birth, Oh great King, with the child whom you are mourning ? How was he related to you in the previous birth, the present birth and will be related in the future one ?

3. Just as the grains of sand come together and separate by the force of the stream of water, so are embodied beings brought together and separated by Time.

4. Just as seeds may or may not produce corn, similarly *Bhūtas* prompted by God's Māyā may or may not produce *Bhūtas*.

5. We, you, the mobile and immobile creatures which are contemporaneous with us, were not so before the present

birth nor are so in the present birth, nor shall be so after death. (Due to the nonexistence of these before and after, they are unsubstantial or unreal like dreams).

6. The Lord of *Bhūtas* who is himself unborn (and therefore imperishable) and has no purpose to achieve, like a playful boy, creates, protects and destroys the *Bhūtas* by means of *Bhūtas* which are created by him and hence dependent on him.

7. Oh King, the body of a son is born from the body (of the mother) through another body (namely that of the father) just as a seed sprouts forth from another seed. But the occupant of the body is eternal like earth and other principles.

8. It is from eternity that this (above-mentioned) distinction between a body and the occupant of the body (the Soul) has been presumed through ignorance, as the distinction between the class or the generic property (*jāti*) and the individuality of a thing (*vyakti*) is conceived as existing in the thing itself (such distinction between interdependants like *jāti* and *vyakti* are untenable).*

Śrī Śuka said :

9. When king Citraketu was thus consoled by the words of the Brāhmaṇa sages, he wiped out with his hand, his

* After verse No. 8, the text before VJ. adds four verses.

(1) Just as the difference or changes due to fuel are wrongly attributed to the fire, similarly the conditions affecting the body, viz., difference, birth, decline, growth and destruction are wrongly attributed to the *Jīva* who is distinct from the body. This misconception is due to *Karma*.

(2) It is due to Jīva's intimate relation to the body and the false identification of the body with the Soul, that the above-mentioned conditions (of the body) appear to be the conditions of the *Jīva* as in a dream. As everything else is a source of fear, one should not ponder over anything leading to evil consequences.

(3) Just as the appearance of a serpent or a tiger or another (frightening) object like it, in a dream, causes fear, as the dream appearance is identified with the reality in a wakeful condition, so is the *Saṁsāra* due to the misconception grown since eternity.

(4) The idea of the world of sons (or relatives) and other possessions depends on the mind. It is due to the influence of the Ego which creates likes and dislikes in the mind and leads to merits and demerits. One should clear away the ignorance in the form of the notions like me and mine, and fix one's mind on the all-powerful Omnipresent Lord Vāsudeva.

face which was withered through grief for his son, and addressed them thus.

The king (Citraketu) said :

10. Who are you both so full of spiritual knowledge, the most worshipful ones among the adorables who have come here disguised as *Avadhūtas* ?

11. For, persons who have realized Brahman and who are dear to the glorious Lord, range over the world in the guise of mad persons, for guiding and counselling sensually-minded people like me.

12. (For example) Sanatkumāra, Nārada, Ṛbhu, Aṅgiras, Devala, Amita, Apāntarātma, Vyāsa, Mārkeṇḍeya and Gautama.

13. Vasiṣṭha, the glorious Paraśurāma, Kapila, Bādarayaṇi (Śuka), Durvāsas, Yājñavalkya, Jātūkarṇya and Āruṇi.

14. Romaśa, Cyavana, Datta, Patañjali, Āsuri, the sage Vedaśiras, the sage Bodhya, and Pañcaśiras.

15. Hiraṇyanābha, Kausalya, Śrutadeva, Ṛtadhvaja—these and other masters of spiritual powers go about in the world with the object of imparting spiritual knowledge.

16. Therefore, you both are the masters of a stupid and ignorant brute like me. Enlighten me with the lamp of your knowledge—me who am plunged into the blinding darkness of ignorance.

Aṅgiras said :

17. Oh King, I am Aṅgiras who blessed you with a son as you longed for one. This is the veritable son of Brahmā, the worshipful divine sage Nārada.

18-19. Finding you, a devotee of the Supreme Person, plunged in the deep impassable darkness of grief for the son, though you are not fit to be so affected, we have arrived here to help you out of it, with our grace. For, you are dear to Brāhmaṇas and votary of the Lord and thus do not deserve to be so despondent.

20. When I visited your house, at that very time (of our first meeting), I would have imparted to you spiritual knowledge. But knowing your insistence and longing for

something else (viz, the birth of a son), I blessed you with a son.

21-22. Now, you experience the agony suffered by persons having sons. In the same way (are the agonies of persons who have) wives, houses, wealth, power and prosperity of various kinds, objects of enjoyment like sound etc., fleeting powers of sovereignty, the earth, kingdom, the army, the treasury, servants, ministers, friends and relations.

23. Oh King Śūrasena, all these are the sources of grief, delusion, fear and affliction, for they are momentary like (the proverbial) city of Gandharvas in the sky, and unreal like a dream, delusion and fancies.

24. They are mental images, for they are perceived without being real or substantial and disappear the next moment. For a man brooding over objects through the force of tendencies of actions (*karma*) in the previous birth, various activities proceed from the mind.

25. In fact, this body of embodied beings is constituted of gross elements, conative and cognitive senses. It is said, by the knowers of the reality, to be the cause of various afflictions and torments to the *Jīva* who identifies itself with its body.

26. Therefore, examining carefully the real nature of the Soul and with concentration of mind, give up the belief in the permanence of the objective world as it implies duality. Betake yourself to renunciation and serenity of the mind*.

---

* Additional verses in VJ.'s text of the Bh. P. :

(1) A king named Bhoja dreamt that he subsisted on the remnant of the food (out of the dishes) of his enemy. He was therefore overcome with nausia, grief, delusion, fear and distress and became utterly miserable.

(2) (In the dream) some (of his enemies) who nursed age-old animosity and vengeance, carried away the objects he enjoyed; some killed his dependents; some abducted his wives while others beheaded him.

(3) Awaking from this dream overflooded with unending miseries, he reflected deeply over it. He got disgusted and renounced his house (worldly life).

(4) Externally appearing as insane, he visualized the Supreme Soul within his heart, free from attachments. Overcoming conflicting states of the mind he established it in the Supreme Brahman called Śrī Nārāyaṇa, untouched by the conditioning perishable body. In this absorbed state of meditation (in a-*samprajñāta-samādhi*), he totally forgot that he was conditioned by the body.

Nārada said :

27. After purifying yourself (i.e. after disposing of the dead body of the child and taking a bath thereafter) accept from me the *Mantropaniṣad* (Vide Infra Ch. XVI, 18-25). By bearing this in mind and meditating over it, you will visualize Lord Saṅkarṣaṇa within seven nights.

28. Oh great King, by resorting to the feet of Saṅkarṣaṇa, ancient votaries of the Lord like god Śiva and others, gave up the illusion of this world which implies duality and attained immediately to his greatness which was neither equalled by nor surpassed by anyone else. You will also attain to that eminence within a short time.

CHAPTER SIXTEEN

(*Citraketu's Realization of Lord Ananta*)

Śrī Śuka said :

1. Then, Oh King, the divine sage Nārada (by his yogic powers) showed the spirit of the departed prince to the relatives who were mourning and spoke to the spirit.

Nārada said :

2. Oh Jīva, God bless you. Have a look at your mother, father, friends and relatives who are deeply afflicted with grief for you.

3. Please enter this body of yours. Surrounded by your friends enjoy pleasures throughout the remaining period of your life—pleasures provided to you by your father and ascend the royal throne.

Jīva said :

4. In what life were these my father and mother, while I was revolving in the cycle of births in the species of gods, subhuman beings and human beings by my *karmas*.

5. For, all persons are by turns related to others as relatives, cousins, enemies, mediators, friends, indifferent men and bitter adversaries.

6. Just as commodities like gold and other articles change hand from one customer to another and one place to another, similarly a *Jīva* wanders from one species of existence to another.

7. Even during the life-time of a person, the relation even of men with animals is temporary. The attachment of mineness lasts so long as the particular relation exists.

8. In the same way, the relation of a *Jīva* who has entered the womb of a particular species is transient. For, by himself, *Jīva* is eternal and as such unrelated to his body and is therefore without attachment (as a son etc.). The sense of belongingness lasts so long as and only with him, with whom he is associated due to his *karma* (and not after death. Therefore grief for me is unnecessary).

9. This Ātman is eternal. He is not subject to decay or change. He is subtle and free from birth. He is the basic support (as the material cause of the universe) of all. He is self-illuminating. Being all-powerful he manifests himself as the universe by the *guṇas* of his Māyā.[289]

10. To him no one is very dear, nor anyone hateful. He has no kith or kin or an alien. He is one, the witness of the working of the minds of friends and foes (who do good or evil).

11. The Ātman does not accept (experience) the good or evil (i.e. pleasure or pain) nor is he the recipient of the fruit of *karmas* (namely kingship). He is a dispassionate witness of cause and effect and not their enjoyer. He is thus unconditioned by body and is independent.

Śrī Śuka said :

12. After explaining thus the spirit departed. The relatives of that *Jīva* then became wonderstruck. They cut asunder their bonds of affection to him and gave up sorrow.

---

289. VJ. explains : The Jīva is eternally related with Hari who by the *guṇas* of his Māyā creates his universe. Hari is eternally connected with all. He is eternal, not conditioned by change or decay, subtle but absolutely one. He perceives everything as he is the Lord of all. Thus the relation of a Jīva with any person is temporary.

13. The relatives took away the dead body and performed the suitable obsequies. They set aside their affection which is so difficult to be rid of, and which causes grief, delusion, fear and distress.

14. The queens who killed the child and whose charms waned due to the infanticide, became ashamed. They performed the expiation for infanticide as enunciated to them by the Brāhmaṇas on the bank of the Yamunā, remembering what the Brāhmaṇas have explained to them, Oh Mahārāja.

15. Citraketu who was thus spiritually awakened by the words (of advice) by the Brāhmaṇa sages, came out of the dark deceptive well in the form of domestic life, just as an elephant extricates himself out of the mire in the lake.

16. Having taken ablution in the Yamunā according to the sacred precepts, and having poured out oblations of water (to the Pitṛs), he, with his senses properly controlled, bowed to the two sons of god Brahmā (viz. Nārada and Aṅgiras) in silence.

17. The venerable sage Nārada gladly taught this great lore to the king who was their devotee and who resorted to them for protection and had fully controlled his mind.

18. "OM ! Salutation unto you, Oh glorious Lord Vāsudeva. We contemplate (mentally pay obeisance to) you. We bow to Pradyumna, Aniruddha and Saṅkarṣaṇa (all the *vyūhas* of the Lord).

19. Obeisance to You who are pure, absolute knowledge, the very embodiment of supreme bliss, delighted with yourself, serene and above the notion of duality.

20. Hail to you who, through realization of your blissful character, kept yourself above the waves (the feelings of love, hate etc.) caused by Māyā. Salutation to the great Hṛṣīkeśa (the Supreme Master of Senses) whose body is the universe.

21. May he protect us—he who shines alone by himself and is beyond the reach of speech and other senses and the mind; who is pure consciousness and has no name or form and who is the cause of the law of causation (and hence above it).

22. Bow to you Supreme Brahman on whom the universe (the product of cause and effect) is based, from whom it evolves and in whom it dissolves and thus pervades everything in the universe, just as products of earth do with reference to the earth.

23. I salute the Brahman which pervades everything from within and without like the sky but to whom the *Prāṇas* (organs of activity) do not touch (by their conative force) nor do the mind, intellect and cognitive senses comprehend him (by their power of cognition).

24. It is only when these—body, senses, vital airs, mind and intellect—are charged by his part or presence (*aṁśa*) that these carry out their functions and not otherwise, just as an unheated piece of iron (does not emit heat or light.) What is called the 'spectator' is another designation of yours in the state of wakefulness (of the Jīva. He has no independent existence apart from you).

25. Salutations to you the Supreme Person, designated by the sacred symbol OM, the possessor of Supreme Might, whose lotus-like feet are adored in great love with the lotus-bud-like joined palms by all the great Sātvatas (votaries of the Lord). I reverentially bow to you, the most excellent controller of all."

Śrī Śuka said :

26. Having taught this prayer-lore to his devotee who sought his protection, Nārada along with Aṅgiras, went to the region of god Brahmā, Oh King.

27. Citraketu observed the course of that lore (of meditation and prayer) with perfect concentration as per instructions of Nārada. For one week he subsisted on water only.

28. Then at the end of the seventh night, the king attained to permanent overlordship of Vidyādharas through the practice of that lore.

29. Then after some days, his mental power became illumined through the practice and repetition of the same lore, and he went near the feet of Śeṣa, the God of gods.

30. He saw the Lord Śeṣa white like a lotus fibre, clad in blue garments and adorned with brilliant crown, armlets,

girdle and wristlets, and with gracious countenance and reddish eyes, attended upon by multitudes of great Siddhas.

31. All his sins having been destroyed at the sight of the Lord, the sage Citraketu whose heart became cleansed of all impurities, approached the Most Ancient Person in silence. Due to surging devotion, his eyes were flowing with tears of love and his hair were standing on ends due to ecstasy, he prostrated himself before him.

32. Repeatedly moistening with his tears of love the altar under the lotus-like.feet of the glorious Lord, and his power of expression was being choked up by his overpowering love and devotion, he was not for a long time able to praise him properly.

33. Then, composing his mind by the force of reason and having restrained the senses from going out to external objects, he addressed the following words to the father of the world, the embodiment of the Sātvata Śāstra, i.e. *Pañcarātra* (or whose body stood described in the *Pañcarātra* scriptures).

Citraketu said :

34. Oh unconquered Lord ! (Despite your unconquerableness) you have been vanquished by self-controlled righteous persons of impartial and unruffled minds. They, in their turn, are conquered by You. You are so very gracious that you bestow your own self upon your devotees whose minds are completely free from desires.

35. Oh glorious Lord ! The creation, preservation and destruction of the universe isyour prowess—a sport. The (so-called) creators of the universe are merely the portion of your portions. They, however, regard themselves severally as creators and vainly vie with one another.

36. You are at the creation, destruction as well as during the intervening period of the subtlest atom as well as (of the universe) of the largest dimensions. But you are (yourself) devoid of this triad of limitation. You are that unchanging constant who exist at the beginning and end as well as in the interim of all created things.

37. The egg of the universe is enveloped by seven sheaths of the earth and other elements etc., each outer envelop being

ten times the extent of the enclosure inner to it. This egg-like universe together with millions and millions of other universes appears just like an atom on your head. Hence, you are called Ananta, the infinite.

38. Oh Controller of the universe ! Those persons are really beasts who, in their thirst for objects of pleasure propitiate the deities concerned (like Indra, who are but your parts only) and not you—for, the blessings (so conferred upon them) come to an end with the extinction of the deities, just as the good fortunes of the followers of a king perish with the fall of that royal house.

39. Oh Supreme Lord ! Even if worldly desires are entreated of you who are pure knowledge and consciousness and not a product of *guṇas*, they do not grow like the fried seeds (which cannot sprout forth). For all the pairs of opposites (e.g. love—hate, leading to rebirth) are the result of *guṇas* (and you are above them).

40. Oh unconquerable one ! When you propounded the pure *Bhāgavata Dharma* (the righteous path leading to the realization of the glorious Lord), you have conquered all (made all your own). For sinless sages (like Sanat-kumāra) who are possessionless and free of desires and find delight in the Supreme Soul, resort to that Dharma (or to you) for Liberation.

41. Here *in the Bhāgavata Dharma* men do not cherish crooked, differential notions such as 'I', 'you', 'mine' and 'yours', (as is in other cults, as that of sacrifice). Whatever (act) is performed with the notion of such differences is impure, perishable and full of sin, (like *hiṁsā*).

42. What good to one's own self or to another can accrue from a *dharma* (path of religion) or what benefit can be gained through a *dharma* which is harmful to oneself and to others. It is irreligion, for pain is caused to oneself through self-mortification and sin is committed by offending others.

43. Your vision by which you expounded the *Bhāgavata-dharma* never goes astray from reality. Hence, the noble Souls who do not regard the multitudes of the mobile and immobile being as different from you follow that *dharma*, Oh Lord.

44. It is no miracle that all the sins committed by men

are annihilated at your sight, for even an outcaste like a Cāṇḍāla becomes liberated from the cycle of birth and death, by hearing your name once only, Oh glorious Lord.

45. Oh Lord, we have got our heart cleansed of all the impurities by your very sight. How could that which the divine sage, your own devotee, has said, turn out to be untrue?

46. Oh Infinite Lord ! As you are the Soul of the world, you know everything that is done in this world by people. You are the Creator and Preceptor of the world. There is nothing new to be specially made known to you, as there is nothing to be revealed to the Sun by the fire-flies.

47. Salutations to you, Oh glorious Lord, who are the master and controller of the creation, sustenance and destruction of all the worlds. You are the purest of the pure (*Paramahaṁsa*). Your real nature is incomprehensible to bad yogins who entertain the notion of difference.

48. The creators of the world (e.g. god Brahmā and other gods who preside over the conative organs) (are activated) when you breathe (become active). When you (wish to) see, the gods (like the Sun who preside over the cognitive organs,) are able to get perception. The globe of this earth is (insignificant) like a mustard seed on your head. My Salutations to you, Oh glorious Lord of a thousand heads.

Śrī Śuka said :

49. Lord Ananta who was thus eulogised, was pleased with him. He spoke out to Citraketu the king of Vidyādharas, Oh scion of the Kuru family (Parīkṣit).

The glorious Lord said :

50. Oh King, it is by the precept (of the means of propitiating me) taught to you by Nārada and Aṅgiras and by the practice of that spiritual lore and by my sight that you have fully achieved your purpose.

51. I am verily all the created beings, their Soul and their support. I am the Veda the Supreme Brahma and both of these are my eternal form.

52. One should understand that his own Self is pervading the whole of the universe (as the subject of experience)

and that the universe is resting on the Ātman (i.e. is superimposed on the Soul) and that both (one's own Self and the universe) are pervaded by me (as the prime cause).

53. Just as in a state of profound slumber, one sees the universe (i.e. the various objects in it) in his own Self, and waking up from the dream, he finds himself alone and in a particular place (of sleeping such as a bed-room).

54. Similarly wakefulness etc. are the conditions of Jīva and are the products of Māyā with reference to Ātman. Therefore, one should remember that Paramātman is only a witness.

55. Recognize me to be that Ātman or Brahman through whom the Jīva in a sleeping condition, regards himself as in deep sleep. I am absolute bliss beyond the range of *guṇas* or the senses.

56. That knowledge is the Supreme Brahma—knowledge which is found in a person who remembers his experiences during sleep and wakefulness—a connecting link as well as the *differentia* between the two states of experience.

57. When the Jīva forgets my real nature, he regards himself as different from me and this is the cause of his Saṁsāra, in which he goes from birth after birth and suffers death after death.

58. Having attained birth in the human species here, where the knowledge of the Self (as detailed in scriptures) and the wisdom, i.e. direct knowledge and perception of the Self, can be developed, he who does not realize me, can never find peace and happiness.

59. Remembering that in the Pravṛtti Mārga (i.e. the path of *karma*) there are great afflictions and contrary results (of the expected fruit), and there is fearlessness, i.e. Liberation (Mokṣa) in the Nivṛtti-Mārga (the path of cessation of activities), a wise man should desist from the path of *karma*.

60. A pair of husband and wife perform (ritualistic) acts for getting pleasure and avoidance of misery. But there is no escape from misery nor the attainment of happiness, as a result of ritualistic performance.

61-62. Having thus realized that the consequences go contrary to expectation of persons who in their pride regard themselves to be clever, and having realized the subtle nature of the Ātman which transcends the three states (viz. state of awakeness, dream and deep sleep), and being completely free (from the desire) for the pleasures of this world and the next, through one's power of discrimination and finding satisfaction and pleasure in one's knowledge and wisdom, a person should devote himself to me (completely).

63. Realization of the unity of the individual spirit and the Supreme Soul is the real objective to be attained through all possible means by yogins whose intellect and power have acquired acuteness through yogic meditation.

64. If you bear in mind my advice and bring that into practice carefully, you will soon be blessed with knowledge and wisdom and attain Liberation, Oh King.

Śrī Śuka said :

65. Having comforted Citraketu in this way, the glorious Lord Hari, the father and the preceptor of the world, and the Soul of the universe, immediately disappeared there while Citraketu was looking on.

CHAPTER SEVENTEEN

(*Citraketu cursed by Pārvatī*)

Śrī Śuka said:

1. Having bowed to the direction in which Lord Ananta disappeared, Citraketu, the Vidyādhara, the sky-ranger went his own way (in the sky).

2-3. Possessed of indefatigable physical power and undiminished acuteness of senses, and eulogised by sages, Siddhas and Cāraṇas as a great Yogī, he (Citraketu), for a period of 1,000 million years, sported in the caverns of the great Kulācala (sumeru) (the boundary mountain), which automatically supplies the desired objects to the occupants. He made the Vidyādhara ladies chant the glories of Lord Hari.

4-5. Once upon a time, while he was going by his resplendent aerial car, gifted to him by Viṣṇu, he saw Lord Śiva surrounded by Siddhas and Cāraṇas and having embraced in his arm the goddess Pārvatī seated on his lap, in the assembly of sages. Approaching near her, he laughed loudly and spoke out within the hearing of the goddess.

Citraketu said :

6. (Look here), here is the preceptor of the world himself, the expounder of Dharma to all embodied beings, the head of the assembly (of sages etc.), sits in a posture coupled with his wife.

7. He has matted hair on his head and performs austere penance. He is the president of the assembly of sages well versed in Vedas, but he sits with his wife on his lap, like a shameless vulgar fellow.

8. Generally, even ordinary people embrace a woman in secluded places, but this observer of great vows indulges in dalliance with his wife, in an open assembly.

Śrī Śuka said :

9. Even Lord Śiva of unfathomable mind laughed out heartily on hearing it, and kept quiet in that assemblage. The members of the assembly also followed his example.

10. The goddess angrily spoke to the impudent Citraketu who was proud of his own self-control, and who passed unbecoming remarks against Lord Śiva, about whose irresistible powers he was ignorant.

Pārvatī said :

11. Is this now the ruler of the world and the punisher thereof? Is he competent to mete out punishment to wicked and shameless fellows like us ?

12. Neither god Brahmā nor the sons of Brahmā like Bhṛgu, Nārada and others, neither Sanatkumāra nor Kapila and Manu comprehended *Dharma* (righteousness), for they raised no objection to Hara's transgression of *dharma*.

13. This impertinent wretched Kṣatriya insults wise gods and sages, and reproves this preceptor and father of the

world whose lotus-like feet are meditated upon by the above-mentioned (great personages), and who is the very embodiment of the highest *dharma*. Therefore, this fellow should be punished.

14. This haughty self-conceited person does not deserve to be allowed to approach the feet of Lord Viṣṇu which are reverently worshipped by pious sages.

15. Oh wicked fellow ! Go forth hence to the most wicked demonic existence of *Asuras* so that you may not again speak ill of the great, Oh child.[290]

Śrī Śuka said :

16. Citraketu who was thus imprecated, got down from the aerial car, and propitiated Satī (Goddess Pārvatī) paying her obeisance with his head bent low, Oh Parīkṣit.

Citraketu said :

17. I accept your curse with my folded palms, Oh Mother. Whatever is pronounced by gods about mortal being is something predestined for him.

18. In this whirling wheel of *Saṁsāra*, a creature, being deluded by ignorance, wanders experiencing pleasure and pain, everywhere, at all times.

19. Neither one's self nor another is the creator of pleasure and pain. It is only the unwise who regards himself or another person as the author of pleasure and pain.

20. (All this Saṁsāra is the product of *Guṇas*). In this stream of *Guṇas*, what is the distinction between a curse and grace? What is the heaven or the hell ? And what is the difference between pleasure and pain ?

21. It is the glorious Lord alone who creates all beings by dint of his Māyā power. To these are ordained bondage and liberation, pleasure and pain, but he himself is above them all.

22. To him none is dear or hateful; none a cousin or a relation; none is friend or an enemy; he is equal to all

290. GS. explains that Pārvatī was really sympathetic towards Citraketu, but the curse was a reproof against his audacity.

everywhere and absolutely pure. He has no attachment for pleasure. How can there be wrath in him ?

23. It is however the outflow of his energy called Māyā manifested in meritorious or sinful acts, that becomes the cause of pleasure and pain, good and bad, bondage and liberation, birth and death of embodied beings, and causes transmigration of the Soul.

24. Therefore, Oh wrathful Goddess, I do not propitiate you for relieving me from your curse. But Oh Satī (Pārvatī), please forgive me for what you consider as an unrighteous expression from me.

Śuka said :

25. Having propitiated Lord Śiva and goddess Pārvatī in this way, Citraketu left by his aerial car, while they looked wondering.

26. Then the glorious god Rudra (Śiva) spoke to Pārvatī while gods, sages, Siddhas and his attendants were listening (reverentially).

Rudra said :

27. Oh beautiful lady (possessor of dainty waist), you have seen the nobleness of the high-souled servants of servants of Hari of miraculous deeds and how they are free from desires (of any kind).

28. All who are devoted to Nārāyaṇa are not afraid of anybody for they see the same Reality in *Svarga*, *Mokṣa* and even in hells.

29. It is through the sporting activities of the Lord that the Soul is invested with a body and experiences pairs of opposites like pleasure and pain, birth and death, grace and curse, through contact with the physical body.

30. The notion of desirability and undesirability with reference to pleasure and pain is certainly illusory and false, and it is the result of man's lack of discrimination and knowledge. For it is like the difference (between the experience of pleasure or pain by seeing oneself to have become a prince or a pauper in a dream) felt within oneself or the imputation of

the notion of a serpent on a garland of flowers (while one is awake).*

31. To persons who are bearing intense devotion to venerable Lord Vāsudeva and whose power lies in spiritual knowledge and renunciation, no object is worth seeking or resorting in this world.

32. Neither I, nor god Brahmā, nor Sanatkumāra or Nārada or the sons of God Brahmā, sages, nor the great gods who are but parts of his parts comprehend his intention. We do not know his real nature though we regard ourselves as independent rulers.

33. To him nobody is beloved or hateful, nobody is his own or an alien. Hari being the Ātman (inner controller) of all beings is the beloved of them all.

34. This highly blessed Citraketu is a beloved follower of the Lord. He looks upon all as equal and is serene. I am also beloved of Lord Viṣṇu. Therefore, I did not get angry with him.

35. You need not, therefore, wonder about (the behaviour of) high-souled men who are devotees of the Supreme person Viṣṇu—the votaries who are tranquil by nature, and regard all beings as equal.

Śrī Śuka said :

36. Having heard the explanatory speech of the glorious Lord Śiva, the goddess Pārvatī got over her feeling of wonder and became appeased and calm in mind, Oh King.

37. Even though the votary of Viṣṇu, Citraketu, was most competent to retaliate the Devī's curse by counter-curse, he accepted it bowing down his head (with great respect and humility),—which is the characteristic of righteousness.

38. Assuming the body of a Dānava, Citraketu was born in the Dakṣiṇāgni of Tvaṣṭṛ, and became famous as Vṛtra. He

* VR. : The *Jīva* is an individual constituted of pure consciousness. The difference as a god or man or a sub-human being with reference to *Jīva* and the desirable and undesirable states (e.g. pleasure and pain, birth and death, grace and curse) are due to the lack of discrimination. It is caused by eternal *Karma* and induces one to identify oneself with the physical body. Moreover, this notion of difference is like pleasant and unpleasant sights in a dream.

was, however, endowed with spiritual knowledge and wisdom (despite his birth as a demon).

39. In this way I have narrated to you everything which you enquired about the cause of Vṛtra's birth as a demon, and his devotion to Hari.

40. Hearing this sacred history of the noble-minded Citraketu and the glory and greatness of votaries of Viṣṇu, one becomes liberated from the bondage (of Saṁsāra).

41. He who gets up early in the morning and recites this episode with reverence, and observing silence, meditates on Lord Hari, attains to the highest region (*Mokṣa*).

CHAPTER EIGHTEEN*

(*The Birth of the Maruts*)

Śrī Śuka said:

1. Pṛśni, the wife of Savitṛ (the fifth son of Aditi) gave birth to three daughters, namely, Sāvitrī[291], Vyāhṛti[292] and Trayī[293] and (nine sons, namely,) Agnihotra[294], Paśu[295], Soma[296], Cāturmāsya[297] and the five great sacrifices[298].

* In the introduction of this chapter, ŚR. states that this chapter is in continuation of the first six chapters in which the progeny of the first four sons of Aditi has been enumerated. He underscores the allegorical significance of this chapter by explaining what deities are described here.

291. The deity presiding over the holy Gāyatrī Mantra.

292. The deity presiding over the three mystical syllables, viz., *Bhūḥ*, *Bhuvaḥ* and *Svar* usually repeated after OM. These are prefixed to the Gāyatrī Mantra. They stand for the earth, the intermediate region and the heaven.

293. The deity presiding over the three Vedas, viz., Ṛgveda, Yajurveda and Sāmaveda.

294. The deity presiding over the acts of offering oblations into the sacred fire.

295. The presiding deity of animal sacrifices.

296. The deity presiding over the Soma Sacrifice.

297. The presiding deity over the three Cāturmāsya sacrifices performed at the beginning of the three main seasons, viz., the summer, the rainy season and the winter.

298. The names of the five great sacrifices (*Mahāmakha*) are as follows:

2. Oh dear Parīkṣit ! Siddhi, the wife of Bhaga (the sixth son of Aditi), brought forth three sons, namely, Mahiman, Vibhu and Prabhu, and a beautiful pious daughter called Āśis.

3. Out of the four wives of *Dhātṛ* (the seventh son of Aditi) Kuhū[299] bore Sāyam[300]; Sinīvālī[301] Darśa[302]; Rākā[303] Prātar[304]; Anumati[305] Pūrṇamāsa[306] respectively.

4. Samanantara or Vidhātṛ (the eighth son of Aditi) begot on Kriyā the Fire-gods called Purīṣya[307]. Carṣaṇī was the spouse of Varuṇa (the ninth son of Aditi. He is the deity presiding over water). To her was reborn Bhṛgu (the son of Brahmā).

5-6. Vālmīki, another son of Varuṇa, was a great Yogī. They say that he was born from an ant-hill. The sages Agastya and Vasiṣṭha were born of Mitra and Varuṇa who, in a jar, deposited their semen that was discharged at the sight of and in the vicinity of the celestial damsel Urvaśī. Mitra (the 10th son of Aditi) begot through Revatī three sons, namely, Utsarga, Ariṣṭa, and Pippala.

7. We are told that the king of gods, Indra, (the 11th

---

(1) *Brahmayajña* : Propitiation of the ancient sages. It consists of teaching and chanting the Vedas.

(2) *Pitṛyajña* : Grateful acknowledgement of our debt to our departed forefathers. This includes *tarpaṇa* or pouring water as oblations in their memory and for their gratification.

(3) *Devayajña* : Propitiation of gods through *homa* (pouring oblations in the sacred fire uttering their names).

(4) *Bhūtayajña* : Offering a portion of our food to all sub-human beings in acknowledgement of our debt to them.

(5) *Nṛyajña* : Worship of our fellow beings. It consists of offering food and shelter to an *atithi* (A traveller staying for only one day).

These five daily sacrifices are binding on every householder (Vide Manu 3.70-71).

299. The deity presiding over the last night of a dark fortnight.

300. The presiding deity over the evening.

301. The deity presiding over the 14th night of a dark fortnight.

302. The presiding deity over the last day of a dark fortnight.

303. The presiding deity of the last night of the bright fortnight.

304. The presiding deity of the morning.

305. The deity presiding over the 14th night of a bright fortnight.

306. The deity presiding over the last day of a bright fortnight.

307. The five deities presiding over the sacred fires known as Purīṣya.

son of Aditi) procreated through Paulomī or Śacī three sons, namely, Jayanta, Ṛṣabha and the third Mīḍhusa, Oh child !

8. Urukrama who was god Viṣṇu who appeared as Vāmana through his own divine Māyā (and who was the 12th son of Aditi) begot on his wife Kīrti, a son called Bṛhacchloka who was the father of Saubhaga and other sons.

9. We shall narrate in detail later (in Skandha VIII) the feats, excellences and the deeds of the high-souled son of Kaśyapa, namely, Vāmana, and also how he incarnated as the son of Aditi.

10. Now, I shall describe to you the sons of the sage Kaśyapa from his spouse Diti. Among them were born the great devotees of Viṣṇu, namely, the glorious Prahlāda and Bali.

11. Diti had two sons, namely, Hiraṇyakaśipu and Hiraṇyākṣa who were respected by Daityas and Dānavas. They were described (formerly in Skandha III).

12-15. The wife of Hiraṇyakaśipu was a Dānava lady called Kayādhu. She was the daughter of Jambha and was given in marriage to Hiraṇyakaśipu. She gave birth to four sons, namely, Saṁhrāda the eldermost, and Anuhrāda, Hrāda and Prahlāda. Their sister was Siṁhikā by name. She got from Vipracitti a son called Rāhu whose head was lopped off by Hari with his disc (Sudarśana) while he (Rāhu) was drinking ambrosia. Kṛti the wife of Saṁhrāda gave birth to Pañcajana. Dhamanī the wife of Hrāda bore Vātāpi and Ilvala. It was Ilvala who cooked Vātāpi for the celebrated guest Agastya.

16. Anuhrāda brought forth through his wife Sūrmyā two sons Bāṣkala and Mahiṣa. The son of Prahlāda was Virocana who had from his spouse Devī, a son called Bali.

17. From Bali, a hundred sons out of whom Bāṇa was the eldest, were born to (Bali's queen) Aśanā. We shall recount later on (in Skandha VIII) the glory of Bali which deserves celebration.

18. Having propitiated god Śiva, Bāṇa attained the first place among his attendants. The glorious god Śiva is by his side and He is still guarding his capital city.

19. Diti had sons called Maruts. They were fortynine in number. All of them were childless and they were brought over by Indra and were converted to his own class of gods.

The King (Parīkṣit) said :

20. Oh Preceptor, how did Indra convert their inborn demonic nature to godhood ? What obligations did they render to Indra which made him convert them into gods.

21. Oh worshipful sage, these other sages along with me, earnestly desire to know the details. You should therefore expound that to us.

Sūta said :

22. Oh Śaunaka, having heard that speech of Viṣṇurāta (king Parīkṣit), Śuka, the son of sage Bādarāyaṇa (Vyāsa), greeted it with heart full of joy, as it was full of earnestness and was brief yet pregnant with significance. The Omniscient Śuka spoke as follows :

Śrī Śuka said :

23. Diti whose sons were slain by Viṣṇu as the ally of Indra, in the background, was burning with wrath enkindled by grief and she began to ponder.

24. "When can I get happy sleep after bringing about the death of the hard-hearted wicked sensual Indra, the cruel murderer of his brothers.

25. The body which is addressed as "A Lord or a Ruler", goes also under the name of worms (becomes full of worms after burial), excrement (if the body is eaten up by carnivorous animals or birds of prey), and ashes (if it is cremated). He (Indra) who seeks to injure other beings for such a body, does not know self-interest, for it leads to hell.

26. By what means can I get a son who will quell the pride of Indra who wrongly presumes that this body is eternal and who is very arrogant (of unrestrained heart) ?"

27-28. With this object in view, she many times served what was wished by her husband. By her service, affection, modesty, self-control, intense devotion, by her charming sweet words as well as by her winning smiles and side glances, she who was intimate with the knowledge of human nature, captivated his heart.

29. Thus enchanted by the sly, clever woman, Kaśyapa, though learned, became powerless (against her charms). He

succumbed to her and acquiesced in her request. Such stupefaction by women is not to be wondered at.

30. At the beginning of creation, Prajāpati found that beings entertained no attachment (and the work of creation was not possible), god Brahmā (then) converted half of his body into a woman who leads astray the judgments of men.

31. The worshipful Kaśyapa who was thus waited upon by his wife, was highly pleased with Diti. With a hearty laugh, he greeted Diti with delight (and said).

Kaśyapa said:

32. Ask for a boon Oh beautiful lady with shapely thighs. Oh faultless one, I am pleased with you. When husband is pleased with his wife, what object in this or in the next world, is unattainable?

33-34. It has been declared that the husband alone is the supreme deity in the case of women.

For the glorious Lord Vāsudeva, the husband of the goddess Śrī, who is in the heart of all beings, is worshipped in the guise of different deities by men who ascribe to him different names (e. g. Indra, Varuṇa) and forms (wielder of the Vajra, or of a noose). But he is worshipped by women in the form of their husbands.

35. Therefore, Oh lady of beautiful waist, chaste women who are desirous of their welfare, worship with unswerving devotion their husband as the image of god and the Soul of the world.

36. I who am worshipped by you with so much devotion and with such superb faith, shall accomplish for you your desired object, Oh blessed lady—an object which is very difficult to be atained by unchaste women.

Diti said:

37. "Oh Brāhmaṇa sage, if you are conferring a boon on me, I pray for an immortal son who will slay Indra, for he (Indra) caused both of my sons killed and I have become a lady whose sons are dead."

38. Hearing her speech, the Brāhmaṇa became dispirit-

ed and repented (as follows): "Alas! What a great unrighteousness and sin have overtaken me today!

39. Alas! Today I have fallen a victim to sense gratification. I allowed my heart to be captivated by Māyā (deluding power) in the form of a woman. Vile as I am, I shall certainly fall in the abysmal hell.

40. What fault is there in the case of the woman who followed the natural tendencies of women? Alas! Fie upon me who am ignorant about my self-interest and lost the control of my senses.

41. Who can fathom the motives of the actions of women whose countenance is beautiful like the fully bloomed autumnal lotus, whose speech is like ambrosia to the ear but whose heart is sharp like a razor-blade.

42. Women whose minds are determined to achieve their own objective have no one really dear. For serving their own purpose, they will kill or cause to be killed their husband, son or brother.

43. I have promised that I shall give her a son. That promise should not prove untrue. But Indra does not deserve death. Under these circumstances the following expedient appears proper.

44. Oh descendant of the Kurus! Considering thus, the worshipful son of Marīci (Kaśyapa) showed some indignation and condemning himself said.

Kaśyapa said:

45. Oh blessed lady, if you carefully observe this vow for one complete year, a son will be born to you who will be the slayer of Indra, or a friend of gods (if this vow is not properly observed).

Diti said:

46. Oh Brāhmaṇa sage! I hereby undertake to observe the vow. Explain to me what acts are obligatory and what are prohibited for me, and also the acts which (are neither obligatory nor prohibitive but which) do not violate the vow.

Kaśyapa said:

47. You should not injure any of the living beings. You should not curse or tell a lie. You should not pare your nails or cut your hair. You should not touch an impure and inauspicious thing.

48. You should not take bath into water by plunging in it. You should not get angry or speak with wicked men. You should not put on unwashed garments nor should wear a garland worn by others.

49. You should not eat food which has remained after being eaten by others; nor food offered to the goddess Bhadrakālī or to seven Mātṛkās or eaten by ants. You should not eat nonvegetarian food or food brought by a Śūdra. You should not take food which is seen by a woman in monthly course. You should not drink water with your folded palms.

50. You must not go out with remnants of food sticking in the mouth or without rinsing the mouth with water. You should not stir out in the evening with dishevelled hair, unadorned or without the upper garment. You should not be unrestrained in speech.

51. You should not sleep without washing your feet or in an impure condition or with wet feet. (You should not go to bed) with your head to the North or to the West. You should not sleep with others or without any clothes. You should not remain asleep at dawn and dusk.

52. Putting on washed garments, always pure and furnished with all auspicious things, you should worship god Viṣṇu, goddess Śrī, cows and Brāhmaṇas before you take breakfast in the morning.

53. You should worship women whose husbands are alive, by offering them garlands, sandal-paste, food and ornaments. Having worshipped your husband, you should wait upon him and contemplate that your husband's energy is present in your womb.

54. If you will observe this vow called Puṁsavana (yielder of a son) for the period of one year without any flaw, you will beget a son who will be the slayer of Indra.

55. Diti agreed to that. She conceived from Kaśyapa and strictly (began to) observe the vow, Oh king.

56. Having come to know the intention of his maternal aunt the sly foresighted Indra waited upon Diti who was staying in a hermitage, (under the pretext of) rendering service to her.

57. At the appointed time he always brought flowers, fruits, sacred sticks, kuśagrass, leaves, shoots, earth and water from the forest.

58. Oh King, in this way the crooked Indra, desiring to find out some flaw in the course of the observance of vows of the lady who had undertaken them, served her like a hunter who puts on the guise of a deer.

59. Indra who was intent on detecting a weak point in her observance of vows, could not find it. He became intensely anxious as to how he could succeed (in securing his good).

60. Once in the evening, Diti who was fatigued with the observance of that austere vow and deluded by fate, slept with the remnants of food in the mouth (without rinsing her mouth with water), and with unwashed feet.

61. Getting this opportunity, Indra who was expert in Yoga entered the womb of Diti by his deluding power of Yoga, while Diti was unconscious in sleep.

62. With his Vajra he cut in seven parts the foetus which was brilliant like gold. While it was crying he said 'Don't cry," and cut each of that piece into seven again.

63. While they were being rent, all of them folded their palms and appealed to him "Oh Indra, we are Maruts, your brothers. Why do you wish to kill us ?"

64. "Don't be afraid, Brothers, you are for me", said Indra to the Maruts who as a class had unswerving loyalty to him as his attendants.

65. The foetus in the womb of Diti did not die through the grace of Lord Viṣṇu even though it was repeatedly hacked with Vajra,* just as you were saved from the missile of Aśvatthāman.

66. If a person worships but once the Ancient Person Viṣṇu, he attains to the self-same form as that of Viṣṇu, whereas the great god Hari was worshipped by Diti for a period slightly less than one year.

67. Along with Indra the Maruts became in all fifty gods. Removing the stigma of maternal heredity, they were made participants in Soma-drinking by Indra.

68. After getting up, Diti saw her sons brilliant like fire in the company of Indra. The faultless lady felt highly gratified.

69. She asked Indra, "Child, desiring a son which would strike terror in the sons of Aditi, I observed this vow which was most difficult.

70. I expected to have one son. How is it that I got seven times seven (fortynine)? Oh Son, if the truth is known to you, please tell me, but don't tell a lie."

Indra said:

71. Oh mother, having learnt about your determination, I approached you. Detecting a flaw in the observance of your vow, I who did not care for righteousness and was bent on achieving my object, slashed the foetus.

72. I hacked the foetus in seven ways and there were seven sons. Each of them was cut in seven; but they did not die.

73. Having seen that greatest miracle, I came to the conclusion that this must be some indescribable incidental Siddhi achieved through the worship of Lord Viṣṇu.

74. Those who without entertaining any blessings propitiate the Lord, do not wish the attainment of even Mokṣa, are declared as clever in accomplishing their objects.

75. After propitiating the Ruler of the World who is one's own Soul and is a bestower of his own Self, what wise man would seek contact with *guṇas* (worldly objects)? For (the products) the *guṇas* are available even in hell.

76. Therefore, Oh Mother, it behoves you to forgive this act of wickedness on my part which I, as a fool, committed to the worshipful ones. Fortunately the foetus has become alive again (after death).

Śrī Śuka said:

77. Indra, the god of heaven, was permitted (to go) by her who was sincerely pleased with him. He, along with Maruts, bowed to her and went to the heaven.

78. In this way, I have narrated to you in details what you had asked me, namely, the auspicious birth of the Maruts. Now tell me what else I should relate to you.

CHAPTER NINETEEN

(*The Details of the Vow called Puṁsavana*)

The King (Parikṣit) asked :

1. I wish to know, Oh Brāhmaṇa Sage, the details of the vow called *Puṁsavana* which you have mentioned, as Lord Viṣṇu is propitiated thereby.

Śrī Śuka said :

2. With the permission and consent of her husband a woman should begin on the 1st day of the bright half of Mārgaśīrṣa this observance of vow which is calculated to confer all desires on one.

3. She should listen to the narrative about the birth of Maruts and consult the Brāhmaṇas. Cleansing her teeth white and having taken a bath, she should put on two white garments. Adorning herself with ornaments, she should worship Lord Viṣṇu along with Śrī in the morning, before taking the breakfast.

4. (She should pray as follows:) "Oh Lord of accomplished desires, I bow to you who, being endowed with enough of all things, are (hence) above wants and expectations. Salutations to you, the Lord of Lakṣmī, the master of all mystic powers.

5. Oh Lord ! Possessor of excellences like supreme grace, fortune, prowess, glory, energy and other divine attributes as you are, you are the real omnipotent Supreme Ruler of the world.

6. Oh Divine consort of Viṣṇu, the supreme deluding power of the Lord, you possess the same characteristics as those of the Supreme Person Viṣṇu. Be propitious unto me, Oh Almighty Goddess. Oh Mother of the universe, I bow to you.

7. I offer worship to the glorious Lord designated by the sacred syllable OM, the Lord who is the Supreme Person, most mighty, the Lord of Mahālakṣmī, along with his highest potencies.

Invoking daily god Viṣṇu by chanting the aforesaid *mantra*, one should offer, with concentrated mind, articles of worship such as water for washing his (Viṣṇu's) hands and feet, and rinse his (Viṣṇu's) mouth and water for taking bath, silken garments, the sacred thread, ornaments, sandal-paste, flowers, incense, light, food and other articles.

8. Out of the food left after offering it to Viṣṇu, twelve oblations of that food should be offered to the fire with the *mantra* "Salutation to the glorious Supreme Person (Viṣṇu) of unlimited powers and denoted by the sacred syllable OM. I offer these oblations to you along with Lakṣmī."

9. If one is desirous of securing all worldly prosperity, one should always devoutly worship goddess Lakṣmī and Lord Viṣṇu who confer boons and both of whom are the fountain-heads of all blessings.

10. She should prostrate herself before them just like a rod on the ground, with her heart submissive in devotion. She should repeat the (abovementioned) *mantra* for ten times and sing (the following) hymn:

11. "Both of you are the Lords of the universe, the ultimate cause of the world. This is verily the subtle Prakṛti, your deluding potency (Māyā) too formidable to be overcome.

12. You are directly her Supreme Ruler, the Supreme Person. You are the embodiment of all sacrifices while she is the sacrificial performance. She is activity itself while you are the enjoyer of the fruit thereof.

13. This goddess is the manifestation of *guṇas*, while you are the cause of that manifestation and the enjoyer of the *guṇas*. You are the Soul, the inner controller of all embodied beings, while Śrī is the body, senses and the inner organ. The glorious Lakṣmī represents the name and form, while you are their support and their illuminator.

14. Inasmuch as both of you Supreme Rulers confer boons on the three worlds, Oh Lord of hallowing renown, may my great desires be fulfilled."

15. Eulogizing thus the Lord of Śrī along with Śrī who confers boons, one should remove all articles used in worship. Having offered water to rinse the mouth (to the deities), one should continue to worship. (known as *uttara-pūjā*)

16. She should then praise with the above hymn, with her mind merged in devotion, Smelling the remnants of the offerings to fire, she should again worship Hari.

17. Identifying with great devotion her husband with Lord Viṣṇu, she should serve him with various objects dear to him. The husband who is loving by nature, should himself help in all the activities of his wife, whether they be great or small, pertaining to the worship of God.

18. It is enough if this vow is observed by one of the couple (husband and wife). If the wife is incapable (for reasons of health) or disqualified (due to monthly course), the husband should observe it with concentrated mind.

19. This vow pertaining to Viṣṇu, if once undertaken, should not be violated under any circumstances. Every day she should worship with devotion Brāhmaṇas and women whose husbands are alive, by offering them wreaths of flowers. sandal-paste, food and ornaments, and should also worship Lord Viṣṇu.

20. After requesting the deity to retire to his abode, one should eat what was offered to the deity, for self-purification and attainment of all desires.

21. After performing such process of worship for a period of twelve months, the pious lady should observe fast on the last day of the month of Kārttika.

22. When the morrow dawns, she should touch water (take bath) and duly worship Lord Kṛṣṇa as before. The husband should offer twelve oblations according to *pārvaṇa-sthālīpāka vidhāna* (a kind of sacrificial performance) of rice cooked in milk and mixed with ghee, (in the sacrificial fire).*

23. Having reverentially accepted the blessings pronounced by the Brāhmaṇas who are pleased, and having devoutly

---

* The text of the Bh.P. used by VR. adds :

"Looking upon Brāhmaṇas as the embodiments or forms of the Supreme Soul, she should serve meals to them with devotion and should give to them sesamum seeds coated with jaggery and fried grains, and drinking vessels full of water."

paid obeisance to them by bowing the head, she should take meals with their permission.

24. After feeding the preceptor first along with the relatives, the husband, with his speech restrained, should give the remnants of the *caru*, which is capable of conferring good progeny and ensuring good fortune, to his wife.

25 A man who observes this vow of the Almighty God with due formalities, gets his desired object. A woman who observes this will get good fortune, wealth, progeny, longevity to her husband (throughout her life), glory and a good house.

26-27. An unmarried girl will get a husband possessing all good characteristics. A widow will be rid of her sins and attain to Liberation. A woman who loses her children in death) will get long-lived children. A woman if ill-fated in spite of wealthy condition, becomes blessed with good fortune and if ugly looking, becomes beautiful. A chronic patient of long period gets free from disease, and becomes energetic and virile in his senses and activities. If it is repeated at the time of auspicious ceremonies, it gives eternal and infinite satisfaction to forefathers and divinities.

28. If the Fire-God, the goddess Lakṣmī and Lord Viṣṇu are pleased after the completion of *Homa* (sacrifice), they confer all desired objects. Oh King, I have narrated to you the auspicious story of the birth of Maruts and the great vow observed by Diti.

ANCIENT INDIAN TRADITION & MYTHOLOGY

Translated by
A BOARD OF SCHOLARS

Edited by
Prof. J.L. SHASTRI

VOLUME 9

ANCIENT INDIAN TRADITION AND MYTHOLOGY SERIES

[PURĀNAS IN TRANSLATION]

Volumes Released

ŚIVA 1-4
LIṄGA 5-6
BHĀGAVATA 7-11
GARUḌA 12-14
NĀRADA 15-19
KŪRMA 20-21
BRAHMĀṆḌA 22-26
AGNI 27-30
VARĀHA 31-32
BRAHMA 33-36
VĀYU 37-38
PADMA 39-48
SKAṆDA, PARTS I-XVIII, 49-66

Volumes Under Preparation

SKANDA, PARTS XIX-XXIII
BHAVIṢYA
BRAHMAVAIVARTA
DEVĪBHĀGAVATA
KĀLIKĀ
MĀRKAṆḌEYA
MATSYA
VĀMANA
VIṢṆU
VIṢṆUDHARMOTTARA

THE BHĀGAVATA-PURĀṆA

Translated and Annotated by

Dr. G. V. TAGARE

PART III

MOTILAL BANARSIDASS PUBLISHERS
PRIVATE LIMITED • DELHI

First Edition: Delhi, 1976
Reprint: Delhi, 1987, 1994, 2003

ISBN: 81-208-0313-2

Also available at:

MOTILAL BANARSIDASS

41 U.A. Bungalow Road, Jawahar Nagar, Delhi 110 007
8 Mahalaxmi Chamber, 22 Bhulabhai Desai Road, Mumbai 400 026
236, 9th Main III Block, Jayanagar, Bangalore 560 011
120 Royapettah High Road, Mylapore, Chennai 600 004
Sanas Plaza, 1302 Baji Rao Road, Pune 411 002
8 Camac Street, Kolkata 700 017
Ashok Rajpath, Patna 800 004
Chowk, Varanasi 221 001

UNESCO COLLECTION OF REPRESENTATIVE WORKS—Indian Series.
This book has been accepted in the Indian Translation Series of the UNESCO Collection of Representative Works, jointly sponsored by the United Nations Educational, Scientific and Cultural Organization (UNESCO) and the Government of India

Printed in India
BY JAINENDRA PRAKASH JAIN AT SHRI JAINENDRA PRESS,
A-45 NARAINA, PHASE-I, NEW DELHI 110 028
AND PUBLISHED BY NARENDRA PRAKASH JAIN FOR
MOTILAL BANARSIDASS PUBLISHERS PRIVATE LIMITED,
BUNGALOW ROAD, DELHI 110 007

PUBLISHER'S NOTE

The purest gems lie hidden in the bottom of the ocean or in the depth of rocks. One has to dive into the ocean or delve into the rocks to find them out. Similarly, truth lies concealed in the language which with the passage of time has become obsolete. Man has to learn that language before he discovers that truth.

But he has neither the means nor the leisure to embark on that course. We have, therefore, planned to help him acquire knowledge by an easier course. We have started the series of Ancient Indian Tradition and Mythology in English Translation. Our goal is to universalize knowledge through the most popular international medium of expression. The publication of the Purāṇas in English Translation is a step towards that goal.

PREFACE

The present Volume contains the *Bhāgavata Purāṇa* Part III (Skandhas 7-9) in English translation. It is the eighth in the series of fifty Volumes on *Ancient Indian Tradition and Mythology.*

The project of the series was envisaged and financed in 1970 by Shri Sundarlal Jain, the Veteran enterprizer in the field of Oriental Publication and the leading partner Messrs Motilal Banarsidass. Hitherto nine Volumes of the Series, including the present one, (that is, four Vols. of the *Śiva Purāṇa,* two Vols. of the *Liṅga Purāṇa* and three Vols. of the *Bhāgavata Purāṇa,* Skandhas 1-9) have been published and released for sale.

The present translation is based on the Sanskrit text of the *Bhāgavata Purāṇa* published by Messrs Kṣemarāja Śrīkṛṣṇadāsa Veṅkaṭeśvara Press, Bombay. This text, constructed on the Collation of Mss. and supported by the oldest Commentator Śrīdhara Svāmin, is fairly accurate. But we have also recorded the translation of all the additional verses accepted as genuine in the authoritative commentaries of Rāmānuja and Madhva Schools, that are not found in the text of Śrīdhara Svāmin.

The *Bhāgavata Purāṇa* deals with a variety of subjects—geographical, historical, philosophical, religious and the like which need elucidation. This task could not be accomplished by a mere translation. We have, therefore, provided footnotes on the topics. On the philosophical verses, especially, we have recorded different interpretations of the commentators belonging to different schools of thought, viz. those of Śaṅkara, Rāmānuja, Madhva, Nimbārka, Vallabha and Caitanya (Gauḍīya School of Vaiṣṇavism) and also two eminent Marathi Commentators—Kṛṣṇa Dayārṇava and Ekanātha. In the accomplishment of this task we have also utilized the commentaries published in the Bhāgavata Vidyā Peeth, Ahmedabad Edition and the Vrindavana edition of this Purāṇa.

In order to help the reader understand the background of the subject matter we have prefixed to part I a critical and comparative introduction which discusses, among other topics, the date, authorship, philosophy, religion, general characteristics and the commentators of this Purāṇa. A List of Abbreviations is also prefixed to Part I of the Purāṇa while a general index will be included in the last part of this work.

Before closing, it is our pleasant duty to put on record our sincere gratitude to Dr. S.K. Chatterjee, Dr. V. Raghavan, Dr. R.N. Dandekar, Shri K.R. Kripalani, and the authorities of the UNESCO for their kind encouragement and valuable help which render this work more valuable to scholars than it would otherwise have been. We must also thank the learned translator and annotator Dr. G.V. Tagare for his untiring zeal and sustained efforts in bringing out this Volume within scheduled time, in spite of untold obstacles.

Finally, we avail of this opportunity to state that any critical suggestion and advice for improvement are welcome and will receive proper consideration from us.

—Editor

CONTENTS

SKANDHA VII

Chapters

1. Conversation between Yudhiṣṭhira and Nārada Jaya and Vijaya cursed 885
2. Hiraṇyakaśipu consoles his mother and Kinsmen 891
3. Hiraṇyakaśipu's Penance—Brahmā grants Boons 898
4. Oppression of Hiraṇyakaśipu and Description of Prahlāda's devotion 903
5. The Life of Prahlāda. Hiraṇyakaśipu attempts to kill Prahlāda 909
6. Prahlāda's teaching 916
7. Prahlāda, enlightened in mother's womb 922
8. Death of Hiraṇyakaśipu and praise of Nṛsiṁha 932
9. Prahlāda eulogizes Nṛsiṁha 941
10. Prahlāda enthroned. The conquest of Tripura 954
11. The Eternal path of Religion 962
12. Inquiry into the right conduct (Duties of Brahmacārins and Vānaprasthas) 968
13. The Code of conduct for saṁnyāsins and a dialogue between Avadhūta and Prahlāda 973
14. The duties of a householder 979
15. Exposition of right conduct (concluded) 985

SKANDHA VIII

1. Description of Manvantaras 997
2. The Elephant leader seized by the Alligator 1002
3. Liberation of the Mighty Elephant 1006
4. Liberation of the Lord of Elephants 1013
5. Description of V and VI Manvantaras—Brahmā Hymns the Lord 1017
6. Mount Mandara Transported for Churning the Ocean 1025
7. The Churning of the Sea for Nectar 1030
8. The Lord's Manifestation as Mohinī (The Enchantress) 1037

9. Distribution of Nectar by Mohinī 1044
10. A Battle between Gods and Asuras 1048
11. End of the Battle between Gods and Asuras at Nārada's Mediation 1053
12. Lord Śiva Fascinated by Mohinī 1059
13. Description of the future Manvantaras 1065
14. Duties of Manus and their functionaries 1069
15. Bali's Conquest of the Svarga (celestial Region) 1071
16. Instruction in the observance of Payovrata to Aditi 1075
17. Manifestation of the Lord as Vāmana 1083
18. The Lord incarnates as Vāmana. Visit to Bali's Sacrifice 1087
19. Vāmana's request for three paces of land—Śukra's opposition 1092
20. Manifestation of the Cosmic form by Viṣṇu 1098
21. Bali bound Down 1102
22. A Dialogue between Bali and Vāmana 1106
23. Bali free from bonds, enters Sutala 1111
24. The Fish incarnation of Lord Viṣṇu 1116

Skandha IX

1. The story of King Sudyumna 1125
2. History of Karūṣa and other four sons of Manu 1130
3. The story of Cyavana and Sukanyā 1134
4. The account of Nābhāga and Ambarīṣa 1138
5. Protection of Durvāsas. The story of Ambarīṣa (concluded) 1148
6. History of Ikṣvāku's posterity 1152
7. The Story of King Hariścandra 1159
8. The story of King Sagara 1164
9. The descent of the Gaṅgā, the story of Kalmāṣapāda 1170
10. The story of Rāma 1177
11. The story of Rāma (concluded) 1186
12. Description of Ikṣvāku's Race (concluded) 1190
13. Description of the Race of Nimi 1193
14. Description of the Lunar Race 1196
15. The story of Paraśurāma. Sahasrārjuna slain 1204

16.	The story of Paraśurāma (concluded)	1209
17.	The Lunar Dynasty—The Descendants of Āyu, the son of Purūravas	1214
18.	History of Nahuṣa's Line—The story of Yayāti	1217
19.	Yayāti's Retirement and Final Emancipation	1223
20.	The History of Pūru's race—Birth of Bharata	1227
21.	The Race of Bharata—The History of Rantideva	1232
22.	The History of the Lunar Race—The Royal Dynasties of Pāñcāla, Magadha and Kuru	1236
23.	History of the Dynasties of Anu, Druhyu, Turvasu and Yadu	1242
24.	History of the Race of Yadu	1247

SEVENTH SKANDHA

CHAPTER ONE

Conversation between Yudhiṣṭhira and Nārada : Jaya and Vijaya cursed

The King (*Parīkṣit*) *said* :

1. How is it that the glorious Lord who is by nature impartial and friendly to all beings, killed Daityas for the sake of Indra, as if He was impelled by partiality, Oh Brāhmaṇa sage ?

2. Being transcendental to *Guṇas* (He is above love and hate). He is the very embodiment of perfect bliss. He has no selfish ends to be served from the host of gods, nor does He entertain any fear from Asuras and nor does He cherish any hatred towards them.

3. Oh highly fortunate one, this has been our great doubt about the excellences of Lord Nārāyaṇa. Your Worship should please dispel it.

Śrī Śuka said :

4. Oh great King, you have asked a good question. The life of Hari is miraculous and mysterious. It contains the glories of the devotees of the Lord and promotes devotion unto Him intensely.

5. The legendary story of Hari which is highly meritorious is sung by sages like Nārada and others. After paying obeisance to Kṛṣṇa-Dvaipāyana Vyāsa, I shall narrate to you that.

6. Though the Lord who is transcendental to Prakṛti, attributeless, unborn and unmanifest, enters into the *guṇas* of his own Māyā. He assumed the role of the chastiser to those who deserved punishment (i.e. became the cause of enmity between gods and demons).

7. *Sattva*, *Rajas* and *Tamas* are the attributes of *Prakṛti* and not of the *Ātman*, nor is there a synchronous increase or decrease of them.

8. During the period of the ascendancy of *Sattva*, he enters into the bodies of celestials and sages, and He thus intensifies their power. During the preponderance of *Rajas* he does so for Asuras. During the dominance of *Tamas*, he fosters Yakṣas and Rākṣasas. It is in conformance with the Time-spirit that this happens. (Not that God is partial).

9. Like fire (in the wood), space i.e. *Ākāśa* (in a pitcher), he appears in many forms or bodies without being distinguished from the body occupied by him. It is only the discerning who, after meticulous investigation (by introspection) into the *Ātman* as residing in themselves, realize Him (as being distinct from *guṇas* and their products).

10. When the Supreme Self desires to create cities, i.e. bodies, for enjoyment of the *Jīva*, he creates separately *Rajas* (which was in a state of equilibrium) and impels it to act with dominant force. When the Lord desires to sport Himself in multifarious bodies, he makes the *Sattva* act. When he desires to go to sleep, i.e. to withdraw the universe within himself, he sets in motion the *Tamas*.

11. Oh King, this infallible Creator and Controller of the universe, through the instrumentality of *Prakṛti* and *Puruṣa*, creates the Present Time which acts as their supporting associate. The entity that is designated as Time, promotes the power of *Sattva*. Due to the fostering of *Sattva* by Time, the Lord of extensive fame, the Controller of Time, appears as a friend of gods (whose dominant characteristic is *Sattva*) and destroys the enemies of gods who are dominated by *Rajas* and *Tamas*. (It is due to his presence that Time has the potency to achieve this).*

12. Oh King, on this very topic was narrated a legend by the divine sage Nārada, when he was respectfully questioned by Yudhiṣṭhira formerly, in the great Rājasūya Sacrifice.

13-14. Having seen the most marvellous absorption of *Śiśupāla*, the king of Cedi, in Lord Vāsudeva at the great

* VR.: Supreme Soul creates the Present Time which, bein pervaded by Him, is like His body. He then brings forth *Prakṛti* an *Puruṣa*—the sentient and the insentient phenomena. When it is the tim for protection through *Sattva guṇa*, the Lord impels the Time to increas the power of gods only and defeat the Asuras who are dominated b *Rajas* and *Tamas*.

sacrifice called Rājasūya the king Yudhiṣṭhira, the son of Pāṇḍu, became astonished in his mind, and asked the divine sage who was sitting there, in the presence of the sages.

Yudhiṣṭhira said :

15. Oh, it is extremely marvellous that Śiśupāla, the hater of Vāsudeva was absorbed into Vāsudeva, the Supreme Reality, as such merger is very difficult even to those who are exclusively devoted to Him.

16. Oh Sage, all of us are solicitous to know (the explanation of) this mystery, for Vena who used to revile the Lord was cursed to hell[1] by Brāhmaṇas.

17. The wicked son of Damaghoṣa, Śiśupāla was wrathful and jealous about Kṛṣṇa since his childhood-lisping up to this time. Even so was the wicked Dantavaktra.

18. Why is it that the tongue of those who constantly blasphemed Viṣṇu who is the immutable transcendental Brahman, was not affected with white leprosy or that they did not enter the blinding darkness of hell?

19. How is it that they were so easily absorbed into his Lordship of incomprehensible nature, even while all people were looking on?[2]

20. This (miracle) confuses my intellect and makes it unsteady like the flame of a lamp flickering before the wind. Your worshipful self should please explain to me the reason of this most wonderful event.

Śrī Śuka said :

21. Hearing that speech (query) of the king, the worshipful sage Nārada was pleased, and addressing to him, he recounted the episodes connected with this event while the members of the assembly were listening

Nārada said ;

22. Censure and eulogy, respectful and disrespectful treatments are meant for this body which is brought forth

1. GS. explains that Vena was killed. He did not go to hell.

2. ŚR. points out that though Dantavaktra was not absorbed at that time, his future merger with Vāsudeva was astrologically predicted and is hence treated as a *fait accompli*, by Nārada.

through want of discrimination and ignorance between *Prakṛti* and *Puruṣa*, Oh King.

23. By the false notion of identity between the body and the Soul, arises the misapprehension of one's being different from others. It leads to the concept of individual distinctness expressed by the words "I" and "Mine" and (gives rise to) the feeling of pain under punishment and harsh words.

24. The killing of creatures is the destruction of the body which they have identified with the Soul and the notion of idividuality (i.e. 'I' and 'Mine'). But the Lord is without a second and the Soul of all. Being absolute, he has no such attachment (or the sense of individuality), he chastises the wicked for their good and not out of malice. How could harmfulness (*Hiṁsā*) be attributed to Him ?

25. Therefore one should concentrate one's mind on Him either through constant hostility or through devotion characterised by absence of malice or enmity or through fear or love. By this concentration, a person will perceive nothing else but the Lord.

26. It is my definite conclusion that just as a mortal being attains identification and concentration with the Lord by cherishing enmity, he does not (with that intensity and to that extent) attain absorption through devotion.[1]

27. A worm shut up by a wasp (in its hole or nest) on a wall, broods over it (the wasp) so intensely and continuously through hatred and fear that it gets transformed into a form like a wasp.

28. Thus those who cherish enmity against the glorious Supreme Ruler Kṛṣṇa who appears a human being through his Māyā power, attain to him as their sins are washed off by their constant meditation upon him through hatred or fear.

29. Many persons have attained unto union with the Supreme Lord after being purified of all the impiety by concentrating their mind on the Lord through love, hatred, fear, affection and devotion.

30. Gopīs (wives of cowherds) through love, Kaṁsa through fear, Śiśupāla and other kings through hatred, Vṛṣṇis

1. VJ. & VC. point out that this verse does not advocate hatred as the best form of devotion, though superficially it appears to do so.

through kinship, you Pāṇḍavas through friendship and affection, and we sages through devotion (attained identity with him), Oh King.

31. Vena does not fall under any of the five categories of devotees of the Supreme Man. One should therefore fix one's mind on Kṛṣṇa by any one of the means (detailed above).

32. Oh Pāṇḍava, Śiśupāla and Dantavaktra, the sons of your maternal aunt, were the foremost attendants of Viṣṇu; but they fell down from that position through the curse of a Brāhmaṇa.

Yudhiṣṭhira said :

33. It appears certainly incredible that those who are exclusively devoted to Hari, were compelled to be born again. Therefore (please tell us) whose curse it was and what was the nature of the imprecation which overpowered the servants of Hari.

34. The residents of the city or region called Vaikuṇṭha are of pure sāttvic form and are devoid of material body, senses and the like. You should narrate to us how it led to the assumption of corporeal existence (in the case of such residents of Vaikuṇṭha).

Nārada said :

35. Once upon a time, Sanandana and others (Sanaka etc.) the sons of Brahmā, went to the region of Viṣṇu, by chance, while they were ranging at will, through the three worlds.

36. Though they were born earlier than elders like Brahmā's sons (such as Marīci and others), they looked like children of five or six years in age. All of them had no garments (and were completely nude). Thinking them to be kiddies those two door-keepers (of Viṣṇu) prevented them (from entering).

37. Being enraged at this, they cursed, "Both of you (doorkeepers) are fools. You do not deserve to live near the feet of Lord Viṣṇu (much less to serve him) as his feet are completely free from *Rajas* and *Tamas*. Hence, immediately turn into the most sinful form of Asuras."

38. While both of them were falling down from their place due to this curse, they were addressed by the merciful sages, "Both of you will be fit to return to your region (Vaikuṇṭha) after three births".

39. Both of them were born as the sons of Diti. The elder was Hiraṇyakaśipu and the younger brother was Hiraṇyākṣa. Both of them were respected by Daityas and Dānavas.

40. Hiraṇyakaśipu was killed by Hari assuming the Man-Lion form. Hiraṇyākṣa was killed by Viṣṇu incarnating in a boar form while lifting up the earth (sunken into the cosmic waters).

41. Hiraṇyakaśipu adopted various devices to torture his son Prahlāda to death, as he wished to kill him for his (Prahlāda's) love and devotion to Viṣṇu.

42. Despite his endeavours to kill Prahlāda, he could not do so, as Prahlāda identified himself with the soul of all beings; was serene and looked upon all as being Brahman (and therefore equal). He was also surcharged and covered with Lord Viṣṇu's power.

43. Thereafter, both of them were born as Rākṣasas as the sons of Keśinī and Viśravas. They were Rāvaṇa and Kumbhakarṇa, the tormentors of all the worlds.

44. Even in that incarnation, Viṣṇu became Rāma, the descendant of Raghu, and killed them for redeeming them from the curse. You will hear the prowess of Rāma from the lips of Mārkaṇḍeya, Oh King.

45. That very pair was born as Kṣatriya, as the sons of your maternal aunt. Now (not they but) their sins (and their present body, as the consequence of the curse) being destroyed by Sudarśana disc of Kṛṣṇa, they are now rescued from the curse.

46. Both of them were led to absorption in Kṛṣṇa (Acyuta), through their contemplation (of Kṛṣṇa) intensified by the bitterest enmity. They have again returned to Hari's presence, as attendants of Viṣṇu.

Yudhiṣṭhira asked :

47. How is it that Hiraṇyakaśipu came to cherish hatred towards his high-souled beloved son? And how did Prahlāda

happen to devote his mind exclusively to Hari ? Please tell me this in detail. Oh worshipful sage.

CHAPTER TWO

Hiraṇyakaśipu consoles his mother and kinsmen

Nārada narrated :

1. When Hari, who had assumed the form of a boar, thus killed his brother Hiraṇyākṣa (out of partiality to gods), Hiraṇyakaśipu was agitated with wrath and grief, Oh King.

2. Trembling with rage, biting his lips, and with eyes fiercely blazing with anger, he looked at the sky which appeared full of smoke; he spoke thus.

3. Looking fierce with his terrible big teeth, frowning look, and terrific looking face with knit eyebrows, he raised his trident in the assembly of Dānavas and addressed them as follows.

4-5. "Oh Dānavas and Daityas, Oh Dvimūrdhan (two-headed demon), Oh three-eyed one, Śambara, hundred-armed one, horse-headed one, Namuci, Pāka, Ilvala, Vipracitti, Puloman, Śakuna and others ! Listen to my words and then immediately execute them. Do not delay.

6. My beloved brother was killed by insignificant enemies through Hari who, though impartial, sided with them through their services (to Him).

7. He (Viṣṇu) was originally pure and impartial but through his assumption of the form of a boar by his Māyā, he has fallen away from his original nature. Like a child, he sides with him who serves him. His mind is unstable.

8. I shall satisfy my brother who is thirsting for blood, with the profuse blood (of Viṣṇu) with his neck cut off by my trident, and thus I shall relieve my grief.

9. When the crafty adversary (whose actions are inscrutable) is destroyed, the residents of heavens (gods) whose very

life is Viṣṇu, will wither away like branches of a tree the roots of which are cut.

10. (While I am accomplishing this), you immediately repair to the earth which has been made prosperous by Brāhmaṇas and Kṣattriyas. Slaughter down those who are engaged in austere penance, sacrifice, Vedic studies, observance of religious vows and acts of charity.

11. Viṣṇu owes his existence to (lit. has for his roots in) the religious performance of Brāhmaṇas, for he Himself is the sacrifice and personified righteousness. He is the ultimate resort of gods, sages, manes and beings.

12. Repair to those regions wherein dwell the Brāhmaṇas, cows, (recitation of) Vedas, (proper observance of the duties of) Varṇas and Āśramas. Devastate that country with fire, and cut down (the trees etc. useful for sacrifice)."

13. In this way, they respectfully accepted the order of their master, bending their heads. Being innately disposed to indulge in harassment of others, they wrought havoc among subjects (on the earth).

14. They set fire to towns, villages, cow-pens, gardens, parks and fields, hermitages and mines, farmers' settlements, villages at the foot of mountains, cow-herd settlements and even capital cities.

15. Some knocked down and dismantled with spades bridges, ramparts and towers. Some with an axe in hand cut down fruit-bearing trees (serving as food to others). Some set on fire the houses of the people with flaming torches.

16. When people were thus constantly harassed by the followers of Hiraṇyakaśipu, the king of the demons, (sacrifices could not be performed and) gods (who starved due to non-receipt of their share in sacrificial oblations) deserted heaven, and wandered over the earth unperceived.

17-18. (Though himself deeply) aggrieved, Hiraṇyakaśipu offered oblations of water to the spirit of his deceased brother, and performed other funeral rites. He consoled the sons of his brothers, viz., Śakuni, Śambara, Dhṛṣṭa, Bhūta-Santāpana, Vṛka, Kālanābha, Mahānābha, Hariśmaśru, Utkaca.

19. Hiraṇyakaśipu who knew what was appropriate for a particular occasion and situation (lit. place and time), addre-

ssed the following in soothing words to his nephews (mentioned above) and to their mother (his sister-in-law) Ruṣābhānu and to his own mother Diti, Oh ruler of men.

Hiraṇyakaśipu said :

20. Mother dear ! Oh daughter (-in law) ! Oh sons ! You ought not to lament (the death of) a hero. Praiseworthy and covetable is the death of the brave, while facing the enemy (on the battle-field).

21. The sojourn of beings in this world is like the get-together of travellers in a shed of water-jars (kept on the road-side for travellers to drink), Oh virtuous lady. Similarly, it is by the Providence that creatures are severally brought and are separated by their respective *karmas*.

22.* The Soul is eternal (deathless), immutable, pure, omnipresent, omniscient, the cause of everything, yet distinct from the body, (hence you should not lament for Hiraṇyākṣa thinking him to be dead, separate etc.). Through his Māyā, he creates *guṇas* (such as various species of bodies, pleasure, pain) and assumes various forms.

23-24. Just as even the (reflection of) trees (in water appears to) move when the waters move, or the earth appears to revolve when one's eyes are swimming, the same way, when the mind gets agitated and conditioned by the *guṇas*, the Perfect Person appears similarly conditioned and invested with a material body, even though he is bodiless.

25-26. It is the perversity of the Soul to presume its identification with the material body which does not exist. By this identification and attachment, are caused one's union with the undesirable and separation from the dear ones, and *vice*

* As usual, VR. sets forth the Viśiṣṭādvaita theory of the Soul, viz. *Ātman* that is *jīva* pervades the whole body that he occupies (*sarvaga*) through his knowledge. To enjoy the fruit of his *karma* (whether merit or sin), he activates the *guṇas* (e.g. Sattva). The association of and separation from the body of each *jīva* is due to his *karma*.

But VR. does not explain the get-together and dispersal of several *jīvas* as required by the text of the Bh. P.

VJ. points out that the *jīva's* relation with his body etc. is temporary, but with that of the Lord is constant. It is the Lord who bestows the *jīva* with the mind, senses etc. Hari is the real support of the *jīva*.

versa, *karmas*, and entrance into various species of beings, birth and death, sorrows of various kinds, lack of discernment and discrimination (between the matter and the spirit), brooding over the (objects of senses), forgetfulness about the discrimination between the Soul and the body.

27. In this context, the wise people give as an illustration, the following ancient legend, in the form of a conversation between Yama (the god of death) and the kinsmen of a dead person. Listen to that dialogue carefully.

28. In the country called Uśīnara, there lived a famous king by name Suyajña. When he was killed in the battle by his enemies his kinsmen stood around him.

29-30. He lay on the battlefield with his armour studded with jewels shattered, his ornaments and wreaths of flowers fallen away from his body. His heart was pierced with arrows and his body lay weltering in blood, the hair of the head dishevelled and scattered. His eyes were blown and lips were bitten with rage. His lotus-like face was covered with dust, and his weapons and arms were cut into pieces.

31. Observing their husband, the king of Uśinaras, reduced to that plight by Fate, the queens were deeply grieved. Screaming out 'We are undone, Oh Lord', they violently beat their breasts with their hands now and then, and fell at his feet.

32. Bewailing loudly and bathing the lotus-like feet of their (dead) husband with tears tinted reddish with saffron paste on their breasts, and their hair and ornaments dishevelled and scattered, they wailed so piteously and loudly as to cause heartrending grief in the hearts of the listening persons.

33. "Alas ! Your majesty has been transported to a stage of existence beyond the range of our sight, by the merciless Destiny, Oh Lord. You who were once the giver of livelihood (and happiness) to the people of Uśīnara country, have now been made the cause of their increasing grief, by it.

34. Oh Lord of the earth ! How can we live without you, our best friend and appreciator of merits ? Permit us who are desirous of serving your feet, to follow you wherever you will go (i.e. to die after you)."

35. While they were lamenting thus clasping their dead

husband, and unwilling to allow him to be removed for cremation, the Sun set in the sky.

36. Having heard the wailings of the relatives of the dead (even while he was in his capital), Yama (the god of death) himself approached them, in the form of a boy, and spoke to them.

Yama said :

37. Oh ! How astonishing is the folly of these elderly people who have been daily observing the course of the world (viz. the death of everyone who is born). Though themselves of the same (mortal) nature as that of the dead person, they bewail in vain the man who has returned to the (unmanifest) state from which he has come (originally).[1]

38. Oh ! How blessed-most we are that though abandoned by parents in this world, we do not feel any anxiety. Weak as we are, we are not devoured by (carnivorous animals like) wolves and others. (We feel confident that) he who protects us while (we were) in the womb, shall protect us (in this world).

39. Oh ladies ! The imperishable Lord, at his sweet will, creates, protects and destroys the universe. The wise people call the mobiles and immobiles as mere toys. It is the Lord alone, who is powerful (enough) to preserve and destroy it.

40. Protected by the Lord, one survives even if abandoned by the road side. If ignored by Him, one meets death even while staying at home. A helpless creature can stay alive even in a jungle, if looked after by Him; while a person if destined by Him to die, shall never live even if protected at home (by the use of medicines, incantations etc.).

41. Bodies of all species (including those of gods, subhuman and human beings) come into existence and perish at a particular time according to the *karmas* depending on the subtle body. But the Soul though it inhabits the Prakṛti (the corporal body), is not affected by the attributes of the Prakṛti (body) as he is different from it.

1. Cf. *avyaktādīni bhūtāni vyaktamadhyāni Bhārata / avyaktanidhanānyeva tatra kā paridevanā* // B.G. 2.28.

42. This corporal body of Puruṣa (the Soul or Spirit) is caused by delusion, and being made of *bhūtas*, is different from the Soul, just as a house is different from its dweller. Like bubbles constituted of atoms of water, pots made of earth, gold ornaments made of (solidified) fire, this body formed (out of elements) by Time, undergoes modification and perishes.

43. Just as fire remaining latent in the pieces of wood is distinct from them, or the vital breath existing in the body remains different from it, or the sky pervading all things does not stick to anything, similarly the Soul, the supporter of all the *guṇas*, i.e. their product, e.g. the body, sense organs or who dwells in them, is distinct from them.[1]

44. You fools! This (body called) Suyajña whom you are lamenting, is lying here. He who heard you and then replied, could never be seen by you.

45. Not even the great vital air (*mukhya-prāṇa*) in the body which is called life, is the listener or the speaker. The principle, which is the master and controller of senses, is the real *ātman*, and it is distinct from the body and the life-breath *mukhya prāṇa*).

46. This all-pervasive principle *ātman*, though distinct, assumes different bodies (celestial, human and sub-human), consisting of five elements (*bhūtas*), senses and mind, and regards himself as one with them; and by dint of his power and wisdom, he casts them off (as well).

47. So long as its association with Māyā continues, the *ātman* identifies itself with the subtle body (*liṅga-śarīra*) and feels attachment for it. The bondage of *karma* holds sway over him. It leads to the perversion of the Soul, resulting into misery.

48. It is a false notion and attachment to look upon and speak of (products of) *guṇas* (such as pleasure, pain) as real. Like our fanciful desires and dreams, all sense-experience is unreal.

1. According to VJ. verses 41-43 emphasize the distinction of *Paramātman* from Jīva. In 43, the presence of the *Paramātman* in the body is not the effect of delusion, and as such he is not affected by the *guṇas*.

49. Hence, the knowers of the reality do not grieve for what is eternal (the Soul) or what is transient (e.g. body, sense-organs, objects of pleasure). But the nature of those who are given to grieving, cannot be changed (as they have not imbibed the knowledge of reality).

50. A fowler, created as the destroyer of birds (by God) spread his net in the forest, placing allurements at different places.

51. A pair of *Kuliṅga* birds (sparrows) was seen flying over it. Out of them, the female sparrow was soon allured by the fowler.

52. The queen-bird, being dragged by Time (Destiny), was enmeshed in the net. Seeing her in that miserable condition, the male partner was extremely afflicted. The pitiable mate, being helpless (to rescue her and to control his own grief), lamented over his miserable companion, out of affection :

53. "Oh ! What that merciless yet almighty Providence is going to do with my wife, who herself is pitiable and helpless in every respect, is lamenting for me.

54. May the Deity be pleased to take me also. Of what use is to me the survival of the one (male) half leading a miserable life, after being separated from my better half ?

55. How can I maintain those unfledged motherless young ones ? Those unfortunate children of mine must be waiting for the arrival of their mother."

56. While the male bird, who was grieved at the separation from his wife, was thus lamenting with his voice choked with tears, the fowler, as if impelled by fate, concealed himself close by, and hit the bird with an arrow.

57. So, you foolish ladies who do not foresee your own destruction (death) will never get back your husband, even if you bewail for hundreds of years."

Hiraṇyakaśipu said :

58. While the child was thus admonishing, all the kinsmen (of Suyajña) became astonished, and realized that everything is transient and unreal.

59. Having exhorted them thus, Yama also disappeared at that very spot. The relatives of Suyajña performed his funeral rites.

60. Hence you need not grieve for yourself or for others. In the case of ignorant beings, the differentiation between one's own self and another or what belongs to one's own self and another, is due to the false notion of distinction between one's own self from another (and the consequent attachment for one's own body and property)."

Nārada said :

61. Having heard the speech of the king of Daityas (Hiraṇyakaśipu) Diti, along with her daughter-in-law, immediately stopped sorrowing for her son and steadied her heart by fixing it on Reality.

CHAPTER THREE

Hiraṇyakaśipu's Penance—Brahmā grants Boons

Nārada said :

1. Oh King (Yudhiṣṭhira) ! Hiraṇyakaśipu wished to be invincible, unaffected by old age and death, unrivalled and the absolute ruler of all the worlds.

2. With his arms stretched upwards, eyes fixed in the sky and (all the while) standing on the tips of his big toes, Hiraṇyakaśipu (with the abovementioned desire) performed penance of a severe type, in the valley of mount Mandara.

3. Like the Sun radiating fiery rays at the time of the destruction of the world, he shone with the brilliant splendour of his matted hair. While he was thus engaged in austerities, gods (who disappeared out of fear) returned to their (former) abodes (in heaven).

4. As a result of his (severe) penance, smoky fire emanated from the crown of his head. It spread in all directions

and scorched the higher, middle and lower regions of the universe.

5. Rivers and oceans were agitated; the earth along with its continents and mountains quaked (violently); planets and stars fell down (from their orbits); all the ten directions were ablaze.

6-7 Being scorched (with that fire), gods deserted the heaven and went to the region of god Brahmā, and implored to the creator of the world : "Oh god of gods, Lord of the universe! Being burnt (severely afflicted) with the penance of Hiraṇyakaśipu, the king of Daityas, we are unable to stay in the Heaven. Oh great god! If it pleases you, please bring about its pacification (extinction) before all the people (or regions) who worship you, are not destroyed, Oh Supreme Lord!

8. Do you not know his intention of performing this severely austere penance? (If not) be pleased to listen to it as reported by us.

9-10 'Having created this universe of mobiles and immobiles by dint of his penance and Yogic meditation, the creator of the universe occupies his throne (position) exalted over all regions. I too will attain a similar high position for me, by my ever-increasing devotion to asceticism and Yogic concentration. For Time and Soul are eternal.

11. Otherwise, by the power of my penance, I shall reverse the old order of the universe and make it as it was not before (making sins result in happiness, meritorious deeds lead to miseries. The *Asuras* will be exalted to Svarga and gods and sages driven to Pātāla). What have I to do with the positions of Dhruva, Viṣṇu and others which are abolished by Time, at the end of *a Kalpa*?[1]

12. We heard it reported that, it is with that determination, he (Hiraṇyakaśipu) undertook those rigorous religious austerities. Oh Lord of the three worlds! Now you may please do promptly whatever is proper.

13. Your exalted position as Parameṣṭhī promotes the growth, welfare, prosperity, good fortune and victory of the twice-born ones and cows, Oh Lord of the universe."

1. The realm of Viṣṇu is eternal. But Hiraṇyakaśipu being of demonic and *Tāmasa* intellect thought it to be perishable.

14. Thus respectfully requested by gods, Brahmā, the glorious, self-originated god, accompanied by Bhṛgu, Dakṣa and others, went to the hermitage of the king of Daityas.

15. But (at first) they could not find him as he was covered with an ant hill, grass and bamboos and as his skin, fat, flesh and blood were eaten up on all sides, by ants.

16. Brahmā (the swan-riding god) was surprised on seeing Hiraṇyakaśipu tormenting the world with his religious austerities (while lying concealed thus) like the Sun (scorching the world though) covered with clouds. Laughing aloud, he spoke :

Brahmā said :

17. Arise, arise, Oh Son of Kaśyapa ! May good betide you ! You have accomplished the purpose of your penance. I, the bestower of boons, have come here (to confer any boon you ask of me). Ask for any boon desired by you.

18. I have seen your extremely wonderful fortitude and patience. Though your body is eaten up by gnats, your life resides in your bony skeleton only.

19. None of the sages of yore has performed such austere penance, nor shall others do it in future. Who can verily sustain his life without (drinking a drop of) water for a hundred celestial years ?[1]

20. By this resoluteness of yours which is hard to practise even by those (great sages) who control their mind, and by your firmness in austere penance, I am conquered by you, Oh son of Diti.

21. I shall bestow on you, Oh leader of Asuras, all the blessings. The sight of an immortal god like me will not be unfructuous and in vain for you (who are but) a mortal.

Nārada said :

22. Having spoken to him (Hiraṇyakaśipu) thus, the first-born god Brahmā sprinkled on the body (of Hiraṇyakaśipu) which was eaten up by ants, celestial water from his

1. Human year of 360 days corresponds to 1 day of gods. Thus, one celestial year=360 human years. 100 celestial years=36,000 human years.

Kamaṇḍalu (earthen or wooden water pot) charged with unfailing potency.

23. From the ant-hill covered with bamboos, there arose, like fire from fuel, a youth of adamantine frame of the body, perfect in all limbs, endowed with energy and power, and with complexion like molten gold.

24. Finding god Brahmā seated on his swan, and stationed in the sky, he was transported with joy at this sight, and reverentially touched the ground with his head.

25. Rising up, he saw the god Brahmā with his own eyes. Reverentially he folded his hands in a suppliant position. With his eyes full of tears of joy, and with his hair standing on their ends, he expressed the following prayer with his voice choked with tears of joy.

Hiraṇyakaśipu said :

26-27.* "Bow to the all-pervading Supreme Lord, the support of the *guṇas—sattva*, *rajas* and *tamas*, who, being self-luminous, manifested by his own splendour (power), this universe which was enveloped in intense *tamas* (not darkness), produced by Time, at the time of the periodic destruction of the universe (at the end of each *Kalpa*), and who, assuming the three *guṇas* of *Prakṛti* creates, protects and destroys this universe.

28** Salutations to the Primary Cause (the instrumental cause of the universe who is knowledge and wisdom *incarnate*, and who (as the material cause) becomes manifest through the modifications, viz., vital airs (*prāṇa*), senses (*indriya*), mind and intellect.

29. You govern the mobiles and immobiles through the chief *Prāṇa* (chief of the five vital airs) and hence, you are the protector of all the creatures, the controller of the mind, and

* VR. notes that due to the *tāmasa* nature of Hiraṇyakaśipu, he wrongly thinks god Brahmā to be the Almighty Lord. VJ. also points out that the attributes used here are inapplicable to the four-faced god Brahmā but are proper for Hari who, as an *antaryāmin*, dwells in all and controls Brahmā.

** VJ. shows that the attributes mentioned herein are applicable both to the Supreme Lord and to god Brahmā.

life principles, of the heart and the sense-organs. You are the *mahat* (and) as such the ruler of the elements (*bhūtas*), their *guṇas* (objects such as sound, touch etc.) as well as their *vāsanās* (sense-impressions).

30. Through your body consisting of the three Vedas, and the sacrificial lore, requiring four officiating priests (viz. Hotṛ, Adhvaryu, Udgātṛ and Brahmā), you perform the seven types of sacrifices (such as *Agniṣṭoma*, *Atyagniṣṭoma*, *Uktha*, *Ṣoḍaśī*, *Atirātra*, *Āptoryāma* and *Vājapeya*). You are the Soul of all living beings. You are indivisible, without a beginning and end, and unlimited by time and place, the Omniscient Indwelling Soul and Controller.

31. You alone are the unwinking Time. You reduce the duration of the life of men by units of time called *lava*, *nimeṣa* and others. You are the immutable Soul, the occupant of the most exalted position, the birthless, all-pervading principle, the supporter and controller of all living beings.

32* Neither cause nor effect, or neither mobiles nor immobiles are apart from you. All the branches of knowledge (viz. Vedas and upa-Vedas) and arts (auxiliaries of Vedic studies e.g. phonetics, grammar, prosody etc.) it, this shining are your forms. You are the great Brahmā containing within egg of the universe. You are beyond (transcendental to) Prakṛti consisting of three *guṇas*.

33** Oh all-pervading Lord! This gross manifested universe is your body through which you enjoy the objects of

* VJ. points out that the attributes in this verse are applicable to the Supreme Lord and this verse is a eulogy of the Inner Controller (*antar-yāmin*).

"No mobiles and immobiles of the past, present and future can stand outside and unsupported by you. Both the *parā* and *aparā vidyās* abide in your body and are the means of knowing you. You are perfect and beyond the reach of the three stages, viz. wakefulness, sleep and dream.

** This verse sums up both the gross and subtle forms of Brahmā —VR.

VJ. The words *hiraṇya-garbha* etc. show that the universe is Hari's gross form, in which he enjoys supreme bliss and not misery, or pain like Devadatta (an ordinary man).

As usual VJ. gives two interpretations, one applicable to Hari and the other to Brahmā—

senses, life-breath (vital energy) and the mind, remaining all the while established in your original most exalted state. You are the unmanifest (subtle) *ātman* and the most ancient Supreme Person.

34. Salutation to the glorious Lord who has pervaded the whole of the universe by His infinite, unmanifest form and who is possessed of powers called *cit* or *vidyā* and *acit* or *māyā*.

35. Oh greatest among the bestowers of boons ! If you are to confer on me my desired boons, may my death not take place at the hands of any being created by You, Oh Lord.

36-37. Let me not meet death indoors or out of doors; during night or at day time, by the hand of any other (being created by you) or by means of weapons; let there be no death to me either on the earth or in the sky, either by men or beasts; by gods, demons and big serpents; by beings whether living or dead. Grant me matchlessness in fight and the sole absolute rulership of all embodied beings.

38. (Lastly) confer on me the great position and power you enjoy among all the guardians of the world. Kindly grant me the undiminishing glory and unfailing mystical powers enjoyed by those whose power lies in asceticism and Yoga."

CHAPTER FOUR

Oppression of Hiraṇyakaśipu and Description of Prahlāda's devotion

Nārada said :

1. Thus solicited, Brahmā who was extremely pleased with the austere penance of Hiraṇyakaśipu, granted on him the boons which are very rarely obtained by anyone.

(1) "Oh Hari, you are the most ancient person in Vaikuṇṭha. This gross manifested universe" etc.

(2) "Oh god Brahmā, you are the Soul (*purāṇa*—one bound to the body) the four-faced god who does "not incarnate (*avyakta*)", the rest as above.

Brahmā said :

2. "My dear child! These boons that you seek of me are very rarely to be obtained by men. I, however, confer them on you, even though they are very difficult to be secured."

3. Then the glorious almighty god of unfailing grace, who was worshipped by the king of Asuras, departed while being extolled by lords of creation (*Prajāpatis* like Marīci and others).

4. The demon who was thus blessed with the boons, assumed a resplendent golden body. Constantly remembering the killing of his brother (by Viṣṇu), he cherished hatred towards the glorious Lord.

5-7. The great Asura subjugated and brought under his control all directions, the three worlds, gods, Asuras, the kings of men, Gandharvas, Garuḍa-like birds, serpents, demi-gods (like Siddhas, Cāraṇas, Vidyādharas); (he subdued) sages, Lords of manes (*Pitṛs*), Manus, Yakṣas, *Rākṣasas*, chiefs of *Piśācas*, *Pretas* and *bhūtas* (goblins, evil spirits etc.); having vanquished and brought under his sway all the chiefs of living beings, the conqueror of the universe forcibly usurped the regions (and offices) of the protectors of the world, along with their glory.

8-11. He established himself in the celestial region which was beautified with the charming heavenly pleasure-garden (*Nandana*). He took up his residence in the palace of the great Indra, (which was) constructed by Viśvakarman, as the very centre of affluence, wealth and prosperity of the three worlds (*OR* the abode of the Lakṣmī of the three worlds). There, the flight of steps are built of coral, the pavement consists of precious emeralds, the walls of crystals and the rows of columns were of *lapis lazuli*. The canopies are of artistic workmanship; the seats were wrought with rubies; beddings white as the foam of milk, were fringed with wreaths of pearls; the heavenly damsels (of pearl-like teeth) filling the mansion here and there (everywhere), with the sweet jingling sound of their anklets (*nūpuras*), see the reflections of their faces on the floors of precious stones.

12. In that palace of Mahendra, the mighty, proud yet magnanimous Hiraṇyakaśipu, the vanquisher and the absolute ruler of the world, enjoyed himself. He ruled with a strong

iron hand, making the oppressed gods and others worship his feet respectfully.

13. With the exception of the three gods (Brahmā, Viṣṇu and Śiva) all the Lokapālas (guardians of the world like Indra), with tributes and presents in their hands, waited upon him (Hiraṇyakaśipu) who was (always) intoxicated with strong-flavoured wines and had his reddish eyes rolling due to inebriation, yet who was the receptacle of penance, *Yoga*, power and energy, Oh King.

14. Viśvāvasu, Tumburu, I and others (had to) give musical performance in the presence of him who had forcibly established himself on the throne of Mahendra. Gandharvas, Siddhas, sages, Vidyādharas, and celestial nymphs eulogised him, Oh descendant of Pāṇḍu.

15. By his majestic lustre, he alone appropriated the portions of oblations offered in sacrifices with generous sacrificial gifts, performed by persons of various *Varṇas* (classes of society) and *āśramas* (stages in life).

16. The earth with all the seven continents yielded harnest without ploughing (and other agricultural operations). The heaven offered him whatever he desired, and the sky presented him various wonderful objects.

17. Oceans (lit. mines of precious stones) full of salt water, wine, clarified butter, sugarcane juice, curds, milk and nectar-like (sweet) water, along with their wives (rivers falling in them) bore, on the crest of their waves, heaps of jewels.

18. Mountains along with their caverns afforded him pleasure-grounds. Trees bore fruits and flowers in all seasons. Singly he combined in himself all the different functions of Lokapālas (such as showering, burning, evaporating etc.).

19. He who became the sole, absolute ruler of the world after vanquishing all the directions, enjoyed as much as he liked, pleasures dear to him. But having no control over senses, he was not satiated thereby.

20. In this way, a long period (of more than seventy-one *Yugas*) passed. With the imprecation of a Brāhmaṇa (Sanaka) hanging over his head, he became inebriated with

power and pelf. In his arrogance, he violated the injunctions of the *śāstras*.

21. Being extremely afraid of his harsh punishments and stern rule, all the inhabitants of the world, along with their protective deities, sought shelter with the unfailing Lord Viṣṇu, as they got no protection anywhere else.

22. (They prayed) "Salutation to that direction where resides Hari, the Soul and sovereign ruler of the universe—the direction (region) after reaching which, pure and tranquil recluses do not return (to the mundane existence)."

23*. Having thus controlled their minds and meditating over the Lord with concentrated attention, they shed off their sins. Foregoing their sleep and subsisting on air only, they prayed Lord Viṣṇu.

23-A** (Additional verse in VJ.'s text).

24. A voice emanating from no visible form, deep like the rumbling of clouds and completely filling all the quarters of heaven with its reverberations, was heard by them, assuring protection to the righteous.

25. They heard: "Oh foremost among the gods ! Be not afraid. Good betide you all. A sight of myself (as well as the hearing of my voice) is the means to attain all blessings to all creatures.

26. The wickedness and oppression of this wretched Daitya is already known (to me). I shall mete out a suitable pacification (death) to him. Wait till that period.

27. When a person cherishes hatred to gods, the Vedas, cows, Brāhmaṇas, the righteous people, religion and Me, he verily perishes in no time.

* VJ. : In this way, feeling confident in mind that the Lord will protect them and with concentrated attention (thus controlling their external and internal senses) and subsisting on air (and controlling the vital breath—*prāṇa*) and foregoing sleep (thus controlling their bodies), they repeated the following *mantra*.

**A (1) Hail to the Supreme Person endowed with six excellences, who is the Inner Controller of all, Omniscient and extremely merciful, and who is absolute knowledge and bliss *incarnate*, a resort affording absolute protection.

28. When he (Hiraṇyakaśipu) will maliciously seek to injure his own son, the serene high-souled Prahlāda who cherishes no enmity against anyone, I shall slay him despite his power derived from Brahmā's boons."

Nārada said:

29. Thus assured (addressed) by the Father (and the protector) of the world, the inhabitants of heaven (gods) bowed down to hin. With all their anxieties allayed, they returned, deeming that the demon is (as good as) killed.

30. The king of Daityas had four extremely marvellous sons. Prahlāda who was the worshipper of the Exalted Being was preeminent amongst them by his virtues.

31. He was full of reverence to Brāhmaṇas and was possessed of noble character, true to his word, self-controlled, and like Paramātman, he was the best friend and well-wisher of all.

32. Like a servant, he bowed at the feet of noble Souls. Like a father he was kind to the poor and needy. With equals, he was affectionate like a brother. He looked upon his elders as his masters. Though he was highly endowed with learning, munificence, personal charms and high lineage, he was completely free from pride and arrogance.

33. In dangers and calamities, his mind (always) remained unruffled. He cherished no desire for enjoyments, heard (as obtainable in the next world) or seen (in this world), as he regarded them to be unreal. He had controlled his senses, vital airs (the life-breath), body and intellect. He completely controlled his desires and kept his mind calm and serene. Though he was a demon by birth, he was devoid of demonic characteristics.

34. Oh King ! The excellent qualities of the Lord or of his devotees are now and again extolled by the wise. Even now they are not obscured as is the case with the excellences of the Lord.

35. In assemblies, where the discourses on the appreciation of the righteous take place, gods, Prahlāda's sworn enemies, cite him as a model (of piety and righteousness). What to speak about the devotees of Viṣṇu like you ?

36. Prahlāda had a natural love and devotion to the glorious Lord Vāsudeva. Hence it is impossible to describe his innumerable qualities. The description of his nobleness of Soul (and greatness) is only suggestive (and not exhaustive).

37. Even as a child, he set aside his toys. His mind being completely absorbed in the Lord, he appeared as a dunce. As his Soul (mind) was possessed by Kṛṣṇa, as though like a spirit, its coveted treasure, he did not know the matter-of-fact world (as known to ordinary persons, but was full of his presence). (His Soul was completely absorbed in the contemplation of Kṛṣṇa who was his only object of attraction).

38. Being folded in the embrace of Viṣṇu (i.e. finding himself fully identified with the Lord), he was not conscious of his acts such as sitting, walking, eating, sleeping, drinking or speaking.

39. Sometimes his consciousness would get mixed with anxiety for the Lord, and being agitated, he cried. Sometimes he would laugh in the excitement of his meditation about him; sometimes he would sing loudly.

40. Sometimes he shouted at the top of his voice. Sometimes, banishing all the sense of bashfulness, he would dance about. Sometimes, being filled with thoughts about him and feeling absorbed in him completely, he would imitate him.

41. Sometimes, with his hair standing on end, he would sit silent as if (deeply) satisfied with the Divine touch. (as if the Lord manifested himself in his heart and touched him with his hand). Sometimes, his eyes were half-closed and steady, with tears of joy and love flowing out.

42. By the service of the lotus-like feet of Lord of hallowing glory (Viṣṇu) which he acquired while in association with the Lord's devotees who claim nothing as their own, he attained supreme happiness not only to himselt but often imparted that felicity to the minds of others which were polluted and miserable by bad company.

43. To his son, who was such a great devotee of the Lord, magnanimous and a highly noble Soul, that Hiraṇyakaśipu tried to do harm, Oh king.

Yudhiṣṭhira said:

44. Oh divine sage of excellent vows ! We desire to know from you why the father meted out ill-treatment to his son who was so pure, innocent and righteous.

45. Fathers affectionate to their sons do remonstrate their disobedient sons for the sake of imparting education but never harm any like an enemy.

46. How much less would they do so in the case of such sons who are so obedient, righteous and regard the father as a deity.

Oh Brāhmaṇa sage, be pleased to satisfy our curiosity as to how the hatred of the father towards his son culminated in the father's attempt on the life of his son (or became the cause of the father's death), My Lord.

CHAPTER FIVE

The Life of Prahlāda

Hiraṇyakaśipu attempts to kill Prahlāda

Nārada said :

1. As is reported, the glorious Kāvya (Śukra) was selected by demons to fill the office of the royal priest. His two sons, Śaṇḍa and Amarka, stayed near the palace of the king of Daityas.

2. They taught the course of studies (in politics and such other sciences) to Prahlāda and other eligible Asura students sent to them by the king, even though Prahlāda was expert in philosophy.

3. Whatever was taught there by the teacher, he (carefully) listened and reproduced it. But he did not approve of the teaching that was on the false notion of distinguishing between (man and man) as friends and enemies.

4. Oh Pāṇḍava, once upon a time, the king of Asuras seated the child on his lap and asked him, "What do you regard as good, my child ?"

Prahlāda replied :

5. Oh Prominent Asura ! To embodied beings who are always mentally harassed with the false notion of 'I' and 'Mine', I regard that it is in their interest that they should abandon the hidden-well-like household which is degrading to the Soul and should enter into the woods and seek shelter with Hari.

Nārada said :

6. Having heard the words of his son which were in favour of the hostile party, he laughed (derisively) and exclaimed : "How the understanding of children gets perverted through contact with others (inimical element) !"

7. Let the child be so carefully guarded in his preceptor's house, that this intellect should not be vitiated by Brāhmaṇas who are the partisans of Viṣṇu *in cognito*.

8. When brought home (from the palace of Hiraṇya-kaśipu), the royal priests of Daityas sent for him. Praising him in soft words, they enquired of him in coaxing terms and in a conciliatory tone.

9. "Oh child Prahlāda ! May you be happy ! Please tell (us) the truth; do not tell a lie. What caused this perversion of intellect which is beyond (i.e. not found in) boys of your age ?

10. Is this change (distraction) in your mind brought out by others ? Or has it taken place automatically due to your innate nature ?

Prahlāda said :

11. Obeisance to the glorious Lord whose deluding power (Māyā) has created the wrong concept that 'this is mine' and 'this is another's', found in men whose intellect is deluded by Māyā.[1]

12. When He is favourable, the beast-like understanding apprehending differentiation that "This is different (from me) and I am different (from him)", comes to an end.

1. VJ. attributes this delusion to the Lord. "vimohitetyanenā pīśvara-kartṛtvaṁ jñāyate /"

13. It is the Supreme Soul which is looked upon as one's own Self and another, by stupid people to whom His ways are inscrutable and indescribable. (It is however no wonder.) Even god Brahmā and other exponents of the Veda, are stupefied when they enquire about his nature. It is that Soul who has changed my mind (and outlook).

14. Oh Brahman ! Just as a piece of iron within the vicinity of a magnet is automatically attracted towards it, my mind, of its own accord (without any ostensible reason), is gravitated to Lord Viṣṇu.

Nārada said :

15. Having spoken (explained) as above, the highly intelligent Prahlāda stopped (speaking). Reproaching him threateningly, the wretched royal servant got enraged (and ordered):

16. "Who is there ? Bring me a cane. This boy brings disreputation to us. The fourth expedient (corporal punishment) has been prescribed in the Śāstras, in case of such a wickedminded fellow who ruins his family.

17. This boy is like a thorny tree grown in the forest of sandal trees in the form of Daityas. He serves as a handle to Viṣṇu who is (like) an axe cutting the roots of that forest."

18. Intimidating him with various expedients like threats (corporal punishment and others), they made Prahlāda to learn (the text dealing with) the first three objects of human life (viz. *dharma*, *artha* and *kāma*).

19. Later on, the teacher was convinced that Prahlāda had mastered (known) the four branches in political strategy (viz. *sāma*, *dāna*, *daṇḍa* and *bheda*). After Prahlāda's mother bathed, dressed and adorned him, he was brought to the presence of the king of Daityas.

20. The Asura (Hiraṇyakaśipu) greeted with blessings his child who lay prostrate at his feet. For a long time he hugged him in his arms and felt deep satisfaction and happiness.

21. Placing him on the lap and smelling the crown of his head, he bathed him with tears. Oh Yudhiṣṭhira, then he spoke to the child of cheerful countenance.

Hiraṇyakaśipu said:

22. "My dear child Prahlāda ! Please recite some excellent passages that you have learnt well from what your teacher has taught you up to this time, Oh long-lived one !"

Prahlāda said:

23-24. "There are nine forms of devotion to Lord Viṣṇu—(1) to hear the names, episodes etc. of Viṣṇu, (2) to sing of his name and glories, (3) to Remember him (his name), (4) to render service unto him, (5) to worship him, (6) to pay obeisance to him, (7) to dedicate all one's actions to him, (8) to confide to him as a friend, (9) to offer one's body and belongings to his service and care. I regard it as the highest type of learning, if one offers himself completely to the Lord and performs this nine-fold devotion[1] (regards complete dedication as the condition precedent of real devotion)."

25. Hearing these words of his son, Hiraṇyakaśipu, with his lips quivering with rage, reproached Śukra's son (the preceptor's son) as follows :

26. "You wretch of a Brāhmaṇa ! What does this mean ? Wicked fellow ! You sided with the enemies and disregarding me completely, you have taught some non-sense to the child.

27. There are wicked persons in this world who assume a friend's garb, but their friendship is treacherous. Their sin (sinfulness) becomes manifest in due time, like the grave diseases of sinners."[2]

Preceptor's (Śukra's) son said :

28. What this son of yours speaks is not taught by me or by any person. Oh foe of Indra ! It is his innate intelligence ! Oh king ! Please control your anger. Do not lay the blame on us.

1. JG. has given a long but excellent exposition of Bhakti and its nine forms which deserve perusal in the original.

2. ŚR. quotes a *smṛti* text according to which certain types of sinners, e.g., murderer of a Brāhmaṇa, a habitual drunkard, a debaucherous person violating his teacher's bed have to suffer from heinous diseases even after completing their term in hell. The question is repeated by VC., VD., GD. and others.

Nārada said :

29. When he was thus replied by (Prahlāda's) preceptor, the Asura (Hiraṇyakaśipu) again asked his son : "If this perverted understanding has not been caused by the teaching of your preceptor, whence has it come, you inauspicious boy ?"

Prahlāda said :

30. (Unswerving attachment and) firm fixation of the mind on Kṛṣṇa does not arise through (the advice of) another, or of one's own accord, or by mutual efforts in the case of those who are firmly devoted to their household (as if it were a sacred vow). Nor (is it engendered) in persons who have not controlled their senses, and who now and again enter the darkness of Saṁsāra, and who again and again ruminate (repeatedly experience) what they have enjoyed (in former births).

31. They whose heart is polluted (by their attachment to worldly objects) do not know Viṣṇu, to be their (real) objective in life and goal. For they look up for guidance to those who regard the external objects as their aim in life, and are like the blind persons led by the blind. They are tied down (like beasts) with Lord Viṣṇu's long rope in the form of Vedic injunctions prescribing rites to be performed for future good. (These persons are like persons who go to the east in search of an object lost in the west).

32. So long as persons do not seek bath in the dust on the feet of those noble Souls (the devotees of Viṣṇu) who have shed off attachment to worldly objects, the mind of such persons cannot touch (reach) the feet of Lord Viṣṇu (the Lord of long strides as Trivikrama or the Lord of infinite prowess), the object of which is the cessation of *Saṁsāra* (the cycle of births and deaths and the miseries involved)."[1]

33. Hardly did the son (Prahlāda) stop speaking, when

1. ŚR. states : Unless one secures the grace of such exalted Souls, the exact implication of Vedānta and the consequent liberation is impossible.

GS. also agrees with this view.

GD. and BP. state that hereby Prahlāda suggests that it was through Nārada's grace that he got this spiritual revelation.

Hiraṇyakaśipu with his mind blinded with rage, hurled him from his lap, down to the ground.

34. Overwhelmed with unbeareble (violent) wrath, and with eyes reddened with anger, he ordered, "This boy deserves capital punishment. Let him be executed immediately. Oh Nairṛtas, take him away from my presence.

35. This (boy) is verily the murderer of my brother. For this wretched fellow, deserting his own well-wishers, worships like a slave the feet of Viṣṇu, the assassinator of his paternal uncle.

36. Or even to Viṣṇu what good purpose can he serve, I doubt; for even as a child of five, he forfeited his parental affection which is so hard to sever.

37. If beneficial, even a stranger should be treated as a child, like medicine (though the medicinal herbs grow into the forest—outside and away from one's home—they are preserved at home). If a son begotten by one's own self becomes inimical (works against one's interest) he should be treated like a disease. One should amputate that part of the body which is injurious to the body as a whole, if by removing it, the rest (of the body) can live in happiness.

38. Like an uncontrolled sense-organ, in the case of a sage, he is a veritable enemy masquerading as a friend (son). He should be disposed of by all expedients, e.g. administering poison in food, killing him while sitting unguarded or while asleep."

39-40 Commanded thus by their master, the demons with sharp teeth, terrific faces and reddish hair and beard, armed themselves with tridents, and giving out terrible yells and shouting "Cut him, kill him", pierced Prahlāda in all the vital parts with their tridents while he was sitting quietly.

41. All their attempts on (the life of) Prahlāda proved fruitless and ineffectual, like the pious acts of a person with no past meritorious deeds to his credit; for Prahlāda's mind was in communion with the glorious Lord who is the Soul of all beings, the incomprehensible Supreme Brahman.

42. When that attempt was thwarted, the king of demons grew alarmed and he persistently devised other expedients to kill Prahlāda, Oh Yudhiṣṭhira.

43-44. When the Asura could not kill his innocent son by employing elephants guarding the quarters, great serpents, by use of black magic, by hurling him down from mountain peaks, by using illusive powers (*māyā*), by confining him in dark holes (silos), administering him poison, by starvation, by exposing him to snow, winds, by throwing him in fire and by throwing mountains on him, he was plunged in the deepest anxiety and could not think of any other (effective) measure to kill him.

45. (Hiraṇyakaśipu thought to himself). "This boy has been severely reproached by me now and again. Measures to kill him were also adopted. But by dint of his own power and energy, he has survived unaffected by those tortures and black spells.

46. He is not away from my presence. Though he is still a boy, his mind is not daunted (through my fear). He is so powerful that he will not forget (and forgive) my unrighteousness (and maltreatment) like Śunaḥśepa.[1]

47. He is of immeasurable prowess; he entertains fear from nobody as if he is immortal. It is certain that my death will take place by confronting him or possibly it may not (overtake at all)."

48. In this anxious mood, he was sitting with his countenance pale and downcast, when Śaṇḍa and Amarka, the two sons of Śukra spoke to him in private, as follows:

49. "You have single-handedly conquered the three worlds by terrifying all the Lokapālas (guardian deities of the world) by merely contracting your eye-brows. For such a (powerful) Lord as you are, we see no reason for anxiety. The behaviour of children should not be seriously judged as good or bad.

50. Keep him bound down by the noose of Varuṇa so that he should not run away out of fear, till your teacher Śukra returns. A man's understanding may improve with advancement of age and service of the noble ones."

1. This refers to the legend of Śunaḥśepa in the *Aitareya Brāhmaṇa*. Śunaḥśepa disowned his father Ajīgarta for selling him for sacrifice to Hariścandra and adopted another—Viśvāmitra—*gotra*.—ŚR.

51. Expressing his assent to the proposals of the preceptor's sons, he ordered, "The duties prescribed for royal householders be taught to him."

52. Oh King ! Then they taught in serial order the details only of *Dharma*, *Artha*, *Kāma*, to Prahlāda who was both modest and obedient.

53. (Though taught systematically), Prahlāda did not approve of the teaching of only the first three objects of human life (as mentioned above), as this instruction was meant for those who were interested in pairs like attachment and hatred, and in the enjoyment of objects of senses.

54. When the teacher was not present (at his class) due to some household duties, he was invited by the school-companions of his age who found opportunity for play (and merry-making).

55. Responding to their call in sweet words, the wise Prahlāda, knowing their attachment to him, spoke to them with a smile, out of grace.

56-57. Out of great regard for him, all the boys whose minds were not vitiated by the advice or actions of persons (teachers) who were given to worldly enjoyments and were subject to love, hate etc., set aside all their play-things. With their eyes and hearts fixed on him, they sat round him. The Asura (Prahlāda) who was a great devotee of Viṣṇu and full of compassion and friendship, addressed them.

CHAPTER SIX

*(Prahlāda's Teaching)**

Prahlāda said:

1. In this world, a wise person should (begin to) practise the righteous duties leading to god-realization, since his

* The text of VJ. gives the following additional five verses :
Prahlāda said :
(1) Alas ! You children ! Please listen to my words of advice which will lead to your happiness in every way. Consider (see and

very childhood; for birth in the human species is not easily attained. Even though it (human life) is transient, it alone can help us to achieve the desired object (viz. Liberation).

2. It is, therefore, advisable that a person should approach the feet of Viṣṇu in this very birth as he is the (real) Ruler, Well-wisher and the very beloved Soul of all beings. (Hence one should adopt the course leading to the attainment of his feet.)

3. Oh descendants of Diti ! Being (closely) related to the body, pleasure, like pain, derived from objects of senses, comes to the lot of embodied beings in all species of life (including sub-human beings) through divine dispensation, without any special effort for it.

4. No endeavours, therefore, should be made to seek sensual pleasures, for, that leads to sheer waste of life. Moreover, by such efforts, the *summum bonum*, viz. attainment of the lotus-like feet of Viṣṇu, is not secured. OR Just as one can attain the Supreme Bliss by resorting to the lotus-like feet of

think) of your friends who are no more. Do not get blind by playfulness and follow a wrong path.

(2) Boys of yore did not lose their minds completely in sports. From the time of their birth (or since their childhood), they were desirous of seeking knowledge about the Supreme Soul and final liberation (*mokṣa*). Whatever has been taught to us by teachers (Śaṇḍa and Amarka, regarding the first three goals of life viz. *dharma*, *artha* and *kāma*) is not acceptable, inasmuch as it represents wrong objectives (which involves us in *saṁsāra*) as the desirable aims in life.

(3) If a person who is engrossed in the sleep of ignorance is not wakened up to reality by the precept of a teacher, that precept or doctrine should not be believed, as such a teacher is like a blind person leading other blind persons.

(4) Who is an enemy or an indifferent person or a friend in the case of *Ātman* or my case ? (None). The same is the case with you. What is the propriety of studying politics ? Prosperity and adversity are caused by the Supreme Divine Agency.

(5) Such a person is very rare to be found as does not violate the righteous course leading to the accomplishment of the desire to realize the Supreme Soul—a person who is not under the control of his senses (which are born with him) or his own people (e.g. sons, relatives, friends) and who has transcended his natural (spiritual) blindness and who by following the *Nivṛttidharma* (path of renunciation), becomes proper (eligible) for this as well as the next world.

Mukunda (Viṣṇu) one cannot obtain this Bliss through such efforts for sensual pleasure).

5. Therefore, having fallen into this fear (-ful *saṁsāra*), a clever person should endeavour to attain that blessed state (of security, viz. *mokṣa*) immediately while one's body is in sound condition and is not yet incapacitated.

6. The span of human life is (limited to) one hundred years only. Half of that life (viz. fifty years) is wasted away in the case of a man who has not subdued himself (his senses and mind); for consigned to (and absorbed in) the blinding darkness of ignorance, he lies asleep at night.

7. (Out of the balance of fifty years) twenty years are lost while he is ignorant in childhood and is absorbed in play in boyhood; and twenty (more) years are wasted when his body is overwhelmed with senility and is rendered unfit.

8. Maddened and (deeply) attached to household life due to the forcible pull of desires (of sensual pleasures) which are difficult to be fulfilled, and under the powerful delusion (of one's ego and belongings expressed by 'I' and 'Mine'), he misspends the remaining portion of his life.*

9. What person who has not conquered his senses can have the power to liberate his own self; who is attached to his house-hold (including wife, children and property) and is tightly bound down with unbreakable ties of love and affection (to them).

10. Who indeed would forego his thirst (passion) for wealth which is dearer than life itself—wealth which thieves (in the house broken by them), servants (while on duty) and merchants (while accompanying their merchandise or cargo) barter in exchange of their life.

11. How can a man renounce his beloved sympathetic wife while remembering his dalliance with her in privacy and her sweet consultation and counsel? (How can one do so)

* 8-A Additicnal verse in VJ.'s text :

See (take into account) also the conflicts of opinions or quarrels of our householders even though related (to each other)—householders who desire to follow the course of *saṁsāra* with efforts which are detrimental to the attainment of final beatitude (and not a single moment is left for spiritual progress—VJ.).

with his friends while being tied down with bonds of friendship and with his sweet-lisping children to whom his heart is deeply attached ?

12. Remembering his sons and his beloved daughters (who are staying away in the houses of their fathers-in-law), his brothers, sisters and poor helpless parents, his houses furnished with beautiful abundant furniture, hereditary professions or vocations and his cattle (horses, elephants etc.) and retinue of servants, how can one go away from them ?

13. Like a silk-worm (which gets imprisoned by enveloping itself in a sheath without any outlet), he, due to his unsated desires and through boundless infatuation, goes on performing actions out of cupidity (in the hope of accomplishing them), holding pleasures relating to sex and palate in high estimation.—How can he become disgusted with the world (and renounce all worldly attachment) ?

14. The careless fellow, deeply attached to his family, does not realize that his turn of existence in this world is being wasted away, and that the purpose of his life (viz. attainment of the highest bliss by devotion to God) is being thwarted in his efforts to maintain his family. Though he is afflicted by three types of misery everywhere, he is not disgusted with the world (worldly objects) as he feels that his family is the (source of) delight to him.

15. With his heart always ever set on amassing wealth and knowing full well the punishment meted out here and the consequences of the sin hereafter, the householder of unsubdued senses and with desires unsated, misappropriates another's wealth.

16. Even a person noted for his erudition in scriptures, who is bent on maintaining his family in the manner described above, is not verily capable of realizing his own Self (*OR* of realizing himself as to who he is and what he is committing etc.). (Then what of you ?) Oh descendants of Danu ! He (even if he be well-versed in *Śāstras*) whose mind is corrupted with the notion of difference between one's own and another's ("mine and yours") enters the dark hell even as an ignorant person.

17. For the poor fellow whoever he be, who has become

a tool of amusement like a toy deer (or a monkey) for (the entertainment of) lascivious women, and who has forged fetters for himself, in the form of progeny, will not be able to liberate himself at any time.

18. Therefore, Oh descendants of Diti, avoiding from a distance the association with Daityas whose minds are absorbed in (enjoyment of) objects of senses, approach for refuge the most ancient God Nārāyaṇa who is the veritable Supreme bliss (liberation) coveted by recluses who have renounced all association with the world.

19. Being the very Soul of all (mobile and immobile) creatures, and being omnipresent and all-pervading, there is not much trouble and exertion in propitiating the unfailing Lord Viṣṇu, Oh sons of Asuras!

20-21. It is none else than the only one Supreme Soul (Brahman) that the Almighty, immutable Ruler who exists in and pervades the higher and the lower order of beings commencing from the immovables (e.g. vegetations etc.) and culminating in god Brahmā, in all the transformations of elements (the inanimate world of matter or ***bhūtas***) in ***bhūtas*** (gross elements e.g. the sky, the wind), in *guṇas* (like sattva) in Pradhāna (the stage in which all *guṇas* are in a state of equilibrium)[1] and in Principles like *Mahat*[2] (which are evolved due to the uneven mixture of guṇas).

22 He, as the Inner Controller (of every being) is the seer, the enjoyer and as such is indicated as 'the pervader'. He is also the object of perception, the objective world enjoyed and is described as 'the pervaded'. He is, however, beyond description, and undifferentiated (though he is spoken of as being different).

23* The Supreme Lord is essentially pure consciousness and absolute bliss. But he conceals his glorious Lordly nature

1. *guṇa-sāmya*—(i) The primordial matter, Pradhāna—ŚR., SD., GD., BP. etc.
(ii) At the time of the Pralaya—VJ.

2. *guṇa-vyatikara*—(i) The evolute *Mahat*—ŚR., SD., GD., BP. etc.
(ii) At the time of the creation of the world—VJ.

VR. puts forward the Viśiṣṭādvaita theory re: God and the world as follows:

The Lord has *Jīva* as his special body and the perceptible inanimate or unconscious world as the gross body. Being incomparable, he is One by his Māyā Power which gives rise to *guṇas*—the creation of the world.

24. Therefore, eschewing out your demonic nature, show kindness and friendliness to all beings, whereby Lord Viṣṇu (God transcendental to sense perception) will be pleased.

25. When the Lord of infinite excellences, the Prime Cause of all, is pleased, what can there be unattainable (to his devotees)? What is the use to us of the objects of human life: Dharma (*artha* and *kāma*) which accrue of their own accord by the product of *guṇas* (designated as Providence, the result of one's past deeds)? Of what attraction is the *Mokṣa* (Final Liberation) which is so covetable to all,—to us who sing of the glory of his feet and taste the nectar-like sweetness thereform?

26. The triad of the highest purposes of human life, viz. *dharma* (religious merits), *artha* (attainment of wealth) and *kāma* (fulfilment of desires), the spiritual lore, the ritualistic lore, logic, politics and various means of livelihood—I regard all these, the subject matter of the Vedas, as true—only if it serves as the means of offering one's self to the Supreme Person who is the true friend of all. (Otherwise they are meaningless).

27. It is traditionally reported that Lord Nārāyaṇa, the companion of (the sage) Nara, imparted to Nārada this pure and sanctifying knowledge which is so difficult to obtain. It will, however, be attainable to those who have bathed their bodies in the dust of the lotus-like feet of the absolutely devoted votaries of the Lord—votaries who are devoid of all desires except God-realization.

Supreme Being who enters the body to support it but is unaffected by the modifications of the body and hence immutable. The Lord is perfect in his six excellences and he controls the *jīva* according to his *karma*.

VJ. He is within everything an *antaryāmin*, Inner controller. He pervades them from outside, in the form of Time. Under another designation Brahman, he is the one who is indicated both as pervader and the pervaded. He cannot be defined like a material object like a pitcher. Though Omnipresent he is invisible as he is concealed by Māyā or Prakṛti who is the source of Sattva and other attributes so essential for creation.

28. It is from the (sage) Nārada who has realized God that I heard (learnt) formerly this knowledge with the immediate apprehension of truth as well as teaching in the pure course of righteous duties and devotion to the Lord.

Sons of Daityas said :

29. Oh Prahlāda ! You and we do not know any other person except the sons of preceptor (Śukrācārya,) as our teachers, as they have been our masters since our childhood.[1]

30. Association with the great (sages) is extremely difficult for a child who is (brought up) in the harem. Please remove our doubt by confiding us with some evidence to give credence to your version, Oh gentle one.

CHAPTER SEVEN

Prahlāda, enlightened while in mother's womb

Nārada continued :

1. When he was thus questioned by the sons of Daityas, the great Asura devotee of the Lord smiled and remembering my teaching, replied to them as follows :

Prahlāda narrated :

2. When our father (Hiraṇyakaśipu) repaired to Mount Mandara to practise religious austerities, the gods made great preparations to wage war against the Dānavas.

3. Indra and other gods began to say thus : "It is really fortunate that the sinful Hiraṇyakaśipu, the scourge of the world, has been eaten up by his own sins, as a serpent is nibbled away by ants."

4. Having heard of the tremendous military preparations of the gods, leaders of Asura forces capitulated when attacked, and fled in terror to all directions.

1. We who are engaged in our studies are not seeking God—VJ.

5. All of them were so anxious and in haste to save their lives that they paid no heed to their wives, sons, friends, relatives, house, cattles and other belongings.

6. Desirous of total victory, the gods ransacked and devastated the king's palace, while Indra seized the chief Queen, my mother.

7. Fortunately, by a happy chance, the divine sage Nārada arrived there and saw her being carried away on the road while she was trembling (with fear) and crying like a female osprey.

8. Peremptorily he intervened, "Oh Lord of gods ! You should not carry away this innocent woman. Leave her, Oh blessed one, Let go this chaste lady who is the wife of another person."

Indra replied :

9. "There lies in her womb an unbearable force—the seed of the enemy of gods (Hiraṇyakaśipu). Let her stay in my custody till her delivery. I shall accomplish my purpose (by killing the new-born child) and then let her go."

Nārada said :

10. "This (child in the womb) is sinless and an eminent devotee of the Lord. This follower of Ananta is essentially so powerful by his excellences, that he will not meet death at your hands."

11. When addressed thus, Indra respected the words of the divine sage (Nārada) and set her at liberty. He circumambulated her out of devotion to the beloved votaries of the infinite Lord and returned to heaven.

12. Thereupon the sage brought our mother to his hermitage. He consoled her and said, "Oh my daughter, stay here till the return of your husband."

13. Agreeing to that proposal, she, being free from fear (from all quarters) dwelt in the hermitage (lit. presence) of Nārada while the king of Daityas did not return from his terrible austere penance.

14. That pious pregnant lady waited upon the sage with utmost devotion for the well-being of the foetus in the womb and the boon of delivery at any time desired by her.

15. Possessed of that Spiritual Power, the kind-hearted sage granted her both (the boons), and for assuaging her grief and with a view to communicating it to me, he imparted her instruction in the essence of righteousness (viz. devotion unto the Lord) and pure knowledge (regarding the nature of the Soul and the non-Soul).

16. (The memory of) that teaching however faded away in the case of my mother due to the lapse of a long time (that intervened), and also due to her being (after all) a woman. But being specially favoured by the sage, it (the recollection of the precepts) has not left me even up to this moment.

17. If you have faith in my words, even your intellect and understanding will be capable of destroying the (false ego of) identification of the Self with the body etc.[1] Just as that sense has been generated in me through faith, it will appear in the case of women and children as well.

18. Just as, through the agency of (eternal) Time which is capable of bringing about modifications, the six transformations, (viz. birth, existence, growth, ripeness, decay and destruction) are found in the case of fruits of a tree (while they are on the tree which lasts much longer), six modifications beginning with birth are observed in relation to the body (so long as it is associated with the Soul) but not to the Soul (which is eternal and unchangeable).

19. The Soul[2] is eternal (not subject to creation and destruction), undeteriorating (free from decay), pure (untouched by love, hate etc.), one (without second), the seer

1. *vaiśāradī dhī*—(1) More keen intelligence in grasping the reality—VR.

(2) Knowledge about God—VJ.

(3) Intelligence directed to God—VC, SD, GD.

2. *ātmā*—VR. takes this as *jīva* (individual soul) while VJ. understands *Paramātman* (Supreme Soul) by this term and interprets:

VR: This verse describes the essential nature of *Jīvātman* in the liberated stage. As distinguished from the body the *Jīva* is eternal, subject to no deterioration or modifications, untainted by the *guṇas* of *Prakṛti*, one as it is of the nature of consciousness running through all bodies, knowing its own body, self-conscious, the support of the body, senses etc., the cause of the movement of bodies (the motive force behind them), all-

(the intelligent subject), the support (of the universe), the immutable, self-effulgent, the primary cause (of the world), the all-pervading, untouched (by anything) and perfect (or uncovered by Māyā).

20. With the help of the twelve supreme characteristics mentioned above, the learned person should renounce the wrong notions of 'I and Mine' with reference to one's body and belongings, as the notion arises out of delusion (and ignorance).

pervading through his power of knowledge, unassociated with another *jīva*, and uncovered (with nothing to hide his real nature).

VJ. takes together vv. 19 and 20 and interprets:

(19) Paramātman is eternal by his very nature, suffering from no loss of any member of the body, pure as he is free from the influence of *avidyā*, attachment etc., the Supreme-most and hence the One, knower of the nature of the body, the support of everything else, subject to no modification or change either due to his innate nature or through the influence of others, Self-seeing (Self-conscious of his Brahmahood), absolutely independent, all-pervading, unattached as he is above *Prakṛti*, not affected (by external forces, not subject to ignorance or other obscuring factors (19).

(20) He who realizes the *ātman* (the Supreme Soul) by these twelve distinguishing characteristics would (automatically) give up the false notions of 'I' and 'Mine' with respect to one's body (and property etc.) caused by delusion and ignorance.

VC. states: For, the purification of oneself is caused by the form of devotion called meditation (*cintana*). The Supreme Soul that is to be meditated is described as follows. VC. here quotes ŚR. verbatim.

SD. explains a few adjectives differently! *Kṣetrajña*—Knowing all (*vyaṣṭi-samaṣṭi*) bodies aggregatively and dis-aggregatively. *āśraya*—the material and instrumental cause for the creation, sustenance etc. of all mobile and immobiles. *Avikriya*—essentially unchangeable but by his eternal powers of mobility and immobility brings about the creation and destruction like the spreading out and withdrawing of the limbs of the tortoise.

SD. contradicts VR. by asserting that this verse does not refer to *jīva* (*jīva-paro nāyam ślokaḥ*).

GD. explains that though the characteristics of *jīva* and *Paramātman* are different, *jīvātman* is a part (*aṁśa*) of *Paramātman* and as such there is non-difference between them. This non-difference between the two is implied in this verse. The explanation of the epithets is the same as that of ŚR.

21* Just as a metallurgist specialised in gold extraction out of ore, is able to obtain gold from gold-bearing rocks found in gold-fields, by using the requisite processes (of smelting etc,), similarly a person expert in the spiritual lore (including the causal relations, will be able to attain to Brahmahood in the fields in the form of the bodies (of different *jīvas*), through the different processes of realizing the Soul (*ātman*).

22. (After analysis of the whole creation and reducing it to fundamental Principles), Teachers of yore (like Kapila and others) have stated that there are eight Prakṛtis (viz. the Primordial matter or *mūla Prakṛti*, *Mahat* (Principle of cosmic Intelligence) *ahaṁkāra* (ego, I-ness) and five subtle elements, three (viz. *sattva*, *rajas* and *tamas*) as their *guṇas* (modes of *Prakṛti*), and sixteen modifications (viz. five gross elements, ten conative and cognitive senses and mind) but the Person or Soul is one, co-ordinating them all.

23. The body is the combination of these all. It is twofold—mobile and immobile. It is here (in the body) that the Soul is to be sought and discriminated, by a process of elimination (viz. This is not the Soul; it is not it).

24. By means of abstract deliberation of the positive and negative concomitance (the omnipresence of the Spirit yet its distinctness from others), by his power of discrimination, and with purified mind and patient reflection over the phenomena of creation, sustenance and the destruction of the universe, that the Soul is to be realized.

25.** The states of wakefulness, dream and deep sleep

* (1) VR: The person who realizes the true nature of the Soul as distinguished from the body, not only attains the knowledge of the Suprememost Person, but realizes the true essential nature.

(2) *adhyātma-vid*—One who is well versed in Vedānta-śāstra with reference to the Soul; realizes in practice the *Sāttvic* virtues; expert in the knowledge about elements.

SD: This verse deals with the knowledge of three Principles viz. non-sentient (universe), the sentient (the Soul) and God who, being different from these, controls them.

SD: It is the God or Brahman who is within all, is to be propitiated by all, through all forms of devotion.

** VJ. takes *buddhi* as *jīva* and interprets: "Guided and prompted by the Supreme Lord, the *jīva* experiences the states of wakefulness etc. The presiding Lord who assumes different forms, e. g. *Viśva*, *Taijasa* and *Prājña* is different from *jīva*."

are the functions of the intellect (*buddhi*). He who is cognisant of (lit. experiences) these (three states) is the transcendent person (who is distinct from the body, senses, the mind etc.), the witness (of these all).

26.* Just as one perceives (the presence of) the wind by means of the different fragrant particles with which it is laden, due to the association of those particles with it (in spite of its distinctness from those particles), one should realize the essential nature of the Soul (*ātman*) by the transformations of the intellect which are associated with it, but are repudiated as not being the attributes of the Soul but of the intellect, and are permeated with three *guṇas*, and born of actions or *karmas* (even though due to his association with intellect—*buddhi*—the Soul appears to be characterised by the modification of the *buddhi*.)

27. The *saṁsāra* comes into being through the 'gates' of the intellect (*buddhi*) as it is perpetuated (lit. is fast bound) by the modifications and activities of *buddhi*. It is rooted in ignorance, and as such is unreal. It, however, is regarded as the dream (state) of man.**

28*** Hence you should at the outset, burn down the seed (viz. *avidyā* of the *karmas* which are motivated by the three

* As in v. 25 VJ., interprets *buddhi* as *jīva* and tries to substantiate the *Dvaita* thesis that the *jīva* is different from *Paramātman*. To summarize his gloss: The *jīva* (individual Soul) is different from the Lord who possesses three forms viz., *Viśva*, *Taijasa* and *Prājña*. He directs the three states (e.g. wakefulness, dream and deep sleep). The three states and their *guṇas* characterised by the colours white, black and yellow distinguish the grades of *jīvas*. To the ignorant, the Lord seems like a *jīva*. But the intelligent people (*prājñajanāḥ*) perceive him to bethe same consciousness and the bliss incarnate.

** The text of VJ. gives the following additional verse:

As all the actions are created by the mind and are of momentary nature, they resemble the things in dream and wakeful states. They cause grief, delusion and fear to the person experiencing them (which would not have happened had they been unreal).

*** According to VR. the seed of *karmas* is 'the mistake of the body for the Soul'. The way to burn down this seed is to put an end to the stream of *buddhi*.

guṇas. This causes the cessation of the functioning (lit. current) of *buddhi*. (This is) *Yoga*—the way of merger with the Lord.

29. Out of the thousands of expedients (for annihilating the seed of *karmas*), the one specifically inculcated by the venerable sage Nārada is the proper performance of the acts which will automatically generate deep love and devotion directly unto the Supreme Lord.

30-31. (This is achieved) by rendering devout service to the preceptor (or by a sincere desire to listen devoutly to the teaching of the preceptor), by offering all one's earnings to him, by associating one's Self with pious devotees of the Lord, and by propitiating the Lord, by reverential liking for listening to the stories of the Lord, by extolling his excellent attributes and glorious deeds, by meditating on his lotus-like feet and by seeing and worshipping his images.

32. With an implicit belief in the presence of the venerable Supreme Lord Hari in all created beings, one should treat them with due respect at heart, and (as far as possible) offer them their desired objects.

33. In this way devotion unto the Supreme Lord Vāsudeva is practised by persons who have conquered the group of six passions (viz. lust, anger, greed, delusion, pride, jealousy) or of six senses (external five cognitive senses and mind—the internal one). It is by (such) devotion that one develops (devotional love) unto the Lord.

34. When he hears (lit. having heard) the accounts of his great deeds, uncomparable attributes (e.g. love towards devotees) and his heroic exploits (e. g. killing of Rāvaṇa) unachievable by others but carried out by him through his incarnations (like Rāma, Kṛṣṇa) assumed by him in sport, he (the devotee) with his hair standing on end through rapturous delight, and in a voice choked with tears, sings loudly with an open throat, shouts and dances.

35. When like a person possessed by an evil spirit, he sometimes bursts out into laughter here and screams out there;

VJ: Saṁsāra is due to wrong identification of the *jīva* with the body or the Lord. To burn down the seed of *Saṁsāra* the stream of *buddhi* should be directed to find delight into Lord Nārāyaṇa.

now he meditates, now he bows down to the people. Frequently he breathes heavily and with his mind absorbed in *ātman*, losing his sense of bashfulness, he utters loudly, "Oh Hari ! Lord of the Universe ! Oh Nārāyaṇa".

36. (It is) then that a man is setfree from all bondages. His mind and body is attuned to the Lord through contemplation over his pastimes and sportive actions. The seed of ignorance and the consequent (latent) desires being burnt down, by the great device ofdevotion, he attains to Lord Nārāyaṇa (from Whom there is no return to *saṁsāra*.)

37. In the case of embodied beings whose hearts are polluted (with worldly attachment, love etc.), mental communion with Adhokṣaja[1] is the means of breaking the rolling wheel (cycle) of births and deaths. The (spiritually) wise people regard it as the absolute bliss of absorption in *Brahman*. Therefore, you do worship the Lord residing in your heart.

38. Oh children of Asuras ! What extraordinary effort is required in worshipping Lord Hari Who abides in your heart like space, and Who is your own Self and an intimate friend ? What is the good of acquiring the objects of senses which are commonly attained to by all embodied beings ?

39. Wealth, a wife, cattles, sons and others (kinsmen) houses, landed property (or the earth), elephants, treasures, luxuries of life and all desired objects are evanescent. How much pleasure can all these fleeting objects afford to one whose life may cease at any moment ?

40. In the same way, definitely susceptible to destruction are the heavenly worlds which are attained to by performance of sacrifices. They are excelled by others (in merit and affluence). Nor are they unpolluted (as they excite jealousy) —Therefore for the purpose of realizing the Self, do you worship the Supreme Lord with absolute, desireless devotion. For no fault in the Lord has been discerned by the Vedas or the Smṛtis.

1. (i) VJ. reads *adhokṣajālāpam* for *adhokṣajālambham* and states that this verse describes that the narration of and conversation about the glories of the Lord, leads to the bliss of final emancipation.

(ii) ŚR. notes v. l. *adhokṣajālambaṃ* 'Taking resort to god Viṣṇu.'

41. In this world a person who supposes himself to be learned and wise, many times performs (Vedic, ritualistic and other) actions with the aim of obtaining it (sensual pleasure), but invariably reaps fruit quite contrary to it.

42. The expectation of a person in undertaking the performance of some religious action is for obtaining happiness and release from miseries. But due to this desire or action he who was (full of happiness due to his desirelessness (i. e. before he was possessed with the desire of happiness or the performance of the action) encounters nothing but misery due to his desires.

43. The physical body for (the happiness of) which a man desires to secure objects of enjoyment by performance of actions actuated by motives, is transient and factually belongs to others (as food for carnivorous beasts and birds of prey). It passes away and (again) returns (to the Soul).

44. How much more so must be one's progeny, wives, houses, wealth and such other things (and in the case of kings their) kingdom, treasury, elephants, ministers, servants and relatives—(all of) which are indirectly connected (through one's body) and whom he regards as his own.

45* The Soul himself is an ocean of eternal bliss. To him, of what interest are these flimsy things (enumerated above) which are sure to perish along with the body—contemptible things which appear covetable as *Puruṣārtha* (ideal in life), but which actually lead to undesirable ends (like hell).

46. Oh Asuras ! Consider to what extent can self-interest (pleasure) be derived through sexual enjoyment etc.[1] by embodied beings who have been suffering miseries from their past actions since their conception (in their mother's womb and other further stages of life in this world till death).

47. The embodied being, with his body obedient to his dictates, begins to perform actions (meritorious or sinful) as

* To those who argue that Lord Viṣṇu assumes incarnation in physical bodies for sensual enjoyment, the verse replies: Hari who is by nature consciousness and bliss is not interested in physical pleasures of the *jīva* (individual Soul)—VJ.

1 ŚR. remarks: There is no scope for enjoyment of pleasures under the circumstances.

a consequence of which he extends (builds) a body (of his next incarnation)—(the process continues *ad infinitum*) as both body and *karmas* are promoted through ignorance.

48. Therefore, even though wealth, enjoyment and acts of righteousness (the three *Puruṣārthas*) are easily available to the devotees of Hari as they depend on Hari, you should, without cherishing any desire (for them), worship Lord Hari, your very Soul who is perfectly desireless.

49. The Supreme Ruler Hari, the beloved Ātman, the controller and indwelling Soul (*antaryāmin*) of all beings (whose bodies are) created out of the gross elements (e.g. the earth, water etc.) which (in their turn) are evolved by Him.

50. It is by resorting to the feet of Mukunda (Lord Viṣṇu) that a god, an *asura* (a demon), a human being, a *yakṣa* or a *gandharva*—whoever he be—becomes blessed like us.

51-52. Oh Asura boys ! It is not the (eminence of) birth as a member of the twice-born family or as a god or as a sage that is sufficient for the propitiation of Hari. Neither righteous conduct, nor extensive knowledge nor charity nor penance, or performance of sacrifices, cleanliness (of body and mind) nor observance of vows is enough for His grace. Lord Hari is pleased through pure (unalloyed) devotion. All the rest is sheer mockery.

53. Hence, Oh descendants of Danu, you focus your devotion on the Almighty Lord Hari who is the Soul of all created beings, by considering everything else as (dear as) your own selves.

54. (Through such devotion) the descendants of Diti (demons), Yakṣas, Rākṣasas, women, Śūdras (low caste people), cowherds (like Ābhīras etc.), birds. beasts and even sinful *jīvas* have attained to immortality (the self-same nature as Acyuta).

55. Unswerving absolute devotion to Govinda (Lord Viṣṇu) which requires viewing His presence in and regard for every creature (mobile or immobile)—this alone has been enunciated in the *Śāstras* as the highest *Puruṣārtha* of man in this world.

CHAPTER EIGHT

Death of Hiraṇyakaśipu and Praise of Nṛsiṁha

Nārada continued :

1. Now, all the Daitya boys listened to the exhortation of Prahlāda and accepted it due to its faultlessness, but not so the teaching of their preceptors.

2. Thereupon, when the son of the preceptor Śukrācārya observed that their mind was exclusively bent on realization of a single purpose (viz. Lord Hari), he got alarmed and immediately he made a factual report of the state of affairs to the king (Hiraṇyakaśipu).

3. Hearing that unpleasant and unbearable misdemeanour on the part of his son, the Daitya, with his body trembling under the impulse of rage, made up his mind to finish with his son.

4-5. Severely reprimanding Prahlāda in a harsh language, though he did not at all deserve it, Hiraṇyakaśipu, cruel by nature as he was, glared askance at him with a wicked look, and heaving heavily like a serpent trodden under foot, he thundered at Prahlāda who, in perfect self-control, stood bent with modesty and with his hands folded.

6. "Oh ill-mannered, stupid wretch, a bane of my family! I shall today despatch you to the abode of Yama, as you have become an obstinate transgressor of my commands.

7. "You stupid fellow ! Relying on whose power did you undauntedly violate my command—I, at whose wrath, all the three worlds along with their guardian deities tremble with fear ?"

Prahlāda replied :

8. He is verily the source of power not only of me, Oh King, but of yours as well as of all other mighty beings. He is that force that keeps under control all creation, high and low, mobile and immobile, beginning from god Brahmā.

9. He is the Supreme Lord, the Eternal Time (—spirit), of mighty strides and of great prowess. He is the very essence of the mental and organic power, courage, intelligence, physical

power and that of sense organs. He is the Supreme Controller of the three *guṇas*. He alone creates, protects and destroys this universe by His potencies.

10. Do you give up this Asura (demonic) nature of yours. Keep your mind equable and serene. There are no (external) enemies except one's uncontrolled mind which goes astray. Know that equipoised mind (looking on friends and foes equably) is the highest form of propitiating the Infinite Lord.

11. Some persons (like you) regard themselves as conquerors of the ten cardinal points, even though they have not, in the first place, controlled the six robbers (viz. five senses and the mind) plundering within. Enemies are born due to one's delusion. How could there be external enemies to the wise who have subdued their mind, and look up all embodied beings as equal.

Hiraṇyakaśipu said :

12. Oh dull-witted fellow! It is obvious that you want to court death. You are, therefore, bragging beyond limits. The words of people who are desirous of death, are certainly incoherent.

13* Hiraṇyakaśipu : Oh unfortunate boy! Where is the Lord of the universe, if there be any other than I ?

Prahlāda : He is everywhere (Omnipresent).

Hiraṇyakaśipu : How is it that He is not seen in this pillar ?

(Prahlāda observes the pillar and bowing down exclaims :)

"Yes, He is seen."

14. "As you are vaunting too much, I now sever your head from the trunk. Let Hari whom you trust as a protector, save you."

* Ś.R. treats this as a dialogue between Hiraṇyakaśipu and Prahlāda. Other commentators treat this as the speech of Hiraṇya alone. "Where is the Lord of the universe, if there be any other than I ? Oh wretched boy! If he be omnipresent how is it that he is not seen in this pillar ?"

15. Thus he repeatedly tormented in rage, his son, a great devotee of the Lord, with reproachful words. (Finding his son gazing at the pillar respectfully with folded hands.) the extremely powerful great Asura, grasping his sword, sprang from his high seat (throne), and knocked the pillar with his fist.

16. Instantaneously there arose in the pillar an immensely terrific crash which rent asunder the shell of the cosmic egg. Hearing the sound as it reached their abodes, god Brahmā and others suspected that to be the time of *Pralaya* when their regions collapse, Oh child ! (Yudhiṣṭhira).

17. Hearing that unprecedented mysterious sound, while proceeding in long strides to kill his son forcibly, he failed to detect within the assembly hall, the source of that crash, at which the leaders of demonic forces were terrified.

18. In order to prove true the utterance of his devotee[1] and to vindicate His (omni-) presence in all creatures and things, He manifested Himself in the pillar of the assembly hall assuming an extremely wonderful form which was neither human nor beastly.

19. Looking (circumspectly) on all sides (for the source of that uncanny roar), he beheld this being coming out from the pillar. (Being astonished, he said to himself:) 'He is neither a beast nor a man. How wonderful is this Man-lion form!'

20. While Hiraṇyakaśipu was musing thus (about the strange figure), there stood before him the extremely terrible form of the Man-lion with his eyes fierce like molten gold, and his face majestic with dazzling hair of his mane.

1. ŚR. applies this expression to all devotees including Prahlāda, Sanaka, Nārada, Hiraṇyakaśipu and god Brahmā. Prahlāda said that Lord Hari was in the pillar pointed out by Hiraṇyakaśipu and he came out of that pillar. Sanaka stated the termination of his curse after three births of Jaya and Vijaya and to fulfil that Viṣṇu incarnated to finish the demonic birth. Nārada's words to Indra about the invincibility of Prahlāda were proved as Hiraṇyakaśipu was not allowed to kill him. Hiraṇyakaśipu's request for the conditions under which he was not to die were satisfied, and god Brahmā's boon to Hiraṇyakaśipu was respected by Viṣṇu in Nṛsiṁha form.

21. He had terrible tusks, a tongue sharp like the blade of a razor, and waving like a sword; his face struck terror with its knitted (frowning) eye-brows; His ears were motionless and erect. His mouth and nostrils were open and amazing like a mountain-cavern. He appeared terrible with his parted jaws.

22. He touched the heavens with his stature. He had a short thick neck, broad chest and slender waist. He was covered with hair white like lunar rays, and hundreds of hands on either side, armed with claws.

23. He was unassailable and he put to flight Daityas and Dānavas with all the choicest weapons peculiar to him (e.g. the Sudarśana disc) as well as to others (e.g. the *vajra*—the thunderbolt).

"Most probably this expedient for my death has been thought out by Hari, the master of the great potency of illusion. But of what avail are his endeavours against me ?"

24. Musing thus to himself, the foremost of (lit. the elephant among) the Daityas, armed with a mace (*gadā*) dashed against Nṛsiṁha (the Man-lion) with a roar. But just like a moth falling into the fire, the *Asura* disappeared in the effulgent nimbus of Nṛsiṁha.

25. There was nothing astonishing in the disappearance of the *asura* (the personified *tamas*) into effulgence of *Sattva* incarnate (viz. Nṛsiṁha) who formerly (at the time of creation) drank up all the *Tamas* (darkness). Then attacking Nṛsiṁha in rage, the great Asura struck him with the mace of tremendous force.

26. Like Garuḍa seizing a big serpent Nṛsiṁha (who was the wielder of a mace) caught hold of the Asura along with his mace while he was fighting. While the Asura was being played with by Nṛsiṁha, he slipped out of his hand like a serpent escaping from the clutches of Garuḍa.

27. Oh Yudhiṣṭhira! Gods and the protectors of all the spheres who were driven out of their abodes (by the Asura) and who concealed themselves behind the curtains of clouds, looked upon this escape as an evil turn (against their interest). The great Asura who freed himself from Nṛsiṁha's hands,

thought Nṛsiṁha to be apprehensive of his prowess. Feeling no fatigue in fighting, he armed himself with a sword and shield, and vehemently assailed Nṛsiṁha again.

28. While the Asura was moving up and down with the speed of a hawk, brandishing his sword and shield, leaving no weak point exposed, Hari roared forth a terrific and shrill peal of laughter, and with great rapidity, seized the Asura whose eyes blinked (by Hari's roaring laughter and dazzling splendour).

29. Just as a serpent would seize a mouse, Hari caught hold of the Asura who, afflicted with the tight hold (of Hari) was trying in every way to escape. At the door (on the threshold) of the assembly-hall, he laid him on his thighs, and though the demon's skin remained unscratched by (Indra's) thunderbolt, He sportingly tore him with his claws as Garuḍa does to the most poisonous serpents. (In this way, all the conditions of god Brahmā's boon were observed while killing Hiraṇyakaśipu).

30. His indignant and terrific eyes were too difficult to gaze at. He was licking the corners of his wide open mouth with his tongue. His face and mane were reddish due (to the stains of) the drops of blood. (Thus) he resembled a lion wearing the garland of the entrails of an elephant after killing it.

31. Throwing aside Hiraṇyakaśipu whose lotus-like heart was broken open, with his pointed claws, Nṛsiṁha who had a number of stout arms, struck down with his claws, weapons and heels, thousands of his (Hiraṇyakaśipu's) followers who closed on him from all sides with their arms lifted (to strike him).

32. The rain-clouds shaken by (the movements of) his mane scattered away (exposing to gods the full view of the battle below). Being outshone by his dazzling eyes, the lustre of the planets got eclipsed. Tossed by his breath, the oceans became turbulent. Terrified at his stunning roar, the elephant guards of the cardinal points wailed loudly.

33. Overcrowded with the aerial cars which were tossed up by the hair of his mane, the firmament was pushed up (from its original position). The earth got sorely pressed down under his (overwhelmingly heavy) steps. By his velo-

city, mountains were uprooted. Both the sky and the quarters were eclipsed by his dazzling splendour.

34. Then he occupied the excellent throne in the assembly-hall (out of curiosity and wonder at the affluence of his servant — the erstwhile Hiraṇyakaśipu). The Lord displayed such concentrated effulgence that no enemy remained in sight. Yet his indignation was not abated, and his countenance appeared so terrific that nobody dared approach him.

35. Hearing that the foremost of Daityas, the veritable brain-fever to the three worlds, has been slain by Hari in a combat, celestial women whose faces were blooming with overwhelming joy, repeatedly poured down upon him showers of flowers.

36. At that time, the whole firmament became crowded with rows of celestial cars of gods who were eager to see him. Heavenly drums and tabors were sounded. Prominent Gandharvas sang and their women danced.

37-39. Oh child! Resorting to that assembly, gods headed by Brahmā, Indra, Śiva and others, sages, manes (*Pitṛs*), demigods like Siddhas, and Vidyādharas, great Nāgas, Manus (who preside over aeons called *Manvantaras*), Prajāpatis (lords of creation), celestial musicians like Gandharvas, Apsaras and Cāraṇas, other demi-gods like Yakṣas, Kimpuruṣas, Vetālas and illustrious Kinnaras and all the attendants of the Lord like Sunanda, Kumuda—all these placed their folded hands to their heads (to pay respects), and from a distance not far from him, severally offered their prayers to the Man-Lion of dazzling splendour, Who was seated (on the throne).

Brahmā said:

40. I bow down to propitiate the Infinite Lord (unlimited by Time, Space etc.) of incomprehensible limitless powers, of marvellous potency and hallowing deeds, who, out of sports, brings about the creation, maintenance and destruction of the universe through the instrumentality of the *guṇas*, and yet himself remains undecayed and unchanged.

Śrī Rudra said:

41. The termination of the cycle of one thousand Yugas is the proper time for the exhibition of Your wrath. (If it be against Hiraṇyakaśipu) this puny demon lies slain. Oh Lord who is affectionate to his devotees ! Hiraṇyakaśipu's son your devotee, has approached you. Please protect him (now).

Indra said:

42. Oh Supreme Lord ! (As you are our in-dwelling controller and as such the real enjoyer of sacrificial oblations), in protecting us and securing our shares in sacrifices, it is (really) your own share that you have recovered (from the Daityas). The lotus of our heart, Your own abode, which was (till now) seized with the fear of the demon (and was thus crampled), got bloomed forth by You. Oh Lord ! Of what account is this sovereignty of three worlds which is to be devoured by Time ? To those who wish to serve You, Oh Man-lion, even liberation from Saṁsāra is of little consideration. What of other objectives in human life (like *Dharma*, *Artha* and *Kāma*) ?

Sages said :

43. (We pay obeisance to You) Oh Most Ancient Person, You taught us the Supreme form of penance, viz. meditation on Your glory, whereby You evolved this universe that lay latent in You. But it was completely obstructed by this demon. By assuming this form of Man-lion for the protection (of Your devotees), You have permitted us to perform it again, Oh protector of Your refugees.

The manes (*Pitṛs*) *said* :

44. This Asura forcibly misappropriated and swallowed up the balls of rice reverentially offered to us by our off-spring at the time of the *Śrāddha* ceremony, and gulped the water mixed with sesamum seeds proffered to us at the time of ablutions in sacred water. We bow to (You) Lord Nṛsiṁha, the Protector of the righteousness, Who (as it were) restored to us those offerings out of the fat of the Asura's belly split open with Your claws.

Siddhas said :

45. We humbly salute You, Lord Nṛsiṁha, who tore down with your claws this wicked demon who, by the force of his *Yoga* and penance, robbed us of our mystic powers acquired by us through Yoga, and was puffed up with pride for his various achievements.

Vidyādharas said :

46. This ignorant fellow, being elated with his physical power and valour, prohibited us the use of our *vidyā* (the power of becoming invisible etc.) acquired by us through Yogic concentration of various types. We ever respectfully bow to You who, assuming, by Your Māyā power, the form of the Man-lion, slew him like a beast in the encounter.

Nāgas (serpents) said :

47. Salutations unto You Who brought delight to our women by tearing open the chest of this wicked demon who wrested the jewels from our hoods, and abducted our gem-like beautiful wives.

Manus said:

48. We are Manus, the executors of Your commands. Oh Lord, all the bounds of social order (viz. the duties prescribed for different classes—*varṇas*, and stages in life—āśramas) have been violated by Diti's son (Hiraṇyakaśipu). Now that the wicked fellow is withdrawn (killed) by you, Oh Lord, what service should we render unto You? Be pleased to command us, Your servants.

Prajāpatis said :

49. Oh Supreme Lord ! We, the Lords of creation, are Your creatures. This demon, due to whose restrictions, we could not verily procreate beings, now lies definitely slain with his bosom split open by You. Oh embodiment of pure *Sattva*, Your incarnation itself is auspiciousness for the world.

Gandharvas said :

50. Oh Lord ! We are Your artistes—singers, dancers and actors. He who by dint of his prowess, might and energy

subjugated us to his service, has been reduced to this condition (death) by You. Can anyone straying away from the path of righteousness attain happiness?

Cāraṇas said :

51. Now that this Asura, the thorn in the heart of the righteous, has been removed (killed) by You, we take shelter under Your lotuslike feet which is the means of emancipation from *Saṁsāra*, Oh Hari.

Yakṣas said :

52. By performing actions pleasing to You, we attained prominence amongst Your followers (servants). But here we were subjected to the position of palanquine bearers by this son of Diti. Being aware of the agony caused by him to the world, You finished with him (lit: reduced him to his five constituent elements), Oh Narahari, the twentyfifth principle (controlling the twentyfour principles[1] responsible for the evolution and involution of the universe).

Kimpuruṣas said :

53. We are (after all) Kimpuruṣas (insignificant beings), but you are the most exalted person, the Almighty Ruler. When denounced by the pious and the good, this wicked fellow was (as good as) dead.

Vaitālikas said :

54. We used to get great worship and respect and wealth by singing of Your pure, sanctifying glory in assemblies and sacrificial sessions. This wicked fellow harshly deprived us of it. We are glad that You have exterminated him like a disease.

1. The following is the usual list of Principles according to Sāṅkhyas: *Puruṣa*, *Prakṛti*, *Mahat*, *Ahaṁkāra* (ego), 5 subtle elements, 10 *indriyas* (sense organs), the mind and 5 gross elements. Out of these Prakṛti is uncreated; the seven from *Mahat* are both created and creative; the rest sixteen are created. Puruṣa according to Sāṅkhyas is neither created nor creative. (But *Bhāgavata* invests Puruṣa with all powers of creation.)

Kinnaras said :

55. Oh Master ! We hosts of *Kinnaras* are Your servants who were forced to labour hard without remuneration by this Daitya. Oh Hari, the wicked fellow is now slain by Your Lordship. Oh Lord Narasiṁha ! Henceforth You be the source of our prosperity.

Viṣṇu's attendants said :

56. Oh protector ! It is today that we have seen this wonderful half-human and half-leonine form which is an auspicious blessing to all worlds. Oh Lord ! (Now) we know that this (Hiraṇyakaśipu) was Your own servant cursed by Brāhmaṇas (Sanaka and others) and (we realize that) death done to him was bestowal of Your grace (on him).

CHAPTER NINE

Prahlāda eulogizes Nṛsiṁha

Nārada continued :

1. Thus all gods and others headed by Brahmā and Rudra dared not go near him who was still possessed (under the influence) of wrath and (hence) unapproachable.

2. The goddess Śrī (who always attends upon Lord Viṣṇu) was personally sent to his presence. But at the sight of the monstrous manifestation, unseen and unheard of before, she was afraid, and did not approach.

3. God Brahmā (ultimately) deputed Prahlāda who was standing near-by, (saying), "Oh dear child, you (at least) approach and propitiate the Lord who has been angry with your father."

4. Consenting (to Brahmā's proposal) the child, a great devotee of the Lord, slowly approached him, and folding his palms together, he prostrated himself on the ground before him, Oh king.

5. Seeing the child fallen at his feet, the Lord was thoroughly overwhelmed with compassion. Raising him up, he placed on his head, his lotus-like hand which dispels the fear of those whose minds are fraught with the fear of the serpent in the form of Kāla (Death, Time, the Destroyer).

6. At the touch of his hand, all the inauspiciousness (in the form of impressions left by past actions) in Prahlāda was washed out, and the highest knowledge of the Supreme Brahman instantly dawned upon him. He meditated upon the lotus like feet of the Lord in his heart. Being deeply gratified at heart, the hair of his body stood on their ends (through joy); his heart got drenched (with devotion) and his eyes were overflowing with tears of joy.

7. Fixing on him his heart and eyes with perfect mental concentration and composure, he praised Nṛsiṁha in inarticulate words in a voice choked with emotion (love).

Prahlāda said :

8. Is it possible that I who belong to a ferocious race (of Asuras), am eligible to praise Lord Hari when hosts of gods headed by Brahmā and others, contemplative sages and wise Siddhas whose minds are constituted of the products of *Sattva* (such as righteousness, knowledge and penance) have not been able, even to this moment, to propitiate him by their streams of prayers, glorifying his many excellences (couched in figurative language.).

9. As the Almighty Lord was pleased with the leader of the elephant-herd[1] due to his (whole-hearted unswerving) devotion (unto him), I presume that affluence, noble lineage, beauty, austerities, learning, keenness of senses, complexion, prowess, physical power, determined exertions, intelligence and the eight-fold process of Yoga are of little avail in propitiating the Supreme Person.

10. I consider that a man of the *cāṇḍāla* (the lowest) caste, who has thoroughly dedicated his mind, speech, deed,

1. This refers to the episode of 'the elephant and the crocodile' described infra VIII. 2-4 (Chapters).

wealth and his very life itself to the Lord,[1] is superior to a Brāhmaṇa endowed with the twelve qualities (mentioned in the above verse or enumerated in verses noted below[2]) but is averse to the lotus-like feet of Lord Viṣṇu (the lotus-naveled god); for the Cāṇḍāla (devotee) sanctifies his (whole) race but not so the Brāhmaṇa even though he is highly respected[3] (by the public).

11. The Supreme Lord is perfect in (the realization of) his blissful nature. Hence he does not expect any respect and worship for himself, from the ignorant (as all of us are before him). He is merciful and therefore he accepts it. For whatever respect (-ful worship) is offered unto the Lord, is returned to the devotee himself, just as the decoration of one's countenance goes to enhance the beauty of the face reflected in the mirror.

12. Therefore, despicable (by birth) as I am, I shall sing of the glory of the Supreme Ruler with all my heart and to the best of my understanding, without any fear or diffidence (about my intelligibility). It is by delineating the glory of the Lord that a man who has entered into *Saṁsāra* (a product of *guṇas*) due to the influence of Avidyā[4] (nescience), will be purified.

13. Oh Almighty Ruler! All these gods such as Brahmā and others who are (now) terrified, are merely the executors

1. VR. brings in the Prapatti doctrine of Rāmānuja herein. He raises the objection that due to the association of *bhakti* (devotion) to Vedānta, only the first three castes (Brāhmaṇa, Kṣattriya and Vaiśya) are eligible for it. The Bh. P. implies *Prapatti* (complete surrender to the Will of the Lord)—here for all people, irrespective of castes and sex.

2. ŚR. and other annotators quote from Sanatsujātīya (in M.Bh.) the following list:

Righteousness, piety (*sattva*), self-control, austerities, non-jealousy, modesty (*hrī*), forbearance, tolerance or envylessness, performance of sacrifices, charity, courage and Vedic-learning—these are the twelve vows to be observed by a Brāhmaṇa.

3. *bhūrimānaḥ* who is puffed up with pride (ŚR., VD., GS., VR. etc.).

4. *ajayāpraviṣṭaḥ*—who has entered into the human body, a product of *guṇas* due to the force of *prakṛti*—VR.

of the orders of Your Lordship who is a receptacle of pure *Sattva* and not like us Asuras (who are Your inimical-devotees). The sportive activities of the glorious Lord through his beautiful incarnations, are conducive to not only the well being and prosperity of the world but also for the conferment of the blissful experience of Your sports (and not for striking terror).

14. Now that You have slain the demon today, You be pleased to withdraw Your wrath (wrathful attitude). Even a pious man is delighted at the destruction of a scorpion or a serpent. All the people have now attained to peace and tranquillity and are waiting (for the subsidence of Your anger). All the people will remember this form of Yours for deliverance from fear, Oh Nṛsiṁha. (Hence the recollection of Your form being enough, there is no need to continue Your angry mood).

15. (As far as I am concerned), I am not at all afraid of Your (present) form with the most ferocious countenance (with a formidable mouth and tongue), Sun-like dazzling eyes and frightful knitting of eyebrows, fearful tusks and the garland of the entrails (of my father) and the mane and conical ears soaked in blood. Nor (am I afraid of) the roar that terrified the elephants guarding the cardinal points, or of Your pointed claws that tore up the enemy, Oh Invincible Lord!

16. I am (really) afraid of the unbearable miseries involved in the inexorable and terrible cycle of transmigrations (*saṁsāra*), Oh Lord (who is) compassionate to the miserables. Bound down with (the fetters in the form of my past) actions, I am thrown in the midst of ferocious ones (Daityas). Oh most merciful Lord ! When will You be pleased to recall me to Your feet, which is the sole asylum of all beings and is the Final Emancipation ?

17. Inasmuch as I am being scorched with the fiery sorrows of separation from the dear ones and association with unpleasant situations and persons, during the course of my transmigrations in different types of births (like celestials, subhuman beings), and the so-called cure from miseries entails miseries, I am wandering about in *Saṁsāra* falsely identifying

me with the body, Oh Almighty Lord ! Be pleased to enlighten me in the remedy (for emancipation from *Saṁsāra*), viz. the method of serving You.

18. Oh Nṛsiṁha ! I (who am thus enlightened in the way of serving You) shall be completely free from (the influence of) *guṇas* (like love, hatred etc.) and associating myself with the enlightened ardent devotees who resort to the asylum of the pair of Your feet, I shall easily tide over all miseries, singing constantly all the while the marvellously sportive activities of my beloved Friend and the Supreme Deity extolled before by god Brahmā.

19. Oh Nṛsiṁha ! In this world, the parents are not (real) protectors of children. Medicine is not the remedy to the suffering patient (who may succumb to death despite medical care). To a person drowning in the sea, a boat is not a (sure) help (as he may go down with it). In the case of embodied beings who (not being favoured with your grace) are disregarded by you, and are afflicted in this *saṁsāra*, whatever remedy (against the misery) is regarded as easy, proves to be temporarily effective[1].

20. Whatever agent, whether ancient (like god Brahmā) or modern (like a human father) and possessing a characteristic nature (dominated by *Sattva* etc.) is prompted to create or transform a thing into whatever form, from whatever source and for whatever cause or purpose, irrespective of its time, instrumentality, its relatedness to anyone or its separation from anything else—all these are (identical with) you (and none else).

21. When Māyā, with its *guṇas* (like Sattva and others), is prompted into action by the Time-Spirit through the gracious approval of the Supreme Man (who is only) a part of yours, it creates the subtle astral body which is predominated by the Mind. It is evolved out of *karmic* activities. It is unconquerable and is predisposed to the performance of ritualistic Vedic

1. ŚR. alternatively : Is there any easy remedy in the case of those embodied beings who, not being favoured . . . . etc.

VR. supports this but to him *tanubhṛtām* = those who are solely devoted to the nourishment of the body.

rites.[1] It is the wheel of *Saṁsāra* which consists of sixteen spokes (in the form of mind, ten cognitive and conative sense-organs and five subtle elements) offered for *Jīva's* enjoyment by *Avidyā* (nescience). What person standing apart from you (i.e. not devoted to you) can (hope to) transgress this, Oh Unborn Lord!

22. Oh Almighty Lord! You have by your inherent power (in the form of consciousness), always kept under perfect control the properties of *Buddhi* or intellect[2] (such as pleasure, pain, love, avarice etc.) Oh Supreme Controller (of the universe), you are the Time-Spirit who as the director of Māyā, exercise full control over the powers of causal relations[3]. Such as you are, be pleased to take me unto your proximity as I have sought your protection. I have been thrown by the Unborn (*avidyā*) into the wheel (of *saṁsāra*) of sixteen spokes and am being crushed in it.

23. The people of this world yearn for longevity, affluence and glory of the celestial guardians of different worlds. But, Oh Lord, I have seen how they were swept away by the contraction of my father's eyebrow knitted in wrathful laughter. But even he has been disposed of by you.

24. Therefore, I who know the consequences of the blessings coveted by embodied beings do not seek long life, wealth, glory, sensual pleasure (of anybody) right from those of god Brahmā. Nor do I aspire after the mystic powers which are destroyed by You in the form of the Time-Spirit of immense

1. *chandomayam*—Full of desires characterised by mental resolves and suspicions—VJ.

VR. contradicts that the word *chandas* is never used in the sense of desire.

The import of the verse according to VJ.: It is impossible to transgress the wheel of *saṁsāra* except through the grace of Lord Hari attained through devotion. People of uncontrolled mind find it hard to secure that grace.

2. *ātma-guṇa*—(i) Properties inherent in one's body—VR.

(ii) Birth, death and such other conditions of the body—VJ.

(iii) Properties of jīva e.g. pleasure, pain, affection, greed—GD.

All *jīvas* like god Brahmā and others and their qualities—SD.

3. *visṛjya-visarga-śaktiḥ*: (*i*) effects and their means—ŚR.

(ii) *jīvas* and *Prakṛti*—VR.; *jīva and Māyā*—SD.

(iii) The world consisting of men, gods etc. and the creation—VJ.

prowess. Do be pleased with me to place me by the side of your servants.

25. Where are the pleasures which are pleasant merely to hear of, but are unreal like the mirage ? Where is this body which is the nursery of all diseases? (Such a body is incapable of enjoying the so-called pleasures). The people, however, knowing this all as they do, are too engrossed to quench the fire of desires with drops of honey-like pleasures so difficult to obtain, to get disgusted with this world. (How wonderful is the working of your Māyā !).

26. What a world of difference there is, Oh Lord, between me, born out of *rajas* in the family of demons (lit. non-gods) dominated with *tamas*, and your immense grace (towards me) ! You were pleased to place your lotus-like palm graciously only on my head but not on that of gods Brahmā, Śiva and the goddess Lakṣmī.

27. Inasmuch as you are the Soul, well-wisher and friend of the world, this notion of inferiority and superiority which is entertained by ordinary beings cannot be there in your case. But your grace, like the favour bestowed by the wish-yielding heavenly tree, depends proportionately on the service performed. Your grace (leading to righteousness etc.) varies directly as per service rendered to you, and not on the ground of superiority and inferiority.

28. Oh Lord ! This *saṁsāra* is like a well infested with a serpent in the form of birth (and death). People desirous of sensual pleasures are falling into it. Due to the force of association, I was about to fall headlong along with them, but was regarded as his own by the divine sage Nārada and (in the way as you favoured me with your grace), was favoured (with knowledge) formerly (while I was in my mother's womb). Thus, how can I possibly give up the service of your servants (devotees) ?

29. When my father, intent upon doing evil, took up a sword and threatened me, "If there be any God other than I, let him protect you while I cut off your head", your act of saving my life and execution of my father was, I think, accomplished to vindicate the word (curse) of the sage (Sanaka, Sanandana etc.), Oh Infinite Lord.

30.* It is you alone who are (manifest as) this universe. You exist independently (as the cause) of the universe at the beginning before it came into being, and stay as such in the middle (while the cosmos exists), and after its dissolution as well. Having created this (universe which is the) product of (the permutation and combination of) the *guṇas*, by dint of your *māyā*, you re-enter it and appear as many (as protector and destroyer) through them.

31.** Oh Lord ! You are verily none else but this universe consisting of cause and effect. But you are, however, different from it (as you exist independently before the creation and after the destruction of the universe). Hence the notion of distinction between 'this is mine and this is another's, is nothing but an illusion (and as such) unreal. A thing which depends for its creation, destruction, subsistence and manifestation on another is really identical with it, just as a tree (the effect) is the same as the seed (the cause) which is essentially the same as the earth and its subtle cause.***

32. Having withdrawn this universe within yourself by your own agency, and being above desires, you lie on the cosmic waters of the Deluge, absorbed in enjoying your own essential blissfulness, and in perfect rest (inactivity). With your eyes closed in Yogic meditation which transcends sleep by your self-illumination, you stay in the fourth state which lies beyond the three states of wakefulness, dream and deep sleep. Therein you neither cognize *Tamas* (the characteristic of deep sleep), nor enjoy any *guṇas* (objects of senses).

* (i) You constitute the entire world consisting of the conscious (individual selves) and the unconscious matter. You maintain your separateness in the beginning, the end and the middle of the universe.—VR.

(ii) The *Śāstras* have conclusively proved your separate existence at the creation, destruction and during the sustenance of the universe—VJ.

(iii) As a matter of fact, *rajo-guṇa* is the creator, *tamoguṇa*, the destroyer, and *sattva guṇa* the sustainer of the universe but (in spite of) your unconcerned entry into them, you are called the slayer (of Hiraṇyakaśipu) —VC.

** Cf. supra 1.6

*** VR.: Oh Lord ! This world consisting of sentients and non-sentients is yourself as you are the cause of it and are non-different from it. The notion that the individual Soul is the same as the Controlling Lord (*Īśvara*)

33. The universe is the body of Him (i.e. Yours) who through His potency called the Time-Spirit, prompted into action the modes of *Prakṛti* (viz. *sattva*, *rajas* and *tamas* which combine and create the universe). While He, i.e. You lay in the bed of the serpent Śeṣa on the cosmic waters of the Deluge, and while Your *Yogic* trance was coming to a close, there sprouted forth from Your navel, like a banyan tree from a tiny seed, a large lotus which was (erstwhile) lying hidden in You.

34. The wise seer (Brahmā) who was born of that lotus, did not see anything else than the lotus. Considering that You who were the seed (material cause) pervading his self internally, were outside himself, could not discover You though he immersed himself into the inundatory waters for a hundred years. Oh how can one find out the seed when the sprout shoots forth from it.

35. That self-born god (Brahmā) was greatly astonished (at his failure to discover the 'seed'), Oh Lord. (He reverted to his place). Seated in the lotus and performing austere penance, he got his heart thoroughly purified in due course. He realized You as pervading in the subtlest form, his own Self consisting of *bhūtas* (elements), *indriyas* (cognitive and conative sense-organs) and heart, just as a discriminating person perceives subtle smell pervading the earth.

is unreal, meaningless and is due to *Avidyā*, just as the notion of the identity of the soul and the body is illusory. So is the identification of the Soul with God. That which causes the origination, sustenance, destruction and manifestation of anything is identical with its material cause, just as the divisions of time are not different from the eternal flow of time or the tree is not different from the soil which germinates the seed.

ŚR., VR. etc. interpret *vasu* as subtle elements and *kāla* as the earth, the basis of blue colour etc.

(ii) SD. regards that this verse asserts the difference-cum-non-difference relation between the world and the *Brahman*. That on which the origination, maintenance, manifestation and destruction of a thing depends is both different and identical with it, as a plant is both different and not different from the soil from which it grows.

(iii) GD. emphasizes that this world of causal relationship is identical with the Lord. He is essentially transcendental to the world (*Prapañca*). The whole world being the Lord's and identical with him, the notion of difference is unreal.

36. In the same way, Brahmā visualized You as the Supreme (cosmic) person endowed with thousands of faces, feet, heads, thighs, noses, mouths, ears, eyes and decorated with rich ornaments and furnished with weapons. The disposition of Your various limbs was indicated by different parts of the universe (nether world and other regions). You assumed this form by Your *Māyā* power. And he (Brahmā) was filled with great joy.

37. Assuming the form of a horse-necked god, Your worshipful self killed the extremely powerful enemies of the Vedas, Madhu and Kaiṭabha by name who were the very embodiments of *rajas* and *tamas*. You thus restored the corpus of the Vedas to him (Brahmā). The Vedas declare that Your most beloved person consists of pure *Sattva*.

38. In this way, Oh Supreme Person, You incarnate Yourself, as a human or a subhuman being, as a sage or a god, or as a fish and protect the world, and kill the enemies of the people. You uphold the path of righteousness suitable to that particular Yuga (epoch). You remain unmanifest in the Kali age and hence You are designated *Triyuga*.

39. Oh Lord of Vaikuṇṭha ! This mind of mine, vitiated as it is by sins, extroversion, extremely morbid, lustfulness and afflicted with joy, grief and three yearnings (for progeny, prosperity and popularity), finds no interest in Your stories. How can I, a poor wretch with such a mind, contemplate on Your essential nature ?

40. Oh Acyuta ! My ungratified palate drags me in one direction and sexual desire (lit. the genital organ) pulls me to a different direction, while the senses of touch, hearing and the abdomen gravitate me to some other direction. My olifactory sense, the constantly moving eye and faculties of action draw me in different directions—all these pull (in different directions) like a number of co-wives dragging their lord of the house (to their bed-rooms).

41. Be pleased to cast a gracious look at these ignorant people who, as a consequence of their actions, have fallen in the Vaitaraṇī[1] in the form of *Saṁsāra* and are frightened extre-

1. *Vaitaraṇī*—a mythological river bordering on the region of Yama, the god of death. It is full of blood, bones, hair etc. and rushes very rapidly and hence unfordable.

mely with the terror of successive births, deaths and sufferings (from want of food), and who entertain the notions of friendship to bodies whom they consider their own and enmity towards others. Out of compassion for their plight, be pleased to protect them by ferrying them today across the *saṁsāra*-Vaitaraṇī, Oh Lord who stays beyond (*saṁsāra*) !

42. Oh Lord ! You are the father (creator and guide) of all. What exertion could there be in lifting up these ignorant people (from *saṁsāra*) to You who are the cause of the creation, sustenance and destruction of the universe ? Oh friend of the afflicted ! It is quite meet that the great should verily be gracious unto the ignorant. To us who already serve Your beloved devotees such rescuing from *saṁsāra* is immaterial (as we are sure to be liberated. It is to others that you be pleased to show Your favour).

43. As my mind is immersed in the rare nectar of your prowess, I am not at all afraid of the (so-called) unfordable Vaitaraṇī, Oh Supreme Lord ! I feel grieved for these ignorant fellows who being averse (to this nectar of singing the great deeds of the Lord) carry on the burden of the family etc. in the hope of securing pleasures caused by objects of senses, which again are illusory.

44. Oh Lord, sages, desirous of self-emancipation, generally meditate on you silently in solitude. But they are indifferent to the interests of others. Leaving aside these helpless creatures, I do not long to attain the final beatitude for me alone. Nor do I see any refuge other than you for these, who are wandering in *saṁsāra*.

45. The so-called pleasures of a householder's life such as sexual intercourse and others are positively insignificant, contemptible and leading to a chain of miseries like the scratching of one itching hand with another. Lascivious people though subjected to various miseries, are never satiated (by enjoying the pleasures) in this world. It is only some person endowed with strength of mind and wisdom who (through your grace) (can repress their passion of lust like the temptation to scratch (an itching limb).

46. Oh Inner Controller ! Means conducive to the attainment of emancipation, viz. observance of the vow of

silence, listening to sacred books, performance of austerities, studies of spiritual texts, discharging one's religious duties, exposition of the *Śāstras*, living in solitude, chanting of the Lord's name and concentration of mind in *Yoga*—all these generally become only the means of livelihood for those whose senses are uncontrolled (and who wish to sell these for worldly gains). In the case of hypocrites it is doubtful whether these might be of any use even for earning the livelihood (as they are likely to be exposed easily.

47. The Vedas have revealed your two symbolic forms, the cause and effect (or the *Prakṛti* and the atoms) which are like the seed and (its) sprout. You are devoid of any form or colour, yet the universe of causal relation is not other than (different from) you. It is by means of the Yoga of Devotion that persons who have controlled their senses, can visualize you directly, both in the cause and its consequence, just as people can perceive fire in (the friction of) the two pieces of wood. Knowledge about you cannot be attained by any other means. (Hence you are pervading everything as its cause).

48. You are (the elements such as the air, fire, earth, sky, water and objects of senses (viz. sound, touch, sight, taste, and smell), the (five) vital airs, the cognitive and conative organs, the heart, the intellect and the Ego (or deities presiding over senses and the mind). Everything possessed of qualities[1] (gross) or devoid of qualities (subtle) is you. There is nothing other than you even if it be conveyed by Mind or Speech, Oh great Lord!

49. Neither these *guṇas* (viz. *sattva*, *rajas* and *tamas*) nor the deities presiding over the *guṇas* or endowed with *guṇas* such as *Mahat* and others (viz. *mahat*, *ahaṁkāra*, five subtle and five gross elements, and ten *indriyas*—cognitive and conative senses) nor the mind etc. nor the various beings including gods and mortals—all these having a beginning-and an end—comprehend you, Oh most highly praised God. It is, therefore, that wise men endowed with high intellect, after careful deliberation (of this) give up the study of the Vedas (and other acts

1. VJ.: *saguṇa*—The *Jīva* in *saṁsāra*—possessed of qualities and *viguṇa*—the emancipated Soul or anything devoid of qualities.

prescribed therein), and worship you alone with concentrated mind.

50. Therefore, Oh most worshipful Lord! How can a person cherish devotion to you who are the goal of the highest order of ascetics (the *parama-haṁsas*), without the (following) six constituents of worship, viz., (1) paying obeisance to the Lord, (2) singing of his glory, (3) offering of all acts to the Lord, (4) waiting on you (worship in the form of service), (5) meditation on the feet of the Lord and (6) listening to the recital of stories of the Lord.

Nārada said :

51. When, in spite of the Lord's transcendence to attributes, the excellences of the Lord were highly extolled with deep reverence and devotion by his devotee Prahlāda, the Lord was pleased with him. Restraining his anger, he spoke to Prahlāda who was respectfully bowing to Him.

The Lord said :

52. "Oh gentle Prahlāda ! May good betide you ! Oh the best among the Asuras ! I am verily pleased with you. Ask whatever boon you like. I am the bestower of all the desires of men.

53. For, Oh long-lived one, even a glimpse of Mine is difficult to get to those who have not propitiated me. Having but once visualized me, a being never suffers an affliction any more.

54. Hence noble and pious Souls who are highly fortunate and are desirous of attaining bliss, try to propitiate me with all their heart, as I am the Lord (and bestower) of all blessings."

Nārada said :

55. Even though Prahlāda, the best of Asuras, was thus tempted with boons which excite allurement in all beings, he desired none of them, as he was exclusively devoted to the Lord (expecting no reward for his unflinching devotion).

CHAPTER TEN

Prahlāda enthroned. The conquest of Tripura

Nārada said :

1. The child, Prahlāda who looked upon all that (offer of boons etc.) as an impediment to the practice of *Bhakti-Yoga* (*Yoga* of Devotion), slightly smiled, and addressed Lord *Nṛsiṁha* (the Lord of the sense organs) as follows:

Prahlāda said :

2. Pray, do not tempt me who am addicted by nature (lit. birth) to pleasures, with (the promise of) those boons. Being afraid of contacts with them and in (sheer) disgust of them, I have resorted to you with the desire of securing liberation (from *saṁsāra*).

3. Oh Lord! Meseems it is with the desire of ascertaining the characteristics of a real servant or devotee that your worship directed me to choose objects of pleasure which are the seeds of the transmigration of the Self (*saṁsāra*) and are like so many knots binding the heart.

4. Otherwise that (offer) would have been impossible from you who are full of mercy, Oh Father of all![1] He who hankers after blessings from you, is but a merchant, and not a real servant (devotee)[2].

5. Verily he is not a real servant who desires to secure worldly pleasures (in return for services) from his master. Nor is he a real master who grants such comforts to play the lord upon his servant.

6. But I am your devotee who cherishes no desire and you are the Master who expect nothing (from your servant). Here, between us, there is no object (to be gained) as between the king and his servant.

1. Some editions add here:
naṣṭa-dṛṣṭes tamasyāndhe tvamekaḥ pāradarśanaḥ/
You are the only guide to lead across to the other shore of the ocean of *saṁsāra*, the people who have lost their eye-sight in blinding darkness.

2. After this line Andhra edition adds:
Sa vai svāmī, sa vai bhṛtyo, guṇalubdhau na kāmukau !
Verily he is the master and he is the servant. They are so due to their appreciation of qualities, but not for any gain or pleasure.

7. Oh foremost one among the bestowers of boons ! If (at all) You (want to) confer any boons on me, Oh Lord, I seek of your Worship the boon that no desire should germinate in my heart.

8. For, with the rise of desires, the (powers of) the senses, the mind, the vital air, the Soul, righteousness, fortitude, judgment, modesty, prosperity, energy, memory and truth come to an end (once for all).

9. When a man gets rid of desires fixed (deep) in the heart, then alone he becomes fit to attain to thy status, Oh lotus-eyed Lord.

10. (Now I remember the *Mantra* to which I was initiated by Nārada).

Salutations to You, Oh Almighty Lord, the Supreme Person, the High-Souled One, Hari, the wonderful lion, Supreme Brahman and Paramātman.

Lord Nṛsiṁha said :

11. Those who are exclusively devoted to Me like you, never expect from Me any blessing in this or in the next world Still (it is my order that you shall enjoy throughout this *Manvantara* the luxuries of the overlordship of the Daityas here.

12. You continue to enjoy listening to my stories so dear to you. Realize within your own heart Me, the Lord present in all beings, and the presiding deity of sacrifices. Dedicating all your activities to Me, worship Me, in meditation.

13. Having exhausted your merit by enjoying pleasure and sin by doing meritorious actions (or by *prāyaścitta*—expiatory rites) and given up your body in course of time, and spread such extremely pure renown as to be sung in heaven, you shall attain to Me completely liberated from all bonds.

* Here ŚR. quotes Kaṭha Upa. 2.3. 14—
Yadā sarve pramucyante kāmā ye'sya hṛdi śritāḥ/
atha martyomṛto bhavatyatra Brahma samaśnute//
When one gets rid of all the desires residing (fixed) in one's heart, the mortal becomes immortal immediately and attains oneness with Brahman in this very life.

14. A person who recites this song (prayer) sung by you to Me and remembers you and Me, becomes free from the bondage of *karman* in due course.

Prahlāda said:

15-17. Oh Supreme Lord ! The Lord of those who graciously confer boons ! I seek from you this boon that my father, ignorant of Your being the Divine Light, and with his mind overwhelmed (lit. pierced through) with indignation, reviled you who are the veritable Father of the World and the Master, by calling You the murderer of his brother, and through wrong outlook, behaved sinfully to me, Your devotee. May (my father) be absolved of the terrible sins which are too difficult to be crossed, even though he must have been purified when he was glanced at by you who are compassionate to the afflicted.

The Lord said :

18. Oh sinless righteous saint ! Inasmuch as you, the purifier of the family, have been born in his house, your father along with twentyone generations of his fore-fathers stands absolved of all sins[1].

19. Wherever my devotees, extremely serene, impartial in outlook, noble in character and of pious behaviour, are present, they sanctify that country (along with its inhabitants) even if it be sinful like that of *Kīkaṭa*.

20. Oh Lord of Daityas ! They (My devotees) who, out of devotion unto Me, have become devoid of desires[2] (which are at the root of anger, violence etc.), do not trouble any creature in any category of beings, high or low, by any means.

1. ŚR. explains that as Hiraṇyakaśipu was the 3rd in generation from god Brahmā, here the twentyone generations of his previous birth are implied.

VC. adds: Twentyone generations of forefathers in your (Prahlāda's) twentyone previous incarnations are included here.

2. mad-bhāvena gataspṛhaḥ—Realizing my presence everywhere, they entertain no jealousy against anyone—VJ.

21. In this world, there are men who follow your way of life and become My devotees. But certainly, you stand as a model to all my devotees.

22. Oh child Prahlāda ! (As a formality) perform the obsequies of your father who has been thoroughly purified through contact with My person (and has become hence sinless). Now, being blest with you as a pious son, he will certainly attain to higher worlds.

23. As directed by exponents of the Vedas, you occupy the throne of your father. Concentrating your mind on Me, carry out your duties with complete devotion to Me, Oh child !

Nārada said :

24. In compliance of the command of the Lord, Prahlāda also performed all the funeral rites of his father. And he was installed as a king by excellent Brāhmaṇas (and governed as per instructions of the Lord.)

25. Seeing the countenance of the Man-Lion Hari graciously pleased, Brahmā who was surrounded with gods, praised Him with holy Vedic hymns and submitted (as follows):

Brahmā said :

26. Oh God of gods ! The Supreme Ruler of all! The Creator of all beings! Oh the First born one! It is fortunate that You have slain the wicked demon, the tormentor of the world.

27. It was this demon who, having secured boons from me, could not be killed by anyone of my creation. Being arrogant with (the powers acquired by) penance and *Yoga* and with prowess he violated the code of righteousness.

28. Luckily, his son, though a child, is a pious Soul and a great devotee of Yours. Fortunately he has been saved by You from death, and he has now attained to You.

29. Oh Lord ! He who, with concentrated mind, contemplates on this form of Yours, will be protected on all sides from fear—even from the god of death wishing to kill one.

Nṛsiṁha said :

30. Oh lotus-born god ! No such boon is to be conferred by you on Asuras. A boon bestowed on those who are cruel by nature, is harmful like feeding serpents with milk.

Nārada said :

31. Oh king Yudhiṣṭhira! Having spoken thus, Lord Hari Who is normally invisible to all beings and Who was worshipped by god Brahmā, vanished on that very spot.

32. Then Prahlāda worshipped god Brahmā, Śiva, Prajāpatis and gods—all of whom were parts of the Almighty Lord—and bowed them with his head.

33. Thereafter, the lotus-seated god Brahmā, together with sages headed by Śukra, crowned Prahlāda as the Lord of Daityas and Dānavas.

34. Then, having felicitated Prahlāda and bestowed their highest blessings on him, the gods headed by Brahmā who were worshipped by him again, returned to their respective places, Oh King.

35. In this way, the two attendants of Viṣṇu (Jaya and Vijaya) who were born as sons to Diti (due to the imprecation of Brāhmaṇas) were killed by Hari. present in their heart due to the hostile attitude adopted by them towards Hari.

36. And due to the curse of a Brāhmaṇa, both of them were born again as the demons Kumbhakarṇa and Rāvaṇa of ten heads, who were killed by Rāma's arrows.

37. While lying on the field of battle with their hearts pierced with Rāma's arrows, both of them quitted their physical bodies with their hearts fixed on Him (Rāma), as (it happened) in their previous birth (as Hiraṇyākṣa and Hiraṇyakaśipu).

38. Both of those (attendants of Viṣṇu) were now born here as Śiśupāla and Dantavakra. It is in Your very presence that they merged in Lord Hari by entertaining continuous enmity towards Him.

39. Kings who were the enemies of Kṛṣṇa shed off, at the end of their life, whatever sins they have committed in the previous life, and become like unto Him through constant meditation like a caterpillar which, through constant brooding, is transformed into a wasp.

40. Just as votaries of the Lord, through their unflinching devotion to Hari attain to perfect identity with Him, (inimical) kings like Śiśupāla and others, through their constant brooding over Him (as their enemy) attained to similarity of form like Him.

41. I have answered to you in details all the queries made by you and also the identity with Hari attained by His enemies like the son of Damaghoṣa (Śiśupāla).

42. This is the sacred story of the (Man-lion) incarnation of the noble-souled Kṛṣṇa, the devotee of Brāhmaṇas —a story (containing the narration) of slaying the two ancient Daityas (viz. Hiraṇyākṣa and Hiraṇyakaśipu).

43-44. This narration includes the life (and character) of Prahlāda, the great votary of the Lord, and (a detailed description of) his devotion, knowledge non-attachment and also of the true nature and an account of the glorious deeds of Hari who is the Lord of the creation, maintenance and the destruction (of the universe). (It describes) the great revolutions in the positions of gods and demons in course of time.

45. In this chronicle has been described the righteous path of the devotees of the Lord which leads to the attainment of (one-ness with) Him; and all topics relating to the soul (spiritual knowledge) have been thoroughly discussed.

46. Whoever, after reverentially listening to this holy narrative of the heroic deeds of Viṣṇu, recites it to others is liberated from the bonds of Karmas (good or bad).

47. Whoever peruses piously with concentrated mind the sportive actions of Lord Viṣṇu (the Most Ancient Person) in assuming the Lion form and slaying Hiraṇyakaśipu, the leader of the legions of demons, and listens to (lit. having listened to) the (recital of the) hallowing glory of the demon Hirayṇyakaśipu's son (Prahlāda), the foremost among the righteous, attains to the region (Mokṣa) which is beyond the range of fear.

48. (Oh Yudhiṣṭhira!) You are certainly immensely more fortunate in this world (as compared with Prahlāda etc. his spiritual preceptor Nārada, as well as your forefathers and other great sages) inasmuch as great sages who sanctify the world, pay visit to you from all quarters, and the

Supreme Brahman Himself, concealing His greatness in the guise of a human being, resides with you in your houses.

49. This Kṛṣṇa who is your dear friend and well-wisher, your maternal uncle's son, your very adorable self, guide and advisor carrying out your behests (as your representative or charioteer), is verily the *Brahman* who is the embodiment of the ecstatic experience of the absolute Supreme bliss (unconditioned by any *upādhi*) which is sought after by the great.

50. May Lord Kṛṣṇa, the Lord of the Sātvatas whose direct essential nature has not been actually comprehended or described with their intellect by gods like Śiva and Brahmā, and who has been devoutly worshipped by us through silent meditation and renunciation, be gracious unto us. [The Supreme Brahman does not reside in Prahlāda's palace. Nor do sages go there to have an audience with him. Nor does He act like a cousin. Hence, Oh Yudhiṣṭhira and Pāṇḍavas, you are immensely more fortunate than Prahlāda and we.]

51. Oh Yudhiṣṭhira ! he is that very Lord who, in days of yore, extended the glory of god Rudra as it was eclipsed by Maya, the master of innumerable delusive powers.

The King (Yudhiṣṭhira) asked :

52. Be pleased to describe to us in which action Maya destroyed the glory of god Śiva and the way in which Lord Kṛṣṇa (re-established and) enhanced it.

Nārada said :

53. Asuras who were completely vanquished in the battle by gods who were strengthened by Lord Kṛṣṇa, sought the refuge of Maya the Supreme Preceptor of all conjurors (experts in the arts of illusion or magic).

54. The master-conjuror constructed three (flying-fortress-like) cities made of gold, silver and iron respectively. Their movements (arrival and departure) were undetectable and the (war) materials and equipments provided therein were beyond the conception of gods (And he handed these over to Asuras).

55. Remembering their old hostility, the leaders of Asura armies destroyed the three worlds along with the rulers,

themselves remaining invisible with the help of those (flying) cities, Oh King.

56. Oh King, thereupon all residents of the three worlds, along with their rulers, approched god Śiva and prayed, "Be pleased, Oh God, to protect us, Your own people (who are practically) destroyed by Asuras residing in three (flying) cities.

57. Out of grace unto the celestials, the almighty god Śiva reassured the gods not to be afraid, and fitted an arrow (charged with mystic powers) to his bow, and discharged the missile at the (flying) cities.

58. Fiery arrows, like streams of rays emanating from the orb of the Sun, shot forth from that shaft and the cities, being screened by them, became invisible.

59. Struck with those shafts, all the citizens of those cities, fell dead. But the great *Yogī* Maya brought them and put them into a well of nectar (excavated by him in the cities).

60. At the touch of the resuscitating fluid prepared by him (Maya), they sprang to life with adamantine bodily frames endowed with extraordinary vigour, like fires of the lightening tearing open the clouds.

61. Finding god Śiva (the bull-bannered god) frustrated in his undertaking and dejected, this Lord Viṣṇu devised an expendient for it.

62. This Lord Viṣṇu assumed the form of a cow and Brahmā became the calf. Entering the cities at midday, he drank out the nectar from the well of that (immortalizing) fluid.

63-65. Though witnessing it, the Asuras (guarding the well) became too bewildered to prevent it. Knowing that and remembering that it was destined to be so, Maya, the past-master in devising expedients addressed the following (words) to the guards of that well of nectar who were stricken with grief : "No one whether a god, a demon, a man or any other being is capable of thwarting what has been ordained by Fate regarding one's own Self or another or of both."

Then by His own potencies, He (Lord Kṛṣṇa) devised the equipment of battle (war-materials) for god Śiva.

66. By means of His powers like righteousness, wisdom, renunciation, affluence, asceticism, knowledge, action and others, (He created for god Śiva) a chariot, a charioteer, the flag, horses, a bow, an armour, shafts and others.

67-68. Clad in the armour and seated in the chariot, god Śiva took up his bow and arrow. At noon, at the auspicious time, called *Abhijit*, Hara (Śiva) fixed the shaft to the bow and burnt down the three impregnable cities. Kettle-drums were sounded in the sky which was crowded with hundreds of celestial cars.

69. Gods, sages, manes (*pitṛs*) and leaders of Siddhas shouted "Victory" in joyous exclamation, and poured showers of flowers. The troupes of celestial nymphs danced in ecstasy.

70. Having thus burnt down the three (flying) cities, the venerable god Śiva (destroyer of cities) returned to his own residence while being praised by Brahmā and others.

71. Such and others are the exploits of this Hari who with his Māyā Potency imitates the human form (i.e. way of life) that the heroic achievements of the Preceptor (or father) of the world which purify the worlds are sung by sages. What else should I relate next ?

CHAPTER ELEVEN

The Eternal Path of Religion

Śrī Śuka said :

1. Having heard the narrative—so highly praised in the assemblies of the righteous and devotees of the Lord like (god Brahmā and others—of Prahlāda (the ruler of Daityas), the leader of illustrious devotees of the Lord, whose, mind was absorbed in the meditation of God Viṣṇu, Yudhiṣṭhira was filled with delight. He again made a further query of Nārada, the son of the self-created god Brahmā.

Yudhiṣṭhira said :

2. I am anxious to hear from you, Oh Omniscient sage the eternal Law—the righteous course of conduct prescribed for men—enjoining the duties to be performed by persons belonging to different classes of society (*varṇa*) and stages in life (*āśrama*) —the observance of which (*Dharma*) leads one to attain knowledge and devotion.

3. Your worshipful self is the son of no other than the highest deity, Brahmā, the Lord of all created beings. Out of his sons, you have been the most beloved one by virtue of your asceticism, Yogic powers and meditation of the Lord, Oh Brahman ! (You must, therefore, have learnt from him the secret of *dharma*).

4. Merciful, pious, tranquil Brāhmaṇas like you who are devoted exclusively to Nārāyaṇa know the highest secret of Dharma but not others (the so-called Law-givers—*Smṛtikāras*).

Nārada said :

5. Saluting the venerable birthless God Nārāyaṇa, the source of Dharma, I shall explain to you the Eternal Law as I heard it from (His) Nārāyaṇa's lips.

6. He incarnated along with his part-manifestation Nara, as the son of Dharma and Mūrti, the daughter of Dakṣa. He still continues to perform penance for the welfare of the people, at the hermitage at Badarikā.

7. For Lord Hari, the embodiment of all Vedas, is the source of *Dharma*; *Smṛtis* are codified by those who knew him. And it is by abiding by that *Dharma* that one's Soul gets pleased, Oh King.[1]

8-12. (1) Truthfulness, (2) mercy, (3) asceticism, (4) purity, (5) endurance, (6) power of discrimination between right and wrong, (7-8) control of mind and the senses, (9) non-violence, (10) celibacy, (11) charity, (12) the study of Vedas or repetition internally of prayers to god, (13) straight-

1. *Vedo'khilo dharma-mūlaṁ Smṛti-śīle ca tad-vidām /*
ācāras caiva sādhūnām atmanas tuṣṭir eva ca // —Manu-Smṛti
Śrutiḥ smṛtiḥ sadācāraḥ svasya ca priyam ātmanaḥ /
samyak-saṅkalpajaḥ kāmo dharma-mūlam idaṁ smṛtam //
—Yājñavalkaya-smṛti

forwardness, (14) contentment, (15) service unto thou who regard all beings as equals, (16) gradual withdrawal from worldly activities, (17) Observation of the fruitlessness of human actions, (18) refraining from useless talk, (19) investigation of the nature of the Soul (and its distinctness from the body), (20) equitable distribution of food, eatables etc. among creatures according to their worth (and needs), (21) to look upon them, especially human beings as one's own self and as the deity, Oh Pāṇḍu's son (Yudhiṣṭhira); (22) hearing (the holy name or stories of the Lord), (23) chanting of his name, (24) contemplation on, (25) service of, (26) worship of, (27) Bowing to, (28) rendering service to God, (29) behaving as his friend and (30) dedication of oneself to Hari who is the goal of the noble Souls—these thirty characteristics are said to constitute the highest *dharma* of all human beings whereby the Soul of the Universe is propitiated and pleased, Oh King.

13. He is called a *dvija* or twice-born one whose (sixteen) purifying rites (accompanied by recitation of *mantras*) have been performed without any break in succession, and to whom god Brahmā has designated as such. Performance of sacrifices, study of scriptures and charity are prescribed for all twice-born classes (viz. Brāhmaṇa, Kṣattriya and Vaiśya) who are of pure birth and conduct. It is for these that duties incumbent on different stages in life (*āśrama*) are prescribed.

14. Scriptural study and others (such as teaching, performance of sacrifice, charity and acceptance of gifts) six (in all) are prescribed for the Brāhmaṇas. Non-acceptance of gifts is laid down for the other (Kṣattriyas). The means of livelihood of a king who protects his subjects, is derived from taxes levied on subjects, with the exception of Brāhmaṇas (who were exempted from taxation).

15. The Vaiśya is to maintain himself by agriculture (cattle-breeding) and trade, and should follow the Brāhmaṇas. A Śūdra is to render service to the twice-born castes whose means of livelihood constitute his means of subsistence also.

16. Means of livelihood for Brāhmaṇas is of four types: (1) various occupations (e. g. agriculture, cattle breeding), (2) acceptance of articles modestly (without asking any one for anything), (3) begging for grain from door to door like

Yāyāvaras (vagrant mendicants) and (4) gleaning grains of corn from the leftover of the threshing floor in the field (*śila*) or of the market place (*uñcha*)—these types are in the ascending order of preference.

17. With the exception of Kṣattriyas[1], no person born in a lower class should adopt the vocation ordained for the higher class under normal circumstances (lit. when not threatened with serious danger. The Kṣattriyas can adopt Brahmanical means of livelihood, except that of accepting charitable gifts). In times of danger anybody (belonging to any class) may resort to any profession(prescribed for any class).

18. A person may sustain his life by following the vocations or professions (technically) known as *ṛta*, *amṛta*, *mṛta*, *pramṛta* or *satyānṛta*, but should never lead a dog's life (*śvavṛtti*) (even) for preserving one's life.

19-20. The gleaning of corn from the leftovers of field or of the marketplace is called *ṛta*; whatever is given to one unsolicited is known as *amṛta*; *mṛta* is daily begging, and *pramṛta* means cultivation; trading is *satyānṛta* (a mixture of truth and falsehood), while rendering service to the low-born is *śva-vṛtti*. A Brāhmaṇa and a Kṣattriya should always shun that 'dog mode of life' which is detested by all; for a Brāhmaṇa is an embodiment of all the Vedas and Kṣattriya (the ruler) is the personification of all deities.

21. Control over mind and senses, asceticism, purity, contentment, forbearance and forgiveness, straightforwardness, knowledge, compassion, fervent devotion to Lord Viṣṇu and truthfulness are the characteristics of a Brāhmaṇa.

22. Valour, prowess, fortitude, adventurous spirit, liberality, self-control, forgiveness, devotion to Brāhmaṇas, majestic graciousness and defence of the weak, constitute the characteristics of a Kṣattriya.

23. Devotion unto gods, teachers and Lord Viṣṇu, maintenance (and achievement) of three objectives in life (viz. *dharma*, *artha* and *kāma*), faith in *Śāstras*, constant effort (in making money) and skill in transactions, form the characteristics of the Vaiśyas.

1. With the exception of Kṣattriyas, other lower *varṇas* (viz. Vaiśyas and Śūdras) may follow the professions of the higher classes—VJ.

24. Submissiveness, purity, faithful (lit. untreacherous) service of the master, performance of the five daily sacrifices by bowing down only (without uttering the *mantras*) abstention from theiving, truthfulness[1] and protection of the cattle and the Brāhmaṇas—these are the characteristics of the Śūdras.

25. Th duties of women who look upon their husband as a (veritable) god are: rendering service to the husband, compliance to his wishes, friendliness to his relatives and ever-observance of the same vows as those of their husband.

26-27. A pious lady should keep the house clean by sweeping and plastering (with cowdung), and decorating it with auspicious coloured diagrams and pictures on the floor. She should adorn her person with ornaments and clean clothes and always keep the utensils etc. in the house clean and polished. She should, at every time, abide by the desires, great or small, of her husband with modesty, self-control and address him lovingly in true yet pleasant words.

28. Contented (with what she has), not covetous, diligent, knowing what is *dharma* (righteousness), sweet yet true in speech, careful, pious, affectionate—thus she should serve her husband who is not fallen (by committing any of the five major sins, viz. murder of a Brāhmaṇa, drinking liquor, theft, adultery with his preceptor's wife and fellowship with a criminal of above type).

29. A woman who, as goddess Lakṣmī would do unto Lord Hari, serves her husband with a single-minded devotion, regarding him as Lord Viṣṇu, would like Lakṣmī in the company of Lord Viṣṇu, rejoice hereafter in the region of Hari (Vaikuṇṭha) along with her husband who (through her devotion) has attained the resemblance of Hari (in form).

30. The means of livelihood of mixed castes[2] such as the *antyajas* (the low-born ones) *antevāsīyas* (communities living at

1. v.l. *mauḍhya* in VJ. which he explains as the cutting of hair, moustaches, nails etc.

2. ŚR. states that children born of a marriage between a woman of a higher caste and a man from a lower caste are *pratiloma* and are regarded as a low-born *antyaja*. Those castes are as follows: Washermen, Workers in leather, Naṭas (ropedancers), Buruḍas (basket-makers), Kaivartas (fishermen), Medas (followers of degraded positions and Bhillas (Bhils—a mountain tribe).

the farther end of a village such as *cāṇḍāla*, Mātaṅga and Pukkasa) are the hereditary callings followed by their respective families, provided it is not robbery and any sinful vocation[1].

31. In every age the *dharma* (the course of duties) of people is generally determined by their innate nature (according as they are predominantly *sāttvic*, *rājasa* or *tāmasa*). Sages—the Vedic seers—have regarded that (particular) course of *dharma* as conducive to happiness (of persons with such natures) both here and hereafter.

32. One who follows a vocation determined as suitable to his special nature (as determined by his caste) and does his duty, goes on relinquishing that type of work suitable to his disposition) and gradually attains to the state of the attributeless *ātman*.

33. A field which is constantly sown with seeds automatically becomes unfertile. It is unsuitable for sowing seeds again and if seed be sown, it perishes.

34. Similarly the mind, the seat of desires, becomes sated and disgusted by overindulgence in pleasures, but not by drops of enjoyments, like fire with drops of clarified butter.

35. If what has been described as the characteristic of a particular caste or class in the sociey be found in another person belonging to a different community, then the latter should be distinctly designated as coming under the class.

1. *Śreyān sva-dharmo viguṇaḥ paradharmāt svanuṣṭhitāt* /

B.G.325; 18.47

CHAPTER TWELVE

Inquiry into the Right Conduct.

(Duties of Brahmacārins and Vānaprasthas)

Nārada continued :

1. A Brahmacārin should dwell in the house of his preceptor. He should be self-controlled and comply with what is agreeable to the preceptor. He should behave humbly like a servant, and entertain very strong affection to his teacher.

2. In the morning and in the evening, he should wait upon the preceptor and worship the Fire-god, the Sun-god and other prominent deities. Observing perfect silence at both the twilights (and in the mid-day), he should repeat the *Gāyatrī mantra* with concentrated mind (while performing *Sandhyā*).

3. If (and when) called by his preceptor, he should study the Vedas (at his feet) with a perfect concentration and disciplined manner. He should bow down to his (teacher's) feet with his head, both at the beginning and the completion of the lesson.

4. With his hair braided, he should wear a *mekhalā* (a girdle of *muñja* grass), the deer-skin and (two pieces of) cloth, the sacred thread (*yajñopavīta*) and carry with him a staff and a *kamaṇḍalu* (water-pot of gourd) and a handful of *darbha* grass as prescribed (in the *Śāstras*[1]).

5. He should beg alms both in the morning and in the evening, and offer it to his teacher. If permitted, he should partake of the food, if not (as a test or a punishment or as occasionally required on days of observing fast), he should fast.

6. He should be of a good character, moderate in eating, alert and prompt (in work), of reverential faith in *Śāstras* and self-controlled. It is only when absolutely necessary and to that much extent only (e. g. getting alms) that he should deal

1. According to Śāstras, a Brāmaṇa pupil should carry a staff of *Palāśa* tree, a Kṣattriya of a *Bilva* tree and a Vaiśya of the *Audumbara* (Indian fig) tree.

with women or with those who are influenced (lit. enslaved) by women.

7. A person other than a householder, who has taken the great vow of celibacy, should avoid all talk with young women. For the senses are (by nature) so powerful and violent that they carry away the mind of even a recluse (*Yati* who is expected to be perfectly self-controlled).

8. A youthful Brahmacārin (student) should not allow a personal service, e. g. combing his hair, massaging, bathing and anointing his person, done by women from his teacher's family, especially if they are young.

9. For verily a young woman is (like) a fire and a man like pot containing clarified butter. One should avoid (the company of) one's daughter in a secluded place, and at other times he should remain with her so long as the work or duty demands it (even in public places).

10* So long as by self-realization one has not firmly determined that his body, senses or the universe etc. are illusory

*VR (I): (So long as Īśvara keeps this body (which is the illusion of the Soul) capable of doing work, the notion of duality (viz. one is a god or a man or a Brāhmaṇa) is found to persist and leads to illusions, he should not give up the duties laid down in *Sāstras*.

Or

(II) Even though one realizes that his Self is distinct from his body, he, so long as he persists to live in his body, should not give up the duties prescribed for him in the *Sāstras* so long as he is able to discharge them.

VJ. states that the world is real and so long as God keeps the *jīva* in a worldly knowledge which is unreal and not true, the perverse notions shall persist and bondage of the world due to ignorance shall continue.

VC.: What danger is there to self-controlled man who has abandoned the company of relatives? (The reply:) Even though one has renounced worldly objects, so long as one has not completely wiped out one's affinity to them from the mind, the notion of duality shall not cease to persist.

GD.: Even though a man is an *aṁśa* (a part) of the blissful Lord, he experiences the contrarity viz. miseries of hell etc.

BP.: So long as the notion of duality persists one should not give up the duties laid down in the *Śāstras*.

and the *jīva* has not attained perfect mastery over himself by identifying himself with the Supreme Lord, the notion of duality (between a man and woman) will continue to persist (provoking thereby the desire to enjoy) through false attribution of *guṇas*.

11. All these (instructions contained from verses 6 to 10) are laid down for the householder, and much more so, even in the case of Saṁnyāsin (a recluse). A householder who is expected to be with his wife at particular period of time, may optionally stay with his preceptor.

12. Those who have taken the vow of Brahmcharya (celibacy) should avoid the use of collyrium, unguents, massage of the body, dealings with women, painting or viewing pictures of women, meat, spirituous liquor (in the case of those who are permitted to drink, honey in the case of Brāhmaṇas), garlands. sandal pigment and ornaments.

13. In this way, having stayed in the preceptor's house, a *dvija* (a twice-born-Ārya) should study and understand to the best of his ability and to the extent of his requirements, the meaning of three Vedas (Ṛk, Sāman and Yajus), along with their (six) auxiliaries[1] and the *Upaniṣads* (Vedānta, philosophical treatises).

14. Having presented, if at all he can afford to do so, with what is desired by his preceptor (as "fee for the course") and having obtained his permission, he (the student) should enter the householder's life, or retire to the forest (for performing penance etc.), or renounce the world to wander as a *Yati* (recluse), or stay with his preceptor (as a lifelong Brahmacārin).

15. He should look upon (conceive) Lord Viṣṇu as if having entered into the fire, the preceptor, himself and the elements (e. g. the earth, the fire) together with all creatures sheltered in Him; for He is their Inner Controller, even though

1. These are intended as aids for the correct pronunciation, and interpretation of the Vedic texts and the correct applications of the *Mantras* in the religious rites. The *aṅgas* are six in number, viz. 1. *Śikṣā*—'Phonetics, the science of proper articulation and pronunciation. 2. *Kalpa* (application) ritual or ceremonial, 3. *Vyākaraṇa* 'Grammar' 4. *Nirukta* 'Etymological explanation of difficult Vedic words'. 5. *Chandas*—'Science of prosody', 6. *Jyotiṣa*—astronomy.

the Lord (having already pervaded these from within and without) does not actually enter.

16. A person belonging to the order of Brahmacharya, Vānaprastha (an anchorite), a saṁnyāsin (a recluse) or a householder who contemplates thus (the omnipresence of the Lord), and follows the course of duties ordained for his particular *āśrama* (stage of life), realizes what is required to be known, and attains to the Supreme Brahman.

17. I shall now explain to you the code of conduct approved by the sages and prescribed for Vānaprasthas (anchorites), by observing which, a sage easily attains Maharloka, the heaven of sages.

18. An anchorite should not eat the product of cultivation (e.g. rice, wheat) or anything (like fruits, roots etc.), which though not a product of tillage, ripened before time. He should not partake of food cooked on fire. He should subsist on what is ripe or cooked by rays of the Sun.

19. He should prepare *caru*[1] and *puroḍāśa*[2] of corn wild growth (Nīvāra) and of a permanent nature. When he procures new and fresh eatables, he should reject the old ones (stored by him).

20. It is just for the preservation of the (sacred) fire that he should take shelter in a house or cottage or a cave in mountains. He himself should bear exposure to snow, wind, fire, rain and heat of the Sun.

21-22. The anchorite with matted hair (on the head) should wear (without shaving) the hair on his body, moustaches, beard and nails and dirt (not properly washed). He should take with him *kamaṇḍalu* (a pot of water), deer-skin, staff, bark-garments and utensils of fire worship. The sage should thus wander in the forest for twelve, eight, four, two or one year, i. e. to that length of time which the mind does not get perverted through the (severity of) austerities.

1. *caru*—An oblation of rice, barley and pulse boiled for presentation to the gods and the manis. *ASD*. p. 204.

2. *puroḍāśa*—Boiled rice rounded into a cake and usually divided into parts which are kept in separate receptacles for offering to different deities.

23. If (after the period of stay in the forest) he finds that, owing to ill health (diseases) or old age, he is incapable of pursuing his courses of duties (as a Vānaprastha) or prosecuting his studies in philosophy, he should adopt the vow of fasting etc. (If he is capable, he should become a *saṁnyāsin*—a recluse).

24. (Before beginning the fast) he should withdraw and deposit the sacred fires (e. g. *āhavanīya* and others) within his Self. He should renounce the notions of 'I' and 'Mine', and should merge the constituents of his body in their own causes (viz. the sky, the air and other three elements).

25. A self-controlled man should merge the cavities in his body (e. g. eyes, ears, nostrils) into the sky (the element-the *mahābhūta* called *ākāśa*), his exhalations (vital-breaths) into the air, the temperature of his body into the fire, (fluids like) blood, phlegm and pus into the water and the rest (hard substances like bones, muscles etc.) into the earth--thus assigning them each to its respective origin. (Thus he should merge his gross body).

26. He should consign his speech along with the organ of speech to the Fire, even his hands and handicraft to Indra, his feet along with (the power of) locomotion to Viṣṇu, the organ of pleasure (along with the power of procreation) to Prajāpati (deity presiding over procreation).

27. (He should merge) the organ of defecation and act of excretion in Mṛtyu (the god of death) directing these organs to their proper places (viz. the deities presiding over those particular organs); his auditory sense along with (its object), sound into (deities presiding over) cardinal points; and his tactual organ along with its tactility to the *ātman* or wind-god).

28. Oh King, he should deposit his eyes (eye-sight) and the colours and forms (the objects of the eye) with the Sun-god, the tongue or its objects of taste such as sweet, bitter etc. in water (or god Varuṇa), and the olifactory sense along with its objects i. e. various smells, with the Earth.

29. He should merge his mind along with its desires and objects in the Moon-god, the intelligence and the objects to be grasped by it in the highest god Brahmā. He should

consign actions with self-consciousness to god Rudra through whose instrumentality the activities actuated by the notions of 'I-ness' and 'Mine-ness' proceed. He should merge his chitta (reason, heart) along with *Sattva* in *Kṣetrajña* (Hiraṇyagarbha) and *Vaikārika ahaṁkāra* along with *guṇas* in the Supreme Brahman).

30. He should then dissolve the earth into water, absorb water into fire, fire into the air and the air into the ether. The ether or *Ākāśa* is to be merged into the principle called ego (*aham*), and that into *Mahat* (the principle of cosmic Intelligence), and that into the unmanifested *Prakṛti* and that unmanifest *Pradhāna* into *Paramātman* (the Supreme Soul).

31. Having thus realized the Soul as identical with Paramātman, and nothing but indestructible consciousness and becoming free from the notion of duality[1], he should cease to function like fire that has consumed its own source (fuel).

CHAPTER THIRTEEN

The Code of Conduct for Saṁnyāsins
and a dialogue between Avadhūta and Prahlāda

Nārada continued :

1. If a person is thus capable and fit (physically and mentally), he should take to the life of a vagrant recluse. Owning nothing else except his body, he should observe the rule of staying one night in a village, and thus wander over the earth, being totally desireless.

2. If at all he is to wear a piece of cloth, it should be a strip of cloth just sufficient to cover his private parts. Uuless there is some serious danger, he should not take anything which has been renounced except the staff and other emblems (e. g.kamaṇḍalu-water-pot) characteristic of a *saṁnyāsin*.

1. *advaya*—with the faith that there is no independent absolute thing other than Hari.

3. Delighted in his own Self and seeking no shelter, he should wander all alone as a mendicant subsisting on alms. He should be friendly to all beings, serene and devoted exclusively to Nārāyaṇa.

4* He should visualize this universe in the immutable *ātman* (Self) who is beyond (and distinct from) cause and effect and should perceive the Self as the Supreme Brahman present everywhere in the universe, (a product) of causes and consequences.

5. During the mediate state between sleep and wakefulness, one should concentrate on the soul within, and should try to perceive the true nature of the Self. He should look upon bondage and emancipation as merely illusory and not real.

6. He should welcome neither death, which is inevitable, nor life that is transitory. But he should simply wait for the Time which brings about the birth and death of beings (and that of one's body as well.

7. He should not be attached to *Śāstras* dealing with topics other than *ātman*. Nor should he try to maintain himself by following any profession (like astrology, medicine practised by him as a *gṛhastha*). He should avoid all form of disputation. He should not persistently adhere to any party.

8. He should not attract students. Nor should he study numerous books[1] (lest they should cause confusion or distraction). He should not undertake the exposition of some sacred text[2]. Nor should he take up the establishment of any institution or monastery.

9. The duties etc. prescribed for the order of recluses (*saṁnyāsins*) are not meant for securing religious merit in the case of the noble-souled ones (*Paramahaṁsas*) who are of serene and equable minds (The rules are to be observed till the recluse realizes the highest wisdom). Thereafter he may

* VR. asserts the Viśiṣṭādvaita position: *Paramātman* is distinct from the Sentient (*Cid*) and the Non-Sentient (*Acid*). By nature he is free from modifications. He (the recluse) should look upon the universe as the inseparable body of Paramātman Who is the Inner Controller.

1. Books not dealing with Vedānta.
2. Texts other than those on Vedānta—VD.

continue to practise the rules (for setting up an ideal life before the public) or discard them.

10. One whose external signs of being a recluse are not evident but continues his purpose (i. e. concentration with the Self), may, though learned, show himself (i. e. behave externally like) a mad person or an ignorant child; though highly intelligent and wise, he should appear to be dumb in the eyes of the public.

11. On this point an old historical (-cum-legendary) account has been traditionally handed down as an illustration. It is the conversation between Prahlāda and a sage Dattātreya[1] observing the *Ajagara*[2] mode of life.

12-13. While Prahlāda, the beloved (devotee) of the Lord, accompanied by a few ministers, was touring through various worlds with a view to acquaint himself with the true nature of the people, he happened to see on the top of the Sahyādri (Western *ghats*) on the bank of the Kāverī, some person lying on bare ground, his pure effulgence being concealed under a coat of dust covering all the part of his body.

14. By his actions, appearances, words of external emblems indicative of his caste (*varṇa*) and stage in life (*āśrama*), people could not recognize him who or what he was and what he was not.

15. Having bowed the sage by touching his feet with his head and having worshipped him with due formalities, the Asura, (himself) a prominent votary of the Lord, who was curious to know (the truth about) him, (the sage) asked him the following question.

16. "You have a robust body like an industrious person who enjoys a luxurious life. Wealth accrues to persons

1. Vide Supra 1.3.11. The Lord incarnated as Datta, the son of Atri and Anasūyā, and taught spiritual lore to king Alarka and Prahlāda.

2. *Ajagara* is a python which is supposed to swallow what comes its way, without making any move on its part. As described in the illustration of Dattātreya below, a person who has adopted the vow of leading Python's way of life, has just to lie on the bare ground under the sky waiting for his death without making any movement—throwing his body at the mercy of the fate. His object is to enjoy all the fruits of his *karmas* then and there before falling away of his body.

who are industrious and comforts and luxuries can be afforded by moneyed people. Indeed only the bodies of those who are given to luxurious life become corpulent and not otherwise.

17. Lying supine without doing any work as you do, Oh Brahman, you obviously possess no wealth which is the source of enjoyment (of a luxurious life). If you think proper (to disclose), please tell us how your body is corpulent despite your non-indulgence in luxuries and lack of comforts.

18. Learned, capable, clever, possessing wonderfully sweet power of speech and of equable temper as you are, how is it that you lie down (doing nothing) simply looking on that other people are exerting themselves."

Nārada said :

19. Being thus questioned by Prahlāda, the king of Daityas, the great sage, being magnetized by his nectarlike speech, smilingly spoke to him.

The Brāhmaṇa said :

20. Oh foremost of Asuras ! Your honour is esteemed by all great and learned people. By your spiritual insight you certainly know this, viz. the consequences of activity for (obtaining) worldly objects and of renouncing them.

21. Due to your absolute and pure devotion, the glorious Lord Nārāyaṇa always abides in your heart. He dispels your ignorance like unto the Sun dispersing darkness.

22. We (I) however, shall (try to) answer your questions according to what I have traditionally learnt (about them). For you deserve respect from those who desire to purify their hearts.

23. Being (induced) to do various actions by powerful desire which is never satiated by enjoyment of suitable objects, and thus becomes the source of the stream of births (and deaths), I was forced to take birth in various species.

24. While wandering (through various types of existence) by force of *karmas*, and through sheer providence, I was brought to the human form of existence which is a gate-way to heaven or final emancipation or to sub-human life or to human life again.

25. Having observed the frustrations and failures of married couples while performing actions for securing happiness and avoiding pain in this life as well, I retired from worldly-activities.

26. Happiness is the essential nature of the Soul[1]. It is manifested after withdrawal and cessation of all activities. Having perceived that enjoyments and experiences are fanciful creations of the mind I lie down (supine enjoying whatever is ordained for me by destiny).

27. Having forgotten that this blissful nature is inherent in one's self, a man is verily enmeshed into *saṁsāra* which is terrible (owing to birth, death and other miseries) and strange (as it consists of birth in celestial, subhuman, human and other-species).

28. He who (being ignorant of his innate blissful state) thinks of finding his object (happiness) elsewhere (outside his Self), is like an ignorant fellow who with a desire to get water (to quench his thirst) leaves water (near him but) covered with acquatic weeds and other overgrowth and runs after the mirage.

29. The body and sense-organs are controlled by Destiny. All the actions and efforts repeatedly done through their instrumentality for securing his happiness and removing his miseries by a luckless person, become fruitlesss.

30. (Granting that a man's efforts are successful) what pleasure can be derived from the hard-earned wealth and desired objects obtained with great difficulty to a mortal (obsessed with the fear of death) and plagued by (lit. not immune from) three types of miseries such as bodily ailments and others.

31. I perceive the agonies and tensions of wealthy covetous persons who have no control over themselves, and who have lost their sleep, out of fear, as they are suspicious of everybody on all sides.

32. I observe that those who are anxious about their life and wealth, entertain fear from kings, robbers, enemies, their

1. VJ. thinks that the grace of the Lord is necessary for the realization of His bliss.

kinsmen, birds and beasts, beggers, Time and themselves, at every moment.

33. (Therefore) a wise man should give up longings for life and property which are the source of sorrow, infatuation, fear, anger, attachment, despondency, over-exertions and such other (troubles).

34. In this world the bee and the big python are our best teachers, for following their example we have attained renunciation and contentment.

35. I have learnt renunciation of all worldly objects from the bee, the gatherer of honey, for any other person may kill the lord and usurp the hard-earned money like honey after killing the bees.

36. Being free from all desires and with contented mind, I accept what is brought to me by providence. If not, I lie inactive like a big serpent for many days, depending on my power.

37. Sometimes I eat scant food; sometimes I enjoy a heavy meal irrespective of the sweetness or otherwise of the food. Sometime I partake of highly rich and dainty dishes and sometimes worthless food.

38. At some places I eat food, that is offered to me with respect and sometimes with irreverence. Sometimes I do justice to food after eating; sometimes I eat food by day or by night as it is offered to me by chance.

39. Remaining contented in mind, I enjoy what is ordained by fate, and I wear linen garments or silks or deer-skin or rags or any other (fabric) that is offered to me.

40. Sometimes I sleep on the bare ground; sometimes on grass or on a heap of leaves or on a slab of stone or in ashes; sometimes I lie inside a mansion on a rich bed over a precious bedstead as desired by God (or other people).

41. Sometimes I take bath with my body anointed with fragrant pigments. I put on rich garments and wear garlands and ornaments. Sometimes I ride in a chariot or on an elephant or on a horse and sometimes I wander stark-naked like an evil spirit, Oh king.

42. I neither revile nor praise people who are of diverse

nature. I pray for their welfare and bless them with their union with the Almighty Lord Viṣṇu.

43. One should oblate (merge) one's notion of diversity in the mental faculty that perceives such differences, that mental faculty into mind which mistakes the unreal for the real, the mind into the *sāttvic ahaṁkāra* and should absorb that *ahaṁkāra* through *mahat* in the Māyā regularly.

44. The sage who perceives the Reality, should merge that Māyā into the realization of his soul. Being devoid of all desires, he should establish himself in self-realization and cease all activities.

45. In this way I have described to you my way of life which is closely guarded as a secret, though it is far different from secular and Śāstric canons of behaviour. (I have thus frankly explained this to you) as you are the beloved of God.

Nārada said :

46. Having heard the code of conduct of the highest order of recluses, the Lord of Asuras (Prahlāda) worshipped him respectfully. Being pleased in mind he bade good-bye, and returned home.

CHAPTER FOURTEEN

(The Duties of a householder)

Yudhiṣṭhira said :

1. Oh celestial sage, please explain to me that course of conduct by which a householder like me whose mind is clouded with attachment to house and property, will attain to the above state of emancipation (*mokṣa*) without difficulty.

Nārada said :

1-A (VRs' text adds) : Even though you know it, you have asked this question for the good of the world, Oh king.

I shall explain to you how the duties of a householder lead one to the state of actionlessness (or attainment of *Jñāna-yoga*.

2. Staying in the household and performing duties (such as *sandhyā*, worship and five *mahā-yajñas*) laid down for a householder as direct offering to Lord Vāsudeva (without expecting any return for it), one should wait upon great sages in order to learn truth.

3. Devoutly listening to the nectar-like sweet stories of the incarnations of Viṣṇu during the leisure time after performance of duties he should constantly be associated with (lit. surrounded by) persons who are tranquil by nature.

4. Through companionship with saintly people, he should gradually release himself from attachment to himself, his wife, his sons etc. which are in the process of being separated from him, and should rise above them like a person awakened from a dream (does in the case of objects seen in the dream).

5. A wise man should be disinterested in and dispassionate to his body and house, but should attend to it to the extent to which it is indispensable. Simulating attachment to them, a man should transcend his status as an ordinary human being and be a recluse. *Or* (carry out his duties in life).

6. Being free from attachment to himself and his property, he should acquiesce in what his kinsmen, parents, sons, brothers and other well-wishers propose and desire.

7. A wise man should carry out his duties while enjoying what he gets from the heaven (e. g. crops due to rain fall), from mines (e. g. gold, precious stones etc.) and what he gets accidentally by wind fall, as all wealth is created by god Viṣṇu (and is obtained through his grace).

8. Embodied beings can lay claim to that much wealth as is just necessary for filling his belly. He who lays claims on the surplus is a thief and deserves punishment.

9. One should look upon beasts, camels, donkeys, monkeys, rats, serpents, birds and flies like one's own sons (and hence these should not be driven out of the house or fields if they enter and begin to eat), for there is very little difference between them and his sons.

10. Even though a man be a householder, he should not put in extraordinary trouble for getting the three *puruṣārthas*. He should enjoy what is afforded to him by providence according to its place and time.

11. He should duly share his objects of enjoyment with all down to dogs, sinners and people belonging to the lowest strata of the society (lit. who dwell at the end of a village). He should allow his wife whom he ardently claims as his own, to receive guests (unmindful of his inconvenience. ŚR warns that this should not be misconstrued).

12. He who can forego his claim on his wife for whose sake he should lay down his life or would kill his father or preceptor (if he suspects them about their contacts with her) has conquered (secured the grace of) the unconquerable Lord Viṣṇu.

13. How despicable is the body that is convertible into worms (if buried), excretion (if eaten up by carnivorous animals) or ashes (if cremated) ! Equally despicable is (the body of) a wife which contributes to its erotic pleasures ! How great is the Soul which pervades the whole of the sky !

14. A wise person should maintain his livelihood by food, after offering oblations to the deities in five *mahā-yajñas* and should relinquish the notion of his claim of what remains as surplus. Thus he would attain to the position of *paramahaṁsas*.

15. A man should worship the *antaryāmin* (the Inner Controller) daily by sharing what he has obtained in his own vocation, with gods, sages, human beings, other living beings, *pitṛs* and his own self.

16. If he possesses all the required materials as well as the requisite qualifications for performing sacrifices, he should worship the Lord according to the procedure laid down in the Śrauta and Kalpa Sūtras.

17. But verily, this Venerable Lord, the Enjoyer of Sacrifice is not propitiated to that extent by oblation offered through the (sacrificial) fire as through (morsels of food offered to Him) through the mouths of Brāhmaṇas, Oh King.

18. One should, therefore, worship this Inner Controller (God) through the Brāhmaṇas, gods presiding over five *Mahā-yajñas* as also through mortals like human beings and

other creatures, by offering them objects of enjoyment, according to their respective order, after (feeding) the Brāhmaṇas.

19. If sufficiently rich, a twice-born person (Brāhmaṇa, Kṣattriya and Vaiśya) should perform according to his means, the *Śrāddha*, i. e. *Mahālaya* in honour of his (departed) parents as well as their kinsmen and others, in the dark half of Bhādrapada.

20-23. He should (also) perform their *Śrāddha* at the time of the summer and winter solstices (*ayanas*), and the vernal and autumnal equinoxes (*viṣuva*), during the division of time called Vyatipāta; on the day when a *tithi* i.e. the lunar day begins and ends between two sun-rises (technically known as *dinakṣaya*); during the lunar and solar eclipses; on the twelfth lunar day, and when the constellations known as Śravaṇa, Dhaniṣṭhā and Śata-tārakā are on the ascendance; on the third day in the bright half of Vaiśākha (i. e. on *Akṣaya tṛtiyā*); on the ninth lunar day in the bright half of Kārttika (known as *Akṣaya-navamī*); on the four *Aṣṭakas* (eighth lunar day in the dark halves) during the seasons called *Hemanta* and *Śiśira* (i.e. on the eighth day in the dark half of the months of Mārgaśīrṣa, Pauṣa, Māgha and Phālguna); on the seventh day in the bright half of the month of Māgha; on the fullmoon day when the constellation Maghā is ascendant (which is in the month of Māgha) on days when the constellations associated with the names of other (lunar) months are ascendant on a full moon day, or even when the moon rises one digit less than the full on that day; on any twelfth lunar day when the constellations Anurādhā, Śravaṇa and the three constellations beginning with the word Uttarā (viz. Uttarāṣāḍhā, Uttarā Bhādrapadā and Uttarā Phālgunī) are ascendant; or when the eleventh lunar day (of any month) is associated with (any of) these three constellations; (and lastly) on any day when the constellation under which a person was born or the constellation called Śravaṇa is ascendant.

24. These are very auspicious times which are conducive to the attainment of prosperity to men on these days. On these days a person should, by every means, try to perform pious acts to the best of his abilities. Thus his merits become most effectual and contribute to his longevity.

25. On these days, performance of ablutions, muttering prayer or *mantra* (*Japa*), oblations to fire, observance of a sacred vow, worship of gods and Brāhmaṇas and gifts donated in the names of manes, gods, men and creatures bear everlasting fruit.

26. Oh King, *Śrāddhas* should be performed when it is the time of the purificatory rites observed in the behalf of himself, his wife or children; as well as at the time of the cremation of a dead body or on the death anniversary of a person; and at the time of any other function like marriage.

27. Now I shall narrate to you the (holy) places which enhance religious merits and other good. That is the most sacred place where a worthy and virtuous recipient is found.

28. For he (such worthy recipient) is the very image of the Almighty Lord in whom abides the whole creation—mobile and immobile. That is the hallowed spot where Brāhmaṇas characterised by penance, knowledge and kindness dwell.

29. All the places where the image of Hari or Śāligrāma is found (or wherever the worship of Lord Hari is being done) that place is the abode of blessings; and the regions through which rivers like the Gaṅgā and others celebrated in Purāṇas flow.

30. And lakes like Puṣkara and others are situated; and places inhabited by venerable sages and spots known as Kurukṣetra, Gayā, Prayāga (the confluence of the Gaṅgā and the Yamunā) the hermitage of Pulaha known as Śālagrāma Kṣetra.

31. Forest like Naimiṣa (modern Nimsar) Kanyātīrtha (Cape Comerin), the holy bridge built by Rāma at Rāmeśvara, Prabhāsa, and Dvārakā, Vārāṇasī, Mathurā, the lake Pampā and Bindusara where stood the hermitage of Kardama the father of Kapila.

32. The Hermitage of Nārāyaṇa (Badarikāśrama), the Alakanandā, Citrakūṭa where stood the hermitage of Rāma and Sītā and such other places; all principal mountain ranges such as Mahendra (Eastern Ghāṭs), Malaya (Western Ghāṭs) and others, Oh King.

33. Those are the sacred-most spots where the idols of Hari are installed. He who is desirous of blessings, should constantly sojourn at these places. Righteous duties per-

formed here yield fruits thousand times more than what accrues at other places.

34. The foremost judges of worthy recipients and wise people have decided that in this world Hari and Lord Hari alone is the only worthy recipient. Oh Lord of the earth, everything mobile and immobile is constituted of him.

35. Accordingly, Oh King, even though gods, sages, worthy persons, such as the sons of god Brahmā and others were present at your Rājasūya sacrifice, Lord Kṛṣṇa was conclusively selected as deserving the first place in the adoration at the sacrifice, owing to his worthiness.

36. The great tree in the form of the universe (Brahmāṇḍa) is crowded with multitudes of *jīvas* and is very extensive, but Acyuta, being the root of that tree, Hari's worship brings gratification to all the *jīvas* and to one's own soul.

37. The dwellings (bodies) in the form of those of men, sub-human beings, sages and gods have been created by him. He dwells in these bodies in the form of *jīva* and hence he is called Puruṣa (the Dweller of habitations or Inner Controller).

38. In these bodies, the Lord is present (i. e. manifests himself) in different degrees (of intelligence, wisdom etc.). Hence, even though every man is a worthy recipient, he is proportionately so according to the manifestation of the Soul (i. e. spiritual wisdom, penance etc.) in him.

39. Oh King, wise sages took into account the mutual hatred, disregard among men in the Tretā and other ages, and have therefore instituted Hari's idols for worship, and other religious duties.

40. Some persons with perfect devotion in the worship of Hari propitiate him thereby, but to some the worship of Hari, even though performed, is not fruitful as they hate the Lord in the form of his creation.

41. Oh Lord of Kings, even amongst men Brāhmaṇa is regarded as the really worthy recipient as he bears in him the body of Hari, viz. the Vedas, along with the virtues of penance, learning and contentment.

42. Oh King, the Brāhmaṇas who purify the three worlds by the dust of their feet form really the Supreme Deity of Lord Kṛṣṇa who is the Soul of the universe.

CHAPTER FIFTEEN

Exposition of right Conduct (Concluded).

Nārada said :

1. Some Brāhmaṇas (*gṛhasthas*) are devoted to rituals prescribed for their particular *āshrama*, some (*vānaprasthas*), are bent on performing austere penance, others (*brahmacārins*) to the study of the Vedas, some to the teaching and exposition of the Vedas, while some to spiritual enlightenment, (as in the case of *saṁnyāsins*) and some to perfection in *Yoga*.

2. A person desirous of attaining eternally lasting merit should offer the gifts of food etc. intended for manes—(*pitṛs*) and those meant for gods, to persons who are solely devoted to spiritual knowledge, and in their absence to others according to their merits.

3. One should feed two Brāhmaṇas in rites connected with gods, three for ceremonies (*Śrāddha*) intended for (*pitṛs*) or may feed one only in each. Even though a person is very affluent, he should not invite a large number.

4. If invitations are given on a large scale, and food etc. is distributed among relatives, conditions regarding proper place, time, piety, devotion, proper materials, worthy recipients etc. are not properly observed.

5. When proper time and place offers itself, food proper for sages and offered to god Hari, if given with proper formalities and devotion to a worthy person, yields desired objects and everlasting fruit.

6. While distributing food to gods, sages, *pitṛs*, beings and one's relatives, one should look upon these all as identical with the Supreme Person.

7. A person who knows the essence of *dharma* should not give (serve) flesh (non-vegetarian food), nor should eat it at the time of *Śrāddha*, for there is no real gratification in slaughter of animals (flesh); for there is supreme satisfaction with the type of food proper for sages.

8. For those persons who desire to follow the right course of conduct, there is no supreme *dharma* other than

abstinence from violence to living beings caused by thought, word and deed.

9. Some persons who are well-versed in sacrificial lore and who have spiritual wisdom, become desireless and offer the ritualistic sacrifices requiring external actions, into the fire of self-control kindled by spiritual knowledge.

10. Living beings become apprehensive on seeing a person who performs sacrifices with gross materials. (They say) "This cruel man, not grasping the spirit of the rules prescribed for *Yajñas*, and thirsting after my life, will surely kill me".

11. Therefore, a person knowing the real path of righteousness should be satisfied with the hermit's fare providentially obtained by him, and should every day carry on the prescribed daily and occasional duties.

12. A man versed in righteousness should steer clear of the five forms (branches) of *adharma* (impiety), viz. *vidharma*, *paradharma*, *ābhāsa*, *upamā*, *chala*, regarding them all as *adharma* (impiety).

13. *Vidharma* is that which, though practised as a *dharma*, obstructs real *dharma* (e.g. black-magic of the *tantras*). *Para dharma* is the course of conduct ordained for another (varṇa or *āśrama* (e.g. Fighting in the case of Brāhmaṇas). *Upadharma* is the heresy opposing the Vedas (e.g. path or duties prescribed in *āgama*) or hypocrisy, while *chala* is the distortion of the text showing apparent conformity to the letter of the scriptures or quibbling.

14. The course of conduct different from the duties (prescribed by Vedas for different *varṇas*—classes in society—and *āśramas*—stages in life) but adopted according to one's fancy (e.g. the *avadhūta* mode of life is (*dharma-*) *ābhāsa*. Who would regard *dharma* which is agreeable to his innate disposition, as not conducive to his (inner) peace and prosperity !

15. An indigent person should not try to earn money either for the sake of charitable donations etc. or for the maintenance of his life. Effortless state of one who ceases from activities becomes his means of subsistence, as in the case of the (proverbial) Python.

16. How can the happiness enjoyed by a self-contented person cherishing no desires and delighted in his own self, be obtained by a person who, actuated by passion and covetousness, runs in all directions in quest of wealth.

17. All directions are full of happiness to a man who is ever contented in his mind, just as the feet protected by shoes have complete safety against gravels, thorns and others.

18. With what will not a self-contented man pull on—say even with water ? Due to beggarly yearnings for the pleasures of the sex and tongue, a man behaves like a dog.

19. The spiritual power, learning, (power accrued from) penance, and glory of a discontented Brāhmaṇa leak away (and are exhausted) and his spiritual knowledge is also dissipitated.

20. A person may cease to feel the sexual urge due to intensity of hunger and thirst (as these are much more powerful), he may see the end of anger when its fruit (revenge) is achieved. But he never sees the end of avarice even after conquering all the quarters and enjoying the sovereignty of the world.

21. There are a number of learned scholars of extensive knowledge, capable of dispelling the doubts of others and leaders of assemblies who have fallen down (into deep hell) through discontent.

22. One should overcome passion by foregoing the desire of love for it, anger by eschewing desire; greed, by looking upon wealth and worldly things as evil; and fear, by the perception of the truth (about the objects of fear).

23. (He should conquer) grief and delusion by realizing the distinction between the Self (*ātman*) and the non-self (*anātman*); hypocrisy, by association with the great; interruption to *Yoga* (mental concentration) by observing silence; and violence to other beings, by bodily inactivity (to secure merit, wealth etc.).

24. He should overcome troubles given by other beings by cherishing compassion (even towards the trouble-makers); and those caused by destiny or gods by equipoise and concentration of the mind; the ailments of the body by the force of

Yoga (*prāṇāyāma* and other *Yogic* expedients); and sleep by recourse to *sāttvic* food.

25. He should vanquish *rajas* and *tamas* by *sattva*, and *sattva* by complete withdrawal of attachment (and activity for it). A man can easily overpower all these above-mentioned through intense devotion to the spiritual preceptor.

26. The spiritual guide is verily the Venerable Lord Himself who imparts to a man the light of knowledge. But the spiritual knowledge or learning of a person who entertains the perverted notion that his preceptor is an ordinary mortal, is as useless as the bath of an elephant (which besmears itself with dust immediately after the bath).

27. For the spiritual preceptor whom people regard as merely a human being, is directly the Almighty God, the Supreme Ruler both of *Prakṛti* and *Puruṣa* (matter and the individual Soul) and His feet are sought after by masters of *Yoga*.

28. All the precepts ordained (for performance of sacrifices etc.) are intended for one purpose, viz. restraint of six passions (e.g, desire, anger and others or alternatively five senses and the mind). If they do not lead to the accomplishment of *Yoga* (viz. *dhyāna*, *dhāraṇā* and *samādhi*) all the above is a source of sheer (fruitless) labour.

29. Just as the rewards and procurements of agriculture and other pursuits do not bear the fruits of *Yoga* (viz. Final Emancipation from *saṁsāra*), the performance of sacrifices and undertakings for public welfare (e. g. construction of tanks etc.) will lead to evil results in case of a person whose mind is attached to external objects (of worldly nature).

30. He who has resolved to subjugate his mind should dissociate himself from all attachments and belongings; he should become a recluse and live alone in secluded place, eating moderately what he gets as alms.

31. One should arrange his seat in a clean hallowed level place and seat himself in an erect, stable, comfortable posture, repeating silently the sacred syllable Om, Oh King.

32. With his gaze fixed on the tip of his nose one should control one's breath (*prāṇa* and *apāna*—inhalation and exhalation) by inhailing, suspending and exhaling his breath till his mind gives up desires.

33. A wise man should retrieve his ever-roving mind smitten with desires from whatever external object it goes and confine it into his heart.*

34. A recluse who strives to exercise such control day and night, finds in a short period that his mind attains quiescence like fire for lack of fuel.

35. When the mind, not agitated by desires and passions, and with its activities calmed down, is touched by the ecstasy of the realization of the Brahman, it never responds to external objects in *saṁsāra*.

36. If a recluse who has formerly renounced his house which is a nursery of *dharma*, *artha* and *kāma* (three objects of human life) again takes to the householder's life and enjoys them, the shameless fellow (is like a man who) is swallowing up his vomited food.

37. If those who have regarded their own body as distinct from Soul, mortal and reducible to excrement (if the body is eaten up by a carnivorous animal), worms (if interred in a grave), and ashes (if cremated on a pyre), highly extol it as if it is the *Ātman*, such persons are the vilest ones.

38-39. Avoidance of religious rites and duties in the case of *gṛhastha*, non-observance (of the vow of celibacy, studies etc.) in the case of a *brahmacārin*, residence in an inhabited locality in the case of ascetics performing penance, and lack of self-control in the case of recluses (*saṁnyāsins*)—all these are the accursed banes of their respective *āśramas* as these certainly reduce their *āśramas* to mockery. Out of compassion, one should neglect these fellows who are deluded by the illusive power (Māyā) of the Almighty God.

*

(1) *Śucau deśe pratiṣṭhāpya sthiram āsanam ātmanaḥ /*
nātyucchritaṁ nātinīcaṁ cailājinakuśottaram //

B.G. 6.11

(2) *Samaṁ kāya-śiro-grīvaṁ dhārayannacalaṁ śiraḥ /*
samprekṣya nāsikāgraṁ svaṁ diśścānavalokayan //

B.G. 6.13

(3) *Yato yato niścarati manaś cañcalam asthiram /*
tas tato niyamyaitad ātmanyeva vaśaṁ nayet //

B.G. 6.26

40. If a person realizes his Self as Supreme Brahman, all the traces of attachment are shaken off from his mind by that spiritual knowledge. (It is not known) with what ulterior motive or for whom does this addict to worldly pleasures nourishes his body.

41. The wise say that this body is a chariot, the senses are the horses, mind, the controller of senses[1], is the reins, the objects of senses are the paths, intellect (reasoning faculty) is the charioteer, and the heart (power is the all-embracing cordage created by God.

42. The ten vital breaths[2] from the axis, *Dharma* and *Adharma* its two wheels, the Soul who identifies himself with the body due to Ego (*ahaṁkāra*) is the owner (occupant) of the chariot. They say that the sacred syllable OM is the bow[3], the pure Self is the arrow and Paramātman (the Supreme Soul) is the target.

43-44. Love, hatred, greed, sorrow, infatuation, fear, pride, haughtiness, disgrace, jealousy, deceitfulness, violence, envy, passion, negligence, hunger, sleep—these and the like are the enemies to be vanquished. These are born of *rajas* and *tamas* and rarely from *sattva*. (At the time of concentration of the mind, the appearance of ideas of doing good is also a distraction and hence inimical.

45. While yet he continues to hold the chariot in the form of human body with all its constituent parts (the sense organs) under his control, he, deriving his strength from Lord Viṣṇu, and wielding the sword of spiritual knowledge sharpened through the service of the highly exalted Souls, should put an end to all the (aforesaid) enemies. Enjoying to his utmost satisfaction the highest bliss of the Self, he should attain (perfect) tranquillity and cast off this (body).

1. *ātmānaṁ rathinaṁ viddhi Śarīraṁ ratham eva tu |*
buddhiṁ tu sārathiṁ viddhi, manaḥ pragrahom eva ca |
Indriyāṇi hayānāhur viṣayāṅś teṣu gocarān ||
—*Kaṭha Upa.* 1.3.3-4
2. They are: Prāṇa, Apāna, Samāna, Vyāna and Udāna, Nāga, Kūrma, Kṛkala, Devadatta and Dhanañjaya.
3. Cf. *Praṇavo dhanuḥ śaro hyātmā—Muṇḍaka Upa.* 2.2.4.

46. Otherwise, these wicked horses in the form of senses and the (feeble) charioteer take the careless and unwary occupant astray to the path of *Pravṛtti* and land him among a band of robbers, viz., objects of sense-enjoyment. Those robbers hurl him among with the horses and the charioteer in the deep well of blinding darkness in the form of *saṁsāra* beset with the terrible fear of death.

47. Acts prescribed in the Vedas are of two kinds : *Pravṛtta* (leading to enjoyment of worldly life) and *Nivṛtta* (leading to spiritual life). By performance of *Pravṛtta karma* a person is born again in *saṁsāra*, while by *Nirvṛtta karma* he attains to immortality (*Mokṣa*).

48-49. Ritual (like *Śyena-yāga*) to destroy the enemies and sacrifices involving slaughter of animals, *Agnihotra* (maintenance of daily domestic sacrificial worship), *Darśa* (sacrifice to be performed on the New Moon day), *Paurṇimāsyā* (sacrifice on the Full Moon day), *Cāturmāsya* (a sacrifice to be performed at the beginning of a quarter—four monthly division—of the year), animal-sacrifice, Soma-sacrifice, *Vaiśvadeva* (oblations to the *Viśvadevas* offered before taking meals) and *Bali-haraṇa* (symbolic offer of food to demigods, household divinities, men and other creature) are known as sacrificial acts; while construction of temples, gardens, tanks or wells and booths supplying water to men and animals, form (what is known as) *Pūrta* acts. Both of these (*iṣṭa* and *pūrta*) are included under *Pravṛtta karma*.

50-51. (The gradual ascension of the departed soul is marked by the subtle modifications of materials of his astral body *liṅga śarīra* which is supposed to be escorted by the deities presiding over), the smoke, the night, the dark half of the month, the *dakṣiṇāyana* (representing the Sun's apparent movement to the South of equator), the orb of the Moon. (After enjoying the fruit of his action, the path of descent of that *jīva* is through) the New Moonday, annual plants and creepers, food grains and the semen (resulting thereby)—this is the *path of Pitṛs* which leads to birth again. Having gone through these stages one by one, a *jīva* is born again in this world[1].

1. The belief in the journey of the Soul by the Path of *Pitṛs* (*pitṛ*.

52. A twice-born person (viz. Brāhmaṇa, Kṣattriya and Vaiśya) who is consecrated with the sixteen purificatory rites from *garbhādhāna* to the funeral obsequies, oblates all his activities as sacrifice into his five cognitive senses kindled by the light of spiritual wisdom.

53. He offers (i.e. merges) the senses into the mind or the thinking faculty full of thoughts, the mind born of *Vāikārika* (*sāttvic*) *ahaṁkāra* into the Speech; the speech into the body of articulate sounds (which go to form Speech), and that collection of sounds into *Praṇava OM*; he should merge that into *Bindu*, the *Bindu* into *Nāda*, the *Nāda* into *Prāṇa* (vital breath) and *Prāṇa* in the Supreme (*Brahman*).

54-55. The path wherein the progress is watched by deities presiding over Fire, the Sun, the Day Time, the Evening (close of the day), the bright fortnight, the full Moon day, *Uttarāyaṇa* (the period when the Sun appears to move to the North of the equator), god Brahmā.[1] (Brahmā's region marks the highest point in the ascent of the departed Soul. After the termination of the person of enjoyment in the *Brahma loka* he proceeds to) *Viśva* (when the Soul identifies himself with gross matter), *Taijasa* (wherein the Soul merges the gross into the subtle *upādhi*, and with his subtle *upādhi* is absorbed into Kāraṇa *upādhi* he becomes) *Prājña*, (after merging of *Kāraṇa upādhi* he becomes) the Turīya (when he is mere witness of all the states) —all these stages being absorbed into one he becomes Pure Self, i.e. is liberated. This path is known as the path of gods (*deva-yāna*). Going through these stages serially, this propitiator of the (Supreme) Self being established into the Supreme Self attains to perfect tranquillity and never returns (to *saṁsāra*)[2]

yāṇa) is very old. In fact the above verses echo *verbatim Chāndogya Upa.* 5.10. 3-6.

Also : *Dhūmo rātris tathā kṛṣṇaḥ ṣaṇmāsā dākṣiṇāyanam /*
tatra Cāndramasaṁ jyotir Yogī prāpya nivartate //

—B.G. 8.25.

1. *agnir jyotir ahaḥ śuklaḥ ṣaṇmāsā uttarāyaṇam /*
tatra prayātā gacchanti Brahma Brahma-vido janāḥ //

—BG. 8.24.

2. VJ. states that every higher stage is more blessed than the former. When he ultimately attains to the Supreme Self, he becomes established in perfect bliss whence there is no return to *Saṁsāra*.

56. He who, through Śāstric point of view, distinctly and correctly understands these paths of *Pitṛs* and gods as created by the Vedas, does not get deluded[1] (and does not fall down to a lower stage in life), even though he still abides in this (physical) body.

57.* For, the knower of the path factually constitutes whatever exists before the creation and after the extinction of the body; he himself is whatever is outside the body (external world to be enjoyed) and inside the body (the enjoyer of the world), what is high and low, knowledge and the object of knowledge, the world and the object denoted by it, darkness as well as light.

58.** Just as a reflection, though logically disproved in everyway, is supposed to be something real, so objects which are cognised by senses are imagined to be really existent. But their objective reality is difficult to be proved.

59.*** (Here the unreality of the body is logically proved). This "shadow" (-like psycho-physical organism called

1. Is not attached to either of the paths—S.D.

* VR. : Before the creation and after the destruction of the universe in and out of the living beings during the tenure of the universe whatever exists high or low, consciousness (Jīva) and the insentient things to be known, the word and the thing described darkness (*Mūla Prakṛti*) and light (*Samaṣṭi-jīva*)—these all are *Paramātman*.

** VR. interprets *ābhāsa* as (1) the visible physical body and (2) the body in the dream state and gives two explanations:

(1) The actual body though continues to be undestroyed does not deserve to be regarded as *Puruṣārtha*. So are the objects of senses, unworthy of pursuit as objects of human life (*Puruṣārtha*).

(2) Just as the body in the dream state disappears at the time of waking, so is the body in the waking state unreal as the eternal qualities of the Soul are not found therein.

B.P. and SD. seem to accept this interpretation.

VJ states the *dvaita* point of view as follows:

The body which is *pratibimba* is (as per *smṛti* texts) *Vastu* as the Supreme Self, abides in it. The body and other objects have a real existence as god and nobody else can create them.

*** VR. : The shadow of trees etc. which are products of the elements like the earth and other lements is neither their collection nor modification; it is neither apart from the tree nor connected with it but is impermanent (*anitya*); so is relation of the body and the *ātman*. The body is not the *ātman*.

VJ. interprets *chāyā* as an aspect of state. He explains, "As none else but god has created everything in this universe it is real; for the *bhūtas* are neither a collection, compound or the modification of other *bhūtas* e.g. the earth or water etc.

body which is regarded as a combination of five elements such as the earth and others) is nothing of (unrelated to) the earth and other elements; for it is neither a collection or a mixture nor a compound or modification. It is neither of them separately or conjointly. Hence, it is unreal.

60. (He now shows that the constituents making up the body are unreal). The ingredients or "the roots" of the body, viz. the five gross elements being themselves composed of components, cannot exist apart from their subtle forms (*tanmātras*) which form their components. And when the whole i.e. combination of constituents) proves to be unreal, the parts (or constituents) *ipso facto* cease to be real.

61. Objection : In case the existence of an individual *avayavin* is denied, the identity of the same individual at different stages in life or periods of time cannot be recognized. The reply :

When there is no difference in Paramātman, it is through similarities between the successive appearances that the mistake in identification will take place while the influence of *avidyā* survives. The force of Śāstric injunctions and prohibition is similar to the distinction between wakefulness and sleep, both perceived during the dream-stage[1].

62* A contemplative sage who, through the realization of the Self comprehends the unity of *Bhāva*[2] (thought), *Kriyā*[2] (action) and *Dravya*[2] (materials) of the *ātman*, shakes off the three dreamy states, viz., wakefulness, dream and sleep.

63. Bhāvādvaita (non-duality of thought) is the comprehension of the essential one-ness of cause and effect like that in the thread and cloth (woven out of thread), their difference being unreal.

64. Oh Yudhiṣṭhira (son of Pṛthā Kuntī) ! The resignation of all acts performed through the instrumentality of

1. VR. : The injunctive and interdictory orders in the Śāstric texts may be binding till this body lasts, just as the distinction between the state of wakefulness and sleep in dreams lasts till the dream continues.

2. The terms are defined in the following verses.

* VJ. : A sage who comprehends the meaning of *Śāstras* knows the identity (*advaita*) in *Bhāva*, *Kriyā* and *Dravya*.

thought, words and deeds directly to the Supreme Brahman himself, is the *Kriyādvaita* (non-duality of action).

65. The *Dravyādvaita* (non-duality of substances) is the realization of *artha* and *kāma* (wealth, property and desire) of one's own self and his wife, children as well as all other embodied beings.

66. Except in the case of calamity (i.e. normally) one should perform one's duties with the materials the acquisition of which is permitted by whatever means, from whatever source and at whatever time and place, (to the man's class and stage in society).

67. Oh King! He who abides by these and other duties prescribed for him in the Vedas and is deeply devoted to Lord Kṛṣṇa, attains to the Lord's realm (or state of godhood) even though he be staying at home.

68. Oh King of kings! Just as you (and your brothers) tided over a series of unsurmountable difficulties by the grace of the Lord and have performed sacrifices after conquering the guardian-elephants of all quarters, so you may cross over this *saṁsāra* through the grace of Lord Kṛṣṇa, the saviour of all.

69. In the previous Mahākalpa, I was born as a Gandharva named Upabarhaṇa and was highly respected among the Gandharvas.

70. Being an amiable person with beautiful appearance, comeliness, sweet in speech and fragrance, I was a favourite with women. I was always intoxicated and extremely lascivious.

71. Once upon a time, in a sacrifice performed by gods Gandharvas (celestial musicians) and Apsaras (heavenly damsels) were invited by the Prajāpatis (Lords of creations) to chant verses in honour of Lord Hari.

72. On coming to know of that invitation, I, in the company of women, went there (drunk) singing (profane songs). Being informed of my contemptuous conduct the creators of the universe cursed with their ascetic power: "Being bereft of your glory, do you be born instantly as a Śūdra, as you have behaved disrespectfully."

73. At first I was born of a female-servant. Even in that birth through my reverential service to and association

with sages who had realised Brahman, I became (lit. attained the status of being) Brahmā's son.

74. The righteous course of conduct prescribed for house-holders and which is capable of destroying sins, has been described to you in details. Following this course, a householder easily attains to the goal of a *saṁnyāsin*, viz. *Mokṣa* (Liberation).

75. In this world you are certainly highly fortunate inasmuch as sages who sanctify the world come to your house where the Supreme Brahman disguised in a human form resides (with you).

76. This (Lord Kṛṣṇa) is verily the Supreme Brahman who is the embodiment of the realization of the ecstatic bliss of eternal emancipation which is sought after by great sages. This venerable Lord is your beloved friend, maternal cousin, your most adorable preceptor, your (very) Soul, and the executor of your commands.

77. May this Lord of Sātvatas (Lord Kṛṣṇa) be propitious unto us—Lord Kṛṣṇa whose essential form (nature) could not be adequately (comprehended and) described with their intellectual faculties even by great gods like Śiva, Brahmā and others, and who is worshipped by us in silence, devotion and tranquillity.

Śrī Śuka said :

78. Hearing the above discourse of the divine sage Nārada, the foremost one of Bharatas (Yudhiṣṭhira) was highly delighted and overwhelmed with devotional love worshipped Kṛṣṇa.

79. The sage who was duly worshipped, took leave of Kṛṣṇa and Yudhiṣṭhira. Yudhiṣṭhira was highly amazed to learn that Kṛṣṇa was the Supreme Brahman.

80. Thus the genealogy of the different dynasties of the daughters of Dakṣa have been severally described to you, and gods, Asuras, human beings and other mobile and immobile creation in the world are included in these (dynasties).

SKANDHA EIGHTH

CHAPTER ONE

Description of Manvantaras

The King (Parīkṣit) requested :

1. Here (in the 7th book) I have heard from you, in details, the history of the dynasty of Svāyambhuva Manu in which were born the progenitors of the universe like Marīci and others and their progeny. Now relate to us, Oh preceptor, the history of other Manus[1].

2. Oh Brahman ! Be pleased to relate to us who are (eagerly) listening, the history of all those Manu-epochs (wherein) wherever the incarnations and great exploits of Hari, the greatest of the great, are sung by the wise.

3. Do you also tell (in details), what Lord Hari, the creator and protector of the universe has accomplished in the past Manvantara, is doing in the present one, and will work in the Manu-epochs to come, Oh Brahman.

The sage (Śuka) replied :

4. In this current *Kalpa* (—Brahmā's day), six Manu-epochs beginning with Svāyambhuva have elapsed. Of these, the first Manvantara (Svāyambhuva) has been described to you, along with the creation of gods and other creatures, during this period.

5. The Lord incarnated as (Yajña) the son of (Svāyambhuva) Manu's daughter Ākūti to enlighten her in the righteous path and as (Kapila) the son of (the same) Manu's daughter Devahūti for imparting spiritual wisdom.

1. GS. adds :
v.l. the second half of this verse :
atra dharmās' ca vividhās' cātur varṇyā'śritāḥ subhāḥ /
Here various courses of righteous and auspicious duties pertaining to four *varṇas* are described.

6. I have previously (in Skandha III) narrated to you the work done by venerable Kapila. I shall (now) relate to you, Oh Chief of Kurus, what the glorious Lord Yajña did.

7. Being indifferent and unattached to sensual enjoyment, and having abdicated his kingship, Lord Svāyambhuva Manu, the spouse of Śatarūpā, entered the forest, along with his queen, to practice penance.

8. Touching the ground with one foot (standing on one leg) for one hundred years, on the bank of the Sunandā, he practised terribly austere penance, Oh Bhārata, and chanted the following (prayer :).

*Manu said**

8A. With his vision uninterrupted, this Vāsudeva dwells in all bodies. He does not perceive the (evolution, continuance and dissolution of) universe with the help of another. He is the cause of the (sentient and nonsentient) universe. Hence his vision (and power of controlling from within).

9.** By him the universe is endowed with consciousness, but unto whom (none in) the universe (can) impart consciousness. He remains awake (as a witness) while the universe is in sleep (even during *Pralaya*). No creatures can know him but he knows all. (He is the *ātman*).

10.*** Whatever is animate (and inanimate) in this uni-

* The next verses are based ou Upaniṣadic texts and are known as *Mantropaniṣad*.

** It is the Sun which prompted by Hari gives light and heat to the universe, and from which, *tapas*, the root cause of all power becomes possible. Even the Sun does not know Lord Hari who remains awake while it (the Sun) sets. But Hari knows it fully—VJ.

*** (i) Everything sentient and insentient in the universe has been penetrated and controlled (from within) by the Supreme Soul who is its main support. Do not think that there is anything absolutely independent of and existing separately from Him. Everything belongs to Him. Do not covet for anything as it depends (for its very existence) upon Him only.—VR.

(ii) The whole of the universe (beginning with the Sun) consisting of the created and yet-to-be-created mobile and immobile objects in the range of *Prakṛti*, is the abode of the Lord (who is their creator). Therefore,

verse,—the whole universe is pervaded by the Supreme Soul. Therefore you should make your living by whatever has been allotted to you by him (or what is given to you, after offering it to him[1]). Do not covet another person's riches.[2]

11. Resort to the self-illuminating Lord who is the abode (the Inner Controller) of all beings and yet unconcerned and aloof from them like Suparṇa (or the bird of beautiful wings, the symbol of *Ātman*, the companion of *jīva* in *Upaniṣads* like the Muṇḍaka 3.1.1), whom though he sees all, no eye (created being) can see (as he is beyond sense-perception), and whose vision (knowledge) never vanishes, (as he is knowledge incarnate).

12. The attributes like beginning, middle and the end cannot be predicated of him (being present in all), he has none that is his own or as belonging to another. (Being all-pervading) the distinction of 'in-ness' and 'out-ness' is not-applicable to him. All these stages (of creation, subsistence and destruction) are attributable to the universe which is his manifestation. Hence, he is the Reality, the supreme truth, the great Perfect Brahman.

13. He (the Supreme Being) has the universe as his body (or he contains the universe within himself at the time of the Deluge) He has innumerable designations. He is the Absolute Ruler, the Supreme Truth, self-effulgent, uncreated, eternal ancient Being. By his (Māyā) Potency, which is also uncreated, he brings about the creation (sustenance and destruction) of this (universe). By his eternal knowledge and wisdom, he sets aside Māyā and remains actionless (in his original state as *Brahman*).

14. (As the Lord initiates action e.g. creation of the universe etc. just to return to actionlessness) so the sages wish

Oh mind, be satisfied, maintain yourself with whatever has been given to you by Him. Do not covet for His omniscience and absolute blissfulness. Nor long for what the Lord has given to another person—VJ.

(iii) Everything in the universe is created by the Lord for His sport. Even if you possess abundant wealth. maintain yourself like a worker getting his wages after giving the 1st priority to His service (and that of His devotees). —VC.

1. Even the wealth in your house belongs to God—GS.
2. This is a *verbatim* reproduction of *Īśa Upa*. 1.

to undertake the religious duties with the object of attaining to actionlessness[1] or Liberation (*Mokṣa*). For, a person who performs actions (dedicating them to the Lord) generally attains to *Mokṣa* (lit. stage of actionlessness).

15. The Supreme Lord of glorious powers engages himself in acts, but is not attached to them, for through realization (of the blissful nature) of his Self, he has all his objects achieved. Hence, those who follow him do not come to grief.

16. I (Svāyambhuva Manu) take shelter in the Almighty Lord who (out of grace) engages himself in activities (such as creation etc. of the universe or follows the path of Veda in his incarnations as Rāma, Kṛṣṇa etc.) yet is absolutely free from egotism as he is full of wisdom. Being Perfect, he is above all cravings (for blessings etc). Being himself the Master, he is not impelled by others; he is yet steadfast in the path of action (according to the incarnation taken by him) as he has to set an example to people and he is the exponent of the path of righteousness

Śrī Śuka said :

17. Seeing him thus repeating the *Mantropaniṣad* (the mystical prayer based on *Upaniṣadic* texts) in meditation, Asuras and Rākṣasas fell upon him to devour him out of hunger.

18. The all-pervading Hari in the form of Yajña, seeing them determined to kill Manu, killed them with the help of gods known as Yāma (who were his sons), and ruled over the Heaven (as the Indra thereof).[2]

19. The second Manu was Svārociṣa, the son of Fire God. He had Dyumat, Suṣeṇa, Rociṣmat as his prominent sons.

1. v.l. *Karma-hantave* : for the destruction of *karmas*.

2. Bh.P. 12.7.15 mentions that each Manvantara is presided over by a Manu as its head, a group of gods (the Manu's sons), an Indra, seven sages and an incarnation of Lord Viṣṇu. Thus in the first Manvantara Svāyambhuva (the son of Brahmā) was the Manu; the gods were known as Yāma; Yajña was the incarnation of Lord Viṣṇu who officiated as Indra also; and the seven sages were Marīci, Atri, Aṅgirā, Pulaha, Kratu, Pulastya and Vasiṣṭha.

20. There Rocana was the Indra, and the gods were (his sons) Tuṣita,and others (Toṣa, Pratoṣa, Santoṣa, Bhadra, Śānti, Iḍaspati, Idhma, Kavi, Vibhu, Svahna, Sudeva, Rocana as listed in the fourth Skandha). The seven sages, well-versed in the Vedas and the knowledge of Brahman, were Ūrja (son of Vasiṣṭha), Stambha (son of Kāśyapa) and others (prāṇa, Bṛhaspati, Datta (son of Atri), Atri, Cyavana as enumerated in the *Harivaṁśa*).

21. From the sage Veda-Śiras and through his wife Tuṣitā by name, the Lord Viṣṇu was born and was well known as Vibhu.

22. Eighty-eight thousand sages who have undertaken the vow of austerities, followed his vow of celibacy, as he was celibate since boyhood.

23. The third Manu was by name Uttama, the son of Priyavrata. He had sons prominent among whom were Pāvana, Sṛñjaya, Yajñahotra, Oh King.

24. In that Manvantara, Pramada and other seven sons of Vasiṣṭha were the seven sages. The three groups of gods were Satya, Vedaśruta and Bhadra, and Satyajit was the Indra.

25. The glorious Supreme Lord was born from Dharma through his wife Sunṛtā and became known as Satyasena. Satyavrata gods were also born along with him.

26. As a friend of the Indra Satyajit, he killed wicked Yakṣas and Rākṣasas who practised hypocrisy and were of bad character, and also the hosts of evil spirits who harmed living beings.

27. The fourth Manu was by name Tāmasa, and was the brother of Uttama. He had ten sons such as Pṛthu, Khyāti, Nara, Ketu and others.

28. In the Manvantara called Tāmasa, the gods were of three groups, Satyaka, Hari and Vīra, and the Lord of the Heavens was Triśikha, and the seven sages were Jyotis, Dhāma and others (namely Pṛthu, Kāvya, Caitra, Agni, Dhanada, and pīvara according to *Harivaṁśa*).

29. The gods were called Vaidhṛti, as they were the sons of Vidhṛti, Oh King. They, with their own intellectual

power, retained the Vedas which were lost in the course of time.

30. In that Manvantara was born Lord Hari from Harimedhas through Hariṇī, and he rescued the big elephant from the grip of an alligator.

The King Requested :

31. Oh son of Vyāsa, we are desirous of hearing from you how Hari delivered the abovementioned King of Elephants seized by the alligator.

32. Wherever the Supreme Lord Hari of most hallowed renown is sung, that story is extremely sacred, praiseworthy, auspicious and contributory to our welfare.

Sūta said :

33. When the son of Vyāsa was urged to continue the narration by King Parīkṣit, who had determined to die of starvation, Śuka congratulated the king with delight and continued (his narration) in the assembly of sages who were listening with rapt attention, Oh Brāhmaṇas.

CHAPTER TWO

The Elephant Leader seized by the Alligator

Śrī Śuka said :

1. Oh King, there was a mountain well known as Trikūṭa. The beautiful mountain was ten thousand *yojanas* in height and was surrounded by the milky ocean.

2. It was wide on all sides to the same extent as its height. It had three peaks of gold, silver and iron (respectively) wherewith it illuminated the milky ocean, the cardinal points and the sky.

3. (It stood radiating its charms) in all directions by its other summits which were variegated (in colours) with precious stones and mineral ores, and were covered with clusters of

trees, creepers and shrubs of various kinds, and was resounded with the cascades of mountain torrents.

4. With its feet washed by the waves of milk on all sides, it makes the earth appear dark-green with its rocks and pebbles of emeralds.

5. Its valleys were resorted to by sporting *Siddhas*, *Cāraṇas*, *Gandharvas*, *Vidyādharas*, big serpents, *Kinnaras* and *Apsaras* (celestial nymphs).

6. While its caves were resonant with the echoes of the music (of *Kinnaras* etc.), proud lions suspecting it to be due to the presence of a rival lion, impatiently roared back in indignation towards them.

7. It appeared picturesque (lit. was adorned) with valleys infested with herds of wild beasts of various kinds. In its celestial gardens abounding in a variety of trees, birds of sweet voice were warbling.

8. It appeared beautiful with streams and lakes of crystal waters, with banks covered with (sparkling) sand of jewels and precious stones. Their waters became highly fragrant by the bathing of celestial women in them, and the breezes blowing over them were charged with sweet scent.

9. In one of the valleys of that mountain, there is a garden called *Ṛtumat* belonging to the glorious highsouled god Varuṇa, which was the sporting ground of celestial ladies.

10-14. On all sides, it was adorned with celestial trees ever laden with fruits and blossoming flowers such as *Mandāras*, *Pārijātas*, *Pāṭalas*, *Aśokas*, *Campakas*, mangoes (of various species), *Priyālas*, bread fruit (Jack-fruit) trees, *Amrātakas* as well as with *Kramukas* (arecas), cocoanut trees, date-palms, *Bījapūrakas* (citrons), *Madhūkas*, *Śāla* trees, tala (palmyras) *Tamālas*, *Asanas*, *Arjunas*, *Ariṣṭas* (soap-berries) *Udumbaras* (Indian fig trees), *Plakṣas*, banyan trees, *Kiṁśukas*, sandal trees, Neem trees, *Kovidāras*, *Saralas* (pine trees?), *Deodars*, grape vines, sugar-canes, plantains, rose-apples, plum-trees, *Akṣas*, the yellow myrobalan, Emblic myrobalan trees and was surrounded by *Bilva*, *Kapittha* (wood apple tree), *Jambīra*, *Bhallātaka* (the marking-nut plant) and others. In that garden there was an extensive lake resplendent with golden lotuses.

15. It looked excellently beautiful with the splendour of

lilies and various species of lotuses such as *Utpala*, *Kalhāra* and *Śatapatra* (white, blue and ordinary types). It was resonant with (the ceaseless) humming of intoxicated bees and with melodious notes of warbling birds.

16. It was swarmed with aquatic birds like swans, ducks called *Kāraṇḍava*, ruddy geese (*Cakravāka*) and cranes. It was resounded with the cries of water-fowls *Koyaṣṭis* and *Dātyūha* (the gallinules).

17-19. It's waters were covered with filaments of lotuses shaking with the movement of the fishes and tortoises. It was surrounded with trees and plants such as *Kadambas*, canes, *Nalas* (a variety of reed) and *Nīpas* (a kind of *Kadamba*), *Vañjulaka*, *Kurbaka*, *Aśoka*, *Śirīṣa*, *Kuṭaja*, *Aṅguda*, *Kubjaka*, *Svarṇa-yūthi* (yellow jasmine), *Nāga*, *Punnāga*, *jātis*, *millikā*, *Śatapatras*, *Mādhavī Jālaka* and other creepers.

It appears superbly beautiful with other trees growing on its banks, and bearing fruits and flowers throughout all seasons.

20. Once upon a time, there came in that garden the leader of a herd of elephants dwelling in the forest over the mountains. It was ranging about in the company of female elephants breaking and treading down thorny shrubs and clusters of various types of bamboos and canes (on their way).

21. Even at the scent of that King-elephant, lions, big elephants, carnivorous animals like tigers, rhinoceroses, huge serpents, white and black Śarabhas (an extinct animal more powerful than the lion), *Camarīs* (female yaks) take to flight through sheer terror.

22. It is by its sufference that weaker animals like wolves, boars, bisons, bears, procupines, baboons, hyenas and monkeys as well as the deer, hares range about without fear.

23-24. The elephant which was exuding the temporal fluid as a consequence of which he was attended by swarms of blackbees feeding on that intoxicating fluid, was surrounded by (a herd of) elephants, male and female, and was followed by their young ones. Being oppressed with the heat of the Sun, and scenting from a distance the breeze blowing from the lake—(and hence) laden with the pollen of lotuses—he, with his eyes rolling under intoxication and accompanied by his herd, all panting for water, speedily approached the vicinity of the lake, shaking by its huge weight the mountain on all its sides.

25. Plunging into the lake, he, with the tip of his trunk, drank to his fill the translucent, nectarlike water perfumed with the pollen of golden and blue lotuses. Bathing himself with the waters of the lake, he became refreshed.

26. The proud yet compassionate elephant, like unto a house-holder, made his female mates and young ones drink water and bathe, spraying them with the cool water by means of his trunk. Being deluded by the *Māyā* power of the Lord, the poor creature could not foresee the (impending) peril.

27. There, some powerful alligator, directed by the will of the Providence, indignantly caught hold of the elephant by the leg, Oh King. Finding himself caught up into this calamity by the will of the Lord, the mighty elephant exerted himself to his utmost capacity (to extricate himself from the hold of the alligator).

28. Noticing that the leader of their herd is being dragged with powrful force, and is rendered helpless, the female elephants, with their minds perplexed, began merely to shriek. The other elephants, though helping him from behind and sides, did not succeed in their attempts to rescue him.

29. In this way, while the mighty elephant and the powerful alligator were struggling, the former trying to drag the other outside the water and the latter pulling him inside, one thousand years rolled by. Finding them equally powerful, even the gods marvelled greatly at this (tough fight).

30. In this way, due to his being dragged into the water and harassed for a very long period, the energy, strength and vitality of that king elephant became greatly depleted, while the very reverse of it took place in the case of the acquatic animal (the alligator).

31. When that mighty elephant, dependent on his physical strength only thus found himself in the peril of life and absolutely helpless and incapable of rescuing himself, he pondered over for a long time, and through the will of the Lord, arrived to the following conclusion.

32. "These elephants, my own kinsfolk are not able to liberate me in this plight. What to speak of these poor she-elephants ! Caught up and bound down as I am in the snare of the Providence, in the form of this alligator, I shall now approach the Supreme Lord who is the last resort of all.

33. We seek refuge in that indescribable Supreme Lord through fear of whom even the (God of) Death flies away, and who, when resorted to as an asylum, protects in every way the affrighted fugitive, vehemently pursued with irresistible force by the mighty serpent (in the form) of Death."

CHAPTER THREE

The Liberation of the Mighty Elephant

Śrī Śuka said :

1. Having thus decided by force of his reason and concentrated his mind within (the region of) his heart, he began to repeat mentally the (following) prayer which he learnt by heart in his previous birth (as Indradyumna).[1]

The Lord of Elephants Prayed:

2. (Due to my leg being caught by the alligator) I can but mentally offer my salutations to the glorious Lord denoted by the sacred syllable OM—the Lord who is the source of animation to all this intelligent (and non-intelligent) creation, who enters all bodies as their cause both as *Prakṛti* and *Puruṣa* and who is the Supreme Lord of all (including great gods like Brahmā).

3. I seek asylum unto the Self-created Being in whom this universe exists and from whom as the natural course, it is evolved and by whose instrumentality it is brought about and

1. Vide *infra* Ch. IV. 7-12.

who constitutes the universe itself,[1] but who is totally different from and transcendental to this phenomenal existence (the effect) as well as its cause (*Prakṛti*).

4. May the self-illuminating Lord protect me—the Lord who is beyond revealing agencies (such as the eyes etc.) as their illuminator; Who as a disinterested witness, observes with his unobstructed vision, both the cause and the effect, this universe superimposed on him by his deluding potency (*Māyā*) both in its occasional manifested form (at the time of the creation) and the occasional unmanifested form at the time of destruction).

5* When, due to the force of time (the period of two *parārdhas*, the life-period of Brahmā), all the (fourteen) worlds along with their guardian deities are reduced to the state of five gross elements (of which they are constituted and when all the causes (viz. the principles such as the *Mahat*, *ahaṁkāra* upto gross elements) become dissolved (into *Prakṛti* or Primordial matter), there prevailed (nothing but) profound incomprehensible and unfathomable darkness (called *Prakṛti*. May that Omnipresent Lord who through its *Prakṛti's* substratum) is not affected by it and who sheds his lustre all round (even beyond that darkness) protect me.

6. Not even gods and sages (with all the predominance of *Sattva guṇa*) could comprehend his real nature. How is it possible for a creature (like me dominated by *rajas* and *tamas*) to understand and describe it? (To gods, sages and us) his nature and course of conduct is difficult to understand and

1. Though Hari and the universe are different, He is identified with it as the universe is under His perfect control; Who is superior (and transcendental) to this phenomenal world as well as from those who have attained Liberation—VJ.

*VR. : *tamas*—the extremely subtle sentient material (*cid-dravya*) that exists after the dissolution of the universe (*tamaḥ śabdaḥ niratiśaya-sūkṣma-daśāpanna-cid-dravya-vāci*). So also BP.

Para abhivirājate—The Lord, as a controller of this *tamas* or subtle composite principle, exists in His glory. VR. derives *para* from *Pṛ* to protect.

VJ. : *Pare abhivirājate*—Who through His form called Time, stays self-refulgent in the region least affected by and thus beyond *tamas*

JG. : —*Para*—In the great Vaikuṇṭha regions.

describe, like the real identity of an actor playing different roles to an ordinary spectator. May he rescue me.

7. My asylum is that Lord for the realization of whose most auspicious nature, the exceedingly pious contemplative sages, have given up all attachment (to their wives, children and also to objects of senses like sound, fragrance etc.) and having identified their Self with the Self of all beings and thus being benevolently disposed to all, perform in a faultless manner extraordinary austerities (such as *Brahmacarya*—celibacy and others) in the forests.

8. The Lord is not conditioned by birth (as a consequence of past actions). He has no *Karma*—(bondage), no name or form (as a result of past *Karmas* as in the case of ordinary beings). However, for the sake of creation and destruction of the world, he assumes them from time to time by his *Māyā*-Potency (or will Power).

9. I bow again and again to that Supreme Lord, the Brahman of infinite potencies, Who, (though) devoid of forms, possesses innumerable forms and performs miraculous activities.

10. I pay obeisance to the Lord who is self-luminous (and as such requires no other light to reveal him); who is the witness (and hence the revealer) of all; and the controller of all beings; I bow to him who is absolutely beyond the ken of speech, mind and its powers.

11. Salutations to him who can be realized by the wise, through purity of the mind developed by cessation (of activities or dedication to the Lord) of Karmas, (and by observance of *nivṛtti* (*dharma* characterised by devotion); Who is the Lord (and hence the bestower) of *Mokṣa* and who is the blissfulness of the final beatitude *incarnate*.

12* I bow to him who assumes the (three) attributes *sattva*, *rajas* and *tamas*, and appears as serene, terrible, and immersed in ignorance; who is devoid of differentiating characteristics, equal to all, and an embodiment of pure consciousness.

*VJ. classifies the various incarnations of Viṣṇu on *guṇa* basis and offers them salutations. He regards the last epithet—*jñānaghana*—as a refutation of the formlessness of Viṣṇu (*arūpasya śūnyatvaṁ nivārayati*)

13* I bow to you who are the controller of all, the only knower of the psycho-physical organism (called *kṣetra*), a witness (to everything). You are the source of all Jīvas, and even that of *Prakṛti* (the primordial cause) as you exist before all.

14. I pay my obeisance to you, who perceive all senses along with their objects; who are indicated (as the basis) by all cognitive activities; whose existence is suggested by the shadowy, unreal phenomenal existence (*ahaṁkāra* and other principles) like that of a material body by its reflection, as it is you who are reflected in every phenomenon.

15. I bow again and again to you who are the cause of everything, but yourself are without a cause; who are the wondrous cause (inasmuch as you produce the effect—viz. assuming the form of the world—without undergoing any change in you); who are the great ocean wherein all *Āgamas* (like the *pañcarātra*) and the Vedas meet (and are directed to you); who are the embodiment of *Mokṣa* (Liberation) and (hence) the ultimate resort of the great.

16.** I salute to you who are the fire of knowledge and consciousness lying hidden in the *Araṇī* (the pieces of wood for kindling sacrificial fire by friction) in the form of *guṇas*; whose will (to create the universe) manifests itself through the commotion (caused by the disturbance in the equilibrium) of *guṇas*; who, out of your own will, reveal yourself to those who, (through the renunciation of *Karmas* or dedication of Karmas to God), meditate on the true (nature of the) soul and have risen above the prescriptions and prohibitions enjoined by *Āgamas*.

VR: *interprets*:

Salutations to you who (at the time of the destruction of the universe) have drunk up (withdrawn within you) the fire of the aggregate of all *jīvas* lying hidden in the *Prakṛti*

* Salutations to You to Whom the *kṣetrajña* (individual soul) is like a body, the Supreme Ruler of all beings, the Witness to all: Who are the Inner Controller (of all); and Who are self-existent (not created by any other cause) and are the primary material cause (of all) as well.—VR.

** VJ. reads a combination of vv. 16 and 18.

(constituted of three *guṇas*); whose will to create begins to function (at the time of the creation of the world) leading to the commotion in *Prakṛti* and *jīvas*; who grants Liberation (*Mokṣa*) to his votaries; whose being beyond the comprehension of speech and mind, stands self-revealed.

17. Hail to you who are yourself not only eternally free, but who, out of boundless grace, promptly[1] (without any idleness in such matters) and absolutely severe the bonds of *Avidyā* or *Saṁsāra* which have fettered creatures like me, (now) completely submitted to your mercy. I bow to you who, by a part of your being, exist in all embodied beings as their inner controller[2] and are capable of directing them all, even though you are infinite (and spatially unlimited)

18. Bow to you who (though the inner controller of all beings) are difficult to be attained by persons who are attached to their bodies, sons, kinsmen, household, wealth and people, as you are devoid of any association with *guṇas*. You are constantly meditated upon in their hearts by souls unattached to their bodies, etc. I bow to you who are an embodiment of pure knowledge, the most omnipotent Ruler of all.

19. May the Lord of infinite mercy (at least) rescue me (from the clutches of the alligator or *Saṁsāra*)—The Lord, by worshipping whom persons desirous of religious merits, sensual objects, affluence, wealth or Liberation (from *saṁsāra*), gain not only their coveted goal but also have other unexpected blessings and undeteriorating (divine) body conferred upon them.

20. His votaries of unflinching constant devotion and even those who have taken refuge with the Lord (or His devotees full of spiritual wisdom) do not seek any boon (from him), but are immersed in the ocean of bliss, while singing his most miraculous and auspicious deeds.

21. I offer my hymn of prayer unto that absolutely perfect imperishable First Principle, the all-pervading highest

1. *ālayāya*—By resorting to whom the devotee never meets destructions —VR.

2. *Svāṁśena sarvatanubhṛt* etc.: Who are realized as being identical with the *jīva* in the heart of every being as the *jīva* is essentially a part of your body—VR.

Brahman, the Supreme Ruler (even of great gods like Brahmā), unmanifest and beyond the range of senses, as it is very remote and subtle, yet is accessible (to his devotees) through internal (path of *bhakti*) *yoga*.

22-24. May the Lord, manifest himself (for my Liberation)[1]—

22. The Lord by whose single minutest modicum of energy (all the) gods headed by Brahmā, the Vedas, the worlds, the mobile and immobile creation of distinct (yet) infinite variety of forms, are created.

23. From that self resplendent Lord issues forth (and is again withdrawn) the stream of *guṇas*[2] and their products such as the intellect, the mind, the senses and aggregates of gross bodies (like those of gods and others), even as sparks and flames go forth from the self-shining Fire-god and rays emanate from the self-luminous sun and are withdrawn again into them constantly.

24. Verily he is neither god nor demon; neither a human being nor a sub-human creature (a bird, a beast etc.); he is neither a famale nor a male nor an important person or an a-sexual being; he is neither an attribute (*guṇa*) nor an action (*Karma*); he is neither effect nor cause; he is the substratum of what is left after negating these all and yet constitutes them all (by his *Māyā*).

25. I do not wish (to get my body) extricated from the clutches of the alligator and) to survive here (in this body). What interest have I with this elephant-life which is enveloped internally and externally with the darkness of ignorance? I crave for emancipation (lifting up of) from that Veil of ignorance which shrouds the spiritual light of the Soul, and which cannot be destroyed merely by (lapse of) time but only by the knowledge of the (*Ātman*).

1. (i) May remove all obstacles in my God-realization—VR. (ii) May relieve me from the misery of *saṁsāra*—VJ. (iii) SD., GD., BP. follow ŚR.

2. This asserts the eternality of the stream of the universe (*guṇa—saṁpravāhaḥ...anena jagat-Pravāhasya nityatvaṁ jñāpitam*)—VJ.

26* Being thus desirous of getting liberated I (who do know the Lord) simply bow down to that all pervading spirit, who is the creator of the universe; whose body is the universe and yet who is beyond and other than it; who uses the universe as his instrument, yet is the soul of it (as its Inner controller); who is unconditioned by birth and is the highest resort of all.

27. I have bowed[1] unto the Lord of *yoga* (who confers the fruit of *yogic* practice), whom the *yogins* visualize in their hearts purified by burning down of their *Karmas* by *yoga* (or devotion unto the Lord).

28. I salute to you again and again. The force of your three-fold power (of three *Guṇas* viz. *sattva, rajas* and *tamas*) is irresistible; who manifest yourself as the object of all senses; who protect those who have resorted to you for shelter and are of unfathomable powers; whose path is inaccessible to those whose senses are directed to external objects.

29. I have sought the protection of the Lord whose glory is unsurpassable and enveloped by whose Māyā power expressed as the ego-sense, this Jīva does not realize (the real nature of) his self.

Śrī Śuka said:

30. When all these gods like Brahmā and others who identified themselves with their special forms and attributes (such as four-headedness, three-eyedness in the case of gods Brahmā, Śiva etc.) did not approach (to rescue) the Lord of elephants who thus glorified the Supreme Lord as being devoid of (and hence without any reference to) any particular form or attribute,[2] Lord Hari, being the Soul (ātman) of all,

* Being desirous of removing the veil of ignorance that obscures the vision of the soul, I bow to You Who are the Wealth or the highest goal in the life (of people) in the universe, who enter the universe to protect it: Whose manifestation is not conditioned by Karmas, yet is full of good attributes; Who are absolutely inaccessible I merely bow to Him as I do not know any other way of propitiating Him—VR.

1. The yogic way being now impossible I can simply bow to Him —VR.

2. And as he has under-rated gods like Brahmā in verse 22 above —GS.

and the embodiment of the aggregate of all gods, manifested himself there.

31. Knowing that the elephant was in that distressed condition and having heard his hymn of prayer (mentally addressed to him), the Lord, the abode of the universe, equipped with his weapon the discus *sudarśana* and riding *Garuḍa*, the embodiment of the (*sāma-*) *veda* (and capable of ranging anywhere with any speed according to his will) and accompanied by celestials singing his praise, instantaneously appeared on the spot, where the Lord of elephants was (in that wretched plight).

32. Beholding in the sky Lord Hari, seated on *Garuḍa* and with his discus upraised (in his hand), the elephant, though greatly distressed, as he was seized by a very powerful alligator inside the lake, lifted up his trunk holding a lotus (as an offering for worshipping his feet!) and uttered with great difficulty the words "Oh glorious Lord Nārāyaṇa!" the Father (or Preceptor) of all the universe! I (reverentially) bow to you."

33. Seeing the elephant greatly afflicted, Lord Hari, the birthless God (feeling the speed of *Garuḍa* as too slow) at once alighted (from *Garuḍa*), and immediately dragging out the elephant out of the lake along with the alligator, out of compassion, rescued the lord of the elephants from its jaws by rending them open with the discus, while gods stood simply looking on.

CHAPTER FOUR

Liberation of the Lord of Elephants

Śrī Śuka continued :

1. Then (seeing the rescue of the lord of elephants), gods headed by Brahmā and Śiva, sages and Gandharvas extolled that mighty deed of Hari, and discharged a shower of flowers on him.

2. Celestial kettle-drums were sounded, the Gandharvas danced and sang; sages, Cāraṇas and Siddhas eulogised the Supreme Person.

3. Verily, he who was (till then) the alligator, instantly assumed the most wonderful form. He was Hūhū, the foremost among the Gandharvas, who was thus redeemed from the curse of the Sage Devala.[1]

4. He bowed down to the eternal Supreme Lord of excellent renown with his head, and he chanted the praise of his worth extolling (innumerable) virtues and sacred episodes of that abode of glory.

5. Being favoured by the Lord with his grace, he was purged of all sins. Going round the Lord (reverentially) and paying him obeisance, he repaired to his own region (of Gandharvas) in the very presence of all the people.

6. By virtue of his being touched by the Lord, the lord of elephants became completely free from the bondage of ignorance, and attained to the form resembling that of the Lord (Viṣṇu) clad in yellow garments and endowed with four arms.

7 It is traditionally reported that he was in his previous birth a king of the Pāṇḍya country wellknown as Indradyumna—the foremost among the Draviḍa people—and devotedly attached to the austere observance of Viṣṇu-worship.

8. Once upon a time, the king who, as an ascetic, wearing matted locks of hair, was staying in his hermitage on the Malaya mountain, had undertaken the vow of silence. At the appointed hour of the propitiation of the Lord, he took his bath and began to worship with due formalities, the imperishable supreme Ruler, Lord Hari.

9. (It is reported that) by chance there arrived (at his hermitage) the celebrated sage Agastya accompanied by hosts

1. ŚR. narrates the cause of the curse as follows:—Once while Hūhū was indulging in watersport with his women in a lake, the sage Devala entered the same lake for bath. Hūhū was upset and he pulled Devala by his leg. The sage cursed him to be an alligator. When entreated, Devala advised him to seize the lord of elephants that way, so that Lord Hari will emancipate him and he would be reinstated to his original position automatically.

of his disciples. Finding Indradyumna seated in solitude and remaining silent (without showing the courtsey of greeting orally) and without paying the due homage (usual formalities of receiving a guest of honour) the sage flared up in rage.

10. He pronounced the following imprecation on the king : "This sinful, uncultured, wicked soul has today insulted a Brāhmaṇa (like me). He is dull-witted like an elephant. Let him be born in the species of elephants steeped in blinding darkness of ignorance."

Śrī Śuka said :

11. Oh king ! Having uttered this curse, the venerable Agastya went way along with his followers. The royal sage Indradyumna, on his part, considered the incident to be the will of the Providence.

12. He entered the species of elephants which obscures the knowledge of the self. But by virtue of his propitiation of Hari the reminiscence of his past life remained unblurred (even while he was an elephant).

13. Having thus rescued the lord of the herd of elephants and accompanied by him after elevating him to the position of his attendant, the lotus-navelled god (Viṣṇu) seated on Garuḍa repaired to his region Vaikuṇṭha, while Gandharvas, Siddhas and gods were glorifying his miraculous feat.

14. This glorious deed of Kṛṣṇa (Viṣṇu), viz. The Liberation of King of elephants, has been narrated to you by me, Oh great king. Listening to this leads to heaven, confers glory, removes the sins of the Kali age and destroys the effect of bad dreams of the hearers, Oh great Kuru.

15. Persons belonging to the twice-born castes desiring to secure their welfare, get up early in the morning, and purifying themselves (after taking a bath) recite this sacred narration (of the liberation of the elephant king) for obliterating the effects of bad dreams (and securing their welfare).

16. It was while all creatures were listening that the Omnipresent Lord Hari who embodies all creation, being highly pleased with the Lord of elephants, addressed the following (words) to him; Oh the best of Kurus.

17-24. Rising up at the close of the latter part of the night i.e. at dawn (known as *Brāhma muhūrta*), and after purifying themselves (by taking a bath), those who, with concentrated mind, remember me, you, this lake, the mountain (*Trikūṭa*) along with its caves and valleys and the forest (covering them), the clusters of canes and *Kīcaka* bamboos, the heavenly trees, the (three) mountain peaks, the abodes of Brahmā, Śiva and myself, the ocean of milk, my favourite resort, the resplendent Śveta-dvīpa (My beloved place), the Śrivatsa mark (the characteristic curl of hair) on my breast, the Kaustubha gem, and the garland known as Vaijayantī, my weapons, the mace called Kaumodakī, the discus Sudarśana, the conch Pāñcajanya, my vehicle Garuḍa, the king of birds, Lord Saṅkarṣaṇa who is my subtle emanation, goddess Śrī (Lakṣmī) who rests on my bosom, god Brahmā, the divine sage Nārada, god Śiva and (my devotee) Prahlāda, and all my deeds performed during my incarnations as Fish, Tortoise, Boar and others—listening to which confers infinite merit (to the hearers), the Sun-god, the Moon-god, the Fire-god, the sacred syllable OM, the Eternal Truth, the unmanifest (*Prakṛti*), Cows and Brāhmaṇas, the eternal path of religion (consisting of devotion unto the Lord, the daughters of Dakṣa who are the wives of Dharma, Soma and Kaśyapa, the rivers—the Gaṅgā, the Sarasvatī, the Nandā, the Yamunā, the White elephant of Indra (Airāvata), Dhruva, the Seven Brāhmaṇa Sages and great men of hallowed fame, (such as Nala, Yudhiṣṭhira, Janaka, the king of Videha)—all these being my forms, those who remember them, become free from all sins.

25. Oh dear Gajendra ! To those who, after getting up at dawn (after the expiry of night), pray to me with the hymn (composed by you), I promise to keep their memory unclouded at the time of their death.

Śrī Śuka said :

26. Having addressed thus, Lord Viṣṇu (the Lord of senses) blew his excellent conch (*Pāñcajanya*) gladdening thereby the host of gods and mounted his carrier Garuḍa, the king of birds.

CHAPTER FIVE

Description of V and VI Manvantaras—Brahmā Hymns the Lord.

Śrī Śuka said :

1. I have narrated to you, Oh King, the sacred story of the liberation of the Lord of elephants which destroys all sinful deeds. Now listen to the account of the Manu-period presided over by Raivata.

2-3. The fifth Manu, Raivata by name, was the brother of Tāmasa. Bali, Vindhya and others, the eldest of whom was Arjuna, were his sons. Vibhu was the Indra, Bhūtaraya and others were the gods, while Hiraṇyaromā, Vedaśiras, Ūrdhvabāhu and others were the Sages[1], Oh king.

4. Vikuṇṭhā was the wife of Śubhra; with a portion of his energy, Lord Vaikuṇṭha was born of these of his own accord, along with great gods known as Vaikuṇṭhas.

5. It was at the request of his spouse, the goddess Ramā (Lakṣmī) and with a view to please her that he created his realm known as Vaikuṇṭha[2] which is highly respected by all the worlds.

6. His prowess (viz. restoring to their original position his attendants who, by the curse of Sanatkumāra, became demons called Hiraṇyākṣa and Hiraṇyakaśipu—vide Skandha III), excellences (such as friendliness to Brāhmaṇas), and his great prosperity have been described to you. (But I could not do so adequately as) he who would be able to describe the excellences of Viṣṇu fully may as well count all the particles of the dust on the entire earth.[3]

7-8. The sixth Manu was known as Cākṣuṣa, the son of Cakṣus; his sons were Puru, Puruṣa, Sudyumna and others. Mantradyumna was the Indra, and the hosts of gods were headed by Āpya. The (seven) Sages were, Oh king, Haviṣmat,

1. GS quotes Harivaṁśa and gives Devabāhu, Sudhāman, Parjanya and Mahāmuni as the names of the remaining (seven) Sages of the *Raivata Manvantara*.

2. GS adds : The Vaikuṇṭha region being eternal, its 'creation' is 'manifestation' only.

3. An echo of RV. 1.154. *Vide infra* 8.23. 29.

Vīraka and others (viz. Sumedhas, Anuttama, Madhu, Atināman, Sahiṣṇu).

9. In this Manvantara, the glorious Lord of the worlds appeared, by a ray of his essential nature, as Ajita, the son of Vairāja and Sambhūti.

10. By him, the nectar as secured for gods, by getting the sea (of milk) churned, while he supported, in the form of the (Divine) Tortoise, the Mount Mandara while it was whirling in the waters of the sea.

The King enquired :

11-12. Be pleased to describe to me Oh Brāhmaṇa Sage, this most wonderous deed of the glorious Lord : as to how the ocean of milk was got churned by the Lord, as also the object (said) of doing so, and why he had to support the mount (Mandara) assuming the form of an acquatic animal (a tortoise); how the nectar was obtained by gods and what else happened at that time (in connection with this event).

13. My heart which has been tormented for a long time by afflictions (of three types) does not get satiated, when you describe in details, the great glory of the Lord of Sātvatas (Kṛṣṇa).

Sūta said:

14. Being thus respectfully requested. the venerable son of Vyāsa (viz. Śuka) appreciated the (king's) query and began to describe in details the prowess of Lord Hari, Oh Brāhmaṇas.

Śrī Śuka said :

15-16. When formidably assailed with sharp weapons by Asuras in battles, gods were killed in large numbers, and they did not revive, and when due to the curse of the sage Durvāsas,[1]

1. ŚR & GS mention the following incident (from the *Brahma Vaivarta Purāṇa*) as the cause of the curse. Once while the sage Durvāsas was wearing a garland gifted to him by Lord Viṣṇu, Indra riding his Airāvata elephant, passed by him. Out of courtesy and with a view to bless Indra with permanent sovereignty of the three worlds, Durvāsas presented the garland to him. Out of arrogance, Indra threw it on the

the three worlds along with Indra were deprived of their glory and wealth, all sacrificial performance and other religious rites ceased to be performed.

17. Seeing this (state of affairs), the hosts of gods headed by the great Indra and Varuṇa met in a conference for mutual consultations, but failed to arrive at a conclusion.

18. All of them went to the court of Brahmā, situated on a crest of mountain Meru. Bowing god Brahmā humbly, they submitted to him all their grievances.

19-20. Observing that gods like Indra, Vāyu and others are bereft of power, energy and splendour and the people (practically) devoid of auspiciousness, and the Asuras (proportionally) better-off, he, with a concentrated mind contemplated the Supreme Person, and with a cheerful countenance, the great Venerable Brahmā addressed the gods as follows:

21. "Let us all—I who am but a portion of the Lord, and Asuras, human beings, sub-human creation like birds, beasts, trees and sweat-born beings (like lice, bugs etc.) who are the progeny of Marīci (and others) who in turn are just a modicum of his energy approach for refuge to him, the imperishable Lord.

22. According to his view-point, none deserves to be killed or protected; no party is worth neglecting or supporting. It is for the creation, subsistence and destruction of the world that he assumes the attributes *sattva*, *rajas* and *tamas* at the proper time.

23. And the present is an opportune time for his creation and protection of the universe for which he has assumed the Sattva attribute for the creation of embodied beings. Let us therefore, approach the Preceptor of the world for protection. Being beloved of gods, he will do whatever is good for us, his devotees."

Śrī Śuka said :

24. Having thus spoken to the gods, god Brahmā, accom-

head of his elephant. The animal in its turn, lifted it from its head and trampled it under its feet. Seeing the gift of the Lord so treated, Durvāsas got enraged and cursed him to be bereft of wealth along with his kingdom of the three worlds.

panied by celestials, went directly to the abode of the unconquerable Lord which lies beyond the region of darkness, Oh destroyer of enemies.

25. There, with the concentration of all his senses (including the mind), he, in the divine (or Vedic) language, addressed the following hymn of praise, to him whose essential form was not seen as yet, but about whom much was heard formerly, Oh king.

Brahmā said :

26. "We bow to the Supreme God, Who is changeless, eternally true, infinite (in time and space), beginningless, present in (everybody's) heart, unconditioned, incomprehensible quicker than the mind and beyond the range of words (indescribable).

27. We go (as a refuge) to him Who is the knower of the vital airs, the mind, the intellect and the soul; Who appears as senses and their objects; Who is devoid of sleep and is bodyless (and hence) imperishable; Who is all-pervasive like the sky, and is unaffected by the darkness of *avidyā* and the sunshine of *Vidyā*;[1] Who is free from desire and other attributes of *Jīva* and who manifests himself in every *Yuga*.

28. I seek asylum in that Deity, the Truth, which the Vedas call as the axle (the main support) of the lightening-like fast rotating wheel of life (i. e. This ever-changing body and other accessories of the Soul), owned by the *Jīva* (who is, in reality birthless). The wheel is propelled by Māyā (the beginningless deluding potency of the Lord). It (the wheel) has mind as its chief component and consists of fifteen spokes (viz. Ten sense organs and five vital breaths—*prāṇas*), three naves (viz. the three *guṇas—sattva, rajas* and *tamas*) and eight fellies* (in the form of eight-fold *Prakṛti* consisting of five elements, the mind, the intellect and the ego).

1. VJ.—*gṛdhra*—covetous of everything, hence *jīva* who like vulture has two wings, viz. *Vidyā* and *Avidyā*.

* VJ. regards deva, asura, humans and other classes of beings as the fellies.

29* Let us bow to him Who has seated himself by the side of Jīva (as the Inner controller) or Who is seated on Garuḍa[1] ever ready to protect his devotees; Who is essentially pure bliss or knowledge[2], beyond the range of darkness or Prakṛti; Who is invisible, beyond the range of all *lokas*; Who is changeless and limitless in time and space; to whom wise men resort through (the chariot in the form of) the discipline of *Yoga*.

30. Let us pay obeisance to the Supreme Ruler Who treats all beings alike (without any partiality); Who has subdued his Māyā along with the (three) *guṇas*—the Māyā which nobody could cross and which has deluded the people so much (that identifying themselves with their bodies) they do not know their true self.

31.** Even we, gods and sages who are created by his favourite body consisting of pure *sattva*, are unable to comprehend his subtle essence, though it is manifest as Light within and as existence without. How (is it possible that) Asuras and others who are dominated by other attributes viz. *rajas* and *tamas* can do so?

32. (Henceforth the *vairāja* form of the Lord is eulogised). May that Lord, the Supreme person, the veritable, absolute Brahman itself, be propitious unto us—The Lord who has created as his feet, this earth which supports the four-

* VJ : I seek refuge in the supreme Deity Who is represented by the syllable (OM); Who is beyond the darkness of ignorance and *prakṛti*. It is beyond the ken of the world, un-revealed and limitless (or comprised of innumerable syllables). Intelligent persons worship and meditate upon Him with great devotion. He is seated on His vehicle the *jīva*.

ananta-pāram (i) Being an embodiment of the Vedas He cannot be comprehended by words and their connotations (ii) He is all pervading yet cannot be seen anywhere by all. They contemplate Him as an *antar-yāmin* (inner controller)—SD. SD interprets *a-Loka* as 'The realm of A i.e. Viṣṇu, Hence Vaikuṇṭha.

1. *upa-suvarṇam*—who occupies a region full of light like gold—VR.
2. *eka-varṇam*—
(i) Constituted of Pure Sattva—VR, JG.
(ii) Who is constituted of the only one syllable *OM*—VJ, VC.
(iii) Constituted of Pure Bliss—GD.

**Though out of His grace He created us both inside and outside with His *sattva* attribute, we, the gods and sages, are unable to comprehend—VJ.

fold creation of beings[1] and yet is completely self dependent, and the Master of infinitely great powers.[2]

33. May that absolute and perfect *Brahman* of immense spiritual powers be gracious unto us—The *Brahman* whose seminal fluid is water, of so much enormous power that it became the source of existence, subsistence and prosperity of the three worlds, as well as all guardian deities.

34. May that Lord of unlimited spiritual glory be propitiated unto us—The Lord whose mind (as declared by the Vedas) is Soma, Who is the food and hence the strength and life of celestials, and Who (due to the nourishing power of his ambrosial rays) is the ruler of the vegetable kingdom and the creator of all living beings (as they subsist on the vegetables and plants).

35 May that most glorious Lord bestow his grace unto us—the Lord whose mouth is the Fire; Who is the source (and hence the bestower) of wealth, (or who takes to gods their respective oblations offered in sacrifices), and Who is engendered for (the performance of) sacrificial rituals (prescribed in the Vedas), and Who abides in the stomach (as the gastric fire) digesting the food, and in the sea (as submarine fire) consuming its (watery) subsistence.

36. May that Lord of infinite glory be propitious unto us—The Lord whose eye is the sun-god; Who is the presiding deity of the path of gods (*devayāna*) leading ultimately to Liberation; Who is the very personification of the triad of Vedas (viz. *ṚK*, *Yajus* and *Sāman*); Who is regarded as the seat of Brahman (as Brahman is meditated upon in relation to the Sun); Who represents not merely the entrance to the path of Liberation but to immortality itself; Who (however as a symbol of Time) is death *incarnate* (as Time terminates everything.)

37. May the Lord of unlimited powers be graciously inclined towards us—The Lord from Whose breath was born *Vāyu* (the air) which is the vital air (*Prāṇa*), who animates the

1. *caturvidha-sargaḥ*—The four categories of beings are viviparous, oviparous, the sweat-born and the plant-world.

2. *mahā-vibhūtiḥ*—Having power over *Mahā-Lakṣmī*, the presiding deity of wealth. May all of us be affluent in every respect—GD.

mobile and immobile creation, and became their mental energy, physical power and potency of the sense-organs, and to whom, we, the presiding deities (of cognitive and conative senses) follow as the retinue goes after an emperor.

38. May that Deity of infinite glory confer favour upon us—The Deity from whose ears were evolved the cardinal points; from whose heart, the pores in the body, and from whose navel were created the (five) vital airs (*Prāṇa*), the senses and organs of the body (*Indriyas*), the mind and the other (five semi-vital airs[1] carrying on) the functions of the body and the sky which supports these all.

39. May the Lord of unlimited glory be favourably disposed to us—the Lord from Whose strength was born the great Indra, from Whose grace the (various) gods; from Whose wrath sprang up god Śiva, the Lord of mountains; from Whose intellect came forth god Brahmā; from the appertures in Whose bodies were created the Vedas and the sages, and from whose generative organ, the god Prajāpati.

40. May that most glorious Lord be propitious unto us —The Lord from Whose bosom came forth the goddess Śrī (the goddess of wealth and beauty); from Whose shadow, the manes (*Pitṛs*); from Whose breast, Dharma (the presiding Deity of righteousness) and from Whose back was born *Adharma* (the evil spirit of unrighteousness); from Whose head evolved the heaven (*svarga*), and from Whose sportive actions, the celestial damsels (*apsaras*).

41. May the Lord of supreme glory bestow his grace on us—The Lord from Whose mouth sprang up the Brāhmaṇas and Vedas of mystic significance; from Whose arms were born Kṣatriyas and the power (to govern); from Whose thighs came forth Vaiśyas and skill in business of agriculture and from Whose feet were born the Śūdras and the vocation of service (other than Vedic studies)[2]

42. May the Lord of infinite powers be gracious unto us—the Lord from Whose lower lip came forth avarice, from

1. These are *Nāga*, *Kūrma*, *Kṛkala*, *Devadatta* and *Dhanañjaya* (vide Supra 3.6.9).

2. Śr notes v.l. *urvor viśoṅghrer abhavaṁśca śūdrāḥ* 'The Vaiśya class was born from His thighs and the Śūdras from His feet.'

Whose upper lip affection; from Whose nose emanated splendour, from Whose touch, the desire to rear up and to tend animals; from Whose eye-brows sprang up Yama, the god of death; from Whose eye-lashes was born the Time-spirit (Kāla).

43. May that most glorious Lord be graciously disposed towards us—The Lord by Whose *yoga-māyā*, the *śāstras* declare are created the five gross elements, the Time (Life-Span), the destiny (effects of acts of past life), qualities[1] (or the modes of *Prakṛti* e.g. *Sattva*, *rajas*) and this phenomenal world all of which are too difficult to comprehend, and which should be renounced by the wise as mere *māyā*.

44. I bow to him Whose energy (in the form of *guṇas* like *Sattva* etc.) is quiescent; Whose mind is thoroughly full of his natural supreme bliss, and hence Who is not attached (even in his mind) to the products of the *guṇas* created by Māyā and Whose sportive activities are like the air (which moves everywhere but is attached to nothing anywhere).

45. You being such (as described above), be pleased to reveal to us your lotus-like smiling countenance in such a way as it will come within the range of our sense of perception, for we have completely surrendered ourselves to you and are eager to have a look at you.

46. For the glorious Lord assumes different forms from time to time, according to his will (or the will of his devotees), and accomplishes feats which are beyond our capacity, Oh Omnipresent God.

47. In the case of embodied beings whose minds are attached to pleasures, their acts require great trouble (for performance) but bear little or no fruit at all (in return). But that is not the case with us who dedicate all our actions to you (We require less trouble to perform the act, and get substantial fruit in return, and it is never futile).

48. Even the slightest resemblance of action, if dedicated to the Lord, never becomes futile (but brings substantial results); for the Lord loves and wishes well of such person (who has resigned himself to him and his actions, therefore, will not be futile).

1. VJ. *guṇāḥ* etc.: devotion etc., or colours. The *v.l.* *vāśeṣam*-The Nature, Jīva, time etc.—VJ.

49. Just as watering the root of trees proves nourishing to its trunk and branches, similarly the propitiation of Lord Viṣṇu leads to the propitiation of all gods and of one's self also.

50. I bow to you, the infinite Lord whose nature and deeds are extremely difficult to comprehend; you are devoid of all attributes, and yet are the master of all qualities, and who at present are established in *sattva.*

CHAPTER SIX

(*Mount Mandara Transported for Churning the Ocean*)

Śrī Śuka said:

1. Oh king! Thus praised by the hosts of gods, the glorious Lord Hari, the supreme Ruler, manifested Himself to them with the effulgence of a thousand suns rising simultaneously.

2. By that very glaring effulgence, all gods got their eyes so much dazzled that they could not perceive the sky, the cardinal points, the earth and even themselves. How could they see the omnipresent Lord?

3. The glorious god Brahmā along with Śiva, beheld that immaculate Form, dark like emerald (blue like sapphire), with eyes reddish like the interior of a lotus.

4. It was clad in bright yellow silken garment (*Pītāmbara*) shining like burning gold, graceful and lovely in every limb, with beautiful countenance and attractive eyebrows.

5. It was adorned with a crown crested with highly precious gems and a pair of armlets (keyūras one on each arm); Its cheeks illumined by the bright splendour of the pendant ear-rings, added to the beauty of its lotus like countenance.

6. It was adorned with an ornamented girdle, bracelets, necklace and pair of anklets. It was wearing the deco-

rative *Kaustubha* gem, the goddess Lakṣmī, and a wreath of sylvan flowers (on its breast).

7. It was attended upon by its missiles like *Sudarśana* and others in their personal form. Brahmā, the foremost among the gods, along with god Śiva, and with hosts of celestials, lay prostrate before him on the ground, and eulogized the Supreme Person (as follows);

Brahmā said:

8.* I offer my obeisance again and again to you of whom birth, subsistence and destruction are beyond predication; who transcends the (three) *guṇas*; who is the ocean of (absolute) bliss attainable in the Final Beatitude; who is the subtlest of the subtle, yet whose glory is immeasurable and powers unlimited.

9. Oh Supreme Person! This form of yours is ever worthy to be adored by those who aspire after the (highest) bliss, through methods prescribed in the Vedas and *tantras* (like *pañcarātra*). Oh Creator and Protector of the universe! In this form of yours which pervades the universe, I see (simultaneously) all the three worlds as well as ourselves.

10. In you who are self-dependent, the universe abided in you at the beginning; in you, it exists in the middle and it will be absorbed in you (after its dissolution) in the end. Just as the earth persists (as the material cause) in the beginning, the middle and the end of a pot, similarly you are the beginning, the middle and the end of this universe.[1]

11. Through your Māyā—potency which absolutely depends on you, you have created the universe, and subse-

*VJ : Again and again I salute to you who are *Aja* (Birthless-*Viṣṇu*), the creation, subsistence and dissolution of the universe, the very personification of various attributes (e.g. *Ānanda*, *Vijñāna*), the ocean of bliss impossible to those who identify themselves with the physical body, and of limitless glory.

1. VJ differs : According to VJ. God is not the material cause but the supreme cause on which other causes depend. The particle *ca* in VJ's text indicates that if Brahman be the material cause even non-sentient material world would be sentient. VR. accepts God as the material cause of the universe, but God is unaffected by changes (*upādānatve'pi tasya nirvikāratvam*),

quently have entered into it (as its Inner Controller). The thoughtful people who are well-versed in *Śāstras* and who have (controlled and) concentrated their minds, perceive through their mind that you are not affected by *guṇas*, even though you abide in them (i.e. in the universe which is the product of *guṇas* in which you have entered).

12. It is a well-known fact that, by adopting proper means, men get fire from wood (by friction of wooden pieces —*araṇis*), nectar i.e. milk from the cows, food and water from the earth (by agriculture and digging) and livelihood by working (in a profession or vocation), similarly thoughtful people, through their intelligence perceive You in (the world which is) the product of *guṇas* and describe you accordingly.

13. Oh Lord! Having seen You graciously (and thus fulfilling) our desire for a long time, we feel extremely blissful as elephants distressed by forest-conflagration do, on reaching the waters of the *Gaṅgā*, Oh Lord with a lotus in your navel.

14. Such as You are (as described above), do fulfill our desire for which we, the guardians of the Worlds have approached Your feet. Oh Lord (the pervader of the universe from inside and outside)! You witness everything. What is there to be made known to you from outside by others ?

15. To You, I, Śiva, gods (and other beings), Dakṣa (and other Lords of creation)—We all are like sparks of fire emanating from fire (and appearing distinct from fire, though originally they are one). Separate as we are, what do we know of (the way to) our welfare? Oh Lord ! Be pleased to advise us what may be beneficial to Brāhmaṇas and gods.

Śrī Śuka said:

16. Being thus prayed (and extolled) by Brahmā and others, and with a full understanding of their hearts, the Lord, in a voice like the rumbling of clouds, addressed the gods who, controlling their senses perfectly, stood with folded palms.

17. Although the Lord alone was capable to accomplish the object of the gods, he, being desirous of indulging in sportful activities like the churning of the ocean and others, addressed them as follows:

The Lord said:

18. Hello ! Brahman, Śiva, gods and demigods ! Listen attentively to my speech, so that all of you will attain welfare and desired object.

19. You do go just now and conclude a peace-treaty with the Daityas and Dānavas who are favoured by time, till you find that growth (prosperous time) has now returned (till Fortune smiles on you).

20. When an object to be achieved is important, an alliance should be entered into, even with enemies. When once, you have accomplished your purpose, you may behave as a serpent does with a mouse.[1]

21. Without any delay, efforts should be made to produce the nectar, by drinking which a being in the jaws of death will become immortal.

22-23. Having thrown all kinds of plants, grasses, creepers and herbs in the sea of milk, and making mount Mandara as the churning rod and Vāsuki (the king of snakes) as the churning rope, you churn the ocean well assiduously with My help. The Daityas shall undergo the trouble of churning while you shall reap the fruit thereof.

24. Oh gods! You agree to whatever desire the Daityas express. All objects are not successfully achieved through anger (and confrontation), as through conciliatory methods.

25. You need not be afraid of the Kālakūṭa poison that will come out of the (churned) sea (for god Śiva will drink it). You should not evince any desire or covetousness (for the objects churned out) or express any anger if Daityas do so.

Śrī Śuka said:

26. After instructing the gods in this way, the glorious Supreme Person, the Ruler (of the universe) who acts according to his own free will, disappeared from their view, Oh king.

27. Having bowed down to the Venerable Lord (who

1. ŚR.—Just as a serpent caught in box by a snake-charmer formed friendship with a mouse outside (to make a hole into that box). When the serpent creeps out of that box, it eats up that mouse. Similarly you should behave now.

had disappeared), god Brahmā and Śiva returned to their respective regions, while gods approached Bali (the king of demons).

28. The praiseworthy king of Daityas who knew the opportune time when to wage war, and when to make peace, restrained his generals, who got excited at the sight of their enemies in that unprepared condition.

29. Then (the gods) approached Bali, the son of Virocana, seated (on a throne) and guarded by Asura generals, endowed with the highest royal splendour after the conquest of the three worlds.

30. The highly intelligent Indra consoled Bali with many soft words, and spoke to him everything as per briefings of the Supreme Man.

31. The (oral) proposal was acceptable to Bali and to other Asura rulers like Śambara, Ariṣṭanemi and other residents of Tripura who were present.

32. Then gods and Asuras reached an agreement, and after contracting a friendly alliance, they made great efforts for obtaining the nectar, Oh tormentor of enemies.

33. Then, being arrogantly proud (of their physical strength), they (gods and demons) forcibly pulled out the mount Mandara. Shouting lustily, they with their *Parigha*-like long and powerful arms, proceeded to take it to the sea.

34. Being thoroughly exhausted by carrying the heavy burden, Indra, Bali and other gods and demons became unable to take it any further and helplessly left it on the way.

35. While the mountain of gold was falling there, it crushed to death under its weight many gods and demons.

36. Knowing that they (gods and demons) had got their arms, thighs and necks broken and were dispirited and nervous, the Eagle-bannered Lord manifested himself there.

37. Having seen the gods and Dānavas (demons) have been crushed by the falling of the mountain, he, by his mere glance, restored gods to life as if they were unhurt.

38. Sportively, with one hand, he placed the mountain on Garuḍa, and mounting it (Garuḍa), he went to the sea surrounded by the hosts of gods and demons.

39. Having taken down the mountain from his shoul-

ders and placing it near the water (of the sea) Garuḍa, the best and foremost among birds, being discharged by Lord Hari, went his way.

CHAPTER SEVEN

The Churning of the Sea for Nectar

Śrī Śuka said :

1-2. They (gods and demons) invited Vāsuki, the king of serpents, agreeing to give him his due share in the proceeds (lit. fruit viz. nectar arising out of that churning). They bound him round the mountain (*Mandara*) like a churning cord. Joyfully yet with a firm determination, they began (to churn the ocean) for the nectar. At first, Lord Hari took hold of the head-side (of the serpent) and gods followed him.

3-4. The lords of the demons did not approve of this act of the Supreme Person. We, who have mastered the Vedic lore and *śāstric* studies and are well-known for our noble birth and deeds, will not hold the tail, that dirty, inauspicious limb of the serpent. (Protesting thus) they stood aloof in silence Seeing that, the Supreme Person, smilingly left off the fore part (of Vāsuki), and took hold of his tail along with the gods.

5. Having thus defined their positions, the sons of Kāśyapa (both gods and demons), began to churn the sea of milk with utmost exertion, for the sake of nectar (*amṛta*).

6. Oh delight (descendant) of Pāṇḍu ! While the sea was being churned, the mountain being unsupported (from below), sank down into the water, due to its own weight, despite the efforts of the mighty ones (gods and demons) to hold it up.

7. Finding their manly efforts frustrated by the much more powerful Providence, they became extremely dejected at heart, and their countenances grew pale.

8. Noticing the set-back caused by the Lord of obstacles,

The Lord of infinite prowess and unfailing determination, assumed the wonderful form of a gigantic tortoise and diving deep into the water bore up the mountain (on its back).

9. Beholding the great mountain being so raised up, the gods and demons proceeded to churn up the sea. The Lord bore the mountain on its back which was, like another big continent, eight hundred thousand *Yojanas* in extent.

10. Supporting on his back the revolving mountain (which was set in motion and was) shaking by the velocity of the powerful arms of the chiefs of gods and demons, (the Lord, incarnated as) the First Tortoise of immeasurable power, regarded the circular motion of the mountain as pleasant scratching of his back, Oh dear King!

11. (Finding the need for still more vigorous efforts) with a view to invigorate their strength and energy, Lord Viṣṇu entered into the Asuras in his demonic form (i. e. his *rājasic* nature); He stimulated the power and energy of the hosts of gods by entering into them in his godly form (i. e. his *sāttvic* nature and into Vāsuki in the form of suspended consciousness (his *tāmasic* form).

12. The Lord of one thousand arms stood like another king of mountains, and stabilised the big mount Mandara by placing one hand over it. The gods headed by Brahmā, Lord Śiva and Indra in the heaven eulogised him and showered him with flowers.

13. Strengthened by the Supreme Lord as pressing the churning rod from above, supporting it from below in the form of a tortoise, entering into the bodies of gods and demons, the mountain (churning rod), and the serpent (the churning cord) the gods and demons lustily and joyously churned the ocean with the great mountain so violently, that all the crocodiles (and other acquatic animals) were greatly agitated.

14. The demons headed by Pauloma, Kāleya, Bali, Ilvala, and others whose splendour and energy was marred with the fire and smoke gushing forth from the thousand fearful eyes and nostrils of that big serpent, became like the *Sarala* trees consumed by forest conflagration.

15. Over the celestials whose splendour was dimmed by the flaming breaths of Vāsuki and whose clothes, excellent

garlands, coats and faces became smoky in colour, the clouds, under the control and (direct command) of the Lord copiously poured showers, and (cool) breezes, impregnated with the waves of the sea, began to blow.

16. When no nectar could come out from the sea, though it was vigorously churned that way (as described above), by the leaders of the hosts of gods and demons, the Unconquerable Lord began to churn it himself.

17. When the Lord, dark blue like clouds, wearing brightly shining garment of golden hue, adorned with a pair of ear-rings, flashing like lightning, with glossy wavy locks of hair on the head, wearing *vanamālā* (a garden of sylvan flowers), with eyes reddish like red lotus, churned the ocean, supporting the mount Mandara from below, and holding in his triumphant arms vouchsafing protection to the worlds, the serpent, he shone like another rival mountain.

18. From the ocean that was being churned and (as a consequence of which) teeming shoals of fishes, crocodiles, sea serpents, and tortoises and whales, sea elephant, alligators and whale-eater *timiṅgalas* got agitated, there issued forth the most deadly poison called *Halāhala*.

19. As that effervescent, irresistible unbearable poison of deadly force spread in each and every direction, above and below, creatures along with their leaders became terribly afraid, and for want of protection flew to Lord Sadāśiva for protection.

20. Beholding that foremost of gods seated along with his divine Consort on the mountain (Kailāsa) for the creation (or prosperity) of the three worlds, and practising penance, so agreeable to sages, for their final Liberation, and thus setting up an ideal before them, they (the celestial patriarchs) paid obeisance to him and offered their prayer.

The Lords of Created Beings said :

21. Oh God of gods ! Oh Supreme God ! Oh Creator, the very soul of beings ! Be pleased to save us who have sought shelter in you, from the poison that is burning the three worlds.

22. You alone are the Almighty Ruler capable of causing bondage and emancipation of the whole worlds, the wise

adore you as such, and as the father (or preceptor) who removes the afflictions of those who seek refuge in you.

23. Oh all pervading Lord! When you, through your own Potency consisting of three *guṇas*, undertake to create, preserve and destroy the universe, Oh self-seeing perfect Lord, you assume (severally) the appellations Brahmā, Viṣṇu and Śiva.

24. You are that Supreme mysterious Brahman, the creator of beings, of the higher (gods) and the lower order (sub-human beings). You are the supreme soul who appear as the universe by means of your various powers (such as *Sattva, Rajas* and *Tamas*). Hence you are the Controller and Master of the Universe.

25. You are the source of the Word (*Vedas*) and (hence you stand self-revealed); you are the prime cause of the universe (viz. the principle *mahat*), the soul (the cosmic ego or *ahaṁkāra*); the three *guṇas* (viz. *sattva, rajas* and *tamas*) which bring forth the Vital airs (*prāṇas*), cognitive and conative sense-organs (*indriyas*) and the material object (*dravya*) and the essential nature (*Sva-bhāva*) of everything, you are the Time spirit (causing commotion and imbalance of *guṇas*), the will to create (*kratu*), the Truth, the (cosmic) Order, the righteousness. The *śāstras* declare that *Pradhāna* constituting of the three *guṇas* is based on (and supported by) you, (or the Praṇava consisting of three syllables A U M reveals you) *

**This verse is variously interpreted* :—

(i) VR : They say that You are the authority of *śāstras*, the cause of the world, the Supreme Self Who is of the nature of vital breath (*prāṇas*), senses, the five elements (*bhūtas*) whose body is Time, the Brahman, The Inner Controller of all, *dharma* (religiousness or to be adored with piety) and the three-syllabled (AUM) *praṇava* is regarded as representing You.

(ii) VJ : You are the root-cause of understanding; You are the promoter of life (senses etc), Your Will is the Truth itself; You are of the nature of existence (*sat*) consciousness (*cit*) and bliss (*ānanda*); You are the *dharma* as You preserve the (social) order; You are designated by the letter OM (as stated by *upaniṣads*).

(iii) SD : *Kratu—Pravṛtti dharma*—leading to worldly life.

Satya & ṛta—Nivṛtti dharma—leading to renunciation of worldly life.

(iv) GD: *satya—factual statement*—Truth.

ṛta—sweet speech.

dharma—sacrifices and other rituals.

26. Oh Creator of the universe ! Fire which represents, gods in its person (as the distributor of sacrificial offerings to gods) is your mouth; the wise know that the earth is your lotus-like feet; Time is the motion, the cardinal points, the ears, and Varuṇa (the Lord of waters) the palate, of you who are the soul (the Inner controller) of all gods.

27. The sky represents your navel; the wind, your breath, the sun, your eyes, water, (your semen; the support of all *jīvas* (individual souls) elevated (like that of god Brahmā) and ordinary (like those of sub-human beings), is your ego; *Soma* or the Moon-god, your mind, and the heavens, your head.

28. The seas symbolize your abdomen, the mountains your bones ; all plants and herbs your hair; the Vedic metres seven humours in your body; the *dharma* as enunciated in the Vedas your heart, Oh embodiment of the three Vedas.

29. Oh Lord ! the five upanisads[1] (the sacred hymns or *mantras* known as *Tatpuruṣa*, *Aghora*, *Sadyojāta*, *Vāmadeva*, and *Īśāna*) from which the collection of thirty eight *mantras* evolve, denote your (five) faces; that self-effulgence constituting the supreme principle which is designated as *Śiva* is your (real) absolute state.

1 : The text of the five *mantras* or *upaniṣads* are as follows :

(i) *Tat puruṣāya vidmahe, Mahādevāya dhīmahī* |
tanno Rudraḥ pracodayāt ||

(ii) *Aghorebhyo'tha ghorebhyo ghora-ghora-tarebhyaḥ* |
sarvatas sarva-sarvebhyo namas te astu Rudra-rūpebhyaḥ |

(iii) *sadyo-jātaṁ prapadyāṁ sadyo jātāya vai namaḥ* |
bhave bhavenāti-bhave bhajasva māṁ bhavod-bhavāya namaḥ |

(iv) *Vāmadevāya namo, jyeṣṭhāya namo, Rudrāya namaḥ, Kālāya namaḥ, kala-vikaraṇāya namo bala-vikaraṇāya namo, bala-pramathanāya namas sarva-bhūta-damanāya namo, manonmanāya namaḥ* ||

(v) *Īśānas sarva-vidyānām Īśvaras sarva-bhūtānāṁ, Brahmā'dhipatir Brahmaṇo' dhipatir Brahmā Śivo me astu sadāśivam* ||

VD. has given the details how these five *mantras* or *upaniṣads* are broken up into thirty-eight *mantras*.

For exemple, from the 1st *upaniṣad Tatpuruṣāya* evolve the following *mantras* :—

(1) *Tat-puruṣāya vidmahe śāntyai* |
(2) *Mahādevāya dhīmahī Vidyāyai* |
(3) *tanno Rudraḥ Pratiṣṭhāyai* |
(4) *Pracodayāt dhṛtyai* |

30. Your shadow is seen in the waves of unrighteousness (such as hypocrisy, covetousness (by which destruction is caused; your (three) eyes are *sattva*, *rajas* and *tamas* (which bring about the creation of the universe); Oh Lord, the eternal Veda mainly composed in meters (like Gāyatrī, Triṣṭubh) stand for your glance; for you are the omniscient[1] propounder of the *śāstric* lore.

31. Oh Lord of mountains! Your supreme effulgence where the modes of *Prakṛti* like *sattva*, *rajas* and *tamas* have no place, and which is nothing but the supreme Brahman transcending all distinctions and differentiations, is absolutely inacessible to all the guardian deities of various spheres and to Brahmā, Viṣṇu[2] and Indra.

32. That you destroyed Kāma (the god of Love), the sacrifice (of Dakṣa), Tripuras—the three cities (constructed by Maya) subdued the god of death, consumed the (Halāhala) poison (which is as good as consumed as you are certain to drink it up just now) and killed innumerable trouble-makers of living beings, is not so much praiseworthy, on your part, as your unawareness of the razing down of this universe—your own creation by the sparks emanating from the fire in your own (third) eye (you remaining absorbed in deep meditation)[3]

33. Shameless are they who talk nonsense that you are always accompanied by (your consort) Umā of whom you are (excessively) enamoured, though (actually) the pair of your feet are contemplated in their hearts by the world's preceptors who are absorbed in the spiritual bliss of the soul. (They are certainly brazen-faced) who (glibly) prate that you are a ferocious and murderous denizen of the funeral-place when you are a performer of austere penance (as an ideal to the

1. for *saṅkhyātmanaḥ*—VJ reads *sākṣāt Manuḥ* 'Manu' himself Who enunciated the *śāstras* represents Your glance, from which originated the divine sage, by your free will.

2. Vaikuṇṭha :—VR explains that here the Supreme Soul is eulogised. As he abides in Rudra, He i.e. the Supreme Soul is rightly regarded as inaccessible to Vaikuṇṭha or upendra.

3. VJ :—states that the praise of Hara is really that of Hari, as mentioned in 'Hari, 'the soul of all is pleased hereby' *sarvātmā prīyate Hariḥ*).

sages) ! Never can such (people lost to shame) understand your sportive ways.

34. Even god Brahmā and others are incapable of accurately comprehending your essential nature, much less are they able to praise you who are all-pervading and transcendental to *Prakṛti* (The primordial nature) lying beyond the causal relation. How is it possible for us (the recentmost) creation of the creations (like Marīci and others) of Brahmā to extol you ? The prayer offered by us (to the best of our ability) is limited to our (meagre) capacity[1].

35. Oh Supreme Lord ! What we behold is only your (apparent) visible form, but not the trancendental one. (We however, consider ourselves blessed even with this). Though your activities are unmanifest, this manifestation of yours is meant for the weal (and protection) of the world.

Śrī Śuka said :

36. Observing the calamity of those (gods other beings) and being overwhelmed with compassion for them, the Deity, the friend of all beings, spoke thus unto his beloved consort Satī (i.e. Umā) (lest his beloved Umā should prohibit him from drinking the *Halāhala* poison).

Lord Śiva said :

37. "Oh ! What a pity ! Behold, Oh Bhavānī ! What calamity has befallen these creatures from the poison *Kālakūṭa*, produced from the churning of the sea of milk.

38. Certainly, it behoves me now to offer protection to these who are anxious to save their lives; for the protection of the afflicted is the sole concern (duty) of those who are powerful.

39-40. Saintly persons protect (the lives of) beings by sacrificing their own lives which they regard as transient. Oh auspicious lady ! Lord Hari, the soul of all (creatures), is pleased with the man who extends mercy to created beings who, being deluded by the illusive potency of the Supreme Self, become the enemies of each other. When the glorious

1. Our praise is an expresssion of our earnest devotion. VJ.

Lord Hari is pleased, I feel delighted along with the mobile and immobile creation. I, therefore, swallow up (the whole of) this poison. May blessings (and happy life) proceed from me to all the creatures."

Śrī Śuka said :

41. Having thus persuaded his consort, Pārvatī, the glorious Lord Śiva, who confers Bliss upon (or protects) the universe, proceeded to swallow up the poison; She, too, being aware of his prowess, expressed her approbation.

42. The liquid-poison (the concentrated impurities of the churned sea) showed its power even in his case inasmuch as, it reduced his throat blue, though it became an ornament of that benevolent Deity.

43. Generally righteous persons become afflicted at the torments and troubles of other people; for that (mitigation of those troubles) constitutes the highest type of worship of the Supreme Person, the Soul of the Universe.

44. Observing the wonderful feat (of swallowing up of the deadly poison) of Lord Śiva, the God of gods who fulfills the desires of his devotees, all creatures, Dakṣa's daughter (his consort Satī), god Brahmā and Viṣṇu eulogised him.

45. What (negligible) little poison leaked down from his palms while drinking, was conserved by scorpions, serpents, poisonous herbs and plants, cobras and other biting animals like dogs, jackals etc.).

CHAPTER EIGHT

The Lord's Manifestation as Mohinī (The Enchantress)

Śrī Śuka said :

1. When the (Kālakūṭa) poison was drunk up by god Śiva (whose emblem is the bull), these celestials and demons felt (relieved and) delighted, and began to churn the sea with

(redoubled) force. Out of that churning emerged *Surabhi* (the wish-yielding cow).

2. The sages, the expounders of the *Vedas* (who devote themselves to sacrifices) accepted it (*Surabhi* which supplied materials like milk, ghee, useful for sacrifices) for (obtaining) sacred oblations in sacrificial performances which constitutes the path of gods (leading to the region of Brahman).

3. After this came out a horse named *Uccaiḥśravas* which was radiantly white like the moon. Bali expressed his desire for it (and took possession of it) but not Indra, as per instructions given by the Lord.

4. Next sprang forth the majestic (moon-white) elephant called Airāvata which, by its four tusks (huge like peaks of mountains) eclipsed the splendour and beauty of the white (snowy) mountain, Kailāsa, (the abode) of the glorious god Śiva.

5. Out of the (churned) ocean, came out a jewel called *Kaustubha*, a precious stone of ruby type. Hari expressed his desire to have that jewel as an adornment for his chest.

6. Thereafter, arose the (celestial tree) *Pārijāta* the ornament of the heavenly region,—a tree capable of conferring eternally all the objects desired by the supplicants just as your honour (Parīkṣit) does on the earth.

7. Next to that came out the *Apsaras* (celestial nymphs) adorned with gold necklaces (and other ornaments), clad in excellent raiments, who delight the denizens of heaven with their charming gait, sportive movements and bewitching glances.

8. And thereafter was manifested goddess Lakṣmī, the very embodiment of Affluence (Śrī), the delight of Lord Hari (Ramā), who is (absolutely) devoted to the glorious Lord. She illumined with her splendour all the quarters (making people residing therein desirous to have affluence), even as the flash of lightening does against the crystalline reflector like mountain Sudāmā.

9. With their minds agitated by the excellence of her glorious beauty, graceful mobility, youthful age and brilliant complexion, all of them including gods, demons and human

beings, cherished a desire for her (in the form of affluence as they know her to be the mother of the three worlds).

10. The great Indra offered her a highly wonderful seat, while principal rivers, in their personal form, brought sacred waters in gold pitchers (for her ablutions).

11. The earth supplied all the herbs and plants required for her ablutions: cows, the five sacred articles (such as milk, curd, ghee constituting the *pañcagavya*) and the spring, all kinds of fruits and flowers produced in the vernal months of *Caitra* and *Vaiśākha*.

12. (With these articles) the seers laid down the procedure of Śāstric rites for her ablutions; while the Gandharvas began to sing auspicious song (in mellifluous notes), and celestial damsels well-versed in dancing, danced and sang.

13. The (presiding deities of) clouds poured forth the sounds of musical instruments like *mṛdaṅga*, *paṇava*, *muraja*, *ānaka* and *gomukha* (various kinds of drums, kettle drums etc.) and produced notes of conchs, flutes, string instruments like *viṇā* in a loud fan-fare.

14. Thereafter, while Vedic hymns were being chanted by Brāhmaṇas, elephants supporting the four quarters, bathed with gold pots filled with sacred waters, the virtuous (sacred) goddess Śrī who was holding a lotus in her hand.

15. (When her bath was over) the ocean presented her two pieces of yellow silk raiments (one for the lower part of the body and one for the upper). Varuṇa offered her the garland Vaijayantī—by sucking honey from which the black-bees got intoxicated.

16. Viśvakarmā, the progenitor, presented her with various wonderful ornaments; Sarasvatī, a necklace of pearls; and Brahmā, a lotus and serpents, a pair of ear-rings.

17. Thereafter, when the auspicious *mantras* for averting evils were chanted and the benedictions were given (by Brāhmaṇas)[1], the goddess Śrī took in her hand a garland of (blue) lotuses with a swarm of black bees loudly humming about it. Her exceedingly beautiful countenance beaming with

1. *Kṛta-svastyayana* —The Comm. note the pun on *Svastyayana* : Śrī who has her permanent abode (*ayana*) on the auspicious bosom of Lord Viṣṇu (*Svasti*).

a bashful smile and with the dangling of ear-rings pressed against her lovely cheeks, she set out (in search of her Lord).

18. With a pair of symmetrical, big breasts (closely touching each other) pasted with sandal and saffron, and a beautifully slender waist, she shone like a moving creeper of gold while she moved through the big assembly, making sweet jingling sound of her anklets.

19. She (The goddess Śrī) the embodiment of Affluence was looking out for a resort (viz. a husband) absolutely faultless, eternal and endowed with everlasting excellences, but she could not get one among the *gandharvas*, *yakṣas*, demons, *siddhas*, *cāraṇas*, celestials and others (in that assembly).

20. (The goddess Lakṣmī[1] in the form of Affluence says to herself.)

"Verily a person possessing asceticism has no control over his anger (e.g. the sage Durvāsas); (similarly) someone is endowed with wisdom but is not above attachment (e.g. Bṛhaspati or Śukra—the preceptors of gods and demons); some possess greatness but have no control over libidinousness (e.g. god Brahmā or Soma); how can a person (like Indra) who depends for his protection on others (or who is deprived of his position by others i.e. enemies) can be a ruler?

21. Righteousness is found in some but they lack compassion for other beings (e.g. Paraśurāma); some others have liberality but that is not conducive to Final Liberation (e.g. King Śibi); some are endowed with virility and prowess, which are subject to the ravages of Time; while the other who is (like Sage Sanaka completely free from attachment to *guṇas*, will have no place for (i.e. will have nothing to do with) the other person (even his wife, as he is always absorbed in meditation).

22. In some person there is a long life but they are not of amiable nature (liked by women, as, like Mārkaṇḍeya, they are always self-controlled); even that virtue is found in some but the duration of their life is unknown; in some (e.g. god Śiva) there is both (longevity and amiability) but even

1. VD. explains that a great goddess like Lakṣmī possessed the knowledge of the past, present and the future. Hence she rejects persons though not present in the assembly.

he is inauspicious (as he stays in funeral grounds). And he who is exceedingly auspicious (as well as long living and lovable) but he (being self-satisfied) does not care for me".

23. Coming to this conclusion (after deliberation), she elected as her spouse, Lord Viṣṇu (Mukunda) who was most worthy due to his everlasting excellences, absolute independence and desirelessness, who is transcendental to the *guṇas* of *Prakṛti* and was sought by all spiritual powers and (hence) was coveted by her even though he is disinterested in all.[1]

24. She placed on his shoulders (round his neck) the beautiful garland of blooming lotuses, resounding with the hum of intoxicated black bees. She stood by him silently waiting (for his grace). She indicated through her eyes blooming with a bashful smile that she attained to his bosom, her permanent resting place.

25. Lord Hari, the Father of the Three worlds offered his bosom as the permanent abode to Śrī (the celebrated consort and beloved of Hari), the mother of the three worlds who was the very embodiment of affluence and fortune or the source of all prosperity and riches. Being thus established (permanently and cosily), she promoted the welfare of all her creatures, the three worlds along with their rulers, by her compassionate and benign glances.

26. There was a loud chorus of the music and melodious notes issuing from the singing and dancing of the Gandharvas (lit. the followers of celestials) along with their wives (celestial damsels) and of the musical instruments such as conchs, trumpets, and drums (which were being played in its accompaniment).

27. Showering flowers on him, all progenitors of the worlds headed by Brahmā, Rudra, and Aṅgiras began to chant the glories of the All-pervading Lord in sacred hymns descriptive of his excellences and of appropriate import.

28. Being looked upon (with Grace) by Śrī, the gods,

1. ŚR. adds : Lakṣmī thought that though Viṣṇu is not interested in others due to His immersion in eternal spiritual bliss, He would not neglect her after marriage, as He entertains the Siddhis. She would consider herself blessed in His service. There is no propriety in marrying ordinary persons.

progenitors of the worlds along with their creation, became endowed with virtuous nature and other excellences, and attained the supreme-most felicity.

29. When the Daityas and Dānavas were disregarded by the goddess Lakṣmī, they became dispirited, voluptuous, indolent and devoid of the sense of shame, Oh king.

30. Thereupon, arose the presiding deity of wine, Vāruṇī by name, in the form of a girl with lotus-eyes. The Asuras verily took hold of her, by the consent of Lord Hari.

31. As the sea was being churned by the sons of sage Kāśyapa (viz. gods and demons) with a desire to get the nectar there appeared a highly wonderful personage.

32. His (pair of) arms were long and muscular (stout); his neck was adorned with three lines as on a conch; his eyes were reddish; complexion bluish (like a cloud); youthful in age; wearing a wreath and adorned with all ornaments.

33. Clad in yellow garment, the broad-chested person was adorned with ear-rings of highly polished jewels; his hair were soft, glossy and curly even to their ends; that charming person walked with a lion-like gait.

34. Adorned with bracelets and bearing (in his hands) a jar full of nectar, he was indeed a direct manifestation of a minute portion of a ray of the most glorious Lord Viṣṇu.

35-37 He was the well-known Dhanvantari, the Father (or revealer) of the Science of Medicine (lit. Science of life) who is a recipient of a special share in sacrificial offerings. Beholding him and the jar brimming with nectar (in his hands), all the demons, being covetous of appropriating all the products (of the churned ocean) to themselves, forcibly snatched away the jar (from him). As the jar containing nectar was thus being forcibly taken away by the Asuras, the gods, being dejected at heart sought refuge with lord Hari. Observing their pitiable condition described above, the glorious Lord who confers the desired objects to his servants (votaries), consoled them (thus): "Do not feel dejected. Both by sowing dissensions among the Asuras and by assuming the form of Mohinī (a charming damsel) through my deluding Yogic power, I shall accomplish your object"

38. With their hearts burning with the desire of grab-

bing the nectar, there arose a quarrel among them, each clamorously saying, "I must get it first", "my priority first", "Not you", "Not you".

39. "Gods too, who contributed their labour (efforts) to achieve this (production of nectar) deserve their due share in this (nectar) just as in a *Satra-yāga* all the performers of the sacrifice participate equally in the merit accruing from it). This is the eternal Law."

40. Oh king! In this way the weaker demons who got jealous of the stronger ones who usurped the jar (of nectar) constantly protested to them.

41 In the meanwhile, the Supreme Ruler Viṣṇu who knows all expedients, assumed an extremely wonderful form of a young damsel (charming) beyond the power of words.

42. The form (of the damsel) was attractive to the eyes. It was blue like a lotus, in complexion, beautiful in every limb. Its ears were symmetrical and adorned with ear-rings. Its countenance had beautiful cheeks and a shapely nose.

43. Its waist was slender due to the heavy breasts developed by blooming youth. Its eyes looked frightened (as if) by the humming of the black-bees attracted by the fragrance of its mouth.

44. It wore on its profuse mass (locks) of hair a wreath of blooming *Mallikā* (a kind of jasmine) flowers. Its shapely neck was beautified by a necklace and her beautiful arms were decked with armlets.

45. It appeared enchanting due to her girdle enhancing the beauty of islet-like big hips covered with shining (spotless) cloth. A pair of anklets making a jingling sound while walking decorated its feet.

46. By its bashful smiles, dancing eye-brows and amorous glances, it constantly provoked passion in the hearts of the Daitya generals.[1]

1. VJ's text continues this chapter to the end of the next one. Thus ŚR's 9th chapter corresponds to VJ's 8th chapter.

CHAPTER NINE

Distribution of Nectar by Mohinī

Śrī Śuka continued :

1. The Asuras who renounced the spirit of mutual friendship, reproached each other (for the nectar). Adopting the ways of robbers (with a determination to secure the nectar) they were snatching the jar of nectar from each other when they happened to behold the approaching damsel (the Mohinī-form of Viṣṇu).

2. "Oh what a graceful form! What exquisite splendour ! What a charming youthfulness !" With such passion enkindled in their hearts, they ran up to her and began to enquire.

3. "Who are you Oh damsel, with eyes like lotus-petals? Whence have you come ? What do you intend to do (What is the object of your visit)? Tell us whose daughter you are. You are as it were churning (agitating) our minds, Oh lady with shapely thighs !

4. Not that we do not know (i. e. we do know definitely) that you are not touched by the celestials, Daityas, Siddhas, Gandharvas, Cāraṇas or (even by) guardians of the worlds. How then (could it be) by human beings ?

5. Oh lady with beautiful brows ! Indeed ! you must have been certainly deputed by the merciful Lord of the universe to give delight to the senses and minds of all embodied beings. Is it not so ? or have you come of your own accord ?

6. Oh proud lady with a beautiful waist ! (Deputed by the Lord as you are) ! As such it behoves you to bring about amity and happiness among us who, though kins, have turned out to be enemies by jealously contending to obtain one common object.

7. As the sons of the sage Kaśyapa, we are all brothers and have displayed our prowess. Be pleased to distribute the prize (the nectar) equitably, so that there will be no ground for a quarrel.

8. When approached with this request by the Daityas, Lord Hari who assumed the form of that damsel by his delu-

ding Potency (*Māyā*), just laughed, and addressed them as follows, looking at them (all the while) with captivating side-long glances.

The Lord said :

9. How is it that you, the sons of the (great) sage Kaśyapa,[1] associate yourselves with a wanton woman like me? Certainly, no wise man reposes trust in women.

10. Oh enemies of celestials! The wise people say that the friendship of wolves and especially of way-ward women who are always on the look-out for ever-new victims (and men), is momentary (and unreliable).

Śrī Śuka said :

11. By such of her jocular and enticing remarks, the Asuras (were tempted to feel) reassured in their minds. They gave out an incomprehensible yet significant laugh, and handed over the jar of nectar to her.

12. Thereupon, taking the charge of the jar of nectar, Hari spoke in a tone brightened up with a gentle smile: "If you (unanimously and whole-heartedly) are ready to accept whatever I do, whether right or wrong, in any way (I please), (then and then only) I shall (undertake to) distribute the nectar among you".

13. On hearing her speech, the leaders of the Asuras, incapable of comprehending the depth and significance of her words, agreed to her condition saying "Be it so".

14. Thereupon having observed a fast[2] (as per Mohinī's instruction) they took their bath. After offering oblations to the fire, and having distributed (food etc.) to cows,

1. VD. dissolves: *Kaśyapa-dāyāda*—into Kaśya-pa-dāya-ada—who are in the habit of and deserving to be served with wine. "Why do you want nectar ?" VC. "You, sons of a great sage like Kaśyapa ! The father a great sage and the sons hunt after wanton women !" This is the sarcastic joke.

2. *Upoṣya*—VC. states that they had already observed a fast for the auspicious act of drinking nectar. But a quarrel broke out among themselves for settling which Mohinī became the mediator. After entrusting the jar of nectar to her, they took their bath.

Brāhmaṇas and other beings, they got performed the rite of *Svastyayana* (recitation of benedictory verses and offer of blessings) by Brāhmaṇas.

15. Wearing brand new clothes according to their (individual) choice, and gorgeously adorning their person with ornaments, all of them entered upon (and squatted) on (the seats of) *Kuśa* grass the ends which pointed to the east.

16-17. When the gods and demons (sons of *Diti*) were sitting with their faces to the east in that hall fragrant with incense, decorated with wreaths of flowers and illuminated with lamps, there entered, with the jar of nectar in hands, she (Mohinī) with beautiful, round, symmetrical thighs, of gait slow due (to the weight of) her bulky hips covered with brilliant silk raiment, eyes swimming as if through inebriation, of pitcher-like big breasts, warbling (as it were) with the jingling of her gold anklets, Oh King.

18. Ogling Her, the veritable supreme Deity, as a compeer to goddess Śrī[1] (or Lakṣmī in beauty), with a winning countenance, having beautiful ears adorned with gold ear-rings, shapely nose and charming cheeks, the gods and demons were completely enchanted by her glances accompanied with captivating smiles while her brassiere (the cloth cover of her breasts) slipped (exposing her breasts).

19. Considering that it is unfair to offer nectar to demons who like serpents are wicked by nature, Lord Viṣṇu did not distribute it to Asuras.

20. Arranging them both in separate rows, the Lord of the world made them sit in their respective rows.

21. Taking the Jar of nectar and beguiling the demons by charming movements of brows, bashful smiles, play with garment and ornaments, sweet flattering words, he made gods who were sitting at a distance, to drink the nectar which prevents old age and death.

22. Oh King! The Asuras abided by the pledge given

1. **Śrī-Sakhīm—GS. observes that though Viṣṇu was a male companion of Śrī, he acted like a female friend to serve the interests of his devotees.**

by them. Out of covetous lust for her and feeling it below their dignity to quarrel with a lady, they kept quiet.

23. They cherished unbounded attachment and lustful longing for her and were too nervous to affect it adversely. Being restrained by the high reverence shown to them by her ("Let the niggardly gods drink first. Sensible people like you should wait a bit") they uttered nothing unpleasant.

24. Disguising himself in the garb of celestials, Rāhu entered (stealthily) in the row of gods (between the sun and the moon) and drank the nectar but was indicated (exposed with gestures) by the sun and the moon (who feared him as more powerful than they).

25. Just while he (Rāhu) was drinking, Hari (swiftly) severed his head with his discus of razor-like sharpness so his headless trunk to which nectar did not touch, fell down dead.

26. His head (however) attained immortality upon which the Birthless Lord conferred planet-hood But cherishing (this old) enmity, he assails the sun and the moon on the new-moon-day and the full-moon-day (respectively whenever he gets an opportunity).

27. When gods had almost consumed the nectar, the glorious Lord Hari, the creator and protector of the world (renouncing his female form) reassumed his own form, while the Asura chiefs kept looking on (agape).

28. In this way, even though (the factors such as) time, place, instrument (apparatus), activity and the objective of the hosts of gods and demons were the same, there was divergence in the fruit (reaped). Out of them, gods easily obtained the fruit viz. the nectar, due to their resort to the dust of the lotus-feet of the Lord, while the Daityas did not.

29. Whatever is done by men with their life, wealth, senses, mind and words for their own person, progeny etc., becomes futile as a consequence of entertaining the idea of difference and distinction. But whatever is done by employing the same set of means dedicating them to the Lord without cherishing the sense of difference, is crowned with success like watering the roots of a tree (reaches to all its branches, leaves etc.).

CHAPTER TEN

A Battle between Gods and Asuras

Śrī Śuka continued:

1. In this way, Oh King, though Dānavas and the Daityas were careful and put in their best of efforts (in churning the ocean), they did not obtain the nectar because they had turned away their face from Lord Vāsudeva.

2. Having accomplished the production of ambrosia and having made his votaries, the gods, to drink of it, the Lord rode on the back of Garuḍa and flew away while all beings were simply looking on (agape).

3. Seeing the best luck (in succeeding to drink the nectar) of their enemies and being unable to tolerate it (out of jealousy), the sons of Diti (*Daityas*) attacked gods with their weapons uplifted.

4. With their power increased by drinking of nectar and depending on the feet of Lord Nārāyaṇa as their asylum, all the gods retaliated unanimously with their weapons.

5. There, on the shore (of the Milky Sea) was fought the fiercest and the most bloody battle called (after the belligerents as) the *Devāsura* battle (the report or sight of) which made the hair stand on end, Oh King!

6. There (on the sea-shore) the enemies with their minds full of wrath clashed (against each other) on the battle field and struck one another with swords, arrows and various other weapons.

7. Terrific was the noise caused by the blasting of conchs and trumpets, beating of tabors, drums and *Ḍamarus* and of the trumpeting elephants, neighing horses, rattling chariots and shouting soldiers.

8. In that battle, warriors in chariots clashed with car-warriors, foot-soldiers with foot-soldiers, horses with horses and elephants with elephants.

9. Some soldiers fought riding camels, some on elephants while others on donkeys, some on white-faced bears, while others on tigers and monkeys.

10. Some fought (while sitting) on the back of Kites,

vultures, cranes, on hawks and *bhāsas* (a kind of bird), whales (*Timiṅgalas*) and *Śarabhas* (eightfooted animal capable of killing a lion), bisons, rhinoceros, bulls, buffalos and *Aruṇas.*

11. Some fought (riding) on the backs of jackals, rats, chameleons, hares and men; some others on goats and sheep, deer and swans, while others on hogs.

12. Some fought riding birds of land and of water and others on animals of deformed shape. Warriors on both the sides penetrated more deeply and further still.

13-15. Like two oceans swarming with sea-monsters shone the two (warring) armies of Deva and Dānava worriors with their ranks of fighters distinguished by their flags of different colours, by their spotlessly white umbrellas with highly precious handles studded with diamonds, diamond handled fans made of feathers of peacock tails and *chowries*; with their upper garments and turbans waved up by winds and with their burnished armours and ornaments glittering brightly and their sharp weapons sparkling in the rays of the sun.

16-17. In this battle the commander-in-chief of the Asura force was Bali, the son of Virocana whose aerial car was called Vaihāyasa. It was manufactured by Maya and was capable of flying to any place at the occupant's will. It was equipped with all war-materials and weapons. Oh King, it was full of wonder that it surpassed all imagination and description (or could not be accurately located due to its unpredictable and quick movements); sometimes it was visible and sometimes invisible.

18. Surrounded by the commanders of Asura forces, Bali occupied that foremost aerial car. With *chowries* being waved on either side and with a white umbrella, he shone like a rising moon.

19-22 On all sides around him, in their respective aerial cars, attended various squadron-leaders of Asuras such as Namuci, Śambara, Bāṇa, Vipracitti, Ayomukha, Dvi-mūrdha (A two-headed demon), Kālanābha, Praheti, Heti, Ilvala, Śakuni, Bhūta-santāpa (the tormentor of all beings), Vajra-daṁṣṭra, Virocana, Hayagrīva, Śaṅku-Śiras, Kapila, Megha-dundubhi, Tāraka, Cakra-dṛk, Śumbha, Niśumbha, Jambha, Utkala, Ariṣṭa, Ariṣṭanemi, Maya, the Lord of the three flying cities and other demon (tribes) such as Pauloma, Kāleya, Nivāta-Kavaca and others.

23. Without receiving any share in the *soma* or nectar, they had only to undergo hardships and exertions (for churning out the nectar). All of them had mostly vanquished the gods, just at the beginning of the battle.

24. Roaring loudly like lions, they blasted their loud-sounding conchs. Perceiving his foes so proud (and confident of their strength), Indra, the killer of the demon Bala, became extremely enraged.

25. The king of heaven (Indra) who rode Airāvata, the elephant supporting the eastern direction, shone like the sun (the Lord of the day) rising on the eastern mountains with cascades (of water) gushing down.

26. Around Indra stood gods in their respective vehicles, with flags and wielding various weapons. There were the guardians of the world like Vāyu (the Wind-god), Agni (the fire-god), Varuṇa (the Lord of waters) and others along with their followers.

27. Assaulting each other violently and reviling one another in biting terms, cutting to the quick, they rushed forward challenging each other and engaged in duels.

28. Bali fought with Indra, Guha conflicted with Kārttikeya; Varuṇa contended with Heti, and the Sun-god with Praheti, Oh King.

29. Yama on his part combated with Kāla-nābha, Viśvakarmā verily gave battle with Maya; Śambara battled with Tvaṣṭṛ and Virocana with Savitṛ.

30. Namuci took up arms against Aparājita, the pair of Aśvinī-Kumāras against Vṛṣaparvā, the Sun-god alone against the hundred sons of Bali of whom Bāṇa was the eldest.

31. *Soma* (the Moon-god) gave battle with Rāhu; Anil (the wind-god) with Puloman; the mighty goddess Bhadrakālī with Niśumbha and Śumbha.

32. Vṛṣākapi combated with Jambha, Vibhāvasu with the demon Mahiṣa, Ilvala along with Vātāpi with the sons of god Brahmā (such as Marīci and others), Oh Vanquisher of enemies.

33. Durmarṣa fought with Kāmadeva (the god of Love),

Utkala with (seven) Mother-goddesses; Bṛhaspati fought with Śukra, and Śanaiścara (the presiding deity of the planet Saturn) with Naraka.

34. Maruts contended with Nivāta-Kavaca demons, the Vasu-gods with the Kāleya-tribe of Daityas, (gods called) Viśve-devas with the sons of Puloman and the (eleven) Rudra-gods with Krodhavaśa serpents.

35. In this way, in the battle wherein Asuras (demons) as well a leaders of gods were fighting in duels and collectively in as body, approached one another and with the desire of gaining victory, violently struck one another with sharp arrows, swords and iron clubs and javelins.

36. They chopped off the heads of each other with (weapons called) *bhuśuṇḍi* (a fire-arm), discuses, maces, lances, battle axes, *Śaktis*, *Ulmukas* (fire-brands) *prāsas* (a barbed missile) *Bhallakas*, (long swords), *parighas* (iron bars), *mudgaras* (hammer-shaped weapons), and *bhindipālas* (small javelins).

37. Elephants and horses (along with their riders), warriors riding chariots and foot-soldiers, riders of various animals and conveyances were cut down to pieces, their arms, thighs, necks and legs were hacked and hewn; their flags, bows, coats of armour and ornaments were torn and tattered.

38. Heavy dust that was raised by trampling and pounding under feet the battle-ground, and the dashing of the wheels of the chariot against it, enveloped the quarters, the sky, and the sun, but settled down to the ground by profuse flood of spouts of blood (of the wounded warriors—the spouts of blood reaching up to heaven drenching the clouds of dust).

39. That battle-field appeared bright as it was thickly strewn with heads from which the diadems and ear-rings were forcibly shaken off (and fallen), with eyes blood-shot with wrath, and tightly closed lips bitten with anger, long and stout arms decorated with ornaments and still clasping the weapons and thighs shapely like elephant's trunk.

40. The headless trunks of the warriors sprang to their feet and (as if) perceiving through the eyes of their fallen heads, rushed on the battle-field onwards the opposing warriors with their arms uplifted in their powerful arms.

41. Bali discharged at Indra ten arrows, three at the elephant Airāvata, four (one arrow each) at the four guards of Airāvata, and one at the conductor of the elephant.

42. Just with a smile, the prompt and valorous Indra cut them in the transit with equal number of sharp Bhalla arrows, even before they could reach him.

43. Observing his excellent skill (in archery) Bali, being intolerant, took in his hand a *Śakti* (a dart-like missile) dazzling like a big meteor. But Indra cut it while it was in the hands of Bali.

44. Then in a serial order Bali took up a *Śūla* (a spear), a *prāsa* (a barbed missile), a *tomara* (an iron club) and *ṛṣṭi* (a double-edged sword). But whatever weapon Bali took, the mighty Indra cut it all.

45. The Asura (Bali) then disappeared and created his demonic illusion. Oh King! there appeared a mountain over the head of the celestial army.

46. From the mountain fell down the trees burning with forest-conflagration, and rocks with chisel-pointed ends descended therefrom crushing the hostile forces to powder.

47. From that mountain rushed forth large serpents, cobras, scorpions, lions and tigers and boars crushing down big elephants.

48. Loudly shouting 'cut down', 'Break asunder' hundreds of naked female Rākṣasīs (ogresses), armed with pikes, appeared along with multitudes of Rākṣasas. Oh King.

49. Large roaring clouds with deep, terrific thunder and blown by stormy wind, rained live coals of fire.

50. A wide spread formidable fire driven by powerful gales and most terrible like the *fire* at the end of the universe, was created (with his black magic) by the demon (Bali) and it began to burn the army of gods.

51. Then there appeared all around them an ocean transgressing all its limits and looked terrible on account of the waves and whirlpools tossed by strong gales.

52. While such terrific illusions were being conjured up by Daityas, powerful in black magic, and dangerous because of their invisible movements, the celestial soldiers stood appalled and despondent.

53. Oh King ! Indra and other gods did not know how to counteract this illusion when the glorious Lord, the creator of the universe was contemplated and he manifested himself.

54. With his feet tender as young leaves, placed across the shoulders of *Garuḍa* (of beautiful wings), he appeared clad in yellow silken garments, with his eyes like a pair of budding lotuses. He wielded eight weapons in his hands. He wore the resplendent Śrī (*Śrī-vatsa* mark) on his bosom, and the *Kaustubha* gems round his neck, an invaluable crown and a pair of priceless ear-rings as well.

55. Hardly did he enter the battle-fields the illusion conjured up by the (black magic) tricks of the Asuras disappeared by the greatness of the destroyer of all types of *māyās* just as a dream breaks up on the return of wakefulness, the very recollection (remembrance) of Hari, put an end to difficulties.

56. Perceiving that Hari arrived on the battle-field on his Garuḍa, Kālanemi who was riding a lion, whirled his javelin aloft and hurled it at him. Playfully seizing it as it was about to fall on the head of Garuḍa, he killed the enemy (Kālanemi) along with his animal with that very weapon.

57. Assaulting the Lord by whose discus the over-powerful Mālī and Sumālī fell down with their head severed on the battle-field. Mālyavān (another Asura General) was about to strike Garuḍa on the head with his heavy mace when Hari, the Supreme-most person, lopped off the head of the enemy who was roaring loudly.

CHAPTER ELEVEN

End of the Battle Between Gods and Asuras at Nārada's Mediation

Śrī Śuka said :

1. Then, having recovered their minds (and *morale* from the impact of demonic illusions) through the great divine grace of the Supreme Person, Indra, Vāyu and other gods

severely hit back each one of the demons who massively assailed them before, in that very battle.

2. When the glorious Indra, being enraged at Bali, the son of Virocana, raised up his Vajra (thunderbolt), all creatures cried out, "Alas! Ha Ha" (lest it should kill Bali).

3. Despising contemptuously the noble-minded, well-equipped Bali who was moving (fearlessly) in the great battle facing Indra, Indra—the wielder of Vajra, spoke to him as follows:

4. "Just as a roguish conjuror makes gullible persons as if blind-folded by his conjuring tricks (and incantations) and robs them of their money, you desire to conquer us, the masters of such Māyās (black magic and illusory tricks) with your Māyā, Oh fool.

5. Those who by their illusive powers (or by unfaithful cunning observances of vows) wish to ascend to the celestial world or desire to transcend it to go to still higher regions (viz. Liberation), I shall oust such ignorant rogues from the post occupied by them previously and definitely throw them downward still (with no hopes of rising up).

6. Oh dull-witted fellow! I, that very Indra, shall, with my *Vajra* (thunderbolt) of hundred joints, remove the head of yours, so adept in black magic and evil spells. Show your valorous prowess with the help of your clansmen".

Bali responded

7. "To those whose previous acts became fruitful through the impelling of Time (Destiny) who participate in the battle, fame, victory, defeat and death come all in due course.

8. Therefore wise, thoughtful people realize that all the above (victory, defeat etc.) are controlled by Time and they neither get elated with joy or downcast with grief. You all are, however, ignorant about this (truth).

9. Inasmuch as you regard yourself as the agent of this (victory, defeat etc.), you deserve to be pitied by good people (for your foolishness) and as such, we do not accept your words (howsoever cutting to the quick (they be)".

Śrī Śuka said:

10. Having thus retorted to the Lord of gods, the valorous Bali, the vanquisher of warriors, struck again with Nārāca arrows drawn to the ear, Indra who was in retaliation previously hit back with reproachtul words.

11. The god Indra who was thus reproached by the enemy who expressed (nothing but) the truth, did not however tolerate the retort like an elephant pricked with a goad.

12. Indra, the conqueror of enemies, discharged at him, his unfailing weapon *Vajra* (thunderbolt). And down fell Bali on the ground, along with his (aerial) car like a mountain with its wings severed.[1]

13. Seeing his friend fallen down, Jambha, the friend and well-wisher of Bali, attacked Indra with a view to carry out his duty as a friend, even though his friend was fallen.

14. Riding his lion, the extremely powerful Jambha approached Indra and raising his mace (*gadā*) impetuously struck him on the neck and the elephant as well.

15. Stunned and tormented by the stroke of the mace, the elephant was deeply distressed and touching the ground with its knees, it fell into a swoon.

16. Thereupon, a chariot yoked with a thousand horses was brought by Mātali. The Lord of gods left the elephant and got into the chariot.

17. Expressing his appreciation at the (prompt) services rendered by the Charioteer (Mātali) smiling, Jambha, the most prominent Dānava, struck him with a burning javelin.

18. Screwing up all his fortitude, Mātali bore up the extremely unbearable pain of the dart. Greatly enraged at it, Indra sundered off the head of Jambha with his *Vajra* (thunderbolt).

19. Having heard from Sage Nārada, the report of Jambha being killed (in the battle), his kinsmen Namuci, Bala, Pāka rushed to the battle field in great haste.

1. In the Vālmīki Rāmāyaṇa *Sundara* 1. 124-33 we are told that in the *Kṛta* age mountains had wings which Indra clipped. Only Maināka was saved by Vāyu in repayment of which obligation he allowed Hanumān to rest during his jump to Laṅkā and told him of the clipping.

20. Cutting Indra to the quick by biting, harsh words, they covered him with volleys of arrows as clouds would do to a mountain, with a down-pour of rain.

21. In that battle, the light-handed Bala struck simultaneously all the thousand horses of Indra with as many arrows.

22. It was certainly an achievement of a marvellous feat in the battle, when Pāka simultaneously fitted and discharged two hundred arrows and struck Mātali with a hundred and all the parts of the chariot with a hundred shafts.

23. With fifteen big arrows furnished with golden hilts, Namuci shot Indra and roared in the battle like a thundering rain-charged cloud.

24. Like clouds obscuring the sun in the rainy season, the Asuras screened off on all sides Indra, along with his chariot and charioteer, with net-works of arrows.

25. Not being able to behold Indra and (considering themselves as) being leaderless and vanquished by the inimical forces, the hosts of celestials and their followers became bewildered and shrieked out like merchants in a ship wrecked on the high seas.

26. Thereupon issued out Indra along with his chariot, horses, flag and charioteer from the cage of arrows. Indra appeared brilliant like the sun illuminating the cardinal points, the sky and the earth, with his effulgence, at the close of the night.

27. Observing his army overpowered by enemies in the battle, the god, the wielder of *Vajra* (thunderbolt) vehemently lifted up his thunderbolt (determined) to strike down the enemy.

28. With that very eight-edged weapon he (simultaneously) sundered the heads of Bala and Pāka, striking terror into the hearts of the kinsmen who stood (simply) looking on, Oh King (Parīkṣit).

29. On perceving their death and being overwhelmed with grief, revenge and rage, Namuci, determined to kill Indra, put forth a mighty exertion.

30. Catching hold of a javelin made of iron, furnished with gold, he attacked Indra in rage, threatening loudly,

"Now you are killed". He hurled it at the King of gods and roared like a lion.

31. Even as it was dashing with terrific speed through the sky, Indra shattered it into thousand pieces with his arrows. The lord of the celestials, out of rage, struck him with his *Vajra* (thunderbolt) on the neck with a view to chop off his head.

32. The thunderbolt that was discharged with great vehemence did not pierce his skin. It was certainly the most wonderful that the *Vajra* (the thunderbolt) that killed the extremely powerful Vṛtra, was baffled by the skin of Namuci's neck.

33. Indra apprehended fear from the enemy from whom even Vajra (thunderbolt) was baffled. What has happened through the Destiny, has deluded the whole of the world.

34. It is by this thunderbolt that, in days of yore, I carried out the severance of wings of mountains which taking to their wings at will, settled anywhere on the earth, causing destruction to people, by their weight.

35. It was by this *Vajra* that Vṛtra, the very embodiment of the power of the austere penance of Tvaṣṭṛ, was split asunder, and also other mighty (persons) whose skin could not be scratched by all other missiles.

36. Such *Vajra*, when hurled by me at an insignificant Asura, became baffled and ineffective. Useless has become the spiritual energy of the Brāhmaṇa (with which it was invested). It has become (nothing but) a stick which I won't handle any more".

37. To Indra who was thus pondering in dejection, a voice from heaven said, "This demon should not be killed by weapons wet or dry.

38. He has been conferred a boon by me that he would not meet death from wet or dry things. Hence, you have to think out some other expedient (for killing) the enemy".

39. Hearing the heavenly voice, Indra composed his mind and contemplated. It occurred to him (lit. he saw) that foam (of the sea) was the (real) expedient which comprises both the conditions (of being wet *and* dry).

40. With the foam which was neither dry nor wet (but

was both simultaneously) he chopped off the head of Namuci.[1] Hosts of sages sang his eulogies and showered the Lord of gods with flowers.

41. The chief of Gandharvas, Viśvāvasu and Parāvasu gave musical concert. Gods beat big drums and celestial nymphs danced with joy.

42. Other gods like Vāyu, Agni, Varuṇa and others destroyed their opponents with volleys of missiles, just as lions would kill the deer.

43. The divine sage Nārada who was deputed to celestials by god Brahmā, on perceiving the slaughter of Dānavas, prevented them (from that genocide, with the following words):

Nārada said:

44. "Supported as you were by the arms of Lord Nārāyaṇa, nectar was secured by you. You are also favoured by goddess Śrī (the consort of Nārāyaṇa). Hence you now cease from fighting."

Śrī Śuka said:

45. Paying due respect to the words of the sage Nārada, they controlled the impetuosity of their rage. All of them returned to heaven, all the while being praised by their attendants.

46. The survivors of the battle carried the still unconscious Bali to the western mountain (of the setting sun) as per Nārada's advice.

47. Śukrācārya (the preceptor of Daityas) restored to life (all the Daityas) whose limbs were intact, and necks in existence (unbroken), by means of his secret science of restoring life (*saṁjīvani vidyā*).

48. Bali regained his consciousness and other faculties at the touch of Śukra's hand. Being endowed with the reality about the nature of the world, Bali suffered no depression, even though he was defeated.

1. *apām phenena Namuceḥ Śira Indrodavartayaḥ* RV 8.14.13, AV. 20.29.3.

CHAPTER TWELVE

Lord Śiva Fascinated by Mohinī

The son of Bādarāyaṇa (Śrī Śuka) said :

1-2. When god Śiva (the bull-bannered god) heard that Lord Hari infatuated the Dānavas in a female form and made the hosts of gods to drink the nectar, he ascended his bull along with goddess Pārvatī, and surrounded by all the hosts of goblins, paid a visit to the region where god Viṣṇu (the killer of Madhu) was residing, with a view to see him.

3. God Śiva (the source of the world) who along with his consort Umā (Pārvatī) was reverentially received by the Lord (Viṣṇu) and was seated comfortably, returned his respects with compliments and spoke smilingly.

Śrī Mahādeva said:

4. "Oh God of gods! Pervader of the universe ! The Lord of the Universe of which you are the embodiment ![1] You are the soul, the source[2] and the controller of all things.

5.* Your honourable self is that *Brahman* which is the Reality and pure consciousness—the *Brahman* wherefrom proceed the beginning (the emergence), the end (the destruction), the middle (the sustenance) of this universe, but who, due to his being unchangeable is not affected by these (changes) ; who constitutes this, the external thing (or the object to be enjoyed) as well as 'I', the other (the enjoyer of that object).

6. Meditative sages desirous of (attaining) the final beatitude do not seek any other blessings. They renounce attachment to both (this and the other world) and adore your lotus-feet.

7.** You are that perfect Brahman, immortal, attribute-

1. *Jagan maya*—Whose body is constituted of the sentients and non-sentients in the universe—VR.

2. *hetu*—The efficient cause and not extraneous ones like *adṛṣṭa*—VJ.

* Deleted by VJ.

** Acc. to VR. Brahman being the material cause is not different from everything else.

less and hence untouched by misery; absolutely and essentially blissful but not subject to modifications. Though one without a second, you are distinct from everything else. You are the cause of the origin, maintenance and dissolution of the universe, and the controller of all *jīvas*. Though sought after by them, you expect nothing from them.

8. You alone are one, both gross and subtle, the cause and the effect. Just as there is no difference in the sub-effect called gold whether moulded (into an ornament) or (kept) unmodified (in its original form)[1] it is through ignorance that difference is superimposed on you, by people. The attribution of difference is due to *guṇas* or modifications, and you are absolutely free from them.

9.* Some (viz. the followers of the Vedānta) regard you to be the *Brahman*; while others (i.e. Mīmāṁsakas). consider you to be *Dharma*. Some (i.e. Sāṁkhyas) think you to be the Supreme Controller transcendental to both *Prakṛti* and *Puruṣa*. Others (the followers of the *Pāñcarātra* school) regard you as one endowed with nine powers,[2] while some others (followers of Yoga) know you to be the Supreme Person (*Mahā-puruṣa*), (while) you are changeless and self-dependent absolute.

10. Neither I nor god Brahmā (whose duration of life is of two *parārdha* years), nor sages of whom Marīci is the chief, though created from the *Sattva* quality, can comprehend the (real nature of the) universe created by you (much less your real nature). Oh Lord, how can demons and human beings and others whose minds are deluded by Māyā and who

1. VR. regards this view as that of Vaiśeṣikas who, through ignorance, believe that this universe exists independent of Brahman.

VJ. takes *vihata* as a v.l. for *vihita* and states 'inasmuch as difference is overlaid on you through ignorance, it is *ipso facto* destroyed i.e. null and void'.

* VJ thinks that the theories about God mentioned here are held by the followers of Vedānta and of Smṛtis, Purāṇas, Pañcarātra and by Ekāntins who regard God as *Mahāpuruṣa* who is changeless and absolute.

2. ŚR. enumerates the powers of the Lord as follows :
Vimalā, ut-karṣiṇī, Jñāna, Kriyā, Yoga, Prahvī, Satyā, Īśānā, Anugrahā

are of inauspicious *rājasic* and *tāmasic* origins,[1] or whose behaviour is wicked due to the influence of *rajas* aud *tamas*, can understand(You or Your creation comprehensively).

11. You are essentially knowledge itself. As such you know everything—(such as) all of your own work, the creation, continuance and destruction of the universe, the activities of beings, their bondage and emancipation from the mundane existence. Just as, Vāyu (the air) enters everything mobile and immobile as well as the sky, you, being the soul of everything and the very knowledge itself, pervade everything.

12. Your incarnations, while indulging in sportive activities with *guṇas*, have been witnessed by me. As such, I desire to behold that form of a young damsel assumed by you.

13. As we have a great curiosity, we have eagerly come to see that (female) form whereby Daityas were fascinated and gods were enabled to drink nectar.

Śrī Śuka said :

14. Being thus entreated by god Śiva, the wielder of the trident, Lord Viṣṇu gave out a hearty laugh, and replied in words pregnant with deep meaning.

The Lord replied :

15. When the jar of nectar passed (into the possession of the Daityas), the female form was assumed by me for exciting the curiosity of Daityas (and thus beguiling them) with a view to accomplish the interests of gods.

16. Oh! The best of gods! As you are curious to see it, I shall presently reveal to you that form which excites amorous passions and which is highly appreciated by passionate persons.

Śrī Śuka said :

17. While speaking thus, the venerable Lord immediately vanished at that very spot, while god Śiva, the Source of the Universe, along with his spouse Umā, waited there wistfully casting his glances in all directions.

18. Thereupon in a garden among trees blossoming with variegated flowers and reddish foliage, he saw a lovely

1. *abhadraṁ rājasaṁ ca tāmasaṁ ca vṛttam utpattir yeṣāṁ te*. ŚR.

damsel with a girdle round her waist clothed with a brilliant silken raiment, engaged in playing with a ball.

19. At every step she appeared as if getting broken in her waist, by the heavy weight of her big breasts, shaken by her movements of bending and rising along with the movements of the bounding ball, as well as with the weight of her precious solid pearl necklaces, and was taking her foliage-like tender feet here and there (from place to place).

20. Due to the quick (impredictabte) movements of the ball in different directions, the pupils of her longish unsteady eyes appeared agitated. Her countenance appeared all the more beautiful with her cheeks shining with the resplendent pair of ear-rings and with her dark glossy tresses.

21. With her beautiful left hand she was tightening her loosened silken raiment and her dishevelling braids of hair and was hitting the ball with the other hand, she appeared as if enchanting the world with her own deluding powers.

22. Beholding her playing with the ball, the god lost his balance of mind by her side glances, accompanied with a covert smile caused by some slight bashfulness, while sporting with the ball. His mind became agitated by the exchange of mutual gazing of the woman. He became oblivious of himself, of his consort Umā and of his own attendants.

23. When the ball slipped from her hand and went to a long distance and she ran after it while the wind blew away her fine silken garment along with the girdle. And indeed (even) god Śiva stood gazing.

24. Beholding that exquisitely charming damsel with such winsome side glances and enchanting the heart, god Śiva fixed his heart on her indeed, when she showed to be enamoured of him through her ogling.

25. Being deprived of his wisdom, sense of decency and discernment, by her, and overcome with erotic passions evoked by her, he lost his sense of shame and approached her even while (his divine consort) Pārvatī stood gazing.

26. Seeing him approaching, she, being stripped of clothes, became extremely abashed. She concealed herself behind the tree laughing but did not linger (anywhere).

27. The divine Śiva whose senses (control of mind)

were robbed away[1] (by the damsel) and was overpowered by passions, pursued her as the leader of elephant would follow a she-elephant.

28. Running after her with great speed, and seizing her by the locks of her hair, he dragged her near him and hugged her in his arms, despite her unwillingness.

29. Being closely embraced by god Śiva, like unto a she-elephant by an elephant, she wriggled to and fro (within his arms) and got her hair dishevelled.

30. Having extricated herself from the arms of the great god, she ran away fast, despite her big hips, as she was the Māyā (deluding potency) created by the Lord, Oh dear king.

31. Being completely overwhelmed with passion, like that by his enemy, the above-described Rudra followed the footsteps of the damsel, created by Lord Viṣṇu of miraculous exploits.

32. While running after her, the semen of Śiva of unfailing procreative capacity, went on escaping like that of a big bull-leader of a herd pursuing a fecundable cow or as that of a rutting leader-elephant running after a fertilizable she-elephant.

33. Oh ruler of the earth! The various places on earth where the seed of that great-souled god fell, became the areas of silver and gold ores.

34.* Thus in the course of his pursuit (of the damsel), god Śiva was found (pursuing her) on the banks of the rivers and lakes on the mountains, in forests and gardens and wherever sages lived.

35. When his semen was completely escaped, he realized that he had been befooled by the Māyā of God Viṣṇu and he recovered himself completely from that delusion, Oh great king.

36. They say that god Śiva who thus fully realized the greatness of Lord Viṣṇu, his own soul, and the soul of the

1. VJ.'s v.l. *pramathitendriyaḥ*—whose senses were extremely provoked.

* GS. remarks that hereby Lord Viṣṇu demonstrated to the sages how even god Śiva had fallen from his yogic status, and thus indirectly emphasized that they should keep themselves aloof from women.

Universe, did not regard it (his being deluded) as in any way wonderful in the case of the Lord of incomprehensible prowess.

37. Perceiving that Śiva is unaffected by remorse and the sense of shame, Lord Viṣṇu (the slayer of demon Madhu) was highly pleased, and assuming his male form, he addressed him thus.

The Lord said :

38. I am glad that even though you have been deluded by my (irresistible) Māyā (deluding potency) in the form of a damsel, Oh dear one ! you, of your own accord, have recovered your normal state of passionlessness or ego-lessness born of devotion (which is impossible in the case of any other god. Hence I address you as) the greatest god.

39. What man, with the exception of you, whence once caught in the snare of delusion, can overcome My Māyā which brings forth various objects (of enjoyment) and becomes extremely difficult to get over, by persons lacking in self-control.

40. This Māyā consisting of attributes (viz. *Sattva*, *rajas* and *tamas*) functions under my control (who am the Time-spirit,) for the purpose (of creation, maintenance and destruction of the universe), by means of the parts (such as *rajas*, *sattva* and *tamas*). She shall not henceforth overpower you.

Śrī Śuka said :

41. In this way, he (god Śiva) who was honoured by an embrace by Lord Viṣṇu bearing the Śrīvatsa mark on the bosom, took his leave of him, (respectfully) circumambulated him and returned to his own abode along with his retinue.

42. Later on, while being eulogized by great sages, the glorious god Śiva (the source of the Universe) lovingly spoke to his spouse Pārvatī about the Māyā which was a part of the Soul (of the Universe, viz.) Lord Viṣṇu, Oh scion of Bharata.

43. "Have you observed the deluding potency of the Unborn Supreme Person, the transcendental Deity whereby

I, prominent one of his digits (rays), became helpless and succumbed to delusion ? What to speak of others who are not the masters of their own selves ?

44. He is that same Eternal Ancient Person, unaffected by Time, and incomprehensible to the Vedas,—The Person about whom you enquired of me at the end of my deep *yogic* meditation which lasted one thousand years."

Śrī Śuka said :

45. Oh Child ! In this way has been related to you the exploit of Lord Viṣṇu, the wielder of Śārṅga bow by whom the great mount (Mandara) was supported on his back while the ocean was being churned (for getting the nectar).

46. Never and in no way shall fail the exertions of a person who constantly chants or listens to the account of this (glorious deed of Hari), or the chanting of the glorious attributes of the Lord of excellent renown relieves one of all the troubles of *saṁsāra*.

47. I bow unto the feet of the Lord who though beyond the reach of the evil ones, is accessible through devotion; who, deluding the enemies of gods by assuming the disguise of a young damsel, made the foremost of gods who resorted to him to drink the nectar churned out of the (milky) sea, and who fulfils all the desires of those who approach him (for asylum).

CHAPTER THIRTEEN

Description of the Future Manvantaras

Śrī Śuka resumed:

1. The present, seventh Manu is known as Śrāddhadeva. He is the son of Vivasvān. Now hear from me the names of his sons.

2. They are Ikṣvāku, Nabhaga, Dhṛṣṭa, Śaryāti, Nariṣyanta, Nābhāga and the seventh is called Diṣṭa.

3. Karuṣa, Paruṣa and the tenth is known as Vasumān—these are the ten sons of Vaivasvata Manu, Oh tormentor of the enemies.

4. The (twelve) Ādityas, the (eight) Vasus, the (eleven) Rudras, the (ten) Viśvedevas, the (forty-nine) Maruts (wind-god), two Aśvinī-kumāras, the (three) Ṛbhus are (the seven grades of) gods and their Indra (ruling god) is Purandara, Oh King.

5. Kaśyapa, Atri, Vasiṣṭha, Viśvāmitra, Gautama, Jamadagni and Bharadvāja—These seven are regarded as the seven (principal) sages.

6. Even in this Manvantara, there was the incarnation of the Lord, born of Kaśyapa and Aditi. Lord Viṣṇu, assuming the form of a dwarf, was born as the youngest son of Aditi.

7. The (first) seven Manvantaras have been described to you briefly by me. Now I shall narrate to you the future ones, associated with the powers (incarnations) of Viṣṇu.

8. Vivasvān had two wives, both being the daughters of Viśvakarman. They were Sandhyā and Chāyā about whom I have spoken to you, Oh king of kings.[1]

9. Some say that he had a third wife called Vaḍavā.[2] Out of the three wives, the children of Saṁjñā were three—Yama, Yamī and Śrāddhadeva. Now listen to the names of Chāyā's children—

10. Sāvarṇi, the daughter Tapatī who became the wife of Saṁvaraṇa and the third son Śanaiścara (the presiding deity of the planet Saturn). The two Aśvinīkumāras were the sons of Vaḍavā.

11. When the eighth Manvantara will set in, Sāvarṇi will be the Manu. Nirmoka, Virajaska and others are the sons of Sāvarṇi, Oh King.

12. Then (in the 8th Manvantara), Sutapas, Virajas and Amṛta-prabhas are going to be the gods. Their ruling god (Indra) will be Bali, the son of Virocana.

13. Having donated the whole of this earth to Viṣṇu who begged for only three paces of land (in this Manvantara), he will relinquish his eminent position of Indra (attained by

1. *Vide Supra* 6.6. 40-41.

2. But according to the Bh. P. *Supra* 6.6.40 Saṁjñā assumed the form of Veḍavā and gave birth to Aśvinī kumāras.

him through Viṣṇu's grace in the next *Manvantara*), and will attain to final beatitude.

14. That same Bali who was bound down by the Lord who, when pleased, installed him in the Nether world Sutala which is superior to the *Svarga* in splendour—still rules there like the king of the heavenly regions.

15-16. Gālava, the glorious (Paraśu-) Rāma, Aśvatthāman, the son of Droṇa, Kṛpa, Ṛṣyaśṛṅga and our father the venerable Bādarāyaṇa—these will be the seven sages. Even now they continue to occupy their own hermitages through their *yogic* powers.

17. The Lord will incarnate with the name Sārvabhauma, from Devaguhya and Sarasvatī (as his parents). The powerful Lord will wrest Indrahood from Purandara and confer it on Bali.

18. The ninth Manu will be Dakṣa-Sāvarṇi who will be born of Varuṇa. Bhūtaketu, Dīptiketu and others[1] will be his sons, Oh King.

19. Pāras and Marīcigarbhas and others (viz. Sudharmans)[2] will be (the three categories of) gods then. It is traditionally reported that Adbhuta will be the Indra. Then there will be the seven sages of whom Dyutimat[3] is prominent.

20. A ray of the Lord will incarnate under the name Ṛṣabha from Āyuṣmat and Ambudharā (as his father and mother). Adbhuta, the Indra, will enjoy the three worlds conquered (for him) by Ṛṣabha.

21. The tenth Manu will be Brahma-sāvarṇi, the great son of Upaśloka. His sons are Bhūriṣeṇa and others while Haviṣmat and others will be prominent Brāhmaṇa (sages).

22. Haviṣmān, Sukṛti, Satya, Jaya, Mūrti will be (some of) the Brāhmaṇa (sages) then. Suvāsana and Viruddha are the gods, and Śambhu is the Lord of gods.

1. VP. 3.2.22 adds Dhṛtaketu, Nirāmaya, Pañca-hasta and Pṛthuśrava to this list.

2. VP. 3.2.20-21 adds this third category and each category will consist of 12 gods.

3. The VP. 3.2.22 gives the complete list as follows :
Dyutimat, Savana, Bhavya, Vasu, Medhātithi, Jyotiṣmān and Satya.

23. The Lord, with a part of his Self, will be born in the house of Viśvasṛj (Prajāpati) through Viṣūci, and be known as Viśvaksena. He will make friends (render help to Śambhu (the then Indra).

24. The self-controlled Dharma-sāvarṇi will be the eleventh Manu who will have ten sons as Satyadharma and others.

25. The (categories of) gods will be Vihaṅgamas, Kāmagamas and Nirvāṇarucis. Their ruler Indra will be Vaidhṛta, while Aruṇa and others[1] will be the (seven) sages.

26. The ray (part) of Hari known as Dharmasetu, the son of Āryaka through Vaidhṛta, will sustain and protect the three worlds.

27. Oh King, the twelfth Manu will be Rudra-sāvarṇi and his sons will be Devavān, Upadeva, Devaśreṣṭha and others.

28. Then Ṛtadhāman will be the Indra and the (groups of) gods will be Harita and others.[2] And the (seven) sages will be Tapo-mūrti, Tapasvin, Āgnīdhraka and others.[3]

29. A part of Hari, by name Svadhāman, the mighty son of Satya-sahas and Sūnṛtā will protect this period of Manu.

30. The thirteenth Manu will be the self-controlled Devasāvarṇi and the sons of Devasāvarṇi are Citrasena, Vicitra and others.

31. The (classes of) gods will be designated as Sukarmạ and Sutrāma[4] and Divaspati. Then Nirmoka, Tattvadarśin and others will be the (seven sages[5]).

32. The ray of Lord Hari, the master of *yoga*, will be

1. GS quotes from the *Harivaṁśa* the following sages implied in *ādi* : Haviṣmān, Vapuṣmān, Aruṇa, Anagha, Urudhī, Niścara and Agnitejas.

2. VP. 3.2.33 enumerates Harita, Rohita, Sumanas, Sukarman and Surāpa as the five groups (*gaṇas*) of gods.

3. The list in VP. 3.2.34 includes Tapasvin, Sutapas, Tapomūrti, Taporati, Tapo-dhṛti, Tapo-dyuti and Tapo-dhana.

4. VP. 3.2.37-39 adds Sudharman as the third class and each class consists of 33 gods.

5. The list in VP (above) differs. It consists of Nirmoha, Tattvadarśin, Niṣprakampya, Nirutsuka, Dhṛtimān, Avyaya and Sutapas.

born as the son of Devahotra through Bṛhatī and will procure the kingdom of three worlds to the Indra, Divaspati.

33. They say that Indra-sāvarṇi will come as the fourteenth Manu, and the sons born of him will be Uru, Gambhīrabuddhi and others.

34. The (categories of) gods will be Pavitra, Cākṣuṣa and others[1], while Śuci will be the Indra. Agnibāhu, Śuci, Śuddha, Māgadha and others will be the (seven sages).[2]

35. Then Hari will incarnate as the son Satrāyaṇa and Vitānā, and will be called Bṛhadbhānu. He will continue the course of sacrificial rituals, Oh great King.

36. These fourteen Manu periods relating to the past, present and future have been described to you, Oh king. It is by these (Manu periods) that the Kalpa comprising one thousand yugas, is measured.

37*. A person who narrates or listens to the narration of the story of the fourteen Manus will find Viṣṇu gracious unto him.

CHAPTER FOURTEEN

Duties of Manus and Their Functionaries

The King (Parikṣit) asked :

1. Be pleased to explain to me, Oh worshipful sage, how and by whom are these Manus and others employed for the execution of what (particular) function during the Manvantaras.

The sage (Śuka) replied :

2. Oh King! Manus, sons of Manus, Sages, Indras,

1. VP. adds Kaniṣṭha, Bhrājata and Vācāvṛddha as three categories. (i.e. in all five)—Ibid 3.2.41.

2. VP. adds Agnīdhra, Yukta and Jita and completes the list of seven sages.—Ibid 3.2.42.

* A probable interpolation recorded in the Bombay edition (e.g. D.S. Yande's edition of the Bh. P.).

gods—all these (five categories of functionaries) are under the control of the Supreme Person.

3. Directed by the aforesaid forms of the Supreme Person such as the incarnation called Yajña and others, Manu and other functionaries carry on the work of the world.

4. At the end of the quartet of *yugas* (i. e. at the beginning of the new *Kṛta-yuga*), the sages, by dint of their asceticism and penance, saw the corpus of the *Vedic* texts 'swallowed up' by Time, through the help of which the Eternal Law (Religion) becomes known.

5. Then Manus are instructed by Hari in the path of righteousness, characterised by four feet (viz. penance, bodily and mental purity, compassion and truth). Remaining controlled in mind, they propagate the path of righteousness all over the world during their period, Oh King.

6. The protectors of the subjects (viz. the sons of Manu) themselves and through their descendants protect the path of righteousness (*dharma*)—and the earth—to the end of that Manvantara, while gods along with others who are eligible for sacrificial shares, enjoy their shares in the sacrificial oblations.

7. Enjoying the excellent affluence and fortune of the three worlds conferred upon him (out of grace) by the Supreme Lord, Indra protects the three worlds and sends down at will showers of rain.

8. Assuming in every *Yuga*, the form of Siddhas (like Sanaka) the sages (like Yājñavalkya) and masters of Yoga (like Datta), Hari teaches the paths of knowledge (*Jñāna*), action (*Karman*) and *Yoga* (respectively).

9. He carried out the work of creation by assuming the form of *Prajāpatis* (Progenitors of the world like Marīci). He kills robbers etc. by appearing as an independent monarch. And possessing different characteristics, in the form of Time, he destroys all.

10. The Lord is never perceived, though praised highly by the people who are deluded by the Māyā (consisting) of various names and forms. Nor is he realized by various systems of philosophy.

11. The measures of the minor *Kalpas* (forming one

day of Brahmā) which are the subdivisions of the great *Kalpa* (the lifetime of Brahmā) have been described to you. Those well-versed in ancient lore state that this *Kalpa* consists of fourteen *Manvantaras*.

CHAPTER FIFTEEN

Bali's Conquest of the Svarga (Celestial Region)

The King Parīkṣit said:

1. For what purpose did Lord Hari, though himself the Supreme Ruler, beg like a miserable fellow, three paces of land from Bali? Why did he bind him down even though he got his object sought for?

2. This we desire to know thoroughly as it is highly surprising to us that the Lord of sacrifices, (though) Perfect (in all respects within himself), begged like a destitute and (subsequently) bound down (with fetters) the innocent (donor).

Śrī Śuka said:

3. Being deprived of his splendour, wealth as well as his life through being defeated by Indra in a battle, Bali was revived by Śukra and other members of the Bhṛgu clan, Oh king. The noble-minded Bali, with utmost faith, resorted to the Bhṛgus as a disciple, offering them whatever they desired.

4. The Brāhmaṇas of the Bhṛgu clan, endowed as they were with extra-ordinary powers and were pleased with him, consecrated him with the great sacred ablution (called *aindra*—Pertaining to Indra) with due formalities, (as prescribed in the *Bahvṛc Brāhmaṇa*), and desirous as he was of conquering the celestial region, made him perform the *Viśvajit* sacrifice.[1]

1. This order of 'consecration' (*abhiṣeka*) and performance of sacrifice is given by G.S. In the *Viśvajit* sacrifice the sacrificer has to give all wealth (after separating the share of the eldest son and land). —Kane's *Hist. of Dh. Śāstra* II. ii. 1212, Fn. 2644.

5-6. From the sacrificial fire duly worshipped with oblations, there emerged a chariot strengthened with gold plates, horses of the same colour (green) as those of Indra, a banner blazing the emblem of a lion, a celestial bow fastened with plates of gold, a pair of inexhaustible quivers full of arrows, a divine coat of mail. His grandfather (Prahlāda) conferred on him a wreath of never-fading flowers and Śukra (his preceptor), a conch.

7. Thus with all the military equipment procured for him by Brāhmaṇas, and having got the *Svastyayana* (auspicious rites) performed through them, Bali circumambulated them respectfully, paid obeisance to them and taking his leave of Prahlāda, bowed down to him.

8-9. Ascending into the celestial chariot conferred upon him by the Bhṛgus (Śukra and his clansmen, by performing the sacrifice), the mighty (chariot) warrior Bali, wearing that excellent wreath, put on his armour, armed himself with the bow, the sword and tied up the (inexhaustible) quivers. With his arms radiant with gold armlets and with dazzling ear-rings (of the shape of an alligator) he shone like the fire blazing in its sacrificial place, when he mounted the chariot.

10-11. Accompanied by his retinue and commanders of (other) Daitya legions who were his equals in command, prowess and splendour, and were (as if) drinking the skies and burning the quarters with (their glaring) eyes, and leading the surrounding mighty Daitya army, he marched against the highly prosperous capital of Indra, shaking as it were the heaven and the earth (by its thumping march).

12. The city appeared beautiful with its splendid gardens and parks like Nandana and others, resonant with its warbling pairs of birds and humming intoxicated black-bees.

13. (It looked charming) with the celestial trees whose branches were heavily laden with tender foliage, fruits and blossoms of flowers, with lotus-ponds thereof, full of acquatic birds like swans, cranes, ruddy geese (*Cakrāhva*), and ducks and young celestials, damsels engaged in watersports with gods therein.

14. It was girt on all sides by the heavenly Gaṅgā (Mandākinī) as its moat. It was surrounded with fortifica-

tions of gold, shining like fire and was provided with high towers.

15. Constructed by Viśvakarmā, the entrance and doors of the houses were fitted with panels of gold while the city-gates were of crystals and all the roads were well laid down.

16. It appeared beautiful with its assembly halls, quadrangles and streets; it was full of trillions of mansions (or heavenly cars); the quadrangles were paved with precious stones and platforms were studded with diamonds and corals.

17. There young damsels of eternal youth and unfading beauty (ever) appearing sixteen years of age, wearing purest raiment, appeared resplendent like fires ablaze with flames.

18. Breezes wafting the fragrance of wreathes of fresh flowers dropped down from the braids of hair of the heavenly damsels blow through its streets.

19. The beloveds of gods (Heavenly nymphs) pace through the streets, covered with whitish fragrant fumes of the *aguru* (a kind of sandal-wood) that escape through the gold-windows (of houses).

20. It was covered with pearl-canopies and flag-staffs studded with precious stones, and balconies decorated all around with buntings. It was resonant with notes of peacocks, pigeons, hummings of black-bees and appeared gay and auspicious by the sweet songs of celestial damsels.

21. It was pleasing to the mind with its sounds of *mṛdaṅga*, conchs, drums and kettle-drums, as also with the sweet rhythmic sound of lutes, *murajas*, *ṛṣṭis* (kind of musical instruments) and flutes regulated to the beat of the cymbals, with dances accompanied with orchestral music and songs of demigods (such as Gandharvas, Kinnaras) and had surpassed with its effulgence, the presiding deity of lustre.[1]

22. The impious, wicked, the cruel to other beings, the rogues, the proud, the lustful and the avaricious have no access to it; only those who are free from these defects can reach it.

23. (Bali) the commander-in-chief of that army, laid siege to the capital of gods with his forces and blew his

1. v.l. The presiding deities of the sun and other planets.

tremendously sounding conch conferred on him by his preceptor, striking terror in the hearts of Indra's women.

24. Comprehending the full implications of the supreme efforts of Bali, Indra, accompanied by all the legions of gods (approached) his preceptor (Bṛhaspati) and spoke to him as follows :

25. "Worshipful Sir ! Tremendous are the (military) preparations of Bali, our old arch-enemy. Me-thinks, they are (now) irresistible. By what energy has he become so overwhelmingly powerful?

26. None is able by any means whatever to approach him or withstand him. He is swallowing the world with his mouth, licking (as it were) the ten quarters, and burning them down by his fiery eyes. He has emerged against us like the fire of dissolution consuming the universe.

27. Be pleased to disclose to me the cause of the irresistibleness of my foe, whereby he derived this energy, mental courage and physical power and prowess and was enabled to make such tremendous efforts.

The Preceptor (Bṛhaspati) Explained :

28. "I know, Oh Indra, the cause of this growth of power of your enemy. It is due to the infusion of spiritual energy in their disciple by those experts in Vedic lore, the Bhṛgus (in exchange of the surrender of all his property to them).

29. With the exception of the Almighty Ruler Hari neither your compeer nor you can stand before him (for confrontation) like human beings before the god of death.

30. Therefore, all of you should now quit the celestial region and go in hiding, biding your favourable time which would bring in the decline of your enemy.

31. With the spiritual power of the Brāhmaṇas, he is getting stronger still and is now of irresistible prowess. (In due course) by insulting those very Brāhmaṇas, he will meet destruction along with his kith and kin."

32. Having thus received a wise counsel after mature deliberation from their preceptor who viewed (the reality of the situation in the proper perspective) gods, being capable of assuming any form they like, vacated the celestial region.

33. When the gods disappeared, Bali, the son of Virocana established himself in the capital of gods and brought under control all the three worlds.

34. Bhṛgus who were affectionate to their disciple who had (now) conquered the universe, and who was devoted to them, made him perform one hundred horse sacrifices (to stabilise his Indra-hood).

35. By virtue of his greatness in the performance of one hundred horse-sacrifices he diffused his reputation, already known all over the three worlds, in all quarters and shone like the moon, the lord of stars.

36. Considering himself as one who had accomplished all his desires, the noble-minded Bali enjoyed the highly prosperous royal fortune blessed upon him by Brāhmaṇas.

CHAPTER SIXTEEN

Instruction in the observance of Payovrata to Aditi

Śrī Śuka said :

1. When her sons thus disappeared and the celestial regions were arrogated to themselves by Daityas (Diti's son), Aditi, the mother of gods, was tormented like a helpless person.

2. Once, rising from his spiritual meditation of a long duration, the worshipful sage Kāśyapa (Aditi's husband) visited her hermitage which was cheerless and gloomy (devoid of joyful atmosphere).

3. Oh best of Kurus ! Received (by his wife) with due formalities and occupying the seat (offered by her), he spoke thus to his wife, whose countenance was mournful.

4. Oh auspicious lady ! I trust nothing inauspicious has befallen[1] the Brāhmaṇas in the world, of late. I believe nothing calamitous has happened to Dharma. I hope that

1. For *āgatam*, VR reads *gavām* : 'in the case of the cows as well'.

misfortune has not overtaken the people who are subject to the whims of death.[1]

5. Or was there any obstruction in carrying out righteous duties with respect to *Dharma*, *Artha and Kāma* in your household where people who do not follow the practice of *yoga*, get the fruits thereof (by disinterested performance of prescribed house-hold duties), Oh mistress of the household.

6. I believe guests, having visited your house, have not gone back, at any time, without being duly received with courtesies like going forth to welcome them, as you might have been engaged in household duties.

7. If new-comers visiting a house go away from it without being honoured with the offer of water at least, such houses are certainly no better than the dens of big jackals.

8. Have not the sacred fires been offered oblations at the proper time on any day by you, as your mind must have been stricken with anxiety due to my departure, Oh fair lady !

9. The Brāhmaṇa and the (sacrificial) fire by worshipping whom a householder attains to regions (like *svarga*) yielding all the desired objects, are verily the mouth of Lord Viṣṇu, the soul of all gods.

10. Oh high-minded lady ! Are all your sons doing well and happy? I perceive through your outward expressions (like pale-facedness) that your heart is not at ease.

Aditi replied :

11. Oh Brahman ! It is all well with the twice-born persons (like Brāhmaṇas), cows; so is the case with righteousness and with this person (me). Oh Lord of the house ! This house (of yours) is the most excellent source of the three objectives of human life (viz. *dharma*, *artha* and *kāma*).

12. It is due to my devoted contemplation about your worshipful self that nothing is lacking and the sacrificial fires, guests, servants and mendicants desirous of getting something, are properly attended to.

13. Oh worshipful lord ! What desire cherished in my

1. VJ. takes *chandānuvartinaḥ* as an adj. qualifying *mṛtyu* implying 'through the god of death who acts according to whim'.

heart can remain unfulfilled when you, the lord of creation and the guardian of the well-being of my children in this way, advise me on religious matters.

14. Oh son of Marīci ! All these beings imbrued predominantly with *sattva*, *rajas* and *tamas* severally are born of your mind or body. (It is quite natural that) you are therefore equally attached to them all. But even the Supreme Lord (who creates the whole of the universe has special attachment to his devotees.

15. Oh Lord ! Be pleased to think of the well being of mine who have been serving you, Oh excellent observer of vows ! We (I and my sons) have been deprived of our wealth and have been ousted from our abodes by the sons of my rival (Diti). Kindly protect us, Oh Lord !

16. Being deprived of my power, splendour, glory and place of residence by powerful enemies, I have been exiled and have consequently immersed in a sea of calamities.

17. Oh foremost guardian of our welfare ! Be pleased to think out such effective device by your intellect as will enable my sons to recover them all.

Śrī Śuka said :

18. Kāśyapa who was thus entreated by Aditi, spoke to her as if with a bit of smile : "Oh how mighty is the power of Lord Viṣṇu's delusive potency (*māyā*) ! The whole world is bound down with affection.

19. There is absolutely no relation between the material body which is different from the soul and the soul who transcends *Prakṛti*. Whose and who are the husband, sons and other relatives ? Delusion alone is the cause of this attachment.

20. Worship therefore the Supreme Person, the glorious Lord Janārdana, the all-pervading God who resides in the heart of all beings, and is the Father and Preceptor of the Universe.

21. Lord Hari is merciful unto the afflicted and shall grant all your desires (even if there may be some deficiencies in devotion). Unfailingly fruitful is the devotion unto

the Lord (and not to any other god). This is my conviction (about the efficacy of devotion).

Aditi requested :

22. By what procedure I should worship the Protector of the world so that he, of effective mental resolve, may grant me my desired object, Oh Brahman !

23. Be pleased to instruct me, oh best of Brāhmaṇas, in that method of worshipping the Lord whereby He will be immediately pleased with me who am sunk in despondency along with my children.

Kaśyapa said :

24. The worshipful Lotus-born god Brahmā was accosted for this by me when desirous of progeny. As narrated by him, I shall now explain to you the sacred vow that leads to the propitiation of Lord Viṣṇu (Keśava.)

25. Subsisting purely on milk during the first twelve days of the bright half of the month of Phālguna, one should worship the Lotus-eyed Lord Viṣṇu with the utmost devotion.

26. On the day preceding the new moon (when the moon rises with a scarcely visible crescent) one should besmear one's body with earth, turned over by the wild-boar, if available and take bath. While standing in the middle of the current, he should recite the following *mantra* :

27. "Oh goddess ! You were lifted up from Rasātala (the nether-most region) by the Lord (assuming the form of) the Primitive Boar, with a view to secure a place (for living beings). I respectfully bow to you. Be pleased to absolve me of all my sins".

28. After completing one's daily routine of religious duties, with a serene and concentrated mind, one should worship God either in an image, or on a consecrated altar or in the sun, water, fire or even in the preceptor. (For invoking the diety, the following nine *Mantras* are to be recited).

29. Obeisance to you the glorious Lord, the Supreme Person, the greatest of the great, the abode of all created beings, (and hence called) the all-pervading Vāsudeva the witness (to all and everything).

30. Salutations to the unmanifest[1] and the subtle, who is both Prakṛti (Primordial matter) and Puruṣa (the spirit)—pervading them as their *antar-yāmin* (the indwelling Principle), who comprehends twenty-four Principles[2] and is the founder of the Sāṁkhya system.[3]

31*. Hail to you who have two heads, three **feet, four** horns; who confer fruit of sacri**fices etc.**, the possessor of seven hands, who are **himself** the sacrifice and the soul of the three *Vedas* (**or** are described in three *Vedas*).

32**. I bow to you who are Śiva (all auspiciousness) and Rudra. Hail to you the (wielder) of Śakti (Power).

1. Cf. Muṇḍaka up. 1.1.6.

2. These principles are subsidiary causes and as his attributes they do not exist separately. VC. thinks that the 24 *guṇas* are the categories of *Vaiśeṣikas* and may mean *Sāṅkhyatattvas* also.

3. VJ. reads : *guṇasaṁsthāna-hetave*.

* (i). ŚR compares this verse with the famous description of the Fire-god *Catvāri Śṛṅgā trayo asya pādā* etc. in the RV 4.58.3 and quotes Yāska's explanation as follows :

Two heads—the rites called *prāyaṇīya & Udayanīya*.

The three feet—three *savanas* or pressing out of the *soma* juice which is to be done in the morning, at midday and in the evening.

Four horns—the four *Vedas*.

Seven arms—the seven Vedic metres (*chandas*) viz. Gāyatrī, Triṣṭubh, Anuṣṭubh, Bṛhatī, Paṅkti, Jagatī and Uṣṇik.

(ii) VJ. has accepted the above explanation of the metaphorical description but the 2nd line : 'Salutation to Lord Viṣṇu who is the *antaryāmin* (*ātmane*) of the performers of *Soma* sacrifice as enjoined in the Vedas (*Trayī Vidyā*).

(iii) VR. gives a totally different interpretation.

The whole universe of name and form is an attribute of the Lord. He is metaphorically described as a bull (Vṛṣabha) with four horns viz., names (nouns), verbs, indeclinables and prefixes (*nāma-ākhyāta-nipāta-upasargāḥ*). The three feet are three divisions of time : past, present and future; the two heads are : the essential attribute (*pravṛtti-nimitta*) and that in which the attribute lies (*tadāśrayaḥ*). The seven hands are the seven cases of declension (of nouns etc.). The Lord is known through *Vedas*. Hence he is the soul of the *Vedas*. He is Viṣṇu or sacrifice (*Yajño vai Viṣṇuḥ*) through whom men can extend the performance of sacrifice (*tantave*).

** VR regards Viṣṇu as the *antaryāmin* of Rudra (and other gods) as he is the real creator, protector and destroyer of the world.

Salutation to you the master of all *lores*[1] or knowledge and the Protector of all created beings.

33. Obeisance to *Hiraṇyagarbha* (god Brahmā), *Prāṇa* (i.e. *sūtrātman*, the soul of the subtle cosmic body), the soul of the universe. Hail to you, the embodiment of the highest powers acquired by *yoga* and the source of *yoga* (*yogic* lore).

34. Salutations to you the First (Eternal) God. I bow to you who are the witness (to everything). Hail to you the omniscient sage Nārāyaṇa and to Nara who are the manifestations of Hari.

35. Bow to you whose person is dark like emerald in complexion and who have been the master of the goddess Śrī. Salutation to you, Oh Keśava, the wearer of yellow garment.

36. You are the conferer of all boons to people. Hence you are most sought for, Oh most prominent bestower of blessings. It is hence that wise men adore the dust of your feet for the final beatitude.

37. May that glorious Lord be gracious to me—the Lord who is worshipped by gods and Lakṣmī, as if they desired to have the fragrance of His Lotus-like feet.

38. Having reverentially established the presence of Viṣṇu, the Lord of Senses, before one's self, by invoking him with these *mantras*, one should with faith, worship him, by offering water for washing the feet (*pādya*), for *ācamana* (sipping and rinsing the mouth) and other formalities of reception.

39. One should worship the Lord with fragrant sandal paste, flowers and other articles of worship and should perform his sacred ablution (*abhiṣeka*) with milk. He should then adore him by beautifying his person with clothes, sacred thread, ornaments and with water for again washing his feet and sipping water as *ācamana*, burning fragrant incense etc. before him, reciting all the while the twelve-syllabled *mantra* : OṀ NAMO BHAGAVATE VĀSUDEVĀYA.

40. If one can afford it (lit. If there is sufficient wealth), one should offer fragrant, white rice cooked

1. *Sarva-vidyādhipataye*—The preceptor of the knowledge which helps to achieve the four *puruṣārthas*—GD.

in milk, mixed with ghee and raw sugar, as an offering (*naivedya*) to him, and should pour it as oblations into the sacred fire chanting the root *mantra* (viz. the above-mentioned *mantra* of twelve syllables)[1].

41. One may give this offering (of boiled rice) to God to a devotee (of the Lord) or should eat it oneself. Having offered water as *ācamana* one should offer betel-leaves (with all the components like areca-nut powder, cardamom seeds, cloves etc.) finally.

42. One should chant this *mantra* (within one's mind) one hundred and eight times, and praise God with panygerics. Circumambulating him by the right side, one should prostrate one's self before him like a rod, with delight.

43. Reverentially placing on one's own head the remnants (flowers etc.) of the worship, one should pray the Deity to retire. One should then feed at least a couple of Brāhmaṇas with rice cooked in milk (and mixed with gur etc.).

44-45. Obtaining the assent of the Brāhmaṇas who are duly honoured (by giving betel-leaves, gift of money etc.), one should partake of the remaining food in company of his dear ones. On the night of the first day, one should observe strict continence. And on the next morning, he should take bath. Keeping himself undefiled according to the procedure laid down, and with composed and concentrated mind, he should perform the ablution of the deity with milk, and worship him (and as per details of worship given above) and thus observe the vow every day), till the period of the observance is completed.

46. Subsisting on milk-food and with full faith and devotion in the worship of Viṣṇu, one should continue to observe this vow. He should offer oblations to the sacred fire as before, and give food to the Brāhmaṇas as well.

1. With due respect to all these commentators, the translator feels that due to the obvious influence of the *Pañcarātra* on these verses, the *mūla-mantra* must be OṀ NAMO NĀRĀYAṆĀYA and NOT *Oṁ Namo Bhagavate Vāsudevāya*, though consistency in *Mantras* is essential.

47. In this way, observing the vow of 'subsistence on milk' from day to day, he should, for a period of twelve days, perform the propitiation of Lord Hari, offering oblations to the sacred fire, worship of the image and gratification of Brāhmaṇas (with food, gift of money etc.).

48. Beginning from the first day (of the bright half of the month of Phālguna) to the thirteenth, he should observe strict continence, sleep on bare ground and take bath three times a day (viz. in the morning, at midday and in the evening).

49 He should avoid speaking the untruth and on unholy topics (as well as with evil persons). He should refrain from pleasures of high or low order; he should abstain from injury to any being, and be absolutely devoted to Vāsudeva only.

50. On the thirtieth day, he should arrange for the ablution of Lord Viṣṇu with five substances (viz. milk, curds, ghee, honey and sugar which are collectively known as *pañcāmṛta*) according to the procedure laid down in the *Śāstras*, and under the guidance of the experts in them.

51-52. Without any mean miserliness in expending money, he should perform the worship of Viṣṇu on a grand scale. For the sake of Viṣṇu who pervaded all light, he should cook rice in milk (mixed with ghee etc.) and with fully concentrated and serene mind he should offer oblations to the sacred fire, and through it propitiate the Supreme Man. He should also offer food of excellent quality (containing articles of six types of tastes and free from any impurity or non-vegetarian food) which may be enjoyable and gratifying to the Supreme Person.

53. He should then gratify the learned preceptor (who conducted the worship) as well as those who carried out the sacrificial part, with articles of dress, ornaments and cows. He should note that to be also the propitiation of Lord Hari.

54. Oh lady with charming smiles! One should then cater to them dainty food of high quality as also to other Brāhmaṇas who might have come there, according to one's (financial) capacity.

55. One should then give *dakṣiṇā* (gift for performing

religious rites) according to merits, to the preceptor as well as to other Brāhmaṇas. One should also gratify with food etc. all those who have assembled there, including *caṇḍālas*.

56. Having gratified all indigent, blind, pitiable persons with food and understanding that that gratification is the real propitiation of Viṣṇu, one should lastly enjoy the food along with one's relatives.

57. Every day the worship of the Lord should be conducted with dancing, instrumental and vocal music, recitation of glorifying hymns and benedictory sayings and narration of the holy episodes of the Lord.

58. This is called *Payovrata*, the most excellent vow for propitiating the Supreme Person. What has been explained to me by god Brahmā has been communicated to you.

59. Oh most fortunate lady ! By properly and correctly observing this vow, and with your heart full of purity and devotion, and mind under control, worship Lord Keśava.

60. This is traditionally regarded as the perfect (or the essence of all kinds of) sacrifice and the perfect vow (the essence of all vows). This is the essence of penance and donations which leads to the gratification of the Lord, Oh fair lady !

61. That by which god Viṣṇu, the Supra-Sensuous deity, is propitiated are the real *Niyamas* (restraints of the mind), and the excellent *yamas* (controls of bodily discipline), the real penance, gifts, vow and sacrifice.

62. Therefore, Oh fair lady, with utmost self-discipline and devotion, you observe this vow, being pleased wherewith the Lord shall soon confer your cherished boons on you.

CHAPTER SEVENTEEN

The Manifestation of the Lord as Vāmana

Śrī Śuka said :

1. Aditi who was thus instructed by her husband Kaśyapa diligently observed this (*payovrata*) vow consecutively for twelve days, Oh king !

2. Having controlled the wild horses of her sense-organs through (the power of) her mind and with her reasoning power as the charioteer, she meditated with undivided mind and intellect upon the Supreme Person, the Controller, of the universe.

3. Concentrating her mind with her one-pointed reason on the glorious Lord Vāsudeva, the soul of all beings, Aditi verily observed the *Payovrata*.

4. (On completion of the observance) Oh child Parīkṣit, the Almighty Lord, the Eternal (First) Person manifested himself before her (in a form) clad in yellow garment with four arms wielding in (three of) them a conch, a discus and a mace.

5. On beholding him suddenly in a visible form, she was overwhelmed with love, and reverentially laid herself prostrate on the ground before him, like a rod.

6. She rose up and with folded palms stood before him to praise him but (being overwhelmed with love she could not do so. With her eyes overflowing with tears of joy, she remained silent. Her hair were standing on their ends all over her person, and her limbs were trembling with ecstatic joy at his sight.

7. Oh Scion of the Kuru race! The goddess Aditi looked at him affectionately as if drinking up that consort of Lakṣmī, the Lord of the universe and of the sacrifice, with her eyes, while she praised him slowly in a faltering voice, full of love.

Aditi began :

8. Oh Lord of sacrifices (who confer the fruit of sacrifices upon the performers)! Oh sacrifice incarnate! Oh imperishable Lord, at whose feet holy waters (like the Gaṅgā) resort, Oh Lord of hallowed glory, the hearing of whose name is auspicious[1] and whose very appearance relieves the sins and inequities of those who seek refuge in you, You are

1. *tīrtha-śrava-nāmadheyam*
The ears (of persons) who are devoted to *Śāstric* studies and who listen to Śāstras, become auspicious on hearing your Name, Oh Lord.—VJ.

the protector of the afflicted. Be pleased to secure (our) happiness (to us).

9. I bow down to you, Oh Lord Hari who are very great, immanent in the universe, and yet assume at your free will the *guṇas* (the modes of *prakṛti* and other powers of the *Māyā*) for the creation, maintenance and destruction of the universe, and are still self-poised (well established in your grandeur without the least disturbance), and who have completely dispelled the darkness (of ignorance, *tamas* or *māyā*) within yourself, by your eternal, perfect wisdom.

10. The longest life-span (viz. two *parārdha* years like that of god Brahmā), body (possessing power, beauty etc.) as desired, unparalleled fortune, dominance in the celestial regions, the earth and the nether world, all the mystic powers attained by *yoga*, the three principal objects in human life (viz. *dharma*, *artha* and *Kāma*), and even the absolute (highest) knowledge—all these are attained from you by men, if you are pleased. What to speak of an insignificant blessing like victory over a rival (co-wife and her progeny) ?

Śrī Śuka said :

11. Oh King ! Thus eulogised by Aditi, the lotus-eyed glorious Lord Viṣṇu, who resides in the heart of all created beings spoke to her as follows : Oh scion of the Bharata race !

The glorious Lord replied :

12. Oh mother of gods ! Known to me is your long cherished desire concerning your sons, who have been robbed of their glory and fortune by their enemies, and have been expelled from their homes.

13. You long to stay with your sons who, after, thoroughly vanquishing the vain-glorious mighty Asura chiefs on the battle field, have recovered their fortune and glory.

14. You desire to behold the wives of the enemies approaching the dead bodies of their husbands and bewailing, when they (enemies of your sons) are killed in battle, by your sons, of whom Indra is the eldest.

15. You wish to see that your sons have retrieved all

their glory and fortune and are extremely prosperous, and having re-established themselves in the heavenly regions, are enjoying themselves in sports.

16. Oh goddess ! In my opinion those leaders of Asura forces are, for the most part, now invincible; for they are now protected by favourable time and spiritually powerful Brāhmaṇas (or spiritually powerful Brāhmaṇas are gracious unto them). Application of prowess, (even on my part) will not be conducive to happiness, under these circumstances.

17. In spite of this, Oh noble lady, an expedient (to restore your former glory etc.) must be thought out by me inasmuch as I am gratified by your observance of the (*payovrata*) vow. My propitiation which results in conferment of the desire motivating it, should not prove futile.

18. By the correct observance of the *payovrata* vow, I have been properly worshipped and agreeably praised by you, for the protection of your children. Establishing myself in the austere penance (the procreative energy) of Kaśyapa, the Son of Marīci (your husband), I shall assume your son-hood by a ray of mine, and shall protect your sons.

19. Conceiving in your mind that I, of such (as is at present) form, am abiding in your husband, attend to your husband, the sinless lord of creation, Kaśyapa (and get conceived).

20. This secret should never be divulged to another person under any circumstances, even though you are interrogated. Everything will turn out well, but this secret of gods must be thoroughly guarded, Oh divine lady.

Śrī Śuka said :

21-22. Having addressed (her) thus, the Lord (immediately) disappeared on that very spot. Being bestowed with an extremely rare boon viz. the birth of Lord Hari through her, Aditi, feeling as if her object had been accomplished, betook herself to her husband with great devotion. Kaśyapa verily came to perceive that through his meditational *yoga*.

23. The sage of unfailing insight (knowledge) cognised the penetration of Lord Hari's ray within him. (Though to him both the *devas* and *asuras*, being his sons were equal) he,

with his mind serene and concentrated, deposited in Aditi that semen (charged with Hari's rays and) conserved through a long penance, just as the wind (to which all are equal) places (frictional) fire in the wood.

24. God Brahmā, knowing the presence of that eternal glorious Lord in Aditi's womb, began to praise him, in esoteric terms.

God Brahmā said :

25. Victory to you, Oh glorious Lord who are widely extolled in the Vedas and are of mighty prowess[1] ! My salutation to you, the protector of the Brāhmaṇas (and the Vedas). I bow to you again and again, you, the master of three *guṇas*.

26. I bow to you who were in the womb of Pṛśni (i. e. Pṛśni's son) and are revealed in the Vedas. You are the Maker of all, and contain all three worlds in your navel. You transcend the three worlds and still as *antaryāmin* (indwelling-soul) you enter and stay within all living beings and are all-pervading.

27. You who are called the Supreme Person of infinite powers, are the beginning, the end and the middle of the universe. Oh Ruler of the Universe ! Being the Time-Spirit you carry away with you everything in the universe like a deep stream of water sweeping away everyting that falls into it.

28. Verily, you are competent to create all beings, mobile or immobile as well as even the Lords of creations. Like a boat unto a person about to drown in water, you are the main supporter of gods (residents of the celestial world) who have fallen from the heaven, Oh Lord !

CHAPTER EIGHTEEN

The Lord incarnates as Vāmana. Visit to Bali's sacrifice

Śrī Śuka said :

1. The Lord whose glorious acts and powers were thus extolled, by god Brahmā and who is above birth and death

1. *Urukrama* : *Or* in anticipation of the Lord's future feat : Oh Lord of wide strides.

manifested himself through Aditi, in a form endowed with four arms wielding (in each) a conch, a mace, a lotus and a discus, clad in yellow garment and with eyes wide like a lotus.

2. Bright dark-blue in complexion, and with the splendour of his lotus-like face enhanced with the lustre of his alligator-shaped ear-rings, the Supreme Person, with the Śrīvatsa mark on his chest, was adorned with bracelets, armlets, a shining diadem, a girdle and a pair of beautiful anklets.

3. Irradiated with his special splendid *Vanamālā* (wreath of forest flowers) resonant with a swarm of humming bees and with the *Kaustubha* gem suspended from his neck, Lord Hari dispelled with his splendour the gloom in the house of Kaśyapa, the Lord of Creation, with his effulgence.

4. At that time, the cardinal points became clear and bright; lakes and ponds became translucent; all the creatures became jubilant; the seasons exhibited their characteristic efflorescence; joy reigned in the heaven, the mid air, the earth, gods (whose tongue is fire), kine, the three twice-born classes and mountains.

5. On the twelfth day of the bright half of the month of Bhādrapada when the moon was within the mansion called *Śravaṇa*, and the auspicious time was the *Abhijit* (the first *aṁśa* of *Śravaṇa*), the Lord incarnated (on the earth) and all constellations of stars (e.g. Aśvinī), planets etc. (by their auspicious influence) indicated his descent to be beneficial.

6. That twelfth day (of the bright half of Bhādrapada), when the sun attained the meridian, and the birth of Lord Hari took place, is known to people as *Vijayā* (the victorious).

7. Conchs were blown and big drums, kettle-drums, tabors and *paṇavas* (a kind of musical instrument) were sounded. There was the tumultuous sound of various musical instruments.

8. The celestial damsels being highly delighted danced and prominent Gandharvas (like Hāhā, Hūhū) sang. Sages, gods, Manus, *manes* and fire-gods extolled the Lord.

9-10. Hosts of *Siddhas* and *Vidyādharas*, along with *Kimpuruṣas* and *Kinnaras*, *Cāraṇas*, *Yakṣas* and *rakṣas*, *suparṇas* (eagles), best of serpents, and the attendants of gods sang and danced. Highly extolling the Lord, they showered flowers on the hermitage of Aditi and its premises.

11. Beholding that Supreme Person as born from her womb, Aditi was astonished and was transported with joy. Amazed at the assumption of a human form by his *yogic Māyā* Power, even Kaśyapa, the Lord of Creation hailed him 'May you be victorious'.

12. With that very form, decorated with ornaments and endowed with weapons which Hari, of unmanifest consciousness, manifested to them, hc (instantly) transformed Himself in a dwarf Brāhmaṇa boy like a wonderfully active actor, while the parents were simply looking on.

13. Seeing (the transformation of the Lord as) the dwarf Brāhmaṇa boy, all great sages were delighted and with Kaśyapa, the Lord of creation, as their head, got performed all the religious rites and observances (from those beginning with the birth e. g. *jātakarman* and other).

14*. While his sacred thread ceremony (*Upanayana*) was being performed, the sun-god (the presiding deity of *Gāyatrī Mantra*) taught him the *Gāyatrī Mantra*; Bṛhaspati, the preceptor of gods, gave him the sacred thread, and Kaśyapa, the cord of *muñja* grass to be tied round his waist.

15*. The Earth-goddess conferred the skin of black-antelope on him,.while Soma, the Lord of plant and herbs offered the sacred staff. The mother covered his nudity with a piece of cloth, and heavens gave an umbrella to the Lord of the Universe.

16*. God Brahmā presented him a water pot (of gourd or wood) and the seven sages, the *darbha* grass. The goddess Sarasvatī gave a rosary of beads to the Immortal Supreme Soul.

17*. When his initiation-ceremony (sacred-thread-inves-

14-17* The list of deities who presented Vāmana different articles differs in other *Purāṇas*. Thus in *Matsya P.* 245-85 we find the black antelope skin given by Brahmā, the sacred thread by Bṛhaspati, the sacred staff by Marīci, Kamaṇḍalu by Vasiṣṭha, a bunch of Kuśa grass by Aṅgiras, rosary of beads by Pulaha, a pair of white garments by Pulastya. The four Vedas, Sāṁkhya, Yoga and other Śāstras attended upon Vāmana.

titure ceremony) was over, Kubera, King of Yakṣas gave him a begging-bowl with words "This is for him". And the veritable Mother-goddess Satī (Umā) herself served him the alms.

18. Thus honoured by all, the newly initiated eminent Brāhmaṇa boy, with his splendid Brahmanic (divine) effulgence, surpassed the whole assembly of Brāhmaṇa-sages.

19. The twice-born boy instituted the sacred fire (on the altar) enkindling it, duly worshipping it by placing the *Kuśa* grass around it in their proper places (*paristīrya*), and oblated into the fire the sacred sticks (daubed with ghee—the *samidhs*).

20. Having learnt that Bali, of enormous wealth and power, was engaged as a sacrificer in a horse-sacrifice conducted by the Brāhmaṇas of the Bhṛgu clan, he (Vāmana) concentrating in himself all the power, proceeded (from the hermitage of Aditi) to that place (of Bali's sacrificial hall), bending down the earth at every step, on account of his weight.

21. The sacrificial priests of the Bhṛgu clan who were conducting the best of sacrifices (viz. a horse-sacrifice) of Bali on the northern bank of the Narmadā, at a spot called *Bhṛgu-Kacchaka* (near modern Broach in Gujarat), beheld him (Vāmana) approaching them, brilliant like the sun risen just near them.

22. Oh King, their glory being eclipsed by the effulgence of Vāmana, the priests conducting the sacrifice, the sacrificer Bali and the members of the sacrificial assembly began to conjecture (among themselves) whether he (Vāmana) was the Sun-god himself or was the Fire-god or the (great) sage Sanatkumāra himself, coming with a view to observe the sacrifice.

23. While the Bhṛgus along with their disciples were thus variously expressing their surmise about him, Lord Vāmana carrying with him his umbrella, sacred staff, and water-bowl full of water, entered the pandal of the horse-sacrifice.

24-25. Noticing the entry of Lord Hari, a dwarfish Brāhmaṇa boy with the (outward) appearance of a *Brahmacā-*

rin assumed with his *Māyā* powers, having the zone of *Muñja*-grass tied round his waist, and wearing as an upper garment a deer-skin in the fashion of the sacred thread (over his shoulder) and matted hair, the Bhṛgus along with their disciples and fires (fire-gods) as well, shrank before his divine lustre, and standing up to honour him, accorded unto him reception with all the due formalities.

26. Overjoyed to see his charming personality worth seeing, with limbs proportionate to his form, the sacrificer himself offered him a suitable seat.

27. According him courteous welcome, Bali washed the feet of the Lord, and worshipped him who is attractive to the minds of those who have abjured all attachment.

28. Bali, the knower of the path of righteousness, placed (sprinkled) on his head the water with which he washed his feet, and hence had become most auspicious and capable of removing all the sins of the people, and which Lord Śiva (the Lord of mount *Kailāśa*) the god of gods and the wearer of the crescent of the moon on his forehead, received on his head with utmost devotion.

Bali said :

29. (Hearty) welcome to you. I pay my obeisance to you. Oh Brahman ! (Be pleased to tell us) what we should do for you. Oh noble Sir, I deem that you are the very embodiment of the penance of all Brāhmaṇa sages.

30. (Fully) satisfied are all our fore-fathers today. Our family and house have been purified. This very sacrifice has been successfully performed inasmuch as your worship has visited our house.

31. The sacrificial fires of mine whose sins have been completely annihilated by the waters used for washing your feet, stand properly worshipped with oblations, according to sacriptural injunctions. This land of our has been purified by your tiny feet, Oh son of a Brāhmaṇa !

32. Oh son of a Brāhmaṇa ! Methinks you have come to seek something. Be pleased to accept from me whatever you desire, Oh Brahmacārin ! Oh most worshipful Brāhmaṇa !

Duly accept from me either the earth, gold, a well-furnished house, delicious food and drink or possibly even a girl or prosperous villages, horses, elephants or chariots, Oh Brāhmaṇa.

CHAPTER NINETEEN

Vāmana's request for three paces of Land—Śukra's opposition

Śrī Śuka said :

1. Hearing the above-mentioned speech of Bali, the son of Virocana, which was in accordance with the prescribed path of righteousness, pleasing yet true, the glorious Lord was pleased with him. Welcoming him, He spoke.

The glorious Lord said:

2. Oh Lord of men! This speech of yours is courteous, true, worthy of your family (traditions), full of righteousness contributory to your glory, as the descendants of Bhṛgu race are your guides in matters temporal, while in matters spiritual your quiescent grand-father, the eldest member of the family (viz. Prahlāda) is your authority.

3. No such niggardly person was born in this family who ever refused to donate (anything) to Brāhmaṇas or was so miserly as going back upon his promise to give.

4. Never there was any such coward king in your family who at the time of religious donations turned this face against persons who, deserving the gift, had requested for it, or who, at the time of battle, showed their backs to worthy foes who challenged them in fight. In your family, Prahlāda shines forth in his unsullied faultless glory like the moon in the firmament.

5. In this family was born Hiraṇyākṣa who, armed with his mace, travelled alone over this earth for the conquest of all directions i.e. of (the entire earth) and did not meet any rival (equal to him in valour).

6. When faced by him (Hiraṇyākṣa), at the time of lifting up of the earth (from the *rasātala*), Viṣṇu (in the Boar-

incarnation) vanquished him with great difficulty, but frequently remembering his great bravery, did not regard himself as the victor (subsequently).

7. Hearing the report of his (Hiraṇyākṣa's) death, his brother Hiraṇyakaśipu got enraged and went, of yore, to the region of Hari, for killing[1] the slayer of his brother.

8. Beholding him (Hiraṇyakaśipu) rushing toward himself with a spear in hand, like the god of death, Viṣṇu, who knows the (suitability of) Time, and is the foremost one among the masters of marvellous illusive powers[2], pondered over the matter.

9. 'Wherever I go, he will certainly follow me as the (god of) death does unto living beings. I shall, therefore, enter his heart, inasmuch as his vision is confined to external things (or affairs)'.

10. Taking this decision, Viṣṇu, with a disturbed mind (as a matter of fact, with a calm and undisturbed mind) concealed his subtle body in the breath of the enemy who was rushing at him, and entered his body through his nostrils (without being known by him), Oh ruler of Asuras !

11. Having ransacked his vacant residence and not being able to find him, the warrior[3] got enraged and roared loudly. He searched for Viṣṇu, the heaven and the earth, the cardinal points and the sky, the subterranean regions and the seas, but could not find him anywhere.

12. As he did not perceive him, he said positively, "The whole of the universe has been closely searched by me. The murderer of my brother must have certainly gone to the place (viz. the region of death) from which no man returns (he being ever liberated from Saṁsāra must have returned to his original nature which is *brahma-hood*).

13. In this world, the persistence in enmity continues only so far i.e. to the extent of, the death of, the (inimical) embodied beings. Anger (the cause of enmity) which is engendered through ignorance is fostered by egotism.

1. As a matter of fact for knowing Him (GS).

2. *māyāvināṁ varaḥ*—The bestower of boons like liberation from saṁsāra.—VJ.

3. *Vīra*—One devoid of knowledge (*vigatam īraṁ jñānaṁ yasya*)—VD.

14. Your father Virocana, the son of Prahlāda was so devoted to Brāhmaṇas that when so requested by celestials in the disguise of twice-born ones (Brāhmaṇas), knew their real nature (as enemies), and still conferred his lease of life upon them.

15. Your worship resorted to the righteous course of conduct followed by householders, Brāhmaṇas, your valorous forefathers and others of wide reputation.

16. Oh Lord of Daityas ! You are the foremost one among the bestowers of boons. From you, I seek a small piece of land three paces in length measured with my feet.[1]

17. Even though you are a liberal Lord of the earth, I do not seek anything else from you, Oh king ! For a learned person who accepts a gift just limited to his (actual) requirements, does not contaminate any sin.

Bali said :

18. Oh Brāhmaṇa's son ! Your words are commendable in the case of the aged. You are, however, a child, of childlike (undeveloped) intelligence[2], as such, you do not know your self-interest.

19. Having propitiated me, the sole supreme ruler of the world, with courteous words, you seek only three paces (feet) of land, out of lack of intelligence[3] or knowledge, when I am capable of gifting a continent.

20. A person who approaches me (for a gift) should not (have the occasion or need to) approach another for begging. Hence, Oh Brāhmaṇa boy ! Accept from me freely, at will[4] as much land as is sufficient for you to maintain your livelihood (decently).

1. This motif of the Vāmana story is traceable to the Vedic symbolism of Viṣṇu measuring out three *lokas* in three strides. Vide RV 1.22.17 also 1.154.2, 1.155.4. Vāmana is the unmanifest principle, while Viṣṇu or Virāṭ is manifest.

2. ŚR states that as a matter of fact the 2nd line should read : *tvaṁ bālo'bāliśā-matiḥ* "You are *a-bāliśa*—whose intelligence is fully developed and as such you consider the interests of your devotees and seek no personal interest." (As you are perfect there is no scope for any personal want).

3. ŚR. : the words in the 2nd line *yo'buddhimān* should be split as '*yo Buddhimān*, "Intelligent as you are" etc.

4. *Kāmam*—By stretching your stride as much as possible—ŚR. Vāmana complies.

The Lord replied :

21. All the desired-most objects (or lands) that are available in the three worlds cannot be enough to satisfy a person who has not subdued his senses or the mind, Oh King !

22. He who is dissatisfied with three feet of land, cannot have his desire fulfilled with an island—continent consisting of nine *Varṣas* (sub-continents), as he will crave to possess all the seven island-continents.

23. We heard the report that Pṛthu, the son of Vena[1], Gaya[2] and other kings who were the Lords of the seven continents (*dvīpas*) never reached the end of their thirst for more, despite their possession of the hoards of wealth and desired objects.

24. A contented person leads a happy life with whatever comes to his lot by chance, while a discontented person who has no control over himself, is never satisfied even if the three worlds be possessed by him.

25. It is said that non-contentment with reference to wealth and objects of enjoyment, is the cause of the transmigration of man in this world, and that contentment with what one happens to get by (one's predestined) luck, is the way to emancipation (from *saṁsāra*).

26. The spiritual glory of a Brāhmaṇa who is satisfied with what he obtains through chance, enhances. It, however, is extinguished through lack of contentment, like fire with water.

27. Prominent among the bestowers of boons as you are, I, hence, seek only three feet of land from you. I shall have my purpose (of depriving you of everything) accomplished

1. *Vainya*—Pṛthu, son of Vena. He was churned out of the hand of the dead body of Vena. He "milked" the earth of food-stuffs. His reign was a golden period. He performed a horse-sacrifice. Installing his son Vijitāśva on the throne, Pṛthu retired to forest and performed penance and merged in *parabrahman*.

—*Mbh. Śānti* 59.98-128; 227. 49-56.

VP. 1.22, The *Bh. P. Supra* 4th *skandha*.

2. *Gaya*—An ancient king-sage (*rājarṣi*) who performed many sacrifices (*Mbh. vana* 75,18). He gifted away all land to Brāhmaṇas (*Mbh. Śānti* 234.25). He earned reputation and wealth by visiting sacred places and temples in India. (*Mbh.Vana.* 94.18).

with that much only. For the desirability of wealth is limited to the extent of its usefulness.

Śrī Śuka said :

28. When addressed thus, Bali laughingly spoke, "Take it as much as desired". He then took in his hand his jar of water to donate the land (with due religious formalities) to Vāmana.

29. Śukra, the foremost among the knowers (of politics) apprehending the (inner) design of Viṣṇu, forewarned his disciple who was about to gift the land to Viṣṇu.

Śukra said :

30. Oh son of Virocana ! This dwarf is no other than the eternal divine Lord Viṣṇu who is born of Kaśyapa and Aditi, with the object of accomplishing the purpose of gods.

31. I do not approve of the promise given by you without foreseeing the consequent calamities (implicit in your promise). A great disaster has befallen the Daityas.

32. This Hari who has assumed the form of a *Brahmacārin* through his delusive powers (*māyā*) will dispossess you of your position, sovereignty, fortune, splendour, world-wide reputation and learning and pass it on to Indra.

33. Assuming his cosmic form, co-extensive with the universe, he will occupy all these (three) regions with three steps. Having conferred everything that you own, upon Viṣṇu, how are you going to exist, oh fool !

34. Where is the space left for the third foot when the all-pervading Viṣṇu covers the whole of the earth in one foot, and the heaven with another, and occupies the intervening space by his body ? (Thus you cannot fulfil your promise.)

35. Me-thinks your permanent place lies in the hell, the destination of those who do not redeem their pledge, since even you will not be able to fulfil your promise.

36. They (i.e. the wise) do not commend that gift as good if it endangers the means of livelihood of the donor. For in this world, charitable gifts, performance of sacrifices, austere penances and religious acts can be performed by persons with means of subsistence.

37. A person who divides his wealth in five shares (and invests it) for the purpose of religious acts, glory, getting economic return, personal pleasure and provision of one's relatives, becomes happy here and hereafter.

38. If you feel uneasy about the break of promise hear from me, Oh best of the Asuras ! the decision of the seers of the *Ṛgveda* on this point (about truth and falsehood). Whatever is promised by uttering the sacred syllable *Om*, is the truth and whatever is denied by expressing a 'No' is untruth.

39. It is sung (in the *Śruti* texts) that one should know that truth is the flower and fruit of the tree of this body. When the tree does not survive that (viz. the fruits and flowers i.e. the truth) ceases to be. Hence, *anṛta* (viz. not giving away all one's possessions) is the root-mainstay of the body.

40. Just as a tree that is uprooted, dries up and dies in a short time, so does the body which has lost its support of *anṛta*, undoubtedly dry up soon.

41. The Vedic text *parāg riktam* etc. means that which is expressed by the assenting syllable *Om* carries away wealth to a long distance, and leaves one incomplete (bereft of wealth).

A person verily becomes poorer to that extent to which he agrees to give by uttering the syllable *Om* (yes). A donor who agrees to give everything to the mendicant cannot find sufficient for his personal enjoyment (subsistence).

42. Therefore, the term 'No' which is regarded as *anṛta* means fullness to oneself (as his wealth is unspent), and adds to his wealth (as due to the consciousness of his deficiency, he tries to get more wealth from others). But if a person who makes a false statement all the while by saying 'No' (refusing to give), gets a bad name, and is as good as dead though breathing.

43. False statements are not condemnable when made to women (while courting), in jokes, in arranging marriages, for obtaining one's livelihood, for saving one's own life in danger, in protecting cows and Brāhmaṇas and where violence (to another) is anticipated.

CHAPTER TWENTY

Manifestation of the Cosmic Form by Viṣṇu

Śrī Śuka said :

1. Bali, the Lord of the household, who was thus addressed by his family-preceptor, remained silent for a moment and (weighing the consequences) with careful mind, he submitted as follows :

Bali said :

2. What has been stated by your worship, is true. It is the duty of householders to see that the wealth, enjoyment (of life) good reputation and the means of livelihood are not adversely affected by anything.

3. Having promised the Brāhmaṇa once that I shall give, how can I, the descendant of Prahlāda, out of greed for wealth, refuse, like a gambler, to give.

4. The earth has verily said : There is no greater heinous unrighteousness than falsehood. I am capable of bearing anything else except a man given to uttering falsehood.

5. I am not so much afraid of the (tortures of) hell, poverty, ocean of misery, displacement from (my present) status and even death, as I am of cheating a Brāhmaṇa.

6. In this world, wealth (and as a matter of fact) everything else abandons a dying man. (Why should not one give it away while alive ? If only a part is given and the recipient Brāhmaṇa is not satisfied, the gift becomes fruitless). What is the propriety of that charitable act unless the recipient Brāhmaṇa is satisfied thereby ?

7. Righteous souls like sage Dadhyañc[1], king Śibi[2] and others accomplish the well-being of creatures by sacrificing their lives which are so difficult to give up; what consideration is there for the earth and other things (which are less important than life) ?

1. A famous sage, Son of Bhṛgu—Handed over his body to gods for preparation of *Vajra* (the weapon of Indra) out of his bones.—*Mbh. Vana* 100.21 *Śalya* 51.29-32.

2. An ancient royal sage who submitted his body to a hawk (Indra) to save a dove (fire-god)—*Mbh. Vana* 197. 21.28.

8. Time has swallowed up the enjoyment of the earth and the position in the next world of the kings of Daityas who (while alive) enjoyed the earth and were ever successful in war. But (it could) not do so to the glorious renown achieved by them on the earth, Oh Brāhmaṇa.

9. Oh Brāhmaṇa Sage ! Those who lay down their lives without retreating from the battlefield are easily available, but not so the donors who, when approached by worthy recipients, reverentially give away their wealth.

10. Poverty and affliction in consequence of satisfying the desires of (ordinary) supplicants, appear graceful to a magnanimous and merciful soul. Need it be said that it is much more so in cases like yours who know the *Brahman* or Vedas ? Hence, I shall bestow upon the *Brahmacārin* what he wants.

11. Let him be Viṣṇu, the bestower of boons whom your worshipful self, conversant with the procedure laid down in the Vedas, so reverentially worship by performance of various kinds of sacrifices (with *Soma* or without *Soma*) or let him be an enemy. I shall confer upon him the land desired for by him, Oh sage !

12. Even if he unrighteously binds me down—an innocent sinless person, I shall do no harm unto him, a cowardly enemy disguised as a Brāhmaṇa.

13. If he be really Viṣṇu of hallowed renown he would not forfeit his fame (by deceiving me thus). He will take away the land by killing me on the battlefield or lie down killed by me.

Śrī Śuka said :

14. The preceptor Śukra, being impelled by Providence, pronounced the following curse upon his noble-minded disciple who placed no faith in his words, and would not abide by his command, but wanted to be true to his promise.

15. "You who are highly conceited as being learned and obstinate. and show disregard to us by transgressing our orders, shall, in no time, fall down from your royal splendour".

16. Though cursed thus by his preceptor, the great Bali did not swerve from the truth and worshipping Vāmana,

he gave away the land with due formality of pouring water (from his right palm in solemn confirmation of the gift).

17. The royal consort Vindhyāvalī, adorned with a costly pearl necklace, came there and brought a gold jar full of water to wash Vāmana's feet.

18. The sacrificer himself gladly washed the glorious feet of the Lord, and sprinkled on his head, the waters which are capable of sanctifying the whole of the universe.

19. In the heaven, all the hosts of gods, Gandharvas, Vidyādharas, Cāraṇas applauded that act of worship, and extolled the Asura King and his straightforwardness and overcome with joy, showered flowers over him.

20. Thousands of kettledrums were sounded; Gandharvas and Kimpuruṣas sang that a most difficult act has been done by this noble-minded Bali, in that, he knowingly bestowed the (sovereignty of the) three worlds upon his enemies.

21. That dwarf form of that infinite Hari, comprising as it is of three *guṇas*, miraculously expanded to such an extent as to include that earth, the heaven, the cardinal points, the space between the heaven and the earth, cavities and hells, oceans, the sub-human beings, human beings, gods and sages and everything else.

22. Bali along with the sacrificial priests, the president of the sacrificial assembly, and its members, saw on the body of the Great Spirit comprising of all the *guṇas*, the whole of the universe made up of three *guṇas*, and consisting of elements, the senses with their objects (of enjoyment), the mind and the *jīvas* (individual souls).

23. Bali whose army was like that of Indra espied on the cosmic form of the Lord the *rasātala* (the sub-terranean regions) at the sole of his feet, the earth resting on his feet, mountains on the shanks, birds on his knee-joints, the group of wind-gods (*maruts*) on the thighs of the Supreme Person.

24. He beheld the two twilights (deities presiding over the dawn and the dusk) on the garments of the all-pervading Lord, the lords of creation in his genital organ, *Asuras* of which he was the chief in the anus, the firmament in the navel, the

seven seas in his sides, and the string of constellations on the chest of the Lord of very colossal strides.

25-26. Oh Child! He saw (the presiding deity of *Dharma* in the heart of the slayer of Mura (Viṣṇu), *Ṛta* (Divine Law) and *Satya* (Truth) on his breasts, the Moon-god in the mind, the goddess *Śrī* with a lotus in her hand resting on his bosom, and all the *Sāma*-hymns, articulate sounds in his throat, all the celestials with Indra as their chief on his arms, the cardinal points in his ears, and the heaven on (the crown of) his head, the clouds in the mass of his hair, the vital breath in his nostrils, the Sun-god in his eyes, and the Fire-god in his mouth.

27. He saw the Vedas in his speech, Varuṇa the Lord of waters in his palate, the interdicting and prescriptive parts (of the scriptures) in his eye-brows, the day and night on his eyelashes, Anger on his forehead, greed on the lower lip of the Supreme Person.

28. Oh King! He saw the passion of Love in his sense of touch, water in his semen, *Adharma* (the spirit of unrighteousness) on his back, sacrificial activity in his steps, Death in his shadow, *Māyā* in his laughter, and various species of herbs in the hair on his body.

29. The warrior Bali beheld the rivers in his arteries, rocks in the nails, god Brahmā in his *Buddhi* (intellect), the hosts of gods and sages in his vital breaths, all creatures mobile and immobile on his person.

30. Perceiving all this universe resting in the Person of the Lord, all the Asuras lost their consciousness, Oh child!

The *Sudarśana* discus of unbearable velocity, force and effulgence, the *Śārṅga* bow twanging like rumbling clouds.

31. The *Pāñcajanya* conch of deep sound like the roar of thunder, the mighty mace of Viṣṇu called *Kaumodakī*, the sword called *Vidyādhara* (otherwise known as Nandaka) paired with a shield called *Śatacandra* (as it was set with hundred moonlike studs), and the two excellent quivers with inexhaustible stock of arrows, (all in personem).

32. His chief attendants headed by Sunanda, accompanied by the guardians of the worlds, waited upon the Lord. Adorned with shining diadem, armlets, a pair of alligator-

shaped ear-rings, the *Śrī-Vatsa* mark, in foremost of all jewels *Kaustubha*, girdle, clad in yellow silk garment.

33. Adorned with the *Vanamālā* (a wreath of forest-flowers) hovered round by bees, the Divine Lord of mighty strides, shone in great brilliance.

Oh King! He coverd the earth of Bali with one foot; He occupied the sky with his body and the quarters with his arms.

34. As he covered the celestial region with another step there was not the slightest space left for the third as the second step of the Lord of wide strides extended higher and higher beyond *Maharloka*, *Janaloka*, *Tapoloka* upto Satyaloka—the region of god Brahmā.

CHAPTER TWENTY-ONE

Bali Bound Down

Śrī Śuka said :

1. On beholding that the foot of the Lord had reached (his region) *satya-loka* and finding himself enveloped in and the effulgence of his region eclipsed by the brilliant lustre of his moon-like (toe-) nails, lotus-born god Brahmā and also great sages like Marīci, sages of great vows (of life-long celebacy like Nārada) and *yogins* (of the path of knowledge) like Sanandana, came forth to receive him.

2. (The presiding deities of) the Vedas and the subsidiary Vedas (viz. *āyur-veda* the science of medicine, *Dhanur-veda* the military science, *Gāndharva veda* the science of music, *Sthāpatya veda* the science of Engineering), *Niyamas* and *yamas*[1], science of Logic (*Sāṁkhya* and *Mīmāṁsā*), History (viz. the *Rāmāyaṇa* and the *Mahābhārata*), six auxiliaries of Vedas,[2]

1. Vide *Supra* Bh. P. 4.22.24.

2. viz. (1) *Śikṣā*—phonetics or Science of proper articulation and pronunciation (2) *Chandas*—science of Prosody, (3) *Vyākaraṇa*—Grammar, (4) *Nirukta*--Etymology of Vedic words, (5) *Jyotiṣa*—Astronomy, (6) *Kalpa*—code of rituals.

Purāṇas and *Saṁhitās* (sacred texts like *Pāñcarātra Saṁhitā*, *Brahma-saṁhitā*, *Garga-saṁhitā* and others) who had burnt down their impurities of sins by the fire of spiritual knowledge enkindled by the wind of *Yoga*, approached and bowed down at the foot of the Lord, by virtue of meditating which they would attain to the region of god Brahmā which is not accessible by the path of *Karmas* (religious, ritualistic acts).

3. Thereupon, the lotus-born god Brahmā, of extremely pure reputation, brought water to worship Viṣṇu's foot raised upto his region. Devoutly worshipping his feet, he sang out his praise, for he himself was born out of the lotus that adorns his navel.

4. The water that was poured out of the *Kamaṇḍalu* (water-jug) of god Brahmā, for washing the feet of the Lord of mighty strides, and being purified thereby, became the heavenly river in the sky. Like the pure hallowing renown of the Lord, it sanctifies the three worlds as it falls from the sky, and flows through them from the heavens.

5. God Brahmā and other protectors of the worlds, along with their followers, reverentially brought articles of worship to their Lord who had withdrawn his all-pervading form in a limited personality (viz. that of Vāmana).

6. With water brought for worship, with garlands of flowers and divinely fragrant sandal-paste and pigment, with burning of fragrant incense and lights, parched grains of paddy, unbroken rice, fruits and sprouts.

7. With songs of praise, shouts of victory announcing his prowess and greatness, with dancing performances, playing of musical instruments and presentation of vocal music and sounds of conchs and kettle drums.

8. Jāmbavān, the king of bears, with the speed of the mind, proclaimed with beating of drums in all directions, the victory of the Lord and the great festive occasion.

9. Finding that under a deceitful pretext of a request of three feet of land, the entire earth was taken away (fraudulently) from their master who was engaged in a sacrifice, the Asuras flared up and said to each other.

10. "Certainly this is not even a Brāhmaṇa by mere caste, (even a lowly Brāhmaṇa will not commit such a fraud).

He is Viṣṇu, the prominent one among the masters of illusive powers (and conjuring tricks). Disguising himself as a Brāhmaṇa, he desires to accomplish the objective of gods.

11. We stand cheated of everything by this enemy who assuming the disguise of a *Brahmacārin* came for begging, while our master has laid down his powers of punishment during the period of this sacrifice.

12. Being a person vowed to observe (perpetual) truthfulness, and especially when consecrated for performing sacrifice, it is not possible to utter falsehood for our master who is friendly to Brāhmaṇas full of compassion.

13. It is, therefore, our sacred duty to kill him (Vāmana) and serve the cause of our master." Saying thus the followers of Bali, Asuras, took up their arms.

14. Thus being enraged, all of them, armed with spears (*śūla*) and sharp-edged steel-bars[1] (*paṭṭiśa*) rushed to strike at Vāmana (the Dwarf), even though Bali did not wish it.

15. Seeing the generals of the Daitya army attacking Vāmana, Viṣṇu's attendants laughed at them, and thwarted them (Asuras' attack) with their arms uplifted.

16-17. Nanda, Sunanda, Jaya, Vijaya, Prabala, Bala, Kumuda, Kumudākṣa, Viśvaksena, the king of birds—Garuḍa, Śrutadeva, Puṣpadanta and Sātvata—each of them possessing the strength of ten thousand elephants, advanced to kill the Asura army.

18. Seeing his people being massacred by the followers of Viṣṇu, and remembering the curse of Śukra (his preceptor), Bali prevented them from fighting, although they were enraged.

19. "Oh Vipracitti ! Oh Rāhu ! Oh Nemi ! Listen to my speech ! Please do not fight; retreat. This period is not favourable unto us.

20. Oh Daitya comrades ! No human being is powerful enough to overcome Him with human prowess, as he is the master (chief cause) who distributes pleasure and pain to all creatures.

1. *paṭṭiśo lohadaṇḍo yas tīkṣṇadhāraḥ kṣuropamaḥ—Vaijayantī* quoted in ASD p. 310.

21. The glorious Lord who was formerly in favour of our prosperity and against that of the celestials, is today disposed to do quite the reverse of it.

22. No person can verily overcome the Time-spirit by physical power, expert advisers, intelligence, fortresses, mystic formulae, medicine etc. and by expedients like *sāma, dāna, daṇḍa and bheda*).

23. These attendants of Hari have many times been vanquished by you, when Fortune was favourable to you. Today those very attendants are roaring after vanquishing you in the battle.

24. If the Providence becomes favourable (again), we shall again defeat them. Therefore wait for the favourable Time, which will turn to be advantageous to us."

Śrī Śuka said :

25. Hearing the directive (speech) of their leader, the generals of the Daitya and Dānava forces, beaten by the attendants of Viṣṇu entered the *Rasātala* (nether world).

26. On the very day of extracting Soma juice in the sacrifice, Garuḍa, king of birds, the son of Tārkṣya, informed of the desire of the Lord[1], bound down Bali with the noosecords of Varuṇa.

27. When the king of Asuras was thus being taken prisoner by Viṣṇu of superior power, there arose a loud outcry on earth, in the sky and in all directions.

28. Glorious Lord Vāmana addressed to Bali who, though bound down by the noose of Varuṇa and bereft of royal splendour, was of balanced and stable mind, and of noble reputation, Oh King !

29. "Oh Asura ! you have given me three paces of land. The entire earth (world) has been covered by two steps, Please provide space for the third.

1. ŚR explains : The Lord wanted to shower grace on Bali by depriving him of all his property and freeing him from his egoistic claim on his body. Or the Lord wanted to lower Bali's position to exhibit Bali's greatness etc.

30. As this entire land as far as the sun warms it by its rays, and the moon and the stars illuminate it, and as far as the rain-god was sending showers of water, was yours.

31. With one step I have covered the region of the earth, the sky and the quarters by my body, the celestial regions were covered by the second step as witnessed by you.

32. If you are not able to give what is promised, it is inevitable that your stay should be in the hell. Hence, you do enter the hell as approved of by your spiritual preceptor.

33. All the aspirations of that person fail. The celestial region is far away (from him). He falls down into hell who deceives a person seeking his help, by failing to give what is promised.

34. Proud of your riches as you were, you deceived me with the words "I shall give you" (three paces of land). Suffer, therefore, for some years in hell as a punishment for uttering falsehood."

CHAPTER TWENTYTWO

A Dialogue between Bali and Vāmana

Śrī Śuka said :

1. Oh King ! Even though Bali was thus (humiliatingly) insulted by the glorious Lord and though he was made to swerve from the truth, Bali remained firm in mind, and gave this dignified reply.

Bali submitted :

2. Oh god of excellent renown ! Your worship regards the promise given by me as false. (It is you who fraudulently disguised yourself as a dwarf at the time of begging, and deceitfully manifested a different form at the time of the implementation of promise). In spite of this, I shall be true to my word so that I should not be regarded as a cheat. Be pleased to place your third step on my head (as the possessor

of wealth is more valuable than the wealth possessed) Oh Prominent one among gods !

3. Displaced as I am from my (sovereign) position, I am not so much afraid of hell or of being bound down with (Varuṇa's) noose, or of insuperable calamities or of financial difficulties or of any punishment from you as from ignoble reputation (viz. Bali was a deceitful person).

4. Methinks punishment meted out by the worthiest person is the most praiseworthy reward to men, as neither mother nor father nor brother or friends can deal such punishment.

5. In the guise of an enemy, you are certainly the highest preceptor (and hence benefactor) of us, the Asuras, inasmuch as you gave an insight in this fall to us, who were blinded by pride and arrogance caused by different factors (such as valour, wealth etc.)

6. As it is wellknown, many Asuras, by cherishing deep rooted enmity to You attained to that high position (emancipation from *Saṁsāra*) which only *yogins* with unserving devotion can reach.

7. Hence, I feel neither much ashamed nor afflicted that I have been taken prisoner and have been bound down with the noose of Varuṇa, by your worship of miraculous feats.

8. My grand-father, Prahlāda who is highly esteemed by your devotees, and whose excellent reputation of saintliness is manifest, was subjected to various cruel tortures by his own father Hiraṇyakaśipu, because he was your enemy.

9. What is the use of the body which abandons one ultimately (at the time of death ? Of what worth are the robbers, designated as one's own people (e.g. sons, kith and kin), who take away our property ? Of what purpose is the wife who is the cause of transmigration in the *Saṁsāra* ? What is the use of houses to a mortal ? It is sheer waste of life here.

10. Having come to this definite decision, my eminent grand-father (Prahlāda) of unfathomable wisdom, and the prominent-most saintly person, disturbed by the company of worldly people, resorted to your lotus-like feet which are eternal and which offer immunity from fear (from any quarter), even though you were the destroyer of his relatives and partisans.

11. It is through sheer good luck that I too am brought to the presence of Yourself—You who are the destroyer of both subtle and gross bodies (of beings and thus grant liberation) and that I am forcibly made to give up my wealth (and glorious position). And it is wealth (and position) that deprives man of his judgement and makes him incapable of understanding the uncertainty of life, due to its being within clutches of death.

Śrī Śuka said :

12. While he (Bali) was addressing thus, Prahlāda, beloved of the glorious Lord, appeared (on the scene) like the full moon above the horizon, Oh foremost of Kurus !

13. Bali, having an army like that of Indra, noticed his grand-father, of majestic stature, charming appearance, with eyes large like (a pair of) lotuses, with long arms (reaching his knees), clad in yellow silken garments, bright dark in complexion yet radiant in his native effulgence.

14. Bali, being bound down with the noose of Varuṇa could not offer him worshipful reception as before. He reverentially bowed him with his head, and with his eyes full of tears, he hung his head with shame[1] (as he remembered his egoistic actions).

15. Seeing the Protector of righteous persons sitting there, and being attended upon by his followers like Sunanda, Nanda and others, the noble-minded Prahlāda approached him and paid obeisance to him, placing his head down on the ground, while his eyes were over-whelmed with tears, and hair stood on their ends (through ecstasy).

Prahlāda said :

16. It is fortunate (and not derogatory) that the exalted position of Indra that you yourself bestowed on Bali has been retaken from him by you. I consider that great divine grace has been shown unto him (Bali) in that he has been relieved of his fortune which infatuates the mind and bewilders the soul.

1. GS attributes this to Bali's sense of guilt for forgetting the teaching of Prahlāda about humility and his disparaging remarks to Vāmana.

17. By wealth, even a self-controlled learned person gets deluded (and forgets the essential nature of the soul, even though known previously). How can an ordinary person comprehend properly the course leading to the realization of the soul, when possessed of wealth ? Hence I offer my obeisance to you (who have rendered a gracious obligation on Bali by divesting him of his wealth and glory), Oh Nārāyaṇa, the controller of the Universe and witness unto all the worlds.

Śrī Śuka said :

18. It was in the very presence of Prahlāda who stood with folded palms that god Brahmā (who emerged from the golden egg) addressed Viṣṇu, the slayer of demon Madhu, Oh King !

19. Seeing her husband so bound down, Bali's saintly wife (Vindhyāvalī), was overwhelmed with fear. With folded palms, she bowed down to Vāmana (the younger brother of Indra), and with face drooping down in supplication burst forth in appeal (And god Brahmā respected her by giving her the priority in communicating with the Lord).

Vindhyāvalī appealed :

20. You have created these three worlds (the earth, the heaven and the subterranean region) for your own divine sport. But other persons of perverted mentality arrogate proprietory rights over it (as did Bali when he says that he has donated the three worlds as a gift and shall redeem his pledge by offering his head for the third step when as a matter of fact, he is not the master of his body, much less of the universe). You are the creator, protector and destroyer of the universe. To such as you are, what these shameless persons in whom the sense of being independent agents has been implanted by you (through your Māyā), are capable of offering ? Oh Lord ! Be pleased to be gracious unto dull-witted Bali and setting him free from bonds, protect him.

God Brahmā said :

21. Oh Creator of living beings ! Oh Controller of all creatures ! Oh God of gods immanent in the Universe ! Be

pleased to release Bali, as he is deprived of everything and he does not deserve confinement.

22. He has gifted to you the entire earth and the higher worlds that he acquired through his pious actions. Everything owned by him including his body has been donated by him to you, without the least flinching of the mind.

23. If a person with sincere and guileless mind, offers water for washing your feet and worships them devoutly with (simple) *dūrvā* (Panic) grass he attains to the highest place (Liberation from *saṁsāra* or a place in your region, Vaikuṇṭha). Then why does Bali who has gifted to you the three worlds gleefully without the least hesitation, should suffer this calamity ?

The Lord replied :

24. Oh Brahman ! I take away the wealth (fortune etc.) of a person to whom I show my Grace. For being infatuated with wealth and power, a person becomes bereft of humility and shows disrespect to the world and (even) to me.

25. It is only by a lucky chance that the individual Soul, not being his own master and passing through various species of existence according to the fruits of his action, happens to be born as a human being.

26. It should be regarded as my Grace in that particular respect, if he, in the human stage of life, is not affected by pride for his lineage, achievements, youth, beauty, learning, authority, affluence and such other circumstances (and I am not constrained to deprive them of wealth etc.).

27. My devotee should not get infatuated with pride and feel lack of humility due to high birth etc. which are obstructive to the attainment of final bliss.

28. This Bali, the leader of Dānavas and Daityas and capable of enhancing their glory, has vanquished the unconquerable Māyā (deluding power of the Lord) and hence, he is not infatuated even in distress.

29-30. He has been deprived of his wealth, dislodged from his sovereign position, insulted, reproached and fettered by his enemies, abandoned by his kith and kin, and subjected to torture, remonstrated and cursed by his spiritual preceptor, but he remained firm in his vow, and did not deviate from the truth. True to his word as he is, he did not swerve from the truth, despite my misleading him by specious arguments about *Dharma* (righteousness).

31. A position very difficult even for immortal celestials to attain, has been conferred upon him by me. (But as he desired Indra-hood) he will be the Indra under my protection in the period (*Manvantara*) presided over by the Manu Sāvarṇi (after which he will attain that position).

32. Till then, let him live (as a ruler) in *Sutala* which is constructed (more beautifully than the celestial region) by Viśvakarman (the architect of gods). There, under my gracious surveillance, the residents are not subjected to anxieties, diseases, fatigue, laziness, defeat (from internal or external enemies) or other troubles.

33. Your Majesty Indrasena (Bali) ! May good betide you ! Accompanied by your relatives and kinsmen, proceed to *Sutala*—a region worthy of being aspired after even by celestial beings.

34. Even the *Lokapālas* (Protectors of the worlds) shall not (be able to) vanquish you. What of others ? My discus (*Sudarśana*) will put an end to the Daityas who will (dare to) transgress your commands.

35. I shall protect you along with your followers, retinue and property, in every respect. You will always find me present there, Oh great warrior !

36. If any demoniac ideas occur to you due to the company of Dānavas and Daityas, they shall immediately disappear at the sight of my glory and prowess.

CHAPTER TWENTY-THREE

Bali, free from bonds, enters Sutala

Śrī Śuka said :

1. The magnanimous Bali who was highly respected by all righteous persons, joined his palms, and with his eyes flowing with tears and throat choked with emotion, submitted in falter-

ing accents to Lord Viṣṇu, the ancientmost person who addressed him (as reported in the previous chapter).

Bali said :

2*. How wonderful! Even an attempt made to offer you obeisance was efficacious enough to accomplish the blessings coveted by your devotees who resorted to you for protection. This unique Grace has never been obtained by the protectors of the world as well as by gods (who are of *Sāttvic* disposition) before. It has been conferred upon a wretched asura (of a *rājasic* nature).

Śrī Śuka said :

3. Having addressed thus, Bali, bowed down to Lord Hari, god Brahmā along with Śiva. Being free from bondage, Bali was highly pleased and he entered the *Sutala* region along with his Asuras.

4. Restoring (the kingdom of) the celestial region to Indra in this way, and having thus fulfilled the desire of Aditi, the Lord ruled over the whole of the world.

5. Seeing that his grandson Bali, the scion of his family, freed from bondage and the recipient of the Grace of the Lord, Prahlāda, full of devotion spoke as follows :

Prahlāda said :

6. Neither god Brahmā, nor goddess Śrī or god Śiva ever received such a Grace. How can others (Indra etc.) obtain it? You whose feet are worshipped by persons adored by the world have become the protector of the fortress of us, the Asuras.

7. Oh Lord that affords shelter! Brahmā and other celestials have attained greatness (prosperity and power) by virtue of their enjoyment of the honey in the lotuslike feet of yours. (I, however, wonder) why we, of crooked behaviour and belonging to ferocious races, are made the recipients of your gracious look.

*SD : If mere attempt to bow down is so efficacious, how much more fruitful must be the worship etc. of Lord Hari.

8. Oh how miraculous are your acts and behaviour ! You have created the worlds as the sportive activity of your inconceivable *yoga-māyā*; you are omniscient, nay the veritable in-dwelling soul of all, and hence, view all equally. Even though you are fond of your devotees, there is no partiality in your nature, you are just like the wish-yielding tree, by nature.

The Lord replied :

9. Child Prahlāda ! May you be blessed ! Go happily to your residence in *Sutala* along with your grandson, and enhance the happiness of your kith and kin.

10. You will always see me there standing with a mace in hand, and the bonds of your karmas will be snapped by the highest bliss of seeing me.

Śrī Śuka said :

11-12. With their palms folded and head bowed down, pure-minded Prahlāda, the Supreme Commander of all the Asura forces, along with Bali, respectfully accepted the command of the glorious Lord. Circumambulating the Eternal Person, they bowed again, and with his permission entered the 'Great cavity' (of *Sutala*), Oh King.

13. Thereafter, Oh King ! Lord Viṣṇu whose abode is cosmic waters, and who removes the sins of his votaries, spoke to Śukra who was sitting near, among the sacrificial priests, in that assembly of experts in Vedas.

14. "Oh Brahman ! Do you now make up for the interruption and deficiency in the sacrificial act that was being performed by your disciple. Whatever defects remain in religious performances are rectified even by the look of Brāhmaṇas (much more so if actually performed by them)."

Śukra replied :

15. How can there be any deficiency in ritualistic performance, where you, the presiding Lord of all religious acts, the master of sacrifice who confer their fruit on performers, the sacrifice itself incarnate, are worshipped with complete devotion ?

16. The recital of Your Name rectified all the defects arising out of (wrong pronunciation and intonation of) ***mantras*** (Vedic verses to be chanted at the time of sacrifices), wrong ritualistic procedure, in-opportuneness of time and unsuitability of place or in the provision of materials for sacrifices.[1]

17. Still, however, as, Oh Mighty Lord, You insist on it, I shall carry out your behest. For what constitutes obedience to your commands, is (in itself) the highest beatitude of human beings.

Śrī Śuka said :

18. Gladly accepting Hari's mandate, the worshipful sage Śukra, with the assistance of other Brāhmaṇa sages, rectified the deficiencies in Bali's sacrifice.

19. In this way, having begged the earth (as well as celestial regions) from Bali, Lord Hari disguised as a dwarf, gave back to his brother, the great Indra, the celestial region (as well as the earth) which was usurped from him by his enemies.

20-21. Then for accomplishing the pleasure of Kaśyapa and Aditi, and for the well-being of all creatures, god Brahmā, the head of all the Protectors of the world (*Prajāpatis*) together with gods, sages, manes and Manu and his sons with Dakṣa, Bhṛgu, Aṅgiras, as well as with Kumāra and god Śiva, crowned Vāmana as the King (and protector) of all the worlds, and the guardians of the worlds.

22-23. For the sake of the prosperity of all, god Brahmā installed Vāmana, the younger brother of Indra as the protector of all Vedas, gods, *dharma* (righteousness), glory, affluence, auspicious vows and of the celestial regions as well as of *Mokṣa* (Liberation of *Saṁsāra*). Oh King, all created beings thereby felt extremely delighted.

24. Then with the approval of god Brahmā, Indra accompanied by the Protectors of the world, placed Vāmana at their head, carried him to heaven, in a suitable celestial car.

1. Cf. the famous verses quoted by VD.
yasya smṛtyā ca nāmoktyā tapo-yajña-kriyādiṣu |
nyūnaṁ sampūrṇatāṁ yāti tam vande harim acyutam ||

25. With the sovereignty of the three worlds restored to him, and being free from fear due to his being protected by the arms of Vāmana, Indra who was endowed with supreme glory, felt highly delighted.

26-27. Eulogising that extremely miraculous great deed of Viṣṇu and praising Aditi, god Brahmā, Śiva, Kumāra, sages headed by Bhṛgu and others, and masses, all beings, Siddhas, all beings moving in aerial cars, repaired to their respective abodes, Oh King.

28. I have recounted to you everything pertaining to the episode of the Lord of Mighty wide Strides which destroys all the sins of the listener to this story, Oh delight of the Kuru family !

29*. A mortal being who presumes to recount completely and exhaustively the glories of Lord Viṣṇu with mighty wide strides, is like unto a person who would count all the particles of dust on the earth. About such a person the seer of the mantra (RV. 1.1.54.1 etc.) asks, 'Is there born now or likely to be born (in future) such a person (who can do so)? (The answer is 'No').

30. A person who listens to the account of this incarnation of Lord Hari, the god of gods of miraculous deeds, attains to the highest stage (of Liberation from *Saṁsāra*).

31. If this story is recited repeatedly during the performance of religious observance to propitiate gods, masses and men, the learned declare that that observance is auspiciously well-done.

**Viṣṇor nu kaṁ vīryāṇi pra vocam*
—RV. 1. 154-1a: AV. 7. 26-1a
VS. 5. 18a, TS. 1.2.13.9a etc.

CHAPTER TWENTY-FOUR

*The Fish Incarnation of Lord Viṣṇu**

The King said :

1. Venerable Sir ! I now desire to hear from you the story of the first incarnation of Lord Hari of miraculous exploits, wherein he assumed the form of a fish, through his deluding potency (Māyā).

2. Why did the Supreme Lord, like one subject to (laws of) *Karma*, assume the form of a fish which is disgustible to the world, as being of *tāmasic* nature and unbearable.

3. It behoves you, Oh worshipful Sir, to tell us everything in details (as it took place), as the actions of the Lord of hallowing renown, are conducive to the happiness of all people.

Sūta said :

4. When requested thus by Parīkṣit (One protected by Viṣṇu i.e. Kṛṣṇa[1]), the venerable Śuka, the son of Bādarāyaṇa,

*The deluge is a part of race-memory in different parts of the world. It testifies to the sub-mergence of some parts of the world under water, at some distant period in the past, and the memory persisted among Hebrews, Assyrians, Hindus etc. The different periods of such deluges in different parts of the world (for example the Nohaic Flood which lasted for about 371 to 376 days was in West Asia round Mt. Ararat (The Old Testament-Genesis Chs. 6, 7, 8.) Also vide T.A. Bryant's *The New Compact Bible Dictionary*, pp. 176-178; 403-4 Special Crusade Edition), while the Indian deluge was in the Himalayan region and it lasted throughout one *Kalpa*, shows that there was really no universal flood, though it appeared to be so to the people in the affected area which was their "world" in ancient times. In India the deluge is described in the *Śatapatha* Br. 1.8.6 the *MBH Vana* 187, *Agni P.* 2, *Matsya P.* 1 & 2. The *Śatapatha* tradition seems to be the earliest and is followed by *MBH* where *Manu*. the saviour of the fish. was at Badari and the locale of the flood was the Himalayan region, but with the Bh. P., King Satyavrata, the saviour of the fish (and a future Manu) was a Draviḍa King who got the fish in the river *Kṛta-mālā* in Tamil Nadu. The brief statement in the *Agni P.* makes Manu perform penance on the bank of *Kṛta-mālā*, while in the *Matsya P.* 1. 17-18 Manu went to Malaya (Kerala) where in his own hermitage the small fish fell from above. The symbolism of the fish is explained by V.S. Agrawala in *M.P.—a study*, pp. 4-8 with which one may not agree, as it presumes an advanced knowledge in Embryology in that *Purāṇic* era (Gupta Period).

1. Vide Supra 1.12.7-11.

began to narrate the history of Lord Viṣṇu as he acted in the form of a fish.

Śrī Śuka said :

5. (The object of incarnations in general :) When the Almighty Lord desires to protect cows, Brāhmaṇas, gods, righteous persons, the Vedas and the laws of *Dharma* (righteousness) and *Artha* and other *Puruṣārthas*, he assumes a body.

6. (This incarnation is not disgustible.) The Supreme Lord moves like vital airs through higher and lower beings. But Himself being transcendental to *guṇas* (attributes), he is not affected by the *guṇas* of Prakṛti and hence by the highness or lowness of status.

7. At the close of the last Kalpa (known as *Brāhma*), there was a periodic deluge caused by (the sleep that overcame) *Brahmā*.[1] At that time, Oh King, the worlds known as *Bhū* (this earth) and other (higher) worlds were submerged under the sea.

8. A mighty demon called Haya-grīva (one with the neck and head of a horse) who was in the vicinity of Brahmā, carried away the Vedas which (unconsciously) escaped from the mouth of Brahmā who was overcome with sleep under the influence of Time, and desired to go to bed.

9. Noticing that (clandestine) act of Hayagrīva the king of Dānavas, the glorious Supreme Lord Hari, assumed the form of a small glittering fish.

10. In that Kalpa, a great royal sage, by name Satyavrata who was absolutely devoted to Nārāyaṇa, was practising austerities, subsisting on water only.

11. That very person (who was then called King Satyavrata) is well known as Śrāddha-deva, the son of Vivasvat and was installed as Manu by Lord Hari, in this great Kalpa.

1. While commenting on verse No. 46, ŚR raises there a pertinent point as to the nature of this Deluge. He states that as the world was submerged within seven days without the usual draught of 100 years, and having fire from above (the sun) and from below (Śeṣa's poison), this must be *an illusory* deluge shown to Satyavrata by the Lord. This has been echoed by GS. on this verse and by VD elsewhere.

12. One day while he was offering libations of water (to sages and manes) in the river Kṛtamālā[1], a certain tiny fish was noticed in the water in the hollow of his folded palms.

13. Satyavrata, the King of Draviḍa land, was about to drop the small fish along with the water in the cavity of his folded palms.

14. To that extremely compassionate king, the fish piteously implored, "Oh king, kind unto the afflicted! How is it that you are throwing a poor helpless creature like me, into the waters of river when I am afraid of acquatic animals who kill their own species.

15. Not knowing that it was Lord Viṣṇu who, out of affection, assumed the form of a fish to confer Grace on him, he made up his mind to Protect the tiny fish.

16. Hearing the piteous appeal of the fish, the merciful king placed it in his water-jar (*Kamaṇḍalu*) and carried it to his hermitage.

17. Growing there in that jar of water (*Kamaṇḍalu*) in one night, and finding the space therein insufficient, she said to the king.

18. "I am not able to accommodate myself in this jar (Kamaṇḍalu) with difficulty. Be pleased to provide for me sufficiently spacious abode, wherein I can live comfortably."

19. He took the fish out of that jar (*Kamaṇḍalu*) and placed it in a big earthen pot for waterstorage (or a well). When thrown therein it grew to the dimensions of three cubits within a *muhūrta* (48 minutes).

20. (The fish requested :) "This reservoir is not sufficient to accommodate me comfortably. As I have adopted you as my protector, please provide me with a more spacious place.

21. Bringing that fish from the reservoir, the king threw it into a lake. Occupying the whole (expanse of the) lake with its body, it grew into a monstrous fish.

22. (The fish requested) "I am an acquatic animal, Oh king! The waters of this lake are not sufficient for my comfor-

1. The river Vaiga in Tamil Nadu. It rises in the Malaya mountain and the holy city of Madura is situated on it—GDAMI, p. 104.

table stay. Be pleased to place me in a pool of inexhaustible storage of water, making arrangement of my safe transit to it."

23. Thus requested, the king carried the fish to various pools of inexhaustible stores of water (each bigger and deeper than the former). When the fish went on growing coextensive with the expanse of the lake, he threw it at last, into the sea.

24. While he was being thus deposited into the sea, he spoke to the king as follows : "Oh heroic king ! It is not proper that you throw me here, as extremely powerful alligators and other acquatic animals will eat me."

25. Being deluded by the fish with the expression of charming words, Satyavrata enquired, "Who are you who beguile us in the form of a fish?"

26. Never such acquatic animal possessing such (miraculous) power and capacity has been seen or heard by us, inasmuch as you fill a lake of one hundred *yojanas* (i.e. 800 miles) in extent, in a single day.

27. Certainly you must be the Imperishable, glorious Lord, Nārāyaṇa or Hari Himself who assumed the form of an acquatic creature for showing Grace unto living beings.

28. Oh Supreme-most Person ! I bow to you who are the Master of the creation, protection and the destruction of the Universe. Oh all-pervading Lord ! You are the real self, the goal and the refuge to us, your votaries, who approach you for protection.

29. All your sportful incarnations are meant for the prosperity and well-being of created beings. I wish to know the main purpose for assuming this form by your worshipful self.

30. Oh Lotus-eyed Lord ! Seeking resort to your feet—you who are the friend and dear soul of all—shall never be futile, as to those others who look upon the body as their soul For you have manifested your miraculous form to us.

Śrī Śuka said :

31. To king Satyavrata who was addressing him in this way, the lord of the Universe who assumed the body of a fish as he desired to sport in the ocean of deluge at the end of

Yuga (which was about to take place), but who, being fond of his exclusive, unflinching votaries, wished to accomplish the good of king and spoke as follows :

The Glorious Lord said :

32. Oh vanquisher of enemies ! On the seventh day from today, all the three worlds, viz. the terrestrial world, the celestial region and space (aerial region) between the two, will be submerged in the ocean of deluge.

33. While the worlds will be sinking in the waters of the deluge, a spacious boat despatched by me will approach you.[1]

34-35. In the meanwhile, you take with you all herbs and plants and seeds of various types (both of inferior and superior qualities) and surrounded by seven sages and accompanied by all varieties of animals, you will board that spacious ship and shall fearlessly sail over the one undivided ocean[2] completely devoid of light but illuminated with the effulgence of sages (to guide you).

36. While the boat will toss hither and thither by strong gales, I shall be near you. You moor it fast to my horn with a big serpent (Vāsuki, as a rope).

37. Oh King ! While the night of god Brahmā lasts, I shall move (through the ocean) dragging the ship with you and the sages on board.

38. In reply to your well-reasoned questions, you will find revealed in your heart, through my Grace, my real greatness, which is designated as Supreme Brahman".

39. Having instructed the King in this way, Lord Hari disappeared. Satyavrata waited for the period about which Lord Viṣṇu forewarned him.

1. In the Bible story of the Flood or Deluge, God gave Noah exact instructions for building the Ark (Genisis 6.14-16). God led Noah and his family as well as pairs of animals into the Ark and shut the door of the Ark (Genisis 7.16). In *MBH Vana* .187.31 the king is asked to build a strong ship.

2. *Ekārṇava*—The original ocean of infinite waters, the source of cosmic creation. In Bh. P. *supra* 3.8.23, it is called *yugānta-toya*. In Harivaṁśa the terms Mahārṇava, Ekārṇava, Agādha, Stabdha Salila are used.

40. Spreading the *darbha* grass with their points towards the east, the royal sage sat with his face to the North-East meditating over the feet of Lord Hari in the fish-form.

41. Then the ocean was seen overflowing its boundaries and inundating the earth on all sides, and seemed to be increasing in volume by the heavy downpour from great clouds.

42. While musing over the command of the Lord, he saw the arrival of a boat. Taking with him all the plants and herbs, he boarded the ship alongwith the prominent Brāhmaṇa sages.

43. Being pleased with him, the sages advised him : "Oh King ! Meditate upon Lord Viṣṇu (Keśava). He will be our saviour from this calamity, and bring about our happiness."

44. Thereupon when the Lord was contemplated upon by the King (as per advice of the sages), there appeared in that vast ocean, a golden fish with one horn and body one hundred thousand *yojanas* in dimensions.

45. Having moored the ship to the horn of that fish with the serpent (-King Vāsuki) as the rope, as per previous instructions of Lord Hari, the King felt highly delighted, and praised Lord Viṣṇu (The slayer of the demon Madhu) as follows :

The King said :

46.* Your Lordship is our highest preceptor[1] Who confer on us Liberation from *Saṁsāra*—we, whose[2] knowledge

*ŚR. shows that this is not only not the Final Deluge (*mahāpralaya*), but not even a periodic one. But just as sage Mārkaṇḍeya was shown the scene of Deluge in this very (Vaivasvata) Manvantara, King Satyavrata was shown the Deluge with a view to initiate him in the spiritual knowledge. BP. however, controverts this and basing himself on *Laghu-Bhāgavata* subscribes to the theory of two fish-incarnations just as there had been two boar-incarnations.

matsyo'pi prādur abhavad dviḥ kalpe'smin varāhavat |
ādau svāyambhuvīyasya daityam ghnanāharat śrutiḥ |

He further quotes *Viṣṇudharmottara* for support. The main objection of ŚR i.e. the impossibility of a real Deluge *within seven days*, without any famine etc., is not met by the critics of ŚR.

1. *Paramo gurur bhavān*: The seven sages were Satyavrata's preceptors and the Lord was the preceptor of these sages. Hence the Lord is the "Grand-sire" (preceptor) of Satyavrata—VC.

2. *anādyavidyā,...saṁvidaḥ* : whose knowledge about the supreme soul and soul *as they are*, is obscured by our date-less ignorance whereby we wrongly identify the body with the soul—VR. By *'ātma-saṁvit'* VJ, understands 'the knowledge of the Supreme Soul' JG. interprets *'avidyā'* as the Lord's Deluding Potency (Māyā).

about the soul is screened (and hence obscured) by Nescience (*avidyā*) which is beginningless, are subjected to suffer the three types of afflictions in this *Saṁsāra* rooted in that very Nescience. It is through your Grace that we take shelter in You[1] and attain to realize You.

47. This category of beings (subject to the cycle of births and deaths) is ignorant (as he identified body with the soul) and is fettered with (and hence subject to the fruits of) his actions. With the desire of enjoying pleasures (derivable from objects of senses), he performs acts with great pains. By adoring you the wrong notion (consisting of the identity of the body and the soul *or* 'in doing Karma') is shaken off. May he, being our preceptor, cut off the knot of false notion (or attachment) in our heart.

48. May that Imperishable Supreme Ruler (of the Universe), our preceptor's preceptor be our preceptor, by serving (adoring) whom, a person (desirous of Liberation from *Saṁsāra*) purges the *tāmasic* dirt from himself and regains its original (blissful) character just as a lump of gold or silver becomes purified of the dross, by being blown into the fire and recovers its original colour and nature.

49. I seek asylum in that Supreme Lord (whose Grace is so unlimited that) not even one out of ten thousand parts of his Grace, the gods, preceptors and all people combined together can, by themselves, show to a person (their devotee).

50. Just as a sightless person is called upon to lead the blind, a spiritually unenlightened person is made the preceptor of ignorant people. Like the light of the sun, you are self-illuminating and providing light to all our senses or are (capable of direct perception). Hence, we have sought you as a preceptor and guide, with the desire of knowing our way and destination.

51. A (spiritually ignorant) person imparts wrong instructions to another person (leading to wealth and

1. *yadṛcchayehopasṛtā* : To whom people attain to after resorting to and through spiritual preceptors.—VR. VR. insists that it is through God's Grace that one comes in contact with spiritual preceptors. But VJ thinks that the very birth in the human species is due to His Grace secured by meritorious acts in the previous births.

gratification of lust) whereby the follower is sure to land in the insuperable darkness (in the form of *Saṁsāra*). You, however, impart eternal unfailing knowledge (of the soul) in the light of which, a person can easily and definitely attain to his (spiritual) goal.

52. To all the people in the world, you (alone) are certainly a friendly well-wisher, the beloved Supreme Ruler, the very soul, the preceptor, the spiritual wisdom itself and the goal to be realized. But people of 'blind' intellect and understanding, who are deeply rooted in worldly desires, cannot see you even though you exist in their very heart.

53. For the sake of spiritual awakening and guidance, I resort to you, the Almighty Ruler, adorable even to gods and worthy of being sought by all. Oh Lord! Cut asunder the knots (of egotism, ignorance etc.) in my heart, with your words shedding light on the (spiritual) truth and reveal unto me your own self.

Śrī Śuka said :

54. To the king who was praying thus, the glorious Lord, the ancient-most person who was sporting in the ocean in the form of a fish, imparted the highest truth.

55. He revealed to the royal sage Satyavrata the divine compilation of Purāṇa[1] (known as the *Matsya Purāṇa*) dealing with the Sāṅkhya system of Philosophy, and the science and practice of Yoga, and also instructed him in the secret lore about the soul.

56. Seated on board the ship along with the sages, the king listened to the discourse on the real nature of the soul and the Eternal Brahman so expounded to them by the glorious Lord as to leave no (shadow of) doubt about it.

1. The *Matsya p.*, in its preamble, (ch. 2.22-24) makes Manu ask the Fish all the topics covered in a *purāṇa* e.g.

utpattiṁ pralayañ caiva vaṁśān manvantarāṇi ca /
vaṁśyānu-caritañ caiva bhuvanasya ca vistaram //

But *MBH Vana* 187 is silent on this point. The word *mātsya purāṇa* etc. in 187.57 means 'the episode of Fish incarnation' narrated in MBH.

57. To god Brahmā who was awkened after the end of the Pralaya (Deluge), Lord Hari restored the Vedas after killing the demon Hayagrīva.

58. That King Satyavrata who was thus blessed with discriminating knowledge and spiritual wisdom, has become Vaivasvata Manu in this Kalpa, through the Grace of Viṣṇu.

59. He who listens to the great story consisting of the dialogue between the royal sage Satyavrata and Viṣṇu who, through his Māyā, assumed the form of a horned fish, stands absolved of all sins.

60. A person who, every day, extols this incarnation of Lord Hari, finds that all his desires are accomplished here, and he attains to the Final Beatitude (hereafter).

61. I do bow unto the Lord who is the cause of everything and who disguised himself as a fish[1] in the cosmic waters of the Deluge, and killing the demon (Hayagrīva), restored to Brahmā the corpus of the *Śruti* texts which were stolen away from his mouths (by Hayagrīva) when his (Brahmā's) powers became dormant in sleep and who imparted the knowledge of Brahman to Satyavrata and the seven sages.[2]

1. GS. on the authority of VC. states that this fish of a curved body is called *āḍi* in common parlance.

2. Curiously enough as a *phala-śruti* of this *skandha*, VD quotes a *purāṇic* story of a king Viṣṇujit who was absolved of the sin of killing a Brāhmaṇa by listening to the VIII Skandha of the *Bhāgavata Purāṇa*.

SKANDHA NINTH

CHAPTER ONE

The story of King Sudyumna

The King (*Parīkṣit*) *requested* :

1. All the Manu-epochs (*Manvantaras*) described by you and the (account of) glorious heroic feats of Lord Hari of infinite prowess and energy, achieved during those epochs as narrated by you, have been heard by me.

2-3. I learnt from you that he who, at the end of the last *Kalpa*, was the royal sage named Satyavrata, the King of Draviḍas (or Draviḍa country), attained spiritual knowledge by worshipping the Supreme Person, has verily become a Manu (Śrāddhadeva), the Son of Vivasvat; I have also heard from you the (history of) his sons, the kings, of whom Ikṣvāku was prominent.

4. Be pleased to describe to us in details, Oh Brahman, the history of the race and the deeds of those belonging to that line, separately, as we are ever eager to listen to them, Oh highly blessed sage.

5. Kindly relate unto us the heroic exploits of all those kings of hallowed (or sanctifying) renown who belonged to the past, who will rule in future and who belong to the present age.

Sūta said :

6. When accosted in these words by king Parīkṣit, in the assembly of the exponents of Vedas and Brahman, venerable Śuka, the expert in the highest form *dharma*[1] proceeded to narrate in details.

1. This *dharma* is 'the extolling the excellences of the Lord' according to VR, while 'Protection of the subjects is *the* dharma of crowned kings' (VJ).

Śrī Śuka said :

7. Oh chastiser of enemies ! Listen to the main events in the history of the race of Manu (in brief), for it will not be possible to describe it in details for centuries together.

8. At the end of the *Kalpa*, there was only the Supreme Person, who is the Soul of all beings high and low. There was neither universe nor anything else.

9. From his navel sprouted forth the calyx of a gold lotus wherein was born the self-created four-faced god Brahmā, Oh mighty king.

10. From his mind was born Marīci and from Marīci was born Kaśyapa. From Kaśyapa and his wife Aditi, the daughter of Dakṣa (Prajāpati) was born a son called Vivasvat.

11. From Vivasvat and his wife Saṁjñā was born Śrāddha-deva, the Manu and through his wife Śraddhā, the self-controlled eminent Śrāddhadeva begot the (following) ten sons :

12. (Namely) Ikṣvāku, Nṛga, Śaryāti, Diṣṭa, Dhṛṣṭa, Karūṣaka, Narīṣyat, Pṛṣaddhra, Nabhaga, Kavi.

13. It is reported that in the beginning, when Manu was childless, the worshipful and (spiritually) powerful Vasiṣṭha performed a sacrifice, in honour of Mitra and Varuṇa.

14. In that sacrifice, Śraddhā, the wife of Manu who was observing the *payo-vrata* vow, approached the *Hotṛ*-priest, paid obeisance to him and begged for the birth of a daughter.

15. The *Hotṛ* (the reciter of Vedic *mantras* in a sacrifice) who was directed by the *Adhvaryu* (the officiating head sacrificial priest), was brooding over the request of Śraddhā. The Brāhmaṇa (contemplating over her request) with full concentration of mind, offered oblations while uttering the mystic word—*Vaṣaṭ* (and propitiated the fire).

16. As a consequence of the dereliction of duty on the part of the *Hotṛ* (the reciter of *mantras*), a daughter named Ilā was born. Not being much delighted at the sight of the daughter (when the sacrifice was performed for the birth of a son), Manu addressed the preceptor (as follows) :

17. "Worshipful Sir, what is this that the act (of sacrificer) performed by the expert exponents of Vedas has led to

the contrary result? Ah! What a pity! There should not have been such a reversal (in the fruit) of Vedic *Mantras*.

18. You are experts in the knowledge and sacrificial application of the *Mantras* and are self-disciplined. You have burnt down all your sins by your austerities. What is the cause of the failure of this expectation. This is as impossible as falsehood in the case of gods. (Just as what gods think or say turns out to be true, your will power should have similarly prevailed)".

19. Hearing this (complaining) speech (of Manu), the worshipful great-grandfather[1] Vasiṣṭha came to know the transgression committed by the reciter of *mantras* (*Hotṛ*) and replied to Vaivasvata Manu (the son of the Sun, Vivasvat).

20. "This frustration of your expectation is due to the dereliction of duty on the part of the *Hotṛ*. Yet by virtue of my spiritual power, I shall accomplish your object of having a good son".

21. The adorable Vasiṣṭha of great renown, determined thus and with the desire of securing manhood to Ilā prayed Lord Viṣṇu, The Eternal Person.

22. The glorious Lord Hari, The Ruler (of the universe), being pleased with Vasiṣṭha, conferred on him the boon sought for (by him). In virtue of that boon, Ilā became Sudyumna, the foremost among men.

23. On one occasion, riding a horse of Sindhu breed, and accompanied by a few ministers, he went on a hunting expedition in a forest, Oh great king.

24. Clad in an armour and arming himself with a beautiful bow and extremely wonderful arrows, the hero went to the northern direction, in pursuit of the game (a deer).

25. It is reported that the prince entered a forest on the foothills of mount Meru, where the glorious Lord Śiva sports amorously with his Spouse Umā.

1. It should have been grand-father's grand-father as can be seen from the following genealogy of Śuka from Vasiṣṭha:

Vasiṣṭha—Śakti—Parāśara—Vyāsa—Śuka but if *pra-pitāmaha* is to be defended (as VD does it) by saying that the father and the son are to be regarded as one as per the Śruti text *ātmaiva putranāmā'si*, the chain of identity will reach to Śuka also.

26 Hardly did Sudyumna, that vanquisher of inimical warriors, enter the forest, when he found himself transformed into a woman and the horse into a mare, Oh king.

27. Noticing a change of sex in themselves, all his followers became dejected at heart and began to stare at each other.

King Parīkṣit asked :

28. Oh venerable Sir ! How is it that the region came to acquire such power ? Who made it so ? Be pleased to answer this query, as our curiosity has become intense.

Śrī Śuka said :

29. On one occasion, sages, who were strict observers of sacred vows, came to that region (Ilāvṛta) to pay visit to god Śiva, the lord of mount Kailāsa, dispelling darkness from all quarters (with their spiritual lustre).

30. Having seen them, goddess Pārvatī, who was then ungarmented, got extremely abashed, and quickly getting up from her consort's lap, put on her raiments immediately.

31. Noting the union of the divine couple in amorous enjoyment, the sages instantly turned back and proceeded to the hermitage of Nara and Nārāyaṇa.

32. Then, with a desire to satisfy his divine beloved, the glorious god Śiva announced : 'Whoever enters this region, shall (automatically and instantly) turn into a veritable woman.

33. Hence all males avoid going to that forest since then. She (Sudyumna, now a woman Ilā) went on wandering from one forest to another, accompanied by her retinue.

34. Now beholding that excellent young woman surrounded by ladies, (leisurely) wandering on the precincts of his hermitage, god Budha (the presiding deity of the planet Mercury) conceived an amorous passion for her.

35. That lady with beautiful eyebrows, in her turn, reciprocated his love and sought him, the son of King Soma, as her husband. He begot on her a son named Purūravas.

36. We hear it reported that King Sudyumna of Manu's

race who was thus transformed into a woman, happened to remember Vasiṣṭha, his family preceptor.

37. (As soon as he was thus remembered, Vasiṣṭha appeared on the scene). Seeing that sad plight of Sudyumna, Vasiṣṭha was overwhelmed with compassion. Being deeply moved, and wishing to restore the manhood of Sudyumna, he approached (appealed to) god Śaṅkara.

38. Being pleased with Vasiṣṭha and with a view to grant his prayer as well as to retain the veracity of his own utterance, the glorious god Śiva spoke as follows, Oh King.

39. 'Sudyumna who is born of your race, shall be a man for one month and a woman for another month alternately. May he protect the earth at his will, under this arrangement'[1].

40. Having accomplished his desire of restoration to manhood through the grace of his preceptor, he ruled over the earth under the above-mentioned arrangement. But his subjects did not approve of it.

41. He got three sons, Utkala, Gaya and Vimala. They became righteous rulers of the Deccan (the southern region including Mahārāṣṭra).

42. With the ripeness of the age, King Sudyumna, the ruler over pratiṣṭhāna[2] handed over (the kingdom of) the earth to (his son) Purūravas, and went to forest (for performance of penance).

1. The story is briefly mentioned in *MBH. Ādi* 75.16, *Anu* 147. 26, *Liṅga P.* 1.65.

2. Most probably *Jhusi* opposite to Allahabad across the Gaṅgā. Mentioned in *MBH Vana.* 85.76. According to *Liṅga P.*I.65 the kingdom of Ikṣvākus was divided among Sudyumna's sons, while according to Vasiṣṭha's advice, the son of Ilā (the female transformation of Sudyumna) Purūravas, was given Pratiṣṭhānapura as he had no hereditory rights on the kingdom of *Ikṣvāku.* But Bh.P. 9.2.2 shows that Ikṣvāku was born, when Sudyumna left for the forest.

D.P. Mishra's conjectural identification of this Pratiṣṭhāna with 'Ortospana' (near Kabul—'nearer Bactria, the home province of Purūravas') of Greek writers deserves consideration. Vide *studies—Proto. Hist. of Ind.* pp. 116-17.

CHAPTER TWO

History of Karūṣa and other four sons of Manu

Śrī Śuka said :

1. When his son Sudyumna thus left (for the forest), Manu, the son of Vivasvat, being desirous of begetting a son performed penance for a hundred years, on the bank of the Yamunā.

2. Thereafter he worshipped Lord Hari (by performing a sacrifice) for (male) progeny; and he had ten sons, Ikṣvāku being the eldest, all resembling himself.

3. Manu's (eighth) son, Pṛṣadhra, was entrusted with the duty of protecting the cows, by his preceptor (as Vasiṣṭha found him competent to tend the bulls). Vigilantly he tended the cows at night, remaining alert in the posture called *Vīrāsana* (kneeling on one knee).

4. On one occasion, while it was raining at night, a tiger made its way into the cowpen. Cows which were lying there, got panicky and springing to their feet, ran about in that enclosure.

5-6. The powerful tiger seized one of the cows, and she, overwhelmed with fear, screamed loudly. It is reported that when Pṛṣadhra heard that screaming in agony, he rushed in haste in that direction, with a sword in hand. In the darkness of night, when even stars were invisible due to clouds, he unwittingly chopped off the head of a tawny coloured cow, believing it to be a tiger.

7. The tiger too got its ear severed with the end of the sword in that stroke, but escaped in extreme panic, dripping blood all the way.

8. Pṛṣadhra, the destroyer of inimical warriors, who believed that the tiger had been killed, found, at the close of night, to his sore grief, that a reddish-brown cow had been killed by him, in the (darkness of) night.

9. To Pṛṣadhra who has unknowingly committed the sin of killing a cow, Vasiṣṭha, the family preceptor (instead of advising him the expiatory rite or procedure for such unwitting acts) pronounced the following imprecation : "In conse-

quence of this (thoughtless) act, you shall be not even the vilest of Kṣattriyas but a veritable Śūdra."

10. When cursed in this way by the family preceptor, the great warrior accepted it (respectfully) with folded palms. He observed the vow of life-long celibacy—a vow so esteemed by sages.

11. Being exclusively and absolutely devoted to the glorious Lord Vāsudeva, the absolutely pure (blemishless), transcendental, universal Spirit, he became a friend and a well-wisher of all beings, impartial to all.

12-13. Completely devoid of attachment, with a serene mind, and with all senses under full control, bereft of all possessions, maintaining himself on whatever came to him by chance (without asking for it), fixing his mind in the Supreme Soul, satiated in spiritual knowledge[1], and absorbed in meditation, he roamed about the earth, presenting an appearance of a blind and deaf dunce.

14. Leading this way of life, he happened to enter a forest where, seeing the outbreak of forest-conflagration, he silently allowed his body to be consumed by it and became one with the transcendental Brahman.

15. And the younger son Kavi[2] (even as a child) had no desire for worldly objects. Renouncing the kingdom along with the relatives, he enthroned the self-effulgent Supreme Person in his heart and repairing to the forest, even in his boyhood, ultimately attained to the Supreme Brahman.

16. From Karūṣa, the son of Manu, was descended the Kṣatriya clan called Kārūṣas who ruled over the northern regions, were friendly to Brāhmaṇas and devoted to righteousness.

17. The Kṣatriya clan called Dhārṣṭa was born from Dhṛṣṭa but attained Brāhmaṇahood (Brahmanical virtues and way of life) on the earth. In the race of Nṛga, Nṛga had a son Sumati whose son was Bhūtajyoti to whom was born a son, Vasu.

1. v.l. *jñāna-hṛṣṭa*—Delighted in spiritual knowledge.

2. VJ. takes *Kavi* 'wise' as the adj. qualifying Pṛṣadhra and treats this verse as a further elucidation of the above (12-13) verses. (*uktameva vivṛṇoti*).

18. Vasu had a son Pratīka whose son Oghavān was the father of a son called Oghavat and a daughter named Oghavatī whom Sudarśana married.

19. Citrasena who was born from Nariṣyanta had a son called Dakṣa. Dakṣa's son was Mīḍhvān of whom was born Kūrca who had a son called Indrasena.

20. Indrasena's son was Vītihotra who got a son named Satyaśravas who, on his part, had Uruśravas as his son. Devadatta was born from Uruśravas.

21. The venerable fire-god Agni himself was born as a son of Uruśravas, and was called Agniveśya. He became famous as a great sage Kānīna or Jātukarṇya.

22. From Agniveśya descended a Brāhmaṇa clan known as Agniveśyāyana, Oh king. The race of Nariṣyanta has been thus described in details. Now listen to the line of Diṣṭa.

23. Nābhāga, another son of Diṣṭa (different from the one to be described later[1]) became a *Vaiśya* by following the profession (agriculture, cow-tending etc.) of that class. His son was Bhalandana whose son was Vatsaprīti.

24. Prāṁśu was the son of Vatsaprīti. Prāṁśu's son is wellknown as Pramati; whose son was Khanitra[2], Khanitra's son was Cākṣuṣa, the father of Viviṁśati.

25. Rambha[3] was the son of Viviṃśati. Rambh's son was the religious Khaninetra, and Karandhama was Khaninetra's son, Oh great king.

26. His son was Avīkṣit. His son Marutta became a sovereign of the whole of the globe of the earth—the same sovereign for whom the great *yogin*, Saṁvartta, the son of sage Aṅgiras, performed sacrifices.

27. Nobody else has ever performed a sacrifice so gloriously as did Marutta. All the utensils therein were of pure gold, and whatever other materials were used in his sacrifice, were auspicious and beautiful.

28. Indra (drank so much *Soma* in that sacrifice that he) became inebriated and Brāhmaṇas were oversatisfied with the gifts (*dakṣiṇā*). Marut-gods served food (in that sacrifice), and

1. Vide infra ch. 4.
2. VR. reads 'Svamitra'.
3. VR. reads 'Dambha'.

the whole fraternity of gods (Viśvedevāḥ) were the members of the sacrificial assembly.[1]

29. Marutta had a son called Dama whose son was Rājyavardhana; his son was Sudhṛti and Nara was born as a son of Sudhṛti.

30. His son was Kevala whose son was Bandhumān of whom was born Vegavān. Bandhu was his (Vegavān's) son. Of Bandhu was born the king of the earth Tṛṇabindu.

31. Being an abode of praiseworthy qualities, a prominent heavenly damsel Alambuṣā resorted to him (as his wife), and bore him a number of sons and a daughter known as Iḍaviḍā (v. l. Ilavilā).

32. The sage Viśravas begot on her a son known as Kubera (the donor of wealth). From his father who was a master of *yogas*, Kubera received the Supreme Lore (about the soul).

33. The sons of this king were Viśāla, Śūnyabandhu, and Dhūmraketu. Visāla was the founder of a dynasty and built the city of Vaiśālī.

34. His (Viśāla's) son was Hemacandra, whose son was Dhūmrākṣa. From his son Saṁyama were born Kṛśāśva and Devaja[2].

35. From Kṛśāśva was born Somadatta who, by performing horse-sacrifices, worshipped the Supreme Person, the presiding deity of sacrifices[3] and attained to the foremost (highest goal through the support of the master of *yoga*.

1. This is nothing but an echo of:
marutaḥ pariveṣṭāro maruttasyāvasan gṛhe |
āvikṣitasya kāma-prer viśvedevāḥ sabhāsada iti ||
—*Ait. Br.* 8.21.14, *Śat.Br.* 13.5.4.6. *MBH* 12.29.18.
The same is repeated in *MBH Droṇa* 55.43-44.

2. But according to VR & VJ. Dhūmrākṣa's son was Sahadeva and Kṛśāśva was Sahadeva's son.

3. *Iḍaspati* (1) The Supreme Person to be propitiated by performing *Iḍā Homa*—VR.
(2) Overlord of the earth (Iḍā)—VR.
(3) The Lord who gives us food—VJ.
(4) The Lord bestower of the Power of speech—VJ.

36. Somadatta's son was Sumati, whose son was Janamejaya. These rulers of the kingdom of Vaiśāli held up the glory (glorious tradition of Tṛṇabindu).

CHAPTER THREE

The story of Cyavana and Sukanyā

Śrī Śuka continued :

1. It is reported that Manu's son, king Śaryāti was the master of the Vedic lore and it was he who, in the sacrificial session of the Aṅgiras, authoritatively explained the procedure of the ritualistic course of the second day (of that session).

2. He had a daughter Sukanyā by name, whose eyes were beautiful like lotuses. Accompanied by her, he went to the hermitage of the sage Cyavana.[1]

3. Surrounded by her maids (of honour), she was leisurely wandering in the forest enjoying the sight of beautiful trees, when she happened to notice a pair of glow-worm-like luminous objects, in the hole of an ant-hill.

4. Impelled by her fate, she, in her childish innocence, perforated the pair of shining objects with a thorn, and blood flowed profusely out of them.

5. That very moment instantly, there was obstruction in the lower passage of his soldiers (stoppage of the excretion

1. A sage of Bhṛgu Clan. *MBH. Vana* chs 122, 123 & 124 give how he was blinded by Sukanyā and was pacified when Sukanyā married him, and how at his request the celestial physicians Aśvinīkumāras rejuvenated him in consideration of a share in Soma-drinking, and how he petrified Indra's arm when in protest against Aśvinikumāra's share in Soma, Indra attacked with his Vajra. The story is repeated in the *Devī Bhāgavata* Skandha VII. Chs. 2-7. In that story Sukanyā deliberately perforates the eyes of Cyavana in spite of his warning. A number of verses are common to *MBH. Vana*, the *Bh.P.* and the *Devī Bhāgavata*, possibly all borrowing from a common source which supplied the story background for RV. 1. 116 (A hymn to AŚVINS).

and urination). Observing that, the royal sage was astonished and enquired of his men.

6. 'Has any of you given offence or done wrong to Cyavana, the descendant of the Bhṛgus. Obviously, someone of us must have profaned his hermitage'.

7. Being terrified, Sukanyā confessed to her father. "Something has been done by me in ignorance, inasmuch as a pair of glittering objects were unknowingly pierced by me".

8. Hearing the words of his daughter, Śaryāti was seized with fear. He slowly tried to appease the sage, lying hidden in the ant-hill.

9. Having ascertained the desire of the sage, the king gave (in marriage) his daughter to the sage. Having thus extricated himself from the scrape, and taking his leave (of the sage), he proceeded to his capital cautiously.

10. Having obtained the extremely wrathful Cyavana as her husband, Sukanyā who (studied and) understood his mentel proclivities, won him over by meticulously careful obedience.

11. After a lapse of some time after this, the twingods Aśvinikumāras visited his hermitage. Worshipping them (with due formalities as guests), he earnestly requested, "Oh ye celestial physicians ! Be pleased to restore to me my youth.

12. Even though you are not eligible to share the Soma-juice, I shall bear you both gobletfuls of Soma in the Soma sacrifice. Be pleased to bestow on me that youthfulness and beauty, covetable to young damsels."

13. "Assuredly" approved the foremost of physicians rejoicing at his offer. "May your worship be pleased to plunge in this pool created by Siddhas."

14. With these words, Cyavana, whose body was stricken with old age and was all over covered with protuberant veins, and appeared repulsive due to his wrinkles and grey hairs, was made to enter the pool by the pair of Aśvin gods.

15. There emerged three men (from that pool)—all bewitchingly beautiful, captivating to women, adorned with lotus-garlands and ear-rings, clad in rich garments, resembling each other in form.

16. Finding them all resembling each other in form, resplendent like the sun, the chaste lady Sukanyā, being unable to distinguish as to who her husband was, sought refuge with Aśvinikumāras (to help her in knowing the husband, by standing apart).

17. Being pleased with her fidelity to her husband, the Aśvinikumāras pointed out her husband. Taking leave of the sage, they left for the celestial region, in their heavenly car.

18. One day, king Śaryāti, intending to perform a sacrifice, went to the hermitage of Cyavana, and found a man glorious like the Sun, by the side of his daughter.

19. When the daughter bowed down to him (to pay respect), the king was not much pleased in his mind about her, and instead of giving the usual benedictions, censured her.

20. "What have you intended to do? Your husband, a sage respectfully saluted by all the world, is deceived by you, inasmuch as abandoninig the aged husband falsely approved by you, you have resorted to a way-farer as your paramour, you unchaste woman!

21. How is it that your mentality stooped to such low wickedness? Otherwise, you are born in a noble family of righteous persons, and this is a vile stigma on the family. You have lost your sense of shame and are harbouring a paramour, hurling thereby the families of your father and husband into the dark depth of hell."

22. To her father who was thus indicting her, Sukanyā, of pure gentle smiles, replied slightly laughting, "Father! This is your son-in-law Cyavana, the delight (or descendant) of Bhṛgu".

23. Then she reported to her father how he (Cyavana) came to regain his youth and beautiful looks. Full of astonishment and being extremely pleased with her, he embraced his daughter.

24. Cyavana made the heroic king Śaryāti to perform a Soma sacrifice, in which by dint of his personal ascetic powers, he bore a cup of Soma to the pair of Aśvinikumāras, even though they were not entitled for a share in Soma till then.

25. The irascible Indra was instantly enraged and raised his Vajra (thunderbolt) to kill him. But Cyavana, a descendant of Bhṛgus, petrified Indra's arm along with the Vajra.

26. Thenceforth, all of them (gods) agreed to give a share in Soma juice to Aśvinikumāras who, being physicians, were previously excluded from the oblations of Soma to them.

27. Śaryāti had three sons—Uttāna-barhis, Ānarta and Bhūriṣeṇa. Revata was born of Ānarta.

28. Building a city called Kuśasthalī, in the middle of the sea, he occupied it and ruled over the country called Ānarta (and adjoining territories), Oh subduer of enemies.

29-30. One hundred excellent sons, of whom Kakudmin was the eldest, were born to him. Taking with him his daughter Revatī Kakudmī went to god Brahmā for cousulting him for a suitable husband to his daughter. The region of Brahmā was then open. As a musical concert of Gandharvas, was going on, he did not get opportunity (to speak to god Brahmā) and waited for a moment.

31. After the conclusion of the musical programme, he bowed down to god Brahmā (the first created god), and told the object of his visit. Hearing that, god Brahmā laughed loudly and said.

32. "Oh King! Suitors that you had in your mind, have already been swallowed up by Time long ago. We do not even hear of their sons, grandsons, great-grandsons. Nay, not even their *gotras* (races).

33-35. The time calculated as thrice nine (i. e. twenty-seven) revolutions of the group of four *yugas* has now elapsed. Therefore, now you go back and offer this jewel of a daughter to the extremely mighty Baladeva, the ray of the God of gods, and a jewel among men. The glorious Lord, the creater of all beings, the chanting and hearing of whose name is meritorious, has incarnated on the earth by his own *aṁśa* (ray) for lightening the burden of the earth". When thus commanded, he bowed down to the unborn god Brahmā, and returned to his capital which was already abandoned by his brothers, out of fear of *yakṣas*, who were scattered all over the quarters (different parts of the earth).

36. Having given in marriage his extremely beautiful daughter to the mighty Balarāma, the king repaired to the hermitage of Nārāyaṇa, known Badarī, to perform austerities.

CHAPTER FOUR

The Account of Nābhāga and Ambarīṣa

Śrī Śuka continued :

1. Nābhāga was the son of Nabhaga. He was the youngest (of the brothers), the most learned and wise, and had spent (an unduly) long time as a celibate (in his teacher's hermitage). When he returned (from the hermitage of the preceptor and demanded his share of the ancestral property), they gave him their father (a commitment of father's maintenance) as his share of hereditary property, (as they have shared among themselves the whole of their father's estate presuming that Nābhāga would remain life-long celibate, and never return).

2. "Brothers ! What have you alotted as my share (in the ancesral propetrty) ?" (Nābhāga asked) (We forgot you then *or* Hearing of your renunciation, no share was set aside in the division of the property). 'Now, however, we give father (maintenance of father) as your share'[1] (replied the brothers). (Nābhāga went to his father and told him), "My elder brothers have alotted you as my share in the family property, dear father". The father told, "Do not place any faith in their words, Oh child"[2] (I am not a property to be enjoyed, but am a life-long commitment for maintenance).

1. "Let us go to father. If father asks us to give you a share, we shall"—VR.

VJ reads : *bhajāna pitaram* : 'If you want a share, go to your father, propitiate him and ask for your share. We also shall come and ask him'.

2. Do not entertain any desire for a share in the family property —VR.VJ.

3. (But for your maintenance, I advise). These (neighbouring) intelligent descendants of the Aṅgiras family are now engaged in a sacrificial session (of a long duration). But on every sixth day, they get confounded about the exact procedure ordained for the sacrifice, Oh learned son.

4-5. You teach those noble-minded (great-souled) Brāhmaṇas the two hymns (sūktas) celebrating the *Viśvedevas*[1]. When (after completion of the sacrifice), they will ascend to heaven, they will bestow upon you all their wealth that remains unspent after the sacrificial session. Hence you approach them (the Aṅgirases). He abided by his father's advice. They donated to him all the wealth that remained after the sacrificial session and went to heaven.

6. While he was about to accept that wealth, a certain man, of black complexion (Rudra), came from the north and claimed, "All this wealth in the premises of this house is mine".

7. Then replied the descendant of Manu, "This is mine inasmuch as it is given to me by the sages (who performed the sacrifice)". "Let this question (dispute) between us be referred to your father." Accordingly Nābhāga asked his father.

8. (His father replied), "On a certain occasion, sages have offered all that remains in the sacrificial hall as Rudra's share.[2] The god deserves (has a rightful claim on) the whole of that wealth."

9. (On return) Nābhāga bowed to him (Rudra) and reported, "Oh Lord ! My father said that all this is your property. Oh Brahman ! I propitiate you by bowing (apologizing with) my head low respectfully.

10. Rudra said, "Since what was spoken by your father was according to (the canons of) religion and you too speak the truth, I shall impart to you, the seer of Vedic *mantras*, spiritual knowledge about the Eternal Brahman.

10A. One should never, even under duress, speak the untruth. Nor should one covet another man's property. I

1. The Sūktas are :
   (1) *idam itthā raudraṁ gūrtavācaḥ* — RV.10.61.1
   (2) ye yajñena dakṣiṇayā samaktāḥ — RV.10.62.1
2. *Vide Supra* Bh.P. 4.6.53. ŚR supports this by the Śruti text : *ucchoṣaṇa-bhāgo vai rudraḥ* /

am extremely pleased with truthfulness and a truthful person is liked (desired) by me.

11. Please accept this wealth, the remainder of my sacrifice, which is granted to you". Saying this the glorious Lord Rudra, who is kind to the truthful, disappeared.

12. He who remembers this sacred story[1] with full concentration, both in the morning and in the evening, becomes blessed with spiritual wisdom, well-versed in the Vedic *mantras*, and attains his good (Liberation from Saṁsāra) or the true knowledge of Ātman as it is.

13. From Nābhāga was born Ambarīṣa who was an eminent devotee of Lord Viṣṇu and had realized fully the Brahman. He was so virtuous that even the imprecation of the Brāhmaṇa Durvāsas which was never ineffective before, could not touch him.

The King (Parīkṣit) asked :

14. Worshipful Sir ! I am eager to hear the story of that intelligent royal sage against whom the Brāhmaṇa's curse (in the form of the destructive female deity) which is irresistible, could not prevail.

Śrī Śuka said :

15-16. The highly fortunate Ambarīṣa inherited the earth with all its seven continents, inexhaustible fund of wealth, and incomparable power and glory in this world—all of which is extremely difficult for men to attain. But he regarded all this as unreal as a dream. He understood correctly the perishability of wealth, and that it ultimately leads man to darkness (of hell).

17. He attained to such a supreme devotion to the glorious Lord Vāsudeva, and so much friendly affection toward his pious devotees, as to regard this universe as a clod of earth —(what to speak of his kingdom ?)

18. He engaged his mind (in meditating) on the lotus-like feet of Lord Kṛṣṇa, his speech in singing of the excellences of Lord Viṣṇu (Vaikuṇṭha), his hands in services e.g. cleansing

1. As ŚR. points out this story of Nābhāga is based on a legend of the same person recorded in the *Bahvṛc Brāhmaṇa*.

the temple of Hari and such other duties, and his ears (sense of hearing) in listening to excellent stories of the Imperishable Lord.

19. He employed his eyes (faculty of seeing) in beholding the images and shrines of god Viṣṇu (Mukunda), his tactile sense in embracing the persons of the servants of gods, his olifactory sense in smelling the fragrance of the Tulasī leaves dedicated to his feet, and his tongue (sense of taste) to what is offered to the Lord.

20. He used his feet in walking to the holy places hallowed with Lord Hari's feet, his head to bow down to the feet of god Viṣṇu (Hṛṣīkeśa), his own desire in the humble services of the Lord, and not for the fulfilment of his worldly desires—All he did for enhancing his fondness or devotion to those who have resorted to the Lord of excellent renown.

21. In this way, he dedicated all his acts and round of duties to the glorious Lord Viṣṇu, the Supreme Ruler who bestows the fruits of the performance of sacrifices, every day. Placing his faith in the presence of the Lord in all beings (or beings devoted to Viṣṇu with their heart and soul[1]), and according to the advice of those who were devoted to the Lord and Brāhmaṇas (like his family preceptor Vasiṣṭha), he ruled over the earth.

22. He worshipped the Supreme Ruler, the presiding Deity of the Sacrifice, by performing horse-sacrifices in which all the 'limbs' (detailed parts of the sacrifice) were duly conducted and sumptuous sacrificial fees were paid befitting his great affluence. He performed these sacrifices under the guidance of great sages like Vasiṣṭha, Asita and Gautama in a desert place called Dhanva in the opposite direction of the current of the river Sarasvatī, (changing the venue of sacrifice along its banks from its mouth towards its source upwards.)

23. In his sacrifices, the sacrificial priests and members of the sacrificial assembly were so richly attired (and adorned), and through wonder or meticulous care in carrying out their

1. GS, GD quote the ideal devotion of *gopīs* in this context :
tan-manaskās tadālāpās tad-viceṣṭās tadātmikāḥ !
tad-guṇāneva gāyantyo nātmāgārāṇi sasmaruḥ !! Bh.P.10.30.44

duties, they forgot to wink and looked like the celestials (in form, dress ornaments and unwinkingness).

24. The heavenly region which is so dear to immortal gods was not coveted by his men, as (subjects) they constantly listened to and sang the glorious deeds of Lord Viṣṇu of excellent renown.

25. To them (his subjects) who visualized Lord Viṣṇu in their hearts, objects of pleasure which are not easily accessible even to Siddhas (who are endowed with mystic powers), did not fascinate and gladden, as they (objects of pleasure) are (as if) thrown into the shade by the essential blissfulness of self-realization (enjoyed by them).[1]

26. In this way the king, by his path of devotion combined with austerities, propitiated Lord Hari by abiding by the ordained course of duties, and gradually dissociated himself from all attachments.

27. He developed the sense of unreality of (and hence did not cherish any attachments to) his palaces, queens, sons, relatives, excellent elephants, chariots, horses, foot-soldiers, his inexhaustible (quantity of) jewels, ornaments, arms etc. and to his unlimited treasures.

28. Being pleased with his unflinching single-minded devotion, Lord Hari assigned to him, for the protection of his servant (devotee) his discus Sudarśana which struck terror in inimical forces.

29. With a desire to propitiate Lord Kṛṣṇa (Viṣṇu), the hero, along with his chief queen of a similar pious disposition, undertook the vow of observing a fast on the *Dvādaśī* day (viz. twelfth day of the dark and the bright half of every lunar month), for the period of one year.

30. At the close of the observance of the vow, in the month of Kārttika, he observed fast for three previous con-

1. Not that Ambarīṣa did not desire the objects of sense-pleasure due to their scarcity. They were in abundance as they were impelled and brought about by His essential greatness, though they were difficult for even Siddhas to obtain. He, however, was not enamoured of them as he saw Lord Viṣṇu in his heart—VJ.

secutive nights.[1] On one *Dvādaśī*, he took his bath in the Yamunā and worshipped Lord Hari in the forest-grove of the (demon) Madhu (the site of future Mathurā).

31-32. After performing the ablution of Hari according to the procedure laid down for the *Mahābhiṣeka* (royal coronation type ablution or a bath in which two thousand *palas* of gold is gifted) along with abundantly rich variety of accessories and ornaments, sandal paste, flowers, offerings and other articles of worship, he adored Lord Viṣṇu with a mind completely absorbed in him, and worshipped highly virtuous[2] Brāhmaṇas even though they had already accomplished their desire.

33-34A. He donated and sent to the houses of pious Brāhmaṇas six hundred million cows of good disposition and attractive appearance, all young and yielding milk in abundance. Their horns were encased in gold and hoofs plated in silver, and all were covered with rich cloth. They were gifted along with their calves and other necessary accessories (such as bells, pots for milking etc).

34B-35. Having first fed Brāhmaṇas with sweet and wholesome dish of excellent quality, and with the permission of those Brāhmaṇas who received their desired objects he (King Ambarīṣa) was making preparations of breaking his fast, when there arrived an unexpected guest who was no other than the venerable sage Durvāsas himself.

36. The king received his guest respectfully, by rising from his seat and proferring a respectable seat and other articles of worship, and bowing down to his feet, he requested him to take meals.

1. In the vow known as *Ekādaśī-vrata*, one has to take no meals at night on the 10th day, to observe complete fast on the 11th day and after breaking fast in the morning of the 12th day, observe fast at night.

2. *mahābhāga* :

VD. quotes a definition of *mahābhāga Brāhmaṇas*

tapo-vidyā-dayā-yuktā hari-niṣṭhaika-cetasaḥ |
pratigraha-nivṛttā ye mahābhāgā dvijāḥ smṛtāḥ ||

'Those who are engaged in penance, learning and merciful activities and whose minds are solely and unflinchingly devoted to Lord Hari, and who have ceased to accept gifts, are regarded as *mahābhāga* (highly virtuous) Brāhmaṇas.

37. Gladly accepting the invitation, he went to perform the prescribed religious duties (of the mid-day). Contemplating over the Suprme Brahman, he plunged in the holy waters of the Yamunā.

38. (As it is necessary to break the fast of *ekādaśī* during the period of *dvādaśī* and) as only half of a *muhūrta* (twenty-four minutes) remained of the *dvādaśī* day to expire in which one has to conclude the fast, the king, who was conversant with the religious technicalities, consulted the Brāhmaṇas (as to what righteous course be adopted) in that critical condition (involving conflict of duties).

39. (The king placed his dilemma before the Brāhmaṇas): (On the one hand) there is sin in transgressing a Brāhmaṇa (if I take meals before feeding the invited guest), and (on the other hand) it is sinful not to break a fast during the *dvādaśī* period. (Advise me) what course would be conducive to my good, and unrighteousness should not touch me.

40. I shall conclude the observance of the fast by sipping water only. For taking of water has been declared by Brāhmaṇas as breaking the fast but at the same time it is no eating at all."[1]

41. Coming to this conclusion, the royal sage took in some water, and waited for the return of the Brāhmaṇa contemplating in his mind the Imperishable Lord (Viṣṇu) all the while, Oh best of Kurus.

42. After finishing the necessary religious duties (of the midday), sage Durvāsas returned from the bank of the Yamunā. He was greeted by the king. But he knew by his intellectual (intuitional) power, the action of the king (viz. breaking of the fast by drinking water).

43. With his limbs quaking through intense wrath, and with his face crooked with knitting of brows (in anger), and being extremely angry, he expostulated the king who stood with folded palms (respectfully).

44. "Oh ! Look at the transgression of the established religious practice committed by this wicked fellow maddened

1. ŚR. quotes *Śruti* text in support :
apośnāti tannaivāśitam naivānaśitam

with his wealth, who regards himself as God and is devoid of any devotion to Viṣṇu.

45. Having extended an invitation to receive his hospitality to me who came to him as an unexpected guest, he himself took his meals without serving me food. (To the king) I show you forthwith the consequence of your misdeed."

46. Saying these words and extremely flared up with rage, he pulled out a matted hair (from his head), and created out of it a female spirit, (fierce) like the fire at the time of the destruction of the universe (to kill him).

47. Seeing the female evil spirit rushing toward him with a sword in hand, emitting fire, and making the earth quake under her feet (as she advanced), the king did not at all stir from his place.

48. The discus Sudarśana that was previously commissioned for protecting his servant (Ambarīṣa) by the Noble-souled Supreme Person, burnt down that evil spirit even as a fire would burn an angry serpent.

49. When Durvāsas saw that all his efforts (against Ambarīṣa) became infructuous, and that the discus was advancing towards him, he got frightened and ran in different directions, to save his life.

50. The discus of the Lord closely pursued him even as a forest conflagration with its flames thrown up follows a serpent. Observing it so close behind him, he took to his heels with a desire to enter one of the caves of mount Meru.

51. He fled to different quarters, the sky, the earth, the nether-world, the (seven) seas, to guardian deities of different regions, and to the celestial region. But wheresoever he ran, he saw the Sudarśana of unbearable splendour close on his heels.

52. When he could not find a protector anywhere, he became terrified at heart, and trying to seek asylum, approached god Brahmā appealing to him, "Oh Creator (of the Universe)! Oh self-born god! Protect me from the discus of Hari—the unvanquished god.

Brahmā said :

53. At the close of the divine sport (of the creation etc. of the universe), at the end of the period called *dviparārdha*

(when Brahmā's span of life ends), my own sphere, along with the whole of the Universe shall vanish (come to an end), by mere contraction of the brow of god Viṣṇu, the Soul of the Time-Spirit wishing to burn it all.

54. I, god Śiva, Dakṣa, Bhṛgu and others, and prominent Lords of created beings (*Prajāpatis*), rulers of goblins and of gods—all of us being subject to his Command, bear on our heads (most respectfully), the divine law for the welfare of the world. (Hence our inability to give you asylum).

55. Being thus refused protection by Brahmā, and being scorched by the discus of Lord Viṣṇu Durvāsas approached god Śiva on mount Kailāsa, for seeking asylum.

Śrī Rudra said :

56.* We cannot prevail against the Supreme Lord, oh child. In that Supreme Ruler great gods like god Brahmā who comprise the universe in their body, are nothing but ordinary *jīvas*; there are thousands of other such Brahmāṇḍas which are born as well as dissolved in the course of time. We are just wandering in transmigration in them.

57-58. I, Sanatkumāra, Nārada, the worshipful god Brahmā, Kapila, the sage Apāntaratamas,[1] Devala, Dharma,

*(i) We are not capable of protecting you against the discus of the Lord Who deserves to be sought after by us. In this universe we who regard ourselves as masters of (our) regions, are wandering (like insects). Thousands of such Brahmāṇḍas appear, when He wills to create, and are dissolved, when He wishes to withdraw—VR.

(ii) We are powerless in affording you protection. At the time of creation numerous deities like me are born from Hari, the Perfect Bliss and are no more at the time of the destruction of the Universe. There are crores of other such Brahmāṇḍas which form the bodies of so many Brahmās in which we and unintelligent beings wander in transmigration. May that Supreme Ruler be your Saviour—Not we—VJ.

(iii) Therefore you seek resort in that Lord Viṣṇu—SD.

(iv) *tāta*—Term of endearment as Durvāsas was a part of ray of god Śiva—GD.

1. A great sage born when god Viṣṇu uttered the word *bhū*. He was absolutely free from the inner darkness or ignorance about the soul. Hence his name is also known as *Sārasvata* as he was born out of the speech (*Sarasvatī*) of the Lord.

—*MBH.Śānti* 349. 38-39.

Āsuri and other leaders of Siddhas who are perfect in wisdom (have seen the other end) of whom Marīci is prominent, all of us are enveloped in Māyā, and we cannot comprehend his Māyā.

59. This is the weapon of the Supreme Ruler of the Universe. It is unbearable and irresistible even to us. You seek refuge in Lord Hari. He will make you happy.

60. Being thus disappointed, Durvāsas went to the region of the Lord called Vaikuṇṭha where Lord Viṣṇu abides along with goddess Śrī.

61. Scorched with the fire emanating from the weapon of the unconquerable Lord, he fell trembling at the feet of Viṣṇu and appealed, "Oh Imperishable, Infinite Lord! You are the goal aspired after by the righteous. Oh Almighty God! You are the protector of the Universe. Oh Protect me who am an offender.

62. Being ignorant of Your Supreme glory, an offence against your dear one has been committed by me. Be pleased to absolve me of that sin, as even a being in hell is released by uttering Your name (what of wiping out this sin?).

The Lord replied :

63. Oh Brāhmaṇa! I am completely under the control of my devotees. I am like one who has no self-dependence. My heart is won over and hence is in possession of my righteous devotees, and I am the beloved of them.

64. To my devotees, I am the Supreme goal, (hence) apart from my righteous devotees, I do not covet even my person (myself), or even (my consort) Goddess Śrī[1] who is absolutely faithful to Me.

65. How can I abandon (to their fate) my devotees who have renounced their wives, homes, sons, kith and kin, their very life, property, (their good in) this world and the next, and resorted to me as their protector.

66. These righteous people who have completely dedicated their hearts to me and entertain impartiality of outlook to all, have enthralled me by their devotion, even as good wives do by their devotion to virtuous husbands.

1. The highest glory of eternal six excellences—VD.

67. So thoroughly satisfied are they in rendering service to me that they do not long for the four types of Liberations such as *Salokatā*—co-residence with the Lord in his region and others[1] which are easily available by my worship. How can they covet for other positions or things which are subject to ravages of time.

68. Righteous people (are so beloved to me that they as if) constitute my heart. I am (reciprocally so much dear to them that I form) their heart. They do not recognize anything beside me. Nor do I know anything else than them.

69. I shall therefore tell you a remedy. Listen to it, Oh Brāhmaṇa. You should verily approach him (Ambarīṣa) on account of whom the act of violence has rebounded against you. The energy discharged against pious people boomerangs against and harms its own author.

70. Asceticism and learning are both for the spiritual good of the Brāhmaṇas but those very powers when mishandled by the indisciplined ones produce the contrary results.

71. Hence, Oh Brāhmaṇa ! May good betide you. You go to King Ambarīṣa, the son of Nābhāga. Apologize and seek forgiveness of that great king. Then alone you can get peace and relief.

CHAPTER FIVE

Protection of Durvāsas. The story of Ambarīṣa Concluded

Śrī Śuka said :

1. Being thus commanded by the glorious Lord, Durvāsas who was afflicted by the discus Sudarśana, returned to Ambarīṣa, and sought protection at his feet (by touching them) remorsefully.

1. The remaining three are : *Samīpatā*—Proximity to the Lord, *Sarūpatā*—resemblance in form with the Lord, *Sāyujyatā*—complete identification or absorption in the Deity.

2. Observing the act (of supplication and touching his feet) by Durvāsas, Ambarīṣa felt ashamed at the touch of his feet (by the sage), and being overwhelmed with deep compassion, prayed to the missile of Lord Hari.

Ambarīṣa prayed :

3. You are the glorious Fire-god, the Sun-god, Soma (or Deity presiding over the moon), the Lord of luminaries (constellations of stars, planets). You are (the elements like) water, the earth, the sky, the air. You are the subtle elements and the senses (or the objects of the senses and fire etc. function due to your power).

4. Oh Sudarśana ! I pay my respects to you who are of thousand spokes and so dear to The Imperishable Lord. You are the destroyer of all missiles, and protector of the earth. May you be propitious to the Brāhmaṇa.

5. You are the righteousness (*dharma*) itself, the Divine Law (*ṛta*) and the Truth (incarnate). You are the sacrifice, and you are the presiding Deity of the Sacrifice who enjoys the oblations. You are the protector of regions, the soul (the Inner Controller) of all; you are the splendour and energy of the Supreme Person.

6. Oh beautifully centred discus ! (Nobody being able to glorify you adequately) I simply utter the word "Bow" to you who are the defender of the injunctions of the Divine Law (ominous and destructive like) a comet unto the unrighteous and the Asuras, the Protector of the three worlds, endowed with purest splendour, of quick speed like the flight of thought and of miraculous deeds.

7. Oh Lord of speech ! By your splendour (constituted) of righteousness, darkness of ignorance obscuring the vision (or the knowledge of the Deity) has been dispelled, and the light (of god-realization) has been flashed and preserved, for the noble-souled righteous people. This entire universe, gross or subtle, high or low has been lighted by you (through the sun, the moon and other luminaries). Your greatness is simply unfathomable.

8. Oh Invincible one ![1] when discharged by the blemi-

1. v.l. *ūrjita* : the (army) of mighty Daityas and Dānavas.

shless Lord, you enter the army of the Daityas and Dānavas and severing (incessantly) their arms, bowels, thighs and feet and necks, you shine irresistible in battles.

9. Oh protector of the world ! You who overcome all (enemies in battle), have been commissioned by the wielder of the mace (Lord Viṣṇu) for the annihilation of the wicked. Therefore, for the sake of the prosperity of our family, be pleased to grant welfare (protection) to the Brāhmaṇa (Durvāsas). That will be your grace unto us (otherwise we shall be responsible for committing the sin of killing a Brāhmaṇa)

10. If a charitable gift has been donated (by us), or a sacrifice has been performed, or our righteous duty has been properly executed, or if our family regards Brāhmaṇas as our gods, may this Brāhmaṇa be free from his distress.

11. If the glorious lord, the sole abode of all excellent qualities be pleased with us due to our looking upon (regarding) all beings as possessing souls like us (or his Spirit), may this Brāhmaṇa get rid of his distress and anxiety.

Śrī Śuka said :

12. While the king was thus praying to Viṣṇu's discus Sudarśana, which was scorching the Brāhmaṇa on all sides, it subsided at the request of the king.

13. Being relieved of the scorching heat of the fire of the missile (Sudarśana), Durvāsas felt comfortable. Bestowing on him the highest blessings, he praised the king.

Durvāsas said :

14. "Oh ! How wonderful ! I have witnessed today the magnanimity of servants of the Infinite Lord in that you wish for the well-being of a person who has offended you, Oh king.

15. What is difficult to be achieved for those righteous persons or what is impossible to give up in the case of those noble-souled persons, who have treasured up (and made their own) the glorious Lord Hari, the leader of the Sātvatas.

16. Can there be any deficiency or unfulfilment in the case of the servants of the Lord of the hallowing feet (to which

even holy rivers resort for purification) by listening to the name of whom a man is absolved of all sins and impurities.

17. Oh King ! I am highly favoured by you in that, exceedingly merciful as you are, you ignored the wrong done by me, and have completely saved my life."

18. The king who did not take any food but waited in expectation of the sage's return, clasped his feet, conciliated him, and made him accept the meal.

19. Having enjoyed the hospitality and the food that was suitable to all tastes and (thus) gratifying all desires) and was served with respect and care, he felt himself thoroughly gratified, and courteously requested the king to take his meals.

20. "I am thoroughly pleased with you, and have been laid under great obligations by the sight, touch, conversation as well as by the hospitality-offered with full devotion to the Lord—of a great votary of the Lord (like you).

21. The celestial damsels will often sing of this noble behaviour (act) of yours (in heaven), and this earth (the whole world) will extol this highly hallowing glory of yours."

Śrī Śuka said :

22. Having thus praised the king, Durvāsas who was highly satisfied, took his leave of him and through ethereal space went to the region of Brahmā[1] which lasts for two *Parārdha* years.[1]

23. A complete year elapsed since the departed sage Durvāsas did not return. It is reported that during this period, the king who longed to see him returned, subsisted simply on water.

24. After the departure of Durvāsas, Ambarīṣa ate the (remnant of the) food that was rendered extremely holy by being partaken of by the Brāhmaṇa (Durvāsas). Pondering over the calamity on Durvāsas and his final release and his own fortitude, he considered all that being due to the power of the Supreme Person.

25. The king Ambarīṣa who was thus endowed with such ennumerable excellent qualities, continued in his devotion

1. *ahaitukam*—where dry rationalists have no place—GS.

of the Lord by dedicating all his acts suitable to his own caste and stage of life to the Supreme Soul, Brahman designated as Vāsudeva. By virtue of such (firm) devotion, he came to regard all positions upto the part of god Brahmā as hellish.

26. In course of time, Ambarīṣa entrusted his kingdom to his sons whose disposition and character were similar to him, and entered the forest. Concentrating his mind wholly on Vāsudeva, his own soul, he destroyed (became free from) the current of guṇas viz. *Saṁsāra* or transmigration of the soul.

27. He who glorifies this sacred story of king Ambarīṣa or ponders over it, becomes a devotee of Lord Viṣṇu.

27A. Those who listen to the story of the noble-souled Ambarīṣa, all of them attain to Liberation from Saṁsāra through the devotion to and by the Grace of Lord Viṣṇu.

CHAPTER SIX

*History of Ikṣvāku's Posterity**

The Story of Saubhari

Śrī Śuka said :

1. Virūpa, Ketumān and Śambhu were the three sons of Ambarīṣa. From Virūpa was born Pṛṣadaśva whose son was Rathītara.

*This chapter gives the first twenty generations of the Solar race :

Manu
Ikṣvāku

Nimi — Janaka
Vikukṣa alias Śaśāda
Daṇḍaka

Śaśāda → Purañjaya (Kakutstha) → Anenas → Pṛthu → Viśvarandhi → Candra → Yuvanāśva → Śabasta → Śābasti → Bṛhadaśva → Kuvalayāśva (Dhundhumāra) → Dṛḍhāśva → Haryaśva → Nikumbha → Barhaṇāśva → Kṛśāśva Senajit → Yuvanāśva → Māndhātṛ (Trasaddasyu).

2. When requested for the continuation of the family of Rathītara, Aṅgiras begot by the wife of Rathītara who was childless, a number of sons, possessing the lustre of the Vedic lore.

3. Though these were born from the wife of Rathītara, they were known as belonging to the family of Aṅgiras (instead of that of Rathītara); they became the leaders of other sons of Rathītara as they were Brāhmaṇas endowed with the characteristic qualities of Kṣattriyas.

4. While Manu was sneezing his son Ikṣvāku was born from his nostrils. Of the hundred sons of Ikṣvāku, Vikukṣi, Nimi and Daṇḍaka were the eldest.

5. Of these one hundred sons, twentyfive became monarchs in (the principalities lying in) the east of Āryāvarta[1], twentyfive became rulers in the West (of Āryāvarta), three in the middle (of that tract), and the rest in other directions (north, south and other directions).

6. Once, on the occasion of *aṣṭaka-Śrāddha*[2] Ikṣvāku ordered his son, "Oh Vikukṣi! Hurry up and bring meat suitable for the purpose of *Śrāddha*. Don't delay, please."

7. Saying 'Be it so' (in compliance of his father's order), the hero went to the forest, and killed beasts suitable for religious rites. Being fatigued and hungry, he unwittingly ate a hare.

8. He brought the remaining flesh to his father. When Ikṣvāku requested the family preceptor (Vasiṣṭha) to sprinkle it with water, he refused saying that it was contaminated, and hence unsuitable for religious rites.

9. Having ascertained from his son the perpetration of the (sacrilegious) act as reported by his family preceptor the king, out of anger, exiled from his land, his son who violated the restrictions of the rite.

1. The sacred land between the Vindhya and the Himālayas—ŚR.

2. (A *Śrāddha* to be performed on the seventh, eighth, ninth and the thirteenth day of dark and bright halfs of the lunar months).

GS quotes :

saptamyādi-trayaṁ caiva tathā caiva trayodaśī !
catasras tvaṣṭakāḥ proktāḥ sarvapakṣād viśeṣataḥ !!

10. The king discussed with his preceptor Vasiṣṭha about the nature of the Truth. As a consequence of it, Ikṣvāku became established in *Jñāna-yoga* (path of knowledge). And casting off this physical body, he attained to what was the highest (*Brahman*).

11. Vikukṣi who came to be known as Śaśāda (the eater of a hare) returned after the demise of his father, and while ruling over the earth, he worshipped Lord Hari with (the performance) of sacrifices.

12. His son Purañjaya (conqueror of a city) was called Indravāha (one borne by Indra), and was also named as *Kakutstha* (one seated on the hump of a bull). Now listen to (what) deeds earned for him these designations.

13. At the end of the Kṛta Age (or at the beginning of the Tretā age)[1], there was a battle between gods and Dānavas— a battle that was fierce like the *Pralaya*, at the end of world. This hero (Purañjaya) was sought as an ally by gods who were defeated by Daityas.

14. ('I shall kill the demons if Indra agrees to be my mount' on this condition) Indra was sought to be a mount. According to the advice of Lord Viṣṇu, the god of gods and the soul of the universe, Indra assumed the form of a big bull (to carry Purañjaya).

15. Accoutered in a coat of mail and armed with a celestial bow and sharp arrows, he, being eager to fight, mounted the bull and occupied his seat on its hump, while he was being extolled by gods.

16. Strengthened with the spiritual energy of Lord Viṣṇu, the Inner Controller, the Supreme Soul, he besieged the town of the Daityas in the west, with the army of gods.

17. He engaged them in a fierce battle which made hair stand on end. Whosoever of the Daityas dared to face in the battle, he despatched them to the god of death with his *bhalla* arrows.

18. While the Daityas were being killed, they avoided the range of the flight of his arrows which were unbearable

1. *Kṛtānta* — Both the meanings of the pun on *Kṛtānta* are accepted.

like the fire that consumes the universe at the end of *yugas* and fled to their region (the subterranean world).

19. Having conquered the splendid city and all its wealth, the royal sage gave it all to Indra, the wielder of the thunderbolt. Hence he was designated with the epithets (mentioned above).

20. Purañjaya had a son called Anenas (the sinless). His son was Pṛthu whose son was Viśvarandhi (v. l. Viśvagandha) His son was Candra whose son was Yuvanāśva.

21. His son was Śābasta who built the city called Śābasti. Bṛhadaśva was the son of Śābasta; thence (the next generation) was Kuvalayāśva.

22. For achieving the well-being of sage Utaṅka, the powerful king, surrrounded by his twentyone thousand sons, killed the demon called Dhundhu.

23. He, thereby, became celebrated as Dhundhumāra. All of his sons except the three who survived, were burnt by the fire that emanated from the mouth of Dhundhu.

24. The surviving sons were Dṛḍhāśva, Kapilāśva and Bhadrāśva, Oh descendant of Bharata. Dṛḍhāśva's son was Haryaśva whose son is remembered at Nikumbha.

25-26. Barhaṇāśva was the son of Nikumbha. His (Barhaṇāśva's) son was Kṛśāśva whose son was Senajit. To him was born Yuvanāśva who, being childless, repaired to the forest, along with his hundred wives, in despair. The merciful sages took pity on him, and with great concentration of mind, they conducted for him a sacrifice, specially dedicated to Indra.

27. (Once) being thirsty at night, the king entered the sacrificial hall. Finding all the Brāhmaṇas in the hall asleep, he himself drank the water consecrated with *mantras* (and meant for the queen).

28. On getting up (at dawn), the Brāhmaṇas found the pitcher of (consecrated) water empty. Then, Oh king, they enquired whose work it was that the water meant for begetting a male issue, was drunk.

29. Then, having come to know that it was drunk by the king who was (as if) impelled by God, they bowed down to the Almighty Lord (with the words) "The power of the Providence is really Supreme and irresistible".

30. It is reported that after the expiry of the due period (of nine months), the son of Yuvanāśva who (later) became the sovereign monarch of the globe of the earth, was born splitting open the right side of his belly.

31. 'The child is incessantly crying[1]. Whom will it suck ?' (asked the Brāhmaṇas anxiously 'He will suckle me. Oh child, do not cry; saying this, Indra (who was propitiated with a sacrifice for its birth) put (in his mouth) his index finger (which was dripping with nectar.)

32. Through the grace of gods and that of Brāhmaṇas, his (Māndhātṛ's) father did not die. Yuvanāśva attained to the Final Beatitude, there (in that very hermitage) through his penance.

33. Indra gave him *Trasad-dasyu* (The terror of evil-doers) as another epithet. For enemies of gods and men like Rāvaṇa and others trembled at the mention of his name and were perturbed.

34. In due course, Māndhātā, the son of Yuvanāśva became the universal monarch, and being infused with the Spiritual power and glory of the Imperishable Lord (Viṣṇu), solely ruled over the world consisting of seven island-continents.

35. A knower of the Self as he was, he performed a number of sacrifices with liberal gifts and *dakṣiṇās*, and thereby worshipped the Supreme Deity of the sacrifices, the Lord who represents all gods (in his person) and who, through his being the inner Controller of all *antaryāmins* is beyond the ken of senses.

36. Materials of sacrifices, *mantras* (recited in the course of the sacrifice), the sacrificial procedure, the sacrifice proper, the performer of sacrifice and priests participating in the sacrifice, the merit accruing from the sacrifice, time and place of sacrifice—all these are his constituents. (In fact, the whole of the universe is constituted of him. Him he worshipped through sacrifices.

37. The point at which the sun rises, to the point where it sets—the whole of the region lighted by the sun is

1. The child which wishes to suck the breast of his mother is incessantly crying—VJ.

regarded as the land (kingdom) of Māndhātṛ, the son of Yuvanāśva.

38. The king begot on Bindumatī, the daughter of Śaśabindu, (three sons, viz.) Purukutsa, Ambarīṣa and Mucakunda, the yogin. Their fifty sisters sought the sage Saubhari[1] as their husband.

39-40. Submerged in the waters of the Yamunā, and practising austere penance, Saubhari happened to observe the happy state of the king of fishes engaged in coition (with a female partner), and he was affected with that passionate desire, and (approaching the king) requested him for a girl. (The king) replied, "Oh Brahman, you can freely have any daughter, provided she selects you of her own accord voluntarily.

41. The sage realized the ruse and said to himself, 'Considering that I, being far advanced in age, grey-haired, covered with wrinkles, with a head unstable and shaking (all the while), will be repulsive and disagreeable to women, I have been (politely) refused by the king.

42. I shall make myself so (attractively) beautiful that I shall be covetable even to celestial nymphs; not to speak of daughters of lords of human beings. The spiritual master (Saubhari) became thus determined (and by his power of asceticism, he became so actually).

43. He was ushered in by the chamberlain, in the richly magnificent and luxurious harem reserved for the princesses. And Lo! That one suitor was sought after and courted as a husband by all the fifty princesses.

44. Throwing to winds (forgetting) their mutual sisterly affection, there arose a great controversy among them about securing him (as a husband). Their hearts being fixed upon him, each one of them argued, "He is suitable in beauty and form only to me, and not to anyone of you (at all)".

45-46. Saubhari, well-versed in the *Ṛgveda* (and master of powerful *mantras*) enjoyed for a long period his life with

1. *Saubhari*—The story, how the old sage Śaubhari married all the fifty daughters of the emperor Māndhātṛ seems to be popular in the epic period, and is found in *Viṣṇu P.* 4.2.3, *Garuḍa P.* 1.138. In fact the whole of that chapter seems to be based on this chapter of the Bh.P.

them (the princesses of Māndhātṛ) in mansions furnished by the power of his inexhaustible penance, with invaluable paraphernalia and furnishings such as highly costly beds, seats, rich clothes, ornaments, baths, articles of beautifications (pigments etc.), sweet dishes, wreaths and flowers, waited upon by men and women adorned with precious ornaments, and resonant with warbling birds, humming bees and singing panegyrists. He revelled with them delightfully in various gardens studded with pools of translucent waters, and in parks full of scented flowers (like Kalhāra).

47. Observing his affluent state of house-holder's life, Māndhātā, the master of the entire earth consisting of seven island-continents, was so astonished that he ceased to feel the obstinate pride of universal sovereignty.

48. Although he was enjoying various objects of pleasure with deep attachment to his houses which were full of various kinds of pleasure[1], Saubhari did not feel sated like a fire fed with drops of ghee.

49. On one occasion, while he was sitting (all alone), Saubhari, the great preceptor of *Ṛgveda*, became conscious of his ascetic degeneration (spiritual oblivion) caused by his observation of the sexual pleasure of the fish.

50. 'Alas ! Look at the ruinous fall of mine—an ascetic of pious conduct, conforming strictly to vows, due to my noticing (the sexual intercourse of) the acquatic animals, under waters, my asceticism[2] which I observed for a long time, was lost.'

51. A person desirous of liberation from *Saṁsāra*, should, with all his heart and soul, avoid association with all who follow married life. He should endeavour not to permit his senses to external objects. Leading a life in solitude, he should fix his mind on the Infinite Ruler (of the universe). If occasion arises, he should associate himself with saintly persons who observe vows (of celibacy etc.) and are devoted to the Lord.

1. VR. reads *nānā-mukhaiḥ* : 'Through many sets of senseorgans'. Saubhari assumed various bodies simultaneously to enjoy through multiple-sets of senseorgans, all the objects of pleasure fully.

2. *brahma—Brahman*, the Supreme Spirit I used to meditate upon for a long time past, was completely forgotten—VR.

52. I was an ascetic without any companion. But due to my association with the fish under water, I became fifty (by marrying fifty wives[1]). (By procreating hundred sons per wife) I became five thousand. I cannot reach the end of desires about them, or I do not see any limit to my wishes relating to man and wife, or this world and the next. I have lost my judgment due to the *guṇas* of *Māyā*. I have come to believe that achievement of worldly objects are the real goal in life.

53. Continuing in the householder's stage of life for some (more) time, he felt disinclination (to that life), and adopted the life of a *Vānaprastha* (*nyāsa*). He repaired to the forest and was followed by his fifty wives who looked upon their husband as God.

54. The self-controlled sage performed there a severely austere penance which reduced his body (to a skeleton), and got absorbed along with the fires (like *gārhapatya*) into the Supreme Soul (and was liberated from *saṁsāra*).

55. Noticing the absorption of their husband in the Supreme Brahman, his wives too followed him through his spiritual power (and attained Liberation from *Saṁsāra*) just as flames become extinguished with a subsided fire.[2]

CHAPTER SEVEN[3]

The Story of King Hariścandra[3]

Śrī Śuka said :

1. The celebrated Ambarīṣa, who was the most excellent son of Māndhātṛ, was adopted as his son by his grandfather.

1. GS : I assumed fifty forms for simultaneous association with fifty wives.

2. VJ's Text does not end this chapter here.

3. This chapter deals with the following generations of Kings of the Solar race :

Māndhātṛ (mentioned in the last ch.)→Purukutsa→Trasaddasyu II→Anaraṇya→Haryaśva→Aruṇa→Tribandhana→Satyavrata alias Triśaṅku →Hariścandra→Rohita

This line is confirmed in the VP. 4.3.

The rivalry between Vasiṣṭhas and Viśvāmitras is as old as the *Ṛgveda*. Here the story is based on the famous Śunaḥśepa legend in the

(Yuvanāśva). His (Ambarīṣa's) son was Yauvanāśva whose son was Hārīta. These are the three important members (and the first three branches of the Māndhātṛ family).

2. Narmadā (a Nāga princess) was given by her Nāga brothers to Purukutsa (the eldest son of Māndhātṛ). As directed by the serpent-King (Vāsuki), she took him (Purukutsa) to the nether-world called *Rasātala*.

3. Infused with the spiritual energy of god Viṣṇu, Purukutsa killed Gandharvas who deserved to be slain. He received a boon from the Nāgas that those who remember this story (of emancipation of Nāgas from Gandharvas) would be immune from the fear of serpents.

4. Purukutsa's son was Trasaddasyu (the second[1]) who was the father of Anaraṇya. His son was Haryaśva whose son was Aruṇa. Aruṇa's son was Tribandhana.

5-6. Tribandhana's son Satyavrata became celebrated as Triśaṅku.[2] He was reduced to the status of a Cāṇḍāla by the curse of his father, but by dint of the spiritual power of Viśvāmitra, he ascended heaven along with his (physical) body, where he is still seen in the sky. When he was made to fall with his head downward by gods, he (Viśvāmitra) stopped him in the mid-air by the spiritual force (of Viśvāmitra).

7. Triśaṅku's son was Hariścandra on account of whom[3] a continuous fight lasting for many years took place

Aitareya Brāhmaṇa. The way in which this Hariścandra treated Varuṇa is different from that of the Hariścandra who sold himself to keep his promise to Viśvāmitra. Two contradictory legends are grafted on the same Hariścandra ! The MBH and VP. corroborate the 'Triśaṅku' legend!

1. 'Trasad-dasyu' is the name of Māndhātṛ also. Vide supra. 9.6.33

2. ŚR. explains: He is called Triśaṅku—one in whom are embedded three darts in the form of three offences, viz. abduction of a Brāhmaṇa girl from her marriage pandal, killing the cow of his preceptor Vasiṣṭha, eating meat before its consecration with water. He quotes a verse from the *Harivaṁśa* enumerating these transgressions :

pituṣ cā'paritoṣeṇa gururdogdhrīvadhena ca /
aprokṣitopayogācca trividhas te vyatikramaḥ //

3. This refers to the persecution of Hariścandra by the sage Viśvāmitra who deprived Hariścandra of everything as a sacrificial fee for conducting a Rājasūya sacrifice. When Vasiṣṭha learnt of this, he cursed Viśvāmitra to be a crane (āḍi) while Viśvāmitra retaliated by imprecating him to be a heron (*baka*). They fought for years in these forms—ŚR.

between Vasiṣṭha and Viśvāmitra in the form of birds (viz. a crane (āḍī, Viśvāmitra) and a heron (Vasiṣṭha).

8. He (Hariścandra) being issueless became dejected in mind. On the advice of Nārada, he resorted to god Varuṇa with the request, "Oh Varuṇa, Bless me with a son.

9. "If he grows to be a warrior, I shall worship you by sacrificing him to you". 'Be it so', replied Varuṇa in granting him the boon. And a son called Rohita was born to him, through the grace of Varuṇa.

10. Varuṇa demanded, "Now a son is born to you, worship me by sacrificing that child". Hariścandra replied, "When a (prospective) victim crosses the first ten days of his life, it becomes fit for sacrificial purpose."

11. When the time limit of ten days was over, Varuṇa arrived and asked the king to worship him (with that child). Hariścandra replied, "It is after dentition that an animal becomes fit for sacrifice."

12. "(After the dentition of the child, Varuṇa appeared again and) said, "Now that the teeth have appeared, do you worship me with the child ?" "But the victim will be fit for sacrifice when its teeth have fallen."

13. (Varuṇa appeared again and (demanded, "The teeth of the sacrificial animal have fallen, now worship (me with him)". "But a victim becomes pure when its teeth grow again." replied Hariścandra.

14. "Now that (the teeth) have grown again, sacrifice it now to me", said Varuṇa. To him replied Hariścandra, "Oh King ! When a Kṣatriya victim is (of the age of) wearing an armour, he is regarded as a pure animal fit for sacrifice."

15. In this way due to affection for his son and with his mind overpowered with (paternal) love, he went on deceiving by postponements (of sacrifice), and the god waited.

16. Rohita who, by then, came to know what (type of) act his father intended to do, and desirous of saving his life, escaped to the forest with a bow in hand.

17. Having come to learn that his father is possessed by Varuṇa and has developed *mahodara* (a disease called 'Dropsy'), Rohita was returning to the capital when Indra forbade him to do so (lest he should be sacrificed).

18. Indra advised Rohita to travel all over the earth, as visiting the holy places and ablutions in sacred waters are meritorious, and Rohita stayed in the forest that year.

19. Assuming the form of an old Brāhmaṇa, Indra visited him in the second, third, fourth and fifth year and tendered him the same advice.

20. Having wandered in the forest for the sixth year, Rohita returned to his capital (and on way) purchased the middle son (the second son by name Śunaḥśepa) from Ajīgarta (of the Bhṛgu clan).

21-23. Handing over Śunaḥśepa as a sacrificial animal to his father, Rohita bowed down to him. King Hariścandra of great glory, worshipped Varuṇa and other gods with human sacrifice and became free from dropsy, and his stories came to be sung in the assemblies of the great. In that sacrifice Viśvāmitra was the high priest (*hotṛ*), the self-controlled (or one who has realized the self), Jamadagni officiated as *adhvaryu*, Vasiṣṭha became the Brahmā, and the sage Ayāsya sang the Sāman hymns. Being pleased with him, Indra gifted to him a gold chariot.

24-25A. The greatness of Śunaḥśepa will be recounted later on (in ch. 16). Being highly pleased to notice the resoluteness deriving its strength from firmness in truth of both the king and the queen, he (Viśvāmitra) imparted to them the unobstructed knowledge of the ultimate truth.

25B-27*. (In meditation) fusing his mind (the root-

* The gists of the explanations of different commentators are as follows :

(1) VR. : Hariścandra in his meditation identified the mind with the earth and the earth with water . . . so on up to *Tāmasic* Ego into *Pradhāna* which contains *Mahat* in itself. Having contemplated the Intelligent principle in it (i.e. by contemplating the *pratyagātman* as being characterised by devotion-cum-knowledge — *upāsanātmaka-vidyā-viśiṣṭam pratyagātmānam anusandhāya ityarthaḥ*/), and burning down by that knowledge the wrong notions of the identification of the body with the soul, absolute independence of *ātman* (*svatantrātmā'bhimāna-rūpam*), and discarding it by realising the limitations of that aspect of devotion-cum-knowledge, and becoming free from the bondage of *karmas* (merits and sins), he realised his blissful nature of the soul which is beyond description (either as a man or a god or a sub-human being etc. or in usual terms of name and form), stayed in his own essential nature (transcend sin etc.).

cause of *Saṁsāra*[1]) into the earth (which is another designation for food which constitutes and hence modifies the mind[2]), the earth into water, water into fire, fire into the air, the air into ether or space, and that into the Tāmasic aspect of Ego (which is the source of all elements), the *Tāmasic* ego into the *mahat* (the principle of cosmic intelligence), but of the intellectual and objective aspects of the *Ātman*, he contemplated the intellectual or knowledge aspect into the *Mahat* ignoring the objective aspect, and thereby burnt down completely the Nescience (that obscured the soul). Through his intelligent consciousness of the absolute bliss of *Nirvāṇa*, he transcended that aspect also, and completely severed off the bondage (such as identification of the soul with the body), and stood in his own essential nature which is beyond the range of description and abstract reasoning.

(II) VJ : Agreeing with ŚR about the procedure of merging of the mind into the earth etc. upto *Mahat* which is presided over by the four-faced god Brahmā, wherein lies the Intelligent principle of which the presiding deity is Sarasvatī; contemplating over this and destroying all the bondages, he stayed in his natural stage of knowledge and blissfulness which is beyond my i.e. human power of description or reasoning capacity.

(III) SD : The fickleness of the mind depends on the food eaten. Thus the mind being identical with the food which grows out of the earth and hence one with it for the control of the mind, he meditated it as identical with the earth. This procedure goes upto *Mahadātman* : but SD states *mahadātman* means *Pradhāna* which is the soul or cause of *Mahat*. *Jñānakalā=Buddhi*, 'Intelligence'. Though it is *jaḍa* (unconscious), it is associated with the knower i.e. *Jīva* and hence called *Jñānakalā*. Contemplating over the distinction between *jīvātman* and *buddhi* and burning down (dispelling) the ignorance i.e. the false identification of the soul with body, mind, intelligence etc., and thus discarding intelligence and distinguishing *Pradhāna* from the self, he became liberated from bondage of *karmas*.

(IV) BP. takes *jñānakalā* as the power of knowledge of jīva (*jñāna-śabda-vācya-jīvasya vidyā-śakti* / Hence—*upāsanāviśiṣṭa-pratyagātma*.

1. *mano-mūlo hi saṁsāraḥ* ! Śruti text quoted by ŚR and GS.
2. *anna-mayaṁ he saumya manaḥ* ! —Chāndogya up. 6.6.5 6.7.6.
— quoted by commentators.

CHAPTER EIGHT[1]

The Story of King Sagara[2]

Śrī Śuka said :

1. Harita was the son of Rohita; from Harita was born Campa who built up the city of Campā.[3] Campa's son was Sudeva whose son was Vijaya.

2. Vijaya's son was Bharuka (Bhiruka, Ruruka in other *purāṇas*). From him was born Vṛka whose son was Bāhuka. This king, being deprived of his kingdom by his enemies, repaired to the forest along with his wife.

3. When the queen was about to immolate herself in fire along with the (body of the) old king who died, she was prevented (from ascending the funeral pyre) by sage Aurva who knew about her pregnancy.

4. Having come to know of this (her pregnancy), she was administered poison (mixed) with food by her co-wives (to kill her alongwith the child). But he (the son) was born along with it (poison). Hence, this highly glorious son was named *Sa-gara* (born with poison).

1. This chapter deals with the following rulers of the solar race in a chronological order :
Rohita (mentioned in ch.7)→Harita→Campa (also known as *Cañcu* in *Vāyu P.* 3.88.119 and other *purāṇas*)→Sudeva→Vijaya→Bharuka→(also called Ruruka, Karuka, Bhiruka in other *purāṇas*)→Vṛka→Bāhuka→Sagara →(Asamañjasa→*Aṁśumān* mentioned only). The *Matsya* group of Purāṇas (viz. Matsya, Padma and Agni) drop all kings between Rohita and Vṛka, possibly being unimportant.

2. The Sagar legend is very popular with all the *purāṇas*, vide *Vāyu* 3.88.123-167, *Brahmāṇḍa* III. chs 47-55, *Matsya* briefly in 12.39-43, *Śiva-Umā Saṁhitā*. 38.29-57, and Textual similarity (including repetition of identical verses) in three different groups of *purāṇas* leads one to assume a common source which though not extant now, can be reconstructed.

3. A site at a distance of four miles to the west of Bhagalpur. It was the capital of Aṅga, of which Karṇa was the King at the time of MBH. Even then, it was a place of pilgrimage (*MBH. Vana* 85, 14-15). It is full of ancient Buddhist and Jain relics as it was sacred to both the sects due to the association of the founders of their sects and other famous teachers of their sects. The Chānd Sadāgar and Behulā episode is supposed to have happened here and a fair in honour of Behulā is held here.

5A. Sagara became a universal monarch. It is his sons who excavated the sea (and hence it became known after them as *Sāgara*).

5B to 7A. He conquered Tālajaṅghas[1], Yavanas[2], Śakas[3], Haihayas[4] and Barbaras[5], but to honour the promise given by his preceptor Aurva, he did not massacre them, but caused them to wear loathsome dress and appearance; some were got clean-shaven; some were left with beards and moustaches only (with no hair on the head); some had only hair on the head (but with clean-shaven face); some had only half-shaven heads; some were made to remove the under-garment, while others, of the upper garment[6].

7B & 8. In accordance with the guidance in *yoga* given by Aurva, he (sagara) worshipped by horse-sacrifices Lord Hari, the very Soul of all Vedas and of gods, who was his own self and the Supreme Ruler. God Indra stole away the sacrificial animal (the horse consecrated for sacrifice), and let free (to wander all over the earth).

9. In compliance of their father's command, the proud sons of (Sagara's queen) Sumati, excavated the earth on all sides, in search of the horse.

1. A famous *Kṣattriya* clan known after its founding father Tālajaṅgha, a descendant of Śaryāti—*MBH. Anu* 30.7 also *Vana* 106.8

It was one of the five clans of Haihayas.

2. The Ionians; the Indo-Greeks who settled in the former NWF. provinces and the adjoining parts.

3. Śakas or Scythians came from the valleys of the Oxus and the Jaxartes and they conquered a part of Western India and settled there.

4. Haihayas were a branch of the Yādava clan. They ruled at Māhiṣmatī, near modern Māndhatā in Nimar District M.P., on the Narmadā.

5. D.C. Sircar identifies these as a people of the country called Varvara or Barbara which lay in the lower valley of the Indus, where the city of Barbara was probably founded by Alexander. Sircar rejects S. Levi's identification with Barbaria of the *Periplus*, the Coast of Somali on the Gulf of Aden. (SGAMI p. 233). The close association of Śakas and Barbaras in *Purāṇas* suggests their geographical proximity, which rules out S.Levy's suggestion of its location in Africa.

6. This is an explanation of the fashions of dress and hair-cut of these extra-Indian tribes, whose war-like qualities (*Kṣatriyatva*) are tacitly admitted, but are relegated to non-Indian status.

10-11. They saw the horse in the north-eastern direction near the sage Kapila. "Here is the thief, the horse-lifter, who sits with his eyes closed. Let this wicked fellow be killed forthwith." Shouting thus, those sixty thousand (sons of Sagara) with their arms lifted, attacked him when the sage opened his eyes.

12. (Firstly) Being deprived of their good sense through the deceptive influence of Indra and now being (as good as) dead through the transgression (insult) committed by them against a great personage (like the sage Kapila), they were reduced to ashes in a moment by the fire that emanated from their own bodies.[1]

13. It is not correct to say that the sons of the emperor were burnt down through the wrath of the sage (Kapila). How can *Tamas* in the form of anger be imagined in the case of that sage who was abode of pure *Sattva* (undiluted by *Rajas* and *Tamas*) and whose person purified the whole universe? It is as impossible as the sticking of the particles of the earthly dust to the sky.

14. It is his promulgation in the form of *Sāṅkhya* system of philosophy, which serves here as a strong and safe boat by means of which a person desirous of Liberation (from *Saṁsāra*) crosses this sea in the form of *Saṁsāra* which is so difficult to cross, and is a road (destined) to death. How can there exist at all the sense of difference (as between a friend or a foe) in the omniscient sage who is no other than the Supreme Lord?

15. He who is (wrongly) called Asamañjasa ('unreasonable' but was actually very reasonable and virtuous) was the son of the king (Sagara) born of his queen Keśinī. His son named Aṁśumān engaged himself in achieving his grandfather's interest.

16. Asamañjasa showed himself outwardly as being unreasonable. He was in his former birth a *yogī* who deviated from his *yogic* path on account of evil association, and was born now with the recollection of the past life. (He dissociated himself from all).

1. According to *Śiva P. Umā-saṁhitā* 38.53-54. only four sons, viz. Harṣaketu, Suketu, Dharmaratha and Pañcajana were spared.

17. He used to behave in a manner censured (by people) in this world, and committed acts unliked by his kith and kin. (For example) he hurled children in the Śarayu while they were playing and thus harassed the public.

18. As he conducted himself in this way, he was abandoned (transported beyond his kingdom) setting aside his parental affection. By his yogic power he showed them all the children alive and then he departed (from Ayodhyā).

19. Having seen all the children returned alive, hale and hearty, the citizens of Ayodhyā were astonished Oh King ! But king Sagara was however, filled with remorse.

20. Aṁśumān, being commanded by the king to find out the sacrificial horse, went along the path dug out by his uncles and perceived the horse near a heap of ashes.

21. Seeing there Lord Viṣṇu in the form of a sage named Kapila, sitting nearby, Aṁśumān folding his palms and bowing down respectfully, prayed him with concentrated mind.

Aṁśumān prayed :

22*. Neither through his concentration of mind in spiritual meditation nor through his capacity of abstract reasoning could Brahmā, even to this day, either perceive you or comprehend you as being transcendental to himself.[1] How is it possible for others like us, who belong to different species

*(i) VR.: Not even *yogins* can clearly realize, even to this day, the essentially true nature of you, the Supreme Soul, in spite of their attempts through concentration of mind in spiritual meditation or through their reasoning capacity. How can other persons like us who are not *yogins* but are creations of *Hiraṇya-garbha* (god Brahmā) and others, who, in their turn, are products of your mind, body, intellect, comprehend your true nature.

(ii) VJ.: The unborn god Viriñci (Brahmā) could not, to this day, perceive you to be a part or ray (*aṁśa*) of the Supreme Soul. Due to your infinite nature, he cannot correctly comprehend you directly or indirectly through his power of mental concentration in spiritual meditation. How can others—other than Viriñci—who are devoid of meditational power and reasoning capacity, comprehend you ? For these derive their knowledge through their sense-organs which are presided over by Marīci and other Lords of creations, who, in their turn, are the products of Viriñci's body and mind.

1. *ātmanaḥ param*—Brahmā's predecessor, father, Lord Viṣṇu.

of beings (such as gods, sub-human beings and human beings), and who, being later creations from his mind, body and intellect (and as such are the products of *Sattva*, *Tamas* and *Rajas*), are devoid of the light (of spiritual wisdom), to realize or comprehend you.

23*. The embodied beings[1] (such as gods, men) whose understanding is deluded by your Māyā and who, being dominated by the three *guṇas* (*sattva*, *rajas* and *tamas*) can cognise (lit. get light of wisdom on) external objects only, do not know you, (even though you) abide in them (as their Soul, the Indwelling controller). What they perceive are only products of *guṇas*, the objects of senses, while they are in the waking and dreaming states, and utter darkness (total ignorance), when (immersed) in deep sleep.

24. How can an ignorant person like me reflect upon you who are an embodiment of knowledge (and hence not an object of knowledge), and capable of being contemplated only by sages like Sanandana who have by their power (or since their very inception) destroyed the *guṇas* of Māyā, and the resultant notion of difference and delusion.

25.** We salute to you, the Ancient-most Eternal Person Whose assumption of the (present) body is for the sake of

*(i) VR. : The corporeal beings, being under the dominance of three *guṇas*, see i.e. brood over *guṇas* or objects of senses, or perceive the body which is the product of *tamas* i.e. *pradhāna*, but not the indwelling soul, as they can cognise external objects only.

(ii) VJ. : The embodied beings are classified according to the dominance of three *guṇas* viz. *sattva*, *rajas* and *tamas*. Out of them, human beings, being dominated by *rajas*, are intent on the first three objectives of human life (*dharma*, *artha*, *Kāma*) and hence perceive objects of senses, and are not interested in *Mokṣa*. The Asuras are dominated by *Tamas*, and have their minds deluded by Māyā, the binding power of Hari, and they see. i.e. experience the blinding darkness of hell. These are ignorant about their soul, and do not perceive Lord Viṣṇu who dwells in them.

1. *dehabhājaḥ*—Gods, men etc. who identify their bodies with the Soul—GD.

**VJ. : Who are not affected by the *guṇas* of Māyā (e.g. *Sattva*) and are devoid of *Karmas* and the material body (evolved out of *guṇas*); who are different from Brahman (*sat*) and material atoms (*asat*); your assumption of the body being for showering grace on the people (by imparting knowledge) and not as a result of *karmas*. Hence, you are above miseries.

imparting spiritual wisdom, but Who, (as a matter of fact), are absolutely free from (the laws of) cause and effect or from merits and demerits, and are devoid of (material) body, actions (*karmas*), name and form which are the products of the *guṇas* of Māyā, Oh Serene Sage.[1]

26. In this world, a creation of your Illusive Power (Māyā), people whose intellect is deluded by their being steeped in lust, greed, envy and infatuation, presume that houses and other objects of senses are real and wander in *Saṁsāra*.

27. Oh glorious Lord ! The very Soul of all beings ! Today, simply by seeing (meeting) you, the strong bondage (lit. cord) of our delusion (in identification of the body with the Soul), which is the root-cause of our desires (for objects of pleasure), actions (striving for securing them), the sense-organs (the tools of such actions), is cut asunder.

Śrī Śuka said :

28. The illustrious sage Kapila whose glory was thus eulogised, blessed Aṁśumān mentally, and addressed to him as follows, Oh King.

The glorious sage (Kapila) said :

29. "Oh child ! This is the horse, the (consecrated) sacrificial beast of your grand-father. It may (now) be taken away (by you). These are your forebears who are reduced to ashes, and deserve (need) to be purified by the waters of the Gaṅgā and by nothing else."

30. Aṁśumān circumambulated Kapila, and securing his grace by bowing him down with his head, brought the sacrificial horse. Sagara completed the remaining part of the sacrifice with that (consecrated) animal.

31. Having entrusted the kingdom to Aṁśumān, Sagara who became free from all cravings and from bond of attach-

1. *OR* (1) Oh Sage, who have subdued Māyā and have been devoid of *guṇas*.

(2) Oh Sage in whom Māyā, its *guṇas* (and their products etc.) have been quiet and ineffective—ŚR.

ment (or the false identification of the body with soul) attained to the highest goal (Liberation from *Saṁsāra*) by following the spiritual course taught to him by the sage Aurva.

CHAPTER NINE*

The Descent of the Gaṅgā[1]; *The Story of Kalmāṣa-pāda*

Śrī Śuka said :

1. (Like his grandfather Sagara) Aṁ umān (also renounced his kingdom in favour of his son Dilīpa), and practised penance for a long time, with the desire of bringing the Gaṅgā down on the earth. But he was not successful (in his mission). In course of time, he passed away.

2. His son Dilīpa also proved unsuccessful, and met death (in his attempt to bring down Gaṅgā). His son Bhāgīratha performed very severe austerities.

3. The goddess (Gaṅgā) manifested herself to him and said, "I am pleased (with your penance). I shall bestow on you the boon (desired by you)." Being assured thus, the king bowed low (in humility), and submitted to her his object (of performing the penance).

* This chapter describes the Solar race from King Aṁśumān to Khaṭvāṅga. The genealogy (or rather the chronological order of kings) is as follows :

Aṁśumān→ Dilīpa →Bhagīratha→Śruta→Nābha→Sindhu-dvīpa→ Ayutāyu → Ṛtuparṇa → Sarvakāma→ Sudās → Saudāsa (Kalmāṣapāda) →Aśmaka→Mūlaka (Nārīkavaca) → Daśaratha→Aiḍāvīḍa→ Viśvasaha→Khaṭvāṅga (Bh.P. omits the name of King Ambarīṣa Nabhāgi, the descendant of Śruta, vide *VP*.4.4.36, *Śiva P.Umā* 39. 9-10 *Vāyu P*. 3.88, 169-71.)

1. The Descent of the Gaṅgā is another popular legend recorded in the *MBH. Vana*. chs. 108, 109, *Bhīṣma* 6.28-50; Vālmiki *Rāmāyaṇa—Bāla* Sargas 43-44; *Brahmāṇḍa* P. II.56. 34-50.

It is probably a race-memory how three generations of the Solar race tried to irrigate the parched plains of the kingdom of Ayodhyā.

4. (She replied:) "Is there anyone capable of sustaining my force while I descend on the earth. Otherwise, I shall penetrate the crust of the earth and go down to Rasātala, the 6th sub-terranean region, Oh King.

5. Besides, I am not willing to go to the earth. Men will wash of their sins in me. Where (and how) can I absolve myself of that sin ? Some remedy on this should also be considered, Oh King."

Bhagīratha said :

6* "Righteous persons who have renounced actions (for obtaining worldly objects), and have controlled their sense-organs, and persons devoted to the contemplation of Brahman, (or prominent knowers of Brahman), are themselves capable of purifying the world. By the contact of their body (while bathing in you) they will annihilate your sins, as Lord Hari, the destroyer of sins, abides in them.

7. God Rudra, who is the very Soul of corporeal beings, and in Whom is woven this universe, warp and woof, as threads are interwoven in a piece of cloth, will bear your force."

7A. Having heard this speech of Bhagīratha, Gaṅgā advised, "In that case, propitiate the great god Śiva, for sustaining the velocity of my waters."

8. Having spoken thus,[1] the king propitiated god Śiva by his penance. Within a short period (of penance), Lord Śiva was also highly pleased with him.

9. Granting the prayer of the King with the words, "Be it so", Lord Śiva who is always benevolent to the world, carefully bore on his head the Gaṅgā whose waters are hallowed by the feet of Hari.

*VJ : Pious persons endowed with quiescence, self-control etc., completely free from desires (for heaven, pleasures etc.), thoroughly devoted to meditation of Brahman and thus established in Brahman and purifiers of the world, will annihilate your sins by their physical contact (e.g. washing hands or feet in your waters or by ablutions).

VR and GD. : As Lord Hari, the destroyer of sins, abides in them, the question of transfer of your sins by them to others does not arise, as Hari annihilates the sins altogether.

1. v.l. : *tac chrutvā*—Hearing this—VR.

10. The royal sage Bhagīratha led Gaṅgā, the purifier of the Universe, to the spot where the bodies of his fore-fathers (great-grand-uncles), lay reduced to ashes.

11. (Closely on the heels of) Bhagīratha who rode (in advance) in a chariot speeding with the velocity of the wind she rushed after him, hallowing the countries or regions (through which she flowed), and bathed the burnt-up sons of Sagara (with her waters).

12. The sons of Sagara, though struck down by their offence against a Brāhmaṇa (sage Kapila), attained to the celestial regions simply through the contact of her waters with their ashes.

13. Merely by the contact of her waters with the ashes to which their bodies were reduced, the sons of Sagara ascended the heaven. What need be said in case of those who observe religious vows and serve her with faith ?

14. What has been glorified above about (the hallowing power of) the heavenly river is not very miraculous, inasmuch as She springs from the lotus-like feet of the Infinite Lord (Viṣṇu) and puts an end to *Saṁsāra.*

15. Concentrating their minds properly with faith in Him, pure-minded sages shed off their contacts with (and attachment to) the three *guṇas* of *Prakṛti* (and its product—their body,—misidentified with the soul)—which is so very difficult to cast off—and have instantly attained identity with Brahman.

16. Śruta was born from Bhagīratha who had another son named Nābha. His son was Sindhudvīpa from whom was born Ayutāyu.

17. Ayutāyu's son was Ṛtuparṇa, a friend of Nala who, in exchange of imparting the secret technique of the play of dice to Nala, learnt from him the equestrian science (the secret of managing horses). His (Ṛtuparṇa's) son was Sarvakāma.

18. From his loins was born Sudās whose son was the husband of Madayantī, Oh King. People called him Mitrasaha, and rarely as Kalmāṣapāda. He became a demon through the curse of Vasiṣṭha, but remained issueless in consequence of his own act.

King (*Parīkṣit*) *asked* :

19. We wish to know the reason or the occasion of the pronouncement of the curse by preceptor Vasiṣṭha on the great-souled son of Sudās. Be pleased to narrate it to us, if there be no secret about it.

Śrī Śuka said :

20. As the tradition goes, king Saudāsa (the son of Sudās) happened to kill a certain demon, while on hunting expedition. He allowed his brother to escape. He (the Rākṣasa's brother) went away with a determination to wreak revenge.

21. Remembering the offence (of killing his brother) committed by the king, and disguising himself as the cook of the king in the palace, he dressed human flesh and presented it for service to the king's preceptor Vasiṣṭha, who came there to dine.

22. Perceiving easily that a prohibited article of food (human flesh) was about to be served to him, the venerable sage flared up in rage, and cursed the king, "You will turn into an ogre by this improper act of yours."

23. Having come to know that, that act (serving of human flesh) was committed by a demon (and that the king was innocent), he limited the duration of his curse to (a period of twelve years. But (in the meanwhile) Saudāsa took water into the hollow of his joined palms and was ready to counter-curse his preceptor (who uttered the unjustifiable imprecation).

24. He was however prevented (from cursing his preceptor) by (his queen) Madayantī. The king found that all the cardinal points, the sky, the earth were all instinct with life. (And lest he should injure living beings), he let the water be charged with wrathful *mantras*, fall on his own feet (and thus justified his epithet—*mitra-saha*, indulgent towards friends).

25. Changed into a demonic state, and with both of his feet turned black (by the water charged by him with a curse), he happened to see a forest-dwelling couple of Brāhmaṇas in the act of sexual intercourse.

26. Overpowered with hunger, he caught hold of the Brāhmaṇa, when his wife helplessly appealed to him, "Your honour is not a born ogre. You are veritably a great hero (a chariot-warrior) belonging directly to the race of Ikṣvākus.

27. Oh warrior ! You are the husband of Madayantī. It does not behove you to perpetrate unrighteous deeds. Be pleased to restore to me who am desirous of having a child, the Brāhmaṇa, my husband, who has not accomplished his purpose.

28. Oh King ! This human body is capable of securing all the objects (*puruṣārthas*) in human life. Hence the destruction of this body is called the total destruction of all purposes.

29. This Brāhmaṇa is learned and endowed with asceticism, virtuous character and other qualities. He desires to propitiate Brahman which is designated as *Mahā-puruṣa* (Viṣṇu) who abides in all beings as their Inner Controller, but lies obscured in them on account of *guṇas*.

30. This being the case, how does this prominent Brāhmaṇa sage deserve death at the hands of a great royal sage like you, even as the death of a son at the hands of the father, Oh knower of the righteous path ?

31. Your worship is respected by the righteous. How do you approve of the death of the righteous, sinless (innocent) *Śrotriya* who is well-versed in the Vedas (or innocent like a child in the womb), any more than killing of a cow.

32. If he is to be your victim, please devour me first, inasmuch as I shall not live without him for a minute, and am as good as dead."

33. Disregarding the piteous appeal of the helpless bewailing Brāhmaṇa woman, Saudāsa deluded by (his preceptor's) curse, devoured the Brāhmaṇa, as a tiger would prey upon a beast.

34. Finding her impregnator (husband) eaten up by a cannibal, the Brāhmaṇa woman lamented herself. Flying in a rage, the chaste lady uttered the imprecation on the king.

35. "You wicked fellow ! Inasmuch as my husband has been devoured by you while I was afflicted with sexual desire, your death too is indicated to follow while engaged in sexual intercourse, you foolish one."

36. Having thus cursed king Mitrasaha, the woman who was determined to attain to the region of her husband, consigned to flames his bones in a burning fire, and followed the course of her husband (by immolating herself to fire).

37. When freed from the curse at the end of the twelfth year, he (Saudāsa) proceeded to have sexual intercourse (with his queen), but the queen who knew well the imprecation of the Brāhmaṇa lady prevented him from that attempt.

38. Thenceforth, he gave up all pleasures with women and he remained issueless by this act. It was with his consent that the sage Vasiṣṭha begot an issue on queen Madayantī.

39. For seven years she carried the foetus and did not deliver. Vasiṣṭha then hit her abdomen with a stone, and the son so born came to be known as Aśmaka.

40. From Aśmaka was born Mūlaka who was protected on all sides (from Paraśurāma) by women, and hence he is called *Nārī-kavaca* (women-armoured). He is called Mūlaka as he was the root of further pro-creation of the Kṣatriya race, when it was being exterminated by Paraśurāma.

41. From Mūlaka sprang forth Daśaratha of whom a son, Aiḍaviḍa was born. His son was King Viśvasaha whose son Khaṭvāṅga became the sovereign ruler of the world.

42. Being entreated by gods, the invincible king killed a number of demons in the battle. Learning (from gods) that only one *muhūrta* (48 minutes) of his life is left, he hurried back to his capital (in a celestial car) and concentrated his mind on the Supreme Lord.

43. (He mused to himself). Neither my life nor my sons, nor my wealth nor the earth, nor my empire or my queens are dearer to me than the Brāhmaṇa race who form our family-deities.

44. Not even in my childhood, my mind ever took delight in unrighteousness. I did not look upon anything other than the Lord of hallowed reputation (Viṣṇu) as the reality.

45. A boon of my choice was offered for bestowal on me by gods, the rulers of the three worlds. But as I contemplate on the creator of all beings, I do not seek any object of desire.[1]

1. As the boon will come in the way of my realization of the Lord —VR. Gd. BP.

46. The celestials themselves have got their minds and senses distracted (by objects of senses), and do not realize the beloved, eternal Soul who stays established in their own heart. Need it be said that human and other beings, characterised by *rajas* and *tamas*, can never do so.

47. I shall give up, through deep devotion to the Creator of the Universe, attachment to *guṇas* (the product of *guṇas* viz. the object of senses) which has been firmly fixed in the mind, by the very nature of things, but which are the creation of the Illusive Power (Māyā) of the Lord, and hence are as unreal and transitory as the city of Gandharvas in the sky, and take asylum in him.

48. Having determined thus by his reasoning capacity and intellect, which was attracted towards himself (and thus possessed) by Lord Nārāyaṇa, he discarded ignorance[1] and the consequent false notions of the identity of the body with Soul and attained to his essential nature (which is Brahmahood).

49.* (The state) that is the Supreme Brahman which is very subtle but not a void[2] though it is as good as intangible, as it is beyond the rage of expression, and which the devotees of Lord Viṣṇu sing as the glorious Lord Vāsudeva.

Any act except the propitiation of Hari, is not acceptable to me as it is not conducive to Liberation—VJ.

1. *hitvānyabhavam ajñānam*—Having given up his body.—VR.

*VJ. : The stage to which Vedantins call the Supreme Brahman, the *yogins* describe as very subtle, beyond the ken of senses like the sky. Some non-vedic thinkers (viz. the Buddhists, especially the followers of Mādhyamika school) assume it as void; but it is really positive (and not void) and which the followers of the Pañcarātra school (Sātvatas) call Lord Vasudeva.

JG. With his intellect (mind) possessed by Nārāyaṇa, Khaṭvāṅga attained to Brahmā's region in a *muhūrta*.

2. BP. *aśūnya*—(i) Proved as positively existent and not non-existent like horns of a hare.

(ii) *Śūnya* is destitute of *guṇas*, attributeless. *a-śūnya* means full of infinite excellences, conducive to the good of all or devoid of *guṇas* which deserve to be discarded.

Sva-bhāva : The *brahmabhāva* implies devoted service to the Lord as of a chaste woman to her husband.

CHAPTER TEN[1]

The Story of Rāma[2]

Śrī Śuka continued :

1. To king Khaṭvāṅga was born Dīrghabāhu, whose son was Raghu of extensively spread renown. From him sprang the emperor Aja of whom Daśaratha was born.

2. When earnestly prayed by celestials this[3] glorious Lord Hari, directly and entirely composed of Brahman[4] Itself, divided Himself in four parts, and was born as Daśaratha's sons under the designations Rāma, Lakṣmaṇa, Bharata and Śatrughna—himself in its entirety as Rāma and as his rays (*aṁśa*) in Lakṣmaṇa, Bharata and Śatrughna.

3. His life and works have been described in details and also heard by sages who have clearly understood the Truth.

1. This chapter covers only five generations :
Khaṭvāṅga (mentioned in ch. 9) → Dīrghabāhu → Raghu → Aja → Daśaratha→Rāma.

2. The Rāma legend is one of the most popular ones in Brahmanism, Buddhism and Jainism. Limiting ourselves to Brahmanical Sanskrit epics or *Purāṇas*, the most important source is Vālmīki's *Rāmāyaṇa*. Its critical edition (M.S. University, Baroda) shows that the Rāma legend is better preserved in the *MBH Vana* 274-293 (also ch. 148-152, *Sabhā* 50, *Droṇa*, 59) than in the vulgate of *Vālmīki Rām*. The spurious nature of many cantos, the *Bāla* and *Uttara Kāṇḍas*, is now established. We find Rāma legend in *Padma P.*, *Pātāla khaṇḍa* chs. 1-68 (Rāma's Aśvamedha), and ch. 116-117 (a slightly different version in prose and verse); *Garuḍa P.*I.143, *Nārada P.* I.79.7-26; II. 75, *Agni P.* Chs. 5-11; *Skandha P. Brahma khaṇḍa—Dharmāraṇya* ch. 30; *Vāyu P.III*.88.183r197; *Devī Bhāgavata* III. chs. 21-30 and in *Upapurāṇas* like *Nṛsiṁha* chs. 47-52, *Saura* ch.30 and later versions like *Adhyātma* and *Ānanda Rāmāyaṇas*. The Rāma problem is extensively studied by Indian and Western scholars. (vide A.D. Pusalkar: *Studies in Epics and Purāṇas*, pp. 189-205). A comparison of Rāma legend in the Bh.P. with those in the above *Purāṇas* is beyond the scope of this work. But the special feature of the legend in the Bh. P. is the non-mention of fire-ordeal of Sītā after the conquest of Laṅkā, and at the time of horse-sacrifice afterwards. After her abandonment by Rāma, Sītā does not return to Ayodhyā, but after entrusting her children to sage Vālmīki, meditating on Rāma she enters in a cavity in the earth never to return.

3. This whom you have witnessed in your mother's womb—GS.

4. The main subject or import of the Vedas—VJ.

The story of the Lord of Sītā might have been listened by you many times.

4. May that Lord of the Kosala (country) protect us—the Lord who gave up his kingdom for honouring the pledge given by his father, and wandered from forest to forest on his lotus-feet that were too tender to bear the touch of the palms of his beloved Sītā (who pressed and massaged them to relieve their fatigue), and whose fatigue from journey was soothed by the leader of the monkeys (Hanumān or Sugrīva) and his younger brother Lakṣmaṇa; the Lord who constructed a bridge at the request of the deity presiding over the ocean, which was terrified at the display of his frowning eyebrows, excited by his wrath at the separation from his beloved, caused (by Rāvaṇa who was incited to do so) by disfiguring of Śūrpaṇakhā (by Lakṣmaṇa's mutilating her nose and ears), and thus who was like a conflagration to the forest (in the form) of the wicked (demons).

5. During the sacrificial session of Viśvāmitra, prominent demons and nocturnal predators like Mārīca and others were (single-handedly) despatched by him while Laksmaṇa was simply witnessing.

6. In the hall specially erected for Sītā's free election of her (prospective) husband, wherein were assembled eminent warriors of the world, Rāma, like unto a cub of an elephant sportively picking up a sugar-cane, lifted up the formidable bow of god Śiva which required three hundred bearers to bring it (at the hall), strung it, drew it and broke it in the middle, oh King.

7. Having won (as a prize) Śrī, the beautiful goddess of prosperity, who had already a place of honour on his bosom, —but is now called Sītā, who was eminently suitable to him in beauty, virtues, disposition, age and form, Rāma, on his way (to Ayodhyā), humbled down the overbearing pride and arrogance of Paraśurāma, the chief of Bhṛgus who extirpated the Kṣatriya race from the earth thrice seven times.

8. He honoured with his head (bent low) the order of his henpecked father who was bound by the noose of truthfulness (pledge to grant two boons to Kaikeyī who now demanded kingdom for her son and banishment of Rāma to forest). With

his spouse, he relinquished his kingdom, wealth, his beloved relations (like his mother etc.), friends and palace and left for the forest just as a *yogin* who has renounced all attachments, would give up his body.

9. While (armed) with an irresistible bow in his hand, he went about leading a hard life (in the forest as a model for mankind to follow), he got mutilated the features of the wicked-minded sister of Rāvaṇa (viz. Śūrpaṇakhā who wanted to devour Sītā with a view to enjoy amorous life with Rāma etc.), and killed fourteen thousand of her kinsmen of whom Khara, Triśiras and Dūṣaṇa were prominent.

10. Being enticed away from his hermitage on seeing a miraculous (golden) form of a deer (assumed by Mārīca), who was so deputed by the Ten-necked demon Rāvaṇa whose passion (for Sītā) was inflamed by listening to the description of Sītā's beauty, Rāma quickly slew Mārīca with an arrow, even as god Rudra (or Vīrabhadra) despatched Dakṣa (or Lord Nṛsiṁha killed Hiraṇyakaśipu), Oh Lord of men.

11. When, during his absence (from the hermitage) in the forest, the princess of Videha (Sītā) was abducted by the vilest demon Rāvaṇa like a wolf (stealthily carrying away a sheep), Rāma, being separated from his beloved, wandered in the forest with his brother Lakṣmaṇa simulating pitiable helplessness[1] demonstrating (to the world) the tragic fate of those who are attached to women.

12*. Rāma, whose feet are adored by gods Brahmā and Śiva even though he assumed the human form, then performed (like a son) the prescribed formal obsequies of Jaṭāyu (the king of vultures) who laid down his life (in attempting to free Sītā) for Rāma's sake; he then slew the demon Kabandha[2]

1. VJ. quotes a 'Smṛti' text which denies the possibility of affliction in the omnipresent Almighty Rāma. He feigned affliction for the public. VC. quotes *Rāma-tāpanī UP*. 1.1 and denies the possibility of affliction in Rāma, the veritable *Para-Brahman* Himself. Rāma simply gave support to *Vipralambha Śṛṅgāra-rasa*.

*Not found in VJ's text.

2. He was originally a Gandharva Prince Viśvāvasu who was blessed with immortality by god Brahmā. He arrogantly attacked Indra who, with his Vajra squeezed his head and thighs into his body. When he beg-

(whose head was in his chest and who attempted to seize Rāma and Lakṣmaṇa with his hands); he made an alliance with the monkeys. When Vāli was killed, He learnt the whereabouts of his beloved (Sītā). He then reached the shores of the ocean (near Laṅkā) with his forces of monkey chiefs (Sugrīva, Hanumān etc.).

13. (When, even after a fast of consecutive three nights, the presiding deity of the sea did not present himself, Rāma flared up in anger). The sea (its presiding deity) with alligators and acquatic animals in whom got panicky and bewildered, at the cast of his side-glance in apparent anger, and with its roar hushed up in terror, assumed a (human) form and taking on his head articles of worship approached his (Rāma's) lotus-like feet and spoke as follows :

14. "We, dull witted fellows, did not know you definitely to be the Immutable, Eternal (First) Person, the overlord of the Universe, Oh Supreme Lord. You are the Lord of *Prakṛti* (the source of *guṇas*), from the *Sattva-guṇa* out of which are evolved the celestials, from the *rajas*, the *prajāpatis* (Lord of creation) and from *tamas*, the goblin-leaders and other evil spirits.

15. May you be pleased to cross me at your sweet will. Do kill Rāvaṇa, the excreation of Viśravas who makes the three world shriek (in fear). Regain your consort, Oh hero! (Although my waters will not obstruct your movements) do construct a bridge here for the spread of your glory which (future) kings, conquerors of the quarters (world) reaching here, will sing."

16. Having constructed a bridge across the sea with mountain peaks of various sizes, covered with trees the branches of which were shaken off by monkey chiefs, Rāma, the foremost in the Raghu's race, under the supervision and guid-

ged for livelihood, he was given two long arms and a mouth on the belly. He was asked to stay near Mātaṅgāśrama in Krauñcāraṇya—a part of Daṇḍakāraṇya. When Rāma and Lakṣmaṇa came after Jaṭāyu's funeral, he caught hold of them. Rāma and Lakṣmaṇa cut his hands. He asked who they were and then told them his life story and fell dead. When they cremated his body, a Gandharva King (Kabandha's former self) rose in the air, advised Rāma to go to Sugrīva for more information about Sītā.—*Vālmīki Rām.*· *Araṇya Kāṇḍa*—Sargas 70-72.

ance of Vibhīṣaṇa, and accompanied by the forces of Vānara chiefs like Sugrīva, Nīla, Hanumān, entered Laṅkā which was already burnt by (Hanumān) previously.

17. Like a river churned up by herds of elephants, the city of Laṅkā was in a state of commotion when its playgrounds, barns and granaries, treasuries, doorways, citygates, assembly-halls, roofs, balconies and pigeon-cots were barricaded and besieged by the armies of the monkey-chiefs, and platforms, flagstaffs, gold-vases (on either sides of entrances) and public squares were destroyed.

18. Observing the state of siege, the king of Rākṣasas (Rāvaṇa) despatched against them all his followers like Nikumbha, Kumbha, Dhūmrākṣa, Durmukha, Surāntaka, Narāntaka and others, and his sons Indrajit, Prahasta, Atikāya, Vikampana and others, and finally (his brother) Kumbhakarṇa.

19. Accompanied by Sugrīva, Lakṣmaṇa, Hanumān, Gandhamāda, Nīla, Aṅgada, Jāmbavān the bear, Panasa and others, Rāma marched against the Rākṣasa army impenetrable on account of its weaponry like swords, spikes, bows, *prāsas* (darts), double-edged swords, lances, arrows, iron clubs and long swords.

20. Aṅgada and all the generals of Rāma's forces fell upon the Rākṣasa army consisting of battalions of elephants, infantry, chariots and cavalry, and engaged them in duels and struck them down with trees, rocks, maces and arrows, as their Lord Rāvaṇa had lost his auspicious luck by the touch of Sītā (in abduction).

21. Perceiving the destruction of his armies, Rāvaṇa, the king of Rākṣasas, got enraged. Ascending his aerial car Puṣpaka, he attacked Rāma who rode resplendent in a refulgent chariot brought from the celestial region by Mātali (the charioteer of god Indra). Rāvaṇa struck Rāma with sharp arrows with horse-shoe-shaped heads.

22. Rāma scolded him : "You, excretion of a maneater ! During our absence our beloved was taken away by you, a wicked fellow, even as a dog (steals away things when the house-owner is away). To you, a shameless fellow, I, like the god of death of irresistible power meting out the puni-

shment to the perpetrator of a sin for his act, shall award the fruit of your detestable action, just now."

23. Reproaching Rāvaṇa thus, Rāma shot his arrow that was already fixed on the bow. It pierced Rāvaṇa's heart as if with the impact of the thunderbolt. Like a meritorious person whose balance of good acts is exhausted, Rāvaṇa fell from his aerial car, with blood gushing out of his ten mouths, while his partisans cried out 'Alas !'.

24. Thousands of Rākṣasa women (whose husbands were killed[1]) along with Mandodarī (Rāvaṇa's chief queen) came out of Laṅkā and rushed to the battle-field[1] wailing loudly.

25. They embraced their respective relatives who were struck down by Lakṣmaṇa's arrows. Beating themselves (their breasts with their own hands), those helpless ladies lamented loudly.

26. "Alas ! Oh Rāvaṇa ! Oh Lord ! The terror of the world ! Undone we are ! Bereft of you, now trampled over by the enemies, to whom can Laṅkā look up for protection ?

27. Oh highly blessed glorious Lord ! Being overwhelmed with the passion of love, you did not estimate and anticipate the potential superforce of Sītā's virtue whereby you have been reduced to this wretched condition.

28. Widowed is Laṅkā and we as well, Oh delight of your family ! Your body has become now food for vultures, your soul fit for hell."

Śrī Śuka said :

29. Under instructions from Rāma, the king of Kośalas Vibhīṣaṇa performed the prescribed funeral rites known as 'sacrifice to manes', of his relatives.

30. Thereafter, the glorious Lord Rāma caught sight of Sītā sitting under a *Śiṁśipā* tree, in the retreat of the Aśoka forest. She was emaciated and suffering from the (mental) agony, due to her separation from him.

1. Although commentators like GS., VR., GD. and BP. insist that those thousands of Rākṣasa women went to the spot where Rāvaṇa fell, the above translation is justifiable as correct, in view of the next verse—The translator

31. Perceiving his most beloved wife in that helpless condition, Rāma was moved with compassion, even though her lotus-like face began to blossom with delight, at the sight of his own self.

32-33-34-A. Having conferred on Vibhīṣaṇa the sovereignty over Laṅkā, and Lordship over the Rākṣasas, and the life-span of a *Kalpa* (a period of the life span of fourteen Manus), the glorious Lord placed her in the aerial car Puṣpaka and accompanied by brothers (Lakṣmaṇa and adopted brother Sugrīva) and Hanumān, Rāma ascended Puṣpaka. As he had completed the vow (of forest-dwelling for fourteen years), he returned to his capital (Ayodhyā), being showered on the way with flowers offered by the presiding deities of various regions, and his glorious deeds being joyously sung by gods like Brahmā and others.

34-B-36. When Rāma heard that his brother put on bark-garments only, and subsisted on barley seeds boiled in cow's urine, had grown matted hair and slept on bare ground with Kuśa grass spread over it, being extremely merciful by nature, he was deeply distressed.

37-39. Hearing of the arrival of his elder brother Rāma, Bharata took over his head the pair of wooden sandals (given to him as a token of love by Rāma) proceeded from his camp at Nandigrāma[1], along with citizens, his cabinet ministers and family preceptors. With vocal and instrumental music and in company of knowers of the Vedas loudly singing Vedic hymns, with flags of guilt edges and chariots plated with gold, and decked with beautiful banners of various colours, with gold caparisoned noble horses and warriors clad in gold armours, with artisans of different guilds and prominent courtesans and servants following on foot, and taking with him the royal insignia (such as white umbrella, chowries etc.), and valuable articles of various kinds (as presents), Bharata fell at his feet with his heart melted in tears of affection.

40. Bharata placed before him the pair of Rāma's sandals (carried on his head so far), and stood before him with

1. Modern Nandgaon, close to Bharata Kuṇḍa, eight or nine miles South of Fyzabad (U.P.)—N.L.De—GDAMI, p. 138.

folded palms, and eyes full of tears. Rāma embraced him with his arms for a long time bathing him with waters that flowed from his eyes.

41. Rāma along with Sītā and Lakṣmaṇa paid personal obeisance to the worthiest of the Brāhmaṇas, and he (in turn) was bowed down by his subjects.

42. Seeing that their (real) lord had returned after the lapse of a long period, the subjects of northern Kosala, waving their upper garments and showering them with flowers, danced in joy.

43. Bharata carried the pair of sandals (of Rāma); Vibhīṣaṇa along with Sugrīva wielded chowries (cāmaras) and a fan (on his either side); Hanumān, the son of the wind god, held up the umbrella.

44. Śatrughna (the youngest brother of Rāma) held a a bow and a pair of quivers, Sītā, a waterpot of gourd, Aṅgada, the sword, Jāmbuvān, the king of bears, his gold plated shield, Oh King.

45. Occupying a seat in the Puṣpaka, attended to by prominent courtesans (mentioned above), and extolled by bards, the glorious Lord Rāmacandra shone like a rising moon in the midst of planets, Oh King.

46-47. Greeted by his brothers, Rāma also entered his festive capital city. Entering the palace, he paid due respects to the wife of his preceptor (or Kaikeyī and Sumitrā), his own mother, Kausalyā, the preceptors and elderly persons, his friends and younger (brothers etc.), and was worshipped by them in return. Sītā, the princess of Videha, and Lakṣmaṇa paid respect with due formalities.

48. Just as (dead) bodies get up after the return of the vital principle (life), the mothers were as if inspired with life when their sons returned. They placed their respective sons on their lap, and bathed them in the flood of their tears, and shed off their grief (of separation for their sons).

49. Having got removed (cut off) Rāma's matted locks of hair, the preceptor Vasiṣṭha, along with elderly persons, sprinkled over him the waters of the four seas, holy rivers etc., as the coronation ceremony even as Bṛhaspati did, as per procedure laid down in *Śāstras*, to Indra.

50. Having taken a full bath including his head (the matted hair whereof were dressed off), Rāma, attired richly and adorned with wreaths of flowers and ornaments, appeared resplendent with his elegently dressed and richly adorned (younger) brother and his consort Sītā.

51. When respectfully requested with a bow (to occupy the throne) by his brother Bharata, Rāma accepted the throne and protected in a fatherly way, his subjects who were devoted to their righteous duties according to the characteristics of their respective class in society (*varṇa*) and stage in life (*āśrama*). The subjects on their part regarded him as their father.

52. While Rāma, a king, expert in Dharma (Law and righteous duties of everyone) ruled and brought happiness to every being, the period of his reign was like the *Kṛta* Age (the Golden Age) even though actually the Age called Tretā was then, current.

53. (During his reign) forests, rivers, mountains, subcontinents, continents and seas—all yielded whatever was desired by the subjects, Oh prominent Bhārata.

54. While Rāma, (the incarnation of) Lord Viṣṇu was the king, there was no trouble from anxieties, diseases, old age, fatigue, pain, sorrow, fear, exhaustion. Even death did not take the toll of unwilling persons.

55. Strict in the observance of the vow of having only one wife throughout his life, leading a pious life of a royal sage, and of pure character, he himself performed strictly his duties as a householder, teaching thereby (a model life) to the world.

56. By her deep love, obedience, pious character, disciplined modesty, intelligence and bashfulness, the chaste queen Sītā who understood the mind of her Lord, captivated Rāma's heart.

CHAPTER ELEVEN

The Story of Rāma (concluded)

Śrī Śuka said :

1. The glorious Lord Rāma who was educated in his preceptor's academy[1], worshipped his ownself, viz. the Supreme Lord (Viṣṇu) who represents all gods in his person, by performing sacrifices with excellent materials.[2]

2. (When the sacrifice was concluded), the Lord donated as sacrificial fee the eastern direction (eastern part of his empire) to the *Hotṛ* (the sacrificial priest who recites the *mantras* from the *Ṛgveda*), the Southern quarter to the sacrificial priest called *Brahmā*, the Western part to the *adhvaryu* (reciter of *Sūktas* from the *Yajurveda*), northern direction (northern part of his empire) to the priest that sang *Sāma* hymns in the sacrifice.

3. To his preceptor (Vasiṣṭha), he gave as grant the remaining portion of the land at the centre, considering a Brāhmaṇa who is devoid of any craving or desire, deserves all this.

4. In this way he was left with his clothes and ornaments (that were on his person), while the queen Sītā (princess of Videha) had only those ornaments which were essential for a lady whose husband is alive (the rest, she distributed to Brahmaṇa ladies).

5. Perceiving this affection of the Lord who treated Brāhmaṇas as gods, the Brāhmaṇas were highly pleased and with their hearts overwhelmed with affection, returned all the gifts to him and said :

6. "Oh illustrious Lord ! What is it that you have not given to us when entering into our hearts you dispel the darkness (of ignorance) by your effulgence, Oh ruler of the world.

7. We bow down to you, Oh Rāma who regard Brāhmaṇas as gods, and whose intelligence (i.e. knowledge) is boundless and unrestricted. You are the leader of those

1. *ācāryavān*, cf.
ācāryavān puruṣo veda—Chāndogya up. 6.14.2
2. Conducted by excellent sage like Vasiṣṭha—VR.

possessing excellent renown. Your feet are being meditated upon by sages and recluses".

8 Once upon a time, while Rāma went about in disguise and unnoticed at night, with a desire to know the pulse of the public, he overheard somebody speaking with reference to his queen Sītā.

9. "I would not accept you a wicked, unchaste woman who lived in the house of a stranger. Rāma, an exorbitant doter of that woman Sītā, might be retaining her, but I am not Rāma to have you again."

10. In this way, Sītā was abandoned by her husband who was afraid of the myriad-tongued, ignorant, unplacative public. She arrived at the hermitage of Vālmīki, the son of Pracetas.

11. Then being pregnant, in due course, she gave birth to twins—sons who came to be called Kuśa and Lava. The sage Vālmīki performed their purificatory rites (*jātakarma*).

12. Lakṣmaṇa had two sons known as Aṅgada and Citraketu (Candraketu, Cakraketu), and Bharata's sons were Takṣa and Puṣkala, Oh protector of the earth.

13-14. The sons of Śatrughna were Subāhu and Śrutasena. During the course of the conquest of directions (i.e. of the world) Bharata slew Gandharvas by tens of millions and collecting their wealth, he handed it over to the king Rāma. Śatrughna slew the demon Lavaṇa[1], the son of Madhu and built up a city called Mathurā, on the site of Madhuvana.

15. Sītā who was forsaken by her husband, entrusted both of her sons to the sage (Vālmīki), and meditating upon the feet of Rāma, she entered into the bowels of the earth—so goes the tradition.

16.* Hearing of that news (about Sītā) and remembering of her various excellent virtues, (even) that glorious Lord Rāma was not able to restrain his grief, despite his attempts (to suppress it) by force of reason.

17. The attachment between men and women in this way brings (in its train) fear and affliction everywhere—even

1. Although Bh.P. calls him a demon, it means an unfriendly king, for his father Madhu was not a demon (vide infra 9.24.5).

*Deleted in VJ.'s text.

in the case of rulers of the world. What needs be said of ordinary persons whose minds are fixed on their house-hold (or of a common house-holder whose mind is attached to his house and property).

18. Thereafter the Lord (Rāma) led a life of strict continence, and continued to offer oblations to the sacrificial fire, for thirteen thousand years, without any interruption.

19. Leaving behind him in the heart of his devotees who meditate upon his foliage-like tender feet which were (once) pricked with thorns in the Daṇḍaka forest, Rāma then repaired to his own self-luminous region.

20. Rāma assumed this (human) form as a sport at the request of gods. His prowess (or essential nature) is free from (i.e. has no) equals or superiors. (Glorification of feats like) the destruction of Rākṣasas with multitudes of missiles or the construction of a bridge across the sea are no great praise in the case of Rāma. (It was only his sportive action). Were the monkeys his real helpmates in exterminating the enemies? (No).

21. I seek asylum with Rāma, the chief of Raghus, as my protector, whose pure glory efficacious enough to destroy all sins and serving as decorative ornaments to the elephants supporting the cardinal points (i.e. has spread all over the world)—is sung even today by sages (like Mārkaṇḍeya) in royal courts (as that of Yudhiṣṭhira), and whose lotus-like feet are adored by the crowns of the rulers of the celestial world (e.g. Indra), and Lord of wealth (Kubera) or by Protectors of the earth).

22. All the residents of the Kosal country by whom he was touched, seen, seated (by the side) or followed, attained to that region (*Mokṣa*) where persons expert in *yoga* go.

23* Oh King! A person who treasures up in his mind the story of Rāma, (heard) through his ears, and exercises

*VJ : 'By merely listening to the name of Rāma, one becomes free from the bondage of *karma*. He quotes the following verse indicating how the whole world was imbued with Rāma, when Rāma was ruling:

rāmo rāmo rāma iti sarveṣām abhavattadā /
sarvo Rāma-mayo loko yadā Rāmas tva pālayat //

This verse is quoted by VD also.

control over his passions, becomes free from the bondage of *Karmas* (and is liberated from *Saṁsāra*).

The King (Parīkṣit) asked :

24. How did the glorious Lord Rāma behave with his brothers and relatives ? How did he conduct himself ? How did they (his kith and kin), his subjects and citizens of Ayodhyā (reciprocally) behave with their ruler ?

Śrī Śuka replied :

25. When the coronation was over, Rāma, the sovereign ruler of the three worlds, directed his brothers to conquer (and protect) all the four quarters (i.e. countries all over the world). He granted audience to all his people, and looked after the capital city along with his attendants.

26. With its streets besprinkled with water perfumed with sandal etc. and with fragrant drops of ichor exuded from the temples of elephants in rut, the city appeared to be exceedingly intoxicated with rapturous joy[1] at the return of its master.

27. It was beautified with gold domes (lit. pitchers) set on the crests of mansions, towers, assemblies, shrines, temples as well as with flags.

28. (The city was decorated) with (auspicious) arches erected with banana trees surrounded by (branches of) areca-nut trees, (or decorations consisting of bunches of fruits and plantains) banners of fancy cloth, mirrors, canopies and wreaths of flowers.

29. With articles of worship (and presents) in their hands, citizens approached him at various places and conferred blessings on him and prayed, "Be pleased to protect the earth which you lifted up formerly (in your boar-incarnation)".

30. Perceiving (hearing) that their Lord had arrived after a lapse of a long period, his subjects—both men and women—left their household duties, and with a desire to see him directly, climbed up to the tops of their houses, but though their eyes remained unsatisfied with viewing the lotus-eyed Rāma, they showered him with flowers.

1. v.l. *Vāśita-gāmiva*—like a cow overwhelmed with passion

31-32. Thereafter, the Lord entered his own residence which was once occupied by his predecessor-kings. It was rich in unlimited treasures of every kind, and was furnished with invaluable articles of furniture, coverings etc. It was beautified with doors the thresholds of which were of coral, and with rows of pillars of *Vaiḍūrya* (cat's-eye) gems, reflecting (mirror like) floors of emeralds and walls of shining crystals.

33-34. It was decorated with garlands of various colours and kinds, with banners and buntings, with cloths, gems canopies and pearls brilliant like intelligence or at places the columns of *vaidūrya* (cat's eye) were decorated with brilliant pearls and equipped with all beautiful covetable objects. It was full of fragrance of incenses and lights and was decorated with flowers. It was provided with the services of men and women who being beautiful like gods, enhanced the charm of ornaments (they put on) themselves.

35. It is reported that in that palace the glorious Lord Rāma, the chief of spiritually wise persons who find bliss in their own self, enjoyed himself with his affectionate darling Sītā.

36. Rāma whose foliage-like tender feet are contemplated upon by men, enjoyed for a great number of years all the pleasures at the proper time, without causing any violation of righteousness.

CHAPTER TWELVE

The Description of Ikṣvāku's Race[1] (*concluded*)

Śrī Śuka said :

1. From Kuśa's (Rāma's son's) loins sprang up Atithi who gave birth to Niṣadha, whose son was Nabha. Nabha's son was Puṇḍarīka from whom was born Kṣemadhanvā.

1. This chapter gives a chronological statement of the kings in the Ikṣvāku family which will end with Sumitra (118th king), as follows: (The list differs in some respects from Pargiter's Table of Royal Genealogies in AIHT.)

2. His son was Devānīka who had a son called Anīha, whose son was Pāriyātra. His son was Bala from whom was born Sthala[1] (Cala), and his son Vajra-nābha was born from an *aṁśa*—ray—of the Sun-god.

3. His son was Khagaṇa from whom Vidhṛti was born as a son. From Vidhṛti sprang Hiraṇyanābha who became a preceptor of *yoga* and a pupil of Jaimini.[2]

4. It was from Hiraṇyanābha that the sage Yājñavalkya of Kosala got instructions in *yoga* pertaining to the science of the soul (spiritual lore), which leads to the attainment of great mystical powers (*siddhis*), and cuts asunder the knot of ego or ignorance in the heart.

5. Hiraṇyanābha's son was Puṣya from whom was born Dhruvasandhi. His son was Agni-varṇa, the father of Śīghra who had Maru as his son.

6. It is this Maru who, having perfect mastery over *yoga*, is still residing at a village called Kalāpa[3] and at the end of Kali Age, he will revive the extinct solar race again.

Kuśa→Atithi→Niṣadha→Nabha→Puṇḍarīka→Kṣema-dhanvā→Devānika →Anīha→Pāriyātra→Bala→Sthala→ Vajranābha → Khagaṇa → Vidhṛti →Hiraṇyanābha→Puṣya → Dhruvasandhi → Sudarśana → Agnivarṇa → Śīghra→Maru→Praśruta→Sandhi→Amarṣaṇa→Mahasvān→ Viśvasāhva →Prasenajit → Takṣaka → Bṛhadbala (contemporary of Pāṇḍavas, but an ally of Kauravas; killed by Abhimanyu) → Bṛhadgaṇa → Urukriya → Vatsavṛddha→Prativyoma→Bhānu→Divāka → Sahadeva → Bṛhadaśva→ Bhānumān→Pratīkāśva→Supratīka→Marudeva→Sunakṣatra → Puṣkara →Antarikṣa→Sutapas→Amitrajit→Bṛhadvāja → Barhis → Kṛtañjaya → Raṇañjaya → Sañjaya → Śākya → Śuddhoda→ Lāṅgala → Prasenjit→ Kṣudraka→Raṇaka→Suratha→Sumitra (kings from Bṛhadbala onwards ruled in the Kali Age).

1. GS.GD.BP. take Bala & Sthala as father and son. B.P. specifically states : *Balasya Sthala-nāmā putro' bhavad ityarthaḥ.*

2. Can this be the author of the Sūtras of Pūrvamīmāṁsā or the pupil of Vyāsa as Hiraṇyanābha's 14th descendant Bṛhadbala was a contemporary of Pāṇḍavas ? He is probably some ancient sage of the same name.

3. *Kalāpa-grāma* : A village situated near Badarikāśrama vide *Bh. P.* 10.87.7. From *Nārada* P. II. 67.6 it appears that Nārada and other sages were residents of this place. Here Maru and Devāpi, the last kings of the Solar and Lunar races, perform penance and wait to re-establish their dynasties at Ayodhyā and Hastināpura after Kalki, the tenth incarnation of Viṣṇu, has established social and religious order. According to the

7. Maru's son was Pra-Suśruta (or Suśruta), whose son was Sandhi, his son Amarṣaṇa, who gave birth to Mahasvān, from whom was born Viśvasāhva.

8. Viśvasāhva's son was Prasenajit whose son was Takṣaka; his son was Bṛhadbala who was killed in the battle by your father (Abhimanyu).

9. These are the kings of the Ikṣvāku race in the past. Now listen to the names of kings who are yet to come in future. Bṛhadbala will have (?) a son by name Bṛhadraṇa[1].

10. Bṛhadraṇa's son will be Urukriya, whose son will be Vatsa-vṛddha; from him will spring Prativyoma whose son will be Bhānu; Bhānu's son will be Divāka the leader of the celestial army.

11. Divāka's son will be the great hero Sahadeva whose son will be Bṛhadaśva of whom will be born Bhānumān. Bhānumān's son will be Pratīkāśva whose son will be Supratīka.

12. From him will be born Marudeva, whose son will be Sunakṣatra. Thence will be Puṣkara whose son will be Antarikṣa; his son will be Sutapas, the father of Amitrajit.

13. From him will be born Bṛhadraja, whose son will be Barhis; thence Kṛtañjaya, whose son will be Raṇañjaya; thence will be born Sañjaya.

14. From him will be born Śākya; of him Śuddhoda from whom in turn will spring Lāṅgala; thence will be Prasenajit from whom will be born Kṣudraka.

15. From Kṣudraka will spring Raṇaka who will have a son called Suratha. Suratha's son Sumitra will be the last scion—These will be the kings descended in the race of Bṛhadbala.

16. The race of Ikṣvākus will end up with Sumitra for when he ascends the throne, the race of Ikṣvāku will be terminated and extinct in the Kali age.

Vāyu P. 91.7, Kalāpa is near Meru where Purūravas and Ūrvaśi honeymooned. N.L. De on the authority of Col. Raper locates it near the source of Sarasvatī—a tributary of the Alakanandā, in Badrīnath in Garhwal—*GDAMI* P 84.

1. If Bṛhadbala is killed by Abhimanyu, Bṛhadraṇa must have been born after the Bhārata war at the most, while Śuka is narrating these two generations after the Bhārata war—The Translator.

CHAPTER THIRTEEN[1]

The Description of the Race of Nimi[2]

Śrī Śuka continued :

1. After commencing the session of a sacrifice, Nimi, the son of Ikṣvāku invited Vasiṣṭha to officiate as a sacrificial priest (*ṛtvij*). He, on his part, replied, "Oh king! I have been already requested by Indra (to conduct his sacrifice).

2. After completing his sacrifice, I shall return (to look after your sacrifice). Wait till then for me". The house-

1. This chapter gives the genealogy of Nimi, the second son of Ikṣvāku, the original founder of the Janaka dynasty of Mithilā. The genealogy is practically the same as in *Vāyu P.* 91 and *Viṣṇu P.* 4.5.1-34. It is as follows :

Nimi→Janaka alias Mithi (*Vāyu* P.89.5)→Udāvasu→Nandivardhana →Suketu→Devarāta→Bṛhadratha→Mahāvīrya→ Sudhṛti→ Dhṛṣṭaketu→Haryaśva→Maru → Pratīpaka → Kṛtiratha → Devamīḍha→ Visṛta → Mahādhṛti → Kṛtirāta → Mahāromā → Svarṇaromā→ Hrasvaromā → *Sīradhvaja* (Sītā's father)→ Kuśadhvaja → Dharmadhvaja→

Kṛtadhvaja | Mitadhvaja
Keśidhvaja | Khāṇḍikya

(Keśidhvaja) ↓

Bhānumān→Śatadyumna→Śuci→Sanadvāja → Urdhvaketu →Aja →Purujit → Ariṣṭanemi → Śrutāyu → Supārśvaka → Citraratha → Kṣemardhi→ Samaratha → Satyaratha → Upaguru → Upagupta→ Vasvananta→Yuyudha→Subhāṣaṇa→Śruta Jaya → Vijaya →Ṛta→ Śunaka → Vītahavya→Dhṛti→Bahulāśva→Kṛti→Mahāvaśī.

2. Nimi (v.l.Nemi) is a famous philosopher-king more popular with non-Brahmanical sects which are anti-sacrifice and pro-recluse types of life. Restricting ourselves to the Brahmanical *purāṇas*, we find the Nimi-legend in *Matsya.* P. 61.32-34, *Vāyu* P. 89.1-4. (The whole chapter tallies with the Bh.P.), *Viṣṇu p.* 4.5.1-15 (the whole prose chapter seems to be the basis of this ch. in the Bh.P.), *Vālmīki Rām. Uttara.* 55-4-21 and canto 57. The curse-episode whereby Nimi left off his physical body and refused to return seems to be an effort at popular etymologies of the capital town "Mithilā" of the country 'Videha', and the word 'Nimiṣa' (winking of the eyes). The special feature of the Mithilā kings was their expertise in philosophy and *yoga* which as *Viṣṇu P.* 4.5.34 puts it : *prāyeṇaite ātma-vidyāśrayiṇo bhūpālā bhavanti.* Generally these kings resorted to the science of the Soul (spiritual lore).' The Bh. P. in the last verse of this ch. endorses the same view, though it gives the credit to the grace of Yājñavalkya, the expert yogin.

holder (Nimi, the performer of the sacrifice) kept silent. He (Vasiṣṭha) finished the sacrifice of Indra.

3. Nimi, himself a thoughtful philosopher, knew how life is transitory and proceeded with the sacrifice with the help of other sacrificial priests, while his preceptor did not return (was absent).

4. The preceptor returned after concluding Indra's sacrifice. Perceiving this disobedience on the part of his disciple, he cursed : 'Let the body of Nimi who conceitedly regards himself as a learned man, fall'.

5. Nimi reciprocated the imprecation of his preceptor who violated the path of righteousness : "May your body fall, as you do not know what is *dharma* due to covetousness".

6. With these words Nimi, who was proficient in spiritual lore cast off his body. My great grand-father[1] Vasiṣṭha was born of Urvaśī from Mitra and Varuṇa.

7. Preserving Nimi's body in fragrant balms, the great sages, at the conclusion of the sacrificial session, spoke to the celestials who assembled there for the sacrifice.

8. "If ye Lords are (propitiated and) pleased, the body of the king be resuscitated". "Amen ! Be it so", said the gods. The soul of Nimi resorted to his *liṅga-Śarīra* and spoke loudly, "Let me have no bondage of the physical body".

9. Being afraid of separation from it, sages do not wish to have any contact (or union) with the body, but they devote themselves to the lotus-like feet of Hari (to escape from *Saṁsāra*).

10. I am not desirous of re-entering into the body which brings misery, grief and fear. It is because of the physical body that the death threatens the *jīva* on all sides and the peril of death is everywhere, as the fish have water on all sides.

Gods said :

11. "Oh incorporal Nimi ! May you live at your free will in the eyes of embodied beings." Nimi thus took his

1. Actually 'great-great-grandfather'. The genealogy being—Vasiṣṭha→Śakti→Parāśara→Vyāsa→Śuka.

place in the bodies of creatures, and is indicated by the opening and closing of eyelids.

12. Considering the fearful consequences of anarchy on the human beings, the great sages churned the body of Nimi and a son was born of him.

13. On account of this miraculous birth (or by being the founder of a dynasty), he became known as *Janaka* and was called "Vaideha" as he was produced from a life-less body or an incorporal being, and 'Mithila' ('Mithi' in other *Purāṇas*) as he got his birth out of churning (of Nimi's body). And the city of Mithilā was built up by him.[1]

14. Janaka's son was Udāvasu of whom was born Nandivardhana; his son was Suketu (Sukeśa) who gave birth to Devarāta, Oh King !

15. From him was born Bṛhadratha, whose son was Mahāvīrya, the father of Sudhṛt; from him sprang up Dhṛṣṭaketu; his son was Haryaśva, whose son was Maru.

16. Maru's son was Pratīpaka whence was born Kṛti; his son was Devamīḍha whose son was Viśruta, the father of Mahādhṛti.

17. His son was Kṛtirāta whose son was Mahāromā; his son was Svarṇaromā from whom was born Hrasvaromā.

18. From him sprang up Sīradhvaja, who while ploughing the earth for sacrifice, Sītā (the consort of Rāma) was born (discovered) at the point of the ploughshare. He is hence remembered as Sīra-dhvaja[2] (one whose plough gave him celebrity like a flag).

19. From him was born Kuśadhvaja, whose son was Dharmadhvaja. He (Dharma) had two sons called Kṛtadhvaja and Mitadhvaja.

20. From Kṛtadhvaja, Keśidhvaja, and from Mitadhvaja, Khāṇḍikya were born. The son of Kṛtadhvaja was expert in the spiritual lore, Oh King.

1. Cf. *Vālmīki Rām.—Uttara* 57. 19 & 20.
mathanān Mithir ityāhur jananāj Janako'bhavat / 19
yasmād Videhāt sambhūto Vaidehas tu tataḥ smṛtaḥ / 20

2. VD. quotes a legend from *Adbhuta Rāmāyaṇa*, according to which Sītā was originally in the womb of Mandodarī who deposited the foetus in the Kurukṣetra (?) and was discovered by Hrasvaromā.

21. Khāṇḍikya was proficient in the path of action (*karma-mārga*), but being afraid of Keśidhvaja, he ran away (leaving his country), Keśidhvaja had a son called Bhānumān whose son was Sudyumna.

22. His son was Śuci, whose son was Sanadvāja; from Sanadvāja was born Ūrdhvaketu whose son was Aja, who had Purujit as his son.

23. His son was Ariṣṭanemi whose son was Śrutāyu; his son Supārśvaka gave birth to Citraratha, whose son Kṣemardhi was the king of Mithilā.

24. From him Samaratha whose son was Satyaratha; from him sprang Vpaguru whose son was Upagupta who was an *aṁśa* of the Fire-god.

25. His son was Vasvananta, whose son was Yuyudha, from whom was born Subhāṣaṇa; his son was Śruta whose son was Jaya, the father of Vijaya. His son was Ṛta.

26. From him was born Śunaka, whose son was Vītahavya, from whom was born Dhṛti. From Dhṛti was born Bahulāśva, whose son was Kṛti noted for great self-control.

27. These are verily the kings of Mithilā who were all proficient in the Science of the Soul (Spiritual lore) through the grace of Yājñavalkya the master of *yoga*. Even though they led the life of householders, they were above the conflicting pairs like pleasure and pain, etc.

CHAPTER FOURTEEN

The Description of the Lunar Race

Śrī Śuka Said :

1. After this (description of Mithilā kings), now listen to the hallowing race of Soma (the moon-god), in which will be glorified celebrated kings of auspicious fame, like Purūravas, the son of Ilā (*Aila*),[1] Oh King.

1. Although *Purūravas* is regarded as the son of Ilā, Manu's daughter, it is probable that this human founder of the Lunar race hailed from Ilāvṛta, the region round-about mount Meru.
Madhye tvilāvṛtaṁ nāma mahā-Meroḥ samantataḥ /—*Matsya P.* 113.19.

2. The creator (god Brahmā), born out of the lotus which was grown out of the deep pool-like navel of the Supreme Person of innumerable (lit. thousands of) heads, had a son called Atri, who was equal to his father in excellent qualities.

3. Wonderfully enough a Son called Soma was born out of his tears of joy, and hence he became an embodiment of nectar. He was appointed as the protector (or king) of Brāhmaṇas, (medicinal) plants and herbs and hosts of constellations and stars, by god Brahmā.

4. After conquering the three worlds, he worshipped Lord Viṣṇu by performing a Rājasūya sacrifice. Out of high notions about self-importance, he forcibly abducted Tārā,[1] the wife of Bṛhaspati.

5. Even though he was repeatedly and earnestly requested by Bṛhaspati, the preceptor of gods, out of arrogance, he refused to restore her (to Bṛhaspati). On this issue was fought a battle between gods and demons.

6. Out of hatred against Bṛhaspati, Śukra along with Asuras, espoused the cause of Soma, the Lord of stars, while god Śiva surrounded by his hosts of goblins took the side of Bṛhaspati, his preceptor's son.[2]

7. The great Indra, accompanied by all the hosts of gods, followed his preceptor (Bṛhaspati). Thus, for the sake of Tārā, a great battle was fought, resulting in the destruction of gods and demons.

8. The Creator of the Universe (god Brahmā) was then appealed to in this matter by Aṅgiras (Bṛhaspati's father). Brahmā threatened Soma and made him restore Tārā to her husband who found her to be pregnant.

9. (Bṛhaspati ordered Tārā): "Cast off, uproot from my field (i.e. get aborted) what has been sown there by others

Roughly this corresponds to the region round modern Pamirs. Purūravas and his descendants had contacts with 'gods' who are now identified as Aryans who inhabited the northern part of *Pamirs* or Uttara Kuru—vide D.P.Miśra—*Proto. Hist. of India*, ch.I.

1. This is a symbolism, rooted in the vedic doctrine of Soma. For details vide Agrawal—*M.P. A study*, pp. 130-31.

2. God Śiva's preceptor was sage Aṅgiras, the father of Bṛhaspati —ŚR.

(or enemies), oh wicked-minded woman. I shall not reduce you to ashes as you are a woman, and I am desirous of having an issue (through you)[1], oh good lady !"

9A. To her was born a son of golden complexion, the destroyer of Dasyus (or evil beings).

10. Overwhelmed with shame, Tārā delivered a son who was lustrous like gold in complexion.[2] And both Bṛhaspati, the son of Aṅgiras, and Soma desired to have the son as his own (as a *kṣetraja* son—born of his field, viz. wife in the case of the former, and as a *vīryaja* son—born of his own semen—in the case of the latter)[3]

11. While they (Bṛhaspati and Soma) were wrangling vociferously, "This (son) is mine and not yours", sages and gods enquired (of Tārā), but through sense of shame, she kept mum.

12. Enraged at the sham modesty of his mother (Tārā), the son exploded, "Why don't you speak, you woman of immoral behaviour ? Confess to me immediately your sin".

12A.* (Although you deserve that punishment) I shall not burn you to ashes (with a curse) for concealing your sinful act (as after all you are my mother). But god Brahmā censured the audacious reviler in her presence.

13. God Brahmā then invited her aside, and consoling her in camera, he (sympathetically) enquired. With great hesitation and slowly, she confessed in a low tone, "Soma's." And immediately Soma took possession of the child.

14. The self-born god (Brahmā) gave the child the name Budha (the intelligent and wise). By the penetrating intelligence and deep wisdom of his son Budha, the moon-god, the king of stars, became highly delighted.

15-16. As already narrated (vide Supra 9.1.35) 'Purūravas was born of Budha and Ilā. On hearing of the personal charms, excellences, generosity, nobility of character, affluence

1. And as there is no son to ensure the continuity of my family—VR.

2. v.l. *janaka-prabham*—was like his father in complexion and beauty.

3. With due respect to these annotators, I fail to understand why god Brahmā took Tārā into confidence to ascertain who was the real father of the child.—The Translator.

* This verse is noted by VR also.

and deeds of valour as extolled by the celestial sage Nārada in the palace of Indra (the king of gods), the celestial nymph Ūrvaśī was afflicted by shafts of the god of love, and she approached Purūravas.[1]

17. Being reduced to the status of human beings due to the curse of Mitra and Varuṇa, and hearing (the report that) that great personage was beautiful like the god of Love incarnate, she mustered sufficient courage, and presented herself to his presence.

18. With his eyes fully blooming with great joy at her sight, and with his hair standing on their end (with ecstatic delight), the king spoke to her softly in winsome words.

The King said :

19. Welcome is your arrival, Oh beautiful lady. Be pleased to take a (comfortable) seat. What can we do for you ? Enjoy yourself fully with me. Let our mutual enjoyment of love last for innumerable years.

Ūrvaśī replied :

20. "Whose mind and eye will not be attracted by and fixed on you, oh charming Prince ? Having caught a glimpse of

1. This story (of Purūravas and Ūrvaśī) is an elaboration of the dialogue between Purūravas and Ūrvaśī recorded in RV. 10.95. Many verses from that *Sūkta* are assimilated *verbatim* in the Bh.P. e.g. RV. 10.95. 1, 14, 15. The textual similarity has been noted by all commentators. VJ. however is more elaborate in this respect. Even an ordinary reader will hear the echo of RV.10.95.1 (repeated in *Śatapatha Br.* 11.5.1-6)

haye jāye manasā tiṣṭha ghore /
vacāṁsi miśrā kṛṇavāvahai nu //

in *Bh.P.*9.14.34

aho jāye tiṣṭha tiṣṭha ghore na tyaktum arhasi /
māṁ tvam adyāpyanirvṛtya vacāṁsi kṛṇavāvahai //

If we accept the hypothesis of Rajaram Shastri Bhagawat who, in 1907, showed in his *Key to Interpret Veda*, that Devas were a race of men and Indra their leader's designation (and there is no reason to disbelieve it as scholars like R.N.Dandekar, D.D.Kosambi endorsed it independently), and M.Ali's identification of Kirghizia, Samarkand (Sogdiana of the Greeks) and Turkemenistan with *Deva-loka* (*The Geography of the Purāṇas, pp.* 63-83), the contract marriage between a lady from Ur (Ūr-vaśī) and a king hailing from Ilāvṛta—Aila Purūravas, appears quite a human episode with historical basis. The geographical vicinity of his kingdom to Deva-loka made it possible for him and his descendants to fight as allies of Indra.

your bosom (lit. having approached your bosom) I become overpowered with the desire of enjoying life with you, and lose the control over my mind.

21. Oh King ! Be pleased to protect the two lambs as my pledges. Oh respector of the respectable ! I shall enjoy life fully with you. For he who (by his qualities of beauty etc.) appears praise-worthy (to a woman) is remembered (ordained in the *Smṛti* texts) as acceptable to women.

22. Oh warrior King ! My food will consist of ghee only. And I shall not see you without clothes except on the occasion of sexual intercourse." The noble-minded king agreed to the conditions.

23. "Oh what elegant form ! How noble sentiment, that enchants the entire humanity ! What man will not attend upon a goddess who presents herself of her own accord."

24. In her company she offered him all pleasures worthy of him. The eminent person (king Purūravas) enjoyed with her at will, and to the full, in the pleasure gardens of gods such as Caitraratha (the garden of Kubera).

25. Enjoying amorous pleasures with the goddess (or the queen) whose person was fragrant like lotus-filaments, and being enraptured by the sweet smell of her mouth, he revelled many years delightfully with her.

26. Not seeing Ūrvaśī (in his court) and feeling, "My assembly does not look very charming without Ūrvaśī," Indra directed Gandharvas (to bring her).

27. Approaching at dead of night when the world was steeped in darkness, and through their Māyā, they stole the two rams which were pledged for safe custody with the king, by his queen Ūrvaśī.

28. Hearing the bleating of her son-like rams, as they were being carried away, queen Ūrvaśī lamented loudly, "I am undone by this sheepish husband, lacking in manliness but posing vaingloriously as a hero.

29. Trusting in him, I am ruined and despoiled of my children (—like lambs) by robbers. Like a woman who is full of fear at night, he sleeps terror-stricken at night, and poses himself as a man when it is (broad) day (—light).

29A. Let me be free ! Leave me immediately ! Take away your arm that clasps around me. He is too timid to leave me, and cunning, and addicted to licentious sexual pleasure only."

30. Being pierced with these verbal shafts, and like an elephant pricked with goads, he caught hold of his sword and sallied forth in rage, in the dead of night, even though he was naked.

31. The Gandharvas let go the two rams, but flashed out light like lightning, when she caught a glimpse of her husband in a nude state, coming with the two rams (and thus left him).

32. Not finding his wife in the bed, Purūravas, the son of *Ilā*, became despondent. His heart being fixed on her, he was beside himself (with affliction). He ranged over the world (in search of her), like a mad man.

33. (In the course of his wanderings, one day) he happened to see her along with her five female companions with their countenances blooming with delight, on the bank of the Sarasvatī, in Kurukṣetra. Purūravas addressed her the following (persuasive) charming words (recorded in the *Sūkta*, RV 10.95 which is adapted here as follows) :

34. "Oh my beloved wife ! Do stop awhile, wait. Oh cruelhearted one ! It does not behove you to abandon me without giving me pleasure of your company to my satisfaction (*or* unsated as I am of the pleasures of your company, you ought not to relegate me to terrible misery). Let us (at least) have some (heart to heart) talk.[1]

35. If this beautiful body of mine[2] which has been drawn away to such a far off distance by you, be not the recipient of your favours, it will fall down dead here only,

1. Cf. RV. 10.95.1.

2. Cf. RV.10.95.14. VJ. reads 'Sudevo'yam' for *Sudeho'yam*, which opens RV 10.95.14 (*Sudevo atra prapatet*). VJ. explains the Ṛk rather than this verse *Sudeva*—This human body which is the tool or means of getting knowledge (*gati-lakṣana-jñāna-sādhanam*).

VR. explains the v.l. *Sudevo'yam* : Here Purūravas addresses his own soul—the Inner Controller. He construes *gṛdhra* (greedy, voracious) as the adj. qualifying *Vṛkas*—wolves in the form of sense-organs which afflict the individual soul.

and wolves and vultures will prey upon it, Oh my queen (Oh goddess).

Ūrvaśī replied :

36. Do not die. You are a man (as such you must be courageous). Let not these wolves (in the form of passionately craving senses) devour you today (Control your senses). The heart of women like the heart of wolves is friendly to none.[1]

37. Women are merciless, cruel, jealous and mind no risk for the object of their love. Even for a trifling matter, they will kill their trustful husband or unsuspecting brother.

38. After inspiring confidence in gullible persons (through deceitful behaviour), they snap asunder all friendly relations. The unchaste women, being wantonly wayward in behaviour, hunt (long) after a new lover (every now and then).

39. My lord, at the end of the year, you will stay with me for one night. You will have other children also, (in addition to the one I carry).

40. Noticing that the queen was pregnant, he returned to his capital. At the end of the year, he came back again to find Ūrvaśī, as the mother of a hero.

41. Full of delight to have her again, he spent that night with her. Then finding him disheartened at the prospect of impending separation, Ūrvaśī advised him :

42. "You propitiate these Gandharvas (by praise), and they will be pleased to give me unto you."

Being pleased with his laudatory prayer, the Gandharvas donated him a fire-vase (for fire-worship which will lead him to the region of Ūrvaśī) Oh King. (Being blinded with passion) he believed that fire-vessel to be (the means of securing) Ūrvaśī, and roved in the forest with it, only to discover it to be a vase for carrying fire, and not Ūrvaśī.

43. Depositing the vase in the forest, he returned to his palace, and contemplated throughout the night on Ūrvaśī. In

1. The veres echoes the text of RV. 10.95.15 while VV. 36-39 explain it. Cf.

Purū-ravo mā mṛthā, mā pra papto
mā tvā vṛkāso aśivāsa u kṣan /
na vai straiṇāni sakhyāni santi
sālāvṛkāṇām hṛdayāneytā //—RV. 10.95.15

the meanwhile (the Kṛta age ended and) the Tretā Age set in, and the knowledge of trinity of Vedas which contained prescriptions, for the ritualistic performance of sacrifices, revealed itself in his mind.

44. Returning to the spot (in the forest) where the firevase was kept (by him), he noticed an *aśvattha* (Peepal) tree grown out from the 'womb' of the *Śamī* tree. With a desire to attain to the region of Ūrvaśī, he made two *araṇis* (churning sticks) out of them (with a view to enkindle fire by friction).

45. Reciting the *mantra* 'Ūrvaśyām urasi Purūravāḥ' (Purūravas is on Ūrvaśī), the powerful king contemplated the lower piece of *araṇi* (churning stick) as Ūrvaśī and the upper *araṇi* to be himself, and the intermediate piece between them as their issue (son), (the king churned out the fire while saying the *mantra* prescribed for such frictional fire).

46. By that friction of churning was enkindled a fire (flame) which is called *Jātaveda* (that from which wealth and every enjoyable object is produced). It was consecrated by the method prescribed in the three Vedas. It assumed three forms[1]—*āhavanīya*, *gārhapatya* and *dakṣiṇāgni*. As it, with its three forms, leads to the celestial regions, it was adopted as his son by the king Purūravas.

47. Wishing to attain to the region of Ūrvaśī he, (Purūravas), worshipped with that sacrificial fire (produced by attrition from *araṇis*) the glorious Lord Hari, who is the presiding Deity of sacrifices and is Supra-sensuous and who represents all gods in His Person.

48. Formerly (in the Kṛta Age), there was only one Veda viz. the sacred syllable *OM* which formed the basis of all speech; there was but one God Nārāyaṇa and no other; there was only one Fire (and not three) and only one caste viz. *Haṁsa*.

49. (In the Kṛta Age), all people had the predominance

1. These are the three forms of householder's perpetual sacrificial fires : The *āhavanīya* is the eastern. The *Gārhapatya* is another perpetual fire transmitted from one generation to another and from this, fires for sacrificial purposes are lighted; the *dakṣiṇāgni* is the sacred fire placed to the south.

of *Sattva* and hence were devoted to spiritual meditation. In the Tretā Age, *rajas* being the dominant quality, the path of ritualistic acts based on the three Vedas became evolved. Since the time of Purūravas, when the Tretā Age dawned, there came into existence the trinity of the Vedas (and the path of ritualistic action based on them), Oh King. As the King accepted the Fire-god as his son (i.e. maintained the sacrificial fire like unto his son), the king attained to the realm of Gandharvas.

CHAPTER FIFTEEN

The Story of Paraśurāma. Sahasrārjuna Slain

Śrī Śuka said :

1. Purūravas, the son of Ilā, had six sons by Ūrvaśī, Oh King. They were Āyu, Śrutāyu, Satyāyu, Raya, Vijaya and Jaya.

2. Śrutāyu's son was Vasumān; Śrutañjaya was Satya's son. Raya's son was Eka, and Jaya's son was Amita.

3. Vijaya had a son called Bhīma whose son was Kañcana from whom was born Hotraka. His son was Jahnu who took all the waters of the Gaṅgā in his folded palms, and drank up the whole river. Jahnu's son was Puru, whose son was Balāka and his son was Ajaka.

4. From him (Ajaka) was born Kuśa who had four sons viz. Kuśāmbu, Tanaya (v. l. Mūrtaya), Vasu and Kuśanābha. Kuśāmbu's son was Gādhi.

5. A Brāhmaṇa called Ṛcīka sought Gādhi's daughter, princess Satyavatī in marriage. Considering that the bridegroom was unworthy of her, king Gādhi spoke to Ṛcīka of the Bhṛgu clan :

6. "We belong to the race of Kuśa, and as such one thousand horses white and bright like the moon, but with one black ear be given as the dowry for the girl."

7. When he was thus replied, he understood the intention of Gādhi. Having approached Varuṇa, he brought and delivered the required horses of the said description and married that lovely princess.

8. The sage Ṛcīka was solicited by his wife and by his mother-in-law both of whom were desirous of having a son. He prepared *Caru*—an oblation of rice, barley and pulse boiled in butter and milk for presentations to gods—consecrated them severally—the one, for his wife, with *Brāhma mantras*, and the other, for his mother-in-law, consecrated with *Kṣātra mantras*. And then the sage went for having his bath.

9. In the meanwhile (during his absence), Satyavatī, was requested by her mother (to give her) the *Caru* (sacrificial boiled rice) meant for Satyavatī herself, considering that to be superior. She gave that *Caru* (meant for herself) to her mother, and ate the one apportioned for her mother.

10. On learning of this (exchange of *Carus*), the sage told his wife, "Alas! What grievous mistake you have committed! Your son will be a terrible chastiser (like god of death), and your brother will be a prominent knower of *Brahman* (the Vedas or the Supreme Deity).

11. Propitiated by persuasive prayer that such eventuality should not materialise, sage Ṛcīka of the Bhṛgu clan said, "If so, your grandson will be of that nature". Then Jamadagni was born.

12. Then Satyavatī was transformed into a very sacred river Kauśikī, the sanctifier of the world. The tradition goes that Jamadagni married Reṇukā, the daughter of (King) Reṇu.

13. They say that several sons like Vasumat and others were begotten on her by the sage Jamadagni of the Bhṛgu clan. The youngest of them born was the great celebrity Rāma (Paraśu-rāma).

14*. They say that he was a ray (*aṁśa*) of Vāsudeva (Lord Viṣṇu) and the exterminator of the Haihaya clan. He

*The Bh.P. contains two main legends from the life of Paraśurāma viz. 1. The slaying of Kārtavīrya or Sahasrārjuna and 2. Beheading his mother and brothers and reviving them.

The legends of Paraśurāma narrated here are found in *MBH Ādi*. 2.4-7 64.4; *Āśvamedhika* chs. 29 & 30 and in *Brahmāṇḍa P.* II.26-40.

is said to have rendered this earth devoid of Kṣatriyas twenty-one times.

15. He destroyed the wicked Kṣatriya race turned inimical to Brāhmaṇas, and constituted as if a burden to the earth. Even on the slightest provocation or commission of a slight offence, he killed the Kṣattriyas enveloped by (i.e. full of) *rajas* and *tamas*.

The king (Parīkṣit) asked :

16. What offence against that glorious sage (Paraśu-rāma) was committed by Kṣatriyas of uncontrolled nature that led to the repeated extermination of the entire Kṣatriya race (by him) ?

Śrī Śuka narrated :

17. Arjuna, a prominent Kṣatriya and the ruler of Haihayas (a branch of Yādavas) propitiated Datta (Dattā-treya), a partial (*aṁśa*) incarnation of Lord Nārāyaṇa, by rendering to him various acts of service (and worship).

18-19. Through him (Datta's grace), he secured a thousand arms, unassailable formidability against the enemies, uninterrupted and insuperable power of senses and organs, splendour, affluence, glory, prowess, fame, physical strength, mastery over *yoga* including supreme spiritual powers characte-rised by the capacity to assume atomic size etc. His move-ments and speed being thus unimpeded, he moved about the world free as a wind.

20. While sporting in the waters of the Narmadā, in company of (lit. surrounded by) jewel-like (charming) women, and wearing the Vaijayantī wreath (of nine well-known gems) he, being intoxicated with pride, obstructed the course of the river with his one thousand arms.

21. (Rāvaṇa was on his expedition of the world con-quest and was camping on the bank of the Narmadā, near Māhiṣmatī, Sahasrārjuna's capital and was then engaged in worship). Finding his encampment flooded with the waters of the river flowing in the opposite direction, Rāvaṇa, the tenheaded demon, who regarded himself as the only hero in the world,

did not tolerate that (display of) prowess (by Sahasrārjuna).

22. When Rāvaṇa (tried to attack him during the water-sports and thus) offended Sahasrārjuna, he (Rāvaṇa) was sportively seized in the very presence of women, and was kept captive like a monkey at his capital Māhiṣmatī and was (ultimately) let off as a worthless fellow.

23. On one occasion, while Arjuna was on a hunting expedition in an impassable forest, he perchance, happened to come to the precincts of the hermitage of the sage Jamadagni.

24. Through the grace of his Kāmadhenu (wish-yielding cow), the sage whose wealth was (nothing but his) penance, however, offered a warm reception (with due formalities) to the king, his ministers, men in his army and even the animals that carried them.

25. Finding the affluence of the sage far surpassing his own, the warrior who was accompanied by his Haihaya clansmen, cherished covetousness for the wish-yielding cow which was essential for maintaining sacrificial fires (*agni-hotra*), and did not appreciate the warm hospitality.

26. Out of arrogance and pride, he commanded his men to take away the sage's cow of plenty (which yielded milk, ghee etc. as oblations to sacrificial fires), and they forcibly carried off the screaming cow and her calf to (the king's capital) Māhiṣmatī.

27. After the king's departure, (Paraśu)-Rāma arrived at the hermitage. Being informed of the act of wickedness of the king, he got enraged like a serpent that is hit.

28. Equipping himself with his formidable axe, a bow with quivers and a shield, the irresistible hero rushed after him like a lion chasing a king elephant of a herd.

29. As Arjuna was entering his capital, he noticed the prominent Bhṛgu, Paraśurāma bearing a bow and armed with arrows and an axe, wearing a black deer-skin and with matted hair resplendent like the sun, rushing (after him) with an irresistible force.

30. (To oppose him) Arjuna directed seventeen very formidable divisions (*akṣauhiṇī*)[1] consisting of elephants, chari-

1. For the details of the strength of an *akṣauhiṇī* vide Bh.P.VII.I.P. 71 ftn. No. 271.

ots, cavalry and infantry equipped with maces, swords, arrows, javelins, *Śataghnīs* (a rocket-like missile or a cylindrical block of wood studded with iron pikes) and darts or lances (*Śaktis*). But the glorious Lord Rāma singlehandedly slaughtered them all.

31. In whatever direction, Rāma, the destroyer of hostile forces, moved with the velocity of the wind and mind, striking down with his axe, there fell down on the ground enemies with their arms, thighs and necks chopped off and their charioteers and animals slain.

32. Perceiving that his army is laid low on the battlefield in the mire caused by streams of blood, with their shields, flags, bows and bodies minced down by the axe and shafts of Rāma, the Haihaya King Arjuna, rushed forward in rage.

33. Now Arjuna (being thousand-armed) simultaneously fitted shafts on five hundred bows in order to discharge them at Rāma. But Rāma, the undisputed leader of all whoever wielded missiles, with one bow in his hand at once—synchronously—cut down all Arjuna's bow and arrows with his shafts.

34. In that fight, while Arjuna was rushing towards Rāma uprooting rocks and trees with his (numerous) hands (to hurl them at Rāma), Rāma forestalled him and quickly cut down his arms like the hoods of serpents, with his axe of a hard and sharp edge.

35. After lopping off all his arms, Rāma chopped off Arjuna's head like the peak of a mountain. When their father was thus killed, Arjuna's ten thousand sons ran away in panic.

36. Rāma, the subduer of hostile forces, restored the cow (essential for the maintenance of *Agnihotra*) along with her calf. Returning to his hermitage, he duly presented the afflicted cow to his father.

37. Rāma, described to his father and brothers (Arjuna's moves) and his exploits; but the sage Jamadagni (disapprovingly) remarked :

38. "(Dear) Rāma ! Oh Rāma of mighty arms ! You have committed a sin. You have unnecessarily killed a king (a god among men) who represents all gods in his person.

39. Oh dear child ! We are Brāhmaṇas ! We have become objects of veneration and worship through forbearance,

just as god Brahmā, the creator of the world, has attained to the status of Parameṣṭhī (the supreme ruler of the world) through forgiveness.

40. It is on account of forgiveness and patience that the Brāhmanic glory shines like the splendour of the sun. Even glorious Lord Hari, the Ruler of the Universe, become seasily pleased with persons of forgiving spirits.

41. Slaying of a king whose head is consecrated in coronation, is more heinous than that of killing a Brāhmaṇa. Oh child ! Now expiate your sin by bathing in holy waters, devoting your mind (all the while) to Lord Viṣṇu (*Acyuta*)."

CHAPTER SIXTEEN

The Story of Paraśurāma[1] (*concluded*)

Śrī Śuka continued:

1. Rāma who was thus admonished by his father, consented (with words) "Be it so". After spending one year in visiting holy places, he returned to his hermitage, Oh princes of the Kuru race !

1. The legend of Paraśurāma ends in this chapter. The Bh.P., like the MBH, seems to be composed under the influence of Bhṛgus and this legend may be called the Bhṛgu version of the feud between the Bhṛgus and Haihayas. Bhṛgus (Greek: Phrugus) as the name of the clan suggests, probably hailed from Phrygia in Western Asia Minor. From the Purāṇic accounts, they seem to have settled on the Western Coast in India and Bhṛgukaccha (Broach, Gujrat), Śūrpāraka (Sopārā, Thana District, Maharashtra) appear to be the centres of their settlement. They were a sea power. Till the time of Kṛtavīrya (Arjuna's father), Bhṛgus and Haihayas seemed to be on good terms. But the Haihayas' policy of expansion had long back alerted Bhṛgus, and their leaders contracted matrimonial alliances with the royal houses of Kānyakubja and Ayodhyā by the marriage of Ṛcīka and Jamadagni with the princesses thereof. Arjuna, Kṛtavīrya's son was an able, ambitious ruler. He seems to have raided Jamadagni's 'hermitage' (!)—if a centre which can receive and feed a king and his army in a royal way, and if its affluence surpasses a sovereign emperor's palace, can be called so—probably to forestall Bhṛgu

2. On one occasion, when Reṇukā went to the Gaṅgā (for bringing water), she happened to see Citraratha, the king of Gandharvas, adorned with a wreath of lotuses, sporting with celestial nymphs (in the water).

3. Reṇukā who came to the river to fetch water, conceived just a passing longing for Citraratha, and forgot the time fixed for the *Homa* (sacrificial worship) while gazing at the sporting king.

4. Realizing the delay caused thereby, and being afraid of the sage's (Jamadagni's) curse, she hastened back, kept the pitcher of water before him, and remained standing with folded palms.

5. Gathering the faithlessness of his wife, the sage got enraged and commanded, "Oh sons ! Kill this sinful woman". Despite this order, none obeyed.

6. Rāma who was fully aware of the powers of the sage through his spiritual meditation and penance, promptly despatched his brothers along with his mother, when directed to do so by his father.

7. Jamadagni, the son of Satyavatī, was pleased with him (Paraśurāma) and asked him to seek a boon. Rāma re-

designs just on the borders of his kingdom. Though under the able leadership of Rāma, the northern allies of Bhṛgus including kings of Vaiśālī, Videha, Kānyakubja and Ayodhyā defeated Haihayas probably in twenty-one battles, and though Rāma was able to kill Arjuna in a surprise attack while the latter was returning from his hunting expedition, the Bhṛgus had ultimately to migrate to the north India and spread along the southern part of the western coast of India. Whatever may be the actual historical facts of this traditional feud, it was *not* a contest between Brāhmaṇas and Kṣatriyas on caste basis, as some misrepresent it. For, right from the days of Cyavana Bhārgava, Bhṛgus had marriage alliances with Kṣattriyas, and Rāma's mother, Rama's grandmother (Ṛcīka's wife) were Kṣattriya princesses. The real cause was economic and political rivalry, and attempts of Haihayas to spread their kingdom to the Doab and other parts of northern India. After Paraśurāma's retirement, Haihayas consolidated their position in Malwa, Rajasthan and Western India and carried their raids against Ayodhyā, Kānyakubja, Kosal and Kāśī. As irony of fate would have it, the last Haihaya prince Vītihotra on the throne of Benares, had to seek refuge with a Bhārgava sage and Vīti-hotra became a Brāhmaṇa. After him little is heard about Haihayas—*Vedic Age*, pp.283-87 (History and Culture of Indian People Vol.I).

quested the boon that all those who had been killed, should be restored to life, and should not remember who slew them.

8. Immediately they got up hale and hearty as if from a sound sleep. Rāma had killed his kith and kin (mother and brothers), as he had known the spiritual power of his father.

9. Oh king ! The sons of Arjuna who, being vanquished by the valour of Rāma, had fled, continued to brood over the killing of their father (by Rāma) and found no mental peace anywhere.

10. On one occasion, when Paraśurāma along with his brothers had left for the forest, they (the sons of Arjuna), desirous of avenging (for the killing of their father by Rāma), found a (favourable) opportunity, and entered the hermitage.

11. Determined to murder Jamadagni, they saw the sage sitting with his mind concentrated upon the glorious Lord of excellent renown, in the sacrificial hall, and killed him.

12. Though piteously entreated by the helpless mother of Paraśurāma, those hard-hearted dregs of the Kṣatriya community, forcibly severed his head and carried it away.

13. Overwhelmed with grief and deep anguish, and beating herself with her own hands, the chaste lady Reṇukā screamed loudly, "Oh Rāma ! Rāma ! come (quickly) Oh child".

14. Hearing from afar, a distressful call "Oh Rāma", Rāma hastened to the hermitage to find his father killed.

15. Overwhelmed and confounded with sorrow, rage, impetuosity, affliction and intense grief, Rāma bewailed "Oh saintly father ! Oh righteous-most sire ! Leaving us behind here, you proceeded to heaven."

16. After lamenting thus, Paraśurāma entrusted the body of his father to his brothers. Taking his axe with him, he determined to exterminate the Kṣatriya race entirely.

17. Sallying forth to the city of Māhiṣmatī, the splendour of which was already lost due to the murder of a Brāhmaṇa (Jamadagni), he built up (as it were) a huge mountain of the heads of the sons of Sahasrārjuna in the heart of the city.

18-19. With the blood of those (Haihayas), he created a terrible river which aroused fear in the heart of the enemies of Brāmaṇas. When the Kṣatriyas had taken to wicked (inauspicious) ways, he made the murder of his father as a cause of action and completely annihilated the Ksatriyas thrice seven times[1] from the earth, and caused (the creation of) pools of blood[2] in Samantapañcaka(Kurukṣetra) Oh King.

20. Recovering the head of his father (taken away by the sons of Arjuna), he joined it to the trunk of his father's body. Keeping it on the Kuśa grass, he worshipped by performing sacrifices, the Deity, his own Soul, who represents all gods in his person.

21. (It is verily reported that) as *dakṣiṇā* (gift for performance of sacrifices), he gave the eastern quarter (the eastern part of the earth) to the *Hotṛ*, the southern quarter to the *Brahmā*, the western direction to the *Adhvaryu* and the northern direction to the *Udgātṛ*.

22. To others he donated (lands in) the intermediate quarters, and the central portion of the earth to sage Kaśyapa, Āryāvarta (region between the Himalayas and the Vindhya mountain) to the sacrificial supervisors (*upadraṣṭas*) and the land lying beyond that to *Sadasyas* (judges or superintendents of sacrifices.).

23. Having washed off all his sins in the conclusive ablution at the end of the sacrifice in the river Sarasvatī, the embodiment of the Veda, he shone resplendent like the sun with clouds dispelled.

24. Having regained his (spiritual) body characterised by pure consciousness, Jamadagni became the seventh star[3] in the sphere of sages in the sky (*Ursa Major*), and was worshipped by Rāma.

25. (It is said that) verily this son of Jamadagni, the glorious Rāma of lotus-like eyes, will be the propagator of the

1. ŚR informs us that according to tradition, Reṇukā beat her breast twenty one times, and hence Rāma destroyed Kṣatriyas as many times.

2. VR. states that the v.l *hradān nava* is wrong, as the place is called *S(y)amanta-pañcaka* and not *S-navaka* and the MBH. *Ādi.* records *S-pañcaka* as the name 2.4-11.

3. VC. gives the list of seven sages presiding over the seven stars in the constellation *Ursa Major* as follows : Kāśyapa, Atri, Vasiṣṭha, Viśvāmitra, Gautama, Bharadvāja and Jamadagni.

Vedas—one of the seven sages, the authorities over the Vedas —in the coming *Manvantara*.

26. Even today he resides on the Mahendra mountain. He has laid down the rod of punishment, and is now perfectly serene in mind. His deeds are being sung by Siddhas, Gandharvas and Cāraṇas.

27. In this way, the glorious Lord Hari, the Ruler of the world, the very Soul of (all beings in) the Universe incarnated Himself in the Bhṛgu clan, and lightened the burden of the earth by killing several times the *Kṣatriyas* (or lords of men).

28. Gādhi (the King of Kānyakubja) begot a son (Viśvāmitra) whose superb majestic personality was brilliant like a blazing fire. By virtue of his asceticism and austere penance, he transcended his *Kṣatriya* status and attained the glory of Brahmanism.

29. Viśvāmitra had a hundred sons. Out of them Madhucchandas was the middle, but all of them are known by the same (group) name Madhucchandas, Oh King !

30. Having adopted as his son Śunaḥśepa, the son of Ajīgarta of the Bhṛgu clan, who was given to him by gods and hence named as *Devarāta*, he told his sons, "Let this (Śunaḥśepa) be regarded by you as your eldest (brother).[1]

31. It was verily the same person who was sold as a human 'sacrificial beast' (victim) for the sacrifice of Hariścandra[2] and who through his prayer[3] to gods and Lords of creation (like Varuṇa) was released from the bondage of cords (that tied him to the sacrificial post).

32. He who was protected and given by gods in the sacrifice offered to Varuṇa, came to be known as *Devarāta* among the Gādhi family and that ascetic was known as Śunḥśepa in the family of Bhṛgus.

33. The brothers who were elder than Madhucchandas did not approve of it (the order of Viśvāmitra to recognize

1. As ŚR. points out, this explains why Devarāta is one of the *Pravara*'s of the Kauśika *Gotra*, even thougn as a rule a *Pravara* belongs to the same *Gotra*.

2. Vide Supra 9.7. 20-21.

3. e.g. Sūktas like RV. 1.25.

Devarāta as their eldest brother). The enraged sage cursed them, "Ye wicked fellows! Be ye all *mlecchas* (outcast barbarians)".

34. It is reported that, thereupon Madhucchandas along with his fifty brothers submitted, "we shall accept the status and abide by whatever you command us."

35. To the seer of Vedic *mantras* (Śunaḥśepa) they told him, "We are all your younger brothers." And thus they recognized him as their eldest brother. Viśvāmitra (being highly pleased) said to his sons, "As you have maintained my respect as your father, and have made me worthy as a father with heroic sons, may you all be blessed with progeny".

36. "Oh descendents of Kauśika family, this Devarāta is one of you (as a scion of your family); obey his orders." Viśvāmitra had also other sons viz. Aṣṭaka, Hārīta, Jaya, Kratumat and others.

37. In this way the Kauśika family came to be divided into different branches through the sons of Viśvāmitra, and it had another different *Pravara* due to the adoption of Devarāta.[1]

CHAPTER SEVENTEEN

The Lunar Dynasty—The Descendants of Āyu, the Son of Purūravas[2]

Śrī Śuka said :

1-3. Āyu who was the son of Purūravas, had the following (five) sons—Nahuṣa, Kṣattravṛddha, the valiant Raji, Rambha and Anenas. Now, Oh emperor, listen to the

1. It appears that there had been different Viśvāmitras in widely distant ages. e.g. Viśvāmitra, the father of Śakuntalā, Viśvāmitra the teacher of Daśaratha's son Rāma, Viśvāmitra the contemporary of Hariścandra, Jamadagni and Śunaḥśepa, and Viśvāmitra and the Dāśarājña. The Purāṇas, however, have rolled these distinct personalities into one, and have caused confusion and chaos among the students of Purāṇas. It is true that there was some rivalry between the Viśvāmitras and Vasiṣṭhas in the RV, but the Purāṇas have added a lot of new material unknown to the Vedas and the Brāhmaṇas.

2. This chapter gives the genealogy of Purū-ravas—especially of the minor branches from Āyu, the son of Purūravas. The history of the descendants of the following four sons of Āyu viz. Kṣattravṛddha, Rambha, Raji and Anenas is given in this chapter. The history of the main line from Nahuṣa is detailed in the following chapters.

genealogy of Kṣattravṛddha : He had a son Suhotra, who had three sons—Kāśya, Kuśa and Gṛtsamada. From Gṛtsamada was born Śunaka whose son sage Śaunaka was the most prominent authority on the *Ṛgveda* (among its followers).

4. Kāśya begot Kāśī, whose son Rāṣṭra was the father of Dīrghatamas. Dhanvantari, the founder of the science of Medicine (*Āyurveda*) was the son of Dīrghatamas.

5. He was a ray (*aṃśa*) of Lord Vāsudeva, the receiver of offerings in sacrifices. His son was Ketumān who gave birth to Bhīmaratha.

6. From him (Bhīmaratha) was born Divodāsa whose son Dyuman was also remembered as Pratardana. He is also called Śatrujit, Vatsa and Ṛtadhvaja. He is celebrated as Kuvalayāśva as well. Of him were born Alarka and others.

7. No king other than Alarka enjoyed (the sovereignty over) this earth for sixty-six thousand years and still preserved his youthfulness (throughout this period).

8. To Alarka was born Santati whose son was Sunītha. From Sunītha sprang up Suketana whose son was Dharmaketu; of him was born Satyaketu.

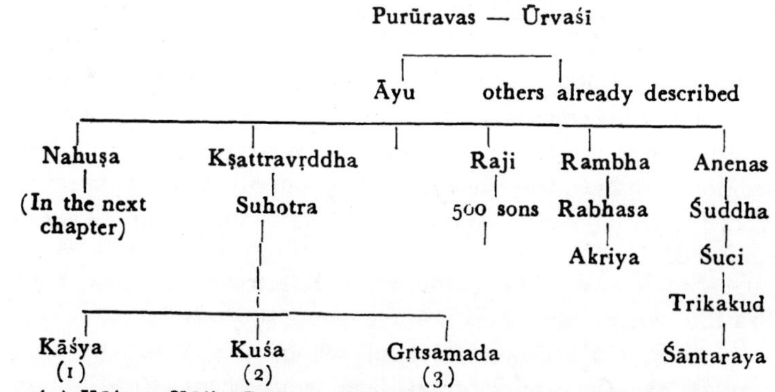

(1) Kāśya→Kāśi→Rāṣṭra→Dīrghatamas→Dhanvantari→Ketumān→Bhīmaratha→ Divodāsa→ Pratardana → Alarka→ Santati→ Sunitha → Suketana→Dharmaketu→Satyaketu→Dhṛṣṭaketu→Sukumāra→ Vītihotra →Bharga→Bhārga-bhūmi.

(2) Kuśa→Prati (Kṣatra)→Sañjaya→Jaya → Kṛta→ Haryaśva → Sahadeva→Jaya (-sena) → Saṅkṛti→Jaya→Kṣātradharmā

(3) Gṛtsamada→Śunaka→Śaunaka.

9. Satyaketu's son was Dhṛṣṭaketu of whom was born Sukumāra, the lord of the earth; his son was Vītihotra whose son was Bharga; his son Bhārgabhūmi became a king.

10. The above-mentioned kings are the descendants of Kāśi in the lineage of Kṣattravṛddha.

(Now the genealogy of Rambha, the fourth son of Āyu). The son of Rambha was Rabhasa whose son was Gambhīra from whom was born Akriya.

11. Through Akriya's queen started the line of Brāhmaṇas. Now listen to the line of Anenas (the fifth son of Āyu). Anenas' son was Śuddha of whom was born Śuci. His son was Trikakud, also known as Dharma-sārathi.

12. Of him was born Śānta-rayas who being selfcontrolled (or knower of the Soul) had almost accomplished his objective (viz. Final beatitude and was not interested in continuing his race). Raji (the third son of Āyu) had five hundred sons, endowed with immense prowess.

13-16. Entreated by gods, Raji slaughtered the demons and restored the celestial kingdom to Indra. But Indra being afraid of Prahlāda and others, again returned the kingdom of heaven to Raji, clasped his feet and placed himself under Raji's protection (as his son). When the father (Raji) died, his sons, even though solicited (by Indra), refused to return the celestial kingdom to him. (On the contrary) they appropriated to themselves shares oblated in sacrifice (for Indra). Bṛhaspati, then offered oblations to fire (with malevolent purpose against the sons of Raji and made them stray from the path of religion) and Indra slew them one and all as they swerved from the path (of righteousness) and not a single son (of Raji) survived.[1]

From Kuśa, the grandson of Kṣattravṛddha, was born Prati, of whom sprang up Sañjaya whose son was Jaya.

17. Jaya's son was Kṛta, of whom was born the king Haryavana. His son was Sahadeva, who begot Hīna, whose son was Jayasena.

18. Jayasena's son was Saṅkṛti whose son Jaya, who, himself a great (chariot-) warrior, followed religiously ordained

1. This episode is confirmed in the *Vāyu P.*92.76-99; *Matsya P.* 24. 34-48.

path of Kṣattriyas. The kings belonging to the line of Kṣattravṛddha have been described. Now listen to the genealogy of Yayāti, the son of Nahuṣa.

CHAPTER EIGHTEEN

The History of Nahuṣa's Line—The Story of Yayāti[1]

Śrī Śuka said :

1. Just as an embodied being is endowed with six senses (five senses *plus* the inner organ, the mind) King Nahuṣa had the following six sons—Yati, Yayāti, Saṁyāti, Āyati, Viyati and Kṛti.

2. Being aware of the consequences of the acceptance of the rulership of a kingdom, Yati did not desire sovereignty offered to him by his father, for (he knew that) by shouldering kingship, a person does not realize his own self.

3. When, due to his misdemeanour towards Indra's queen, Indrāṇī, Nahuṣa was dethroned from his position (as the ruler of the celestial world) and was converted verily into a boa-constrictor by the Brāhmaṇa-sages, Yayāti became a king.

4. Appointing his four younger brothers to govern over the kingdom in four directions (each in one direction), he married the daughter of Śukra (the preceptor of Asuras) and

1. The Yayāti legend—the exchange of Yayāti's age with the youth of his son and his memorable words at the return of the youth and reacceptance of his age at the time of renunciation :

> *na jātu kāmaḥ kāmānām upabhogena śāmyati* /
> *haviṣā kṛṣṇa-vartmeva bhūya evābhivardhate* //

have been immortalized in *MBH. Adi.* chs. 76-81, *Matsya P.* chs. 30-35 *Padma P.Bhūmi.* chs. 76-83 (with a Vaiṣṇavite colouring), the *Vāyu P.* ch.93. The legend in its modern garb is still very popular and a Marāṭhī novel on this legend received a Bhāratīya Jñānapīṭha Award—the most honoured and covetable prize in India, this year.

of Vṛṣaparvā, the king of Asuras and thus protected the earth (from his capital).

King Parīkṣit enquired :

5. The venerable Śukra was a Brāhmaṇa sage while Yayāti, the son of king Nahuṣa, was a Kṣattriya by caste. Why and how could such an irregular marriage against the caste-order between a Kṣatriya man and a Brāhmaṇa girl come about ?

Śrī Śuka replied :

6-7. On one occasion, in the company of a thousand lady-friends and Devayānī, the preceptor's daughter, Śarmiṣṭhā, the princess of the great Dānava king Vṛṣaparvā who, though of the weaker sex was imperious by nature, was promenading in the pleasure garden of her capital which was full of blooming flower-trees, and charming with pools, the sandy banks and lotus beds of which were full of sweet humming of bees.

8. Arriving at a pool of water, those lotus-eyed girls left their silken garments on its bank and engaged themselves in water sports sprinkling each other with water.

9. Perceiving that god Śiva accompanied by his Consort Pārvatī, was riding that way on his bull, the ladies forthwith rushed out of the water, and hastened to put on their garments, out of bashfulness.

10. Not knowing that the garments belonged to the preceptor's daughter, Śarmiṣṭhā wore it, thinking it to be her own. Getting enraged thereby, Devayānī spoke as follows :

11. "Oh ! Behold the impropriety of this slave-girl in that, like a bitch carrying away the oblation (meant for gods) in a sacrifice, she wore the garment which was to be put on by us.

12. By us Brāhmaṇas (like god Brahmā, Prajāpatis like Marīci) has been created this universe through the power of our asceticism and penance; we constitute the mouth of the Supreme Person (i.e. we are born from god's mouth and as such are superior to all, as he gets propitiated when we are feasted to our satisfaction). By us the light of the Supreme

Brahman is conserved (as an object of adoration) in our hearts, and the blessed path of Vedic religion is shown by us.

13. To us (Brāhmaṇas) the Lords of gods, protectors of the world, and even the most purifying, glorious Lord Viṣṇu, the Soul of the Universe and the abode of goddess Śrī, pay homage and praise.

14. And among such Brāhmaṇas, we are the descendants of Bhṛgu. Her father, a demon, is our disciple. This unchaste girl has put on the dress meant for us like a Śūdra bearing (reciting) the Veda—(a privilege of the twice-born castes).

15. Thus attacked, Śarmiṣṭhā who angrily sighed heavily like a hissing female serpent, bit her lips and retorted to the spiritual preceptor's daughter who was reproaching her with words of abuse.

16. "Oh! Beggar-maid, ignoring your own (menial) position, you are vainly boasting yourself. Do you not wait at our house-(door) like a crow or a dog (for crumbs of food)?"

17. Having reproached the good daughter of her preceptor with such and other harsh words, Śarmiṣṭhā snatched away all her cloths and pushed her into a well.

18. It is traditionally told that when Śarmiṣṭhā returned home, Yayāti who was on the hunting expedition, wanted to drink water, and happened, by chance, to come to that well where he saw her (Devayānī).

19. The merciful king gave his upper garment to the girl who was stark naked, and holding her hand by his own, he lifted her out of water.

20. Devayānī, the daughter of Uśanas (i. e. Śukra) spoke to the king in words steeped in genuine love: "Oh King! You have accepted my hand, Oh conqueror of inimical cities!"

21. "As my hand has now been accepted by you once, let no one else now take it. This relation of ours is ordained providentially and not through human agency, Oh valiant warrior. It is hence that I could have this sight of yours while clinging to the (walls of the) well.

22. Oh King of powerful arms ! No Brāhmaṇa is destined to accept my hand due to the (reciprocal curse of Kaca the son of Bṛhaspati whom I imprecated initially".[1]

23. Yayāti found that the unexpected event was brought about by his destiny and being conscious that now his heart was attached to her, accepted her proposal.

24. When the valiant king departed, Devayānī went to her father crying (all the while) and reported to him all that was said and done by Śarmiṣṭhā.

25. The glorious sage Śukra was deeply agitated at heart. Disparaging the profession of a priest and commending the way of life of a pigeon (which freely gathers its food in the forest—technically known as *Uñccha-vṛtti*—"maintenance by gleaning), he went out of the city (Vṛṣaparvā's capital) along with his daughter.

26. Knowing that his intention is to conspire and bring victory to the enemies viz. gods, Vṛṣaparvā propitiated his preceptor by falling prostrate at his feet on the way.

27. The glorious Śukra, the descendent of Bhṛgu whose anger lasts hardly for half a moment, spoke to his disciple Vṛṣaparvā, "Oh King ! Let the desire of her (Devayānī) be satisfied because I cannot brook to let her alone."

28. When Vṛṣaparvā agreed with the words, "Be it so", and awaited (to hear Devayānī's desire), Devayānī disclosed what was in her mind. "Wherever I shall go after being given away by my father in marriage, let her (Śarmiṣṭhā) follow me along with her companions (as attendants)."

29. Realizing the peril (involved in the departure of Śukra) to her people, and the importance of the matter, she (Śarmiṣṭhā) along with her thousand lady-companions, attended upon Devayānī like a menial.

1. According to *MBH. Ādi.* chs. 76-77 Kaca, the son of Bṛhaspati could successfully learn the *Sañjīvanī Vidyā* from Śukra through the special favour of Devayānī. At the time of departure Devayānī proposed to marry him. But he rejected her on the ground that being his preceptor's daughter she is like a sister to him. Enraged at this, Devayānī cursed him that his *vidyā* will be futile. Kaca reciprocated the curse (that no Brāhmaṇa would marry her).

30. Having given in marriage his daughter along with Śarmiṣṭhā to Yayāti, the son of Nahuṣa, Śukra warned him, "Oh king ! Never take Śarmiṣṭhā to share the bed with you."

31. On one occasion, seeing Devayānī blessed with a son, the chaste lady Śarmiṣṭhā, at the period proper for conception, courted her friend's (Devayānī's) husband secretly (for children).

32. The king, being well-versed in *Dharma-śāstra*, realized it to be his sacred duty to comply with the request of the princess (Śarmiṣṭhā) who solicited him for progeny, and he followed the course ordained for him by Destiny, though he remembered the warning of Śukra.

33. Devayānī gave birth to Yadu and Turvasu, while Śarmiṣṭhā, the daughter of Vṛṣaparvā, had three sons—Druhyu, Anu, and Pūru.

34. Learning about the pregnancy of the Asura princess from her husband, proud Devayānī, being offended with her husband (through jealousy and pride), was overwhelmed with rage and proceeded to her father's house.

35. The passionate king followed his beloved to reconcile her with words of appeasement and winsome promises, but was not able to please her, even by shampooing her feet.

36. Flying in rage, Śukra cursed him, "You liar ! Woman-addict ! Let the decrepitude of old age which disfigures men overtake you, you stupid fellow !"

37. Yayāti urged, "Oh Brāhmaṇa Sage ! I am not till today sated with enjoyment of pleasure with your daughter". (Śukra replied) "In that case, you may exchange it (your old age) with the (youth of) anyone else who is willing to accept it."

38-39. Having secured this arrangement (as a way out of the curse), Yayāti addressed to his eldest son : "Oh my child Yadu ! Please accept this decrepitude of age caused by your maternal grand-father, and give me your youth in exchange. Dear child ! I am not yet satisfied with enjoyment of pleasures. I would like to enjoy for a few more years, with your youth."

Yadu replied :

40* "I dare not accept and live with the old age which overtook you in the middle of life, (for) a man cannot attain to desirelessness without an actual experience of the worldly pleasures first."

41. Turvasu, Anu, and Druhyu were then requested (one by one) by the father. But they did not know what was righteousness and regarded transient things (like youth) as eternal, and refused his proposal, Oh scion of Bharata.

42. He requested his son Pūru who was the youngest in age but seniormost in virtues. "Oh child ! It does not behove you to refuse my request as was done by your elder brothers".

Pūru said :

43. "Oh lord of men ! What man on earth is capable of repaying fully the obligations of his father, the procreator of his body, and through whose grace one can attain the highest (objective in life) ?

44. The best son is he who accomplishes the task in anticipation of the expectation of his father. The mediocre is one who complies when expressly told by his father. The lowest type is he who obeys but with irreverence. And he who disobeys is the excretion of his father."

45. In this way, Pūru gladly accepted the old age of his father. With his youth, Yayāti also enjoyed pleasures at his sweet will.

46. As a lord of the seven continents of the earth, he protected his subjects well like a father, and with his senses unimpaired, he gratified his desires (by enjoying pleasures) to his heart's content.

47. His beloved Devayānī every day heightened his love by affording pleasures to him by her thought, word and deed, and by offering objects of enjoyment in privacy.

* Yadu was very pious (*infra* 10.1.2). VC defends Yadu's disobedience thus: Yadu wanted to devote himself to the services of the Lord at the earliest. That mental stage is possible only after actual experience of worldly pleasures for some days. Acceptance of Yayāti's age would postpone that mental stage and consequently the life devoted to the services of the Lord. Between Service to the Lord and disobedience to father, the former is preferable according to Dharma. Marvellous defence !

48. By performance of sacrifices with profusely liberal gifts, Yayāti worshipped Lord Hari (Destroyer of all miseries and sins) the Presiding Deity of sacrifices, the God who represents all gods in Himself, and is an embodiment of all Vedas.

49. On Hari is superimposed this universe as a row of clouds on the sky and which, like a dream or an illusion or a fancy now appears to be different (in names, forms etc.) and now ceases to be (in dreamless sleep or after the deluge of the world).

50. Enthroning in his heart the Almighty Lord Vāsudeva who is abiding in the hearts of all as the Indweller, he (Yayāti) worshipped the subtlemost Nārāyaṇa without cherishing any desire for blessings.

51. Yayāti, the emperor of the entire earth, did not feel sated even though he enjoyed pleasures for thousands of years through his (five) wicked senses of which his mind was the sixth.

CHAPTER NINETEEN

Yayāti's Retirement and Final Emancipation

Śrī Śuka said :

1. (While) Yayāti, the woman-dominated addict, was enjoying the pleasures of senses in this way, he became aware of his spiritual fall (negligence of the Self) and being disenchanted (with worldly pleasures), narrated the following parable to his beloved Devayānī.

2. "Oh Devayānī ! Please listen to this history of a passionate person on this earth, whose life and conduct were just like mine, and whose lot was deplored by self-controlled people residing in forests.

3. A certain goat, while seeking all alone for an object dear to him, in a jungle, happened to see a goat fallen into a well as a result of her fate.

4. Cherishing lust for her, the goat thought out a way to lift her up and digging out the earth on the bank with the tips of his horns, he made a way out for her.

5-6. It is said that after getting out of the well, the beautiful she-goat loved him (as her husband). Observing that she had selected a stout, finely bearded, lovable he-goat possessing great venereal strength and expert in the art of sexual intercourse, a number of other she-goats desirous of having a mate, wooed him. That he-goat possessed as he was by the devil of sexual passion, excited the passion of that flock of she-goats and revelled with them all alone, and thus failed to realize and think about his own self.

7. Seeing him enjoying himself with another most beautiful she-goat, the female-goat that formerly suffered a fall in the well, did not tolerate that act of the he-goat.

8. Being distressed, she left her mate who was wicked-hearted, a false lover posing as a friend, and professing love only for a moment, but really given to the gratification of his senses, and went to her master.

9. Even that goat too, being a woman-addict, felt aggrieved and followed her to reconcile her, but in spite of his bleating with erotic eloquence he failed to win her over on the way.

10. There, her master, a certain Brāhmaṇa, castrated the dangling scrotum of that goat. But in the interest (of the she-goat), he, being a master of (such) expedients sewed back the amputated limb.

11. Having got his testicles (along with his capacity of sexual enjoyment) restored, the goat, though enjoyed pleasures for a long time with the she-goat found in the well, does not feel satiated with sexual pleasures even today.

12. In the same way, Oh lady with beautiful eyebrows, I, a person of poor intellect, am chained down by your love, Oh gracious lady. Being infatuated by your charms, I do not know (the nature of) my Self.

13. All the food-grains, all gold, animals and women cannot yield satisfaction (to the degree of satiation) to the mind of a person subjected to cravings and passions.

14. Never, never does passion get satiated with the en-

joyment of its sense-objects. (On the contrary) like a fire fed with oblations of ghee, it grows again in intensity.

15. When one does not cherish inauspicious attitudes (e. g. of hatred, partiality) to living beings, and looks upon all with equality, all the directions are full of bliss to him (i.e. he is blessed with happiness from all quarters).

16. A person desirous of happiness (untarnished by misery), should instantly give up thirst (for happiness) which is difficult to get rid of by evil-minded persons, and which does not get worn out even if one's body gets withered with age, and which is a source of endless misery.

17. A person should not sit very close in privacy (lit. share the same seat in private) to his mother, sister or daughter. For the senses (as a whole) are so powerful that they lead astray even a wise (learned) man.

18. It is for complete one thousand years that I have been enjoying repeatedly and incessantly the objects of pleasures. Still every time (I enjoy them), the hankering after them grows (apace).

19. Therefore giving up this (thirst for enjoyment) and concentrating my mind on the *Brahman* and freeing myself from the pairs of opposites (pleasure-pain etc.) and the notion of egotism (I and mine), I shall lead a life in forest.

20. Knowing the unreality (momentariness) of what is seen (the kingdom or pleasures in this world) and what is heard (from the *Vedas* about the pleasures and positions promised in the next world), one should not brood over them or enjoy them. For, in that lies the transmigration of the soul, and the loss of (the real knowledge of) the soul. Such a knower realizes the Ātman".

21. Having addressed thus to his wife (Devayānī), Yayāti, the son of Nahuṣa, returned his youth to Pūru, and becoming free from desires, accepted the decrepitude of his old age from him.

22. He appointed Druhyu to rule over the South-eastern region (of his kingdom), Yadu in the South, Turvasu in the west and Anu in the north.

23. Having consecrated Pūru, the worthiest of them all, as the sovereign ruler of the earth and the subjects, he placed

the elder brothers under his control and then repaired to the forest.

24. Just as a bird leaves its nest as soon as it gets full-fledged, he instantly shed off the six-fold objects of pleasures enjoyed through his senses and mind, for a considerable number of years (or) controlled his senses and mind.

25*. Freeing himself completely from all attachments and shedding off his subtle body constituted of three *guṇas* by virtue of his spiritual power of self realization, the celebrated king Yayāti became absorbed[1] in the Supreme Brahman unsoiled by Māyā (or any impurity) and designated as Vāsudeva—a state attained by the devotees of the Supreme Lord.

26. Hearing that parable, Devayānī regarded it as an incentive to follow a path of renunciation, and a jocular story told out of agony of separation between a man and his wife.

27-28. Realizing that the association of friends and relatives is brought about by *Māyā* (according to their *karma*)[1] and is controlled by the Almighty Lord, and thus is as temporary as those of travellers attending a watering place (to drink water on the way), Devayānī, the scion of the Bhṛgu race, gave up attachment to everything and everywhere regarding it as unreal as dreams. She concentrated her mind on Kṛṣṇa (i. e. Lord Viṣṇu) and shuffled off her (subtle) body (and became liberated).

29. I bow to you the glorious Lord Vāsudeva, the cause of the Universe, the abode of all beings (or the Inner Controller of all) perfectly serene and all-pervading. Salutations to you.

* VJ. By his direct perception of the Self, he shed off his egotism caused by three *guṇas* or the threefold misery caused by them and became liberated—a stage reached by following the *Bhāgavata dharma*.

1. VR. He approached the stage of Mokṣa, for according to the *Mahābhārata*, he spent some period in the celestial world.

CHAPTER TWENTY

The History of Pūru's race—Birth of Bharata[1]

Śrī Śuka said :

1. I shall now narrate to you the history of Pūru's line wherein you are born, Oh descendant of Bharata. In this family sprang up many royal sages and Brāhmaṇas who propagated their own lines.

2. Janamejaya was born of Pūru; Janamejaya's son was Pracinvān. His son was Pravīra who begot Namasyu. To him was born Cārupada.

3. Sudyu sprang from Cārupada; Sudyu had a son Bahugava; thence was born Saṁyāti; his son was Ahaṁyāti whose son was Raudrāśva.

4-5. Raudrāśva begot on a celestial nymph Ghṛtāci ten sons viz. Ṛteyu, Kukṣeyu, Sthaṇḍileyu, Kṛteyu, Jaleyu, Santateyu, Dharmeyu, Satyeyu, Vrateyu and the youngest known as Vaneyu—even as ten sense organs (both conative and cognitive) are evolved from the chief vital air, the Soul of the world.

6. From Ṛteyu was born Rantibhāra. He had the following three sons viz. Sumati, Dhruva and Apratiratha. Kaṇva was the son of Apratiratha, Oh King !

7. Kaṇva's son was Medhātithi. From him were originated Praskaṇva and other Brāhmaṇa clans. Sumati had a son called Raibhya, and Duṣyanta was regarded as his son.

8-9. While on a hunting excursion, (king) Duṣyanta happened to visit the hermitage of Kaṇva. Having seen a beautiful damsel beautifying the surroundings with her effulgence, and enchanting like the Māyā of the Lord, he instantaneously got infatuated. And though surrounded by some of his soldiers, he spoke to that charming lady.

1. This chapter gives the following descendants of Pūru up to Vitatha as follows :
Pūru→Janamejaya→ Pracīnvān → Pravīra → Namasyu →Cārupada → Sudyu → Bahugava→ Saṁyāti→Ahaṁyāti→Raudrāśva→Ṛteyu→Rantibhāra→Sumati→Raibhya→Duṣyanta→Bharata→Bharadvāja→Vitatha. The story of Duṣyanta, Śakuntalā and the birth of Bharata is given in details in *MBH Ādi*. Chs. 69-74.

10. Overjoyed at her very sight, he felt all his fatigue relieved. Tormented by sexual passion, he smilingly asked her, in soft words.

11. "Who are you, Oh beautiful lady (with eyes like lotus-petals)? Whose daughter are you, Oh charming damsel? what is your object in staying in a tenantless forest?

12. Oh lady of a beautiful waist! As I perceive it, you are obviously a girl from a royal family. For the mind of the descendants of Pūru, hardly finds delight in unrighteous paths."

Śakuntalā replied :

13. "As the venerable sage Kaṇva knows it, I am the daughter of Viśvāmitra, abandoned by my mother Menakā in the forest. What should we do for you, Oh warrior?

14. Be pleased to take a seat, Oh lotus-eyed one, and accept our hospitality. Enjoy the boiled rice of wild paddy. You may stay here, if it pleases you."

Duṣyanta said :

15. "Oh lady of beautiful eyebrows! Born as you are in the line of Kuśika, all this (hospitality) is quite proper and natural. Maidens of royal families select of their own accord, their life-mates".

16. When she consented to it, he married Śakuntalā duly according to Gāndharva custom prescribed (for Kṣatriyas) in *Dharmaśāstra*, as the king was expert in the knowledge of what should be done at particular time and place according to Dharma.

17. The royal sage of unfailing procreative capacity, deposited his semen in his queen. Next morning he returned to his capital. In due course, she was delivered of a son.

18. Kaṇva carried out the appropriate religious rites of the boy, in the forest. With his tremendous strength, the child used to catch hold of lions and played with them.

19. Taking with her, her son who was born of a portion of Lord Hari, and was of invincible prowess, the excellent lady sought the audience of her royal consort.

20. When the king did not accept his wife and child, though both of them were blameless and irreproachable, an

incorporal voice from heaven announced, while all beings were listening.

21. "The mother is simply a receptacle. The son belongs to his father alone, of whom he is born. Nay, the father is himself (no other than) the son. Therefore, Oh Duṣyanta, bring up your son. Do not neglect Śakuntalā.

22. Oh King, a son who propagates the line of the family takes away his father out of the abode of Yama.[1] You have deposited Bharata in the foetus (i.e. you are the real father). What Śakuntalā stated is the truth.[2]

22A. Bring up your son Bharata who is imbued with a ray of Vāsudeva. He is friendly towards Brāhmins, true to his promise, capable of knowing and appreciating virtues and excellences and enhancing your reputation.

22B. He is possessed of superior energy, is generous, grateful and ready to wait upon the elders." Hearing this incorporal voice from the heaven, the king accepted his son.

23. When the father (Duṣyanta) expired, he (Bharata) became an emperor of great renown. The great glory of Bharata who was born from the ray of Lord Hari, is still eulogised on the earth.

24. He had the sign of discus on right palm and that of a lotus on the soles of his feet. That powerful king, the sole emperor of the earth was consecrated (on the throne) by the performance of *Mahābhiṣeka.* He performed many sacrifices.

25. With fifty-five sacrificial horses he performed (horse) sacrifices along the course of the Gaṅgā (from its source to the sea) with Dīrgha-tamas (the son of Mamatā) as his sacrificial priest.

26. Along the course of the Yamunā, he tied seventy-eight sacrificial horses (i. e. performed seventyeight horse-sacrifices on the bank of the river as it flows to join the Gaṅgā), liberally distributing wealth (among the Brāhmaṇas).

1. v.l. : In case of dispute between the father and the mother both claiming the child, the father's claim is upheld by Yama (Dharmaśāstra).

2. Cf. *MBH Ādi.* 74. 110-111. is *verbatim* the same.

bhastrā mātā pituḥ putro yena jātaḥ sa eva saḥ /
bharasva putraṁ Duṣyanta māvamaṁsthāḥ Śakuntalām //
retodhāḥ putra unnayati naradeva Yamakṣayāt /

The sacred fire of Bharata, the son of Duṣyanta was set up on an exceedingly excellent place where the thousand Brāhmaṇas (engaged in the sacrifice) divided among themselves cows (gifted by Bharata), each receiving his share of thirteen thousand eightyfour (*Badva*[1]) cows.

27. Having thus tied to the sacrificial post one hundred and thirtythree horses, he sprang a surprise on the earthly kings. The son of Duṣyanta surpassed gods with his affluence, and he became one with Viṣṇu who is adorable to gods.

28. At the conclusion of the sacrificial ritual *maṣṇāra*[2] (or at a sacred place called Maṣṇāra), he donated as gift, fourteen lakhs of elephants of the *mṛga* type[3] black in colour, with their white tusk plated with gold.[4]

29. No king of the past could accomplish the great eminence of Bharata. Nor can kings of the future do so any more than one can reach the celestial world by hands.

30. During his expedition for the conquest of the world, he defeated the tribes Kirātas, Hūṇas, Yavanas, Āndhras, Kaṅkas, Khaśas and Śakas and killed the Mleccha kings who were inimical to Brahmins or Vedas.

31*. By sending messengers, he restored to the gods, the celestial damsels who were formerly abducted to Rasātala by Asuras, after vanquishing the gods and occupying various parts of that region.

32. While he ruled, both heaven and earth supplied desires and needs of his subjects. His sovereignty extended all over the world for thrice nine thousand (27000) years.

1. ŚR quotes the definition of *badva* : *iyaṁ ca badva-saṅkhyā ślokena saṅgṛhyate* :

catur-daśānāṁ lakṣāṇāṁ saptādhika-śatāṁśakaḥ /
badvaṁ caturaśītyagra-sahasrāṇi trayodaśa //

2. No commentator from ŚR to BP is sure of the exact significance of the word *maṣṇāra*. VJ : 'At the conclusion of a particular observance (*vrata*) called *Maṣṇāra*.' All of them state that (alternatively) Maṣṇāra is the name of a holy place.

3. The elephants are of the three types : *bhadra*, *mandra* and *mṛga*.

4. Cf. *Ait. Br.* 8.23.3. VD. regards these elephant-types as belonging to the region of the Himalayas, Vindhya and Sahyādri respectively.

* Vanquishing the Asuras, he repatriated gods to their respective regions and restored to their husbands the celestial damsels who were carried away by demons celled Paṇis—VJ.

33. The tradition goes that the emperor realized that his sovereignty the fame of which had spread over all the worlds, his imperial glory and affluence, his unchallenged authority and implicit obedience to commands, nay even his life and sense-organs were unreal and so he renounced the world.

34. He had three queens all from the state of Vidarbha. When he remarked that his sons did not look like him, they, being afraid of being abandoned by him (suspecting their character), killed them all.

35. When his family line was (in the danger of being) extinct, the Marut gods gave him Bharadvāja as a son, when the emperor was propitiating them with sacrifice *Marutstoma* (for getting a son).

36. When Mamatā, the wife of his brother (Utathya), was pregnant, Bṛhaspati attempted to have a sexual intercourse with her, and was prevented (by the child in the womb with strong loud protests). He (Bṛhaspati) cursed the child in the womb (to become blind). He discharged per force his semen (in her), but the blind child in the womb prevented its entry by his foot. The seed that fell out on the ground assumed the form of a child.

37. To Mamatā who wanted to give away that child as she was terribly afraid of being abandoned by her husband, gods spoke the following verse which contains the etymology of the name of the child (which is nothing but the quarrel between Bṛhaspati and Mamatā each throwing the responsibility of bringing up that child on the other).

38. (SR. records this controversy between Mamatā and Bṛhaspati as follows):

(Said Bṛhaspati :) "Oh foolish woman ! Nourish (this child). (If you say that you are afraid of your husband that is baseless as) this child is born of us two brothers (by me through the *Kṣetra* viz. the wife of my brother)!" (Replied Mamatā) "Bṛhaspati ! You nourish this child because he is born of us two (when you raped me)". Saying these words (*bhara dvājam*) both the parents went away (abandoning the child). Hence he is called *Bhara-dvāja*.

39. Though urged by gods (to bring up the child), they thought him as a useless son and abandoned him. The Maruts nourished the child and it was given to Bharata when his family was going to be extinct. (*Vitatha* should be regarded as the name of Bharadvāja, after his adoption by Bharata).

CHAPTER TWENTYONE

The Race of Bharata[1]. *The History of Rantideva*[2]

Śrī Śuka said :

1. Vitatha (Bharadvāja) had a son Manyu who begot (five sons) viz. Bṛhatkṣatra, Jaya, Mahāvīrya, Nara, Garga. Nara's son was Saṅkṛti.

2. Saṅkṛti had two sons—Guru and Rantideva, Oh delight of the Pāṇḍu family ! The glory of Rantideva is eulogised in this world as well as in heaven.

3-4. By giving away wealth which came his way without efforts (like the sky) thinking it to be momentary, he became hungry and destitute of everything (including provision even for the evening). While the hero suffered hardships along with his family, fortyeight days passed during which he could not get even water to drink. In the morning (of the fortyninth day), he happened to get by chance ghee, rice cooked in milk, (*saṁyāva*) (an article of food consisting of wheat-flour, raw-sugar, ghee and milk) along with water.

5. He whose family was distressed and trembling due to utter starvation and parched with thirst, was about to partake of it (the food) when a Brāhmaṇa guest arrived, just at the time of their breaking the fast.

1. As ŚR points out, although Bharadvāja was originally a Brāhmaṇa, he became Kṣattriya after his adoption by Bharata. He is thenceforth known as Vitatha and he continued Bharata's race.

2. The Rantideva episode and especially his refusal to attain to Mokṣa but wish to live here in order to relieve the misery of all beings (vv 12, 13 below) are similar to the Bodhisattva ideal of Buddhists.

6. As he visualized Hari everywhere (and in everybody), he received the Brāhmaṇa with reverence and faith, gave him his share of food. The Brāhmaṇa took his meal and went his way.

7. While he was about to partake of the remaining food which was distributed among themselves, another stranger—now a Śūdra—arrived. He gave him the portion of the food so distributed, contemplating all the while on Lord Hari, Oh king of the earth.

8. When the Śūdra departed, another stranger surrounded by a pack of hounds approached him and requested, "Oh King ! May food be served to me alongwith my dogs, who are hungry".

9. The king received them kindly and gave to him respectfully whatever food that remained with him, and bowed to the dogs and the master of those hounds.

10-11. Now some water, just sufficient to quench the thirst of one person, remained. While he was about to drink it, a Cāṇḍāla came up and requested, "Give water to me who am a low caste person". Hearing his pitiful request uttered with great pains and exhaustion, the king who was deeply moved and tormented with compassion, uttered the following nectar-like speech.

12. "I do not seek from the Almighty Lord the highest position attended with eight spiritual powers (e. g. *Aṇimā*, *Laghimā*, etc. detailed in the *Yogasūtras*), nor emancipation from *saṁsāra*; I would rather prefer to dwell in all beings and undergo sufferings for them, whereby they may be free from miseries.

13. By offering water which was essential to save the life of an unfortunate creature who craved for life, my personal hunger, thirst, exhaustion of limbs, distress, languor, grief, despondency and delusion—all have disappeared."

14. Expressing such nobility of heart, the king who was compassionate by nature and full of fortitude, gave that water to the Cāṇḍāla, though he himself was on the point of death through thirst.

15. To him, the Lords of the Three worlds (e. g. God Brahmā and others) who bestow fruits on those who seek them,

and who visited him in those illusory forms (a short while ago) under instructions from Lord Viṣṇu, revealed themselves to him.

16. The king being entirely free from attachments, cherished no desires. Bowing down to them all, he concentrated his mind on glorious Lord Vāsudeva with utmost devotion, and sought no boons from them.

17. Concentrating his mind on the Almighty Lord as the only support, and cherishing no desire for any fruit (in return) therefrom, *Māyā* the deluding potency of the Lord constituted of three *guṇas* (automatically) dissolved (disappeared altogether) like a dream, in the case of Rantideva, Oh king.

18. By virtue of close association with him, all *yogins* who followed closely Rantideva (i. e. his path of intense, selfless devotion) became absolutely devoted to Lord Nārāyaṇa.

19-20. From Garga was born Śini who begot Gārgya. In this way, a Brāhmaṇa family-line started from a Kṣatriya race. From Mahāvīrya sprang Duritakṣaya whose sons were Trayyāruṇi, Kavi and Puṣkarāruṇi. They attained to the state of Brāhmaṇahood. Bṛhat-kṣattra had a son, who built the city of Hastināpura.

21. Hastin begot Ajamīḍha, Dvimīḍha and Purumīḍha. The descendants of Ajamīḍha were Brāhmaṇas like Priyamedha and others.

22. From Ajamīḍha was born (another son) Bṛhadiṣu whose son was Bṛhad-dhanu. His son was Bṛhatkāya whose son was Jayadratha.

23. He (Jayadratha) begot Viśada from whom sprang up Senajit. His sons were Rucirāśva, Dṛḍhahanu, Kāśya and Vatsa.

24. Rucirāśva's son was Pāra whose son was Pṛthuṣeṇa. Pāra's son was Nīpa to whom were born a hundred sons.

24A. Among them one was Aṇuha, the eldest was Satyaka, Oh King.

25. That Nīpa begot on Kṛtvī, the daughter of Śuka[1],

1. ŚR. VR. VC. BP. quote from HV (*Harivaṁśa*) ch. 18 and explain that when Śuka left home even before his *upanayana* (investiture of the sacred thread) ceremony, to lead a perpetually celibate life, he left

Brahmadatta. That *yogī* procreated through his wife Gau (Sarasvatī) a son called Viśvaksena.

26. According to the advice and guidance of sage Jaigīṣavya, he wrote a work on the *yoga*-system. He begot Udaksvan from whom sprang Bhallāda. These are the descendants of Bṛhadiṣu.

27. Dvimīḍha had a son called Yavīnara whose son was Kṛtimān by name. His son was Satyadhṛti whose son Dṛḍhanemi was the progenitor of Supārśva.

28-29. From Supārśva was born Sumati whose son was Sannati. His son was Kṛti who learnt yoga under Hiraṇyanābha, and sang the six earlier *saṁhitās* of the *Sāma-veda*[1] (divided them separately). He begot Nīpa from whom was born Ugrāyudha. His son was Kṣemya; his son Suvīra from whom was born Ripuñjaya.

30. His son was Bahuratha. Purumīḍha (Dvimīḍha's younger brother) had no child. Ajamīḍha begot on Nalinī, a son called Nīla whose son was Śānti.

31. From Śānti was born Suśānti, whose son was Puruja, from whom Arka was born. His son was Bharmyāśva who had five sons beginning with Mudgala.

32-33. Yavīnara, Bṛhadiṣu, Kāmpilya and Sañjaya were the (remaining four) sons (of Bharmyāśva). Bharmyāśva said, "These five sons of mine are capable (and enough) to

behind his shadow for the consolation of his father who married and had five sons and one daughter. The daughter is named *Kīrti-matī* and not Kṛtvī as here. *Devī Bhāgavata* I.19.39-43 rejects the shadow theory and states that as per Janaka's advice Śuka married pīvarī, a daughter of Pitṛs and had four sons (names differ from the HV), and a daughter Kīrti who was married to Anu, the son of king Vibhrāj. I think JG is correct in regarding this Śuka as a different person, not so much because JG quotes the authority of the *Brahmavaivarta P.* where Śuka is said to have been born as a boy of twelve years, who, renouncing the world, straightway walked out of home, but the tenor of the text of the Bh.P., shows that according to Śuka the narrator of the Bh. P. this Śuka, father of Kṛtvī, is altogether different, merely a name-sake.

1. v.l. *jagan ḍvi-ṣat*—Twelve earlier *saṁhitās* of the Sāma Veda (BP) and BP quotes VP. which credits him with saying (mastering and teaching) twenty-four *saṁhitās* :

Hiraṇya-nābho yogam adhyāpayāmāsa |
yaścaturviṁśatim prācya-sāmnāṁ cakāra saṁhitām ||

protect five countries. And hence they came to be known as Pāñcālas. From Mudgala originated a clan of Brāhmaṇas named Maudgalya.

34. A twin was born of Mudgala, the son of Bharmyāśva; (out of the twin) the male child was Divodāsa and the female child, Ahalyā. She had from (her husband) Gautama, a son called Śatānanda.

35-36. Śatānanda's son Satyadhṛti was expert in Military Science. His son was Śaradvān. They say that at the sight of Urvaśī, the seed of Śaradvān (emanated and) fell on a clump of reeds. From the semen was produced an auspicious twin. Finding the twin children during the course of hunting, Śantanu picked them out of compassion. The male child came to be known as Kṛpa, while the female child Kṛpī became the wife of Droṇa.

CHAPTER TWENTYTWO

The History of the Lunar Race.[1] *The Royal Dynasties of Pāñcāla, Magadha and Kuru*

Śrī Śuka said :

1-2. From Divodāsa was born Mitreyu, whose sons were Cyavana, Sudāsa, Sahadeva and Somaka. Somaka had a hundred sons of whom Jantu was the eldest, and Pṛṣata, the youngest. His son was Drupada whose daughter was Draupadī, and sons were Dhṛṣṭadyumna and others.

1. This chapter gives the genealogies of the following branches of the lunar race :

i. *Pāñcālas* A. *South Pāñcālas*

Ajamīḍha→Bṛhadiṣu→Bṛhad-dhanus → Bṛhatkāya→Jayadratha Viśada←Senajit→Rucirāśva→Pṛthuṣena→Para→Nīpa→ Brahmadatta→ Viṣvaksena→Udaksvana→Bhallāda.

B. *North Pāñcālas*

Ajamīḍha→Nalini→Nīla→Śānti→ Suśānti→Puruja → Arka→ Bharmyāśva→Mudgala→ Divodāsa → Mitreyu → Cyavana → Sudās→ Sahadeva→Somaka→Jantu→Pṛṣata→Drupada

3. From Dhṛṣṭadyumna appeared Dhṛṣṭaketu. These are the descendants of Bharmyāśva, also known as Pāñcālakas or Pāñcāla. Ajamīḍha had another son Ṛkṣa from whom was born Saṁvaraṇa.

4. Saṁvaraṇa begot on Tapatī, the daughter of the Sun-god, Kuru, the Lord of the Kurukṣetra. Kuru had Parīkṣit (the first, an ancestor of the hearer of the Bh. P.) Sudhanu, Jahnu and Niṣadhāśva as his sons.

5. From Sudhanu was born Suhotra whose son was Cyavana, his son was Kṛti, the father of Uparicara Vasu. From him were born Bṛhadratha and other sons.

6. (Out of them) Kuśāmba, Matsya, Pratyagra, Cedipa and others were the rulers of the Cedi country (Modern Bundelkhand and the region roundabout). From Bṛhadratha was born Kuśāgra whose son was Ṛṣabha.

7. Ṛṣabha begot Satyahita, whose son was Puṣpavān. His son was Jahu. Bṛhadratha had two parts (of a child) born by another wife.

8. Those parts were thrown away by the mother. A demoness Jarā, out of sport had joined them muttering the words 'Live ! Live. And lo ! A son called Jarāsandha (one joined by Jarā) appeared.

9. Of him was born Sahadeva whose son was Somāpī, who begot Śrutaśravas. (Out of the sons of Kuru) Parīkṣit was childless. The son of Jahnu was Suratha.

2. *Magadha*

Vasu Uparicara→Bṛhadratha→Kuśāgra → Ṛṣabha → Puṣpavān → Satyahita→Jahu→Jarāsandha→Sahadeva→Somāpi

3. *Pauravas*

Bharata adopted Bharadvāja and named him 'Vitatha' → Manyu→ Bṛhatkṣatra→Hastin→Ajamīḍha→Ṛkṣa→Saṁvaraṇa→Kuru→

|　　　　　　　　　　　　|

Dvimīḍha　　　　　　**Parīkṣit I→**

Jahnu → Suratha → Vidūratha → Sārvabhauma→Jayasena→Rādhika→ Ayuta → Krodhana → Devātithi → Ṛṣya→ Dilīpa→Pratīpa→Śantanu→ Vicitravīrya → Dhṛtarāṣṭra → Yudhiṣṭhira→ (Abhimanyu)→Parīkṣit II (the remaining line is a prediction).

4. **Dvimīḍhas**

Dvimīḍha→ Yavīnara→Kṛtimān → Satyadhṛti → Dṛḍha-nemi→ Supārśva→Sumati→Sannatimān→Kṛti→Nīpa→Ugrāyudha→Kṣemya→ Suvīra→Ripuñjaya→Bahuratha.

10. Suratha's son was Vidūratha, from whom was born Sārvabhauma. His son was Jayasena, whose son was Rādhika; from whom appeared Ayuta.

11. From him sprang up Krodhana whose son was Devātithi. His son was Ṛṣya, from whom was born Dilīpa. He had a son Pratīpa.

12. He (Pratīpa) had three sons—Devāpi, Śantanu and Bālhīka. Devāpi abdicated his ancestral throne and repaired to forest (for his spiritual advancement).

13-14. (After Devāpi's departure to forest) Śantanu who was formerly designated as Mahābhiṣa (a great physician), came to the throne. Whomsoever he touched with his hand—even if he be old—got rejuvenated again. And the old man got immediate and complete relief (from all ailments). By virtue of this (miraculous) gift, he was called Śantanu. When the rain-god did not rain for twelve years in his kingdom,

15. Śantanu was advised by Brāhmaṇas that inasmuch as he, though a younger brother, enjoyed the kingship (superseding his elder brother) and had become a *parivettā*[1] (a usurper), and for the prosperity of the capital and the kingdom, he should immediately restore the kingdom to his elder brother, Devāpi (when alone it will rain).

16. When thus addressed (advised) by Brāhmaṇas, he conciliated him (Devāpi) and persuaded him to accept the kingdom. Devāpi, however, was made to go astray from the path of Vedas by the words of Brāhmaṇas who were deputed by his ministers (especially by his minister (Aśma-rāva).

17. When Devāpi spoke blasphemously about the Vedas (and their teachings), the god Indra released the showers (as Devāpi proved apostate to the Vedic religion, and ceased to have a right to rule). Devāpi (realized his mistake and adopted the path of *yoga* and resorted to Kalāpagrāma.

1. ŚR quotes the following definition of *Parivettā* from a *Smṛti* text :

dārā'gnihotra-saṁyogaṁ kurute yo' graje sthite |
parivettā sa vijñeyaḥ, parivittis tu pūrvajaḥ ||

He who accepts a wife or *Agni-hotra* (fire-worship) before his elder brother does so, is called *parivettā* and the brother so superseded *Parivitti*.

18-20. When Lunar race gets extinct in the Kali age, he will (re-) establish it at the advent of the next age. From Bāhlīka was born Somadatta who had three sons viz. Bhūri, Bhūriśravas and Śala. Śantanu's son by Gaṅgā was the self-controlled Bhīṣma who was the most eminent among all the experts in *dharma-śāstra*, a great devotee of the Lord, a wise and learned person, a leader of a battalion of warriors by whom even Parśurāma (his preceptor in the science of arms) was pleased with his art and skill in fighting. Śantanu begot on Satyavatī[1], the daughter of the chief of Dāśas, a son called Citrāṅgada.

21. Her younger son was Vicitra-vīrya. Citrāṅgada was killed (in a duel with a Gandharva, called Citrāṅgada). Through her, from Parāśara, descended directly a digit or a ray of Lord Hari as her son (in the person of Kṛṣṇa Dvaipāyana).

22-24. The sage Kṛṣṇa Dvaipāyana is the protector of the Vedas from whom I learnt this *Śrīmad Bhāgavata*. In supersession of his own disciples such as Paila and others (vide Supra 1. 4. 21-22), the venerable sage Bādarāyaṇa preferred me, his son, as I was very serene by nature and recited (taught) to me this esoteric and sacred text (viz. the *Bhāgavata Purāṇa*. Then Vicitravīrya married two princesses of Kāśī, Ambā and Ambālikā both of whom were taken away by force (by Bhīṣma) from their *svayaṁvara*. Vicitravīrya was too much attached to them, and caught pthysis and died (in his youth).

25. When requested by his mother[2] (Satyavatī), Bādarāyaṇa (Vyāsa) procreated from the fields (i. e. wives) of his childless brother (Vicitravīrya)—Dhṛtarāṣṭra, Pāṇḍu and Vidura[3]

1. According to *MBH Adi* 63.50-69 she was the daughter of king Uparicara Vasu (vide V.5 above) developed in the womb of a celestial nymph Ārdrikā, cursed to be a female fish. She was brought up by the chief of fishermen and known as 'Satyavatī' due to her uprightness and moral virtues.

2. ŚR. quotes a religious injunction that one has to comply with such requests when instructed by elders.

3. Vidura's mother was not Vicitravīrya's wife, but a maid servant of the widowed queen Ambikā who deputed her as her substitute to Vyāsa —*MBH Adi* 1.94-96.

26. Dhṛtarāṣṭra had a hundred sons by his wife Gāndhārī. Of them, Duryodhana was the eldest. They had also a daughter, by name Duḥśalā.

27. To Pāṇḍu who was prohibited from sexual intercourse by a curse, three great (chariot-) warriors, the eldest of whom was Yudhiṣṭhira (Bhīma and Arjuna being the next two) were procreated on Kuntī from Dharma (the god Yamadharma), the wind-god and Indra.

28. Nakula and Sahadeva were born from (the loins of Aśvinī-kumāras) through Mādrī (Pāṇḍu's second wife). Draupadī had five sons,) one from each of her five husbands)—all of them your uncles (or who were the manes in their former life).

29-31. (Through Draupadī) Prativindhya was born from Yudhiṣṭhira; Śrutasena, from Bhīma; Śrutakīrti from Arjuna, Śatānīka from Nakula. Śrutakarmā was the son of Sahadeva. The other sons of the Pāṇḍavas were as follows: Yudhiṣṭhira begot Devaka on Pauravī; Bhīma had Ghaṭotkaca by Hiḍimbā and Sarvagata by Kālī. Vijayā, the daughter of Parvata, gave birth to a son Suhotra from Sahadeva.

32. Nakula begot Nirāmitra on Kareṇumatī. So also Arjuna had Irāvān from Ulūpī and Babhruvāhana by (Citrāṅgadā) the princess of the Maṇipura king. But he was adopted as a son by his (maternal) grandfather (as that was the condition precedent of the marriage, technically called *putrikāsuta*) [1]

33. Your father Abhimanyu was born of Subhadrā. He was a hero who vanquished all *ati-rathis* (a chariot-warrior who defeats innumerable enemies on the battlefield). You are born of Uttarā from him.

34. When all the Kauravas were slain, (Aśvatthāman) the son of Droṇa discharged the missile called *Brahmāstra*.

1. VR., GD., BP.VD. quote the condition:

abhrātṛkām pradāsyāmi tubhyaṁ kanyām alaṅkṛtām |
asyāṁ yo jāyate putraḥ sa me putro bhaviṣyati ||

'I give in marriage my daughter duly decorated with ornaments, on condition that, as she has no brother, the son that will be born to her will be my son.

You were rescued alive from the god of death by the spiritual prowess of Lord Kṛṣṇa.

35. Oh child! You have the following four sons, the eldest of whom is Janamejaya, the rest being Śrutasena, Bhīmasena and Ugrasena—all of whom are valiant.

36. Knowing that you have met death from Takṣaka's bite, he (Janamejaya) will get enraged, and will commit as oblations to fire, serpents in the serpent-sacrifice.

37. Having conquered the earth on all sides, and appointing Tura, the son of Kavaṣa, as the sacrificial priest, Janamejaya, the performer of *aśvamedha* (horse-sacrifice), will worship the Lord by performance of many sacrifices.

38. Janamejaya's son Śatānīka will learn the three Vedas as well as the knowledge of religious rites from Yājñavalkya, the technique of the use of missiles (from Kṛpa), and the knowledge about the self (the spiritual science) from Śaunaka.

39. His son will be Sahasrānīka whose son will be Aśvamedhaja; his son will be Asīma-Kṛṣṇa, whose son will be Nemi-cakra.

40. When Hastināpura will be washed away by the floods of the river (Gaṅgā), he will settle down at Kauśāmbī (Kosam, near Allahabad). He will have Citraratha as his son, of whom a son Kaviratha will be born.

41. From Kaviratha will appear Vṛṣṭimān (as the son) from whom will be born king Mahīpati. Sunītha will be his son. He will have a son Nṛcakṣus whose son will be Sukhīnala.

42. His son will be Pariplava, whose son will be Medhāvī who will have Sunaya as his son. Thence will be born Nṛpañjaya, from whom will be Dūrva, who will beget Timi.

43. From Timi will be born Bṛhadratha whose son will be Sudāsa, the father of Śatānīka. From Śatānīka will spring Durdamana whose son will be Bahīnara.

44. His son will be Daṇḍapāṇi who will beget Nimi. From him will be born king Kṣemaka. In this way the lineage of Brāhmaṇa-cum-Kṣatriya (Lunar race from which Brāhmaṇa and Kṣatriya races started) which has been honoured and praised by gods and sages has been described to you.

45. When the lunar race reaches king Kṣemaka, it will

be extinct in the Kali age. Now I shall describe to you the future kings of the Magadha country.

46. The son of Sahadeva (Jarāsandha's successor—son) will be Mārjāri whose son will be Śrutaśravas. Thence will be Ayutāyu, whose son will be Niramitra.

47. His son will be Sunakṣatra, from whom will be born Bṛhatsena—his son will be Karmajit. Thence will be Sṛtañjaya, from whom will appear Vipra, the father of Śuci.

48. Then will follow Kṣema whose son will be Suvrata. His son will be born Dharmasūtra whose son will be Śama. Thence will be Dyumatsena from whom will be born Sumati, whose son will be Subala.

49. Thence will be Sunītha of whom Satyajit, the father of Viśvajit will be born. From Viśvajit will be born Ripuñjaya. The kings of Bṛhadratha dynasty will reign for one thousand years.

CHAPTER TWENTY-THREE

The History of the Dynasties of Anu, Druhyu, Turvasu and Yadu[1]

Śrī Śuka continued :

1. Anu (the son of Yayāti) had three sons—Sabhānara, Cakṣu and Parokṣa. From Sabhānara was born Kālanara, whose son was then Sṛñjaya.

1. For the clear understanding of the Purāṇic history the genealogies of different branches of the Lunar race are given below : These names indicate Successors to the thrones—not necessarily sons.

Anu-s —I *Branch*

Anu→Sabhānara→Kālanara→Sṛñjaya→Janamejaya→ Mahāśīla→ Mahāmanas→Uśīnara→Śibi→Kaikeya

— *II Branch*

Titikṣu→Ruṣadratha→Hema→Sutapas→ Sutapā-Bali → Aṅga → Khanapāna→Diviratha→Dharmaratha →Romapāda→ Caturaṅga→Pṛthulākṣa Campa → Bṛhatkarman → Bṛhadratha → Bṛhadbhānu → Bṛhanmanas→

2. His son was Janamejaya, who begot Mahāśīla and his son was Mahāmanas. Uśīnara and Titikṣu were the sons of Mahāmanas.

3-4. Uśīnara had four sons—Śibi, Vana, Śami and Dakṣa. Śibi's four sons were Vṛṣādarbha, Suvīra, Madra and Kaikeya. Titikṣu's son was Ruśadratha, and his son, Hema. Hema's son was Sutapas from whom Bali was born.

5. On the wife of king Bali (who was childless), the sage Dīrghatamas begot six sons beginning with Aṅga, Vaṅga, Kaliṅga and also those called by the names Suhma, Puṇḍra and Āndhra.

6. These six established principalities in eastern provinces were known after their names (respectively). From Aṅga was born Khanapāna whose son was Diviratha.

7. His son was Dharmaratha whose son Citraratha had no issue. He was also known as Romapāda and was a friend of Daśaratha (king of Ayodhyā).

8-10. Daśaratha gave his daughter Śāntā (in adoption) whom Ṛṣyaśṛṅga married. When Indra did not release showers of rain, beautiful courtesans enticed away that son of a female deer, by means of dancing, vocal and instrumental music, coquettish behaviour, embraces and presents and brought him (to the king). By conducting a sacrifice (Iṣṭi) in honour of Indra, he (propitiated Indra and) secured progeny

Jayadratha → Vijaya → Dhṛti → Dhṛtavrata→Satkarman→Adhiratha→ Karṇa→Vṛṣasena

Druhyu-s

Druhyu→Babhru→Setu→Ārabdha→Gāndhāra→Dharma→Dhṛta→ Durmanas→Pracetas→Prācetas

Turvasu-s

Turvasu→Vahni→Bharga→Bhānumān→Tribhānu → Karandhama →Maruta→Duṣyanta.

Yadus: *Haihaya Branch*

Yadu→Sahasrajit→ Śatajit → Haihaya → Dharmanetra → Kunti→ Sohañji→Mahiṣman→Bhadrasena-ka→Durmada→ Dhanaka→Kṛtavīrya →Arjuna→Jayadhvaja→Tālajaṅgha→Vītihotra

Yadu : Main Branch

Yadu→Kroṣṭā→Vṛjinvan→Svāhi → Ruśeku → Citraratha → Śaśabindu → Pṛthuśravas → Dharma → Uśanas → Rucaka →Jyāmagha → Vidarbha

to Romapāda (who was childless). Daśaratha who was issueless was also blessed with children by a similar sacrifice. Caturaṅga was born from Romapāda, whose son was Pṛthulākṣa.

11. Pṛthulākṣa had (three) sons viz. Bṛhadratha, Bṛhatkarmā and Bṛhadbhānu. From the first (Bṛhadratha), was born Bṛhan-manas, from whom Jayadratha appeared.

12. He begot on Sambhūti (a son called) Vijaya from whom appeared Dhṛti. Thence Dhṛtavrata whose son was Satkarmā, from whom was born Adhiratha.

13. While playing on the bank of the Gaṅgā the king found a son encased in a (floating) box, abandoned by Kuntī, as he was born before her marriage. Being issueless, he brought him up as his son.

14. Vṛṣasena was the son of Karṇa who became a king. Druhyu (another son of Yayāti) had a son called Babhru, whose son was Setu.

15. His son was Ārabdha; his son, Gāndhāra, whose son was Dharma. Dharma's son was Dhṛta of whom Durmanas was the son. His son was Pracetas who had a hundred sons.

16. They became the rulers of the Mlecchas, and established themselves in the northern region. Turvasu (another son of Yayāti) had a son called Vahni of whom Bhaga was born. His son was Bhānumān.

17. His (Bhānumān's) son was Tribhānu whose son was the noble-hearted Karandhama. His son was Marut. He was childless and adopted Duṣyanta of the Pūru line, as his son.

18-19. That Duṣyanta, being desirous of (one more) kingdom, returned again to his family (as Pūru's descendant). I shall now describe to you the dynasty of Yadu, the eldest son of Yayāti—a dynasty of great religious merits and capable of removing sins. A man who listens to the account of the (family-line of) Yadu is absolved of all sins.

20-21. It was in this dynasty that the Supreme Soul incarnated, assuming a human form. It is reported that Yadu had four sons—Sahasrajit, Kroṣṭṛ, Nala and Ripu. The son of the first (Sahasrajit) was Śatajit. He had (three) sons—Mahāhaya, Veṇuhaya and Haihaya.

22. Haihaya's son was Dharma, whose son was Netra,

the father of Kunti. From Kunti was born Sohañji whose son was Mahiṣmān; his son was Bhadrasenaka.

23. Bhadrasena's sons were Durmada and Dhanaka, the father of Kṛtavīrya. Kṛtāgni, Kṛtavarmā and Kṛtaujāḥ also were the sons of Dhanaka.

24. Arjuna, the son of Kṛtavīrya became the lord of seven continents. He became extremely proficient in Yoga through the grace of Dattātreya, himself a ray of Lord Hari.

25. Other rulers of the earth cannot definitely reach the status of Kārtavīrya, in point of performance of sacrifices, munificent donations, asceticism, spiritual (*yogic*) powers, scholarship, valour, victories etc.

26. For eighty five thousand years, with unabated strength . . .

26A. Arjuna ruled his kingdom always remembering Lord Hari. . .with no dimunition in wealth of memory[1], he enjoyed the inexhaustible (fund) of objects of six senses (including the mind, as the sixth).

27. Out of his thousand sons, only five survived the battle (with Paraśurāma). They were Jayadhavja, Śūrasena, Vṛṣabha, Madhu and Ūrjita.

28. From Jayadhvaja was born Tālajaṅgha, who had hundred sons. The family of Tālajaṅghas was destroyed by the prowess of Sagara (the Aurva).

29. Vītihotra was the eldest of Tālajaṅgha's sons. Of Madhu (the son of Kārtavīrya Arjuna) was born Vṛṣṇi[2]. Madhu had hundred sons of whom Vṛṣṇi was the eldest. Hence the family came to be known after Vṛṣṇi.

30. Hence they came to be designated as Mādhavas, Vṛṣṇis and Yādavas, Oh king. Of Kroṣṭṛ, the son of Yadu, appeared Vṛjinavān.

31. He had a son Svāhi whose son was Ruśeku.[3] His son was Citraratha from whom was born a great *yogin* Śaśabindu

1. v.l. *anaṣṭa-Viṣṇu-smaraṇaḥ* — who never forgot to remember Hari any time.

2. VR. notes a v.l. according to which 'Vītihotra's son was Madhu from whom Vṛṣṇi was born'. The text here creates some confusion, in this half line.

3. 'Uruśaṅku, according to V.R. He notes 'Kuśeku' as a v.l.

of great affluence and luxurious life, as well as endowed with great moral virtues.

32. He was the master (possessor) of fourteen great jewels[1] and the sole sovereign ruler of the entire globe of the earth and of very great renown. He had ten thousand wives.[2]

33-34. By them he procreated a million sons. Of these, six were very prominent. Out of them, the son of Pṛthuśravas was known as Dharma. His son was Uśanas, a performer of one hundred horse-sacrifices (*aśvamedhas*). His son was Rucaka who had five sons. Listen (to their account).

35-36. They were called Purujit, Rukma, Rukmeṣu, Pṛthu and Jyāmagha. Jyāmagha who married Śaibyā, was childless, but he dared not take another wife through the fear (of Śaibyā). Once he brought from the enemy's house a girl for enjoyment. Seeing her in (her husband's) chariot, Śaibyā got enraged with her husband.

37. 'Who is this girl made to occupy my place in the chariot, you deceitful rogue'? (demanded Śaibyā). When he replied, "Your daughter-in-law", she smiled and spoke.

38. "I am a barren woman. How can a co-wife be my daughter-in-law?" "Oh queen! She will be suitable for marriage to the son who is to be born of you".

39. (ŚR gives a dramatic description of the situation). 'The king was perspiring and quaking through the fear of his wife. But he had all the while propitiated the fraternity of gods—*Viśvedevas*—and his manes, who approvingly blessed him) 'Amen', said the Viśvedevas and manes. After some time Śaibyā became pregnant (even after her menopause), and was

1. SR. quotes from *Mārkaṇḍeya purāṇa* the following list of jewels(i.e., excellent things) : An elephant, a horse, a chariot, women, an arrow, treasury, a garland of flowers, dress, wish-yielding tree, a Śakti (javelin), a noose, a gem (i.e.Ruby diamond), an umbrella and an aerial car.

2. VD. accepts this v.l. of ŚR :

tasya patnī-sahasrasya daśāsan sumahāyaśāḥ /

I accepted it as it is more clear than *patnīsahasrāṇāṁ daśānām* /

delivered of an auspicious son called 'Vidarbha', and he married the chaste girl who was already accepted as a daughter-in-law.[1]

CHAPTER TWENTY-FOUR

The History of the Race of Yadu[2]

Śrī Śuka said :

1. Vidarbha begot on her (Bhojyā) two sons by name Kuśa and Kratha, and the third one Romapāda who was the delight of the Vidarbha family.

1. All commentators quote Parāśara who declared Jyāmagha as the most hen-pecked husband. But even Parāśara in VP.4.12.12 remarks 'About Jyāmagha (his henpeckedness) the following verse is recited', so the verse :

bhāryāvaśyās tu ye kecid bhaviṣyantyathavā mṛtāḥ !
teṣāṁ tu Jyāmaghaḥ śreṣṭhaś Śaibyāpatir abhūn nṛpaḥ//

—VP.4.12.13 seems to be a traditional quotation.

2. The genealogies of the royal houses described in this chapter are given in order to clarify their mutual relations : They are the successors to the throne, not necessarily the sons of the predecessor

(1) *CEDI* (Vaidarbhas or Kaiśikas)

Vidarbha→Kuśa→Romapāda→Babhru→Kṛti→Uśika→ Cedi → Caidya etc.

(2) *CEDI-PA-S* (Vāsavas or Cedipas)

Vasu-Uparicara→Cedipa or Pratyagra→Damaghoṣa→Śiśupāla→Dhṛṣṭaketu.

(3) *YĀDAVAS*

Vidarbha→Kratha→Kunti→Dhṛṣṭi→Nivṛti→Daśārha→Vyoman→ Jīmūta → Vikṛti → Bhīmaratha → Navaratha → Daśaratha →Śakuni → Karambi→Devarāta→Devakṣatra→Madhu→ Kuruvaśa → Puruhotra → Anu I—Āyu→Sātvata.

(4) *SĀTVATAS*

Sātvata→Andhaka I→ Kukura→Vahni→Kapotaroman → Viloman →Anu II→Andhaka II→Dundubhi→ Aridyota → Punarvasu→Āhuka—Ugrasena→Kaṁsa

2. Romapāda's son was Babhru, from whom was born Kṛti. His son was Uśika from whom proceeded (the line of) kings like Caidya and others (i.e. Damaghoṣa etc.)

3. Kratha (the second son of Vidarbha) had a son called Kunti, from whom was born Dhṛṣṭi (Vṛṣṇi) whose son was Nirvṛti (Vidhṛti). From him sprang a son named Daśārha, whose son was Vyoma.

4. His son was Jīmūta whose son was Vikṛti, the father of Bhīmaratha. His son was Navaratha, from whom was born Daśaratha.

5. From his son Śakuni was born Kerambhi from whose loins appeared Devarāta. His son was Devakṣatra. From him was born Madhu, whose son was Kuruvaśa of whom was born Anu.

6-8. Anu's son was Puruhotra whose son was Āyu from whom Sātvata was born. Sātvata had seven sons—Bhajamāna, Bhaji, Dīpta, Vṛṣṇi, Devavṛdha, Andhaka, Mahābhoja, Oh noble king! Bhajamāna's sons were Nimloci, Kiṅkiṇī and Dhṛṣṭi, through one wife, while by another wife, he had three sons viz. Śatājit, Sahasrājit and Ayutājit, Oh Lord.

9-11. Babhru was the son of Devāvṛdha in eulogizing whom the following couplet is recited :

(5) *SATVATAS*

Sātvata → Mahābhoja → Bhajamāna II → Vidūratha → Śūra I→ Śini→Svayambhoja→Hṛdika—Devamīḍha→Śūra II→Vasudeva→Kṛṣṇa

(6) *VṚṢṆIS*

Vṛṣṇi I married to Gāndhārī :→Sumitra→Nimna—Satrājit—Bhaṅgakāra→Sabhākṣa.
(Satrājit | Prasena)

Vṛṣṇi I married to Mādrī :→Yudhājit→Vṛṣṇi II (Pṛṣṇi)
(Vṛṣṇi II | Śvaphalka | Akrūra etc.)
((Pṛṣṇi) | Citraka | Pṛthu etc.)

Vṛṣṇi I→Devamīḍha→Śūra II→Vasudeva→ Kṛṣṇa → Sāmba→ Vajra.

Vṛṣṇi→Śini II→Satyaka→Yuyudhāna→Jaya→ Kuṇi → Asaṅga → Yugandhara.

Vṛṣṇi I — Śini I.

"Just as we hear from far afar, so we see (them) from near. Babhru is the greatest among human beings while Devāvṛdha is just like gods (lit. equal in comparison with gods). Through the spiritual guidance of Babhru and Devāvṛdha fourteen thousand and sixty-five men attained immortality (liberation from *saṁsāra.*)."

Mahābhoja (the seventh son of Sātvata) was pious, and religious-minded. Kings born in his family-line were (known as) Bhojas.

12. Vṛṣṇi's son was Sumitra, whose son was Yudhājit, Oh chastiser of enemies. His son was Śini who had Anamitra as his son. From Anamitra appeared Nimna.

13. Satrājit and Prasena were the two sons of Nimna. Another Śini, a son of Anamitra had a son Satyaka.

14. Satyaka's son was Yuyudhāna whose son was Jaya from whom was born Kuṇi. His son was Yugandhara. Anamitra had another son named Vṛṣṇi.

15. Vṛṣṇi had two sons—Śva-phalka and Citraratha. Śva-phalka begot on Gandinī twelve famous sons (in addition to Akrūra), but Akrūra was the foremost of them all.

16-17. (The names of those sons are :) Āsaṅga, Sārameya, Mṛdura, Mṛduvid, Giri, Dharmavṛddha, Sukarmā, Kṣetropekṣa, Arimardana, Śatrughna, Gandhamāda and Pratibāhu. They had a sister called Sucīrā. Akrūra also had two sons—

18. Viz. Devavān and Upadeva. Citraratha had sons such as Pṛthu, Vidūra and many others—all descendants of Vṛṣṇi.

19. Andhaka[1] had four sons : Kukura, Bhajamāna, Śuci and Kambalabarhiṣa. Kukura's son was Vahni, whose son was Viloma.

20. He had a son Kapotaroma whose son was Anu. His friend was Tumbaru (the famous celestial musician. From Anu was born Andhaka, from whom was born Dundubhi. His son was Aridyota, the father of Punarvasu.

21. Punarvasu had a son called Āhuka, and a daugh-

1. On the strength of VP.4.14.12 ŚR gives the name Andhaka, though Bh.P. does not mention his name.

ter named Āhukī. Āhuka's sons were Devaka and Ugrasena. Devaka had four sons :

22. Viz. Devavān, Upadeva, Sudeva, Deva-vardhana. They had seven sisters such as Dhṛtadevā and others, Oh King !

23. (In addition to Dhṛtadevā) the sisters were Śāntidevā, Upadevā, Śrīdevā, Devarakṣitā, Sahadevā and Devakī all of whom Vasudeva (Kṛṣṇa's father) married.

24. Kaṁsa, Sunāma, Nyagrodha, Kaṅka, Śaṅku, Suhū, Rāṣṭrapāla, Sṛṣṭi and Tuṣṭimān were the sons of Ugrasena.

25. The daughters of Ugrasena were Kaṁsā, Kaṁsāvatī, Kaṅkā, Śarabhū, Rāṣṭrapālikā, and they were the wives of Vasudeva's younger brothers.

26. Śūra was born of Vidūratha (the son of Citraratha). His son was Bhajamāna of whom was born Śini. From him was born Svayambhoja whose son was Hṛdika.

27. Hṛdika's sons were Devabāhu, Śatadhanu, and Kṛtavarmā. Śūra (sena) was the son of Devamīḍha (who, as explained by ŚR on the strength of Parāśara i. e. VP to be the fourth son of Hṛdika[1]). Māriṣā was Śūra's wife.

28-30. He begot on her ten sons of spotless character viz. Vasudeva, Devabhāga, Devaśravas, Anaka, Sṛñjaya, Śyāmaka, Kaṅka, Śamīka, Vatsaka, Vṛka. They call Vasudeva, the father of Hari (lit. the source of Hari's birth), as Ānakadundubhi, as the celestial kettledrums (*dundubhis*) and still bigger drums (Ānakas) were sounded at his (auspicious) birth. And their five sisters Pṛthā, Śrutadevā, Śrutakīrti, Śrutaśravas.

31. And Rājādhidevī were his five daughters. (Pṛthā's) father Śūra gave her in adoption to his friend Kunti who was childless,

32. From the sage Durvāsas whom she pleased (by her services), she obtained the lore (*mantras*) of invoking gods (*Devahutī Vidyā*). For testing the efficacy of that lore, she invoked the lustrous sun.

1. The name however does not appear in the text of the VP.4.14.24 in the Gita Press edition. Saṁvat 2026. But ŚR clearly states :

Devamīḍhasya yaḥ Śūro nāma Putras tasya Devamīḍho Hṛdikasyaiva sutas tathā'ha Parāśaraḥ / and quotes VP. 4.14.24 etc.

33. She was astounded to see the (sun)-god appearing instantly in her presence. (Being embarrassed, apologetically) she said, "It is just for testing the efficacy of the lore that the *mantra* was used. Excuse me, Oh god, and (kindly) go your way."

34. 'The sight of gods is never fruitless, Oh lady! I shall beget a son for you, and see to it that your virginity is unimpaired, Oh girl of beautiful waist!'

35. Assuring her thus, the sun-god impregnated her and returned to the firmament. She instantly gave birth to a son who was (brilliant) like another sun.

36. Being afraid of a public censure, she abandoned him (in a box) in the river. Your really valorous great grandfather Pāṇḍu married her.

37. Vṛddhaśarmā of Kāruṣa dynasty married Śrutadevā of whom was born Dantavakra, one of the Diti's sons (viz. Hiraṇyākṣa) who was formerly attendant of god Viṣṇu, called Vijaya but cursed by the sage (Sanaka).

38. Dhṛṣṭaketu of Kekaya family wedded Śrutakīrti and had five sons in the Kekaya family.

39. Jayasena begot by Rājādhidevī two sons viz. Vinda and Anuvinda. Damaghoṣa, the king of Cedi, married Śrutaśravā.

40. Śiśupāla was her (Śrutaśravā's) son. Thus the (account of his) birth is narrated. By Kaṁsā, Devabhāga had two sons, Citraketu and Bṛhadbala.

41. Devaśravas had by Kaṁsavatī two sons—Suvīra and Iṣumān, while Ānaka begot on Kaṅkā (two sons viz.) Satyajit and Purujit.

42. Sṛñjaya procreated from Rāṣṭrapālī, Vṛṣa, Durmarṣaṇa and other sons, while Śyāmaka had Harikeśa and Hiraṇyākṣa by Śūrabhūmī.

43. Vatsaka begot on a celestial nymph Miśrakeśī, Vṛka and other sons, while Vṛka had by his wife Durvākṣī sons such as Takṣa, Puṣkara, Śāla and others.

44. By Sudāminī, Śamīka had Sumitra, Arjunapāla and other sons, while Kaṅka begot on Karṇikā, Ṛtadhāman and Jaya.

45. Ānakadundubhi (Vasudeva) had Pauravī, Rohiṇī, Bhadrā, Madirā, Rocanā, Ilā and Devakī (and others) as wives. Out of them Devakī was prominent.

46. By Rohiṇī, Vasudeva procreated Bala, Gada, Sāraṇa, Durmada, Vipula, Dhruva, as well as Kṛta and others.

47. Vasudeva's sons by Pauravī were Subhadra, Bhadravāha, Durmada, Bhadra as well as others beginning with Bhūta, all together being twelve (in number).

48. Nanda, Upananda, Kṛtaka, Śūra and others were the chidren of (Vasudeva's wife) Madirā, while Kausalyā gave birth to one son Keśin, the delight of his family.

49. Rocanā bore (to Vasudeva) Hasta, Hemāṅgada and other sons. He begot on Ilā, Uruvalka and other chiefs of Yadus.

50. Ānakadundubhi (Vasudeva) had only one son Vipṛṣṭha from Dhṛtadevā, while the sons of Sāntidevā were Śrama, Pratiśruta and others, Oh king !

51. Ten kings beginning with Kalpavarṣa were the sons of Upadevā; while Śridevā had six sons viz. Vasu, Haṁsa, Suvaṁśa and (three) others.

52-53. By Devarakṣitā, he got nine sons such as Gada and others. While he begot eight sons on Sahadevā. Of them, Puruviśruta was most prominent. Just as God Dharma procreated eight Vasus, the noble-minded Vasudeva begot on Devakī eight sons.

54. They were Kīrtimat, Suṣeṇa, Bhadrasena, Ṛju, Sammardana, Bhadra and Saṅkarṣaṇa who was Śeṣa, the Lord of Serpents.

55. Their eighth son was verily Lord Hari himself. And the highly fortunate Subhadrā, your grand mother was their daughter, Oh King !

56. Whenever there is deterioration in righteousness and waxing of sinfulness, the glorious Lord Hari incarnates himself.[1]

57. Oh King ! No cause except his will-power (*Māyā*) can be attributed for the appearance or deeds of the Lord

1. Cf. *yadā yadā hi dharmasya glānir bhavati Bhārata |*
abhyutthānam adharmasya tadātmānaṁ sṛjāmyaham || Bh. GĪTĀ

who is the all-pervading Lord of the universe, the Suprememost, detached and impartial Witness.

58. The activity of the Lord through his Māyā brings about the birth, continuation and destruction of the *jīva* (an embodied soul). The recession of Māyā is his Grace, which leads to self-realization.

59. He endeavoured to lighten the burden of the earth which was being over-run by Asuras in the guise of kings leading Akṣauhiṇīs of army.

60. The glorious Lord Viṣṇu (Slayer of demon Madhu) accompanied by Saṅkarṣaṇa (Balarāma) achieved feats which the Lords of gods could not comprehend, even by thought or imagination.

61. For conferring grace on his devotees, he spread his hallowing glory which will also remove the misery, sorrow and ignorance of those who will be born in (the impending) Kali age.

62. Having but once slightly tasted with the joined palms in the form of ears, from the sacredmost stream of his glory, which is sweet like nectar to the ears of the righteous people, a person shakes himself free from tendencies to *Karmas*.

63-64. Lord Kṛṣṇa whose sportive acts were ever eulogised by (the members of the clans like) Bhojas, Vṛṣṇis, Andhakas, Madhus, Śūrasenas and Daśārhas as well as Kauravas, Sṛñjayas and Pāṇḍavas, delighted the entire humanity with his affectionate smiles and glances, with his sublime speech and his valorous sportive actions and personality, charming in every respect.

65. Drinking (as it were) with their eyes, his countenance appearing most beautiful with ears ornamented with alligator-shaped ear-rings and with brilliant cheeks, a face beaming with graceful sportive smiles, an eternal seat of ecstasy—men and women[1] steeped in delight, are never satiated but grow angry with Nimi (who causes winking and thus deprives them of their happiness and joy).

1. VC. insists that these were cowherd women of Vṛndāvana and not others, and men were Kṛṣṇa's mates like Subala and quotes *Ujjvalanīlamaṇi* as an authority on this.

66. He manifested himself with his own form, but later on assuming the human form, he went from his father's house to Vraja. He enhanced its prosperity. He killed all the enemies; he married a number of wives and begot hundreds of sons through them. He worshipped the Supreme person (who is himself) by performing numerous sacrifices, and promulgated thereby the Vedic path that leads to him, amongst the people.

67. Desiring to reduce the heavy burden of the earth, he struck down with his glance the legions of kings in the battle resulting from the internal feuds of the Kuru clans, but (gave credit of victory to Arjuna) by proclaiming the victory (as if) won by Arjuna; he then enlightened Uddhava in the secrets of the highest Truth, and retired to his Supreme Abode.